International GAAP® 2014

Generally Accepted Accounting Practice under International Financial Reporting Standards

Martin Beyersdorff
Mike Bonham
Wei Li Chan
Tony Clifford
Angela Covic
Matthew Curtis
Tai Danmola
Mike Davies
Tim Denton
Lara Duveen
Joanna Frykowska
Omar Halloum
Billy Hamilton
Bernd Kremp
Emily Moll
Richard Moore
Victoria O'Leary
Margaret Pankhurst
Alexandra Poddubnaya
Hedy Richards
Tim Rogerson
Serene Seah-Tan
Anna Sirocka
Michael Varila
Tracey Waring
Matt Williams
Mathias Zeller

WILEY

This edition first published in 2014 by John Wiley & Sons Ltd.

http://www.internationalgaap.com

Registered office
John Wiley & Sons Ltd, The Atrium, Southern Gate, Chichester, West Sussex, PO19 8SQ, United Kingdom

For details of our global editorial offices, for customer services and for information about how to apply for permission to reuse the copyright material in this book please see our website at www.wiley.com

ISBN 978-1-118-75785-7 (paperback)
[EY personnel only ISBN 978-1-118-75781-9]

ISBN 978-1-118-75782-6 (ebk)
ISBN 978-1-118-75783-3 (ebk)
ISBN 978-1-118-75784-0 (ebk)

A catalogue record for this book is available from the British Library.

Printed and bound by CPI Group (UK) Ltd, Croydon, CR0 4YY

This book is printed on acid-free paper responsibly manufactured from sustainable forestry.

About this book

International GAAP® 2014 has been fully revised and updated in order to:

- Examine practical issues arising from the adoption of IFRS 10 (*Consolidated Financial Statements*), IFRS 11 (*Joint Arrangements*), IFRS 12 (*Disclosure of Interests in Other Entities*), IFRS 13 (*Fair Value Measurement*) and IAS 19 Revised (*Employee Benefits*).
- Address amended standards and new interpretations issued since the preparation of the 2013 edition.
- Include a completely new chapter on the expected changes in hedge accounting under IFRS 9 (*Financial Instruments*).
- Explain the many initiatives that are currently being discussed by the IASB and by the IFRS Interpretations Committee and the potential consequential changes to accounting requirements. In particular, projects on revenue recognition, financial instruments, insurance contracts, leases and the conceptual framework for financial reporting may all result in significant changes to current accounting practice.
- Provide insight on the many issues relating to the practical application of IFRS, based on the extensive experience of the book's authors in dealing with recent day-to-day issues.

The book is published in three volumes. The 51 chapters – listed on pages ix to xi – are split between the three volumes as follows:

- Volume 1 - Chapters 1 to 20,
- Volume 2 - Chapters 21 to 39,
- Volume 3 - Chapters 40 to 51.

Each chapter includes a detailed list of contents and list of illustrative examples.

Each of the three volumes contains the following indexes covering all three volumes:

- an index of extracts from financial statements,
- an index of references to standards and interpretations,
- a general index.

Preface

Not long before last year's edition of this book went to press, the IASB announced that convergence between IFRS and US GAAP was no longer to be a primary objective. In response, we voiced the fear that this might set back the achievement of a single set of high-quality global standards for financial reporting, whilst expressing the hope that, over the longer term, such convergence was not merely desirable but possible, if not inevitable.

One year on, the outlook for convergence is mixed. The IASB is clearly determined to set its own agenda. There could be no clearer indication of this than the recent publication for comment of an IASB-only discussion paper proposing potentially significant changes to the Conceptual Framework for Financial Reporting. On the other hand, the general message from the IASB appears to be that, while convergence with US GAAP is not an explicit aim, unnecessary divergence is to be avoided. For its part, the FASB seems equally resolved to avoid unnecessary divergence from IFRS. Its chairman Russell Golden has recently made it clear that the FASB will evaluate and consider IFRS as the starting point for implementing improvements to US GAAP, and promote global alignment where this is in the best interests of capital market participants.

The IASB's discussion paper also appears to acknowledge some of the criticisms levelled at IFRS in the wake of the financial crisis. For example, a possible new, and more 'prudent', approach to liability recognition is explored. The IASB also indicates that a mixed measurement model (one that measures some assets and liabilities at historical cost and others at fair value) will continue for the foreseeable future, and – more significantly – that the choice of model should have regard to its effect on the volatility of the income statement.

Some of the more vocal criticism of IFRS has come from within the EU, with some proposing that the EU should either adopt IFRS on a more selective basis, or even take primary responsibility for setting accounting standards. In our view, either approach would represent a regrettable and retrograde step, significantly damaging to the credibility of IFRS and the quest for a global accounting framework more generally. We are reassured that such suggestions have gained no significant political traction and that the EU appears instead to be focussing on how it might influence the IASB in a more effective and unified way.

As more and more countries, with different traditions of financial reporting and enforcement, join the IFRS fold, so the challenge of consistent application of IFRS – essential for its credibility – increases. We believe that *International GAAP*, now in its ninth edition, plays an important part in this. Our team of authors and reviewers hails from all parts of the world, and includes not only our global technical experts but also many senior client-handlers. This gives us an in-depth knowledge of practice in many different countries and industry sectors, enabling us to go beyond mere recitation of the requirements of standards to explaining their application in many varied situations.

Whilst we promote the consistent application of IFRS where we can, we also acknowledge areas where more than one legitimate interpretation can be found in practice. We therefore welcome the recent announcement by the IASB and IOSCO of a more proactive and collaborative approach to ensuring that the IASB continues to produce high-quality standards that can be, and are, consistently applied and enforced. We hope that these efforts will focus on significant practice issues and retain the principles-based approach of IFRS that, in our view, is one of its major strengths.

****

We are deeply indebted to many of our colleagues within the global organisation of EY for their selfless assistance and support in the publication of this book. It has been a truly international effort, with valuable contributions from EY people around the globe.

Our thanks go particularly to those who reviewed, edited and assisted in the preparation of drafts, most notably: Justine Belton, Richard Bembridge, Larissa Clark, Dennis Deutmeyer, Michael Elliott, Charles Feeney, Sabrina Frey, Martin Friedhoff, Peter Gittens, Paul Hebditch, Mike Herbst, Guy Jones, Ryan Kaye, Kevin Kispert, Steinar Kvifte, Twan van Limpt, Michiel van der Lof, James Luke, Santosh Maller, Steve Martin, Robert McCracken, Joseph McGrath, John O'Grady, Eric Ohlund, Danita Ostling, Ruth Picker, Christoph Piesbergen, Jeffrey Rosen, Gerard van Santen, Thomas Sciametta, Alison Spivey, Dusanka Stevanovic, Paul Sutcliffe, Leo van der Tas, Lynda Tomkins, Hans van der Veen, Arne Weber, Allister Wilson and Luci Wright.

Our thanks also go to everyone who directly or indirectly contributed to the book's creation, including the following members of the Financial Reporting Group in the UK: Denise Brand, Rob Carrington, Robin Chatterjee, Larissa Connor, Julie Dempers, Marianne Dudareva, Rabindra Jogarajan, Sharon Johal, Dean Lockhart, Sharon MacIntyre, Amanda Marrion and Claire Taylor.

We also thank Jeremy Gugenheim for his assistance with the production technology throughout the period of writing.

London,
October 2013

Martin Beyersdorff
Mike Bonham
Wei Li Chan
Tony Clifford
Angela Covic
Matthew Curtis
Tai Danmola
Mike Davies
Tim Denton
Lara Duveen
Joanna Frykowska
Omar Halloum
Billy Hamilton
Bernd Kremp
Emily Moll
Richard Moore
Victoria O'Leary
Margaret Pankhurst
Alexandra Poddubnaya
Hedy Richards
Tim Rogerson
Serene Seah-Tan
Anna Sirocka
Michael Varila
Tracey Waring
Matt Williams
Mathias Zeller

Lists of chapters

Volume 1

The lists of chapters in volumes 2 and 3 follow overleaf.

Volume 2

Volume 3

Volume 3

Abbreviations

The following abbreviations are used in this book:

Professional and regulatory bodies:

AASB	Australian Accounting Standards Board
AcSB	Accounting Standards Board of Canada
AICPA	American Institute of Certified Public Accountants
AOSSG	Asian-Oceanian Standard-Setters Group
APB	Accounting Principles Board (of the AICPA, predecessor of the FASB)
ARC	Accounting Regulatory Committee of representatives of EU Member States
ASAF	Accounting Standards Advisory Forum
ASB	Accounting Standards Board in the UK
ASBJ	Accounting Standards Board of Japan
CASC	China Accounting Standards Committee
CESR	Committee of European Securities Regulators, an independent committee whose members comprised senior representatives from EU securities regulators (replaced by ESMA)
CICA	Canadian Institute of Chartered Accountants
EC	European Commission
ECB	European Central Bank
ECOFIN	The Economic and Financial Affairs Council
EFRAG	European Financial Reporting Advisory Group
EITF	Emerging Issues Task Force in the US
EPRA	European Public Real Estate Association
ESMA	European Securities and Markets Authority (see CESR)
EU	European Union
FAF	Financial Accounting Foundation
FASB	Financial Accounting Standards Board in the US
FCAG	Financial Crisis Advisory Group
FEE	Federation of European Accountants

FSB	Financial Stability Board (successor to the FSF)
FSF	Financial Stability Forum
G4+1	The (now disbanded) group of four plus 1, actually with six members, that comprised an informal 'think tank' of staff from the standard setters from Australia, Canada, New Zealand, UK, and USA, plus the IASC
G7	The Group of Seven Finance Ministers
G20	The Group of Twenty Finance Ministers and Central Bank Governors
GPPC	Global Public Policy Committee of the six largest accounting networks
HKICPA	Hong Kong Institute of Certified Public Accountants
ICAI	Institute of Chartered Accountants of India
IASB	International Accounting Standards Board
IASC	International Accounting Standards Committee. The former Board of the IASC was the predecessor of the IASB
IASCF	International Accounting Standards Committee Foundation (predecessor of the IFRS Foundation)
ICAEW	Institute of Chartered Accountants in England and Wales
ICAS	Institute of Chartered Accountants of Scotland
IFAC	International Federation of Accountants
IFRIC	The IFRS Interpretations Committee (formerly the International Financial Reporting Interpretations Committee) of the IASB
IGC	Implementation Guidance Committee on IAS 39 (now disbanded)
IOSCO	International Organisation of Securities Commissions
IPSASB	International Public Sector Accounting Standards Board
IPTF	International Practices Task Force (a task force of the SEC Regulations Committee)
IVSC	International Valuation Standards Council
JWG	Joint Working Group of Standard-setters that comprised representatives from the IASC, the FASB, and eight other international bodies. The purpose of the (now disbanded) group was to develop an integrated and harmonised standard on financial instruments – a task they were unable to complete
RICS	Royal Institution of Chartered Surveyors
SAC	Standards Advisory Council, predecessor of the IFRS Advisory Council which provides advice to the IASB on a wide range of issues
SEC	Securities and Exchange Commission (the US securities regulator)
SIC	Standing Interpretations Committee of the IASC (replaced by IFRIC)
TEG	Technical Expert Group, an advisor to the European Commission

Accounting related terms:

ADS	American Depositary Shares
AFS	Available-for-sale investment
ARB	Accounting Research Bulletins (issued by the AICPA)
ARS	Accounting Research Studies (issued by the APB)
ASC	Accounting Standards Codification™. The single source of authoritative US GAAP recognised by the FASB, to be applied to non-governmental entities for interim and accounting periods ending after 15 September 2009
CCIRS	Cross Currency Interest Rate Swap
CDO	Collateralised Debt Obligation
CGU	Cash-generating Unit
CU	Currency Unit
DD&A	Depreciation, Depletion and Amortisation
DPF	Discretionary Participation Feature
E&E	Exploration and Evaluation
EBIT	Earnings Before Interest and Taxes
EBITDA	Earnings Before Interest, Taxes, Depreciation and Amortisation
EIR	Effective Interest Rate
EPS	Earnings per Share
FAS	Financial Accounting Standards (issued by the FASB). Superseded by Accounting Standards Codification™ (ASC)
FC	Foreign currency
FIFO	First-In, First-Out basis of valuation
FRS	Financial Reporting Standard (issued by the ASB)
FTA	First-time Adoption
FVLCD	Fair value less costs of disposal
FVLCS	Fair value less costs to sell (following the issue of IFRS 13, generally replaced by FVLCD)
GAAP	Generally accepted accounting practice (as it applies under IFRS), or generally accepted accounting principles (as it applies to the US)
HTM	Held-to-maturity investment
IAS	International Accounting Standard (issued by the former board of the IASC)
IBNR	Incurred but not reported claims
IFRS	International Financial Reporting Standard (issued by the IASB)
IPO	Initial Public Offering

IPR&D	In-process Research and Development
IPSAS	International Public Sector Accounting Standard
IRR	Internal Rate of Return
IRS	Interest Rate Swap
JA	Joint Arrangement
JCA	Jointly Controlled Asset
JCE	Jointly Controlled Entity
JCO	Jointly Controlled Operation
JO	Joint Operation
JV	Joint Venture
LAT	Liability Adequacy Test
LC	Local Currency
LIBOR	London Inter Bank Offered Rate
LIFO	Last-In, First-Out basis of valuation
NCI	Non-controlling Interest
NBV	Net Book Value
NPV	Net Present Value
NRV	Net Realisable Value
OCI	Other Comprehensive Income
PP&E	Property, Plant and Equipment
R&D	Research and Development
SCA	Service Concession Arrangement
SE	Structured Entity
SFAC	Statement of Financial Accounting Concepts (issued by the FASB as part of its conceptual framework project)
SFAS	Statement of Financial Accounting Standards (issued by the FASB). Superseded by Accounting Standards Codification[tm] (ASC)
SPE	Special Purpose Entity
SV	Separate Vehicle
TSR	Total Shareholder Return
VIU	Value In Use
WACC	Weighted Average Cost of Capital

References to IFRSs, IASs, Interpretations and supporting documentation:

AG	Application Guidance
AV	Alternative View
B, BCZ	Basis for Conclusions on IASs
BC	Basis for Conclusions on IFRSs and IASs
DI	Draft Interpretation
DO	Dissenting Opinion
DP	Discussion Paper
ED	Exposure Draft
IE	Illustrative Examples on IFRSs and IASs
IG	Implementation Guidance
IN	Introduction to IFRSs and IASs

Authoritative literature

The content of this book takes into account all accounting standards and other relevant rules issued up to September 2013. Consequently, it covers the IASB's *Conceptual Framework for Financial Reporting* and authoritative literature listed below.

References in the main text of each chapter to the pronouncements below are generally to the versions of those pronouncements as approved and expected to be included in the Blue Book edition of the Bound Volume 2014 International Financial Reporting Standards IFRS – Consolidated without early application – Official pronouncements applicable on 1 January 2014, to be published by the IASB.

References to those pronouncements below which have an effective date after 1 January 2014 (such as IFRS 9 – *Financial Instruments*) are to the versions of those pronouncements as denoted by the ISBN references noted below. These are expected to be included in the Red Book edition of the Bound Volume 2014 International Financial Reporting Standards IFRS – Official pronouncements issued at 1 January 2014, to be published by the IASB.

References in the main text to pronouncements that applied only to periods beginning before 1 January 2014 are generally denoted by the last version of the Blue Book edition of the Bound Volume in which they were included. For example, IAS 27 (2012) refers to IAS 27 – *Consolidated and Separate Financial Statements*, which was included in the Blue Book edition of the Bound Volume 2012 International Financial Reporting Standards IFRS – Consolidated without early application – Official pronouncements applicable on 1 January 2012.

US GAAP accounting standards are organised within a comprehensive FASB Accounting Standards Codification[tm], which is now the single source of authoritative US GAAP recognised by the FASB to be applied to non-governmental entities and has been applied in this publication.

† The standards and interpretations marked with a dagger have been withdrawn or superseded.

IASB Framework

The Conceptual Framework for Financial Reporting

International Financial Reporting Standards (2014 Bound Volume)

IFRS 1	First-time Adoption of International Financial Reporting Standards
IFRS 2	Share-based Payment
IFRS 3	Business Combinations
IFRS 4	Insurance Contracts
IFRS 5	Non-current Assets Held for Sale and Discontinued Operations

IFRS 6	Exploration for and Evaluation of Mineral Resources
IFRS 7	Financial Instruments: Disclosures
IFRS 8	Operating Segments
IFRS 10	Consolidated Financial Statements
IFRS 11	Joint Arrangements
IFRS 12	Disclosure of Interests in Other Entities
IFRS 13	Fair Value Measurement

International Financial Reporting Standards (mandatory after 1 January 2014)

IFRS 9	Financial Instruments	ISBN 978-1-907026-51-5
	Mandatory Effective Date and Transition Disclosures (Amendments to IFRS 9 and IFRS 7)	ISBN 978-1-907877-48-3

International Accounting Standards (2014 Bound Volume)

IAS 1	Presentation of Financial Statements
IAS 2	Inventories
IAS 7	Statement of Cash Flows
IAS 8	Accounting Policies, Changes in Accounting Estimates and Errors
IAS 10	Events after the Reporting Period
IAS 11	Construction Contracts
IAS 12	Income Taxes
IAS 16	Property, Plant and Equipment
IAS 17	Leases
IAS 18	Revenue
IAS 19	Employee Benefits
IAS 20	Accounting for Government Grants and Disclosure of Government Assistance
IAS 21	The Effects of Changes in Foreign Exchange Rates
IAS 23	Borrowing Costs
IAS 24	Related Party Disclosures
IAS 26	Accounting and Reporting by Retirement Benefit Plans
IAS 27	Separate Financial Statements
IAS 28	Investments in Associates and Joint Ventures
IAS 29	Financial Reporting in Hyperinflationary Economies
IAS 32	Financial Instruments: Presentation
IAS 33	Earnings per Share
IAS 34	Interim Financial Reporting
IAS 36	Impairment of Assets
IAS 37	Provisions, Contingent Liabilities and Contingent Assets
IAS 38	Intangible Assets
IAS 39	Financial Instruments: Recognition and Measurement
IAS 40	Investment Property
IAS 41	Agriculture

IFRS Interpretations Committee Interpretations

	IFRIC 1	Changes in Existing Decommissioning, Restoration and Similar Liabilities
	IFRIC 2	Members' Shares in Co-operative Entities and Similar Instruments
†	IFRIC 3	Emission Rights
	IFRIC 4	Determining whether an Arrangement contains a Lease
	IFRIC 5	Rights to Interests arising from Decommissioning, Restoration and Environmental Rehabilitation Funds
	IFRIC 6	Liabilities arising from Participation in a Specific Market – Waste Electrical and Electronic Equipment
	IFRIC 7	Applying the Restatement Approach under IAS 29 *Financial Reporting in Hyperinflationary Economies*
	IFRIC 9	Reassessment of Embedded Derivatives
	IFRIC 10	Interim Financial Reporting and Impairment
	IFRIC 12	Service Concession Arrangements
	IFRIC 13	Customer Loyalty Programmes
	IFRIC 14	IAS 19 – The Limit on a Defined Benefit Asset, Minimum Funding Requirements and their Interaction
	IFRIC 15	Agreements for the Construction of Real Estate
	IFRIC 16	Hedges of a Net Investment in a Foreign Operation
	IFRIC 17	Distributions of Non-cash Assets to Owners
	IFRIC 18	Transfer of Assets from Customers
	IFRIC 19	Extinguishing Financial Liabilities with Equity Instruments
	IFRIC 20	Stripping Costs in the Production Phase of a Surface Mine
	IFRIC 21	Levies

Standing Interpretations Committee Interpretations

	SIC-7	Introduction of the Euro
	SIC-10	Government Assistance – No Specific Relation to Operating Activities
†	SIC-12	Consolidation – Special Purpose Entities
†	SIC-13	Jointly Controlled Entities – Non-Monetary Contributions by Venturers
	SIC-15	Operating Leases – Incentives
	SIC-25	Income Taxes – Changes in the Tax Status of an Entity or its Shareholders
	SIC-27	Evaluating the Substance of Transactions Involving the Legal Form of a Lease
	SIC-29	Service Concession Arrangements: Disclosures
	SIC-31	Revenue – Barter Transactions Involving Advertising Services
	SIC-32	Intangible Assets – Web Site Costs

IASB Exposure Drafts

ED/2010/13	Hedge Accounting
ED/2011/6	Revenue from Contracts with Customers
ED/2012/1	Annual Improvements to IFRSs 2010-2012 Cycle
ED/2012/2	Annual Improvements to IFRSs 2011-2013 Cycle
ED/2012/3	Equity Method: Share of Other Net Asset Changes (Proposed amendments to IAS 28)
ED/2012/4	Classification and Measurement: Limited Amendments to IFRS 9 (Proposed amendments to IFRS 9 (2010))
ED/2012/5	Clarification of Acceptable Methods of Depreciation and Amortisation (Proposed amendments of IAS 16 and IAS 38)
ED/2012/6	Sale or Contribution of Assets between an Investor and its Associate or Joint Venture (Proposed amendments to IFRS 10 and IAS 28)
ED/2012/7	Acquisition of an Interest in a Joint Operation (Proposed amendment to IFRS 11)
ED/2013/3	Financial Instruments: Expected Credit Losses
ED/2013/4	Defined Benefit Plans: Employee Contributions (Proposed amendments to IAS 19)
ED/2013/5	Regulatory Deferral Accounts
ED/2013/6	Leases
ED/2013/7	Insurance Contracts
ED/2013/8	Bearer Plants (Proposed amendments to IAS 16 and IAS 41)

IFRS Interpretations Committee Exposure Drafts

DI/2012/2	Put Options Written on Non-controlling Interests	ISBN 978-1-907877-61-2

IASB Discussion Papers

DP/2013/1	A Review of the Conceptual Framework for Financial Reporting	ISBN 978-1-909704-04-6

Other IASB publications

IFRS for SMEs	International Financial Reporting Standard (IFRS) for Small and Medium-sized Entities (SMEs)	ISBN 978-1-907026-16-4
Feedback Statement	IFRS Practice Statement: Management Commentary – A Framework for Presentation	ISBN 978-1-907026-56-0
	Agenda Consultation 2011 (December 2012)	
Report and Feedback Statement	Post Implementation Review: IFRS 8 Operating Segments (July 2013)	

Chapter 21 Capitalisation of borrowing costs

List of examples

Chapter 21 Capitalisation of borrowing costs

1 INTRODUCTION

A common question when determining the initial measurement of an asset is whether or not finance costs incurred on its acquisition or during the period of its construction should be capitalised. There have always been a number of strong arguments in favour of the capitalisation of directly attributable finance costs. For example, it is argued that they are just as much a cost as any other directly attributable cost; that expensing finance costs distorts the choice between purchasing and constructing an asset; that capitalising the costs leads to a carrying value that is far more akin to the market value of the asset; and that the financial statements are more likely to represent the true results of the project.

In accounting periods commencing prior to 1 January 2009, entities were permitted to capitalise borrowing costs as an alternative to expensing them in the period they were incurred. However, in March 2007, the IASB issued a revised version of IAS 23 – *Borrowing Costs* – mandating capitalisation of borrowing costs directly attributable to the acquisition, construction or production of a qualifying asset. This was done to achieve convergence with the main principle in US GAAP. *[IAS 23.BC2].* It thereby eliminated some (but not all) of the differences with Topic 835 – *Interest* – in the FASB Accounting Standards Codification (ASC 835, formerly FASB Statement No. 34 – *Capitalization of Interest Cost* (SFAS 34)).

The revised standard applied for the first time to accounting periods commencing on or after 1 January 2009, although early implementation was permitted. *[IAS 23.29].* In this chapter we consider the requirements of this revised standard.

2 THE REQUIREMENTS OF IAS 23

2.1 Core principle

IAS 23 requires borrowing costs to be capitalised if they are directly attributable to the acquisition, construction or production of a qualifying asset (whether or not the funds have been borrowed specifically). These borrowing costs are included in the cost of the asset; all other borrowing costs are recognised as an expense in the period in which they are incurred. *[IAS 23.1, 8]*.

2.2 Scope

IAS 23 deals with the treatment of borrowing costs in general, rather than solely focusing on capitalising borrowing costs as part of the carrying value of assets.

The standard does not deal with the actual or imputed costs of equity used to fund the acquisition or construction of an asset. *[IAS 23.3]*. This means that any distributions or other payments made in respect of equity instruments, as defined by IAS 32 – *Financial Instruments: Presentation*, are not within the scope of IAS 23. Conversely, interest and dividends payable on instruments classified as financial liabilities would appear to be within the scope of the standard (see 4.2 below).

3 QUALIFYING ASSETS

IAS 23 defines a qualifying asset as 'an asset that necessarily takes a substantial period of time to get ready for its intended use or sale'. *[IAS 23.5]*.

Assets that are ready for their intended use or sale when acquired are not qualifying assets. *[IAS 23.7]*.

IAS 23 does not define 'substantial period of time' and this will therefore require the exercise of judgement after considering the specific facts and circumstances. However, an asset that normally takes twelve months or more to be ready for its intended use will usually be a qualifying asset.

The standard indicates that, depending on the circumstances, the following may be qualifying assets: manufacturing plants, power generation facilities, investment properties, inventories and intangible assets. *[IAS 23.7]*.

3.1 Inventories

Inventories are considered qualifying assets under IAS 23 as long as they meet the definition of a qualifying asset and require a substantial period of time to bring them to a saleable condition. However, an entity is not required to apply the standard to inventories that are routinely manufactured or otherwise produced in large quantities on a repetitive basis even if they take a substantial period of time to get ready for sale. *[IAS 23.4(b), BC6]*.

Therefore an entity may choose whether to apply the requirements of IAS 23 to such inventories as a matter of accounting policy. This optional scope exemption has been allowed because of the difficulty of calculating and monitoring the amount to be capitalised. There are many examples of such inventories, including large manufactured or constructed items that take some time to complete but are basically sold as standard items, such as aircraft and large items of equipment or food and drink that take a long time to mature, such as cheese or alcohol that matures in bottle or cask.

Conversely, IAS 23 is required to be applied to bespoke inventories (i.e. those made according to the unique specifications of a particular customer) that are occasionally manufactured or produced on a single item by item basis and take a substantial period of time to get ready for sale.

3.2 Assets measured at fair value

IAS 23 does not require entities to capitalise interest relating to assets measured at fair value that would otherwise be qualifying assets, for example, biological assets. *[IAS 23.4(a)]*. If the assets are held under a fair value model (or a fair value less costs to sell model) with all changes going to profit or loss, then capitalisation would not affect measurement in the statement of financial position and would involve no more than a reallocation between finance costs and the fair value movement in profit or loss. However, this scope exemption is optional and would still allow an entity to choose whether to apply the requirements of IAS 23 to such assets as a matter of accounting policy.

IAS 23 does not restrict the exemption to assets where the fair value movement is taken to profit or loss. Assets measured at fair value that fall under the revaluation model of IAS 16 – *Property, Plant and Equipment* – are also eligible for this scope exemption even though the revaluation gain or loss goes to other comprehensive income, not profit or loss (see Chapter 18). While such assets may be subject to the scope exemption, the revaluation model in IAS 16 is only applied subsequent to initial recognition. *[IAS 16.31]*. Therefore, such assets might be qualifying assets at initial recognition, but subject to the scope exemption subsequently.

For example, assume that an entity borrows specific funds to construct a building, that the building is a qualifying asset and that the entity has a policy of revaluing all its land and buildings. When the constructed building is initially recognised, it will be measured at cost, which would include the directly attributable borrowing costs. *[IAS 16.15, 16(b)]*. Assume that the entity subsequently renovates the building, that the renovation takes a substantial amount of time to complete and that those costs qualify for capitalisation under IAS 16. Since the asset is being revalued it would fall under the scope exemption in IAS 23. Therefore, the entity would not be required to capitalise any directly attributable borrowing costs relating to this subsequent renovation even if it takes a substantial amount of time to complete.

3.3 Construction contracts

IAS 11 – *Construction Contracts* – allows borrowing costs to be treated as contract costs when they can be attributed to contract activity and allocated to specific contracts (see Chapter 23). *[IAS 11.18]*. If an entity includes borrowing costs in its IAS 11 contract costs, it will affect the classification of those costs when they are recognised in profit or loss. It does not preclude the borrowing costs from being capitalised in accordance with IAS 23, if the criteria for capitalisation in the standard are met.

The reference to IAS 23 in paragraph 18 of IAS 11 was deleted because the IASB argued that it is unnecessary to refer to IAS 23, as attributing borrowing costs to construction contracts is really a matter of identifying the contract costs and does not affect the recognition of borrowing costs as specified in IAS 23. *[IAS 23.BC27]*.

3.4 Financial assets

IAS 23 excludes all financial assets (including equity accounted investments) from the definition of qualifying assets. *[IAS 23.7]*.

4 DEFINITION OF BORROWING COSTS

4.1 The definition of borrowing costs in IAS 23

Borrowing costs are interest and other costs incurred by an entity in connection with the borrowing of funds. *[IAS 23.5]*. Borrowing costs are defined in the standard to include:

- interest expense calculated using the effective interest method as described in IAS 39 – *Financial Instruments: Recognition and Measurement*;
- finance charges in respect of finance leases recognised in accordance with IAS 17 – *Leases*; and
- exchange differences arising from foreign currency borrowings to the extent that they are regarded as an adjustment to interest costs (see 5.4 below). *[IAS 23.6]*.

The standard addresses whether or not to capitalise borrowing costs as part of the cost of the asset. *[IAS 23.8-9]*. The identification and measurement of finance costs are not dealt with in IAS 23 (see 4.2 below).

4.2 Other finance costs

IAS 23 does not address many of the ways in which an entity may finance its operations or other finance costs that it may incur. For example, the standard does not address any of the following:

- the many derivative financial instruments such as interest rate swaps, floors, caps and collars that are commonly used to manage interest rate risk on borrowings;
- gains and losses on derecognition of borrowings, for example early settlement of directly attributable borrowings that have been renegotiated prior to completion of an asset in the course of construction;
- dividends payable on shares classified as financial liabilities (such as, certain redeemable preference shares) that have been recognised as an expense in profit or loss; and
- the unwinding of discounts that may be included within the caption 'finance costs' in an entity's income statement.

IAS 23 does not preclude the classification of costs, other than those it identifies, as borrowing costs. However, they must meet the basic criterion in the standard, i.e. that they are costs that are directly attributable to the acquisition, construction or production of a qualifying asset, which would, therefore, preclude treating the unwinding of discounts as borrowing costs. In addition, as in the case of exchange differences, capitalisation of such costs should be permitted only 'to the extent that they are regarded as an adjustment to interest costs' (see 5.4 below). *[IAS 23.6(e)]*.

The eligibility of these other finance costs for capitalisation under IAS 23 is discussed at 5.5 below.

5 BORROWING COSTS ELIGIBLE FOR CAPITALISATION

5.1 Directly attributable borrowing costs

Borrowing costs are eligible for capitalisation if they are directly attributable to the acquisition, construction or production of a qualifying asset. *[IAS 23.10]*.

The standard starts from the premise that directly attributable borrowing costs are those that would have been avoided if the expenditure on the qualifying asset had not been made. *[IAS 23.10]*. Recognising that it may not always be easy to identify a direct relationship between particular borrowings and a qualifying asset and to determine the borrowings that could otherwise have been avoided, the standard includes separate requirements for specific borrowings and general borrowings.

5.2 Specific borrowings

If an entity borrows funds specifically to obtain a qualifying asset, the borrowing costs that are directly related to that qualifying asset can be readily identified. *[IAS 23.10]*. The borrowing costs eligible for capitalisation would be the actual borrowing costs incurred during the period. *[IAS 23.12]*.

Entities frequently borrow funds in advance of expenditure on qualifying assets and may temporarily invest the borrowings. The standard makes it clear that any investment income earned on the temporary investment of those borrowings needs to be deducted from the borrowing costs incurred and only the net amount capitalised (see Example 21.2 below). *[IAS 23.12-13]*.

There is no restriction in IAS 23 on the type of investment in which the funds can be invested but, in our view, to maintain the conclusion that the funds are specific borrowings, the investment must be of a nature that does not expose the principal amount to the risk of not being recovered. The more risky the investment, the greater is the likelihood that the borrowing is not specific to the qualifying asset. If the investment returns a loss rather than income, such losses are not added to the borrowing costs to be capitalised.

5.3 General borrowings

IAS 23 concedes that there may be practical difficulties in identifying a direct relationship between particular borrowings and a qualifying asset and in determining the borrowings that could otherwise have been avoided. *[IAS 23.11]*. This could be the case if the financing activity of an entity is co-ordinated centrally, for example, if an entity borrows to meet its funding requirements as a whole and the construction of the qualifying asset is financed out of general borrowings. Other circumstances that may cause difficulties are identified by the standard as follows:

- a group has a treasury function that uses a range of debt instruments to borrow funds at varying rates of interest and lends those funds on various bases to other entities in the group; or
- loans are denominated in or linked to foreign currencies and the group operates in highly inflationary economies or there are fluctuations in exchange rates. *[IAS 23.11]*.

In these circumstances, determining which borrowing costs are attributable to the acquisition of a qualifying asset may be difficult and require the exercise of judgement. *[IAS 23.11]*.

When general borrowings are used in part to obtain a qualifying asset, IAS 23 requires the application of a capitalisation rate to the expenditure on that asset in determining the amount of borrowing costs eligible for capitalisation. However, the amount of borrowing costs capitalised during a period cannot exceed the amount of borrowing costs incurred during that period. *[IAS 23.14]*.

The capitalisation rate applied should be the weighted average of the borrowing costs applicable to the borrowings of the entity that are outstanding during the period, other than borrowings made specifically for the purpose of obtaining a qualifying asset. *[IAS 23.14]*. The capitalisation rate is then applied to the expenditure on the qualifying asset.

Expenditure on a qualifying asset includes only that expenditure resulting in the payment of cash, the transfer of other assets or the assumption of interest-bearing liabilities. Such expenditure must be reduced by any progress payments and grants received in connection with the asset. The standard accepts that, when funds are borrowed generally, the average carrying amount of the asset during a period, including borrowing costs previously capitalised, is normally a reasonable approximation of the expenditure to which the capitalisation rate is applied in that period. *[IAS 23.18]*.

The standard does not provide specific guidance regarding interest income earned from temporarily investing excess general funds. However, any interest income earned is unlikely to be directly attributable to the acquisition or construction of a qualifying asset. In addition, the capitalisation rate required by IAS 23 focuses on the borrowings of the entity outstanding during the period of construction or acquisition and does not include temporary investments. As such, borrowing costs capitalised should not be reduced by interest income earned from the investment of general borrowings nor should such income be included in determining the appropriate capitalisation rate.

In some circumstances all borrowings made by the group can be taken into account in determining the weighted average of the borrowing costs. In other circumstances only those borrowings made by individual subsidiaries may be taken into account. *[IAS 23.15]*. It is likely that this will largely be determined by the extent to which borrowings are made centrally (and, perhaps, interest expenses met in the same way) and passed through to individual group companies via intercompany accounts and intra-group loans. The capitalisation rate is discussed further at 5.3.2 below.

5.3.1 Definition of general borrowings

As noted at 5.3 above, determining general borrowings will not always be straightforward and, as a result, the determination of the amount of borrowing costs that are directly attributable to the acquisition of a qualifying asset is difficult and the exercise of judgement is required.

In July 2009, the Interpretations Committee received a request for guidance on what borrowings comprise 'general borrowings' for the purpose of capitalising borrowing costs in accordance with IAS 23. The request asked for guidance on the treatment of general borrowings used to purchase a specific asset other than a qualifying asset.

The Interpretations Committee noted that paragraph 14 of IAS 23 states that '[t]o the extent that an entity borrows funds generally and uses them for the purpose of obtaining a qualifying asset, the entity shall determine the amount of borrowing costs eligible for capitalisation by applying a capitalisation rate to the expenditures on that asset. The capitalisation rate shall be the weighted average of the borrowing costs applicable to the borrowings of the entity that are outstanding during the period, other than borrowings made specifically for the purpose of obtaining a qualifying asset.'

The Interpretations Committee also noted that because paragraph 14 refers only to qualifying assets:

- some conclude that borrowings related to specific assets other than qualifying assets cannot be excluded from determining the capitalisation rate for general borrowings; and
- others note the general principle in paragraph 10 that the borrowing costs that are directly attributable to the acquisition, construction or production of a qualifying asset are borrowing costs that would have been avoided if the expenditure on the qualifying asset had not been made.

Consequently, the Interpretations Committee concluded that any guidance it could provide would be in the nature of application guidance rather than an interpretation. In light of this and because the IASB was due to consider whether to add this issue to the annual improvements project, the Committee decided not to add the issue to its agenda.[1]

The IASB subsequently considered the issue of whether debt incurred specifically to acquire a non-qualifying asset could be excluded from general borrowings but, as IAS 23 excludes only debt used to acquire qualifying assets from the determination of the capitalisation rate, decided not to include this issue in its annual improvements process.[2]

Another question that arises is whether a specific borrowing undertaken to obtain a qualifying asset ever changes its nature into a general borrowing. Differing views exist as to whether or not borrowings change their nature throughout the period they are outstanding. Some consider that once the asset for which the borrowing was incurred has been completed, and the entity chooses to use its funds on constructing other assets rather than repaying the loan, this changes the nature of the loan into a general borrowing. However, to the extent that the contract links the repayment of the loan to specific proceeds generated by the entity, its nature as a specific borrowing would be preserved. Others take the view that once the borrowing has been classified as specific, its nature does not change while it remains outstanding. Management will therefore need to exercise judgement in determining its policy and assessing the nature of the loans when construction activity is completed.

5.3.2 Calculation of capitalisation rate

As the standard acknowledges that determining general borrowings will not always be straightforward, it will be necessary to exercise judgement to meet the main objective – a reasonable measure of the directly attributable finance costs.

The following example illustrates the practical application of the method of calculating the amount of finance costs to be capitalised:

Example 21.1: Calculation of capitalisation rate (no investment income)

On 1 April 2014 a company engages in the development of a property, which is expected to take five years to complete, at a cost of £6,000,000. The statements of financial position at 31 December 2013 and 31 December 2014, prior to capitalisation of interest, are as follows:

	31 December 2013	31 December 2014
	£	£
Development property	–	1,200,000
Other assets	6,000,000	6,000,000
	6,000,000	7,200,000
Loans		
5.5% debenture stock	2,500,000	2,500,000
Bank loan at 6% p.a.	–	1,200,000
Bank loan at 7% p.a.	1,000,000	1,000,000
	3,500,000	4,700,000
Shareholders' equity	2,500,000	2,500,000

The bank loan with an effective interest rate at 6% was drawn down to match the development expenditure on 1 April 2014, 1 July 2014 and 1 October 2014.

Expenditure was incurred on the development as follows:

	£
1 April 2014	600,000
1 July 2014	400,000
1 October 2014	200,000
	1,200,000

If the bank loan at 6% p.a. is a new borrowing specifically to finance the development then the amount of interest to be capitalised for the year ended 31 December 2014 would be the amount of interest charged by the bank of £42,000 ((£600,000 × 6% × 9/12) + (£400,000 × 6% × 6/12) + (£200,000 × 6% × 3/12)).

However, if all the borrowings were general (i.e. the bank loan at 6% was not specific to the development) and would have been avoided but for the development, then the amount of interest to be capitalised would be:

$$\frac{\text{Total interest expense for period}}{\text{Weighted average total borrowings}} \times \text{Development expenditure}$$

Total interest expense for the period

	£
£2,500,000 × 5.5%	137,500
£1,200,000 (as above)	42,000
£1,000,000 × 7%	70,000
	249,500

Therefore the capitalisation rate would be calculated as:

$$\frac{249{,}500}{3{,}500{,}000 + 700{,}000} = 5.94\%$$

The capitalisation rate would then be applied to the expenditure on the qualifying asset, resulting in an amount to be capitalised of £41,580 as follows:

	£
£600,000 × 5.94% × 9/12	26,730
£400,000 × 5.94% × 6/12	11,880
£200,000 × 5.94% × 3/12	2,970
	41,580

If the 5.5% debenture stock were irredeemable then it would be excluded from the above calculation as it could no longer be a borrowing that could have been avoided. The calculation would be done using the figures for the bank loans and their related interest costs only.

In this example, all borrowings are at fixed rates of interest and the period of construction extends at least until the end of the period, simplifying the calculation. The same principle is applied if borrowings are at floating rates i.e. only the interest costs incurred during that period, and the weighted average borrowings for that period, will be taken into account.

Note that the company's shareholders' equity (i.e. equity instruments – see further discussion in 5.5.4 below) cannot be taken into account and at least part of the outstanding borrowings is presumed to finance the acquisition or construction of qualifying assets – unless they are specific borrowings used to obtain other qualifying assets (see discussion in 5.3.1 above).

The above example also assumes that loans are drawn down to match expenditure on the qualifying asset. If, however, a loan is drawn down immediately and investment income is received on the unapplied funds, then the calculation differs from that in Example 21.1. This is illustrated in Example 21.2.

Example 21.2: Calculation of amount to be capitalised – specific borrowings with investment income

On 1 April 2014 a company engages in the development of a property, which is expected to take five years to complete, at a cost of £6,000,000. In this example, a bank loan of £6,000,000 with an effective interest rate at 6% was taken out on 31 March 2014 and fully drawn. The total interest charge for the year ended 31 December 2014 was consequently £270,000.

However, investment income was also earned at 3% on the unapplied funds during the period as follows:

	£
£5,400,000 × 3% × 3/12	40,500
£5,000,000 × 3% × 3/12	37,500
£4,800,000 × 3% × 3/12	36,000
	114,000

Consequently, the amount of interest to be capitalised for the year ended 31 December 2014 is:

	£
Total interest charge	270,000
Less: investment income	(114,000)
	156,000

5.3.3 Accrued costs and trade payables

As noted in 5.3 above, IAS 23 states that expenditure on qualifying assets includes only that expenditure resulting in the payment of cash, the transfer of other assets or the assumption of interest-bearing liabilities. *[IAS 23.18]*. Therefore, in principle, costs of a qualifying asset that have only been accrued but have not yet been paid in cash should be excluded from the amount on which interest is capitalised, as by definition no interest can have been incurred on an accrued payment. The same principle can be applied to non-interest bearing liabilities e.g. non-interest-bearing trade payables.

The effect of applying this principle is often merely to delay the commencement of the capitalisation of interest since the capital expenditure will be included once it has been paid in cash. In most cases it is unlikely that the effect will be material as the time between accrual and payment of the cost will not be that great. An example of this is retention money that is not generally payable until the asset is completed.

5.3.4 Assets carried below cost in the statement of financial position

An asset may be recognised in the financial statements during the period of production on a basis other than cost, i.e. it may have been written down below cost as a result of being impaired. An asset may be impaired when its expected ultimate cost, including costs to complete and the estimated capitalised interest thereon, exceed its estimated recoverable amount or net realisable value (see 6.2.1 below).

The question then arises as to whether the calculation of interest to be capitalised should be based on the cost or carrying amount of the asset. In this case, cost should be used, as this is the amount that the entity or group has had to finance. In the case of an impaired asset, the continued capitalisation based on the cost of the asset may well necessitate a further impairment.

5.4 Exchange differences as a borrowing cost

An entity may borrow funds in a currency that is not its functional currency e.g. a US dollar loan financing a development in a company which has the Russian rouble as its functional currency. This may have been done on the basis that, over the period of the development, the borrowing costs, even after allowing for exchange differences, were expected to be less than the interest cost of an equivalent rouble loan.

IAS 23 defines borrowing costs as including exchange differences arising from foreign currency borrowings to the extent that they are regarded as an adjustment to interest costs. *[IAS 23.6(e)]*. The standard does not expand on this point. In January 2008, the Interpretations Committee considered a request for guidance on the treatment of foreign exchange gains and losses and on the treatment of any derivatives used to hedge such foreign exchange exposures. The Interpretations Committee decided not to add the issue to its agenda because:

- the standard acknowledges that judgement will be required in its application and appropriate disclosure of accounting policies and judgements would provide users with the information they need to understand the financial statements; and
- the IASB had considered this issue when developing the new IAS 23 and had decided not to provide any guidance.[3]

In our view, as exchange rate movements are partly a function of differential interest rates, in many circumstances the foreign exchange differences on directly attributable borrowings will be an adjustment to interest costs that can meet the definition of borrowing costs. However, care is needed if there are fluctuations in exchange rates that cannot be attributed to interest rate differentials. In such cases, we believe that a practical approach is to limit exchange losses taken as borrowing costs such that the total borrowing costs capitalised do not exceed the amount of borrowing costs that would be incurred on functional currency equivalent borrowings.

If this approach is used and the construction of the qualifying asset takes more than one accounting period, there could be situations where in one period only a portion of foreign exchange differences could be capitalised. However, in subsequent years, if the borrowings are assessed on a cumulative basis, foreign exchange losses previously expensed may now meet the recognition criteria. The two methods of dealing with this are illustrated in Example 21.3 below.

In our view, whether foreign exchange gains and losses are assessed on a discrete period basis or cumulatively over the construction period is a matter of accounting policy, which must be consistently applied. As alluded to above, IAS 1 – *Presentation of Financial Statements* – requires clear disclosure of significant accounting policies and judgements that are relevant to an understanding of the financial statements (see 7.2 below).

Example 21.3: Foreign exchange differences in more than one period

Method A – The discrete period approach

The amount of foreign exchange differences eligible for capitalisation is determined for each period separately. Foreign exchange losses that did not meet the criteria for capitalisation in previous years are not capitalised in subsequent years.

Method B – The cumulative approach

The borrowing costs to be capitalised are assessed on a cumulative basis based on the cumulative amount of interest expense that would have been incurred had the entity borrowed in its functional currency. The amount of foreign exchange differences capitalised cannot exceed the amount of foreign exchange losses incurred on a cumulative basis at the end of the reporting period. The cumulative approach looks at the construction project as a whole as the unit of account ignoring the occurrence of reporting dates. Consequently, the amount of the foreign exchange differences eligible for capitalisation as an adjustment to the borrowing cost in the period is an estimate, which can change as the exchange rates vary over the construction period.

An illustrative calculation of the amount of foreign exchange differences that may be capitalised under Method A and Method B is set out below.

	Year 1	Year 2	Total
	$	$	$
Interest expense in foreign currency (A)	25,000	25,000	50,000
Hypothetical interest expense in functional currency (B)	30,000	30,000	60,000
Foreign exchange loss (C)	6,000	3,000	9,000
Method A – Discrete Approach			
Foreign exchange loss capitalised – lower of C and (B minus A)	5,000	3,000	9,000
Foreign exchange loss expensed	1,000	–	–
Method B – Cumulative Approach			
Foreign exchange loss capitalised	5,000 *	4,000 **	9,000
Foreign exchange loss expensed	1,000	(1,000)	–

* Lower of C and (B minus A) in Year 1

** Lower of C and (B minus A) in total across the two years. In this example this represents the sum of the foreign exchange loss of $3,000 capitalised using the discrete approach plus the $1,000 not capitalised in year 1.

5.5 Other finance costs as a borrowing cost

5.5.1 Derivative financial instruments

The most straightforward and commonly encountered derivative financial instrument used to manage interest rate risk is a floating to fixed interest rate swap, as in the following example.

Example 21.4: Floating to fixed interest rate swaps

Entity A has borrowed €4 million for five years at a floating interest rate to fund the construction of a building. In order to hedge the cash flow interest rate risk arising from these borrowings, A has entered into a matching pay-fixed receive-floating interest rate swap, based on the same underlying nominal sum and duration as the original borrowing, that effectively converts the interest on the borrowings to fixed rate. The net effect of the periodic cash settlements resulting from the hedged and hedging instruments is as if A had borrowed €4 million at a fixed rate of interest. Prior to IAS 39, entities simply recognised, on an accruals basis, each periodic net cash settlement in profit or loss.

These instruments are not addressed in IAS 23. IAS 39 sets out the basis on which such instruments are recognised and measured. See Chapter 48 regarding how to account for effective hedges and the conditions that these instruments must meet.

An entity may consider that a specific derivative financial instrument, such as an interest rate swap, is directly attributable to the acquisition, construction or production of a qualifying asset. If the instrument does not meet the conditions for hedge accounting then the effects on income will be different from those if it does, and they will also be dissimilar from year to year. What is the impact of the derivative on borrowing costs eligible for capitalisation? In particular, does the accounting treatment of the derivative financial instrument affect the amount available for capitalisation? If hedge accounting is not adopted, does this affect the amount available for capitalisation?

The following examples illustrate the potential differences.

Example 21.5: Cash flow hedge of variable-rate debt using an interest rate swap

Entity A is constructing a building and expects it to take 18 months to complete. To finance the construction, on 1 January 2013, the entity issues an eighteen month, €20,000,000 variable-rate note payable, due on 30 June 2014 at a floating rate of interest plus a margin of 1%. At that date the market rate of interest is 8%. Interest payment dates and interest rate reset dates occur on 1 January and 1 July until maturity. The principal is due at maturity. On 1 January 2013, the entity also enters into an eighteen month interest rate swap with a notional amount of €10,000,000 from which it will receive periodic payments at the floating rate and make periodic payments at a fixed rate of 9%, with settlement and rate reset dates every 30 June and 31 December. The fair value of the swap is zero at inception.

On 1 January 2013, the debt is recorded at €20,000,000. No entry is required for the swap on that date because its fair value was zero at inception.

During the eighteen month period, floating interest rates change as follows:

	Cash payments	
	Floating rate on principal	Rate paid by Entity A
Period to 30 June 2013	8%	9%
Period to 31 Dec 2013	8.5%	9.5%
Period to 30 June 2014	9.75%	10.75%

Under the interest rate swap, Entity A receives interest at the market floating rate as above and pays at 9% on the nominal amount of €10,000,000 throughout the period.

At 31 December 2013, the swap has a fair value of €37,500, reflecting the fact that it is now in the money as Entity A is expected to receive a net cash inflow of this amount in the period until the instrument is terminated. There are no further changes in interest rates prior to the maturity of the swap and the fair value of the swap declines to zero at 30 June 2014. Note that this example excludes the effect of issue costs and discounting. In addition, it is assumed that, if Entity A is entitled to, and applies, hedge accounting, there will be no ineffectiveness.

The cash flows incurred by the entity on its borrowing and interest rate swap are as follows:

	Cash payments		
	Interest on principal	Interest rate swap (net)	Total
	€	€	€
30 June 2013	900,000	50,000	950,000
31 Dec 2013	950,000	25,000	975,000
30 June 2014	1,075,000	(37,500)	1,037,500
Total	2,925,000	37,500	2,962,500

There are a number of different ways in which Entity A could calculate the borrowing costs eligible for capitalisation, including the following.

(i) The interest rate swap meets the conditions for, and entity A applies, hedge accounting. The finance costs eligible for capitalisation as borrowing costs will be €1,925,000 in the year to 31 December 2013 and €1,037,500 in the period ended 30 June 2014.

(ii) Entity A does not apply hedge accounting. Therefore, it will reflect the fair value of the swap in income in the year ended 31 December 2013, reducing the net finance costs by €37,500 to €1,887,500 and increasing the finance costs by an equivalent amount in 2014 to €1,075,000. However, it considers that it is inappropriate to reflect the fair value of the swap in borrowing costs eligible for capitalisation so it capitalises costs based on the net cash cost on an accruals accounting basis. In this case this will give the same result as in (i) above.

(iii) Entity A does not apply hedge accounting and considers only the costs incurred on the borrowing, not the interest rate swap, as eligible for capitalisation. The borrowing costs eligible for capitalisation would be €1,850,000 in 2013 and €1,075,000 in 2014.

In our view, all these methods are valid interpretations of IAS 23 and the preparer will need to consider the most appropriate method in the particular circumstances.

In particular, if using method (ii), it is necessary to demonstrate that the gains or losses on the derivative financial instrument are directly attributable to the construction of a qualifying asset. In making this assessment it is necessary to consider the term of the derivative and this method may not be appropriate if the derivative has a different term to the underlying directly attributable borrowing.

Based on the facts in this example, method (iii) appears to be inconsistent with the underlying principle of IAS 23 – that the costs eligible for capitalisation are those costs that could have been avoided if the expenditure on the qualifying asset had not been made – and is not therefore appropriate. *[IAS 23.10].* However, it may not be possible to demonstrate that the gains or losses on a specific derivative financial instrument are directly attributable to a particular qualifying asset, rather than being used by the entity to manage its interest rate exposure on a more general basis. In such a case, method (iii) may be an appropriate method to use.

Note that method (i) would not be permitted under US GAAP which prohibits the capitalisation of the gain or loss on the hedging instrument in a cash flow hedge. Instead, ASC 815 states that '[i]f the variable-rate interest on a specific borrowing is associated with an asset under construction and capitalized as a cost of that asset, the amounts in accumulated other comprehensive income related to a cash flow hedge of the variability of that interest shall be reclassified into earnings over the depreciable life of the constructed asset, because that depreciable life coincides with the amortization period for the capitalized interest cost on the debt.'[4] For fair value hedges, however, under US GAAP derivative gains and losses (arising from the effective portion of a derivative instrument that qualifies as a fair value hedge) are considered to be part of the capitalised interest cost. *[IAS 23.BC21].*

Whichever policy is chosen by an entity, it needs to be consistently applied in similar situations.

5.5.2 Gains and losses on derecognition of borrowings

If an entity repays borrowings early, in whole or in part, then it may recognise a gain or loss on the early settlement. Such gains or losses include amounts attributable to expected future interest rates; in other words, it includes an estimated prepayment of the future cash flows under the instrument. The gain or loss is a function of relative interest rates and how the interest rate of the instrument differs from current and anticipated future interest rates. There may be circumstances in which a loan is repaid while the qualifying asset is still under construction. IAS 23 does not address the issue.

In our view, gains and losses on derecognition of borrowings are generally not eligible for capitalisation. It would be extremely difficult to determine an appropriate amount to capitalise and it would be inappropriate thereafter to capitalise any interest amounts (on specific or general borrowings) if doing so would amount to double counting. Decisions to repay borrowings early are not usually directly attributable to the qualifying asset but to other circumstances of the entity.

The same approach would be applied to gains and losses arising from a refinancing when there is a substantial modification of the terms of borrowings.

5.5.3 Gains or losses on termination of derivative financial instruments

If an entity terminates a derivative financial instrument, for example, an interest rate swap, before the end of the term of the instrument, it will usually have to either make or receive a payment, depending on the fair value of the instrument at that time. This fair value is typically based on expected future interest rates; in other words it is an estimated prepayment of the future cash flows under the instrument.

The treatment of the gain or loss for the purposes of capitalisation will depend on the following:

- the basis on which the entity capitalises the gains and losses associated with derivative financial instruments attributable to qualifying assets (see 5.5.1 above); and
- whether the derivative is associated with a borrowing that has also been terminated.

Entities must adopt a treatment that is consistent with their policy for capitalising the gains and losses from derivative financial instruments that are attributable to qualifying investments (see 5.5.1 above).

The accounting under IAS 39 will differ depending on whether the instrument has been designated as a hedge or not; in the former case, and assuming that the borrowing has not also been repaid, the entity will usually continue to account for the cumulative gain or loss on the instrument as if the hedge were still in place. In such a case, the amounts that are reclassified from other comprehensive income will be eligible for capitalisation for the remainder of the period of construction.

If the entity is not hedge accounting for the derivative financial instrument, but considers it to be directly attributable to the construction of the qualifying asset then it will have to consider whether part of the gain or loss relates to a period after construction is complete.

If the underlying borrowing is also terminated then the gain or loss will not be capitalised and the treatment will mirror that applied on derecognition of the borrowing, as described in 5.5.2 above.

5.5.4 Dividends payable on shares classified as financial liabilities

An entity might finance its operations in whole or in part by the issue of preference shares and in some circumstances these will be classified as financial liabilities (see Chapter 43). In some circumstances the dividends payable on these instruments would meet the definition of borrowing costs. For example, an entity might have funded the development of a qualifying asset by issuing redeemable preference shares that are redeemable at the option of the holder and so are classified as financial liabilities under IAS 32. In this case, the 'dividends' would be treated as interest and meet the definition of borrowing costs and so should be capitalised following the principles on specific borrowings discussed in section 5.2 above.

Companies with outstanding preference shares which are treated as liabilities under IAS 32 might subsequently obtain a qualifying asset. In such cases, these preference share liabilities would be considered to be part of the company's general borrowings. The related 'dividends' would meet the definition of borrowing costs and could be capitalised following the principles on general borrowings discussed in section 5.3 above.

Capitalisation of such 'dividends' would not apply to these shares if they were irredeemable, unless, consistent with section 5.3 above, they are directly attributable to a qualifying asset. However, if such instruments are treated as general borrowings and are irredeemable, it would generally be difficult to demonstrate that such borrowings could have been avoided if the expenditure on a qualifying asset had not been made and so capitalisation would not be appropriate.

Capitalisation of dividends or other payments made in respect of any instruments that are classified as equity in accordance with IAS 32 is not appropriate as these instruments would not meet the definition of financial liabilities. In addition, as discussed in 2.2 above, IAS 23 does not deal with the actual or imputed cost of equity, including preferred capital not classified as a liability. *[IAS 23.3]*.

5.5.5 Unwinding discounts on provisions classified as finance costs in profit or loss

Many unwinding discounts are treated as finance costs in profit or loss. These include discounts relating to various provisions such as those for onerous leases and decommissioning costs. These finance costs will not be borrowing costs under IAS 23 because they do not arise in respect of funds borrowed by the entity that can be attributed to a qualifying asset. Therefore, they cannot be capitalised.

5.6 Capitalisation of borrowing costs in hyperinflationary economies

In situations where IAS 29 – *Financial Reporting in Hyperinflationary Economies* – applies, an entity needs to distinguish between borrowing costs that compensate for inflation and those incurred in order to acquire or construct a qualifying asset.

IAS 29 states that '[t]he impact of inflation is usually recognised in borrowing costs. It is not appropriate both to restate the capital expenditure financed by borrowing and to capitalise that part of the borrowing costs that compensates for the inflation during the same period. This part of the borrowing costs is recognised as an expense in the period in which the costs are incurred.' *[IAS 29.21]*.

IAS 23 specifies that when an entity applies IAS 29, the borrowing costs that can be capitalised should be restricted and the entity must expense the part of borrowing costs that compensate for inflation during the same period. *[IAS 23.9]*.

Issues relating to exchange differences that do not arise in hyperinflationary situations and their eligibility for capitalisation are discussed at 5.4 above.

5.7 Group considerations

5.7.1 Borrowings in one company and development in another

A question that often arises in practice is whether it is appropriate to capitalise interest in the group financial statements on borrowings that appear in the financial statements of a different group entity from that carrying out the development. Based on the underlying principle of IAS 23, capitalisation in such circumstances would only be appropriate if the amount capitalised fairly reflected the interest cost of the group on borrowings from third parties that could have been avoided if the expenditure on the qualifying asset were not made.

Although it may be appropriate to capitalise interest in the group financial statements, the entity carrying out the development should not capitalise any interest in its own financial statements as it has no borrowings. If, however, the entity has intra-group borrowings then interest on such borrowings may be capitalised in its own financial statements.

5.7.2 Qualifying assets held by joint ventures

A number of sectors carry out developments through the medium of joint arrangements (see Chapter 12) – this is particularly common with property developments. In such cases, the joint arrangement may be financed principally by equity and the joint operators or joint venturers may have financed their participation through borrowings.

In situations where the joint arrangement is classified as a joint venture in accordance with IFRS 11 – *Joint Arrangements*, it is not appropriate to capitalise interest in the joint venture on the borrowings of the venturers as the interest charge is not a cost of the joint venture. Neither would it be appropriate to capitalise interest in the financial statements of the venturers, whether separate or consolidated financial statements, because the qualifying asset does not belong to them. The investing entities have an investment as a financial asset (i.e. an equity accounted investment), which is excluded by IAS 23 from being a qualifying asset (see 3.4 above).

In situations where the joint arrangement is classified as a joint operation in accordance with IFRS 11 and the operators are accounting for their share of the assets, liabilities, revenue and expenses, then the operators should capitalise borrowing costs incurred that relate to their share of any qualifying asset. Borrowing costs eligible for capitalisation would be based on the operator's obligation for the loans of the joint operation and any direct borrowings of the operator itself if the operator funds part of the acquisition of the joint operation's qualifying asset.

6 COMMENCEMENT, SUSPENSION AND CESSATION OF CAPITALISATION

6.1 Commencement of capitalisation

IAS 23 requires that capitalisation of borrowing costs commence when:

(a) expenditures for the asset are being incurred;

(b) borrowing costs are being incurred; and

(c) activities that are necessary to prepare the asset for its intended use or sale are in progress. *[IAS 23.17].*

The standard is explicit that only those expenditures on a qualifying asset that have resulted in payments of cash, transfers of other assets or the assumption of interest-bearing liabilities, may be included in determining borrowing costs. Such expenditures must be reduced by any progress payments and grants received in connection with the asset. *[IAS 23.18].*

The activities necessary to prepare an asset for its intended use or sale can include more than the physical construction of the asset. Necessary activities can start before the commencement of physical construction and include, for example, technical and administrative work such as obtaining permits. This does not mean that borrowing costs can be capitalised if it is not certain that permits that are necessary for the construction will be obtained. No cost could be considered 'directly attributable' prior to this point.

Borrowing costs may not be capitalised during a period in which there are no activities that change the condition of the asset. For example a house-builder or property developer may not capitalise borrowing costs on its 'land bank' i.e. that land which is held for future development. Borrowing costs incurred while land is under development are capitalised during the period in which activities related to the development are being undertaken. However, borrowing costs incurred while land acquired for building purposes is held without any associated development activity represent a holding cost of the land and hence would be considered a period cost (i.e. expenses as incurred). *[IAS 23.19].*

An entity may make a payment to a third party contractor before that contractor commences construction activities. It is unlikely to be appropriate that capitalisation of borrowing costs should commence in the event of such a prepayment until that contractor commences activities that are necessary to prepare the asset for its intended use or sale.

Kazakhmys' policy describes the period during which borrowing costs are capitalised, as well as noting that it uses either an actual rate or a weighted average cost of borrowings.

Extract 21.1: Kazakhmys PLC (2012)

Notes to the consolidated financial statements [extract]

3. Summary of significant accounting policies [extract]

(u) Borrowing costs

Borrowing costs directly relating to the acquisition, construction or production of a qualifying capital project under construction are capitalised and added to the project cost during construction until such time as the assets are considered substantially ready for their intended use i.e. when they are capable of commercial production. Where funds are borrowed specifically to finance a project, the amount capitalised represents the actual borrowing costs incurred. Where surplus funds are available for a short term from money borrowed specifically to finance a project, the income generated from the temporary investment of such amounts is also capitalised and deducted from the total capitalised borrowing cost. Where the funds used to finance a project form part of general borrowings, the amount capitalised is calculated using a weighted average of rates applicable to relevant general borrowings of the Group during the year. All other borrowing costs are recognised in the income statement in the period in which they are incurred using the effective interest rate method.

Borrowing costs that represent avoidable costs not related to the financing arrangements of the development projects and are therefore not directly attributable to the construction of these respective assets are expensed in the period as incurred. These borrowing costs generally arise where the funds are drawn down under the Group's financing facilities, whether specific or general, which are in excess of the near term cash flow requirements of the development projects for which the financing is intended, and the funds are drawn down ahead of any contractual obligation to do so.

6.2 Suspension of capitalisation

IAS 23 states that capitalisation should be suspended during extended periods in which active development is interrupted. *[IAS 23.20].* However, the standard distinguishes between extended periods of interruption (when capitalisation would be suspended) and periods of temporary delay that are a necessary part of preparing the asset for its intended purpose (when capitalisation is not normally suspended). *[IAS 23.21].*

Capitalisation continues during periods when inventory is undergoing slow transformation – the example is given of inventories taking an extended time to mature (presumably such products as Scotch whisky or Cognac, although the relevance of this may be limited as these products are likely to meet the optional exemption for 'routinely manufactured' products – see 3.1 above). Similarly, capitalisation would continue in the case of a bridge construction delayed by temporary adverse weather conditions, where such conditions are common in the region. *[IAS 23.21].* Borrowing costs incurred during extended periods of interruption caused, for example, by a lack of funding or a strategic decision to hold back project developments during a period of economic downturn are not considered a necessary part of preparing the asset for its intended purpose and should not be capitalised.

6.2.1 *Impairment considerations*

When it is determined that capitalisation is appropriate, an entity continues to capitalise borrowing costs that are directly attributable to the acquisition, construction or production of a qualifying asset as part of the cost of the asset even if the capitalisation causes the expected ultimate cost of the asset to exceed its recoverable amount or net realisable value.

If the carrying amount of the qualifying asset exceeds its recoverable amount or net realisable value (depending on the type of asset), the asset must be written down in accordance with the relevant IFRS. If the asset is incomplete, this assessment is performed by considering the expected ultimate cost of the asset. *[IAS 23.16]*. The expected ultimate cost must include costs to complete and the estimated capitalised interest thereon.

IAS 36 – *Impairment of Assets* – will apply if the qualifying asset is property, plant and equipment accounted for in accordance with IAS 16 or if the asset is otherwise within the scope of IAS 36 (see Chapter 20). For inventories that are qualifying assets, the requirements of IAS 2 – *Inventories* – on net realisable value will apply (see Chapter 22).

6.3 Cessation of capitalisation

The standard requires capitalisation to cease when substantially all the activities necessary to prepare the qualifying asset for its intended use or sale are complete. *[IAS 23.22]*.

An asset is normally ready for its intended use or sale when the physical construction of the asset is complete, even though routine administrative work might still continue. If minor modifications, such as the decoration of a property to the purchaser's or user's specification, are all that are outstanding, this indicates that substantially all the activities are complete. *[IAS 23.23]*. In some cases there may be a requirement for inspection (e.g. to ensure that the asset meets safety requirements) before the asset can be used. Usually 'substantially all the activities' would have been completed before this point in order to be ready for inspection. In such a situation, capitalisation would cease prior to the inspection.

When the construction of a qualifying asset is completed in parts and each part is capable of being used while construction continues on other parts, capitalisation should cease for the borrowing costs on the portion of borrowings attributable to that part when substantially all the activities necessary to prepare that part for its intended use or sale are completed. *[IAS 23.24]*. An example of this might be a business park comprising several buildings, each of which is capable of being fully utilised while construction continues on other parts. *[IAS 23.25]*. This principle also applies to single buildings where one part is capable of being fully utilised even if the building as a whole is incomplete.

For a qualifying asset that needs to be complete in its entirety before any part can be used as intended, it would be appropriate to capitalise related borrowing costs until all the activities necessary to prepare the entire asset for its intended use or sale are substantially complete. An example of this is an industrial plant, such as a steel mill, involving processes which are carried out in sequence at different parts of the plant within the same site. *[IAS 23.25]*.

7 DISCLOSURE REQUIREMENTS

7.1 The requirements of IAS 23

An entity shall disclose:

- the amount of borrowing costs capitalised during the period; and
- the capitalisation rate used to determine the amount of borrowing costs eligible for capitalisation. *[IAS 23.26].*

AngloGold Ashanti discloses in its 'tangible assets' note its capitalisation rate used to determine its borrowing costs. The amount of borrowing costs capitalised during the period is disclosed within the table of movements in property, plant and equipment that precedes this narrative disclosure.

Extract 21.2: AngloGold Ashanti Limited (2012)

GROUP – NOTES TO THE FINANCIAL STATEMENTS [extract]

15. Tangible assets [extract]

(2) The weighted average capitalisation rate used to determine the amount of borrowing costs eligible for capitalisation was 6.54% (2011: 6.86%). Interest capitalised relates to the Tropicana project in Australia.

7.2 Disclosure requirements in other IFRSs

In addition to the disclosure requirements in IAS 23, an entity may need to disclose additional information in relation to its borrowing costs in order to comply with requirements in other IFRSs. For example, disclosures required by IAS 1 – *Presentation of Financial Statements* – include:

- the nature and amount of material items included in profit or loss;
- the measurement bases used in preparing the financial statements and other accounting policies used that are relevant to an understanding of the financial statements (see an example at Extract 21.1 above); and
- the significant judgements made in the process of applying an entity's accounting policies that have the most significant effect on the recognised amounts (e.g. criteria in determining a qualifying asset, including definition of 'substantial period of time'). *[IAS 1.97, 117, 122].*

As noted in 5.4 above, the Interpretations Committee considered a request for guidance on the treatment of foreign exchange gains and losses and on the treatment of any derivatives used to hedge such foreign exchange exposures.

The Interpretations Committee decided not to add the issue to its agenda but concluded both that (i) how an entity applies IAS 23 to foreign currency borrowings is a matter of accounting policy requiring an entity to exercise judgement and (ii) IAS 1 requires disclosure of significant accounting policies and judgements that are relevant to an understanding of the financial statements.[5] The requirements of IAS 1 are discussed in Chapter 3.

References

1 *IFRIC Update*, July 2009.
2 *IASB Update*, July 2009.
3 *IFRIC Update*, January 2008.
4 FASB Accounting Standards Codification 815-30-35-45, *Forecasted Interest Payment Capitalized as a Cost of an Asset Under Construction* (formerly EITF 99-9, *Effect of Derivative Gains and Losses on the Capitalisation of Interest*, FASB, July 1999, para. 6.).
5 *IFRIC Update*, January 2008.

Chapter 22 Inventories

Chapter 22 Inventories

1 INTRODUCTION

Under IFRS the relevant standard for inventories is IAS 2 – *Inventories.* The term 'inventories' includes raw materials, work-in-progress, finished goods and goods for resale, although the standard does not include all instances of these categories; some are covered by other standards, for example growing crops are covered by IAS 41 – *Agriculture* (see Chapter 38). This chapter deals only with the inventories within the scope of IAS 2. Long-term contracts and the associated work in progress are the subject of a separate standard, IAS 11 – *Construction Contracts* – which is dealt with in Chapter 23.

Under the historical cost accounting system, costs of inventories comprise expenditure which has been incurred in the normal course of business in bringing the product or service to its present location and condition. All costs incurred in respect of inventories are charged as period costs, except for those which relate to those unconsumed inventories which are expected to be of future benefit to the entity. These are carried forward, to be matched with the revenues that they will generate in the future. Under the historical cost system, inventories in the statement of financial position have characteristics similar to those of prepaid expenses or property, plant and equipment – they are effectively deferred costs.

When IAS 2 was revised in 2003 all references to matching and to the historical cost system were deleted, even though historical cost was retained as the main measurement method for IAS 2 inventories. However, there have been no recent developments suggesting a move away from this widely accepted and traditional cost-based inventory measurement model to one based on fair value. The Exposure Draft *Revenue from Contracts with Customers* only applies when there is a contract with a customer.[1] It will therefore have an impact on accounting for construction contracts currently accounted for under IAS 11 (see Chapter 23) but will not apply to inventory in the absence of a contract, e.g. a forward purchase with a prepayment by the purchaser.

2 THE SCOPE OF IAS 2

IAS 2 applies to all inventories in financial statements except work-in-progress arising under construction contracts including directly related service contracts (both of which are dealt with by IAS 11, see Chapter 23), financial instruments (see Chapters 40 to 50), and biological assets related to agricultural activity and agricultural produce at the point of harvest (see Chapter 38). *[IAS 2.2]*.

Agricultural produce that has been harvested by the entity from its biological assets is in scope; it is initially recognised at its fair value, less costs to sell at the point of harvest, as set out in IAS 41 (see Chapter 38). This figure becomes the cost of inventories at that date for the purposes of IAS 2. *[IAS 2.20]*.

The measurement provisions of IAS 2 do not apply to the measurement of inventories held by:

(a) producers of agricultural and forest products, agricultural produce after harvest, and minerals and mineral products, to the extent that they are measured at net realisable value in accordance with well-established practices in those industries. When such inventories are measured at net realisable value, changes are recognised in profit or loss in the period of the change *[IAS 2.3]*. This occurs, for example, when agricultural crops have been harvested or minerals have been extracted and sale is assured under a forward contract or a government guarantee, or when an active market exists and there is a negligible risk of failure to sell *[IAS 2.4]*; and

(b) commodity broker-traders who measure their inventories at fair value less costs to sell. If these inventories are measured at fair value less costs to sell, the changes are recognised in profit or loss in the period of the change. *[IAS 2.3]*. Broker-traders are those who buy or sell commodities for others or on their own account and these inventories are principally acquired with the purpose of selling in the near future and generating a profit from fluctuations in price or broker traders' margin. *[IAS 2.5]*.

In both cases, the standard stresses that these inventories are only scoped out from the measurement requirements of IAS 2; the standard's other requirements, such as disclosure, continue to apply. Fair value and net realisable value (NRV) are discussed at 3.1 below.

Inventories are defined by IAS 2 as:

(a) assets held for sale in the ordinary course of business;

(b) assets in the process of production for such sale; or

(c) assets in the form of materials or supplies to be consumed in the production process or in the rendering of services. *[IAS 2.6]*.

Inventories can include all types of goods purchased and held for resale including, for example, merchandise purchased by a retailer and other tangible assets such as land and other property held for resale, although investment property accounted for under IAS 40 – *Investment Property* – is not treated as an inventory item. The term also encompasses finished goods produced, or work in progress being produced by the entity, and includes materials and supplies awaiting use in the production process. If the entity is a service provider, its inventories may be intangible (e.g. the costs of the service for which the entity has not yet recognised the related revenue). *[IAS 2.8]*. The inventory of service providers will probably consist mainly of the labour costs of the people providing the service. There is a separate standard, IFRS 5 – *Non-current Assets Held for Sale and Discontinued Operations* – that governs the accounting treatment of non-current assets held for sale, for example a group of assets held for sale such as a business being disposed of. An entity would apply IFRS 5 to any inventories that form part of a disposal group. IFRS 5 is discussed in Chapter 4.

2.1 Scope issues: IAS 2 or another IFRS

2.1.1 Core inventories and spare parts – IAS 2 or IAS 16

In certain industries, for example the petrochemical industry, certain processes or storage arrangements require a core of inventory to be present in the system at all times. For example, in order for a crude oil refining process to take place, the plant must contain a certain minimum quantity of oil. This can only be taken out once the plant is abandoned and could then only be sold as sludge. Similarly, underground gas storage caves are filled with gas but a substantial part (perhaps say 25%) of that gas can never be sold as its function is to pressurise the cave, thereby allowing the remaining 75% to be extracted. Even though the gas will be turned around on a continuing basis, at any one time 25% of it will never be available to sell and cannot be recouped from the cave.

It is our view that if an item of inventory is not held for sale or consumed in a production process, but is necessary to the operation of a facility during more than one operating cycle, and its cost cannot be recouped through sale (or is significantly impaired), this item of inventory should be accounted for as an item of property, plant and equipment (PP&E) under IAS 16 – *Property, Plant and Equipment.* This applies even if the part of inventory that is deemed to be an item of PP&E cannot be separated physically from the rest of inventory.

These matters will always involve the exercise of judgement, however, in the above instances, we consider that:

(i) the deemed PP&E items do not meet the definition of inventories;

(ii) although it is not possible to physically separate the chemicals involved into inventory and PP&E categories, there is no accounting reason why one cannot distinguish between identical assets with different uses and therefore account for them differently. Indeed, IAS 2 does envisage such a possibility when discussing different cost formulas; *[IAS 2.25]*.

(iii) the deemed PP&E items are necessary to bring another item of PP&E to the condition necessary for it to be capable of operating in the manner intended by management. This meets the definition of the costs of PP&E on initial recognition in IAS 16; *[IAS 16.16(b)]*.

(iv) recognising these items as inventories would lead to an immediate loss because these items cannot be sold or consumed in a production process, or during the process of rendering services. This does not properly reflect the fact that the items are necessary to operate another asset over more than one operating cycle.

Scope questions may also arise in relation to spare parts. Many entities carry spare parts for items of PP&E, some of which may be used over more than one period. As part of the *Annual Improvements to IFRSs 2009-2011 Cycle* issued in May 2012, the IASB clarified IAS 16 to state that spare parts are classified as inventory unless they meet the definition of PP&E. The recognition of spare parts as PP&E is discussed further in Chapter 18 at 3.1.1.

2.1.2 Broadcast rights – IAS 2 or IAS 38

Broadcasters purchase programmes under a variety of different arrangements. Often they commit to purchasing programmes that are at a very early stage of development, perhaps merely being concepts. The broadcaster may have exclusive rights over the programme or perhaps only have the rights to broadcast for a set period of time or on a set number of occasions. IFRS is not clear on how these rights should be classified and when they should be recognised.

We believe that an entity may either treat these rights as intangible assets and classify them under IAS 38 – *Intangible Assets*, see Chapter 17 at 11.5, or classify them as inventory under IAS 2. Such rights would certainly seem to meet the definition of inventory under IAS 2. Given that the acquisition of these rights is a part of the cost of the broadcaster's programming schedule, they meet the general IAS 2 definition in that they are:

(a) held for sale in the ordinary course of business;

(b) in the process of production for such sale; or

(c) in the form of materials or supplies to be consumed in the production process or in the rendering of services. *[IAS 2.6]*.

When classified as inventory the rights will need to be disclosed within current assets, even if the intention is not to consume them within 12 months. *[IAS 1.68]*. As with costs of other inventory the cash outflow from acquisition will be classified as an operating cash flow and the expense will be presented within cost of sales when the right is consumed.

There is also the issue of the timing of recognition of these rights. In accordance with paragraph 4.4 of the *Conceptual Framework for Financial Reporting* an asset is a resource controlled by an entity from which future economic benefits are expected to flow to the entity. Hence it is necessary to determine when control is obtained. Under IFRS, executory contracts where both parties are still to perform (such as purchase orders where neither payment nor delivery has yet been made) do not generally result in the recognition of assets and liabilities. When a broadcaster initially contracts to purchase a programme it will not generally result in immediate recognition of an asset relating to that programme. At this point there will not normally be an asset under the control of the broadcaster. Factors that may be relevant in determining when the entity controls an asset include whether:

- the underlying resource is sufficiently developed to be identifiable (e.g. whether the manuscript or screenplay has been written, and whether directors and actors have been hired);

- the entity has legal, exclusive rights to broadcast, which may be in respect of a defined period or geographic area;
- there is a penalty to the licensor for non-delivery of the content;
- it is probable that content will be delivered; and
- it is probable that economic benefits will flow to the entity.

Where there is difficulty in determining when control of the asset is obtained it may be helpful to assess at what point any liability arises, since a liability will generally indicate that an asset has been acquired. In practice an entity might recognise an asset and liability for a specific broadcast right on the following trigger dates:

- when a screening certificate is obtained;
- when programming is available for exhibition;
- the beginning of the season;
- the beginning of the license period; or
- the date the event occurs (e.g. game-by-game basis).

The issue of when a licensor recognises revenue on the sale of such broadcast rights is covered in Chapter 28 at 5.10.

3 MEASUREMENT

The standard's basic rule is that inventories are measured at the lower of cost and net realisable value, apart from those inventories scoped out of its measurement requirements as explained above. *[IAS 2.9]*. Net realisable value is 'the estimated selling price in the ordinary course of business less the estimated costs of completion and the estimated costs necessary to make the sale.' *[IAS 2.6]*. Fair value is defined, as in IFRS 13 – *Fair Value Measurement*, as 'the price that would be received to sell an asset or paid to transfer a liability in an orderly transaction between market participants at the measurement date.' *[IAS 2.6]*. The standard points out that net realisable value is an entity-specific value, the amount that the entity actually expects to make from selling that particular inventory, while fair value is not. Therefore, net realisable value may not be the same as fair value less costs to sell. *[IAS 2.7]*. This is illustrated in the following example in which net realisable value is based on estimated future sales prices of the product.

Extract 22.1: AngloGold Ashanti Limited (2012)

Notes to the AngloGold Ashanti Limited Integrated Report 2012 [extract]

1.2 Significant accounting judgements and estimates [extract]

Use of estimates [extract]

Stockpiles, metals in process and ore on leach pad [extract]

Costs that are incurred in or benefit the production process are accumulated as stockpiles, metals in process and ore on leach pads. Net realisable value tests are performed at least annually and represent the estimated future sales price of the product, based on prevailing and long-term metals prices, less estimated costs to complete production and bring the product to sale.

Care must be taken if an entity asserts that net realisable value is significantly higher than fair value. This can happen if there has been a downturn in a cyclical business such as real estate and may indicate that the selling price has declined and time taken to dispose of assets has increased. Net realisable value is discussed at 3.4 below.

This basic measurement rule inevitably raises the question of what may be included in an inventory's cost.

3.1 What may be included in cost?

The costs attributed to inventories under IAS 2 comprise all costs of purchase, costs of conversion and other costs incurred in bringing the inventories to their present location and condition. *[IAS 2.10]*. These costs include import duties and other unrecoverable taxes, transport and other costs directly attributable to the inventories. Trade discounts and similar rebates should be deducted from the costs attributed to inventories. *[IAS 2.11]*. For example a supplier may pay to its customer an upfront cash incentive when entering into a contract. This is a form of rebate and the incentive should be accounted for as a liability by the customer until it receives the related inventory, which is then shown at cost net of this incentive.

Costs of conversion include direct costs such as direct labour and materials, as well as an allocation of fixed and variable production overheads. It must be remembered that the inclusion of overheads is not optional. Overheads may comprise indirect labour and materials or other indirect costs of production. For the most part there are few problems over the inclusion of direct costs in inventories although difficulties may arise over the inclusion of certain types of overheads and over the allocation of overheads into the inventory valuation. Overhead costs must be apportioned using a 'systematic allocation of fixed and variable production overheads that are incurred in converting materials into finished goods'. *[IAS 2.12]*. Overheads should be allocated to the cost of inventory on a consistent basis from year to year, and should not be omitted in anticipation of a net realisable value problem.

Variable production overheads are indirect costs that vary with the volume of production such as indirect material and indirect labour. *[IAS 2.12]*. Fixed production overheads are indirect costs that remain relatively constant over a wide range of production, such as building and equipment maintenance and depreciation, and factory management expenses. The allocation of fixed production overheads is based on the normal capacity of the facilities. Normal capacity is defined as 'the production expected to be achieved on average over a number of periods or seasons under normal circumstances, taking into account the loss of capacity resulting from planned maintenance.' *[IAS 2.13]*. While actual capacity may be used if it approximates to normal capacity, increased overheads may not be allocated to production as a result of low output or idle capacity. In these cases the unrecovered overheads must be expensed. Similarly, in periods of abnormally high production, the fixed overhead absorption must be reduced, as otherwise inventories would be recorded at an amount in excess of cost. *[IAS 2.13]*.

In computing the costs to be allocated via the overhead recovery rate, costs such as distribution and selling must be excluded, together with cost of storing raw materials and work in progress, unless it is necessary that storage costs be incurred prior to further processing, which may occasionally be the case (see 3.1.1 below).

The assumptions about normal levels of activity relate to all costs including direct costs. Although determining the normal level of activity when allocating overheads is a judgemental area, it is relatively straightforward when dealing with the manufacturing and processing of physical inventory. It is far harder to establish what this can mean in the context of service industries where the 'inventory' is intangible and based on work performed for customers that has not yet been recognised as income. There really is no equivalent to the normal capacity of production facilities in these cases. However, the standard still requires the inclusion of attributable overheads, and entities must take care to establish an appropriate benchmark to avoid the distortions that could occur if overheads were attributed on the basis of actual 'output'.

Extract 22.2 below shows how Syngenta AG describes its inventory valuation policies.

Extract 22.2: Syngenta AG (2012)

Notes to the Syngenta Group Consolidated Financial Statements [extract]

2. Accounting policies [extract]

Inventories

Purchased products are recorded at acquisition cost while own-manufactured products are recorded at manufacturing cost including a share of production overheads based on normal capacity. Cost is determined on a first-in-first-out basis. Allowances are made for inventories with a net realizable value less than cost, or which are slow moving. Net realizable value is the estimated selling price in the ordinary course of business, less the estimated costs of completion and costs to sell. Costs to sell include direct marketing, selling and distribution costs. Unsalable inventories are fully written off.

IAS 2 mentions the treatment to be adopted when a production process results in the output of more than one product, for example a main product and a by-product. If the costs of converting each product are not separately identifiable, they should be allocated between the products on a rational and consistent basis; for example this might be the relative sales value of each of the products. If the value of the by-product is immaterial, it may be measured at net realisable value and this value deducted from the cost of the main product. *[IAS 2.14]*.

Other costs are to be included in inventories only to the extent that they bring them into their present location and condition. An example is given in IAS 2 of design costs for a special order for a particular customer as being allowable, *[IAS 2.15]*, and as a result other non-production overheads may possibly be appropriately included. However a number of examples are given of costs that are specifically disallowed. These include:

(a) abnormal amounts of wasted materials, labour, or other production costs;

(b) storage costs, unless those costs are necessary in the production process prior to a further production stage;

(c) administrative overheads that do not contribute to bringing inventories to their present location and condition; and

(d) selling costs. *[IAS 2.16]*.

3.1.1 Storage and distribution costs

Storage costs are not permitted as part of the cost of inventory unless they are necessary in the production process. *[IAS 2.16(b)]*. This appears to prohibit including the costs of the warehouse and the overheads of a retail outlet as part of inventory, as neither of these is a prelude to a further production stage.

Where it is necessary to store raw materials or work in progress prior to a further processing or manufacturing stage, the costs of such storage should be included in production overheads. For example, it would appear reasonable to allow the costs of storing maturing stocks, such as cheese, wine or whisky, in the cost of production.

Although distribution costs are obviously a cost of bringing an item to its present location, the question arises as to whether costs of transporting inventory from one location to another are eligible.

Costs of distribution to the customer are not allowed; they are selling costs and the standard prohibits their inclusion in the carrying value of inventory. It therefore seems probable that distribution costs of inventory whose production process is complete should not normally be included in its carrying value. If the inventory is transferred from one of the entity's storage facilities to another and the condition of the inventory is not changed at either location, none of the warehousing costs may be included in inventory costs. The same argument appears to preclude transportation costs between the two storage facilities.

A question arises about the meaning of 'production' in the context of large retailers, for example supermarkets. As the transport and logistics involved are essential to their ability to put goods on sale at a particular location in an appropriate condition, it seems reasonable to conclude that such costs are an essential part of the production process and can be included in the cost of inventory.

The circumstances of the entity may warrant the inclusion of distribution or other costs into cost of sales even though they have been excluded from the cost of inventory. *[IAS 2.38]*. Disclosure is discussed at 6 below.

3.1.2 General and administrative overheads

IAS 2 specifically disallows administrative overheads that do not contribute to bringing inventories to their present location and condition. *[IAS 2.16]*. Other costs and overheads that do contribute are allowable as costs of production. There is a judgement to be made about such matters, as on a very wide interpretation any department could be considered to make a contribution. For example, the accounts department will normally support the following functions:

(a) production – by paying direct and indirect production wages and salaries, by controlling purchases and related payments, and by preparing periodic financial statements for the production units;

(b) marketing and distribution – by analysing sales and by controlling the sales ledger; and

(c) general administration – by preparing management accounts and annual financial statements and budgets, by controlling cash resources and by planning investments.

Only those costs of the accounts department that can be allocated to the production function can be included in the cost of conversion. Part of the management and overhead costs of a large retailer's logistical department may be included in cost if it can be related to bringing the inventory to its present location and condition. These types of cost are unlikely to be material in the context of the inventory total held by organisations. In our view, an entity wishing to include a material amount of overhead of a borderline nature must ensure it can sensibly justify its inclusion under the provisions of IAS 2 by presenting an analysis of the function and its contribution to the production process similar to the above.

3.1.3 Borrowing costs

IAS 2 states that, in limited circumstances, borrowing costs are to be included in the costs of inventories. *[IAS 2.17]*. IAS 23 – *Borrowing Costs* – requires that borrowing costs be capitalised on qualifying assets but the scope of that standard exempts inventories that are manufactured in large quantities on a repetitive basis. *[IAS 23.4, 8]*. In addition, IAS 23 clarifies that inventories manufactured over a short period of time are not qualifying assets. *[IAS 23.7]*. However, any manufacturer that is producing small quantities over a long time period has to capitalise borrowing costs. This is further discussed in Chapter 21.

IAS 2 also states that on some occasions, an entity might purchase inventories on deferred settlement terms, accompanied by a price increase that effectively makes the arrangement a combined purchase and financing. Under these circumstances the price difference is recognised as an interest expense over the period of the financing. *[IAS 2.18]*.

3.1.4 Service providers

IAS 2 deals specifically with the inventories of service providers – effectively their work-in-progress. For this type of business, IAS 2 requires the labour and other costs of personnel directly engaged in providing the service, including supervisory personnel and attributable overheads, to be included in the cost of inventories. However, labour and other costs relating to sales and general administrative personnel must be expensed as incurred. Inventories should not include profit margins or non-attributable overheads. *[IAS 2.19]*. As discussed in 3.1 above, service providers may find it a challenge to establish 'normal capacity' for the purposes of allocating attributable overheads.

3.1.5 Forward contracts to purchase inventory

The standard scopes out commodity broker-traders that measure inventory at fair value less costs to sell from its measurement requirements (see 2 above). If a broker-trader had a forward contract for purchase of inventory this contract would be accounted for as a derivative under IAS 39 – *Financial Instruments: Recognition and Measurement* – since it would not meet the normal purchase or sale exemption (see Chapter 42 at 5.2) and when the contract was physically settled the inventory would likewise be shown at fair value less costs to sell. *[IAS 2.3(b)]*. However, if such an entity were not measuring inventory at fair value less costs to sell it would be subject to the measurement requirements of IAS 2 and would therefore have to record the inventory at the lower of cost and net realisable value. This raises the question: what is cost when such an entity takes delivery of inventory that has been purchased with a forward contract?

On delivery, the cash paid (i.e. the fixed price agreed in the forward contract) is in substance made up of two elements:

(i) an amount that settles the forward contract; and

(ii) an amount that represents the 'cost of purchase', being the market price at the date of purchase.

This 'cost of purchase' represents the forward contract price adjusted for the derivative asset or liability. For example, assume that the broker-trader was purchasing oil and the forward contracted price was $140 per barrel of oil, but at the time of delivery the spot price of oil was $150 and the forward contract had a fair value of $10 at that date. The oil would be recorded at the fair value on what is deemed to be the purchase date of $150. The $140 cash payment would in substance consist of $150 payment for the inventory offset by a $10 receipt on settlement of the derivative contract, which would be separately accounted for. This is exactly the same result as if the entity had been required to settle the derivative immediately prior to, and separate from, the physical delivery of the oil.

If the entity purchasing the oil in the example above is not a broker-trader, and the acquisition meets the normal purchase or sale exemption given in IAS 32 – *Financial Instruments: Presentation*, the purchase of oil would be recognised at the entity's cost thereof, in terms of IAS 2, that is $140 per barrel of oil.

3.1.6 Drug production costs within the pharmaceutical industry

After the development stage, pharmaceutical companies often commence production of drugs prior to obtaining the necessary regulatory approval to sell them. As long as the regulatory approval has been applied for and it is believed highly likely that this will be successfully obtained then it is appropriate to be recognising an asset and classifying this as inventory. Prior to this application for regulatory approval being made any costs would need to be classified as research and development costs rather than inventory and the criteria within IAS 38 assessed to determine if capitalisation was appropriate (see Chapter 17 at 6.2.3).

3.2 Cost measurement methods

IAS 2 specifically allows the use of the standard cost method, or of the retail method, provided that the chosen method gives a result which approximates to cost. Standard costs should take into account normal levels of materials and supplies, labour, efficiency and capacity utilisation. They must be regularly reviewed and revised where necessary. *[IAS 2.21]*. Normal levels of activity are discussed in 3.1 above.

The retail method is typically used in businesses with high volumes of various line items of inventory, where similar mark-ups are applied to ranges of inventory items or groups of items. It may be unnecessarily time-consuming to determine the cost of the period-end inventory on a conventional basis. Consequently, the most practical method of determining period-end inventory may be to record inventory on hand at selling prices, and then convert it to cost by adjusting for a normal margin.

A judgemental area in applying the retail method is in determining the margin to be removed from the selling price of inventory in order to convert it back to cost. The percentage has to take account of circumstances in which inventories have been marked down to below original selling price. Adjustments have to be made to eliminate the effect of these markdowns so as to prevent any item of inventory being valued at less than both its cost and its net realisable value. In practice, however, entities that use the retail method apply a gross profit margin computed on an average basis appropriate for departments and/or ranges, rather than applying specific mark-up percentages. This practice is, in fact, acknowledged by IAS 2, which states: 'an average percentage for each retail department is often used'. *[IAS 2.22].*

Items that are not interchangeable and goods or services produced for specific projects should have their costs specifically identified, *[IAS 2.23]*, and these costs will be matched with the goods physically sold. In practice this is a relatively unusual method of valuation, as the clerical effort required does not make it feasible unless there are relatively few high value items being bought or produced. Consequently, it would normally be used where the inventory comprised items such as antiques, jewellery and automobiles in the hands of dealers. This method is inappropriate where there are large numbers of items that are interchangeable, as specific identification of costs could distort the profit or loss arising from these inventories. *[IAS 2.24].*

Where it is necessary to use a cost-flow assumption (i.e. when there are large numbers of ordinarily interchangeable items), IAS 2 allows either a FIFO (first-in, first-out) or a weighted average cost formula to be used. *[IAS 2.25].*

(a) *FIFO* – In the vast majority of businesses it will not be practicable to keep track of the cost of identical items of inventory on an individual unit basis; nevertheless, it is desirable to approximate to the actual physical flows as far as possible. The FIFO method probably gives the closest approximation to actual cost flows, since it is assumed that when inventories are sold or used in a production process, the oldest are sold or used first. Consequently the balance of inventory on hand at any point represents the most recent purchases or production. *[IAS 2.27].* This can best be illustrated in the context of a business which deals in perishable goods (e.g. food retailers) since clearly such a business will use the first goods received earliest. The FIFO method, by allocating the earliest costs incurred against revenue, matches actual cost flows with the physical flow of goods reasonably accurately. In any event, even in the case of businesses which do not deal in perishable goods, this would reflect what would probably be a sound management policy. In practice, the FIFO method is generally used where it is not possible to value inventory on an actual cost basis;

(b) *Weighted average* – This method, which like FIFO is suitable where inventory units are identical or nearly identical, involves the computation of an average unit cost by dividing the total cost of units by the number of units. The average unit cost then has to be revised with every receipt of inventory, or alternatively at the end of predetermined periods. *[IAS 2.27].* In practice, weighted average systems are widely used in packaged inventory systems that are computer controlled, although its results are not very different from FIFO in times of relatively low inflation, or where inventory turnover is relatively quick.

LIFO (last-in, first-out), as its name suggests, is the opposite of FIFO and assumes that the most recent purchases or production are used first. In certain cases this could represent the physical flow of inventory (e.g. if a store is filled and emptied from the top). However it is not an acceptable method under IAS 2. LIFO is an attempt to match current costs with current revenues so that the profit and loss account excludes the effects of holding gains or losses. Essentially, therefore, LIFO is an attempt to achieve something closer to replacement cost accounting for the statement of profit or loss, whilst disregarding the statement of financial position. Consequently, the period-end balance of inventory on hand represents the earliest purchases of the item, resulting in inventories being stated in the statement of financial position at amounts which may bear little relationship to recent cost levels. Unlike under IFRS, LIFO is allowable under US GAAP, and is popular in the US as the Internal Revenue Service officially recognises LIFO as an acceptable method for the computation of tax provided that it is used consistently for tax and financial reporting purposes.

The standard makes it clear that the same cost formula should be used for all inventories having a similar nature and use to the entity, although items with a different nature and use may justify the use of a different cost formula. *[IAS 2.25]*. For example the standard acknowledges that inventories used in one operating segment may have a use to the entity different from the same type of inventories used in another operating segment. However, a difference in geographical location of inventories (or in their respective tax rules) is not sufficient, by itself, to justify the use of different cost formulas. *[IAS 2.26]*.

An entity may choose, as a result of particular facts and circumstances, to change its cost formula, for instance, from a FIFO-based cost formula to a weighted average cost formula. The change in a cost formula represents a change in the basis on which the value of the inventory has been determined, rather than a change in valuation of the inputs used to determine the cost of the inventory. An accounting policy is defined in IAS 8 – *Accounting Policies, Changes in Accounting Estimates and Errors* – as including specific bases applied by an entity in preparing and presenting financial statements. Therefore a change in the cost formula represents a change in accounting policy which should only be made if it results in the financial statements providing reliable and more relevant information. If material, the change in accounting policy will have to be dealt with as a prior period adjustment in accordance with IAS 8 (see Chapter 3 at 4.4).

3.3 Transfers of rental assets to inventory

An entity may, in the course of its ordinary activities, routinely sell items that had previously been held for rental and classified as property, plant and equipment. For example, car rental companies may acquire vehicles with the intention of holding them as rental cars for a limited period and then selling them. IAS 16 requires that when such items become held for sale rather than rental they be transferred to inventory at their carrying value. *[IAS 16.68A]*. Revenue from the subsequent sale is then recognised gross rather than net, as discussed in Chapter 18 at 7.2.

3.4 Net realisable value

IAS 2 carries substantial guidance on the identification of net realisable value, where this is below cost and therefore inventory must be written down.

The cost of inventory may have to be reduced to its net realisable value if the inventory has become damaged, is wholly or partly obsolete, or if its selling price has declined. The costs of inventory may not be recovered from sale because of increases in the costs to complete, or the estimated selling costs. *[IAS 2.28]*. However the costs to consider in making this assessment should only comprise direct costs to complete and sell the inventory and will not include any profit margin on these activities.

Selling costs are excluded from the cost of inventory and are expensed as incurred; of course, the selling price takes account of the expected costs of sale. Selling costs include direct costs that are only incurred when the item is sold, e.g. sales commissions, and indirect costs, which are those overheads that enable sales to take place, including sales administration and the costs of retail activities. If inventory is not impaired then the distinction between direct and indirect costs is not relevant as both are expensed as incurred. *[IAS 2.16]*. It is clear that costs to be reflected in the write down to NRV must be incremental but Paragraph 28 does not distinguish between direct and indirect costs. This allows for different interpretations. In practice there may be few incremental increases in indirect costs that will cause inventory to be sold at a loss.

Writing inventory down to net realisable value should normally be done on an item-by-item basis. IAS 2 specifically states that it is not appropriate to write down an entire class of inventory, such as finished goods, or all the inventory of a particular segment. However, it may be necessary to write down an entire product line or group of inventories in a given geographical area if the items cannot be practicably evaluated separately. Service contracts usually accumulate costs on a contract-by-contract basis and net realisable value must be considered on this basis. *[IAS 2.29]*.

Estimates of net realisable value must be based on the most reliable evidence available and take into account fluctuations of price or cost after the end of the period if this is evidence of conditions existing at the end of the period. *[IAS 2.30]*. A loss realised on a sale of a product after the end of the period may well provide evidence of the net realisable value of that product at the end of the period. However if this product is, for example, an exchange traded commodity, and the loss realised can be attributed to a fall in prices on the exchange after the period end date, then this loss would not, in itself, provide evidence of the net realisable value at the period end date.

Estimates of net realisable value must also take into account the purpose for which the inventory is held. Therefore inventory held for a particular contract has its net realisable value based on the contract price, and only any excess inventory held would be based on current market prices. If there is a firm contract to sell and this is in excess of inventory quantities that the entity holds or is able to obtain under a firm purchase contract, this may give rise to a liability that should be provided for in accordance with IAS 37 – *Provisions, Contingent Liabilities and Contingent Assets* (see Chapter 27). *[IAS 2.31]*.

IAS 2 explains that materials and other supplies held for use in the production of inventories are not written down below cost if the final product in which they are to be used is expected to be sold at or above cost. *[IAS 2.32]*. This is the case even if these materials in their present condition have a net realisable value that is below cost and would therefore otherwise require write down. Thus, a whisky distiller would not write down an inventory of grain because of a fall in the grain price, so long as it expected to sell the whisky at a price which is sufficient to recover cost. If a decline in the price of materials indicates that the cost of the final product will exceed net realisable value then a write down is necessary and the replacement cost of those materials may be the best measure of their net realisable value. *[IAS 2.32]*. If an entity writes down any of its finished goods, the carrying value of any related raw materials must also be reviewed to see if they too need to be written down.

Often raw materials are used to make a number of different products. In these cases it is normally not possible to arrive at a particular net realisable value for each item of raw material based on the selling price of any one type of finished item. If the current replacement cost of those raw materials is less than their historical cost, a provision is only required to be made if the finished goods into which they will be made are expected to be sold at a loss. No provision should be made just because the anticipated profit will be less than normal.

When the circumstances that previously caused inventories to be written down below cost no longer exist, or when there is clear evidence of an increase in net realisable value because of changed economic circumstances, the amount of the write-down is reversed. The reversal cannot be greater than the amount of the original write-down, so that the new carrying amount will always be the lower of the cost and the revised net realisable value. *[IAS 2.33]*.

3.5 Consignment stock and sale and repurchase agreements

A seller may enter into an arrangement with a distributor where the distributor sells inventory on behalf of the seller. Such consignment arrangements are common in certain industries, such as the automotive industry. IAS 18 – *Revenue* – requires entities to recognise revenue (and therefore derecognise inventory) only if the substantial risks and rewards of ownership have been transferred to the customer.

Similarly, entities may enter into sale and repurchase agreements with a customer where the seller agrees to repurchase inventory under particular circumstances. For example the seller may agree to repurchase any inventory that the customer has not sold to a third party after six months. IAS 18 gives some guidance on when revenue can be recognised in these types of transaction in the illustrative examples to the standard. Recognition of revenue for consignment sales and sale and repurchase transactions is considered in Chapter 28 at 5.1.

There is no other specific guidance on these types of inventories in IFRS and so entities need to ensure they adopt an appropriate and consistent accounting policy for derecognising inventory and recognising revenue that reflects the commercial substance of these transactions.

Extract 22.3: Volkswagen AG (2012)

Notes to the consolidated financial statements of the Volkswagen Group as of December 31, 2012 [extract]

Accounting policies [extract]

Revenue and expense recognition [extract]

Income from assets for which a Group company has a buy back obligation is recognized only when the assets have definitively left the Group. If a fixed repurchase price was agreed when the contract was entered into, the difference between the selling and repurchase price is recognized as income ratably over the term of the contract. Prior to that time, the assets are carried as inventories in the case of short contract terms and as leasing and rental assets in the case of long contract terms.

The entity will also have to consider appropriate disclosure for material amounts of inventory that is held on consignment or sale and return at a third party's premises.

4 REAL ESTATE INVENTORY

4.1 Classification of real estate as inventory

Many real estate businesses develop and construct residential properties for sale, and these developments often consist of several units. The strategy is to make a profit from the development and construction of the property rather than to make a profit in the long term from general price increases in the property market. The intention is to sell the property units as soon as possible following their construction and the sale is therefore in the ordinary course of the entity's business. When construction is complete it is not uncommon for individual property units to be leased at market rates to earn revenues to partly cover expenses such as interest, management fees, and real estate taxes. Large-scale buyers of property, such as insurance companies, are often reluctant to buy unless tenants are *in situ*, as this assures immediate cash flows from the investment.

It is our view that if it is in the entity's ordinary course of business (supported by its strategy) to hold property for short-term sale rather than for long-term capital appreciation or rental income, the entire property (including the leased units) should be accounted for and presented as inventory. This will continue to be the case as long as it remains the intention to sell the property in the short term. Rent received should be included in other income as it does not represent a reduction in the cost of inventory.

Investment property is defined in IAS 40 as 'property ... held ... to earn rentals or for capital appreciation or both, rather than for ... use in the production or supply of goods or services or for administrative purposes; or ... for sale in the ordinary course of business.' *[IAS 40.5]*. Therefore in the case outlined above, the property does not meet the definition of investment property. Properties intended for sale in the ordinary course of business – no matter whether leased out or not – are outside the scope of IAS 40. However, if a property is not intended for sale, IAS 40 requires it to be transferred from inventory to investment property when there is a change in use. The change can be evidenced by the commencement of an operating lease to another party (see Chapter 19 at 9).

4.2 Costs of real estate inventory

4.2.1 Allocation of costs to individual units in multi-unit developments

A real estate developer of a multi-unit complex will be able to track and record various costs that are specific to individual units, such as individual fit out costs. However there will also be various costs that are incurred which are not specific to any individual unit, such as the costs of land and any shared facilities, and a methodology will be required to allocate these costs to the individual units. This will of course impact the profit that is recognised on the sale of each individual unit.

There are two general approaches to this allocation, both of which we believe are acceptable under IAS 2. The first approach is to allocate these non-unit specific costs based on some relative cost basis. A reasonable proxy of relative cost is likely to be the size of each unit and hence an appropriate methodology would be to allocate the non-unit specific cost per square metre to the individual units based upon the floor area of each unit. Another proxy of (total) relative cost may be the use of the specific cost of each unit. Marking up the specific cost that is attributable to each unit by a fixed percentage so as to cover and account for the non-unit specific costs would also seem reasonable. This relative cost approach is consistent with the guidance under IAS 2 in respect of allocation of overheads which requires a 'systematic allocation of variable and production overheads'. *[IAS 2.12]*.

The second approach would be to allocate these non-unit specific costs based on the relative sales value of each unit. This methodology is specifically referred to by the standard in the context of where a production process results in more than one product being produced simultaneously. *[IAS 2.14]*. This latter approach will lead to a more consistent profit margin being achieved on the sale of each unit.

Whichever approach is adopted it must be used consistently. In addition the developer should initially, as far as is practicable, segregate the non-unit specific costs between any commercial, retail and residential components before applying these methodologies.

4.2.2 Property demolition and operating lease costs

During the course of a property redevelopment project, an existing building may need to be demolished in order for the new development to take place. Should the cost of the existing building that will be demolished be capitalised as part of the construction cost for the new building to be erected on the same piece of land, or should the cost of the original building be derecognised and charged to profit or loss?

In all such cases judgement must be made on the basis of the particular facts involved, as the exact circumstances of the entity will bear upon the decision. There are three distinct scenarios to consider:

(a) the entity is the owner-occupier, in which case the matter falls under IAS 16;

(b) the entity holds the property to earn rentals, in which case the matter falls under IAS 40;

(c) the entity sells such properties in its normal course of business.

IAS 2 defines inventories as assets (a) held for sale in the ordinary course of business; or (b) in the process of production for such sale; or (c) in the form of materials or supplies to be consumed in the production process or in the rendering of services. *[IAS 2.6]*. The cost of inventories must comprise all costs of purchase, costs of conversion and other costs incurred in bringing the inventories to their present location and condition. *[IAS 2.10]*.

If it is the strategy of the developer to sell the developed property after construction, the new development falls within the scope of IAS 2, as it would be considered held for sale in the normal course of business by the developer. The cost of the old building as well as demolition costs and costs of developing the new one would be treated as inventory, but must still be subject to the normal 'lower of cost and net realisable value' requirements.

In our view a similar approach can be applied to lease costs for the land upon which a building is being constructed. The amount that can be included in inventory will depend on whether the entity considers the land lease to be a finance lease or an operating lease.

- If it is a finance lease, depreciation is an example of a fixed cost that can be considered a cost of conversion. *[IAS 2.12]*. IAS 2 states that, in limited circumstances, borrowing costs are to be included in the costs of inventories. *[IAS 2.17]*. It is quite possible that buildings constructed for disposal under a finance lease could meet these criteria. See the discussion at 3.1.3 above.
- If the entity considers it to be an operating lease, the operating lease costs could be considered costs of conversion.

  Alternatively, the entity could consider that the operating lease costs are for the right to control the land during the lease period rather than costs in bringing this inventory to any particular condition, in which case it may be appropriate to expense the costs.

5 RECOGNITION IN PROFIT OR LOSS

IAS 2 specifies that when inventory is sold, the carrying amount of the inventory must be recognised as an expense in the period in which the revenue is recognised.

Judging when to recognise revenue (and therefore to charge the inventory expense) is one of the more complex accounting issues that can arise, particularly in the context of extended payment arrangements and manufacturer financing of sales to customers. In some industries, for example automobile manufacturing and retailing, aircraft manufacturing, railway carriage manufacturing and maintenance, and mobile phone handset retailing, it is customary for the goods concerned to be subject to extended and complex delivery, sales and settlement arrangements. For these types of transactions, the accounting problem that arises principally concerns when to recognise revenue, the consequent derecognition of inventory being driven by the revenue recognition judgement, not vice-versa.

Revenue recognition is dealt with in Chapter 28, to which reference should be made in considering such issues.

Inventory that goes into the creation of another asset, for instance into a self-constructed item of property, plant or equipment, would form part of the cost of that asset. Subsequently these costs are expensed through the depreciation of that item of property, plant and equipment during its useful life. *[IAS 2.35].*

Any write-downs or losses of inventory must be recognised as an expense when the write-down or loss occurs. Reversals of previous write-downs are recognised as a reduction in the inventory expense recognised in the period in which the reversal occurs. *[IAS 2.34].* An entity cannot continue to recognise inventory over which it has no control as an asset, because it has not, for some reason, recognised revenue.

6 DISCLOSURE REQUIREMENTS OF IAS 2

The financial statements should disclose:

(a) the accounting policies adopted in measuring inventories, including the cost formula used;

(b) the total carrying amount of inventories and the carrying amount in classifications appropriate to the entity;

(c) the carrying amount of inventories carried at fair value less costs to sell;

(d) the amount of inventories recognised as an expense during the period;

(e) the amount of any write-down of inventories recognised as an expense in the period;

(f) the amount of any reversal of any write-down that is recognised as a reduction in the amount of inventories recognised as expense in the period;

(g) the circumstances or events that led to the reversal of a write-down of inventories; and

(h) the carrying amount of inventories pledged as security for liabilities. *[IAS 2.36].*

IAS 2 does not specify the precise classifications that must be used to comply with (b) above. However it states that 'information about the carrying amounts held in different classifications of inventories and the extent of the changes in these assets is useful to financial statement users', and suggests suitable examples of common classifications such as merchandise, production supplies, materials, work-in-progress, and finished goods. *[IAS 2.37].*

Extract 22.4 below shows how the Unilever Group disclosed the relevant information.

Extract 22.4: Unilever N.V. (2012)

Notes to the consolidated financial statements [extract]

12. Inventories [extract]

Inventories	**€ million 2012**	€ million 2011
Raw materials and consumables	**1,517**	1,584
Finished goods and goods for resale	**2,919**	3,017
	4,436	4,601

Inventories with a value of €143 million (2011: €158 million) are carried at net realisable value, this being lower than cost. During 2012, €131 million (2011: €99 million) was charged to the income statement for damaged, obsolete and lost inventories. In 2012, €71 million (2011: €43 million) was utilised or released to the income statement from inventory provisions taken in earlier years.

The amount of inventory recognised as an expense in the period is normally included in cost of sales; this category includes unallocated production overheads and abnormal costs as well as the costs of inventory that has been sold. However, the circumstances of the entity may warrant the inclusion of distribution or other costs in cost of sales. *[IAS 2.38]*. Hence when a company presents its profit or loss based upon this function of expense or 'cost of sales' method it will normally be disclosing costs that are greater than those that have previously been classified as inventory, but this appears to be explicitly allowable by the standard.

Extract 22.5 below shows how Stora Enso classified its inventories in its 2012 financial statements.

Extract 22.5: Stora Enso Oyj (2012)

Notes to the Consolidated Financial Statements [extract]

Note 17 Inventories

	As at 31 December	
EUR million	**2012**	**2011**
Materials and supplies	343.8	400.6
Work in progress	80.3	68.7
Finished goods	703.9	713.0
Spare parts and consumables	282.6	275.2
Other inventories	16.5	27.7
Advance payments and cutting rights	147.8	150.1
Obsolescence allowance – spare parts and consumables	–98.3	–87.6
Obsolescence allowance – finished goods	–14.7	–14.9
Net realisable value allowance	–4.4	–4.1
Total	**1 457.5**	**1 528.7**

Some entities adopt a format for profit or loss that results in amounts other than the cost of inventories being disclosed as an expense during the period. This will happen if an entity presents an analysis of expenses using a classification based on the nature of expenses. The entity then discloses the costs recognised as an expense for raw materials and consumables, labour costs and other costs together with the amount of the net change in inventories for the period. *[IAS 2.39]*.

Formats for the presentation of profit or loss are discussed in Chapter 3.

References

1 Exposure Draft – *Revenue from Contracts with Customers,* revised November 2011.

Chapter 23 Construction contracts

List of examples

Chapter 23 Construction contracts

1 INTRODUCTION

IAS 11 – *Construction Contracts* – deals with the accounting treatment of revenues and costs arising from construction contracts. Like a number of other older standards that have not yet been revised significantly by the IASB (IAS 11 was last revised in 1993), the focus is on the income statement and the basis on which income and expenditure should be recognised. The IASB, in conjunction with the FASB, is developing a new revenue recognition standard. In June 2010, the Boards issued the first Exposure Draft on revenue recognition entitled *Revenue from Contracts with Customers*. After considerable debate, a revised Exposure Draft was issued in November 2011. This joint project and the Exposure Drafts are discussed in Chapter 28 and, as highlighted in that Chapter, the proposals could significantly affect the manner in which revenue is recognised under construction contracts. The IASB's intention is that any standard that results from this project will replace both IAS 18 – *Revenue* – and IAS 11, as well as those Interpretations that address revenue-related matters (e.g. IFRIC 15 – *Agreements for the Construction of Real Estate*).

1.1 Scope and definitions of IAS 11

IAS 11 applies to accounting for construction contracts in the financial statements of the contractor. *[IAS 11.1]*.

A construction contract is defined as follows:

> 'a contract specifically negotiated for the construction of an asset or a combination of assets that are closely interrelated or interdependent in terms of their design, technology and function or their ultimate purpose or use.' *[IAS 11.3]*.

The meaning of 'specifically negotiated for the construction of an asset' has been considered by the Interpretations Committee. Although IFRIC 15 has been written in the specific context of the construction of real estate, it includes an analysis of the distinguishing features of construction contracts and it is, therefore, more generally relevant in determining whether any contract that involves the construction of an asset is within the scope of IAS 11 or is a sale of goods, and within the scope of IAS 18 and IAS 2 – *Inventories* (see 1.2 below).

Something that may be accounted for as a single construction contract can comprise a number of different elements. Single constructions could include a bridge, a building, a dam, a pipeline, a road, a ship or a tunnel. Other single contracts include groups of inter-related assets such as an oil refinery or complex pieces of plant and equipment. *[IAS 11.4]*. Whether a contract is, in fact, a single construction contract or one that should be separated into components, each of which is dealt with individually, is one of the more difficult and subjective areas of contract accounting and one that has also been considered by the Interpretations Committee (see 2 below).

Contracts for services directly related to construction contracts are covered by IAS 11 and not by IAS 18. These include contracts for the services of project managers and architects. Contracts for the demolition and restoration of assets and restoration of the environment after an asset is demolished are also construction contracts. *[IAS 11.5]*.

IAS 11 does not specify any minimum period of duration for a construction contract. This means that any such contract which starts and ends in two different reporting periods will need to be accounted for under this standard. The standard identifies two specific types of construction contract:

> 'A *fixed price contract* is a construction contract in which the contractor agrees to a fixed contract price, or a fixed rate per unit of output, which in some cases is subject to cost escalation clauses;
>
> 'A *cost plus contract* is a construction contract in which the contractor is reimbursed for allowable or otherwise defined costs, plus a percentage of these costs or a fixed fee.' *[IAS 11.3]*.

These types determine the basis on which income is recognised, as discussed at 3.3.1 below.

Contracts that contain elements of both types, e.g. a cost plus contract that has an agreed maximum price, will have to be analysed in order to determine when to recognise contract revenue and expenses. *[IAS 11.6]*.

1.2 Whether an arrangement is a construction contract

Determining whether an arrangement is a construction contract is critical as this determines whether revenue is recognised using the percentage of completion method under IAS 11. Otherwise arrangements are governed by IAS 18, and revenue is not recognised until the risks and rewards of ownership and control have passed. In developing IFRIC 15, the meaning of the term 'construction contract' as defined in IAS 11 was addressed, which helps to clarify the scope of this standard.

IAS 11 defines a construction contract as 'a contract specifically negotiated for the construction of an asset or a combination of assets ...'. *[IAS 11.3]*.

Although IFRIC 15 provides guidance in the particular context of real estate, as described below, it can be applied by analogy to other arrangements that do not include real estate. IFRIC 15 is discussed further in Chapter 28 at 5.12.

Under the Interpretation:

- an agreement for the construction of real estate meets the definition of a construction contract when the buyer is able to specify the major structural elements of the design of the real estate before construction begins and/or specify major structural changes once construction is in progress, whether or not it exercises that ability. When IAS 11 applies, the construction contract also includes any contracts or components for the rendering of services that are directly related to the construction of the real estate. *[IFRIC 15.11]*.
- an agreement for the construction of real estate in which buyers have only limited ability to influence the design of the real estate, for example to select a design from a range of options specified by the entity, or to specify only minor variations to the basic design, is an agreement for the sale of goods and therefore within the scope of IAS 18. *[IFRIC 15.12]*.

Within a single agreement, an entity may contract to deliver goods or services in addition to the construction of real estate (for example a sale of land or provision of property management services – see 3.3.8 below). Such an agreement may need to be split into separately identifiable components, which may include one for the construction of real estate. The fair value of the total consideration received or receivable for the agreement must be allocated to each component. *[IFRIC 15.8]*. The Basis for Conclusions to the Interpretation points to IFRIC 12 – *Service Concession Arrangements* – and IFRIC 13 – *Customer Loyalty Programmes* – for guidance on allocating the fair value. *[IFRIC 15.BC11]*. In these Interpretations it is based on the fair values of the separate components. The segmentation of contracts is discussed below at 2.

The Interpretation assumes that there is revenue to be recognised, i.e. it assumes that the entity retains neither continuing managerial involvement to the degree usually associated with ownership nor effective control over the constructed real estate to an extent that would preclude recognition of some or all of the consideration as revenue. *[IFRIC 15.7]*.

It can be seen that, with these types of contracts in general, there is a range of contractual arrangements for similar products from, at one end, sales of 'off the shelf' items through to large projects where a similar type of asset is constructed to a purchaser's specification. Determining whether an arrangement is a construction contract, which should be accounted for under IAS 11, or a sale of goods, which should be accounted for under IAS 18, is relatively simple in arrangements at either end of this spectrum but can be less clear in other cases.

An example of an entity whose activities cover this range is Vestas Wind Systems A/S whose revenue recognition policy is as follows:

> *Extract 23.1: Vestas Wind Systems A/S (2012)*
> **Notes to the Consolidated Accounts**
> **1. Group accounting policies** [extract]
> **Income statement** [extract]
> **Revenue** [extract]
>
> Revenue comprises sale of wind turbines and wind power systems, aftersales service and sale of spare parts.
>
> Sale of individual wind turbines and small wind power systems based on standard solutions (supply-only and supply-and-installation projects) as well as spare parts sales are recognised in the income statement provided that risk has been transferred to the buyer prior to the year end, and provided that the income can be measured reliably and is expected to be received. Contracts to deliver large wind power systems with a high degree of customisation are recognised in revenue as the systems are constructed based on the stage of completion of the individual contract (turnkey projects). Where the profit from a contract cannot be estimated reliably, revenue is only recognised equalling the expenses incurred to the extent that it is probable that the expenses will be recovered.

1.3 Service concession agreements

Service concession agreements commonly include the construction of an asset followed by a period in which the constructor maintains and services that asset; this secondary period may include asset replacement and refurbishment as well as service elements. Alternatively, the contract might provide for the refurbishment of an existing infrastructure asset together with related services. These agreements provide particular accounting difficulties because they combine contract accounting issues and issues arising from a number of other accounting standards including IAS 11, IAS 17 – *Leases* – and IAS 18. The accounting issues raised by IFRIC 12 are discussed further in Chapter 26.

2 COMBINATION AND SEGMENTATION OF CONTRACTS

IAS 11 should be applied separately to each construction contract. *[IAS 11.7]*. However, in order to reflect the substance of the transaction it may be necessary for a contract to be sub-divided and the standard to be applied individually to each component, or for a group of contracts to be treated as one.

IAS 11 provides guidance in three separate cases. The first is where a single contract covers the construction of a number of separate assets, each of which is in substance a separate contract, i.e.

(a) separate proposals have been submitted for each asset;

(b) the contractor and customer have negotiated separately for each asset and can accept or reject that part of the contract relating to each asset; and

(c) the costs and revenues relating to each asset can be identified. *[IAS 11.8]*.

The second case is effectively the reverse of the first and deals with situations where in substance there is only a single contract with a customer, or a group of customers. This group of contracts should be treated as a single contract where:

(a) the group of contracts is negotiated as a single package;
(b) the contracts are so closely interrelated that they are, in effect, part of a single project with an overall profit margin; and
(c) the contracts are performed concurrently or in a continuous sequence. *[IAS 11.9].*

The third case is where a contract anticipates the construction of a further asset at the customer's discretion. Whether these options should be accounted for in combination with, or separately from, the original contract is discussed at 2.1 below.

One clear weakness of IAS 11 is that it contains little guidance on combining and segmenting contracts. It really only considers the issues in very clear-cut circumstances, i.e. where a number of separate contracts have been negotiated as a single package or where a series of separate contracts have been subsumed within a single contract document but where the individual contracts should be dealt with separately. There is no further guidance in the standard on whether or how individual contracts or groups of contracts should be segmented or combined and contract revenue and costs recognised on the basis of the individual segments or combined contracts. These treatments can have a major effect on the recognition of income. Segmenting a contract can affect the profile of income recognition, perhaps allowing earlier recognition of revenue. If a series of contracts is negotiated as a package with the objective of achieving an overall profit margin, this will not be reflected if the individual contracts are accounted for separately. Inappropriate combining of the segments of a contract could result in the timing of profits or losses not being recognised on the basis required by the standard.

The Interpretations Committee has discussed whether some of the detailed guidance under US GAAP for combining and segmenting contracts (ASC 605-35) should be incorporated into IAS 11 but concluded that it was not appropriate to do so. The Interpretations Committee members were not aware of any significant divergence in practice. They also concluded that, because of differences between the two standards, full convergence of the conditions for combining and segmenting construction contracts could not be achieved simply through interpretation.[1] Therefore these differences will remain until the proposed new revenue recognition model, which is being jointly developed by the IASB and the FASB, comes into effect.

In the meantime the segmentation and combination of construction contracts should be assessed in accordance with paragraphs 8 and 9 of IAS 11, as described above.

2.1 Options for the construction of an additional asset

Another area where it is necessary to consider whether contracts should be combined is in contract options and additions. Once again, combining of contracts is important because of its potential impact on the recognition of revenue and profits on transactions. If the optional asset is treated as part of the original contract, contract revenue will be recognised using the percentage of completion method over the combined contract.

IAS 11 considers the circumstances in which a contract gives a customer an option for an additional asset (or is amended in this manner) and concludes that this should be treated as a new contract if:

(a) the asset differs significantly in design, technology or function from the asset or assets covered by the original contract; or

(b) the price of the asset is negotiated without regard to the original contract price. *[IAS 11.10]*.

This means, for example, that the contract for an additional, identical asset would be treated as a separate contract if its price was negotiated separately from the original contract price. Costs often decline with additional production, not only because of the effects of initial costs but also because of the 'learning curve' (the time taken by the workforce to perform activities decreases with practice and repetition). This could result in a much higher profit margin on the additional contract. If, for example, a government department takes up its option with a defence contractor for five more aircraft, in addition to the original twenty-five that had been contracted for, but the option was unpriced and the new contract is priced afresh, then it cannot be combined with the original contract regardless of the difference in profit margins. Note that this conclusion appears consistent with US GAAP, which would only allow contracts not executed at the same time to be combined if they were negotiated as a package in the same economic environment. This means that the time period between the commitments of the parties to the individual contracts must be reasonably short.[2] Although 'short' is not defined, it is unlikely to cover a period of several years, as could happen in defence contracting.

The combining of contracts may also have unexpected results. If, for example, an entity has a contract with a government to build two satellites and a priced option to build a third, it may be obliged to combine the contracts at the point at which the option is exercised. This could well be in a different accounting period to the commencement of the contract. Using the rules outlined in 3.3.3 below, there will be a cumulative catch-up of revenue, and probably also of profits. In subsequent periods results will be based on the combined contracts.

3 CONTRACT REVENUE, COSTS AND EXPENSES

3.1 Contract revenue

Contract revenue comprises the amount of revenue initially agreed by the parties together with any variations, claims and incentive payments as long as it is probable that they will result in revenue and can be measured reliably. *[IAS 11.11]*. The standard states that such revenue is to be measured at the fair value of the consideration received and receivable. In this context, 'fair value' includes the process whereby the consideration is to be revised as events occur and uncertainties are resolved. These may include contractual matters such as increases in revenue in a fixed price contract as a result of cost escalation clauses or, when a contract involves a fixed price per unit of output, contract revenue may increase as the number of units is increased. Penalties for delays may reduce revenue. In addition, variations and claims must be taken into account. *[IAS 11.12]*. If deferred payments are due after completion of the contract, for example retention payments, such payments will be brought into account at their present value. Similarly if advance payments are received, and these constitute financing transactions, it may be appropriate to accrue interest on them (see Chapter 28 at 5.1.4).

Variations are instructions by the customer to change the scope of the work to be performed under the contract, including changes to the specification or design of the asset or to the duration of the contract. Variations may only be included in contract revenue when it is probable that the customer will approve the variation and the amount to be charged for it, and the amount can be measured reliably. *[IAS 11.13]*.

Given the extended periods over which contracts are carried out and changes in circumstances prevailing whilst the work is in progress, it is quite normal for a contractor to submit claims for additional sums to a customer. Claims may be made for costs not included in the original contract or arising as an indirect consequence of approved variations, such as customer caused delays, errors in specifications or design and disputed variations. Because their settlement is by negotiation, which can in practice be very protracted, they are subject to a high level of uncertainty; consequently, no credit should be taken for them unless negotiations have reached an advanced stage such that:

- it is probable that the customer will accept the claim; and
- the amount that it is probable will be accepted by the customer can be measured reliably. *[IAS 11.14]*.

This means that, as a minimum, the claims must have been agreed in principle and, in the absence of an agreed sum, the amount to be accrued must have been carefully assessed.

Contracts may provide for incentive payments, for example, for early completion or superior performance. They may only be included in contract revenue when the contract is at such a stage that it is probable the required performance will be achieved and the amount can be measured reliably. *[IAS 11.15]*.

Where contract revenue is denominated in a foreign currency it will be necessary to apply an appropriate exchange rate to record that revenue in the functional currency of the entity concerned. IAS 21 – *The Effects of Changes in Foreign Exchange Rates* – requires that foreign currency transactions be recorded at the spot exchange rate at the date of a transaction. *[IAS 21.21]*. Where work is performed on a steady basis over a period of time it may be appropriate to use an average exchange rate for that period.

IAS 11 does not provide explicit guidance on how to incorporate the effect of foreign currency denominated contracts when costs and revenues are denominated in different currencies. For example, an entity with a functional currency of GBP sterling may construct an asset where the revenues received are denominated in US dollars and some of the costs are denominated in Euros. IAS 11 requires an entity to apply percentage of completion when it can establish a reliable estimate of costs and revenues. At the reporting date, costs and revenues (still to be recognised) are generally translated using the spot exchange rate on that date in line with the requirements of IAS 21. Where revenue and costs are denominated in different currencies and are translated at their respective spot rates, this may affect the calculated percentage of completion where the entity determines the stage of completion using the proportion of total costs incurred to date compared to the total estimated contract costs (see 3.3.2 below). Where there is evidence that a different foreign exchange rate provides for a better estimate, an entity applies such other rate provided it can be supported by market information. In such cases, disclosures about management judgments would be necessary in the financial statements.

Progress billings and cost accruals incurred during construction will be recognised at the spot rate on the date the transaction occurs, which may differ from the spot rate at the end of the reporting period. Any remeasurement at the reporting date is presented in profit or loss with other foreign exchange gains or losses.

Changes in foreign exchange rates will only affect the calculated percentage of completion where it is measured using the proportion of total costs incurred to date compared to the total estimated contract costs. Entities using an alternative basis for determining the percentage of completion, such as a survey of the work performed, will not be impacted.

3.2 Contract costs

Contract costs are those that relate directly to the specific contract and to those that are attributable to contract activity in general that can be allocated to the contract. In addition, they include costs that are specifically chargeable to the customer under the terms of the contract. *[IAS 11.16].*

Directly related costs include: *[IAS 11.17]*

(a) direct labour costs, including site supervision;

(b) costs of materials used in construction;

(c) depreciation of plant and equipment used on the contract;

(d) costs of moving plant, equipment and materials to and from the contract site;

(e) costs of hiring plant and equipment;

(f) costs of design and technical assistance that is directly related to the contract;

(g) the estimated costs of rectification and guarantee work, including expected warranty costs; and

(h) claims from third parties.

If the contractor generates incidental income from any directly related cost, e.g. by selling surplus materials and disposing of equipment at the end of the contract, this is treated as a reduction in contract costs. *[IAS 11.17].*

The second category of costs comprises those attributable to contract activity in general that can be allocated to a particular contract. These include design and technical assistance not directly related to an individual contract, insurance, and construction overheads such as the costs of preparing and processing the payroll for the personnel actually working on the contract. These must be allocated using a systematic and rational method, consistently applied to all costs having similar characteristics. Allocation must be based on the normal level of construction activity. *[IAS 11.18].*

There are various costs that, in most circumstances, are specifically precluded by IAS 11 from being attributed to contract activity or allocated to a contract. These include general administration costs, selling costs, research and development costs and the depreciation of idle plant and equipment that is not used on a particular contract. *[IAS 11.20]*. However, the entity is allowed to classify general administration costs and research and development as contract costs if they are specifically reimbursable under the terms of the contract. *[IAS 11.19-20]*. An example is given by EADS, which discloses the following:

> *Extract 23.2: EADS N.V. (2012)*
>
> **Notes to the Consolidated Financial Statements** [extract]
>
> 2.1 **Basis of Presentation** [extract]
>
> 2. **Summary of significant accounting policies** [extract]
>
> **Research and development expenses** [extract]
>
> Research and development expenses – Research and development activities can be (i) contracted or (ii) self-initiated.
>
> (i) Costs for contracted research and development activities, carried out in the scope of externally financed research and development contracts, are expensed when the related revenues are recorded.

Chapter 23

Costs may be attributed to a contract from the date on which it is secured until its final completion. Additionally, costs relating directly to the contract, which have been incurred in gaining the business, may be included in contract costs if they have been incurred once it is probable the contract will be obtained. These costs must be separately identified and measured reliably. *[IAS 11.21]*. This is not dissimilar to the general rules for recognition of an asset. An asset is defined in the Framework as 'a resource controlled by the entity as a result of past events and from which future economic benefits are expected to flow to the entity'. *[Framework.4.4]*. Therefore, we believe that this should be read restrictively and that these costs should not be recognised until they can themselves be seen as an asset of the entity through its control of the future economic benefits from the contract.

An example is from Balfour Beatty plc, which expenses pre-contract costs until it is *virtually certain* that a contract will be awarded.

> *Extract 23.3: Balfour Beatty plc (2012)*
>
> **Notes to the Financial Statements** [extract]
>
> **1.8 Pre-contract bid costs and recoveries** [extract]
>
> Pre-contract costs are expensed as incurred until it is virtually certain that a contract will be awarded, from which time further pre-contract costs are recognised as an asset and charged as an expense over the period of the contract. Amounts recovered in respect of pre-contract costs that have been written off are deferred and amortised over the life of the contract.

Costs that have been written off cannot be reinstated if the contract is obtained in a subsequent period. *[IAS 11.21]*.

Costs incurred in securing a contract include such things as the building of models (including computer modelling exercises) for tender purposes, travelling costs of technicians to survey sites, technical tendering costs, and similar expenses relating specifically to a given contract.

3.2.1 Borrowing costs

Borrowing costs may be specific to individual contracts or attributable to contract activity in general. IAS 23 – *Borrowing Costs* – requires capitalisation of borrowing costs that are directly attributable to the acquisition, construction or production of qualifying assets. [IAS 23.8].

During its debates on accounting for service concessions, the Interpretations Committee concluded that the 'amount due from customers' asset is a financial asset within the scope of IAS 32 – *Financial Instruments: Presentation*. This asset is not a qualifying asset for the purposes of capitalisation of borrowing costs because the treatment requires interest income to be imputed (see Chapter 26 at 4). [IFRIC 12.BC58]. Therefore, once revenue is recognised on work that has been performed, capitalisation of borrowing costs will cease. Only contract costs that related to future activity could be a qualifying asset. In June 2005, the Interpretations Committee decided not to prepare an Interpretation to this effect, stating that it 'was not aware of any evidence that the conclusion was of major importance outside the service concession sector'. The Interpretations Committee noted that it would reconsider this decision if the responses to the draft Interpretations on service concession arrangements indicated otherwise.[3] It did not reconsider. IFRIC 12 was issued in November 2006; the position taken with regard to amounts due from customers, i.e. that they are financial assets, remains unchanged and there has been no other comment on the matter.

The Interpretations Committee's conclusion is significant for all entities engaged in construction contracts if these are deemed to fall under IFRIC 12 and if, under this Interpretation, the operator has a financial asset rather than an intangible asset. Borrowing costs will only be capitalised under IFRIC 12 if the operator has an intangible asset. [IFRIC 12.22]. Where the operator has a financial asset the borrowing costs will need to be expensed and, in addition, part of the contract revenue will be taken as finance income, as income is accreted on the carrying value of the financial asset. [IFRIC 12.BC58]. This changes the profile of income recognition. The implications of this conclusion outside service concessions remain unclear.

3.3 The recognition of contract revenue and expenses

If the basic rule of accounting for inventories were applied to contracts, it would result in an annual income statement that reflected only the outcome of contracts completed during the year. In a contracting company this might bear no relation to the company's actual level of activity for that year. IAS 11 therefore requires revenue and expenses to be recognised on uncompleted contracts in order to present a consistent view of the results of the company's activities during the period and from one period to the next. The underlying principle in IAS 11 is that, once the outcome of a construction contract can be estimated reliably, revenue associated with the construction contract should be recognised by reference to the stage of completion of the contract activity at the end of the reporting period. [IAS 11.22]. The standard does not define the attributable profit in a contract, which will therefore be the balancing figure once revenue and expenses are known.

If it is anticipated that the contract will be loss-making, the expected loss must be recognised immediately. This is described further in 3.3.6 below.

3.3.1 *Types of construction contract*

IAS 11 identifies two types of construction contract, fixed price and cost plus contracts.

3.3.1.A Fixed price contracts

In the case of a fixed price contract, the standard states that the outcome of a construction contract can be estimated reliably when all the conditions discussed below are satisfied.

- First, it must be probable that the economic benefits associated with the contract will flow to the entity, which must be able to measure total contract revenue reliably. As discussed further below, these conditions will usually be satisfied when there are adequate contractual arrangements between the parties;
- Second, both the contract costs to complete the contract and the stage of contract completion at the end of the reporting period must be able to be measured reliably; and
- Third, the entity must be able to identify and measure reliably the contract costs attributable to the contract so that actual contract costs incurred can be compared with prior estimates. *[IAS 11.23].* This means that it must have adequate reporting and budgeting systems.

3.3.1.B Cost plus contracts

Cost plus contracts are not subject to all of the same uncertainties as fixed price contracts. As with any transaction, it must be probable that the economic benefits associated with the contract will flow to the entity in order to recognise income at all. In most contracts this will be evidenced by the contract documentation. The fundamental criterion for a cost plus contract is the proper measurement of contract costs. Therefore, the contract costs attributable to the contract, whether or not specifically reimbursable, must be clearly identified and measured reliably. *[IAS 11.24].*

3.3.2 *The stage of completion method*

There are certain general principles that apply whether the contract is classified as fixed cost or as cost plus. Recognition of revenue is by reference to the 'stage of completion method', also known as the 'percentage of completion method'. Contract revenue and costs are recognised as revenue and expenses in profit or loss in the period in which the work is performed. Any anticipated excess of contract costs over contract income (i.e. a loss on the contract) is recognised as soon as it is anticipated. *[IAS 11.25-26].*

This does not mean that contract activity is necessarily based on the total costs that have been incurred by the entity. Contract costs that relate to future contract activity (i.e. that activity for which revenue has not yet been recognised) may be deferred and recognised as an asset as long as it is probable that they will be recovered. This point is made explicitly by Royal BAM Group nv in Extract 23.5 below. These costs are usually called contract work in progress. *[IAS 11.27].* An example of this may be materials purchased and stored for future use on a contract. Otherwise, contract costs are recognised in the profit or loss as they are incurred.

Importantly, this does not mean that an entity can determine what it considers to be an appropriate profit margin for the whole contract and spread costs over the contract so as to achieve this margin, thereby classifying deferred costs as work in progress. As noted at 3.3 above, IAS 11 defines revenue and contract costs and not attributable profit. The standard does not seek to achieve a uniform profit margin throughout the contract, unless, of course, it is a cost plus contract.

An entity does not adjust the cumulative revenue it has recognised if it transpires in a subsequent period that there are doubts about the recoverability of an amount it has recognised as revenue and it consequently has to make provision against its debtor. Instead the amount that is no longer considered recoverable is written off as an expense. *[IAS 11.28]*.

In order to be able to recognise revenue, the construction entity must be able to make reliable estimates of its income and costs. It is usually possible to do so once the parties have agreed to a contract that establishes both parties' enforceable rights, the contract consideration and the manner and terms of settlement. However, the entity must also be able to review and, where necessary, revise, the estimates of contract revenue and contract costs as the contract progresses. This means that the entity must have an effective system of internal financial budgets and reporting systems. *[IAS 11.29]*.

The standard allows the stage of completion of a contract to be determined in a number of ways, including:

- the proportion that contract costs incurred for work performed to date bear to the estimated total contract costs;
- surveys of work performed; or
- completion of a physical proportion of the contract work. *[IAS 11.30]*.

These could, of course, give different answers regarding the stage of completion of a contract as demonstrated in the following example.

Example 23.1: Determination of revenue

A company is engaged in a construction contract with an expected sales value of £10,000. It is the end of the accounting period during which the company commenced work on this contract and it needs to compute the amount of revenue to be reflected in the profit and loss account for this contract.

Scenario (i) Stage of completion is measured by the proportion that contract costs incurred for work performed to date bear to the estimated total contract costs

The company has incurred and applied costs of £4,000. £3,000 is the best estimate of costs to complete. The company should therefore recognise revenue of £5,714, being the appropriate proportion of total contract value, and computed thus:

$$\frac{4{,}000}{7{,}000} \times 10{,}000 = 5{,}714$$

Scenario (ii) Stage of completion is measured by surveys of work performed

An independent surveyor has certified that at the period-end the contract is 55% complete and that the company is entitled to apply for cumulative progress payments of £5,225 (after a 5% retention). In this case the company would record revenue of £5,500 being the sales value of the work done. (If it is anticipated that rectification work will have to be carried out to secure the release of the retention money then this should be taken into account in computing the stage of completion – but the fact that there is retention of an amount does not, in itself, directly impact the amount of revenue to be recorded.)

Scenario (iii) Stage of completion is measured by completion of a physical proportion of the contract work

The company's best estimate of the physical proportion of the work it has completed is that it is 60% complete. The value of the work done and, therefore, the revenue to be recognised is £6,000.

Note that in each of the above scenarios the computation of the amount of revenue is quite independent of the question of how much (if any) profit should be taken. This is as it should be, because even if a contract is loss-making the sales price will be earned and this should be reflected by recording revenue as the contract progresses. In the final analysis, any loss arises because costs are greater than revenue, and costs should be reflected through cost of sales. Different methods of determining revenue will, as disclosed above, produce different results, which highlights the importance of disclosing the method adopted by the entity.

Where an entity uses a method of determining stage of completion, other than by measuring the proportion of costs incurred to date compared to the total estimated contract cost, an entity may find that the profit margin recognised is not in line with expectations due to the timing of the recognition of costs. For example, a survey of work performed may indicate that the work is 70% complete, but significantly more costs may have been incurred, resulting in a lower than expected profit margin. It is not clear within IAS 11 how such costs could be treated as work in progress. Likewise, if costs incurred are lower than expected, it would normally be inappropriate for entities to accrue for costs not yet incurred. In this circumstance, entities may need to reassess whether the method selected for determining the stage of completion is the most appropriate. The method chosen should accurately reflect progress in the contract and should be applied consistently.

An entity that discloses that it uses a variety of methods to determine revenue is EADS, as shown in the following extract.

Extract 23.4: EADS N.V. (2012)

Notes to the Consolidated Financial Statements [extract]

2.1 **Basis of Presentation** [extract]

2. **Summary of significant accounting policies** [extract]

Revenue recognition [extract]

For construction contracts, when the outcome can be estimated reliably, revenues are recognised by reference to the percentage of completion ("PoC") of the contract activity by applying the estimate at completion method. The stage of completion of a contract may be determined by a variety of ways. Depending on the nature of the contract, revenue is recognised as contractually agreed technical milestones are reached, as units are delivered or as the work progresses. Whenever the outcome of a construction contract cannot be estimated reliably – for example during the early stages of a contract or when this outcome can no longer be estimated reliably during the course of a contract's completion – all related contract costs that are incurred are immediately expensed and revenues are recognised only to the extent of those costs being recoverable ("early stage method of accounting"). In such specific situations, as soon as the outcome can (again) be estimated reliably, revenue is from that point in time onwards accounted for according to the estimate at completion method, without restating the revenues previously recorded under the early stage method of accounting. Changes in profit rates are reflected in current earnings as identified. Contracts are reviewed regularly and in case of probable losses, loss-at-completion provisions are recorded. These loss-at-completion provisions in connection with construction contracts are not discounted.

By contrast, many entities use just one principal method to calculate the percentage of completion.

The Royal BAM Group considers contract costs incurred as a proportion of total costs.

Extract 23.5: Royal BAM Group nv (2012)

3. **Summary of significant accounting policies** [extract]

3.10 Construction contracts [extract]

The Group uses the 'percentage of completion method' to determine the appropriate amount to be recognised in a given period. The stage of completion is measured by reference to the contract cost incurred as a percentage of total actual or estimated project cost. Revenues and result are recognised in the income statement based on this progress.

Projects are presented in the balance sheet as receivables from or payables to customers on behalf of the contract. If the costs incurred (including the result recognised) exceed the invoiced instalments, the contract will be presented as a receivable. If the invoiced instalments exceed the costs incurred (including the result recognised) the contract will be presented as a liability.

Contracts containing the construction of a project and the possibility of subsequent long-term maintenance of that project as separate components, or for which these components could be negotiated individually in the market, are accounted for as two separate contracts. Revenue and results are recognised accordingly in the income statement as construction contracts for third parties or the rendering of services respectively.

The Taylor Wimpey Group relies on surveys of work completed.

Extract 23.6: Taylor Wimpey plc (2012)

Notes to the Consolidated Financial Statements for the year to 31 December 2012 [extract]

1. Significant accounting policies [extract]

Revenue

(d) Contracting work and social housing contracts

Where the outcome of a construction contract can be estimated reliably, revenue and costs are recognised by reference to the stage of completion of the contract activity at the balance sheet date. This is normally measured by surveys of work performed to date. Variations in contract work, claims and incentive payments are included to the extent that it is probable that they will result in revenue and they are capable of being reliably measured.

Where the outcome of a construction contract cannot be estimated reliably, contract revenue is recognised to the extent of contract costs incurred that it is probable will be recoverable. Contract costs are recognised as expenses in the period in which they are incurred. When it is probable that total contract costs will exceed total contract revenue, the expected loss is recognised as an expense immediately.

There are, of course, other ways of measuring work done, e.g. labour hours, which depending upon the exact circumstances might lead to a more appropriate basis for computing revenue.

The above examples apply only to fixed-price contracts. Where a contract is on a cost-plus basis, it is necessary to examine the costs incurred to ensure they are of the type and size envisaged in the terms of the contract. Only once this is done and the recoverable costs identified can the figure be grossed up to arrive at the appropriate revenue figure.

If the stage of completion is determined by reference to the contract costs incurred to date, it is fundamental that this figure includes only those contract costs that reflect work actually performed so far. Any contract costs that relate to future activity on the contract must be excluded. This includes the costs of materials that have been delivered to a contract site or set aside for use in a contract but not yet installed, used or applied during contract performance, unless the materials have been made especially for the contract. Payments made to subcontractors in advance of work performed under the subcontract would similarly not relate to work performed to date and have to be excluded. *[IAS 11.31]*.

Example 23.2: Determination of revenue – exclusion of unapplied costs

The circumstances are as in Scenario (i) of Example 23.1 above. The entity has incurred and applied costs of £4,000. £3,000 is the best estimate of costs to complete. If the costs incurred to date included, say, £500 in respect of unapplied raw materials, then the revenue to be recognised falls to £5,000 being:

$$\frac{\text{costs incurred and applied}}{\text{total costs}} = \frac{(4{,}000 - 500)}{7{,}000} \times 10{,}000 = 5{,}000$$

3.3.3 *Changes in estimates*

The percentage of completion method is applied on a cumulative basis in each accounting period to the current estimates of contract revenues and costs. The effect of any changes in estimates of revenue and costs, or the effect of any change in the estimate of the outcome of a contract, must be treated as a change in accounting estimate, in accordance with IAS 8 – *Accounting Policies, Changes in Accounting Estimates and Errors*. The revised estimates must be used in determining the amount of revenue and expenses recognised in profit or loss in the period in which the change is made, and in subsequent periods. *[IAS 11.38]*.

Where an entity makes assumptions about the future, and is subject to major sources of estimation uncertainty at the end of the reporting period, that have a significant risk of resulting in a material adjustment to the carrying amounts of assets and liabilities within the next financial year, this must be disclosed. *[IAS 1.125]*. An example of an entity that makes disclosures about the uncertainties is Petrofac.

Extract 23.7: Petrofac (2011)

Notes to the Consolidated Accounts [extract]

2 **Summary of significant accounting policies** [extract]

Significant accounting judgements and estimates [extract]

Estimation uncertainty

The key assumptions concerning the future and other key sources of estimation uncertainty at the statement of financial position date, that have a significant risk of causing a material adjustment to the carrying amounts of assets and liabilities within the next financial year are discussed below:

- project cost to complete estimates: at each statement of financial position date the Group is required to estimate costs to complete on fixed-price contracts. Estimating costs to complete on such contracts requires the Group to make estimates of future costs to be incurred, based on work to be performed beyond the statement of financial position date. This estimate will impact revenues, cost of sales, work-in-progress, billings in excess of costs and estimated earnings and accrued contract expenses
- onerous contract provisions: the Group provides for future losses on long-term contracts where it is considered probable that the contract costs are likely to exceed revenues in future years. Estimating these future losses involves a number of assumptions about the achievement of contract performance targets and the likely levels of future cost escalation over time US$ nil (2010: US$2,523,000).

3.3.4 The determination of contract revenue and expenses

It is now possible to see how these features of accounting for construction contracts are put together to calculate the timing and measurement of contract revenue and expenses throughout the term of a construction contract, as in the following example, based on the Illustrative Examples in IAS 11:

Example 23.3: Cumulative example – the determination of contract revenue and expenses

The following example illustrates the determination of the stage of completion of a contract and the timing of the recognition of contract revenue and expenses, measured by the proportion that contract costs incurred for work performed to date bear to the estimated total contract costs.

A construction contractor has a fixed price contract to build a bridge. The initial amount of revenue agreed in the contract is €9,000. The contractor's initial estimate of contract costs is €8,000. It will take 3 years to build the bridge.

By the end of year 1, the contractor's estimate of contract costs has increased to €8,050.

In year 2, the customer approves a variation resulting in an increase in contract revenue of €200 and estimated additional contract costs of €150. At the end of year 2, costs incurred include €100 for standard materials stored at the site to be used in year 3 to complete the project.

The contractor determines the stage of completion of the contract by calculating the proportion that contract costs incurred for work performed to date bear to the latest estimated total contract costs. A summary of the financial data during the construction period is as follows:

	Year 1 €	Year 2 €	Year 3 €
Initial amount of revenue agreed in contract	9,000	9,000	9,000
Variation	–	200	200
Total contract revenue	9,000	9,200	9,200
Contract costs incurred to date	2,093	6,168	8,200
Contract costs to complete	5,957	2,023	–
Total estimated contract costs	8,050	8,200	8,200
Estimated profit	950	1,000	1,000
Stage of completion	26%	74%	100%

The constructor uses the percentages calculated as above to calculate the revenue, contract costs and profits over the term of the contract. The stage of completion for year 2 (74%) is determined by excluding from contract costs incurred for work performed to date the €100 of standard materials stored at the site for use in year 3.

The amounts of revenue, expenses and profit recognised in profit or loss in the three years are as follows:

	To date	Recognised in prior years	Recognised in current years
Year 1			
Revenue (9,000 × 26%)	2,340	–	2,340
Expenses	2,093	–	2,093
Profit	247	–	247
Year 2			
Revenue (9,200 × 74%)	6,808	2,340	4,468
Expenses (6,168 incurred less 100 of materials in storage)	6,068	2,093	3,975
Profit	740	247	493
Year 3			
Revenue (9,200 × 100%)	9,200	6,808	2,392
Expenses	8,200	6,068	2,132
Profit	1,000	740	260

3.3.5 *Inability to estimate the outcome of a contract reliably*

When the outcome of a construction contract cannot be estimated reliably, an entity will first of all have to determine whether it has incurred costs that it is probable will be recovered under the contract. It can then recognise revenue to the extent of these costs. Contract costs should be recognised as an expense in the period in which they are incurred, *[IAS 11.32]*, unless, of course, they relate to future contract activity, such as materials purchased for future use on the contract as explained at 3.3.2 above.

It is often difficult to estimate the outcome of a contract reliably during its early stages. This means that it is not possible to recognise contract profit. However, the entity may be satisfied that some, at least, of the contract costs it has incurred will be recovered and it will be able to recognise revenue to this extent.

Chapter 23

If it is probable that total costs will exceed total revenues, even if the outcome of the contract cannot be estimated reliably, any expected excess of contract costs must be expensed immediately. *[IAS 11.33]*. The standard also identifies a number of situations that may give rise to irrecoverable contract costs that must be recognised as expenses immediately. There may be deficiencies in the contract, which means that it is not fully enforceable. Other problems may be caused by the operation of law, such as the outcome of pending litigation or legislation or the expropriation of property. The customer or the contractor may no longer be able to meet their obligations or the contractor may be unable for some reason to complete the contract. *[IAS 11.34]*.

If these uncertainties that prevent the outcome of the contract being estimated reliably are resolved, revenue and expenses are recognised by the stage of completion method. *[IAS 11.35]*.

3.3.6 Loss-making contracts

As soon as the entity considers that it is probable that the contract costs will exceed contract revenue it must recognise immediately the expected loss as an expense. It is irrelevant whether work has commenced on the contract or the stage of completion of contract activity. In addition, the entity may not take into account any anticipated profits on other contracts with the same customer unless all of these contracts are treated as a single construction contract. *[IAS 11.36-37]*.

3.3.7 Contract inefficiencies

IAS 2 explicitly excludes from the costs of inventories 'abnormal amounts of wasted materials, labour or other production costs'. *[IAS 2.16(a)]*. There is no such requirement in IAS 11 and this is reflected in a degree of uncertainty about how to account for inefficiencies and 'abnormal costs' incurred during the course of a construction contract. If such costs are simply added to the total contract costs, this may affect the stage of completion if contract activity is estimated based on the total costs that have been incurred (see 3.3.2 above).

It is clear in principle that abnormal costs and inefficiencies that relate solely to a particular period ought to be expensed in that period as they are not 'costs that relate directly to the specific contract'. *[IAS 11.16(a)]*. The issue is often a practical one of how to distinguish such costs from revisions of estimates that can more reasonably be treated as contract costs.

Usually, inefficiencies that result from an observable event can be identified and expensed. If a major supplier collapses and the materials from another source are more expensive, this may be an inefficiency that ought to be expensed, as well as being one where the costs ought to be identifiable without undue difficulty. By contrast, an unexpected increase in costs of materials unrelated to such an event may be a revision to the estimate of costs. There are more marginal situations. A load of bricks may develop an off colour and not be suitable for their designated purpose. This is a natural, but intermittent defect that builders must face and here it is much less clear whether it is an inefficiency or change in estimate. In any particular case an assessment may have to be based on the significance to the project. It is relatively easy to distinguish cases at either extreme but much less so when the issues are marginal, where judgement will have to be exercised.

Note that this must be distinguished from cost increases that will result in the contract becoming loss-making, as these must be expensed immediately (see above).

3.3.8 Contracts that contain sales of assets and construction contracts

In some real estate markets an entity may enter into a contract to construct a building on land that the entity owns and then – after construction is complete – to deliver the entire property to a customer.

If the contract can be segmented into a construction contract and the sale of the land, the delivery of land follows the revenue recognition guidance of IAS 18 for sale of land. The construction of the building follows the revenue recognition guidance of IAS 11 or IAS 18 as appropriate, as it may be necessary to apply IFRIC 15's guidance to the construction of the building (see 1.2 above). The effect of this can be seen below:

Example 23.4: Segmented construction contract

On 1 January 2014, entity A entered into a contract to construct a building on a piece of land it has acquired and, when construction is complete, to deliver the entire property to a customer. A applies the percentage of completion method to account for contract revenues and expenses. The relative percentage of cost incurred is considered a reliable method for measuring the progress of the contract.

- Total cost of land: €2m
- Estimated total cost of construction: €8m
- Estimated total cost of contract: €10m
- Agreed sales price of the completed building: €11m

Construction has commenced and at the end of the reporting period (31 December 2014) total construction costs incurred amount to €2m.

Entity A considers that the amount of revenue in the contract attributable to the construction is €8.5m and the amount to the sale of land is €2.5m.

The percentage completion of the construction contract is 25% – calculated as €2m costs incurred as a proportion of the €8m estimated total cost of construction.

Accordingly, as at 31 December 2014 the following amounts are recorded:

Revenue	(€8.5m × 25%)	€2.13m
Contract expense		€2.00m
Gross amount due from customer	(Revenue of €2.13m)	€2.13m
Inventory	(Cost of the land)	€2.00m

The revenue and cost relating to the land will be recognised when the revenue recognition criteria of IAS 18 are met – this is often when legal title passes.

4 DISCLOSURE REQUIREMENTS OF IAS 11

IAS 11 has detailed and onerous disclosure requirements. The following disclosures must be given by entities in respect of construction contracts:

(a) the amount of contract revenue recognised as revenue in the period;

(b) the methods used to determine the contract revenue recognised in the period; and

(c) the methods used to determine the stage of completion of contracts in progress. *[IAS 11.39]*.

The standard includes in its Appendix an example of accounting policy disclosures, shown below.

Example 23.5: Disclosure of accounting policies

Revenue from fixed price construction contracts is recognised on the percentage of completion method, measured by reference to the percentage of labour hours incurred to date compared to estimated total labour hours for each contract.

Revenue from cost plus contracts is recognised by reference to the recoverable costs incurred during the period plus the fee earned, measured by the proportion that costs incurred to date bear to the estimated total costs of the contract.

The following is the accounting policy of Thales, which also refers to the treatment of the related balances in the balance sheet.

Extract 23.8: Thales (2012)

Notes to the Consolidated Financial Statements [extract]

1. ACCOUNTING POLICIES [extract]

i) Revenues [extract]

Construction contracts

A construction contract is a contract specifically negotiated for the construction of an asset or of a group of assets, which are interrelated in terms of their design, technology, function, purpose or use.

According to its characteristics, a notified construction contract can either be accounted for separately, be segmented into several components which are each accounted for separately, or be combined with another construction contract in progress in order to form a single construction contract for accounting purposes in respect of which revenues and expenses will be recognised.

Sales and expenses on construction contracts are recognised in accordance with the technical percentage of completion method. However, when there is no significant time difference between technical percentage of completion and contractual dates of transfer of ownership, the percentage of completion is determined according to the contractual transfer of ownership.

Penalties for late payment or relating to improper performance of a contract are recognised as a deduction from sales. In the balance sheet, provisions for penalties are deducted from assets related to the contract.

Expected losses on contracts are fully recognised as soon as they are identified.

Selling, administrative and interest expenses are directly charged to the profit and loss account in the financial year in which they are incurred.

Estimates of work remaining on loss-making contracts do not include sales from claims made by the Group, except when it is highly probable that such claims will be accepted by the customer.

> Progress payments received on construction contracts are deducted from contract assets as the contract is completed. Progress payments received before the corresponding work has been performed are classified in "Advances received from customers on contracts" in balance sheet liabilities.
>
> The cumulative amount of costs incurred and profit recognised, reduced by recognised losses and progress billings, is determined on a contract-by-contract basis. If this amount is positive it is categorised as "Construction contracts: assets" in balance sheet assets. If it is negative it is categorised as "Construction contracts: liabilities" in balance sheet liabilities.

EADS identifies different features by which its contract revenue is recognised, as disclosed in Extract 23.4 above.

In the case of contracts in progress at the end of the reporting period, an entity should disclose each of the following:

(a) the aggregate amount of costs incurred and recognised profits (less recognised losses) to date;

(b) the amount of advances received; and

(c) the amount of retentions. *[IAS 11.40]*.

Retentions, progress billings and advances are defined as follows:

> 'Retentions are amounts of progress billings which are not paid until the satisfaction of conditions specified in the contract for the payment of such amounts or until defects have been rectified. Progress billings are amounts billed for work performed on a contract whether or not they have been paid by the customer. Advances are amounts received by the contractor before the related work is performed.' *[IAS 11.41]*.

In addition, an entity should present:

(a) the gross amount due from customers for contract work as an asset for all contracts in progress for which costs incurred plus recognised profits (less recognised losses) exceed progress billings (i.e. the net amount of costs incurred plus recognised profits, less the sum of recognised losses and progress billings); and

(b) the gross amount due to customers for contract work as a liability for all contracts in progress for which progress billings exceed costs incurred plus recognised profits (i.e. the net amount of costs incurred plus recognised profits, less the sum of recognised losses and progress billings). *[IAS 11.42-44]*.

The following example is based on the Illustrative Examples in IAS 11, and serves to illustrate the financial statement disclosure requirements of the standard as they apply to the various circumstances that might arise concerning construction contracts. It is followed by an example of the disclosures in practice from the financial statements of Thales.

Example 23.6: Disclosure of numerical information regarding construction contracts

A contractor has reached the end of its first year of operations. All its contract costs incurred have been paid for in cash and all its progress billings and advances have been received in cash. Contract costs incurred for contracts B, C and E include the cost of materials that have been purchased for the contract but which have not been used in contract performance to date.

For contracts B, C and E, the customers have made advances to the contractor for work not yet performed.

The status of the entity's five contracts in progress at the end of year 1 is as follows:

Contract	**A**	**B**	**C**	**D**	**E**	**Total**
Contract revenue recognised in accordance with IAS 11.22 (see 3.3 above)	145	520	380	200	55	1,300
Contract expenses recognised in accordance with IAS 11.22 (see 3.3 above)	110	450	350	250	55	1,215
Expected losses recognised in accordance with IAS 11.36 (see 3.3.6 above)	–	–	–	40	30	70
Recognised profits less recognised losses	35	70	30	(90)	(30)	15
Contract costs incurred in the period	110	510	450	250	100	1,420
Contract costs incurred recognised as contract expenses in the period in accordance with IAS 11.22	110	450	350	250	55	1,215
Contract costs that relate to future activity recognised as an asset in accordance with IAS 11.27	–	60	100	–	45	205
Contract revenue	145	520	380	200	55	1,300
Progress billings (IAS 11.41: see above)	100	520	380	180	55	1,235
Unbilled contract revenue	45	–	–	20	–	65
Advances (IAS 11.41: see above)	–	80	20	–	25	125

The amounts to be disclosed in accordance with IAS 11 are as follows:

Contract revenue recognised as revenue in the period	1,300
Contract costs incurred and recognised profits (less recognised losses) to date	1,435
Advances received	125
Gross amount due from customers for contract work (presented as an asset)	220
Gross amount due to customers for contract work (presented as a liability)	(20)

These amounts are calculated as follows:

Contract	**A**	**B**	**C**	**D**	**E**	**Total**
Contract costs incurred	110	510	450	250	100	1,420
Recognised profits less recognised losses	35	70	30	(90)	(30)	15
	145	580	480	160	70	1,435
Progress billings	100	520	380	180	55	1,235
Due from customers	45	60	100	–	15	220
Due to customers	–	–	–	(20)	–	(20)

The amount disclosed in accordance with IAS 11.40(a) (the aggregate amount of costs incurred and recognised profits (less recognised losses) to date) is the same as the amount for the current period because the disclosures relate to the first year of operation.

Thales discloses its contracts in progress at the year end as follows:

Extract 23.9: Thales (2012)

Notes to the Consolidated Financial Statements [extract]

Note 16 Construction contracts [extract]

This note is related to contracts accounted for under IAS 11.

	31/12/2012	**31/12/2011**
Construction contracts: assets	**2,082.6**	2,305.3
Construction contracts: liabilities	**(1,345.0)**	(1,355.6)
Net	**737.6**	949.7

This balance is analyzed as follows:

	31/12/2012	**31/12/2011**
Work in progress on construction contracts	**1,087.6**	1,287.2
Unbilled receivable on construction contracts	**1,337.4**	1,369.7
Reserves for losses at completion on construction contracts[(a)]	**(737.7)**	(884.6)
Other reserves on construction contracts	**(949.7)**	(822.6)
Total	**737.6**	949.7
Advances received from customers on construction contracts	**3,546.3**	3,341.9

(a) *The variations of reserves for losses at completion between 2011 and 2012 are mainly explained by the utilization of reserves booked during the previous years.*

Chapter 23

References

1 *IFRIC Update*, February 2005, p.5.
2 *FASB ASC* 605-35-25-8.
3 *IFRIC Update*, June 2005, p.6.

References

Chapter 24 Leases

List of Examples

Chapter 24 Leases

1 INTRODUCTION

IAS 17 – *Leases* – has been in place for many years, having been originally issued in September 1982. So have its equivalent standards around the world, SFAS 13 – *Accounting for Leases* (1976) – in the US (now ASC 840) and SSAP 21 – *Accounting for leases and hire purchase contracts* (1984) – in the UK.

Although a lease is an agreement that gives a lessee the right to use an asset for an agreed period of time in return for a payment or series of payments, companies are required in certain circumstances to capitalise assets in their statements of financial position, together with the corresponding obligations, irrespective of the fact that legal title to those assets is vested in another party.

The term 'lease' also applies to arrangements that do not take the form of leases. Instead, they essentially combine rights to use assets and the provision of services or outputs, for agreed periods of time in return for a payment or series of payments, e.g. outsourcing arrangements that include the provision of assets and services. Entities have to consider the substance of these arrangements to see if they are, or contain, leases. If so, then the elements identified as a lease will be subject to the requirements of IAS 17.

The IASB and the FASB have developed proposals under which the rights and obligations arising under lease contracts will, with few exceptions, be recognised in the statements of financial position of lessees and many lessors. An Exposure Draft (ED) was issued in August 2010 but many proposals proved very contentions. The IASB and FASB agreed to publish a revised ED which was not reissued until May 2013. The current state of the project is discussed at 10 below.

2 WHAT IS A LEASE?

IAS 17 defines a lease as 'an agreement whereby the lessor conveys to the lessee in return for a payment or series of payments the right to use an asset for an agreed period of time.' *[IAS 17.4]*. The standard applies to agreements that transfer the right to use assets even though substantial services by the lessor may be called for in connection with the operation or maintenance of such assets. It does not apply to agreements that are contracts for services that do not transfer the right to use assets from one contracting party to the other. The definition of a lease includes contracts for the hire of an asset that contain a provision giving the hirer an option to acquire title to the asset when agreed conditions have been complied with (sometimes known as hire purchase contacts). *[IAS 17.6]*.

In recent years new types of arrangements have arisen that do not take the legal form of leases. They take many forms, but essentially combine rights to use assets and the provision of services or outputs, for agreed periods of time in return for a payment or series of payments. These issues are dealt with in IFRIC 4 – *Determining whether an Arrangement contains a Lease* – which is considered further in 2.1 below. Some of the arrangements under service concession arrangements give rise to further accounting issues that have been separately addressed by the Interpretations Committee; service concessions have been excluded from the scope of lease accounting and are discussed in Chapter 26.

The SIC had previously considered whether all transactions in the legal form of a lease should be considered under IAS 17. The results of these deliberations, SIC-27 – *Evaluating the Substance of Transactions Involving the Legal Form of a Lease,* are covered in 2.2 below.

2.1 Determining whether an arrangement contains a lease

IFRIC 4 notes that arrangements have been developed in recent years that do not take the legal form of a lease but that nevertheless convey rights to use items for agreed periods of time in return for a payment or series of payments. *[IFRIC 4.1]*. IFRIC 4 has the objective only of dealing with the practical issues that arise when applying IAS 17 to arrangements that are not (or do not contain) leases in form: how to identify an arrangement that is in substance a lease, when to make the assessment and how to measure the lease element. *[IFRIC 4.5]*. The Interpretation does not provide any guidance for determining lease classification under IAS 17, *[IFRIC 4.2]*, (in other words, it could be a finance lease or an operating lease under IAS 17), nor does it expect the guidance to extend the scope of that standard. If an arrangement turns out to contain a lease or licence of a type excluded from the scope of IAS 17 (see 3.1.1 below), the Interpretation does not apply. Service concession arrangements to which IFRIC 12 – *Service Concession Arrangements* – applies are also out of scope (see Chapter 26). *[IFRIC 4.4]*.

The Interpretation addresses some more traditional forms of arrangement that are also within its scope. It considers the accounting implications of the following, in all of which an entity (the supplier) conveys a right to use an asset to another entity (the purchaser), together with related services or outputs:

- outsourcing arrangements, including outsourcing of the data processing functions of an entity;
- arrangements in the telecommunications industry, where suppliers of network capacity enter into contracts to provide purchasers with rights to capacity; and
- take-or-pay and similar contracts, in which purchasers must make specified payments regardless of whether they take delivery of the contracted products or services (e.g. where purchasers are committed to acquiring substantially all of the output of a supplier's power generator). *[IFRIC 4.1]*.

The Interpretations Committee concluded that an arrangement of one of these types could be within the scope of IAS 17 if it met the definition of a lease, e.g. if it conveyed to the lessee the right to use an asset for an agreed period of time in return for a payment or series of payments. *[IFRIC 4.BC2].* IAS 17 applies to the lease element of the arrangement notwithstanding the related services or outputs because IAS 17 applies to 'agreements that transfer the right to use assets even though substantial services by the lessor may be called for in connection with the operation or maintenance of such assets.' *[IAS 17.3].* This is regardless of the fact that the arrangement is not described as a lease and is likely to grant rights that are significantly different from those in a formal lease agreement.

2.1.1 Identification of an asset

The first condition that must be met to determine whether an arrangement is, or contains a lease is that fulfilment of the arrangement depends on a specific asset or assets. *[IFRIC 4.6].*

IAS 17 applies only to an arrangement in which there is a 'right to use an asset', so an arrangement will not contain a lease unless it depends on a specific asset or assets.

A specific asset that is explicitly identified by the arrangement will not be the subject of a lease if the arrangement is not dependent on the asset. If the seller is required under the arrangement to deliver a specified quantity of goods or services and has the right or ability to provide those goods using other assets not specified in the agreement, the arrangement will not contain a lease. *[IFRIC 4.7].*

However, an arrangement may still contain a lease if a specific asset is not explicitly identified but it would not be economically feasible or practical for the supplier to provide the use of alternative items. For example, the supplier may only own one suitable asset. *[IFRIC 4.8].*

Some arrangements may allow the supplier to replace the specified asset with a similar asset if the original asset is unavailable (e.g. because it is unexpectedly inoperable). The Interpretations Committee takes the view that as such a requirement is in effect a warranty obligation it does not preclude lease treatment. *[IFRIC 4.7].*

To take a relatively simple example, an arrangement in which an entity (the purchaser) outsources its product delivery department to another organisation (the supplier) will not contain a lease if the supplier is obliged to make available a certain number of delivery vehicles of a certain standard specification and the supplier is a delivery organisation with many other vehicles available. However, if the supplier has to supply and maintain a specified number of specialist vehicles in the purchaser's livery, then this arrangement is more likely to contain a lease. The latter arrangement may be commercially more akin to outsourcing the purchaser's acquisitions of delivery vehicles rather than its delivery functions. Similar issues would have to be taken into account if data processing functions are outsourced as these may require substantial investment by the supplier in computer hardware dedicated to the use of a single customer.

Where arrangements are likely to contain leases (delivery vehicles in livery, dedicated hardware), the purchaser cannot be unaware that there are specific assets underlying the service. There would have been negotiations between supplier and purchaser that would probably be reflected in the contract documentation. By contrast, if the purchaser does not know what assets are used to provide the service (beyond the fact that they are trucks and computers, of course), and in the circumstances it is reasonable not to know, it is plausible that there is no underlying lease in the arrangement. This remains true even if the supplier has dedicated specific assets to the service being provided and expects their cost to be recouped during the course of the contractual relationship.

2.1.2 Parts of assets and the unit of account

IFRIC 4 notes that some arrangements transfer the right to use an asset that is a component of a larger asset but the issue of whether and when such rights should be accounted for as leases is not dealt with in the Interpretation. The Interpretation does not attempt to address whether there is any conceptual difference between, say, using a quarter of the capacity of a whole pipeline and all of the capacity of a pipeline a quarter of the size. It states merely that 'arrangements in which the underlying asset would represent a unit of account' in either IAS 16 – *Property, Plant and Equipment* – or IAS 38 – *Intangible Assets* – are within the scope of the Interpretation. *[IFRIC 4.3]*. 'Unit of account' presumably means an asset whose cost, replacement, impairment and depreciation are separately accounted for under one of these standards (see Chapters 17 and 18). However, the opposite is not necessarily the case. It does not mean that a component of one of these assets cannot be the underlying asset.

There are many arrangements in practice that demonstrate this issue. For example, a plant may contain more than one production unit or line that might be regarded as a single 'component' (because each makes the same product) or alternatively each of its units or lines might be regarded as separate 'components'. Depending on other aspects of the arrangement, a particular production line may be the asset that is the subject of a lease, if the supplier cannot transfer production to a different line to supply the goods.

Similar examples from the telecommunications industry include fibre optical cable, satellite and wireless tower arrangements. Fibre agreements vary from those that allow use of the whole cable, through those that specify the wavelength or spectrum within a fibre to the most common arrangements which are essentially for transmission capacity within the vendor's fibre cable or network. As a result, arrangements have to be examined carefully to determine if they do specify an asset. Generally, a portion of a larger asset that is not physically distinct is not considered to be a specified asset.

2.1.3 The arrangement conveys a right to use the item

In order to contain a lease, the arrangement must convey a right to use the asset. *[IFRIC 4.6]*. An arrangement does not convey the right to use an asset unless the purchaser has the right to control the use of the underlying item, which depends on any one of the following conditions being met: *[IFRIC 4.9]*

(a) The purchaser has the ability or right to operate the asset or direct others to operate the asset in a manner it determines while obtaining or controlling more than an insignificant amount of the output or other utility of the asset;

(b) The purchaser has the ability or right to control physical access to the underlying asset while obtaining or controlling more than an insignificant amount of the output or other utility of the asset; or

(c) Facts and circumstances indicate:

  (i) it is remote that one or more parties other than the purchaser will take more than an insignificant amount of the output or other utility that will be produced or generated by the asset during the term of the arrangement: and

  (ii) the price that the purchaser will pay for the output is neither contractually fixed per unit of output; nor equal to the current market price per unit of output as of the time of delivery of the output.

Therefore, control of the asset may be obtained in circumstances in which an entity obtains 'more than an insignificant amount of the output' but *only* if it has the ability or right to operate (or direct others to operate) the asset in a manner that it determines or if it can control physical access to the asset.

When the arrangement involves a single purchaser taking substantially all of the output from a specific asset other than at market price and the price varies other than in response to market price changes, the variability ('off-market' nature) is regarded by IFRIC 4 as indicating that payment is being made for the right to use the asset rather than for the actual use of or output from the asset. In these circumstances the arrangement would also convey the right to use the asset, even though the purchaser would neither have the ability or right to operate the asset or direct others to operate the asset in a manner it determines nor have the ability or right to control physical access to the underlying asset.

The effects of this are demonstrated by the following examples. Example 24.1 is based on an illustrative example in IFRIC 4. *[IFRIC 4.IE1-2]*.

Example 24.1: An arrangement that contains a lease

A production company (the purchaser) enters into an arrangement with a third party (the supplier) to supply a minimum quantity of gas needed in its production process for a specified period of time. The supplier designs and builds a facility near to the purchaser's plant to produce the gas and maintains ownership and control over all significant aspects of operating the facility. The agreement provides for the following:

- The facility is explicitly identified in the arrangement, and the supplier has the contractual right to supply gas from other sources, although supplying gas from other sources is not economically feasible or practicable;

- The supplier has the right to provide gas to other customers and to remove and replace the facility's equipment and modify or expand the facility to enable the supplier to do so. However, at inception of the arrangement, the facility is designed to meet only the purchaser's needs and the supplier has no plans to modify or expand the facility;
- The supplier is responsible for repairs, maintenance and capital expenditures;
- The supplier must stand ready to deliver a minimum quantity of gas each month;
- On a monthly basis, the purchaser will pay a fixed capacity charge and a variable charge based on actual production taken. The purchaser must pay the fixed capacity charge irrespective of whether it takes any of the facility's production. The variable charge includes the facility's actual energy costs, which comprise approximately 90 per cent of the facility's total variable costs. The supplier is subject to increased costs resulting from the facility's inefficient operations;
- If the facility does not produce the stated minimum quantity, the supplier must return all or a portion of the fixed capacity charge.

The arrangement contains a lease within the scope of IAS 17. An asset (the facility) is explicitly identified in the arrangement and fulfilment of the arrangement is dependent on the facility. While the supplier has the right to supply gas from other sources, its ability to do so is not substantive. The purchaser has obtained the right to use the facility because, on the facts presented – in particular, that the facility is designed to meet only the purchaser's needs and the supplier has no plans to expand or modify the facility – it is remote that one or more parties other than the purchaser will take more than an insignificant amount of the facility's output and the price the purchaser will pay is neither contractually fixed per unit of output nor equal to the current market price per unit of output as of the time of delivery of the output.

Having concluded that the arrangement contains a lease, it is then necessary to classify it as an operating or a finance lease. Identifying the relevant lease payments is dealt with below.

The next two examples illustrate arrangements that do not contain a lease. The first, Example 24.2, illustrates two of the concepts in IFRIC 4. It describes circumstances in which an arrangement does not contain a lease because no specific asset has been identified. The significance of the control concept is shown in the second example based on the second illustrative example in IFRIC 4. *[IFRIC 4.IE3-4].*

Example 24.2: Arrangements that do not contain leases

(a) Take-or-pay contract that does not depend on a specific asset

A purchaser enters into a take-or-pay contract to buy industrial gases from a supplier. The supplier is a large company operating similar plants at various locations. The amount of gas that the purchaser is committed to buy is roughly equivalent to the total output of one of the plants. Because a good distribution network is available, the supplier is able to provide gas from various locations to fulfil its supply obligation.

In this example, the arrangement does not depend on a specific asset. This is because it is economically feasible and practical for the supplier to fulfil the arrangement by providing use of more than one plant. A specific asset has therefore not been identified either explicitly or implicitly.

Payments under the contract may be unavoidable because it is a take-or-pay arrangement and the purchaser may in fact take all of the output of a single plant but the arrangement does not convey a right to use the asset. The purchaser does not have the right to control the use of the underlying asset. It does not have the ability or right to operate the asset in a manner it determines (or to direct others to do so on its behalf), and it does not control physical access. The arrangement does not contain a lease.

(b) The right to control the use of an underlying asset is not conveyed

A manufacturing company (the purchaser) enters into an arrangement with a third party (the supplier) to supply a specific component part of its manufactured product for a specified period of time. The supplier designs and constructs a plant next to the purchaser's factory to produce the component part. The designed capacity of the plant exceeds the purchaser's current needs, and the supplier maintains ownership and control over all significant aspects of operating the plant.

The supplier's plant is explicitly identified in the arrangement, but the supplier has the right to fulfil the arrangement by shipping the component parts from another plant owned by the supplier. However, to do so for any extended period of time would be uneconomical. The supplier must stand ready to deliver a minimum quantity. The purchaser is required to pay a fixed price per unit for the actual quantity taken. Even if the purchaser's needs are such that they do not need the stated minimum quantity, they still pay only for the actual quantity taken.

The supplier has the right to sell the component parts to other customers and has a history of doing so by selling in the replacement parts market, so it is expected that parties other than the purchaser will take more than an insignificant amount of the component parts produced at the supplier's plant.

The supplier is responsible for repairs, maintenance, and capital expenditures of the plant.

This arrangement does not contain a lease. An asset (the plant) is explicitly identified in the arrangement and fulfilment of the arrangement is dependent on the facility. While the supplier has the right to supply component parts from other sources, the supplier would not have the ability to do so because it would be uneconomical. However, the purchaser has not obtained the right to use the plant because it does not control it, for the following reasons:

(a) the purchaser does not have the ability or right to operate or direct others to operate the plant or control physical access to the plant; and

(b) the likelihood that parties other than the purchaser will take more than an insignificant amount of the component parts produced at the plant is more than remote, based on the facts presented.

(c) the price paid by the purchaser is fixed per unit of output taken but see the following section where this is discussed further.

2.1.4 Fixed or current market prices and control of the asset

The third control condition states that an arrangement will not contain a lease notwithstanding that a purchaser takes all but an insignificant amount of the output or other utility if the price is contractually fixed per unit of output. We consider that by this the Interpretation means absolutely fixed, with no variance per unit based on underlying costs or volumes, whether discounts or stepped pricing.

In the manufacturing industry 'lifetime' agreements with step pricing between the supplier and the purchaser are not uncommon. The parties to the agreement agree in advance on progressive unit price reductions on achievement of specified production volume levels, reflecting the supplier's increasing efficiencies and economies of scale. These types of contracts should be closely analysed, especially to see whether one of the other two conditions, the 'right to operate the asset' or the 'right to control the physical access to the asset', is met before concluding that the arrangement contains a lease.

'Current market price per unit of output' means that the cost is solely a market price for the output of the asset without any other pricing factors. A 'market price per KWH plus x per cent change in the price of natural gas' would not be the current market price per unit of the output of the asset. Price increases based on a general index such as a retail and prices index are unlikely to result in a current market price for the output in question.

Example 24.3: Fixed prices per unit

Purchaser P and supplier S enter in a parts supply agreement for the lifetime of the finished product concerned. S uses tooling equipment that is specific to the needs of P. The tooling is explicitly identified in the agreement and S could not use an alternative asset. The estimated capacity of the tooling equipment is 500,000 units which corresponds to the total production of the finished product units over its life cycle. P takes substantially all of the output produced by S using the specific tooling.

Purchaser P and supplier S agree on the following unit price reductions in the parts supply agreement to reflect S's increasing efficiencies and economies of scale:

- from 0 to 100,000 units, price per each unit €150;
- from 100,001 to 200,000, price per each unit €140;
- from 200,001 to 300,000, price per each unit €135;
- from 300,001 to 400,000, price per each unit €132;
- above 400,000 price per each unit €130.

The fulfilment of the arrangement depends on the use of a specific asset, the tooling. P has obtained the right to use the tooling because, on the facts presented, the likelihood is remote that one or more parties other than the P will take more than an insignificant amount of the tooling's output. As the estimated capacity of the tooling equipment corresponds to the total production of the finished product units produced by P, P takes substantially all of the output produced using that tooling.

However, stepped pricing does not mean price 'fixed per unit of output' and, particularly as the stepped pricing is agreed in advance, it is not equal to the current market price per unit as of the time of delivery of the output. The arrangement contains a lease within the scope of IAS 17. The purchaser will have to determine whether it is a finance or operating lease.

2.1.5 When to assess the arrangements

IFRIC 4 states that assessing whether an arrangement contains a lease should be made at the inception of the arrangement, which is the earlier of the date of the arrangement and the date of commitment by the parties to the principal terms of the arrangement, on the basis of all the facts and circumstances. A reassessment of whether the arrangement contains a lease should be made only if: *[IFRIC 4.10]*

(a) there is a change in the terms of the contract, except for a renewal or extension of the arrangement;

(b) a renewal option is exercised or an extension is agreed, unless these had been taken into account in the original assessment of the lease term in accordance with IAS 17; *[IAS 17.4]*

(c) there is a change in whether or not the arrangement depends on specified item; or

(d) there is a substantial physical change to the specified assets.

Changes to estimates, for example of the amount of output that would be taken by the purchaser, would not trigger a reassessment. *[IFRIC 4.11].*

If the arrangement is reassessed and found to contain a lease or vice versa then lease accounting will be applied or discontinued as from the time that the arrangement is reassessed, or renewal option exercised when this was not previously anticipated, as described in (b) above. *[IFRIC 4.11].* The exercise of renewal options is discussed at 3.2.3 below.

2.1.6 Separation of leases from other payments within the arrangement

If an arrangement contains a lease, both parties to the arrangement are to apply IAS 17 to the lease element of the arrangement unless it is an arrangement that is not within IAS 17's scope (see 3.1 below). Other elements of the arrangement must be accounted for in accordance with the appropriate standards. *[IFRIC 4.12]*.

It must be stressed that this means that the lease element of the arrangement may be classified as an operating or finance lease. Therefore, having identified the lease payments, the entity may still classify the arrangement as an operating lease if it does not transfer substantially all the risks and rewards incidental to ownership of an asset (see 3.2 below). *[IAS 17.4, 8]*.

In order to apply IAS 17, the payments and other consideration under the arrangement must be separated at inception or on reassessment between those for the lease of the asset (that will meet the definition of minimum lease payments, see 3.4.3 below) and those for other services and outputs. IFRIC 4 requires this to be done on the basis of their relative fair values. *[IFRIC 4.13]*. This may require the purchaser to use estimation techniques – this appears to be somewhat of an understatement as, unless the price to be paid for both elements is clear and they have both been negotiated at market value, it will always be necessary to use some form of estimation. The Interpretation suggests that it may be possible to estimate either the lease payments (by comparison with similar leases that do not contain other elements) or the other elements (using comparable arrangements) and then deduct the estimated amount from the total under the arrangement. *[IFRIC 4.14]*.

This is not a straightforward exercise and the Interpretation does not go into any further detail as to how it would be carried out. There may be no market-based evidence of fair value of the underlying assets because of their specialised nature or because they are rarely sold, in which case it will be necessary to use valuation techniques. Discounted cash flow projections based on estimated future cash flows that will be generated by specialised assets may be difficult to obtain, although it should be possible to make some form of estimate, if need be with the assistance of valuation experts. The service elements within these agreements are by no means standardised and it may not be easy to identify comparable arrangements. The exercise will be complicated by the fact that the fair value of a bundle of services is not necessarily the same as the aggregation of their individual fair values and making such an assumption could lead to an overstatement of the service element and consequent understatement of the fair value of the lease element or *vice versa*. The discount rates should reflect current market assessments of the uncertainty and timing of the cash flows, i.e. the risk inherent in the separate elements of the transaction. There are usually very different risk profiles for the provision of services and for leasing assets. If, as suggested by the Interpretation, the entity estimates one of the elements under the arrangement and derives the other by deduction, i.e. it uses a residual method, it will always be necessary to carry out a 'sense check' on the derived payments.

IFRIC 4 suggests that only in rare cases will a purchaser conclude that it is impracticable to separate the payments reliably. In the case of a finance lease, the entity should recognise an asset at an amount equal to the fair value of the underlying asset that it has identified as the subject of the lease, as described in 2.1.1 above. A liability should be set up at the same amount as the asset. The entity would impute a finance charge based on the purchaser's incremental borrowing rate of interest (see 3.4.5 below) and, from this, compute the reduction in the liability as payments are made. *[IFRIC 4.15]*. Presumably the Interpretations Committee considers that the entity's incremental borrowing rate would have to be used because, if it were possible to determine the interest rate implicit in the lease, the arrangement would not be one in which it was impracticable to separate the payments reliably.

What this means, of course, is that an entity may be required to account for an asset held under a finance lease when it is, in fact, unable to identify the lease payments. It is to be hoped that the application of the control model means that this will not often happen in practice as control is more likely to result in an entity being able to identify the underlying payment streams.

If the lease is assessed as an operating lease, applying the Interpretation might affect the recognition of costs and revenue over the term of the arrangement. IAS 17 requires lessors and lessees to recognise operating lease payments on a straight-line basis over the lease term unless another systematic basis is more representative (see 5.1.2 below) and this may not be in line with the payments for the lease element so some adjustments might be required. *[IFRIC 4.BC39]*.

See below for disclosure implications if the arrangement is deemed to contain an operating lease and the purchaser concludes that it is impracticable to separate the payments reliably.

2.1.7 Disclosure requirements

IAS 17 required a general description of the lessee's material leasing arrangements, *[IAS 17.31(e)]*, which will require disclosure of the details of major transactions that have fallen within IFRIC 4.

There are no specific disclosure requirements if the arrangements are assessed as containing finance leases as these arrangements are deemed to be within the scope of IAS 17 and therefore within its disclosure requirements (see 9 below).

However, if it were considered to be an operating lease, the Interpretation may result in additional disclosures, because IAS 17 specifies that the lessor and lessee should disclose the future minimum lease payments. Although the arrangements discussed in the Interpretation typically represent significant future commitments, purchasers are not required to disclose them in the financial statements unless they fall within IAS 17. The Interpretations Committee argues that bringing such arrangements within the scope of IAS 17 will provide users of financial statements with relevant information that is useful for assessing the purchaser's solvency, liquidity and adaptability. *[IFRIC 4.BC39]*.

As long as the entity is able to distinguish the lease payments from other elements of the lease, then the disclosed information will relate only to the lease element of the arrangement. There appears to be no intention to require entities to disclose the service (executory) element of arrangements. However, if the arrangement is one of those in which it is impracticable to separate the payments reliably, the Interpretation requires disclosure of all payments under the arrangement separately from other minimum lease payments, together with a statement that the disclosed payments also include payments for non-lease elements in the arrangement. *[IFRIC 4.15]*.

2.2 Transactions that are not, in substance, leases

While there are some arrangements that contain leases that are not formally lease contracts, the reverse is also true: there are some 'lease agreements' that are not, in substance leases. These issues are addressed by SIC-27.

Essentially, SIC-27 deals with the issue of how to evaluate the substance of transactions, or a series of linked transactions, in the legal form of a lease. The main purpose of the Interpretation is to reinforce the principle of substance over form, and to ensure that, where appropriate, a series of linked transactions should be accounted for as one transaction. If the transaction does not meet the definition of a lease under IAS 17, SIC-27 deals with the extent to which the arrangement gives rise to other assets and liabilities of the reporting entity, the reporting of any other obligations and the recognition of fee income. *[SIC-27.2]*.

An entity may enter into a transaction or a series of structured transactions (an arrangement) with an unrelated party or parties (an investor) that involves the legal form of a lease. Although the details may vary considerably, a typical example involves an entity leasing or selling assets to an investor and leasing the same assets back. The lease and leaseback transactions are often entered into so that the investor may achieve a tax advantage. *[SIC-27.1]*. In recent years these arrangements have become less common as taxation authorities in various jurisdictions have restricted the tax benefits. The following example illustrates an arrangement that does not, in substance, involve a lease under IAS 17: *[SIC-27.A2(a)]*.

Example 24.4: Substance of an arrangement

Entity A leases a specialised asset that it requires to conduct its business to an Investor and leases the same asset back for a shorter period of time under a sublease. At the end of the sublease period, Entity A has the right to buy back the rights of the Investor under a purchase option. If Entity A does not exercise its purchase option, the Investor has options available to it under each of which it receives a minimum return on its investment in the headlease – the Investor may put the underlying asset back to Entity A, or require it to provide a return on the Investor's investment in the headlease.

The arrangement achieves a tax advantage for the Investor who pays a fee to Entity A and prepays the lease payment obligations under the headlease. The agreement requires the amount prepaid to be invested in risk-free assets and, as a requirement of finalising the execution of the legally binding arrangement, placed into a separate investment account held by a Trustee outside of the control of the entity.

Over the term of the sublease, the sublease payment obligations are satisfied with funds of an equal amount withdrawn from the separate investment account. Entity A guarantees the sublease payment obligations, and will be required to satisfy the guarantee should the separate investment account have insufficient funds. Entity A, but not the Investor, has the right to terminate the sublease early under certain circumstances (e.g. a change in local or international tax law causes the Investor to lose part or all of the tax benefits, or Entity A decides to dispose of (e.g. replace, sell or deplete) the underlying asset) and on payment of a termination value to the Investor. If Entity A chooses early termination, then it would pay the termination value from funds withdrawn from the separate investment account, and if the amount remaining in the separate investment account is insufficient, the difference would be paid by Entity A.

A series of transactions that involve the legal form of a lease should be accounted for as one transaction when the overall economic effect cannot be understood without reference to the series of transactions as a whole. All aspects and implications of an arrangement should be evaluated to determine the substance of the arrangement, with greater weight given to those aspects and implications that will have an economic effect in practice. The accounting should reflect the substance of the arrangement. *[SIC-27.3,4]*.

2.2.1 The arrangement

First, it must be part of a single 'arrangement'; a series of transactions may be closely interrelated, negotiated as a single transaction, and take place concurrently or in a continuous sequence. *[SIC-27.3]*.

Second, there must be indicators that individually demonstrate that an arrangement may not, in substance, involve a lease under IAS 17. SIC-27 states that in circumstances such as those in Example 24.4 above, these indicators are as follows:

(a) the entity retains all the risks and rewards of ownership and there is no significant change in its rights to use the asset;

(b) the primary reason for the arrangement is to achieve a particular tax result, and not to convey the right to use an asset; and

(c) the options on which the arrangement depends are included on terms that make their exercise almost certain (e.g. a put option that is exercisable at a price sufficiently higher than the expected fair value when it becomes exercisable). *[SIC-27.5]*.

In other words, the entity retains more rights than it would in a straightforward sale and finance leaseback. In the example, for instance, it retains all of the residual interests in the asset. The investor has no interest at all in the underlying asset while a lessor under a finance lease will often retain title and some residual value in the asset. The investor has only entered into the transaction to obtain a tax benefit.

2.2.2 Accounting for assets and liabilities arising under the arrangement

The balances arising under the arrangement (in the example these comprise the separate investment account and the lease payment obligations under the sublease) must be assessed to see whether they represent assets and liabilities of the entity. SIC-27 refers to definitions of assets and liabilities and guidance in the *Conceptual Framework for Financial Reporting ('Framework')*. *[Framework 4.4-19]*. It argues that:

(a) the investment account is not an asset of the entity because it cannot control it;

(b) there is only a remote risk that the entity will have to pay out under the guarantee or reimburse the entire amount of any fee received; and

(c) once the arrangement has been set up and the initial payments have been made, no further cash flows will be made by the entity.

The entity cannot use the cash in the investment account for its own benefit, nor can it prevent it being used to make lease payments to the investor. The lease payments will be satisfied solely from funds withdrawn from the separate investment account established with the initial cash flows. In the example, the terms of the arrangement require that a prepaid amount is invested in risk-free assets that are expected to generate sufficient cash flows to satisfy the lease payment obligations. *[SIC-27.6]*. This also demonstrates, *inter alia*, that the entity is not, in substance, entering into a financing arrangement, as it has no need of the funds.

Care must be taken to ensure that the assets in which the prepayment is invested are in fact 'risk-free' and this will have to be monitored throughout the arrangement. A consequence of the financial crisis in 2008 was that it revealed that many so-called 'AAA' or 'risk-free' assets, including sovereign debt, were not risk-free, leaving entities exposed to shortfalls in the cash held in the investment account for which they may have had to make provision.

Other obligations of the entity, including any guarantees provided and obligations incurred on early termination, should be accounted for under IFRS 4 – *Insurance Contracts*, IAS 37 – *Provisions, Contingent Liabilities and Contingent Assets* – or IAS 39 – *Financial Instruments: Recognition and Measurement* (or IFRS 9 – *Financial Instruments* – if the entity has applied that standard), depending on the terms of the arrangement. *[SIC-27.7]*. Therefore, if Entity A were to elect to terminate the arrangement, it would have to provide for its exposure in excess of the available funds in the investment account.

2.2.3 Fee income

SIC-27 addresses the recognition of fee income. There are many factors that could affect the economic substance and nature of the fee and it may not be appropriate to recognise it in its entirety at the inception of the agreement if the entity has significant future performance obligations, retained risks or a significant risk of repayment. Factors to be taken into account include:

(a) obligations that are conditions of earning the fee so that entering into the agreement is not the most significant act required by the arrangement;

(b) limitations are put on the use of the underlying asset that lead to significant changes in the entity's rights to use the asset, e.g. the entity's right to deplete or sell it or pledge it as collateral;

(c) the possibility of reimbursing any amount of the fee and possibly paying some additional amount is not remote. This occurs when, for example:

    (i) the underlying asset is essential for the entity's business, in which case there is a possibility that the entity may be prepared to pay to terminate the arrangement early and be required to repay all or part of the fee; or

    (ii) the possibility that there are insufficient assets in the investment account to meet the lease payment obligations is not remote, and therefore it is possible that the entity may be required to pay some additional amount. This may occur if the entity is required, or has some or total discretion, to invest in assets carrying more than an insignificant amount of risk (e.g. currency, interest rate or credit risk). *[SIC-27.8]*.

An entity must now take great care before it considers any investment as carrying an insignificant amount of risk.

2.2.4 Presentation and disclosure requirements.

The fee must be presented in the income statement based on its economic substance and nature. *[SIC-27.9].* The entity must disclose the following in each period that an arrangement exists:

An entity has to make the disclosures that are necessary to understand the arrangement and the accounting treatment adopted, including the following:

(a) a description of the arrangement including:
  (i) the underlying asset and any restrictions on its use;
  (ii) the life and other significant terms of the arrangement;
  (iii) the transactions that are linked together, including any options; and

(b) the accounting treatment of any fee received, the amount that has been recognised as income in the period, and the line item of the income statement in which it is included.

These disclosures should be provided individually for each arrangement or in aggregate for each class of arrangement. A class is a grouping of arrangements with underlying assets of a similar nature. *[SIC-27.10, 11].*

3 SCOPE AND DEFINITIONS OF IAS 17

3.1 Scope of IAS 17

The standard applies in accounting for all leases other than:

- lease agreements to explore for or use minerals, oil, natural gas and similar non-regenerative resources (see Chapter 39); and
- licensing agreements for such items as motion picture films, video recordings, plays, manuscripts, patents and copyrights.

The standard should not be applied to the measurement by:

- lessees of investment property held under finance leases;
- lessors of investment property leased out under operating leases, as in these cases IAS 40 – *Investment Property* – applies (see Chapter 19);
- lessees of biological assets held under finance leases; or
- lessors of biological assets leased out under operating leases, as in these cases IAS 41 – *Agriculture* – applies (see Chapter 38). *[IAS 17.2].*

3.1.1 Leases and licences

IAS 17 does not define a licensing agreement so the distinction between 'leases' and 'licensing agreements' is not clear. This is not helped by the fact that the agreements may be economically similar. Further, while the examples of licensing agreements excluded from the scope of IAS 17 (motion picture films, video recordings, plays, manuscripts, patents and copyrights) are specific intangible assets, IAS 17 does not exclude leases of intangible assets from its scope. IAS 38 by contrast, excludes from its scope 'lease agreements', stating 'this standard shall be applied in accounting for intangible assets, except intangible assets that are within the scope of another Standard.' *[IAS 38.2]*. It emphasises that 'if another Standard prescribes the accounting for a specific type of intangible asset, an entity applies that Standard instead of this Standard. For example, this Standard does not apply to... leases that are within the scope of IAS 17, Leases.' *[IAS 38.3]*.

IAS 17 does not apply to agreements that are contracts for services that do not transfer the right to use assets from one contracting party to the other. A conventional licence over an intangible asset (such as a film or video) commonly gives a non-exclusive right of 'access' to show or view the video simultaneously with many others but not a 'right of use' of the original film or video itself because the licensee does not control that asset. Arguably, this puts such a conventional licence outside the scope of IAS 17. There is a similar argument underlying IFRIC 4 that is considered further in 2.1 above.

3.1.2 Arrangements over intangible assets

IAS 17 applies to leases over intangible assets although there are additional issues when the right is not tangible.

First, the 'right' in question must be an asset that meets the definition of an intangible asset in IAS 38. Second, because many of these rights are either acquired for an up-front sum or for a series of periodic payments and by definition the period covered by the payments equals the life of the right, there is divergence in practice in how to account for them, i.e. whether they are leases (and if so, whether finance or operating leases) or whether they are acquisitions of assets on deferred payment terms.

Many intangible assets are capable of being subdivided with the part subject to the lease itself meeting the definition of an intangible asset; see Chapter 17 at 2.1. If the rights are exclusive, the part will meet the definition of an intangible asset because it is embodied in legal rights that allow the acquirer to control the benefits arising from the asset. For example, an entity might sell to another entity rights to distribute its product in a particular geographical market. If the right is not on an exclusive basis then it may not be within scope of IAS 38, e.g. it may be a licensing agreement as discussed above. Other arrangements may, on analysis, prove to be for services and not for a right of use of an intangible asset.

Note that it is irrelevant to the analysis whether the original right is recognised prior to the arrangement in the financial statements of the lessor.

Rights that do meet the definition of an intangible asset usually have a finite life, e.g. a radio station may acquire a licence that gives it a right to broadcast over specified frequencies for a period of seven years. Yet the underlying asset on which the right depends exists both before and after the 'right' has been purchased and may have an indefinite life, as is the case with the broadcast spectrum. Many intangible rights can be purchased for an upfront sum, which will be accounted for as the acquisition of an intangible asset that is capitalised at cost. As an alternative to up-front purchase, an entity may pay for the same right in a series of instalments over a period of time. Does it become an operating lease because it is only a short period out of the life of the underlying asset? Usually the answer is no: these rights will not be accounted for as operating leases by comparison to the total life of the underlying asset as the arrangement is over *right* in question. If the arrangement is considered to be a lease, then it will be accounted for in accordance with IAS 17, whatever the pattern of payment.

If, rather than as a lease, the arrangement is seen as the acquisition of an asset on deferred payment terms, the effective interest rate method is mandated. The effective interest rate is the rate that exactly discounts estimated future cash payments or receipts through the expected life of the financial instrument or, when appropriate, a shorter period, to the carrying amount of the financial asset or financial liability. This will take account of estimated future cash payments or receipts through the expected life of the financial instrument, to the extent required by IAS 39 or IFRS 9, which may include some of the 'contingent' payments that are excluded from the measurement of finance leases (see 3.5 below).

Therefore, there are arguments as to whether there are assets and liabilities to be recognised and, even if recognition is accepted, measurement depends on the view that is taken of the applicable standard. In the absence of a clear principle, there is bound to be diversity in practice.

Lessor's leases of intangible assets are excluded from the scope of the proposed lease ED, discussed at 10 below. Lessee's leases of intangible assets would not have to be accounted for in accordance with the proposals.[1] It is assumed that entities will be allowed as an accounting policy election to account for them under the leases standard.

3.2 Lease classification

3.2.1 Finance and operating leases

A finance lease is a 'lease that transfers substantially all the risks and rewards incidental to ownership of an asset', and an operating lease is 'a lease other than a finance lease', *[IAS 17.4]*, i.e. a lease that does not transfer substantially all the risks and rewards incidental to ownership.

The individual circumstances of a lessor and lessee may differ in respect of a single lease contract. As a result, it is perfectly possible that the application of the definitions to the different circumstances of the lessor and lessee may result in the same lease being classified differently by them. For example, a lease may be classified as an operating lease by the lessee and as a finance lease receivable by the lessor if it includes a residual value guarantee provided by a third party. *[IAS 17.9]*. These are discussed further under 3.4.6 below.

3.2.2 Determining the substance of transactions

The classification of leases adopted in the standard is based on the extent to which the risks and rewards incidental to ownership of a leased asset lie with the lessor or the lessee. 'Risks include the possibilities of losses from idle capacity or technological obsolescence and of variations in return due to changing economic conditions. Rewards may be represented by the expectation of profitable operation over the asset's economic life and of gain from appreciation in value or realisation of a residual value.' *[IAS 17.7]*.

Some national standards include the rebuttable presumption that the transfer of substantially all of the risks and rewards occurs if, at the inception of the lease, the present value of the minimum lease payments amounts to substantially all (normally 90% or more) of the fair value of the leased asset. IAS 17 provides no numerical guidelines to be applied in classifying a lease as either finance or operating. It seems that it was a conscious decision of the (then) IASC Board not to refer to a percentage such as 90% in the standard, as it wanted to avoid the possibility of lease classification being reduced to a single pass or fail test.

Instead, the standard takes a more principles-based substance over form approach. It makes the statement that the classification of a lease depends on the substance of the transaction rather than the form of the contract, and lists a number of examples of situations that individually or in combination would normally lead to a lease being classified as a finance lease: *[IAS 17.10]*

(a) the lease transfers ownership of the asset to the lessee by the end of the lease term;

(b) the lessee has the option to purchase the asset at a price which is expected to be sufficiently lower than the fair value at the date the option becomes exercisable such that, at the inception of the lease, it is reasonably certain that the option will be exercised (frequently called a 'bargain purchase' option);

(c) the lease term is for the major part of the economic life of the asset even if title is not transferred;

(d) at the inception of the lease the present value of the minimum lease payments amounts to at least substantially all of the fair value of the leased asset; and

(e) the leased assets are of a specialised nature such that only the lessee can use them without major modifications being made.

All of these are indicators that the lessor will only look to the lessee to obtain a return from the leasing transaction, so it can be presumed that the lessee will, in fact, pay for the asset.

Although the first criterion refers to title being transferred, it is clear from the standard that title does not have to be transferred to the lessee for a lease to be classified as a finance lease. *[IAS 17.4]*. The point is that the lease will almost certainly be classified as a finance lease if title does transfer.

'Fair value' is defined as the amount for which an asset could be exchanged or a liability settled, between knowledgeable, willing parties in an arm's length transaction (see 3.4.2 below). *[IAS 17.4]*. IFRS 13 – *Fair Value Measurement* – does not apply because the IASB states that IAS 17 uses 'fair value' in a way that differs in some respects from the definition in the IFRS. *[IFRS 13.6, IAS 17.6A]*.

Options such as those referred to under (b) are common in lease agreements. The bargain purchase option is designed to give the lessor its expected lender's return but no more (comprising interest on its investment perhaps together with a relatively small fee), over the life of the agreement.

Criteria (c) and (d) above also include the unquantified expressions 'major part of' and 'substantially all', which means that judgement must be used in determining their effect on the risks and rewards of ownership. By contrast, in US GAAP the equivalent to (c) above in ASC 840 (formerly SFAS 13) does quantify when a lease will be a capital lease, (the equivalent of a finance lease). In ASC 840, if the lease term is equal to 75% or more of the estimated economic life of the leased asset, the lease will normally be a capital lease (there is an exception if the beginning of the lease term falls within the last 25% of the total estimated economic life of the leased property, including earlier years of use, where this criterion is not used for purposes of classifying the lease).[2] However in practice, if the lease is for the major part of the economic life of the asset then it is unlikely that the lessor will rely on any party other than the lessee to obtain its return from the lease. This would still not be conclusive evidence that the lease should be classified as a finance lease. There could be other terms that indicate that the significant risks and rewards of ownership rest with the lessor, e.g. lease payments might be reset periodically to market rates or there might be significant technological, obsolescence or damage risks borne by the lessor.

Similarly, whilst (d) above refers to the present value of the minimum lease payments being at least 'substantially all of the fair value of the asset', it does so without putting a percentage to it. We have already speculated as to why this may be; nevertheless, we see no harm in practice in applying the '90% test' described above as a rule of thumb benchmark as part of the overall process in reaching a judgement as to the classification of a lease. Clearly, though, it cannot be applied as a hard and fast rule.

For an example of the 90% test, see Example 24.7 at 3.4.9 below. In that example, the present value of the minimum lease payments is calculated to be 92.74% of the asset's fair value; as this exceeds 90%, this would normally indicate that the lease is a finance lease. Nevertheless, the other criteria discussed above would need to be considered as well.

Consequently, we would stress that the 90% test is not an explicit requirement of the standard and should not be applied as a rule or in isolation, but it may be a useful tool to use in practice in attempting to determine the economic substance of a lease arrangement.

The standard then goes on to list the following indicators of situations that, individually or in combination, could also lead to a lease being classified as a finance lease: *[IAS 17.11]*

(a) if the lessee can cancel the lease, the lessor's losses associated with the cancellation are borne by the lessee;

(b) gains or losses from the fluctuation in the fair value of the residual fall to the lessee (for example, in the form of a rent rebate equalling most of the sale proceeds at the end of the lease); and

(c) the lessee has the ability to continue the lease for a secondary period at a rent which is substantially lower than market rent.

IAS 17 notes that these examples are only indications and are not always conclusive. A right to purchase the residual asset for its fair value or an expectation to pay substantially all of the fair value of the asset if contingent rents are taken into account will not necessarily give the lessee substantially all of the risks and rewards of ownership. *[IAS 17.12]*.

In our view, other considerations that could be made in determining the economic substance of the lease arrangement include the following:

- are the lease rentals based on a market rate for use of the asset (which would indicate an operating lease) or a financing rate for use of the funds, which would be indicative of a finance lease? and
- is the existence of put and call options a feature of the lease? If so, are they exercisable at a predetermined price or formula (indicating a finance lease) or are they exercisable at the market price at the time the option is exercised (indicating an operating lease)?

Note that these two considerations mean that an arrangement for the whole of an asset's useful life may be an operating lease, as may an agreement in which the lessee has a right to obtain title to the asset at market value.

3.2.3 Changes to lease terms and provisions

Lease classification is made at the inception of the lease, which is the earlier of the date of the lease agreement or of a commitment by the parties to the principal provisions of the lease. *[IAS 17.4]*. Lease classification is only changed if, at any time during the lease, the lessee and the lessor agree to change the provisions of the lease (without renewing it) in such a way that it would have been classified differently at inception had the changed terms been in effect at that time. *[IAS 17.13]*. 'Renewing' in this context refers to the lessee and lessor entering into an agreement for a new lease that supersedes the existing lease between the two parties. 'Renewing' should also be distinguished from exercising a renewal option and thereby extending the lease for an additional period. If the lease does contain a renewal option it will be taken into account in assessing the initial lease classification (see above).

This section addresses changes to the terms of leases and changes to assessments and estimates connected with lease accounting and whether or not they will change the initial classification of the lease. In particular it considers:

(a) a modification to the terms of an existing lease;

(b) what happens if the lessee exercises an option in the original lease whose exercise was not considered probable at inception; or

(c) how to take account of a change in estimates such as the useful life or residual value.

While all of these may affect accounting for the lease, nothing that falls within (b) or (c) will affect the way in which the lease is classified, i.e. they will not change an operating lease into a finance lease or vice versa.

Modifications to the terms of an existing lease ((a) above) affect the risks and rewards incidental to ownership of the asset by changing the terms and cash flows of the existing lease. The revised agreement resulting from the modification is considered as a new agreement and should be accounted for appropriately, as a finance or operating lease, prospectively over the remaining term of the lease.

The second category ((b) above) relates to circumstances such as exercising an option to extend the lease or purchase the underlying asset, when these options were included in the original lease but whose exercise were not considered probable at its inception. Changes in circumstances or intentions do not give rise to a new classification of a lease for accounting purposes, provided that the circumstances or intentions concerned do not indicate that the initial lease classification was not based on the substance of the lease arrangement at the time it was entered into, in which case the initial lease classification would be an error. This category of change is more likely to occur in the context of a lease originally classified as an operating lease.

Changes in estimates (for example, changes in estimates of the economic life or of the residual value of the leased item) or changes in circumstances (for example, default by the lessee – category (c) above) do not result in the lease being reclassified for accounting purposes. *[IAS 17.13]*. This is of particular relevance given the requirement in IAS 16 that the residual value and useful life of an asset must be reviewed at least at each financial year end. *[IAS 16.51]*. These changes principally affect accounting by lessors. How lessors account for residual values, including reductions in the amounts they expect to receive, is discussed at 4.2.3 below.

A lessee can negotiate a new lease with the lessor that has no effect on the existing lease. This new lease is often referred to as a 'renewal'. It will be accounted for as a new lease on its own terms.

Example 24.5: Lease classification

Consider the following scenarios:

(a) Entity A leases a motor vehicle from Entity B for a non-cancellable three-year period. At the inception of the lease, the lease was assessed as an operating lease. The lease did not contain any explicit option in the lease contract to extend the term of the lease. After 2 years, Entity A applies to Entity B to extend the lease for a further two years after the initial three-year period is complete. This extension is granted by the leasing company on an arm's length basis.

Entity A's negotiations result in a renewed (i.e. new) lease, not a change in the provisions of the original lease. This does not affect the classification of the original lease. Although the date of inception of the new lease would be the date on which negotiations were completed, the new lease would not be accounted for until its commencement, which will be after the termination of the original lease.

(b) Entity C leases a machine tool from Entity D for 5 years, expecting to purchase a new asset after the lease expires. After 3 years, Entity C concludes that it is more economically viable for it to lease the asset from Entity D for a total of 8 years. The lessor agrees to revised lease terms and the lease is extended by 3 years, giving a total term of 8 years. At the same time the lease payments for years 4 and 5 are revised so that Entity C will pay a new rental for each of the years 4 to 8.

This is a lease modification as it has resulted in a change to the terms of the original lease. The entity will have to assess whether the revised lease is an operating or finance lease.

(c) Entity E leases an asset from Entity F for 10 years. The lease includes a purchase option under which Entity E may purchase the asset from Entity F at the end of the lease. The exercise price is fair value. Entity E is required to give notice of its intention to purchase no later than the end of the eighth year of the lease (since this arrangement allows Entity F time to market the leased asset for sale). On inception, Entity E classifies the lease as an operating lease, believing it was not reasonably certain that it would exercise the option. Near the end of the eighth year of the lease, Entity E serves notice that it will purchase the asset, thereby creating a binding purchase commitment.

Entity E exercises an option that was not considered reasonably certain at inception; this is a change in estimate and does not affect lease classification. Many entities would consider the arrangement to be executory at the time that the notice is given even though there is a legal obligation to make the option payment (see Chapter 27 at 2.2.1.A) and therefore would account for the purchase option only when it is exercised.

IAS 17 does not give any guidance on how to assess whether modified lease terms give rise to a new classification or on how to measure modifications of leases if changes affect the value of the assets and liabilities for both lessor and lessee. These issues are discussed at 6 below. Sections 6.1.1 and 6.1.2 below discuss how to assess whether the classification has changed, based on the revised cash flows, and how to account for the reclassification. Example 24.22 at 6.1.1 below describes circumstances in which a lease term is extended mid-term, changing the cash flows over the remainder of the original lease term as well as requiring the lessee to make payments during the extended term.

If lease terms are modified but the classification does not change, the entity will still have to account for the modified cash flows. How to account for the changes if a finance lease remains a finance lease is discussed at 6.1.3 below. Accounting for changes to the terms of operating leases, where those changes do not result in reclassification, is considered at 6.1.5 below.

3.3 Leases of land – finance or operating leases?

Land normally has an indefinite economic life and, until IAS 17 was amended in 2009, all leases over land were classified as operating leases unless title was expected to pass to the lessee by the end of the lease term. The standard now requires an entity to assess the classification of leases over land as finance or operating leases in accordance with the general rules in paragraphs 7-13 that are described above. Many leases include elements for both land and buildings and both parts must be considered separately as discussed in 3.3.4 below.

The standard includes a reminder that 'in determining whether the land element is an operating or a finance lease, an important consideration is that land normally has an indefinite economic life'. *[IAS 17.15A]*. A lease term for the major part of the economic life of the asset can indicate that a lease is a finance lease, even if title is not transferred, *[IAS 17.10]*, and by repeating this in the amendment the IASB is stressing that this particular feature of finance leases is not likely to be met.

The Board expected the amendment to affect lease classification of land, noting that it will be an improvement in accounting for leases and the significance of this issue in countries in which property rights are obtained under long-term leases. *[IAS 17.BC8E]*. In these jurisdictions these interests are frequently purchased for single lease premiums in a manner comparable to the purchase of a freehold, although there may also be a small annual rent payable (e.g. a 'ground rent' in the UK). The Basis for Conclusions suggests that the lessee in leases of this type 'will typically be in a position economically similar to an entity that purchased the land and buildings. The present value of the residual value of the property in a lease with a term of several decades would be negligible. The Board concluded that accounting for the land element as a finance lease in such circumstances would be consistent with the economic position of the lessee.' *[IAS 17.BC8C]*. Therefore, the fact that land has an indefinite life will be assessed alongside other features that distinguish finance leases from operating leases. As well as considering whether the minimum lease payments amount to substantially all of the fair value, it is necessary to consider whether the lease includes other features that indicate that the significant risks and rewards of ownership rest with the lessor rather than the lessee. These include significant contingent rentals, rentals that are reset to market rates and fair value purchase options, all of which could indicate that the lease is an operating lease.

Some have questioned whether a purchase of a right to use land could ever be classified as a fixed asset, i.e. as PP&E under IAS 16 or an intangible asset under IAS 38, especially in circumstances in which the right can be extended indefinitely, as happens in some jurisdictions. The Interpretations Committee has noted that a lease could be indefinite with extensions or renewals so the fact that the right to use could have an indefinite period does not prevent it from qualifying as a lease in accordance with IAS 17. In the particular country, entities can purchase a right to exploit or build on land that can be extended indefinitely, subject to government rights to take back possession at the end of the term or otherwise with compensation. The Committee concluded that the particular arrangement should be classified as a lease. However, because the circumstances were specific to a jurisdiction, the Committee decided not to take the matter onto its agenda.[3]

An advantage of classifying certain land leases as finance leases is that they can then be presented in the financial statements as property, plant and equipment. Under the previous standard, unless title to the land transfers to the lessee, premiums paid for a leasehold interest in land always represented pre-paid lease payments to be amortised over the lease term in accordance with the pattern of benefits provided. *[IAS 17 (2008).14]*. This treatment is now reserved for pre-paid land rentals that are not classified as finance leases. An example would be a lease premium that comprises ten year's prepaid rentals, which is most unlikely to be classified as a finance lease.

A company that reclassified land leases as finance leases as a result of the change to IAS 17 is Wm Morrison Supermarkets PLC.

Extract 24.1: Wm Morrison Supermarkets PLC (2011)

Consolidated financial statements under International Financial Reporting Standards [extract]
Group accounting policies [extract]
Long-leasehold land

The amendment to IAS 17 Leases is effective for annual periods beginning on or after 1 January 2010. During the period, the Group has reassessed the classification of unexpired land leases between operating and finance leases. Leases newly classified as finance leases have been accounted for retrospectively in accordance with IAS 8 Accounting policies, changes in accounting estimates and errors, and the required disclosures have been made.

The adoption of the amendment to IAS 17 Leases has resulted in a) derecognising long-lease land premiums previously classified within non-current asset lease prepayments, and the current element classified within debtors; and b) recognising a corresponding increase in the closing net book value of leasehold land and buildings to reflect the carrying value of the leased assets. The impact on previously disclosed costs and net book value for each of the balance sheet dates of 30 January 2011, 31 January 2010 and 1 February 2009 is detailed in notes 11 and 15.

The Group has assessed the present value of future minimum lease payments and considers these obligations to be immaterial for disclosure.

The depreciation rate on the newly classified leases is consistent with the annual amortisation charge incurred on the previous lease prepayments. Therefore there is no impact on profit for the period for the year ended 30 January 2011, or reserves of comparative periods.

There is no impact on earnings per share previously disclosed.

Notes to the Group financial statements [extract]
11 Property, plant and equipment [extract]

Leasehold land and buildings have been restated for the comparative periods as a result of an amendment to IAS 17 Leases. At 30 January 2011, the effect is a decrease of £271m (2010: £257m; 2009: £250m) to non-current asset lease prepayments and an increase to closing net book value of leasehold land and buildings of £273m (2010: £259m; 2009: £251m).

3.3.1 Lessors and land leases

Lessors selling a leasehold interest in land, where the interest is classified as a finance lease, can recognise a profit on disposal of that interest. In other words, they may recognise a receivable under a finance lease rather than the land itself and recognise a profit on disposal.

The previous requirement to treat all leases over land as operating leases probably had a more profound effect on lessors than lessees. Lessors selling a leasehold interest, no matter how long its term, were apparently unable to treat the element of the proceeds that related to the land as anything other than prepaid rent to be spread on a straight-line basis over the lease term. This did not apply to the sale of a leasehold interest in any property if that was defined as an interest under a finance lease. The issues of separating the leasehold interests in land and properties are discussed at 3.3.4 below.

The lessee could not classify its prepaid lease premium as 'property, plant and equipment' and could not revalue it, unless the interest met the definition of investment property (see 3.3.5 below) but it indubitably had acquired an asset that would be amortised over its useful life.

3.3.2 Measurement of operating leases over land

Prepayments that are classified as operating leases over land and buildings will continue to be disclosed as current or non-current assets, as appropriate, in the entity's statement of financial position. If certain costs arise at the inception of the lease that are necessary to consummate the agreement and enable a lessee to exercise its rights under the lease agreement, these costs are incurred as a direct result of the lease. Therefore, it is appropriate to consider these as lease-related costs that should be subject to the same accounting treatment as prepaid lease payments. Initial direct costs of leases are discussed at 3.4.8 below.

3.3.3 Presentation of operating leases over land

The following is an example of presentation of pre-paid operating leases in the statement of financial position, together with the supporting note.

Extract 24.2: VTech Holdings Ltd. (2011)

Consolidated Financial Statements [extract]
Consolidated Balance Sheet [extract]
As at 31 March 2011

	Note	**2011** **US$ million**	2010 US$ million
Non-current assets			
Tangible assets	7	**78.4**	81.4
Leasehold land payments	8	**5.0**	4.9
Investments	9	**0.2**	0.2
Deferred tax assets	10(b)	**5.4**	5.6
		89.0	92.1

Notes to the Financial Statements [extract]

Principal Accounting Policies [extract]

J Leases [extract]

Leasehold land payments are up-front payments to acquire long-term leasehold interests in land. These payments are stated at cost and are amortised on a straight-line basis over the respective period of the leases.

8 Leasehold Land Payments

	Note	**2011** **US$ million**	2010 US$ million
Net book value at 1 April		**4.9**	2.2
Transfer from tangible assets		**–**	2.8
Amortisation	2	**(0.1)**	(0.1)
Effect of changes in exchange rates		**0.2**	–
Net book value at 31s March		**5.0**	4.9
Leasehold land payments in respect of:			
Owner-occupied properties		**5.0**	4.9

3.3.4 Separating land and buildings

A characteristic of property leases in some jurisdictions (such as the UK) is that it is not possible to lease a building without leasing the land on which it stands – under UK property law all such leases are leases of land and everything attached to it. There is no separate fair value for the land and buildings elements as they cannot be disposed of separately and the IASB noted that in substance such leases may differ little from buying a property. *[IAS 17.BC5].* The standard states explicitly that the land and buildings elements of leases are considered separately for the purposes of lease classification. *[IAS 17.15A].* Each part must be classified as an operating or finance lease in the same way as leases of other assets. This does not apply to leases of investment properties where there is no requirement to separate the land and buildings elements; see 3.3.5 below.

Before the amendment to IAS 17 allowing land leases to be accounted for as finance leases, initial classification was based on whether or not title passed. Where title to the land did not pass and it had an indefinite economic life, the land was normally classified as an operating lease while the buildings element was be an operating lease or finance lease according to the classification in the standard. *[IAS 17 (2008).15]*. The initial classification now depends on the individual assessment of both land and buildings parts of the lease.

Entities may need to make the allocation between the land and buildings elements even if both are clearly finance leases as there could be a difference in amortisation methods, although this would be very unusual. *[IAS 17.BC8F]*. Much more common is a difference in useful economic life, where an entity takes out a lease for land and buildings where the term is longer than the useful life of any building on the land, e.g. a lease of 75 years over land on which there is a building that has a remaining useful life of 30 years.

If either or both parts of the lease might comprise a finance lease, the minimum lease payments need to be allocated between the land and buildings elements in proportion to the respective fair values of the leasehold interest in the land and buildings elements at the inception of the lease. The minimum lease payments must, of course, include any up-front payments, such as the payment for a lease premium. *[IAS 17.16]*.

The allocation of the minimum lease payments should be weighted to reflect the fair value of the land and buildings components to the extent they are the subject of the lease. This means that the amount that is being allocated is the lessee's leasehold interest in the land and buildings and the compensation received by the lessor, not the relative fair values of the land and buildings. The amount for which the land could be purchased at the inception of the lease is not the same as the value of that interest to the lessee. As land has an indefinite life, the value to the lessor may not be significantly affected by the grant of the lease. *[IAS 17.BC9-11]*.

The standard addresses the fact that it may not be possible to determine the fair values of the elements at inception and allows the following:

- if it is difficult or impossible to allocate the payments between the two elements, then the entire lease may be classified as a finance lease unless it is obvious that both the land and buildings elements are operating leases; *[IAS 17.16]*
- if the land element is immaterial, the lease may be treated as a single unit and classified as a finance or operating lease. The economic life of the entire leased asset will be the economic life of the buildings. *[IAS 17.17]*.

Some examples of the ways in which these exemptions may operate in practice are as follows:

Chapter 24

Example 24.6: Leases of land and buildings

Consider the following scenarios:

- Company A leases a building (and the underlying land) for 10 years. The remaining economic life of the building when the lease is entered into is 30 years. The lease is for considerably less than the economic life of the building so it is clear that both the land and buildings elements are operating leases and no separation is necessary.
- Company B takes on a 30-year lease of a new building and the underlying land. It is on a retail park and almost all of the value is ascribed to the building as land values are low. Although the building has a fabric life of 60 years, its economic life is estimated to be 30 years, after which it is expected to be technologically obsolete. The lease is for most of the economic life of the buildings and the present value of the minimum lease payments amounts to substantially all of the fair value of the building. It is not legally possible to lease the building without leasing the underlying land or, therefore, to estimate the relative fair values reliably. In any event, the lessor retains the residual value in the land and the lessee's interest in the land alone must be insignificant. The entire lease is accounted for as a finance lease with an economic life of 30 years.
- Company C takes out a 25 year non-cancellable lease of premises in the centre of a major town where land values are high. There are upward-only rent reviews every 5 years. It is a modern building that may have a remaining economic life of 35 years (or perhaps more, as the building has a fabric life of 60 years) and the land is clearly valuable to the lessor, who will want a reasonable return from it over the lease term. In this case the interest in the building may or may not be a finance lease and the lessee's leasehold interest in the land is not insignificant. Company C will have to undertake a valuation exercise to determine the allocation of minimum lease payments between the land and building elements of the lease in order to determine whether or not it has finance or operating leases over the land and buildings.

There will be many circumstances in which it is unclear whether the lessee has a finance or operating lease over land and buildings. In such cases it will probably be necessary to obtain the help of a valuation expert.

There are four elements that need to be taken into account in the apportionment: the value within the lease of the buildings and the land, and the residual value of both buildings and land. In the UK, The Royal Institution of Chartered Surveyors has produced an information paper analysing the apportionments based on these elements for lease classification under IFRSs, which could be of more general interest.[4] The principal steps are as follows:

(a) assess the freehold value of the land and buildings;

(b) apportion the freehold value between the value within the lease and the residual (reversionary) value;

(c) apportion the freehold value between land and buildings by calculating the value of one or other interest (usually, in practice, the building element) and deducting this from the value obtained in (b) to obtain the other;

(d) apportion the value of the buildings element calculated at (c) between the residual and the value within the lease;

(e) the value within the lease (b) can now be allocated between the buildings element (calculated at (d)) and the land element ((b) less (d)); and

(f) apportion minimum lease payment between land and buildings in the ratio in (e) above.

This methodology makes it possible to calculate the implicit interest rate separately for the building as all elements needed for the calculation are known (fair value of the building, value of its residual and an appropriate proportion of the rentals paid).[5]

3.3.5 Leases and investment properties

IAS 17 requires leases to be separated into land and building components, subject to this being possible or the land element being immaterial. If the interest is an investment property carried at fair value in accordance with IAS 40, there is no requirement to separate the land and buildings elements of the lease. *[IAS 17.18].*

Once the lessee has classified an operating lease property interest as if it were held under a finance lease, it must apply the fair value model and it must continue to do so even if subsequent changes in circumstances mean that the property interest is no longer an investment property to the lessee. IAS 17 gives two examples:

(a) the lessee occupies the property, in which case it is transferred to owner-occupied property at fair value at the date of change of use; or

(b) the lessee grants a sublease over substantially all of its property interest to an unrelated third party. It will treat the sublease as a finance lease to the third party even though the interest may well be accounted for as an operating lease by that party. *[IAS 17.19].*

In some arrangements, a developer may acquire a headlease over land and sell its rights under that same headlease. In these circumstances the developer may apply an IAS 40 analysis and treat the transaction as a purchase and sale of the same investment property. However, this does depend on the disposal in substance of the same asset as the one that has been acquired.

Under IAS 17 and IAS 40, entities are allowed to treat interests under operating leases as investment properties as long as they apply the fair value model (see Chapter 19). Until both IAS 17 and IAS 40 were amended in 2003, IFRS did not permit an interest in property held under an operating lease to be classified as an investment property. This was of great significance to the property industry in places such as the UK, where long leasehold interests in property are common, and to other jurisdictions such as Hong Kong where there are no freehold interests. In the UK these leasehold interests are normally acquired for an up-front premium that, if not recognised as an investment property asset, would have to be treated as a prepayment and gradually amortised. The amortisation of the prepayment would have effectively forced these entities to depreciate assets that would not otherwise have been depreciated (investment properties are not depreciated under IAS 40).

3.4 Defined terms

3.4.1 Inception and commencement of the lease

The standard distinguishes between the inception of the lease (when leases are classified) and the commencement of the lease term (when recognition takes place). The *inception* of the lease is the earlier of the date of the lease agreement and the date of commitment of the parties to the principal terms of the lease. This is the date on which a lease is classified as a finance or operating lease and, for finance leases, the date at which the amounts to be recognised at commencement are determined. [IAS 17.4]. The *commencement* of the lease term is the date on which the lessee is entitled to exercise its right to use the leased asset and is the date of initial recognition of the assets, liabilities, income and expenses of the lease in the financial statements. [IAS 17.4]. This means that the entity makes an initial calculation of the assets and liabilities under a finance lease at inception of the lease but does not recognise these in the financial statements until the commencement date, if this is later. These amounts may in some circumstances be revised.

It is not uncommon for these two dates to be different, especially if the asset is under construction. Lease payments may be adjusted for changes in the lessor's costs during the period between inception and commencement. The lease may allow for changes in respect of costs of construction, acquisition costs, changes in the lessor's financing costs and any other factor, such as changes in general price levels, during the construction period. Changes to the lease payments as a result of such events are deemed to take place at inception of the lease, i.e. are taken into account in establishing, at inception, whether it is a finance or operating lease. [IAS 17.5]. In other words, if the final cost of the asset, and hence its fair value, is not known until after the date of inception, hindsight is used to establish that fair value.

The fair value may be known at inception but payment delayed until commencement, which may happen with large but routinely constructed assets such as aircraft or railway locomotives. The lease liability will increase between the date of inception and the date of commencement, taking account of payments made and the interest rate implicit in the lease (see 3.4.5 below). Although IAS 17 does not address this, the lessee will add the increase in the liability until the commencement date to the asset. It is not a finance cost on the liability (no liability is recognised prior to commencement) and nor need it be an expense. It is not appropriate to recognise at commencement the liability that was calculated at inception as that would change the interest rate implicit in the lease.

The standard also considers what will happen if the lease terms are changed so radically (but without entering into a new lease agreement) that it would have been classified in a different way, e.g. it would have been a finance lease instead of an operating lease. Such changes could happen at any stage during the lease (see 3.2.3 above) but if they happen in the period between inception and commencement, the lease will be classified at inception in accordance with the revised terms as if they had existed as at that date. Accounting for modifications is discussed at 6 below.

3.4.2 Fair value

Fair value is defined as the amount for which an asset could be exchanged or a liability settled, between knowledgeable, willing parties in an arm's length transaction. [IAS 17.4]. In practice, the transaction price, i.e. the purchase price of the asset that is the subject of the lease, will be its fair value, unless there is evidence to the contrary. IFRS 13 does not apply because IAS 17 uses 'fair value' in a way that differs in some respects from the definition in the IFRS. [IFRS 13.6, IAS 17.6A]. As a result lessees and lessors are also exempt from IFRS 13's disclosure requirements.

3.4.3 Minimum lease payments

The minimum lease payments are the payments over the lease term that the lessee is or can be required to make, excluding contingent rent, costs for services and taxes to be paid by and reimbursed to the lessor, together with:

(a) for a lessee, any amounts guaranteed by the lessee or by a party related to the lessee;

(b) for a lessor, any residual guaranteed to the lessor by:

  (i) the lessee or by a party related to the lessee; or

  (ii) a third party unrelated to the lessor who is financially capable of discharging the obligations under the guarantee.

The lessee may have an option to purchase the asset at a price that is expected to be sufficiently lower than the fair value at the date the option becomes exercisable so that, at the inception of the lease, it is reasonably certain to be exercised. In this case the minimum lease payments comprise the minimum payments payable over the lease term to the expected date of exercise of this purchase option and the payment required to exercise it. *[IAS 17.4]*.

3.4.4 Lease term and non-cancellable period

The lease term is the non-cancellable period for which the lessee has contracted to lease the asset, together with any further terms for which the lessee has the option to continue to lease the asset, with or without further payment, if it is reasonably certain at the inception of the lease that the lessee will exercise the option. *[IAS 17.4]*. A non-cancellable lease is either a lease that has no cancellation terms or one that has terms that effectively force the lessee to continue to use the asset for the period of the agreement. Therefore, a lease is considered to be non-cancellable if it can be cancelled only:

(a) on the occurrence of a remote contingency;

(b) with the permission of the lessor;

(c) if the lessee enters into a new lease with the same lessor for the same or an equivalent asset; or

(d) if the lessee is required to pay additional amounts that make it reasonably certain at inception that the lessee will continue the lease. *[IAS 17.4]*.

An example of (d) is a requirement that the lessee pays a termination payment equivalent to the present value of the remaining lease payments.

3.4.5 Interest rate implicit in the lease and incremental borrowing rate

The interest rate implicit in the lease ('IIR') is the discount rate that, at the inception of the lease, causes the aggregate present value of

(a) the minimum lease payments; and

(b) the unguaranteed residual value

to be equal to the sum of the fair value of the leased asset and any initial direct costs of the lessor. Example 24.7 at 3.4.9 below illustrates the calculation of the implicit interest rate.

If it is not practicable to determine this then the lessee may use its incremental borrowing rate of interest, which it is the rate of interest the lessee would have to pay on a similar lease or, if that is not determinable, the rate that, at the inception of the lease, the lessee would have to pay to borrow over a similar term, and with a similar security, the funds necessary to purchase the asset. *[IAS 17.4]*.

3.4.6 Residual value

The guaranteed residual value is:

(a) for a lessee, the part of the residual value that is guaranteed by itself or by one of its related parties. The amount of the guarantee is the maximum amount that could, in any event, become payable; and

(b) for a lessor, it is the part of the residual value that is guaranteed by the lessee or by a third party unrelated to the lessor who is financially capable of discharging the obligations under the guarantee.

The lessor's unguaranteed residual value is any part of the residual value of the leased asset, the realisation of which is not assured or is guaranteed solely by a party related to it. *[IAS 17.4]*.

If the net present value of the residual value of an asset is significant and is not guaranteed by the lessee or a party related to it, then the lease is likely to be classified as an operating lease. The risks of recovering the significant residual value will be the lessor's; consequently it is unlikely that 'substantially all' of the risks and rewards of ownership will have passed to the lessee. There are frequently problems of interpretation regarding the significance of residual values in lease classification. Lessees may find it difficult to obtain information in order to calculate the unguaranteed residual values. However, lessees may guarantee all or part of the residual value of the asset and this has to be taken into account in the lease classification.

3.4.6.A Residual value guarantors

A lessee and lessor may legitimately classify the same lease differently if the lessor has received a residual value guarantee provided by a third party. *[IAS 17.9]*. Residual value guarantors undertake to acquire the assets from the lessor at an agreed amount at the end of the lease term because they can dispose of the assets on a ready and reliable market. As a result, the lease is an operating lease for the lessee and a finance lease for the lessor. Residual value guarantors may be prepared to take the residual risk with many types of assets as long as there is a second-hand market. This is particularly common with vehicle leases where there is an efficient second-hand market, including price guides, many car dealers and car auctions.

3.4.7 Contingent rents

Contingent rents, which are excluded from minimum lease payments, are defined in the standard as that portion of the lease payments that are not fixed in amount, but are based on a factor other than just the passage of time (for example, percentage of sales, amount of usage, price indices, market rates of interest). *[IAS 17.4]*.

Contingent rents are embedded derivatives, as defined by IAS 39 (or IFRS 9, should the entity apply that IFRS), and in principle within the scope of that standard. An embedded derivative is a component of a hybrid or combined instrument that also includes a non-derivative host contract; it has the effect that some of the cash flows of the combined instrument vary in a similar way to a stand-alone derivative. In other words, it causes some or all of the cash flows that otherwise would be required by the contract to be modified according to a specified underlying. *[IAS 39.10]*. Embedded derivatives have to be separated from the host contract and recognised separately in the financial statements of the entity unless they are closely related to the economic characteristics and risks of the host contract. *[IAS 39.11]*.

IAS 39 specifically identifies the examples of contingent rents referred to in IAS 17 as being 'closely related' to the lease contract and hence not separately accounted for. *[IAS 39.11, AG33(f)]*. This means that lessees continue to expense such contingent payments as they arise.

However, other types of contingent rent could be embedded derivatives, e.g. an index that relates to inflation in another economic environment. *[IAS 39.AG33(f)]*. In the case of more complex lease terms, reference should be made to IAS 39 paragraphs 10 to 13 and Section 5 of Chapter 42.

A lease is classified as a finance lease if it transfers substantially all the risks and rewards incidental to ownership. *[IAS 17.8]*. Contingent payments will be taken into account in assessing whether substantially all of the risks and rewards of ownership have been transferred; e.g. property rentals that are periodically reset to market rates would tend to indicate that risks and rewards rest with the lessor – see the discussion at 3.2.2 above. This still leaves open to debate whether a particular 'contingency' is in fact contingent or is so certain that it ought to be reflected in the minimum lease payments for the purposes of classifying the lease. In practice this will always be based on an assessment of the individual circumstances.

Lessees under finance leases need to disclose the minimum lease payments payable under finance leases and contingent rents recognised as an expense in the period (see 9.2 below). *[IAS 17.31(b), (31)(c)]*. Some argue that once the contingency has occurred, it is no longer contingent and should be included in the disclosure of future minimum lease payments. This argument arises most often in the context of operating leases (see below).

3.4.7.A Contingent rents and operating leases

IAS 17 specifies that lessees expense contingent rents relating to finance leases in the period in which they are incurred. *[IAS 17.25]*. However, the Standard is not explicit in the treatment of contingent elements of operating lease rentals.

In its May 2006 meeting, the Interpretations Committee considered whether an estimate of contingent rents should be included in the total operating lease payments or lease income to be recognised on a straight line basis over the lease term. It concluded that current practice was to exclude such amounts (which is consistent with our view of the issue) and did not, therefore, add the matter to its agenda for further consideration. Accordingly, lease payments or receipts under operating leases may exclude contingent amounts. However, the area remains contentious and practice undoubtedly varies. Views are divided on whether minimum lease payments determined at the inception of the lease are revised on the occurrence of the contingency, e.g. whether minimum lease payments change when there are rent revisions that are stipulated in the original lease agreement, either for straight-line recognition or disclosure purposes.

Contingent property rents are common. They usually fall into one of two categories: rents that vary in accordance with an index (e.g. a cost or retail price index) or those that vary with turnover or a similar contingency. In the case of contingencies based on an index, the treatments found in practice include:

(a) excluding all contingent payments from measurement and disclosure

If the initial payment before any indexation changes was 100 per year, continue to recognise as minimum lease payments of 100 per year throughout the term; or

(b) reflecting all contingencies that have occurred in future minimum lease disclosures.

This is on the basis that the contingency has occurred and IAS 17 specifies disclosure of *future* minimum lease payments. If at the end of year 1, the index was 2.5, the minimum lease payments for disclosure purposes would be 102.5 for each remaining year of the lease term. Alternatively, some might apply the same rate (i.e. 2.5%) or an estimate of future rates to the initial payment when disclosing the amounts for subsequent periods.

Some differentiate between rent reviews that are upward only (or, in principle, downward only) and those that will vary according to the index. They would take into account in calculating the minimum lease payments upward-only increases in accordance with (b) above but would exclude from those that may be upward or downward, on the basis that these are truly contingent. Lease disclosures relating to minimum lease payments and contingent rents are discussed at 9.3 below.

3.4.8 Initial direct costs

Initial direct costs are incremental costs that are directly attributable to negotiating and arranging a lease, except for such costs incurred by manufacturer or dealer lessors. *[IAS 17.4].*

If the lessee incurs costs that are directly attributable to activities it has performed to obtain a finance lease, these are added to the amount recognised as an asset. *[IAS 17.24].* IAS 17 is silent on the treatment of initial direct costs of operating leases but there seems to be no restriction, in principle, to an entity selecting a policy of recognising initial direct costs as assets and amortising them, as appropriate, over the lease term.

Initial direct costs of lessors include amounts such as commissions, legal fees and internal costs that are incremental and directly attributable to negotiating and arranging a lease. Internal costs must exclude general overheads such as those incurred by a sales or marketing team. *[IAS 17.38].* Lessors must add internal direct costs to the carrying value of leased assets under both finance and operating leases – see 4.2 and 5.2 below – unless they are manufacturer and dealer lessors, in which case they must be expensed – see 4.4 below.

3.4.9 *Calculation of the implicit interest rate and present value of minimum lease payments*

The following example illustrates the calculation of the implicit interest rate and present value of minimum lease payments:

Example 24.7: Calculation of the implicit interest rate and present value of minimum lease payments

Details of a non-cancellable lease are as follows:

(i) Fair value = €10,000

(ii) Five annual rentals payable in advance of €2,100

(iii) Lessor's unguaranteed estimated residual value at end of five years = €1,000

The implicit interest rate in the lease is that which gives a present value of €10,000 for the five rentals plus the total estimated residual value at the end of year 5. This rate can be calculated as 6.62%, as follows:

Year	Capital sum at start of period	Rental paid	Capital sum during period	Finance charge (6.62% per annum)	Capital sum at end of period
	€	€	€	€	€
1	10,000	2,100	7,900	523	8,423
2	8,423	2,100	6,323	419	6,742
3	6,742	2,100	4,642	307	4,949
4	4,949	2,100	2,849	189	3,038
5	3,038	2,100	938	62	1,000
		10,500		1,500	

In other words, 6.62% is the implicit interest rate that, at the inception of the lease, causes the aggregate present value of the minimum lease payments (€10,500) and the unguaranteed residual value (€1,000) to be equal to the fair value of the leased asset. Lessor's initial direct costs have been excluded for simplicity.

This implicit interest rate is then used to calculate the present value of the minimum lease payments, i.e. €10,500 discounted at 6.62%. This can be calculated at €9,274, which is 92.74% of the asset's fair value, indicating that the present value of the minimum lease payments is substantially all of the fair value of the leased asset and a finance lease is therefore indicated.

It would be appropriate for the lessee to record the asset at €9,274 as the present value of the minimum lease payments is lower than the fair value and this would take account of the lessor's residual interest in the asset.

The lessor will know all of the information in the above example, as it will have been used in the pricing decision for the lease. However, the lessee may not know either the fair value or the unguaranteed residual value and, therefore, not know the implicit interest rate. In such circumstances the lessee will substitute a rate from a similar lease or its incremental borrowing rate. The lessee is also unlikely to know the lessor's initial direct costs even if the other information is known, but this is unlikely to have more than a marginal effect on the implicit interest rate.

3.5 Leases as financial instruments

In accordance with the accounting model in IAS 17, a finance lease is essentially regarded as an entitlement to receive, and an obligation to make, a stream of payments that are substantially the same as blended payments of principal and interest under a loan agreement. Consequently, the lessor accounts for its investment in the amount receivable under the lease contract rather than the leased asset itself. An operating lease, on the other hand, is regarded primarily as an uncompleted contract committing the lessor to provide the use of an asset in future periods in exchange for consideration similar to a fee for a service. The lessor continues to account for the leased asset itself rather than any amount receivable in the future under the contract.

Accordingly, a finance lease is regarded as a financial instrument and an operating lease is not, except as regards individual payments currently due and payable. *[IAS 32.AG9].*

In general the lease rights and obligations that come about as a result of IAS 17's recognition and measurement rules are not included within the scope of IAS 39 (or IFRS 9, should an entity apply that standard, as it incorporates IFRS 9's scope). Finance lease assets and liabilities are not necessarily stated at the same amount as they would be if they were measured under IAS 39. The most obvious differences are those between the implicit interest rate and the effective interest rate. The IIR (as described in 3.4.5 above) is the discount rate that, at the inception of the lease, causes the aggregate present value of the minimum lease payments (receivable during the non-cancellable lease term and any option periods that it is reasonably certain at inception the lessee will exercise) and the unguaranteed residual value to be equal to the sum of the fair value of the leased asset and any initial direct costs of the lessor. *[IAS 17.4].* The effective interest rate, by contrast, is the rate that exactly discounts estimated future cash payments or receipts through the expected life of the financial instrument (see Chapter 46 at 6). *[IAS 39.9].* The latter may include payments that would be considered contingent rentals, and hence excluded, from the calculation of the IIR and may take account of cash flows over a different period.

However, the following aspects of accounting for leases are within IAS 39's scope: *[IAS 39.2(b)]*

(a) finance lease payables recognised by a lessee are subject to the derecognition provisions (see 4.3.1 below);

(b) lease receivables recognised by a lessor, which are subject to the derecognition and impairment provisions of IAS 39 (see 4.3.2 below); and

(c) derivatives that are embedded in leases are subject to IAS 39's embedded derivatives provisions (see 3.4.7 above). *[IAS 39.2(b)].*

IAS 39 (or IFRS 9) has little impact on traditional, straightforward leases. However, its requirements will have to be considered in many more complex situations and in relation to sub-leases and back-to-back leases, as described in 8 below.

4 ACCOUNTING FOR FINANCE LEASES

Lessees recognise finance leases as assets and liabilities in their statements of financial position at the commencement of the lease term at amounts equal at the inception of the lease to the fair value of the leased item or, if lower, at the present value of the minimum lease payments. In calculating the present value of the minimum lease payments the discount factor is the interest rate implicit in the lease, if this is practicable to determine; if not, the lessee's incremental borrowing rate should be used. Any initial direct costs of the lessee are added to the asset. *[IAS 17.20, 21]*. 'Fair value' and 'minimum lease payments' are defined in 3.4.2 and 3.4.3 above.

The fair value and the present value of the lease payments are both determined as at the inception of the lease. At commencement, the asset and liability for the future lease payments are recognised in the statement of financial position at the same amount. *[IAS 17.22]*. Both asset and liability must be recognised separately, with an appropriate distinction between current and non-current liabilities being made. *[IAS 17.23]*. The terms and calculations of initial recognition by lessees are discussed further in 4.1 below.

Lease payments made by the lessee are apportioned between the finance charge and the reduction of the outstanding liability. The finance charge should be allocated to periods during the lease term so as to produce a constant periodic rate of interest on the remaining balance of the liability for each period. *[IAS 17.25]*. This is covered in 4.1.2 below.

Lessors recognise assets held under a finance lease as receivables in their statement of financial positions and present them as a receivable at an amount equal to the net investment in the lease. *[IAS 17.36]*. Lessors who are not manufacturers or dealers include costs that they have incurred in connection with arranging and negotiating a lease as part of the initial measurement of the finance lease receivable. Initial recognition by lessors, which is in many respects a mirror image of lessee recognition, follows at 4.2 below. The recognition of finance income and other issues in connection with subsequent measurement of the lessor's assets arising from finance leases is dealt with in 4.2.1 to 4.2.4 below. The consequences of terminating a finance lease are described in 4.3.

Manufacturer or dealer lessors have specific issues with regard to recognition of selling profit and finance income. These are dealt with at 4.4 below.

4.1 Accounting by lessees

4.1.1 Initial recognition

At commencement of the lease, the asset and liability for the future lease payments are recorded in the statement of financial position at the same amount, which is an amount equal to the fair value of the leased asset or the present value of the minimum lease payments, if lower, with initial direct costs of the lessee being added to the asset. *[IAS 17.22]*. An example of the calculation is given in Example 24.7 above.

4.1.2 Allocation of finance costs

The standard requires that lease payments should be apportioned between the finance charge and the reduction of the outstanding liability. The finance charge should be allocated to periods during the lease term so as to produce a constant periodic rate of interest on the remaining balance of the liability for each period. *[IAS 17.25]*.

Example 24.8: Allocation of finance costs

In Example 24.7 above, the present value of the lessee's minimum lease payments was calculated at €9,274 by using the implicit interest rate of 6.62%. The total finance charges of €1,226 (total rentals paid of €10,500 less their present value of €9,274) are allocated over the lease term as follows:

Year	Liability at start of period	Rental paid	Liability during period	Finance charge (6.62% per annum)	Liability at end of period
	€	€	€	€	€
1	9,274	2,100	7,174	475	7,649
2	7,649	2,100	5,549	368	5,917
3	5,917	2,100	3,817	253	4,070
4	4,070	2,100	1,970	130	2,100
5	2,100	2,100	–	–	–
		10,500		1,226	

The standard notes that, in practice, when allocating the finance charge to periods during the lease term some form of approximation may be used to simplify the calculation. *[IAS 17.26]*. However, it provides no guidance as to the methodology that should be applied in allocating finance charges to accounting periods.

Two methods that are used as approximations are the 'sum of the digits' ('rule of 78') or simply taking the finance costs on a straight line basis over the lease term. The 'sum of digits' is based on allocating the finance charge based on the cumulative number of payments still outstanding as illustrated in the example below. These are progressively easier to apply but also give progressively less accurate answers. There is, therefore, a trade-off to be made between the costs versus benefits of achieving complete accuracy, but in making this trade-off, the question of materiality is important. If differences between allocated finance charges under each method are immaterial, the simplest method may be used for convenience. The converse also applies and, of course, a number of individually immaterial differences may in aggregate be material. The following example illustrates the implicit interest rate and sum of the digits methods of allocating finance charges to accounting periods.

Example 24.9: Sum-of-digits allocation as compared to implicit interest rate

Continuing the lease example from Example 24.7 above, the sum of the digits method calculation is as follows:

Year	Number of rentals not yet due	×	total finance charge / sum of number of rentals	=	Finance charge per annum
					€
1	4	×	€1,226 ÷ 10	=	490
2	3	×	€1,226 ÷ 10	=	368
3	2	×	€1,226 ÷ 10	=	245
4	1	×	€1,226 ÷ 10	=	123
5	–	×	€1,226 ÷ 10	=	
	10				1,226

We can now compare the finance charges in each of the five years under the implicit interest rate (IIR) as calculated in Example 24.7 and sum of the digits methods:

	Annual finance charge		Annual finance charge as % of total rentals	
	IIR	Sum of the digits	IIR	Sum of the digits
Year	€	€	%	%
1	475	490	39	40
2	368	368	30	30
3	253	245	20	20
4	130	123	11	10
5	–	–	–	–
	1,226	1,226	100	100

As can be seen above, in situations where the lease term is not very long (typically not more than seven years) and interest rates are not very high, the sum of the digits method gives an allocation of finance charges that is close enough to that under the implicit interest rate method to allow the simpler approach to be used.

4.1.3 *Recording the liability*

The carrying amount of the liability will always be calculated in the same way, by adding the finance charge (however calculated) to the outstanding balance and deducting cash paid. The finance charge depends on the method used to apportion the finance costs. If the IIR method is used, the liability in each of the years, as apportioned between the current and non-current liability, is as follows:

Example 24.10: Lessee's liabilities and interest expense

The entity entering into the lease in Example 24.7 will record the following liabilities and interest expense in its statement of financial position:

Year	Liability at end of period	Current liability at end of period	Non-current liability at end of period	Interest expense (at 6.62%) for the period
	€	€	€	€
1	7,649	1,732	5,917	475
2	5,917	1,847	4,070	368
3	4,070	1,970	2,100	253
4	2,100	2,100	–	130
5	–	–	–	–
				1,226

4.1.4 *Accounting for the leased asset*

At commencement of the lease, the asset and liability for the future lease payments are recorded in the statement of financial position at the same amount, with initial direct costs of the lessee being added to the asset. *[IAS 17.22]*. These are costs that are directly attributable to the lease in question and are added to the carrying value *[IAS 17.24]* in an analogous way to the treatment of the acquisition costs of property, plant and equipment.

Accounting for the leased asset follows the general rules for accounting for property, plant and equipment or intangible assets. A finance lease gives rise to a depreciation expense for depreciable assets as well as a finance expense for each accounting period. The depreciation policy for depreciable leased assets should be consistent with that for depreciable assets that are owned, and the depreciation recognised should be calculated in accordance with IAS 16 and IAS 38. *[IAS 17.27]*. The useful life is the estimated remaining period, from the commencement of the lease term but without the limitation of the lease term, over which the entity expects to consume the economic benefits embodied in the asset. This is different to the economic life which takes account of the period of time for which the asset is economically usable by one or more users and would therefore include additional lease terms with the same or different lessees. *[IAS 17.4]*. If there is reasonable certainty that the lessee will obtain ownership by the end of the lease term, the period of expected use is the useful life of the asset. *[IAS 17.28]*. IAS 17 does not address the situation in which an entity expects to extend a lease but it is not reasonably certain at inception that it will do so. In our view, the entity is not precluded from depreciating assets either over the lease term or over the shorter of the asset's useful life and the period for which the entity expects to extend the lease. See also Chapter 18 at 5.4.

Because the interest expense and depreciation must be calculated separately and are unlikely to be the same it is not appropriate simply to treat the lease payments as an expense for the period. *[IAS 17.29]*. This is demonstrated in the following example.

Example 24.11: Lessee's depreciation and interest expense

The entity that has entered into the lease agreement described in Example 24.7 will depreciate the asset (whose initial carrying value, disregarding initial direct costs, is €9,274) on a straight-line basis over five years in accordance with its depreciation policy for owned assets, i.e. an amount of €1,855 per annum. The balances for asset and liability in the financial statements in each of the years 1-5 will be as follows:

Year	Carrying value of asset at end of period	Total liability at end of period	Total charged to income statement*	Lease payments
	€	€	€	€
1	7,419	7,649	2,330	2,100
2	5,564	5,917	2,222	2,100
3	3,709	4,070	2,108	2,100
4	1,854	2,100	1,985	2,100
5	–	–	1,855	2,100
			10,500	10,500

* The total charge combines the annual depreciation of €1,855 and the interest calculated according to the IIR method in Example 24.8, which is in aggregate the initial carrying value of the asset of €9,274 and the total finance charge of €1,226, i.e. the total rent paid of €10,500. Note that this example assumes that the asset is being depreciated to a residual value of zero over the lease term, which is shorter than its useful life, so IAS 16's requirement to reconsider the residual value and useful life at least at each financial year end is unlikely to have an effect. *[IAS 16.51]*.

An entity applies IAS 36 – *Impairment of Assets* – to determine whether the leased asset has become impaired in value (see Chapter 20). *[IAS 17.30]*.

Leased assets may also be revalued using the revaluation model but the entire class of assets (both owned and those held under finance lease) must be revalued. *[IAS 16.36]*. See Chapter 18 at 6.5.

Whilst it is not explicit in IAS 16, in our view, to obtain the fair value of an asset held under a finance lease for financial reporting purposes, the assessed value must be adjusted to take account of any recognised finance lease liability. The mechanism for achieving this, which is mainly an issue for investment properties, is set out in detail in Chapter 19 at 6.7.

4.2 Accounting by lessors

Under a finance lease, a lessor retains legal title to an asset but passes substantially all the risks and rewards of ownership to the lessee in return for a stream of rentals. In substance, therefore, the lessor provides finance and expects a return thereon.

The standard requires lessors to recognise assets held under a finance lease in their statement of financial position as a receivable at an amount equal to the net investment in the lease. *[IAS 17.36]*. The lease payments received from the lessee are treated as repayments of principal and finance income. *[IAS 17.37]*. Initial direct costs may include commissions, legal fees and internal costs that are incremental and directly attributable to negotiating and arranging the lease. They do not include general overheads such as the costs of the sales and marketing departments. They are included in the measurement of the net investment in the lease at inception and reflected in the calculation of the implicit interest rate. *[IAS 17.38]*.

The recognition of finance income should be based on a pattern reflecting a constant periodic rate of return on the lessor's net investment outstanding in respect of the finance lease. *[IAS 17.39]*.

4.2.1 The lessor's net investment in the lease

The lessor's gross investment in the lease is the aggregate of the minimum lease payments receivable by the lessor under a finance lease and any guaranteed and unguaranteed residual value to which the lessor is entitled. The net investment in the lease is the gross investment discounted at the interest rate implicit in the lease, *[IAS 17.4]*, i.e. at any point in time it comprises the gross investment after deducting gross earnings allocated to future periods.

The lessor's gross investment is, therefore, the same as the aggregate figures used to calculate the implicit interest rate and the net investment is the present value of those same figures – see 3.4.9 and Example 24.7 above.

Therefore, at inception, the lessor's net investment in the lease is the cost of the asset as increased by its initial direct costs. The difference between the net and gross investments is the gross finance income to be allocated over the lease term. Example 24.12 below illustrates this point.

4.2.2 Allocation of finance income

The lessor recognises finance income based on a pattern reflecting a constant periodic rate of return on the lessor's net investment outstanding in respect of the finance lease. *[IAS 17.39]*. Lease payments, excluding costs for services, are applied against the gross investment in the lease to reduce both the principal and the unearned finance income. *[IAS 17.40]*. The standard does not refer to the use of approximations by lessors and, accordingly, the alternative methods described in 4.1.2 above should not be used unless the differences are clearly immaterial.

Example 24.7 at 3.4.9 can be examined from the lessor's perspective:

Example 24.12: The lessor's gross and net investment in the lease

The lease has the same facts as described in Example 24.7, i.e. the asset has a fair value of €10,000, the lessee is making five annual rentals payable in advance of €2,100 and the total unguaranteed estimated residual value at the end of five years is estimated to be €1,000. The lessor's direct costs have been excluded for simplicity.

The lessor's gross investment in the lease is the total rents receivable of €10,500 and the unguaranteed residual value of €1,000. The gross earnings are therefore €1,500. The initial carrying value of the receivable is its fair value of €10,000, which is also the present value of the gross investment discounted at the interest rate implicit in the lease of 6.62%.

Year	Receivable at start of period	Rental received	Finance income (6.62% per annum)	Gross investment at end of period	Gross earnings allocated to future periods	Receivable at end of period
	€	€	€	€	€	€
1	10,000	2,100	523	9,400	977	8,423
2	8,423	2,100	419	7,300	558	6,742
3	6,742	2,100	307	5,200	251	4,949
4	4,949	2,100	189	3,100	62	3,038
5	3,038	2,100	62	1,000	–	1,000
		10,500	1,500			

The gross investment in the lease at any point in time comprises the aggregate of the rentals receivable in future periods and the unguaranteed residual value, e.g. at the end of year 2,, the gross investment of €7,300 is three years' rental of €2,100 plus the unguaranteed residual of €1,000. The net investment, which is the amount at which the debtor will be recorded in the statement of financial position, is €7,300 less the earnings allocated to future periods of €558 = €6,742.

4.2.3 Residual values

Residual values have to be taken into account in assessing whether a lease is a finance or operating lease as well as affecting the calculation of the IIR and finance income.

- Unguaranteed residual values have to be estimated in order to calculate the IIR and finance income receivable under a finance lease. Any impairment in the residual must be taken into account; this is illustrated in 4.2.3.A below.
- Residual values can be guaranteed by the lessee or by a third party. The effects of third party guarantees on risks and rewards are described in 3.4.6.A above.
- The terms of a lease guarantee can affect the assessment of the risks and rewards in the arrangement as in the example in 4.2.3.B below.
- A common form of lease requires the asset to be sold at the end of the lease term. The disposition of the proceeds has to be taken into account in assessing who bears residual risk, as described in 4.2.3.C below.

4.2.3.A *Unguaranteed residual values*

Income recognition by lessors can be extremely sensitive to the amount recognised as the asset's residual value. This is because the amount of the residual directly affects the computation of the amount of finance income earned over the lease term – this is illustrated in Example 24.13 below. The standard gives no guidance regarding the estimation of unguaranteed residual values but it does require them to be reviewed regularly. If there has been a reduction in the estimated value, the income allocation over the lease term is revised and any reduction in respect of amounts accrued is recognised immediately. *[IAS 17.41]*.

Example 24.13: Reduction in residual value

Taking the same facts as used in Example 24.12 above, the lessor concludes at the end of year 2 that the residual value of the asset is only €500 and revises the income allocation over the lease term accordingly. It continues to apply the same implicit interest rate, 6.62%, as before.

Year	Receivable at start of period	Rental received	Finance income (6.62% per annum)	Gross investment at end of period*	Gross earnings allocated to future periods	Receivable at end of period
	€	€	€	€	€	€
2	8,423	2,100	419	6,800	471	6,329
3	6,329	2,100	280	4,700	191	4,509
4	4,509	2,100	160	2,600	31	2,569
5	2,569	2,100	31	500	–	500

* The gross investment in the lease now takes account of the revised unguaranteed residual of €500, rather than the original €1,000.

The lessor will have to write off €413, being the difference between the carrying amount of the receivable as previously calculated in Example 24.12 and the revised balance above (€6,742 – €6,329). This is the present value as at the end of year 2 of €500 and represents the part of the unguaranteed residual written off.

Impairment of lease receivables is within the scope of IAS 39 *[IAS 39.2(b)]* and this methodology is required by IAS 39 paragraph 63, described in 4.3.2.A below.

4.2.3.B *Residual values guaranteed by the lessee*

Although a lessee may give a residual value guarantee in a lease, the lease itself may be structured so that the most likely outcome of events relating to the residual value indicates that no significant risk will attach to the lessee.

Example 24.14: A lease structured such that the most likely outcome is that the lessee has no significant residual risk

Brief details of a motor vehicle lease are:

Fair value – €10,000
Rentals – 20 monthly payments of €300, followed by a final rental of €2,000

At the end of the lease, the lessee sells vehicle as agent for the lessor and if sold for:

(i) more than €3,000, 99% of the excess is repaid to the lessee; or

(ii) less than €3,000, lessee pays the deficit to the lessor up to a maximum of 0.4 pence per mile above 25,000 miles p.a. on average that the leased vehicle has done.

The net present value of the minimum lease payments excluding the guarantee amounts to €7,365.

This lease involves a guarantee by the lessee of the residual value of the leased vehicle of €3,000, as a result of (ii) above. However, the guarantee will only be called on if both:

(a) the vehicle's actual residual value is less than €3,000; and

(b) the vehicle has travelled more than 25,000 miles per year on average over the lease term.

Further, the lessee is only liable to pay a certain level of the residual; namely, €100 for each 2,500 miles above 25,000 miles that the vehicle has done.

One could argue that the guarantee should be assumed to apply only to the extent that experience or expectations of the sales price and/or the mileage that vehicles have done (and the inter-relationship between these) indicate that a residual payment by the lessee will be made and if this best estimate is that a zero or minimal payment will be made, this should be used for the purposes of lease classification. This would be applying the principles in IAS 37 to the calculation of the liability. However, IAS 17 states that the amount of the guarantee is 'the maximum amount that could, in any event, become payable'. Therefore, the standard appears to require the maximum guarantee of €3,000 to be taken into account.

By taking the maximum guarantee into account, the present value of the minimum lease payments might equal the fair value of the asset. This does not necessarily mean that the lease will automatically fall to be treated as a finance lease. This depends on the substance of the arrangement and the entity might take account of the residual it estimates it will actually pay in making this assessment. Another interpretation is given in Example 24.16 below, in which the entity capitalises the full residual guarantee and factors the amount that it expects to recover into the residual value of the asset.

4.2.3.C Rental rebates

IAS 17 suggests that an indicator that the lease is a finance lease is that 'the gains or losses from the fluctuation in the fair value of the residual accrue to the lessee (for example, in the form of a rent rebate equalling most of the sales proceeds at the end of the lease)'. *[IAS 17.11]*. This is because a lessee that obtains most of the sales proceeds has received most of the risks and rewards of the residual value in the asset. This would indicate that the lessor has already been compensated for the transaction and hence that it is a finance lease.

Other leases require the asset to be sold at the end of the lease but the lessor receives the first tranche of proceeds and only those proceeds above a certain level are remitted to the lessee. These arrangements may have a different significance as the lessor may be taking the proceeds to meet its unguaranteed residual value. Lessors are prepared to take risks on residual values of such assets if there is an established and reliable market in which to sell them. This could mean that the gains or losses from the fluctuation in the fair value of the residual do not fall predominantly to the lessee and, in the absence of other factors, could indicate that it is an operating lease.

Example 24.15: Rental rebates

The lease arrangements are as in Example 24.14, except that at end of the lease, the lessee sells the vehicle as agent for the lessor, and if it is sold for

(i) up to £3,000, the guaranteed residual value, all of the proceeds are received by the lessor; or

(ii) more than £3,000, 99% of excess is repaid to the lessee. The lessee does not have to make good any deficit, should one arise.

In this example, it appears that the lessor is using the sale proceeds to meet its unguaranteed residual value but it is also taking the first loss provision. Only thereafter does the lessee gain or lose from the fluctuations in the fair value. The lessee's minimum lease payments have a net present value of €7,365, it has not guaranteed the residual value at all and is not exposed to any risk of any fall in value, although it may benefit from increases in the fair value in excess of €3,000. On balance this indicates that the arrangement is an operating lease.

4.2.4 *Disposals by lessors of assets held under finance leases – measurement*

If a lessor is to dispose of an asset under a finance lease that is classified as held for sale, or is included in a disposal group that is so classified, it is to apply the requirements of IFRS 5 – *Non-current Assets Held for Sale and Discontinued Operations* – to the disposal. *[IAS 17.41A]*. The 'asset under a finance lease' is the receivable from the lessee, which is not a financial asset under IAS 39; see 3.5 above for an analysis of the extent to which assets and liabilities under leases are within scope of that standard. This means that measurement as well as classification of the asset under the finance lease is within scope of IFRS 5, unlike financial assets within scope of IAS 39 that are subject only to its classification rules. Once classified as held for sale, it must be measured at the lower of carrying amount and fair value less costs to sell. Any residual interest in the leased asset, which is accounted for under IAS 16 or IAS 38, is clearly within scope of IFRS 5. IFRS 5's requirements are dealt with in Chapter 4.

4.3 Termination of finance leases

The expectations of lessors and lessees regarding the timing of termination of a lease may affect the classification of a lease as either operating or finance. This is because it will affect the expected lease term, level of payments under the lease and expected residual value of the lease assets.

Termination during the primary lease term will generally not be anticipated at the lease inception because the lessee can be assumed to be using the asset for at least that period. In addition, early termination will be unlikely because most leases are non-cancellable. A termination payment is usually required which will give the lessor an amount equivalent to most or all of the rental receipts which would have been received if no termination had taken place, which means that it is reasonably certain at inception that the lease will continue to expiry.

However, there are consequences if the lease is terminated. The issues for finance lessees and lessors are discussed in the following sections.

4.3.1 *Termination of finance leases by lessees*

Finance lease payables recognised by a lessee are subject to the derecognition provisions of IAS 39 (or IFRS 9, should the entity apply that standard). *[IAS 39.2(b)]*.

IAS 39 requires an entity to derecognise (i.e. remove from its statement of financial position) a financial liability (or a part of a financial liability) when, and only when, it is 'extinguished', that is, when the obligation specified in the contract is discharged, cancelled, or expires. *[IAS 39.39]*. This will be achieved when the debtor either:

- discharges the liability (or part of it) by paying the creditor, normally with cash, other financial assets, goods or services; or
- is legally released from primary responsibility for the liability (or part of it) either by process of law or by the creditor. *[IAS 39.AG57]*.

The difference between the carrying amount of a financial liability (or part of a financial liability) extinguished or transferred to another party and the consideration paid, including any non-cash assets transferred or liabilities assumed, is recognised in profit or loss.

In order to identify the part of a liability derecognised, an entity allocates the previous carrying amount of the financial liability between the part that continues to be recognised and the part that is derecognised based on the relative fair values of those parts on the date of the repurchase. *[IAS 39.41-42]*. Derecognition of part of a lease liability will most likely come about in the context of a lease renegotiation, discussed at 6 below.

The derecognition of financial liabilities under IAS 39 is dealt with in Chapter 47 at 6.

4.3.1.A Early termination by lessees

Except as part of a renegotiation or business combination or similar larger arrangement, early termination of a finance lease results in derecognition of the capitalised asset by the lessee, with any remaining balance of the capitalised asset being written off as a loss on disposal. Any payment made by the lessee will reduce the lease obligation that is being carried in the statement of financial position. If either a part of this obligation is not eliminated or the termination payment exceeds the previously existing obligation, then the remainder or excess will be included as a gain or loss respectively on derecognition of a financial liability.

A similar accounting treatment is required where the lease terminates at the expected date and there is a residual at least partly guaranteed by the lessee. For the lessee, a payment made under such a guarantee will reduce the obligation to the lessor as the guaranteed residual would obviously be included in the lessee's finance lease obligation. If any part of the guaranteed residual is not called on, then the lessee would treat this as a profit on derecognition of a financial liability.

The effect on the derecognition of the capitalised asset will depend on the extent to which the lessee expected to make the residual payment as this will have affected the level to which the capitalised asset has been depreciated. For example, if the total guaranteed residual was not expected to become payable by the lessee, then the depreciation charge may have been calculated to give a net book value at the end of the lease term equal to the residual element not expected to become payable. If this estimate was correct then the remaining obligation will equal the net book value of the relevant asset, so that the gain on derecognition of the liability will be equal to the loss on derecognition of the asset.

Example 24.16: Early termination of finance leases by lessees

In Example 24.15 above there is effectively a guarantee of a residual of €3,000 dependent on the mileage done by the leased vehicle. Assuming that the lease is capitalised as a finance lease, if the lessee considers at the lease inception that the guarantee will not be called on, then he will depreciate the vehicle to an estimated residual value of €3,000 over the lease term. In the event that his estimate is found to be correct, then the loss on disposal of the asset at its written down value will be equal and opposite to the gain on derecognition of the lease obligation of €3,000. However, if, for example, €1,000 of the guarantee was called on, whereas the lessee had estimated that it would not be, then the net book value of €3,000 and the unused guarantee of €2,000 will both be derecognised and a loss of €1,000 will be shown on disposal of the vehicle.

4.3.2 *Termination and impairment of finance leases by lessors*

Although lease receivables are not financial instruments within scope of IAS 39 (or IFRS 9, if applied), the carrying amounts recognised by a lessor are subject to the derecognition and impairment provisions of those standards. Generally, a financial asset is derecognised when the contractual rights to the cash flows from that asset have expired. *[IAS 39.17]*. This will apply to most leases at the end of the term when the lessor has no more right to cash flows from the lessee.

If the cash flows from the financial asset have not expired, it is derecognised when, and only when, the entity 'transfers' the asset within the specified meaning of the term in IAS 39, and the transfer has the effect that the entity has either:

(a) transferred substantially all the risks and rewards of the asset; or

(b) neither transferred nor retained substantially all the risks and rewards of the asset and has not retained control of the asset. *[IAS 39.20]*. If the rights to the cash are retained then there are other tests that must be met. *[IAS 39.19]*.

These requirements are relevant to common lease situations such as sub-leases and back-to-back leases, dealt with in 8 below. Derecognition of financial assets is a complex area discussed in Chapter 47.

4.3.2.A *Impairment of lease receivables*

If a lease receivable is impaired, for example, because the lessee is in default of lease payments, the amount of the impairment is measured as the difference between the carrying value of the receivable and the present value of the estimated future cash flows, discounted at the implicit interest rate used on initial recognition. Therefore, if the lessor makes an arrangement with the lessee and reschedules and/or reduces amounts due under the lease, the loss is by reference to the new carrying amount of the receivable, calculated by discounting the estimated future cash flows at the original implicit interest rate. *[IAS 39.63]*. This methodology has been used in Example 24.13 at 4.2.3.A above.

4.3.2.B *Early termination of finance leases for lessors*

Any termination payment received by a lessor on an early termination will reduce the lessor's net investment in the lease shown as a receivable. If the termination payment is greater than the carrying amount of the net investment, the lessor will account for a gain on derecognition of the lease; conversely, if the termination payment is smaller than the net investment, a loss will be shown.

Losses on termination in the ordinary course of business are less likely to arise because a finance lease usually has termination terms so that the lessor is compensated fully for early termination and the lessor has legal title to the asset. The lessor can continue to include the asset in current assets as a receivable to the extent that sales proceeds or new finance lease receivables are expected to arise. If the asset is then re-leased under an operating lease, the asset may be transferred to property, plant and equipment and depreciated over its remaining useful life. There is no guidance about the amount at which the asset is recognised in PP&E. Although the net investment (i.e. the lease receivable recognised by the lessor) is not a financial instrument within scope of IAS 39, *[IAS 39.2(b)]*, in general we expect that entities would use the carrying amount of the net investment as the cost of the reacquired item of PP&E. However, in the absence of authoritative guidance we would expect there to be divergence in practice. If the asset is designated as held for sale then the requirements of IFRS 5 will apply (see Chapter 4). The aspects of lease assets and liabilities that are within scope of IAS 39 are described at 3.5 above.

4.4 Manufacturer or dealer lessors

Manufacturers or dealers often offer customers the choice of either buying or leasing an asset. While there is no selling profit on entering into an operating lease because it is not the equivalent of a sale, *[IAS 17.55]*, a finance lease of an asset by a manufacturer or dealer lessor gives rise to two types of income:

(a) the profit or loss equivalent to the profit or loss resulting from an outright sale of the asset being leased, at normal selling prices, reflecting any applicable volume or trade discounts; and

(b) the finance income over the lease term. *[IAS 17.43]*.

If the customer is offered the choice of paying the cash price for the asset immediately or paying for it on deferred credit terms then, as long as the credit terms are the manufacturer or dealer's normal terms, the cash price (after taking account of applicable or volume discounts) can be used to determine the selling profit. *[IAS 17.42]*. However, in many cases such an approach should not be followed as the manufacturer or dealer's marketing considerations often influence the terms of the lease. For example, a car dealer may offer 0% finance deals instead of reducing the normal selling price of his cars. It would be wrong in this instance for the dealer to record a profit on the sale of the car and no finance income under the lease.

The standard, therefore, requires sales revenue to be based on the fair value of the asset (i.e. the cash price) or, if lower, the present value of the minimum lease payments computed at a market rate of interest. As a result, if artificially low rates of interest are quoted, selling profit is restricted to that which would apply if a commercial rate of interest were charged. *[IAS 17.44-45]*. The cost of sales is reduced to the extent that the lessor retains an unguaranteed residual interest in the asset. *[IAS 17.44]*.

Initial direct costs should be recognised as an expense in the income statement at the inception of the lease. This is not the same as the treatment when a lessor arranges a finance lease where the costs are added to the finance lease receivable; the standard argues that this is because the costs are related mainly to earning the selling profit. *[IAS 17.46]*. If the manufacturer or dealer is in the (relatively unlikely) position of incurring an overall loss because the total rentals receivable under the finance lease are less than the cost to it of the asset then this loss should be taken to profit or loss at the inception of the lease. IAS 17 assumes that the manufacturer or dealer will have a normal implicit interest rate based on its other leasing activity. However, in other situations where the manufacturer or dealer does not conduct other leasing business, an estimate will have to be made of the implicit rate for the leasing activity.

5 ACCOUNTING FOR OPERATING LEASES

5.1 Operating leases in the financial statements of lessees

IAS 17 requires lease payments under an operating lease, excluding costs for services such as insurance and maintenance, to be recognised as an expense on a straight-line basis over the lease term unless another systematic basis is representative of the time pattern of the user's benefit, even if the payments are not on that basis. *[IAS 17.33, 34]*. Generally, the only other acceptable bases are where rentals are based on a unit of use or unit of production.

IAS 17 requires a straight line recognition of the lease expenses even when amounts are not payable on this basis. This does not require the entity to anticipate contingent rental increases, such as those that will result from a periodic re-pricing to market rates or those that are based on some other index (see 3.4.7 above). However, lease payments may vary over time for other reasons that will have to be taken into account in calculating the annual charge. Described in more detail below are some examples: leases that are inclusive of services, leases with increments intended to substitute for inflation and security deposits made with lessors that attract low or no interest. Lease incentives are another feature that may affect the cash flows under a lease; they are dealt with in more detail in 5.1.4 (for lessees) and 5.2.2 (for lessors) below.

5.1.1 Leases that include payments for services

There is a wide range of services that can be subsumed into a single 'lease' payment. For a vehicle, the payment may include maintenance and servicing. Property leases could include cleaning, security, reception services, gardening, utilities and local and property taxes. Single payments for operating facilities may include lease payments for the plant and the costs of operating them, as discussed in the context of IFRIC 4; see Example 24.2 above. IAS 17 says in the definition of minimum lease payments that the costs of services should be excluded to arrive at the lease payments. *[IAS 17.4]*. This is straightforward enough if the payments are made by the lessor and quantified in the payments made by the lessee. It will be somewhat less so if, for example, the lessor makes all maintenance payments but does not specify the amounts; instead, payments are increased periodically to take account of changes in such costs. In such a case the lessee will have to estimate the amount paid for services and deduct them from the total. The remaining payments, which relate solely to the right to use the asset, will then be spread on a straight line basis over the non-cancellable term of the lease.

5.1.2 Straight-line recognition over the lease term

Operating lease payments must be recognised on a straight line basis over the lease term, unless another systematic basis is more representative of the time pattern of the user's benefit. *[IAS 17.33]*. There are some lease payments that increase annually by fixed increments intended to compensate for expected annual inflation over the lease period. There has been debate as to whether such increases must also be taken on a straight-line basis over the non-cancellable lease term.

In considering the issue, the Interpretations Committee noted that IAS 17 does not incorporate adjustments to operating lease payments to reflect the time value of money. Except in those cases where another basis is more appropriate, it requires all operating leases to be taken on a straight-line basis. They concluded that to allow recognition of these increases on an annual basis would be inconsistent with the treatment of other operating leases.[6]

Some leases allow for an annual increase in line with an index but with a fixed minimum increment. As discussed in 3.4.7 above, contingent rents are excluded from the lease payments but the fixed minimum increment will have to be spread so as to take the payments on a straight line basis over the lease term.

Example 24.17: Operating lease expenses with fixed annual increment

Entity A leases a property at an initial rent of €1,000,000 per annum. The lease has a non-cancellable term of 30 years and rent increases annually in line with the Retail Prices Index (RPI) of the country in which the property is situated but with a minimum increase of 2.5% (the estimated long-term rate of inflation in the country in question) and a maximum of 5% per annum.

The annual increase of 2.5% must be taken into account in calculating the operating lease payment charged to profit or loss. On a straight-line basis this will be €1,463,000 per annum. Therefore, by the end of year 15 (at which point the amounts payable under the lease will exceed the straight-lined amount) the entity will have paid rentals of €15 million, charged €22 million to income and will be recording an accrual of €7 million.

If the increase in the RPI exceeds 2.5% these additional amounts will be charged to income as contingent rents.

5.1.3 Notional or actual interest paid to lessors

Lessees are sometimes required to place security deposits with lessors that are refunded at termination to the extent that they have not been utilised by the lessor. Lessees receive either no or a reduced rate of interest. In accordance with IAS 39, the lessee initially measures the deposit at fair value and subsequently at amortised cost (assuming that the deposit is classified as a loan and receivable *[IAS 39.46]*) using the effective interest method; accordingly interest income is recognised through profit and loss over the useful life of the deposit. *[IAS 39.9]*. At inception of an operating lease, the difference between the nominal value of the deposit and its fair value should be considered additional rent payable to the lessor. This will be expensed on a straight-line basis over the lease term.

Example 24.18: Operating lease expenses reflecting interest payments to the lessor

A lessee makes an interest-free security deposit of €1,000 on entering into a five year lease. It assesses an appropriate rate of interest for the deposit to be 4% and accordingly the fair value of the deposit at inception is €822. On making the deposit, it will record it as follows:

Year		€	€
1	Security deposit	822	
	Advance rentals	178	
	Cash		1,000

During the five years of the lease, it will record interest income and additional rental expense as follows:

Year	Interest income	Rental expense	Difference
1	33	(36)	(3)
2	34	(35)	(1)
3	36	(36)	–
4	37	(36)	1
5	38	(35)	3
	178	(178)	

5.1.4 Lease incentives – accounting by lessees

Incentives that may be given by a lessor to a lessee as an incentive to enter into a new or renewed operating lease agreement include an up-front cash payment to the lessee or the reimbursement or assumption by the lessor of costs of the lessee, such as relocation costs, leasehold improvements and costs associated with a pre-existing lease commitment of the lessee. Alternatively, the lessor may grant the lessee rent-free or reduced rent initial lease periods. *[SIC-15.1]*.

The consensus reached by the SIC in Interpretation SIC-15 – *Operating Leases – Incentives* – was that all incentives for the agreement of a new or renewed operating lease should be recognised as an integral part of the net consideration agreed for the use of the leased asset, irrespective of the incentive's nature or form or the timing of payments. *[SIC-15.3]*. The lessee should recognise the aggregate benefit of incentives as a reduction of rental expense over the lease term, on a straight-line basis unless another systematic basis is representative of the time pattern of the lessee's benefit from the use of the leased asset. *[SIC-15.5]*. Finally, SIC-15 requires costs incurred by the lessee, including costs in connection with a pre-existing lease (for example, costs for termination, relocation or leasehold improvements), to be accounted for by the lessee in accordance with the IAS applicable to those costs, including costs which are effectively reimbursed through an incentive arrangement. *[SIC-15.6]*.

Chapter 24

The following two examples based on those the Illustrative Examples to SIC-15 illustrate how to apply the Interpretation:

Example 24.19: Accounting for lease incentives under SIC-15

Example 1

An entity agrees to enter into a new lease arrangement with a new lessor. As an incentive for entering into the new lease, the lessor agrees to pay the lessee's relocation costs. The lessee's moving costs are €1,000. The new lease has a term of 10 years, at a fixed rate of €2,000 per year.

The lessee recognises relocation costs of €1,000 as an expense in Year 1. Both the lessor and lessee would recognise the net rental consideration of €19,000 (€2,000 for each of the 10 years in the lease term, less the €1,000 incentive) over the 10 year lease term using a single amortisation method in accordance with SIC-15. *[SIC-15. 4, 5]*.

Example 2

An entity agrees to enter into a new lease arrangement with a new lessor. The lessor agrees to a rent-free period for the first three years. The new lease has a term of 20 years, at a fixed rate of $5,000 per annum for years 4 through 20.

Net consideration of $85,000 consists of $5,000 for each of 17 years in the lease term. Both the lessor and lessee would recognise the net consideration of $85,000 over the 20-year lease term using a single amortisation method. *[SIC-15.4,5]*.

One point about SIC-15 that has attracted considerable debate is its requirement to spread incentives over the lease term. The validity of this has been questioned if rentals are re-priced to market rates at periodic intervals. It is argued that in these circumstances the rent-free period is being given solely to compensate for an above-market rental in the primary period.

The Interpretations Committee rejected this view in April 2005. It did not accept that the lease expense of a lessee after an operating lease is re-priced to market ought to be comparable with the lease expense of an entity entering into a new lease at that same time at market rates. Nor did it believe that the re-pricing itself would be reflective of a change in the time patterns of the lessee's benefit from the use of the leased asset.[7] In other words, incentives are seen in the context of the total cash flows under the lease and, except where the benefit of the lease is not directly related to the time during which the entity has the right to use the asset, IAS 17 requires these to be taken on a straight line basis.

There is a similar argument when lessees contend (as they often do) that they should not be obliged to spread rentals over a void period as they are not actually benefiting from the property during this time – it is a fit-out period or a start-up so activities are yet to increase to anticipated levels. However, the argument against this is really no different to the above: the lessee's period of benefit from the use of the asset is the lease term, so the incentive cannot be taken over the initial period. This was reinforced by the Interpretations Committee in July 2008, when it noted that IAS 16 and IAS 38 require an entity to recognise the use of productive assets using the method that best reflects 'the pattern in which the asset's future economic benefits are expected to be consumed by the entity', *[IAS 16.60, IAS 38.97]*, but IAS 17 refers to the time pattern of the user's benefit. *[IAS 17.33]*. Therefore, any alternative to the straight-line recognition of lease expense under an operating lease must reflect the time pattern of the use of the leased property rather than the amount of use or other factor related to economic benefits.[8] The Interpretations Committee has not shown any indication that it is prepared to accept economic arguments for other than straight-line treatment.

5.1.5 Onerous contracts

IAS 37 prohibits the recognition of provisions for future operating losses *[IAS 37.63]* but the standard specifically addresses the issue of onerous contracts. It requires that if an entity has a contract that is onerous, the present obligation under the contract should be recognised and measured as a provision. *[IAS 37.66]*.

The standard defines an onerous contract as 'a contract in which the unavoidable costs of meeting the obligations under it exceed the economic benefits expected to be received under it'. *[IAS 37.10]*. This is taken to mean that the contract itself is onerous to the point of being directly loss-making, not simply uneconomic by reference to current prices. A common example of an onerous contract seen in practice relates to operating leases for the rent of property, and the standard includes the following example: *[IAS 37 IE Example 8]*

Example 24.20: An onerous contract

An entity operates profitably from a factory that it has leased under an operating lease. During December 20X0 the entity relocates its operations to a new factory. The lease on the old factory continues for the next four years, it cannot be cancelled and the factory cannot be re-let to another user.

Present obligation as a result of a past obligating event	The obligating event is the signing of the lease contract, which gives rise to a legal obligation.
Transfer of economic benefits in settlement	When the lease becomes onerous, a transfer of economic benefits is probable. Until then, the entity accounts for the lease by applying IAS 17.
Conclusion	A provision is recognised for the best estimate of the unavoidable lease payments *[IAS 37.5(c), 14, 66]*.

Care must be taken to ensure that the lease itself is onerous. If an entity has a number of retail outlets and one of these is loss-making, this is not sufficient to make the lease onerous. However, if the entity vacates the premises and sub-lets them at an amount less than the rent it is paying, then the lease becomes onerous and the entity should provide for its best estimate of the unavoidable lease payments. This will include the difference between the lease and sub-lease payments, together with provision as appropriate for any period where there is no sub-tenant.

The accounting for onerous contracts is discussed in more detail in Chapter 27 at 6.2.

5.2 Operating leases in the financial statements of lessors

5.2.1 Accounting for assets subject to operating leases

Lessors should present assets subject to operating leases in their statement of financial position according to the nature of the asset, i.e. usually as PP&E or as an intangible asset. Lease income from operating leases should be recognised in income on a straight-line basis over the lease term, unless another systematic basis is more representative of the time pattern in which, the standard states, 'use benefit derived from the leased asset is diminished'. *[IAS 17.49, 50]*. Generally, the only other basis that is encountered is based on unit-of-production or service.

Lease income excludes receipts for services provided such as insurance and maintenance. IAS 18 – *Revenue* – provides guidance on how to recognise service revenue – see Chapter 28. Costs, including depreciation, incurred in earning the lease income are recognised as an expense. *[IAS 17.51]*. Initial direct costs incurred specifically to earn revenues from an operating lease are added to the carrying amount of the leased asset and allocated to income over the lease term in proportion to the recognition of lease income. *[IAS 17.52]*. This means that the costs will be depreciated on a straight-line basis if this is the method of recognising the lease income, regardless of the depreciation basis of the asset.

The depreciation policy for depreciable leased assets is to be consistent with the entity's policy for similar assets that are not subject to leasing arrangements and calculated in accordance with IAS 16 or IAS 38, as appropriate. *[IAS 17.53]*. If the lessor does not use similar assets in its business then the depreciation policy must be set solely by reference to IAS 16 and IAS 38. This also means that the lessor is obliged in accordance with IAS 16 to consider the residual value and economic life of the assets at least at each financial year-end. *[IAS 16.51]*. There are similar requirements in the case of intangible assets, although IAS 38 notes that they rarely have a residual value. *[IAS 38.100]*. These matters are discussed in Chapters 17 and 18. These assets are also tested for impairment in a manner consistent with other tangible and intangible fixed assets; IAS 17 refers to IAS 36 (discussed in Chapter 20) in providing guidance on the need to assess the possibility of an impairment of assets. *[IAS 17.54]*.

5.2.2 Lease incentives – accounting by lessors

In negotiating a new or renewed operating lease, a lessor may provide incentives for the lessee to enter into the arrangement. In the case of a property lease, the tenant may be given a rent-free period but other types of incentive include up-front cash payments to the lessee or the reimbursement or assumption by the lessor of lessee costs such as relocation costs, leasehold improvements and costs associated with a pre-existing lease commitment of the lessee. Interpretation SIC-15 states that the lessor should recognise the aggregate cost of incentives as a reduction of rental income over the lease term, on a straight-line basis unless another systematic basis is representative of the time pattern over which the benefit of the leased asset is diminished. *[SIC-15.4]*. The SIC rejected the argument that lease incentives for lessors are part of the initial direct costs of negotiating or arranging the contract; instead concluding that they are in substance, related to the amount of consideration received by the lessor for the use of the asset. This view was confirmed in the IASB's 2003 revision of IAS 17, which requires initial direct costs to be capitalised as part of the carrying value of the asset – see 3.4.8 above. Lessor accounting is, therefore, the mirror image of lessee accounting for the incentives, as described in 5.1.4 above.

5.3 Payments made in connection with the termination of operating leases

Payments for terminating operating leases or payments between a lessee and a third party regarding a lease are extremely common but not all are directly addressed by either IAS 17 or SIC-15. In addition, neither statement addresses payments made between a lessee and a third party in connection with a lease. The following example addresses a variety of payments that might arise in connection with terminating an operating lease over a property:

Example 24.21: Payments made in connection with terminating an operating lease

	Treatment in the financial statements of		
Transaction	*Lessor*	*Old tenant*	*New tenant*
Lessor pays			
Old tenant – lessor intends to renovate the building.	Expense immediately, or Capitalise as part of the carrying amount of the leased asset if the payment meets the definition of construction costs in IAS 16 (note 1)	Recognise income immediately (note 1)	
Old tenant – new lease with higher quality tenant	Expense immediately)	Recognise income immediately (note 1)	
New tenant – an incentive to occupy	Prepayment amortised over the lease term on a straight line basis under SIC-15 (see 5.2.2 above)		Deferred lease incentive amortised over the lease term on a straight line basis under SIC-15 (see 5.1.4 above).
Building alterations specific to the tenant with no further value to the lessor after completion of the lease period.	Prepayment amortised over the lease term on a straight line basis under SIC-15 (see 5.2.2 above)		Leasehold improvements capitalised and depreciated. Deferred lease incentive amortised over the lease term on a straight line basis under SIC-15 (see 5.1.4 above).

Transaction	*Lessor*	*Old tenant*	*New tenant*
Old tenant pays			
Lessor, to vacate the leased premises early	Recognised as income immediately to the extent not already recognised (note 2)	Recognised as expense immediately to the extent not already recognised (note 2)	
New tenant to take over the lease		Recognise as an expense immediately (note 3)	Recognise as income immediately, unless compensation for above market rentals, in which case amortise over expected lease term (note 3)

Transaction	*Lessor*	*Old tenant*	*New tenant*
New tenant pays			
Lessor to secure the right to obtain a lease agreement	Recognise as deferred revenue under IAS 17 and amortise over the lease term on a straight line basis (see 5.2.1 above)		Recognise as a prepayment under IAS 17 and amortise over the lease term on a straight line basis (see 5.1.2 above).
Old tenant to buy out the lease agreement		Recognise as a gain immediately (note 4)	Recognised as an intangible asset with a finite economic life (note 4)

Note 1 A payment by a lessor to a lessee to terminate the lease is not dealt with under IAS 17 or SIC-15. If the lessor's payment meets the definition of a cost of an item of PP&E, which might be the case if the lessor intends to renovate, it must be capitalised. *[IAS 16.7]*. If not, the payment will be expensed, as it does not meet the definition of an intangible asset in IAS 38. *[IAS 38.8]*. As the lessee has no further performance obligation the receipt should be income.

Note 2 A payment made by the lessee to the lessor to get out of a lease agreement does not meet the appropriate definitions of an asset in IAS 16 or IAS 38 and does not fall within IAS 17 as there is no longer a lease – the payments are not for the use of the asset. Therefore it should be expensed. Similarly, from the lessor's perspective, income should be recorded.

Note 3 A payment made by an existing tenant to a new tenant to take over the lease would also not meet the definition of an asset under IAS 16 or IAS 38 (see notes above) and falls outside IAS 17 as the lease no longer exists. The old tenant must expense the cost. The new tenant will recognise the payment as income except to the extent that it is compensation for an above-market rental, in which case the treatment required by SIC-15 for a lease incentive must be applied and it will be amortised over the lease term (see 5.1.4 above).

Note 4 The new tenant has made a payment to an old tenant, and while it is in connection with the lease arrangements, it is not directly related to the actual lease as it was made to a party outside the lease contract. Therefore it cannot be accounted for under IAS 17. The old tenant will treat the receipt as a gain immediately. Any remaining balances of the lease will be removed and a net gain (or loss) recorded. The payment by the lessee will generally meet the definition of an intangible asset in IAS 38 and therefore will be amortised over the useful life, usually the term of the lease. However, if other conditions and circumstances in the arrangement mean that this definition is not met, the payment will be expensed in the period in which it is incurred.

5.3.1 Compensation for loss of profits

Compensation amounts paid by lessors to lessees are sometimes described as 'compensation for loss of profits' or some similar term. This is a method of calculating the amount to be paid and the receipt is not a substitute for the revenue or profits that the lessee would otherwise have earned. The description will not affect the treatment described above.

6 MODIFYING THE TERMS OF LEASES

Lessees may renegotiate lease terms for a variety of reasons. They may wish to extend the term over which they have a right to use the asset or to alter the number of assets that they have a right to use. They may consider that the lease is too expensive by comparison with current market terms. The renegotiations may deal with several such issues simultaneously.

Lessors may also renegotiate leases, for example one lessor may sell the lease to another that offers to provide the lease service more cheaply to the lessee, usually because the new lessor's transactions have different tax consequences. Lease contracts may allow for changes in payments if specified contingencies occur, for example a change in taxation or interest rates.

6.1 IAS 17 and accounting for renegotiations

The standard has little to say on the consequences of such renegotiations. It states:

> 'If at any time the lessee and the lessor agree to change the provisions of the lease, other than by renewing the lease, in a manner that would have resulted in a different classification of the lease ... if the changed terms had been in effect at the inception of the lease, the revised agreement is regarded as a new agreement over its term.' *[IAS 17.13].*

As described at 3.2.3 above, the consequences of a different classification are clear. A revised agreement that is reclassified (e.g. an operating lease is reassessed as a finance lease or *vice versa*) is accounted for prospectively in accordance with the revised terms. However, IAS 17 leaves many questions of application unanswered. It provides no practical guidance on what to take into account to determine whether there would have been a different classification. It does not explain how to account for the consequences of modifications, whether or not they would lead to a different classification. These matters are described below.

Other changes to lease terms that do not lead to reclassification but that nevertheless need to be accounted for, for example variations due to changes in rates of taxation or interest rates, are discussed in 6.1.4 below.

Changes in estimates, for example changes in estimates of the economic life or of the residual value of the leased item, or changes in circumstances, for example default by the lessee, do not result in a different classification. *[IAS 17.13]*. Changes in estimates also include the renewal of a lease or the execution of a purchase option, if these were not considered probable at the inception of the lease (see 3.2.3 above).

6.1.1 Determining whether there is a different classification

IAS 17 states that, if the terms of a lease are modified so that the revised terms would have resulted in a different classification of the lease had they been in effect at inception, the revised agreement is regarded as a new agreement over its term. *[IAS 17.13]*.

The modification must, therefore, be one that affects the risks and rewards incidental to ownership of the asset by changing the terms and cash flows of the existing lease, for example a renegotiation that changes the duration and/or the payments due under the lease.

One of the indicators used in practice is an assessment of the net present value of the minimum lease payments and whether or not these amount to substantially all of the fair value of the leased asset. An entity might use this test to help assess whether the revised lease is a finance or operating lease, in conjunction with a reassessment of the other factors described at 3.2.2 above. Therefore, the entity might use one of the following methods to calculate the net present value:

(a) recalculate the net present value based on the revised lease term and cash flows (and revised residual value, if relevant), which will result in a different implicit interest rate to that used in the original calculation;

(b) take into consideration the changes in the agreement but calculate the present value of the asset and liability using the interest rate implicit in the original lease. This approach, which is consistent with the remeasurement of the carrying value of financial instruments applying the effective interest rate method, as required by IAS 39, *[IAS 39.AG8]*, will result in a 'catch up' adjustment as at the date of the reassessment; or

(c) consider the revised agreement to be a new lease and assess the classification based on the terms of the new agreement and the fair value and useful life of the asset at the date of the revision. The inference of this method, unlike (a) and (b), is that the entity already considers that there is likely to be a new classification to the lease, based on an assessment of other factors.

A lessee under an operating lease will be able to apply methods (a) and (c) but (b) will not be available to it unless it has sufficient information to be able to calculate the IIR at the inception of the original lease. Lessees that are party to more complex leases or sale and leaseback arrangements are more likely to have the necessary information available to them.

Each of these three approaches is likely to lead to a different net present value for the minimum lease payments.

It must be stressed that all features of any arrangement must be considered in order to assess whether or not the modified lease transfers substantially all of the risks and rewards of ownership.

They are compared in the following example.

Example 24.22: Modifying the terms of leases

Details of a non-cancellable lease taken out on the first day of the year are as follows:

(i) Fair value = €25,000

(ii) Estimated useful life of asset = 8 years

(iii) Five annual rentals payable in advance of €4,200

(iv) At the end of year 5, the asset must be sold and all proceeds up to €8,292 taken by the lessor. If any amount in excess of €8,292 is received, 99% of the excess is repaid to the lessee.

The lease does not contain any renewal options.

The lessee assesses this as an operating lease because the terms suggest that substantially all of the risks and rewards of ownership have not been transferred to it – the lease term is only 62.5% of the useful life of the asset and there is clearly significant residual value.

At the end of year 2, the parties renegotiate the lease, with the changes coming into effect on the first day of year 3. The lease term is to be extended for a further two years, making the term seven years in total. Payments for the four years 3-6 have been reduced to €4,000 and €1,850 is payable for year 7. At the time of the renegotiation the estimated fair value of the asset is €17,500 and its residual value at the end of year 7 is €1,850.

The implicit interest rate in the original lease can be calculated because the maximum amount receivable by the lessor on the sale of the asset at the end of the lease term is the residual value (on the assumption that the lessor disregards any potential upside in its contingent 1%); the IIR is 5.92%, as follows:

Year	Capital sum at start of period	Rental paid	Capital sum during period	Finance charge (5.92% per annum)	Capital sum at end of period
	€	€	€	€	€
1	25,000	4,200	20,800	1,231	22,031
2	22,031	4,200	17,831	1,056	18,887
3	18,887	4,200	14,687	869	15,556
4	15,556	4,200	11,356	672	12,028
5	12,028	4,200	7,828	464	8,292
		21,000		4,292	

This supports the lessee's assessment that this is an operating lease as the present value of the minimum lease payments is €18,780, which is 75% of the fair value of the asset at the commencement of the lease.

Chapter 24

If these revised terms had been in existence at inception then the implicit interest rate and NPV calculation would have been as follows. This corresponds to (a) above.

Year	Capital sum at start of period	Rental paid	Capital sum during period	Finance charge (4.10% per annum)	Capital sum at end of period
	€	€	€	€	€
1	25,000	4,200	20,800	853	21,653
2	21,653	4,200	17,453	715	18,168
3	18,168	4,000	14,168	581	14,749
4	14,749	4,000	10,749	441	11,190
5	11,190	4,000	7,190	294	7,484
6	7,484	4,000	3,484	143	3,627
7	3,627	1,850	1,777	73	1,850
		26,250		3,100	

The NPV of the lessee's minimum lease payments is €23,603 which is 94% of the fair value of the asset at the commencement of the lease. The lease would be classified as a finance lease.

Method (b) results in the following calculation:

Year	Capital sum at start of period	Rental paid	Capital sum during period	Finance charge (5.92% per annum)	Capital sum at end of period
	€	€	€	€	€
1	25,000	4,200	20,800	1,231	22,031
2	22,031	4,200	17,831	1,056	**18,887**
3	**17,566**	4,000	13,566	803	14,369
4	14,369	4,000	10,369	613	10,982
5	10,982	4,000	6,982	414	7,396
6	7,396	4,000	3,396	201	3,597
7	3,597	1,850	1,747	103	1,850
		26,250		4,421	

The present value of the total payments over the revised lease term at the original discount rate is €22,585, which is 90.3% of the fair value of the asset at commencement of the lease. In addition, the residual value of €1,850 would have had a present value of only €1,237; it is a feature of the methodology that the present value of the lease payments and the present value of the residual do not add up to the fair value of the asset at inception. In order to make the computation, an adjustment is made to the capital amount as at the date that the lease is renegotiated. The outstanding amount is recomputed from €18,887 (the balance at the end of year 2 calculated using the original assumptions) to €17,566, the amount that corresponds to the new assumptions. Note that it is not relevant that the method results in a change to the 'capital sum' of only 7% ((18,887–17,566) ÷ 18,887). The assessment is based on the net present value of the minimum lease payments over the lease term and other features of the revised agreement.

If method (c) is applied, the modified lease is considered as if it were a new five year lease. The IIR calculated prospectively over the remaining term is now 6.13%:

Year	Capital sum at start of period	Rental paid	Capital sum during period	Finance charge (6.13% per annum)	Capital sum at end of period
	€	€	€	€	€
3	17,500	4,000	13,500	827	14,327
4	14,327	4,000	10,327	633	10,960
5	10,960	4,000	6,960	426	7,386
6	7,386	4,000	3,386	207	3,593
7	3,593	1,850	1,743	107	1,850
		17,850		2,200	

The present value of the remaining payments is €16,126, which is 92.15% of the fair value of the asset (€17,500) at the date of entering into the new lease.

In this example, all three methods result in a present value of the minimum lease payments that exceeds 90% but this would not, of course, always be the case.

6.1.2 *Accounting for reclassified leases*

IAS 17 states that the revised agreement is treated as a new agreement over its term.

If the original lease was a finance lease and the revised lease is an operating lease, then the balances relating to the finance lease must be derecognised. For the lessee, this involves derecognising both the asset (which will have been depreciated up to the point of derecognition over the shorter of the useful life or the lease term) and the finance lease liability. Finance lease derecognition is discussed further at 4.3 above.

If the original lease was an operating lease and the revised lease is a finance lease, then any balances resulting from recognising the lease cost on a straight line basis will be expensed and the balances relating to the finance lease must be recognised for the first time.

Although the standard says that 'the revised agreement is regarded as a new agreement over its term,' *[IAS 17.13]*, this refers to classification; there is no consensus regarding the measurement of assets and liabilities as at this point.

The most obvious interpretation is that the revised lease is accounted for as a new lease as from the date on which the terms were changed, based on the fair value of the assets as at the date of revision. The assets and liabilities under the finance lease would be recognised initially as in method (c) in Example 24.22 above, which calculates the assets and liabilities as if the revised agreement were a new lease as from the date of reassessment.

This is consistent with using either method (a) or method (c) in 6.1.1 above to help determine the revised classification. However, some consider that the new lease can be recognised using method (b) above, by taking into consideration the changes in the agreement but calculating the present value of the asset and liability by using the interest rate implicit in the original lease. This uses an accepted methodology and is consistent with the fact that there has, in fact, only been a change to the original terms and not a completely new lease; it also has the advantage that the revised fair value of the assets does not have to be known. In the facts as in

Example 24.22 above, this means that the asset and liability would be recorded at €17,566. In the specific example, this is close to the fair value of the asset at the time of the renegotiation.

If the original lease agreement and the revised lease agreement are both finance leases, then the modification will have accounting consequences that are discussed in the following section.

6.1.3 Accounting for modifications to finance leases

If the rights under a finance lease have changed without a change in the classification, these changes to lease term and cash flows must be accounted for. Once again, the accounting consequences are not dealt with by IAS 17.

The two most obvious methods of calculating the impact of the changes are as follows:

(a) Even though the classification has not changed, the revised agreement is accounted for as if it were a new lease. The calculation will be based on the fair value and useful life of the asset at the date of the revision.

(b) Use the original IIR to discount the revised minimum lease payments and (for a lessee) adjust any change in lease liability to the carrying amount of the asset. Lessors will adjust the carrying value of the asset, taking gains or losses to income. As noted before, this approach is consistent with the requirements of IAS 39 when the effective interest rate method is applied and the cash flows change. *[IAS 39.AG8].*

These are described in 6.1.1 and Example 24.22 above (method (c) and method (b)). For lessees, both of these methods will affect the carrying value of the asset and hence its future amortisation.

Another method that might be considered is to reflect changes prospectively over the remaining term of the lease; this is only likely to be appropriate if the cash flows are modified but all other rights remain unchanged. Some of the circumstances in which such changes can arise are considered at 6.1.4 below.

Example 24.23: Accounting for lease modifications

The details of a lease are as in Example 24.22 above, except that the lease has an original duration of six years with an annual rent of €4,200, rather than five years. The present value of the minimum lease payments is €21,931, which is 87.72% of the fair value of the leased asset, calculated as follows:

Year	Capital sum at start of period	Rental paid	Capital sum during period	Finance charge (5.92% per annum)	Capital sum at end of period
	€	€	€	€	€
1	21,931	4,200	17,731	1,050	18,780
2	18,780	4,200	14,580	863	15,443
3	15,443	4,200	11,243	666	11,909
4	11,909	4,200	7,709	456	8,165
5	8,165	4,200	3,965	235	4,200
6	4,200	4,200	0	0	0
		25,200		3,270	

The directors of the entity assess this as a finance lease, taking account of all of the circumstances surrounding the agreement. The entity capitalise the asset at €21,931 at commencement of the lease and recognise an equivalent liability.

At the end of year 2, the lease term is extended for a further year, making the term seven years in total. Payments for the four years 3-6 are reduced to €4,000 and €1,850 is payable for year 7.

The asset (which has a useful life to the lessee of six years) has been depreciated on a straight line basis for two years and its carrying amount is €14,620, while the lessee's lease liability (as calculated above) is €15,443:

(a) If the modification is treated as a new lease, it will be accounted for as follows, using the revised fair value of €16,126 and IIR of 6.13% calculated at Example 24.22(c) above:

Year	Capital sum at start of period	Rental paid	Capital sum during period	Finance charge (6.13% per annum)	Capital sum at end of period
	€	€	€	€	€
3	16,126	4,000	12,126	743	12,868
4	12,868	4,000	8,868	543	9,412
5	9,412	4,000	5,412	331	5,743
6	5,743	4,000	1,743	107	1,850
7	1,850	1,850	0	0	0
		17,850		1,724	

Therefore, the entity will derecognise both the leased asset of €14,620 and liability of €15,443, recognising a net gain of €823. The new asset of €16,126 will be depreciated prospectively over the remaining life of 5 years.

(b) If the modification is accounted for by restating the liability using the original IIR of 5.92%, the liability will be €16,178 calculated as follows:

Year	Capital sum at start of period	Rental paid	Capital sum during period	Finance charge (5.92% per annum)	Capital sum at end of period
	€	€	€	€	€
3	16,178	4,000	12,178	721	12,899
4	12,899	4,000	8,899	526	9,425
5	9,425	4,000	5,425	322	5,747
6	5,747	4,000	1,747	103	1,850
7	1,850	1,850	0	0	0
		17,850		1,672	

The entity will increase the lease liability by €735 (from €15,443 to €16,178) but it will increase the asset's carrying mount by the same amount from €14,620 to €15,355 which will be depreciated prospectively over the asset's remaining life of 5 years.

6.1.4 *Tax and interest variation clauses and similar modifications*

The relationship between leasing and taxation is frequently complex. It depends on whether tax deductions or taxable income are based on amounts receivable or payable in accordance with the lease or on the amounts that are taken to the income statement. It further depends on the availability of tax deductions for the cost of leased assets and who is able to claim these deductions. Some lessors draw up leases that are based on a post-tax return that takes account of these factors. These leases include tax variation clauses that enable lessors to change the amounts receivable from the lessee so that their post-tax return remains constant. The rental could be adjusted in a number of different ways, e.g. a new fixed payment, an up-front sum or an adjustment on a rental-by-rental basis.

The variations are unlikely of themselves to change the lease classification because their potential impact will have been taken into account in making that original assessment. Nor are they likely to lead to an impairment of the lessor's finance lease asset (assuming that it is a finance lease) as the profitability of the lease (on a post-tax basis) is unaffected.

IAS 17 does not refer to variation clauses so the question is whether the change is a variety of contingent rent, defined by the standard as that portion of the lease payments that is not fixed in amount but is based on a factor that varies other than with the passage of time, such as percentage of sales, amount of usage, price indices or market rates of interest, *[IAS 17.4]*, or another type of event. Contingent rent is recognised when it is incurred. This means that a reduction in rentals because of a reduction in rates of taxation would be a negative contingent rent.

However, it is also argued that the effect of the change in tax rates is far more like the lease modifications described at 6.1.3 above and there is some merit in this argument. As a result, some lessors take the view that the most relevant method of accounting for the changes is to use the original IIR to discount the revised minimum lease payments, taking the change in value of the finance lease asset to income (this is method (b) as described in 6.1.3). If rental payments decrease because the revised rate of taxation is lower, lessors applying this approach will recognise a loss on remeasuring the asset.

Leases may also contain interest variation clauses which adjust the rental by reference to movements in bank base rates or similar. As market rates of interest are specific examples of contingent rent in the standard, they must be accounted for as such. These movements could be positive or negative over the lease term.

6.1.5 Accounting for changes to the terms of operating leases

Lessees may renegotiate terms with lessors, e.g. in circumstances in which the lessee has financial difficulties or where there is evidence that the lease terms are at higher than market rates.

Operating leases may include explicit or implicit options to extend the lease and the extension may have different payment terms. If there is a formal option, the lessee might be required to give notice to the lessor of its intention to extend at a set date before the lease expires. There may be similar arrangements with purchase options.

If the lessee renews a lease or exercises a purchase option, it does not have to re-assess the classification of a lease if the renewal and exercise were not considered probable at the inception of the lease (see 3.2.3 above). There may still be accounting consequences in connection with spreading the lease costs because of IAS 17's requirement to take lease costs on a straight line over the lease term, save in unusual circumstances (see 5.1.2 above).

The revised terms should be taken into account prospectively from the date of the agreement. There are good arguments against any alternative treatment. A catch-up adjustment as if the new terms had always existed is not consistent with the fact that the modification is a change in estimate and these are normally accounted for prospectively.

Accounting for the original lease until its expiry and then treating the modification (e.g. the extended term) as if it were a new lease may be an attractive option as it avoids any change if there are straight line prepayments or accruals; these will reduce to zero at the end of the original lease term. However, it is inconsistent with the fact that there has been a contractual modification to the existing lease.

The lessee now has a contractual obligation to continue the lease and the effect on any existing straight line prepayment or accrual should be taken into account. Both previously recognised amounts and aggregate future minimum lease payments should be recognised on a straight-line basis prospectively over the remaining revised lease term, whether or not the original lease contract contained a renewal option.

Because these modifications are given to tenants in financial difficulties, any asset that is being spread forward may need to be assessed for impairment.

7 SALE AND LEASEBACK TRANSACTIONS

These transactions involve the original owner of an asset selling it to a provider of finance and immediately leasing it back. The lease payment and the sale price are usually interdependent because they are negotiated as a package. These parties will be termed the seller/lessee (the original owner) and buyer/lessor (the finance provider) respectively. Sometimes, instead of selling the asset outright, the original owner will lease the asset to the other party under a finance lease and then lease it back. Such a transaction is known as a 'lease and leaseback' and has similar effects so for these purposes is included within the term 'sale and leaseback'.

Sale and leaseback transactions are a fairly common feature in sectors where entities own many properties, such as the retail and hotel industries. Many parties are involved as buyer/lessors, not only finance houses and banks but also pension funds and property groups. From a commercial point of view, the important point of difference lies between an entity that decides that it is cheaper to rent than to own – and is willing to pass on the property risk to the landlord – and an entity which decides to use the property as a means of raising finance – and will therefore retain the property risk. However from the accounting point of view, a major consideration is whether a profit can be reported on such transactions.

The buyer/lessor will treat the lease in the same way as it would any other lease that was not part of a sale and leaseback transaction. The accounting treatment of the transaction by the seller/lessee depends on the type of lease involved, i.e. whether the leaseback is under a finance or an operating lease. *[IAS 17.58]*.

7.1 Sale and finance leaseback

In order to assess whether the leaseback is under a finance lease, the seller/lessee will apply the qualitative tests in IAS 17 that are described at 3.2.2 above. If a sale and leaseback transaction results in a finance lease, any excess of sales proceeds over the carrying amount should not be recognised immediately as income by a seller/lessee. Instead, the excess is deferred and amortised over the lease term. *[IAS 17.59]*. It is inappropriate to show a profit on disposal of an asset which has, in substance, been reacquired by the entity under a finance lease. The lessor is providing finance to the lessee with the asset as security. *[IAS 17.60]*. The asset will be restated to its fair value (or the present value of the minimum lease payments, if lower) in exactly the same way as any other asset acquired under a finance lease.

Example 24.24: Sale and finance leaseback – accounting for the excess sale proceeds

An asset that has a carrying value of €700 and a remaining useful life of 7 years is sold for €1,200 and leased back on a finance lease. This is accounted for as a disposal of the original asset and the acquisition of an asset under a finance lease for €1,200. The excess of sales proceeds of €500 over the original carrying value should be deferred and amortised (i.e. credited to profit or loss) over the lease term.

The net impact on income of the charge for depreciation based on the carrying value of the asset held under the finance lease of €171 and the amortisation of the deferred income of €71 is the same as the annual depreciation of €100 based on the original carrying amount.

In 2007 the Interpretations Committee considered the related area of sale and repurchase options, concluding that IAS 17 itself contains 'the more specific guidance with respect to sale and leaseback transactions'.[9] However, many still consider that there is an alternative treatment which is more consistent with the substance of the arrangement and with the approach in SIC-27 described at 2.2 above, which deals with transactions that have the form but not the substance of leases. It follows the standard's description of the transaction as 'a means whereby the lessor provides finance to the lessee, with the asset as security'. *[IAS 17.60]*. The previous carrying value is left unchanged, with the sales proceeds being shown as a liability to be accounted for under IAS 39. The creditor balance represents the finance lease liability under the leaseback. This is consistent with IAS 18 which states that a transaction is not a sale and revenue is not recognised if the entity retains significant risks of ownership. *[IAS 18.16]*. By definition the entity will have retained the significant risks and rewards, because it now holds the asset under a finance lease.

Both methods of accounting for sale and leaseback transactions are seen in practice. Therefore, an entity should select a treatment as a matter of accounting policy and apply it consistently.

If the sales value is less than the carrying amount then the apparent 'loss' need not be taken to income unless there has been an impairment under IAS 36. *[IAS 17.64]*. There may be an obvious reason why the sales proceeds are less than the carrying value; for example, the fair value of a second-hand vehicle or item of plant and machinery is frequently lower than its book value, especially soon after the asset has been acquired by the entity. This fall in fair value after sale has no effect on the asset's value-in-use. This means that, in the absence of impairment, a deficit (sales proceeds lower than carrying value) will be deferred in the same manner as a profit and spread over the lease term.

7.2 Operating leaseback

If a sale and leaseback transaction results in an operating lease, and it is clear that the transaction is established at fair value, any profit or loss should be recognised immediately. If the sale price is below fair value, any profit or loss should be recognised immediately unless the loss is compensated by future lease payments at below market price, in which case it should be deferred and amortised in proportion to the lease payments over the period for which the asset is expected to be used. If the sale price is above fair value, the excess over fair value should be deferred and amortised over the period for which the asset is expected to be used. *[IAS 17.61-63].*

The rationale behind these treatments is that if the sales value is not based on fair values then it is likely that the normal market rents will have been adjusted to compensate. For example, a sale at above fair value followed by above-market rentals is similar to a loan of the excess proceeds by the lessor that is being repaid out of the rentals. Accordingly, the transaction should be recorded as if it had been based on fair value.

However, this will not always be the case. Where the sales value is less than fair value there may be legitimate reasons for this to be so, for example where the seller has had to raise cash quickly. In such situations, as the rentals under the lease have not been reduced to compensate, the profit or loss should be based on the sales value.

The standard includes an Appendix, which comprises the following table of the standard's requirements concerning sale and leaseback transactions, and is aimed at providing guidance in interpreting the various permutations of facts and circumstances that are set out in the requirements.

Sale price established at fair value (paragraph 61)	*Carrying amount equal to fair value*	*Carrying amount less than fair value*	*Carrying amount above fair value*
Profit	no profit	recognise profit immediately	not applicable
Loss	no loss	not applicable	recognise loss immediately
Sale price below fair value (paragraph 61)			
Profit	no profit	recognise profit immediately	no profit (note 1)
Loss *not* compensated by future lease payments at below market price	recognise loss immediately	recognise loss immediately	(note 1)
Loss compensated by future lease payments at below market price	defer and amortise loss	defer and amortise loss	(note 1)

Sale price above fair value (paragraph 61)	Carrying amount equal to fair value	Carrying amount less than fair value	Carrying amount above fair value
Profit	defer and amortise profit(note 3)	defer and amortise profit (note 3)	defer and amortise profit (note 2)
Loss	no loss	no loss	(note 1)

Note 1 These parts of the table represent circumstances that would have been dealt with under paragraph 63 of the Standard. Paragraph 63 requires the carrying amount of an asset to be written down to fair value where it is subject to a sale and leaseback.

Note 2 The profit would be the difference between fair value and sale price as the carrying amount would have been written down to fair value in accordance with paragraph 63.

Note 3 Any excess profit (the excess of sale price over fair value) is deferred and amortised over the period for which the asset is expected to be used. Any excess of fair value over carrying amount is recognised immediately.

IAS 17's disclosure requirements for lessees and lessors apply equally to sale and leaseback transactions. The requirement of the standard for lessees to give a general description of their significant leasing arrangements will lead to the disclosure of unique or unusual provisions of the agreement or terms of the sale and leaseback transactions. *[IAS 17.35(d), 65]*. Furthermore, sale and leaseback transactions may meet the separate disclosure criteria for 'exceptional items' set out in IAS 1 – *Presentation of Financial Statements* (see Chapter 3). *[IAS 17.66]*.

Sale and leaseback arrangements may also include features such as repurchase options. These are not addressed by IAS 17 and are discussed below.

7.3 Sale and leaseback arrangements including repurchase agreements and options

IAS 17 does not deal explicitly with the function of options in the context of sale and leaseback arrangements, where circumstances could be complex and there may be a variety of options that may affect the overall assessment of the lease.

The Interpretations Committee considered whether these arrangements would have to meet the derecognition criteria in IAS 18 in order to recognise the sale of the asset. If this were the case then it would be unlikely that the seller/lessee would ever achieve derecognition. Arguably the vendor would retain effective control through continuing managerial involvement to the degree usually associated with ownership. It might also retain the significant risks and rewards of ownership, e.g. through fixed price repurchase terms that allowed it to retain the rewards but not the risks of ownership. *[IAS 18.14]*.

The Interpretations Committee concluded that there was no such requirement as IAS 17 itself contained 'the more specific guidance with respect to sale and leaseback transactions'. However, these transactions may be outside the scope IAS 17 because they do not 'convey a right to use an asset' as defined by SIC-27 and IFRIC 4, whose requirements are described at 2.1 above. If the purchaser/lessor does not have a right of use, the transaction is outside the scope of IAS 17 and the sale and leaseback accounting in IAS 17 should not be applied.

The Interpretations Committee considered that 'significantly divergent interpretations do not exist in practice on this issue and that it would not expect such divergent interpretations to emerge'. Consequently, The Interpretations Committee decided not to take the issue onto its agenda.[10]

The Interpretations Committee considers, therefore, that entities should use IFRIC 4 and SIC-27 to analyse whether or not the arrangement contains a lease and then apply IAS 18 to determine whether or not there is revenue relating to the transaction. SIC-27 is helpful in the analysis; it includes the following indicators that an arrangement is not in substance a lease:

(a) the entity retains all the risks and rewards of ownership and there is no significant change in its rights to use the asset; and

(b) the options on which the arrangement depends are included on terms that make their exercise almost certain (e.g. a put option that is exercisable at a price sufficiently higher than the expected fair value when it becomes exercisable). *[SIC-27.5]*.

In practice entities may well have obtained the same answer by moving straight to IAS 18 and applying a 'risks and rewards' analysis, rather than considering whether the arrangement contains a lease, which could explain the lack of divergence in practice.

7.3.1 Sale and leaseback arrangements with put and call options

If a lease arrangement includes an option that can only be exercised by the seller/lessee at the then fair value of the asset in question, the risks and rewards inherent in the residual value of the asset have passed to the buyer/lessor. The option amounts to a right of first refusal to the seller/lessee.

Where there is both a put and a call option in force on equivalent terms at a determinable amount other than the fair value, it is clear that the asset will revert to the seller/lessee. It must be in the interests of one or other of the parties to exercise the option so as to secure a profit or avoid a loss, and therefore the likelihood of the asset remaining the property of the buyer/lessor rather than reverting to the seller must be remote. In such a case, this is a bargain purchase option and the seller/lessee has entered into a finance leaseback.

However, the position is less clear where there is only a put option or only a call option in force, rather than a combination of the two. Where there is only a put option by the buyer/lessor, the effect will be (in the absence of other factors) that the seller/lessee has disposed of the rewards of ownership to the buyer/lessor but retained the risks. This is because the buyer/lessor will only exercise his option to put the asset back to the seller/lessee if its value at the time is less than the repurchase price payable under the option. This means that if the asset continues to rise in value the buyer/lessor will keep it and reap the benefits of that enhanced value; conversely if the value of the asset falls, the option will be exercised and the downside on the asset will be borne by the seller/lessee.

Chapter 24

This analysis does not of itself answer the question whether the deal should be treated as an operating or financing leaseback. The overall commercial effect will still have to be evaluated, taking account of all the terms of the arrangement and by considering the motivations of both of the parties in agreeing to the various terms of the deal; in particular it will need to be considered why they have each agreed to have this one-sided option.

Where there is only a call option exercisable by the seller/lessee, the position will be reversed. In this case, the seller/lessee has disposed of the risks, but retained the rewards to be attained if the value of the asset exceeds the repurchase price specified in the option. Once again, though, the overall commercial effect of the arrangement has to be evaluated in deciding how to account for the deal. Emphasis has to be given to what is likely to happen in practice, and it is instructive to look at the arrangement from the point of view of both parties to see what their expectations are and what has induced them to accept the deal on the terms that have been agreed. It may be obvious from the overall terms of the arrangement that the call option will be exercised, in which case the deal will again be a financing arrangement and should be accounted for as such. For example, the exercise price of the call option may be set at a significant discount to expected market value, the seller/lessee may need the asset to use on an ongoing basis in its business, or the asset may provide in effect the only source of the seller/lessee's future income. Equally, the financial effects of *not* exercising the option, such as continued exposure to escalating costs, may make it obvious that the option will have to be exercised (so-called 'economic compulsion').

The following is an example of a sale and leaseback deal where the seller has a call option to repurchase the asset but has no commitment to do so:

Example 24.25: Sale and leaseback transaction involving escalating rentals and call options

Company S sells a property to Company B for £100,000,000 and leases it back on the following terms:

Rental for years 1 to 5	£1,475,000per annum
Rental for years 6 to 10	£2,900,000per annum
Rental for years 11 to 15	£5,500,000per annum
Rental for years 16 to 20	£10,800,000per annum
Rental for years 21 to 25	£19,100,000per annum
Rental for years 26 to 30	£30,025,000 per annum
Rental for years 31 to 35	£45,150,000 per annum
Rental thereafter	open market rent

Rentals are payable annually in advance.

Company S has a call option to buy back the property at the following dates and prices:

At the end of year 5	£125,000,000
At the end of year 10	£150,000,000
At the end of year 15	£168,000,000
At the end of year 20	£160,000,000
At the end of year 25	£100,000,000

Company B has no right to put the property back to Company S.

An analysis of the economics of this deal suggests that whilst Company S has no legal obligation to repurchase the property, there is no genuine commercial possibility that the option will not be exercised. This is because the rentals and option prices are structured in such a way as to give the buyer of the property a lender's return whilst, at the same time, there is no commercial logic for the seller not to exercise the option at year 25, if not earlier. Exercising the option at the end of year 25 will mean that Company S will regain ownership of the property and will have had the use of the £100,000,000 at an effective rate of approximately 6% per annum; failure to exercise the option will mean additional lease obligations of £375,875,000 over the ten years from years 25 to 35, followed by the obligation to pay market rents thereafter.

8 SUB-LEASES AND BACK-TO-BACK LEASES

8.1 Introduction

Sometimes there are more parties to a lease arrangement than simply one lessor and one lessee. This section relates to situations involving an original lessor, an intermediate party and an ultimate lessee. The intermediate party is unrelated to both lessor and lessee and may be acting either as both a lessee and lessor of the asset concerned or, alternatively, as an agent of the lessor in the transaction.

Both sub-leases and back-to-back leases involve the intermediate party acting as both lessor and lessee of the asset. The difference between the two arrangements is that, for a back-to-back lease, the terms of the two lease agreements match to a greater extent than would be the case for a sub-lease arrangement. This difference is really only one of degree. The important decision to be made concerns whether the intermediate party is acting as both lessee and lessor in two related but independent transactions or whether the nature of the interest is such that it need not recognise the rights and obligations under the leases in its financial statements.

8.1.1 The original lessor and the ultimate lessee

The accounting treatment adopted by these parties will not be affected by the existence of sub-leases or back-to-back leases. The original lessor has an agreement with the intermediate party, which is not affected by any further leasing of the assets by the intermediate party unless the original lease agreement is thereby replaced.

Similarly, the ultimate lessee has a lease agreement with the intermediate party. The lessee will have use of the asset under that agreement and must make a decision, in the usual way, as to whether the lease is of a finance or operating type under the requirements of IAS 17.

8.1.2 The intermediate party

It is common for entities whose business is the leasing of assets to third parties to finance these assets themselves through leasing arrangements. There are also arrangements in which a party on-leases assets as an intermediary between a lessor and a lessee while taking a variable degree of risk in the transaction. The appropriate accounting treatment by the intermediate party depends on the substance of the series of transactions. Either the intermediate party will act as lessee to the original lessor and lessor to the ultimate lessee or, if in substance it has transferred the risks and rewards of ownership, it may be able to derecognise the assets and liabilities under its two lease arrangements and recognise only its own commission or fee income.

In order to analyse the issues that may arise, the various combinations of leases between lessor/intermediate and intermediate/lessee are summarised in the following table:

	Lessor	Intermediate party		Lessee
	Lease to Intermediate	*Lease from Lessor*	*Lease to Lessee*	*Lease from Intermediate*
(1)	Operating lease	Operating lease	Operating lease	Operating lease
(2)	Finance lease	Finance lease	Operating lease	Operating lease
(3)	Finance lease	Finance lease	Finance lease	Finance lease

Only in unusual circumstances could there be an operating lease from the lessor to the intermediate and a finance lease from the intermediate to the lessee. The intermediate would have to acquire an additional interest in the asset from a party other than the lessor in order to be in a position to transfer substantially all of the risks and rewards incidental to ownership of that asset to the lessee.

There are no significant accounting difficulties for the intermediate party regarding (1), an operating lease from the lessor to the intermediate and from the intermediate to the lessee. The intermediate may be liable to the lessor if the lessee defaults, in which case it would have to make an appropriate provision, but otherwise both contracts are executory and will be accounted for in the usual way.

In situation (2), the intermediate will record at commencement of the lease term an asset acquired under a finance lease and an obligation to the lessor of an equal and opposite amount. As it has granted an operating lease to the lessee, its risks and rewards incidental to ownership of the asset exceed those assumed by the lessee under the lease. It is appropriate for the intermediate party to record a fixed asset, which it will have to depreciate as set out in 4.1.4 above.

However, under scenario (3), the intermediate is the lessee under a finance lease with the lessor and lessor under a finance lease with the lessee. Its statement of financial position, *prima facie*, records a finance lease receivable from the lessee and a finance lease obligation to the lessor. Both of these are treated as if they are financial instruments for derecognition purposes (see 3.5 above for the circumstances in which lease assets and liabilities are within scope of IAS 39).

The intermediate may be in a position to derecognise its financial asset and liability if it transfers to the lessor the contractual right to receive the cash flows of the lessee and thereby extinguishes its liability under the lease. *[IAS 39.18]*. However, it is more likely that it retains the contractual right to receive the cash flow under the lease and takes on a contractual obligation to pay the cash flows to the lessor. In accordance with the derecognition rules in IAS 39 it can derecognise its asset and liability if, and only if, it meets certain criteria, which are summarised below and described in detail in Chapter 47.

In the context of leases, the most important of these conditions is that the intermediate has no obligation to pay amounts to the lessor unless in collects equivalent amounts from the lessee. *[IAS 39.19]*. If the ultimate lessee defaults on its lease obligations (for whatever reason), the original lessor must have no recourse against the intermediate party for the outstanding payments under the lease if derecognition is to be appropriate. Another important factor is what happens if the original lessor defaults, for example through insolvency. The analysis will also have to take account of the following conditions for derecognition of a financial asset in IAS 39 (or IFRS 9 if the entity applies that standard):

(a) the entity (i.e. the intermediate party) is prohibited by the terms of the transfer contract from selling or pledging the original asset; and

(b) the entity has an obligation to remit any cash flows it collects without material delay. Investment in cash or cash equivalents is permitted, but interest earned must be passed to the eventual recipients. *[IAS 39.19]*.

If all of these factors indicate that the intermediate party has derecognised its interest in the two leases, i.e. commercially it is acting merely as a broker or agent for the original lessor, it should not include any asset or obligation relating to the leased asset in its statement of financial position. The income received by such an intermediary should be taken to profit or loss on a systematic and rational basis – the discussion of the recognition of fee income in SIC-27, as discussed in 2.2 above, may be helpful. If, on the other hand, the intermediate party is taken to be acting as both lessee and lessor in two independent although related transactions, the assets and obligations under finance leases should be recognised in the normal way.

It should not be inferred from the above discussion that all situations encountered can be relatively easily analysed. In practice this is unlikely to be the case, as the risks and rewards will probably be spread between the parties involved. This is especially likely where more than the three parties discussed above are involved. Therefore, even if the arrangements meet the definition of a 'transfer' under IAS 39, the intermediate may have retained some of the risks and rewards of ownership or control of the asset and it may be necessary to recognise other assets and liabilities in this respect. The complex area concerning derecognition of financial assets is dealt with in Chapter 47.

9 DISCLOSURES REQUIRED BY IAS 17

This section deals only with the disclosure requirements of IAS 17 and those of other accounting standards to which it specifically refers. Disclosures required by SIC-27 are dealt with in 2.2 above.

9.1 Disclosures relating to financial assets and liabilities

Because finance lease assets and obligations and individual payments currently due and payable under operating leases are financial assets and liabilities, lessees and lessors must make the disclosures required by IFRS 7 – *Financial Instruments: Disclosures*. This principally applies to the general requirements regarding classification and disclosure of financial assets and liabilities in the statement of financial position and disclosure of interest income and expense, together with other gains and losses arising from financial instruments, whether reflected in profit or loss or other comprehensive income. IFRS 7's disclosure requirements are covered in Chapter 50. However, if the lease arrangements contain more complex terms then there may be additional disclosure requirements, which are also summarised in Chapter 50.

9.2 Disclosure by lessees

9.2.1 *Disclosure of finance leases*

As well as meeting the IFRS 7 disclosure requirements, IAS 17 requires lessees to make the following disclosures for finance leases: *[IAS 17.31]*

(a) for each class of asset, the net carrying amount at the reporting date. Assets that are recognised under a finance lease will generally be considered to be the same class of assets with a similar nature that are owned, so there is no need to provide separate reconciliations of movements in owned assets from assets under finance leases;

(b) a reconciliation between the total of future minimum lease payments at the reporting date, and their present value. The minimum lease payments will include adjustments that have been made following a rent review. In addition, an entity shall disclose the total of future minimum lease payments at the reporting date, and their present value, for each of the following periods:

  (i) not later than one year;

  (ii) later than one year and not later than five years;

  (iii) later than five years.

(c) contingent rents recognised as an expense in the period. See 3.4.7 above for a discussion about the meaning for disclosure purposes of future minimum lease payments and contingent rents;

(d) the total of future minimum sublease payments expected to be received under non-cancellable subleases at the reporting date;

(e) a general description of the lessee's material leasing arrangements including, but not limited to, the following:

  (i) the basis on which contingent rent payable is determined;

  (ii) the existence and terms of renewal or purchase options and escalation clauses; and

  (iii) restrictions imposed by lease arrangements, such as those concerning dividends, additional debt, and further leasing.

The following is an example of disclosures made.in practice:

Extract 24.3: Deutsche Telekom AG (2012)

Notes to the Consolidated Financial Statements [extract]

34 Disclosures on leases [extract]

Deutsche Telekom as lessee [extract]

Finance leases. When a lease transfers substantially all risks and rewards to Deutsche Telekom as lessee, Deutsche Telekom initially recognizes the leased assets in the statement of financial position at the lower of fair value or present value of the future minimum lease payments. Most of the leased assets carried in the statement of financial position as part of a finance lease relate to long-term rental and lease agreements for office buildings. The average lease term is 17 years. The agreements include extension and purchase options. Table T129 shows the net carrying amounts of leased assets capitalized in connection with a finance lease as of the reporting date:

T129

	Dec. 31, 2012	Of which: sale and leaseback transactions	Dec. 31, 2011	Of which: sale and leaseback transactions
	millions of €	millions of €	millions of €	millions of €
Land and buildings	792	443	883	493
Technical equipment and machinery	80	0	104	0
Other	7	0	11	0
Net carrying amounts of leased assets capitalized	879	443	998	493

At the inception of the lease term, Deutsche Telekom recognizes a lease liability equal to the carrying amount of the leased asset. In subsequent periods, the liability decreases by the amount of lease payments made to the lessors using the effective interest method. The interest component of the lease payments is recognized in the income statement.

Table T130 provides a breakdown of these amounts:

T130

	Minimum lease payments		**Interest component**		**Present values**	
	Total	Of which: sale and leaseback	Total	Of which: sale and leaseback	Total	Of which: sale and leaseback
	millions of €	millions of €	millions of €	millions of €	millions of €	millions of €
Dec. 31, 2012						
Maturity						
Within 1 year	231	109	95	57	136	52
In 1 to 3 years	408	215	158	99	250	116
In 3 to 5 years	361	202	126	79	235	123
After 5 years	969	566	344	219	625	347
	1,969	**1,092**	**723**	**454**	**1,246**	**638**
Dec. 31, 2011						
Maturity						
Within 1 year	257	108	100	60	157	48
In 1 to 3 years	413	218	177	109	236	109
In 3 to 5 years	363	209	142	90	221	119
After 5 years	1,136	666	399	257	737	409
	2,169	**1,201**	**818**	**516**	**1,351**	**685**

Chapter 24

In addition, the leased asset is accounted for as property, plant and equipment, an intangible asset or other asset of the reporting entity and the requirements for disclosure in accordance with IAS 16 (Chapter 18), IAS 36 (Chapter 20), IAS 38 (Chapter 17), IAS 40 (Chapter 19) and IAS 41 (Chapter 38) are applicable as appropriate. *[IAS 17.32]*.

9.2.2 Disclosure of operating leases

In addition to meeting the requirements of IFRS 7, lessees must make the following disclosures for operating leases: *[IAS 17.35]*

(a) the total of future minimum lease payments under non-cancellable operating leases for each of the following periods:
  (i) not later than one year;
  (ii) later than one year and not later than five years;
  (iii) later than five years.

(b) the total of future minimum sublease payments expected to be received under non-cancellable subleases at the reporting date;

(c) lease and sublease payments recognised as an expense in the period, with separate amounts for minimum lease payments, contingent rents, and sublease payments. See 3.4.7.A above for a discussion about the meaning for disclosure purposes of future minimum lease payments and contingent rents;

(d) a general description of the lessee's significant leasing arrangements including, but not limited to, the following:
  (i) the basis on which contingent rent payable is determined;
  (ii) the existence and terms of renewal or purchase options and escalation clauses; and
  (iii) restrictions imposed by lease arrangements, such as those concerning dividends, additional debt and further leasing.

An example of the disclosures made by a lessee in respect of their obligations under operating leases is as follows.

Extract 24.4: Deutsche Telekom AG (2012)

Notes to the Consolidated Financial Statements [extract]
34 Disclosures on leases [extract]
Deutsche Telekom as lessee [extract]

Operating leases. Beneficial ownership of a lease is attributed to the lessor if this is the party to which all the substantial risks and rewards incidental to ownership of the asset are transferred. The lessor recognizes the leased asset in its statement of financial position. Deutsche Telekom recognizes the lease payments made during the term of the operating lease in profit or loss. Deutsche Telekom's obligations arising from operating leases are mainly related to long-term rental or lease agreements for network infrastructure, cell towers and real estate.

Some leases include extension options and provide for stepped rents. Most of these leases relate to cell towers in the United States.

The operating lease expenses recognized in profit or loss amounted to EUR 2.8 billion in the 2012 financial year (2011: EUR 2.8 billion; 2010: EUR 2.9 billion). Table T131 provides a breakdown of future obligations arising from operating leases:

T131

	Dec. 31, 2012 millions of €	Dec. 31, 2011 millions of €
Maturity		
Within 1 year	**2,385**	2,369
In 1 to 3 years	**4,096**	3,845
In 3 to 5 years	**3,492**	3,085
After 5 years	**7,529**	5,982
	17,502	**15,281**

Future obligations arising from operative leases no longer include capacity contracts on data connections for cell towers in the United States operating segment totalling EUR 2.0 billion (2011: EUR 2.1 billion) from the 2012 financial year onward. Prior-period comparatives have been adjusted with retroactive effect. These obligations are included in other financial obligations.

T-Mobile USA signed an agreement with Crown Castle concerning the leasing and use of cell sites. T-Mobile USA will continue to operate its mobile communications systems at these cell sites and, to the end, lease back the required infrastructure from Crown Castle through operating leases. In return, the owners of the land on which the cell towers are built will no longer receive lease payments from T-Mobile USA for those cell towers which were contributed to the two associates and those that were disposed of.

T-Mobile USA concluded contract extensions and amendments with several cell-site operators in 2012 for the lease of mobile transmission capacity on cell towers. This resulted in an increase of EUR 1.6 billion in operating lease obligations as of December 31, 2012.

9.3 Disclosure by lessors

9.3.1 Disclosure of finance leases

In addition to meeting the requirements in IFRS 7 (see 9.1 above), lessors must disclose the following for finance leases:

(a) a reconciliation between the gross investment in the lease at the reporting date, and the present value of minimum lease payments receivable at the reporting date. In addition, an entity shall disclose the gross investment in the lease and the present value of minimum lease payments receivable at the reporting date, for each of the following periods:
   (i) not later than one year;
   (ii) later than one year and not later than five years;
   (iii) later than five years;

(b) unearned finance income;

(c) the unguaranteed residual values accruing to the benefit of the lessor;

(d) the accumulated allowance for uncollectible minimum lease payments receivable;

(e) contingent rents recognised as income in the period; and

(f) a general description of the lessor's material leasing arrangements. *[IAS 17.47].*

IAS 17 also recommends but does not require disclosure of the gross investment less unearned income in new business added during the period, after deducting the relevant amounts for cancelled leases as a useful indicator of growth. *[IAS 17.48].*

Deutsche Telekom discloses its activities as a finance lessor as follows:

Extract 24.5: Deutsche Telekom AG (2012)

Notes to the Consolidated Financial Statements [extract]
34 Disclosures on leases [extract]
Deutsche Telekom as lessor [extract]

Finance Leases. Deutsche Telekom is lessor in connection with finance leases. Essentially, these relate to the leasing of routers and other hardware which Deutsche Telekom provides to its customers for data and telephone network solutions. Deutsche Telekom recognizes a receivable in the amount of the net investment in the lease. The lease payments made by the lessees are split into an interest component and a principal component using the effective interest method. The lease receivable is reduced by the principal received. The interest component of the payments is recognized as finance income in the income statement. The amount of the net investment in a finance lease is determined as shown as follows:

	Dec. 31, 2012 millions of €	Dec. 31, 2011 millions of €
Minimum lease payments	262	348
Unguaranteed residual value	13	3
Gross investment	275	351
Unearned finance income	(27)	(33)
Net investment (present value of the minimum lease payments)	248	318

The gross investment amount and the present value of payable minimum lease payments are shown as follows:

	Dec. 31, 2012		Dec. 31, 2011	
	Gross investment millions of €	Present value of minimum lease payments millions of €	Gross investment millions of €	Present value of minimum lease payments millions of €
Maturity				
Within 1 year	131	106	139	124
In 1 to 3 years	116	110	168	153
In 3 to 5 years	16	20	41	38
After 5 years	12	12	3	3
	275	**248**	**351**	**318**

According to the framework agreement signed between T-Mobile USA and Crown Castle, 451 cell sites will be leased out to Crown Castle as part of the finance lease.

9.3.2 *Disclosure of operating leases*

Lessors must, in addition to meeting the requirements of IFRS 7, disclose the following for operating leases:

(a) the future minimum lease payments under non-cancellable operating leases in the aggregate and for each of the following periods:

(i) not later than one year;

(ii) later than one year and not later than five years;

(iii) later than five years;

(b) total contingent rents recognised as income in the period; and

(c) a general description of the lessor's leasing arrangements. *[IAS 17.56].*

Deutsche Telekom's lessor interests in operating leases are disclosed as follows.

Extract 24.6: Deutsche Telekom AG (2012)

Notes to the Consolidated Financial Statements [extract]
34 Disclosures on leases [extract]
Deutsche Telekom as lessor [extract]

Operating leases: If Deutsche Telekom is a lessor in connection with operating leases, it continues to recognize the leased assets in its statement of financial position. The lease payments received are recognized in profit or loss. The leases mainly relate to the rental of cell towers and building space and have an average term of 13 years. The future minimum lease payments arising from non-cancelable operating leases are as follows:

	Dec. 31, 2012 millions of €	Dec. 31, 2011 millions of €
Maturity		
Within 1 year	266	374
In 1 to 3 years	371	476
In 3 to 5 years	310	349
After 5 years	676	737
	1,623	**1,936**

In addition, the leased asset is accounted for as a fixed asset of the reporting entity and the requirements for disclosure in accordance with IAS 16 (Chapter 18), IAS 36 (Chapter 20), IAS 38 (Chapter 17), IAS 40 (Chapter 19) and IAS 41 (Chapter 38) as appropriate. *[IAS 17.57].*

10 UPDATING LEASE ACCOUNTING: EXPOSURE DRAFT – LEASES

Lease accounting has always been a convergence project and it became a priority under the revised Memorandum of Understanding in 2008. Although the IASB and FASB issued exposure drafts in August 2010, a revised ED, ED/2013/6 – *Leases* – was not issued until May 2013, an indication of the difficulties faced by standard-setters.

This section describes briefly the requirements of ED/2013/6 ('the ED'). It does not address all aspects of the proposed accounting or the extensive disclosure proposals. Any standard that follows from the ED will not necessarily have the features that are discussed below.

10.1 Introduction

The IASB's *Framework* defines a liability as 'a present obligation of the entity arising from past events, the settlement of which is expected to result in an outflow from the entity of resources embodying economic benefits'. *[Framework 4.4].* It follows that most leases, irrespective of whether finance or operating in nature, contain an unavoidable legal obligation to transfer economic benefits to the lessor, i.e. contain a liability. The Boards argue that the lessee also has an asset, as it is likely both to control and enjoy the future economic benefits embodied in the leased asset, thereby meeting the definition of an asset in the *Framework*. *[Framework 4.4].* It should therefore recognise these rights as an asset (the 'right-of-use asset'). This would have consequential effects on accounting by lessors as this suggests that they have a lease receivable, which represents the right to collect rentals, and a residual asset rather than the asset that is the subject of the lease.

The definition of a lease is largely unchanged; a lease will be defined as a contract in which the right to use an asset (the underlying asset) is conveyed, for a period of time, in exchange for consideration. The consequences of identifying a lease differ fundamentally from IAS 17. If an entity controls an identified asset for any period of time then lease obligations and right-of-use assets will be recognised (there is an exemption for leases of up to 12 months). IAS 17, by contrast, essentially distinguishes quasi-acquisitions of assets (finance leases) from executory contracts (operating leases). The crucial accounting issue, therefore, will be how to distinguish one type of executory contract, the lease, from another type, the service arrangement. Often these will be bundled together in a single arrangement.

Unlike IAS 17, this is not a risks and rewards model, it is about control. IAS 17 attempts to capture the difference between its two models based on the amount of risk and reward borne by each party. Pricing mechanisms can be very important for this purpose e.g. whether payments over the lease term or for the residual interest are based on market prices or are fixed amounts. Under a control model, pricing usually affects measurement of the asset and liability but does not determine whether there is an asset or liability in the first place.

What is being proposed is not a comprehensive fair value approach. The model measures lease obligations and right-of-use assets at the present value of expected lease payments, not at their fair value. Unlike earlier approaches, the Boards have not required separate measurement and accounting for renewal or purchase options and residual value guarantees.

Like IAS 17, the ED requires lessees and lessors to classify leases by type, which determines both the method and timing for recognising lease revenue and expense, but the criteria for classifying leases and the related accounting are different. Leases are classified as either Type A or Type B. Both types will require recognition of assets and liabilities on the statement of financial position. The effect on profit or loss of Type A leases resembles accounting for finance leases under IAS 17. Type B leases are usually land and buildings and the periodic lease expense resembles that of today's operating leases.

10.2 The new lease model

10.2.1 Scope and key concepts

Scope: The following arrangements would not be in scope:[11]

(i) leases for the right to explore for or use natural resources (such as minerals, oil, natural gas and similar non-regenerative resources);

(ii) leases of biological assets;

(iii) leases of service concession arrangements within the scope of IFRIC 12; and

(iv) a lessor's leases of intangible assets.

A lessee's leases of intangible assets would not be required to be accounted for in accordance with the proposed leases standard.[12] It is assumed that entities will be allowed as an accounting policy election to account for them under the leases standard.

Leases of investment property as defined in IAS 40 are in scope of the ED. Entities would no longer be allowed to choose whether or not to recognise these property assets, which means they would have to be carried at fair value if the entity applies that model.

Definition of a lease: a lease will be defined as a contract in which the right to use an asset (the underlying asset) is conveyed, for a period of time, in exchange for consideration. To be a lease, an arrangement will have to meet two criteria:

(1) fulfilment of the contract depends on a 'specified asset' (as described in paragraphs 8-11); and

(2) the contract conveys the 'right to control the use' of the specified asset. Consistent with current standards, a 'specified asset' will be an asset that is implicitly or explicitly identifiable (as described in paragraphs 12-19).[13]

An identified asset: even if an asset is explicitly specified (which is usually the case), the contract will not depend on an asset if the contract provides the supplier with substantive substitution rights (i.e. that allow the supplier to use any one of a number of different assets to fulfil the contract). These will not be leases because they do not depend on the use of an identified asset. It is likely that they would be accounted for as executory arrangements.

A substitution right would be substantive if substitution of the asset is both practical and economically feasible and the asset could be substituted without the customer's consent. Contract terms that allow or require a supplier to substitute other assets only when the underlying asset is not operating properly (e.g. a normal warranty provision) or when a technical upgrade becomes available would not create a substantive substitution right.[14]

Although a physically distinct portion of a larger asset (e.g. a floor in a multi-storey building) could be an identified asset, a non-physically distinguishable portion of an asset (e.g. a capacity portion of a fibre-optic cable) would not qualify and would not be the subject of a lease.[15]

The right to control the use of an identified asset: an entity will have the right if it has the ability to both direct the use of the asset and derive the benefit from its use.[16] An arrangement under which a customer obtains all of the benefit from the use of an asset, but does not direct its use, would not be considered a lease.

The ability to direct the use of the asset would be demonstrated by the ability to make decisions about the use of the asset (e.g. determining how, when and in what manner the asset is used) that significantly affect the benefits received by the customer from the asset. If the customer specifies the quantity and timing of the delivery of goods, this would not, by itself, indicate the customer's ability to direct the use of the asset used to produce or deliver those goods. In contrast, if the vendor operates the asset according to the specific instructions of the customer, the customer has the ability to direct the use of the asset.[17]

Chapter 24

The ability to derive the benefits from use of an asset means obtaining substantially all of the potential economic benefits from its use, whether directly or indirectly, throughout the term of the contract. The economic benefits include its primary output and by-products in the form of products and services. However, the customer will not have this ability if:

- it needs other goods or services provided by the supplier to obtain the benefits and these are not sold separately by the supplier or other suppliers; and
- the asset is incidental to the delivery of services because it can function only with the additional goods or services provided by the supplier.

In such cases, the customer receives a bundle of goods or services that combine to deliver an overall service for which the customer has contracted.[18]

Lease term: this is the non-cancellable period, plus any options where there is a significant economic incentive to extend or not terminate the lease.

The lease proposals should be applied only to periods for which enforceable rights and obligations arise. Lessees and lessors should reassess the lease term only if there has been a change in circumstances so that a lessee would either have, or no longer have, a significant economic incentive to exercise options to extend or terminate the lease.

Factors that might create an economic incentive include those that are part of the contract, e.g. renewal rates priced at a bargain or penalty payments for cancellation or non-renewal. Others are economic penalties such as significant customisation or installation costs (e.g. leasehold improvements) or subleases with longer non-cancellable terms than head leases.

Leases referred to as 'cancellable', 'month-to-month', 'at will', 'evergreen', 'perpetual' or 'rolling' will be subject to the proposal if they create enforceable rights and obligations. A contract (or a period within a contract) is not enforceable when the lessee and the lessor each have the unilateral right, without penalty, to terminate the lease without permission from the other party. An arrangement for which there are enforceable rights and obligations between the lessee and lessor (e.g. the lessee has a renewal option) would meet the definition of a contract and any non-cancellable periods in such leases would be considered part of the lease term.[19]

Lease payments: for lessees and lessors, these will include:[20]

- fixed lease payments less any lease incentives received or receivable from the lessor;
- In-substance fixed lease payments structured as variable payments
- the exercise price of purchase options if there is a significant economic incentive for the lessee to exercise;
- residual value guarantees (lessee only) or fixed payments structured as residual value guarantees (lessor only);
- termination option penalties; and
- variable lease payments that depend on an index or rate.

Variable lease payments: those that depend on an index or a rate should be measured initially based on the spot rate and then reassessed using the period-end index or rate.[21] It is actually being proposed that there be no further increases in the amount of the variable payments rather than making the assumption that there will be no further changes to the index. Therefore, if the payment in year 1 was 100 and the index is 5% at the end of the year, all future lease payments will be 105. The entity will not assume that the index remains at 5%, in which case the future payments would inflate by 5% annually.

Those that are based on performance (e.g. a percentage of sales) or usage (e.g. number of miles flown) of the underlying asset will be recognised as an expense when incurred. For example, a variable payment based on annual sales of a leased store will not be included in the right-of-use asset and liability to make lease payments recognised by the lessee.

Payments must be truly variable to be excluded from the amounts recognised in the statement of financial position. Payments that are contractually described as variable, but in substance are fixed, would be treated as fixed lease payments.[22]

Discount rate: this will be determined on a lease-by-lease basis. The discount rate would be the rate that the lessor charges the lessee if available; otherwise, the lessee would use its incremental borrowing rate. The rate the lessor charges the lessee could be based on:

- the implicit rate in the lease; or
- the property yield.

The lessee's incremental borrowing rate would be the rate of interest that the lessee would have to pay to borrow over a similar term (i.e. the lease term), and with a similar security, the funds necessary to purchase a similar underlying asset.[23]

10.2.2 Classification of leases

Leases will be classified at the lease commencement date as follows:[24]

Type A leases: leases of assets that are not property (e.g. equipment and vehicles) unless one of the following two conditions is met:

- the lease term is for an insignificant part of the total economic life of the underlying asset; or
- the present value of the lease payments is insignificant relative to the fair value of the underlying asset at the commencement date.

Type B leases: leases of property (land, a building or part of a building) unless one of the following two conditions is met:

- the lease term is for the major part of the remaining economic life of the underlying asset; or
- the present value of the lease payments accounts for substantially all of the fair value of the underlying asset at the commencement date.

Chapter 24

If a lessee has a significant economic incentive to exercise an option to purchase the underlying asset, the lease would be classified as Type A.

This distinction is based on the physical nature of the underlying asset which is not usual under current IFRS and has been developed to address the concerns of the property sector. Therefore, the IASB expects most leases of land and buildings will be Type B leases. There will also be guidance if the lease covers more than one asset, economic lives and subleases. The status of other structures such as towers, masts, dams and roads is uncertain as few would consider them to be buildings. Entities always have to be aware of the other conditions; even if they are persuaded that the asset is of Type B, they will still have to consider the lease term and present value of the lease payments; if these are high enough, this could mean that the arrangement defaults to Type A.

Another area that may need clarification is 'insignificant', in the context of leases of assets other than property. The meaning is likely to be subjective and require careful judgement.

Lease classification would not be reassessed after lease commencement unless a new contract is created by a substantive modification to the contract provisions.[25]

10.2.3 The new lease model – accounting by lessees

Initial recognition and measurement: the liability to make lease payments will be based on the present value of the lease payments to be made over the lease term. Variable rents not based on an index or rate (e.g. performance or usage-based payments) would be excluded from the lease liability and would be recognised in profit or loss as incurred. The right-of-use asset will be measured initially at cost and will include the amount of the liability to make lease payments plus any initial direct costs incurred by the lessee. Initial direct costs are direct and incremental to the lease transaction (e.g. commissions, legal fees).[26]

Subsequent measurement: The lease liability for Type A and Type B leases will be accreted using a rate in each period during the lease term that produces a constant periodic discount rate on the remaining balance of the liability,.[27] Lease payments will reduce the lease liability when paid. However, Type A and Type B leases will achieve different expense recognition patterns through the subsequent measurement of the right-of-use asset.

Type A leases

The lessee will:

- amortise the right-of-use asset on a systematic basis that reflects the pattern of consumption of the expected future economic benefits (generally straight-line);
- recognise interest expense using the interest method (i.e. a level effective rate throughout the lease term); and
- reduce the liability for lease payments made.

The amortisation period for most right-of-use assets will be the shorter of the lease term or the life of the underlying asset. If title transfers at the end of the lease term or the lessee has a significant economic incentive to exercise a purchase option, the amortisation period will be the remaining life of the underlying asset.[28]

Because of the consistent interest rate and decreasing liability over the lease term, lessees will recognise higher total periodic expense (i.e. total interest and amortisation expense) in the earlier periods of a lease and lower total periodic expense in later periods. This expense recognition pattern is consistent with the treatment of finance leases under current lease accounting, but would accelerate lease expense for current operating leases.

Type B leases

Lessees would calculate a periodic lease expense amount in a manner that is in some ways similar to today's accounting for operating leases. Throughout the lease term, the periodic lease expense is the greater of:

- the remaining cost of the lease (calculated at the beginning of each period) allocated over the remaining lease term on a straight-line basis, or
- the periodic interest expense taken on the lease liability (using the rate in each period during the lease term that produces a constant periodic discount rate on the remaining balance of the liability).[29]

At each reporting period, the remaining cost of the lease is calculated as follows:

lease payments (determined at the lease commence date),
plus
initial direct costs (determined at the lease commencement date),
minus
the periodic lease cost recognised in prior periods,
minus
any impairment of the right-of-use asset recognised in prior periods,
plus or minus
adjustments to reflect changes that arise from the remeasurement of the lease liability.

If the remaining cost of the lease allocated over the remaining lease term is higher than the periodic interest taken on the lease liability, the change in the right-of-use asset is the difference between the periodic straight-line expense amount and the accretion of the lease liability. If the periodic interest expense taken on the lease liability is higher, there would be no adjustment to the right-of-use asset. This could happen following a significant impairment of the right-to-use asset.

Example 24.26: Type A and Type B charge to profit or loss for lessees

A lessee enters into a 3 year lease under which it will pay €10,000 in year 1, €12,000 in year 2 and €14,000 in year 3. The initial measurement of the right-of-use asset and the liability to make lease payments is €33,000 using a discount rate of approximately 4.24%.

If the asset being leased is a car, the lease is likely to be a Type A lease. If the leased asset is space in an office building, it will probably be a Type B lease.

	Both lease types		Type A lease		Type B lease		
Year	Lease Liability €	Interest expense	Total expense €	ROU asset €	Lease expense €	Change in ROU asset €	ROU asset €
Notes			(a)		(b)	(c)	(d)
Initial	33,000			33,000			33,000
1	24,398	1,398	12,398	22,000	12,000	10,602	22,398
2	13,431	1,033	12,033	11,000	12,000	10,967	11,431
3	–	569	11,569	–	12,000	11,431	–
		3,000	36,000		36,000	33,000	

Notes

(a) The total lease expense under the Type A approach is the sum of the interest expense and the annual amortisation expense of €11,000.

(b) The annual straight-line amount is €12,000 ((10,000 + 12,000 + 14,000)÷3).

(c) Calculated by subtracting the accretion of the lease liability (i.e. the interest expense calculated for the interest/amortisation lease) from the annual lease expense, the straight-line amount calculated above.

(d) Calculated by subtracting the change in the ROU asset from the prior period's closing balance.

Reassessment: lessees must reassess certain key considerations throughout the life of the lease. Reassessment requirements vary, as follows:[30]

	Reassessment indicator
Lease term and purchase options	changes that suggest that a lessee may or may not have a significant economic incentive to exercise (market factors in isolation are not conclusive)
Discount rate	Change in lease payments due to a change in lease term, change to or from a significant economic incentive to exercise or changes in a reference interest rate.
Residual value guarantees	Events or circumstances indicate that there has been a significant change in the amounts expected to be payable

Lessees will remeasure the lease liability and adjust right-of-use asset except:

- any part of the remeasurement arising from a change in an index or a rate attributable to the current period will be recognised in profit or loss; and
- if the right-of-use asset is reduced to zero, a lessee will recognise any remaining amount of the remeasurement in profit or loss

Regardless of the extent of any remeasurement, lease classification will not be reassessed after the commencement date.[31] This means that a lease originally classified as a Type B will not be reclassified to Type A if a long renewal option, not taken into account at commencement, is exercised and this would have changed the initial assessment.

10.2.4 The new lease model – accounting by lessors

Initial recognition and measurement: accounting for Type A leases is similar to accounting for finance leases under IAS 17, although there is a different approach to residual values. Type B leases would be accounted for using a method similar to current operating lease accounting.

Type A leases: the residual asset is an apportionment of cost, unlike IAS 17, where residual interests are treated as future cash flows. In order to avoid the loss of revenue indicated by such an approach, residual assets are accreted upwards over the lease term. A Type A lease could, for example, be a lease that covers two years out of the five years of an asset's useful life so residual assets will be common and significant for equipment leases.

The lessor will, on commencement of the lease:

(i) measure the right to receive lease payments at their present value, discounted using the rate that the lessor charges the lessee. These terms are defined in 10.2.1 above);

(ii) measure the residual asset as an allocation of the carrying amount of the underlying asset. This comprises three amounts:

- (a) the gross residual asset, measured at the present value of the estimated residual value at the end of the lease term, discounted using the rate that the lessor charges the lessee;
- (b) the present value of variable lease payments, which the lessor expects to receive and which have been reflected in the rate the lessor charges the lessee, but which are not included in the lease receivable (e.g. variable lease payments linked to performance); and
- (c) the deferred profit, measured as the difference between the gross residual asset and the allocation of the carrying amount of the underlying asset.

The residual asset will initially be recognised as (a) + (b)–(c),[32]

Subsequent measurement: briefly, the lessor will:

(i) recognise finance revenue on the right to receive lease payments, which will be measured at amortised cost using the rate that produces a constant periodic discount rate on the remaining balance of the receivables;

(ii) measure the gross residual asset by accreting to the estimated residual value at the end of the lease term using the rate that the lessor charges the lessee. The lessor would not recognise any of the deferred profit in profit or loss until the residual asset is sold or re-leased;

(iii) reassess the variable lease payments as required; and

(iv) present the gross residual asset and the deferred profit together as a net residual asset.

The lessor will determine the lease term and lease payments (including lease payments structured as residual value guarantees) using the same principles applied by the lessee, described in 10.2.3 above. A lessor should recognise immediately in profit or loss changes in the right to receive lease payments due to reassessments of variable lease payments that depend on an index or a rate.

Over the term of the lease, the lessor will recognise interest income from the right to receive payments, using as a discount rate the amount that produces a constant periodic rate on the remaining balance of the receivable, taking into consideration the reassessment and impairment requirements as necessary. It will also accrete the gross residual asset using the rate the lessor charges the lessee.[33] These rates will differ to the extent that the lease receivable includes initial direct costs. The carrying amount of the residual asset at the end of the lease term will not represent either the expected value or the amortised cost of the underlying asset at the end of the lease.

Type B leases: lessors will recognise lease payments from Type B leases over the lease term on either a straight-line basis or another systematic basis that better represents the pattern in which income is earned from the underlying asset. Initial direct costs will as an expense over the lease term, on the same basis as lease income, which could be different to the amortisation of the asset.[34]

10.2.5 Other lease arrangements

Short-term leases: the ED includes exemptions for short-term leases. Lessees may elect to recognise lease expenses on a straight-line basis over the lease term for leases with a maximum possible lease term, including any options to renew, of 12 months. Lessors will have a similar election but lease revenue will not have to be recognised straight-line if another systematic and rational basis better represents the pattern of use. The lessee will not recognise any lease-related assets and lease liabilities. A lease will be defined as short-term based solely on whether the maximum possible lease term in the contract, including any options to extend, is less than one year. The entity's intentions, expectations or lease term for accounting purposes will not be considered. Entities will have to make a policy election to use the simplified accounting.[35]

Sale and leaseback transactions: Sale and leasebacks will no longer provide off-balance sheet financing as all leases (other than short-term leases) will be recognised on the statement of financial position. Whether these transactions are accounted for as a sale and a lease, or as a financing transaction, will be based on meeting the conditions for a sale in the revised revenue IFRS (see Chapter 28 at 6). If the arrangement qualifies as a sale and leaseback and the consideration exchanged (i.e. sales price for the sale of the asset and rental rate for the lease) is at fair value, the seller-lessee will recognise a gain or loss. If the consideration is not at fair value, the assets, liabilities, gain or loss will be adjusted to reflect current market rentals.[36] The seller/transferor will account for the lease in accordance with lessee accounting described at 10.2.3 above. Under current accounting, the seller-lessee may be required to defer and amortise some or all of the profit or loss on a sale based on the specific terms of the particular transaction. A transaction that is not a sale will be accounted for as a financing transaction.

10.3 The Conceptual Framework: derecognition and lease accounting

In July 2013 the IASB issued a discussion paper DP/2013/1 – *A Review of the Conceptual Framework for Financial Reporting* – in which it considers whether some arrangements including sale and leaseback transactions might be better reflected by partial derecognition, i.e. by derecognising a component of the original asset. Partial derecognition would affect the amount of asset shown after the arrangement as well as the amount of gain or loss as the entity would not recognise any gain or loss on the retained component.

In accounting for a sale and leaseback transaction under IAS 17, the entity entering into the arrangement (the seller/lessee) either continues to recognise the original asset because it is in substance a financing arrangement or it recognises none of it (full derecognition) as the arrangement is in substance a sale (see 7 above). The revised ED has a similar analysis between transfers that are, or are not, in substance sales but there will be a different result if the transfer meets the criteria to be accounted for as a sale. As all lease arrangements will be on balance sheet under the new proposals, the seller/lessee will derecognise the original asset and recognise the leaseback in accordance with lessee accounting, as described at 10.2.3 above. If the transfer does not meet the sales criteria then the arrangement will be accounted for as a financing arrangement.

Whether the arrangement meets the criteria for derecognition or not, the seller/lessee always retains some degree of continuing interest in the original asset through the leaseback.

Under IAS 17 and the proposals in the ED, the asset is considered to be a single unit of account. The entity either derecognises all of it or continues to recognise all of it. This even applies to the ED's proposals for transfers that are accounted for as sales because the asset under the leaseback is not a component of the original asset, and the gain or loss is measured by reference to the original asset. Yet in principle the rights under the sale and leaseback transaction could be considered as part of the original asset. The entity could 'sell' part of the original asset, while retaining the remainder. Therefore, if a seller/lessee disposed of a machine with a remaining life of ten years and leased it back for six years this could be seen as retaining the rights over the first six years and disposing of the rights over the last four years of the asset's life (i.e. selling them and recognising a gain or loss). The DP does not consider the nature of the deferred gain, so it does not speculate whether the entity is in substance financing the retained portion, nor does it consider in any detail the basis of allocation of the asset or of the consideration received between the two components.

Any decision made by the IASB regarding sale and leaseback transactions depends on its conclusions about the unit of account. The Board also needs to consider whether the component retained should be regarded as continuing to be a component of the original asset, or whether its character has changed so much that it should be regarded as an entirely new asset.[37]

Note that accounting by lessors for Type A leases as proposed under the new lease model is a form of partial derecognition as the residual asset is an apportionment of cost, unlike IAS 17, where residual interests are treated as future cash flows (see 10.2.4 above). The consequence of a partial derecognition model have been complex and controversial, involving accretion of the residual interest as well as deferral of gains relating to the residual.

References

1 Exposure Draft Leases, IASB, May 2013, ED/2013/6, paras. 4, 5.
2 ASC 840-10-25-1.
3 *IFRIC Update*, May 2012.
4 Valuation Information Paper No. 9, The Royal Institution of Chartered Surveyors, May 2006.
5 RICS Valuation Information Paper No. 9, paras. 4.7 and 4.8.
6 *IFRIC Update*, September 2005.
7 *IFRIC Update*, April 2005.
8 *IFRIC Update*, July 2008.
9 *IFRIC Update*, March 2007.
10 *IFRIC Update*, March 2007.
11 ED/2013/6, para. 4.
12 ED/2013/6, para. 5.
13 ED/2013/6, paras. 6-7.
14 ED/2013/6, paras. 8-10.
15 ED/2013/6, para. 11.
16 ED/2013/6, para. 12.
17 ED/2013/6, paras. 13-17.
18 ED/2013/6, paras. 18-19.
19 ED/2013/6, paras. 25-27, B2-B6.
20 ED/2013/6, paras. 39, 70.
21 ED/2013/6, paras. 39(b), 70(b).
22 ED/2013/6, paras. 39(c), 70(c).
23 ED/2013/6, paras. 38, 69, B7-B9.
24 ED/2013/6, paras. 28-35.
25 ED/2013/6, para. 36.
26 ED/2013/6, paras. 38-40.
27 ED/2013/6, para. 41(a).
28 ED/2013/6, paras. 47-49.
29 ED/2013/6, para. 42(b).
30 ED/2013/6, paras. 43-46.
31 ED/2013/6, para. 28.
32 ED/2013/6, para. 71.
33 ED/2013/6, paras. 76-83.
34 ED/2013/6, paras. 93-97.
35 ED/2013/6, paras. 118-120.
36 ED/2013/6, paras. 111-115.
37 Discussion Paper/2013/1, *A Review of the Conceptual Framework for Financial Reporting.* IASB, July 2013, paras. 4.45-4.49, 9.36.

Chapter 25 Government grants

List of examples

Chapter 25 Government grants

1 INTRODUCTION

IAS 20 – *Accounting for Government Grants and Disclosure of Government Assistance* – applied for the first time in 1984. *[IAS 20.41]*. With the exception of an amendment in 2008 requiring entities to quantify the benefit of a government loan at a below-market rate of interest, *[IAS 20.43]*, the standard has survived for all that time without any substantive amendment. The standard pre-dates the IASB's *Conceptual Framework* and, as the IASB itself has noted, it is inconsistent with it,[1] resulting in the recognition in the balance sheet of deferred debits and credits that do not meet the *Framework's* definitions of assets and liabilities and allowing alternatives to initial measurement at fair value that could result in an asset being understated by reference to the *Framework*.

IAS 20 defines government grants in terms of assistance given to an entity in return for meeting certain conditions relating to the operating activities of the entity. *[IAS 20.3]*. SIC-10 *Government Assistance – No Specific Relation to Operating Activities* – was issued in 1998 to clarify that IAS 20 applies even if the only condition is a requirement to operate in certain regions or industry sectors (see 2.2.1 below).

Government grants related to biological assets are excluded from the scope of IAS 20 and are dealt with in IAS 41 – *Agriculture* (see section 5 below and Chapter 38 at 3.3). *[IAS 20.2(d)]*.

A project to revise IAS 20 was deferred in 2006 and, at the time of writing, the lack of any reference to it in the IASB's Work Plan indicates that resumption of this project is not a priority.[2]

1.1 Overview of IAS 20

Government grants are transfers of resources to an entity in return for past or future compliance with certain conditions relating to the entity's operating activities. *[IAS 20.3]*. Such assistance has been available to businesses for many years, although its form and extent will often have undergone changes depending on the priorities of governments over time and from country to country. The purpose of government grants, which may be called subsidies, subventions or premiums, *[IAS 20.6]*, and other forms of government assistance is often to encourage a private sector entity to take a course of action that it would not normally have taken if the assistance had not been provided. *[IAS 20.4]*. As the standard notes, the receipt of government assistance by an entity may be significant for the preparation of the financial statements for two reasons:

- if resources have been transferred, an appropriate method of accounting for the transfer must be found; and
- it is desirable to give an indication of the extent to which an entity has benefited from such assistance during the reporting period, because this facilitates comparison of its financial statements with those of prior periods and with those of other entities. *[IAS 20.5]*.

The main accounting issue that arises from government grants is how to deal with the benefit that the grant represents. IAS 20 adopts an income approach, whereby grants are recognised in profit or loss in the same period as the costs that the grants are intended to compensate. *[IAS 20.12]*. Accordingly, grants relating to specific expenses are recognised in profit or loss in the same period as those expenses, and grants relating to depreciable assets are recognised in profit or loss in the same periods as the related depreciation expense. *[IAS 20.17]*. This approach is applied regardless of whether the benefit is received in the form of cash; by a transfer of a non-monetary asset; or as a reduction of a liability to the government. *[IAS 20.9, 23]*.

The standard recognises that an entity may receive other forms of government assistance, such as free technical or marketing advice and the provision of guarantees, which cannot reasonably have a value placed upon them. Rather than prescribe how these should be accounted for, it requires disclosure about such assistance. *[IAS 20.35, 36]*.

1.2 Terms used in this chapter

The following terms are used in this chapter with the meanings specified:

Term	Definition
Government	Government, government agencies and similar bodies whether local, national or international. *[IAS 20.3]*
Government assistance	Action by government designed to provide an economic benefit specific to an entity or a range of entities qualifying under certain criteria. Government assistance does not include benefits provided only indirectly through action affecting general trading conditions, such as the provision of infrastructure in development areas or the imposition of trading constraints on competitors. *[IAS 20.3]*
Government grants	Assistance by government in the form of transfers of resources to an entity in return for past or future compliance with certain conditions relating to the operating activities of the entity. This excludes those forms of government assistance which cannot reasonably have a value placed upon them and transactions with government which cannot be distinguished from the normal trading transactions of the entity. *[IAS 20.3]* Government grants are sometimes called by other names such as subsidies, subventions, or premiums. *[IAS 20.6]*

Grants related to assets	Government grants whose primary condition is that an entity qualifying for them should purchase, construct or otherwise acquire long-term assets. Subsidiary conditions may also be attached restricting the type or location of the assets or the periods during which they are required to be held. *[IAS 20.3]*
Grants related to income	Government grants other than those related to assets. *[IAS 20.3]*
Forgivable loans	Loans which the lender undertakes to waive repayment under certain prescribed conditions. *[IAS 20.3]*
Fair value	The price that would be received to sell an asset or paid to transfer a liability in an orderly transaction between market participants at the measurement date. *[IAS 20.3, IFRS 13 Appendix A]*
Costs to sell	The incremental costs directly attributable to the disposal of an asset, excluding finance costs and income taxes. *[IAS 41.5]*
Non-monetary government grant	A government grant that takes the form of a transfer of a non-monetary asset, such as land or other resources, for the use of the entity. *[IAS 20.23]*
Biological asset	A living plant or animal. *[IAS 41.5]*

2 SCOPE OF IAS 20

IAS 20 applies in accounting for, and in the disclosure of, government grants and in the disclosure of other forms of government assistance. *[IAS 20.1]*. The distinction between government grants and other forms of government assistance is important because the standard's accounting requirements only apply to the former.

The standard regards the term 'government' to include governmental agencies and similar bodies whether local, national or international. *[IAS 20.3]*.

2.1 Government assistance

Government assistance is defined as action by government designed to provide an economic benefit to an entity or range of entities qualifying under certain criteria (see 3.7 below). *[IAS 20.3]*. Government assistance takes many forms 'varying both in the nature of the assistance given and in the conditions which are usually attached to it'. *[IAS 20.4]*.

However, such assistance does not include benefits provided indirectly through action affecting general trading conditions, such as the provision of infrastructure (e.g. transport, communications networks or utilities) in development areas or that are available for the benefit of an entire local community or the imposition of trading constraints on competitors. *[IAS 20.3, 38]*.

2.2 Government grants

Government grants are a specific form of government assistance. Under IAS 20, *government grants* represent assistance by government in the form of transfers of resources to an entity in return for past or future compliance with certain conditions relating to the operating activities of the entity. *[IAS 20.3].* The standard identifies the following types of government grants:

- *grants related to assets* are government grants whose primary condition is that an entity qualifying for them should purchase, construct or otherwise acquire long-term assets. Subsidiary conditions may also be attached restricting the type or location of the assets or the periods during which they are to be acquired or held; and
- *grants related to income* are government grants other than those related to assets. *[IAS 20.3].*

Government grants exclude:

(a) assistance to which no value can reasonably be assigned, e.g. free technical or marketing advice and the provision of guarantees; and

(b) transactions with government that cannot be distinguished from the normal trading transactions of the entity, e.g. where the entity is being favoured by a government's procurement policy. *[IAS 20.3, 35].*

Such excluded items are to be treated as falling within the standard's disclosure requirements for government assistance (see 2.1 above and 3.7 below).

Loans at below market interest rates are also deemed to be a form of government assistance and the standard requires entities to measure and record the benefit of the below-market rate of interest in accordance with IAS 39 – *Financial Instruments: Recognition and Measurement* – or IFRS 9 – *Financial Instruments* – as appropriate. *[IAS 20.10A].* The accounting consequences are discussed at 3.4 below.

In public-to-private service concession arrangements a government may give certain assets to the operator of the service concession. If the entire arrangement is to be accounted for under IFRIC 12 – *Service Concession Arrangements* – the assets are not a government grant. *[IFRIC 12.27].* Service concessions are discussed in Chapter 26.

While grants of emission rights and renewable energy certificates typically meet the definition of government grants under IAS 20, the rights and certificates themselves are intangible assets. Accounting for emission rights and renewable energy certificates is discussed in Chapter 17 at 11.2 and 11.3.

2.2.1 Grants with no specific relation to operating activities (SIC-10)

SIC-10 – *Government Assistance – No Specific Relation to Operating Activities* – addresses the situation in some countries where government assistance is provided to entities, but without there being any conditions specifically relating to their activities, other than to operate in certain regions or industry sectors. It determined that such forms of government assistance are to be treated as government grants. *[SIC-10.3].* This ruling was made to avoid any suggestion that such forms of assistance were not governed by IAS 20 and could be credited directly to equity.

2.3 Scope exclusions

IAS 20 does not deal with:

(a) accounting for government grants if the entity prepares financial information that reflect the effects of changing prices, whether as financial statements or in supplementary information;

(b) government assistance in the form of benefits that are available in determining taxable profit or loss or are determined or limited on the basis of income tax liability, e.g. income tax holidays, investment tax credits, accelerated depreciation allowances and reduced income tax rates;

(c) government participation in the ownership of the entity; and

(d) government grants covered by IAS 41. *[IAS 20.2].*

The accounting treatment of government assistance either provided by way of a reduction in taxable profit or loss; or determined or limited according to an entity's income tax liability is discussed in the context of investment tax credits at 2.3.1 below and in Chapter 29 at 4.3.

The reason for exclusion (d) above is that the presentation permitted by IAS 20 of deducting government grants from the carrying amount of the asset (see 4.1 below) was considered inconsistent with a fair value model, which can be used in the measurement of biological assets. *[IAS 41.B66].* The IASB decided to deal with government grants related to agricultural activity in IAS 41 rather than initiate a wider review of IAS 20. *[IAS 41.B67].* The requirements of IAS 41 in relation to government grants are set out at 5 below and in Chapter 38 at 3.3.

There are no similar exclusions for government grants in IAS 40 – *Investment Property* – which includes a similar fair value model (see Chapter 19), nor was IAS 20 revised to deal with the matter. This is probably because government grants in the investment property sector are relatively rare compared to the agricultural sector. However, governments do on occasion provide grants and subsidised loans to finance the acquisition of social housing that meets the definition of investment property. The discount on these subsidised loans is now considered to be a government grant, as described at 3.4 below.

2.3.1 Investment tax credits

IAS 20 excludes from its scope government assistance either provided by way of a reduction in taxable profit; or determined or limited according to an entity's income tax liability, citing investment tax credits as an example. *[IAS 20.2(c)].* Investment tax credits are excluded altogether from the scope of IAS 12 – *Income Taxes* – although any temporary differences that arise from them are in the scope of the standard. *[IAS 12.4].* Accordingly, if government assistance is described as an investment tax credit, but it is neither determined or limited by the entity's income tax liability nor provided in the form of an income tax deduction, the requirements of IAS 20 apply.

This raises the question as to how an entity should account for those forms of government incentives for specific kinds of investment that are delivered through the tax system. Typically, a tax credit is given as a deduction from the entity's income tax liability, rather than as a deductible expense in computing the liability. Entitlement to assistance can be determined in a variety of ways. Some investment tax credits may relate to direct investment in property, plant and equipment. Other entities may receive investment tax credits relating to research and development activities. Some credits may be realisable only through a reduction in current or future income taxes payable, while others may be settled directly in cash if the entity does not have sufficient income taxes payable to offset the credit within a certain period. Access to the credit may be limited according to the total of all taxes paid to the government providing the assistance, including payroll and sales taxes in addition to income taxes. There may be other conditions associated with receiving the investment tax credit, and the credit may become repayable if ongoing conditions are not met.

The fact that both IAS 20 and IAS 12 exclude from their scope those investment tax credits that are realisable only through a reduction in current or future income taxes payable does not prohibit an entity from applying either standard in accounting for such credits. Indeed, either IAS 20 or IAS 12 will generally provide an appropriate accounting framework, by analogy under the 'GAAP hierarchy' in IAS 8 – *Accounting Policies, Changes in Accounting Estimates and Errors* (see Chapter 3).

Which standard provides the better accounting model in a particular case is a matter of judgement. In our view, such a judgement would be informed by reference to the specific terms of the arrangement including the following factors:

Feature of credit	**Indicator of IAS 20 treatment**	**Indicator of IAS 12 treatment**
Method of payment	Directly settled in cash where there are insufficient taxable profits to allow credit to be fully offset, or available for set off against payroll taxes, VAT or amounts owed to government other than income taxes payable.	Only available as a reduction in income taxes payable. However, the longer the period allowed for carrying forward unused credits, the less relevant this indicator becomes.
Number of conditions not related to tax position (e.g. minimum employment, operating in a designated geographical area)	Many	None or few
Restrictions as to nature of expenditure	Highly specific	Broad criteria encompassing many different types of expenditure
Tax status of grant income	Taxable	Not taxable

In group accounts, in which entities from a number of different jurisdictions may be consolidated, it is desirable that each particular investment tax credit should be consistently accounted for under either IAS 20 or IAS 12. However, the lack of specific guidance for investment tax credits in IFRS may mean that predominant practice in a particular jurisdiction for a specific type of tax credit differs from predominant practice in another jurisdiction for a substantially similar credit. We believe that, in determining whether IAS 20 or IAS 12 should be applied, an entity should consider the following factors in the order listed below:

- the predominant local treatment for a specific credit in the relevant tax jurisdiction;
- if there is no predominant local treatment, the group wide accounting policy for such a credit;
- in the absence of a predominant local treatment or a group wide accounting policy, the indicators listed in the table above should provide guidance.

This may occasionally mean that an entity operating in a number of territories adopts different accounting treatments for apparently similar arrangements in different countries, but it at least ensures a measure of comparability between different entities operating in the same tax jurisdiction.

The treatment of investment tax credits accounted under IAS 12 is discussed in Chapter 29 at 4.3.

3 RECOGNITION AND MEASUREMENT

3.1 General requirements of IAS 20

IAS 20 requires that government grants should be recognised only when there is reasonable assurance that:

(a) the entity will comply with the conditions attaching to them; and

(b) the grants will be received. *[IAS 20.7].*

The standard does not define 'reasonable assurance', which raises the question of whether or not it means the same as 'probable' (or 'more likely than not' *[IAS 37.15]*). When developing IAS 41 the Board believed that recognition of government grants when there is 'reasonable assurance' was different from the alternative approaches it considered for biological assets, being recognition when 'it is probable that the entity will meet the conditions attaching to the government grant' and 'the entity meets the conditions attaching to the government grant'. *[IAS 41.B70].* The Board also noted that 'it would inevitably be a subjective decision as to when there is reasonable assurance that the conditions are met and that this subjectivity could lead to inconsistent income recognition.' *[IAS 41.B69].* Nevertheless, we would not expect an entity to recognise government grants before it was at least probable that the entity would comply with the conditions attached to them (even though these conditions may relate to future performance and other future events) and that the grants would be received. The standard notes that receiving a grant does not of itself provide conclusive evidence that the conditions attaching to the grant have been or will be fulfilled. *[IAS 20.8].*

After an entity has recognised a government grant, any related contingent liability or contingent asset should be accounted for under IAS 37 – *Provisions, Contingent Liabilities and Contingent Assets. [IAS 20.11].*

Accounting for government grants is not affected by the manner in which they are received, i.e. grants received in cash, as a non-monetary amount, or forgiveness of a government loan, are all accounted for in the same manner. *[IAS 20.9].*

3.2 Non-monetary grants

A government grant in the form of a transfer of a non-monetary asset, such as land or other resources, which is intended for use by the entity, is usually recognised at the fair value of that asset. *[IAS 20.23]*. Fair value is defined in IFRS 13 – *Fair Value Measurement* – which is mandatory for annual periods beginning on or after 1 January 2013 and applies when another IFRS requires or permits fair value measurement, including IAS 20. *[IFRS 13.5, IAS 20.45]*. Fair value is the price that would be received to sell an asset or paid to transfer a liability in an orderly transaction between market participants at the measurement date. *[IAS 20.3, IFRS 13.9]*. The requirements of IFRS 13 are discussed in Chapter 14.

The alternative of recognising such assets, and the related grant, at a nominal amount is permitted. *[IAS 20.23]*. Under IAS 8 – *Accounting Policies, Changes in Accounting Estimates and Errors* – an entity should select an accounting policy and apply it consistently to all non-monetary government grants. *[IAS 8.13]*.

3.3 Forgivable loans

A forgivable loan from government, the repayment of which will be waived under certain prescribed conditions, *[IAS 20.3]*, is to be treated as a government grant when there is reasonable assurance that the entity will meet the terms for forgiveness of the loan. *[IAS 20.10]*.

Example 25.1: Government grant by way of forgivable loan

An entity participates in a government-sponsored research and development programme under which it is entitled to receive a government grant of up to 50% of the costs incurred for a particular project. The government grant is interest-bearing and fully repayable based on a percentage ('royalty') of the sales revenue of any products developed. Although the repayment period is not limited, no repayment is required if there are no sales of the products.

The entity should account for this type of government grant as follows:

- initially recognise the government grant as a forgivable loan;
- apply the principles underlying the effective interest rate method in subsequent periods, which would involve estimating the amount and timing of future cash flows;
- review at each reporting date whether there is reasonable assurance that the entity will meet the terms for forgiveness of the loan, i.e. the entity assesses that the product will not achieve sales. If this is the case then derecognise part or all of the liability initially recorded with a corresponding profit in the income statement; and
- if the entity subsequently revises its estimates of future sales upwards, it recognises a liability for any amounts previously included in profit and recognises a corresponding loss in the income statement.

3.4 Loans at lower than market rates of interest

IAS 20 requires government loans that have a below-market rate of interest to be recognised and measured in accordance with IAS 39 or IFRS 9 as appropriate, i.e. at their fair value. *[IAS 20.10A, IAS 39.43, IFRS 9.5.1.1]*. The loans could be interest-free. The difference between the initial carrying value of the loan (its fair value) and the proceeds received is treated as a government grant.

Example 25.2: Interest-free loan from a government agency

Company A secures an interest-free loan of €1,000 from a local government agency to ensure that the company invests in new equipment at its manufacturing facility. The loan is repayable over five years and carries no interest. Company A can draw down the loan on demonstrating that it has incurred qualifying expenditure on property, plant and equipment.

On initial recognition, the market rate of interest for a similar five year loan with payment of interest at maturity is 10% per year. The initial fair value of the loan is the present value of the future payment of €1,000, discounted using the market rate of interest for a similar loan of 10% for five years. This equates to €621.

The fair value of the government incentive to Company A to invest in its factory is €379, the difference between the total consideration received of €1,000 and the loan's initial fair value of €621. This difference is treated as a government grant.

Subsequently, interest will be imputed to the loan using the effective interest method, taking account of any transaction costs (see Chapter 46 at 3.2.1). The grant will not necessarily be released on a basis that is consistent with the interest expense. The standard stresses that the entity has to consider the conditions and obligations that have been, or must be, met when 'identifying the costs for which the benefit of the loan is intended to compensate'. *[IAS 20.10A]*. This process of matching the benefit to costs is discussed at 3.5 below.

As well as routine subsidised lending to meet specific objectives, loans made as part of government rescue plans are generally within scope of IAS 20 if they are at a lower than market rate of interest. PSA Peugeot Citroën describes the treatment of one such loan in Extract 25.1 below.

Extract 25.1: PSA Peugeot Citroën (2009)

Half-Year Financial Report 2009 [extract]

17.2. REFINANCING TRANSACTIONS [extract]

– EIB loan

In April 2009, Peugeot Citroën Automobiles S.A. obtained a €400 million 4-year bullet loan from the European Investment Bank (EIB). Interest on the loan is based on the 3-month Euribor plus 179 bps. At June 30, 2009 the government bonds (OATs) given by Peugeot S.A. as collateral for all EIB loans to Group companies had a market value of €160 million. In addition, 4,695,000 Faurecia shares held by Peugeot S.A. were pledged to the EIB as security for the loans. The interest rate risk on the new EIB loan has not been specifically hedged.

This new loan is at a reduced rate of interest. The difference between the market rate of interest for an equivalent loan at the inception date and the rate granted by the EIB has been recognised as a government grant in accordance with IAS 20. The grant was originally valued at €38 million and was recorded as a deduction from the capitalized development costs financed by the loan. It is being amortised on a straight-line basis over the life of the underlying projects. The loan is measured at amortised cost, in the amount of €362 million at June 30, 2009. The effective interest rate is estimated at 5.90%.

This will also affect the manner in which arrangements that are similar in substance to loans are accounted for. Governments sometimes allow entities to retain sums that they collect on behalf of the government (e.g. value added taxes) to be retained until a future event, as in the following example:

Example 25.3: Entity allowed to retain amounts owed to government

The local government of an underdeveloped region is trying to stimulate investment by allowing local companies to retain the value added tax (VAT) on their sales. An entity participating in this scheme is entitled to retain an amount up to 40% of its investment in fixed assets. The retained VAT must be paid to the local government after 5 years. The deferred VAT liability is comparable in nature to an interest-free loan. The entity can reasonably place a value on the government assistance using the principles in IAS 39 and the benefit will be accounted for as government grants.

3.5 Recognition in the income statement

Grants should be recognised in the income statement on a systematic basis that matches them with the related costs that they are intended to compensate. *[IAS 20.12]*. They should not be credited directly to shareholders' funds. Income recognition on a receipts basis, which is not in accordance with the accruals accounting assumption, is only acceptable if no basis existed for allocating a grant to periods other than the one in which it was received. *[IAS 20.16]*.

IAS 20 rejects a 'capital approach', under which a grant is recognised outside profit or loss (typically credited directly to equity), *[IAS 20.13]*, in favour of the 'income approach', under which grants are taken to income over one or more periods, because:

(a) government grants are receipts from a source other than shareholders. As such, they should not be credited directly to equity but should be recognised as income in appropriate periods;

(b) government grants are rarely gratuitous. An entity earns them through compliance with their conditions and meeting the envisaged obligations. They should therefore be recognised as income and matched with the associated costs which the grant is intended to compensate; and

(c) as income and other taxes are expenses, it is logical to deal also with government grants, which are an extension of fiscal policies, in the income statement. *[IAS 20.15]*.

IAS 20 envisages that in most cases, the periods over which an entity recognises the costs or expenses related to the government grant are readily ascertainable and thus grants in recognition of specific expenses are recognised as income in the same period as the relevant expense. *[IAS 20.17]*.

Grants related to depreciable assets are usually recognised as income over the periods, and in the proportions, in which depreciation on those assets is charged. *[IAS 20.17]*. Grants related to non-depreciable assets may also require the fulfilment of certain obligations, in which case they would be recognised as income over the periods in which the costs of meeting the obligations are incurred. For example, a grant of land may be conditional upon the erection of a building on the site and it may be appropriate to recognise it as income over the life of the building. *[IAS 20.18]*.

IAS 20 acknowledges that grants may be received as part of a package of financial or fiscal aids to which a number of conditions are attached. In such cases, the standard indicates that care is needed in identifying the conditions giving rise to the costs and expenses which determine the periods over which the grant will be earned. It may also be appropriate to allocate part of the grant on one basis and part on another. *[IAS 20.19]*.

Where a grant relates to expenses or losses already incurred, or for the purpose of giving immediate financial support to the entity with no future related costs, the grant should be recognised in income when it becomes receivable. If such a grant is recognised as income of the period in which it becomes receivable, the entity should disclose its effects to ensure that these are clearly understood. *[IAS 20.20-22]*.

Many of the problems in accounting for government grants relate to that of interpreting the requirement to match the grant with the related costs, particularly because of the international context in which IAS 20 is written. It does not address specific questions that relate to particular types of grant that are available in individual countries.

3.5.1 Achieving the most appropriate matching

Most problems of accounting for grants relate to implementing the requirement to match the grant against the costs that it is intended to compensate. This apparently simple principle can be difficult to apply in practice, because it is sometimes far from clear what the essence of the grant was and, therefore, what costs are being subsidised. Moreover, grants are sometimes given for a particular kind of expenditure that forms an element of a larger project, making the allocation a highly subjective matter. For example, government assistance that is in the form of a training grant could be recognised in income in any of the following ways:

(a) matched against direct training costs;

(b) taken over a period of time against the salary costs of the employees being trained, for example over the estimated duration of the project;

(c) taken over the estimated period for which the company or the employees are expected to benefit from the training;

(d) matched against total project costs together with other project grants receivable;

(e) taken to income systematically over the life of the project, for example the total grant receivable may be allocated to revenue on a straight-line basis;

(f) allocated against project costs or income over the period over which the grant is paid (instead of over the project life); or

(g) taken to income when received in cash.

Depending on the circumstances, any of these approaches might produce an acceptable result. However, our observations on these alternative methods are as follows:

Under method (a), the grant could be recognised as income considerably in advance of its receipt, since often the major part of the direct training costs will be incurred at the beginning of a project and payment is usually made retrospectively. As the total grant receivable may be subject to adjustment, this may not be prudent or may lead to a mismatch of costs and revenues.

Methods (b) to (e) all rely on different interpretations of the expenditure to which the grant is expected to contribute, and could all represent an appropriate form of matching.

Method (f) has less to commend it, but the period of payment of the grant might in fact give an indication (in the absence of better evidence) of the duration of the project for which the expenditure is to be subsidised.

Similarly, method (g) is unlikely to be the most appropriate method *per se*, but may approximate to one of the other methods, or may, in the absence of any conclusive indication as to the expenditure intended to be subsidised by the grant, be the only practicable method that can be adopted.

In some jurisdictions grants are taxed as income on receipt; consequently, this is often the argument advanced for taking grants to income when received in cash. However, it is clear that the treatment of an item for tax purposes does not necessarily determine its treatment for accounting purposes, and immediate recognition in the income statement may result in an unacceptable departure from the principle that government grants should be matched with the costs that they are intended to compensate. *[IAS 20.16]*. Consequently, the recognition of a grant in the income statement in a different period from that in which it is taxed, gives rise to a temporary difference that should be accounted for in accordance with IAS 12 – *Income Taxes* (see Chapter 29). The example below illustrates that the interpretation of the matching requirement in the standard is not always straightforward.

Example 25.4: Grant associated with investment property

The government provides a grant to an entity that owns an investment property. The grant is intended to compensate the entity for the lower rent it will receive when the property is let as social housing at below market rates. That means that future rental income will be lower over the period of the lease which, at the same time, reduces the fair value of the investment property.

If the entity accounts for the investment property under the IAS 40 cost model then it could be argued that the government grant should be recognised over the term of the lease to offset the lower rental income.

Alternatively, if the entity applied the IAS 40 fair value model then the cost being compensated is the reduction in fair value of the investment property. In that case it is more appropriate to recognise the benefit of the government grant immediately.

If, instead of a grant, the government subsidises a loan used by the entity to acquire the property, then the loan will be brought in at its fair value. The difference between the face value and fair value will be a government grant and the arguments above will apply to its treatment.

If the government imposes conditions, e.g. that the building must be used for social housing for ten years, this does not necessarily mean that the grant should be taken to income over that period. Rather, it should apply a process similar to that in Example 25.1 above. The entity assesses whether there is reasonable assurance that it will meet the terms of the grant and, to that extent, treat an appropriate amount as a grant as above. This should be reviewed at each balance sheet date and adjustments made if it appears that the conditions will not be met (see 3.6 below).

In the face of the problems described above of attributing a grant to related costs, it is difficult to offer definitive guidance; entities will have to make their own judgements as to how the matching principle is to be applied. The only overriding considerations are that the method should be systematically and consistently applied, and that the policy adopted in respect of both capital and revenue grants, if material, should be adequately disclosed.

3.5.2 The period to be benefited by the grant

IAS 20 cautions that care is needed in identifying the conditions giving rise to the costs and expenses, which determine the periods over which the grant will be earned. *[IAS 20.19]*. The qualifying conditions that have to be satisfied are not necessarily conclusive evidence of the period to be benefited by the grant. For example, certain grants may become repayable if assets cease to be used for a qualifying purpose within a certain period; notwithstanding this condition, the grant should be recognised over the whole life of the asset, not over the qualifying period.

3.5.3 *Separating grants into elements*

The grant received may be part of a package, the elements of which have different costs and conditions. In such cases, it is common that the elements for which the grant is given are not specifically identified or quantified. It will often be appropriate to treat these different elements on different bases rather than accounting for the entire grant in one way. For example, a grant may be given on the basis that an entity makes approved capital expenditure in a particular area and employs a specified number of local people for an agreed period of time. The amount of grant may be based on the approved capital expenditure but this does not mean that the grant is necessarily treated wholly as a capital grant. It will be necessary to examine the full circumstances of the grant in order to determine its purpose.

In general, the most straightforward way of recognising a grant is by linking it to long-term assets where this is a possible interpretation, particularly where the receipt of the grant depends on the cost of acquisition of long-term assets. However, this approach can only be taken if there is no clear indication to the contrary.

Allocation of a grant between the elements will always be a matter of judgement and entities may place more stress on some features than on others. We believe that the most important consideration where there are significant questions over how the grant is to be recognised, and where the effect is material, is that the financial statements should explicitly state what treatment has been chosen and disclose the financial effect of adopting that treatment.

3.6 Repayment of government grants

A government grant that becomes repayable after recognition should be accounted for as a revision of an accounting estimate. Repayment of a grant related to income should be charged against the related unamortised deferred credit and any excess should be recognised as an expense immediately. *[IAS 20.32].*

Repayment of a grant related to an asset should be recognised by increasing the carrying amount of the related asset or reducing the related unamortised deferred credit. The cumulative additional depreciation that would have been recognised to date as an expense in the absence of the grant should be charged immediately to profit or loss. *[IAS 20.32].*

IAS 20 emphasises that the circumstances giving rise to the repayment of a grant related to an asset may require that consideration be given to the possible impairment of the asset. *[IAS 20.33].*

3.7 Government assistance

As indicated above, IAS 20 excludes from the definition of government grants 'certain forms of government assistance which cannot reasonably have a value placed upon them and transactions with government which cannot be distinguished from the normal trading transactions of the entity'. *[IAS 20.34]*. In many cases the 'existence of the benefit might be unquestioned but any attempt to segregate the trading activities from government assistance could well be arbitrary'. *[IAS 20.35]*. The standard therefore requires disclosure of significant government assistance (see 6.1 below).

Under IAS 20, 'government assistance does not include the provision of infrastructure by improvement to the general transport and communication network and the supply of improved facilities such as irrigation or water reticulation that is available on an ongoing indeterminate basis for the benefit of an entire local community.' *[IAS 20.38]*.

4 PRESENTATION OF GRANTS

4.1 Presentation of grants related to assets

Grants that are related to assets (i.e. those whose primary condition is that an entity qualifying for them should purchase, construct or otherwise acquire long-term assets) should be presented in the balance sheet either: *[IAS 20.24]*

(a) by setting up the grant as deferred income, which is recognised as income on a systematic and rational basis over the useful life of the asset; *[IAS 20.26]* or

(b) by deducting the grant in arriving at the carrying amount of the asset, in which case the grant is recognised in income as a reduction of depreciation. *[IAS 20.27]*.

IAS 20 regards both these methods of presenting grants in financial statements as acceptable alternatives. *[IAS 20.25]*.

A company that adopted the former treatment is Greencore Group, as shown below:

Extract 25.2: Greencore Group plc (2010)

Group Statement of Accounting Policies year ended 24 September 2010 [extract]

Government Grants

Government grants for the acquisition of assets are recognised at their fair value when there is reasonable assurance that the grant will be received and any conditions attached to them have been fulfilled. The grant is held on the Balance Sheet as a deferred credit and released to the Income Statement over the periods necessary to match the related depreciation charges, or other expenses of the asset, as they are incurred.

An example of a company adopting a policy of deducting grants related to assets from the cost of the assets is shown below:

Extract 25.3: AkzoNobel N.V. (2010)

Notes to the consolidated financial statements [extract]

Note 1 Summary of significant accounting policies [extract]

Government grants

Government grants related to costs are deducted from the relevant cost to be compensated in the same period. Emission rights granted by the government are recorded at cost. A provision is recorded if the actual emission is higher than the emission rights granted. Government grants to compensate for the cost of an asset are deducted from the cost of the related asset.

4.1.1 Cash flows

The purchase of assets and the receipt of related grants can cause major movements in the cash flow of an entity. Therefore, such movements are often disclosed as separate items in the cash flow statement whether or not the grant is deducted from the related asset for the purpose of balance sheet presentation. *[IAS 20.28].*

4.2 Presentation of grants related to income

Grants related to income should be presented either as:

(a) a credit in the income statement, either separately or under a general heading such as 'other income'; or

(b) a deduction in reporting the related expense. *[IAS 20.29].*

The standard points out that supporters of method (a) consider it inappropriate to present income and expense items on a net basis and that 'separation of the grant from the expense facilitates comparison with other expenses not affected by a grant'. *[IAS 20.30].* Furthermore, method (a) is consistent with the general prohibition of offsetting in IAS 1 – *Presentation of Financial Statements*. *[IAS 1.32-33].* However, supporters of method (b) would argue that 'the expenses might well not have been incurred by the entity if the grant had not been available and presentation of the expense without offsetting the grant may therefore be misleading'. *[IAS 20.30].* Although the arguments in favour of method (b) are not that convincing (it compares the accounting for the actual facts with that for a scenario that did not take place), the standard regards both methods as acceptable for the presentation of grants related to income. *[IAS 20.31].* When offsetting is permitted by another standard, the general prohibition in IAS 1 does not apply. *[IAS 1.32].* In any case, IAS 20 considers that disclosure of the grant may be necessary for a proper understanding of the financial statements. Furthermore, disclosure of the effect of grants on any item of income or expense, which should be disclosed separately, is usually appropriate. *[IAS 20.31].*

As illustrated below, AB InBev has adopted a policy of presenting grants within other operating income, although not separately on the face of the income statement, rather than as a deduction from the related expense.

Extract 25.4: AB InBev NV (2010)

3. Summary of significant accounting policies [extract]

(X) Income recognition [extract]

Government grants

A government grant is recognized in the balance sheet initially as deferred income when there is reasonable assurance that it will be received and that the company will comply with the conditions attached to it. Grants that compensate the company for expenses incurred are recognized as other operating income on a systematic basis in the same periods in which the expenses are incurred. Grants that compensate the company for the acquisition of an asset are presented by deducting them from the acquisition cost of the related asset in accordance with IAS 20 *Accounting for Government Grants and Disclosure of Government Assistance.*

AkzoNobel N.V. is an example of a company presenting the grant as a deduction from the related expense in the income statement, as illustrated in Extract 25.3 above.

5 GOVERNMENT GRANTS RELATED TO BIOLOGICAL ASSETS

A different accounting treatment to that prescribed in IAS 20 is required if a government grant relates to a biological asset measured at its fair value less costs to sell, in accordance with IAS 41; or a government grant requires an entity not to engage in specified agricultural activity. *[IAS 41.38]*. Government grants involving biological assets should only be accounted for under IAS 20 if the biological asset is 'measured at its cost less any accumulated depreciation and any accumulated impairment losses' (see Chapter 38). *[IAS 41.37-38]*. For government grants relating to biological assets measured at fair value less costs to sell, the requirements of IAS 41 apply as follows.

An unconditional government grant related to a biological asset measured at its fair value less costs to sell is recognised in profit or loss when, and only when, the grant becomes receivable. *[IAS 41.34]*. An entity is therefore not permitted under IAS 41 to deduct a government grant from the carrying amount of the related asset. The IASB determined that any adjustment to the carrying value of the asset would be inconsistent with a fair value model and would give rise to no difference in the treatment of unconditional and conditional government grants, with both effectively recognised in income immediately. *[IAS 41.B66]*.

A conditional government grant related to a biological asset measured at its fair value less costs to sell is recognised only when the conditions attaching to the grant are met. *[IAS 41.35]*. IAS 41 permits an entity to recognise a government grant as income only to the extent that it (i) has met the terms and conditions of the grant and (ii) has no obligation to return the grant. This would generally be later than the point of recognition in IAS 20, where reasonable assurance that these criteria will be met is sufficient. *[IAS 20.7]*. The following example, which is taken from IAS 41, illustrates how an entity should apply these requirements.

Example 25.5: Grant relating to biological assets carried at fair value

Entity A receives a government grant under terms that require it to farm in a particular location for five years. The entire government grant has to be returned if it farms for less than five years. In this case the government grant is not recognised as income until the five years have passed.

Entity B receives a government grant on a similar basis, except it allows part of the government grant to be retained based on the passage of time. Entity B recognises the government grant as income on a time proportion basis.

6 DISCLOSURES

IAS 20 requires that entities should disclose the following information regarding government grants:

(a) the accounting policy, including the method of presentation adopted in the financial statements;

(b) a description of the nature and extent of the grants recognised and an indication of other forms of government assistance from which the entity has directly benefited; and

(c) unfulfilled conditions or contingencies attaching to government assistance that has been recognised. *[IAS 20.39]*.

The extract below illustrates how companies typically disclose government grants under IFRS. It should be noted that disclosures concerning the nature and conditions of government grants are sometimes relatively minimal, possibly because the amounts involved are immaterial.

Extract 25.5: Danisco A/S (2010)

Note 38 – Accounting policies [extract]

Government grants

Government grants, which are disclosed in a note, include grants for research and development, CO2 allowances and investments. Grants for research and development and CO2 allowances are recognised as income on a systematic basis to match the related cost. Investment grants are set off against the cost of the subsidised assets.

33 Government grants

During the financial year ended, Danisco received government grants for research and development of DKK 2 million (2008/09 DKK 3 million) DKK 1 million (2008/09 DKK 9 million) for investments and DKK 6 million (2008/09 DKK 14 million) for other purposes.

Further Danisco was granted quotas of 49,551 tonnes of CO2 allowances (2008/09 610,277 tonnes). The value at grant date was DKK 5 million (2008/09 DKK 88 million), and the quotas match the expected emission tax.

Additional examples of accounting policies for government grants can be found in Extracts 25.2, 25.3 and 25.4 above.

6.1 Government assistance

In addition to the disclosures noted above, for those forms of government assistance that are excluded from the definition of government grants, the significance of such benefits may be such that the disclosure of the nature, extent and duration of the assistance is necessary to prevent the financial statements from being misleading. *[IAS 20.36]*.

References

1 IASB website, *www.iasb.org*, Project Update, July 2010, Amendments to IAS 20 Accounting for Government Grants and Disclosure of Government Assistance (Deferred).

2 *IASB Work Plan as at 30 May 2013*, IASB.

Chapter 26 Service concession arrangements

List of examples

Chapter 26 Service concession arrangements

1 INTRODUCTION

Service concession arrangements are of great complexity, often devised to meet political as well as purely commercial ends. The issues cross the boundaries of a number of accounting standards, and this has made it difficult to devise an adequate accounting model. IFRIC Interpretation 12 – *Service Concession Arrangements* – which took more than three years to develop, was finally approved by the IASB in November 2006.

Service concession arrangements have been developed as a mechanism for procuring public services. Under a service concession arrangement ('SCA'), private capital is used to provide major economic and social facilities for public use. The initial idea was that, rather than having bodies in the public sector taking on the entire responsibility for funding and building infrastructure assets such as roads, bridges, railways, hospitals, prisons and schools, some of these should be contracted out to private sector entities from which the public sector bodies would buy services. This is sometimes referred to as a 'build-operate-transfer' service concession arrangement. *[IFRIC 12.2].* As time has passed, the types of services covered by such arrangements have changed and they no longer necessarily include the construction of a new infrastructure asset. Many service concessions now engage the private sector to bring an existing facility or service up to an agreed standard and continue to maintain it for a contracted period; this type of 'rehabilitate-operate-transfer' service concession arrangement *[IFRIC 12.2]* has covered a range of projects from the refurbishment of social housing and street lighting to major civil engineering projects to restore a city's underground rail system. Another variant involves the handover of an infrastructure asset to a private sector entity but requires the provision of only operational management and maintenance services over the contract term. This last variant, together with the development of similar arrangements between private sector bodies has obscured the boundary between service concessions and outsourcing arrangements.

The accounting challenge is to reflect the substance of these arrangements fairly in the accounts of both of the contracting parties. It would be possible simply to take the contracts at fair value and account for the amounts received as revenue when due under the contract; however, closer analysis may sometimes reveal that this is, in reality, a composite transaction whereby the public sector body is paying for an asset to be constructed or refurbished at the outset and then operated at its direction as well as for services to be provided to the public over the remainder of the concession term. There is the issue of how to account for the operations period of the contract, which may also include asset replacement and refurbishment as well as more obvious provision of services.

The issues raised by service concessions range across a number of accounting standards and interpretations, including IAS 11 – *Construction Contracts*, IAS 16 – *Property, Plant and Equipment*, IAS 17 – *Leases*, IFRIC Interpretation 4 – *Determining whether an Arrangement contains a Lease*, IAS 18 – *Revenue,* IAS 20 – *Accounting for Government Grants and Disclosure of Government Assistance*, IAS 23 – *Borrowing Costs*, IAS 32 – *Financial Instruments: Presentation*, IAS 37 – *Provisions, Contingent Liabilities and Contingent Assets*, IAS 38 – *Intangible Assets* – and IAS 39 – *Financial Instruments: Recognition and Measurement* (or IFRS 9 – *Financial Instruments,* as appropriate), which makes it extremely difficult to develop a coherent accounting model that deals with all of the features of service concessions simultaneously, and from the position of both the private sector (i.e. the 'operator') and public sector (i.e. the 'grantor'). Moreover, entrenched national positions had developed and differing accounting treatments had been widely adopted in various jurisdictions, with or without a basis in specific local accounting standards. For example, in the UK, where there is formal accounting guidance under UK GAAP, operators are required to analyse assets constructed for the concession as property, plant and equipment or as financial assets (receivables due from the public sector body).[1] Indeed, some jurisdictions accepted more than one treatment of broadly similar arrangements, some of which are associated with a taxation basis that has been agreed with the jurisdictional revenue authorities.

In 2001, SIC-29 – *Service Concession Arrangements: Disclosures* – was issued. This did not attempt to address the accounting issues but considered the information that should be disclosed in the notes to the financial statements of an 'operator' and 'grantor' under a service concession arrangement. *[SIC-29.4]*. Its requirements are described further at 6 below.

Since then, the complex accounting issues raised by service concessions have been subject to prolonged debate. The IFRIC (now the Interpretations Committee) began its formal discussions in 2003 but it took until November 2006 to issue IFRIC 12. The Interpretations Committee discussions clearly demonstrate the complexity of the issues and the difficulty in fitting them into the existing accounting framework.

1.1 The Interpretations Committee's approach to accounting for service concessions

The Interpretations Committee limited its guidance to accounting by the operator of the service concession. *[IFRIC 12.4, 9]*. It views the primary accounting determination for the operator as being whether control over the infrastructure assets has been ceded to the operator or whether any new or existing assets under the concession arrangement are controlled by the grantor.

The Interpretations Committee suggests that arrangements where control does not rest with the grantor, and the asset is either derecognised by the grantor or is an asset constructed for the concession that the grantor never controls, can be dealt with adequately by other accounting standards or interpretations. *[IFRIC 12.BC13]*. The interrelationship with other accounting standards is discussed further at 2 below.

Infrastructure assets controlled by the grantor are the subject of IFRIC 12. *[IFRIC 12.7]*. This applies whether the assets are constructed or acquired by the operator for the concession, that become those of the grantor because it controls them, or existing assets that remain under the grantor's control and to which the operator is granted access.

'Control' is therefore a central concept in IFRIC 12. Control is not determined by attributing risks and benefits to identify the 'owner' of the infrastructure. Instead, IFRIC12 regards control in terms of the operator's ability (or lack thereof) to decide how to use the asset during the concession term and how it will be deployed thereafter. Its definition and consequences are discussed further at 3 below.

Thus any infrastructure that remains under the control of the grantor will be accounted for using IFRIC 12. In doing so, the Interpretations Committee establishes a number of principles for accounting by the operator of a concession falling within its scope:

- the infrastructure is not recognised as property, plant and equipment by the operator; *[IFRIC 12.11]*
- the operator recognises revenue from construction services when assets are built or upgraded during the concession term; *[IFRIC 12.14]*
- a financial asset or an intangible asset is recognised as consideration for these construction services, depending upon the way in which the operator is paid for services under the contract; *[IFRIC 12.15]* and
- revenues and costs for the provision of operating services are recognised over the term of the concession arrangement in accordance with IAS 18. *[IFRIC 12.20]*.

The requirement to recognise an asset as consideration for construction services gives rise to two service concession models – the 'financial asset' model or the 'intangible asset' model. These are considered further at 4 below. The recognition of revenue and costs in the operations phase is discussed at 5 below.

2 SCOPE OF IFRIC 12

The Interpretations Committee concluded that the scope should be limited to the accounting by the operator in a public-to-private service concession that meets its control criteria. *[IFRIC 12.4, 5].*

The grantor, including parties related to it, will be considered to control the infrastructure if the arrangement meets two conditions:

(a) the grantor controls or regulates the services that the operator must provide using the infrastructure, to whom it must provide them, and at what price; and

(b) the grantor controls any significant residual interest in the property at the end of the concession term through ownership, beneficial entitlement or otherwise. Infrastructure used for its entire useful life is within the scope of IFRIC 12 if the arrangement meets the conditions in (a). *[IFRIC 12.5, 6].*

The Interpretations Committee was deliberately restrictive in setting the scope of IFRIC 12, on the basis that the above conditions were likely to be met in most of the public-to-private arrangements for which guidance had been sought. The Committee concluded that other standards apply when these conditions are not a feature of the arrangement, *[IFRIC 12.BC 11-13]*, for example arrangements where infrastructure is leased by the operator of the service or where an activity previously undertaken by government is privatised and the infrastructure becomes the operator's property.

Infrastructure assets within scope are those constructed or acquired for the purpose of the concession or existing infrastructure to which the operator is given access by the grantor for these purposes (see 3.3 below). *[IFRIC 12.7].* Accounting is based on who controls the right to use the infrastructure. Crucially, control may be separated from ownership. Therefore, if the grantor controls the infrastructure assets, they should be accounted for according to one of the service concession models (see 4 below).

Arrangements within scope will be those that meet the following criteria:

1. the arrangement is a public-to-private service concession *[IFRIC 12.4]* (2.1 below);
2. the grantor controls or regulates the services *[IFRIC 12.5(a)]* (3.1 below);
3. the grantor controls any significant residual interest *[IFRIC 12.5(b)]* (3.2 below);
4. infrastructure is constructed or acquired (or the grantor provides access to that infrastructure) for the purpose of the service concession *[IFRIC 12.7]* (3.3 below); and
5. the operator has either a contractual right to receive cash from or at the direction of the grantor; or a contractual right to charge users of the service. *[IFRIC 12.16, 17].*

If an arrangement meets all of these criteria then the concession is in scope of IFRIC 12. The last question also determines which of IFRIC 12's accounting models, financial asset or intangible asset, described at 4 below, should be applied.

While the Interpretations Committee expects IFRIC 12 to be applied to arrangements that share the features of the public service obligation (see 2.1.3 below), its application to private-to-private arrangements is neither required nor prohibited. The Basis for Conclusions notes that this could be appropriate under the hierarchy in IAS 8 – *Accounting Policies, Changes in Accounting Estimates and Errors* – if the arrangement were of a similar type and met the control criteria quoted above. *[IFRIC 12.BC14]*. The Interpretation does not expand on the features that could make a private-to-private arrangement 'similar' to a transaction that is within scope.

The Interpretation applies only to accounting by the operator, not the grantor. *[IFRIC 12.9]*. This seems reasonable as most grantors are government bodies who may have their own views about accounting and, as not-for-profit entities, do not necessarily apply IFRS, to the extent that they prepare publicly available financial information at all. *[IFRIC 12.BC15]*. In 2011, the International Public Sector Accounting Standards Board (IPSASB) approved a new standard, IPSAS 32 – *Service Concession Arrangements: Grantor* – that addresses the grantor's accounting in such arrangements using an approach that is consistent with that used for the operator's accounting in IFRIC 12.[2] This chapter does not address accounting by grantors.

The Interpretations Committee's accounting framework for public-to-private arrangements is summarised in the following diagram from Information Note 1 in IFRIC 12. The diagram starts with the presumption that the arrangement has already been determined to be a service concession:

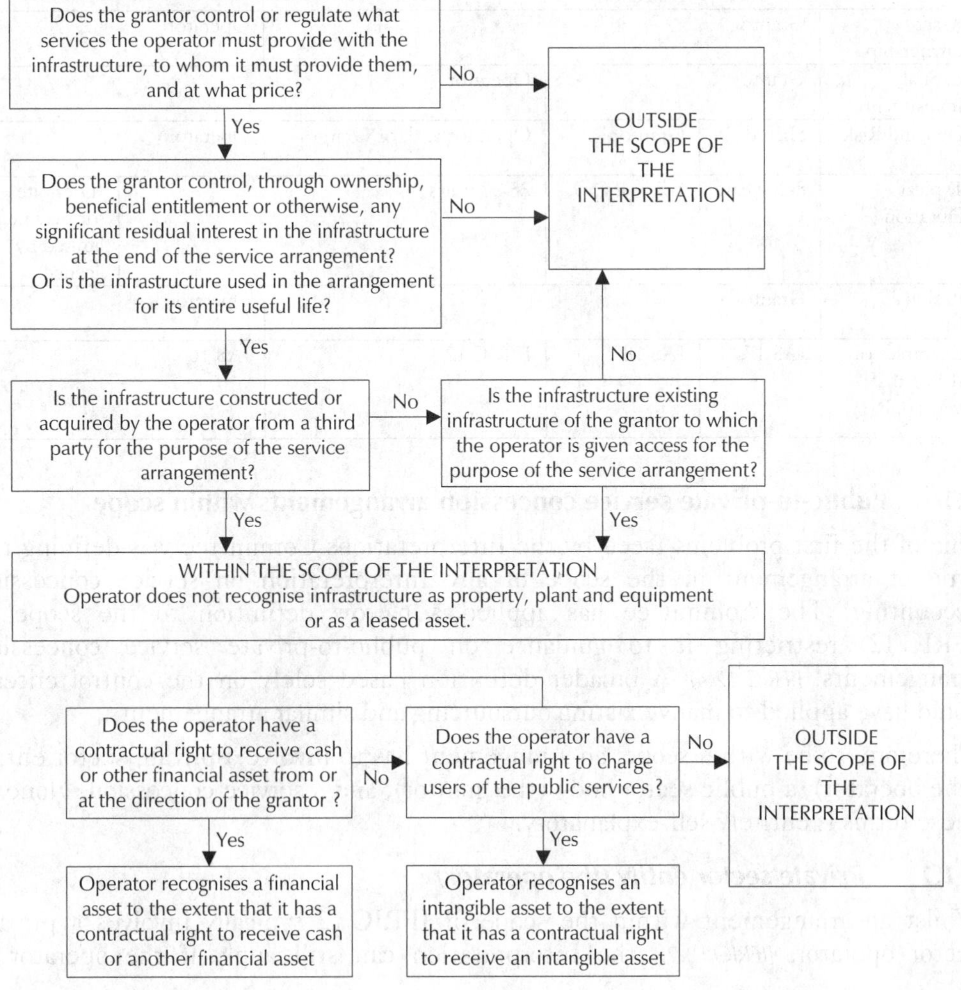

In an attempt to clarify the scope, the Interpretations Committee has produced a table on which the following is based (included as Information Note 2 to IFRIC 12) and which shows a range of arrangements between the public and private sectors. The Interpretations Committee's view is that IFRIC 12 is interpreting IFRSs for the transactions in the middle of this range, where the application of standards is unclear. These are described in the table below as 'Rehabilitate-operate-transfer' and 'Build-operate-transfer' arrangements. The table also demonstrates how other standards, namely IAS 17, IAS 18 and IAS 16, apply to arrangements that do not contain the features of a public-to-private service concession as defined in the Interpretation.

Category	*Lessee*	*Service Provider*			*Owner*	
Typical arrangement types	Lease, e.g. Operator leases assets from grantor	Service and/or maintenance contract (specific tasks e.g. debt collection)	Rehabilitate-operate-transfer	Build-operate-transfer	Build-own-operate	100% Divestment, Privatisation, Corporation
Asset Ownership	Grantor				Operator	
Capital Investment	Grantor		Operator			
Demand Risk	Shared	Grantor	Operator and/or Grantor		Operator	
Typical Duration	8-20 years	1-5 years	25-30 years			Indefinite (or may be limited by licence)
Residual Interest	Grantor				Operator	
Examples of IFRSs that may apply	IAS 17	IAS 18	IFRIC 12		IAS 16	

2.1 Public-to-private service concession arrangements within scope

One of the first problems faced by the Interpretations Committee was defining the type of arrangement in the scope of any Interpretation on service concession accounting. The Committee has applied a narrow definition to the scope of IFRIC 12, restricting it to guidance on public-to-private service concession arrangements. *[IFRIC 12.4]*. A broader definition based solely on the control criteria could have applied to many existing outsourcing and similar arrangements.

Therefore, to be within scope, an arrangement has to involve a private sector entity (the operator), a public sector body (the grantor), and a service concession. None of these terms is entirely self-explanatory.

2.1.1 Private sector entity (the operator)

Whilst an arrangement within the scope of IFRIC 12 typically involves a private sector operator, *[IFRIC 12.2]*, the Interpretation can still apply if the operator is ultimately controlled by the state, provided that it can be demonstrated that it is acting independently and not as an agent for the grantor. *[IFRIC 12.3(b)]*.

Generally, a private sector entity would be expected to be one that was entirely independent of the state. However, there may be circumstances in which an entity is partially or wholly state-owned but allowed autonomy to conduct its own affairs. Entities such as these are common, not only in jurisdictions where there is state ownership of all economic activity. Some governments allow utilities to control most of their own affairs while retaining ownership of the utility. Governments may take total or partial ownership of entities as a means of encouraging economic development but allow the entity control over its contractual arrangements.

If there is a contractual arrangement that in all other respects appears to be the same as a service concession arrangement between a private entity and the public sector, a state-owned operator may be considered as if it were a private sector entity and IFRIC 12 will apply. If the activity of the 'service concession' is regulated only by law rather than in a contractual arrangement between the operator and the grantor, then the arrangement is not within scope (see 2.1.5 below).

2.1.2 Public sector body (the grantor)

The Interpretation identifies the grantor of a service concession arrangement in terms of a public sector body, including a governmental body or a private sector entity to which the responsibility for the public service has been devolved. *[IFRIC 12.3(a)]*.

In its guidance as to what constitutes control over services and prices in paragraph 5(a), described at 2 above, IFRIC 12 extends what might be considered to mean 'public sector':

> '... includes circumstances in which the grantor buys all of the output as well as those in which some or all of the output is bought by other users. In applying this condition, the grantor and any related parties shall be considered together. If the grantor is a public sector entity, the public sector as a whole, together with any regulators acting in the public interest, shall be regarded as related to the grantor for the purposes of this Interpretation.' *[IFRIC 12.AG2]*.

This means that the entire public may be considered as part of the 'public sector' if the grantor purchases all of the output and provides services for free, e.g. health services provided by privately operated hospitals but free at the point of delivery to the patient.

Not every related party of the grantor (as defined in paragraph 9 of IAS 24 – *Related Party Disclosures* – see Chapter 35) need be taken into account in determining whether the grantor controls the service concession. Some services may be provided simultaneously to more than one public sector body but they will only be taken into account together if they operate in concert to control the 'output'. For instance, an entity may provide similar information technology services to several government departments and local government bodies but each contract is negotiated separately; the departments and bodies are not necessarily 'related parties'.

Regulators must be taken into account although they may not be related parties of the grantor as defined by IAS 24, as they may be required to be independent to act in the public interest. If the activities of the operator are regulated, but there is no contractual arrangement between the operator and the grantor, then the arrangement is not within scope (see 2.1.5 below).

Control over services is discussed further at 3.1 below.

2.1.3 Service concession arrangement ('SCA')

IFRIC 12 does not describe the features of a service concession agreement in the scope paragraphs; instead they are included in 'background' information where they help explain what is, and what is not, a public-to-private service arrangement. The main characteristic of a service concession is the public service nature of the obligation undertaken by the operator. The services related to the infrastructure are to be provided to the public as a matter of policy, irrespective of the identity of the party that operates the services. The service concession arrangement contractually obliges the operator to provide the services to the public on behalf of the public sector entity. IFRIC 12 states that 'other common features' are:

'(a) the party that grants the service arrangement (the grantor) is a public sector entity, including a governmental body, or a private sector entity to which the responsibility for the service has been devolved.

(b) the operator is responsible for at least some of the management of the infrastructure and related services and does not merely act as an agent on behalf of the grantor.

(c) the contract sets the initial prices to be levied by the operator and regulates price revisions over the period of the service arrangement.

(d) the operator is obliged to hand over the infrastructure to the grantor in a specified condition at the end of the period of the arrangement, for little or no incremental consideration, irrespective of which party initially financed it.' *[IFRIC 12.3]*.

The meaning of the public service obligation remains somewhat elusive. SCAs fall into two broad categories where the public service obligation can be identified:

1. SCAs that provide services directly to the public (e.g. transport, water supply, sewage, landfills).
2. SCAs where the services 'related to the infrastructure' continue to be provided by the grantor, e.g. the services provided by hospitals, prisons or schools, all of which would usually be considered to be examples of service concession arrangements. However, the infrastructure that is the subject of the contractual arrangement is used to provide services directly to the public, or to a significant part of it.

In other cases, it is far less clear that there is a public service obligation. Some arrangements are controlled by government bodies that may only comprise a few municipal authorities within that jurisdiction. Some European city authorities, for example, control car parking but in the vast majority of cities car parking *per se* is not considered a public service. In these cases the entity simply has to provide services to the grantor through an asset it has constructed and the arrangement may well be the same as those it has with local supermarkets and cinemas. An arrangement to provided parking services with the city authority may meet the control criteria in paragraph 5 of IFRIC 12, described at 3 below but so, too, may a contract to provide parking services with a cinema.

The services may be those that need to be provided to the public as a matter of policy (e.g. the provision of electricity) but the contractual arrangement itself may be unrelated to any public service obligation. There are no services in addition to the provision of power (a combination of assets and services is often thought as typical of SCAs) and the grantor pays for the fixed and variable costs of the power produced, as do many private purchasers of power. Similarly, a public sector water utility might engage a private contractor to build, maintain and operate a water treatment facility; but there are no services in addition to the provision of a functioning facility within the water network.

These outsourcing-type arrangements are examples of perhaps the most problematic boundary, that between IFRIC 12 and IFRIC 4 – *Determining whether an Arrangement contains a Lease*. The Interpretations Committee has attempted to deal with this, not wholly successfully, by introducing an amendment to IFRIC 4 specifically to exclude arrangements falling within the scope of IFRIC 12 from its scope. *[IFRIC 4.4]*. This is discussed at 2.2 below.

2.1.4 Agent type arrangements

A feature of SCAs is that the operator is responsible for at least some of the management of the infrastructure and related services and does not merely act as an agent on behalf of the grantor. *[IFRIC 12.3(b)]*.

For example, an operator constructs and maintains for 25 years a building that will be used for administrative purposes by the Defence Ministry in a particular country. The building does not have any parts dedicated to services provided directly to the public although the service that is provided within the building (national security) may be considered a public service as a matter of policy. At the end of the concession term, the building reverts to the Ministry for a nominal sum. In the interests of national security, all details of the services to be provided are predetermined. In this type of arrangement there may be virtually no scope for the operator to make any management decisions.

This will always be a question of degree and is unlikely to be the crucial feature in making a decision but it may help distinguish SCAs within scope of IFRIC 12 from some of the 'outsourcing' type arrangements discussed at 2.2 below.

2.1.5 A contract with the grantor

An arrangement can only be an SCA if there is a contract with the grantor 'that sets out performance standards, mechanisms for adjusting prices, and arrangements for arbitrating disputes'. *[IFRIC 12.2]*.

If the operator of an asset obtains a licence to provide services but has no contractual obligation to the grantor (including parties 'related' to the grantor in the sense in which the term is used in IFRIC 12, see 3.1 below) then the arrangement will not be within scope. There are many activities that require a formal licence; in some jurisdictions these include licences to operate pharmacies, provide childcare or carry out certain waste disposal activities, any of which could be considered public service obligations in some countries. Obtaining the licence does not bring the activity into scope of IFRIC 12 unless there is a separate contractual arrangement that governs the provision of the service.

Information Note 2 to IFRIC 12, reproduced at 2 above, indicates that there are certain contractual arrangements between grantor and operator that are not within scope of the Interpretation. These include arrangements in which there is a service and/or maintenance contract, i.e. to perform specific tasks, where IAS 18 is the relevant standard. Another example is where the operator leases assets from the grantor, in which case IAS 17 would provide relevant guidance, unless, for example, the lease payments are made as part of a wider service concession, in which case the costs may have to be taken into account as part of the costs of an infrastructure asset (see 3.3 below).

However, the contractual arrangement does not need to be for construction services in respect of any infrastructure. The arrangement may be within scope of IFRIC 12 in respect of post-construction services alone. Accounting for the post-construction period is described at 5 below.

2.2 IFRIC 4 and IFRIC 12: outsourcing arrangements and SCAs

Some features of a service concession arrangement may make it difficult to distinguish from a lease. The concept of an operator's right of 'access to operate the infrastructure' *[IFRIC 12.11]* can appear to be very similar to an arrangement that 'conveys the right to use the asset'. *[IFRIC 4.6(b), 9].* It can therefore be unclear whether the private sector entity is a lessee or the operator of a service concession arrangement.

The guidance presented in Information Note 2 to IFRIC 12 (and reproduced at 2 above) identifies some differences between a leasing arrangement and a service concession, but is not always conclusive. Whilst a service concession will usually require capital investment by the operator and perhaps have a longer duration than a typical lease, under both arrangements control over the asset and its residual interest rests with the grantor. It is therefore necessary sometimes to look beyond the control criteria (discussed at 3 below) to other features of a service concession arrangement to distinguish it from a lease, in particular:

- a service concession contractually obliges the operator to provide services to the public on behalf of the public sector grantor; *[IFRIC 12.3]*
- in contrast to a lease, where the lessee is given a 'right to control the use of the underlying asset' *[IFRIC 4.9]*, the operator in a service concession arrangement is granted access to the infrastructure; but the use to which that asset is applied is governed by the contract with the grantor. *[IFRIC 12.11].*

The Interpretations Committee recognised the risk of confusion and amended IFRIC 4 to exclude arrangements falling within the scope of IFRIC 12 from its scope. *[IFRIC 4.4].* Under IFRIC 12, whilst the operator has rights over the infrastructure, the grantor retains control and therefore the Interpretations Committee concluded that the infrastructure should not be recognised by the operator as property, plant and equipment. *[IFRIC 12.11, BC21, BC22].*

2.2.1 The private sector entity acting as lessor or provider of outsourcing services

While it is evident that IFRIC 4 does not apply to the treatment by the private sector entity of infrastructure assets in public-to-private service concession arrangements that are clearly within scope of IFRIC 12, *[IFRIC 4.4]*, the analysis at 2.2 above does not help if there is doubt as to whether the arrangement ought to fall within scope of IFRIC 12 in the first place. Service concessions are not the only contractual arrangements between the public sector and private sector. There are numerous examples of arrangements in which the grantor controls both the services in and the residual interest in the infrastructure asset but that would be seen as containing leases under IAS 17 by applying an IFRIC 4 analysis (see Chapter 24 at 2.1). Public sector bodies lease buildings or other property, plant and equipment from private sector entities for their own use. The public sector also engages independent subcontractors to outsource the operation of its internal services and functions. Sometimes the leasing of assets and the provision of outsourcing services to government are embodied in the same contract. Examples of outsourcing arrangements include contracts for the provision of building maintenance services, accounting and information technology functions and operating employee cafeteria. *[SIC-29.1]*. It is arguable whether outsourcing-type arrangements were intended to be within scope of IFRIC 12. The Interpretations Committee noted in September 2005 that it would not expect an information technology outsourcing arrangement for a government department to be dealt with under IFRIC 12.[3] The Interpretations Committee presumably concluded that, as an outsourcing arrangement, this more properly fell within IFRIC 4. In our view a distinguishing feature is the purpose to which the leased assets or services is applied. In a service concession arrangement, the private sector operator is contracted to provide services to the public on behalf of the public sector entity. *[IFRIC 12.3]*. By contrast, in a leasing or outsourcing arrangement, the infrastructure is used by the grantor, in order that it can ultimately provide a public service but it is not used itself to provide the service.

This could make a significant difference to the manner in which the arrangement is accounted for. IFRIC 12's control model and IAS 17's risks and rewards tests could result in different assets being recognised in the financial statements of operator and grantor. An arrangement could be accounted for under the financial asset model under IFRIC 12, so the asset would be accounted for as a receivable by the operator, yet considered an operating lease under IAS 17, in which case the operator would consider the asset to be PP&E. The operator may have arrangements on the same terms with private sector bodies and with the public sector. It would appear strange that similar arrangements should be treated differently merely because the customer is a public sector entity. One example is power supply. In many parts of the world, governments have chosen to expand power generation capacity in their countries by entering into contracts with operators. Some of these arrangements have the same features as power supply contracts to private sector purchasers to which IFRIC 4 applies. Commonly, the contract allows for a fixed charge that is payable irrespective of deliveries, which may or may not cover all of the capital expenditure, a variable charge related to the variable costs of generating power and a penalty regime under which part of the fixed cost is refundable. These are the features that are described

Chapter 26

in Chapter 24, Example 24.1, as 'An arrangement that contains a lease'. Providing power is usually considered to be a public service yet the public service element may be irrelevant to the structure of the contract. For example, the operator may have no relationship with the public, instead selling its output to the grantor. The use to which the grantor puts the power need not affect the arrangement; for example, the power could be used solely by Government department buildings, by a government-owned industry, for naval dockyards or it could be put directly into the national electricity distribution network.

In such a case there may be no services in addition to those necessary to maintain the power supply, unlike the much more extensive services that are provided as part of what are usually considered typical SCAs such as hospitals or prisons. By contrast, other 'typical' SCAs such as toll roads and bridges have few associated services but are clearly used directly by the public. This means that the provision of significant ancillary or associated services is not sufficient by itself to distinguish SCAs from other contractual arrangements with grantors. Whether the operator is directly involved in the provision of services *to the public* is an indicator of a service concession rather than a lease.

However, to require a public service to be identified in an arrangement that could equally be a service concession or a lease is not a conclusive test either. The Interpretations Committee was unable to come up with a robust definition of public service obligation. The description of the features of SCAs (discussed at 2.1.3 above), is included in a 'background' section preceding the body of the Interpretation itself. In the period since IFRIC 12 was issued, it has still not proved possible to come up with a workable definition of public service obligation. To some extent this is because the public policy component of its meaning comes from a political or ideological determination of what activities should be provided by the state. This means that there will always be a certain amount of confusion over whether an arrangement that meets the control criteria but that does not appear to contain any obvious public service obligation ought, as a matter of course, to be accounted for under IFRIC 12.

In the end, it is always likely to be a matter of judgement and there will be different views in practice. IFRIC 12 was developed because there are transactions that are so complex that it is very difficult to fit them into an existing accounting model and it is important not to lose sight of this. It appears that it was not the intention of the Interpretations Committee to change the manner in which outsourcing arrangements were accounted for solely because the contracting party is a government body but equally if the control criteria in paragraph 5 of IFRIC 12 apply to these arrangements many companies choose to apply IFRIC 12.

3 THE CONTROL MODEL

A contractual arrangement that is within the scope of IFRIC 12 includes the following features, commonly referred to as the 'control criteria':

(a) the grantor controls or regulates the services that the operator must provide using the infrastructure, to whom it must provide them, and at what price; and

(b) the grantor controls any significant residual interest in the infrastructure at the end of the concession term through ownership, beneficial entitlement or otherwise. *[IFRIC 12.5]*.

The Interpretations Committee considers that, taken together, these conditions identify when the infrastructure is controlled by the grantor for the whole of its economic life, in which case an operator is only managing the infrastructure on the grantor's behalf. *[IFRIC 12.AG6]*. Crucially, it has concluded from this that an infrastructure asset controlled by the grantor cannot be the property, plant and equipment of the operator. *[IFRIC 12.11, BC21, BC22]*.

3.1 Regulation of services

Although there has to be a contract between grantor and operator for the arrangement to be a service concession, the control or regulation of services does not have to be governed by contract – it could include control via an industry regulator. Control also extends to circumstances in which the grantor buys all of the output as well as those in which it is bought by other users. The grantor and any related parties must be considered together. If the grantor is a public sector entity, the public sector as a whole, together with any independent regulators acting in the public interest, are to be regarded as related to the grantor. *[IFRIC 12.AG2]*. 'Price' can mean the amount at which the grantor buys the service or the amount that the operator charges members of the public or a combination of both.

This means that many regulated public utilities (water, sewage, electricity supply etc.) will fall within (a) above. Other arrangements that fall within (a) include public health facilities that are free to users and subsidised transport facilities (rail, some toll roads and bridges) that are partly paid by public sector grant and partly by passenger fares. Of course, all of these will only be within scope of IFRIC 12 if there is also a contract between grantor and operator for the arrangement and any significant residual interest is also 'controlled' by the grantor under (b).

The Interpretations Committee stresses that the grantor does not need to have complete control of the price. It is sufficient for the price to be regulated, which could be by way of a capping mechanism (regulated utilities are usually free to charge *lower* prices). Other 'caps' may not be so apparent. A contract may give the operator freedom to set its prices but any excess is clawed back by the grantor (e.g. through setting a maximum return on an agreed investment in the infrastructure). In such a case, the operator's return is capped and the price element of the control test is substantively met. *[IFRIC 12.AG3]*.

Obviously, it is a requirement to look to the substance of the agreements so a cap that only applies in remote circumstances will be ignored.

Some arrangements only allow the grantor to control prices for part of the life of the infrastructure, particularly if it is a lease-type arrangement. For example, an operator may construct clinical facilities that are used by a government health care provider (the grantor) for a five year contract term. At the end of the term, the grantor may extend the contract by renegotiation. If it does not do so, the operator can run the facilities for private health care. Although the prices are controlled for the first five years, this arrangement is unlikely to meet the control condition in (a) above.

Alternatively, the contract might allow regulation of the prices of some but not all of the services provided with the infrastructure. Judgement is required in determining whether arrangements involving partially regulated assets fall within the scope of IFRIC 12 (see 3.4 below).

3.2 Control of the residual interest

In order for an arrangement to be within scope of IFRIC 12, the grantor must control not only the services provided with the infrastructure but also any significant residual interest in the property at the end of the concession term through ownership, beneficial entitlement or otherwise. *[IFRIC 12.5(b)].* The grantor's control over any significant residual interest should restrict the operator's ability to sell or pledge the infrastructure. The grantor must also have a right of use of the infrastructure throughout the concession term. *[IFRIC 12.AG4].* As discussed below, control over the residual interest does not require the infrastructure to be returned to the grantor. It is sufficient that the grantor controls how access to the infrastructure is awarded after the concession term.

Many infrastructure assets are partially replaced during the course of the concession and the impact of this on condition (b) has been considered. If the operator has to replace part of an item of infrastructure during the life of the concession (for example, the top layer of a road or the roof of a building), the item of infrastructure is to be considered as a whole, so that condition (b) will be met for the whole of the infrastructure, including the part that is replaced, if the grantor has the residual interest in the final replacement of that part. *[IFRIC 12.AG6].*

IFRIC 12 pays little attention to the residual interest. Its application guidance states that 'the residual interest in the infrastructure is the estimated current value of the infrastructure as if it were already of the age and in the condition expected at the end of the period of the arrangement'. *[IFRIC 12.AG4].* This echoes the definition of 'residual value' in IAS 16, but excludes any deduction for the estimated costs of disposal *[IAS 16.6]* (see Chapter 18). However, the Interpretation does not expand on what is regarded as 'significant'. Some infrastructure assets such as toll roads and bridges generate cash flows directly and it may be possible to use estimated future cash flows to calculate the significance of the residual value, whether or not the grantor will charge tolls after reversion of the asset. It may not be possible to base the assessment of 'significance' on the cash flows received by the operator on handing back the asset to the grantor as these may be nominal amounts; indeed, the grantor may pay nothing. In such a case, the remaining useful life of the asset when it reverts may give a good indication, e.g. if a hospital is handed back to the public sector with a remaining useful life of twenty years, this residual interest is likely to be significant.

There are a number of features that indicate whether the grantor controls the residual interest. There are usually several contractual alternatives: the operator is granted a second concession term, a new operator is allowed to acquire the assets or the grantor acquires the assets and brings the arrangement 'in house'. The grantor still controls the residual as it will determine which of these alternatives applies and the option exercise price (if it or a new operator acquires the infrastructure) is irrelevant.

In some arrangements the grantor only has an option to reacquire the asset at the end of the concession term. The operator cannot control the infrastructure until the grantor decides what to do with the option. An option at fair value at the date of exercise may by itself be enough to give the grantor control over the residual under IFRIC 12 if it is sufficient to restrict the operator's ability to sell or pledge the infrastructure. This is a clear difference between a 'risks and rewards' and a 'control' model as under the former, the operator would be seen as keeping the risks and rewards of ownership if another party had the right to acquire the asset at fair value.

Example 26.1: Residual arrangements

A gas transmission system is being operated under a concession arrangement with the State Gas Authority. At the end of the term, the grantor will either acquire the infrastructure assets at their net book value, determined on the basis of the contract, or it may decide to grant a new SCA on the basis of a competitive tender, which will exclude the current operator. If the grantor elects to do the latter, the operator will be entitled to the lower of the following two amounts:

(a) the net book value of the infrastructure, determined on the basis of the contract; and

(b) the proceeds of a new competitive bidding process to acquire a new contract.

Although the operator cannot enter the competitive tender, it also has the right to enter into a new concession term but, in order to do so, it must match the best tender offer made. It has to pay to the grantor the excess of the best offer (b) above the amount in (a); should the tender offer be lower than (a), it will receive an equivalent refund.

In this arrangement, the grantor will control the residual. It can choose to take over the activities of the concession itself or it can allow potential operators, including the incumbent, to bid for a second term. The price that might be received by the operator, or paid by the grantor, is not relevant.

What if the arrangement is for the whole life of the infrastructure? Assets in service concession arrangements may revert to the grantor at the end of the concession term but they may not have much, if any, remaining useful life. Many modern buildings, for example, only have a useful life of thirty years or so and this is a common concession term. Consequently, infrastructure used in a service concession arrangement for its entire useful life ('whole of life infrastructure') is included within the scope of IFRIC 12. *[IFRIC 12.6]*.

The Interpretations Committee noted that one reason for including the 'significant residual interest' requirement was to differentiate between regulated industries and service concession arrangements, thereby seeming to confirm that it had not intended regulated industries to be in scope.[4] The Interpretations Committee considers that privatised regulated industries should generally be out of scope, because they are divestitures or privatisations where it is more appropriate to treat the infrastructure as the property, plant and equipment of the operator. This is indicated in the table included as Information Note 2 to IFRIC 12 (reproduced at 2 above). It is usually the case in a privatisation that the infrastructure only reverts to the grantor in the event of a major breach of the conditions of the regulatory framework as otherwise the right of the operator to provide the regulated services may roll over indefinitely into a new term. In other cases it may require legislative change to bring the assets back into the control of the public sector. This means that the grantor does not control the residual interest in the property as required by IFRIC 12.

GDF SUEZ discloses that some of its concessions are not considered to be within scope of IFRIC 12 as the infrastructure is not returned to the grantor at the end of the contract. These assets (for water and gas distribution) are likely to have a life in excess of the contract term.

Extract 26.1: GDF SUEZ SA (2012)

Notes to the consolidated financial statements [extract]
Note 23 SERVICE CONCESSION ARRANGEMENTS [extract]

The Group manages a large number of concessions as defined by SIC 29 covering drinking water distribution, water treatment, waste collection and treatment, and gas and electricity distribution.

These concession arrangements set out rights and obligations relative to the infrastructure and to the public service, in particular the obligation to provide users with access to the public service. In certain concessions, a schedule is defined specifying the period over which users should be provided access to the public service. The terms of the concession arrangements vary between 10 and 65 years, depending mainly on the level of capital expenditure to be made by the concession operator.

In consideration of these obligations, GDF SUEZ is entitled to bill either the local authority granting the concession (mainly incineration and BOT water treatment contracts) or the users (contracts for the distribution of drinking water or gas and electricity) for the services provided. This right to bill gives rise to an intangible asset, a tangible asset, or a financial asset, depending on the applicable accounting model (see Note 1.4.7 "Concession arrangements").

The tangible asset model is used when the concession grantor does not control the infrastructure. For example, this is the case with water distribution concessions in the United States, which do not provide for the return of the infrastructure to the grantor of the concession at the end of the contract (and the infrastructure therefore remains the property of GDF SUEZ), and also natural gas distribution concessions in France, which fall within the scope of Law No. 46-628 of April 8, 1946.

A general obligation also exists to return the concession infrastructure to good working condition at the end of the concession. Where appropriate (see Note 1.4.7 "Concession arrangements"), this obligation leads to the recognition of a capital renewal and replacement liability.

3.3 Assets within scope

There are two groups of assets within scope of IFRIC 12:

(a) the infrastructure that the operator constructs or acquires from a third party for the purpose of the concession; and

(b) existing infrastructure to which the grantor gives the operator access for the purpose of the concession. *[IFRIC 12.7].*

Generally, 'infrastructure' is interpreted broadly and it is accepted that 'the infrastructure' used to provide services can include moveable assets. Although IFRIC 12 uses the word 'infrastructure' and includes examples traditionally regarded as such (including roads, bridges, hospitals and airports *[IFRIC 12.1]*), the Interpretation is based on the definition of an asset under IFRS ('an asset is a resource controlled by the entity as a result of past events and from which future economic benefits are expected to flow to the entity' *[Framework.4.4]*), and is therefore considered to apply to all assets, including items such as buses or rolling stock.

It is usually relatively straightforward to apply (a) above, infrastructure that the operator constructs or acquires from a third party for the purpose of the concession. However, there are some issues of interpretation relating to infrastructure to which the grantor has given access to the operator for the purpose of the SCA. Infrastructure under (b) above could include other arrangements in the form of leases over assets. As part of a SCA, in addition to receiving payments for the construction and/or operation of the infrastructure, an operator may make lease payments to a grantor, e.g. it may lease the land on which a facility is to be built. These issues are discussed at 3.3.1 below.

A third group of assets comprises property, plant and equipment previously held by the operator and then used in connection with the provision of services under the SCA. The Interpretations Committee's view is that accounting for assets is already covered by existing accounting standards, principally IAS 16, and therefore it does not specify how the operator should account for its previously existing assets that now form part of the infrastructure. *[IFRIC 12.8].* The treatment of existing assets is discussed further at 3.3.2 below.

3.3.1 Payments made by a service concession operator

Assets within the scope of IFRIC 12 include infrastructure that the operator constructs or acquires from a third party for the purpose of the service arrangement and existing infrastructure to which the grantor gives the operator access for the purpose of the service arrangement. *[IFRIC 12.7].* IFRIC 12 contains no explicit guidance regarding periodic payments made in connection with the right to use assets. The issue is whether these costs should be treated as lease costs in accordance with IAS 17, treated as executory in nature with costs expensed as incurred or otherwise recognised as a liability. If they are considered to be within scope of IFRIC 12, what are the accounting consequences? Are they part of the overall consideration paid by the grantor or recognised as an asset and, if an asset, did they form part of the 'concession asset' at the start of the concession, with an obligation to make the related payments?

This has been discussed by the Interpretations Committee for the last three years. No formal decision has been made regarding the treatment of payments that vary in relation to future activity by the purchaser, pending the conclusion to the leasing project as this may affect the treatment of variable payments made under such an arrangement.[5] For fixed payments made by the operator, the Committee decided to proceed with the proposed amendments to the Interpretation discussed at its March and May 2012 meetings.[6] The Committee's tentative conclusion was that these payments will be accounted for under IFRIC 12 unless:

(a) they are payments for the right to use assets that are controlled by the operator, which will be within scope of IAS 17; or

(b) they are payments for a distinct good or service that is separate from the concession arrangement, which should be accounted for under other applicable IFRSs.[7]

Payments that are part of the overall concession agreement but do not fall within these two exceptions will be accounted for as part of the SCA. In this case the accounting treatment will depend on whether the SCA falls within the financial asset model, the intangible asset model or is a hybrid. If the financial asset model applies, payments would be treated as reductions to the overall consideration received and therefore be offset against the financial asset receivable under the SCA. In contrast, under the intangible asset model the payments to the grantor should be recognised as a liability that increases the cost of the concession right asset.[8] This is discussed further at 4.7 below.

3.3.2 Previously held assets used for the concession

IFRIC 12 does not apply to infrastructure held and recognised as PP&E by the operator before entering into the SCA. Because a concession arrangement is characterised by the grantor having control over the infrastructure, on entering the SCA the operator must apply the derecognition requirements of IAS 16 to determine whether it should derecognise those previously held assets. *[IFRIC 12.8]*. The Interpretations Committee's view is that accounting for assets is already covered by existing accounting standards, principally IAS 16, and therefore it is not necessary to specify how the operator should account for its previously existing assets that now form part of the infrastructure. *[IFRIC 12.BC16]*.

The implication is that losing control of a previously held asset by contractually giving control of its use to the grantor may in some circumstances be a deemed disposal of the asset under IAS 16. The existing asset would be derecognised and any consideration received on the disposal recognised at its fair value. *[IAS 16.72]*. This means that the total consideration received under the contract would be disaggregated to calculate the relevant amount receivable for the transfer of the asset to the control of the grantor. See 4.1.1 below for a discussion of the allocation of the consideration, which depends on the accounting model appropriate to the particular SCA. Gains and losses must be calculated as the difference between any net disposal proceeds and the carrying value of the item of PP&E *[IAS 16.71]* and recognised in profit or loss. Derecognition of assets within scope of IAS 16 in general is discussed in Chapter 18 at 7.

The operator may use some of its existing assets for the purpose of the concession without transferring control to the grantor. These are out of scope.

Therefore, an entity may already control assets (which might include assets regarded as infrastructure) that it has constructed and used for its operations before it enters into a concession arrangement. Unless the contract transfers the residual interest in these pre-existing assets to the grantor (and thereby both of the control criteria laid out at 3 above are met), these assets are out of scope of IFRIC 12. The SCA might include, for example, extensions to that asset, upgrades to it and a contractual period of using the infrastructure asset to provide services. In this case, the total consideration payable under the concession will be allocated between the extension, upgrade and operating services within scope of IFRIC 12. Accordingly, construction revenue would be recognised at the time of the extension or upgrade work, with an additional financial asset or intangible asset recognised as appropriate.

3.4 Partially regulated assets

IFRIC 12 notes that it is not uncommon for the use of infrastructure to be partly regulated and partly unregulated and gives examples while noting that these activities take a variety of forms:

'(a) any infrastructure that is physically separable and capable of being operated independently and meets the definition of a cash generating unit as defined in IAS 36 shall be analysed separately if it is used wholly for unregulated purposes. For example this might apply to a private wing of a hospital, where the remainder of the hospital is used by the grantor to treat public patients.

(b) where purely ancillary activities (such as a hospital shop) are unregulated, the control tests shall be applied as if those services did not exist, because in cases in which the grantor controls the services described in paragraph 5, the existence of ancillary activities does not detract from the grantor's control of the relevant infrastructure.' *[IFRIC 12.AG7]*.

In both of these cases, the operator may have a lease from the grantor that gives it a right to use the unregulated asset in question; if so, this is to be accounted for in accordance with IAS 17. *[IFRIC 12.AG8]*. This would be likely to involve using IFRIC 4's principles to distinguish the lease payments from other parts of the service concession arrangement (see Chapter 24 at 2.1).

The Interpretation gives no further guidance on how an entity might interpret the term 'purely ancillary' in evaluating whether an unregulated activity is ignored for the purposes of determining if the control criteria are met or considered to detract from the grantor's control of the asset. The example of a hospital shop is clearly insignificant by virtue of its size relative to the whole hospital, the proportion of cash flows attributable to it and the fact that the existence of a shop has no direct impact on the function of the infrastructure in the provision of regulated services. However, it is not clear at what point a secondary activity would become or cease to be 'purely ancillary'.

In addition, there are many concession agreements that include unregulated services that are neither purely ancillary nor delivered by using a physically separable portion of the total infrastructure, a situation not addressed by AG 7. For example, a grantor may control prices charged to children, pensioners and the unemployed who use a sports facility but the amounts charged to other adults are not controlled. The same swimming pool is being used by all, regardless of the amount that they pay. Alternatively, price regulation could apply only to services provided at certain times of the day rather than to different classes of user. In such cases it will be a matter of judgement whether enough of the service is unregulated in order to demonstrate that the grantor is not considered to control the asset, which would lead to the arrangement as a whole falling out of the scope of IFRIC 12. This assessment will be made at the beginning of the contract and will not be revisited unless errors were made in the original assessment.

However, if it transpires that there are significantly fewer unregulated users than anticipated then it is likely that the contract will be renegotiated. This is because of the public service obligation, which means that the grantor will want the service to continue to be provided to the public albeit under new terms. The new contract may be within scope of IFRIC 12. If a toll bridge has had fewer users than anticipated, the grantor might subsidise the tolls under a new arrangement.

4 ACCOUNTING BY THE CONCESSION OPERATOR: THE FINANCIAL ASSET AND INTANGIBLE ASSET MODELS

The two models in the analysis utilise several decisions of principle:

- the control model applies as described at 3 above, which means that the operator will not recognise infrastructure assets as its property, plant and equipment; *[IFRIC 12.11]* and
- the operator is providing 'construction services' and not, for example, constructing an item of property, plant and equipment for sale. Construction services are to be accounted for separately from 'operation services' in the operations phase of the contract. *[IFRIC 12.13, BC31]*.

There is a third important point of principle: the 'amounts due from customers' asset that arises from the application of the stage of completion method of revenue recognition required by IAS 11 (whose principles are used during the period of construction of the asset) is a financial asset as defined in IAS 32 (see 4.2 below).

4.1 Consideration for services provided and the choice between the two models

Most service concession agreements are for both construction (or upgrade) services and operations services. Operators almost always negotiate a single contract with the grantor and, although the Interpretation does not refer to this, this will usually include a single payment mechanism throughout the concession term (sometimes called a 'unitary payment'). The operator is unlikely to be remunerated separately for its different activities. The payment mechanism often falls into one or other of the following models:

Example 26.2: Payment mechanisms for service concessions

(a) a hospital where the payment is based on the availability of the whole hospital

The unitary payment is based on the full provision of an overall accommodation requirement which is divided into different units, such as hospital wards, consulting rooms, operating theatres, common parts and reception. Availability is defined in terms of being usable and accessible and, includes some associated core services such as heating, power and (in the case of operating theatres) appropriate cleanliness. There is a payment deduction for failure to provide an available unit according to a contractual scale. There are no separate payment streams for any of the non-core services but substandard performance can result in payment deductions.

P = (F × I) – (D + E)
P = unitary payment per day
F = price per day for overall accommodation requirement
I = Indexation increase based on the retail prices index
D = deductions for unavailability
E = performance deductions

The payments for both schemes are not immediately separable between amounts attributable to the construction or other services.

b) a prison where payment is made based on the number of occupied places

The unitary payment is based on the number of occupied places. Occupied means not only that a prisoner is allocated a physical space but the associated core services and minimum requirements must be met in relation to services such as heating, mail delivery and food. No payment is made for unoccupied places. There are no separate payment streams for any of the non-core services (i.e. not associated with the definition of an occupied place) but deductions from the unitary payment can be made for substandard performance of these services.

The unitary payment is based on the following formula:

P = (F × I) – Z
P = unitary payment per place
F = Fixed amount per occupied place per day
I = Indexation increase based on the retail prices index
Z = Performance deductions

IFRIC 12 clarifies the basis on which revenue is recognised in accordance with IAS 11 and IAS 18. It argues that if the operator provides separate services as part of its overall contractual arrangement it will allocate the consideration receivable by reference to their relative fair values. *[IFRIC 12.13].* The exercise to separate the consideration receivable for the separate services (e.g. construction, upgrade or operating services) provided by the operator is expanded at 4.1.1 below. The nature of the consideration determines the accounting model, as described at 4.1.2 below.

Payments usually start only when the infrastructure asset has been completed and accepted as suitable for purpose by the grantor. Operators usually seek payment during the construction phase but whether or not they receive any is inevitably a result of negotiation between the parties. Payments that are received are normally for services provided and not directly to meet construction costs; any amounts received will be allocated to the relevant service activity as described below.

4.1.1 Allocating the consideration

The Interpretation Committee argues that it is a requirement of IAS 18, to separate the construction services that will be accounted for under IAS 11 from the remainder of the contract. Thereafter the separate services within this contract (for example 'upgrade services' or 'operations services') may also be disaggregated on the basis of their 'distinct skills, requirements and risks'. *[IFRIC 12.BC31].* IFRIC 12 argues that the operator might report different profit margins for its construction services within IAS 11 and the other services that are within IAS 18. The inference is that these different margins may also help allocate the total consideration. *[IFRIC 12.BC31].* One must be very cautious here as IAS 11 does not permit an entity to determine what it considers to be an appropriate profit margin for the contract and use this as the basis of recognising revenue and attributable contract costs (unless, of course, it is a cost plus contract, see Chapter 23 at 3.3.1). The profit margin must be a consequence of the different fair values of the separate elements of the contract rather than driving the allocation of the consideration.

An operator may also be contractually required to make payments to the grantor. These may take the form of payments for the right to use assets, for the construction of assets or additional fees for the right to operate the concession. If the SCA falls within the financial asset model, the payments made will reduce the consideration received from the grantor. This is considered further at 4.7 below.

Although there is a single contract and a single payment mechanism, it is often straightforward in practice to identify the underlying cash flows that relate to different activities. This may be on the basis of the original contract negotiations or because the contract contains terms allowing for subsequent price adjustments by 'market testing' or benchmarking. However, the cash flows may not reflect the fair value of the underlying services so care will have to be taken. There will always be practical problems when it comes to apportioning the total contract consideration between the elements of the contract and the allocation will always be a matter of judgement.

4.1.2 Determining the accounting model

IFRIC 12 states that the operator may receive a financial asset or an intangible asset as consideration for its construction services and the asset that it receives determines the subsequent treatment. *[IFRIC 12.15]*.

The Interpretations Committee decided that the boundary between the financial and the intangible asset models should be based on the operator's contractual right to receive cash from, or at the direction of, the grantor. The grantor does not need to pay the cash to the operator directly. Fees or tolls received directly from users are viewed as essentially no more than collections on behalf of the grantor if they are part of an overall arrangement under which the grantor bears ultimate responsibility. If the grantor pays but the amounts are wholly based on usage of the infrastructure and there is no minimum guaranteed payment, the entity has no contractual right to receive cash. Therefore the intangible asset model will apply.

The operator will recognise a financial asset to the extent that it has a contractual right to receive cash or other financial assets from the grantor for the construction services, where the grantor has little, if any, discretion to avoid payment. This is usually because the agreement is legally enforceable. *[IFRIC 12.16]*. The operator will recognise an intangible asset to the extent that it receives a licence to charge users of the public service. *[IFRIC 12.17]*.

Sometimes it is necessary to 'bifurcate' the operator's right to cash flows for construction services into a financial asset and an intangible asset and account separately for each component of the operator's consideration. This, the Interpretations Committee argues, is because the operator is paid for its services partly by a financial asset and partly by an intangible asset. *[IFRIC 12.18]*.

The analysis between the different models can be seen in the following table:

	Arrangement	*Applicable model*
1	Grantor pays – fixed payments	Financial asset
2	Grantor pays – payments vary with demand	Intangible asset
3	Grantor retains demand risk – users pay but grantor guarantees amounts	Financial asset or bifurcated (part financial, part intangible)
4	Grantor retains demand risk – operator collects revenues from users until it achieves specified return	Intangible asset
5	Users pay – no grantor guarantees	Intangible asset

Of the two arrangements in Example 26.2 above, the hospital is an example of (1) above: the payments are contractually fixed if all obligations and services are provided. The prison, as described in Example 26.2 above, would fall within (2) and be accounted for as an intangible asset. However, the prison operator might be paid on a different basis, e.g. it might be paid for 1,000 'available places' and receive this as long as heating and food were capable of being provided. In this case it would be no different to the hospital and be a financial asset. There are, of course, many potential variations and a combination of fixed and variable demand could lead to bifurcation.

Common examples of arrangements that fall within (3) above are transport concessions where the operator collects revenue from users but is entitled to an agreed return on capital invested in the infrastructure. The fees or tolls are considered to be collections on behalf of the grantor. There will be a financial asset to the extent of the guaranteed return. There may be an intangible asset as well if the operator retains a right to collect tolls in excess of the guaranteed amount.

However, arrangements of the type in (4) above remain to be treated as intangible assets even if the overall risk to the operator of not obtaining a specified result is very low. An arrangement that effectively caps revenue collected from users once an agreed level of return is reached, it is argued, is not a contractual right to cash but a right to collect revenues from users and it is not relevant that the risk is low or that the operator will, in effect, get a fixed return. *[IFRIC 12.BC52].*

The following are examples of arrangements that will be accounted for using the intangible asset model:

(a) A municipality grants the operator a contract to treat all of its waste collections for which it will be paid per unit processed. The arrangement does not provide for any guaranteed volume of waste to be treated by the operator (so it does not contain a take-or-pay arrangement) or any form of guarantee by the grantor. Historically, however, the annual volume of waste has never been less than 40,000 tons and the average annual volume over the last 20 years has been 75,000 tons.

(b) An operator enters into a toll bridge concession. The operator is permitted to collect revenues from users or the grantor until it achieves a 6% return on its agreed infrastructure spend, at which point the arrangement comes to an end.

The toll bridge concession may be virtually commercially identical to a transaction that falls within (3), e.g. where the users pay tolls but the grantor guarantees a minimum 6% return. The crucial difference is the grantor's guarantee. Somewhat ironically, the arrangement with the guarantee, which will contain a financial asset, is likely to leave more of the rewards of ownership with the operator than the intangible arrangement in (b) as the operator will be entitled to benefits in excess of the 6% return.

There are jurisdictions where public-to-private contract laws or the concession arrangements themselves allow an operator to ask the grantor for a revision of the tariffs for the public service when the operator's actual return is below initial expectations. Although this feature in the concession arrangement is included to reduce the operator's risk, it only gives the operator a right to re-negotiate and the outcome of that is not certain. As a result, the operator does not have an unconditional right to receive cash and, therefore, the operator may not apply the financial asset model.

Many payment mechanisms include deductions for substandard performance of services. These do not affect the analysis of the contract as a financial asset or intangible asset and are discussed further below.

4.2 The financial asset model

Under the financial asset model, which applies if the entity has a contractual right to receive cash or another financial asset, *[IFRIC 12.16]*, the service element that relates to the construction of the infrastructure asset ('construction services') is accounted for in accordance with IAS 11. The consideration received by the operator for other services is addressed at 5 below.

The Interpretations Committee has argued that the 'amounts due from customers', i.e. those amounts recognised as revenue under IAS 11 from the point of initial recognition of the service concession, net of cash received, are deemed to be financial assets under IAS 32 because they represent contractual rights to receive cash or another financial asset from another entity. *[IAS 32.11]*. This analysis is not affected by the fact that this contractual right may be contingent on performance standards, as in the example of a unitary charge for a hospital in Example 26.2 above. The Interpretations Committee points out that this is no different from other circumstances and other financial assets where the payment depends on the subsequent performance of the asset. *[IFRIC 12.BC44]*.

Should the entity apply IFRS 9, the financial asset would be recognised at amortised cost or at fair value through profit or loss. *[IFRIC 12.24]*. Until it applies that standard, the financial asset will fall into one of the following three categories under IAS 39:

- a loan or receivable;
- an available-for-sale financial asset; or
- at fair value through profit or loss, if so designated on initial recognition.

In the first two cases, interest income will be recognised, calculated using the effective interest method. *[IFRIC 12.25]*.

The financial asset will not be classified as held-to-maturity. *[IFRIC 12.BC61]*.

It is argued that under IAS 39, amounts may only be classified as loans and receivables if the holder will receive 'substantially all of its initial investment, other than through credit deterioration'. *[IAS 39.9]*. In this regard, the potential for variation that exists in any service concession arrangement does not comprise an embedded derivative because it is specific to the parties in the contract. *[IFRIC 12.BC62]*. When the amount to be received by the operator could vary with the quality of services it provided or according to performance or efficiency targets, the arrangement does not contain an embedded derivative. These are non-financial measures and the remainder of the arrangement may still meet the definition of a loan and receivable. Non-compliance with this contractual requirement is a breach of contract and the resulting adjustment of future payments would be considered a penalty which causes forfeiture of some or the entire financial asset but it does not need to be considered part of the original financial asset.

This approach is consistent with general practice for accounting for receivables arising from the sale of goods and services with performance conditions under IASs 11 and 18. The Basis for Conclusions notes that the operator's position is the same as that of any other entity in which payment for goods or services is contingent on subsequent performance of the goods or service sold. *[IFRIC 12.BC44]*. Following this argument, the financial asset is recognised as consideration for delivering construction services and is no different from any other such receivable.

In practice many entities classify IFRIC 12 financial assets as loans and receivables.

Extract 26.2: VINCI SA (2012)

Consolidated financial statements

3 Measurement rules and methods [extract]

3.5 Concession contracts [extract]

In return for its activities, the operator receives remuneration from [...]

- **The grantor: the financial asset model applies.** The operator has an unconditional contractual right to receive payments from the concession grantor, irrespective of the amount of use made of the infrastructure.

  Under this model, the operator recognises a financial asset, attracting interest, in its balance sheet, in consideration for the services it provides (design, construction etc.). Such financial assets are recognised in the balance sheet under "Loans and receivables", in an amount corresponding to the fair value of the infrastructure on first recognition and subsequently at amortised cost. The receivable is settled by means of the grantor's payments received. The financial income calculated on the basis of the effective interest rate, equivalent to the project's internal rate of return, is recognised under operating income.

3.20 Other non-current financial assets[extract]

3.20.2 Loans and receivables at amortised cost [extract]

"Loans and receivables at amortised cost" mainly comprises receivables connected with shareholdings, current account advances to companies accounted for under the equity method or unconsolidated entities, guarantee deposits, collateralised loans and receivables and other loans and financial receivables. It also includes the financial receivables relating to concession contracts and public-private partnerships whenever the concession operator has an unconditional right to receive remuneration (generally in the form of "scheduled payments") from the grantor.

When first recognised, these loans and receivables are recognised at their fair value less the directly attributable transaction costs. At each balance sheet date, these assets are measured at their amortised cost using the effective interest method. In the particular case of receivables coming under the scope of IFRIC 12, the effective interest rate used corresponds to the project's internal rate of return.

If the contract is not classified as a loan and receivable it will most likely be classified as available-for-sale and be accounted for at fair value with changes in value taken to other comprehensive income. These definitions are further described in Chapter 44.

Whichever of these classifications apply, the financial asset will be measured on initial recognition at its fair value, and interest will be calculated on the balance using the effective interest rate method. *[IAS 39.43]*. Revenue will be recognised in accordance with IAS 11 when the contract work is performed using the percentage of completion method. *[IAS 11.26]*. This means that the financial asset will be recognised from the beginning of contract activity.

How to measure this could represent a conundrum: it is necessary to recognise interest (using the effective interest rate method) on the financial asset simultaneously with recognising revenue using the percentage of completion method. Part of what would otherwise have been recognised as construction revenue is now finance income. The Illustrative Example 1 in IFRIC 12, on which Example 26.3 below is based, demonstrates how to avoid this problem by deeming the fair value of the consideration for construction services to be based on construction costs plus a margin. Potential issues with the use of a profit margin have previously been discussed at 4.1.1 above.

Borrowing costs cannot be capitalised under the financial asset model. *[IFRIC 12.22]*.

Example 26.3: The Financial Asset Model – recording the construction asset

Table 1 Concession terms

The terms of the arrangement require an operator to construct a road – completing construction within two years – and maintain and operate the road to a specified standard for eight years (i.e. years 3-10). The terms of the concession also require the operator to resurface the road at the end of year 8. At the end of year 10, the arrangement will end. The operator estimates that the costs it will incur to fulfil its obligations will be:

	Year	**€**
Construction services (per year)	1-2	500
Operation services (per year)	3-10	10
Road resurfacing	8	100

The terms of the concession require the grantor to pay the operator €200 per year in years 3-10 for making the road available to the public.

For the purpose of this illustration, it is assumed that all cash flows take place at the end of the year.

Table 2 Contract revenue

The operator recognises contract revenue and costs in accordance with IAS 11. The costs of each activity – construction, operation, maintenance and resurfacing – are recognised as expenses by reference to the stage of completion of that activity. Contract revenue – the fair value of the amount due from the grantor for the activity undertaken – is recognised at the same time.

The total consideration (€200 in each of years 3-8) reflects the fair values for each of the services, which are:

	Fair value		
Construction	**Forecast cost**	+	**5%**
Operation and maintenance	" "	+	**20%**
Road resurfacing	" "	+	**10%**
Lending rate to grantor	**6.18% per year**		

In year 1, for example, construction costs of €500, construction revenue of €525 (cost plus 5 per cent), and hence construction profit of €25 are recognised in the income statement.

Financial asset

The amount due from the grantor meets the definition of a receivable in IAS 39. The receivable is measured initially at fair value. It is subsequently measured at amortised cost, i.e. the amount initially recognised plus the cumulative interest on that amount calculated using the effective interest method minus repayments.

Table 3 Measurement of receivable

	€
Amount due for construction in year 1	525
Receivable at end of year 1*	525
Effective interest in year 2 on receivable at the end of year 1 (6.18% × €525)	32
Amount due for construction in year 2	525
Receivable at end of year 2	1,082
Effective interest in year 3 on receivable at the end of year 2 (6.18% × €1,082)	67
Amount due for operation in year 3 (€10 × (1 + 20%))	12
Cash receipts in year 3	(200)
Receivable at end of year 3	961

* No effective interest arises in year 1 because the cash flows are assumed to take place at the end of the year.

4.3 The intangible asset model

If the financial asset model does not apply (i.e. there is no contractual right to cash or other financial assets), the operator's consideration for its construction services will be an intangible asset. *[IFRIC 12.15]*. As with the financial asset model, the operator cannot have an item of property, plant and equipment because the physical infrastructure is an asset of the grantor (see 3 above). *[IFRIC 12.11]*. Therefore, the Interpretations Committee has concluded that the right of an operator to charge users of the public service, for example the right to collect tolls from a road or a bridge, meets the definition of an intangible asset, that should be accounted for in accordance with IAS 38. It is, in effect, a licence 'bought' in exchange for construction services. *[IFRIC 12.17]*.

The Interpretations Committee has concluded that an intangible asset will be recorded during the construction phase as activity progresses, representing the operator's right to receive the licence. On this assumption, the entity will account for the construction of the infrastructure asset as follows:

(i) revenue will be measured at the fair value of the intangible asset received. *[IFRIC 12.15]*.

(ii) it will record this contract revenue in accordance with IAS 11 as it provides 'construction services' by constructing the asset. *[IFRIC 12.14]*.

The intangible asset under the concession (the licence received in return for construction services) meets the definition of a qualifying asset because it will not be ready for use until the infrastructure is constructed. Therefore borrowing costs must be capitalised during the period of construction. *[IFRIC 12.22]*. This contrasts with the treatment of borrowing costs under the financial asset model, where capitalisation is forbidden but financial income (the accretion of interest on the financial asset) is recognised.

Furthermore, it is argued that an inevitable consequence of applying the intangible asset model is that there must be an exchange transaction in which the operator receives the intangible right in exchange for its construction services. As this is an exchange of dissimilar assets, revenue must be recognised in accordance with IAS 18, which requires the recognition of revenue and a profit (or loss) based on the fair value of the assets received, unless the fair value of the assets given up can be measured more reliably. *[IFRIC 12.BC32-BC35]*. This means that the operator must establish the fair value of either the intangible asset it receives or the fair value of the construction services it has provided. The following example, based on Illustrative Example 2 in IFRIC 12, indicates how the Interpretations Committee expects this to apply in practice. It assumes that the fair value can be based on the cost of the construction services plus a margin – a similar methodology to that applied for the financial asset model above.

Example 26.4: The Intangible Asset Model – recording the construction asset

Arrangement terms

The terms of a service arrangement require an operator to construct a road – completing construction within two years – and maintain and operate the road to a specified standard for eight years (i.e. years 3-10). The terms of the arrangement also require the operator to resurface the road when the original surface has deteriorated below a specified condition. The operator estimates that it will have to undertake the resurfacing at the end of the year 8. At the end of year 10, the service arrangement will end. The operator estimates that the costs it will incur to fulfil its obligations will be:

Table 1 Contract costs

	Year	**€**
Construction services (per year)	1-2	500
Operation services (per year)	3-10	10
Road resurfacing	8	100

The terms of the arrangement allow the operator to collect tolls from drivers using the road. The operator forecasts that vehicle numbers will remain constant over the duration of the contract and that it will receive tolls of €200 in each of years 3-10.

For the purpose of this illustration, it is assumed that all cash flows take place at the end of the year.

Intangible asset

The operator provides construction services to the grantor in exchange for an intangible asset, i.e. a right to collect tolls from road users in years 3-10. In accordance with IAS 38, the operator recognises the intangible asset at cost, i.e. the fair value of consideration received or receivable.

During the construction phase of the arrangement the operator's asset (representing its accumulating right to be paid for providing construction services) is classified as an intangible asset (licence to charge users of the infrastructure). The operator estimates the fair value of its consideration received to be equal to the forecast construction costs plus 5 per cent margin. The operator also capitalises borrowing costs during the construction phase as required by IAS 23, at an estimated rate of 6.7 per cent:

Table 2 Initial measurement of intangible asset

	€
Construction services in year 1 (€500 × (1 + 5%))	525
Capitalisation of borrowing costs	34
Construction services in year 2 (€500 × (1 + 5%))	525
Intangible asset at end of year 2	1,084

The intangible asset is amortised over the period in which it is expected to be available for use by the operator, i.e. years 3-10. In this case, the directors determine that it is appropriate to amortise using a straight-line method. The annual amortisation charge is therefore €1,084 divided by 8 years, i.e. €135 per year.

Construction costs and revenue

The operator recognises the revenue and costs in accordance with IAS 11 i.e. by reference to the stage of completion of the construction. It measures contract revenue at the fair value of the consideration received or receivable. Thus in each of years 1 and 2 it recognises in its income statement construction costs of €500, construction revenue of €525 (cost plus 5 per cent) and, hence, construction profit of €25.

Toll revenue

The road users pay for the public services at the same time as they receive them, i.e. when they use the road. The operator therefore recognises toll revenue when it collects the tolls.

4.3.1 Amortisation of the intangible asset

The intangible asset will subsequently be accounted for in accordance with IAS 38 *[IFRIC 12.26]*, which means that the amount at which it is measured initially, i.e. after the exchange transaction, is its cost. *[IAS 38.45]*. It will be amortised on a systematic basis over its useful life, using a method that reflects 'the pattern in which the asset's future economic benefits are expected to be consumed by the entity'. *[IAS 38.97]*. This means that the methods permitted by IAS 38 are available (straight line, diminishing balance or unit-of-production). *[IAS 38.98]*. The requirements of IAS 38 are discussed in detail in Chapter 17. Interest methods of amortisation are forbidden. *[IFRIC 12.BC65]*.

The Interpretations Committee expressly considered unit-of-production methods to be appropriate in some circumstances; in March 2006, it was noted in *IFRIC Update* that the Basis of Conclusions had been redrafted to avoid the impression that these methods were not allowed.[9] There were still concerns as a unit-of-production method could result in lower amortisation in the early years of the asset's operation so IAS 38 itself was amended to remove a statement discouraging methods that might have such a result.[10] This clarifies that there is no prohibition when the method is the most appropriate, whatever the resulting profile of amortisation.

Unit-of-production methods are typically considered in the context of toll roads and bridges. Obviously the method might apply if there is a right to charge a specified number of users. Questions still remained as to whether it might also be used if the basis was the estimated number of users, e.g. the number of vehicles that might use a particular road during the concession term.

The remaining issue regarding amortisation methods has been whether they could be based on revenue generated by the asset; this depends on the meaning of 'consumption of economic benefits' in the context of intangible assets with finite lives. In December 2012, the IASB issued an Exposure Draft of proposed amendments to IAS 16 and IAS 38 to clarify that a method of depreciation or amortisation based on the revenue expected to be generated from using the asset in an entity's business is not appropriate. This is because this method reflects a pattern of generation of economic benefits from operating the business (of which the asset is a part), rather than the consumption of the economic benefits embodied in the asset.[11] See Chapter 17 at 9.2.1; this includes Example 17.12 which demonstrates the distorting effects of basing amortisation on revenue. The proposed amendment is currently expected to be issued before the end of 2013.[12] It is expected to require retrospective application.[13]

This does not prevent an entity using a revenue-based method if it can be demonstrated that it is a reasonable approximation to a usage method based on consumption of the asset. This might be the case when there is a linear relationship between usage and revenue, for example when unit prices are stable over the term of the SCA. An expected future reduction in unit selling prices or service output might indicate an expected reduction in the future economic benefits of the asset and so a diminishing balance method of utilisation may be appropriate,[14] but this is not the same as amortising the asset in accordance with expected future revenues. Amortisation would still be determined using estimates of usage of the asset, such as customer numbers.[15]

The choice of amortisation method is a matter of judgement. One of the most fundamental issues, therefore, is whether reasonable estimates can be made, especially in circumstances in which the entity has little or no past experience on which to base its decision about the most appropriate method of amortisation. In the following extract from its accounting policies, GDF SUEZ indicates that it amortises its intangible assets on a straight line basis over the concession term if the pattern of consumption cannot be determined reliably.

Extract 26.3: GDF SUEZ SA (2012)

Notes to the Consolidated Financial Statements [extract]

1.4.4.2 Other intangible assets [extract]

Other internally-generated or acquired intangible assets

Other intangible assets include mainly:

- amounts paid or payable as consideration for rights relating to concession contracts or public service contracts;
- customer portfolios acquired on business combinations;
- power station capacity rights: the Group helped finance the construction of certain nuclear power stations operated by third parties and in consideration received the right to purchase a share of the production over the useful life of the assets. These rights are amortized over the useful life of the underlying assets, not to exceed 40 years;
- surface and underground water drawing rights, which are not amortized as they are granted indefinitely;
- concession assets;
- the GDF Gaz de France brand and gas supply contracts acquired as part of the business combination with Gaz de France in 2008.

Intangible assets are amortized on the basis of the expected pattern of consumption of the estimated future economic benefits embodied in the asset. Amortization is calculated mainly on a straight-line basis over the following useful lives (in years):

	Useful life	
Main depreciation period (years)	Minimum	Maximum
Concession rights	10	65
Customer portfolios	10	40
Other intangible assets	1	40

Some intangible assets with an indefinite useful life such as trademarks and water drawing rights are not amortized.

4.3.2 Impairment during the construction phase

The operator will recognise an intangible right during the construction phase of the arrangement, which is before the asset has been brought into use. There may be other circumstances in which the operator will continue to recognise an intangible asset prior to the service being provided to users. IAS 36 requires any intangible asset that has not yet been brought into use to be tested for impairment annually, irrespective of whether there are any indications of impairment. *[IAS 36.10]*. See Chapter 20 at 2.2.

4.4 Revenue recognition implications of the two models

There are major differences in the way in which revenue is measured under the two models. Under the financial asset model, total revenue over the concession term will be the same as the total cash inflows under the contract. By contrast, the fair value of the intangible asset is recognised as revenue under the intangible asset model, so total revenue measured using this model will be higher by this amount. The consequences of the two models can be demonstrated by the following simple example:

Example 26.5: Revenue under the financial asset and intangible models

An operator builds a road at a cost of 100. The construction profit is 10 and total cash inflows over the life of the concession are 200.

Under the financial asset model, the operator will recognise construction revenue of 110 and a receivable of 110. Of the future cash inflows of 200, 110 will be treated as repaying the receivable, with the remaining 90 being recognised as revenue over the life of the concession. Total revenue will be 200.

Under the intangible asset model, the operator will recognise construction revenue of 110, an intangible of 110, and a construction profit of 10. Over the life of the concession, the intangible asset of 110 would be amortised against revenues (which in this case would be from users) of 200. The net position is the same as in the financial asset case, but total revenues will be 310 rather than 200.

It is fair to say that this proved highly controversial. In fact, the September 2004 *IFRIC Update* stated that 'the majority of the Interpretations Committee strongly disliked this outcome.'[16] However, the Interpretations Committee maintained that this is the appropriate application of accounting standards to the arrangements and is consistent with the treatment generally accorded to barter transactions, *[IFRIC 12.BC35]*, although, of course, there are no other sectors where barter transactions are fundamental to the arrangement. The possible implications for many other transactions with governmental grantors where licences are granted have not been considered.

4.5 'Bifurcation' – single arrangements that contain both financial and intangible assets

As part of its redeliberations, the Interpretations Committee agreed that it may be necessary in certain circumstances to divide the operator's right to cash flows into a financial asset and an intangible asset. *[IFRIC 12.18]*. The *IFRIC Update* (March 2006) reported that 'With this change, the proposed amendment would better reflect the economic reality of concession arrangements: to the extent that the operator is remunerated for its construction services by obtaining a contractual right to receive cash from, or at the direction of, the grantor, the operator would recognise a financial asset and, to the extent that the operator receives only a licence to charge users, it would recognise an intangible asset.'

The Basis for Conclusions to IFRIC 12 explains more of the reasoning and potential impact. In some arrangements both parties to the contract share the risk (demand risk) that the cash flows generated by the project will not be sufficient to recover the operator's capital investment. A common mechanism for achieving this is where the grantor pays partly by a financial asset (i.e. the grantor will pay cash for the services provided) but gives the operator the right to charge for services (i.e. the operator has an intangible asset). The operator's infrastructure asset is to be split into a financial asset component for any guaranteed amount of cash and an intangible asset for the remainder. *[IFRIC 12.18, BC53].*

These are common in transport concessions, e.g. a rail system paid for partly by grantor subsidy and partly by the payment of fares. This gives rise to difficult matters of interpretation. It may not be clear how much of the arrangement is a financial asset and, therefore, where to draw the boundary between the two assets. There may be minor amounts within a contract that fall within another model and entities may conclude that these are *de minimis.*

4.6 Accounting for residual interests

Unless the infrastructure is used in a service concession arrangement for the whole of its useful life (within scope of IFRIC 12 – see 3.2 above), there will be a residual interest at the end of the contract that will be controlled by the grantor. The way in which the grantor controls the residual interest will affect the way in which the operator accounts for it. If the operator has a contractual right to cash (or another financial asset) for the residual interest in the infrastructure, this right will be a financial asset. It will be recognised as part of the consideration for the construction services. *[IFRIC 12.16].* This is unaffected by the basis on which the consideration is calculated.

There are many different arrangements over residual interests in the infrastructure at the end of the concession term but broadly they depend on whether the grantor has a right or an option to acquire the residual interest and on the rights or options of the operator:

(a) The grantor may control the residual via a right to purchase the infrastructure from the operator but this could be at fair value, net book value, a notional amount or zero.

(b) It may only have an option to acquire the assets, on similar bases to (a), but it also has a right to put in place other arrangements, e.g. granting the operator a new term or selecting a new party to take on the assets. Payment might be made by the grantor or by the new operator but always at the direction of the grantor.

(c) The grantor has an option to acquire the assets but if this is not exercised then the operator may retain them.

The implications of grantor options and control of the residual interest have been discussed at 3.2 above.

If the terminal arrangements fall within (a) or (b), the operator will have a contractual right to cash. It will recognise a financial asset, initially at fair value, which will then be accounted for according to the relevant classification under IAS 39 or IFRS 9, as appropriate (see 4.2 above). If the financial asset is classified as a loan and receivable or as available for sale then interest will be calculated using the effective interest rate method. At the end of the contract the residual interest will be stated at the operator's best estimate of the amount receivable.

If the arrangement is of the type described in (c), then the operator's residual interest is not a financial asset. Nor does it have a residual interest in the underlying property, plant and equipment because this is an arrangement within scope of IFRIC 12 and the entity cannot recognise the underlying assets, in whole or in part. *[IFRIC 12.11]*. The only option is to recognise an intangible right to receive cash or the residual interest in the assets. By contrast to the residual financial asset, it is most unlikely that the operator would be able to restate the value of this right over the term to its best estimate of the amount receivable at the end of the contract. IAS 38 only allows intangible assets to be revalued in very restricted circumstances; see Chapter 17 at 8.2.

The operator will have to account for its residual interests as described above based on the contractual rights, whatever model is being applied to its construction services. This is similar to the explicit requirements for upgrade services described at 5.1 below: IFRIC 12 recognises that upgrade services have to be recognised as construction revenue on the basis of their individual contract terms regardless of the model applied. *[IFRIC 12.14]*. The result is that an entity that has recognised an intangible asset for the major part of its construction services might have to recognise a financial asset for the residual interests – or *vice versa* if its construction services have been accounted for as a financial asset. This treatment is a variation of the bifurcation described at 4.5 above except that the financial asset relates only to the residual interest in the infrastructure rather than to a portion of the consideration receivable for the infrastructure as a whole. The residual rights will be taken into account in calculating the revenue receivable under the contract, which are described at 4.2 and 4.3 above.

As the termination arrangements can be complex, care will have to be taken to ensure that the effects are fully analysed.

Chapter 26

Example 26.6: Contractual rights to cash in termination arrangements

The facts of the SCA are as in Example 26.1 above. At the end of the term, the grantor will either pay for the infrastructure assets at their net book value, determined on the basis of the contract, or it may decide to grant a new SCA on the basis of a competitive tender, which will exclude the current operator. If the grantor elects to do the latter, the operator will be entitled to the lower of the following two amounts:

(a) the net book value of the infrastructure, determined on the basis of the contract; and

(b) the proceeds of a new competitive bidding process to acquire a new contract.

Although the operator cannot enter the competitive tender, it also has the right to enter into a new concession term but in order to do so, it must match the best tender offer made. It has to pay to the grantor the excess of the best offer (b) above the amount in (a); should the tender offer be lower than (a), it will receive an equivalent refund.

In this arrangement, the operator has a contractual right to cash that should be recognised as a financial asset. It has a right to receive the lower of (a) and (b). It may *choose* to use its right to cash to settle part or all of the price of a new concession agreement but this does not affect the fact that it has a right to cash. This example also illustrates that calculating the fair value of the contractual right to cash may be complex as it has to take account of a number of different estimates, including the net book value of the infrastructure at the end of the contract, as well as the options available to the parties to the contract.

4.7 Accounting for contractual payments to be made by an operator to a grantor

Many arrangements require an entity to make payments to the grantor during the course of the SCA. These payments take two main forms:

(a) payments related to the use of tangible assets, including:
   (i) payments to the grantor or third parties for making assets available (such as trains and buses) in order to provide the services required by the concession contract;
   (ii) payments to a third party for the construction and making available assets (such as rolling stock) that passes to the grantor at the end of the concession term; and
   (iii) payments to the grantor for making available land on which the infrastructure assets are constructed or situated; or

(b) fees payable to the grantor for the right to operate the concession, which can be described as concession fees, development fees or access charges.

It is possible that some of these payments could be for the right to use assets controlled by the operator itself or the concession payment could relate to a distinct good or service that is separate from the concession arrangement. If so, these payments should be accounted for under other applicable IFRSs and excluded from the IFRIC 12 amounts recorded for the concession. For example, an operator might lease trains from a third party unrelated to the grantor and at the end of the lease term the assets are returned to that lessor. The leases for these trains will be accounted for under IAS 17.

The Interpretations Committee has proposed that the accounting for payments from operators to grantors which fall within the scope of IFRIC 12 (i.e. payments which are not related to the right of use of a tangible asset that meet the definition of a lease and which are not related to goods and services distinct from the SCA) should depend on whether the SCA falls within the financial asset model, the intangible asset model or is a hybrid. This means that the payments will be reflected in the carrying value of the appropriate concession asset:

- if the SCA is accounted for under the financial asset model, then the concession payment is an adjustment to the overall consideration receivable, illustrated at 4.7.2 below;

- if the intangible asset model applies, then the concession payment is part of the cost of acquiring the intangible asset recognised for the right to charge users of the service, illustrated at 4.7.3 below; and
- if the operator has both a right to charge users of the public service and a contractual right to receive cash from the grantor, then the entity should assess the extent to which the concession payment represents an adjustment to the overall consideration receivable or whether it is consideration for the intangible asset element. This is determined by comparing the amount of the contractual right to receive cash from the grantor with the fair value of the operator's services.

As noted at 3.3.1 above, this was the interim conclusion of the Interpretations Committee at its March 2012 meeting, which it repeated in May 2012.[17] However, although there is currently divergence in practice in the way in which these items are accounted for, the Committee's proposals are consistent with the accounting treatment required in other circumstances as well as being in accordance with the existing requirements of IFRIC 12.

The proposals for the financial asset model are predicated on the fact that the operator has a contractual right to receive cash from the grantor and that payments between the parties are all part of this single relationship, however described. In this regard, payments to the grantor will include amounts paid to a related private sector entity to which responsibility for the service has been devolved *[IFRIC 12.3]*.

Under the Interpretations Committee's approach for the intangible asset model, concession payments to the grantor represent consideration for the concession, i.e. part of the cost of the intangible asset recognised. When the payments are linked to the right of use of a tangible asset, but the arrangement does not represent an embedded lease, the payment should be analysed in the same way as a concession fee.[18] It is clearly a requirement of IAS 38 that an intangible asset be recognised when it meets the definition and other recognition criteria (see Chapter 17 at 2 and 3) and it must be recognised at its present value if payment is deferred. *[IAS 38.32]*.

Therefore, fixed fees payable over the life of a concession generate an intangible asset and give rise to a financial liability on inception, as the fixed fee will only be avoided by the operator if it withdraws from the concession, which in most circumstances is contractually and economically unfeasible.

4.7.1 Accounting for variable payments in a service concession

Some contracted payments, particularly concession fees, vary with a measure of usage of the concession asset or with another feature of the arrangement. Whilst the Interpretations Committee was able to reach a consensus on the treatment of concession fees that do not depend on future activity, as noted at 4.7 above, it has found the issue of variable payments more challenging. The Committee recognises that this question is linked to the broader issue of contingent payments for the separate purchase of PP&E and intangible assets outside of a business combination and in January 2013 decided to proceed with the proposed amendments noted above in respect of fixed concession payments and to address separately the question of variable payments.[19]

At the time of writing, the Committee remains unable to reach a consensus on the treatment of payments that vary in relation to future activity, but have tentatively agreed that in all other cases (i.e. where the variable payments do not depend on the purchaser's future activity) that the fair value of those variable payments should be recognised as a liability and included as appropriate in the measurement of the related asset.[20] The Committee's deliberations on the treatment of variable payments for the separate acquisition of PP&E and intangible assets are discussed further in Chapter 17 at 4.5 and Chapter 18 at 4.1.9. At present, the usual treatment for an operator in a service concession is to treat contingent payments that vary in relation to future activity as executory and expense them as incurred.

4.7.2 Accounting for contractual payments under the financial asset model

If the financial asset model applies then the Interpretations Committee proposes that the contractual payment is accounted for as a reduction in the overall consideration received, i.e. it is an adjustment to the fair value of the consideration given by the grantor. Another way of expressing this is that payments from the grantor reduce the financial asset while payments to the grantor increase that asset; both will also affect the amount of interest accrued on the outstanding balance. This applies whether the payment is for the right to use an asset or described as a concession fee. This will not affect the revenue recognised under the contract which depends on the cost of providing the services. This is demonstrated in the following example.

Example 26.7: Contractual payments made to a grantor under the financial asset model

Entity A enters into a 10 year concession agreement requiring it to construct a school and be responsible for operations services (including maintenance, utilities, cleaning and catering). After a 2 year construction period, the entity will receive €300 per year during years 3-10, to operate the asset, after which the concession will cease. The entity must pay €30 per year for the use of the land on which the school is built.

The entity's estimated contract costs and contractual payments are as follows:

	Year	Annual charge €	Total €
Construction services	1-2	500	1,000
Operation services	3-10	100	800
Land use charge	1-10	30	300
Total cash paid	1-10		2,100

The operating cash flows under the contract are as follows:

Year	1 €	2 €	3 €	4 €	5 €	6 €	7 €	8 €	9 €	10 €
Concession consideration	–	–	300	300	300	300	300	300	300	300
Construction costs	(500)	(500)	(100)	(100)	(100)	(100)	(100)	(100)	(100)	(100)
Land use charge	(30)	(30)	(30)	(30)	(30)	(30)	(30)	(30)	(30)	(30)
Net cash flow	(530)	(530)	170	170	170	170	170	170	170	170

The entity estimates that the fair value of its services and total revenue from those services is as follows:

	Fair value			Total
				€
Construction	Forecast cost	+	5%	1,050
Operation and maintenance	" "	+	15%	920
Total revenue				1,970
Lending rate to grantor	5% per year			

Under the financial asset model, the land use charge is treated as an adjustment to the carrying value of the financial asset and is not treated as an expense. Accordingly, the gross concession profit is calculated as follows:

Year	**1**	**2**	**3**	**4**	**5**	**6**	**7**	**8**	**9**	**10**
	€	€	€	€	€	€	€	€	€	€
Concession revenue*	525	525	115	115	115	115	115	115	115	115
Construction costs	(500)	(500)	(100)	(100)	(100)	(100)	(100)	(100)	(100)	(100)
Finance income	13	25	23	20	16	13	10	7	3	–
Concession profit**	38	50	38	35	31	28	25	22	18	15

* Concession revenue comprises revenue from construction and operation and maintenance services

** Concession profit totals €300, which represents the total consideration received for services (€2,400) less the total costs including the land use charge of €2,100. In the income statement this is analysed as:

	€
Concession revenue	1,970
Construction costs	(1,800)
Finance income	130
Total	300

The financial asset is computed as follows, applying an effective interest rate of 5%.

Year	**1**	**2**	**3**	**4**	**5**	**6**	**7**	**8**	**9**	**10**
	€	€	€	€	€	€	€	€	€	€
Opening balance	0	568	1148	1016	881	742	600	455	307	155
Additions	525	525	115	115	115	115	115	115	115	115
Net cash	30	30	(270)	(270)	(270)	(270)	(270)	(270)	(270)	(270)
Finance income*	13	25	23	20	16	13	10	7	3	–
Closing balance	568	1,148	1,016	881	742	600	455	307	155	–

* Finance income is calculated on the average debtor balance outstanding.

In the above example, the land use charge is treated as an adjustment to the carrying value of the financial asset and is not treated as an expense. The effect of paying the land use charge is incorporated into the effective finance cost recognised in the income statement. This is why the total profit is €300, representing the total consideration received for services (€2,400) less the total costs including the land use charge of €2,100. If the land use charge were accounted for separately as an expense, this would not affect contract revenue, which is based on the fair value of the services provided. Instead, the additional cost of €300 would be offset by increasing the amount of finance income over the concession term from €130 to €430 (€130 + €300). It can be demonstrated that this would increase the effective interest rate on the finance debtor from 5% to 15% because only cash inflows from the grantor would be taken into account in the financial asset calculation and not the cash outflows relating to the land use charge. This is clearly an inappropriately high lending rate for this concession arrangement. Of course, in an actual concession agreement the effects of the treatment of such charges is likely to be much less marked but the principle remains the same.

4.7.3 Accounting for contractual payments under the intangible asset model

Under the intangible asset model, concession payments would be treated in accordance with IAS 38 as part of the consideration for the intangible asset.

While lease-type costs and land use charges can be part of any concession arrangement, concession fees (however called) are much more commonly a feature of arrangements which follow the intangible asset model. This is unsurprising as they are in substance payments made by the operator for the right to charge users of the concession infrastructure.

Although the effects on revenue were not addressed directly, the Interpretations Committee did note that the concession payment represents consideration for the concession right (i.e. part of the cost of the intangible asset recognised).[21] It is therefore consistent with this to assume that, as part of the cost of the intangible asset, it should be reflected in the revenue earned for the construction services. This would mean that the fair value of the construction services would include an appropriate margin on top of the concession fee, in the same way as it includes a margin on amounts paid to subcontractors (see 4.3 above).

The illustration below considers how an entity might account for a concession fee under the intangible asset model. The same approach would apply if the payments were for access to the land on which the asset was to be constructed or for an asset used in the delivery of the service.

Example 26.8: Contractual payments made to a grantor under the intangible asset model

Entity B enters into a 10 year concession agreement to construct a toll road and be responsible for operations services. After a 2 year construction period, the entity expects to receive tolls of €300 per year, which it expects to remain at the same level for the duration of the concession. The entity must pay a concession fee of €50 per year in years 5-10.

The entity concludes that the obligation for the concession fee is incurred in year 1 and estimates that its present value is €209. The contract costs and contractual payments are as follows:

	Year	Annual charge €	Total €
Construction services	1-2	500	1,000
Operation services	3-10	100	800
Concession fee	5-10	50	300
Total cash paid	1-10		2,100

The entity assesses the fair value of its intangible asset to be the cost of construction services plus a margin of 5%. This means that it will record construction revenue in years 1 and 2 as follows.

Year	1	2
	€	€
Construction services	500	500
Concession fee	209	–
Total costs	709	500
Revenue	744	525

This means that the entity recognises concession revenue for construction services totalling €1,269 and an intangible asset of the same amount. It concludes that, as usage is expected to be the same throughout the term, the intangible asset should be amortised in equal annual instalments commencing in year 3. The concession gross profit (revenue – contract costs – unwinding discount on the concession fee – amortisation of the intangible asset) is calculated as follows:

Year	1	2	3	4	5	6	7	8	9	10
	€	€	€	€	€	€	€	€	€	€
Concession revenue	744	525	300	300	300	300	300	300	300	300
Construction costs	(709)	(500)	(100)	(100)	(100)	(100)	(100)	(100)	(100)	(100)
Unwinding discount	(10)	(11)	(12)	(12)	(12)	(11)	(9)	(7)	(5)	(2)
Amortisation*	–	–	(159)	(159)	(158)	(158)	(158)	(159)	(159)	(159)
Concession profit**	25	14	29	29	30	31	33	34	36	39

* The amortisation is adjusted for rounding

** Concession profit totals €300, which represents the total consideration received from users for services (€2,400) less the total costs including the concession fee of €2,100. In the income statement this is analysed as:

	€
Concession revenue (744+525+2,400)	3,669
Contract costs	(2,009)
Unwinding discount	(91)
Amortisation	(1,269)
Total	300

5 REVENUE AND EXPENDITURE DURING THE OPERATIONS PHASE OF THE CONCESSION AGREEMENT

So far, we have described the recognition and measurement of the infrastructure asset in the accounts of the operator under the two models. A significant issue in practice is that service concession arrangements are composite transactions. They usually have a long duration (twenty-five to thirty years is not uncommon) during which time the operator has a variety of obligations. These may be in connection with the infrastructure asset itself and include:

- enhancement of the infrastructure or construction of new infrastructure;
- infrastructure components that must be replaced in their entirety;
- infrastructure subject to major cyclical repairs; and
- regular repairs and maintenance.

In addition, many service concession arrangements involve the provision of services. In the case of a hospital, for example, this could include utilities (such as water and electricity) and a wide range of 'soft' services such as cleaning, laundry, meals, portering, security and grounds maintenance, amongst others. All of these might be paid for as a single unitary charge that would probably be adjusted according to performance as in Example 26.2 above. The accounting models for service concessions must be able to deal with all of these issues.

5.1 Additional construction and upgrade services

The concession may include obligations to construct new infrastructure (construction services) or to enhance either new or existing infrastructure to a condition better than at the start of the concession (upgrade services). IFRIC 12 does not deal in detail with the treatment to be adopted other than to say that revenue and costs relating to construction or upgrade services are recognised in accordance with IAS 11. *[IFRIC 12.14]*. This means that all construction or upgrade services are accounted for in accordance with the appropriate model, regardless of when they take place. Contractual obligations to maintain or restore infrastructure may also include an upgrade element. *[IFRIC 12.21]*.

Upgrade or construction services are separate revenue-generating activities. This means that the contract has to require the particular service to be carried out at a specified time. This is not the same as a general requirement to maintain the asset in a specified condition.

It would be unusual for a toll road concession, for example, to require resurfacing to take place according to a predetermined schedule as road surfaces degrade with usage (based on both the number of vehicles and weight per axle) as well as weather conditions. However, the contract might require a new bridge or access road after a specified period of time and either of these could be separate upgrade services.

Upgrade services must be recognised in accordance with IAS 11, using the percentage of completion method and recognising revenue during the construction period, as described at 4.2 and 4.3 above and in Chapter 23 at 3.3.2.

If the financial asset model applies to the upgrade, the entity has to determine the fair value of consideration received for the upgrade services. This may be part of the allocation at inception of the contract, as shown in Example 26.3 above where part of the contract revenue is attributed to road resurfacing, or the contract may specify a separate payment when the upgrade is performed. In the latter case the entity would account for the upgrade service as a separate financial asset once it started to provide the services (e.g. started to build the bridge) which means recognising revenue during construction. If the infrastructure is being accounted for as a financial asset, the entity cannot simply add upgrade-related maintenance costs as incurred to the carrying value of an existing financial asset.

Similar issues for intangible assets are discussed in further detail below. Are the construction services part of the original asset or should they be accounted for as a new asset? If it is a new asset, when should it be recognised?

5.1.1 Subsequent construction services that are part of the initial infrastructure asset

In some circumstances, the 'enhancement' spend is a component of the original intangible asset and should be recognised as part of the exchange transaction to secure the right to charge users described at 4.3 above. An example of this is the common requirement in concession contracts that the operator replace certain items at the operator's cost, whether or not the items concerned have become unserviceable. For example, a water supply operator may be contractually required to replace all lead pipes for environmental and health reasons; similarly, a gas supply operator may be required to replace all cast-iron pipes for safety reasons.

Assuming that the intangible asset model is the relevant one, the first issue is whether these expenditures should be regarded as operating costs (obligations to maintain or to restore the infrastructure) and treated as described at 5.2 below or as an additional cost of the intangible asset. They do not directly increase the future economic benefits of any particular infrastructure asset when the costs are incurred and might therefore be treated as the cost of maintaining the original benefits and expensed. However, unlike most subsequent expenditure on intangible assets, which is not recognised as an asset because it cannot be distinguished from expenditure to develop the business as a whole. *[IAS 38.20]*, it is possible in the case of SCAs to attribute the expenditure directly to the cost of securing a particular intangible asset (the right to operate the concession). The requirement of the operator to incur subsequent expenditure for building, upgrading or maintaining a physical infrastructure asset is embodied in the contract entered into to secure that intangible right. IAS 16 explicitly allows such expenditure to be capitalised as part of an item of property, plant and equipment *[IAS 16.10]* so it would seem that capitalisation is an appropriate treatment.

These features indicate that these expenditures should be included in the measure of the consideration given for the intangible asset and therefore recognised as part of its carrying value on initial recognition. This would require the recognition of a liability for the present value of the best estimate of the amount required to replace the underlying asset, such as the pipes. Note that the revenue earned in the construction phase is based on the fair value of the building or upgrade work performed on initial recognition, in accordance with IAS 11. In other words, the fair value of the 'construction services' may remain unchanged although the entity has accrued additional costs in relation to the other obligations it has assumed in return for securing the right to operate the infrastructure asset and to earn related revenues.

The Interpretations Committee did not address the accounting treatment of subsequent variations in the amount of the liability for the operator's unfulfilled obligations that is recognised as part of the cost of the intangible asset (the licence) e.g. when the estimated amount of the expenditures to be incurred is revised. The situation may be regarded as analogous to the situation addressed by IFRIC Interpretation 1 – *Changes in Existing Decommissioning, Restoration and Similar Liabilities* – where the obligation is recognised as a liability in accordance with IAS 37 and as part of the cost of an asset. *[IFRIC 1.5]*. Therefore, the principles set out in IFRIC 1 – *Changes in Existing Decommissioning, Restoration and Similar*

Liabilities – should be applied, i.e. a change in the measurement of the liability should be added to, or deducted from the cost of the intangible asset, subject to impairment testing and to the extent that the amount deducted from the cost of the asset does not exceed the carrying amount of the intangible asset. The periodic unwinding of the discount must be recognised in income.

5.1.2 Subsequent construction services that comprise a new infrastructure asset

An operator may be contractually entitled to add to or upgrade the infrastructure and from this generate additional revenues. The operator may have a right to extend a distribution network and, under its right to charge for the services, it will obtain revenues from newly connected users. There is an example of such a right in Extract 26.4 below, in which Telenor ASA discloses that it has a right 'to arrange, expand, operate and provide the cellular telephone services in various areas in Thailand'.

Extract 26.4: Telenor ASA (2012)

Notes to the financial statements /Telenor Group [extract]

18. Intangible assets [extract]

DTAC operates under a concession right to operate and deliver mobile services in Thailand granted by CAT Telecom Public Company Limited (CAT). CAT allows DTAC to arrange, expand, operate and provide the cellular telephone services in various areas in Thailand. The concession originally covered a 15-year period but the agreement was amended on 23 July 1993 and 22 November 1996, with the concession period being extended to 22 and 27 years, respectively. Accordingly, the concession period under the existing agreement expires in 2018.

Revenues generated by the new infrastructure will be determined under the terms of the *original* licence granted to the operator. However, in this case there is no pre-existing obligation to incur the cost of the extension work, meaning that it will only be recognised when the expenditure is made. Accordingly, that new cost is not an additional component of the cost of the original intangible asset but will be a new intangible asset in its own right, giving rise to new construction revenues and recognised using the same principles as the original as described at 4.3 above.

5.2 Accounting for the operations phase

Both the financial and intangible asset models apply the same accounting in the operations phase of the SCA. According to the September 2006 *IFRIC Update*, 'the nature of the asset recognised by the operator as consideration for providing construction services (a financial asset or an intangible asset) does not determine the accounting for the operation phase of the arrangement'.[22]

Revenue and costs for the operation services will be recognised in accordance with IAS 18. *[IFRIC 12.20].* This means that most operating and maintenance costs are likely to be executory and will be accounted for as incurred. Contractual obligations, including obligations to maintain, replace or restore infrastructure, are to be recognised and measured in accordance with IAS 37, i.e. once there is a present obligation as a result of a past event, and measured at the best estimate of the expenditure required to settle the present obligation at the reporting date, as shown in Example 26.9 below. These include obligations to restore infrastructure to a specified condition before it is returned to the grantor at the end of the concession. *[IFRIC 12.21]*. These do not include any upgrade element which is treated as an additional construction service (see 5.1 above).

Distinguishing between executory maintenance expenditure and contractual obligations is not always straightforward. A concession arrangement may provide for a specified total amount of expenditure to be incurred by the operator throughout the contract. Sometimes, the contract provides for mechanisms whereby at the end of the contract, any shortfall in the agreed amount is paid in cash to the grantor by the operator. Particularly in the case of older contracts, it is common for the maintenance and repair obligation to be expressed in very general terms such as keeping the infrastructure in 'good working condition' or 'state of the art' working condition. The obligation may include the requirement that the asset be handed over with a certain number of years' useful life remaining.

Local regulations or laws also change over time. Some operators are obliged to report annually to the grantor on the level of maintenance and renewal expenditure incurred during the year and on a cumulative basis from inception of the contract. Sometimes, the operator must report on expected expenditures over some future period of time (e.g. over the next 12 months or two years) as well. In these situations, more often than not the grantor compares the cumulative expenditure at any point in time with either the operator's prior estimates of expenditures or with the level of expenditure that had been anticipated at the outset of the arrangement and was factored into the level of usage charges. In such circumstances, judgement is required in deciding whether expenditure on renewals is an obligation requiring recognition or an executory contract.

Example 26.9: Executory and contractual obligations to maintain and restore the infrastructure

The operator under a water supply service concession is required as part of the overall contractual arrangement to replace four water pumps as soon as their performance drops below certain quality levels. The operator expects this to be the case after 15 years of service. The expected cost of replacing the pumps is CU 1,000. The operator's best estimate is that the service potential of the pumps is consumed evenly over time and provision for the costs is made on this basis from inception of the service concession arrangement until the date of expected replacement. The provision is measured at the net present value of the amounts expected to be paid, using the operator's discount rate of 5%. The amount provided in the first year can be calculated as CU 33.67. Assuming no changes to estimates, in 15 years CU 1,000 would have been provided and would be utilised in replacing the pumps. The provision would be adjusted on a cumulative basis to take account of changes in estimates to the cost of replacement pumps, the manner in which they are wearing out or changes to the operator's discount rate.

The Interpretations Committee has also provided an example in Illustrative Example 2, the intangible asset model, of how operational expenditure might be accounted for in accordance with IAS 37. Although this illustration is in the context of an intangible asset, IAS 37 can apply to maintenance and other obligations whatever model applies. Major maintenance, in this case the requirement to resurface the road, will be recognised as the best estimate of the expenditure required to settle the present obligation at the reporting date and it is suggested that this might 'arise as a consequence of use of the road', therefore increasing in measurable annual increments. *[IFRIC 12.IE19]*. The basis for accounting for such obligations is discussed further in Chapter 27.

Example 26.10: The Intangible Asset Model – recording the operations phase

The terms of the arrangement are the same as in Example 26.4 above. The contract costs and initial measurement of the intangible asset are set out in Table 1 and Table 2 in that example.

Resurfacing obligations

The operator's resurfacing obligation arises as a consequence of use of the road during the operating phase. It is recognised and measured in accordance with IAS 37, i.e. at the best estimate of the expenditure required to settle the present obligation at the reporting date.

For the purpose of this illustration, it is assumed that the terms of the operator's contractual obligation are such that the best estimate of the expenditure required to settle the obligation at any date is proportional to the number of vehicles that have used the road by that date and increases by €17 (discounted to a current value) each year. The operator discounts the provision to its present value in accordance with IAS 37. The income statement charge each period is:

Table 3 Resurfacing obligation

Year	3	4	5	6	7	8	Total
	€	€	€	€	€	€	€
Obligation arising in year (€17 discounted at 6%)	12	13	14	15	16	17	87
Increase in earlier years' provision arising from passage of time	–	1	1	2	4	5	13
Total expense recognised in income statement	12	14	15	17	20	22	100

Overview of cash flows, income statement and statement of financial position

For the purpose of this illustration, it is assumed that the operator finances the arrangement wholly with debt and retained profits. It pays interest at 6.7% a year on outstanding debt. If the cash flows and fair values remain the same as those forecast, the operator's cash flows, income statement and statement of financial position over the duration of the arrangement will be:

Table 4 Cash flows

Year	1	2	3	4	5	6	7	8	9	10	Total
	€	€	€	€	€	€	€	€	€	€	€
Receipts	–	–	200	200	200	200	200	200	200	200	1,600
Contract costs	(500)	(500)	(10)	(10)	(10)	(10)	(10)	(110)	(10)	(10)	(1,180)
Borrowing costs†	–	(34)	(69)	(61)	(53)	(43)	(33)	(23)	(19)	(7)	(342)
Net inflow/ (outflow)	(500)	(534)	121	129	137	147	157	67	171	183	78

† Debt at start of year (table 6) × 6.7%

Table 5 Income statement

Year	1	2	3	4	5	6	7	8	9	10	Total
	€	€	€	€	€	€	€	€	€	€	€
Revenue	525	525	200	200	200	200	200	200	200	200	2,650
Amortisation	–	–	(135)	(135)	(136)	(136)	(136)	(136)	(135)	(135)	(1,084)
Resurfacing expense	–	–	(12)	(14)	(15)	(17)	(20)	(22)	–	–	(100)
Other operating costs†	(500)	(500)	(10)	(10)	(10)	(10)	(10)	(10)	(10)	(10)	(1,080)
Borrowing costs* (table 4)	–	–	(69)	(61)	(53)	(43)	(33)	(23)	(19)	(7)	(308)
Net profits	25	25	(26)	(20)	(14)	(6)	1	9	36	48	78

* Borrowing costs are capitalised during the construction phase

† Table 1

Table 6 Statement of financial position

End of Year	1	2	3	4	5	6	7	8	9	10
	€	€	€	€	€	€	€	€	€	€
Intangible asset	525	1,084	949	814	678	542	406	270	135	–
Cash/ (debt)*	(500)	(1,034)	(913)	(784)	(647)	(500)	(343)	(276)	(105)	78
Resurfacing obligation	–	–	(12)	(26)	(41)	(58)	(78)	–	–	–
Net assets	25	50	24	4	(10)	(16)	(15)	(6)	30	78

* Debt at start of year plus net cash flow in year (table 4)

To make this illustration as clear as possible, it has been assumed that the arrangement period is only ten years and that the operator's annual receipts are constant over the period. In practice, arrangement periods may be much longer and annual revenue may increase with time. In such circumstances, the changes in net profit from year to year could be greater.

5.3 Items provided to the operator by the grantor

Following the basic principles underlying the proposed accounting treatment and under both models, infrastructure items to which the operator is given access by the grantor for the purpose of the service concession are not recognised as its property, plant and equipment. *[IFRIC 12.27]*. This is because they remain under the control of the grantor.

There is a different treatment for assets that are given to the operator as part of the consideration for the concession that can be kept or dealt with as the operator wishes. These assets are not to be treated as government grants as defined in IAS 20. Instead, they are brought into account by the operator at fair value, together with a liability in respect of any unfulfilled obligations assumed in exchange for the assets. *[IFRIC 12.27]*.

What this means is that an operator that has been given a licence or similar arrangement over a piece of land on which a hospital is to be built does not recognise the land as an asset. If, on the other hand, the operator has been given a piece of surplus land on which it can build private housing for sale, it will recognise an asset. The consideration, which is the fair value of that land, will be aggregated with the remainder of the consideration for the transaction and accounted for according to the model being used.

6 DISCLOSURE REQUIREMENTS: SIC-29

IFRIC 12 has no specific disclosure requirements although the disclosure requirements of the various applicable standards (such as IFRS 7 – *Financial Instruments: Disclosures* – and IAS 38) will have to be made as appropriate. SIC-29, which pre-dates IFRIC 12 by several years, includes additional disclosure requirements. It is important to note that the scope of SIC-29 is not defined in terms of IFRIC 12 and is potentially broader than IFRIC 12's scope as described above. It applies to a type of transaction that is described although not really defined and which does not depend on the control criteria described at 3 above. It also applies to both sides of the transaction, whereas IFRIC 12 applies only to the operator under the concession agreement.

SIC-29 describes service concessions as arrangements in which an entity (the operator) provides services on behalf of another entity (the grantor, which may be a public or private sector entity, including a governmental body) that give the public access to major economic and social facilities. The examples of service concession arrangements given by SIC-29 include water treatment and supply facilities, motorways, car parks, tunnels, bridges, airports and telecommunication networks. *[SIC-29.1].*

SIC-29 states that the common characteristic of all service concession arrangements is that the operator both receives a right and incurs an obligation to provide public services. *[SIC-29.3].* It excludes from its scope an entity outsourcing the operation of its internal services (e.g. employee cafeteria, building maintenance, and accounting or information technology functions). *[SIC-29.1].* This means that some of the arrangements that do not include the construction of a major capital asset, as discussed above, may not be caught by the requirements of the SIC, although there is no hard-and-fast dividing line between service concessions and outsourcing arrangements. For example, a contract between a government department and an operator to maintain the existing computer system, including replacement of hardware and software as appropriate, may be outside the scope of SIC-29.

SIC-29 summarises the rights and obligations as follows:

For the period of the concession, the operator has received from the grantor:

(a) the right to provide services that give the public access to major economic and social facilities; and

(b) in some cases, the right to use specified tangible assets, intangible assets, and/or financial assets,

in exchange for the operator:

(a) committing to provide the services according to certain terms and conditions during the concession period; and

(b) when applicable, committing to return at the end of the concession period the rights received at the beginning of the concession period and/or acquired during the concession period. *[SIC-29.2].*

The disclosure requirements in respect of such projects are set out below:

SIC-29 requires disclosure in addition to that required by other standards that may cover part of the transaction, such as IAS 16 (see Chapter 18), IAS 17 (see Chapter 24) and IAS 38 (see Chapter 17). *[SIC-29.5].* All aspects of a service concession arrangement should be considered in determining the appropriate disclosures in the notes to the financial statements. *[SIC-29.6].*

An operator and a grantor should disclose the following in each period:

(a) a description of the arrangement;

(b) significant terms of the arrangement that may affect the amount, timing and certainty of future cash flows (e.g. the period of the concession, re-pricing dates and the basis upon which re-pricing or re-negotiation is determined);

(c) the nature and extent (e.g. quantity, time period or amount as appropriate) of:

  (i) rights to use specified assets;

  (ii) obligations to provide or rights to expect provision of services;

  (iii) obligations to acquire or build items of property, plant and equipment;

  (iv) obligations to deliver or rights to receive specified assets at the end of the concession period;

  (v) renewal and termination options; and

  (vi) other rights and obligations (e.g. major overhauls);

(d) changes in the arrangement occurring during the period; and

(e) how the service arrangement has been classified.

These disclosures should be provided individually for each service concession arrangement or in aggregate for each class of service concession arrangements. A class is a grouping of service concession arrangements involving services of a similar nature (e.g. toll collections, telecommunications and water treatment services). *[SIC-29.6-7].*

IFRIC 12 added a requirement to disclose 'the amount of revenue and profits or losses recognised in the period on exchanging construction services for a financial asset and an intangible asset'. *[SIC-29.6A].*

Vinci has made aggregate disclosures for the principal terms of its arrangements. The following extract is part only of the extensive disclosures that separately address concession arrangements under the financial asset model and mixed model.

Extract 26.5: VINCI SA (2012)

Notes to the consolidated financial statements [extract]

F. Notes on the main features of concession and PPP contracts

25. Controlled subsidiaries' concession contracts – intangible asset model [extract]

25.1 Main features of concession contracts [extract]

The main features of contracts for the concessions operated by controlled subsidiaries and accounted for using the intangible asset model are as follows:

	Control and regulation of prices by concession grantor	**Remuneration paid by**	**Grant or guarantee from concession grantor**	**Residual value**	**Concession end date**	**Accounting model**
Motorway and road infrastructure (including bridges and tunnels)						
ASF Group						
ASF 2,714 km of toll motorways, of which 21 km at project stage (France)	Pricing law as defined in the concession contract. Price increases subject to agreement by grantor	Users	Nil	Infrastructure returned to grantor for no consideration at the end of the contract unless purchased before term by the grantor on the basis of the economic value	2033	Intangible asset
Escota 459 km of toll motorways (France)	Pricing law as defined in the concession contract. Price increases subject to agreement by grantor	Users	Nil	Infrastructure returned to grantor for no consideration at the end of the contract unless purchased before term by the grantor on the basis of the economic value	2027	Intangible asset

	Control and regulation of prices by concession grantor	Remuneration paid by	Grant or guarantee from concession grantor	Residual value	Concession end date or average duration	Accounting model
Parking facilities						
VINCI park 356,726 parking spaces in 164 towns under 366 concession contracts (France and other European countries)	Indexed maximum prices generally set in contracts	Users	If applicable, grants for equipment or operating grants and/or guaranteed revenue paid by grantor	Nil	26 years (weighted average remaining period of concession contracts)	Intangible asset and/or financial asset

25.2 Commitments made under concession contracts – intangible asset model [extract]
Contractual investment, renewal or financing obligations

(in € millions)	31/12/2012	31/12/2011
ASF/Escota	1,869.9	2,429.5
Cofiroute	837.8	906.4
VINCI park	52.6	64.4
Société Concessionnaire Aéroports du Grand Ouest	388.5	350.4
Other	135.3	24.9
Total	**3,284.1**	**3,775.6**

Contractual capital investment obligations for ASF and Escota relate in particular to the relief section on the A9 near Montpellier and the green motorway package.
Cofiroute's contractual capital investment obligations comprise the green motorway package and the investments provided for under the 2011-2014 master plan.
The above amounts do not include obligations relating to maintenance expenditure on infrastructure under concession.
The investments by motorway concession companies (ASF, Escota, Cofiroute and Arcour) are financed by issuing bonds on the markets, taking out new loans from the European Investment Bank (EIB) or drawing on their available credit facilities.

Collateral security connected with the financing of concessions
Some concession operating companies have given collateral security to guarantee the financing of their investments in concession infrastructure. These break down as follows:

(in € millions)	**Start date**	**End date**	Amount
Arcour	2008	2045	600.0
VINCI Park(*)	2006	2026	385.2
Other concession operating companies			109.7

(*) *Including shares in subsidiaries pledged to guarantee a bank loan of €500 million taken out at the end of June 2006.*

Chapter 26

Vinci also disclosed the revenue and profit earned from its concession arrangements. The following extract discloses revenue from concessions as a component of revenue by business line.

Extract 26.6: VINCI SA (2012)

Notes to the consolidated financial statements [extract]

C. Information by operating segment [extract]

1. Revenue [extract]

1.1 Breakdown of revenue by business line

(in € millions)	2012	2011	Change
Concessions	**5,354.0**	**5,296.7**	**1.1%**
VINCI Autoroutes	4,439.3	4,409.0	0.7%
VINCI Concessions	914.7	887.6	3.1%
Contracting	**33,090.2**	**31,495.2**	**5.1%**
VINCI Energies	9,016.6	8,666.5	4.0%
Eurovia	8,746.8	8,721.6	0.3%
VINCI Construction	15,326.8	14,107.2	8.6%
VINCI Immobilier	**810.9**	**698.1**	**16.2%**
Intragroup eliminations	**(621.5)**	**(534.1)**	**16.4%**
Revenue(*)	**38,633.6**	**36,955.9**	**4.5%**
Concession subsidiaries' revenue derived from works carried out by non-Group companies	549.6	690.2	–20.4%
Total revenue	39,183.2	37,646.1	4.1%

(*) Excluding concession subsidiaries' revenue derived from works carried out by non-Group companies.

References

1 FRS 5, *Reporting the substance of transactions*, ASB, April 1994 (with subsequent amendments), Application Note F, *Private finance initiative and similar contracts.*

2 IPSAS 32, *Service Concession Arrangements: Grantor,* International Public Sector Accounting Standards Board, October 2011

3 *IFRIC Update*, September 2005.

4 *IFRIC Update*, September 2005.

5 *IASB Update*, July 2013.

6 *IFRIC Update*, January 2013.

7 *IFRIC Update*, March and May 2012.

8 *IFRIC Update*, March and May 2012.

9 *IFRIC Update*, March 2006.

10 IAS 38 (2007), *Intangible Assets*, IASB, 2007 Bound Volume, para. 98 stated that 'there is rarely, if ever, persuasive evidence to support an amortisation method for intangible assets with finite useful lives that results in a lower amount of accumulated amortisation than under the straight-line method.' This was removed by *Improvements to IFRSs*, May 2008.

11 Exposure Draft ED/2012/5: *Clarification of Acceptable Methods of Depreciation and Amortisation – Proposed amendments to IAS 16 and IAS 38*, IASB, December 2012, para. 98A.

12 *IASB Work Plan – projected timetable as at 29 July 2013*, IASB.

13 ED/2012/5, para. 130G.

14 ED/2012/5, para. 98B.

15 ED/2012/5, paras. BC4-BC7.

16 *IFRIC Update*, September 2004.

17 *IFRIC Update*, March and May 2012.

18 *IFRIC Update*, March 2012.

19 *IFRIC Update*, January 2013.

20 *IASB Update*, July 2013.

21 *IFRIC Update*, March 2012.

22 *IFRIC Update*, September 2006.

Chapter 27 Provisions, contingent liabilities and contingent assets

Chapter 27

List of examples

Chapter 27 Provisions, contingent liabilities and contingent assets

1 INTRODUCTION

1.1 Background

IAS 37 – *Provisions, Contingent Liabilities and Contingent Assets* – applies to all provisions, contingent liabilities and contingent assets, except those relating to executory contracts that are not onerous and those provisions covered by another Standard. *[IAS 37.1]*. Thus, it only deals with provisions that are shown as liabilities in a statement of financial position, since the definition of a provision in IAS 37 is 'a liability of uncertain timing or amount'. *[IAS 37.10]*. IAS 37 does not deal with items termed 'provisions' that reduce the carrying amount of assets such as depreciation, impairment of assets and doubtful debts. *[IAS 37.7]*.

IAS 37 was developed in parallel with the equivalent UK standard, FRS 12 – *Provisions, Contingent Liabilities and Contingent Assets* – under a joint project between the IASC and the UK Accounting Standards Board (ASB). As a result, the two standards were published on the same day in September 1998. There were no differences of substance between the requirements of the two standards – indeed the text is still mostly identical (apart from consequential amendments made to IAS 37 as a result of later standards issued by the IASB) – but FRS 12 includes slightly more guidance on two areas:

- recognition of an asset when a provision is recognised (see 3.3 below); and
- the discount rate to be used in the net present value calculation (see 4.3 below).

For some time the IASB has considered amending IAS 37 and an exposure draft was issued in June 2005. Subsequent deliberation, including round-table meetings held with constituents to discuss their views, resulted in the Board revising its proposals and issuing a second exposure draft in January 2010. In the months that followed, other documents were issued, including:

- a working draft of a proposed new IFRS, combining the original proposals with the exposure draft on measurement and incorporating other amendments identified by the Board during its deliberations;[1] and
- an IASB Staff Paper on discussing the recognition of liabilities arising from lawsuits.[2]

Under the Board's proposals, the terms 'provision', 'contingent liability' and 'contingent asset' (see 1.3 below) would be eliminated. Instead, a new standard would refer simply to 'liabilities'. The only assets addressed by the exposure draft were reimbursement rights. For these, the current recognition requirement of 'virtual certainty' (see 4.5 below) would be removed; such rights being recognised unless they cannot be measured reliably.[3] Items currently meeting the definition of contingent assets in IAS 37 (see 3.2.2 below) were intended to be brought within the scope of IAS 38 – *Intangible Assets*.

Work on the liabilities project was effectively suspended pending the outcome of the Board's 2011 consultation on its future agenda. The IASB indicated that it expected to issue a further exposure draft of the revised standard following the conclusion of that consultation.[4] Instead, in May 2012, the IASB declared its unanimous support to give priority to initiating a research programme to include, among other topics, non-financial liabilities.[5] At the time of writing, no timetable has been established for the start of this research.

1.2 Interpretations related to the application of IAS 37

The Interpretations Committee has issued a number of pronouncements relating to the application of IAS 37 (although one of them was subsequently withdrawn).

1.2.1 IFRIC 1

IFRIC 1 – *Changes in Existing Decommissioning, Restoration and Similar Liabilities* – provides guidance on how to account for the effect of changes in the measurement of existing provisions for obligations to dismantle, remove or restore items of property, plant and equipment. This is discussed at 6.3 below.

1.2.2 IFRIC 3

Another issue considered by the Interpretations Committee was how to account for a 'cap and trade' emission rights scheme. In December 2004, the IASB issued IFRIC 3 – *Emission Rights* – but this was later withdrawn in June 2005. This interpretation, *inter alia*, required that as emissions are made, a liability was to be recognised for the obligation to deliver allowances equal to the emissions that had been made by the entity. Such liability was a provision within the scope of IAS 37, and was to be measured at the present market value of the number of allowances required to cover emissions made up to the end of the reporting period. Accounting for liabilities associated with emissions trading schemes is discussed at 6.5 below.

1.2.3 IFRIC 5

IFRIC 5 – *Rights to Interests arising from Decommissioning, Restoration and Environmental Rehabilitation Funds* – deals with the accounting by an entity when it participates in a 'decommissioning fund', the purpose of which is to segregate assets to fund some or all of the costs of its decommissioning or environmental liabilities for which it has to make a provision under IAS 37. This is discussed at 6.3.3 below.

1.2.4 IFRIC 6

IFRIC 6 – *Liabilities arising from Participating in a Specific Market – Waste Electrical and Electronic Equipment* – provides guidance on the accounting for liabilities for waste management costs. This clarifies when certain producers of electrical goods will need to recognise a liability for the cost of waste management relating to the decommissioning of waste electrical and electronic equipment (historical waste) supplied to private households. This is discussed at 6.7 below.

1.2.5 IFRIC 21

IFRIC 21 – *Levies* – addresses the recognition of a liability to pay a levy imposed by government if that liability is within the scope of IAS 37. It also addresses the accounting for a liability to pay a levy whose timing and amount is certain. See section 6.8 below.

The number of other Interpretations that refer to IAS 37 demonstrates just how pervasive the consideration of non-financial liabilities is in developing accounting practice. For example, IAS 37 is also referred to in IFRIC 12 – *Service Concession Arrangements* (see Chapter 26); IFRIC 13 – *Customer Loyalty Programmes* (see Chapter 28); IFRIC 14 – *IAS 19 – The Limit on a Defined Benefit Asset, Minimum Funding Requirements and their Interaction* (see Chapter 31); and IFRIC 15 – *Agreements for the Construction of Real Estate* (see Chapter 23).

1.3 Terms used in this chapter

The following terms are used in this chapter with the meanings specified:

Term	Definition
Provision	A liability of uncertain timing or amount. *[IAS 37.10]*
Liability	A present obligation of the entity arising from past events, the settlement of which is expected to result in an outflow from the entity of resources embodying economic benefits. *[IAS 37.10]*
Obligating event	An event that creates a legal or constructive obligation that results in an entity having no realistic alternative to settling that obligation. *[IAS 37.10]*
Legal obligation	An obligation that derives from a contract (through its explicit or implicit terms); legislation; or other operation of law. *[IAS 37.10]*
Constructive obligation	An obligation that derives from an entity's actions where: (a) by an established pattern of past practice, published policies or a sufficiently specific current statement, the entity has indicated to other parties that it will accept certain responsibilities; and (b) as a result, the entity has created a valid expectation on the part of those other parties that it will discharge those responsibilities. *[IAS 37.10]*.

Term	Definition
Contingent liability	(a) a possible obligation that arises from past events and whose existence will be confirmed only by the occurrence or non-occurrence of one or more uncertain future events not wholly within the control of the entity; or (b) a present obligation that arises from past events but is not recognised because: (i) it is not probable that an outflow of resources embodying economic benefits will be required to settle the obligation; or (ii) the amount of the obligation cannot be measured with sufficient reliability. *[IAS 37.10]*
Contingent asset	A possible asset that arises from past events and whose existence will be confirmed only by the occurrence or non-occurrence of one or more uncertain future events not wholly within the control of the entity. *[IAS 37.10]*
Onerous contract	A contract in which the unavoidable costs of meeting the obligations under the contract exceed the economic benefits expected to be received under it. *[IAS 37.10]*
Restructuring	A programme that is planned and controlled by management, and materially changes either: (a) the scope of a business undertaken by an entity; or (b) the manner in which that business is conducted. *[IAS 37.10]*.
Executory contract	A contract under which neither party has performed any of its obligations or both parties have partially performed their obligations to an equal extent. *[IAS 37.3]*
Levy	An outflow of resources embodying economic benefits that is imposed by governments on entities in accordance with legislation (i.e. laws and or regulations), other than: (a) those outflows of resources that are within the scope of other Standards (such as income taxes that are within the scope of IAS 12); and (b) fines or other penalties that are imposed for breaches of the legislation. *[IFRIC 21.4]*.
Government	Refers to government, government agencies and similar bodies whether local, national or international. *[IFRIC 21.4]*

2 OBJECTIVE AND SCOPE OF IAS 37

2.1 Objective

The objective of IAS 37 'is to ensure that appropriate recognition criteria and measurement bases are applied to provisions, contingent liabilities and contingent assets and that sufficient information is disclosed in the notes to enable users to understand their nature, timing and amount'. *[IAS 37 Objective]*.

2.2 Scope of IAS 37

The standard is required to be applied by all entities in accounting for provisions, contingent liabilities and contingent assets, except those arising from executory contracts (unless the contract is onerous) and those covered by another standard. *[IAS 37.1]*.

The following table lists the specific types of transaction or circumstances referred to in the standard that might give rise to a provision, contingent liability or contingent asset. In some cases, the transaction is identified in IAS 37 only to prohibit recognition of any liability, such as for future operating losses and repairs and maintenance of owned assets (see 5 below). This chapter does not address those items identified below as falling outside the scope of the standard.

Types of transaction or circumstances referred to	*In scope*	*Out of scope*	*Another standard*
Restructuring costs	•		
Environmental penalties or clean-up costs	•		
Decommissioning costs	•		
Product warranties / refunds	•		
Legal claims	•		
Reimbursement rights	•		
Future operating costs (training, relocation, etc.)	•		
Future operating losses	•		
Onerous contracts	•		
Repairs and maintenance costs	•		
Provisions for depreciation, impairment or doubtful debts		•	
Executory contracts (unless onerous)		•	
Construction contracts		•	IAS 11
Income taxes		•	IAS 12
Leases (unless onerous)		•	IAS 17
Employee benefits		•	IAS 19
Insurance contracts issued by insurers to policyholders		•	IFRS 4
Contingent liabilities acquired in a business combination		•	IFRS 3
Financial instruments and financial guarantees within the scope of IAS 39 and IFRS 9		•	IAS 39 / IFRS 9
Trade payables or accruals		•	

2.2.1 Items outside the scope of IAS 37

2.2.1.A Executory contracts, except where the contract is onerous

The standard uses the term executory contracts to mean 'contracts under which neither party has performed any of its obligations, or both parties have partially performed their obligations to an equal extent'. *[IAS 37.3].* This means that contracts such as supplier purchase contracts and capital commitments, which would otherwise fall within the scope of the standard, are exempt.

This exemption prevents the statement of financial position from being grossed up for all manner of commitments that an entity has entered into, and in respect of which it is debatable whether (or at what point) such contracts give rise to items that meet the definition of a liability or an asset. In particular, the need for this exemption arises because the liability framework on which this standard is based includes the concept of a constructive obligation (see 3.1.1 below) which, when applied to executory contracts would otherwise give rise to an inordinate number of contingent promises requiring recognition or disclosure.

An executory contract will still require recognition as a provision if the contract becomes onerous. *[IAS 37.3].* Onerous contracts are dealt with at 6.2 below.

2.2.1.B Items covered by another standard

Where another standard deals with a specific type of provision, contingent liability or contingent asset, it should be applied instead of IAS 37. Examples given in the standard are:

- construction contracts (dealt with in IAS 11 – *Construction Contracts* – see Chapter 23);
- income taxes (dealt with in IAS 12 – *Income Taxes* – see Chapter 29);
- leases (dealt with in IAS 17 – *Leases* – see Chapter 24). However, the standard states that if operating leases become onerous, there are no specific requirements within IAS 17 to address the issue and thus IAS 37 applies to such leases;
- employee benefits (dealt with in IAS 19 – *Employee Benefits* – see Chapter 31); and
- insurance contracts (dealt with in IFRS 4 – *Insurance Contracts* – see Chapter 51). However, IAS 37 requires an insurer to apply the standard to provisions, contingent liabilities and contingent assets, other than those arising from its contractual obligations and rights under insurance contracts within the scope of IFRS 4. *[IAS 37.5].*

Whilst IAS 37 contains no reference to it, IFRS 3 – *Business Combinations* – states that the requirements in IAS 37 do not apply in determining which contingent liabilities to recognise as of the acquisition date (see 4.9 below and Chapter 9 at 5.6.1). *[IFRS 3.23].*

In addition, the standard does not apply to financial instruments (including guarantees) that are within the scope of IAS 39 and IFRS 9 – *Financial Instruments* (see Chapter 40). *[IAS 37.2].* This means that guarantees of third party borrowings (including those of subsidiaries, associates and joint arrangements) are not covered by IAS 37.

IAS 37 also notes that some amounts treated as provisions may relate to the recognition of revenue, for example where an entity gives guarantees in exchange for a fee, and states that the standard does not address the recognition of revenue. This is dealt with by IAS 18 – *Revenue* (see Chapter 28), and IAS 37 does not change the requirements of that standard. *[IAS 37.6]*.

The standard applies to provisions for restructurings, including discontinued operations. However, it emphasises that when a restructuring meets the definition of a discontinued operation under IFRS 5 – *Non-current Assets Held for Sale and Discontinued Operations*, additional disclosures may be required under that standard (see Chapter 4 at 3). *[IAS 37.9]*.

The standard defines a provision as 'a liability of uncertain timing or amount'. *[IAS 37.10]*. Thus it only deals with provisions that are shown as liabilities in a statement of financial position. The term 'provision' is also used widely in the context of items such as depreciation, impairment of assets and doubtful debts. Such 'provisions' are not addressed in IAS 37, since these are adjustments to the carrying amounts of assets. *[IAS 37.7]*.

2.2.2 Provisions compared to other liabilities

IAS 37 states that the feature distinguishing provisions from other liabilities, such as trade payables and accruals, is the existence of 'uncertainty about the timing or amount of the future expenditure required in settlement'. *[IAS 37.11]*. The standard compares provisions to:

(a) trade payables – liabilities to pay for goods or services that have been received or supplied and have been invoiced or formally agreed with the supplier; and

(b) accruals – liabilities to pay for goods or services that have been received or supplied but have not been paid, invoiced or formally agreed with the supplier, including amounts due to employees (for example, amounts relating to accrued vacation pay). Although it is sometimes necessary to estimate the amount or timing of accruals, the uncertainty is generally much less than for provisions.

IAS 37 also notes that accruals are often reported as part of trade and other payables whereas provisions are reported separately. *[IAS 37.11]*.

For trade payables and their associated accruals, there is little uncertainty regarding either the amount of the obligation (which would be determined by the contracted price for the goods and services being provided) or of the timing of settlement (which would normally occur within an agreed period following transfer of the goods and services in question and the issue of an invoice). In practice, however, contracts can be more complex and give rise to a wide range of possible outcomes in terms of the amount or timing of payment. In these circumstances, the difference between provisions and other liabilities is less obvious and judgement may be required to determine where the requirement to make an estimate of an obligation indicates a level of uncertainty about timing or amount that is more indicative of a provision. Such judgements, if significant to the amounts recognised in the financial statements, would merit disclosure (see Chapter 3 at 5.1.1.B). *[IAS 1.122]*.

One reason why this distinction matters is that provisions are subject to narrative disclosure requirements regarding the nature of the obligation and the uncertainties over timing and amount; and to quantitative disclosures of movements arising from their use, remeasurement or release that do not apply to other payables (see 7.1 below). In fact, although questions of recognition and measurement are important, transparency of disclosure is also a very significant matter in relation to accounting for provisions and ensuring that their effect is properly understood by users of the financial statements.

2.2.3 Distinction between provisions and contingent liabilities

There is an area of overlap between provisions and contingent liabilities. Although contingent liabilities are clearly not as likely to give rise to outflows, similar judgments are made in assessing the nature of the uncertainties, the need for disclosures and ultimately the recognition of a liability in the financial statements. The standard notes that in a general sense, all provisions are contingent because they are uncertain in timing or amount. However, in IAS 37 the term 'contingent' is used for liabilities and assets that are not recognised because their existence will be confirmed only by the occurrence of one or more uncertain future events not wholly within the entity's control. In addition, the term 'contingent liability' is used for liabilities that do not meet the recognition criteria for provisions. *[IAS 37.12]*.

Accordingly, the standard distinguishes between:

(a) provisions – which are recognised as liabilities (assuming that a reliable estimate can be made) because they are present obligations and it is probable that an outflow of resources embodying economic benefits will be required to settle the obligations; and

(b) contingent liabilities – which are not recognised as liabilities because they are either:
   (i) possible obligations, as it has yet to be confirmed whether the entity has a present obligation that could lead to an outflow of resources embodying economic benefits; or
   (ii) present obligations that do not meet the recognition criteria in the standard because either it is not probable that an outflow of resources embodying economic benefits will be required to settle the obligation, or a sufficiently reliable estimate of the amount of the obligation cannot be made. *[IAS 37.13]*.

3 RECOGNITION

3.1 Determining when a provision should be recognised

IAS 37 requires that a provision should be recognised when:

(a) an entity has a present obligation (legal or constructive) as a result of a past event;

(b) it is probable that an outflow of resources embodying economic benefits will be required to settle the obligation; and

(c) a reliable estimate can be made of the amount of the obligation.

No provision should be recognised unless all of these conditions are met. *[IAS 37.14]*.

Each of these three conditions is discussed separately below.

3.1.1 'An entity has a present obligation (legal or constructive) as a result of a past event'

The standard defines both legal and constructive obligations. The definition of a legal obligation is fairly straightforward and uncontroversial; it refers to an obligation that derives from a contract (through its explicit or implicit terms), legislation or other operation of law. *[IAS 37.10]*.

The definition of a constructive obligation, on the other hand, may give rise to more problems of interpretation. A constructive obligation is defined as an obligation that derives from an entity's actions where:

(a) by an established pattern of past practice, published policies or a sufficiently specific current statement, the entity has indicated to other parties that it will accept certain responsibilities; and

(b) as a result, the entity has created a valid expectation on the part of those other parties that it will discharge those responsibilities. *[IAS 37.10]*.

The following examples in IAS 37 illustrate how a constructive obligation is created.

Example 27.1: Recognising a provision because of a constructive obligation

Scenario 1: Environmental policy – contaminated land

An entity in the oil industry operates in a country with no environmental legislation. However, it has a widely published environmental policy in which it undertakes to clean up all contamination that it causes and it has a record of honouring this published policy. During the period the entity causes contamination to some land in this country.

In these circumstances, the contamination of the land gives rise to a constructive obligation because the entity (through its published policy and record of honouring it) has created a valid expectation on the part of those affected by it that the entity will clean up the site. *[IAS 37 IE Example 2B]*.

Scenario 2: Refunds policy – product returns

A retail store has a generally known policy of refunding purchases by dissatisfied customers, even though it is under no legal obligation to do so.

In these circumstances, the sale of its products gives rise to a constructive obligation because the entity (through its reputation for providing refunds) has created a valid expectation on the part of customers that a refund will be given if they are dissatisfied with their purchase. *[IAS 37 IE Example 4]*.

These examples demonstrate that the essence of a constructive obligation is the creation of a valid expectation that the entity is irrevocably committed to accepting and discharging its responsibilities.

The standard states that in almost all cases it will be clear whether a past event has given rise to a present obligation. However, it acknowledges that there will be some rare cases, such as a lawsuit against an entity, where this will not be so because the occurrence of certain events or the consequences of those events are disputed. *[IAS 37.16]*. When it is not clear whether there is a present obligation, a 'more likely than not' evaluation (taking into account all available evidence) is deemed to be sufficient to require recognition of a provision at the end of the reporting period. *[IAS 37.15]*.

The evidence to be considered includes, for example, the opinion of experts together with any additional evidence provided by events after the reporting period. If on the basis of such evidence it is concluded that a present obligation is more likely than not to exist at the end of the reporting period, a provision will be required (assuming that the other recognition criteria are met). *[IAS 37.16]*. This is an apparent relaxation of the standard's first criterion for the recognition of a provision as set out at 3.1 above, which requires there to be a definite obligation, not just a probable one. It also confuses slightly the question of the existence of an obligation with the probability criterion, which strictly speaking relates to whether it is more likely than not that there will be an outflow of resources (see 3.1.2 below). However, this interpretation is confirmed in IAS 10 – *Events after the Reporting Period*, which includes 'the settlement after the reporting period of a court case that confirms that the entity had a present obligation at the end of the reporting period' as an example of an adjusting event. *[IAS 10.9]*.

The second half of this condition uses the phrase 'as a result of a past event'. This is based on the concept of an obligating event, which the standard defines as 'an event that creates a legal or constructive obligation and that results in an entity having no realistic alternative to settling that obligation'. *[IAS 37.10]*. The standard says that this will be the case only:

(a) where the settlement of the obligation can be enforced by law; or

(b) in the case of a constructive obligation, where the event (which may be an action of the entity) creates valid expectations in other parties that the entity will discharge the obligation. *[IAS 37.17]*.

This concept of obligating event is used in the standard when discussing specific examples of recognition, which we consider further at 6 below. However, it is worth mentioning here that this concept, like that of a constructive obligation, is open to interpretation and requires the exercise of judgement, as the obligating event is not always easy to identify.

The standard emphasises that the financial statements deal with the financial position of an entity at the end of its reporting period, not its possible position in the future. Accordingly, no provision should be recognised for costs that need to be incurred to operate in the future. The only liabilities to be recognised are those that exist at the end of the reporting period. *[IAS 37.18]*. It is not always easy to distinguish between the current state at the reporting date and the entity's future possible position, especially where IAS 37 requires an assessment to be made based on the probability of obligations and expectations as to their outcome. However, when considering these questions it is important to ensure that provisions are not recognised for liabilities that arise from events after the reporting period (see Chapter 34 at 2).

Example 27.2: No provision without a past obligating event

The government introduces a number of changes to the income tax system. As a result of these changes, an entity in the financial services sector will need to retrain a large proportion of its administrative and sales staff in order to ensure continued compliance with financial services regulation. At the end of the reporting period, no training has taken place.

In these circumstances, no event has taken place at the reporting date to create an obligation. Only once the training has taken place will there be a present obligation as a result of a past event. *[IAS 37 IE Example 7]*.

IAS 37 prohibits certain provisions that might otherwise qualify to be recognised by stating that it 'is only those obligations arising from past events existing independently of an entity's future actions (i.e. the future conduct of its business) that are recognised as provisions'. In contrast to situations where the entity's past conduct has created an obligation to incur expenditure (such as to rectify environmental damage already caused), a commercial or legal requirement to incur expenditure in order to operate in a particular way in the future, will not of itself justify the recognition of a provision. It argues that because the entity can avoid the expenditure by its future actions, for example by changing its method of operation, there is no present obligation for the future expenditure. *[IAS 37.19]*.

Example 27.3: Obligations must exist independently of an entity's future actions

Under legislation passed in 2013, an entity is required to fix smoke filters in its factories by 30 June 2015. The entity has not fitted the smoke filters.

At 31 December 2014, the end of the reporting period, no event has taken place to create an obligation. Only once the smoke filters are fitted or the legislation takes effect, will there be a present obligation as a result of a past event, either for the cost of fitting smoke filters or for fines under the legislation.

At 31 December 2015, there is still no obligating event to justify provision for the cost of fitting the smoke filters required under the legislation because the filters have not been fitted. However, an obligation may exist as at the reporting date to pay fines or penalties under the legislation because the entity is operating its factory in a non-compliant way. However, a provision would only be recognised for the best estimate of any fines and penalties if, as at 31 December 2015, it is determined to be more likely than not that such fines and penalties will be imposed. *[IAS 37 IE Example 6]*.

The standard expects strict application of the requirement that, to qualify for recognition, an obligation must exist independently of an entity's future actions. Even if a failure to incur certain costs would result in a legal requirement to discontinue an entity's operations, this example states that no provision can be recognised. As discussed at 5.2 below, IAS 37 considers the example of an airline required by law to overhaul its aircraft once every three years. It concludes that no provision is recognised because the entity can avoid the requirement to perform the overhaul, for example by replacing the aircraft before the three year period has expired. *[IAS 37 IE Example 11B]*.

Centrica plc describes its interpretation of the group's obligations under UK legislation to install energy efficiency improvement measures in domestic households in a manner consistent with Example 27.3 above.

Extract 27.1: Centrica plc (Interim results for the period ended 30 June 2013)

NOTES TO THE CONDENSED INTERIM FINANCIAL STATEMENTS [extract]

3. Accounting policies [extract]

(d) Update to critical accounting judgements in applying the Group's accounting policies

Energy Company Obligation

The Energy Company Obligation ('ECO') order requires UK-licensed energy suppliers to improve the energy efficiency of domestic households from 1 January 2013. Targets are set in proportion to the size of historic customer bases and must be delivered by 31 March 2015. The Group continues to judge that it is not legally obligated by this order until 31 March 2015. Accordingly, the costs of delivery are recognised as incurred, when cash is spent or unilateral commitments made resulting in obligations that cannot be avoided. During the period, the Group has entered into a number of contractual arrangements and commitments, and issued a public statement to underline its commitment, to deliver a specific proportion of the ECO requirements. Consequently, the Group's result includes the costs of these contractual arrangement and commitment obligations.

Significantly, however, such considerations do not apply in the case of obligations to dismantle or remove an asset at the end of its useful life, where an obligation is recognised despite the entity's ability to dispose of the asset before its useful life has expired. Such costs are required to be included by IAS 16 – *Property, Plant and Equipment* – as part of the measure of an asset's initial cost. *[IAS 16.16].* Decommissioning provisions are discussed at 6.3 below. A further distinction can be drawn where the requirement to maintain the asset is a contractual obligation, such as when the asset in question is held under an operating lease (see 6.9 below). Accordingly, the determination of whether an obligation exists independently of an entity's future actions can be a matter of judgement that depends on the particular facts and circumstances of the case.

There is no requirement for an entity to know to whom an obligation is owed. The obligation may be to the public at large. It follows that the obligation could be to one party, but the amount ultimately payable will be to another party. For example, in the case of a constructive obligation for an environmental clean-up, the obligation is to the public, but the liability will be settled by making payment to the contractors engaged to carry out the clean-up. However, the principle is that there must be another party for the obligation to exist. It follows from this that a management or board decision will not give rise to a constructive obligation unless it is communicated in sufficient detail to those affected by it before the end of the reporting period. *[IAS 37.20].* The most significant application of this requirement relates to restructuring provisions, which is discussed further at 6.1 below.

The standard discusses the possibility that an event that does not give rise to an obligation immediately may do so at a later date, because of changes in the law or an act by the entity (such as a sufficiently specific public statement) which gives rise to a constructive obligation. *[IAS 37.21].* Changes in the law will be relatively straightforward to identify. The only issue that arises will be exactly when that change in the law should be recognised. IAS 37 states that an obligation arises only when the legislation is virtually certain to be enacted as drafted and suggests that in many cases, this will not be until it is enacted. *[IAS 37.22].*

The more subjective area is the possibility that an act by the entity will give rise to a constructive obligation. The example given is of an entity publicly accepting responsibility for rectification of previous environmental damage in a way that creates a constructive obligation. *[IAS 37.21].* This seems to introduce a certain amount of flexibility to management when reporting results. By bringing forward or delaying a public announcement of a commitment that management had always intended to honour, it can affect the reporting period in which a provision is recognised. Nevertheless, the existence of a public announcement provides a more transparent basis for recognising a provision than, for example, a decision made behind the closed doors of a boardroom.

3.1.2 'It is probable that an outflow of resources embodying economic benefits will be required to settle the obligation'

This requirement has been included as a result of the standard's attempt to incorporate contingent liabilities within the definition of provisions. This is discussed at 3.2 below.

The meaning of *probable* in these circumstances is that the outflow of resources is more likely than not to occur; that is, it has a probability of occurring that is greater than 50%. *[IAS 37.23]*. The standard also makes it clear that where there are a number of similar obligations, the probability that an outflow will occur is based on the class of obligations as a whole. This is because in the case of certain obligations such as warranties, the possibility of an outflow for an individual item may be small (likely to be much less than 50%) whereas the possibility of at least some outflow of resources for the population as a whole will be much greater (almost certainly greater than 50%). *[IAS 37.24]*. With regard to the measurement of a provision arising from a number of similar obligations, the standard refers to the calculation of an 'expected value', whereby the obligation is estimated by weighting all the possible outcomes by their associated probabilities. *[IAS 37.40]*. Where the obligation being measured relates to a single item, the standard suggests that the best estimate of the liability may be the individual most likely outcome. *[IAS 37.40]*. For the purposes of recognition, a determination that it is more likely than not that *any* outflow of resources will be required is sufficient. The measurement of provisions is discussed at 4 below.

3.1.3 'A reliable estimate can be made of the amount of the obligation'

The standard takes the view that a sufficiently reliable estimate can almost always be made for a provision where an entity can determine a range of possible outcomes. Hence, the standard contends that it will only be in extremely rare cases that a range of possible outcomes cannot be determined and therefore no sufficiently reliable estimate of the obligation can be made. *[IAS 37.25]*. In these extremely rare circumstances, no liability is recognised. Instead, the liability should be disclosed as a contingent liability (see disclosure requirements at 7.2 below). *[IAS 37.26]*. Whether such a situation is as rare as the standard asserts is open to question, especially for entities trying to determine estimates relating to potential obligations that arise from litigation and other legal claims (see 6.11 below).

3.2 Contingencies

IAS 37 says that contingent liabilities and contingent assets should not be recognised, but only disclosed. *[IAS 37.27-28, 31, 34]*.

Contingent liabilities that are recognised separately as part of allocating the cost of a business combination are covered by the requirements of IFRS 3. *[IFRS 3.23]*. Such liabilities continue to be measured after the business combination at the higher of:

(a) the amount that would be recognised in accordance with IAS 37, and

(b) the amount initially recognised less, if appropriate, cumulative amortisation recognised in accordance with IAS 18. *[IFRS 3.56]*.

The requirements in respect of contingent liabilities identified in a business combination are discussed in Chapter 9 at 5.6.1.

3.2.1 Contingent liabilities

A contingent liability is defined in the standard as:

(a) a possible obligation that arises from past events and whose existence will be confirmed only by the occurrence or non-occurrence of one or more uncertain future events not wholly within the control of the entity; or

(b) a present obligation that arises from past events but is not recognised because:
   (i) it is not probable that an outflow of resources embodying economic benefits will be required to settle the obligation; or
   (ii) the amount of the obligation cannot be measured with sufficient reliability. *[IAS 37.10].*

At first glance, this definition is not easy to understand because a natural meaning of 'contingent' would include any event whose outcome depends on future circumstances. The meaning is perhaps clearer when considering the definition of a liability and the criteria for recognising a provision in the standard. A possible obligation whose existence is yet to be confirmed does not meet the definition of a liability; and a present obligation in respect of which an outflow of resources is not probable, or which cannot be measured reliably does not qualify for recognition. *[IAS 37.14].* On that basis a contingent liability under IAS 37 means one of the following:

(a) an obligation that is estimated to be less than 50+% likely to exist (i.e. it does not meet the definition of a liability). Where it is more likely than not that a present obligation exists at the end of the reporting period, a provision is recognised. *[IAS 37.16(a)].* Where it is more likely than not that no present obligation exists, a contingent liability is disclosed (unless the possibility is remote); *[IAS 37.16(b)]* or

(b) a present obligation that has a less than 50+% chance of requiring an outflow of economic benefits (i.e. it meets the definition of a liability but does not meet the recognition criteria). Where it is not probable that there will be an outflow of resources, an entity discloses a contingent liability (unless the possibility is remote); *[IAS 37.23]* or

(c) a present obligation for which a sufficiently reliable estimate cannot be made (i.e. it meets the definition of a liability but does not meet the recognition criteria). In these rare circumstances, a liability cannot be recognised and it is disclosed as a contingent liability. *[IAS 37.26].*

The term 'possible' is not defined, but literally it could mean any probability greater than 0% and less than 100%. However, the standard effectively divides this range into four components, namely 'remote', 'possible but not probable', 'probable' and 'virtually certain'. The standard requires a provision to be recognised if 'it is more likely than not that a present obligation exists at the end of the reporting period'. *[IAS 37.16(a)].* Therefore, IAS 37 distinguishes between a 'probable' obligation (which is more likely than not to exist and, therefore requires recognition as a provision) and a 'possible' obligation (for which either the existence of a present obligation is yet to be confirmed or where the probability of an outflow of resources is 50% or less). *[IAS 37.13].* Appendix A to IAS 37, in summarising the main requirements of the standard, uses the phrase 'a possible obligation ... that may, but probably will not, require an outflow of resources'. Accordingly, the definition restricts contingent liabilities to those where either the existence of the liability or the transfer of economic benefits arising is less than 50+% probable (or where the obligation cannot be measured at all, but as noted at 3.1.3 above, this would be relatively rare).

The standard requires that contingent liabilities are assessed continually to determine whether circumstances have changed, in particular whether an outflow of resources embodying economic benefits has become probable. Where this becomes the case, then provision should be made in the period in which the change in probability occurs (except in the rare circumstances where no reliable estimate can be made). *[IAS 37.30]*. Other changes in circumstances might require disclosure of a previously remote obligation on the grounds that an outflow of resources has become possible (but not probable).

Example 27.4: When the likelihood of an outflow of benefits becomes probable

After a wedding in 2014, ten people died, possibly as a result of food poisoning from products sold by the entity. Legal proceedings are started seeking damages from the entity. The entity disputes any liability and, up to the date on which its financial statements for the year ended 31 December 2014 are authorised for issue, its lawyers have advised that is probable that the entity will not be found liable. However, when the entity prepares its financial statements for the year ended 31 December 2015, its lawyers advise that, owing to developments in the case, it is probable that the entity will be found liable.

At 31 December 2014, no provision is recognised and the matter is disclosed as a contingent liability unless the probability of any outflow is regarded as remote. On the basis of the evidence available when the financial statements were approved, there is no obligation as a result of a past event.

At 31 December 2015, a provision is recognised for the best estimate of the amount required to settle the obligation. The fact that an outflow of economic benefits is now believed to be probable means that there is a present obligation. *[IAS 37 IE Example 10]*.

3.2.2 Contingent assets

A contingent asset is defined in a more intuitive way. It is 'a possible asset that arises from past events and whose existence will be confirmed only by the occurrence or non-occurrence of one or more uncertain future events not wholly within the control of the entity'. *[IAS 37.10]*. In this case, the word 'possible' is *not* confined to a level of probability of 50% or less, which may further increase the confusion over the different meaning of the term in the definition of contingent liabilities.

Contingent assets usually arise from unplanned or other unexpected events that give rise to the possibility of an inflow of economic benefits to the entity. An example is a claim that an entity is pursuing through legal process, where the outcome is uncertain. *[IAS 37.32]*.

The standard states that a contingent asset should not be recognised, as this could give rise to recognition of income that may never be realised. However, when the realisation of income is virtually certain, then the related asset is no longer regarded as contingent and recognition is appropriate. *[IAS 37.33]*.

Virtual certainty is not defined in the standard, but it is certainly a much higher hurdle than 'probable' and indeed more challenging than the term 'highly probable', defined in IAS 39 – *Financial Instruments: Recognition and Measurement* – as indicating a much greater likelihood of happening than the term 'more likely than not', *[IAS 39.F.3.7]*, and in IFRS 5 as 'significantly more likely than probable'. *[IFRS 5 Appendix A]*. We think it reasonable that virtual certainty is interpreted as being at least 95% likely to occur.

The standard requires disclosure of the contingent asset when the inflow of economic benefits is probable. *[IAS 37.34]*. For the purposes of the standard 'probable' means that the event is more likely than not to occur; that is, it has a probability greater than 50%. *[IAS 37.23]*. The disclosure requirements are detailed at 7.3 below.

As with contingent liabilities, any contingent assets should be assessed continually to ensure that developments are appropriately reflected in the financial statements. If it has become virtually certain that an inflow of economic benefits will arise, the asset and the related income should be recognised in the period in which the change occurs. If a previously unlikely inflow becomes probable, then the contingent asset should be disclosed. *[IAS 37.35]*.

The requirement to recognise the effect of changing circumstances in the period in which the change occurs extends to the analysis of information available after the end of the reporting period and before the date of approval of the financial statements. In our view, such information would not give rise to an adjusting event after the reporting period. In contrast to contingent liabilities (in respect of which IAS 10 includes as a specific example of an adjusting event 'the settlement after the reporting period of a court case that confirms that the entity had a present obligation at the end of the reporting period' *[IAS 10.9]*), no adjustment should be made to reflect the subsequent settlement of a legal claim in favour of the entity. In this instance, the period in which the change occurs is subsequent to the reporting period. There is also no suggestion that the example in IAS 10 is referring to anything but liabilities. An asset could only be recognised if, at the end of the reporting period, the entity could show that it was virtually certain that its claim would succeed.

3.2.3 *How probability determines whether to recognise or disclose*

The following matrix summarises the treatment of contingencies under IAS 37:

Likelihood of outcome	*Accounting treatment: contingent liability*	*Accounting treatment: contingent asset*
Virtually certain (say, >95% probable)	Not a contingent liability, therefore recognise	Not a contingent asset, therefore recognise
Probable (say, 50-95% probable)	Not a contingent liability, therefore recognise	Disclose
Possible but not probable (say, 5-50% probable)	Disclose	No disclosure permitted
Remote (say, <5% probable)	No disclosure required	No disclosure permitted

The standard does not put a numerical measure of probability on either 'virtually certain' or 'remote', which lie at the outer ends of the range, but we think it reasonable to regard them as falling above the 95th percentile and below the fifth percentile respectively. However, these guidelines are not definitive and each case must be decided on its merits. In any event, it is usually possible to assess the probability of the outcome of a particular event only very approximately.

3.3 Recognising an asset when recognising a provision

In most cases, the recognition of a provision results in an immediate expense in profit or loss. Nevertheless, in some cases it may be appropriate to recognise an asset. These issues are not discussed in IAS 37, which neither prohibits nor requires capitalisation of the costs recognised when a provision is made. It states that other standards specify whether expenditures are treated as assets or expenses. *[IAS 37.8].*

Whilst the main body of IAS 37 is silent on the matter, the standard contains the following example which concludes that an asset should be recognised when a decommissioning provision is established.

Example 27.5: When the recognition of a provision gives rise to an asset

An entity operates an offshore oilfield where its licensing agreement requires it to remove the oil rig at the end of production and restore the seabed. 90% of the eventual costs relate to the removal of the oil rig and restoration of damage caused by building it, with 10% expected to arise through the extraction of oil. At the end of the reporting period, the rig has been constructed but no oil has been extracted.

A provision is recognised in respect of the probable costs relating to the removal of the rig and restoring damage caused by building it. This is because the construction of the rig, combined with the requirement under the licence to remove the rig and restore the seabed, creates an obligating event as at the end of the reporting period. These costs are included as part of the cost of the oil rig.

However, there is no obligation to rectify any damage that will be caused by the future extraction of oil. *[IAS 37 IE Example 3].*

This conclusion is supported by IAS 16, which requires the cost of an item of property, plant and equipment to include the initial estimate of the costs of dismantling and removing an asset and restoring the site on which it is located, the obligation for which an entity incurs either when the item is acquired or as a consequence of having used the item during a particular period for purposes other than to produce inventories during that period. *[IAS 16.16(c), 18].* The treatment of decommissioning costs is discussed further at 6.3 below.

4 MEASUREMENT

4.1 Best estimate of provision

IAS 37 requires the amount to be recognised as a provision to be the best estimate of the expenditure required to settle the present obligation at the end of the reporting period. *[IAS 37.36].* This measure is determined before tax, as the tax consequences of the provision, and changes to it, are dealt with under IAS 12. *[IAS 37.41].*

The standard equates this 'best estimate' with 'the amount that an entity would rationally pay to settle the obligation at the end of the reporting period or to transfer it to a third party at that time'. *[IAS 37.37]*. It is interesting that a hypothetical transaction of this kind should be proposed as the conceptual basis of the measurement required, rather than putting the main emphasis upon the actual expenditure that is expected to be incurred in the future.

The standard does acknowledge that it would often be impossible or prohibitively expensive to settle or transfer the obligation at the end of the reporting period. However, it goes on to state that 'the estimate of the amount that an entity would rationally pay to settle or transfer the obligation gives the best estimate of the expenditure required to settle the present obligation at the end of the reporting period'. *[IAS 37.37]*.

The estimates of outcome and financial effect are determined by the judgement of the entity's management, supplemented by experience of similar transactions and, in some cases, reports from independent experts. The evidence considered will include any additional evidence provided by events after the reporting period. *[IAS 37.38]*.

The standard suggests that there are various ways of dealing with the uncertainties surrounding the amount to be recognised as a provision. It mentions three, an expected value (or probability-weighted) method; the mid-point of the range of possible outcomes; and an estimate of the individual most likely outcome. An expected value approach would be appropriate when a large population of items is being measured, such as warranty costs. This is a statistical computation which weights the cost of all the various possible outcomes according to their probabilities, as illustrated in the following example taken from IAS 37. *[IAS 37.39]*.

Example 27.6: Calculation of expected value

An entity sells goods with a warranty under which customers are covered for the cost of repairs of any manufacturing defects that become apparent within the first six months after purchase. If minor defects were detected in all products sold, repair costs of £1 million would result. If major defects were detected in all products sold, repair costs of £4 million would result. The entity's past experience and future expectations indicate that, for the coming year, 75 per cent of the goods sold will have no defects, 20 per cent of the goods sold will have minor defects and 5 per cent of the goods sold will have major defects. In accordance with paragraph 24 of IAS 37 (see 3.1.2 above) an entity assesses the probability of a transfer for the warranty obligations as a whole.

The expected value of the cost of repairs is:

(75% of nil) + (20% of £1m) + (5% of £4m) = £400,000. *[IAS 37.39, Example]*.

In a situation where there is a continuous range of possible outcomes and each point in that range is as likely as any other, IAS 37 requires that the mid-point of the range is used. *[IAS 37.39]*. This is not a particularly helpful way of setting out the requirement, as it does not make it clear what the principle is meant to be. The mid-point in this case represents the median as well as the expected value. The latter may have been what was intended, but the median could be equally well justified on the basis that it is 50% probable that at least this amount will be payable, while anything in excess of that constitutes a possible but not a probable liability, that should be disclosed rather than accrued. Interestingly, US GAAP has a different approach to this issue in relation to contingencies. FASB ASC Topic 450 – *Contingencies* – states that where a contingent loss could fall within a range of amounts then, if there is a best estimate within the range, it should be accrued, with the remainder noted as a contingent liability. However, if there is no best estimate then the *lowest* figure within the range should be accrued, with the remainder up to the maximum potential loss noted as a contingent liability.[6]

Where the obligation being measured relates to a single item, the standard suggests that the best estimate of the liability may be the individual most likely outcome. However, even in such a case, it notes that consideration should be given to other possible outcomes and where these are predominantly higher or mainly lower than the most likely outcome, the resultant 'best estimate' will be a higher or lower amount than the individual most likely outcome. To illustrate this, the standard gives an example of an entity that has to rectify a fault in a major plant that it has constructed for a customer. The most likely outcome is that the repair will succeed at the first attempt. However, a provision should be made for a larger amount if there is a significant chance that further attempts will be necessary. *[IAS 37.40]*.

4.2 Dealing with risk and uncertainty in measuring a provision

It is clear from the definition of a provision as a liability of uncertain timing or amount that entities will have to deal with risk and uncertainty in estimating an appropriate measure of the obligation at the end of the reporting period. It is therefore interesting to consider how the measurement rules detailed in IAS 37 help entities achieve a faithful representation of the obligation in these circumstances. A faithful representation requires estimates that are neutral, that is, without bias. *[Framework.QC12, QC14]*. The *Conceptual Framework* warns against the use of conservatism or prudence in estimates because this is 'likely to lead to a bias'. It adds that the exercise of prudence can be counterproductive, in that the overstatement of liabilities in one period frequently leads to overstated financial performance in later periods, 'a result that cannot be described as prudent or neutral'. *[Framework.BC3.28]*.

The standard does not refer to neutrality as such; however, it does discuss the concept of risk and the need for exercising caution and care in making judgements under conditions of uncertainty. It states that 'the risks and uncertainties that inevitably surround many events and circumstances shall be taken into account in reaching the best estimate of a provision'. *[IAS 37.42]*. It refers to risk as being variability of outcome and suggests that a risk adjustment may increase the amount at which a liability is measured. *[IAS 37.43]*. Whilst the standard provides an example of a case in which the best estimate of an obligation might have to be larger than the individual most likely outcome, *[IAS 37.40]*, it gives no indication of how this increment should be determined. It warns that caution is needed in making judgements under conditions of uncertainty, so that expenses or liabilities are not understated. However, it says that uncertainty does not justify the creation of excessive provisions or a deliberate overstatement of liabilities. Accordingly, care is needed to avoid duplicating adjustments for risk and uncertainty, for example by estimating the costs of a particularly adverse outcome and then overestimating its probability. *[IAS 37.43]*. Any uncertainties surrounding the amount of the expenditure are to be disclosed (see 7.1 below). *[IAS 37.44]*.

The overall result of all this is somewhat confusing. Whilst a best estimate based solely on the expected value approach or the mid-point of a range addresses the uncertainties relating to there being a variety of possible outcomes, it does not fully reflect risk, because the actual outcome could still be higher or lower than the estimate. Therefore, the discussion on risk suggests that an additional adjustment should be made. However, apart from indicating that the result may be to increase the recognised liability and pointing out the need to avoid duplicating the effect of risk in estimates of cash flows and probability, *[IAS 37.43]*, it is not clear quite how this might be achieved. This leaves a certain amount of scope for variation in the estimation of provisions and is further complicated when the concept of risk is combined with considerations relating to the time value of money (see 4.3.2 below).

4.3 Discounting the estimated cash flows to a present value

The standard requires that where the effect of the time value of money is material, the amount of a provision should be the present value of the expenditures expected to be required to settle the obligation. *[IAS 37.45]*. The discount rate (or rates) to be used in arriving at the present value should be 'a pre-tax rate (or rates) that reflect(s) current market assessments of the time value of money and the risks specific to the liability. The discount rate(s) shall not reflect risks for which the future cash flow estimates have been adjusted.' *[IAS 37.47]*. However, it is worth noting that no discounting is required for provisions where the cash flows will not be sufficiently far into the future for discounting to have a material impact. *[IAS 37.46]*.

IAS 37 gives no guidance as to how these requirements are to be applied. On the other hand, FRS 12 in the UK gives some guidance on the discount rate to be used in the net present value calculation and this is discussed at 4.3.1 below. The main types of provision where the impact of discounting will be significant are those relating to decommissioning and other environmental restoration liabilities. IFRIC 1 addresses some of the issues relating to the use of discounting (in the context of provisions for obligations to dismantle, remove or restore items of property, plant and equipment, referred to as 'decommissioning, restoration and similar liabilities') which are discussed at 6.3.1 below.

4.3.1 Real versus nominal rate

IAS 37 does not indicate whether the discount rate should be a real discount rate or a nominal discount rate (although a real discount rate is referred to in Example 2 in Appendix D which illustrates the narrative disclosure for decommissioning costs). FRS 12 in the UK notes that the discount rate used depends on whether:[7]

(a) the future cash flows are expressed in current prices, in which case a real discount rate (which excludes the effects of general inflation) should be used; or

(b) the future cash flows are expressed in expected future prices, in which case a nominal discount rate (which includes a return to cover expected inflation) should be used.

Either alternative is acceptable under FRS 12, and these methods may produce the same figure for the initial present value of the provision. However, the effect of the unwinding of the discount will be different in each case (see 4.3.5 below). In Extract 27.9 at 6.4 below, BP p.l.c. discloses how its provision for the costs of environmental remediation is estimated using current prices and discounted using a real rate.

4.3.2 Adjusting for risk and using a government bond rate

IAS 37 also requires that risk is taken into account in the calculation of a provision, but gives little guidance as to how this should be done. Where discounting is concerned, it merely says that the discount rate should not reflect risks for which the future cash flow estimates have been adjusted. *[IAS 37.47]*. FRS 12 in the UK suggests that using a discount rate that reflects the risk associated with the liability (a risk-adjusted rate) may be easier than trying to adjust the future cash flows for risk.[8] It gives no indication of how to calculate such a risk adjusted rate, but a little more information can be obtained from the ASB's earlier Working Paper – *Discounting in Financial Reporting*[9] – on which the following example is based.

Example 27.7: Calculation of a risk-adjusted rate[10]

A company has a provision for which the expected value of the cash outflow in three years' time is £150, and the risk-free rate (i.e. the nominal rate unadjusted for risk) is 5%. However, the possible outcomes from which the expected value has been determined lie within a range between £100 and £200. The company is risk averse and would settle instead for a certain payment of, say, £160 in three years' time rather than be exposed to the risk of the actual outcome being as high as £200. The effect of risk in calculating the present value can be expressed as either:

(a) discounting the risk-adjusted cash flow of £160 at the risk-free (unadjusted) rate of 5%, giving a present value of £138; or

(b) discounting the expected cash flow (which is unadjusted for risk) of £150 at a risk-adjusted rate that will give the present value of £138, i.e. a rate of 2.8%.

As can be seen from this example, the risk-adjusted discount rate is a *lower* rate than the unadjusted (risk-free) discount rate. This may seem counter-intuitive initially, because the experience of most borrowers is that banks and other lenders will charge a higher rate of interest on loans that are assessed to be higher risk to the lender. However, in the case of a provision a risk premium is being suffered to eliminate the possibility of the actual cost being higher (thereby capping a liability), whereas in the case of a loan receivable a premium is required to compensate the lender for taking on the risk of not recovering its full value (setting a floor for the value of the lender's financial asset). In both cases the actual cash flows incurred by the paying entity are higher to reflect a premium for risk. In other words, the discount rate for an asset is increased to reflect the risk of recovering less and the discount rate for a liability is reduced to reflect the risk of paying more.

A problem with changing the discount rate to account for risk is that this adjusted rate is a theoretical rate, as it is unlikely that there would be a market assessment of the risks specific to the liability alone. *[IAS 37.47]*. However the lower discount rate in the above example is consistent with the premise that a risk-adjusted liability should be higher than a liability without accounting for the risk that the actual settlement amount is different to the estimate. *[IAS 37.43]*. It is also possible for the adjusted rate to be negative, although in practice the maximum amount a liability could increase to is the nominal amount of the expected future cash flow. It is also difficult to see how a risk-adjusted rate could be obtained in practice. In the above example, it was obtained only by reverse-engineering; it was already known that the net present value of a risk-adjusted liability was £138, so the risk-adjusted rate was just the discount rate applied to unadjusted cash flow of £150 to give that result.

IAS 37 offers an alternative approach – instead of using a risk-adjusted discount rate, the estimated future cash flows themselves can be adjusted for risk. *[IAS 37.47]*. This does of course present the problem of how to adjust the cash flows for risk (see 4.2 above). However, this may be easier than attempting to risk-adjust the discount rate.

FRS 12 expresses this alternative in terms of adjusting the cash flows for risk and then discounting using a risk-free (unadjusted) rate. It suggests that an example of a risk-free rate would be a government bond rate.[11] Presumably, this government bond rate should strictly have a similar remaining term to the liability, although this is not specified in FRS 12. For the purposes of discounting post-employment benefit obligations, IAS 19 requires the discount rate to be determined by reference to market yields at the end of the reporting period on high quality corporate bonds (although in countries where there is no deep market in such bonds, the market yields on government bonds should be used). *[IAS 19.83]*. Although IAS 19 indicates that this discount rate reflects the time value of money (but not the actuarial or investment risk), *[IAS 19.84]*, we do not believe it is appropriate to use the yield on a high quality corporate bond for determining a risk-free rate to be used in discounting provisions under IAS 37. Accordingly, in our view, where an entity is using a risk-free discount rate for the purposes of calculating a provision under IAS 37, that rate should be based on a government bond rate with a similar currency and remaining term as the provision. It follows that because a risk-adjusted rate is always lower than the risk-free rate, an entity cannot justify the discounting of a provision at a rate that is higher than a government bond rate with a similar currency and term to the provision.

Whichever method of reflecting risk is adopted, IAS 37 emphasises that care must be taken that the effect of risk is not double-counted by inclusion in both the cash flows and the discount rate. *[IAS 37.47]*.

In recent years, government bond rates have been more volatile as markets have changed rates to reflect (among other factors) heightened perceptions of sovereign debt risk. The question has therefore arisen whether government bond rates, at least in certain jurisdictions, should continue to be regarded as the default measure of a risk-free discount rate. Whilst the current volatility in rates has highlighted the fact that no debt (even government debt) is totally risk free, the challenge is to find a more reliable measure as an alternative. Any adjustment to the government bond rate to 'remove' the estimate of sovereign debt risk is conceptually flawed, as it not possible to isolate one component of risk from all the other variables that influence the setting of an interest rate. Another approach might be to apply some form of average bond rate over a period of 3, 6 or 12 months to mitigate the volatility inherent in applying the spot rate at the period end. However, this is clearly inappropriate given the requirements in IAS 37 to determine the best estimate of an obligation by reference to the expenditure required to settle it '*at the end of the reporting period*' *[IAS 37.36]* and to determine the discount rate on the basis of '*current market assessments*' of the time value of money. *[IAS 37.47]*.

With 'risk' being a measure of potential variability in returns, it remains the case that in most countries a government bond will be subject to the lowest level of variability in that jurisdiction. As such, it remains the most suitable of all the observable measures of the time value of money in a particular country.

A difficulty that can arise in certain countries is finding a government bond with a similar term to the provision, for example when measuring a decommissioning provision expected to be settled in 30 years in a country where there are no government bonds with a term exceeding 10 years. In such cases, the government bond rate might still be the most reliable measure of the time value of money, although an alternative could be to employ the techniques adopted by actuaries measuring retirement obligations with long maturities, for example by extrapolating current market rates along a yield curve. *[IAS 19.86]*. The difficulties of finding an appropriate discount rate in the context of retirement benefit obligations are discussed in Chapter 31 at 5.2.2.F.

4.3.3 Own credit risk is not taken into account

In considering the risk factors that might give rise to a difference between the actual cash flows required to settle a liability and their previously estimated amounts, an entity would not take into account its own credit risk; that is, the risk that the entity could be unable to settle the amount finally determined to be payable. This is because IAS 37 requires the discount rate to reflect 'the risks specific to the liability'. *[IAS 37.47]*.

In March 2011, the Interpretations Committee decided not to take to its agenda a request for interpretation of the phrase 'the risks specific to the liability' and whether this means that an entity's own credit risk should be excluded from any adjustments made to the discount rate used to measure liabilities. In doing so, the Interpretations Committee acknowledged that IAS 37 is not explicit on the question of own credit risk; but understood that the predominant practice was to exclude it for the reason that credit risk is generally viewed as a risk of the entity rather than a risk specific to the liability.[12]

4.3.4 Pre-tax discount rate

Since IAS 37 requires provisions to be measured before tax, it follows that cash flows should be discounted at a pre-tax discount rate. *[IAS 37.47]*. No further explanation of this is given in the standard.

This is probably because, in reality, the use of a pre-tax discount rate will be most common. Supposing, for example, that the risk-free rate of return is being used, then the discount rate used will be a government bond rate. This rate will be obtained gross. Thus, the idea of trying to determine a pre-tax rate (for example by obtaining a required post-tax rate of return and adjusting it for the tax consequences of different cash flows) will seldom be relevant.

The calculation is illustrated in the following example.

Example 27.8: Use of discounting and tax effect

It is estimated that the settlement of an environmental provision will give rise to a gross cash outflow of £500,000 in three years time. The gross interest rate on a government bond maturing in three years time is 6%. The tax rate is 30%.

The net present value of the provision is £419,810 (£500,000 × 1 ÷ $(1.06)^3$). Hence, a provision of £419,810 should be booked in the statement of financial position. A corresponding deferred tax asset of £125,943 (30% of £419,810) would be set up if it met the criteria for recognition in IAS 12 (See Chapter 29 at 7.4).

Chapter 27

4.3.5 Unwinding of the discount

IAS 37 indicates that where discounting is used, the carrying amount of a provision increases in each period to reflect the passage of time, and that this increase is recognised as a borrowing cost. *[IAS 37.60].* This is the only guidance that the standard gives on the unwinding of the discount. IFRIC 1 in relation to provisions for decommissioning, restoration and similar liabilities requires that the periodic unwinding of the discount is recognised in profit or loss as a finance cost as it occurs. The Interpretations Committee concluded that the unwinding of the discount is not a borrowing cost for the purposes of IAS 23 – *Borrowing Costs* – and thus cannot be capitalised under that standard. *[IFRIC 1.8].* It noted that IAS 23 addresses funds borrowed specifically for the purpose of obtaining a particular asset and agreed that a decommissioning liability does not fall within this description since it does not reflect funds borrowed. Accordingly, the Interpretations Committee concluded that the unwinding of the discount is not a borrowing cost as defined in IAS 23. *[IFRIC 1.BC26].*

However, there is no discussion of the impact that the original selection of discount rate can have on its unwinding, that is the selection of real versus nominal rates, and risk-free versus risk-adjusted rates. The IASB appears to have overlooked the fact that these different discount rates will unwind differently. This is best illustrated by way of an example.

Example 27.9: Effect on future profits of choosing a real or nominal discount rate

A provision is required to be set up for an expected cash outflow of €100,000 (estimated at current prices), payable in three years' time. The appropriate nominal discount rate is 7.5%, and inflation is estimated at 5%. If the provision is discounted using the nominal rate, the expected cash outflow has to reflect future prices. Accordingly, if prices increase at the rate of inflation, the cash outflow will be €115,762 (€100,000 × 1.05^3). The net present value of €115,762, discounted at 7.5%, is €93,184 (€115,762 × 1 ÷ $(1.075)^3$). If all assumptions remain valid throughout the three-year period, the movement in the provision would be as follows:

	Undiscounted cash flows	*Provision*
	€	€
Year 0	115,762	93,184
Unwinding of discount (€93,184 × 0.075)		6,989
Revision to estimate		–
Year 1	115,762	100,173
Unwinding of discount (€100,173 × 0.075)		7,513
Revision to estimate		–
Year 2	115,762	107,686
Unwinding of discount (€107,686 × 0.075)		8,076
Revision to estimate		–
Year 3	115,762	115,762

If the provision is calculated based on the expected cash outflow of €100,000 (estimated at current prices), then it needs to be discounted using a real discount rate. This may be thought to be 2.5%, being the difference between the nominal rate of 7.5% and the inflation rate of 5%. However, it is more accurately calculated using the Fisher relation or formula[13] as 2.381%, being (1.075 ÷ 1.05) – 1. Accordingly, the net present value of €100,000, discounted at 2.381%, is €93,184 (€100,000 × 1 ÷ $(1.02381)^3$), the same as the calculation using future prices discounted at the nominal rate.

If all assumptions remain valid throughout the three-year period, the movement in the provision comprises both the unwinding of the discount and the increase in the level of current prices used to determine the estimate of cost, as follows:

	Undiscounted cash flows	*Provision*
	€	€
Year 0	100,000	93,184
Unwinding of discount (€93,184 × 0.02381)		2,219
Revision to estimate (€100,000 × 0.05)	5,000	4,770
Year 1	105,000	100,173
Unwinding of discount (€100,173 × 0.02381)		2,385
Revision to estimate (€105,000 × 0.05)	5,250	5,128
Year 2	110,250	107,686
Unwinding of discount (€107,686 × 0.02381)		2,564
Revision to estimate (€110,250 × 0.05)	5,512	5,512
Year 3	115,762	115,762

Although the total expense in each year is the same under either method, what will be different is the allocation of the change in provision between operating costs (assuming the original provision was treated as an operating expense) and finance charges. It can be seen from the second table in the above example that using the real discount rate will give rise to a much lower finance charge each year. However, this does not lead to a lower provision in the statement of financial position at the end of each year. Provisions have to be revised annually to reflect the current best estimate of the obligation. *[IAS 37.59]*. Thus, the provision in the above example at the end of each year needs to be adjusted to reflect current prices at that time (and any other adjustments that arise from changes in the estimate of the provision), as well as being adjusted for the unwinding of the discount. For example, the revised provision at the end of Year 1 is €100,173, being €105,000 discounted for two years at 2.381%. After allowing for the unwinding of the discount, this required an additional provision of €4,770.

A more significant difference will arise where the recognition of the original provision is included as part of the cost of property, plant or equipment, rather than as an expense, such as when a decommissioning provision is recognised. In that case, using a real discount rate will result initially in a lower charge to the income statement, since under IFRIC 1 any revision to the estimate of the provision is not taken to the income statement but is treated as an adjustment to the carrying value of the related asset, which is then depreciated prospectively over the remaining life of the asset (see 6.3.1 below).

A similar issue arises with the option of using the risk-free or the risk-adjusted discount rate. However, this is a more complex problem, because it is not clear what to do with the risk-adjustment built into the provision. This is illustrated in the following example.

Example 27.10: Effect on future profits of choosing a risk-free or risk-adjusted rate

A company is required to make a provision for which the estimated value of the cash outflow in three years' time is £150, when the risk-free rate (i.e. the rate unadjusted for risk) is 5%. However, the possible outcomes from which the expected value has been determined lie within a range between £100 and £200. The reporting entity is risk averse and would settle instead for a certain payment of, say, £160 in three years' time rather than be exposed to the risk of the actual outcome being as high as £200. The measurement options to account for risk can be expressed as either:

(a) discounting the risk-adjusted cash flow of £160 at the risk-free (unadjusted) rate of 5%, giving a present value of £138; or

(b) discounting the expected cash flow (which is unadjusted for risk) of £150 at a risk-adjusted rate that will give the present value of £138, i.e. a rate of 2.8%.

Assuming that there are no changes in estimate required to be made to the provision during the three-year period, alternative (a) will unwind to give an overall finance charge of £22 and a final provision of £160. Alternative (b) will unwind to give an overall finance charge of £12 and a final provision of £150.

In this example, the unwinding of different discount rates gives rise to different provisions. The difference of £10 (£22 – £12) relates to the risk adjustment that has been made to the provision. As the actual date of settlement comes closer, the estimates of the range of possible outcomes (and accordingly the expected value of the outflow) and the premium the entity would accept for certainty will converge. As such, the effect of any initial difference related to the decision to apply a risk-free or risk-adjusted rate will be lost in the other estimation adjustments that would be made over time.

4.3.6 The effect of changes in interest rates on the discount rate applied

The standard requires the discount rate to reflect current market assessments of the time value of money. [IAS 37.47]. This means that where interest rates change, the provision should be recalculated on the basis of revised interest rates (see Example 27.11 below).

Any revision in the interest rate will give rise to an adjustment to the carrying value of the provision in addition to the unwinding of the previously estimated discount. The standard requires these movements to be disclosed in the notes to the financial statements (see 7.1 below). [IAS 37.84(e)]. However, the standard does not explicitly say how the effect of changes in interest rates should be classified in the income statement. We believe that this element should be treated separately from the effect of the passage of time, with only the charge for unwinding of the discount being classified as a finance cost. Any adjustment to the provision as a result of revising the discount rate is a change in accounting estimate, as defined in IAS 8 – *Accounting Policies, Changes in Accounting Estimates and Errors* (see Chapter 3 at 4.5). Accordingly, it should be reflected in the line item of the income statement to which the expense establishing the provision was originally taken and not as a component of the finance cost. Indeed, this is the approach required by IFRIC 1 in relation to provisions for decommissioning, restoration and similar liabilities in relation to assets measured using the cost model (see 6.3.1 below). However, in that case the original provision gives rise to an asset rather than an expense, so any subsequent adjustment is not included in profit or loss, [IAS 8.36], but added to or deducted from the cost of the asset to which it relates *[IFRIC 1.5]*. The adjusted depreciable amount of the asset is then depreciated prospectively over its remaining useful life. *[IFRIC 1.7]*. Nevertheless, the effect is distinguished from the unwinding of the discount.

In addition, the standard gives no specific guidance on how or when this adjustment should be made. For example, it is unclear whether the new discount rate should be applied during the year or just at the year-end, and whether the rate should be applied to the new estimate of the provision or the old estimate. IFRIC 1 implies that the finance cost is adjusted prospectively from the date on which the liability is remeasured. Example 1 to IFRIC 1 states that if the change in the liability had resulted from a change in discount rate, instead of a change in the estimated cash flows, the change would still have been reflected in the carrying value of the related asset, but next year's finance cost would have reflected the new discount rate. *[IFRIC 1.IE5]*. This conclusion is consistent with the requirement in IAS 37 for the value of a provision to reflect the best estimate of the expenditure required to settle the obligation as at the end of the reporting period, *[IAS 37.36]*, as illustrated in the following example.

Example 27.11: Accounting for the effect of changes in the discount rate

A provision is required to be set up for an expected cash outflow of €100,000 (estimated at current prices), payable in three years' time. The appropriate nominal discount rate is 7.5%, and inflation is estimated at 5%. At future prices the cash outflow will be €115,762 (€100,000 × 1.05^3). The net present value of €115,762, discounted at 7.5%, is €93,184 (€115,762 × 1 ÷ 1.075^3).

At the end of Year 2, all assumptions remain valid, except it is determined that a current market assessment of the time value of money and the risks specific to the liability would require a decrease in the discount rate to 6.5%. Accordingly, at the end of Year 2, the revised net present value of €115,762, discounted at 6.5%, is €108,697 (€115,762 ÷ 1.065).

The movement in the provision would be reflected as follows:

	Undiscounted cash flows	*Provision*
	€	€
Year 0	115,762	93,184
Unwinding of discount (€93,184 × 0.075)		6,989
Revision to estimate		–
Year 1	115,762	100,173
Unwinding of discount (€100,173 × 0.075)		7,513
	115,762	107,686
Revision to estimate (€108,697 – €107,686)		1,011
Year 2	115,762	108,697
Unwinding of discount (€108,697 × 0.065)		7,065
Revision to estimate		–
Year 3	115,762	115,762

In Year 2, the finance charge is based on the previous estimate of the discount rate and the revision to the estimate of the provision would be charged to the same line item in the income statement that was used to establish the provision of €93,184 at the start of Year 1.

Where market rates of interest are more volatile, entities may decide to reassess the applicable discount rate for a provision during an annual reporting period. Equally, it would be appropriate to revise this assessment as at the end of any interim reporting period during the financial year to the extent that the impact is material.

4.4 Anticipating future events that may affect the estimate of cash flows

The standard states that 'future events that may affect the amount required to settle an obligation shall be reflected in the amount of a provision where there is sufficient objective evidence that they will occur'. *[IAS 37.48].* The types of future events that the standard has in mind are advances in technology and changes in legislation.

The requirement for objective evidence means that it is not appropriate to reduce the best estimate of future cash flows simply by assuming that a completely new technology will be developed before the liability is required to be settled. There will need to be sufficient objective evidence that such future developments are likely. For example, an entity may believe that the cost of cleaning up a site at the end of its life will be reduced by future changes in technology. The amount recognised has to reflect a reasonable expectation of technically qualified, objective observers, taking account of all available evidence as to the technology that will be available at the time of the clean-up. Thus it is appropriate to include, for example, expected cost reductions associated with increased experience in applying existing technology or the expected cost of applying existing technology to a larger or more complex clean-up operation than has previously been carried out. *[IAS 37.49].*

Similarly, if new legislation is to be anticipated, there will need to be evidence both of what the legislation will demand and whether it is virtually certain to be enacted and implemented. In many cases sufficient objective evidence will not exist until the new legislation is enacted. *[IAS 37.50].*

These requirements are most likely to impact provisions for liabilities that will be settled some distance in the future, such as decommissioning costs (see 6.3 below).

4.5 Reimbursements, insurance and other recoveries from third parties

In some circumstances an entity is able to look to a third party to reimburse part of the costs required to settle a provision or to pay the amounts directly to a third party. Examples are insurance contracts, indemnity clauses and suppliers' warranties. *[IAS 37.55].* A reimbursement asset is recognised only when it is virtually certain to be received if the entity settles the obligation. The asset cannot be greater than the amount of the provision. No 'netting off' is allowed in the statement of financial position, with any asset classified separately from any provision. *[IAS 37.53].* However, the expense relating to a provision can be shown in the income statement net of reimbursement. *[IAS 37.54].* This means that if an entity has insurance cover in relation to a specific potential obligation, this is treated as a reimbursement right under IAS 37. It is not appropriate to record no provision (where the recognition criteria in the standard are met) on the basis that the entity's net exposure is expected to be zero.

The main area of concern with these requirements is whether the 'virtually certain' criterion that needs to be applied to the corresponding asset might mean that some reimbursements will not be capable of recognition at all. For items such as insurance contracts, this may not be an issue, as entities will probably be able to confirm the existence of cover for the obligation in question and accordingly be able to demonstrate that a recovery on an insurance contract is virtually certain if the entity is required to settle the obligation. Of course, it may be more difficult in complex situations for an entity to confirm it has cover against any loss. For other types of reimbursement, it may be more difficult to establish that recovery is virtually certain.

Except when an obligation is determined to be joint and several (see 4.6 below), any form of net presentation in the statement of financial position is prohibited. This is because the entity would remain liable for the whole cost if the third party failed to pay for any reason, for example as a result of the third party's insolvency. In such situations, the provision should be made gross and any reimbursement should be treated as a separate asset (but only when it is virtually certain that the reimbursement will be received if the entity settles the obligation). *[IAS 37.56].*

If the entity has no liability in the event that the third party cannot pay, then these costs are excluded from the estimate of the provision altogether because, by its very nature, there is no liability. *[IAS 37.57].*

Extract 27.2 at 4.6 below illustrates how Syngenta classifies amounts recoverable from third parties as separate assets.

In contrast, where an entity is assessing an onerous contract, such as a vacant leasehold property, it is common for entities to apply what looks like a net approach. However, because an onerous contract provision relates to the excess of the unavoidable costs over the expected economic benefits, *[IAS 37.68]*, there is no corresponding asset to be recognised. Accordingly, the amount of the provision is determined net of the cash flows that may be expected to arise from sub-letting the property. This is discussed further at 6.2 below.

4.6 Joint and several liability

It is interesting to contrast the approach of IAS 37 to reimbursements with the case where an entity is jointly and severally liable for an obligation. Joint and several liability arises when a number of entities are liable for a single obligation (for example, to damages), both individually and collectively. The holder of the obligation in these circumstances can collect the entire amount from any single member of the group or from any and all of the members in various amounts until the liability is settled in full. Even when the members have an agreement between themselves as to how the total obligation should be divided, each member remains liable to make good any deficiency on the part of the others. This situation is different from proportionate liability, where individual members of a group might be required to bear a percentage of the total liability, but without any obligation to make good any shortfall by another member. Joint and several liability can be established in a contract, by a court judgment or under legislation.

An entity that is jointly and severally liable recognises only its own share of the obligation, based on the amount it is probable that the entity will pay. The remainder that is expected to be met by other parties is treated only as a contingent liability. *[IAS 37.29, 58].*

The fact that the other third parties in this situation have a direct (albeit shared) obligation for the past event itself, rather than only a contractual relationship with the entity, is enough of a difference in circumstances to allow a form of net determination of the amount to recognise. Arguably, the economic position is no different, because the entity is exposed to further loss in the event that the third parties are unable or unwilling to pay. However, IAS 37 does not treat joint and several liability in the same way as reimbursement, which would have required a liability to be set up for the whole amount with a corresponding asset recognised for the amount expected to be met by other parties.

The extract below illustrates how Syngenta describes its policy for the classification of amounts recoverable from third parties and measurement where liability is joint and several.

Extract 27.2: Syngenta AG (2012)

Notes to the Syngenta Group Consolidated Financial Statements [extract]
2 Accounting policies [extract]
Provisions

A provision is recognized in the balance sheet when Syngenta has a legal or constructive obligation to a third party or parties as a result of a past event, the amount of which can be reliably estimated and it is probable that an outflow of economic benefits will be required to settle the obligation. The amount recognized as a provision is the best estimate of the expenditure required to settle the obligation at the balance sheet date. If the effect of discounting is material, provisions are discounted to the expected present value of their future cash flows using a pre-tax rate that reflects current market assessments of the time value of money and the risks specific to the liability. Where some or all of the expenditures required to settle a provision are expected to be reimbursed by another party, the expected reimbursement is recognized as a separate asset only when virtually certain.

Where Syngenta has a joint and several liability for a matter with one or more other parties, no provision is recognized by Syngenta for those parts of the obligation expected to be settled by another party. Syngenta self-insures or uses a combination of insurance and self-insurance for certain risks. Provisions for these risks are estimated in part by considering historical claims experience and other actuarial assumptions and, where necessary, counterparty risk.

4.7 Provisions are not reduced for gains on disposal of related assets

IAS 37 states that gains from the expected disposal of assets should not be taken into account in measuring a provision, even if the expected disposal is closely linked to the event giving rise to the provision. Such gains should be recognised at the time specified by the Standard dealing with the assets concerned. *[IAS 37.51-52].* This is likely to be of particular relevance in relation to restructuring provisions (see 6.1.4 below). However, it may also apply in other situations. Extract 27.6 at 6.3 below illustrates an example of a company excluding gains from the expected disposal of assets in determining its provision for decommissioning costs.

4.8 Changes and uses of provisions

After recognition, a provision will be re-estimated, used and released over the period up to the eventual determination of a settlement amount for the obligation. IAS 37 requires that provisions should be reviewed at the end of each reporting period and adjusted to reflect the current best estimate. If it is no longer probable that an outflow of resources embodying economic benefits will be required to settle the obligation, the provision should be reversed. *[IAS 37.59]*. Where discounting is applied, the carrying amount of a provision increases in each period to reflect the passage of time. This increase is recognised as a borrowing cost. *[IAS 37.60]*. As discussed at 4.3.5 above, the periodic unwinding of the discount is recognised as a finance cost in the income statement, and it is not a borrowing cost capable of being capitalised under IAS 23. *[IFRIC 1.8]*.

The standard does not allow provisions to be redesignated or otherwise used for expenditures for which the provision was not originally recognised. *[IAS 37.61]*. In such circumstances, a new provision is created and the amount no longer needed is reversed, as to do otherwise would conceal the impact of two different events. *[IAS 37.62]*. This means that the questionable practice of charging costs against a provision that was set up for a different purpose is specifically prohibited.

4.9 Changes in contingent liabilities recognised in a business combination

In a business combination, the usual requirements of IAS 37 do not apply and the acquirer recognises a liability at the acquisition date for those contingent liabilities of the acquiree that represent a present obligation arising as a result of a past event and in respect of which the fair value can be measured reliably. *[IFRS 3.23]*. After initial recognition, and until the liability is settled, cancelled or expires, the acquirer measures the contingent liability recognised in a business combination at the higher of: *[IFRS 3.56]*

(a) the amount that would be recognised in accordance with IAS 37; and

(b) the amount initially recognised less, if appropriate, cumulative amortisation recognised in accordance with IAS 18.

This requirement does not apply to contracts accounted for in accordance with IAS 39 and IFRS 9. See Chapter 9 at 5.6.1.B.

This requirement prevents the immediate release to post acquisition profit of any contingency recognised in a business combination.

5 CASES IN WHICH NO PROVISION SHOULD BE RECOGNISED

IAS 37 sets out three particular cases in which the recognition of a provision is prohibited. They are: future operating losses, repairs and maintenance of owned assets and staff training costs. The Interpretations Committee has also considered repeated requests relating to obligations arising on entities operating in a rate-regulated environment and concluded that there is no justification for the recognition of a special regulatory liability (see 5.4 below). The common theme in these cases is that the potential obligation does not exist independently of an entity's future actions. In other words, the entity is able to change the future conduct of its business in a way that avoids the future expenditure. Only those obligations that exist independently of an entity's future actions are recognised as provisions. *[IAS 37.19]*. This principle is also relevant to determining the timing of recognition of a provision, whereby no liability is recognised until the obligation cannot otherwise be avoided by the entity. Examples include those arising from participation in a particular market under IFRIC 6 (see 6.7 below) and an obligation for levies imposed by government under IFRIC 21 (see 6.8 below).

5.1 Future operating losses

IAS 37 explicitly states that 'provisions shall not be recognised for future operating losses'. *[IAS 37.63]*. This is because such losses do not meet the definition of a liability and the general recognition criteria of the standard. *[IAS 37.64]*. In particular there is no present obligation as a result of a past event. Such costs should be left to be recognised as they occur in the future in the same way as future profits.

However, it would be wrong to assume that this requirement has effectively prevented the effect of future operating losses from being anticipated, because they are sometimes recognised as a result of requirements in another standard, either in the measurement of an asset of the entity or to prevent inappropriate recognition of revenue. For example:

- under IAS 2 – *Inventories* – inventories are written down to the extent that they will not be recovered from future revenues, rather than leaving the non-recovery to show up as future operating losses (see Chapter 22 at 3.4);
- under IAS 11 provision is made for losses expected on construction contracts (see Chapter 23 at 3.3.6); and
- under IAS 36 – *Impairment of Assets* – impairment is assessed on the basis of the present value of future operating cash flows, meaning that the effect of not only future operating losses but also sub-standard operating profits will be recognised (see Chapter 20). IAS 37 specifically makes reference to the fact that an expectation of future operating losses may be an indication that certain assets are impaired. *[IAS 37.65]*.

This is therefore a rather more complex issue than IAS 37 acknowledges. Indeed, IAS 37 itself has to navigate closely the dividing line between the general prohibition of the recognition of future losses and the recognition of contractual or constructive obligations that are expected to give rise to losses in future periods.

5.2 Repairs and maintenance of owned assets

Repairs and maintenance provisions in respect of owned assets are generally prohibited under IAS 37. Under the standard, the following principles apply:

(a) provisions are recognised only for obligations existing independently of the entity's future actions (i.e. the future conduct of its business) and in cases where an entity can avoid future expenditure by its future actions, for example by changing its method of operation, it has no present obligation; *[IAS 37.19]*

(b) financial statements deal with an entity's position at the end of the reporting period and not its possible position in the future. Therefore, no provision is recognised for costs that need to be incurred to operate in the future; *[IAS 37.18]* and

(c) for an event to be an obligating event, the entity can have no realistic alternative to settling the obligation created by the event. *[IAS 37.17]*.

These principles are applied strictly in the case of an obligation to incur repairs and maintenance costs in the future, even when this expenditure is substantial, distinct from what may be regarded as routine maintenance and essential to the continuing operations of the entity, such as a major refit or refurbishment of the asset. This is illustrated by two examples in an appendix to the standard.

Example 27.12: Prohibition on maintenance provisions relating to owned assets

Scenario 1: *Re-lining costs of a furnace*

An entity operates a furnace, the lining of which needs to be replaced every five years for technical reasons. At the end of the reporting period, the lining has been in use for three years. In these circumstances, a provision for the cost of replacing the lining is not recognised because, at the end of the reporting period, no obligation to replace the lining exists independently of the entity's future actions. Even the intention to incur the expenditure depends upon the entity deciding to continue operating the furnace or to replace the lining. Instead of a provision being recognised, the initial cost of the lining is treated as a significant part of the furnace asset and depreciated over a period of five years. *[IAS 16.43]*. The re-lining costs are then capitalised when incurred and depreciated over the next five years. *[IAS 37 IE Example 11A]*.

Scenario 2: *Overhaul costs of an aircraft*

An airline is required by law to overhaul its aircraft once every three years. Even with the legal requirement to perform the overhaul, there is no obligating event until the three year period has elapsed. As with Scenario 1, no obligation exists independently of the entity's future actions. The entity could avoid the cost of the overhaul by selling the aircraft before the three year period has elapsed. Instead of a provision being recognised, the overhaul cost is identified as a separate part of the aircraft asset under IAS 16 and is depreciated over three years. *[IAS 37 IE Example 11B]*.

Entities might try to argue that a repairs and maintenance provision should be recognised on the basis that there is a clear intention to incur the expenditure at the appointed time and that this means it is more likely than not, as at the end of the reporting period, that an outflow of resources will occur. However, the application of the three principles noted above, particularly that an entity should not provide for future operating costs, make an entity's intentions irrelevant. In the example above, recognition was not allowed because the entity could do all manner of things to avoid the obligation, including selling the asset, however unlikely that might be in the context of the entity's business or in terms of the relative cost of replacement as compared to repair. The existence of a legal requirement, probably resulting in the aircraft being grounded, was still not enough. This detachment from intention or even commercial reality, regarded by some as extreme, is most recently exhibited in the Interpretations Committee's approach to the recognition of levies imposed by government under IFRIC 21 (see 6.8 below).

It is interesting, however, that a similar argument had not been used in respect of the recognition of decommissioning costs, where presumably an entity could also avoid such obligations by selling, for example, its oil and gas assets.

The effect of the prohibition on setting up provisions for repairs obviously has an impact on presentation in the statement of financial position. It may not always, however, have as much impact on the statement of comprehensive income. This is because it is stated in the examples that depreciation would be adjusted to take account of the repairs. For example, in the case of the furnace lining, the lining should be depreciated over five years in advance of its expected repair. Similarly, in the case of the aircraft overhaul, the example in the standard states that an amount equivalent to the expected maintenance costs is depreciated over three years. The result of this is that the depreciation charge recognised in profit or loss over the life of the component of the asset requiring regular repair may be equivalent to that which would previously have arisen from the combination of depreciation and a provision for repair. This is the way IAS 16 requires entities to account for significant parts of an item of property, plant and equipment which have different useful lives (see Chapter 18 at 5.1). *[IAS 16.44]*.

5.3 Staff training costs

In the normal course of business it is unlikely that provisions for staff training costs would be permissible, because it would normally contravene the general prohibition in the standard on the recognition of provisions for future operating costs. *[IAS 37.18]*. In the context of a restructuring, IAS 37 identifies staff retraining as an ineligible cost because it relates to the future conduct of the business. *[IAS 37.81]*. Example 27.2 at 3.1.1 above reproduces an example in the standard where the government introduces changes to the income tax system, such that an entity in the financial services sector needs to retrain a large proportion of its administrative and sales workforce in order to ensure continued compliance with financial services regulation. The standard argues that there is no present obligation until the actual training has taken place and so no provision should be recognised. We also note that in many cases the need to incur training costs is not only future operating expenditure but also fails the 'existing independently of an entity's future actions' criterion, *[IAS 37.19]*, in that the cost could be avoided by the entity, for example, if it withdrew from that market or hired new staff who were already appropriately qualified.

This example again illustrates how important it is to properly understand the nature of any potential 'constructive obligation' or 'obligating event' and to determine separately its financial effect in relation to past transactions and events on the one hand and in relation to the future operation of the business on the other. Otherwise, it can be easy to mistakenly argue that a provision is required, such as for training costs to ensure that staff comply with new legal requirements, on the basis that the entity has a constructive obligation to ensure staff are appropriately skilled to adequately meet the needs of its customers. However, the obligation, constructive or not, declared or not, relates to the entity's future conduct, is a future cost of operation and is therefore ineligible for recognition under the standard until the training takes place.

5.4 Rate-regulated activities

Under certain national GAAPs, an entity can defer benefits that would otherwise be included in profit for the period (for example, revenues) or recognise future performance obligations imposed by a regulator as 'regulatory assets' or 'regulatory liabilities' on the basis that the regulator requires it to reduce its tariffs or improve services so as to return the benefit of earlier excess profits to customers. This issue has for a long time been a matter of significant interest as entities in those countries adopt IFRS, because the recognition of these regulatory liabilities is prohibited under IFRS. Just as the ability to charge higher prices for goods services to be rendered in the future does not meet the definition of an intangible asset in IAS 38 (see Chapter 17 at 11.1), the requirement to charge a lower price for the delivery of goods and services in the future does not meet the definition of a past obligating event, or a liability, in IAS 37.

A liability is defined in IAS 37 as 'a present obligation of the entity arising from past events, the settlement of which is expected to result in an outflow from the entity of resources embodying economic benefits'. *[IAS 37.10]*. The return to customers of amounts mandated by a regulator depends on future events including:

- future rendering of services;
- future volumes of output (generally consisting of utilities such as water or electricity) consumed by users; and
- the continuation of regulation.

Similar considerations apply to actions that a regulator may require entities to complete in the future, such as an obligation to invest in equipment to improve efficiency. Other than decommissioning obligations (see 6.3 below), such items do not meet the definition of a liability because there needs to be a present obligation at the end of the reporting period before a liability can be recognised. Such a regulatory obligation that fails to qualify for recognition under IAS 37 is illustrated in Extract 27.1 at 3.1.1 above.

Whilst the requirements of IAS 37 and the *Conceptual Framework* are clear in this respect, their perceived inflexibility in this regard has been identified as a significant barrier that prevents the entities affected by it from adopting IFRS as a whole.[14] In an effort to establish a way for certain liabilities and assets to achieve recognition under very limited circumstances, the IASB issued an exposure draft in July 2009 on rate-regulated activities. However, the IASB discontinued the project in September 2011, on the basis that the complexities of the issue could not be resolved quickly and cited resource constraints. However, it identified the following options which were then presented in its 2011 agenda consultation document:[15]

- a disclosure only standard;
- an interim standard to 'grandfather' previous GAAP accounting practices with some limited improvements;
- a medium-term project focused on the effects of rate-regulation; or
- addressing it as part of a comprehensive project on intangible assets.

In response to the feedback received, the IASB embarked on a two-tier approach. In September 2012 the IASB added to its agenda a comprehensive research project on rate-regulated activities and in December 2012 the IASB decided to develop an interim Standard on the accounting for regulatory deferral accounts that would apply for first-time adopters of IFRS until the completion of the comprehensive project.[16]

The aim of the comprehensive project is to develop a Discussion Paper that will identify and more clearly articulate:[17]

(a) the common features of rate regulation;

(b) whether these common features create economic resources for, or claims against, a rate-regulated entity that should be recognised in IFRS financial statements; and

(c) the information about the consequences of rate regulation that would be most useful for users of IFRS financial statements.

The Exposure Draft, if implemented, would apply only to entities preparing their first set of IFRS financial statements[18] and provide relief from the usual requirements of IFRS only for 'regulatory deferral accounts', which it defines as 'the balance of any expense (income) deferral or variance account that is included in the setting of the future rate(s) by the rate regulator and that would not otherwise be recognised as an asset or a liability in accordance with other Standards'.[19] In addition, the Exposure Draft restricts the scope of any new Standard to those regulatory deferral accounts arising from the entity's rate-regulated activities that meet the following criteria:

(a) an authorised body (the rate regulator) restricts the price that the entity can charge its customers for the goods or services that the entity provides, and that price binds the customers; and

(b) the price established by regulation (the rate) is designed to recover the entity's allowable costs of providing the regulated goods or services.[20]

For eligible balances, the Exposure Draft proposes to:

(a) permit an entity that adopts IFRS to continue to use its previous GAAP accounting policies, as accepted in their local jurisdiction, for the recognition, measurement and impairment of regulatory deferral account balances;[21]

(b) require the entity to present regulatory deferral account balances as separate line items in the statement of financial position and to present movements in those account balances as a separate line item in the statement of profit or loss and other comprehensive income;[22] and

(c) require specific disclosures to identify clearly the nature of, and risks associated with, the rate regulation that has resulted in the recognition of regulatory deferral account balances in accordance with the proposals.[23]

At the time of writing, the IASB expects to issue a Discussion Paper in the last quarter of 2013 and to commence its redeliberations on the Exposure Draft following the end of the consultation period on 4 September 2013.[24]

Until any new standard becomes effective, most regulatory liabilities and assets are still not eligible for recognition under IFRS.

6 SPECIFIC EXAMPLES OF PROVISIONS AND CONTINGENCIES

IAS 37 expands on its general recognition and measurement requirements by including more specific requirements for particular situations, i.e. future restructuring costs and onerous contracts. This section discusses those situations, looks at other examples, including those addressed in an appendix to the Standard and other areas where the Interpretations Committee has considered how the principles of IAS 37 should be applied.

6.1 Restructuring provisions

IAS 37 allows entities to recognise restructuring provisions, but it has specific rules on the nature of obligation and the types of cost that are eligible for inclusion in such provisions, as discussed below. These rules ensure that entities recognise only obligations that exist independently of their future actions, *[IAS 37.19]*, and that provisions are not made for future operating costs and losses. *[IAS 37.63]*.

6.1.1 Definition

IAS 37 defines a restructuring as 'a programme that is planned and controlled by management, and materially changes either:

(a) the scope of a business undertaken by an entity; or

(b) the manner in which that business is conducted'. *[IAS 37.10]*.

This is said to include:

(a) the sale or termination of a line of business;

(b) the closure of business locations in a country or region or the relocation of business activities from one country or region to another;

(c) changes in management structure, for example, eliminating a layer of management; and

(d) fundamental reorganisations that have a material effect on the nature and focus of the entity's operations. *[IAS 37.70]*.

This definition is very wide and whilst it may be relatively straightforward to establish whether an operation has been sold, closed or relocated, the determination of whether an organisational change is fundamental, material or just part of a process of continuous improvement is a subjective judgment. Whilst organisational change is a perennial feature in most business sectors, entities could be tempted to classify all kinds of operating costs as restructuring costs and thereby invite the user of the financial statements to perceive them in a different light from the 'normal' costs of operating in a dynamic business environment. Even though the requirements in IAS 37 prevent such costs being recognised too early, the standard still leaves the question of classification open to judgment. As such there can be a tension between the permitted recognition of expected restructuring costs, subject to meeting the criteria set out at 6.1.2 below, and the general prohibition in IAS 37 against provision for future operating losses, which is discussed above at 5.1.

IAS 37 emphasises that when a restructuring meets the definition of a discontinued operation under IFRS 5, additional disclosures may be required under that standard (see Chapter 4 at 3). *[IAS 37.9]*.

6.1.2 Recognition of a restructuring provision

IAS 37 requires that restructuring costs are recognised only when the general recognition criteria in the standard are met, i.e. there is a present obligation (legal or constructive) as a result of a past event, in respect of which a reliable estimate can be made of the probable cost. *[IAS 37.71]*. The standard's specific requirements for the recognition of a provision for restructuring costs seek to define the circumstances that give rise to a constructive obligation and thereby restrict the recognition of a provision to cases when an entity:

(a) has a detailed formal plan for the restructuring identifying at least:
  (i) the business or part of a business concerned;
  (ii) the principal locations affected;
  (iii) the location, function, and approximate number of employees who will be compensated for terminating their services;
  (iv) the expenditures that will be undertaken; and
  (v) when the plan will be implemented; and

(b) has raised a valid expectation in those affected that it will carry out the restructuring by starting to implement that plan or announcing its main features to those affected by it. *[IAS 37.72]*.

The standard gives examples of the entity's actions that may provide evidence that the entity has started to implement a plan, quoting the dismantling of plant or selling of assets, or the public announcement of the main features of the plan. However, it also emphasises that the public announcement of a detailed plan to restructure will not automatically create an obligation; the important principle is that the announcement is made in such a way and in sufficient detail to give rise to valid expectations in other parties such as customers, suppliers and employees that the restructuring will be carried out. *[IAS 37.73]*.

The standard also suggests that for an announced plan to give rise to a constructive obligation, its implementation needs to be planned to begin as soon as possible and to be completed in a timeframe that makes significant changes to the plan unlikely. Any extended period before commencement of implementation, or if the restructuring will take an unreasonably long time, will mean that recognition of a provision is premature, because the entity is still likely to have a chance of changing the plan. *[IAS 37.74]*.

In summary, these conditions require the plan to be detailed and specific, to have gone beyond the directors' powers of recall and to be put into operation without delay or significant alteration.

The criteria set out above for the recognition of provisions mean that a board decision, if it is the only relevant event arising before the end of the reporting period, is not sufficient. This message is reinforced specifically in the standard, the argument being made that a constructive obligation is not created by a management decision. There will only be a constructive obligation where the entity has, before the end of the reporting period:

(a) started to implement the restructuring plan; or

(b) announced the main features of the restructuring plan to those affected by it in a sufficiently specific manner to raise a valid expectation in them that the entity will carry out the restructuring. *[IAS 37.75]*.

If the restructuring is not started or announced in detail until after the end of the reporting period, no provision is recognised. Instead, the entity discloses a non-adjusting event after the reporting period. *[IAS 37.75, IAS 10.22(e)]*.

The following examples in IAS 37 illustrate how a constructive obligation for a restructuring may or may not be created.

Example 27.13: The effect of timing of the creation of a constructive obligation on the recognition of a restructuring provision

Scenario 1: Closure of a division – no implementation before end of the reporting period

On 12 December 2014, the board of Entity A decided to close down a division. No announcement was made before the end of the reporting period (31 December 2014) and no other steps were taken to implement the decision before that date.

In these circumstances, no provision is recognised because management's actions are insufficient to create a constructive obligation before the end of the reporting period. *[IAS 37 IE Example 5A]*.

Scenario 2: Closure of a division – communication/implementation before end of the reporting period

In another case, the board of Entity B decides on 12 December 2014 to close down one of its manufacturing divisions. On 20 December 2014 a detailed plan for closure was agreed by the board; letters were sent to customers warning them to seek an alternative source of supply and redundancy notices were sent to the staff of the division.

The communication of management's decision to customers and employees on 20 December 2014 creates a valid expectation that the division will be closed, thereby giving rise to a constructive obligation from that date. Accordingly, a provision is recognised at 31 December 2014 for the best estimate of the costs of closing the division. *[IAS 37 IE Example 5B]*.

The standard acknowledges that there will be circumstances where a board decision could trigger recognition, but not on its own. Only if earlier events, such as negotiations with employee representatives for termination payments or with purchasers for the sale of an operation, have been concluded subject only to board approval would the decision of the board create an obligation. In such circumstances, it is reasoned that when board approval has been obtained and communicated to the other parties, the entity is committed to restructure, assuming all other conditions are met. *[IAS 37.76]*.

There is also discussion in the standard of the situation that may arise in some countries where, for example, employee representatives may sit on the board, so that a board decision effectively communicates the decision to them, which may result in a constructive obligation to restructure. *[IAS 37.77]*.

In practice it can be very difficult to determine whether it is appropriate to recognise a provision for the future costs of a restructuring programme. The determination of whether an organisational change is fundamental, material or just part of a process of continuous improvement is a subjective judgment. Once it has been established that the activities in question constitute a restructuring rather than an ongoing operating cost, it can be difficult to determine whether management's actions before the reporting date have been sufficient to have 'raised a valid expectation in those affected'. *[IAS 37.72]*. Even if a trigger point is easily identifiable, such as the date of an appropriately detailed public announcement, it might not necessarily commit management to the *whole* restructuring, but only to specific items of expenditure such as redundancy costs. When the announcement is less clear, referring for example to consultations, negotiations or voluntary arrangements, particularly with employees, judgment is required. Furthermore, taken on its own, the 'valid expectation' test is at least as open to manipulation as one based on the timing of a board decision. Entities anxious to accelerate or postpone recognition of a liability could do so by advancing or deferring an event that signals such a commitment, such as a public announcement, without any change to the substance of their position.

In these situations it is important to consider all the related facts and circumstances and not to 'home in' on a single recognition criterion. The objective of the analysis is to determine whether there is a past obligating event at the reporting date. The guidance in the standard about restructuring, referring as it does to constructive obligations and valid expectations is ultimately aimed at properly applying the principle in IAS 37 that only those obligations arising from past events and existing independently of an entity's future actions are recognised as provisions. *[IAS 37.19]*. In essence, a restructuring provision qualifies for recognition if, as at the reporting date, it relates to a detailed plan of action from which management cannot realistically withdraw.

6.1.3 Recognition of obligations arising from the sale of an operation

IAS 37 has some further specific rules governing when to recognise an obligation arising on the sale of an operation, stating that no obligation arises for the sale of an operation until the entity is committed to the sale, i.e. there is a binding sale agreement. *[IAS 37.78]*. Thus a provision cannot be made for a loss on sale unless there is a binding sale agreement by the end of the reporting period. The standard says that this applies even when an entity has taken a decision to sell an operation and announced that decision publicly, it cannot be committed to the sale until a purchaser has been identified and there is a binding sale agreement. Until there is such an agreement, the entity will be able to change its mind and indeed will have to take another course of action if a purchaser cannot be found on acceptable terms. *[IAS 37.79]*.

Even in cases where it is part of a larger restructuring that qualifies for recognition under IAS 37, an obligation arising from the sale is not recognised until there is a binding sale agreement. Instead, the assets of the operation must be reviewed for impairment under IAS 36. This may therefore mean that an expense is recorded in the income statement; it is just that the expense gives rise to a reduction of the carrying amount of assets rather than the recognition of a liability. The standard also recognises that where a sale is only part of a restructuring, the entity could be committed to the other parts of restructuring before a binding sale agreement is in place. *[IAS 37.79]*. Hence, the costs of the restructuring will be recognised over different reporting periods.

6.1.4 Costs that can (and cannot) be included in a restructuring provision

Having met the specific tests in the standard for the recognition of a restructuring provision at the end of the reporting period, IAS 37 imposes further criteria to restrict the types of cost that can be provided for. Presumably these additional restrictions are intended to ensure that the entity does not contravene the general prohibition in IAS 37 against provision for future operating losses. *[IAS 37.63]*.

A restructuring provision should include only the direct expenditures arising from the restructuring, which are those that are both:

(a) necessarily entailed by the restructuring; and

(b) not associated with the ongoing activities of the entity. *[IAS 37.80]*.

The standard gives specific examples of costs that may not be included within the provision, because they relate to the future conduct of the business. Such costs include:

(a) retraining or relocating continuing staff;

(b) marketing; or

(c) investment in new systems and distribution networks. *[IAS 37.81]*.

Because these costs relate to the future conduct of the business, they are recognised on the same basis as if they arose independently of a restructuring. *[IAS 37.81]*. In most cases, this means that the costs are recognised as the related services are provided.

Example 27.14: Distinguishing restructuring costs from ongoing expenses

On 15 November 2014, management announced its intention to close down its operation in the North of the country and relocate to a new site in the South, primarily to be closer to its key customers. Before the end of the reporting period (31 December 2014), the principal elements of the plan were agreed with employee representatives, a lease signed for a building at the new location, and a notice to vacate the existing facility given to the landlord; all on the basis that production would start at the new location on 31 March 2015 and the existing site would be vacated on 30 April 2015. Production would cease at the existing site on 28 February 2015 to allow plant and equipment to be relocated. Inventory levels would be increased up to that date so that customers could be supplied with goods sent from the Northern facility until 31 March.

Whilst the majority of the 600 existing staff was expected to take redundancy on 28 February 2015, 50 had agreed to accept the entity's offer of relocation, including an incentive of €3,000 each towards relocation costs. Of those employees taking redundancy, 20 had agreed to continue to work for the entity until 30 June 2015, to dismantle plant and equipment at the Northern site; install it at the new facility in the South; and train new staff on its operation. A bonus of €4,500 per employee would be payable if they remained until 30 June. A further 60 had agreed to stay with the entity until 31 March 2015, to ensure that inventory was sent out to customers before the new site was operational, of which 10 would remain until 30 April 2015 to complete the decommissioning of the Northern facility. These employees would also receive a bonus for staying until the promised date.

The announcement of management's decision on 15 November 2014 and the fact that the key elements of the plan were understood by employees, customers and the landlord of the Northern site before the end of the reporting period give rise to a constructive obligation that requires a provision to be recognised at 31 December 2014 for the best estimate of the costs of the reorganisation.

However, only those direct costs of the restructuring not associated with ongoing activities can be included in the provision. For example, as follows:

Chapter 27

Type of expense	Direct cost of restructuring	Associated with ongoing activities
Redundancy payments to 550 staff	•	
Payroll costs to 28 February 2015 (all 600 staff)		•
Relocation incentive of €3,000 per employee (50 staff)		•
Payroll costs – to 31 March 2015 (60 staff dispatching goods)		•
Payroll costs – March to June 2015 (20 staff relocating plant)[Note 1]	•	•
Payroll costs – April 2015 (10 staff decommissioning site)	•	
Costs of dismantling plant and equipment [Note 1]	•	•
Cost of transporting PP&E and inventory to the new site		•
Costs of recruiting and training staff for the Southern site		•
Rent of Northern site to 31 March 2015		•
Rent of Northern site for April 2015	•	
Cost of terminating lease of Northern site	•	
Rent of new site to 31 March 2015 (pre-production)		•
Cost of invoices, forms and stationery showing new address		•

Note 1: Costs relating to dismantling plant and equipment that is no longer intended for use in the business could be regarded as a direct cost of restructuring. However, costs relating to the dismantling and installation of equipment at the new site and training staff to operate it are costs associated with ongoing operations and, therefore, ineligible for inclusion in the restructuring provision.

This example shows that individual classes of expenditure should be disaggregated into components that distinguish those elements associated with ongoing activities. Even if expenditure would not have been incurred without the restructuring activity, its association with ongoing activities means that it is ineligible for inclusion in a provision. IAS 37 requires the cost to be *both* necessarily entailed by the restructuring *and* not associated with the ongoing activities of the entity. *[IAS 37.80]*.

For that reason, whilst the cost of making employees redundant is an eligible restructuring cost, any incremental amounts paid to retain staff to ensure a smooth transition of operations from one location to another are not eligible because they are incurred to facilitate ongoing activities. IAS 19 requires these to be treated as short-term employee benefits to the extent that they are expected to be settled within 12 months after the end of the reporting period.[25] Similarly, whilst the costs of dismantling plant and equipment intended to be scrapped is an eligible restructuring cost, the costs of dismantling plant and equipment intended to be relocated and installed at the new site is ineligible, because it is associated with ongoing activities.

A further rule in IAS 37 is that the provision should not include identifiable future operating losses up to the date of the restructuring, unless they relate to an onerous contract. *[IAS 37.82]*. This means that even if the operation being reorganised is loss-making, its ongoing costs are not provided for. This is consistent with the general prohibition against the recognition of provisions for future operating losses. *[IAS 37.63]*.

The general requirement in the standard that gains from the expected disposal of assets cannot be taken into account in the measurement of provisions, *[IAS 37.51]*, is also relevant to the measurement of restructuring provisions, even if the sale of the asset is envisaged as part of the restructuring. *[IAS 37.83]*. Whilst the expected disposal proceeds from asset sales might have been a significant element of the economic case for a restructuring, the income from disposal is not anticipated just because it is part of a restructuring plan.

6.2 Onerous contracts

Although future operating losses in general cannot be provided for, IAS 37 requires that 'if an entity has a contract that is onerous, the present obligation under the contract shall be recognised and measured as a provision'. *[IAS 37.66]*.

The standard notes that many contracts (for example, some routine purchase orders) can be cancelled without paying compensation to the other party, and therefore there is no obligation. However, other contracts establish both rights and obligations for each of the contracting parties. Where events make such a contract onerous, the contract falls within the scope of the standard and a liability exists which is recognised. Executory contracts that are not onerous fall outside the scope of the standard. *[IAS 37.67]*.

IAS 37 defines an onerous contract as 'a contract in which the unavoidable costs of meeting the obligations under the contract exceed the economic benefits expected to be received under it'. *[IAS 37.10]*. This requires that the contract is onerous to the point of being directly loss-making, not simply uneconomic by reference to current prices.

IAS 37 considers that 'the unavoidable costs under a contract reflect the least net cost of exiting from the contract, which is the lower of the cost of fulfilling it and any compensation or penalties arising from failure to fulfil it'. *[IAS 37.68]*. This evaluation does not require an intention by the entity to fulfil or to exit the contract. It does not even require there to be specific terms in the contract that apply in the event of its termination or breach. Its purpose is to recognise only the unavoidable costs to the entity, which in the absence of specific clauses in the contract relating to termination or breach could include an estimation of the cost of ceasing to honour the contract and having the other party go to court for compensation for the resultant breach.

There is a subtle yet important distinction between making a provision in respect of the unavoidable costs under a contract (reflecting the least net cost of what the entity has to do) compared to making an estimate of the cost of what the entity *intends* to do. The first is an obligation, which merits the recognition as a provision, whereas the second is a choice of the entity, which fails the recognition criteria because it does not exist independently of the entity's future actions, *[IAS 37.19]*, and is therefore akin to a future operating loss.

Example 27.15: Onerous supply contract

Entity P negotiated a contract in 2011 for the supply of components when availability in the market was scarce. It agreed to purchase 100,000 units per annum for 5 years commencing 1 January 2012 at a price of $20 per unit. Since then, new suppliers have entered the market and the typical price of a component is now $5 per unit. Whilst its activities are still profitable (Entity P makes a margin of $6 per unit of finished product sold) changes to the entity's own business means that it will not use all of the components it is contracted to purchase. As at 31 December 2014, Entity P expects to use 150,000 units in future and has 55,000 units in inventory. The contract requires 200,000 units to be purchased before the agreement expires in 2016. If the entity terminates the contract before 2016, compensation of $1 million per year is payable to the supplier. Each finished product contains one unit of the component.

Therefore, the entity expects to achieve a margin of $900,000 (150,000 × $6) on the units it will produce and sell; but will make a loss of $15 ($20 – $5) per unit on each of the 105,000 components (55,000 + 200,000 – 150,000) it is left with at the end of 2016 and now expects to sell in the components market.

In considering the extent to which the contract is onerous, Entity P in the example above should not concentrate solely on the net cost of the excess units of $1,575,000 (105,000 × $15) that it is contracted to purchase but which are expected to be left unsold. Instead, the entity should consider all of the related benefits of the contract, which includes the profits earned as a result of having a secure source of supply of components. Therefore the supply contract is onerous (directly loss making) only to the extent of the costs not covered by related revenues, justifying a provision of $675,000 ($1,575,000 – $900,000).

An example of such a provision is BG Group's capacity contract provisions, which are described in this extract.

Extract 27.3: BG Group plc (2012)

Notes to the accounts [extract]
21 PROVISIONS FOR OTHER LIABILITIES AND CHARGES [extract]
OTHER [extract]

The balance as at 31 December 2012 includes provisions for onerous contracts of $149m (2011: $165m), field-related payments of $53m (2011: $70m), insurance costs of $52m (2011: $53m) and costs associated with acquisitions, disposals and restructuring of $122m (2011: $106m). The payment dates are uncertain, but are expected to be between 2013 and 2018.

A provision for onerous contracts was recognised in 2007 in respect of capacity contracts in the Interconnector pipeline, retained following disposal of the Group's 25% equity in Interconnector (UK) Limited. The obligation associated with these contracts extends to 2018.

6.2.1 Recognition of provisions for vacant leasehold property

The most common example of an onerous contract in practice relates to leasehold property. From time to time entities may hold vacant leasehold property which they have substantially ceased to use for the purpose of their business and where sub-letting is either unlikely, or would be at a significantly reduced rental from that being paid by the entity. In these circumstances, the obligating event is the signing of the lease contract (a legal obligation) and when the lease becomes onerous, an outflow of resources embodying economic benefits is probable. Accordingly, a provision is recognised for the best estimate of the unavoidable lease payments. *[IAS 37 IE Example 8].*

Entities have to make systematic provision when such properties become vacant, and on a discounted basis where the effect is sufficiently material. Indeed, it could be argued that it is not just when the properties become vacant that provision would be required, but that provision should be made at the time the expected economic benefits of using the property fall short of the unavoidable costs under the lease. Although the Interpretations Committee had a preliminary discussion in December 2003 about the timing of recognition and the measurement of a provision for an onerous lease, including its application to other types of executory contracts such as a take or pay contract, it agreed that the issue should not be taken onto its agenda at that time.[26] However, it is sometimes the case in practice that entities interpret the requirements of IAS 37 as meaning that they should only recognise a provision when the properties are vacated.

Nevertheless, where a provision is to be recognised a number of difficulties remain. The first is how the provision should be calculated. It is unlikely that the provision will simply be the net present value of the future rental obligation, because if a substantial period of the lease remains, the entity will probably be able either to agree a negotiated sum with the landlord to terminate the lease early, or to sub-lease the building at some point in the future. Hence, the entity will have to make a best estimate of its future cash flows taking all these factors into account.

Another issue that arises from this is whether the provision in the statement of financial position should be shown net of any cash flows that may arise from sub-leasing the property, or whether the provision must be shown gross, with a corresponding asset set up for expected cash flows from sub-leasing only if they meet the recognition criteria of being 'virtually certain' to be received. Whilst the expense relating to a provision can be shown in the income statement net of reimbursement, *[IAS 37.54]*, the strict offset criteria in the standard (see 4.5 above) would suggest the latter to be required, as the entity would normally retain liability for the full lease payments if the sub-lessee defaulted. However, the standard makes no explicit reference to this issue. It is common for entities to apply a net approach for such onerous contracts under IAS 37. Indeed, it could be argued that because an onerous contract provision relates to the excess of the unavoidable costs over the expected economic benefits, *[IAS 37.68]*, there is no corresponding asset to be recognised. In its 2005 exposure draft of proposed amendments to IAS 37, the IASB confirmed that if an onerous contract is an operating lease, the unavoidable cost of the contract is the remaining lease commitment reduced by the estimated rentals that the entity could reasonably obtain, regardless of whether or not the entity intends to enter into a sublease.[27]

In the past, some entities may have maintained that no provision is required for vacant properties, because if the property leases are looked at on a portfolio basis, the overall economic benefits from properties exceed the overall costs. However, this argument is not sustainable under IAS 37, as the definition of an onerous contract refers specifically to costs and economic benefits *under the contract*. *[IAS 37.10]*.

It is more difficult to apply the definition of onerous contracts to the lease on a head office which is not generating revenue specifically. If the definition were applied too literally, one might end up concluding that all head office leases should be provided against because no specific economic benefits are expected under them. It would be more sensible to conclude that the entity as a whole obtains economic benefits from its head office, which is consistent with the way in which corporate assets are allocated to other cash generating units for the purposes of impairment testing (see Chapter 20 at 4.3.2). *[IAS 36.101]*. However, this does not alter the fact that if circumstances change and the head office becomes vacant, a provision should then be made in respect of the lease.

IAS 37 requires that any impairment loss that has occurred in respect of assets dedicated to an onerous contract is recognised before establishing a provision for the onerous contract. *[IAS 37.69]*. For example, any leasehold improvements that have been capitalised should be written off before provision is made for excess future rental costs. One company which has provided for onerous leases under IAS 37 is Jardine Matheson as indicated by the following extract.

Extract 27.4: Jardine Matheson Holdings Limited (2012)

Notes to the Financial Statements [extract]
34 Provisions

	Motor vehicle warranties US$m	Closure cost provisions US$m	Obligations under onerous leases US$m	Reinstate-ment and restoration costs US$m	Statutory employee entitlements US$m	Others US$m	Total US$m
2012							
At 1st January	23	10	3	39	84	10	**169**
Exchange differences	2	–	–	–	(5)	–	**(3)**
Additional provisions	8	3	1	3	28	3	**46**
Unused amounts reversed	–	(3)	–	(2)	–	(2)	**(7)**
Utilized	(4)	(4)	(1)	–	(1)	(1)	**(11)**
At 31st December	**29**	**6**	**3**	**40**	**106**	**10**	**194**
Non-current	–	–	2	36	93	5	**136**
Current	29	6	1	4	13	5	**58**
	29	**6**	**3**	**40**	**106**	**10**	**194**
2011							
At 1st January	21	10	3	37	68	10	149
Exchange differences	–	–	–	(1)	(1)	–	(2)
Additional provisions	6	4	1	4	20	3	38
Unused amounts reversed	–	(1)	–	(1)	–	(1)	(3)
Utilized	(4)	(3)	(1)	–	(3)	(2)	(13)
At 31st December	23	10	3	39	84	10	169
Non-current	–	–	2	36	70	4	112
Current	23	10	1	3	14	6	57
	23	10	3	39	84	10	169

Motor vehicle warranties are estimated liabilities that fall due under the warranty terms offered on sale of new and used vehicles beyond that which is reimbursed by the manufacturers.

Closure cost provisions are established when legal or constructive obligations arise on closure or disposal of businesses.

Provisions are made for obligations under onerous operating leases when the properties are not used by the Group and the net costs of exiting from the leases exceed the economic benefits expected to be received.

Other provisions principally comprise provisions in respect of indemnities on disposal of businesses and legal claims.

6.2.2 *Recognition of provisions for occupied leasehold property*

The discussion above deals with situations where the leasehold property becomes vacant. However, it does not address the case where the rentals payable for an occupied property increase under the contract or otherwise come to exceed current market rates. As noted above, IAS 37 defines an onerous contract as 'a contract in which the unavoidable costs of meeting the obligations under the contract exceed the economic benefits expected to be received under it'. *[IAS 37.10]*. This requires that the contract is onerous to the point of being directly loss-making, not simply uneconomic by reference to current prices. Thus, if the entity still expects to operate profitably from the leased property over the remaining period of its use, despite these higher rental payments, no provision should be made. If the business operated out of the leased property has become loss-making, and the entity does not expect to be able to improve its operating results to recover the higher rental payments over the remaining period of its use, then a provision may be necessary. However, before a separate provision for an onerous contract is established, IAS 37 requires that an entity should first recognise any impairment loss that has occurred on assets dedicated to the contract. *[IAS 37.69]*.

Tesco PLC includes in its property provisions an amount for the excess of future rents over market value on its loss-making stores.

Extract 27.5: Tesco PLC (2013)

Notes to the Group financial statements [extract]
Note 24 Provisions [extract]

Property provisions comprise obligations for future rents payable net of rents receivable on onerous leases including on vacant property and unprofitable stores, terminal dilapidations and other onerous contracts relating to property. The majority of these provisions are expected to be utilised over the period to 2020.

Tesco also provides for dilapidation costs relating to leasehold properties, which are discussed at 6.9 below.

6.2.3 *When an entity ceases to occupy part of a leased property*

A further complication arises in the case of a leased property when only part of the building under lease is vacated. In our view, despite the fact that the building is leased under a single contract, it is appropriate to regard physically separable parts of that building in isolation when determining whether the lease (or in this case part of it) is onerous. This would appear reasonable in the case of an office block with a number of floors, where it is customary for individual floors to be sub-let to other occupants.

Nevertheless, a distinction needs to be made between physically separable areas of a property that have been vacated (i.e. taken out of use by the lessee) and areas of a property that are being used inefficiently. It would be appropriate to recognise a provision for the rental costs related to a single floor of an office block that has been vacated. However, it would not be appropriate to recognise a provision in respect of an open-plan area that is still partly-occupied, albeit at less than its full capacity.

6.3 Decommissioning provisions

Decommissioning costs arise when an entity is required to dismantle or remove an asset at the end of its useful life and to restore the site on which it has been located, for example, when an oil rig or nuclear power station reaches the end of its economic life.

Rather than allowing an entity to build up a provision for the required costs over the life of the facility, IAS 37 requires that the liability is recognised as soon as the obligation arises, which will normally be at commencement of operations. This is because the construction of the asset (and the environmental damage caused by it) creates the past obligating event requiring restoration in the future. *[IAS 37 IE Example 3].*

The accounting for decommissioning costs is dealt with in IAS 37 by way of an example relating to an oil rig in an offshore oilfield (see Example 27.5 at 3.3 above). A provision is recognised at the time of constructing the oil rig in relation to the eventual costs that relate to its removal and the restoration of damage caused by building it. Additional provisions are recognised over the life of the oil field to reflect the need to reverse damage caused during the extraction of oil. *[IAS 37 IE Example 3].* The total decommissioning cost is estimated, discounted to its present value and it is this amount which forms the initial provision. This 'initial estimate of the costs of dismantling and removing the item and restoring the site' is added to the corresponding asset's cost. *[IAS 16.16].* Thereafter, the asset is depreciated over its useful life, while the discounted provision is progressively unwound, with the unwinding charge shown as a finance cost, as discussed at 4.3.5 above.

The effect of discounting on the statement of comprehensive income is to split the cost of the eventual decommissioning into two components: an expense based on the present value of the expected future cash outflows; and a finance element representing the unwinding of the discount. The overall effect is to produce a rising pattern of cost over the life of the facility, often with much of the total cost of the decommissioning classified as a finance cost.

AngloGold Ashanti's accounting policies and provisions note in respect of decommissioning obligations and restoration obligations are shown in the following extract.

Extract 27.6: AngloGold Ashanti Limited (2012)

GROUP – NOTES TO THE FINANCIAL STATEMENTS [extract]

For the year ended 31 December

1 **Accounting policies** [extract]

1.3 **Summary of significant accounting policies** [extract]

Environmental expenditure

The group has long-term remediation obligations comprising decommissioning and restoration liabilities relating to its past operations which are based on the group's environmental management plans, in compliance with current environmental and regulatory requirements. Provisions for non-recurring remediation costs are made when there is a present obligation, it is probable that expenditure on remediation work will be required and the cost can be estimated within a reasonable range of possible outcomes. The costs are based on currently available facts, technology expected to be available at the time of the clean up, laws and regulations presently or virtually certain to be enacted and prior experience in remediation of contaminated sites.

Contributions for the South African operations are made to Environmental Rehabilitation Trust Funds, created in accordance with local statutory requirements where applicable, to fund the estimated cost of rehabilitation during and at the end of the life of a mine. The amounts contributed to the trust funds are accounted for as non-current assets in the company. Interest earned on monies paid to rehabilitation trust funds is accrued on a time proportion basis and is recorded as interest income. For group purposes, the trusts are consolidated.

Decommissioning costs

The provision for decommissioning represents the cost that will arise from rectifying damage caused before production commences. Accordingly, a provision is recognised and a decommissioning asset is recognised and included within mine infrastructure.

Decommissioning costs are provided at the present value of the expenditures expected to settle the obligation, using estimated cash flows based on current prices. The unwinding of the decommissioning obligation is included in the income statement. Estimated future costs of decommissioning obligations are reviewed regularly and adjusted as appropriate for new circumstances or changes in law or technology. Changes in estimates are capitalised or reversed against the relevant asset. Estimates are discounted at a pre-tax rate that reflects current market assessments of the time value of money.

Gains or losses from the expected disposal of assets are not taken into account when determining the provision.

Restoration costs

The provision for restoration represents the costs of restoring site damage after the start of production. Changes in the provision are recorded in the income statement as a cost of production.

Restoration costs are estimated at the present value of the expenditures expected to settle the obligation, using estimated cash flows based on current prices and adjusted for the risks specific to the liability. The estimates are discounted at a pre-tax rate that reflects current market assessments of the time value of money.

Figures in million (US dollars)		**2012**	2011
27	**Environmental rehabilitation and other provisions** [extract]		
	Environmental rehabilitation obligations [extract]		
	Provision for decommissioning		
	Balance at beginning of year	**240**	213
	Change in estimates(1)	**53**	32
	Acquisition of subsidiary (note 33)	**6**	–
	Unwinding of decommissioning obligation (note 7)	**11**	12
	Translation	**(4)**	(17)
	Balance at end of year	**306**	240
	Provision for restoration		
	Balance at beginning of year	**507**	338
	Charge to income statement	**18**	8
	Change in estimates(1)	**(16)**	180
	Acquisition of subsidiary (note 33)	**34**	–
	Unwinding of restoration obligation (note 7) (2)	**18**	17
	Utilised during the year	**(21)**	(18)
	Translation	**(5)**	(18)
	Balance at end of year	**535**	507
	[...]		

(1) The change in estimates relates to changes in mine plans resulting in accelerated cash flows, changes in economic assumptions and discount rates and changes in design of tailings storage facilities and in methodology following requests from the environmental regulatory authorities. These provisions are expected to unwind beyond the end of the life of mine.

(2) Included in unwinding of restoration obligation is $1m (2011: $2m) which is recoverable from a third party. The asset is included in trade and other receivables.

6.3.1 Changes in estimated decommissioning costs (IFRIC 1)

IAS 37 requires provisions to be revised annually to reflect the current best estimate of the provision. *[IAS 37.59]*. However, the standard gives no guidance on accounting for changes in the decommissioning provision. Similarly, IAS 16 is unclear about the extent to which an item's carrying amount should be affected by changes in the estimated amount of dismantling and site restoration costs that occur *after* the estimate made upon initial measurement. This was addressed by the IASB with the publication of IFRIC 1 in May 2004.

IFRIC 1 applies to any decommissioning, restoration or similar liability that has been both included as part of the cost of an asset measured in accordance with IAS 16 and recognised as a liability in accordance with IAS 37. *[IFRIC 1.2]*. It addresses how the effect of the following events that change the measurement of an existing decommissioning, restoration or similar liability should be accounted for:

(a) a change in the estimated outflow of resources embodying economic benefits (e.g. cash flows) required to settle the obligation;

(b) a change in the current market-based discount rate (this includes changes in the time value of money and the risks specific to the liability); and

(c) an increase that reflects the passage of time (also referred to as the unwinding of the discount). *[IFRIC 1.3]*.

IFRIC 1 requires that (c) above, the periodic unwinding of the discount, is recognised in profit or loss as a finance cost as it occurs. *[IFRIC 1.8]*. The Interpretations Committee concluded that the unwinding of the discount is not a borrowing cost as defined in IAS 23, and thus cannot be capitalised under that standard. *[IFRIC 1.BC26-27]*.

For a change caused by (a) or (b) above, however, the adjustment is taken to the income statement only in specific circumstances. Any revision to the provision (other than to reflect the passage of time) is first recognised in the carrying value of the related asset or in other comprehensive income, depending on whether the asset is measured at cost or using the revaluation model. *[IFRIC 1.4-7]*.

If the related asset is measured using the cost model, the change in the liability should be added to or deducted from the cost of the asset to which it relates. Where the change gives rise to an addition to cost, the entity should consider the need to test the new carrying value for impairment. Reductions over and above the remaining carrying value of the asset are recognised immediately in profit or loss. *[IFRIC 1.5]*. The adjusted depreciable amount of the asset is then depreciated prospectively over its remaining useful life. *[IFRIC 1.7]*. IFRIC 1 includes the following illustrative example.

Example 27.16: Changes in decommissioning costs – related asset measured at cost

An entity has a nuclear power plant and a related decommissioning liability. The nuclear power plant started operating on 1 January 2005. The plant has a useful life of 40 years. Its initial cost was \$120,000,000; this included an amount for decommissioning costs of \$10,000,000, which represented \$70,400,000 in estimated cash flows payable in 40 years discounted at a risk-adjusted rate of 5%. The entity's financial year ends on 31 December.

On 31 December 2014, the plant is 10 years old. Accumulated depreciation is $30,000,000. Because of the unwinding of discount over the 10 years, the decommissioning liability has grown from $10,000,000 to $16,300,000.

On 31 December 2014, the discount rate has not changed. However, the entity estimates that, as a result of technological advances, the net present value of the expected cash flows has decreased by $8,000,000. Accordingly, the entity reduces the decommissioning liability from $16,300,000 to $8,300,000 and reduces the carrying amount of the asset by the same amount.

Following this adjustment, the carrying amount of the asset is $82,000,000 ($120,000,000 – $8,000,000 – $30,000,000), which will be depreciated over the remaining 30 years of the asset's life to give a depreciation expense for 2015 of $2,733,333 ($82,000,000 ÷ 30). The next year's finance cost for the unwinding of the discount will be $415,000 ($8,300,000 × 5%). *[IFRIC 1.IE1-4].*

In illustrating the requirements of the Interpretation, the example in IFRIC 1 reduces the carrying value of the whole asset (comprising its construction cost and decommissioning cost) by the reduction in the present value of the decommissioning provision. The solution set out in the example does not treat the decommissioning element as a separate component of the asset. Had this been the case, the component would have had accumulated depreciation as at 31 December 2014 of $2,500,000 ($10,000,000 × 10/40), giving a carrying amount of $7,500,000 at that date and a gain of $500,000 when reduced by the decrease in the provision of $8,000,000. Accordingly, we believe that the example in IFRIC 1 indicates that it would not be appropriate to recognise any gain until the carrying value of the whole asset is extinguished.

If the related asset is measured using the revaluation model, changes in the liability alter the revaluation surplus or deficit previously recognised for that asset. Changes to the provision are recognised in other comprehensive income and increase or decrease the value of the revaluation surplus in respect of the asset, except to the extent that:

(a) a decrease in the provision reverses a previous revaluation deficit that was recognised in profit or loss;

(b) a decrease in the provision exceeds the carrying amount of the asset that would have been recognised under the cost model; or

(c) an increase in the provision exceeds the previous revaluation surplus relating to that asset,

in which case the change is recognised in profit or loss. Changes in the provision might also indicate the need for the asset (and therefore all assets in the same class) to be revalued. *[IFRIC 1.6].*

The illustrative examples in IFRIC 1 address this alternative.

Example 27.17: Changes in decommissioning costs – related asset carried at valuation

Assume that the entity in Example 27.16 above instead adopts the revaluation model in IAS 16, and its policy is to eliminate accumulated depreciation at the revaluation date against the gross carrying amount of the asset.

The entity first revalues the asset as at 31 December 2007 when the nuclear power plant is 3 years old. The valuation of $115,000,000 comprises a gross valuation of $126,600,000 and an allowance of $11,600,000 for decommissioning costs, which represents no change to the original estimate, after

Chapter 27

the unwinding of three years' discount. The amounts included in the statement of financial position at 31 December 2007 and the related revaluation reserve movements are therefore:

	Net book value	*Valuation*	*Revaluation reserve*
	$'000	$'000	$'000
Cost or valuation	120,000	126,600	6,600
Accumulated depreciation (3/40)	(9,000)	–	9,000
Carrying amount of asset	111,000	126,600	15,600
Original provision	10,000		
Unwinding of discount (3 years @ 5%)	1,600		
	11,600	11,600	
Carrying amount less provision	99,400	115,000	15,600

The depreciation expense for 2008 is therefore $3,420,000 ($126,600,000 ÷ 37) and the discount expense for 2008 is $580,000 (5% of $11,600,000). On 31 December 2008, the decommissioning liability (before any adjustment) is $12,180,000 and the discount rate has not changed. However, on that date, the entity estimates that, as a result of technological advances, the present value of the decommissioning liability has decreased by $5,000,000. Accordingly, the entity adjusts the decommissioning liability to $7,180,000. To determine the extent to which any of the change to the provision is recognised in profit or loss, the entity has to keep a record of revaluations previously recognised in profit or loss; the carrying amount of the asset that would have been recognised under the cost model; and the previous revaluation surplus relating to that asset. *[IFRIC 1.6]*. In this example, the whole of the adjustment is taken to revaluation surplus, because it does not exceed the carrying amount that would have been recognised for the asset under the cost model of $103,000 (see below). *[IFRIC 1.IE6-10]*.

In addition, the entity decides that a full valuation of the asset is needed at 31 December 2008, in order to ensure that the carrying amount does not differ materially from fair value. Suppose that the asset is now valued at $107,000,000, which is net of an allowance of $7,180,000 for the reduced decommissioning obligation. The valuation of the asset for financial reporting purposes, before deducting this allowance, is therefore $114,180,000. The effect on the revaluation reserve of the revision to the estimate of the decommissioning provision and the new valuation can be illustrated in the table below. *[IFRIC 1.IE11-12]*.

	Cost model	*Revaluation*	*Revaluation reserve*
	$'000	$'000	$'000
Carrying amount as at 31 December 2007	111,000	126,600	15,600
Depreciation charge for 2008	(3,000)	(3,420)	
Carrying amount as at 31 December 2008	108,000	123,180	
Revision to estimate of provision	(5,000)		
Revaluation adjustment in 2008		(9,000)	(9,000)
	103,000	114,180	
Provision as at 31 December 2007	11,600	11,600	
Unwinding of discount @ 5%	580	580	
Revision to estimate	(5,000)	(5,000)	5,000
Provision as at 31 December 2008	7,180	7,180	
Carrying amount less provision	95,820	107,000	11,600

These requirements are discussed further in Chapter 18 at 4.3.

As indicated at 4.3.6 above, IAS 37 is unclear whether a new discount rate should be applied during the year or just at the year-end, and whether the rate should be applied to the new estimate of the provision or the old estimate. Although IFRIC 1 requires that changes in the provision resulting from a change in the discount rate is added to, or deducted from, the cost of the related asset in the current period, it does not deal specifically with these points. However, Example 1 in the illustrative examples to IFRIC 1 indicates that a change in discount rate would be accounted for in the same way as other changes affecting the estimate of a provision for decommissioning, restoration and similar liabilities. That is, it is reflected as a change in the liability at the time the revised estimate is made and the new estimate is discounted at the revised discount rate from that point on. *[IFRIC 1.IE5]*.

When accounting for revalued assets to which decommissioning liabilities attach, the illustrative example in IFRIC 1 states that it is important to understand the basis of the valuation obtained. For example:

(a) if an asset is valued on a discounted cash flow basis, some valuers may value the asset without deducting any allowance for decommissioning costs (a 'gross' valuation), whereas others may value the asset after deducting an allowance for decommissioning costs (a 'net' valuation), because an entity acquiring the asset will generally also assume the decommissioning obligation. For financial reporting purposes, the decommissioning obligation is recognised as a separate liability, and is not deducted from the asset. Accordingly, if the asset is valued on a net basis, it is necessary to adjust the valuation obtained by adding back the allowance for the liability, so that the liability is not counted twice. This is the case in Example 27.17 above;

(b) if an asset is valued on a depreciated replacement cost basis, the valuation obtained may not include an amount for the decommissioning component of the asset. If it does not, an appropriate amount will need to be added to the valuation to reflect the depreciated replacement cost of that component. *[IFRIC 1.IE7]*.

6.3.2 *Changes in legislation after construction of the asset*

The scope of IFRIC 1 is set out in terms of any existing decommissioning, restoration or similar liability that is both recognised as part of the cost of the asset under IAS 16; and recognised as a liability in accordance with IAS 37. *[IFRIC 1.2]*. The Interpretation does not address the treatment of obligations arising after the asset has been constructed, for example as a result of changes in legislation. *[IFRIC 1.BC23]*. Nevertheless, in our opinion the cost of the related asset should be measured in accordance with the principles set out in IFRIC 1 regardless of whether the obligation exists at the time of constructing the asset or arises later in its life.

As discussed at 3.3 in Chapter 18, IAS 16 makes no distinction in principle between the initial costs of acquiring an asset and any subsequent expenditure upon it. In both cases any and all expenditure has to meet the recognition rules, and be expensed in profit or loss if it does not. IAS 16 states that the cost of an item of property, plant and equipment includes 'the initial estimate of the costs of dismantling and removing the item and restoring the site on which it is located, the obligation for which an entity incurs either when the item is acquired or as a consequence of having used the item during a particular period for purposes other than to produce inventories during that period.' *[IAS 16.16(c)]*.

When changes in legislation give rise to a new decommissioning, restoration or similar liability that is added to the carrying amount of the related asset, it would be appropriate to perform an impairment review in accordance with IAS 36 (see Chapter 20).

6.3.3 Funds established to meet an obligation (IFRIC 5)

Some entities may participate in a decommissioning, restoration or environmental rehabilitation fund, the purpose of which is to segregate assets to fund some or all of the costs of decommissioning for which the entity has to make a provision under IAS 37. IFRIC 5 was issued in December 2004 to address this issue, referring to decommissioning to mean not only the dismantling of plant and equipment but also the costs of undertaking environmental rehabilitation, such as rectifying pollution of water or restoring mined land. *[IFRIC 5.1]*.

Contributions to these funds may be voluntary or required by regulation or law, and the funds may have one of the following common structures:

- funds that are established by a single contributor to fund its own decommissioning obligations, whether for a particular site, or for a number of geographically dispersed sites;
- funds that are established with multiple contributors to fund their individual or joint decommissioning obligations, where contributors are entitled to reimbursement for decommissioning expenses to the extent of their fund contributions plus any actual earnings on those contributions less their share of the costs of administering the fund. Contributors may have an obligation to make potential additional contributions, for example, in the event of the bankruptcy of another contributor;
- funds that are established with multiple contributors to fund their individual or joint decommissioning obligations when the required level of contributions is based on the current activity of a contributor, but the benefit obtained by that contributor is based on its past activity. In such cases there is a potential mismatch in the amount of contributions made by a contributor (based on current activity) and the value realisable from the fund (based on past activity). *[IFRIC 5.2]*.

Such funds generally have the following features:

- the fund is separately administered by independent trustees;
- entities (contributors) make contributions to the fund, which are invested in a range of assets that may include both debt and equity investments, and are available to help pay the contributors' decommissioning costs. The trustees determine how contributions are invested, within the constraints set by the fund's governing documents and any applicable legislation or other regulations;
- the contributors retain the obligation to pay decommissioning costs. However, contributors are able to obtain reimbursement of decommissioning costs from the fund up to the lower of the decommissioning costs incurred and the entity's share of assets of the fund; and
- the contributors may have restricted or no access to any surplus of assets of the fund over those used to meet eligible decommissioning costs. *[IFRIC 5.3]*.

IFRIC 5 applies to accounting in the financial statements of a contributor for interests arising from decommissioning funds that have both the following features:

- the assets are administered separately (either by being held in a separate legal entity or as segregated assets within another entity); and
- a contributor's right to access the assets is restricted. *[IFRIC 5.4]*.

A residual interest in a fund that extends beyond a right to reimbursement, such as a contractual right to distributions once all the decommissioning has been completed or on winding up the fund, may be an equity instrument within the scope of IAS 39 or IFRS 9, as appropriate, and is not within the scope of IFRIC 5. *[IFRIC 5.5]*.

The issues addressed by IFRIC 5 are:

(a) How should a contributor account for its interest in a fund?

(b) When a contributor has an obligation to make additional contributions, for example, in the event of the bankruptcy of another contributor, how should that obligation be accounted for? *[IFRIC 5.6]*.

6.3.3.A Accounting for an interest in a fund

IFRIC 5 requires the contributor to recognise its obligations to pay decommissioning costs as a liability and recognise its interest in the fund separately, unless the contributor is not liable to pay decommissioning costs even if the fund fails to pay. *[IFRIC 5.7]*.

The contributor determines whether it has control, joint control or significant influence over the fund by reference to IFRS 10 – *Consolidated Financial Statements*, IFRS 11 – *Joint Arrangements* – and IAS 28 – *Investments in Associates and Joint Ventures*. If the contributor determines that it has such control, joint control or significant influence, it should account for its interest in the fund in accordance with those standards (see Chapters 6, 11 and 12 respectively). *[IFRIC 5.8]*.

Otherwise, the contributor should recognise the right to receive reimbursement from the fund as a reimbursement in accordance with IAS 37 (see 4.5 above). This reimbursement should be measured at the lower of:

- the amount of the decommissioning obligation recognised; and
- the contributor's share of the fair value of the net assets of the fund attributable to contributors. *[IFRIC 5.9]*.

This 'asset cap' means that the asset recognised in respect of the reimbursement rights can never exceed the recognised liability. Accordingly, rights to receive reimbursement to meet decommissioning liabilities that have yet to be recognised as a provision are not recognised. *[IFRIC 5.BC14]*. Although many respondents expressed concern about this asset cap and argued that rights to benefit in excess of this amount give rise to an additional asset, separate from the reimbursement asset, the Interpretations Committee, despite having sympathy with the concerns, concluded that to recognise such an asset would be inconsistent with the requirement in IAS 37 that 'the amount recognised for the reimbursement should not exceed the amount of the provision'. *[IFRIC 5.BC19-20]*.

Changes in the carrying value of the right to receive reimbursement other than contributions to and payments from the fund should be recognised in profit or loss in the period in which these changes occur. *[IFRIC 5.9]*.

The effect of this requirement is that the amount recognised in the statement of comprehensive income relating to the reimbursement bears no relation to the expense recognised in respect of the provision, particularly for decommissioning liabilities where most changes in the measurement of the provision are not taken to the profit or loss immediately, but are recognised prospectively over the remaining useful life of the related asset (see 6.3.1 above).

One company that has been affected by the 'asset cap' is Fortum as shown below. In this extract, the company observes that because IFRS does not allow the asset to exceed the amount of the provision, *[IFRIC 5.BC19-20]*, it recognises a reimbursement asset in its statement of financial position that is lower than its actual share of the fund.

Extract 27.7: Fortum Oyj (2012)

Notes to the consolidated financial statements [extract]

1 Summary of significant accounting policies [extract]

1.25 Assets and liabilities related to decommissioning of nuclear power plants and the disposal of spent fuel [extract]

Fortum owns Loviisa nuclear power plant in Finland. Fortum's nuclear related provisions and the related part of the State Nuclear Waste Management Fund are both presented separately in the balance sheet. Fortum's share in the State Nuclear Waste Management Fund is accounted for according to IFRIC 5, Rights to interests arising from decommissioning, restoration and environmental rehabilitation funds which states that the fund assets are measured at the lower of fair value or the value of the related liabilities since Fortum does not have control or joint control over the State Nuclear Waste Management Fund. The related provisions are the provision for decommissioning and the provision for disposal of spent fuel.

[...]

Fortum's actual share of the State Nuclear Waste Management Fund, related to Loviisa nuclear power plant, is higher than the carrying value of the Fund in the balance sheet. The legal nuclear liability should, according to the Finnish Nuclear Energy Act, be fully covered by payments and guarantees to the State Nuclear Waste Management Fund. The legal liability is not discounted while the provisions are, and since the future cash flow is spread over 100 years, the difference between the legal liability and the provisions are material.

34 Nuclear related assets and liabilities [extract]

EUR million	2012	2011
Amounts recognised in the balance sheet		
Nuclear provisions	678	653
Share in the State Nuclear Waste Management Fund	678	653
Legal liability and actual share of the State Nuclear Waste Management Fund		
Liability for nuclear waste management according to the Nuclear Energy Act	996	968
Funding obligation target	996	941
Fortum's share in the State Nuclear Waste Management Fund	956	903

34.1 Nuclear related provisions [extract]

[...] The legal liability by the end of 2012, decided by the Ministry of Employment and the Economy and calculated according to the Nuclear Energy Act, is EUR 996 million (2011: 968). The carrying value of the nuclear provisions in the balance sheet, calculated according to IAS 37, have increased by EUR 25 million compared to 31 December 2011, totalling EUR 678 million on 31 December 2012. The main reason for the difference between the carrying value of the provision and the legal liability is the fact that the legal liability is not discounted to net present value.

The change in the provision for decommissioning is added to the nuclear decommissioning cost and depreciated over the remaining estimated operating time of the nuclear power plant. [...]

Nuclear provisions **EUR million**	**2012**	**2011**
1 January	**653**	**625**
Additional provisions	10	17
Used during the year	–21	–25
Unwinding of discount	36	36
31 December	**678**	**653**
Fortum's share in the State Nuclear Waste Management Fund	678	653

34.2 Fortum's share in the State Nuclear Waste Management Fund [extract]

Fortum contributes funds to the State Nuclear Waste Management Fund in Finland to cover future obligations based on the legal liability calculated according to the Finnish Nuclear Energy Act. The fund is managed by governmental authorities. The carrying value of the Fund in Fortum's balance sheet is calculated according to IFRIC 5 *Rights to interests arising from decommissioning, restoration and environmental rehabilitation funds*.

According to the Nuclear Energy Act, Fortum is obligated to contribute the funds in full to the State Nuclear Waste Management Fund to cover the legal liability.

The Fund is from an IFRS perspective overfunded with EUR 278 million (2011: 250), since Fortum's share of the Fund on 31 December 2012 is EUR 956 million (2011: 903) and the carrying value in the balance sheet is EUR 678 million (2011: 653).

Operating profit for 2012 includes a negative total adjustment of EUR –31 million (2011: –28), since the value of the Fund has increased more than the carrying value of the provision. [...]

34.2.1 Funding obligation target [extract]

The funding obligation target for the each year is decided by the Ministry of Employment and the Economy in December each year after the legal liability has been decided. The difference between the funding obligation target for Fortum and Fortum's actual share of the State Nuclear Waste Management Fund is paid in Q1 each year.

6.3.3.B *Accounting for obligations to make additional contributions*

IFRIC 5 requires that when a contributor has an obligation to make potential additional contributions, for example, in the event of the bankruptcy of another contributor or if the value of the investments held by the fund decreases to an extent that they are insufficient to fulfil the fund's reimbursement obligations, this obligation is a contingent liability that is within the scope of IAS 37. The contributor shall recognise a liability only if it is probable that additional contributions will be made. *[IFRIC 5.10]*.

6.3.3.C *Gross presentation of interest in the fund and the decommissioning liability*

IFRIC 5 requires the contributor to a fund to recognise its obligations to pay decommissioning costs as a liability and recognise its interest in the fund separately, unless the contributor is not liable to pay decommissioning costs even if the fund fails to pay. *[IFRIC 5.7]*. Accordingly, in most cases it would not be appropriate to offset the decommissioning liability and the interest in the fund.

The Interpretations Committee reached this conclusion because IAS 37 requires an entity that remains liable for expenditure to recognise a provision even where reimbursement is available and to recognise a separate reimbursement asset only when the entity is virtually certain that it will be received when the obligation is settled.

[IFRIC 5.BC7]. The Interpretations Committee also noted that the conditions in IAS 32 – *Financial Instruments: Presentation* – for offsetting a financial asset and a financial liability would rarely be met because of the absence of a legal right of set off and the likelihood that settlement will not be net or simultaneous. *[IAS 32.42].* Arguments that the existence of a fund allows derecognition of the liability by analogy to IAS 39; or a net presentation similar to a pension fund, were also rejected. *[IFRIC 5.BC8].*

6.4 Environmental provisions – general guidance in IAS 37

The standard illustrates its recognition requirements in two examples relating to environmental provisions. The first deals with the situation where it is virtually certain that legislation will be enacted which will require the clean up of land already contaminated. In these circumstances, the virtual certainty of new legislation being enacted means that the entity has a present legal obligation as a result of the past event (contamination of the land), requiring a provision to be recognised. *[IAS 37 IE Example 2A].* However, in its discussion about what constitutes an obligating event, the standard notes that 'differences in circumstances surrounding enactment make it impossible to specify a single event that would make the enactment of a law virtually certain. In many cases, it will be impossible to be virtually certain of the enactment of a law until it is enacted.' *[IAS 37.22].* The second example deals with a similar situation, except that the entity is not expected to be legally required to clean it up. Nevertheless, the entity has a widely publicised environmental policy undertaking to clean up all contamination that it causes, and has a record of honouring this policy. In these circumstances a provision is still required because the entity has created a valid expectation that it will clean up the land, meaning that the entity has a present constructive obligation as a result of past contamination. *[IAS 37 IE Example 2B].* It is therefore clear that where an entity causes environmental damage and has a present legal or constructive obligation to make it good; it is probable that an outflow of resources will be required to settle the obligation; and a reliable estimate can be made of the amount, a provision will be required. *[IAS 37.14].*

One company making provision for environmental costs is Syngenta, which describes some of the practical difficulties and uncertainties relating to its measurement in the extract below.

Extract 27.8: Syngenta AG (2012)

Notes to the Syngenta Group Consolidated Financial Statements [extract]

2. Accounting policies [extract]

Environmental provisions [extract]

Provisions for remediation costs are made when there is a present obligation, it is probable that expenditures for remediation work will be required within ten years (or a longer period if specified by a legal obligation) and the cost can be estimated within a reasonable range of possible outcomes. The costs are based on currently available facts: technology expected to be available at the time of the clean up; laws and regulations presently or virtually certain to be enacted; and prior experience in remediation of contaminated sites. Environmental liabilities are recorded at the estimated amount at which the liability could be settled at the balance sheet date, and are discounted if the impact is material and if cost estimates and timing are considered reasonably certain.

19. Provisions [extract]

Movements in provisions for the year ended December 31, 2012 are as follows: [extract]

($m)	January 1	Charged to income	Release of provisions credited to income	Payments	Actuarial (gains)/ losses	Transfers offset in defined benefit pension assets	Currency translation effects/ other	December 31
Environmental provisions	369	4	(3)	(33)	–	–	6	343

25. Commitments and contingencies [extract]

Environmental Matters

In the opinion of Syngenta, it is not possible to estimate reliably the remediation costs that may be incurred in the future for environmental damage that has occurred at sites currently in operation and having no present obligation for environmental damage remediation because it is neither possible to determine a time limit beyond which the sites will no longer be operated, nor what remediation costs may be required upon their eventual closure.

In the USA, Syngenta and/or its indemnitors or indemnitees, have been named under federal legislation (the Comprehensive Environmental Response, Compensation and Liability Act of 1980, as amended) as a potentially responsible party ("PRP") in respect of several sites. Syngenta expects to be indemnified against a proportion of the liabilities associated with a number of these sites by the sellers of the businesses associated with such sites and, where appropriate, actively participates in or monitors the clean-up activities at the sites in respect of which it is a PRP.

If the expenditure relating to an environmental obligation is not expected to be incurred for some time, a significant effect of the standard is its requirement that provisions should be discounted, which can have a material impact. BP sets out its policy in the following extract.

Extract 27.9: BP p.l.c. (2012)

Notes on financial statements [extract]

1. Significant accounting policies [extract]

Environmental expenditures and liabilities

Environmental expenditures that relate to current or future revenues are expensed or capitalized as appropriate. Expenditures that relate to an existing condition caused by past operations and do not contribute to current or future earnings are expensed.

Liabilities for environmental costs are recognized when a clean-up is probable and the associated costs can be reliably estimated. Generally, the timing of recognition of these provisions coincides with the commitment to a formal plan of action or, if earlier, on divestment or on closure of inactive sites.

The amount recognized is the best estimate of the expenditure required. Where the liability will not be settled for a number of years, the amount recognized is the present value of the estimated future expenditure.

36. Provisions [extract]	$ million Environmental
At 1 January 2012	3,264
Exchange adjustments	3
Acquisitions	–
New or increased provisions	1,350
Derecognition of provision for items that cannot be reliably estimated	–
Write-back of unused provisions	(65)
Unwinding of discount	9
Utilization	(841)
Reclassified as liabilities directly associated with assets held for sale	(91)
Deletions	(1)
At 31 December 2012	3,628
Of which – current	1,235
– non-current	2,393

	$ million Environmental
At 1 January 2011	2,465
Exchange adjustments	(4)
Acquisitions	–
New or increased provisions	1,677
Write-back of unused provisions	(140)
Unwinding of discount	27
Change in discount rate	90
Utilization	(840)
Reclassified as liabilities directly associated with assets held for sale	–
Deletions	(11)
At 31 December 2011	3,264
Of which – current	1,375
– non-current	1,889

Provisions not related to the Gulf of Mexico oil spill [extract]

Provisions for environmental remediation are made when a clean-up is probable and the amount of the obligation can be estimated reliably. Generally, this coincides with commitment to a formal plan of action or, if earlier, on divestment or closure of inactive sites. The provision for environmental liabilities has been estimated using existing technology, at current prices and discounted using a real discount rate of 0.5% (2011 0.5%). The weighted average period over which these costs are generally expected to be incurred is estimated to be approximately five years. The extent and cost of future remediation programmes are inherently difficult to estimate. They depend on the scale of any possible contamination, the timing and extent of corrective actions, and also the group's share of liability.

Provisions relating to the Gulf of Mexico oil spill [extract]

Environmental

The amounts committed by BP for a 10-year research programme to study the impact of the incident on the marine and shoreline environment of the Gulf of Mexico have been provided for. BP's commitment is to provide $500 million of funding, and the remaining commitment, on a discounted basis, of $376 million was included in provisions at 31 December 2012. This amount is expected to be spent over the remaining life of the programme.

As a responsible party under the Oil Pollution Act of 1990 (OPA 90), BP faces claims by the United States, as well as by State, tribal, and foreign trustees, if any, for natural resource damages ("Natural Resource Damages claims"). These damages include, among other things, the reasonable costs of assessing the injury to natural resources. BP has been incurring natural resource damage assessment costs and a provision has been made for the estimated costs of the assessment phase. Since May 2010, more than 200 initial and amended work plans have been developed to study resources and habitat. The study data will inform an assessment of injury to the Gulf Coast natural resources and the development of a restoration plan to mitigate the identified injuries. Detailed analysis and interpretation continue on the data that have been collected. The expected assessment spend is based upon past experience as well as identified projects. During 2011, BP entered a framework agreement with natural resource trustees for the United States and five Gulf coast states, providing for up to $1 billion to be spent on early restoration projects to address natural resource injuries resulting from the oil spill, to be funded from the $20-billion trust fund. In 2012, work began on the initial set of early restoration projects identified under this framework. The total amount provided for natural resource damage assessment costs and early restoration projects was $1,486 million at 31 December 2012. Until the size, location and duration of the impact is assessed, it is not possible to estimate reliably either the amounts or timing of the remaining Natural Resource Damages claims other than the assessment and early restoration costs noted above, therefore no additional amounts have been provided for these items and they are disclosed as a contingent liability. See Note 43 for further information.

6.5 Liabilities associated with emissions trading schemes

A number of countries around the world either have, or are developing, schemes to encourage reduced emissions of pollutants, in particular of greenhouse gases. These schemes comprise tradable emissions allowances or permits, an example of which is a 'cap and trade' model whereby participants are allocated emission rights or allowances equal to a cap (i.e. a maximum level of allowable emissions) and are permitted to trade those allowances. A cap and trade emission rights scheme typically has the following features:[28]

- an entity participating in the scheme (participant) is set a target to reduce its emissions to a specified level (the cap). The participant is issued allowances equal in number to its cap by a government or government agency. Allowances may be issued free of charge, or participants may pay the government for them;
- the scheme operates for defined compliance periods;
- participants are free to buy and sell allowances;
- if at the end of the compliance period a participant's actual emissions exceeded its emission rights, the participant will incur a penalty;
- in some schemes emission rights may be carried forward to future periods; and
- the scheme may provide for brokers – who are not themselves participants – to buy and sell emission rights.

In response to diversity in the accounting for cap and trade emission rights schemes, the Interpretations Committee added this matter to its agenda. Accordingly, in December 2004 the IASB issued IFRIC 3 – *Emission Rights* – to address the accounting for emission allowances that arise from cap and trade emission rights schemes.

IFRIC 3 took the view that a cap and trade scheme did not give rise to a net asset or liability, but that it gave rise to various items that were to be accounted for separately:[29]

(a) *an asset for allowances held* – Allowances, whether allocated by government or purchased, were to be regarded as intangible assets and accounted for under IAS 38 – *Intangible Assets.* Allowances issued for less than fair value were to be measured initially at their fair value;[30]

(b) *a government grant* – When allowances are issued for less than fair value, the difference between the amount paid and fair value was a government grant that should be accounted for under IAS 20 – *Accounting for Government Grants and Disclosure of Government Assistance.* Initially the grant was to be recognised as deferred income in the statement of financial position and subsequently recognised as income on a systematic basis over the compliance period for which the allowances were issued, regardless of whether the allowances were held or sold;[31]

(c) *a liability for the obligation to deliver allowances equal to emissions that have been made* – As emissions are made, a liability was to be recognised as a provision that falls within the scope of IAS 37. The liability was to be measured at the best estimate of the expenditure required to settle the present obligation at the end of the reporting period. This would usually be the present market price of the number of allowances required to cover emissions made up to the end of the reporting period.[32]

However, the interpretation met with significant resistance because application of IFRIC 3 would result in a number of accounting mismatches:[33]

- a measurement mismatch between the assets and liabilities recognised in accordance with IFRIC 3;
- a mismatch in the location in which the gains and losses on those assets are reported; and
- a possible timing mismatch because allowances would be recognised when they are obtained – typically at the start of the year – whereas the emission liability would be recognised during the year as it is incurred.

Consequently, the IASB decided in June 2005 to withdraw IFRIC 3 despite the fact that it considered it to be 'an appropriate interpretation of existing IFRSs'.[34] The IASB activated its project on emission trading schemes in December 2007 but work was suspended in November 2010. At the time of writing, users and preparers of financial statements can refer only to the unanimous support of IASB members in May 2012 to giving priority to starting again its research on emission trading schemes.[35] However, the IASB has given no indication of the expected timetable for this research project.[36]

In the meantime, entities can either:

(a) apply IFRIC 3, which despite having been withdrawn, is considered to be an appropriate interpretation of existing IFRS; or

(b) develop its own accounting policy for cap and trade schemes based on the hierarchy of authoritative guidance in IAS 8.

A fuller discussion of the issues and methods applied in practice are covered in Chapter 17 at 11.2.

6.6 Green certificates compared to emissions trading schemes

Some countries have launched schemes to promote the production of power from renewable sources based on green certificates – also known as renewable energy certificates (RECs), green tags, or tradable renewable certificates.

In a green certificates system, a producer of electricity from renewable sources is granted certificates by the government based on the power output (kWh) of green electricity produced. These certificates may be used in the current and future compliance periods as defined by the particular scheme. The certificates can be sold separately. Generally the cost to produce green electricity is higher than the cost of producing an equivalent amount of electricity generated from non-renewable sources, although this is not always the case. Distributors of electricity sell green electricity at the same price as other electricity.

In a typical green certificates scheme, distributors of electricity to consumers (businesses, households etc.) are required to remit a number of green certificates based on the kWh of electricity sold on an annual basis. Distributors must therefore purchase green certificates in the market (such certificates having been sold by producers). If a distribution company does not have the number of required certificates, it is required to pay a penalty to the environmental agency. Once the penalty is paid, the entity is discharged of its obligations to remit certificates.

It is this requirement to remit certificates that creates a market in and gives value to green certificates (the value depends on many variables but primarily on the required number of certificates that have to be delivered relative to the amount of power that is produced from renewable sources, and the level of penalty payable if the required number of certificates are not remitted).

There are similarities between green certificates and emission rights. However, green certificates are granted to generators of cleaner energy as an incentive for 'good' production achieved, irrespective of whether or not there is a subsequent sale of that cleaner energy to an end consumer. For a distributor of energy, a green certificate gives a similar 'right to pollute' as an emission right except that a distributor of energy under a green certificate regime must acquire the certificates from the market (i.e. they are not granted to the distributor by the government). As with emission rights, the topic of green certificates cuts across a number of different areas of accounting, not just provisions. A fuller discussion of the issues and methods applied in practice are covered in Chapter 17 at 11.3.

6.7 EU Directive on 'Waste Electrical and Electronic Equipment'[37] (IFRIC 6)

This Directive regulates the collection, treatment, recovery and environmentally sound disposal of waste electrical or electronic equipment (WE&EE). It applies to entities involved in the manufacture and resale of electrical or electronic equipment, including entities (both European and Non-European) that import such equipment into the EU. As member states in the EU began to implement this directive into their national laws, it gave rise to questions about when the liability for the decommissioning of WE&EE should be recognised. The Directive distinguishes between 'new' and 'historical' waste and between waste from private households and waste from sources other than private households. New waste relates to products sold after 13 August 2005. All household equipment sold before that date is deemed to give rise to historical waste for the purposes of the Directive. *[IFRIC 6.3]*.

The Directive states that the cost of waste management for historical household equipment should be borne by producers of that type of equipment that are in the market during a period to be specified in the applicable legislation of each Member State (the measurement period). The Directive states that each Member State shall establish a mechanism to have producers contribute to costs proportionately 'e.g. in proportion to their respective share of the market by type of equipment.' *[IFRIC 6.4]*.

The Interpretations Committee was asked to determine in the context of the decommissioning of WE&EE what constitutes the obligating event in accordance with paragraph 14(a) of IAS 37 (discussed at 3.1.1 above) for the recognition of a provision for waste management costs:

- the manufacture or sale of the historical household equipment?
- participation in the market during the measurement period?
- the incurrence of costs in the performance of waste management activities? *[IFRIC 6.8]*.

IFRIC 6 was issued in September 2005 and provides guidance on the recognition, in the financial statements of producers, of liabilities for waste management under the EU Directive on WE&EE in respect of sales of historical household equipment. *[IFRIC 6.6]*. The interpretation addresses neither new waste nor historical waste from sources other than private households. The Interpretations Committee considers that the liability for such waste management is adequately covered in IAS 37. However, if, in national legislation, new waste from private households is treated in a similar manner to historical waste from private households, the principles of IFRIC 6 are to apply by reference to the hierarchy set out in IAS 8 (see Chapter 3 at 4.3). The IAS 8 hierarchy is also stated to be relevant for other regulations that impose obligations in a way that is similar to the cost attribution model specified in the EU Directive. *[IFRIC 6.7]*.

IFRIC 6 regards participation in the market during the measurement period as the obligating event in accordance with paragraph 14(a) of IAS 37. Consequently, a liability for waste management costs for historical household equipment does not arise as the products are manufactured or sold. Because the obligation for historical household equipment is linked to participation in the market during the measurement period, rather than to production or sale of the items to be disposed of, there is no obligation unless and until a market share exists during the measurement period. It is also noted that the timing of the obligating event may also be independent of the particular period in which the activities to perform the waste management are undertaken and the related costs incurred. *[IFRIC 6.9]*.

The following example, which is based on one within the accompanying Basis for Conclusions on IFRIC 6, illustrates its requirements.

Example 27.18: Illustration of IFRIC 6 requirements

An entity selling electrical equipment in 2012 has a market share of 4 per cent for that calendar year. It subsequently discontinues operations and is thus no longer in the market when the waste management costs for its products are allocated to those entities with market share in 2014. With a market share of 0 per cent in 2014, the entity's obligation is zero. However, if another entity enters the market for electronic products in 2014 and achieves a market share of 3 per cent in that period, then that entity's obligation for the costs of waste management from earlier periods will be 3 per cent of the total costs of waste management allocated to 2014, even though the entity was not in the market in those earlier periods and has not produced any of the products for which waste management costs are allocated to 2014. *[IFRIC 6.BC5].*

The Interpretations Committee concluded that the effect of the cost attribution model specified in the Directive is that the making of sales during the measurement period is the 'past event' that requires recognition of a provision under IAS 37 over the measurement period. Aggregate sales for the period determine the entity's obligation for a proportion of the costs of waste management allocated to that period. The measurement period is independent of the period when the cost allocation is notified to market participants. *[IFRIC 6.BC6].*

Some constituents asked the Interpretations Committee to consider the effect of the following possible national legislation: the waste management costs for which a producer is responsible because of its participation in the market during a specified period (for example 2014) are not based on the market share of the producer during that period but on the producer's participation in the market during a previous period (for example 2013). The Interpretations Committee noted that this affects only the measurement of the liability and that the obligating event is still participation in the market during 2014. *[IFRIC 6.BC7].*

IFRIC 6 notes that terms used in the interpretation such as 'market share' and 'measurement period' may be defined very differently in the applicable legislation of individual Member States. For example, the length of the measurement period might be a year or only one month. Similarly, the measurement of market share and the formulae for computing the obligation may differ in the various national legislations. However, all of these examples affect only the measurement of the liability, which is not within the scope of the interpretation. *[IFRIC 6.5].*

6.8 Levies imposed by governments

When governments or other public authorities impose levies on entities in relation to their activities, as opposed to income taxes and fines or other penalties, it is not always clear when the liability to pay a levy arises and a provision should be recognised. In May 2013, the Interpretations Committee issued IFRIC 21 – *Levies* – to address this question. *[IFRIC 21.2].* The Interpretation does not address the accounting for the costs arising out of an obligation to pay a levy, for example to determine whether an asset or expense should be recorded. Other standards should be applied in this regard. *[IFRIC 21.3].*

The Interpretation is mandatory for accounting periods beginning on or after 1 January 2014, although earlier application is permitted. *[IFRIC 21.A1].* It requires that, for levies within its scope, an entity should recognise a liability only when the activity that triggers payment, as identified by the relevant legislation, occurs. *[IFRIC 21.8].* A levy is defined as an outflow of resources embodying economic benefits that is imposed by governments on entities in accordance with legislation, other than:

(a) those outflows of resources that are within the scope of other Standards (such as income taxes that are within the scope of IAS 12); and

(b) fines or other penalties that are imposed for breaches of the legislation. *[IFRIC 21.4]*.

In addition to income taxes (see Chapter 29) and fines, the Interpretation does not apply to contractual arrangements with government in which the entity acquires an asset (see Chapters 17 and 18) or receives services; and it is not required to be applied to liabilities that arise from emission trading schemes (see 6.5 above). *[IFRIC 21.5, 6]*.

For levies within the scope of the Interpretation, the *activity* that creates the obligation under the relevant legislation to pay the levy is the obligating event for recognition purposes. *[IFRIC 21.8]*. In many cases this activity is related to the entity's participation in a relevant market at a specific date or dates. The Interpretation states that neither a constructive nor a present obligation arises as a result of being economically compelled to continue operating; or from any implication of continuing operations in the future arising from the use of the going concern assumption in the preparation of financial statements. *[IFRIC 21.9, 10]*.

When a levy is payable progressively, for example as the entity generates revenues, the entity recognises a liability over a period of time on that basis. This is because the obligating event is the activity that generates revenues. *[IFRIC 21.11]*. If an obligation to pay a levy is triggered in full as soon as a minimum threshold is reached, such as when the entity commences generating sales or achieves a certain level of revenue, the liability is recognised in full on the first day that the entity reaches that threshold. *[IFRIC 21.12]*. If an entity pays over amounts to government before it is determined that an obligation to pay that levy exists, it recognises an asset. *[IFRIC 21.14]*.

Example 27.19: A levy is triggered in full as soon as the entity generates revenues

An entity with calendar year end generates revenues in a specific market in 2014. The amount of the levy is determined by reference to revenues generated by the entity in the market in 2013 although the levy is only payable when revenues are generated in 2014. The entity generated revenues in the market in 2013 and starts to generate revenues in the market in 2014 on 3 January 2014.

In this example, the liability is recognised in full on 3 January 2014 because the obligating event, as identified by the legislation, is the first generation of revenues in 2014. The generation of revenues in 2013 is necessary, but not sufficient, to create a present obligation to pay a levy. Before 3 January 2014, the entity has no obligation. In other words, the activity that triggers the payment of the levy as identified by the legislation is the first generation of revenues at a point in time in 2014. The generation of revenues in 2013 is not the activity that triggers the payment of the levy. The amount of revenues generated in 2013 only affects the measurement of the liability. *[IFRIC 21.13, IE1 Example 2]*.

When the legislation provides that a levy is triggered by an entity operating in a market only at the end of its annual reporting period, no liability is recognised until the last day of the annual reporting period. No amount is recognised before that date in anticipation of the entity still operating in the market. Accordingly, a provision would not be permitted to be recognised in interim financial statements if the obligating event occurs only at the end of the annual reporting period. *[IFRIC 21.IE1 Example 3]*. The accounting treatment in interim reports is discussed in Chapter 37 at 9.7.5.

6.9 Dilapidation and other provisions relating to leased assets

As discussed at 5.2 above, it is not appropriate to recognise provisions that relate to repairs and maintenance of owned assets (including assets held under finance leases). However, the position can be different in the case of obligations relating to assets held under operating leases. Nevertheless, the same principles under IAS 37 apply:

(a) provisions are recognised only for obligations existing independently of the entity's future actions (i.e. the future conduct of its business) and in cases where an entity can avoid future expenditure by its future actions, for example by changing its method of operation, it has no present obligation; *[IAS 37.19]*

(b) financial statements deal with an entity's position at the end of the reporting period and not its possible position in the future. Therefore, no provision is recognised for costs that need to be incurred to operate in the future; *[IAS 37.18]* and

(c) for an event to be an obligating event, the entity must have no realistic alternative to settling the obligation created by the event. *[IAS 37.17]*.

Operating leases often contain clauses which specify that the lessee should incur periodic charges for maintenance, make good dilapidations or other damage occurring during the rental period or return the asset to the configuration that existed as at inception of the lease. These contractual provisions may restrict the entity's ability to change its future conduct to avoid the expenditure. For example, the entity might not be able to transfer the asset in its existing condition. Alternatively, the entity could return the asset to avoid the risk of incurring costs relating to any future damage, but would have to make a payment in relation of dilapidations incurred to date. So the contractual obligations in a lease could create an environment in which a present obligation could exist as at the reporting date from which the entity cannot realistically withdraw.

Under principle (b) above, any provision should reflect only the conditions as at the reporting date. This means that a provision for specific damage done to the leased asset would merit recognition, as the event giving rise to the obligation under the lease has certainly occurred. For example, if an entity has erected partitioning or internal walls in a leasehold property and under the lease these have to be removed at the end of the term, then provision should be made for this cost (on a discounted basis, if material) at the time of putting up the partitioning or the walls. In this case, an equivalent asset would be recognised and depreciated over the term of the lease. This is similar to a decommissioning provision discussed at 6.3 above. Another example would be where an airline company leases aircraft under an operating lease, and upon delivery of the aircraft has made changes to the interior fittings and layout, but under the leasing arrangements has to return the asset to the configuration that existed as at inception of the lease.

What is less clear is whether a more general provision can be built up over time for maintenance charges and dilapidation costs in relation to a leased asset. It might be argued that in this case, the event giving rise to the obligation under the lease is simply the passage of time, and so a provision can be built up over time. However, in our view the phrase 'the event giving rise to the obligation under the lease' indicates that a more specific event has to occur; there has to be specific evidence of dilapidation etc. before any provision can be made.

Example 27.12 at 5.2 above dealt with an owned aircraft that by law needs overhauling every three years, but no provision could be recognised for such costs. Instead, IAS 37 suggests that an amount equivalent to the expected maintenance costs is treated as a separate part of the asset and depreciated over three years. Airworthiness requirements for the airline industry are the same irrespective of whether the aircraft is owned or leased. So, if an airline company leases the aircraft under an operating lease, should a provision be made for the overhaul costs? The answer will depend on the terms of the lease.

If the lease requires the lessee to maintain the airworthiness of the aircraft and to return the aircraft at the end of the lease in the same condition as it was taken at inception of the lease, i.e. the aircraft has to be overhauled prior to its return, then the lessee should make provision. In this case the overhaul of the aircraft is a contractual obligation under the lease. The specific event that gives rise to the obligation is each flown hour or cycle completed by the aircraft as these determine the timing and nature of the overhaul that must be carried out. Provision should therefore be made for the costs of overhaul as the obligation towards the lessor arises (typically based upon the specific requirements of each aircraft type such as each flown hour or cycle), with a corresponding expense recognised in the statement of comprehensive income. For certain aircraft types and aircraft leases it is likely that the provision for the costs will be built up and then released, as the expenditure is incurred, a number of times during the term of the operating lease.

However, if the lease does not require the overhaul to be undertaken prior to the return of the aircraft (or require the lessee to make a contribution towards the next overhaul), then no provision should be made as the lessee does not have a contractual obligation to incur these costs that is independent of its own future actions.

The fact that a provision for repairs can be made at all in these circumstances might appear inconsistent with the case where the asset is owned by the entity. In that case, as discussed at 5.2 above, no provision for repairs could be made. There is, however, a difference between the two situations. Where the entity owns the asset, it has the choice of selling it rather than repairing it, and so the obligation is not independent of the entity's future actions. However, in the case of an entity leasing the asset, it can have a contractual obligation to repair any damage from which it cannot walk away.

Extract 27.5 at 6.2.2 above, shows an example of a company that has provided for dilapidation costs.

6.10 Warranty provisions

Warranty provisions are specifically addressed in one of the examples appended to IAS 37. However, it is worth noting that the IASB decided to address the future accounting of warranty costs in its Exposure Draft on Revenue from Contracts with Customers. The revenue recognition project is discussed in Chapter 28.

Example 27.20: Recognition of a provision for warranty costs

A manufacturer gives warranties at the time of sale to purchasers of its product. Under the terms of the contract for sale, the manufacturer undertakes to make good, by repair or replacement, manufacturing defects that become apparent within three years from the date of sale. On past experience, it is probable (i.e. more likely than not) that there will be some claims under the warranties.

In these circumstances the obligating event is the sale of the product with a warranty, which gives rise to a legal obligation. Because it is more likely than not that there will be an outflow of resources for some claims under the warranties as a whole, a provision is recognised for the best estimate of the costs of making good under the warranty for those products sold before the end of the reporting period. *[IAS 37 IE Example 1]*.

The assessment of the probability of an outflow of resources is made across the population as a whole, and not using each potential claim as the unit of account. *[IAS 37.24]*. On past experience, it is probable that there will be some claims under the warranties, so a provision is recognised.

The assessment over the class of obligations as a whole makes it more likely that a provision will be recognised, because the probability criterion is considered in terms of whether at least one item in the population will give rise to a payment. Recognition then becomes a matter of reliable measurement and entities calculate an expected value of the estimated warranty costs. IAS 37 discusses this method of 'expected value' and illustrates how it is calculated in an example of a warranty provision. *[IAS 37.39]*. See Example 27.6 at 4.1 above.

An example of a company that makes a warranty provision is Nokia as shown below:

Extract 27.10: Nokia Corporation (2012)

NOTES TO THE CONSOLIDATED FINANCIAL STATEMENTS [extract]

1. **Accounting principles** [extract]

WARRANTY PROVISIONS

The Group provides for the estimated liability to repair or replace products under warranty at the time revenue is recognized. The provision is an estimate calculated based on historical experience of the level of volumes, product mix, repair and replacement cost.

Use of estimates and critical accounting judgements [extract]

WARRANTY PROVISIONS

The Group provides for the estimated cost of product warranties at the time revenue is recognized. The Group's warranty provision is established based upon best estimates of the amounts necessary to settle future and existing claims on products sold as of each balance sheet date. As new products incorporating complex technologies are continuously introduced, and as local laws, regulations and practices may change, changes in these estimates could result in additional allowances or changes to recorded allowances being required in future periods.

6.11 Litigation and other legal claims

IAS 37 includes an example of a court case in its appendix to illustrate how its principles distinguish between a contingent liability and a provision in such situations. See Example 27.4 at 3.2.1 above. However, the assessment of the particular case in the example is clear-cut. In most situations, assessing the need to provide for legal claims is one of the most difficult tasks in the field of provisioning. This is due mainly to the inherent uncertainty in the judicial process itself, which may be very long and drawn out. Furthermore, this is an area where either provision or disclosure might risk prejudicing the outcome of the case, because they give an insight into the entity's own view on the strength of its defence that can assist the claimant. Similar considerations apply in other related areas, such as tax disputes.

In principle, whether a provision should be made will depend on whether the three conditions for recognising a provision are met, i.e.

(a) there is a present obligation as a result of a past event;

(b) it is probable that an outflow of resources embodying economic benefits will be required to settle the obligation; and

(c) a reliable estimate can be made of the amount of the obligation. *[IAS 37.14]*.

In situations such as these, a past event is deemed to give rise to a present obligation if, taking account of all available evidence (including, for example, the opinion of experts), it is more likely than not that a present obligation exists at the end of the reporting period. *[IAS 37.15]*. The evidence to be considered includes any additional evidence occurring after the end of the reporting period. Accordingly, if on the basis of the evidence it is concluded that a present obligation is more likely than not to exist, a provision will be required, assuming the other conditions are met. *[IAS 37.16]*.

Condition (b) will be met if the transfer of economic benefits is more likely than not to occur, that is, it has a probability greater than 50%. In making this assessment, it is likely that account should be taken of any expert advice.

As far as condition (c) is concerned, the standard takes the view that a reasonable estimate can generally be made and it is only in extremely rare cases that this will not be the case. *[IAS 37.25]*.

Clearly, whether an entity should make provision for the costs of settling a case or to meet any award given by a court will depend on a reasoned assessment of the particular circumstances, based on appropriate legal advice.

6.12 Refunds policy

Example 27.1 at 3.1.1 above reflects an example given in the appendix of IAS 37 of a retail store that has a policy of refunding goods returned by dissatisfied customers. There is no legal obligation to do so, but the company's policy of making refunds is generally known. The example argues that the conduct of the store has created a valid expectation on the part of its customers that it will refund purchases. The obligating event is the original sale of the item, and the probability of some economic outflow is greater than 50%, as there will nearly always be some customers demanding refunds. Hence, a provision should be made, *[IAS 37 IE Example 4]*, presumably calculated on the 'expected value' basis.

This example is straightforward when the store has a very specific and highly publicised policy on refunds. However, some stores' policies on refunds might not be so clear cut. A store may offer refunds under certain conditions, but not widely publicise its policy. In these circumstances, there might be doubt as to whether the store has created a valid expectation on the part of its customers that it will honour all requests for a refund. As with warranty costs (discussed at 6.10 above), the accounting treatment of refunds impinges into the area of revenue recognition and is therefore an element of the project to develop a new standard on Revenue from Contracts with Customers (see Chapter 28).

6.13 Self insurance

Another situation where entities sometimes make provisions is self insurance which arises when an entity decides not to take out external insurance in respect of a certain category of risk because it would be uneconomic to do so. The same position may arise when a group insures its risks with a captive insurance subsidiary, the effects of which have to be eliminated on consolidation. In fact, the term 'self insurance' is potentially misleading, since it really means that the entity is not insured at all and will settle claims from third parties from its own resources in the event that it is found to be liable. Accordingly, the recognition criteria in IAS 37 should be applied, with a provision being justified only if there is a present obligation as a result of a past event; if it is probable that an outflow of resources will occur; and a reliable estimate can be determined. *[IAS 37.14].*

Therefore, losses are recognised based on their actual incidence and any provisions that appear in the statement of financial position should reflect only the amounts expected to be paid in respect of those incidents that have occurred by the end of the reporting period.

In certain circumstances, a provision will often be needed not simply for known incidents, but also for those which insurance companies call IBNR – Incurred But Not Reported – representing an estimate of claims that have occurred at the end of the reporting period but which have not yet been notified to the reporting entity. We believe that it is appropriate that provision for such expected claims is made to the extent that such items can be measured reliably.

6.14 Obligations to make donations to non-profit organisations

When an entity promises to make donations to a non-profit organisation it can be difficult to determine whether a past obligating event exists that requires a provision to be recognised or whether it is appropriate instead to account for the gift as payments are made.

Example 27.21: Accounting for donations to non-profit organisations

An entity decides to enter into an arrangement to 'donate' €1m in cash to a university. A number of different options are available for the arrangement and the entity's management want to determine whether the terms of these options make any difference to the timing, measurement or presentation of the €1m expenditure, as follows:

Option 1:

The entity enters into an unenforceable contract to contribute €1m for general purposes. The benefits to the entity are deemed only to relate to its reputation as a 'good corporate citizen'; the entity does not receive any consideration or significant benefit from the university in return for the donation.

Option 2:

As per Option 1 except the entity publishes a press release in relation to the donation and announcing that payment is to be made in equal instalments of €200,000 over 5 years.

Option 3:
As per Option 2, except that the contract is legally enforceable in the event that the entity does not pay all the instalments under the contract.

Option 4:
As per Option 2, except that the entity is only required to make the donation if the university raises €4m from other sources.

Option 5:
As per Option 2, except that the contract is legally enforceable and the funds will be used for research and development activities specified by the entity. The entity will retain proprietary rights over the results of the research.

The following principles are relevant in determining when a promise to make a donation should be recognised as an obligation:

- to the extent that there is an enforceable contract, the donor should recognise an expense and a liability upon entry into that contract;
- where the agreement is not enforceable, the donor recognises an expense and a liability when a constructive obligation arises. The timing of recognition depends on whether the donation is conditional, whether it is probable that those conditions are substantially met and whether a past event has occurred; and
- if the donor expects to receive benefits commensurate with the value of the donation, the arrangement should be treated as an exchange transaction. Such transactions are in some cases executory contracts and may also give rise to the recognition of an asset rather than an expense.

In cases where the 'donation' is made under an enforceable contract, a present obligation is created when the entity enters into that contract. When payment is required in cash, the signing of an enforceable contract gives rise to a financial liability *[IAS 32.11]* which is measured initially at fair value. *[IAS 39.43].*

Where there is no legal obligation to make the payments, a liability is recognised when a constructive obligation arises. It is a matter of judgement whether and when a constructive obligation exists. In many unenforceable contracts, there is no constructive obligation simply because the contract has been signed; hence the donor would recognise the expenditure when the cash or other assets are transferred.

By contrast, an exchange transaction is a reciprocal transfer in which each party receives and sacrifices approximately equal value. Assets and liabilities are not recognised until each party performs their obligations under the arrangement.

Applying these principles to the options listed in Example 27.21 above:

- In Option 1, the contract is unenforceable, there is no announcement or conditions preceding payment and there is no exchange of benefits. Accordingly, an expense would be recognised only when the entity transfers cash to the university.
- For Option 2, it may be appropriate for the entity to conclude that the entity's announcement of the donation to be paid by instalments indicates that there is a constructive obligation because the entity has a created a valid expectation that it will make all of the payments promised. Alternatively, it could determine that once the first instalment is paid, the entity has created a valid

expectation that it will make the remaining payments. This is a matter of judgement. In this case the entity would recognise an expense and a liability, measured at the net present value of the 5 instalments of €200,000, at the point when it is determined that a constructive obligation exists.

- Option 3 involves an enforceable contract with no exchange of benefits. Therefore a liability and an expense is recognised on signing the enforceable contract, measured at the present value of the 5 instalments of €200,000.
- Under Option 4, the contract is unenforceable and the donation is subject to a condition. In these circumstances, management come to the judgement that no constructive obligation exists until it is probable that the condition is met (which might not be until the additional funds have been collected). Only then would a liability and expense be recognised, measured at the net present value of the €1m promised.
- Option 5 involves an enforceable contract. Therefore a liability is recognised when the contract is signed. In addition, there is an exchange of benefits relating to the research and development activities performed on behalf of the entity. Whether these benefits have a value close to the present value of the 5 instalments of €200,000 is a matter of judgment. If it is determined that this is an exchange transaction, the entity would apply the criteria in IAS 38 to determine whether an asset or expense would be recognised for the related research and development costs (see Chapter 17 at 6.2).

Where the arrangement gives rise to an exchange transaction rather than a donation, the expenditure incurred by the donor is recorded in accordance with the relevant IFRS.

7 DISCLOSURE REQUIREMENTS

A significant distinction between the accounting treatment of provisions and other liabilities, such as trade payables and accruals, is the level of disclosure required.

7.1 Provisions

For each class of provision an entity should provide a reconciliation of the carrying amount of the provision at the beginning and end of the period showing:

(a) additional provisions made in the period, including increases to existing provisions;
(b) amounts used, i.e. incurred and charged against the provision, during the period;
(c) unused amounts reversed during the period; and
(d) the increase during the period in the discounted amount arising from the passage of time and the effect of any change in the discount rate.

Comparative information is not required. *[IAS 37.84]*.

It is not clear whether disclosure (d) allows a single amount to be provided for the sum of the unwinding of the discount and any change in the provision resulting from a reassessment of the discount rate to be used or it requires these amounts to be given separately. However, given our view (discussed at 4.3.6 above) that only the charge for unwinding of the discount should be classified as a finance cost, with any further charge or credit that arises if discount rates have changed being recorded in the same line item that was used to establish the provision, it would make sense to disclose these items separately. This treatment is demonstrated by BP p.l.c. in Extract 27.9 at 6.4 above. It is also interesting that there is no specific requirement in the standard to disclose the discount rate used, especially where the effect of using a different discount rate could be material, such as in the measurement of a decommissioning provision.

One of the important disclosures which is reinforced here is the requirement to disclose the release of provisions found to be unnecessary. This disclosure, along with the requirement in the standard that provisions should be used only for the purpose for which the provision was originally recognised, *[IAS 37.61]*, is designed to prevent entities from concealing expenditure by charging it against a provision that was set up for another purpose.

In addition, for each class of provision an entity should disclose the following:

(a) a brief description of the nature of the obligation and the expected timing of any resulting outflows of economic benefits;

(b) an indication of the uncertainties about the amount or timing of those outflows. Where necessary to provide adequate information, an entity should disclose the major assumptions made concerning future events, as addressed in paragraph 48 of the standard (discussed at 4.4 above). This refers to future developments in technology and legislation and is of particular relevance to environmental liabilities; and

(c) the amount of any expected reimbursement, stating the amount of any asset that has been recognised for that expected reimbursement. *[IAS 37.85]*.

Section D of the implementation guidance to the standard provides examples of suitable disclosures in relation to warranties and decommissioning costs.

Most of the above disclosures are illustrated in the extract below.

Extract 27.11: Roche Holding Ltd. (2012)

Notes to the Roche Group Consolidated Financial Statements [extract]

24. Provisions and contingent liabilities [extract]

Provisions: movements in recognised liabilities in millions of CHF

	Legal provisions	Environ-mental provisions	Restruct-uring provisions	Employee provisions	Other provisions	Total
Year ended 31 December 2011						
At 1 January 2011	781	261	970	253	815	3,080
Additional provisions created	99	8	173	92	533	905
Unused amounts reversed	(35)	(1)	(77)	(8)	(244)	(365)
Utilised during the year	(99)	(9)	(480)	(57)	(303)	(948)
Unwinding of discount	1	7	–	1	6	15
Business combinations						
– Acquired companies	–	–	–	7	1	8
– Contingent consideration	–	–	–	–	82	82
– Contingent consideration utilisation	–	–	–	–	(15)	(15)
Divestment of subsidiaries	–	(1)	(3)	–	–	(4)
Currency translation effects	(1)	–	(17)	1	(8)	(25)
At 31 December 2011	**746**	**265**	**566**	**289**	**867**	**2,733**

Of which						
– Current portion	655	11	376	88	612	1,742
– Non-current portion	91	254	190	201	255	991
Total provisions	**746**	**265**	**566**	**289**	**867**	**2,733**
Year ended 31 December 2012						
At 1 January 2012	746	265	566	289	867	2,733
Additional provisions created	86	317	607	137	509	1,656
Unused amounts reversed	(21)	–	(139)	(9)	(124)	(293)
Utilised during the year	(65)	(15)	(326)	(104)	(318)	(828)
Unwinding of discount	1	7	–	1	3	12
Business combinations						
– Acquired companies	–	–	–	–	–	–
– Contingent consideration	–	–	–	–	1	1
– Contingent consideration utilisation	–	–	–	–	(24)	(24)
Currency translation effects	(19)	(8)	(10)	(1)	(19)	(57)
At 31 December 2012	**728**	**566**	**698**	**313**	**895**	**3,200**
Of which						
– Current portion	703	109	522	91	733	2,158
– Non-current portion	25	457	176	222	162	1,042
Total provisions	**728**	**566**	**698**	**313**	**895**	**3,200**
Expected outflow of resources						
– Within one year	703	109	522	91	733	2,158
– Between one and two years	8	124	103	43	26	304
– Between two and three years	6	112	25	30	98	271
– More than three years	11	221	48	149	38	467
Total provisions	**728**	**566**	**698**	**313**	**895**	**3,200**

Legal provisions

Legal provisions consist of a number of separate legal matters, including claims arising from trade, in various Group companies. The majority of any cash outflows for these other matters are expected to occur within the next one to three years, although these are dependent on the development of the various litigations. Significant provisions are discounted by between 4% and 5% where the time value of money is material.

Legal expenses during 2012 totalled 72 million Swiss francs (2011: 74 million Swiss francs) which reflect the recent developments in various legal matters. Details of the major legal cases outstanding are disclosed below.

Environmental provisions

Provisions for environmental matters include various separate environmental issues in a number of countries. By their nature the amounts and timings of any outflows are difficult to predict. The estimated timings of these cash outflows are shown in the table above. Significant provisions are discounted by between 4% and 6% where the time value of money is material.

As disclosed in Note 7, the restructuring plan to streamline the research and development activities within the Pharmaceuticals Division includes the closure of the US site in Nutley, New Jersey. An expense of 243 million Swiss francs was recorded based on estimates of the additional remediation activities that may be needed before the Nutley site can be sold. Further expenses were also recorded for an increase in the estimated remediation costs for a landfill site near Grenzach, Germany, that was used by manufacturing operations that were closed some years ago.

Restructuring provisions

These arise from planned programmes that materially change the scope of business undertaken by the Group or the manner in which business is conducted. Such provisions include only the costs necessarily entailed by the restructuring which are not associated with the recurring activities of the Group. The timings of these cash outflows are reasonably certain on a global basis and are shown in the table above. These provisions are not discounted as the time value of money is not material in these matters.

The restructuring provisions created in 2012 are primarily related to the plan to streamline the research and development activities within the Pharmaceuticals Division, mainly related to the closure of the US site in Nutley, New Jersey.

Employee provisions

These mostly relate to certain employee benefit obligations, such as sabbatical leave and long-service benefits. The timings of these cash outflows can be reasonably estimated based on past performance and are shown in the table above. Significant provisions are discounted by 6% where the time value of money is material.

Other provisions

The timings of cash outflows are by their nature uncertain and the best estimates are shown in the table below. Significant provisions are discounted by between 2% and 6% where the time value of money is material.

Other provisions in millions of CHF

	2012	2011	2010
Sales returns	503	377	328
Contingent consideration	81	153	132
Other items	311	337	355
Total other provisions	**895**	**867**	**815**

The standard states that in determining which provisions may be aggregated to form a class, it is necessary to consider whether the nature of the items is sufficiently similar for a single statement about them to fulfil the requirements of (a) and (b) above. An example is given of warranties: it is suggested that, while it may be appropriate to treat warranties of different products as a single class of provision, it would not be appropriate to aggregate normal warranties with amounts that are subject to legal proceedings. *[IAS 37.87].* This requirement could be interpreted to mean that in disclosing restructuring costs, the different components of the costs, such as redundancies, termination of leases, etc. should be disclosed separately. However, materiality will be an important consideration in judging how much analysis is required.

As indicated at 6.1.1 above, IAS 37 emphasises that when a restructuring meets the definition of a discontinued operation under IFRS 5, additional disclosures may be required under that standard (see Chapter 4 at 3). *[IAS 37.9].*

7.2 Contingent liabilities

Unless the possibility of any outflow in settlement is remote, IAS 37 requires the disclosure for each class of contingent liability at the end of the reporting period to include a brief description of the nature of the contingent liability, and where practicable:

(a) an estimate of its financial effect, measured in accordance with paragraphs 36-52 of IAS 37 (discussed at 4 above);

(b) an indication of the uncertainties relating to the amount or timing of any outflow; and

(c) the possibility of any reimbursement. *[IAS 37.86]*.

Where any of the information above is not disclosed because it is not practicable to do so, that fact should be stated. *[IAS 37.91]*.

The guidance given in the standard on determining which provisions may be aggregated to form a class referred to at 7.1 above also applies to contingent liabilities.

A further point noted in the standard is that where a provision and a contingent liability arise from the same circumstances, an entity should ensure that the link between the provision and the contingent liability is clear. *[IAS 37.88]*. This situation may occur, for instance, when an entity stratifies a population of known and potential claimants between different classes of obligation, and accounts for each class separately. For example, an entity's actions may have resulted in environmental damage. The entity identifies the geographical area over which that damage is likely to have occurred and recognises a provision based on its 'best estimate' of value of claims it expects to be submitted from residents in that geographical area. In addition, there is a chance (albeit possible rather than probable) that the pollution is found to have had an effect beyond the geographical area established by the entity. As noted at 3.2.1 above, the latter, 'possible but not probable' obligation meets the definition of a contingent liability for which disclosure is required.

Another example of when a provision and a contingent liability may arise from the same circumstance would be where an entity is jointly and severally liable for an obligation. As noted at 4.6 above, in these circumstances the part of the obligation that is expected to be met by other parties is treated as a contingent liability.

It is not absolutely clear what is meant by 'financial effect' in (a) above. Is it the *potential* amount of the loss or is it the *expected* amount of the loss? The cross-reference to the measurement principles in paragraphs 36-52 might imply the latter, but in any event, disclosure of the potential amount is likely to be relevant in explaining the uncertainties in (b) above.

7.3 Contingent assets

IAS 37 requires disclosure of contingent assets where an inflow of economic benefits is probable. The disclosures required are:

(a) a brief description of the nature of the contingent assets at the end of the reporting period; and

(b) where practicable, an estimate of their financial effect, measured using the principles set out for provisions in paragraphs 36-52 of IAS 37. *[IAS 37.89]*.

Where any of the information above is not disclosed because it is not practicable to do so, that fact should be stated. *[IAS 37.91]*. The standard goes on to emphasise that the disclosure must avoid giving misleading indications of the likelihood of income arising. *[IAS 37.90]*.

One problem that arises with IAS 37 is that it requires the disclosure of an estimate of the potential financial effect for contingent assets to be measured in accordance with the measurement principles in the standard. Unfortunately, the measurement principles in the standard are all set out in terms of the settlement of obligations, and these principles cannot readily be applied to the measurement of contingent assets. Hence, judgement will have to be used as to how rigorously these principles should be applied.

7.4 Reduced disclosure when information is seriously prejudicial

IAS 37 contains an exemption from disclosure of information in the following circumstances. It says that, 'in extremely rare cases, disclosure of some or all of the information required by [the disclosure requirements at 7.1 to 7.3 above] can be expected to prejudice seriously the position of the entity in a dispute with other parties on the subject matter of the provision, contingent liability or contingent asset'. *[IAS 37.92]*.

In such circumstances, the information need not be disclosed. However, disclosure will still need to be made of the general nature of the dispute, together with the fact that, and the reason why, the required information has not been disclosed. *[IAS 37.92]*.

In the following extract, Daimler applied this exemption in relation to antitrust investigations by the European Commission into the activities of European vehicle manufacturers.

Extract 27.12: Daimler AG (2012)

Notes to the Consolidated Financial Statements [extract]

28. Legal proceedings [extract]

In mid-January 2011, the European Commission carried out antitrust investigations of European commercial vehicle manufacturers, including Daimler AG. Daimler is taking the Commission's initial suspicion very seriously and is also – parallel to the Commission's investigations – carrying out its own extensive internal investigation to clarify the underlying circumstances. If antitrust infringements are discovered, the European Commission can impose considerable fines depending on the gravity of the infringement. In accordance with IAS 37.92 the Group does not provide further information on this antitrust investigation and the associated risk for the Group, especially with regard to the measures taken in this context, in order not to impair the outcome of the proceeding.

As it can be seen in the above example, an entity applying the 'seriously prejudicial' exemption is still required to describe the general nature of the dispute, resulting in a level of disclosure that many entities might find uncomfortable in the circumstances.

References

1 Working Draft, International Financial Reporting Standard [X] - *Liabilities*, IASB, 19 February 2010.
2 IASB Staff Paper, *Liabilities – IFRS to replace IAS 37 – Recognising liabilities from lawsuits*, IASB, 7 April 2010.
3 *Exposure Draft of Proposed Amendments to IAS 37 Provisions, Contingent Liabilities and Contingent Assets* (IAS 37 ED) *and IAS 19 Employee Benefits* (IAS 19 ED), IASB, June 2005, para 46.
4 Request for Views *Agenda Consultation 2011*, IASB, July 2011, Appendix C.
5 *IASB Update*, May 2012, p. 9.
6 FASB ASC Topic 450, Contingencies, para. 450-20-30-1.
7 FRS 12, *Provisions, Contingent Liabilities and Contingent Assets*, ASB, September 1998, para. 50.
8 FRS 12.49.
9 *Discounting in Financial Reporting*, ASB, April 1997.
10 *Discounting in Financial Reporting*, ASB, April 1997, para. 2.10.
11 FRS 12.49.
12 *IFRIC Update*, March 2011, p. 4.
13 Fisher, Irving PhD. *The Rate of Interest*, New York: MacMillan, 1907.
14 Exposure Draft ED/2013/5: *Regulatory Deferral Accounts*, IASB, April 2013, para. BC15.
15 Request for Views *Agenda Consultation 2011*, IASB, July 2011, Appendix C.
16 ED/2013/5, para. BC10.
17 Request for Information, *Rate Regulation*, IASB, March 2013, Introduction.
18 ED/2013/5, para. C1.
19 ED/2013/5, Appendix A.
20 ED/2013/5, para. 7.
21 ED/2013/5, paras. 4, 5.
22 ED/2013/5, paras. 20, 21.
23 ED/2013/5, para. 22.
24 *IASB Work Plan – projected timetable as at 29 July 2013*, IASB.
25 IAS 19, *Employee Benefits*, Example illustrating paragraphs 159-170.
26 *IFRIC Update*, December 2003, pp. 4-5.
27 *Exposure Draft of Proposed Amendments to IAS 37 Provisions, Contingent Liabilities and Contingent Assets* (IAS 37 ED) *and IAS 19 Employee Benefits* (IAS 19 ED), IASB, June 2005, para. 58.
28 IFRIC 3, *Emission Rights*, IASB, December 2004, para. 6.
29 IFRIC 3.5.
30 IFRIC 3.6.
31 IFRIC 3.7.
32 IFRIC 3.8.
33 *IASB Update*, June 2005, p. 1.
34 *IASB Update*, June 2005, p. 1.
35 *IASB Update*, May 2012, p. 8.
36 *IASB Work Plan – projected timetable as at 29 July 2013*, IASB.
37 Directive 2002/96/EC of the European Parliament and of the Council of 27 January 2003 on waste electrical and electronic equipment and Directive 2003/108/EC of the European Parliament and of the Council of 8 December 2003 amending Directive 2002/96/EC on waste electrical and electronic equipment.

Chapter 28 Revenue recognition

Chapter 28

List of examples

Chapter 28 Revenue recognition

1 THE NATURE OF REVENUE

Until relatively recently, the revenue recognition debate has taken place in the context of the historical cost system. The accounting principles focused on determining when transactions should be recognised in the financial statements, what amounts were involved in each transaction, how these amounts should be classified and how they should be allocated between accounting periods. These principles were reflected in the original version of IAS 18 – *Revenue* – which was issued in 1982, in which revenue was defined as the 'gross inflow of cash, receivables or other consideration arising in the course of the ordinary activities of an entity from the sale of goods, from the rendering of services, and from the use by others of entity resources yielding interest, royalties and dividends'.[1]

Historical cost accounting in its pure form avoids having to take a valuation approach to financial reporting by virtue of the fact that it is transactions-based; in other words, it relies on transactions to determine the recognition and measurement of assets, liabilities, revenues and expenses. Over the life of an entity, its total income will be represented by net cash flows generated; however, because of the requirement to prepare periodic financial statements, it is necessary to break up the entity's operating cycle into reporting periods. The effect of this is that at each reporting date the entity will have entered into a number of transactions that are incomplete; for example, it might have delivered a product or service to a customer for which payment has not been received, or it might have received payment in respect of a product or service yet to be delivered. Alternatively, it might have expended cash on costs that relate to future sales transactions, or it might have received goods and services that it has not yet paid for in cash.

Consequently, the most important accounting questions that have to be answered revolve around how to allocate the effects of these incomplete transactions between periods for reporting purposes, as opposed to simply letting them fall into the periods in which cash is either received or paid. Under historical cost accounting this allocation process is based on two, sometimes conflicting, fundamental accounting concepts: accruals (or matching), which attempts to allocate the costs associated with earning revenues to the periods in which the related revenues will be reported; and prudence (or conservatism), under which revenue and profits are not anticipated, whilst anticipated losses are provided for as soon as they are foreseen, with the result that costs are not deferred to the future if there is doubt as to their recoverability.

As a result, the pure historical cost balance sheet contains items of two types: cash (and similar monetary items), and debits and credits that arise as a result of allocating the effects of transactions between reporting periods by applying the accruals and prudence concepts; in other words, the balance sheet simply reflects the balances that result from the entity preparing an accruals-based profit and loss account rather than a receipts and payments account. A non-monetary asset under the historical cost system is purely a deferred cost that has been incurred before the balance sheet date and, by applying the accruals concept, is expected (provided it passes the prudence test) to give rise to economic benefits in periods beyond the balance sheet date, so as to justify it being carried forward. Similarly, the balance sheet incorporates non-monetary credit balances that are awaiting recognition in the profit and loss account but, as a result of the application of the prudence and/or matching concepts, have been deferred to future reporting periods.

However, financial reporting under IFRS is still not a pure historical cost system; it incorporates a mixed model that embraces both historical costs and fair values. IAS 18 was issued in its original form in 1982 and received its last major revision in 1993. Consequently, it is a standard that is based on historical cost principles, not fair value. Thus, it is a standard that focuses on profit or loss, not assets and liabilities and therefore relies heavily on the concepts of prudence and matching.

The IASB's accounting model has been based on fair values, meaning that gains and losses are determined by reference to the change in fair value that has occurred over the financial reporting period. This approach is evident in a number of standards, including IAS 39 – *Financial Instruments: Recognition and Measurement* – and the IFRS that will replace it, *IFRS 9 – Financial Instruments*, IAS 40 – *Investment Property*, IAS 41 – *Agriculture* – and IFRS 2 – *Share-based Payment*. Because so many standards incorporate the concept of fair value, the IASB in conjunction with the FASB issued IFRS 13 – *Fair Value Measurement* – which defines fair value in most IFRSs including IAS 18, e.g. in measuring the fair value of consideration received. It is clear also that as new standards are developed, greater emphasis will be placed on the balance sheet, with fair value as the relevant measurement attribute.

IAS 18 is therefore based upon concepts that, at least in their strictest sense, are not viewed with much importance by the IASB. In addition the standard does not address many of the complex transactions undertaken by modern business, such as those involving multiple deliverables.

It is therefore not surprising that the IASB and FASB have been working on a joint project to develop a new approach to revenue recognition which is expected to culminate in the issuance of a new revenue standard in the second half of 2013. The new model is discussed at 6 below.

Until the new model comes into effect, the traditional historical cost approach to revenue recognition remains in place for most practical purposes and companies and their auditors will have to continue to live with the inherent weaknesses of IAS 18.

The chapter discusses the subject drawing on both IASB and US pronouncements. For companies reporting under IFRS, IAS 18 is the main source of authoritative guidance on revenue recognition, but several other standards also address revenue recognition issues. These include IAS 11 – *Construction Contracts*, IAS 17 – *Leases*, IFRS 4 – *Insurance Contracts*, SIC-31 – *Revenue – Barter Transactions Involving Advertising Services*, IFRIC 13 – *Customer Loyalty Programmes*, IFRIC 15 – *Agreements for the Construction of Real Estate* – and IFRIC 18 – *Transfers of Assets from Customers.* In most cases, this revenue recognition guidance was developed in order to deal with specific issues on a piecemeal basis, rather than to follow any form of conceptual approach to revenue recognition.

The US, in particular, has a substantial body of literature on revenue recognition that can, on occasion, prove useful when there is no IFRS guidance available (see 4 below). Historically this was particularly relevant for IFRS-reporting companies registered with the US SEC, who wished to avoid as far as possible having IFRS/US GAAP differences. This is now less significant as reconciliation to US GAAP is no longer required. However, such differences are sometimes unavoidable, and it is not always the case that a revenue recognition policy under US GAAP is acceptable under IFRS, and vice versa.

2 THE TIMING OF REVENUE RECOGNITION

Under the historical cost system revenues are the inflows of assets to an entity as a result of the transfer of products and services by the entity to its customers during a period of time. They are recorded at the cash amount received or expected to be received (or, in the case of non-monetary exchanges, at their cash equivalent) as the result of these exchange transactions. However, because of the system of periodic financial reporting, it is necessary to determine the point (or points) in time when revenue should be measured and reported. This has traditionally been governed by what is known as the 'realisation principle', which acknowledges that, for revenue to be recognised, it is not sufficient merely for a sale to have been made; there has to be a certain degree of performance by the vendor as well. Whilst there are many different (and sometime inconsistent) rules for different circumstances, the rules underlying revenue recognition have been developed from two broad approaches to the recognition of revenue: the critical event and the accretion approaches, each of which is appropriate under particular circumstances. These are discussed below.

2.1 The critical event approach

The fundamental approach to revenue recognition under both IFRS and US GAAP has been built on the foundation of critical event theory. The new approach to revenue recognition discussed in 6 below still essentially follows a critical event approach but it is a control-based model rather than one that depends on the transfer of risks and rewards.

The critical event approach is based on the belief that revenue is earned at the point in the operating cycle when the most critical decision is made or the most critical act is performed.[2] In theory, the critical event could occur at various stages during the operating cycle; for example, at the completion of production, at the time of sale, at the time of delivery or at the time of cash collection.

Revenue recognition is subject to a number of measurement uncertainties which could occur at any of these points. As these uncertainties fall away at various stages throughout the operating cycle, it is necessary to identify a point in the cycle at which the remaining uncertainties can be estimated with sufficient accuracy to enable revenue to be recognised. As discussed later in this chapter, the decision is often not straightforward; further complications arise in the case of transactions that involve multiple elements and/or significant post-delivery obligations.

2.1.1 The recognition of revenue at the completion of production

An entity may enter into a firm contract for the production and delivery of a product, where the sales price will have been determined and the selling costs will have already been incurred. Consequently, provided that both the delivery expenses and the bad debt risk can reasonably be assessed, it may be appropriate to report revenue on the completion of production, unless it is a transaction for which the percentage of completion method is mandated by IAS 11 or IAS 18. The completed contract method of recognising revenue on construction contracts is not common and is not permitted under IFRS (construction contracts are discussed in Chapter 23).

It has also become accepted practice in a limited number of industries to recognise revenue at the completion of production, even though a sales contract may not have been entered into. This practice has been adopted, for example, in the case of some agricultural and minerals and mineral products. IAS 2 – *Inventories* – allows commodity broker-traders to carry inventory at net realisable value if it is a 'well-established' practice, as long as changes in net realisable value are recognised in profit or loss in the period of the change. *[IAS 2.3(b)].* IAS 2 specifies that the treatment might be appropriate if, for example, the minerals have been extracted, the sale is assured under a forward contract or a government guarantee, there is an active market and there is a negligible risk of failure to sell. *[IAS 2.4].* Note that this is different to recognising biological products at fair value throughout the period of growth, which is an example of the accretion approach described at 2.2 below that is mandated by IAS 41.

The US FASB's Concepts Statement 5 – *Recognition and Measurement in Financial Statements of Business Enterprises* – allows a similar treatment. It acknowledges that revenue may be recognised on the completion of production of such assets, provided that they consist of interchangeable units and quoted prices are available in an active market that can rapidly absorb the quantity held by the entity without significantly affecting the price.[3]

2.1.2 The recognition of revenue at the time of sale

The point of sale is probably the most widely used basis of recognising revenue from transactions involving the sale of goods. The sale is usually the critical point in the earning process when most of the significant uncertainties are eliminated; the only uncertainties that are likely to remain are those of possible return of the goods (where the customer has the right to do so, thereby cancelling the sale), the failure to collect the sales price (in the case of a credit sale), and any future liabilities in terms of any express or implied customer warranties. Under normal circumstances, these uncertainties will be both minimal and estimable to a reasonable degree of accuracy, based, *inter alia*, on past experience.

However, should revenues be recognised at the time of sale if the sale takes place before production, or if delivery only takes place at some significantly distant time in the future? In practice, the time of sale is generally taken to be the point of delivery; among other reasons, this reflects the law in a large number of jurisdictions, under which title passes to the buyer upon delivery, whether or not payment has been made.

See 3.7 below for a discussion of the principles laid down in IAS 18 for determining when to recognise revenue from a transaction involving the sale of goods.

2.1.3 The recognition of revenue subsequent to delivery

The uncertainties that exist after delivery may be of such significance that recognition should be delayed beyond the normal recognition point.

If the principal uncertainty concerns collectability, it might be appropriate to defer recognition of the whole sale (and not just the profit) until collection is reasonably assured – as is the requirement under US GAAP, discussed below.

The entity may sell its product but give the customer the right to return the goods, e.g. in the case of an online business where the customer is given an approval period of, say, 14 days. Revenue may be recognised on delivery if future returns can be predicted reasonably accurately; otherwise it should be recognised on receipt of payment for the goods, or on customer acceptance of the goods and express or implied acknowledgement of the liability for payment, or after the 14 days have elapsed – whichever is considered to be the most appropriate under the circumstances. Note that entities may have a statutory right to cancel most sales of goods bought online or by mail order without reason; in the EU, customers have 7 days from the date of receipt.

In fact, this is an area where practice has been somewhat inconsistent. A transaction with a right of return is usually accounted for as a sale, whereas revenue from a transaction with a 14-day acceptance period is usually deferred – despite the fact that the transactions are virtually identical in terms of the legal rights and obligations of the parties.

This area of uncertainty is dealt with in US GAAP under Accounting Standards Codification (ASC) 605-15 – *Revenue Recognition – Products* – which states that if an entity sells its product but gives the buyer the right to return the product, revenue from the sales transaction is recognised at time of sale only if *all* of the following conditions are met:[4]

(a) the seller's price to the buyer is substantially fixed or determinable at the date of sale;

(b) the buyer has paid the seller, or the buyer is obligated to pay the seller and the obligation is not contingent on resale of the product;

(c) the buyer's obligation to the seller would not be changed in the event of theft or physical destruction or damage of the product;

(d) the buyer acquiring the product for resale has economic substance apart from that provided by the seller (i.e. the buyer does not merely exist 'on paper' with little or no physical facilities, having been established by the seller primarily for the purpose of recognising revenue);

(e) the seller does not have significant obligations for future performance to directly bring about resale of the product by the buyer; and

(f) the amount of future returns can be reasonably estimated.

Revenue that was not recognised at the time of sale because these conditions were not met should be recognised either when the return privilege has 'substantially expired', or when all the above conditions are met, whichever occurs first.[5]

The ability to make a reasonable estimate of future returns depends on many factors and will vary from one case to the next. US GAAP lists the following factors as being those that might impair a seller's ability to make such an estimate:[6]

(a) the susceptibility of the product to significant external factors, such as technological obsolescence or changes in demand;

(b) relatively long periods in which a particular product may be returned;

(c) absence of historical experience with similar types of sales of similar products, or inability to apply such experience because of changing circumstances; for example, changes in the selling entity's marketing policies or its relationships with its customers; and

(d) absence of a large volume of relatively homogeneous transactions.

The right of return is, therefore, viewed as a significant uncertainty that would preclude recognition under circumstances when the level of returns cannot be estimated. This means, for example, that a 14-day acceptance period would not of itself require deferral of a sale, provided that the 14-day period is normal and routine and the uncertainty related to the returns is not significant.

2.2 The accretion approach

The accretion approach involves the recognition of revenue during the process of production, rather than at the end of a contract or when production is complete. There are four broad areas of entity activity where the application of the accretion approach might be appropriate.

(a) The use by others of entity resources

The traditional accrual basis of accounting recognises revenue as entity resources are used by others; this approach is followed, for example, in the case of rental or interest income. Uncertainty of collection should always be considered, in which case it might be appropriate to delay recognition until cash is received or ultimate collection is assured beyond all reasonable doubt.

(b) Long-term contracts

The second accepted application of the accretion approach may be found in the accounting practice for long-term construction contracts. For example, under IAS 11 the amount of revenue to be recognised on construction contracts is determined according to the 'percentage-of-completion method', whereby contract revenue is matched with the contract costs incurred in reaching the stage of completion, resulting in the reporting of revenue, expenses and profit that can be attributed to the proportion of work completed at each balance sheet date. *[IAS 11.25].* Normally, the main uncertainties in the application of this approach are the estimation of the total costs and the degree of completion attained at the balance sheet date, particularly in the early stages of the contract. However, the selling price is sometimes uncertain as well, owing to contract modifications that give rise to revenue from 'extras'. Accounting for construction contracts is dealt with in detail in Chapter 23.

(c) The rendering of services

This is probably the most widespread example of the application of the accretion approach. For example, IAS 18 requires that when the outcome of a transaction involving the rendering of services can be estimated reliably, revenue is recognised 'by reference to the stage of completion of the transaction at the end of the reporting period' *[IAS 18.20]*, (in other words, using the percentage-of-completion method). This is discussed further at 3.8 below.

(d) Natural growth and 'biological transformation'

Where an entity's activity involves production through natural growth or ageing, the accretion approach suggests that revenue should be recognised at identifiable stages during this process. For example, in the case of livestock, there could be market prices available at the various stages of growth; revenue could, therefore, be recognised throughout the production process by making comparative stock valuations and reporting the accretions at each accounting date.

This is dealt with by IAS 41. The standard requires application of fair value accounting to all 'biological assets', which are defined as being living animals and plants, *[IAS 41.5]*, throughout their period of growth. Entities that undertake agricultural activity are required to measure all biological assets at fair value less costs to sell, *[IAS 41.12]*, whilst all agricultural produce should be measured at fair value less costs to sell, and thereafter inventory accounting under IAS 2 should be applied. Fair value less costs to sell at harvest becomes 'cost' for IAS 2 purposes at the date at which that standard first applies. *[IAS 41.13].*

The change in fair value less costs to sell of biological assets during a period is reported in net profit or loss for the period. *[IAS 41.26]*. However, IAS 41 contains no guidance on revenue recognition. In fact, the term 'revenue' is not mentioned in the entire standard and in the illustration of the statement of comprehensive income set out in the Illustrative Examples to IAS 41, there is no revenue line. IAS 41 amended IAS 18 to exclude from the scope of IAS 18 changes in fair value and initial recognition at fair value of agricultural assets and produce before harvest. Fair value gains and revenue from the sale of biological assets and agricultural produce should not be aggregated as this may result in double counting.

IAS 41 is dealt with in detail in Chapter 38. This includes a discussion of the treatment of fair value movements in the statement of comprehensive income at 5.1.2.

3 THE REQUIREMENTS OF IAS 18

3.1 Scope

Income is defined in the IASB's *Conceptual Framework for Financial Reporting ('Framework')* as increases in economic benefits during the accounting period in the form of inflows or enhancements of assets or decreases of liabilities that result in increases in equity, other than those relating to contributions from equity participants. *[Framework 4.25(a)]*. The revised IAS 18 embraces in its objective the definition of income from the *Framework,* adding that 'revenue is income that arises in the course of ordinary activities of an entity and is referred to by a variety of different names including sales, fees, interest, dividends and royalties'. *[IAS 18 Objective]*. However, having established the link between the *Framework's* definition of income and IAS 18's definition of revenue, IAS 18 reverts to the transactions-based critical event approach for the recognition of revenues derived from the sale of goods.

The standard explains that its objective is to prescribe the accounting treatment of revenue arising from the following types of transactions and events:

(a) the sale of goods;

(b) the rendering of services; and

(c) the use by others of entity assets yielding interest, royalties and dividends. *[IAS 18.1]*.

The term 'goods' includes goods produced by the entity for the purpose of sale and goods purchased for resale, such as merchandise purchased by a retailer or land and other property held for resale. *[IAS 18.3]*.

The rendering of services typically involves the performance by the entity of a contractually agreed task over an agreed period of time. The services may be rendered within a single period or over more than one period. However, some contracts for the rendering of services are directly related to construction contracts, for example, those for the services of project managers and architects. Consequently, revenue arising from these contracts is not specified by IAS 18, but is dealt with in accordance with the requirements for construction contracts in IAS 11 (see Chapter 23). *[IAS 18.4].*

The use by others of entity assets gives rise to revenue in the form of:

(a) interest – charges for the use of cash or cash equivalents or amounts due to the entity;

(b) royalties – charges for the use of long-term assets of the entity, for example, patents, trademarks, copyrights and computer software; and

(c) dividends – distributions of profits to holders of equity investments in proportion to their holdings of a particular class of capital. *[IAS 18.5].*

There are a number of matters that the standard expressly states that it does not deal with, because they are all dealt with in other standards. These are: *[IAS 18.6]*

(a) lease agreements (see IAS 17). However, IAS 17 itself does not apply to licensing agreements for such items as motion picture films, video recordings, plays, manuscripts, patents and copyrights, *[IAS 17.2]*, (see Chapter 24 at 3.1);

(b) dividends arising from investments that are accounted for under the equity method (see Chapters 11 and 12, which address associates and joint arrangements respectively);

(c) insurance contracts within the scope of IFRS 4 (see Chapter 51);

(d) the changes in the fair value of financial assets and financial liabilities or their disposal (see Chapter 46 and 47);

(e) the changes in the value of other current assets;

(f) revenue arising from the initial recognition and from changes in the fair value of biological assets related to agricultural activity (see Chapter 38);

(g) the initial recognition of agricultural produce (see Chapter 38); and

(h) the extraction of mineral ores (see Chapter 39).

3.2 The distinction between income, revenue and gains

The *Framework* explains that its definition of income encompasses both 'revenue' and 'gains'. Revenue arises in the course of the ordinary activities of an entity; as we have seen above it can include sales, fees, interest, dividends, royalties and rent. Gains represent other items that meet the definition of income and may, or may not, arise in the course of the ordinary activities of an entity. Gains include, for example, those arising on the disposal of non-current assets. The definition of income also includes unrealised gains; for example, those arising on the revaluation of marketable securities and those resulting from increases in the carrying amount of long-term assets. *[Framework 4.31].*

The rules on offset in IAS 1 – *Presentation of Financial Statements* – distinguish between revenue and gains. The standard states that an entity undertakes, in the course of its ordinary activities, other transactions that do not generate revenue but are incidental to the main revenue-generating activities. When this presentation reflects the substance of the transaction or other event, the results of such transactions are presented by netting any income with related expenses arising on the same transaction. For example, gains and losses on the disposal of non-current assets, including investments and operating assets, are reported by deducting from the proceeds on disposal the carrying amount of the asset and related selling expenses. *[IAS 1.34]*. IAS 16 – *Property, Plant and Equipment* – has a general rule that 'gains shall not be classified as revenue'. *[IAS 16.68]*. The only exception to this rule is where an entity routinely sells property, plant and equipment (PP&E) that it has held for rental to others, which is discussed further at 5.11.1 below.

IAS 18 explains that revenue includes only the gross inflows of economic benefits received and receivable by the entity on its own account. In practice, the distinction between gross and net revenues is not always straightforward, but there is guidance regarding revenue and agency relationships, which is discussed at 3.3 below.

Amounts collected on behalf of third parties such as sales taxes, goods and services taxes and value added taxes are not economic benefits that flow to the entity and do not result in increases in equity. Therefore, they are excluded from revenue. See 5.8 below for a discussion of some of the factors that need to be considered in determining whether gross or net revenue presentation is appropriate in relation to excise taxes and goods and services taxes.

3.3 Revenue and agency relationships

In an agency relationship, the gross inflows of economic benefits include amounts collected on behalf of the principal and which do not result in increases in equity for the entity. The amounts collected on behalf of the principal are not revenue; instead, revenue is the amount of commission. *[IAS 18.8]*.

The Illustrative Examples to IAS 18 includes guidance to help determine whether an entity is acting as a principal or as an agent. *[IAS 18.IE21]*. An entity is acting as a principal when it has exposure to the significant risks and rewards associated with the sale of goods or rendering of services. There are four criteria that, individually or in combination, indicate that an entity is acting as principal: *[IAS 18.IE21]*

- the entity has the primary responsibility for providing the goods or services to the customer or for fulfilling the order, for example by being responsible for the acceptability of the products or services ordered or purchased by the customer;
- the entity has inventory risk before or after the customer order, during shipping or on return;
- the entity has latitude in establishing prices, either directly or indirectly, for example by providing additional goods or services; and
- the entity bears the customer's credit risk on the receivable due from the customer.

Conversely an entity is acting as agent when it does not have exposure to the significant risks and rewards associated with the sale of goods or rendering of services and this may be evidenced by the entity earning a predetermined amount, perhaps a fixed fee per transaction or a stated percentage of customer billings. *[IAS 18.IE21]*.

This amendment is closely related to the more detailed US GAAP guidance in ASC 605-45 – *Revenue Recognition – Principal agent considerations* – which had been widely used as guidance on agency and gross versus net accounting.

An entity may make sales to parties that are acting as agents. In order to recognise revenue on the sale of goods the seller must have transferred the significant risks and rewards of ownership to the buyer and must not retain either continuing managerial involvement to the degree usually associated with ownership or effective control over the goods sold. *[IAS 18.14(a), 14(b)].* This may not be the case if the buyer is an agent of the seller. For example, revenue from sales to intermediate parties, such as distributors, dealers or others for resale is generally recognised when the risks and rewards of ownership have passed. When the buyer is acting, in substance, as an agent, the sale is treated as a consignment sale, i.e. no revenue is recognised until the goods are sold to a third party. *[IAS 18.IE6, IE2(c)].*

3.4 Income and distributable profits

IFRS, generally, and IAS 18, specifically, do not address the issue of the distribution of profit. Whether or not revenue and gains recognised in accordance with IFRS are distributable to shareholders of an entity will depend entirely on the national laws and regulations with which the entity needs to comply. Thus, income reported in accordance with IFRS does not necessarily imply that such income would either be realised or distributable under a reporting entity's applicable national legislation.

3.5 Measurement of revenue

Revenue should be measured at the fair value of the consideration received or receivable. *[IAS 18.9].* IAS 18 states that the amount of revenue arising on a transaction is usually determined by agreement between the entity and the buyer or user of the asset. This means that it is measured at the fair value of the consideration received or receivable taking into account the amount of any trade discounts and volume rebates allowed by the entity. *[IAS 18.10].* Fair value is as defined in IFRS 13 as 'the price that would be received to sell an asset or paid to transfer a liability in an orderly transaction between market participants at the measurement date.' *[IAS 18.7].* This has replaced the previous definition in IAS 18, which was 'the amount for which an asset could be exchanged, or a liability settled, between knowledgeable, willing parties in an arm's length transaction'. The principal difference between the IFRS 13 definition and that previously in IAS 18 is that the new definition is explicitly an exit value.

Usually, this will present little difficulty, as the consideration will normally be in the form of cash or cash equivalents and the amount of revenue will be the amount of cash or cash equivalents received or receivable. However, if the inflow is deferred, the fair value of the consideration will then be less than the nominal amount of cash received or receivable. IFRS 13 requires an entity to use market participant assumptions in measuring fair value and to prioritise observable inputs over those that are unobservable. Therefore, when an arrangement effectively constitutes a financing arrangement, the fair value of the consideration would market participants' assumptions about the time value of money and the risk associated with the financing arrangement. IFRS 13 does not restrict or prioritise the types of techniques an entity can use to measure fair value. However, IAS 18 requires that the fair value of the consideration be determined by discounting all future receipts using an imputed rate of interest. The imputed rate of interest is the more clearly determinable of either:

(a) the prevailing rate for a similar instrument of an issuer with a similar credit rating; or

(b) a rate of interest that discounts the nominal amount of the instrument to the current cash sales price of the goods or services. *[IAS 18.11]*.

The difference between the fair value and the nominal amount of the consideration is recognised as interest revenue using the effective interest method as set out in IAS 39, paragraphs 9 and AG5 to AG8. *[IAS 18.11, 30(a)]*. The application of the effective interest rate method is discussed in Chapter 46 at 6.

A further issue arises if a company offers prompt settlement discounts to its customers. An example of a prompt settlement discount is a reduction of 5% of the selling price for paying an invoice within 7 days instead of the usual 60 days. In such cases, in order to comply with IAS 18's requirement that revenue should be measured at the fair value of the consideration received or receivable, *[IAS 18.9]*, prompt settlement discounts should be estimated at the time of sale and deducted from revenues.

3.6 Identifying the transaction

IAS 18 states that the recognition criteria of the standard are usually applied separately to each transaction. However, in certain circumstances, it is necessary to apply the recognition criteria to the separately identifiable components of a single transaction in order to reflect the substance of the transaction. *[IAS 18.13]*. This means that transactions have to be analysed in accordance with their economic substance in order to determine whether they should be combined or segmented for revenue recognition purposes. For example, when the selling price of a product includes an identifiable amount for subsequent servicing, that amount is deferred and recognised as revenue over the period during which the service is performed.

Conversely, the recognition criteria are applied to two or more transactions together when they are linked in such a way that the commercial effect cannot be understood without reference to the series of transactions as a whole – as is the case, for example, with the sale of mobile phones combined with related service contracts (the issue of bundled offers in the telecommunications sector is discussed below at 5.7). A further example might be where an entity sells goods and, at the same time, enters into a separate agreement to repurchase the goods at a later date, thus negating the substantive effect of the transaction; in such a case, the two transactions are dealt with together. *[IAS 18.13]*. The following extracts from the revenue recognition policies of Sandvik and Renault illustrate this point:

Extract 28.1: Sandvik AB (2011)

Significant accounting policies [extract]

Revenue [extract]

Revenue from sales and services [extract]

Buy-back commitments may entail that sales revenue cannot be recognized if the agreement with the customer in reality implies that the customer has only rented the product for a certain period of time.

Extract 28.2: Renault SA (2011)

4.2.7.1 Accounting policies and scope of consolidation [extract]

2 – ACCOUNTING POLICIES [extract]

G – Revenues and margin [extract]

Sales of goods and services and margin recognition [extract]

Sales and margin recognition

Sales of goods are recognized when vehicles are made available to the distribution network in the case of non-Group dealers, or upon delivery to the end-user in the case of direct sales. The margin on sales is recognized immediately for normal sales by the Automobile segment, including sales with associated financing contracts that can be considered as finance leases (long-term or with a purchase option). However, no sale is recognized when the vehicle is covered by an operating lease from a Group finance company or the Group has made a buy-back commitment with a high probability of application, when the term of the contract covers an insufficient portion of the vehicle's useful life.

In such cases, the transactions are recorded as operating leases and included in sales of services. The difference between the price paid by the customer and the buy-back price is treated as rental income, and spread over the period the vehicle is at the customer's disposal. The production cost for the new vehicle concerned is recorded in inventories for contracts of less than one year, or included in property, plant and equipment under vehicles leased to customers when the contracts exceed one year. The sale of the vehicle as second-hand at the end of the lease gives rise to recognition of sales revenue and the related margin. The forecast resale value takes account of recent known developments on the second-hand vehicle market but also future anticipated developments over the period in which the vehicles will be sold, which may be influenced by factors both external (economic situation, taxation) and internal (changes in the range, lower manufacturer prices). As soon as a loss is expected on the resale, a provision (if the vehicle is in inventories) or additional depreciation (if the vehicle is included in property, plant and equipment) is recognized to cover the loss. When the overall position of the lease contract (rental income and income on resale) shows a loss, an additional provision is also recorded immediately to cover the future loss.

IAS 18 does not establish criteria for segmenting and combining revenue transactions. However, IAS 11 includes a requirement similar to that of IAS 18 in that it requires companies to apply the standard to separately identifiable components of a single construction contract, or to a group of contracts together, in order to reflect the substance of a contract or a group of contracts. *[IAS 11.7]*. The practical issues in connection with combining and segmenting contracts are considered further in Chapter 23 at 2.

In the absence of any equivalent practical guidance in IAS 18, the criteria set out in IAS 11 may be helpful in determining whether revenue transactions should be combined or segmented. However the underlying principle in IAS 18, which focuses on whether combination or segmentation is necessary to reflect the substance and understand the commercial effect, should remain the primary consideration in making this assessment. *[IAS 18.13]*.

IAS 18 does not provide any additional guidance in identifying the separate components to which revenue should be allocated, nor does it prescribe an allocation method for multiple-component sales. In the specific case of servicing fees included in the price of a product, it notes that part of the revenue should be deferred to meet the expected costs of the service, together with a 'reasonable profit' on those services. *[IAS 18.IE11]*. There is no further explanation of what constitutes a 'reasonable profit', but it is quite clearly not a requirement to allocate revenue on a relative fair value basis. The allocation of revenue can be based on relative fair values or on a residual method. The entity will draw on its experience of transactions with similar customers.

In the case of certain arrangements with multiple deliverables, it may also be helpful (but not required), under the hierarchy in IAS 8 – *Accounting Policies, Changes in Accounting Estimates and Errors*, *[IAS 8.12]*, to refer to the US GAAP guidance codified in ASC 605-25 – *Revenue Recognition – Multiple-Element Arrangements* (previously EITF 00-21), which deals with the issue of separating elements of revenue. See 5.7.1 below for a discussion of how this US GAAP guidance has been applied to recognising revenue on bundled offers in the telecommunications sector.

3.7 The sale of goods

IAS 18 lays down the following five criteria that must be satisfied in order to recognise revenue from the sale of goods: *[IAS 18.14]*

(a) the entity has transferred to the buyer the significant risks and rewards of ownership of the goods;

(b) the entity retains neither continuing managerial involvement to the degree usually associated with ownership nor effective control over the goods sold;

(c) the amount of revenue can be measured reliably;

(d) it is probable that the economic benefits associated with the transaction will flow to the entity; and

(e) the costs incurred or to be incurred in respect of the transaction can be measured reliably.

If the costs incurred cannot be measured reliably, the standard requires that 'any consideration already received for the sale of the goods is recognised as a liability'. *[IAS 18.19]*.

IAS 18 views the passing of risks and rewards as the most crucial of the five criteria, giving the following four examples of situations in which an entity may retain the significant risks and rewards of ownership: *[IAS 18.16]*

(a) when the entity retains an obligation for unsatisfactory performance not covered by normal warranty provisions;

(b) when the receipt of the revenue from a particular sale is contingent on the derivation of revenue by the buyer from its sale of the goods;

(c) when the goods are shipped subject to installation and the installation is a significant part of the contract which has not yet been completed by the entity; and

(d) when the buyer has the right to rescind the purchase for a reason specified in the sales contract and the entity is uncertain about the probability of return.

It is clear that the standard still advocates an earnings process-driven critical event approach to revenue recognition. It is, therefore, necessary to establish at which point in the earnings process both the significant risks and rewards of ownership are transferred from the seller to the buyer and any significant uncertainties (which would otherwise delay recognition) are removed. For example, the responsibilities of each party during the period between sale and delivery should be established, possibly from past practice and by examination of the customer agreements. If the goods have merely to be uplifted by the buyer, and the seller has performed all his associated responsibilities, then the sale may be recognised immediately. However, if the substance of the sale is merely that an order has been placed, and the goods have still to be acquired or manufactured by the seller, then the sale should not be recognised. The following extract from the accounting policies of Atlas Copco illustrates the deferral of revenue recognition until installation is completed in those cases where installation is a significant part of the contract:

Extract 28.3: Atlas Copco Group (2011)

Notes to the Consolidated Financial Statements [extract]

1. **Significant accounting principles, accounting estimates and judgments** [extract]

Revenue recognition [extract]

Goods sold [extract]

Revenue from sale of goods is recognized when the significant risks and rewards of ownership have been transferred to the buyer, which in most cases occurs in connection with delivery. When the product requires installation and that is a significant part of the contract, revenue is recognized when the installation is completed.

The terms of trade, and the associated legal implications, may also be relevant in determining the timing of revenue recognition. The standard assumes that 'in most cases, the transfer of risks and rewards of ownership coincides with the transfer of legal title or the passing of possession to the buyer' but acknowledges that this may not always be the case. The standard recognises that transactions occur where the transfer of risks and rewards of ownership occurs at a different time from the transfer of legal title or the passing of possession. *[IAS 18.15].* Transfer of legal title is, therefore, not a condition for revenue recognition under IAS 18. IAS 18 recognises that, under certain circumstances, goods are sold subject to reservation of title in order to protect the collectability of the amount due; in such circumstances, provided that the seller has transferred the significant risks and rewards of ownership, the transaction can be treated as a sale and revenue can be recognised. *[IAS 18.17].*

This point is reinforced in the introductory paragraph to the Illustrative Examples to IAS 18, which notes that laws in different countries may mean that the recognition criteria in the standard are met at different times. In particular, the law may determine the point in time at which an entity transfers the significant risks and rewards of ownership. Therefore, the illustrative examples need to be read in the context of the laws relating to the sale of goods in the country in which the transaction takes place. *[IAS 18.IE].*

The following extracts from the financial statements of Smith & Nephew and Roche illustrate both the measurement principles of IAS 18 and the application of the critical event approach in determining the timing of revenue recognition:

Extract 28.4: Smith & Nephew plc (2011)

Notes to the Group Accounts [extract]

2.1 Revenue by business segment and geography [extract]

Accounting policy

Revenue comprises sales of products and services to third parties at amounts invoiced net of trade discounts and rebates, excluding taxes on revenue. Revenue from the sale of products is recognised upon transfer to the customer of the significant risks and rewards of ownership. This is generally when goods are delivered to customers. Sales of inventory located at customer premises and available for customers' immediate use are recognised when notification is received that the product has been implanted or used. Appropriate provisions for returns, trade discounts and rebates are deducted from revenue. Rebates comprise retrospective volume discounts granted to certain customers on attainment of certain levels of purchases from the Group. These are accrued over the course of the arrangement based on estimates of the level of business expected and adjusted at the end of the arrangement to reflect actual volumes.

Extract 28.5: Roche Holdings, Inc. (2011)

Notes to the Roche Holdings, Inc. Consolidated Financial Statements [extract]

1. Summary of significant accounting policies [extract]

Revenues

Sales represent amounts received and receivable for goods supplied to customers after deducting trade discounts, cash discounts and volume rebates, and exclude sales taxes and other taxes directly linked to sales. Revenues from the sale of products are recognized upon transfer to the customer of significant risks and rewards. Trade discounts, cash discounts and volume rebates are recorded on an accrual basis consistent with the recognition of the related sales. Estimates of expected sales returns, charge-backs and other rebates, including Medicaid in the United States, are also deducted from sales and recorded as accrued liabilities or provisions or as a deduction from accounts receivable. Such estimates are based on analyses of existing contractual or legislatively mandated obligations, historical trends and RHI's experience. If the circumstances are such that the level of sales returns, and hence revenues, cannot be reliably measured, then sales are only recognized when the right of return expires, which is generally upon prescription of the products to patients. Other revenues are recorded as earned or as the services are performed. Where necessary, single transactions are split into separately identifiable components to reflect the substance of the transaction. Conversely, two or more transactions may be considered together for revenue recognition purposes, where the commercial effect cannot be understood without reference to the series of transactions as a whole.

3.8 The rendering of services

IAS 18 requires that when the outcome of a transaction involving the rendering of services can be estimated reliably, revenue is recognised 'by reference to the stage of completion of the transaction at the end of the reporting period' (in other words, using the percentage-of-completion method) *[IAS 18.20]*. The requirements of IAS 11 are 'generally applicable to the recognition of revenue and the associated expenses for a transaction involving the rendering of services'. *[IAS 18.21]*.

According to IAS 18, the outcome of a transaction can be estimated reliably when all the following conditions are satisfied: *[IAS 18.20]*

(a) the amount of revenue can be measured reliably;
(b) it is probable that the economic benefits associated with the transaction will flow to the entity;
(c) the stage of completion of the transaction at the end of the reporting period can be measured reliably; and
(d) the costs incurred for the transaction and the costs to complete the transaction can be measured reliably.

When the outcome cannot be estimated reliably, revenue is recognised only to the extent of the expenses recognised that are recoverable. *[IAS 18.26]*. During the early stages of a transaction, it is often the case that the outcome of the transaction cannot be estimated reliably. Nevertheless, it may be probable that the enterprise will recover the transaction costs incurred. Therefore, revenue is recognised only to the extent of costs incurred that are expected to be recoverable. As the outcome of the transaction cannot be estimated reliably, no profit is recognised. *[IAS 18.27]*. For an example of this see the Nokia Corporation revenue recognition policy in Extract 28.7 below.

When the outcome of a transaction cannot be estimated reliably and it is not probable that the costs incurred will be recovered, revenue is not recognised and the costs incurred are recognised as an expense. When the uncertainties that prevented the outcome of the contract being estimated reliably no longer exist, revenue is recognised by reference to the stage of completion of the transaction at the balance sheet date. *[IAS 18.28]*.

IAS 18 provides several illustrative examples of transactions involving the rendering of services. It is clear from these examples that the performance of the service is the critical event for revenue recognition. *[IAS 18.IE10-19]*.

The standard claims that an entity is generally able to make reliable estimates after it has agreed to the following with the other parties to the transaction: *[IAS 18.23]*

(a) each party's enforceable rights regarding the service to be provided and received by the parties;
(b) the consideration to be exchanged; and
(c) the manner and terms of settlement.

The standard notes that it is usually necessary for the entity to have an effective internal financial budgeting and reporting system. The entity reviews and, when necessary, revises the estimates of revenue as the service is performed. The need for such revisions does not necessarily indicate that the outcome of the transaction cannot be estimated reliably. *[IAS 18.23]*.

When it comes to determining the stage of completion of a transaction, IAS 18 suggests three methods that may be used: *[IAS 18.24]*

(a) surveys of work performed;
(b) services performed to date as a percentage of total services to be performed; or
(c) the proportion that costs incurred to date bear to the estimated total costs of the transaction. Only costs that reflect services performed to date are included in costs incurred to date. Only costs that reflect services performed or to be performed are included in the estimated total costs of the transaction.

For practical purposes, when services are performed by an indeterminate number of acts over a specified period, the standard states that revenue should be recognised on a straight-line basis over the specified period unless there is evidence that some other method better represents the stage of completion. However, when a specific act is much more significant than any other acts, the standard requires that the recognition of revenue be postponed until the significant act is executed. *[IAS 18.25]*.

What this means in practice can be seen by considering outsourcing arrangements. These are contracts that require services to be provided on an ongoing basis, often for a number of years, rather than the provision of a single service or a number of services that constitute a single project. These arrangements are common across a wide range of services including processing, provision of telecommunications services, general professional advice, help desk support, accounting advice, maintenance or cleaning, The 'service' to which IAS 18's method applies is the individual act, whether it be the individual process, answering the telephone help line or cleaning the office each night. Clearly in most cases it would not be feasible to identify the costs and revenue for each of these acts so revenue is taken on a straight line over the contract term and costs are expensed as incurred.

The entities that provide outsourcing services frequently provide single services as well. The following revenue recognition policy for Cap Gemini illustrates both the treatment of revenue for outsourcing contracts and for its long-term contracts.

Extract 28.6: Cap Gemini S.A. (2011)

6.7 Notes to the consolidated financial statements [extract]

NOTE 1 – ACCOUNTING POLICIES [extract]

E) Recognition of revenues and the cost of services rendered [extract]

The method for recognizing revenues and costs depends on the nature of the services rendered:

a) Time and materials contracts

Revenues and costs relating to time and materials contracts are recognized as services are rendered.

b) Long-term fixed-price contracts

Revenues, including systems development and integration contracts, are recognized using the "percentage-of-completion" method. Costs are recognized as they are incurred.

c) Outsourcing contracts

Revenues from outsourcing agreements are recognized over the term of the contract as the services are rendered. When the services are made up of different components which are not separately identifiable, the related revenues are recognized on a straight-line basis over the term of the contract.

The related costs are recognized as they are incurred. However, a portion of costs incurred in the initial phase of outsourcing contracts (transition and/or transformation costs) may be deferred when they are specific to a given contract, relate to future activity on the contract and/or will generate future economic benefits, and are recoverable.

Nokia provides an illustration of an accounting policy whereby revenue from contracts involving the modification of complex telecommunications equipment is recognised using the percentage-of-completion method:

Extract 28.7: Nokia Corporation (2011)

Notes to the consolidated financial statements [extract]

1. **Accounting principles** [extract]

Revenue recognition [extract]

In addition, sales and cost of sales from contracts involving solutions achieved through modification of complex telecommunications equipment are recognized using the percentage of completion method when the outcome of the contract can be estimated reliably. A contract's outcome can be estimated reliably when total contract revenue and the costs to complete the contract can be estimated reliably, it is probable that the economic benefits associated with the contract will flow to the Group and the stage of contract completion can be measured reliably. When the Group is not able to meet one or more of the conditions, the policy is to recognize revenues only equal to costs incurred to date, to the extent that such costs are expected to be recovered.

Progress towards completion is measured by reference to cost incurred to date as a percentage of estimated total project costs, the cost-to-cost method.

3.9 Exchanges of goods and services

Under IAS 18, when goods or services are exchanged or swapped for goods or services that are of a similar nature and value, the exchange is not regarded as a transaction that generates revenue. The standard notes exchanges of commodities like oil or milk, where suppliers exchange or swap inventories in various locations to fulfil demand on a timely basis in a particular location as examples of this. There are similar reasons behind exchanges of capacity in the telecommunications sector.

If the goods or services exchanged are dissimilar then revenue will be recognised on the transaction. The revenue is measured at the fair value of the goods or services received, adjusted by the amount of any cash or cash equivalents transferred. When the fair value of the goods or services received cannot be measured reliably, the revenue is measured at the fair value of the goods or services given up, adjusted by the amount of any cash or cash equivalents transferred. *[IAS 18.12].*

IFRIC 18, which addresses accounting for transfers of assets from customers, provides guidance in situations where an entity receives an item of PP&E from a customer (or cash for the acquisition or construction of such items) that must then be used by the entity either to connect the customer to a network or to provide the customer ongoing access to a supply of goods or services. *[IFRIC 18.4-6].* These arrangements are relatively common in the utilities and automobile industries. The Interpretation is discussed at 5.14 below.

There are specific requirements for exchanges of fixed assets within scope of IAS 16 or IAS 38 – *Intangible Assets* – described below.

3.10 Exchanges of property plant and equipment and intangible assets

Accounting for exchanges of PP&E is dealt with in IAS 16, which takes a different approach to IAS 18's treatment of exchanges of goods and services. IAS 38 deals with exchanges of intangible assets, and includes the same requirements as IAS 16 with respect to intangible assets. *[IAS 38.45-47].*

IAS 16 stipulates that gains arising from the derecognition of PP&E may not be classified as revenue *[IAS 16.68]* and it is clear that this applies equally to derecognition by way of an exchange, sale and abandonment; this means that an exchange of PP&E does not result in the recognition of revenue. The sole exception is the sale of certain ex-rental assets, discussed at 5.11.1 below. *[IAS 16.68A]*.

IAS 16 does not contain the distinction between similar and dissimilar assets that still remains in IAS 18 in respect of exchanges of goods and services. Instead, IAS 16 requires PP&E acquired in exchange for a non-monetary asset or assets, or a combination of monetary and non-monetary assets, to be accounted for at fair value, unless: *[IAS 16.24]*

(a) the exchange transaction lacks commercial substance, or

(b) the fair value of neither the asset received nor the asset given up is reliably measurable.

The acquired item is measured in this way even if an entity cannot immediately derecognise the asset given up. *[IAS 16.24]*.

The fair value of an asset for which there are no comparable market transactions is reliably measurable if:

(a) the variability in the range of reasonable fair value estimates is not significant for that asset, or

(b) the probabilities of the various estimates within the range can be reasonably assessed and used in estimating fair value. *[IAS 16.26]*.

Note that, while fair value is defined by reference to IFRS 13, these requirements are specific to asset exchanges in IAS 16 and IAS 38. No guidance is given in either IAS 16 or IAS 38 on how to assemble a 'range of reasonable fair value estimates'. Instead, judgement would be needed to determine such a range in light of the requirements of IFRS 13.

If an entity is able to determine reliably the fair value of either the asset received or the asset given up, then the fair value of the asset given up is used to measure the cost of the asset received unless the fair value of the asset received is more clearly evident. *[IAS 16.26]*. If the acquired item is not measured at fair value, its cost is measured at the carrying amount of the asset given up. *[IAS 16.24]*. Exchanges of assets are discussed in Chapter 18 at 4.4.

BP p.l.c. is an example of an entity that discloses an accounting policy for asset exchanges:

Extract 28.8: BP p.l.c. (2011)

Notes on financial statements [extract]

1 Significant accounting policies [extract]

Property, plant and equipment [extract]

Exchanges of assets are measured at fair value unless the exchange transaction lacks commercial substance or the fair value of neither the asset received nor the asset given up is reliably measurable. The cost of the acquired asset is measured at the fair value of the asset given up, unless the fair value of the asset received is more clearly evident. Where fair value is not used, the cost of the acquired asset is measured at the carrying amount of the asset given up. The gain or loss on derecognition of the asset given up is recognized in profit or loss.

IFRS 5 – *Non-current Assets Held for Sale and Discontinued Operations* – lays down additional requirements for assets held for disposal; these requirements include measurement rules that affect the measurement of the amount of the gain on disposal to be recognised. These are discussed in Chapter 4 at 2.2.

3.11 Barter transactions involving advertising services

This is an issue that arose during the dotcom boom of the late 1990s and early 2000s, and is addressed in SIC-31. The issue arises where an entity (the seller) enters into a barter transaction to provide advertising services in exchange for receiving advertising services from its customer. Advertisements may be displayed on the Internet or poster sites, broadcast on television or radio, published in magazines or journals, or presented in another medium. In some cases, no cash or other consideration is exchanged between the entities although in other cases equal or approximately equal amounts of cash or other consideration may pass between them.

IAS 18 specifically addresses the recognition of revenue from advertising commissions, discussed at 5.5 below. It is clear that, under IAS 18, a seller that provides advertising services in the course of its ordinary activities recognises revenue from a barter transaction involving advertising when, amongst other criteria, the services exchanged are dissimilar and the amount of revenue can be measured reliably. *[IAS 18.12, 20(a)].* However, an exchange of similar advertising services is not a transaction that generates revenue under IAS 18.

The Standing Interpretations Committee (SIC) concluded that revenue cannot be measured reliably at the fair value of advertising services received. A seller can only measure revenue reliably at the fair value of the advertising services it provides by reference to non-barter transactions that:

(a) involve advertising similar to the advertising in the barter transaction;

(b) occur frequently;

(c) represent a predominant number of transactions and amount when compared to all transactions to provide advertising that is similar to the advertising in the barter transaction;

(d) involve cash and/or another form of consideration (e.g. marketable securities, non-monetary assets, and other services) that has a reliably measurable fair value; and

(e) do not involve the same counterparty as in the barter transaction. *[SIC-31.5].*

The conditions represent a relatively high hurdle for companies to overcome, and it would seem that in most instances they would find it difficult to be able to recognise any revenue. For example, payments of equal or substantially equal amounts between the entities that provide and receive advertising services do not provide reliable evidence of fair value. An exchange of advertising services that also includes only partial cash payment provides reliable evidence of the fair value of the transaction to the extent of the cash component (except when partial cash payments of equal or substantially equal amounts are swapped), but does not provide reliable evidence of the fair value of the entire transaction.

Barter transactions involving services occur mainly in the media industry. German television corporation, ProSiebenSat.1 discloses the following accounting policy for barter transactions involving advertising:

Extract 28.9: ProSiebenSat.1 Media AG (2011)

Notes to the consolidated financial statements [extract]

[6] Accounting policies [extract]

Recognition of income and expenses [extract]

Revenues from barter transactions are considered revenue-generating transactions only when dissimilar goods or services are exchanged, and the amount of the proceeds and costs, as well as the economic benefit, can be clearly measured. These revenues from barter transactions are measured on the basis of the fair value of the provided (advertising) service, if that fair value can be measured reliably. Barter transactions at the ProSiebenSat.1 Group are primarily trade-off transactions relating to the sale of advertising time.

In our view, SIC-31 was issued as a specific anti-abuse rule that does not have wider implications and should not be applied to other situations by analogy.

3.12 Interest, royalties and dividends

When it is probable that the economic benefits associated with the transaction will flow to the entity and that the amount of revenue can be measured reliably, IAS 18 requires that the revenue arising from the use by others of entity assets yielding interest, royalties and dividends should be recognised as follows: *[IAS 18.29-30]*

(a) *interest:* using the effective interest method as set out in IAS 39, paragraphs 9 and AG5-AG8 and discussed in Chapter 46 at 6;

(b) *royalties:* on an accrual basis in accordance with the substance of the relevant agreement; and

(c) *dividends:* when the shareholder's right to receive payment is established.

When unpaid interest has accrued before the acquisition of an interest-bearing investment, the subsequent receipt of interest is allocated between pre-acquisition and post-acquisition periods; only the post-acquisition portion is recognised as revenue.

There is no distinction between pre- and post-acquisition dividends. IAS 27 – *Separate Financial Statements* – states that an entity is to recognise dividends from subsidiaries, jointly controlled entities or associates in profit or loss in its separate financial statements when its right to receive the dividend is established. *[IAS 27.12]*. Entities determine as a separate exercise whether or not the investment has been impaired as a result of the dividend. IAS 36 – *Impairment of Assets* – includes specific triggers for impairment reviews on receipt of dividends. *[IAS 36.12(h)]*. The treatment of the dividends received is discussed in Chapter 8 at 2.3.

Scrip dividends, whereby new shares are issued to investors in lieu of a cash dividend, are popular in certain jurisdictions. Where the investor has the option to receive cash or the equivalent value in new shares this arrangement is in substance a cash dividend with an immediate reinvestment in shares. If the investment is either an associate or joint venture held at cost under IAS 27, or an investment classified as available for sale under IAS 39 (or IFRS 9 if applied), the scrip dividend will be recorded as revenue in the normal manner when the right to receive payment is established. The debit entry will be recognised as an addition to the investment. However, if the scrip dividend is compulsory with no cash alternative, or where the cash alternative is priced at such an unfavourable rate that an investor would be unlikely to take that option, the arrangement cannot be considered to be in substance a cash dividend with immediate reinvestment. The transaction will not result in economic benefits to the investor and therefore revenue will not be recognised.

Royalties accrue in accordance with the terms of the relevant agreement and are usually recognised on that basis unless, having regard to the substance of the agreement, it is more appropriate to recognise revenue on some other systematic and rational basis. *[IAS 18.33].*

Anglo Platinum provides a straightforward example of accounting policies for dividends, interest and royalties:

> *Extract 28.10: Anglo American Platinum Limited (2011)*
>
> **PRINCIPAL ACCOUNTING POLICIES** [extract]
>
> 11 **Revenue recognition** [extract]
>
> - Dividends are recognised when the right to receive payment is established.
> - Interest is recognised on a time proportion basis, which takes into account the effective yield on the asset over the period it is expected to be held.
> - Royalties are recognised when the right to receive payment is established.

3.13 Uncollectible revenue

Revenue is recognised only when it is probable that the economic benefits associated with the transaction will flow to the entity. Because it is recognised at fair value, the revenue may be lower than the contracted amount, to take account of expected non-recoveries. In some cases, part or all of the revenue may not be recognised until the consideration is received or until an uncertainty is removed as, until then, its receipt is not probable. However, if the collectability of an amount already included in revenue becomes uncertain, the uncollectible amount or the amount in respect of which recovery has ceased to be probable is recognised as an expense, rather than as an adjustment of the amount of revenue originally recognised. *[IAS 18.18, 22, 34].* In other words, bad and doubtful debts are recognised as expenses, not as reductions of revenue.

3.14 Disclosure

IAS 18's disclosure requirements relate to both revenue recognition policies and amounts included in the financial statements under the different categories of revenue. They are set down in the standard as follows: *[IAS 18.35]*

Chapter 28

(a) the accounting policies adopted for the recognition of revenue including the methods adopted to determine the stage of completion of transactions involving the rendering of services;

(b) the amount of each significant category of revenue recognised during the period including revenue arising from:
    (i) the sale of goods;
    (ii) the rendering of services;
    (iii) interest;
    (iv) royalties;
    (v) dividends; and

(c) the amount of revenue arising from exchanges of goods or services included in each significant category of revenue.

The disclosures required under (b) and (c) above may be provided in the notes to the financial statements, rather than on the face of the statement of comprehensive income or separate income statement (if presented).

3.15 Revenue in the statement of comprehensive income

IAS 1 contains minimum requirements for the contents of the statement of comprehensive income. This states that an entity is to present all items of income and expense recognised in a period either in a single 'statement of comprehensive income', or in two statements:

- a statement displaying components of profit or loss (separate income statement); and
- a second statement beginning with profit or loss and displaying components of other comprehensive income (the statement of comprehensive income).

If the second approach applies, the separate income statement will correspond to the income statement required by the previous version of the standard. There are minimum requirements for what must be disclosed on the face of the statement of comprehensive income or separate income statement (if presented). The formats and their requirements are described in Chapter 3. The following must be shown on the face of the statement of comprehensive income or separate income statement (if presented): *[IAS 1.81-82]*

(a) revenue;

(b) finance costs; and

(c) share of the profit or loss of associates and joint ventures accounted for using the equity method.

IAS 1 goes on to state that additional line items, headings and subtotals are to be presented in the statement of comprehensive income and the separate income statement (if presented) when such presentation is relevant to an understanding of the entity's financial performance. Additional line items are included, and the descriptions used and the ordering of items are amended, when this is necessary to explain the elements of financial performance. Factors to be considered include materiality and the nature and function of the components of income and expenses. *[IAS 1.85-86]*.

These requirements provide a company with a substantial amount of flexibility with regard to the presentation of its statement of comprehensive income and separate income statement (if presented). However, they also raise a number of practical questions about the presentation of revenue, such as:

- whether the amount for 'finance costs' be shown net of interest and other finance income; and
- the classification in profit or loss of gains on disposal of PP&E

3.15.1 Interest and other finance income

IAS 18 requires interest income to be disclosed as one of the categories of revenue. *[IAS 18.35(b)]*. It used to be a fairly widespread practice under a number of national GAAPs for companies to show finance costs net of interest and other finance income. However IAS 1 states that income and expenses should not be offset unless required or permitted by a Standard or an Interpretation. *[IAS 1.32]*. 'Finance costs' are listed as one of the line items that must be included on the face of the statement of comprehensive income or separate income statement (if presented). *[IAS 1.82(b)]*. Taken together, these paragraphs preclude an entity presenting 'net finance costs' on the face of the statement of comprehensive income and separate income statement (if presented) without showing separately the finance costs and finance revenue included in the net amount, e.g. by presenting gross interest income and gross interest expense and then striking a sub-total that shows net interest.

The IASB has removed a reference in IFRS 7 – *Financial Instruments: Disclosures* – paragraph IG13 to 'total interest income' as a component of finance costs. This amendment confirmed the IASB's intention that finance income and finance expense be separately disclosed on the face of profit or loss.

IAS 1 permits some gains and losses arising from a group of similar transactions to be reported on a net basis, for example, foreign exchange gains and losses or gains and losses arising on financial instruments held for trading. Such gains and losses are, however, reported separately if they are material. *[IAS 1.35]*.

Although there is no Standard or Interpretation that permits interest income to be offset against interest expense, we believe that net presentation is appropriate in the case of trading activities; in our view, the interest income on financial instruments (e.g. bonds) that are held as trading assets (e.g. by a financial institution) could be included within net trading income.

UBS provide shows interest income and expense gross in the income statement but provides note disclosure on a net basis by business activity.

Extract 28.11: UBS AG (2011)

Financial information [extract]

Consolidated financial statements [extract]

Income statement [extract]

		For the year ended			% change from
CHF million, except per share data	Note	**31.12.11**	31.12.10	31.12.09	31.12.10
Continuing operations					
Interest income	3	**17,969**	18,872	23,461	(5)
Interest expense	3	**(11,143)**	(12,657)	(17,016)	(12)
Net interest income	3	**6,826**	6,215	6,445	10
Credit loss (expense)/recovery		**(84)**	(66)	(1,832)	27
Net interest income after credit loss expense		**6,742**	6,149	4,614	10
Net fee and commission income	4	**15,236**	17,160	17,712	(11)
Net trading income	3	**4,343**	7,471	(324)	(42)
Other income	5	**1,467**	1,214	599	21
Total operating income		**27,788**	31,994	22,601	(13)

Income statement notes [extract]

Note 3 Net interest and trading income [extract]

The "Breakdown by businesses" table below analyzes net interest and trading income according to the businesses that drive it: Net income from trading businesses includes both interest and trading income generated by the Investment Bank, including its lending activities, and trading income generated by the other business divisions; Net income from interest margin businesses comprises interest income from the loan portfolios of Wealth Management & Swiss Bank and Wealth Management Americas; Net income from treasury activities and other reflects all income from the Group's centralized treasury function.

	For the year ended			% change from
CHF million	**31.12.11**	31.12.10	31.12.09	31.12.10
Net interest and trading income				
Net interest income	**6,826**	6,215	6,446	10
Net trading income	**4,343**	7,471	(324)	(42)
Total net interest and trading income	**11,169**	13,686	6,122	(18)
Breakdown by businesses				
Net income from trading businesses[1]	**5,964**	7,508	392	(21)
Net income from interest margin businesses	**4,874**	4,624	5,053	5
Net income from treasury activities and other	**332**	1,554	687	(79)
Total net interest and trading income	**11,169**	13,686	6,122	(18)

Net interest income[2]				
Interest income				
Interest earned on loans and advances[3,4]	**9,925**	10,603	13,202	(6)
Interest earned on securities borrowed and reverse repurchase agreements	**1,716**	1,436	2,629	19
Interest and dividend income from trading portfolio	**5,466**	6,015	7,150	(9)
Interest income on financial assets designated at fair value	**248**	262	316	(5)
Interest and dividend income from financial investments available-for-sale	**615**	557	164	10
Total	**17,969**	18,872	23,461	(5)
Interest expense				
Interest on amounts due to banks and customers[5]	**2,040**	1,984	3,873	3
Interest on securities lent and repurchase agreements	**1,352**	1,282	2,179	5
Interest and dividend expense from trading portfolio	**2,851**	3,794	3,878	(25)
Interest on financial liabilities designated at fair value	**1,993**	2,392	2,855	(17)
Interest on debt issued	**2,907**	3,206	4,231	(9)
Total	**11,143**	12,657	17,016	(12)
Net interest income	**6,826**	6,215	6,446	10

1 Includes lending activities of the Investment Bank
2 Interest includes forward points on foreign exchange swaps used to manage short-term interest rate risk on foreign currency loans and deposits.
3 Includes interest income on impaired loans and advances of CHF 20 million for 2011, CHF 37 million for 2010 and CHF 66 million for 2009.
4 Includes interest income on Cash collateral receivables on derivative instruments.
5 Includes interest expense of Cash collateral payables on derivative instruments.

3.15.2 Gains on disposal of property, plant and equipment and intangible assets

As discussed at 3.2 above, the IASB's *Framework* explains that income includes both 'revenue' and 'gains'. Gains include, for example, those arising on the disposal of non-current assets. IAS 16 and IAS 38 also make it clear that 'gains shall not be classified as revenue'. *[IAS 16.68, IAS 38.113].*

Therefore, gains arising on the disposal of PP&E do not form part of revenue (aside from entities that routinely sell PP&E that it has held for rental to others as discussed at 5.11.1 below). However, in our view, it is acceptable to show such gains net of any losses on disposal as part of income, whilst net losses on disposal should be shown within expenses.

4 REVENUE RECOGNITION UNDER US GAAP

4.1 Applicability of US literature

Although IAS 18 lays down general principles of revenue recognition, there is a lack of specific guidance in relation to matters, such as multiple-element revenue arrangements and industry-specific issues – e.g. those relating to the software industry. The underlying approach to revenue recognition under US GAAP is closely aligned with that of IAS 18, in that it is based clearly on the earnings process and realisation principle, so US revenue recognition guidance may in many instances be compatible with IAS 18. Whilst the US literature does not override the specific requirements of IFRS, some companies might choose to avail themselves of the hierarchy set out in IAS 8 in order to use US GAAP as guidance to formulate appropriate accounting policies with respect to specific transactions. *[IAS 8.12].* However, whilst US GAAP might provide useful guidance in certain instances, the IAS 8 hierarchy does not require companies to refer either to US GAAP or, indeed, any other national GAAP. It is crucial to bear in mind that not all industry practices under US GAAP are permissible under IFRS; for example, utility companies should not adopt a revenue recognition policy that gives rise to regulatory assets/liabilities (although the IASB is considering the treatment of rate-regulated activities – see below at 5.13). Care always needs to be taken to ensure that the adoption of the more detailed US GAAP requirements results in IFRS compliance. It may be the case that the application of the principles in IAS 18 could result in different accounting from that which would be achieved if the detailed rules in US GAAP were applied.

4.2 The general approach to revenue recognition under US GAAP

The accounting literature of US GAAP on revenue recognition includes both broad conceptual discussions and certain industry-specific guidance. If a transaction is within the scope of specific authoritative literature that provides revenue recognition guidance, that literature should be applied. In the absence of authoritative literature addressing a specific arrangement or a specific industry, the SEC staff will consider the existing authoritative accounting standards as well as the broad revenue recognition criteria specified in the FASB's conceptual framework that contain basic guidelines for revenue recognition.[7]

Concepts Statement No. 5 deals with recognition issues primarily from the angle of providing reliability of measurement. However, the broad principle for revenue recognition laid down by Concepts Statement 5 is that revenues are not recognised until they are both realised or realisable and earned.[8] Concepts Statement 5 states that 'an entity's revenue-earning activities involve delivering or producing goods, rendering services, or other activities that constitute its ongoing major or central operations, and revenues are considered to have been earned when the entity has substantially accomplished what it must do to be entitled to the benefits represented by the revenues'.[9] It states that 'the two conditions (being realized or realizable and being earned) are usually met by the time product or merchandise is delivered or services are rendered to customers, and revenues from manufacturing and selling activities and gains and losses from sales of other assets are commonly recognized at time of sale (usually meaning delivery)'.[10] In addition, it states 'if services are rendered or rights to use assets extend continuously over time (for example, interest or rent), reliable measures based on contractual prices established in advance are commonly available, and revenues may be recognized as earned as time passes'.[11]

The SEC staff believes that revenue generally is realised or realisable and earned when all of the following criteria are met:

- persuasive evidence of an arrangement exists;

- delivery has occurred or services have been rendered;
- the seller's price to the buyer is fixed or determinable; and
- collectability is reasonably assured.[12]

Generally, a sales price is not fixed or determinable when a customer has the unilateral right to terminate or cancel the contract and receive a cash refund. A sales price or fee that is variable until the occurrence of future events (other than short-term rights of return that are not considered to be cancellation privileges and fall under the guidance provided within ASC 605-15) generally is not fixed or determinable until the future event occurs. The revenue from such transactions should not be recognised in earnings until the sales price or fee becomes fixed or determinable.[13]

IAS 18 states that revenue can be recognised at the time of sale if only an insignificant risk of ownership is retained, the seller can estimate returns and it provides for them. *[IAS 18.17]*. This means that a retailer who offers refunds if the customer is not satisfied can generally recognise revenue for those sales, provided the retailer has separately provided for the estimated returns.

4.3 US GAAP requirements for multiple-element transactions

One area of US GAAP guidance that is often referred to by IFRS reporters is that relating to transactions that comprise multiple components. The guidance under IFRS is limited. IAS 18 points out that it may be necessary to apply its requirements to separately identifiable components of a single transaction in order to reflect the substance of a transaction. *[IAS 18.13]*. It does not prescribe a method of allocation which means that allocations based on relative fair value or on a residual method could be acceptable, depending on the relevant facts and circumstances. In an example illustrating the need to defer an amount relating to subsequent servicing when this servicing fee is included in the price of a product, the entity is required to defer sufficient revenue to cover the expected costs of the service together with a 'reasonable profit' on these services (see 3.6 above). *[IAS 18.IE11]*.

The key issues relate to how the components within these multiple-element transactions should be broken down (i.e. what is the unit of account?) and when revenue on each element should be recognised.

The primary US GAAP guidance is included within ASC 605-25 although this does not apply to software arrangements which is included within industry specific guidance and briefly explained at 5.6 below.

ASC 605-25 requires that in multiple-element arrangements, the delivered item or items is considered a separate unit of accounting if:[14]

- the delivered item or items have stand-alone value; and
- when a general right of return exists for the delivered item, the delivery or performance of the undelivered item is probable and is substantially under the control of the seller.

Unlike IAS 18, ASC 605-25 provides specific guidance, requiring that the consideration is allocated to components based on their relative selling prices. These selling prices are calculated based upon vendor-specific objective evidence (VSOE), where available, or third party evidence where not available. If neither VSOE nor third-party evidence of selling price exists for a component, the entity should use its best estimate of the selling price for that component, i.e. the price at which the entity would transact if the component were sold by the entity regularly on a stand-alone basis.[15]

Amendments removed the requirement for VSOE of a delivered component before it could be treated as a separate unit of account, and no longer allows the residual method in allocating consideration[16] (i.e. where VSOE was available for the undelivered element but not the delivered element the 'residual' was allocated to the delivered element). These detailed requirements were never included within IFRS. Rather, IFRS reporters have always had to comply with the general principles of IAS 18.

5 PRACTICAL ISSUES

IAS 18 could be said to be one of the few truly principles-based standards in the IFRS literature. However, the broader the principles the more that judgement is required to apply them in practice, with the inevitable result that consistency is not always achieved. Nevertheless, consistency has tended to be achieved over time within specific industries on the basis of principles-based consensuses between the preparer, regulator and auditor communities.

The following table summarises the broad approaches to revenue reporting that would appear to have achieved general acceptance through existing reporting practice. The table indicates the circumstances under which it might be appropriate to apply each of the approaches.

It is essential that each situation is considered on its individual merits, with particular attention being paid to the risks and uncertainties that remain at each stage of the earnings process and the extent to which the amount of revenue can be measured reliably. Revenue recognition will also be affected by the laws in a jurisdiction and by the applicable terms of trade.

The timing of recognition	*Criteria*	*Examples of practical application*
During production (accretion)	Revenues accrue over time, and no significant uncertainty exists as to measurability or collectability. A contract of sale has been entered into and future costs can be estimated with reasonable accuracy.	Most services. The accrual of interest and dividend income. Accounting for construction contracts using the percentage-of-completion method.

At the completion of production	There is a ready market for the commodity that can rapidly absorb the quantity held by the entity; the commodity comprises interchangeable units; the market price should be determinable and stable; there should be insignificant marketing costs involved.	Certain precious metals and commodities.
At the time of sale (but before delivery)	Goods must have already been acquired or manufactured; goods must be capable of immediate delivery to the customer; selling price has been established; all material related expenses (including delivery) have been ascertained; no significant uncertainties remain (e.g. ultimate cash collection, returns).	Certain sales of goods (e.g. 'bill and hold' sales). Property sales where there is an irrevocable contract.
On delivery	Criteria for recognition before delivery were not satisfied and no significant uncertainties remain.	Most sales of goods and some services. Property sales where it is not certain that the sale will be completed.
Subsequent to delivery	Significant uncertainty regarding collectability existed at the time of delivery; at the time of sale it was not possible to value the consideration with sufficient accuracy.	Certain sales of goods and services (e.g. where the right of return exists). Goods shipped subject to conditions (e.g. installation and inspection/performance).
On an apportionment basis (the revenue allocation approach)	Where revenue represents the supply of initial and subsequent goods/services.	Franchise fees. Sale of goods with after sales service.

All the same, because minimal implementation guidance is given in IFRS about the timing of revenue recognition, we have devoted the remainder of this Chapter to the examination of specific areas of revenue recognition in practice that might be open to inconsistent, controversial or varied accounting practices. Some of this comprises a discussion of the issues addressed in the Illustrative Examples to IAS 18, which expands on the principles in the standard. The IFRIC Interpretations that have a particular impact on revenue recognition (IFRIC 13, IFRIC 15 and IFRIC 18) are also discussed below. Many of the issues discussed below relate to specific industries that pose particular revenue recognition problems.

Chapter 28

5.1 Sale of goods

The Illustrative Examples to IAS 18 identifies a number of different arrangements that may affect the point at which the risks and rewards of ownership pass to the buyer. The terms of trade agreed with a customer, as well as the law governing the sale of goods in any particular jurisdiction, must be taken into account.

5.1.1 'Bill and hold' sales

The term 'bill and hold' sale is used to describe a transaction where delivery is delayed at the buyer's request, but the buyer takes title and accepts billing.

Under the guidance provided in the Illustrative Examples to IAS 18, revenue is recognised when the buyer takes title, provided:

(a) it is probable that delivery will be made;

(b) the item is on hand, identified and ready for delivery to the buyer at the time the sale is recognised;

(c) the buyer specifically acknowledges the deferred delivery instructions; and

(d) the usual payment terms apply.

Revenue is not recognised when there is simply an intention to acquire or manufacture the goods in time for delivery. *[IAS 18.IE1].*

5.1.2 Goods shipped subject to conditions

The Illustrative Examples to IAS 18 identify four scenarios where goods are shipped subject to various conditions: *[IAS 18.IE2]*

(a) installation and inspection

Revenue is normally recognised when the buyer accepts delivery, and installation and inspection are complete. Revenue is recognised immediately upon the buyer's acceptance of delivery when:

(i) the installation process is simple in nature, e.g. the installation of a factory-tested television receiver which only requires unpacking and connection of power and antennae; or

(ii) the inspection is performed only for purposes of final determination of contract prices, for example, shipments of iron ore, sugar or soya beans.

(b) on approval when the buyer has negotiated a limited right of return

If there is uncertainty about the possibility of return, revenue is recognised when the shipment has been formally accepted by the buyer or the goods have been delivered and the time period for rejection has elapsed. See the discussion at 2.1.3 above.

(c) consignment sales under which the recipient (buyer) undertakes to sell the goods on behalf of the shipper (seller)

Revenue is recognised by the shipper when the goods are sold by the recipient to a third party.

(d) cash on delivery sales

Revenue is recognised when delivery is made and cash is received by the seller or its agent.

The following extract from the financial statements of Sandvik AB illustrates a revenue recognition policy that reflects some of these requirements:

Extract 28.12: Sandvik AB (2011)

Significant accounting policies [extract]

Revenue [extract]

Revenue from sales and services [extract]

Revenue from the sale of goods is recognized in profit or loss for the year when the significant risks and rewards of ownership have been transferred to the buyer, that is, normally in connection with delivery. If the product requires installation at the buyer, and installation is a significant part of the contract, revenue is recognized when the installation is completed. Buy-back commitments may entail that sales revenue cannot be recognized if the agreement with the customer in reality implies that the customer has only rented the product for a certain period of time.

5.1.3 Layaway sales

The term 'layaway sales' applies to transactions where the goods are delivered only when the buyer makes the final payment in a series of instalments. This is fairly common in the retail sector, e.g. clothing and household goods. Revenue from such sales is recognised when the goods are delivered. However, when experience indicates that most such sales are completed, revenue may be recognised when a significant deposit is received, provided the goods are on hand, identified and ready for delivery to the buyer. *[IAS 18.IE3]*.

5.1.4 Payments in advance

In certain sectors (e.g. furniture and kitchen retail) payment or partial payment is received from the customer when he places his order for the goods. This is often well in advance of delivery for goods which are not presently held in inventory, if, for example, the goods are still to be manufactured or will be delivered directly to the customer by a third party. In such cases, revenue is recognised when the goods are delivered to the buyer. *[IAS 18.IE4]*.

In other sectors – for example, utilities – companies receive advance payments from customers for services to be provided in the future. In some cases, these advance payments are long term in nature. The issue that arises is whether or not interest should be accrued on these advances and, if so, how revenue should be measured in these circumstances.

IAS 18 requires entities to measure revenue 'at the fair value of the consideration received or receivable'. *[IAS 18.9]*. The standard refers to the situations in which an entity either provides interest-free credit to the buyer or accepts a note receivable bearing a below-market interest rate from the buyer as consideration for the sale of goods. If the arrangement effectively constitutes a financing transaction, IAS 18 requires that the entity determine the fair value of the consideration by discounting all future receipts using an imputed rate of interest. *[IAS 18.11]*. Although IAS 18 does not address the reverse situation of the receipt of interest-free advances from customers, a similar rationale may be applied to justify the accruing of interest, i.e. there is a financing element to the transaction and this must be taken account of if revenue is to be measured at the fair value of the consideration at the time the good or service is provided.

However, in drafting IFRIC 18 the Interpretations Committee considered the concept of accruing interest on advance payments received from customers but the majority of respondents commenting on the draft disagreed that this was necessary. The Interpretations Committee subsequently agreed with this majority view and noted that 'paragraph 11 of IAS 18 requires taking the time value of money into account only when payments are deferred'. *[IFRIC 18.BC22]*.

Given this lack of clarity we believe it is a policy choice of whether or not to accrue interest on advance payments received from customers. If interest is accrued it will be calculated based upon the incremental borrowing rate of the entity and revenue will ultimately be recognised based upon the nominal value of the advance payments received from customers plus this accrued interest. Whichever accounting policy is adopted, it should be applied consistently.

5.1.5 Sale and repurchase agreements

Sale and repurchase agreements take many forms: the seller concurrently agrees to repurchase the same goods at a later date, or the seller has a call option to repurchase, or the buyer has a put option to require the repurchase, by the seller, of the goods.

In a sale and repurchase agreement for an asset other than a financial asset, the terms of the agreement need to be analysed to ascertain whether, in substance, the seller has transferred the risks and rewards of ownership to the buyer and hence revenue is recognised. When the seller has retained the risks and rewards of ownership, even though legal title has been transferred, the transaction is a financing arrangement and does not give rise to revenue. Sale and leaseback arrangements, repurchase agreements and options are discussed in Chapter 24 at 7. For a sale and repurchase agreement on a financial asset, IAS 39 applies (see Chapter 47). *[IAS 18.IE5]*.

5.1.6 Instalment sales

The term 'instalment sales' refers to sales where the goods are delivered to the customer, but payment is made by a number of instalments that include financing charges. In such cases, revenue attributable to the sale price, exclusive of interest, is recognised at the date of sale. The sale price is the present value of the consideration, determined by discounting the instalments receivable at the imputed rate of interest. The interest element is recognised as revenue as it is earned, using the effective interest method set out in IAS 39. *[IAS 18.IE8]*. The application of the effective interest rate method is discussed in Chapter 46 at 6.

5.2 Receipt of initial fees

The practice that has developed in certain industries of charging an initial fee at the inception of a service, followed by subsequent service fees, can present revenue allocation problems. This is because it is not always altogether clear what the initial fee represents; it is necessary to determine what proportion, if any, of the initial fee has been earned on receipt, and how much relates to the provision of future services. In some cases, large initial fees are paid for the provision of a service, whilst continuing fees are relatively small in relation to future services to be provided. If it is probable that the continuing fees will not cover the cost of the continuing services to be provided plus a reasonable profit, then a portion of the initial fee should be deferred over the period of the service contract such that a reasonable profit is earned throughout the service period. Accounting for initial fees has proved problematic and the Interpretations Committee has addressed the issue inconclusively – see 5.2.4 below.

5.2.1 Franchise fees

Franchise agreements between franchisors and franchisees can vary widely both in complexity and in the extent to which various rights, duties and obligations are explicitly addressed. There is no standard form of franchise agreement which would dictate standard accounting practice for the recognition of all franchise fee revenue. Only a full understanding of the franchise agreement will reveal the substance of a particular arrangement so that the most appropriate accounting treatment can be determined; nevertheless, the following are the more common areas which are likely to be addressed in any franchise agreement and which will be relevant to franchise fee revenue reporting:

(a) *rights transferred by the franchisor:* the agreement gives the franchisee the right to use the trade name, processes, know-how of the franchisor for a specified period of time or in perpetuity.

(b) *the amount and terms of payment of initial fees:* payment of initial fees (where applicable) may be fully or partially due in cash, and may be payable immediately, over a specified period or on the fulfilment of certain obligations by the franchisor.

(c) *amount and terms of payment of continuing franchise fees:* the franchisee will normally be required to pay a continuing fee to the franchisor – usually on the basis of a percentage of gross revenues.

(d) *services to be provided by the franchisor initially and on a continuing basis:* the franchisor will usually agree to provide a variety of services and advice to the franchisee, such as:

- site selection;
- the procurement of fixed assets and equipment – these may be either purchased by the franchisee, leased from the franchisor or leased from a third party (possibly with the franchisor guaranteeing the lease payments);
- advertising;
- training of franchisee's personnel;
- inspecting, testing and other quality control programmes; and
- bookkeeping services.

(e) *acquisition of equipment, stock and supplies*: the franchisee may be required to purchase these items either from the franchisor or from designated suppliers. Some franchisors manufacture products for sale to their franchisees, whilst others act as wholesalers.

Chapter 28

The Illustrative Examples to IAS 18 includes a broad discussion of the receipt of franchise fees, stating that they are recognised as revenue on a basis that reflects the purpose for which the fees were charged. *[IAS 18.IE18].* The standard states that the following methods of franchise fee recognition are appropriate: *[IAS 18.IE18]*

Supplies of equipment and other tangible assets: the amount, based on the fair value of the assets sold, is recognised as revenue when the items are delivered or title passes.

Supplies of initial and subsequent services: fees for the provision of continuing services, whether part of the initial fee or a separate fee, are recognised as revenue as the services are rendered. When the separate fee does not cover the cost of continuing services together with a reasonable profit, part of the initial fee, sufficient to cover the costs of continuing services and to provide a reasonable profit on those services, is deferred and recognised as revenue as the services are rendered.

The franchise agreement may provide for the franchisor to supply equipment, inventories, or other tangible assets, at a price lower than that charged to others or a price that does not provide a reasonable profit on those sales. In these circumstances, part of the initial fee, sufficient to cover estimated costs in excess of that price and to provide a reasonable profit on those sales, is deferred and recognised over the period the goods are likely to be sold to the franchisee. The balance of an initial fee is recognised as revenue when performance of all the initial services and other obligations required of the franchisor (such as assistance with site selection, staff training, financing and advertising) has been substantially accomplished.

The initial services and other obligations under an area franchise agreement may depend on the number of individual outlets established in the area. In this case, the fees attributable to the initial services are recognised as revenue in proportion to the number of outlets for which the initial services have been substantially completed.

If the initial fee is collectible over an extended period and there is a significant uncertainty that it will be collected in full, the fee is recognised as cash instalments are received.

Continuing Franchise Fees: fees charged for the use of continuing rights granted by the agreement, or for other services provided during the period of the agreement, are recognised as revenue as the services are provided or the rights used.

Agency Transactions: transactions may take place between the franchisor and the franchisee which, in substance, involve the franchisor acting as agent for the franchisee. For example, the franchisor may order supplies and arrange for their delivery to the franchisee at no profit. Such transactions do not give rise to revenue.

In summary, it is necessary to break down the initial fee into its various components, e.g. the fee for franchise rights, fee for initial services to be performed by the franchisor, fair value of tangible assets sold etc. The individual components may be recognised at different stages. The portion that relates to the franchise rights may be recognised in full immediately unless part of it has to be deferred because the continuing fee does not cover the cost of continuing services to be provided by the franchisor plus a reasonable profit. In this case a portion of the initial fee should be deferred and recognised as services are provided. The fee for initial services should only be recognised when the services have been 'substantially performed' (it is unlikely that substantial performance will have been completed before the franchisee opens for business). The portion of the fee which relates to tangible assets may be recognised when title passes. If the collection period for the initial fees is extended and there is doubt as to the ultimate collectability, recognition of revenue should be deferred.

5.2.2 *Advance royalty or licence receipts*

The general guidance relating to licence fees and royalties states that 'fees and royalties paid for the use of an entity's assets (such as trademarks, patents, software, music copyright, record masters and motion picture films) are normally recognised in accordance with the substance of the agreement. As a practical matter, this may be on a straight line basis over the life of the agreement, for example, when a licensee has the right to use certain technology for a specified period of time'. *[IAS 18.IE20]*.

Therefore, under normal circumstances, the accounting treatment of advance royalty or licence receipts is straightforward; under the accruals concept the advance should be treated as deferred income when received, and released to the profit and loss account when earned under the terms of the royalty/licence agreement. Bayer AG provides an example of such an approach:

Extract 28.13: Bayer AG (2012)

Consolidated Financial Statements

Notes [extract]

4. Basic principles, methods and critical accounting estimates [extract]

Net sales and other operating income [extract]

Some of the Bayer Group's revenues are generated on the basis of licensing agreements under which third parties have been granted rights to products and technologies. Payments received, or expected to be received, that relate to the sale or outlicensing of technologies or technological expertise are recognized in profit or loss as of the effective date of the respective agreement if all rights relating to the technologies and all obligations resulting from them have been relinquished under the contract terms. However, if rights to the technologies continue to exist or obligations from them have yet to be fulfilled, the payments received are deferred accordingly. Upfront payments and similar non-refundable payments received under these agreements are recorded as other liabilities and recognized in profit or loss over the estimated performance period stipulated in the agreement.

Companies in the media sector often enter into arrangements in which one party receives upfront sums of a similar nature, e.g. a music company may receive fees from another party for content that will be accessed via the internet, e.g. digital downloading or streaming of music. If so, the same considerations apply and revenue will be recognised when earned under the terms of the royalty or licence agreement. Often the terms of such arrangements call for the music company to make its current product (past recordings) available and may also require that future product be made available to the other party in exchange for an upfront payment (often called a 'minimum guarantee') that is recouped against future amounts owed the music company by the other party. This revenue will generally be recognised over the term of the arrangement. However, in cases where there is no expectation or obligation to provide future content (arrangement is for past recordings only) revenue would generally be recognised by the music company once its product has been made available to the other party. In the latter instance, the arrangement would likely be viewed as an in-substance sale, as discussed below.

Advance royalty or licence receipts have to be distinguished from assignments of rights that are, in substance, sales. The Illustrative Examples to IAS 18 explain in-substance sales as follows:

'An assignment of rights for a fixed fee or non-refundable guarantee under a non-cancellable contract which permits the licensee to exploit those rights freely and the licensor has no remaining obligations to perform is, in substance, a sale. An example is a licensing agreement for the use of software when the licensor has no obligations subsequent to delivery. Another example is the granting of rights to exhibit a motion picture film in markets where the licensor has no control over the distributor and expects to receive no further revenues from the box office receipts. In such cases, revenue is recognised at the time of sale.' *[IAS 18.IE20]*.

Software revenue recognition and the granting of rights to exhibit motion pictures are discussed at 5.6 and 5.10 below respectively, but in-substance sales are not restricted to these sectors. The extract from Bayer AG in Extract 28.13 above indicates that some arrangements in the pharmaceutical sector can be accounted for as in-substance sales.

Licence fees or royalties may be receivable only on the occurrence of a future event, in which case revenue will be recognised only when it is probable that the fee or royalty will be received. This is normally when the event has occurred. *[IAS 18.IE20]*.

This means that advance receipts may comprise a number of components that may require revenue to be recognised on different bases.

5.2.3 Financial service fees

IAS 18 includes a series of illustrative examples that relate to financial service fees, pointing out that the recognition of revenue for financial service fees depends on the purposes for which the fees are assessed and the basis of accounting for any associated financial instrument. *[IAS 18.IE14]*. The description of fees for financial services may not be indicative of the nature and substance of the services provided. Therefore, it is necessary to distinguish between fees that are an integral part of the effective interest rate of a financial instrument, fees that are earned as services are provided, and fees that are earned on the execution of a significant act. The definition of the effective interest rate in IAS 39 refers to IAS 18, (see Chapter 46 at 6) and the Illustrative Examples to IAS 18 make this distinction as follows: *[IAS 18.IE14]*

5.2.3.A Fees that are an integral part of the effective interest rate of a financial instrument

Such fees are generally treated as an adjustment to the effective interest rate. However, when the financial instrument is measured at fair value with the change in fair value recognised in profit or loss the fees are recognised as revenue when the instrument is initially recognised.

- *Origination fees received by the entity relating to the creation or acquisition of a financial asset other than one that under IAS 39 is classified as a financial asset 'at fair value through profit or loss':* Such fees may include compensation for activities such as evaluating the borrower's financial condition, evaluating and recording guarantees, collateral and other security arrangements, negotiating the terms of the instrument, preparing and processing documents and closing the transaction. These fees are an integral part of generating an involvement with the resulting financial instrument and, together with the related transaction costs (as defined in IAS 39), are deferred and recognised as an adjustment to the effective interest rate.

Deutsche Bank discloses a policy that reflects this requirement:

Extract 28.14: Deutsche Bank AG (2012)

Notes to the Consolidated Financial Statements [extract]

01 – Significant Accounting Policies [extract]

Commission and Fee Income [extract]

The recognition of fee revenue (including commissions) is determined by the purpose of the fees and the basis of accounting for any associated financial instruments. If there is an associated financial instrument, fees that are an integral part of the effective interest rate of that financial instrument are included within the effective yield calculation. However, if the financial instrument is carried at fair value through profit or loss, any associated fees are recognized in profit or loss when the instrument is initially recognized, provided there are no significant unobservable inputs used in determining its fair value. Fees earned from services that are provided over a specified service period are recognized over that service period. Fees earned for the completion of a specific service or significant event are recognized when the service has been completed or the event has occurred.

Loan commitment fees related to commitments that are not accounted for at fair value through profit or loss are recognized in commissions and fee income over the life of the commitment if it is unlikely that the Group will enter into a specific lending arrangement. If it is probable that the Group will enter into a specific lending arrangement, the loan commitment fee is deferred until the origination of a loan and recognized as an adjustment to the loan's effective interest rate.

- *Commitment fees received by the entity to originate a loan when the loan commitment is outside the scope of IAS 39 (or IFRS 9, if applied):* If it is probable that the entity will enter into a specific lending arrangement and the loan commitment is not within the scope of IAS 39, the commitment fee received is regarded as compensation for an ongoing involvement with the acquisition of a financial instrument and, together with the related transaction costs (as defined in IAS 39), is deferred and recognised as an adjustment to the effective interest rate. If the commitment expires without the entity making the loan, the fee is recognised as revenue on expiry. Loan commitments that are within the scope of IAS 39 are accounted for as derivatives and measured at fair value.
- *Origination fees received on issuing financial liabilities measured at amortised cost:* These fees are an integral part of generating an involvement with a financial liability. When a financial liability is not classified as 'at fair value through profit or loss', the origination fees received are included, with the related transaction costs (as defined in IAS 39) incurred, in the initial carrying amount of the financial liability and recognised as an adjustment to the

effective yield. An entity distinguishes fees and costs that are an integral part of the effective interest rate for the financial liability from origination fees and transaction costs relating to the right to provide services, such as investment management services.

5.2.3.B Fees earned as services are provided

The following are examples of situations where revenue is recognised over the period of the related service:

- *Fees charged for servicing a loan:* These fees are recognised as revenue as the services are provided.
- *Commitment fees to originate a loan when the loan commitment is outside the scope of IAS 39:* If it is unlikely that a specific lending arrangement will be entered into and the loan commitment is outside the scope of IAS 39, the commitment fee is recognised as revenue on a time proportion basis over the commitment period. Loan commitments that are within the scope of IAS 39 are accounted for as derivatives and measured at fair value.
- *Investment management fees:* Fees charged for managing investments are recognised as revenue as the services are provided. Incremental costs that are directly attributable to securing an investment management contract are recognised as an asset if they can be identified separately and measured reliably and if it is probable that they will be recovered. As in IAS 39, an incremental cost is one that would not have been incurred if the entity had not secured the investment management contract. The asset represents the entity's contractual right to benefit from providing investment management services, and is amortised as the entity recognises the related revenue. If the entity has a portfolio of investment management contracts, it may assess their recoverability on a portfolio basis. Some financial services contracts involve both the origination of one or more financial instruments and the provision of investment management services. An example is a long-term monthly saving contract linked to the management of a pool of equity securities. The provider of the contract distinguishes the transaction costs relating to the origination of the financial instrument from the costs of securing the right to provide investment management services.

5.2.3.C Fees that are earned on the execution of a significant act

The fees are recognised as revenue when the significant act has been completed, as in the examples below.

- *Commission on the allotment of shares to a client:* The commission is recognised as revenue when the shares have been allotted.
- *Placement fees for arranging a loan between a borrower and an investor:* The fee is recognised as revenue when the loan has been arranged.
- *Loan syndication fees:* A syndication fee received by an entity that arranges a loan and retains no part of the loan package for itself (or retains a part at the same effective interest rate for comparable risk as other participants) is compensation for the service of syndication. Such a fee is recognised as revenue when the syndication has been completed.

The following extracts from the financial statements of HSBC Holdings plc and Barclays PLC illustrate the approach followed in practice:

Extract 28.15: HSBC Holdings plc (2011)

Notes on the Financial Statements [extract]

2 Summary of significant accounting policies [extract]

(b) Non-interest income [extract]

Fee income is earned from a diverse range of services provided by HSBC to its customers. Fee income is accounted for as follows:

- income earned on the execution of a significant act is recognised as revenue when the act is completed (for example, fees arising from negotiating, or participating in the negotiation of, a transaction for a third-party, such as the arrangement for the acquisition of shares or other securities);
- income earned from the provision of services is recognised as revenue as the services are provided (for example, asset management, portfolio and other management advisory and service fees); and
- income which forms an integral part of the effective interest rate of a financial instrument is recognised as an adjustment to the effective interest rate (for example, certain loan commitment fees) and recorded in 'Interest income'.

By contrast to the detail disclosed by HSBC Holdings plc, Barclays PLC provides summarised information about its accounting policies and refers directly to IAS 18:

Extract 28.16: Barclays PLC (2011)

Notes to the financial statements [extract]

4 Net fee and commission income [extract]

The group applies IAS 18 *Revenue*. Fees and commissions charged for services provided or received by the Group are recognised as the services are provided, for example on completion of the underlying transaction.

5.2.4 *Initial and ongoing fees received by a fund manager*

Fund managers' activities generate a number of different fees and commissions, including the payment and receipt of initial fees followed by further payments and receipts (so-called 'trail' or 'trailing' commissions) and performance fees depending on the value of investments under management. Various parties have argued that the initial fee should be recognised as revenue when receivable, or alternatively that it should be spread over the estimated life of the investment.

These fees are typically paid by an investor who makes an investment in a fund, and they are non-refundable regardless of how long the investor chooses to remain invested. An investor may pay a non-refundable fee (for example 5% of the initial investment) on investing in a fund and ongoing fees (say 1% of the fund assets per annum) for continuing fund management. Units in the fund may be sold by an adviser from an in-house sales department of the same group as the fund manager or by a separate financial adviser. If they are sold by a separate financial adviser, that adviser will retain the 5% upfront fee. There are considerable difficulties in

Chapter 28

determining the appropriate accounting and they demonstrate a tension between different accounting standards that can lead to different accounting treatments.

The Interpretations Committee has considered on a number of occasions the appropriate accounting for initial fees and trail commissions and failed to come to any conclusion, most recently in July 2008.[17] The Interpretations Committee focused on the accounting treatment by the party that receives the fee, usually the financial adviser to the investor.

Some members of the Interpretations Committee viewed the fact that the upfront fee is the same, regardless of whether it is retained by a separate financial adviser (which is independent of the group that includes the fund manager and therefore has no further involvement with the transaction) or by an adviser from an in-house sales department of the same group as the fund manager, as evidence that upfront services were delivered and that the fair value of those services can be measured reliably. Other members noted that the receipt of a non refundable initial fee does not, in itself, give evidence that an upfront service has been provided or that the fair value of the consideration paid in respect of any upfront services is equal to the initial fee received.[18]

Trail commissions raise additional problems. They are paid periodically in arrears and the amounts payable vary with values (e.g. a percentage of funds under management). In July 2008 the Interpretations Committee was again unable to determine whether there were future services, but revenue recognition remains an issue even if it is assumed that there are no services provided during the arrangement. Some argue that IAS 18 should be used; revenue ought to be taken when the conditions are met as two of the basic criteria for revenue recognition cannot be demonstrated at inception (i.e. that the amount of revenue can be measured reliably and that is probable that the economic benefits associated with the transaction will flow to the entity). *[IAS 18.14]*. Paragraph 20 of the Illustrative Examples notes, in the context of licence fees or royalty whose receipt is contingent on the occurrence of a future event, that revenue is recognised only when it is probable that the fee will be received, which is normally when the event has occurred. *[IAS 18 IE.20]*. Others argue that the initial fee and trail commissions together comprise the revenue earned by the financial advisor. The fair value can be estimated and ought to be recognised at inception, using IAS 39 as the relevant accounting standard.

Similar arrangements can be found in many industries, not all of which are financial services. For example, 'revenue share' arrangements in telecommunications share many features: an upfront commission is paid to the distributor, who receives further sums if the customer remains on the same network tariff. The corresponding treatment of the cost to the operator is also debated: is it an upfront liability as defined by IAS 32 – *Financial Instruments: Presentation* – expensed as incurred and measured using IAS 39 principles, or is it recognised when incurred under IAS 37 – *Provisions, Contingent Liabilities and Contingent Assets*? It is a widespread and complex problem and the arrangements create issues for the entity making the payment as well as the recipient. The Interpretations Committee decided not to add this issue to its agenda. While industry practice varies, some asset management groups take the view that some front-end fees are earned over the period in which it is expected that services will be provided and other fees earned as conditions are met.

Extract 28.17: Henderson Group plc (2011)

2 Accounting policies [extract]

2.1 Significant accounting policies [extract]

Income recognition [extract]

Fee income and commission receivable

Fee income includes management fees, transaction fees and performance fees (including earned carried interest). Management fees and transaction fees are recognised in the accounting period in which the associated investment management or transaction services are provided. Performance fees are recognised when the prescribed performance hurdles have been achieved and it is probable that the fee will crystallise as a result. The Group accrues 95% of the expected fee on satisfaction that the recognition criteria have established a performance fee is due, with the balance recognised on cash settlement.

Initial fees and commission receivable are deferred and amortised over the anticipated period in which services will be provided, determined by reference to the average term of investment in each product on which initial fees and commissions are earned. Other income is recognised in the accounting period in which services are rendered.

In this extract, the company discloses its policy for performance fees. This is another area where practice varies, particularly in interim financial statements; some asset management groups accrue fees on a mark-to-market basis; most take nothing.

5.2.5 Insurance agency commissions

The critical event for the recognition of insurance agency commissions is the commencement of the policy. Hence, the Illustrative Examples to IAS 18 states that insurance agency commissions received or receivable which do not require the agent to render further service are recognised as revenue by the agent on the effective commencement or renewal dates of the related policies. However, when it is probable that the agent will be required to render further services during the life of the policy, the commission, or part thereof, is deferred and recognised as revenue over the period during which the policy is in force. *[IAS 18.IE13].*

Some insurance agency commissions have similar features to the investment fund initial fee and 'trail commissions' noted in the preceding section so there is a similar degree of uncertainty regarding the recognition and measurement of revenue.

5.2.6 Credit card fees

It is common practice in some countries for credit card companies to levy a charge, payable in advance, on its cardholders. Although such charges may be seen as commitment fees for the credit facilities offered by the card, they clearly cover the many other services available to cardholders as well. Accordingly, we would suggest that the fees that are periodically charged to cardholders should be deferred and recognised on a straight-line basis over the period the fee entitles the cardholder to use the card.[19]

5.2.7 Admission, entrance and membership fees

The issue of entrance and membership fees is dealt with briefly in IAS 18's Illustrative Examples, which note that revenue recognition depends on the nature of the services provided. If the fee permits only membership, and all other services or products are paid for separately, or if there is a separate annual subscription, the fee is recognised as revenue when no significant uncertainty as to its collectability exists. If the fee entitles the member to services or publications to be provided during the membership period, or to purchase goods or services at prices lower than those charged to non-members, it is recognised on a basis that reflects the timing, nature and value of the benefits provided. *[IAS 18.IE17]*.

Admission fees to 'artistic performances' and other special events are recognised when the event takes place. Fees may be allocated pro-rata to the services provided if there is a subscription to a number of events. *[IAS 18.IE15]*.

5.3 Subscriptions to publications

Publication subscriptions are generally paid in advance and are non-refundable. As the publications will still have to be produced and delivered to the subscriber, the subscription revenue cannot be regarded as having been earned until production and delivery takes place. This is the approach adopted by IAS 18, which requires that revenue is recognised on a straight-line basis over the period in which the items are despatched when the items involved are of similar value in each time period. When the items vary in value from period to period, revenue is recognised on the basis of the sales value of the item despatched in relation to the total estimated sales value of all items covered by the subscription. *[IAS 18.IE7]*.

Reed Elsevier discloses its policy for recognising revenue from subscriptions as follows:

Extract 28.18: Reed Elsevier (2011)

Combined financial statements [extract]

Accounting policies [extract]

Revenue

Revenue represents the invoiced value of sales less anticipated returns on transactions completed by performance, excluding customer sales taxes and sales between the combined businesses.

Revenues are recognised for the various categories of turnover as follows: subscriptions – on periodic despatch of subscribed product or rateably over the period of the subscription where performance is not measurable by despatch; circulation and transactional – on despatch or occurrence of the transaction; advertising – on publication or over the period of online display; and exhibitions – on occurrence of the exhibition.

Where sales consist of two or more independent components whose value can be reliably measured, revenue is recognised on each component as it is completed by performance, based on attribution of relative value.

5.4 Installation fees

Installation fees are recognised as revenue by reference to the stage of completion of the installation, unless they are incidental to the sale of a product in which case they are recognised when the goods are sold. *[IAS 18.IE10]*. However, in certain circumstances where the installation fees are linked to a contract for future services (for example, in the telecommunications industry: see 5.7 below) it may be more appropriate to defer such fees over either the contract period or the average expected life of the customer relationship, depending on the circumstances.

5.5 Advertising revenue

IAS 18's Illustrative Examples adopt the performance of the service as the critical event for the recognition of revenue derived from the rendering of advertising services. Consequently, media commissions are recognised when the related advertisement or commercial appears before the public. Production commissions are recognised by reference to the stage of completion of the project. *[IAS 18.IE12].* The special case of barter transactions involving advertising services is addressed at 3.11 above.

German television corporation ProSiebenSat.1's revenues are derived mainly from the sale of advertising time on television as disclosed in its accounting policy:

> *Extract 28.19: ProSiebenSat.1 Media AG (2011)*
>
> **Notes to the consolidated financial statements** [extract]
>
> [6] **ACCOUNTING POLICIES** [extract]
>
> **Recognition of income and expenses** [extract]
>
> The ProSiebenSat.1 Group's revenues are mainly advertising revenues derived from the sale of advertising time on television. Advertising revenues are presented net of volume discounts, agency commissions, cash discounts and value-added tax.
>
> Revenues are realized at the time when the service is provided, or when risk is transferred to the client. Revenues are accordingly recognized once the service has been provided, the principle risks and rewards of ownership have been transferred to the buyer, the amount of the proceeds can be measured reliably, an economic benefit from the sale is sufficiently probably and the costs associated with the sale can be measured reliably.
>
> Specifically, advertising revenues from both television and radio are considered realized when advertising spots are broadcasted. Revenues from pay TV activities and from the sale of print products are considered realized when the service is provided. Revenues from the sale of merchandising licenses are realized at the agreed guarantee amount as of the inception of the license for the customer. Revenues from the sale of programming assets and ancillary programming rights are considered realized when the license term for the purchaser of the programming asset has begun and broadcast-ready materials have been delivered to the purchaser.

5.6 Software revenue recognition

The accounting issues in the software services industry relate to when to recognise revenue from contracts to develop software, software licensing fees, customer support services and data services. However, these issues have not been addressed in the IFRS literature. IAS 18 provides only one sentence of guidance: fees from the development of customised software are recognised as revenue by reference to the stage of completion of the development, including completion of services provided for post delivery service support. *[IAS 18.IE19].* Because of the nature of the products and services involved, applying the general revenue recognition principles to software transactions can sometimes be difficult. As a result, software companies have used a variety of methods to recognise revenue, often producing significantly different financial results from similar transactions.

The problem of software revenue recognition was recognised in the US by the FASB and SEC who encouraged the AICPA to provide guidance on software revenue recognition methods. As a result of practical experiences, in 1997 the AICPA issued guidance now codified in ASC 985-605 – *Revenue Recognition – Software.*

Whilst this US GAAP guidance is not mandatory for companies reporting under IFRS, many of them benefit by using the hierarchy in IAS 8 to adopt the US requirements in the absence of an IFRS pronouncement of comparable detail. Set out below is a broad overview of this guidance, but the detailed requirements are beyond the scope of this publication.

5.6.1 The basic principles of ASC 985-605

Software arrangements range from those that simply provide a licence for a single software product, to those that require significant production, modification or customisation of the software. Arrangements may also include multiple products or services. The codified guidance in ASC 985-605 states that if the arrangement does not require significant production, modification or customisation of existing software (i.e. contract accounting does not apply – see below), revenue should be recognised when all of the following criteria are met:[20]

- persuasive evidence of an arrangement exists;
- delivery has occurred (and no future elements to be delivered are essential to the functionality of the delivered element);
- the vendor's fee is fixed or determinable (the 'determinable' criterion relates to the issue as to whether the fee is subject to factors such as acceptance, refund, extended payment terms); and
- collectability is probable (i.e. whether the customer has the ability to pay and will pay).

With respect to 'persuasive evidence of an arrangement', ASC 985-605 requires that if a vendor has a customary practice of obtaining written contracts, revenues should not be recognised until the contract is signed by both parties.[21] Therefore, in the absence of a signed contract, revenue should not be recognised even if the software has been delivered and payment received.

ASC 985-605 states that the fee should be allocated to the various elements based on vendor-specific objective evidence ('VSOE') of fair value, regardless of any separate prices stated within the contract for each element.[22] It requires deferral of all revenue from multiple-element arrangements that are not accounted for using long-term contract accounting if there is insufficient VSOE to allocate revenue to the various elements of the arrangement.

The licence fee under an arrangement with multiple elements should be allocated to the elements according to VSOE. A portion of the licence fee should be allocated to elements that are deliverable on a when-and-if-available basis, whereby a vendor agrees to deliver software only when or if it becomes available while the agreement is in effect. However, absent such features and if all other criteria are met, this means that revenue may be recognised on entering into the arrangement in respect of a licence that allows the customer to use the software for a finite period.

If there is VSOE for the fair values of the undelivered elements in an arrangement, but not for one or more of the delivered elements in the arrangement, that fee can be recognised using the 'residual method'.[23] This means deducting the values for which there is VSOE from the total revenue and treating the remaining balance as the share of revenue for the element for which there is no VSOE. These requirements under US GAAP only apply to sales of computer software which are scoped into ASC 985. The US GAAP requirements in respect of other arrangements were always different to these and were significantly amended in 2008; the revised requirements in ASC 605-25 are described at 4.3 above.

5.6.2 Accounting for software arrangements with multiple elements

Software arrangements may provide licences for many products or services such as additional software products, upgrades/enhancements, rights to exchange or return software, post-contract customer support (PCS) or other services including elements deliverable only on a 'when-and-if-available' basis. These are referred to in US GAAP as 'multiple elements'.

We have noted at 3.6 above that in certain circumstances it is necessary to apply the recognition criteria to the separately identifiable components of a single transaction in order to reflect the substance of the transaction. *[IAS 18.13].* However, IAS 18 does not establish more detailed criteria for identifying components and little guidance on the allocation of revenue to those elements. As such, an entity must use its judgement to select the most appropriate methodology, taking into consideration all relevant facts and circumstances.

Two of the most important rules in ASC 985-605 address discounts and the effects on revenue recognition of VSOE. If there is a discount, ASC 985-605 requires a proportionate amount to be applied to each element included in the arrangement based on relative fair values without regard to the discount. No portion of the discount should be allocated to any upgrade rights and the residual method attributes the discount entirely to the delivered elements.[24]

If there is insufficient VSOE, ASC 985-605 provides that all revenue from the arrangement should be deferred until the earlier of the date on which such sufficient VSOE is obtained or all elements of the arrangement have been delivered.[25]

VSOE is a complex area and there are many detailed rules and requirements that expand the basic points made above and deal with areas such as upgrades, post-contract customer support, extended payment terms, rights of return and services. It is not necessary under IFRS to demonstrate VSOE in order to allocate revenue on the basis of the fair value of individual components.

5.6.3 Accounting for arrangements which require significant production, modification or customisation of software

Where companies are running well-established computer installations with systems and configurations that they do not wish to change, off-the-shelf software packages are generally not suitable for their purposes. For this reason, some software companies will enter into a customer contract whereby they agree to customise a generalised software product to meet the customer's specific requirements. A simple form of customisation is to modify the system's output reports so that they integrate with the customer's existing management reporting system. However, customisation will often entail more involved obligations, e.g. having to translate the software so that it is able to run on the customer's specific hardware configuration, data conversion, system integration, installation and testing.

The question that arises, therefore, is the basis on which a software company recognises revenue when it enters into a contract that involves significant obligations. It is our view that the principles laid down in IAS 11 should be applied in this situation. This is supported by IAS 18, which states that the requirements of IAS 11 are generally applicable to the recognition of revenue and the associated expenses for a transaction involving the rendering of services. *[IAS 18.21]*. Accounting under IAS 11 is described in Chapter 23.

Consequently, where the software company is able to make reliable estimates as to the extent of progress towards completion of a contract, the related revenues and the related costs, and where the outcome of the contract can be assessed with reasonable certainty, the percentage-of-completion method of profit recognition should be applied.

One company that follows this approach is SAP AG:

Extract 28.20: SAP AG (2012)

Notes to the Consolidated Financial Statements [extract]

(3) Summary of Significant Accounting Policies [extract]

(3b) Relevant Accounting Policies [extract]

Revenue Recognition [extract]

Sometimes we enter into customer-specific on-premise software development agreements. We recognize software revenue in connection with these arrangements using the percentage-of-completion method based on contract costs incurred to date as a percentage of total estimated contract costs required to complete the development work. If we do not have a sufficient basis to reasonably measure the progress of completion or to estimate the total contract revenue and costs, revenue is recognized only to the extent of the contract costs incurred for which we believe recoverability to be probable. When it becomes probable that total contract costs exceed total contract revenue in an arrangement, the expected losses are recognized immediately as an expense based on the costs attributable to the contract.

Under ASC 985-605, if an arrangement to deliver software or a software system, either alone or together with other products or services, requires significant production, modification or customisation of software, the entire arrangement should be accounted for in accordance with ASC 605-35 – *Revenue – Construction-Type and Production-Type Contracts.*[26] This will not necessarily have any relevance when applying IFRS as the entity will need to determine the most appropriate accounting policy. These may be the principles in IAS 11.

5.7 Revenue recognition issues in the telecommunications sector

There are significant revenue recognition complexities that affect the telecommunications sector, and about which IFRS is effectively silent. The complexities differ depending upon the type of telecommunications services being considered. Recognition issues may differ between fixed line (principally voice and data) services and wireless (principally mobile voice and data) services. In addition customers may purchase elements of both as part of a bundled package.

A number of general factors underlie the accounting issues. For example: local regulatory laws may dictate the way business is done by the operators; there may be restrictions on the discounting of handsets; handsets may be branded in some countries but not in others; both branded and unbranded handsets may co-exist in the same country; and there may be varying degrees of price protection.

Connection and up-front fees are an issue for both fixed line and mobile operators.

5.7.1 Recording revenue for multiple service elements ('bundled offers')

IAS 18 notes that in some instances revenue is recognised for the separately identifiable components of a single transaction and refers specifically to situations where the selling price of a product includes an identifiable amount for subsequent servicing, in which case that amount is deferred and recognised as revenue over the period during which the service is performed. *[IAS 18.13]*. This is directly relevant to some aspects of multiple deliverable arrangements offerings, where customers are offered a 'bundle' of assets and services.

When a consumer enters into a mobile phone contract with a provider, the contract may be a package that includes a handset and various combinations of talktime, text messages and data allowances (internet access). The bundle may also include fixed line products, such as voice, video and broadband services.

Consumers may pay for their bundle of assets and services in a number of different ways: a payment for the handset (which may be discounted); connection charges related to activation of the handset; monthly fixed or usage-based payments; and prepayments by credit card or voucher. None of these payments may relate directly to the cost of the services being provided by the operator, and operators also may offer loyalty programs that entail the provision of future services at substantially reduced prices.

As there is no specific guidance within IFRS on the subject of multiple deliverable arrangements beyond the brief references in paragraph 13 of IAS 18 referred to above, many companies use the hierarchy in IAS 8 to consider any relevant US guidance. However, it needs to be made clear that whilst US GAAP might provide useful guidance in this area, the IAS 8 hierarchy does not require companies to refer to it.

5.7.1.A Accounting for handsets and monthly service arrangements

Many of the mobile operators that provide handsets to customers who subscribe to service contracts do so at heavily discounted prices or even free of charge. Most telecommunications operators have an accounting policy under which handsets and airtime are separately identifiable components but they apply a form of 'residual method' to the amount of revenue taken for the sale of the handset, recognising no more than the amount contractually receivable for it which may, *inter alia*, be equivalent to the so-called 'cash cap' under US GAAP, now in ASC 605-25-30-5. This states, 'The amount allocable to a delivered item or items is limited to the amount that is not contingent upon the delivery of additional items or meeting other specified performance conditions (the noncontingent amount)'. An example of this is France Télécom's policy with respect to bundled offers:

Extract 28.21: France Télécom (2012)

CONSOLIDATED FINANCIAL STATEMENTS [extract]

NOTE 18 Accounting policies [extract]

18.3 Revenues [extract]

Revenues from the Group's activities are recognized and presented as follows, in accordance with IAS 18:

Separable components of bundled offers [extract]

Numerous service offers on the Group's main markets include two components: an equipment component (e.g. a mobile handset) and a service component (e.g. a talk plan).

For the sale of multiple products or services, the Group evaluates all deliverables in the arrangement to determine whether they represent separate units of accounting. A delivered item is considered a separate unit of accounting if (i) it has value to the customer on a standalone basis and (ii) there is objective and reliable evidence of the fair value of the undelivered item(s). The total fixed or determinable amount of the arrangement is allocated to the separate units of accounting based on its relative fair value. However, when an amount allocated to a delivered item is contingent upon the delivery of additional items or meeting specified performance conditions, the amount allocated to that delivered item is limited to the non-contingent amount. The case arises in the mobile business for sales of bundled offers including a handset sold at a discounted price and a telecommunications service contract. The handset is considered to have value on a standalone basis to the customer, and there is objective and reliable evidence of fair value for the telecommunications service to be delivered. As the amount allocable to the handset generally exceeds the amount received from the customer at the date the handset is delivered, revenue recognized for the handset sale is generally limited to the amount of the arrangement that is not contingent upon the rendering of telecommunication services, i.e. the amount paid by the customer for the handset.

In March 2006, the Interpretations Committee was asked whether:

- the contracts should be treated as comprising two separately identifiable components, i.e. the sale of a telephone and the rendering of telecommunication services, as discussed in paragraph 13 of IAS 18 (under which revenue would be attributed to each component); or
- the telephones should be treated as a cost of acquiring the new customer, with no revenue being attributed to them.

The Interpretations Committee did not take this issue on to its agenda; instead, it published the following 'rejection notice' in the March 2006 issue of IFRIC Update:

'The IFRIC acknowledged that the question is of widespread relevance, both across the telecommunications industry and, more generally, in other sectors. IAS 18 does not give guidance on what it means by "separately identifiable components" and practices diverge.

'However, the IFRIC noted that the terms of subscriber contracts vary widely. Any guidance on accounting for discounted handsets would need to be principles-based to accommodate the diverse range of contract terms that arise in practice. The IASB is at present developing principles for identifying separable components within revenue contracts. In these circumstances, the IFRIC does not believe it could reach a consensus on a timely basis. The IFRIC, therefore, decided not to take the topic onto its agenda.'[27] The new principles are discussed at 6 below.

The Interpretations Committee did not publish its views on how (or whether) revenue ought to be attributed to each component if the transaction is treated as falling under paragraph 13. However, although IAS 18 requires revenue to be measured at its fair value, it is not definitive on the method of allocation. Usually, an allocation of revenue based on relative fair values would be considered an appropriate basis but this is not an explicit requirement and there are other bases allowed in IAS 18 and in IFRS more generally. These are discussed at 3.6 above.

5.7.1.B 'Free' services

'Free' services are often included in the monthly service arrangement for contract subscribers as an additional incentive to encourage subscribers to sign up for a fixed contract period, typically one or two years.

'Free' services can either be provided up-front as inclusive services for a fixed monthly fee, or as an incentive after a specific threshold has been exceeded, intended to encourage subscribers to spend more than their specified amount.

As a result, one of the challenges for mobile operators is the accounting treatment for the 'free' service period. In our opinion, the total amount that is contractually required to be paid by the customer is recognised as revenue rateably over the entire service period, including the period in which the 'free' services are provided.

The following example illustrates the accounting for free minutes granted at subscription date by a mobile operator to a subscriber:

Example 28.1: Accounting for free minutes

An operator enters into a service contract with a customer for a period of 12 months. Under the contract specifications, the customer is offered for the first 2 months 60 free minutes talktime per month and for the remaining 10 months of the contract the customer will pay a fixed fee of €30 per month for 60 minutes of communication per month. The operator considers the recoverability of the amounts due under the contract from the customer to be probable.

In our view, since the free minutes offer is linked to the non-cancellable contract, the fee receivable for the non-cancellable contract is spread over the entire contract term.

Consequently, the fixed fee of €300 (€30 × 10 months) to be received from the subscriber would be recognised on a straight line basis over the 12 month contract period, being the stage of completion of the contract. The operator therefore would recognise €25 each month over the twelve month period (€30 × 10/12 = €25).

France Télécom's accounting policy is as follows.

Extract 28.22: France Télécom (2012)

CONSOLIDATED FINANCIAL STATEMENTS [extract]

NOTE 18 Accounting policies [extract]

18.3 Revenues [extract]

Promotional offers

Revenues are stated net of discounts. For certain commercial offers, where customers are offered a free service over a certain period in exchange for signing up for a fixed period (time-based incentives), the total revenue generated under the contract may be spread over the fixed, non-cancellable period.

5.7.1.C Connection and up-front fees

Connection fees can be a feature of both the wireless (mobile) and the fixed line activities.

When the mobile telecoms industry was in its infancy, upfront costs such as connection fees, contract handling fees, registration fees, fees for changing plans etc., were commonly charged by operators. Such charges have been phased out over the years and are no longer a common feature in a number of markets.

Nevertheless, there are still occasions in which a telecommunications operator charges its subscribers a one-time non-refundable fee for connection to its network. The contract for telecommunications services between the operator and the subscriber has either a finite or an indefinite life and includes the provision of the network connection and ongoing telecommunications services. The direct/incremental costs incurred by the operator in providing the connection service are primarily the technician's salary and related benefits; this technician provides both connection and physical installation services at the same time.

In such cases, the connection service and the telecommunications services have to be analysed in accordance with their economic substance in order to determine whether they should be combined or segmented for revenue recognition purposes. When the connection transaction is bundled with the service arrangement in such a way that the commercial effect cannot be understood without reference to the two transactions as a whole, the connection fee revenue should be recognised over the expected term of the customer relationship under the arrangement which generated the connection. In our view, the expected term of the customer relationship may not necessarily be the contract period, but may be the estimated average life of the customer relationship, provided that this can be estimated reliably.

Vodafone is an example of a company that defers customer connection fees over the period in which services are expected to be provided to the customer, another way of describing the expected life of the customer relationship.

Extract 28.23: Vodafone Group Plc (2013)

A1. Significant accounting policies [extract]

Revenue [extract]

Customer connection revenue is recognised together with the related equipment revenue to the extent that the aggregate equipment and connection revenue does not exceed the fair value of the equipment delivered to the customer. Any customer connection revenue not recognised together with related equipment revenue is deferred and recognised over the period in which services are expected to be provided to the customer.

Charging fees remains relatively common for connection to a fixed telephone line. Although connection fees are commonly recognised over the contract period, upfront recognition of the non-refundable fee may be possible if there is a clearly demonstrable separate service and it is provided at the inception of the contract.

The guidance provided within IFRIC 18 which is explained at 5.14 below may be of some help in identifying what services have been provided in return for the upfront fee, but the Interpretation is not normally directly relevant because the upfront fee is not used to construct PP&E required for connection as envisaged under paragraph 6 of that Interpretation. Nevertheless, it is a common practice amongst fixed line operators to defer activation revenue, as illustrated by the two relevant policies of Telkom Group, which are similar to Vodafone's mobile policies included above:

Extract 28.24: Telkom Group (2012)

Notes to the annual financial statements [extract]

2. Significant accounting policies [extract]

Summary of significant accounting policies [extract]

Fixed-line [extract]

Subscriptions, connections and other usage [extract]

The Company provides telephone and data communication services under post-paid and pre-paid payment arrangements. Revenue includes fees for installation and activation, which are deferred and recognised over the expected customer relationship period.

Deferred revenue and expenses [extract]

Activation revenue and costs are deferred and recognised systematically over the expected duration of the customer relationship because it is considered to be part of the customers' ongoing rights to telecommunication services and the operator's continuing involvement. Any excess of the costs over revenues is expensed immediately.

5.7.2 'Gross versus net' issues

The difficulty of deciding whether to record revenue gross or net is pervasive in the telecommunications sector. The problem occurs because of the difficulty in deciding whether the parties involved in any particular agreement are acting as principal or agent. IAS 18 states that 'in an agency relationship, the gross inflows of economic benefits include amounts collected on behalf of the principal and which do not result in increases in equity for the entity. The amounts collected on behalf of the principal are not revenue. Instead, revenue is the amount of commission'. *[IAS 18.8].*

There is guidance in IAS 18's Illustrative Examples to help determine whether an entity is acting as a principal or as an agent. *[IAS 18.IE21].* This guidance is discussed at 3.3 above but does not necessarily help decide the matter in many telecoms scenarios. A frequent arrangement is where there is data content provided by third parties that is subject to a separate provider agreement.

Content, such as music, navigation and other downloads such as 'apps' can either be included in the monthly price plan, or purchased separately on an *ad hoc* basis. Operators can either develop the content in-house, or use third party providers to offer a range of items to their subscribers, with charges based either on duration (news, traffic updates etc.) or on quantity (number of ringtones, games etc.).

The issue is whether the operator should report the content revenue based on the gross amount billed to the subscriber because it has earned revenue from the sale of the services or the net amount retained (that is, the amount billed to the subscriber less the amount paid to a supplier) because it has only earned a commission or fee. Is the substance of the transaction with the supplier one of buying and on-selling goods or selling goods on consignment (i.e. an agency relationship)? The two most important considerations of those listed in IAS 18's Illustrative Examples paragraph 21, for most of these arrangements, are:

- whether the operator has the primary responsibility for providing the services to the customer or for fulfilling the order, for example by being responsible for the acceptability of the services ordered or purchased by the customer; and
- whether it has discretion in establishing prices, either directly or indirectly, for example by providing additional goods or services.

Inventory risk is unlikely to be relevant for a service provision and credit risk may be only a weak indicator as the amounts are individually small and may be paid to access the download.

Therefore, if the content is an own-brand product or service then the revenue receivable from subscribers should be recorded as revenue by the operator, and the amounts payable to the third party content providers should be recorded as costs.

By contrast, if the content is a non-branded product/service that is merely using the mobile operator's network as a medium to access its subscriber base, then the amounts receivable from subscribers should not be recorded as revenue. The operator's revenue will comprise only the commissions receivable from the content providers for the use of the operator's network.

Vivendi discloses that it bases the decision on whether it is an agent or principal status on who has responsibility for content and setting the price to subscribers, as follows:

Extract 28.25: Vivendi SA (2012)

Notes to the Consolidated Financial Statements [extract]

Note 1. Accounting Policies and Valuation Methods [extract]

1.3. Principles governing the preparation of the Consolidated Financial Statements [extract]

1.3.4. Revenues from operations and associated costs [extract]

1.3.4.3. SFR, Maroc Telecom Group, and GVT [extract]

Content sales

Sales of services provided to customers managed by SFR and Maroc Telecom Group on behalf of content providers (mainly premium rate numbers) are either accounted for gross, or net of the content providers' fees when the provider is responsible for the content and for setting the price payable by subscribers.

5.7.3 Accounting for roll-over minutes

Where an operator offers a subscriber a finite number of call minutes for a fixed amount per period with the option of rolling over any unused minutes, the question arises as to how the operator should account for the unused minutes that the subscriber holds. The operator is not obliged to reimburse the subscriber for unused minutes, but is obliged (normally subject to a ceiling) to provide the accumulated unused call minutes to the subscriber until the end of the contract, after which they expire.

In such cases, revenue is recognised at the time the minutes are used. Any minutes unused at the end of each month should be recognised as deferred revenue.

However, in some instances, the operator has relevant and reliable evidence that shows that a portion of those unused minutes will not be used before the expiration of the validity period. In that case, the operator could consider an alternative revenue recognition policy that would take account of the probability of unused minutes at the end of the validity period in the computation of the revenue per minute used by the subscriber. This would result in allocating a higher amount of revenue per minute used.

When the validity period expires, any remaining balance of unused minutes would be recognised as revenue immediately, since the obligation of the operator to provide the contractual call minutes is extinguished.

5.7.4 Accounting for the sale of pre-paid calling cards

Prepaid cards are normally sold by an operator either through its own sales outlet or through distributors. The communication credit sold with the cards has an expiry date that varies from one operator to another, although, in certain limited jurisdictions, there is no expiry date. For example: prepaid cards may be sold with an initial credit of €10 covering 60 minutes of communication and the credit has a validity period of 90 days from the date of activation. If not used within this period, the credit is lost.

When the cards are sold through distributors, the distributor is usually obliged to sell the cards to the customers at the face value of the card. On sale of the card, the distributor pays the operator the face value less a commission. The distributor has a right to return unsold cards to the operator. Once the distributor has sold the cards, it has no further obligation to the operator.

In our view, when an operator sells calling cards directly, revenue is recognised at the time the minutes are used. Any minutes unused at the end of each month should be recognised as deferred revenue. However, if the operator has relevant and reliable evidence that shows that a portion of those unused minutes will not be used before the expiration of the validity period then it could consider an alternative revenue recognition policy. This would take account of the probability of unused minutes at the end of the validity period in the computation of the revenue per minute recognised as the minutes are used by the customer.

When an operator sells calling cards through a distributor, the revenue is required to be recognised based on the substance of the arrangement with the distributor.

It is usually the case that the distributor is in substance acting as an agent for the operator. The revenue associated with the sale of the calling card is recognised when the subscriber uses the minutes. The difference between the card's usage value, which is charged to the subscriber, and the amount paid to the operator is the distributor's commission.

In our view, unless the distributor is also an operator or the calling card could be used on any operator's network (which is rare), it would be difficult to conclude that the distributor is the principal in the arrangement with the subscriber, because the distributor would not have the capacity to act as the principal under the terms of the service provided by the calling card to the subscriber (see 3.3 and 5.7.2 above).

5.8 Excise taxes and goods and services taxes: recognition of gross versus net revenues

Many jurisdictions around the world raise taxes that are based on components of sales or production. These include excise taxes and goods and services or value added taxes. In some cases, these taxes are, in effect, collected by the entity from customers on behalf of the taxing authority. In other cases, the taxpayer's role is more in the nature of principal than agent. The regulations (for example, excise taxes in the tobacco and drinks industries) differ significantly from one country to another. The practical accounting issue that arises concerns the interpretation of paragraph 8 of IAS 18: should excise taxes and goods and services taxes be deducted from revenue (net presentation) or included in the cost of sales and, therefore, revenue (gross presentation)? *[IAS 18.8].*

Clearly, the appropriate accounting treatment will depend on the particular circumstances. In determining whether gross or net presentation is appropriate, the entity needs to consider whether it is acting in a manner similar to that of an agent or principal.

We believe that there are two main indicators that should be considered when determining whether the entity is acting as principal or agent. An additional two indicators relating to the nature of the tax itself should also be considered to determine whether a net or gross presentation is applicable. No one indicator is considered to be conclusive on its own. These indicators are:

Acting as Principal or Agent:

A whether the entity is exposed to financial risk in relation to the tax (e.g. non-recovery of the tax from the customers); and

B whether the entity has an obligation to change prices in line with changes in the rate or amount of the tax.

Nature of Taxes:

C basis of calculation – whether the tax is levied on sales proceeds or on units of production; and

D point of payment – whether the entity becomes liable to pay the tax at the point of sale or at the time of production.

Whether an entity is acting as principal or agent is a matter of judgement that depends on the relevant facts and circumstances of the particular tax in the country concerned. The factors that should be taken into account in determining gross or net treatment are summarised in the following table.

	Indicator	Circumstances indicating: net revenue recognition	Circumstances indicating: gross revenue recognition
A	Whether the entity is exposed to financial risk in relation to the tax (e.g. non-recovery of the tax from the customers): (i) who benefits from any short term fluctuations? (ii) who bears the inventory risk? (iii) who bears the credit risk?	• The tax is refundable in the event that stock becomes damaged or obsolete, or receivables are not collectible.	• The entity will not be refunded for the tax paid if the stock is not sold or the receivables are not collected.
B	Whether the entity has an obligation to change prices in line with changes in the rate or amount of the tax.	• The tax is included in the selling price and the selling price can never fall below taxes paid. • The entity will change or is required (by law) to change the price of the product to reflect the tax increases but is unable to increase the price above tax increases. • The entity will reduce or is required (by law) to reduce the price of the product to reflect tax decreases.	• The entity has the discretion to determine the final selling price of the products. It bears the tax and makes the decision whether to pass the tax (entire/a portion of it) to the consumer.
C	Basis of calculation – Whether the tax is levied on sales proceeds or on units of production.	• The tax is computed based on the sales price or units sold rather than producing activities.	• The tax is computed based on the number of units produced rather than sold. This suggests that it is a type of production tax.
D	Point of payment – Whether the entity becomes liable to pay the tax at the point of sale or at the time of production. (This is likely to be a weak indicator that should not be considered without additional factors.)	• The tax is payable to the government only when the sale has occurred or the entity is required to make payment to the government at a date relatively close to the point of sale. The closer the payment is to the point of sale the more likely it is that the tax is similar to a sales tax.	• The tax is payable to the government when the unit is produced or the entity is required to make payment to the government at a date relatively close to the point of production. The closer the payment is to the point of production the more likely it is that the tax is a production tax.

Clearly, it is important that companies disclose the policies that they have adopted in accounting for duty. BP is an example of a company that provides disclosure in this area:

Extract 28.26: BP p.l.c. (2012)

Notes on financial statements [extract]

1. Significant accounting policies [extract]

Customs duties and sales taxes

Custom duties and sales taxes which are passed on to customers are excluded from revenues and expenses. Assets and liabilities are recognized net of the amount of customs duties or sales tax except:

- Where the customs duty or sales tax incurred on a purchase of goods and services is not recoverable from the taxation authority, in which case the customs duty or sales tax is recognized as part of the cost of acquisition of the asset.
- Receivables and payables are stated with the amount of customs duty or sales tax included.

The net amount of sales tax recoverable from, or payable to, the taxation authority is included within receivables or payables in the balance sheet.

5.9 Sales incentives

IAS 18 states that 'the amount of revenue arising on a transaction is usually determined by agreement between the entity and the buyer or user of the asset. It is measured at the fair value of the consideration received or receivable taking into account the amount of any trade discounts and volume rebates allowed by the entity'. *[IAS 18.10]*. Consequently, where an entity provides sales incentives to a customer when entering into a contract these are usually treated as rebates and will be included in the measurement of (i.e. deducted from) revenue when the goods are delivered or services provided.

Where the incentive is in the form of cash, revenue will be recognised at a reduced amount taking into account the rebate factor from the cash incentive.

Non-cash incentives take a variety of forms. Where the seller provides 'free postage' this would impose an additional cost on the entity but would not impact revenue. Where the seller provides free delivery and undertakes this service itself, this would either be a separate component of a multiple element transaction to which some of the transaction price should be allocated, or more commonly, where risks and rewards of the good are not transferred to the customer until delivery, the total transaction price will not be recognised until that point.

Non-cash incentives may comprise products or services from third parties. If these are provided as part of a sales transaction they will represent separate components of a multiple element transaction to which revenue must be attributed. The seller will need to determine whether they are acting as agent or principal for that element of the transaction. If the seller is acting as agent and has no further obligations in respect of that component then it will immediately recognise the margin on that element as its own revenue. If acting as principal it will recognise the full transaction price as revenue but it will need to defer any element that relates to the provision of the good or service by the third party if that party still needs to provide that good or service (for example where the incentive is in the form of a voucher that is redeemable by the third party at a later date).

Some of these non-cash incentives that are issued as part of a sales transaction will fall under the scope of IFRIC 13 (see 5.15 below). However even where it may be argued that they do not strictly fall under that Interpretation the main principle of IFRIC 13 (whereby fair value is attributed to the incentive and deferred from revenue until the related obligation is fulfilled) will still be applicable.

If the sales incentive is in the form of a voucher that is issued independently of a sales transaction (e.g. one that entitles the customer to money off if they choose to make a purchase) there will be no impact on revenue. The entity will need to assess whether this results in an onerous contract that would need to be provided for under IAS 37.

Prompt settlement discounts (for example, customers are offered a reduction of 5% of the selling price for paying an invoice within 7 days instead of the usual 60 days) should be estimated at the time of sale and deducted from revenues.

From the perspective of the buyer, cash incentives are accounted for as a liability when received until the buyer receives the goods, pays for the inventory (thereby reducing the cost of goods sold) and meets any additional obligations that might be attached to the incentives. Non-cash incentives, such as gifts, would only be considered part of inventories if they meet the definition of inventories.

Sanofi is an example of a company that provides various forms of sales incentives to its customers:

Extract 28.27: Sanofi (2011)

NOTES TO THE CONSOLIDATED FINANICIAL STATEMENTS

Year ended December 31, 2011 [extract]

B. SUMMARY OF SIGNIFICANT ACCOUNTING POLICIES [extract]

B.14. Revenue recognition

Revenue arising from the sale of goods is presented in the income statement under *net sales*. Net sales comprise revenue from sales of pharmaceutical products, vaccines, and active ingredients, net of sales returns, of customer incentives and discounts, and of certain sales-based payments paid or payable to the healthcare authorities.

Revenue is recognized when all of the following conditions have been met: the risks and rewards of ownership have been transferred to the customer; the Group no longer has effective control over the goods sold; the amount of revenue and costs associated with the transaction can be measured reliably; and it is probable that the economic benefits associated with the transaction will flow to the Group, in accordance with IAS 18 (Revenue). In particular, the contracts between Sanofi Pasteur and government agencies specify terms for the supply and acceptance of batches of vaccine; revenue is recognized when these conditions are met.

The Group offers various types of price reductions on its products. In particular, products sold in the United States are covered by various governmental programs (such as Medicare and Medicaid) under which products are sold at a discount. Rebates are granted to healthcare authorities, and under contractual arrangements with certain customers. Some wholesalers are entitled to chargeback incentives based on the selling price to the end customer, under specific contractual arrangements. Cash discounts may also be granted for prompt payment.

Returns, discounts, incentives and rebates, as described above are recognized in the period in which the underlying sales are recognized as a reduction of sales revenue.

These amounts are calculated as follows:

- Provisions for chargeback incentives are estimated on the basis of the relevant subsidiary's standard sales terms and conditions, and in certain cases on the basis of specific contractual arrangements with the customer. They represent management's best estimate of the ultimate amount of chargeback incentives that will eventually be claimed by the customer.
- Provisions for rebates based on attainment of sales targets are estimated and accrued as each of the underlying sales transactions is recognized.
- Provisions for price reductions under Government and State programs, largely in the United States, are estimated on the basis of the specific terms of the relevant regulations and/or agreements, and accrued as each of the underlying sales transactions is recognized.
- Provisions for sales returns are calculated on the basis of management's best estimate of the amount of product that will ultimately be returned by customers. In countries where product returns are possible, Sanofi has implemented a returns policy that allows the customer to return products within a certain period either side of the expiry date (usually 6 months before and 12 months after the expiry date). The provision is estimated on the basis of past experience of sales returns.

The Group also takes account of factors such as levels of inventory in its various distribution channels, product expiry dates, information about potential discontinuation of products, the entry of competing generics into the market, and the launch of over-the-counter medicines.

In each case, the provisions are subject to continuous review and adjustment as appropriate based on the most recent information available to management.

The Group believes that it has the ability to measure each of the above provisions reliably, using the following factors in developing its estimates:

- the nature and patient profile of the underlying product;
- the applicable regulations and/or the specific terms and conditions of contracts with governmental authorities, wholesalers and other customers;
- historical data relating to similar contracts, in the case of qualitative and quantitative rebates and chargeback incentives;
- past experience and sales growth trends for the same or similar products;
- actual inventory levels in distribution channels, monitored by the Group using internal sales data and externally provided data;
- the shelf life of the Group's products; and
- market trends including competition, pricing and demand;

Non-product revenues, mainly comprising royalty income from licence arrangements that constitute ongoing operations of the Group (see Note C), are presented in *Other revenues.*

5.10 Film exhibition and television broadcast rights

Revenue received from the licensing of films for exhibition at cinemas and on television should be recognised in accordance with the general recognition principles discussed in this chapter.

Contracts for the television broadcast rights of films normally allow for multiple showings within a specific period; these contracts usually expire either on the date of the last authorised telecast, or on a specified date, whichever occurs first. Rights for the exhibition of films at cinemas are generally sold either on the basis of a percentage of the box office receipts or for a flat fee.

IAS 18 states that an assignment of rights for a fixed fee or non refundable guarantee under a non cancellable contract which permits the licensee to exploit those rights freely and the licensor has no remaining obligations to perform is, in substance, a sale. When a licensor grants rights to exhibit a motion picture film in markets where it has no control over the distributor and expects to receive no further revenues from the box office receipts, revenue is recognised at the time of sale. *[IAS 18.IE20]*.

Therefore, it is our view that the revenue from the sale of broadcast, film or exhibition rights may be recognised in full upon commencement of the licence period provided the following conditions are met:

(a) a contract has been entered into;

(b) the film is complete and available for delivery;

(c) there are no outstanding performance obligations, other than having to make a copy of the film and deliver it to the licensee; and

(d) collectability is reasonably assured.

This applies even if the rights allow for multiple showings within a specific period for a non-refundable flat fee and the contract expires either on the date of the last authorised telecast, or on a specified date, whichever occurs first. The sale can be recognised even though the rights have not yet been used by the purchaser. We do not believe it appropriate to recognise revenue prior to the date of commencement of the licence period since it is only from this date that the licensee is able to freely exploit the rights of the licence and hence has the rewards of ownership. *[IAS 18.14(a)]*.

When the licensor is obliged to perform any significant acts or provide any significant services subsequent to delivery of the film to the licensee – for example to promote the film – it would be appropriate to recognise revenue as the acts or services are performed (or, as a practical matter, on a straight-line basis over the period of the licence).

Rights for the exhibition of a film at cinemas may be granted on the basis of a percentage of the box office receipts, in which case revenue should be recognised as the entitlement to revenue arises based on box office receipts.

If the fees only become payable when the box office receipts have exceeded a minimum level, IAS 18 suggests that revenue should not be recognised until the minimum level has been achieved. It states that revenue that is contingent on the occurrence of a future event is recognised only when it is probable that the fee or royalty will be received, in this case normally when the event has occurred. *[IAS 18.IE20]*.

In this instance the guidance in IAS 18 supports deferral until the contingency has occurred. This differs from the arguments based on IAS 32 described in 5.2.4 in the context of initial and ongoing fees, in which the full amount can be recognised at inception and the contingency affects measurement.

5.11 The disposal of property, plant and equipment

IAS 16 requires that the gain or loss arising from the derecognition of an item of PP&E be included in profit or loss when the item is derecognised unless IAS 17 requires otherwise on a sale and leaseback. IAS 16 prohibits recognition of any such gain as revenue *[IAS 16.68]* except in the case of entities that are in the business of renting and selling the same asset (see below).

An item is disposed of when the criteria in IAS 18 for recognising revenue from the sale of goods are met (see 3.7 above). IAS 17 applies to disposal by a sale and leaseback.

[IAS 16.69]. IAS 18's criteria are essentially built around the transfer of significant risks and rewards of ownership. *[IAS 18.14-16].* Although, IAS 18 states that in most cases the transfer of the risks and rewards of ownership coincide with the transfer of legal title, it acknowledges that legal title sometimes passes at a different time. *[IAS 18.15].*

There are two significant points in the earning process that could, depending on the circumstances of the sale, be considered to be the critical event for recognition. The first point is on exchange of contracts, at which time the vendor and purchaser are both bound by a legally enforceable contract of sale, whilst the second possible point of recognition is on completion of the contract, when legal title and beneficial ownership pass.

It is possible that the earnings process is sufficiently complete to permit recognition to take place on exchange of contracts. This is because the selling price would have been established, all material related expenses would have been ascertained and, usually, no significant uncertainties would remain. If, however, on exchange of contracts there are doubts that the sale will ultimately be completed, recognition should take place on the receipt of the sales proceeds at legal completion.

The issue arises most commonly with regard to the sale of real estate, but is not restricted to it. The two approaches had previously been supported by the Illustrative Examples to IAS 18, which stated that, in the case of real estate sales, revenue is normally recognised when legal title passes to the buyer; however, at the same time, it acknowledged that recognition might take place before legal title passes, provided that the seller has no further substantial acts to complete under the contract. *[IAS 18.IE9 (2008)].* This paragraph was deleted with the introduction of IFRIC 15 (discussed at 5.12 below).

The evidence is that some companies delay profit recognition until legal completion, whilst others recognise profit before completion when the significant risks and returns have been transferred to the buyer. In our view, both approaches are acceptable and not affected by the amendment to IAS 18. Care must be taken before recognising profits before completion and it may be that in many cases, legal completion is the more appropriate point at which to recognise revenue. Whichever policy is adopted, it is important to ensure that all of the general conditions in IAS 18 have been met (see 3.7 above).

The two approaches are illustrated in the following extracts:

Extract 28.28: Barratt Developments PLC (2012)

ACCOUNTING POLICIES [extract]

Revenue

Revenue is recognised at legal completion in respect of the total proceeds of building and development. An appropriate proportion of revenue from construction contracts is recognised by reference to the stage of completion of contract activity. Revenue is measured at the fair value of consideration received or receivable and represents the amounts receivable for the property, net of discounts and VAT. The sale proceeds of part-exchange properties are not included in revenue.

Interest income is accrued on a time basis, by reference to the principal outstanding and at the effective interest rate applicable.

> *Extract 28.29: Capital Shopping Centres Group PLC (2011)*
> **2 Accounting policies – group and company** [extract]
> **Revenue recognition** [extract]
> **– Trading property income**
> Revenue on the sale of trading property is recognised when the significant risks and rewards of ownership have been transferred to the buyer. This will normally take place on exchange of contracts.

The gain or loss on derecognition of an item of PP&E is the difference between the net disposal proceeds, if any, and the carrying amount of the item. *[IAS 16.71]*. This means that any revaluation surplus relating to the asset disposed of is transferred within equity to retained earnings when the asset is derecognised and not reflected in profit or loss.

The consideration receivable on disposal of an item of PP&E is recognised initially at its fair value. If payment for the item is deferred, the consideration received is recognised initially at the cash price equivalent. In accordance with IAS 18, the difference between the nominal amount of the consideration and the cash price equivalent is recognised as interest revenue reflecting the effective yield on the receivable (see 3.5 above). *[IAS 16.72]*.

IFRS 5 lays down additional requirements for assets held for disposal; these requirements include measurement rules, which affect the measurement of the amount of the gain on disposal to be recognised. These are discussed in Chapter 4 at 2.2.

5.11.1 Sale of assets held for rental

Until 2008, IAS 16 prohibited classification as revenue of any gains arising from the derecognition of items of property, plant and equipment. *[IAS 16.68]*. However, some entities are in the business of renting and subsequently selling the same asset. The IASB has agreed that the presentation of gross selling revenue, rather than a net gain or loss on the sale of the assets, would better reflect the ordinary activities of such entities. *[IAS 16.BC35C]*.

Therefore IAS 16 was amended to require that where an entity, in the course of its ordinary activities, routinely sells items of PP&E that it has held for rental to others to transfer the assets to inventories at their carrying amount when they cease to be rented and become held for sale. The proceeds from the sale of such assets are recognised as revenue in accordance with IAS 18. IFRS 5 does not apply when assets that are held for sale in the ordinary course of business are transferred to inventories. *[IAS 16.68A]*.

IAS 7 – *Statement of Cash Flows* – has been amended to require presentation within operating activities of cash payments to manufacture or acquire such assets and cash receipts from rents and sales of such assets. *[IAS 7.14]*.

5.12 IFRIC 15 and pre-completion contracts

When and how to recognise revenue is a complex issue in the case of real estate developments where there are agreements for sale to the ultimate buyer prior to the completion of construction. Such 'forward sale' contracts are common in areas such as multiple-unit real estate developments (for example, residential apartment blocks) and commercial property developments where agreements for sale are reached before construction is complete. In these situations, the developers start marketing the development before construction is complete (perhaps even before construction has started, i.e. 'off plan') and buyers enter into agreements to acquire either the entire building or a specific unit within the building development on completion of the construction. The contracts may require the buyer to pay a deposit and progress payments, which are refundable only if the developer fails to complete and deliver the unit. The balance of the purchase price may be payable only when the buyer gains possession, which often coincides with the point at which legal title is transferred to the buyer. However, within this broad framework, the details of the legal rights and obligations might differ quite widely and legal title may transfer at different times, depending on national laws and practices.

5.12.1 Applicable standard: IAS 18 or IAS 11

The first issue that needs to be resolved is which standard is the relevant standard to apply: IAS 18 or IAS 11? IFRIC 15 was issued in July 2008 and applies to the accounting for revenue and associated expenses by entities that undertake the construction of real estate directly or through subcontractors. *[IFRIC 15.4]*. In substance, the Interpretation argues that pre-completion sales contracts typically do not meet the IAS 11 definition of, and are distinguishable from, construction contracts. They are, instead, generally sales of goods for which IAS 18 is the applicable standard. This means that revenue is recognised only when the IAS 18 conditions are met. Such contracts may span more than one accounting period, but this does not, by itself, justify the use of the percentage of completion method. Consequently, there will be differences between IFRS and US GAAP, which requires a percentage of completion method for recognising profit from sales of units in condominium projects or time-sharing interests (provided specified criteria are met), but the Interpretations Committee considers that these differences should be resolved by harmonising standards (see 6 below).

As well as guidance as to the applicable standard, the Interpretation addresses when revenue from the construction of real estate should be recognised. *[IFRIC 15.6]*.

The Interpretations Committee has focused on IAS 11's definition of a construction contract as 'a contract specifically negotiated for the construction of an asset or a combination of assets...'. *[IAS 11.3]*. An agreement for the construction of real estate meets the definition of a construction contract when the buyer is able to specify the major structural elements of the design of the real estate before construction begins and/or specify major structural changes once construction is in progress (whether or not it exercises that ability). *[IFRIC 15.11]*. By contrast, the buyer may only have limited ability to influence the design of the real estate, for example to select a design from a range of options specified by the entity, or to specify only minor variations to the basic design. In practice many agreements only give the buyer the right of choice over a few options, such as types of flooring or kitchen fittings. In this case the agreement is for the sale of goods and is within the scope of IAS 18 rather than IAS 11. *[IFRIC 15.12].*

The analysis assumes that there is revenue to be recognised, i.e. it assumes that the entity retains neither continuing managerial involvement to the degree usually associated with ownership nor effective control over the constructed real estate to an extent that would preclude recognition of some or all of the consideration as revenue. *[IFRIC 15.7].* Examples are agreements in which the entity guarantees occupancy of the property for a specified period, or guarantees a return on the buyer's investment for a specified period. In such circumstances, recognition of revenue may be delayed or precluded altogether. *[IFRIC 15.IE9-10].*

A feature of many of these agreements is that an entity may contract to deliver goods or services in addition to the construction of real estate. *[IFRIC 15.5].* For example, the agreement may include the sale of land or provision of property management services and it may need to be split into its separate components. *[IAS 18.13].* The fair value of the total consideration received or receivable for the agreement is allocated to each component. The entity will apply IFRIC 15 to the component for the construction of real estate in order to determine the appropriate accounting, *[IFRIC 15.8]*, as illustrated in the following flowchart:

Analysis of a single agreement for the construction of real estate

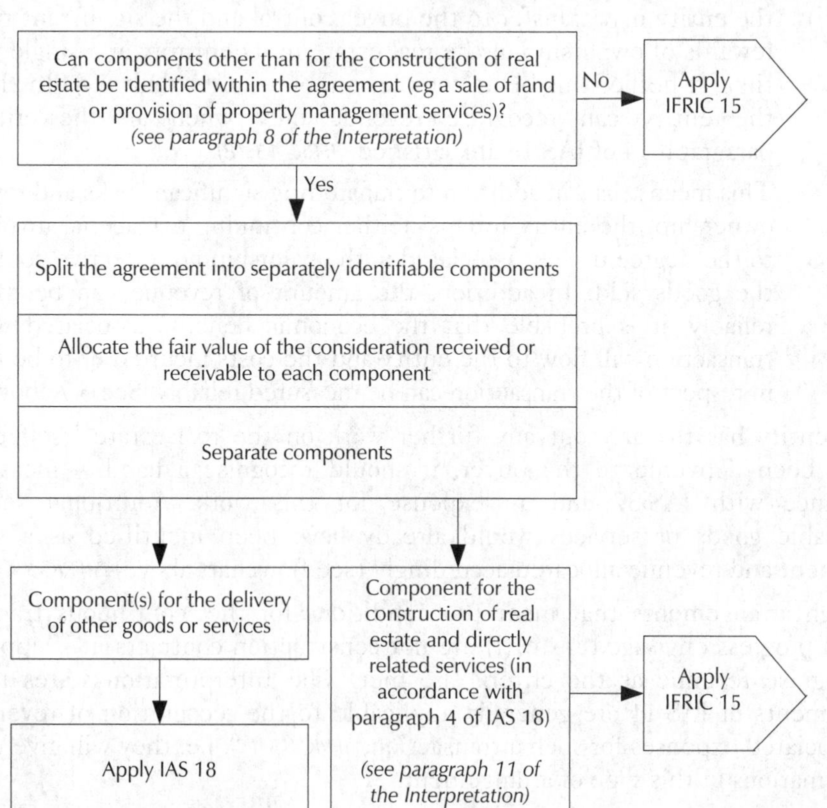

Analysis of the agreement, or the component for the construction of real estate within it, will determine whether it is a construction contract, a contract for services or a contract for the sale of goods:

(a) *the agreement is a construction contract:* if its outcome can be estimated reliably, the entity should recognise revenue by reference to the stage of completion of the contract activity in accordance with IAS 11; *[IFRIC 15.13]*

(b) *the agreement is for the rendering of services*: the entity does not have to acquire and supply construction materials so the agreement may be for services and IAS 18 requires revenue to be recognised by reference to the stage of completion using IAS 11 principles; *[IFRIC 15.15]* (see 3.8 above) or

(c) *the agreement is an agreement for the sale of goods:* if the entity has to provide services and construction materials as part of its contractual obligation to deliver the real estate to the buyer, it is an agreement for the sale of goods to which IAS 18 applies. *[IFRIC 15.16].* There are two alternatives depending on the transfer of control:

    (i) the entity may transfer to the buyer control and the significant risks and rewards of ownership of the work in progress in its current state as construction progresses, i.e. in a process of continuous transfer, and the percentage of completion method will apply; *[IFRIC 15.17]* or

    (ii) the entity may transfer to the buyer control and the significant risks and rewards of ownership of the real estate in its entirety at a single point in time (whether this be at completion, on or after delivery). In this case, the entity can recognise revenue only when all the criteria in paragraph 14 of IAS 18 are satisfied. *[IFRIC 15.18].*

    This means that, in addition to transferring significant risks and rewards of ownership, the entity retains neither continuing managerial involvement to the degree usually associated with ownership nor effective control over the goods sold. In addition, the amount of revenue can be measured reliably, it is probable that the economic benefits associated with the transaction will flow to the entity and the costs incurred or to be incurred in respect of the transaction can be measured reliably. See 3.7 above.

If the entity has to carry out any further work on the real estate itself that has already been delivered to the buyer, it should recognise a liability measured in accordance with IAS 37 and an expense for this work. Additional separately identifiable goods or services would already have been identified as a separate component and revenue allocated accordingly (see flowchart above). *[IFRIC 15.19].*

Although arrangements that meet the conditions for the 'continuous transfer' of work in progress envisaged in (c)(i) are not construction contracts, it is appropriate to recognise revenue as the criteria are met. The Interpretation states that the requirements of IAS 11 are generally applicable to the recognition of revenue and the associated expenses for such a transaction, *[IFRIC 15.17]*, i.e. they will give the best approximations in this type of arrangement.

If a builder/developer 'pre-sells' a development to an institutional investor, this contractual arrangement is usually, in substance, a financing arrangement and the purchaser will not have the right to assume the work in progress. Revenue recognition will normally be deferred until a single point of time (as in (c)(ii) above), such as on completion.[28]

5.12.2 Continuous transfer

Continuous transfer ((c)(i) above) is a concept developed in IFRIC 15; it allows an entity to apply percentage of completion accounting to transactions that would not otherwise qualify for this method, whether under IAS 11 as a construction contract or under IAS 18 as a contract for services. Without continuous transfer, these entities might have has to recognise revenue at a single point in time, e.g. at completion or on delivery.

Some of the features of 'continuous transfer' are described in the Illustrative Examples; they include circumstances in which the buyer has a right to take over the work in progress during construction (albeit with a penalty) and to engage a different entity to complete it. During this process the builder will have access to the land and the work in progress in order to perform its contractual obligations. This access does not necessarily imply that the builder retains continuing managerial involvement to the degree usually associated with ownership to an extent that would preclude recognition of some or all of the consideration as revenue. The builder may have control over the activities related to the performance of its contractual obligation but not over the real estate itself. *[IFRIC 15.IE11]*.

The following example is based on the Illustrative Example 2: *[IFRIC 15.IE6-8]*

Example 28.2: Applying IFRIC 15 to residential real estate

An entity is developing residential real estate and starts marketing individual units (apartments) while construction is still in progress. Buyers enter into a binding sale agreement that gives them the right to acquire a specified unit when it is ready for occupation. They pay a deposit that is refundable only if the entity fails to deliver the completed unit in accordance with the contracted terms. Buyers are also required to make progress payments between the time of the initial agreement and contractual completion. The balance of the purchase price is paid only on contractual completion, when buyers obtain possession of their unit. Buyers are able to specify only minor variations to the basic design but they cannot specify or alter major structural elements of the design of their unit.

(a) In Country A, no rights to the underlying real estate asset transfer to the buyer other than through the agreement. Consequently, the construction takes place regardless of whether sale agreements exist. The terms of the agreement and other facts and circumstances indicate that the agreement is not a construction contract. It is a forward contract that gives the buyer an asset in the form of a right to acquire, use and sell the completed real estate at a later date and an obligation to pay the purchase price in accordance with its terms. Although the buyer might be able to transfer its interest in the forward contract to another party, the entity retains control and the significant risks and rewards of ownership of the work in progress in its current state until the completed real estate is transferred. Therefore, revenue should be recognised at completion as it is only at this point that all of IAS 18's criteria are met.

(b) In Country B, the law requires the entity to transfer immediately to the buyer ownership of the real estate in its current state of completion and that any additional construction becomes the responsibility and property of the buyer as construction progresses. In this case it is possible that the entity transfers to the buyer control and the significant risks and rewards of ownership

> of the work in progress in its current state as construction progresses. For example, if the agreement is terminated before construction is complete, the buyer retains the work in progress and the entity has the right to be paid for the work performed. This might indicate that control is transferred along with ownership. If it does, the entity recognises revenue using the percentage of completion method taking into account the stage of completion of the whole building and the agreements signed with individual buyers.

The Interpretations Committee considered that continuous transfer would not be common. Certain specific agreements were considered in developing the Interpretation that may be examples of continuous transfer. These are agreements defined by law in certain jurisdictions, such as France and Belgium (Vente en l'Etat Final d'Achèvement – otherwise known as 'VEFA' agreements) under which the seller of real estate immediately transfers the rights of ownership of the floor area and existing work to the buyer, and additional construction work becomes the property of the buyer as it is performed.[29] These terms are reflected in the Illustrative Examples.

Since IFRIC 15, was issued, the Interpretations Committee has discussed continuous transfer on three occasions. Identifying those arrangements to which continuous transfer applies is highly contentious and arrangements that might be eligible are apparently more common than the Committee had hoped.

In addition, there are different opinions about how to account for protective rights given to buyers of residential properties when they are obliged to make progress payments during the period of construction. These protective rights may be enforced by relevant public authorities; usually they protect the buyer if the developer defaults, e.g. the public authorities may have the right to appoint another developer.[30] It is not clear whether continuous transfer of control means that the buyer receives control over the part-completed work in progress or the seller loses control and the buyer gains protective rights.

At the same time, but quite independently, the Boards have made tentative decisions about performance obligations where control is passed to the customer over time, which were included in the ED (see 6.6 below). Although this may appear to be a similar concept to continuous transfer, the conditions that would have to be met are different.

Early in 2012, the future of IFRIC 15 was considered by the IASB at the request of the Interpretations Committee. Although the IASB considered a range of options including withdrawing or revising IFRIC 15 (either in line with the revenue proposals or to include indicators and guidance in interpreting IAS 18), the Board's advice to the Committee was to retain IFRIC 15 as drafted.[31] Until these issues are clarified, or until IFRC 15 is superseded by a new revenue IFRS, it seems inevitable that there will continue to be different interpretations in practice.

5.12.3 Separation into components

The following, based on Illustrative Example 1 that accompanies IFRIC 15, *[IFRIC 15.IE1-4]*, helps identify the different elements within these arrangements.

Example 28.3: Applying IFRIC 15 to commercial real estate

An entity buys a plot of land for the construction of commercial real estate. It designs an office block and applies for building permission. The entity markets the office block to potential tenants and signs conditional lease agreements.

(a) It then markets the office block itself to potential buyers and signs with one of them a conditional agreement for the sale of land and the construction of the office block. The buyer cannot put the land or the incomplete office block back to the entity. When the entity receives the building permission and all agreements become unconditional, it constructs the office block.

The agreement should be separated into a component for the sale of land and a component for the construction of the office block. The component for the sale of land is a sale of goods within the scope of IAS 18.

Because all the major structural decisions were made by the entity and were included in the designs submitted to the planning authorities before the buyer signed the conditional agreement, it is assumed that there will be no major change in the designs after the construction has begun. Consequently, the construction of the office block is not a construction contract and is within the scope of IAS 18. Construction takes place on land the buyer owns before construction begins and the buyer cannot put the incomplete office block back to the entity. This indicates that the entity transfers to the buyer control and the significant risks and rewards of ownership of the work in progress in its current state as construction progresses. Therefore, the entity recognises revenue from the construction of the office block by reference to the stage of completion using the percentage of completion method.

(b) Alternatively, assume that the construction of the office block started before the entity signed the agreement with the buyer. In that event, the agreement should be separated into three components: a component for the sale of land, a component for the partially constructed office block and a component for the construction of the office block. The entity should apply the recognition criteria separately to each component. Assuming that the other facts remain unchanged, the entity recognises revenue from the component for the construction of the office block by reference to the stage of completion using the percentage of completion method.

In this example, the sale of land is a separately identifiable component but this will not always be the case. IFRIC 15 notes that in some jurisdictions, a condominium is legally defined as the absolute ownership of a unit based on a legal description of the airspace the unit actually occupies, plus an undivided interest in the ownership of the common elements (that includes the land and actual building itself, all the driveways, parking, lifts, outside hallways, recreation and landscaped areas) that are owned jointly with the other condominium unit owners. The undivided interest in the ownership of the common elements does not give the buyer control over the significant risks and rewards of the land. The right to the unit and the interest in the common elements are not separable. *[IFRIC 15.IE5]*.

5.12.4 Disclosure

IAS 18 has fewer disclosure requirements than IAS 11 and therefore the Interpretations Committee have inserted a number of specific disclosures in IFRIC 15 that are required when these agreements are deemed to be 'continuous transfer' arrangements that are accounted for under IAS 18: *[IFRIC 15.20-21]*

(a) When an entity recognises revenue using the percentage of completion method for agreements that meet all the criteria in paragraph 14 of IAS 18 continuously as construction progresses it should disclose:

   (i) how it determines which agreements meet all the criteria in paragraph 14 of IAS 18 continuously as construction progresses;
   (ii) the amount of revenue arising from such agreements in the period; and
   (iii) the methods used to determine the stage of completion of agreements in progress.

(b) For the agreements described in the paragraph above that are in progress at the reporting date, the entity should also disclose:
   (i) the aggregate amount of costs incurred and recognised profits (less recognised losses) to date; and
   (ii) the amount of advances received.

The guidance in IFRIC 15 replaces the guidance on real estate sales that was previously included in IAS 18's Illustrative Examples. The reference to revenue generally being recognised on the passing of legal title, *[IAS 18.IE9 (2008)]*, has been deleted but of course the general criteria of IAS 18 applicable to the sale of goods (see 3.7 above) will still be applicable.

5.13 Regulatory assets and liabilities

In many countries the provision of utilities (e.g. water, natural gas or electricity) to consumers is regulated by a government agency. Regulations differ between countries but often regulators operate a cost-plus system under which a utility is allowed to make a fixed return on investment. Consequently, the future price that a utility is allowed to charge its customers may be influenced by past cost levels and investment levels.

Under many national GAAPs (including US GAAP) accounting practices have been developed that allow an entity to account for the effects of regulation by recognising a 'regulatory liability' or 'regulatory asset' that reflects the decrease in future prices required by the regulator to compensate for an excessive return on investment, and vice versa where an increase would be permitted.

In July 2009 the IASB issued an Exposure Draft – *Rate-regulated Activities*.[32] This exposure draft favoured the US GAAP approach, requiring an entity to recognise a regulatory asset or regulatory liability in certain circumstances.[33] The Board did not proceed with the ED.

In September 2012, the Board decided to restart its rate-regulated activities project and plans to issue a discussion paper by the end of 2013.[34] As an interim measure, the IASB issued an exposure draft for a standard – *Exposure Draft: Regulatory Deferral Accounts* – to help entities who currently recognise rate-regulated assets and liabilities under their national GAAP adopt IFRS (e.g. Canadian utility entities). The exposure draft proposes to permit a first-time adopter of IFRS to continue to use its previous accounting policies for rate-regulated assets and liabilities, with specific disclosure requirements.

Until any new standard becomes effective, regulatory assets and liabilities are not eligible for recognition under IFRS. For further details see Chapter 17 at 11.1.

5.14 Transfers of assets from customers and IFRIC 18

It is quite common for utilities, in particular, to receive contributions of assets from customers so that they can be connected to networks or receive services from them. IFRIC 18 – *Transfers of Assets from Customers* – provides guidance in these situations.

This Interpretation applies to all agreements under which an entity receives from a customer, or another party, an item of PP&E (or cash to acquire or construct such an asset) that the entity must then use either to connect the customer to a network or to provide the customer ongoing access to a supply of goods or services or both. *[IFRIC 18.3-6]*. The Interpretation does not apply if this transfer is a government grant within the scope of IAS 20 – *Accounting for Government Grants and Disclosure of Government Assistance* – or the asset is used in a service concession within the scope of IFRIC 12 – *Service Concession Arrangements; [IFRIC 18.7]* see Chapters 25 and 26.

A typical arrangement is one in which a builder or individual householder must pay for power cables, pipes, or other connections for water, electricity or other supplies. However, the Interpretation will also apply to many outsourcing arrangements where the existing assets are contributed to the service provider or the customer must pay for assets or both. For example, in an arrangement under which an entity outsources its telephony, it is very common for it to transfer its existing assets to the service provider and for this to be reflected in the contract price.

The following flowchart illustrates the analysis and accounting to be applied under IFRIC 18:

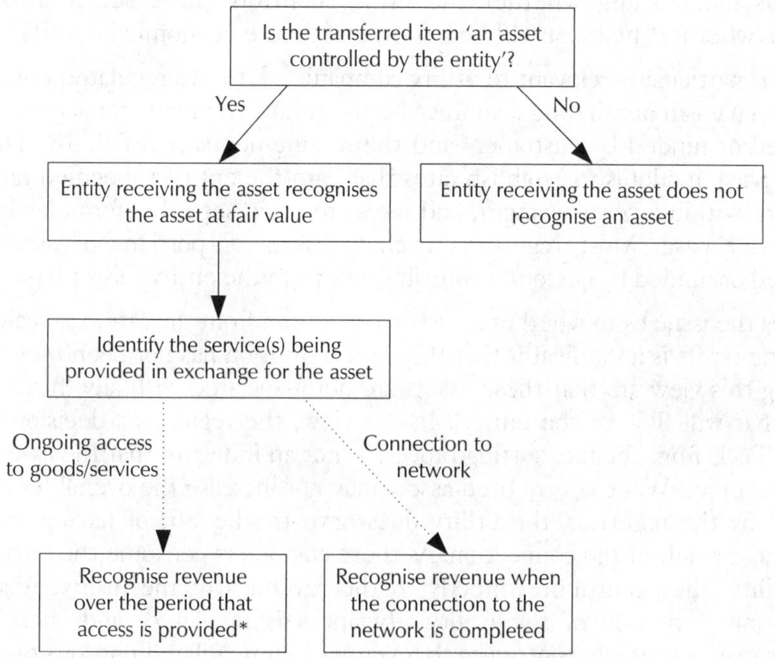

* If the agreement is silent, this is no longer than the life of the related asset.

The first step is to assess whether the item of PP&E received meets the definition of an asset. *[IFRIC 18.9]*. Paragraph 4.4(a) of the *Framework* defines an asset as 'a resource controlled by the entity as a result of past events and from which future economic benefits are expected to flow to the entity.' *[Framework 4.4(a)]*.

In other words, whose asset is it? Something can only be an asset of the reporting entity if that entity controls it. The water pipes put in to connect the new house may be controlled by the householder from the house to the boundary of the property and the utility will control everything from the boundary. Note that a third party that has no direct connection to the ongoing service may have constructed and contributed the asset, e.g. the builder; this does not prevent the arrangement being within scope. In an outsourcing arrangement, the service provider may operate the equipment but may or may not have rights over its maintenance and replacement which will indicate who controls the asset.

Control is not determined solely by the transfer of legal ownership, and will require a careful assessment of the facts and circumstances. Factors that would indicate that the transferred asset is controlled by the receiving entity are that entity's ability to:

- exchange the asset for other assets to deliver the same service;
- employ the asset to produce other goods or services or settle a liability;
- charge a price for others to use it; and
- determine how the transferred asset is operated and maintained and when it is replaced.

As well as establishing whether the entity controls the asset it also needs to determine whether the asset will be a source of future economic benefits.

IFRIC 18 is particularly relevant to utility companies. Utilities regulated under a 'cost of service' mechanism are finding a conflict between how the regulator accounts for items contributed or funded by customers and the requirements of IFRIC 18. The aim of a 'cost of service' model is to establish rates that earn the entity a specified rate of return (or a return within a certain range), and rates are often set using formulas involving an entity's asset base. Most regulators exclude assets or portions of assets that are contributed or funded by customer contributions from the entity's asset base.

This raises the issue as to whether an asset's exclusion from the rate-base calculation for establishing tariffs is an indicator that the asset definition has not been met. Arguments supporting this view are that these assets are not associated with any 'future economic benefits that will flow to the entity'. In our view, the regulator's decision to exclude items of PP&E from the rate setting process is not an indicator that the asset definition has not been met. While contributed assets may not increase the overall level of returns permitted by the regulator, the utility does have the benefit of having an additional customer as a result of the connection. As these customers consume the ongoing service of the utility, they contribute directly to the revenues of the utility. Also, in some markets, only a portion of the utility's business is regulated, and these additional customers may potentially contribute to revenues in unregulated portions of the utility's business. An entity's ability to sell the asset is also an indication that future economic benefits exists. Finally, contributed assets are usually only one of the many differences between the regulated asset and the asset in financial statements prepared under IFRS. For example, regulators may permit capitalisation of expenditure that would be considered repairs or maintenance under IAS 16 and accounted for as an expense.

Any asset transferred to the reporting entity will be measured initially at its fair value, which will become its cost for accounting purposes. *[IAS 18.12, IFRIC 18.11]*. It will be necessary to identify the separate services that are to be provided in exchange for the item of property, plant and equipment. *[IFRIC 18.14]*. This is because revenue needs to be recognised as it is an exchange transaction involving dissimilar goods and services *[IFRIC 18.13]* (see 3.9 above). The nature of the services provided will determine the manner in which revenue is recognised.

The service may simply be connection of the customer to the network. This may be a separately identifiable service if connection represents stand-alone value to the customer. *[IFRIC 18.15]*. Although IFRIC 18 does not provide a definition of stand-alone value, stand-alone selling price is expected to be defined when the new revenue standard is issued in late 2013. The November 2011 Exposure Draft which the IASB and FASB have been re-deliberating, proposes that stand-alone selling price be defined as 'the price at which the entity would sell a good or service separately to the customer'[35] (see 6 below). US GAAP currently has a broader definition of stand-alone value – 'if they are sold separately by any vendor or the customer could resell the delivered item on a stand-alone basis'.[36]

Other factors that could be considered in determining if the connection has stand-alone value are:

- does the customer have a choice of service provider? If there is no choice in providers, this may indicate that connection does not have stand-alone value; and
- if the customer is able to choose the service provider, does the connection allow a future purchaser of the property to avoid connection charges with the new provider (i.e. a connection enhances the value of a property)? A connection that increases a property's value relative to a property that is not connected to the network indicates that the connection has stand-alone value.

Another feature that indicates that the connection is a separately identifiable service is if the fair value of the connection service can be measured reliably. *[IFRIC 18.15]*. This may not always be straightforward, particularly when the connection is not sold separately.

It may be possible to identify the services that the entity is providing in exchange for the contributed asset by looking at how the ongoing goods and services are priced. Would the customer who made the contribution pay the same amount for the ongoing goods and services as others who have not done so? If so, this suggests that connection is the only service provided in exchange for the contributed asset. *[IFRIC 18.17]*. By contrast, a lower price than is available to other customers suggests that the future goods and services are, at least to some extent, provided in return for the contributed asset. *[IFRIC 18.16]*. The existence of any rate regulation, so common in the utilities industry, may make it harder to interpret this indicator. Prices established in a free market can be assumed to approximate a measure of the fair value of the ongoing service. Accordingly, it would be clear that if that price is the same for all customers irrespective of whether they contributed to the cost of the utility's assets, there is no ongoing benefit to those customers that made a contribution. However, where the price charged to customers is regulated, it does not follow that that price is a true measure of the fair value of the ongoing service obligation. In these circumstances, use of ongoing prices as an indicator can be inconclusive.

IFRIC 18 does not attribute a weighting or a priority to any of these features, and as a result, utility entities may find indicators that point to different conclusions. For example, many utilities have a legal obligation to provide ongoing services at set rates to all customers, indicating that the asset has been contributed in exchange for the connection, but the connection service may not have stand-alone value to the customer, which implies the opposite. In our opinion, no individual indicator is definitive and, as such, entities must consider all of them, along with other relevant facts and circumstances and exercise its own judgment in reaching its conclusion.

Once the services that have been provided in return for the asset have been indentified then the fair value of the total consideration received or receivable under the agreement, i.e. including the fair value of the contributed asset, is allocated to each service. *[IFRIC 18.19]*. This enables the entity to determine the period over which the revenue is recognised. If there are no ongoing goods and services provided in exchange, then revenue is recognised as soon as the connection is complete. The revenue for ongoing access will be recognised in accordance with the terms of the agreement if it has a specified term; otherwise the revenue will be recognised over a period not exceeding the useful life of the contributed item of PP&E. *[IFRIC 18.20]*. The following example based on Illustrative Example 3 in IFRIC 18 illustrates issues concerning revenue recognition (rather than asset recognition): *[IFRIC 18.IE6-9]*.

Example 28.4: Recognising revenue when assets are transferred for services

An entity enters into an agreement with a customer involving the outsourcing of information technology (IT) functions. As part of the agreement, the customer transfers ownership of its existing IT equipment to the entity. Initially, the entity must use the equipment to provide the service required by the outsourcing agreement. The entity is responsible for maintaining the equipment and for replacing it when it decides to do so. The useful life of the equipment is estimated to be three years. The outsourcing agreement requires service to be provided for ten years for a fixed price that is lower than the price the entity would have charged if the IT equipment had not been transferred.

These facts indicate that the IT equipment is an asset of the entity, which will recognise the equipment and measure its cost on initial recognition at its fair value, together with a liability to provide the service. Because the price charged for the service is lower than the price the entity would charge without the transfer of the IT equipment, this service is a separately identifiable service included in the agreement. The facts also indicate that it is the only service to be provided in exchange for the transfer of the IT equipment. Therefore, the entity should recognise revenue arising from the exchange transaction when the service is performed, i.e. over the ten-year term of the outsourcing agreement.

Alternatively, assume that after the first three years, the price the entity charges under the outsourcing agreement increases to reflect the fact that it will then be replacing the equipment the customer transferred. In this case, the reduced price for the services provided under the outsourcing agreement reflects the useful life of the transferred equipment. For this reason, the entity should recognise revenue from the exchange transaction over the first three years of the agreement.

IFRIC 12 and IFRIC 13 may be used for guidance on allocating the fair value; in these Interpretations it is based on the fair values of the separate components. *[IFRIC 18.BC19]*. IFRIC 12 is discussed in Chapter 26 and IFRIC 13 at 5.15 below.

The analysis and accounting to be applied when the entity receives cash that it must use to construct or acquire the assets is similar to the above. The entity needs to assess whether the agreement is within scope of the Interpretation and, if so, it will need to assess whether an asset is required to be recognised. The PP&E acquired or constructed will be recognised in accordance with IAS 16 and revenue, at the amount of cash received, will be recognised accordingly to each separately identifiable service provided. *[IFRIC 18.21]*.

5.15 Customer loyalty programmes and IFRIC 13

Customer loyalty programmes are now an integral element of a wide range of businesses – from airlines to retailers, and from consumer credit to mobile telecommunications. Customer loyalty programmes are used by companies to provide incentives to their customers to buy their products or use their services. Customer loyalty is recognised through the grant of award credits, such as 'points' or 'airmiles'; customers can then redeem the award credits for free or discounted goods or services.

The programmes operate in a variety of ways. Customers may be required to accumulate a specified minimum number or value of award credits before they are able to redeem them. Award credits may be linked to individual purchases or groups of purchases, or to continued custom over a specified period of time. A company may operate the customer loyalty programme itself or participate in a programme operated by a third party. The awards offered may include goods and services supplied by the company itself and/or rights to claim goods or services from another vendor. *[IFRIC 13.2]*.

In addressing the issue, the Interpretations Committee has rejected two approaches. It does not accept that an obligation for expenses is recognised as an expense at the time of the initial sale, measured by reference to the amount required to settle it, in accordance with IAS 37. Nor does it consider the accounting should depend on the nature of the customer loyalty programme, e.g. as a marketing expense or revenue, depending on significance. Instead it has concluded that some of the consideration received from the customer should be allocated to the award credits and deferred as a liability until the entity fulfils its obligations to deliver awards to customers. The liability is measured by reference to the value of the award credits to the customer (not their cost to the entity) and recognised as a deferral of revenue (not an expense). In support of this approach, it is argued that:

(a) award credits are an element of the market exchange of economic benefits between the entity and the customer. They represent rights granted to a customer, for which the customer is implicitly paying. They can be distinguished from marketing expenses because they are granted to the customer as part of a sales transaction; and

(b) award credits are separately identifiable from the other goods or services sold as part of the initial sale.

In the Interpretations Committee's view, paragraph 13 of IAS 18 applies if a single transaction requires two or more separate goods or services to be delivered at different times; it ensures that revenue for each item is recognised only when that item is delivered. In contrast, paragraph 19 of IAS 18 applies only if the entity has to incur further costs directly related to items already delivered – for example, to meet warranty claims. In the Interpretation Committee's view, loyalty awards are not costs that directly relate to the goods and services already delivered – rather, they are separate goods or services delivered at a later date. *[IFRIC 13.BC9(a)]*.

Although the issue of customer loyalty programmes was discussed by the US Emerging Issues Task Force, no conclusion was reached. As a result, under US GAAP there is no specific authoritative accounting guidance on accounting for the issue of award credits, and in practice entities commonly recognise an expense on original sale or when the obligation is fulfilled. In the airline sector – where such arrangements are pervasive – the majority of airlines have historically used the first approach.

5.15.1 The scope of IFRIC 13

The Interpretation applies to customer loyalty award credits that an entity grants to its customers as part of a sales transaction (i.e. a sale of goods, rendering of services or use by a customer of entity assets) as a result of which, subject to meeting any further qualifying conditions, those customers can redeem the credits for free or discounted goods and services. *[IFRIC 13.3]*. In other words, it applies to schemes whereby the award credits offered to customers derive from a past transaction. This means that it does not apply to the distribution of 'money off' vouchers or other schemes that do not involve an initial sales transaction.

IFRIC 13 does not specifically address the situation where an operator of a loyalty programme (e.g. an airline) sells award credits to another entity (e.g. a credit card company) and that other entity grants the purchased award credits to its own customers who are also members of the loyalty programme. This type of transaction is a direct sale of the award credits to a third party and therefore is within the scope of IAS 18, as opposed to IFRIC 13. As the cardholders/members can redeem the awards directly with the programme operator, it is our view that the programme operator still has an obligation that should be recognised through the deferral of some or all of the sales proceeds. Furthermore, the award credits granted to programme members directly by the programme operator versus those granted by third parties will, in both cases, have the same rights attaching to them and are indistinguishable from one another in the members' accounts.

Where a programme operator sells its award credits to a third party, it is likely that the sale will involve a number of components. For example, an airline selling its airmiles to a credit card company is likely to be selling both a travel component (for redemption by the third party's customers) and a marketing component for allowing the third party access to its loyalty program and customer base. In determining how much revenue should be recognised on the sale of the airmiles to the third party, the airline should determine how much of the consideration should be attributed to these components, since it is likely that the consideration related to marketing component may not require deferral. This is discussed in more detail in 5.15.3 below.

5.15.2 The requirements of IFRIC 13

Under IFRIC 13, an entity must account for award credits as a separately identifiable component of the sales transaction(s) in which they are granted (the 'initial sale'). The fair value of the consideration received or receivable in respect of the initial sale must be allocated between the award credits and the other components of the sale. *[IFRIC 13.5]*.

IAS 18 does not prescribe an allocation method for multiple-component sales. Its overall objective is to determine the amount the customer is paying for each component, which can be estimated by drawing on the entity's experience of transactions with similar customers. Hence, the Interpretation requires the consideration allocated to award credits to be measured by reference to their fair value.

The Interpretation does not specify whether the amount allocated to the award credits should be:

(a) equal to their fair value (irrespective of the fair values of the other elements); or

(b) a proportion of the total consideration based on the fair value of the award credits relative to the fair values of the other elements of the sale.

The Interpretations Committee noted that IAS 18 does not specify which of these methods should be applied, or in what circumstances and decided that the Interpretation should not be more prescriptive than IAS 18. The selection of one or other method is therefore left to management's judgement.

The measurement of fair value is discussed in more detail in 5.15.3 below.

Since not all award credits will ultimately be redeemed, IFRIC 13 specifies the basis on which revenue should be recognised, depending on whether the awards are supplied by the entity itself or by a third party. If the entity supplies the awards itself, it should recognise the consideration allocated to award credits as revenue when award credits are redeemed and it fulfils its obligations to supply awards. The amount of revenue recognised should be based on the number of award credits that have been redeemed in exchange for awards, relative to the total number expected to be redeemed. *[IFRIC 13.7]*.

The practical application of this approach is illustrated in Example 1 of the Illustrative Examples appended to IFRIC 13, as follows: *[IFRIC 13.IE1-6]*

Example 28.5: Awards supplied by the entity

A grocery retailer operates a customer loyalty programme. It grants programme members loyalty points when they spend a specified amount on groceries. Programme members can redeem the points for further groceries. The points have no expiry date. In one period, the entity grants 100 points. Management expects 80 of these points to be redeemed. Management estimates the fair value of each loyalty point to be $1, and defers revenue of $100.

Year 1

At the end of the first year, 40 of the points have been redeemed in exchange for groceries, i.e. half of those expected to be redeemed. The entity recognises revenue of (40 points ÷ 80 points) × $100 = $50.

Year 2

In the second year, management revises its expectations. It now expects 90 points to be redeemed altogether.

During the second year, 41 points are redeemed, bringing the total number redeemed to 40 + 41 = 81 points. The cumulative revenue that the entity recognises is (81 points ÷ 90 points) × $100 = $90. The entity has already recognised revenue of $50 in the first year, so it recognises $40 in the second year.

Year 3

In the third year, a further nine points are redeemed, taking the total number of points redeemed to 81 + 9 = 90. Management continues to expect that only 90 points will ever be redeemed, i.e. that no more points will be redeemed after the third year. So the cumulative revenue to date is (90 points ÷ 90 points) × $100 = $100. The entity has already recognised $90 of revenue ($50 in the first year and $40 in the second year), so it recognises the remaining $10 in the third year. All of the revenue initially deferred has now been recognised.

The IASB has clarified in *Improvements to IFRSs* issued in May 2010 that when the fair value of the award credit is calculated by reference to the value of the awards for which they could be redeemed, the value of the awards for which they could be redeemed must be adjusted to reflect expected forfeitures, as well as the discounts or incentives that would otherwise be offered to customers who have not earned award credits from an initial sale. *[IFRIC 13.AG2]*. Therefore each loyalty point issued could be redeemed for groceries valued at $1.25 but the fair value of the award credits is calculated at $100 being the 100 points issued multiplied by 80% (given the 20% forfeiture rate) of $1.25.

If a third party supplies the awards, the entity must assess whether it is collecting the consideration allocated to the award credits on its own account (i.e. as the principal in the transaction) or on behalf of the third party (i.e. as an agent for the third party).

(a) If the entity is collecting the consideration on behalf of the third party, it must:

 (i) measure its revenue as the net amount retained on its own account, i.e. the difference between the consideration allocated to the award credits and the amount payable to the third party for supplying the awards; and

 (ii) recognise this net amount as revenue when the third party becomes obliged to supply the awards and entitled to receive consideration for doing so. These events may occur as soon as the award credits are granted. Alternatively, if the customer can choose to claim awards from either the entity or a third party, these events may occur only when the customer chooses to claim awards from the third party.

(b) If the entity is collecting the consideration on its own account, it must measure its revenue as the gross consideration allocated to the award credits and recognise the revenue when it fulfils its obligations in respect of the awards. *[IFRIC 13.8]*.

The practical application of this approach is illustrated in Example 2 of the illustrative examples appended to IFRIC 13, as follows:

Example 28.6: Awards supplied by a third party

A retailer of electrical goods participates in a customer loyalty programme operated by an airline. It grants programme members one airmile with each $1 they spend on electrical goods. Programme members can redeem the airmiles for air travel with the airline, subject to availability. The retailer pays the airline $0.009 for each airmile.

In one period, the retailer sells electrical goods for consideration totalling $1 million and grants 1 million airmiles.

Allocation of consideration to airmiles

The retailer estimates that the fair value of an airmile is $0.01. It allocates to the airmiles 1 million × $0.01 = $10,000 of the consideration it has received from the sales of its electrical goods.

Revenue recognition

Having granted the airmiles, the retailer has fulfilled its obligations to the customer. The airline is obliged to supply the awards and entitled to receive consideration for doing so. Therefore the retailer recognises revenue from the airmiles when it sells the electrical goods.

Revenue measurement

If the retailer has collected the consideration allocated to the airmiles on its own account, it measures its revenue as the gross $10,000 allocated to them. It separately recognises the $9,000 paid or payable to the airline as an expense. If the retailer has collected the consideration on behalf of the airline, i.e. as an agent for the airline, it measures its revenue as the net amount it retains on its own account. This amount of revenue is the difference between the $10,000 consideration allocated to the airmiles and the $9,000 passed on to the airline.

Normally, the deferred consideration will exceed the unavoidable costs of meeting the obligation to supply the awards. However, if at any time the unavoidable costs of meeting the obligations to supply the awards are expected to exceed the consideration received and receivable for them (i.e. the consideration allocated to the award credits at the time of the initial sale that has not yet been recognised as revenue plus any further consideration receivable when the customer redeems the award credits), the entity has onerous contracts. A liability must be recognised for the excess in accordance with IAS 37. The need to recognise such a liability could arise if the expected costs of supplying awards increase, for example if the entity revises its expectations about the number of award credits that will be redeemed. *[IFRIC 13.9]*.

5.15.3 Measuring the fair value of award credits

IAS 18 requires revenue to be measured at the fair value of the consideration received or receivable. *[IAS 18.9]*. Hence the amount of revenue attributed to award credits should be the fair value of the consideration received for them.

IFRIC 13 requires also that the consideration allocated to the award credits must be measured by reference to their fair value. The brief Application Guidance set out in the Appendix to IFRIC 13 notes that this amount is often not directly observable and in such circumstances, it must be estimated. *[IFRIC 13.AG1]*.

This can lead to some confusion as, for example, airlines also sell airmiles/award credits to third parties to use in their marketing programs. However, airlines would not consider the amount for which the credits are sold separately to be the same as the fair value of airmiles issued as part of sale of a ticket. The reason is that when airlines sell airmiles to third parties they are selling both a travel component (for redemption by the third party's customers) and a marketing component for allowing the third party access to their loyalty program and customer base. In such cases these sales would themselves be required to be accounted for under IAS 18 with an estimation required for the two components.

It is expected that in the majority of cases the fair value will need to be estimated. IFRIC 13 sets out in the application guidance that an entity may estimate the fair value of award credits by reference to the fair value of the awards for which they could be redeemed. It goes further and notes that if customers can choose from a range of different awards, the fair value of the award credits will reflect the fair values of the range of available awards, weighted in proportion to the frequency with which each award is expected to be selected. *[IFRIC 13.AG2].*

This means, for example, that airlines may be required to estimate the fair value of an airmile by reference to a weighted average ticket value using an equivalent restricted fare as a proxy for tickets representing the profile of actual redemptions. These would depend on which routes, classes of travel, and the time of flights for which the miles are redeemed. Therefore an airline would be expected to determine the fair value of the airmiles on a basis that is 'weighted in proportion to the frequency with which each award is expected to be selected'. In our view, companies will be required in a number of cases to maintain comprehensive redemption data covering all variables subject to estimation, and that this is likely to place an onerous burden on many companies that grant loyalty awards.

However, the Application Guidance goes on to state that, in some circumstances, other estimation techniques may be available. *[IFRIC 13.AG3].* For example, if a third party will supply the awards and the entity pays the third party for each award credit it grants, it could estimate the fair value of the award credits by reference to the amount it pays the third party, adding a reasonable profit margin. The Application Guidance then ends merely by stating that 'Judgement is required to select and apply the estimation technique that satisfies the requirements of paragraph 6 of the consensus and is most appropriate in the circumstances.' *[IFRIC 13.AG3].* Clearly, this provides preparers with substantial flexibility in choosing the estimation techniques that they apply in practice. At the same time, though, it needs to be recognised that in most cases the amount of revenue that is attributable to the award credits is not directly observable because the award credits are granted as part of a larger sale.

5.16 Revenue recognition from gambling

Many gambling activities are derivative financial instruments if they are legally enforceable, which means they meet the definition of a financial liability. *[IAS 39.11].* These activities are accounted for in accordance with IAS 39 (see Chapter 42). However, some gambling contracts or activities are not in scope of IAS 39, in which case IAS 18 applies and the operator has to assess whether it acts as a principal or an agent.

If the operator is acting as a principal, revenue is recognised gross at the amount collected from players, with prizes awarded to winners classified as an expense.

Presenting revenue on a gross basis may present practical challenges if the entity's systems records information on a net basis. An entity could be, for example, recording net amounts collected from slot machines at the end of each day. Even if the cash flows received are net, an entity that is deemed to be the principal presents revenue on gross basis.

The general criteria in IAS 18 for determining whether an entity is an agent or principal are described in 3.3 above. The most applicable of these indicators to gambling is likely to be the ability of the operator to establish prices but the general characteristics of an agent are also highly relevant. An agent does not have exposure to the significant risks and rewards associated with the rendering of services and the amount the entity earns may be predetermined, being either a fixed fee per transaction or a stated percentage of the amount billed to the customer. *[IAS 18.IE21]*.

When assessing whether the entity is a principal or agent, the following indicators should be considered. These indicators have not been ranked and they are not intended to be exhaustive. This assessment is based on the weight of evidence available. In making this assessment, it is generally helpful to consider the responsibilities of the operator under the contract.

	Indicators that the operator is acting as principal	*Indicators that the operator is acting as an agent*
(a)	The operator has latitude in establishing the prices for players to participate in the game.	The operator does not set the price to enter the game.
(b)	The operator participates in the game.	The operator facilitates the game for the benefit of the players.
(c)	The amount the operator earns is not predetermined, for example, it is not limited to a fixed percentage or fixed amount of the wagers.	The amount the operator earns is predetermined, for example, it may be limited to a predefined percentage or the entity may only be entitled to a fixed amount of the wagers.
(d)	The operator is not required to pay out a prescribed amount of the wagers.	The operator is required, for example, by law or regulation, to pay a prescribed amount (e.g. a fixed percentage) of the wagers.

(a) In some gambling activities, the operator might set the price or the minimum stake for a player to participate. An example could include the sale of bingo cards for a fixed price. This might indicate the operator is the principal. However, in other gambling activity, the price might be set by the players, perhaps by mutual agreement, for example in a game of poker, or be predetermined as part of the game rules. The price might also be set by a regulator, with the operator entitled to a fixed percentage of total amounts wagered, for example, the price to purchase a lottery ticket. This might indicate the operator is not the principal.

(b) In games such as poker, the players play against each other and the operator facilitates the game, for example by providing the venue, the chips, cards and dealer. This might indicate the operator is acting as an agent. In other games, the operator might be a participant (i.e. the players place wagers against the operator). Examples of this include roulette, blackjack and slot machines. In such situations, the operator might be the principal.

(c) Sports betting is commonly performed through a bookmaker or through various online outlets. The bookmaker can accept wagers for different outcomes. If the bookmaker has the option to accept or reject the wagers, it may indicate the operator is the principal.

If the amount to which the operator is entitled is predetermined or capped, it may indicate the operator is an agent. In games such as poker, for example, where players play against each other, the house takes a commission, which might be a set percent of the pot (i.e. combined amount wagered by the players), up to a predetermined maximum amount.

The operator's ability to determine the spread may indicate the operator is the principal. For example, in sports betting the role of the bookmaker is generally to act as a market maker for the wagers, many of which have a binary outcome (e.g. a team either wins or loses) and/or have fixed odds. The bookmaker usually accepts wagers for either outcome and maintains a spread, which ensures a profit for the bookmaker regardless of the outcome of the wager.

(d) A requirement to pay a fixed percentage of all amounts wagered to the winners, either in cash or in kind, may indicate the operator is acting as an agent. However, if that requirement is contained in laws or regulations, the operator may need to look to other indicators to determine whether it is a principal or acting as an agent.

6 REVENUE FROM CONTRACTS WITH CUSTOMERS

The IASB and FASB have been working since 2002 on a joint project on revenue recognition. The Boards issued an Exposure Draft of their proposals in June 2010 but comments revealed complex implementation issues and a series of amendments were made. The Boards re-exposed the proposals in a revised Exposure Draft ED/2011/6 – *Revenue from Contracts with Customers* – in November 2011. The discussion in this section is based on this ED as well as subsequent re-deliberations. At the time of writing, the Boards had substantially completed all re-deliberations and planned to issue a new standard in late 2013.

Although accounting for some transactions may not be significantly changed, it is likely that all entities will be affected by the new guidance. The proposals will also introduce more detailed guidance on accounting for certain transactions, such as multiple-element arrangements, than is currently contained in IAS 18. IFRS reporters that have looked to US GAAP for guidance on these transactions will also need to consider these changes. This is because the proposed model brings the two frameworks together, and reduces the amount of industry-specific guidance currently in US GAAP.

This new model will replace all of the main pronouncements that currently address the recognition of revenue; as well as IAS 18 itself, it will replace IAS 11 (see Chapter 23) and the various Interpretations and SICs that address aspects of revenue recognition, thereby covering customer loyalty programmes (IFRIC 13 – see 5.15 above), agreements for the construction of real estate, in particular agreements that are for the sale of goods and are not in scope of IAS 11 (IFRIC 15, discussed at 5.12 above), transfers of assets from customers (IFRIC 18, discussed at 5.14 above) and SIC 31, which addresses barter transactions in advertising (discussed at 5.5 above).[37]

The Boards are proposing that entities apply the new guidance retrospectively for all periods presented in the period of adoption,[38] although some limited reliefs, e.g. allowing estimations and reducing some disclosures, are expected to be allowed.[39]

The IASB has set an effective date of 1 January 2017, with early adoption permitted (following a reversal of its previous decision not to allow early adoption by existing IFRS preparers).[40]

6.1 Scope

The proposed guidance will apply to all contracts with customers except financial instruments within scope of IAS 39 or IFRS 9, insurance contracts within scope of IFRS 4, lease contracts within scope of IAS 17 and certain non-monetary transactions.[41]

An arrangement is within scope only if there is a contract with a customer.

Contract and customer: A contract is an agreement between two or more parties that creates enforceable rights and obligations, discussed further in the next section.[42] A customer is defined as 'a party that has contracted with an entity to obtain goods or services that are an output of the entity's ordinary activities'. The ED notes that the counterparty to some contracts is not a customer but 'rather a collaborator or a partner that shares with the entity the risks and benefits of developing a product to be marketed'.[43] A contract with a collaborator or a partner will be within scope if the counterparty meets the definition of a customer.[44]

6.1.1 *Summary of the proposed model*

The core principle, according to the Exposure Draft is that entities should recognise revenue to depict the transfer of promised goods or services to customers in an amount that reflects the consideration to which the entity expects to be entitled in exchange.[45]

It is a control-based model rather than one primarily focused on risks and rewards as is the case under IAS 18. This means that the individual performance obligations under a contract with a customer are identified and revenue allocated to these obligations at the outset. Revenue is recognised when control of the related good or service is passed to the customer.

Entities will apply the following five steps to determine the appropriate timing and amount of revenue recognition.[46]

(1) identify the contract with a customer;

(2) identify the separate performance obligations in the contract;

(3) determine the transaction price;

(4) allocate the transaction price to the separate performance obligations in the contract; and

(5) recognise revenue when (or as) the entity satisfies a performance obligation.

6.2 Identify the contract with a customer

An entity must first identify the contract(s). Contracts may be written, verbal or implied, and the entity's business practices and those of the jurisdiction may influence its determination of whether or not a contract exists but they must create enforceable obligations.[47]

The contract must have commercial substance which means that it must be expected to affect the risk, timing or amount of the entity's future cash flows.

The parties must have approved the contract, whether in writing, orally or in accordance with other customary business practices) and be committed to perform their respective obligations.

The entity must be able to identify each party's rights regarding the goods or services to be transferred; and the payment terms for them.[48]

There will be no contract if either party has the unilateral enforceable right to terminate a wholly unperformed contract without compensating the other party or parties.[49]

The Boards are expected to provide more guidance on whether or not there is a contract between two parties and how to account for contract modifications.

6.3 Identify the separate performance obligations in the contract

The entity needs to evaluate the terms of the contract as well as the entity's normal business practices to identify all promised goods and services within the contract, and to determine whether each needs to be treated as a separate performance obligation.[50] Promised goods or services may include, but are not limited to, the following:[51]

(a) goods produced by an entity for sale (for example, inventory of a manufacturer);

(b) goods purchased by an entity for resale (for example, merchandise of a retailer);

(c) providing a service of arranging for another party to transfer goods or services to the customer (i.e. acting as an agent);

(d) standing ready to provide goods or services (for example, when-and if-available software products);

(e) constructing, manufacturing or developing an asset on behalf of a customer;

(f) granting licences or rights to use intangible assets;

(g) granting options to purchase additional goods or services when those options provide the customer with a material right; and

(h) performing a contractually agreed-upon task (or tasks) for a customer.

Promised goods and services are treated as separate performance obligations only if the good or service is 'distinct'.[52] A bundle of promised goods or services will be accounted for as one performance obligation if the entity provides a service of integrating those goods or services into a single item that it provides to the customer.

If the good or service has a different pattern of transfer to the customer from other goods and services in the contract and has a distinct function, then each promised good or service (or a bundle of goods or services, as above) will be accounted for as a separate performance obligation.

A good or service is 'distinct' if the customer can benefit from the good or service either on its own or together with resources that are readily available to the customer (including resources obtained in previous transfers of goods or services or that the customer could purchase separately). For example, a good or service will be distinct if the entity regularly sells it separately.[53]

In July 2012, the Boards discussed whether the concept of 'distinct' ought to be supported by various indicators. It was proposed that the following be added:

- the entity does not provide a significant service of integrating the good or service (or bundle of goods or services) into the bundle of goods or services that the customer has contracted. In other words, the entity is not using the good or service as an input to produce the output specified in the contract;
- purchasing or otherwise the good or service will not significantly affect the other promised goods or services in the contract for the customer;
- the good or service does not significantly modify or customise another good or service promised in the contract;
- the good or service is not part of a series of consecutively delivered goods or services that meet the following two conditions:
  - the promises to transfer those goods or services to the customer are performance obligations that are satisfied over time; and
  - the entity uses the same method for measuring progress to depict the transfer of those goods or services to the customer.[54]

If goods or services are not individually distinct, they are combined with other promised goods or services until the entity identifies a bundle of goods or services that is distinct.

At the same time, they decided to remove the practical expedient proposed in the ED that goods or services that have the same pattern of transfer to the customer could be account for as a single performance obligation.[55] However, the Boards do plan to permit an entity to bundle certain homogeneous goods or services that are delivered consecutively.[56]

6.4 Determine the transaction price

The transaction price is the amount of consideration to which an entity expects to be entitled in exchange for transferring promised goods or services to a customer, excluding amounts collected on behalf of third parties (for example, sales taxes). The transaction price does not include the effects of the customer's credit risk (as discussed at 6.3.1 below).[57]

The entity must assume that the goods or services will be transferred to the customer as promised in accordance with the existing contract and that the contract will not be cancelled, renewed or modified.[58]

6.4.1 Collectability and credit risk

The transaction price is to exclude the effects of a customer's credit risk, so revenue will be based on the amount in the contract without reflecting whether or not the customer has the ability to pay. Entities will present revenue without deducting amounts that may not be collectible.[59]

Respondents to the ED observed that some doubts about collectability could be as a result of variable consideration, which may be reflected in the estimated transaction price as discussed below, rather than an impairment loss. An entity might routinely offer price concessions (or discounts) to its customers. In July 2013, the Boards concluded that the proposed IFRS should include guidance on this point. This will address whether the entity expects to be entitled to an amount that is less than the contractually stated price.[60]

The ED proposes that entities present an allowance for expected impairment losses on a separate line immediately below gross revenue, including recognition of the initial allowance as well as the effects of subsequent changes in collectability.[61]

In a change from the ED, the Boards are suggesting that the effects of customer credit risk (related to contracts with and without significant financing components) should to be presented prominently as a separate line item in expenses in the statement of comprehensive income, rather than adjacent to revenue.[62] This is consistent with the current practice of presenting bad debts as an expense, although few entities present these amounts as a separate line item on the face of the statement of comprehensive income.

6.4.2 Variable consideration

An entity must take account of the effects of variable consideration, the time value of money, non-cash consideration and consideration payable to a customer when determining the transaction price.[63]

If the promised amount of consideration in a contract is variable, an entity must estimate the total amount to which it will be entitled from the customer.[64] The entity should estimate either of the following amounts, depending on which best predicts the amount of consideration to which the entity will be entitled:

a) the probability-weighted amount; or

b) the most likely amount.[65]

The entity must use the same method consistently throughout the duration of the contract.

Rather than a single estimate, the ED requires an entity to identify a range of 'reasonable number of possible consideration amounts', using all the information that is reasonably available to it, including historical, current and forecasted data. This information would typically be similar to that used during the bid and proposal process in establishing prices for promised goods or services.[66]

The estimated transaction price is to be updated at each reporting date.[67] Accounting for changes in the transaction price is discussed at 6.6.1 below.

6.4.3 Refunds

If an entity expects to refund some or all of the consideration that it has received to the customer, the entity must recognise as a refund liability for the amount of consideration that it reasonably expects to refund. The refund liability (and corresponding change in the transaction price) will be updated at each reporting period for changes in circumstances.[68]

6.4.4 *Time value of money*

An entity need only reduce the transaction price for the time value of money if the effect would be significant. The Boards have tentatively decided that, as a practical expedient, an entity will not be required to assess whether a contract has a significant financing component if the period between payment by the customer and the transfer of the promised goods or services to the customer is one year or less.[69] This was confirmed in September 2012, at which time the Boards also clarified that this should also apply to contracts with a duration of greater than one year if the period between performance and payment for that performance is one year or less. In addition, no adjustment should be made to advance payments if the transfer of goods or services is at the discretion of the customer. The proposed revenue standard will not preclude an entity from presenting as revenue interest income that is recognised from contracts with a significant financing component.[70]

6.4.5 *Constraining the cumulative amount of revenue recognised*

The ED proposes that the cumulative amount of revenue the entity recognises to date should not exceed the amount to which the entity was reasonably assured to be entitled.[71] This means that the constraint would be recognised as the entity satisfies its performance obligations (see 6.6 below). During re-deliberations, the Boards tentatively decided that the proposed constraint on recognising variable consideration should be applied by an entity when it estimates the transaction price.[72]

This addresses the maximum revenue but the minimum amount of revenue to be recognised is another potential constraint. The Boards have concluded that some, but not all (i.e. a minimum amount) of variable consideration should be included in the estimate of the transaction price, as long as this would not result in a significant revenue reversal in future. They have also agreed not to specify the circumstances when that minimum amount would be zero, nor to specify an exception for sales-based royalties on licences of intellectual property.[73]

For example, an entity that grants a licence of intellectual property to a customer typically receives royalty payments that are based on the customer's sales of products using the underlying intellectual property. Today, such royalties are considered contingent revenue and are recognised as the customer's sales occur. Under the proposed requirement, the entity may conclude that some portion of this variable consideration is not subject to significant revenue reversal at the time of the transfer of the intellectual property. If so, it would have to include this amount in the transaction price.

This may bring forward the timing of revenue recognition. The estimate will need to be updated each reporting period (see 6.6.1 below).

6.5 Allocate the transaction price to the separate performance obligations

Once the performance obligations are identified and the transaction price determined, the proposed model requires an entity to allocate the transaction price to the performance obligations, usually in proportion to their stand-alone selling prices, that is, on a relative stand-alone selling price basis.[74]

When available, the observable price of a good or service sold separately provides the best evidence of stand-alone selling price.[75] In many situations, stand-alone selling prices will not be readily observable, in which case the entity should estimate the amount for which it would sell each performance obligation on a stand-alone basis. The Exposure Draft gives three examples of possible estimation approaches, including expected cost plus a margin, adjusted market assessment (e.g. estimating what a customer would be willing to pay for the good or service) or a type of residual technique if the standalone selling price of a good or service underlying a separate performance obligation is highly variable. For the residual approach, an entity determines a standalone selling price by reference to the total transaction price less the standalone selling prices of other goods or services in the contract.[76] If the sum of the stand-alone prices exceeds the transaction price, the discount is allocated pro-rata to stand-alone prices unless there is observable selling price information from the entity's own sales that all of the discount should be allocated differently.[77] If the transaction price includes contingent consideration, this will be allocated on the basis of relative stand-alone prices unless the contingent amount relates specifically to one good or service.[78]

In December 2012, the Boards clarified the following:

- an entity should allocate a discount before using a residual approach to estimate a standalone selling price for a good or service with a highly variable or uncertain standalone selling price; and
- an entity can allocate contingent consideration to more than one distinct good or service in the contract.[79]

Changes to the transaction price are discussed at 6.6.1 below.

6.6 Recognise revenue when each performance obligation is satisfied

The ED states that revenue allocated to a particular performance obligation should be recognised when or as the customer obtains control of the promised good or service. The ED argues that the goods and services are assets and control of an asset refers to the ability to direct the use of and obtain substantially all of the remaining benefits from the asset The ED recognises an number of benefits from this 'asset', such as using it to produce goods or provide services (including public services), to enhance the value of other assets, to settle liabilities or reduce expenses, selling or exchanging it, using it to secure a loan or holding it.[80]

If an entity does not satisfy a performance obligation over time, the performance obligation is satisfied at a point in time.[81]

A performance obligation is satisfied continuously over time if:

(a) the entity's performance creates or enhances an asset that the customer controls as the asset is being created or enhanced; or

(b) the entity's performance does not create an asset with alternative use to the entity and at least one of the following conditions is met:

- the customer receives and consumes the benefits as each task is being performed;

- another entity would not need to re-perform all of the task(s) performed to date if that other entity were to fulfil the remaining obligation; and
- the entity has a right to payment for performance to date and it expects to fulfil the contract as promised.[82]

These criteria have since been redrafted to clarify the meaning and prevent difficulties, in particular, when they are applied to contracts solely for services (which include audit services). In pure service contracts, conceptually the asset is consumed as each task is performed and it is difficult to conceive of an alternative use for that asset.[83] The various conditions will be grouped into three criteria, as follows:

(a) the customer is receiving and consuming the benefits of the entity's performance as the entity performs. A customer obtains the benefits of the entity's performance as the entity performs if another entity would not need to substantially re-perform the work the entity has completed to date if that other entity were to fulfil the remaining obligation to the customer;

(b) the entity's performance creates or enhances an asset (e.g. work in progress) that the customer controls as the asset is created or enhanced; or

(c) the entity's performance does not create an asset with an alternative use to the entity and the entity has a right to payment for performance completed to date and it expects to fulfil the contract as promised.

In evaluating (a) above, an entity will have to disregard potential limitations (contractual or practical) that would prevent it from transferring a remaining performance obligation to another entity.[84]

As well as the general indicators that ownership has passed, the ED includes the following indicators that the customer has obtained control at a point in time:

- the entity has a present right to payment;
- the customer has legal title;
- the customer has physical possession;
- the customer has the significant risks and rewards of ownership; or
- the customer has accepted the asset.[85]

Recognising revenue over time is similar to percentage of completion accounting under IAS 11. The ED proposes that the entity use output or input methods to measure the progress towards complete satisfaction of that performance obligation. Output methods recognise revenue on the basis of direct measurements of the value to the customer of the goods or services transferred to date, e.g. surveys of performance completed to date, appraisals of results achieved, milestones reached or units produced.[86] Although the ED suggests that this can be the 'most faithful depiction of the entity's performance', it has the disadvantage that outputs are not always observable.[87]

Input methods recognise revenue on the basis of the entity's efforts or inputs to the satisfaction of a performance obligation, e.g. resources consumed, labour hours expended, costs incurred, time lapsed or machine hours used as a proportion of the total expected inputs. If the entity's efforts or inputs are expended evenly throughout the performance period, it may be appropriate for an entity to recognise revenue on a straight-line basis.[88]

6.6.1 Changes in the transaction price

Any change to the transaction price is allocated to all performance obligations based upon measurement at contract inception, i.e. they are not updated to reflect changes in relative stand-alone selling prices after contract inception. Entities may allocate all of a change in transaction price to specific goods or services only by applying the same principles as for contingent consideration.[89]

The ED states that if the amount of consideration to which an entity expects to be entitled is variable, the cumulative amount of revenue the entity recognises to date must not exceed the amount to which the entity is reasonably assured to be entitled.[90] Constraining the amount of revenue has been the subject of subsequent discussion and the proposed method of recognition has been changed. This is discussed at 6.3.5 above.

6.7 Onerous contracts

The ED proposes that performance obligations satisfied over time that are expected to take more than one year may have to be treated as onerous if the lowest costs of settling them exceed the amount of the transaction price allocated to them. The lowest cost is the lower of the direct costs of satisfying the obligation or the amount the entity would pay to exit the performance obligation, if it is permitted to do so other than by transferring the goods or services. If it is onerous, the entity must recognise a liability and a corresponding expense to the extent the lowest costs exceed the allocated transaction price. The liability for onerous contracts is remeasured at each reporting date using the most current estimates.[91]

Many respondents disagreed with this approach, which could have resulted in onerous performance obligations being recognised for overall profitable contracts. In response, the Boards tentatively decided to remove this requirement from the standard. For IFRS reporters, the requirements of IAS 37 will continue to apply.[92]

6.8 Contract costs

The ED indicates that costs incurred in connection with fulfilling the performance obligations of a contract that are not eligible for capitalisation under another standard (i.e. as inventory under IAS 2, PP&E under IAS 16 or an intangible asset under IAS 38) may give rise to a separate asset if the cost:[93]

- relate directly to the contract or a specific contract under negotiation;
- generate or enhance resources of the entity that will be used in satisfying performance obligations in the future; and
- are expected to be recovered.

The incremental costs of obtaining a contract will be recognised as an asset, unless the amortisation period of the asset would be less than one year. Its amortisation period will depend on the 'pattern of transfer of the goods or services to which the asset relates', which can include an anticipated contract.[94]

6.9 Disclosure requirements

The Exposure Draft also includes a number of new disclosure requirements. The overall disclosure objective is to 'help users of financial statements understand the amount, timing and uncertainty of revenue and cash flows arising from contracts with customers'.[95] Based on this, the ED proposes disclosure of qualitative and quantitative information about all of the following:

(a) its contracts with customers;

(b) the significant judgements, and changes in the judgements made; and

(c) any assets recognised from the costs to obtain or fulfil a contract.[96]

This included a disaggregation of revenue for the period, a reconciliation from the opening to the closing aggregate balance of contract assets and contract liabilities and information about the entity's performance obligations, including additional information about any onerous performance obligations.[97]

On the basis of responses to the ED, the Boards are suggesting that the way in which this information is disclosed be amended. This is discussed below.

6.9.1 Proposed disclosure requirements

In February 2013, the Boards reconsidered the disclosure proposals in the ED, taking account of the responses that they had received. Briefly, they have proposed retaining the qualitative disclosures about performance obligations[98] and significant judgements,[99] but removing the proposed disclosure requirements for onerous performance obligations. This last suggestion is consistent with the decision to base the treatment of onerous contracts on IAS 37 (see 6.7 above).

6.9.1.A Disaggregation of revenue

The Boards had previously proposed in the ED that revenue be presented in categories such as the type of good or service, the country or region, the type of customer and contract, the timing of transfer, the contract duration or the sales channel. These disclosures were intended to illustrate how economic factors affect the nature, amount, timing and uncertainty of revenue.[100]

In the responses, concerns were raised about the level of detail and the Boards have tentatively decided that when determining the level of disaggregation, an entity should consider how management and market participants analyse revenue. Entities should also discuss how their disaggregated revenue disclosures relate to their segment disclosures.[101]

6.8.1.B Reconciliations of contract balance and contract costs

The Boards have tentatively decided to require narrative explanations of changes in contract asset and liability balances, rather than the tabular disclosures they had proposed in the ED. These narrative disclosures include:

- opening and closing balances of an entity's contract assets, contract liabilities and trade receivables (if not disclosed elsewhere);
- an explanation of any unusual or non-recurring changes in contract balances;

- revenue recognised in the current period for performance obligations settled in previous periods; and
- revenue recognised in the current period that had been deferred in previous periods.

The Boards tentatively decided not to require reconciliations of costs to obtain or fulfil a contract. Instead, entities will disclose certain qualitative and quantitative information about the costs to obtain or fulfil a contract.[102]

6.10 Transition and First-time adoption

6.10.1 Transitional requirements

All entities will apply the standard retrospectively. The Boards have tentatively decided to allow either full retrospective application of the new standard or a modified retrospective approach. This is a change from the ED, which allows retrospective application in accordance with IAS 8, with only limited relief available.

Under the modified retrospective approach, entities will:

- present comparative periods under current IFRS revenue requirements;
- apply the new standard to new and existing contracts as at the effective date;
- recognise a cumulative catch-up adjustment to the opening balance of retained earnings at the effective date for existing contracts that still require performance by the entity; and
- disclose all line items in the year of adoption as if they were prepared under current IFRS revenue requirements.[103]

The IASB has set an effective date of 1 January 2017, with early adoption permitted (following a reversal of its previous decision not to allow early adoption by existing IFRS preparers).[104]

6.10.2 First-time adoption

In May 2013, the IASB considered the transition requirements for first-time adopters of IFRS that adopt the new revenue standard on transition to IFRS. The IASB tentatively agreed not to allow them the modified retrospective approach outlined above. Instead, they will be given an optional exemption to ignore, contracts that are completed under legacy revenue requirements before the earliest comparative period.

In addition, the Boards intend to remind first-time adopters that, while contracts may be considered complete for revenue recognition purposes under legacy revenue requirements, on transition to IFRS, provision will need to be made for any onerous contracts in accordance with IAS 37.[105]

6.11 Changes to current practice that would result from the proposed model

There are a number of areas that may be affected by this new model.

- Revenue on construction contracts under IAS 11 is recognised in the period the work is performed. *[IAS 11.26].* The new model will only allow revenue to be recognised when a performance obligation is satisfied which will be when control of the asset has been transferred to the customer. Many construction contracts involve the continual transfer of such rights and work in progress to the customer but there are some that do not, which would lead to later revenue recognition on these.

- An entity will be required to separate contracts into different performance obligations for goods or services that are deemed to be 'distinct', as explained above, and this may well differ to the components that are treated as separate units of account under current practice.
- The model requires an entity to estimate the stand-alone selling prices for separate performance obligations in multiple-element contracts.
- Greater estimation will be required under the new model, especially where there is an element of variable consideration, and in calculating the relative stand-alone selling prices of each of the performance obligations which is the basis by which the transaction price is allocated.
- The disclosures required under the Exposure Draft and expected under the revised ED are more detailed than under IAS 18 and will require more effort to prepare.

References

1 IAS 18 (Original), *Revenue Recognition*, IASC, December 1982, para. 4.
2 John H. Myers, '*The Critical Event and Recognition of Net Profit*', Accounting Review 34, October 1959, pp. 528-532.
3 Concepts Statement No. 5, *Recognition and Measurement in Financial Statements of Business Enterprises*, paras. 83-84.
4 FASB Accounting Standards Codification Revenue Recognition 605-15-25-1.
5 ASC 605-15-25-1.
6 ASC 605-15-25-3.
7 FASB ASC 605-10-S99.
8 SFAC No. 5, para. 83.
9 SFAC No. 5, para. 83(b).
10 SFAC No. 5, para. 84(a).
11 SFAC No. 5, para. 84(d).
12 ASC 605-10-S99.
13 ASC 605-10-S99.
14 ASC 605-25-25-5.
15 ASC 605-25-30-2.
16 These were in ASC 605-25-25-5(b) and 605-25-30-2 prior to amendment by EITF 08-01.
17 *IFRIC Update*, July 2008.
18 *IFRIC Update*, January 2007.
19 This is also the view taken under US GAAP; see ASC 310-20-35-5.
20 ASC 985-605-25-3.
21 ASC 985-605-25-16.
22 ASC 985-605-25-6.
23 ASC 985-605-25-10.
24 ASC 985-605-25-8.
25 ASC 985-605-25-10.
26 ASC 985-605-25-2.
27 *IFRIC Update*, March 2006, Page 7.
28 *IFRIC Update*, May 2008.
29 Agenda Paper 2B to the May 2008 IFRIC meeting, para. 12.
30 *IFRIC Update*, May 2011, November 2012 and Mat 2012.
31 *IASB Update*, February 2012.
32 Exposure Draft, *Rate-regulated Activities*, July 2009.
33 Exposure Draft, *Rate-regulated Activities*, para. 2.
34 www.ifrs.org/current-projects
35 ED/2011/6, Appendix.
36 ASC 605-25-25-5.
37 ED/2011/6, para. C6.
38 ED/2011/6, para. C2.

39 ED/2011/6, para. *C3.*
40 *IASB Update*, February and March 2013.
41 ED/2011/6, para. 9.
42 ED/2011/6, para. 13.
43 ED/2011/6, para. 10.
44 *IASB Update*, January 2013.
45 ED/2011/6), para. IN9.
46 ED/2011/6, para. 4.
47 ED/2011/6, paras. 12-13.
48 ED/2011/6, para. 14.
49 ED/2011/6, para. 15.
50 ED/2011/6, paras. 23-24.
51 ED/2011/6, para. 26.
52 ED/2011/6, para. 27.
53 ED/2011/6, para. 28.
54 *IASB Update,* July 2012.
55 *IASB Update* July 2012, ED/2011/6, para. 30.
56 *IASB Update,* July 2012.
57 ED/2011/6, para. 50.
58 ED/2011/6, para. 51.
59 ED/2011/6, para. 50.
60 *IASB Update,* July 2013.
61 ED/2011/6, para. 69.
62 *IASB Update,* November 2012.
63 ED/2011/6, para. 52.
64 ED/2011/6, para. 54.
65 ED/2011/6, para. 55.
66 ED/2011/6, para. 56.
67 ED/2011/6, para. 54.
68 ED/2011/6, para. 57.
69 ED/2011/6, paras. 58-60.
70 *IASB Update,* September 2012.
71 ED/2011/6, para. 81.
72 *IASB Update* November 2012.
73 *IASB Update* July 2013.
74 ED/2011/6, paras. 70-71.
75 ED/2011/6, para. 72.
76 ED/2011/6, para. 73.
77 ED/2011/6, para. 75.
78 ED/2011/6, para. 76.
79 *IASB Update,* December 2012.
80 ED/2011/6, paras. 31-32.
81 ED/2011/6, para. 34.
82 ED/2011/6, para. 35.
83 *IASB Update,* July 2012.
84 *IASB staff paper, supplement to paper 7C, July 2012.*
85 ED/2011/6, para. 37.
86 ED/2011/6, para. 41.
87 ED/2011/6, para. 41.
88 ED/2011/6, para. 41.
89 ED/2011/6, paras. 77-80.
90 ED/2011/6, para. 81.
91 ED/2011/6, paras. 86-88.
92 *IASB Update,* July 2012.
93 ED/2010/6, para. 91.
94 ED/2010/6, paras. 94-98.
95 ED/2011/6, para. 109.
96 ED/2011/6, para. 109.
97 ED/2011/6, para. 109.
98 ED/2011/6, para. 118.
99 ED/2011/6, paras. 124-127.
100 ED/2011/6, para. 113.
101 *IASB Update,* February 2013.
102 *IASB Update,* February 2013.
103 *IASB Update,* February 2013.
104 *IASB Update,* February and March 2013.
105 *IASB Update,* May 2013.

Chapter 29 Income taxes

List of examples

Chapter 29 Income taxes

1 INTRODUCTION

1.1 The nature of taxation

Accounting for taxation in financial statements must begin with some consideration of the nature of taxation. Although this might appear a simple question, taxation has certain characteristics which set it apart from other business expenses and which might justify a different treatment, in particular:

- tax payments are not typically made in exchange for goods or services specific to the business (as opposed to access to generally available national infrastructure assets and services); and
- the business has no say in whether or not the payments are to be made.

It is held by some that these characteristics mean that taxation is more in the nature of a distribution than an expense – in essence that the government is a stakeholder in the success of the business and participates in its results (generally in priority to other stakeholders).

Adoption of a 'distribution' view of taxation would render irrelevant most of the accounting questions which follow, since these are essentially concerned with the allocation of taxation expense between accounting periods (and to particular components of comprehensive income and equity within the same accounting period). If taxation were regarded as a distribution, however, these questions would not arise, since distributions are recognised when they are made rather than being allocated to accounting periods in the same way as items of expense.

In practice, however, a 'distribution' view of taxation is not adopted.[1] For all practical purposes, taxation is dealt with as an expense of the business, and the accounting standards which have been developed both by the IASB and by national standard setters are based on that premise.

1.2 Allocation between periods

The most significant accounting question which arises in relation to taxation is how to allocate tax expense between accounting periods. The recognition of transactions in the financial statements in a particular period is governed by the application of IFRS.

However, the timing of the recognition of transactions for the purposes of measuring the taxable profit is governed by the application of tax law, which sometimes prescribes an accounting treatment different from that used in the financial statements. The generally accepted view is that it is necessary for the financial statements to seek some reconciliation between these different treatments.

Accordingly IFRS requires an entity to recognise, at each reporting date, the tax consequences expected to arise in future periods in respect of the recovery of its assets and settlement of its liabilities recognised at that date. Broadly speaking, those tax consequences that are legal assets or liabilities at the reporting date are referred to as current tax. The other consequences, which are expected to become, or (more strictly) form part of, legal assets or liabilities in a future period, are referred to as deferred tax.

This is illustrated by Example 29.1, and the further discussion in 1.2.1 and 1.2.2, below.

Example 29.1: PP&E attracting tax deductions in advance of accounting depreciation

An item of equipment is purchased on 1 January 2014 for €50,000 and is estimated to have a useful life of five years, at the end of which it will be scrapped. There is no change to the estimated residual amount of zero over the life of the equipment. The depreciation charge will therefore be €10,000 per year for five years.

The entity is tax-resident in a jurisdiction where the corporate tax rate is 30%. No tax deductions are given for depreciation charged in the financial statements. Instead, the cost may be deducted from taxes payable in the year that the asset is purchased. The entity's profit before tax, including the depreciation charge, for each of the five years ended 31 December 2014 to 31 December 2018 is €100,000. All components of pre-tax profit, other than the accounting depreciation, are taxable or tax-deductible.

The entity's tax computations for each year would show the following (all figures in €s)[2]:

	2014	**2015**	**2016**	**2017**	**2018**
Accounting profit	100,000	100,000	100,000	100,000	100,000
Accounting depreciation	10,000	10,000	10,000	10,000	10,000
Tax depreciation	(50,000)	–	–	–	–
Taxable profit	60,000	110,000	110,000	110,000	110,000
Tax payable @ 30%	18,000	33,000	33,000	33,000	33,000

1.2.1 No provision for deferred tax ('flow through')

If the entity in Example 29.1 above were to account only for the tax legally due in respect of each year ('current tax'), it would report the amounts in the table below in profit or loss. Accounting for current tax only is generally known as the 'flow through' method.

€s	**2014**	**2015**	**2016**	**2017**	**2018**	**Total**
Profit before tax	100,000	100,000	100,000	100,000	100,000	500,000
Current tax	18,000	33,000	33,000	33,000	33,000	150,000
Profit after tax	82,000	67,000	67,000	67,000	67,000	350,000
Effective tax rate (%)	18	33	33	33	33	30

The 'effective tax rate' in the last row of the table above is the ratio, expressed as a percentage, of the profit before tax to the charge for tax in the financial statements, and is regarded as a key performance indicator by many preparers and users of financial statements. As can be seen from the table above, over the full five-year life of the asset, the entity pays tax at the statutory rate of 30% on its total profits of €500,000, but with considerable variation in the effective rate in individual accounting periods.

The generally held view is that simply to account for the tax legally payable as above is distortive, and that the tax should therefore be allocated between periods. Under IAS 12 – *Income Taxes* – this allocation is achieved by means of deferred taxation (see 1.2.2 below).

However, the flow-through method attracts the support of a number of respected commentators. They argue that the tax authorities impose a single annual tax assessment on the entity based on its profits as determined for tax purposes, not on accounting profits. That assessment is the entity's only liability to tax for that period, and any tax to be assessed in future years is not a present liability as defined in the IASB's *Conceptual Framework*. Supporters of flow-through acknowledge the distortive effect of transactions such as that in Example 29.1 above, but argue that this is better remedied by disclosure than by creating what they see as an 'imaginary' liability for deferred tax.

1.2.2 Provision for deferred tax (the temporary difference approach)

Over the last eighty years or so, numerous methods for accounting for deferred tax have evolved and been superseded. The approach currently required by IAS 12 is known as the temporary difference approach, which focuses on the difference between the carrying amount of an asset or liability in the financial statements and the amount attributed to it for tax purposes, known as its 'tax base'.

In Example 29.1 above, the carrying value of the PP&E in the financial statements at the end of each reporting period is:

€s	2014	2015	2016	2017	2018
PP&E	40,000	30,000	20,000	10,000	–

If the tax authority were to prepare financial statements based on tax law rather than IFRS, it would record PP&E of nil at the end of each period, since the full cost of €50,000 was written off in 2014 for tax purposes. There is therefore a difference, at the end of 2014, of €40,000 between the carrying amount of €40,000 of the asset in the financial statements and its tax base of nil. This difference is referred to as a 'temporary' difference because, by the end of 2018, the carrying value of the PP&E in the financial statements and its tax base are both nil, so that there is no longer a difference between them.

As discussed in more detail later in this Chapter, IAS 12 requires an entity to recognise a liability for deferred tax on the temporary difference arising on the asset, as follows.

€s	2014	2015	2016	2017	2018
Net book value	40,000	30,000	20,000	10,000	–
Tax base	–	–	–	–	–
Temporary difference	40,000	30,000	20,000	10,000	–
Deferred tax[1]	12,000	9,000	6,000	3,000	–
Movement in deferred tax in period	12,000	(3,000)	(3,000)	(3,000)	(3,000)

1 Temporary difference multiplied by tax rate of 30%

IAS 12 argues that, taking the position as at 31 December 2014 as an example, the carrying amount of the PP&E of €40,000 implicitly assumes that the asset will ultimately be recovered or realised by a cash inflow of at least €40,000. Any tax that will be paid on that inflow represents a present liability. In this case, the entity pays tax at 30% and will be unable to make any deduction in respect of the asset for tax purposes in a future period. It will therefore pay tax of €12,000 (30% of €[40,000 – nil]) as the asset is realised. This tax is as much a liability as the PP&E is an asset, since it would be internally inconsistent for the financial statements simultaneously to represent that the asset will be recovered at €40,000 while ignoring the tax consequences of doing so. *[IAS 12.16]*.

The deferred tax liability is recognised in the statement of financial position and any movement in the deferred tax liability during the period is recognised as deferred tax income or expense in profit or loss, with the following impact:

€s	2014	2015	2016	2017	2018	Total
Profit before tax	100,000	100,000	100,000	100,000	100,000	500,000
Current tax	18,000	33,000	33,000	33,000	33,000	150,000
Deferred tax	12,000	(3,000)	(3,000)	(3,000)	(3,000)	–
Total tax	30,000	30,000	30,000	30,000	30,000	150,000
Profit after tax	70,000	70,000	70,000	70,000	70,000	350,000
Effective tax rate (%)	30	30	30	30	30	30

It can be seen that the effect of accounting for deferred tax is to present an effective tax rate of 30% in profit or loss for each period. As will become apparent later in the Chapter, there is some tension in practice between the stated objective of IAS 12 (to recognise the appropriate amount of tax assets and liabilities in the statement of financial position) and what many users and preparers see as the real objective of IAS 12 (to match the tax effects of a transaction with the recognition of its pre-tax effects in the statement of comprehensive income or equity).

This tension arises in part because earlier methods of accounting for income tax, which explicitly focused on tax income and expense ('income statement approaches') rather than tax assets and liabilities ('balance sheet approaches'), remain part of the professional 'DNA' of many preparers and users. Moreover, as will be seen later in the Chapter, a number of aspects of IAS 12 are difficult to reconcile to the purported balance sheet approach of the standard, because, in reality, they are relics of the now superseded income statement approaches.

1.3 The development of IAS 12

The current version of IAS 12 was published in October 1996, and has been amended by a number of subsequent pronouncements. IAS 12 is based on the same principles as the US GAAP guidance (FASB ASC Topic 740 *Income Taxes*). However, there are important differences of methodology between the two standards which can lead to significant differences between the amounts recorded under IAS 12 and US GAAP. Some of the main differences between the standards are noted at relevant points in the discussion below.

In December 2010, the IASB issued an amendment to IAS 12 – *Deferred Tax: Recovery of Underlying Assets*. The amendment addresses the measurement of deferred tax associated with non-depreciable revalued property, plant and equipment (PP&E) and investment properties accounted for at fair value (see 8.4.6 and 8.4.7 below).

In addition, the SIC has issued an interpretation of IAS 12, SIC-25 – *Income Taxes – Changes in the Tax Status of an Entity or its Shareholders* (see 10.9 below).[3]

In March 2009 the IASB issued an exposure draft (ED/2009/2 – *Income Tax*) of a standard to replace IAS 12. This was poorly received by commentators and there is no prospect of a new standard in this form being issued in the foreseeable future. However, the ED gives some useful insights into the IASB's thinking on IAS 12, which are referred to where relevant in the text below.

The IASB continues to consider possible limited changes to IAS 12 with the aim of improving it or clarifying its existing provisions. These are discussed further at 7.4.3.A, 8.4.10.A and 15 below.

1.3.1 References to income taxes in standards other than IAS 12

There are numerous passing references in other standards and interpretations to income taxes, the more significant of which are noted at relevant points in the discussion below. In particular, the requirements of IFRS for accounting for income taxes in interim financial statements are discussed in Chapter 37 at 9.5.

2 OBJECTIVE AND SCOPE OF IAS 12

2.1 Objective

The stated objective of IAS 12 is 'to prescribe the accounting treatment for income taxes. The principal issue in accounting for income taxes is how to account for the current and future tax consequences of:

(a) the future recovery (settlement) of the carrying amount of assets (liabilities) that are recognised in an entity's statement of financial position; and

(b) transactions and other events of the current period that are recognised in an entity's financial statements.' *[IAS 12 Objective].*

IAS 12 requires this approach (the 'temporary difference approach') to be adopted, on the grounds that it is inherent in the recognition of an asset or liability that the reporting entity expects to recover or settle the carrying amount of that asset or liability. IAS 12 requires an entity to consider whether it is probable that recovery or settlement of that carrying amount will result in future tax payments larger (or smaller) than they would be if such recovery or settlement had no tax consequences. *[IAS 12.16, 25]*. If it is probable that such a larger or smaller tax payment will arise, in most cases IAS 12 requires an entity to recognise a deferred tax liability or deferred tax asset. This is discussed further at 3 to 9 and 11 below.

IAS 12 also requires an entity to account for the tax consequences of transactions and other events in a manner consistent with the accounting treatment of the transactions and other events themselves. *[IAS 12 Objective]*. In other words:

- tax effects of transactions and other events recognised in profit or loss are also recognised in profit or loss;
- tax effects of transactions and other events in other comprehensive income are also recognised in other comprehensive income;
- tax effects of transactions and other events recognised directly in equity are also recognised directly in equity; and
- deferred tax assets and liabilities recognised in a business combination affect:
  - the amount of goodwill arising in that business combination; or
  - the amount of the bargain purchase gain recognised.[4]

This is discussed in more detail at 10 and 12 below.

Finally the standard deals with:

- the recognition of deferred tax assets arising for unused tax losses or unused tax credits (see 7.4 below);
- the presentation of income taxes in financial statements (see 13 below); and
- the disclosure of information relating to income taxes (see 14 below).

IAS 12 requires an entity to account for the tax consequences of recovering assets or settling liabilities at their carrying amount in the statement of financial position, not for the total tax expected to be paid (which will reflect the amount at which the asset or liability is actually settled, not its carrying amount at the reporting date). This is discussed further at 8.3 below.

IAS 12 may require an entity to recognise tax even on an accounting transaction that is not itself directly taxable, where the transaction gives rise to an asset (or liability) whose recovery (or settlement) will have tax consequences. For example, an entity might revalue a property. If (as is the case in many tax jurisdictions) no tax is payable on the revaluation, one might conclude that it has no tax effect. However, this is not the correct analysis under IAS 12, which focuses not on whether the revaluation itself is directly taxed, but rather on whether the profits out of which the increased carrying value of the property will be recovered will be subsequently taxed. This is discussed further at 8.3 below.

2.2 Overview

The overall requirements of IAS 12 can be summarised as follows:

- determine whether a tax is an 'income tax' (see 4 below);
- recognise income tax due or receivable in respect of the current period (current tax), measured using enacted or substantively enacted legislation (see 5 below), and having regard to any uncertain tax positions (see 9 below);
- determine whether there are temporary differences between the carrying amount of assets and liabilities and their tax bases (see 6 below), having regard to the expected manner of recovery of assets or settlement of liabilities (see 8 below);
- determine whether there are unused tax losses or investment tax credits;
- determine whether IAS 12 prohibits or restricts recognition of deferred tax on any temporary differences or unused tax losses or investment tax credits (see 7 below);
- recognise deferred tax on all temporary differences, unused tax losses or investment tax credits not subject to such a prohibition or restriction (see 7 below), measured using enacted or substantively enacted legislation (see 8 below), and having regard to:
  - the expected manner of recovery of assets and settlement of liabilities (see 8 below); and
  - any uncertain tax positions (see 9 below);
- allocate any income tax charge or credit for the period to profit or loss, other comprehensive income and equity (see 10 below);
- present income tax in the financial statements as required by IAS 12 (see 13 below); and
- make the disclosures required by IAS 12 (see 14 below).

3 DEFINITIONS

IAS 12 uses the following terms with the meanings specified below. *[IAS 12.1, 2, 5, 6].*

Income taxes include all domestic and foreign taxes which are based on taxable profits. Income taxes also include taxes, such as withholding taxes, which are payable by a subsidiary, associate or joint arrangement on distributions to the reporting entity.

Accounting profit is profit or loss for a period before deducting tax expense.

Taxable profit (tax loss) is the profit (loss) for a period, determined in accordance with the rules established by the taxation authorities, upon which income taxes are payable (recoverable).

Tax expense (tax income) is the aggregate amount included in the determination of profit or loss for the period in respect of current tax and deferred tax.

Current tax is the amount of income taxes payable (recoverable) in respect of the taxable profit (tax loss) for a period.

Deferred tax liabilities are the amounts of income taxes payable in future periods in respect of *taxable temporary differences* (see below).

Deferred tax assets are the amounts of income taxes recoverable in future periods in respect of *deductible temporary differences* (see below), together with the carryforward of unused tax losses and tax credits.

Temporary differences are differences between the carrying amount of an asset or liability in the statement of financial position and its *tax base*. Temporary differences may be either:

- *taxable temporary differences*, which are temporary differences that will result in taxable amounts in determining taxable profit (tax loss) of future periods when the carrying amount of the asset or liability is recovered or settled; or
- *deductible temporary differences,* which are temporary differences that will result in amounts that are deductible in determining taxable profit (tax loss) of future periods when the carrying amount of the asset or liability is recovered or settled.

The *tax base* of an asset or liability is the amount attributed to that asset or liability for tax purposes.

4 SCOPE

IAS 12 should be applied in accounting for income taxes, defined as including:

- all domestic and foreign taxes which are based on taxable profits; and
- taxes, such as withholding taxes, which are payable by a subsidiary, associate or joint arrangement on distributions to the reporting entity. *[IAS 12.1-2].*

IAS 12 does not apply to accounting for government grants, which fall within the scope of IAS 20 – *Accounting for Government Grants and Disclosure of Government Assistance*, or investment tax credits. However, it does deal with the accounting for any temporary differences that may arise from grants or investment tax credits. *[IAS 12.4].*

A tax classified as an income tax is accounted for under IAS 12. Taxes other than income taxes are accounted for under IAS 37 – *Provisions, Contingent Liabilities and Contingent Assets.* The classification of a tax as an income tax affects its accounting treatment in several key respects:

- *Deferred tax*

  IAS 12 requires an entity to account for deferred tax in respect of income taxes. IAS 37 has no equivalent requirement for other taxes, recognising only legal or constructive obligations.

- *Recognition and measurement*

  IAS 12 requires tax to be recognised and measured according to a relatively tightly-defined accounting model. IAS 37 requires a provision to be recognised only where it is more likely than not that an outflow of resources will occur as a result of a past obligating event, and measured at the best estimate of the amount expected to be paid.

- *Presentation*

  IAS 1 – *Presentation of Financial Statements* – requires income tax assets, liabilities, income and expense to be presented in separate headings in profit or loss and the statement of financial position. There is no requirement for separate presentation of other taxes, but neither can they be included within the captions for 'income taxes'.

- *Disclosure*

  IAS 12 requires disclosures for income taxes significantly more detailed than those required by IAS 37 for other taxes.

4.1 What is an 'income tax'?

This is not as clear as might at first sight appear, since the definition is circular. Income tax is defined as a tax based on 'taxable profits', which are in turn defined as profits 'upon which income taxes are payable' (see 3 above).

It seems clear that those taxes that take as their starting profit the total net profit or loss before appropriations are income taxes. However, several jurisdictions raise 'taxes' on sub-components of net profit. These include:

- sales taxes;
- goods and services taxes;
- value added taxes;
- levies on the sale or extraction of minerals and other natural resources;
- taxes on certain goods as they reach a given state of production or are moved from one location to another; or
- taxes on gross production margins.

Taxes that are simply collected by the entity from one third party (generally a customer or employee) on behalf of another third party (generally local or national government) are generally not regarded as 'income taxes' for the purposes of IAS 12. This view is supported by the requirement of IAS 18 – *Revenue* – that taxes which are collected from customers by the entity on behalf of third parties do not form part of the entity's revenue *[IAS 18.8]* (and therefore, by implication, are not an expense of the entity either).

In cases where such taxes are a liability of the entity, they may often have some characteristics both of production or sales taxes (in that they are payable at a particular stage in the production or extraction process and may well be allowed as an expense in arriving at the tax on net profits) and of income taxes (in that they may be determined after deduction of certain allowable expenditure). This makes the classification of such taxes (as income taxes or not) difficult – see, for example, the discussion in Chapter 39 at 4.17.

In March 2006 the Interpretations Committee considered whether to give guidance on which taxes are within the scope of IAS 12. The Committee noted that the definition of 'income tax' in IAS 12 (i.e. taxes that are based on taxable profit) implies that:

- not all taxes are within the scope of IAS 12; but
- because taxable profit is not the same as accounting profit, taxes do not need to be based on a figure that is exactly accounting profit to be within the scope of IAS 12.

The latter point is also implied by the requirement in IAS 12 to disclose an explanation of the relationship between tax expense and accounting profit – see 14.2

below. [IAS 12.81(c)]. The Interpretations Committee further noted that the term 'taxable profit' implies a notion of a net rather than gross amount, and that any taxes that are not in the scope of IAS 12 are in the scope of IAS 37 (see Chapter 27).

The Interpretations Committee drew attention to the variety of taxes that exist across the world and the need for judgement in determining whether some taxes are income taxes. The Committee therefore believed that guidance beyond the observations noted above could not be developed in a reasonable period of time and decided not to take a project on this issue onto its agenda.[5]

The Interpretations Committee's deliberations reinforce the difficulty of formulating a single view as to the treatment of taxes. The appropriate treatment will need to be addressed on a case-by-case basis depending on the particular terms of the tax concerned and the entity's own circumstances.

Where a tax is levied on multiple components of net income, it is more likely that the tax should be viewed as substantially a tax on income and therefore subject to IAS 12.

Even where such taxes are not income taxes, if they are deductible against current or future income taxes, they may nevertheless give rise to tax assets which do fall within the scope of IAS 12 (see 7.4 below).

4.1.1 Levies

A number of governments have recently introduced levies on certain types of entity, particularly those in the financial services sector. In many cases the levies are expressed as a percentage of a measure of revenue or net assets, or some component(s) of revenue or net assets, at a particular date. Such levies are not income taxes and should be accounted for in accordance with IAS 37 (see Chapter 27 at 6.8).

4.1.2 Hybrid taxes (including minimum taxes)

Some jurisdictions impose income taxes which are charged as a percentage of taxable profits in the normal way, but are subject to a requirement that a minimum amount of tax must be paid. This minimum may be an absolute amount or a proportion of one or more components of the statement of financial position – for example, total equity as reported in the financial statements, or total share capital and additional paid-in capital (share premium).

Such taxes raise the issue of how they should be accounted for. One view would be that the fixed minimum element is not an income tax and should be accounted for under IAS 37, but any excess above the fixed minimum element is an income tax which should be accounted for under IAS 12.

There is a logical elegance to this approach, but it has the significant practical disadvantage that the future rate of tax accounted for as income tax is unpredictable, as it will depend on the level of profit in future periods. Suppose for example that an entity is required to pay tax at 30% on its taxable profit, but subject to a minimum tax of €100,000 per year. If its taxable profits were €1 million, it would pay tax of €300,000 (€1,000,000 at 30%). Under this approach, this €300,000 would be accounted for as comprising a minimum (non-income) tax of €100,000 and income tax of €200,000. The effective rate of tax accounted for as income tax would be 20% (€200,000/€1,000,000). If, however, the entity's taxable profits were €2,000,000 it would pay tax of €600,000 (€2,000,000 at 30%). In this case, this €600,000 would be accounted for as comprising a minimum (non-income) tax of $100,000 and income tax of €500,000. The effective rate of tax accounted for as income tax would be 25% (€500,000/€2,000,000). This illustrates that, in order to calculate deferred income taxes for the purposes of IAS 12, any future income tax rate would be subject to constant re-estimation, even if the 'headline' rate were a known enacted rate.

Some therefore favour an alternative analysis which would be to consider overall the substance of the tax. Those who take this view would argue that, if it is apparent that the overall intention of the legislation is to levy taxes based on income, but subject to a floor, the tax should be accounted for as an income tax in its entirety, even if the floor would not be an income tax if considered in isolation.

In our view, either of these broad approaches can be adopted so long as it is applied consistently to all taxes of a similar nature in all periods. We would generally expect a common approach to be applied to the same tax in the same jurisdiction.

4.2 Withholding and similar taxes

As noted at 4.1 above, IAS 12 also includes in its scope those taxes, such as withholding taxes, which are payable by a subsidiary, associate or joint arrangement on distributions to the reporting entity. *[IAS 12.2]*. This gives rise to further questions of interpretation.

The most basic issue is what is meant by a 'withholding tax'. This is discussed at 10.3.2 below.

A second issue is whether the scope of IAS 12 covers only taxes on distributions from a subsidiary, associate or joint arrangement, or whether it extends to distributions from other entities in which the reporting entity has an investment. Such an investment will typically be accounted for at fair value under IAS 39 – *Financial Instruments: Recognition and Measurement* – or, where applied, IFRS 9 – *Financial Instruments*.

The rationale for the treatment as income taxes of taxes payable by a subsidiary, associate or joint arrangement on distributions to the investor is discussed further at 7.5 below. Essentially, however, the reason for considering withholding taxes within the scope of income tax accounting derives from the accounting treatment of the investments themselves. The accounting treatment for such investments – whether by full consolidation or the equity method – results in the investor recognising profit that may be taxed twice: once as it is earned by the investee entity concerned, and again as that entity distributes the profit as dividend to the investor. IAS 12 ensures that the financial statements reflect both tax consequences.

Some argue that this indicates a general principle that an entity should account for all the tax consequences of realising the income of an investee as that income is recognised. On this analysis withholding taxes suffered on any investment income should be treated as income taxes. Others argue that the reference in IAS 12 to distributions from 'a subsidiary, associate or joint arrangement' should be read restrictively, and that no wider general principle is implied.

We believe that the first (wider) analysis is more appropriate. Accordingly, an entity should treat as income taxes the withholding taxes that could potentially be suffered on distributions from all investments, not just subsidiaries, associates and joint arrangements. Whether or not any tax liability is recognised will depend on an analysis of the facts and circumstances in each particular case, in particular whether the investment concerned is expected to be recovered through receipt of dividend income or through sale (see 8.3 below).

4.3 Investment tax credits

Investment tax credits are not defined in IAS 12, but for the purposes of the following discussion they are taken to comprise government assistance and incentives for specific kinds of investment delivered through the tax system. Typically, a tax credit is given as a deduction from the tax liability, rather than as a deductible expense in computing the liability. As noted at 4 above, investment tax credits are not within the scope of IAS 12 (although any temporary differences that arise from them are in the scope of the standard). Moreover, government assistance that is either provided by way of a reduction in taxable income, or determined or limited according to an entity's income tax liability, is excluded from the scope of IAS 20. *[IAS 20.2].* Conversely, government assistance that is not determined or limited by reference to an entity's liability to income taxes falls within the scope of IAS 20 (see Chapter 25 at 2.2).

Entities may receive investment tax credits in a variety of ways. Some investment tax credits may relate to direct investment in property, plant and equipment. Other entities may receive investment tax credits relating to research and development activities. Some credits may be realisable only through a reduction in current or future income taxes payable, while others may be settled directly in cash if the entity does not have sufficient income taxes payable to offset the credit within a certain period. Sometimes the level of credit is limited according to total taxes paid (i.e. including taxes such as payroll and sales taxes in addition to income taxes). There may be other conditions associated with receiving the investment tax credit, and the credit may become repayable if ongoing conditions are not met.

The fact that both IAS 20 and IAS 12 exclude from their scope those investment tax credits that are realisable only through a reduction in current or future income taxes payable does not prohibit an entity from applying either standard in accounting for such credits. Indeed, either IAS 12 or IAS 20 will generally provide an appropriate accounting framework, by analogy under the 'GAAP hierarchy' in IAS 8 – *Accounting Policies, Changes in Accounting Estimates and Errors* (see Chapter 3).

Which standard provides the better accounting model in a particular case is a matter of judgement. In our view, such a judgement would be informed by reference to the specific terms of the arrangement including the following factors:

Feature of credit	Indicator of IAS 12 treatment	Indicator of IAS 20 treatment
Method of payment	Only available as a reduction in income taxes payable. However, the longer the period allowed for carrying forward unused credits, the less relevant this indicator becomes.	Directly settled in cash where there are insufficient taxable profits to allow credit to be fully offset
Number of conditions not related to tax position (e.g. minimum employment, operating in a designated geographical area)	None or few	Many
Restrictions as to nature of expenditure	Broad criteria encompassing many different types of expenditure	Highly specific
Tax status of grant income	Not taxable	Taxable

In group accounts, in which entities from a number of different jurisdictions may be consolidated, it is desirable that each particular investment tax credit should be consistently accounted for under either IAS 12 or IAS 20. However, the lack of specific guidance for investment tax credits in IFRS may mean that predominant practice in a particular jurisdiction for a specific type of tax credit differs from predominant practice in another jurisdiction for a substantially similar credit. We believe that, in determining whether IAS 12 or IAS 20 should be applied, an entity should consider the following factors in the order listed below:

- the predominant local treatment for a specific credit in the relevant tax jurisdiction;
- if there is no predominant local treatment, the group-wide accounting policy for such a credit;
- in the absence of a predominant local treatment or a group-wide accounting policy, the indicators listed in the table above should provide guidance.

This may occasionally mean that an entity operating in a number of territories adopts different accounting treatments for apparently similar arrangements in different countries, but it at least ensures a measure of comparability between different entities operating in the same tax jurisdiction. Similar considerations apply in determining the meaning of 'substantively enacted' legislation in different jurisdictions (see 5.1 below).

Where a tax credit is accounted for as income tax, it is generally treated as a discrete tax asset akin to a tax loss. However, where a credit is received in respect of a specific asset, an alternative analysis might be that the effect of a tax credit is to make the asset 'super-deductible' (i.e. eligible for tax deductions in excess of its cost). For example, if an entity pays tax at 30% and is allowed to deduct 100% of the cost of an item of PP&E costing €1,000 from its tax liability, it could be argued that the economic effect is the same as if the entity had been allowed to deduct €3,333 in respect of the asset in computing its taxable profit. The treatment of super-deductible assets is discussed further at 7.2.6 below. However, a credit (where the economic benefit is typically a fixed amount) is not wholly analogous to a 'super-deductible' asset, where the economic benefit of the 'super deduction' could vary in response to changes in the tax rate. For this reason, we believe that it will generally be more appropriate to treat a tax credit that is accounted for as income tax as a discrete tax asset akin to a tax loss.

4.4 Interest and penalties

Many tax regimes provide for interest and/or penalties to be paid on late payments of tax. This raises the question of whether or not such penalties fall within the scope of IAS 12. The issue is primarily one of presentation in the income statement. If such penalties and interest fall within the scope of IAS 12, they are presented as part of tax expense. If they do not fall within the scope of IAS 12, they should be included within profit before tax.

Some argue that penalties and interest have the characteristics of tax – they are paid to the tax authorities under tax legislation and in many jurisdictions are not a tax-deductible expense. Others contend that penalties and interest are distinct from the main tax liability and should not therefore form part of tax expense. Those who hold this view would point out, for example, that under IFRS the unwinding of the discount on discounted items is generally accounted for separately from the discounted expense.

The Interpretations Committee considered this issue in June 2004. It decided not to add the issue to its agenda, given that the disclosure requirements of IAS 12 and IAS 1 provide adequate transparency of these items.[6] The reference to IAS 12 indicates that the Interpretations Committee at the very least does not consider it inappropriate to account for interest and penalties as income taxes under IAS 12. Moreover, in the exposure draft of a possible replacement for IAS 12 issued in 2009, the IASB proposed that an entity should make an accounting policy decision whether to classify interest and penalties payable to tax authorities as tax expense.[7]

In our view:

- Where interest and penalties are not deductible in determining taxable income, there are reasonable grounds for treating them as either part of the tax charge or as an expense in arriving at profit before tax. Entities should determine their accounting policy for such items and apply it consistently.
- Where interest and penalties are tax-deductible, we believe that it is more generally appropriate to treat them as an expense in arriving at profit before tax.

4.5 Effectively tax-free entities

In a number of jurisdictions, certain classes of entity are exempt from income tax, and accordingly are not within the scope of IAS 12.

However, a more typical, and more complex, situation is that tax legislation has the effect that certain classes of entities, whilst not formally designated as 'tax-free' in law, are nevertheless exempt from tax provided that they meet certain conditions that, in practice, they are almost certain to meet. A common example is that, in many jurisdictions, some investment vehicles pay no tax, provided that they distribute all, or a minimum percentage, of their earnings to investors.

Accounting for the tax affairs of such entities raises a number of challenges, as discussed further at 8.5.1 below.

5 CURRENT TAX

Current tax is the amount of income taxes payable (recoverable) in respect of the taxable profit (tax loss) for a period. *[IAS 12.5].*

Current tax for current and prior periods should, to the extent unpaid, be recognised as a liability. If the amount already paid in respect of current and prior periods exceeds the amount due for those periods, the excess should be recognised as an asset. *[IAS 12.12].*

The benefit relating to a tax loss that can be carried back to recover current tax of a previous period should be recognised as an asset. When a tax loss is used to recover current tax of a previous period, an entity recognises the benefit as an asset in the period in which the tax loss occurs because it is probable that the benefit will flow to the entity and the benefit can be reliably measured. *[IAS 12.13-14].*

Current tax should be measured at the amount expected to be paid to or recovered from the tax authorities by reference to tax rates and laws that have been enacted or substantively enacted by the end of the reporting period. *[IAS 12.46].*

5.1 Enacted or substantively enacted tax legislation

IAS 12 requires current tax to be measured using tax rates or laws enacted 'or substantively enacted' at the end of the reporting period. The standard comments that, in some jurisdictions, announcements of tax rates (and tax laws) by the government have the substantive effect of actual enactment, which may follow the announcement by a period of several months. In these circumstances, tax assets and liabilities are measured using the announced tax rate (and tax laws). *[IAS 12.48].*

IAS 12 gives no guidance as to how this requirement is to be interpreted in different jurisdictions and both the IASB and the Interpretations Committee have resisted various requests for it. In most jurisdictions, however, a consensus has emerged as to the meaning of 'substantive enactment' for that jurisdiction (see 5.1.1 below). Nevertheless, apparently similar legislative processes in different jurisdictions may give rise to different treatments under IAS 12. For example, in most jurisdictions, tax legislation requires the formal approval of the head of state in order to become law. However, in some jurisdictions the head of state has real executive power (and could potentially not approve the legislation), whereas in others the head of state has a more ceremonial role (and cannot practically fail to approve the legislation).

The view tends to be that in those jurisdictions where the head of state has executive power, legislation is not substantively enacted until actually enacted by the head of state. Where, however, the head of state's powers are more ceremonial, substantive enactment is generally regarded as occurring at the stage of the legislative process where no further amendment is possible.

5.1.1 Meaning of substantive enactment in various jurisdictions

The following table summarises the meaning of 'substantive enactment' in various jurisdictions as generally understood in those jurisdictions.[8]

Country	Point of substantive enactment
United Kingdom	A Finance Bill has been passed by the House of Commons and is awaiting only passage through the House of Lords and Royal Assent. Alternatively, a resolution having statutory effect has been passed under the Provisional Collection of Taxes Act 1968.
Canada	If there is a majority government, substantive enactment generally occurs with respect to proposed amendments to the Federal Income Tax Act when detailed draft legislation has been tabled for first reading in Parliament. If there is a minority government, proposed amendments to the Federal Income Tax Act would not normally be considered to be substantively enacted until the proposals have passed the third reading in the House of Commons.
Australia	The Bill has passed through both Houses of Parliament (but before Royal Assent).
France	Signature of the legislation by the executive.
Germany	The Bundestag and Bundesrat pass the legislation.
Japan	The Diet passes the legislation.
United States	The legislation is signed by the President or there is a successful override vote by both houses of Congress.
South Africa	Changes in tax rates not inextricably linked to other changes in tax law are substantively enacted when announced in the Minister of Finance's Budget statement. Other changes in tax rates and tax laws are substantively enacted when approved by Parliament and signed by the President.

5.2 Uncertain tax positions

In recording the 'amount expected to be paid or recovered' as required by IAS 12, the entity will need to have regard to any uncertain tax positions. 'Uncertain tax position' is a term not defined in IAS 12, but is generally understood in practice to refer to an item, the tax treatment of which is unclear or is a matter of unresolved dispute between the reporting entity and the relevant tax authority. An uncertain tax position generally occurs where there is an uncertainty as to the meaning of the tax law, or to the applicability of the law to a particular transaction, or both.

Accounting for uncertain tax positions is a particularly challenging aspect of accounting for tax, discussed further at 9 below.

5.3 'Prior year adjustments' of previously presented tax balances and expense (income)

The determination of the tax liability for all but the most straightforward entities is a complex process. It may be several years after the end of a reporting period before the tax liability for that period is finally agreed with the tax authorities and settled.

Therefore, the tax liability initially recorded at the end of the reporting period to which it relates is no more than a best estimate at that time, which will typically require revision in subsequent periods until the liability is finally settled.

Tax practitioners often refer to such revisions as 'prior year adjustments' and regard them as part of the overall tax charge or credit for the current reporting period whatever their nature. However, for financial reporting purposes, the normal provisions of IAS 8 – *Accounting Policies, Changes in Accounting Estimates and Errors* (see Chapter 3) apply to tax balances and the related expense (income). Therefore, the nature of any revision to a previously stated tax balance should be considered to determine whether the revision represents:

- a correction of a material prior period error (in which case it should be accounted for retrospectively, with a restatement of comparative amounts and, where applicable, the opening balance of assets, liabilities and equity at the start of the earliest period presented) *[IAS 8.42]*; or
- a refinement in the current period of an estimate made in a previous period (in which case it should be accounted for in the current period). *[IAS 8.36]*.

In some cases the distinction is clear. If, for example, the entity used an incorrect substantively enacted tax rate (see 5.1 above) to calculate the liability in a previous period, the correction of that rate would – subject to materiality – be a prior year adjustment. A more difficult area is the treatment of accounting changes to reflect the resolution of uncertain tax positions (see 5.2 above). These are in practice almost always treated as measurement adjustments in the current period. However, a view could be taken that the eventual denial, or acceptance, by the tax authorities of a position taken by the taxpayer indicates that one or other party (or both of them) were previously taking an erroneous view of the tax law. As with other aspects of accounting for uncertain tax positions, this is an area where considerable judgement may be required.

5.4 Intra-period allocation, presentation and disclosure

The allocation of current tax income and expense to components of total comprehensive income and equity is discussed at 10 below. The presentation and disclosure of current tax income expense and assets and liabilities are discussed at 13 and 14 below.

6 DEFERRED TAX – TAX BASES AND TEMPORARY DIFFERENCES

All deferred tax liabilities and many deferred tax assets represent the tax effects of temporary differences. Therefore, the first step in measuring deferred tax is to identify all temporary differences. The discussion in section 6 of this Chapter addresses only whether a temporary difference exists. It does not necessarily follow that deferred tax is recognised in respect of that difference, since there are a number of situations, discussed at 7 below, in which IAS 12 prohibits the recognition of deferred tax on a temporary difference.

Temporary differences are differences between the carrying amount of an asset or liability in the statement of financial position and its *tax base*. Temporary differences may be either:

- *taxable temporary differences*, which result in taxable amounts in determining taxable profit (tax loss) of future periods when the carrying amount of the asset or liability is recovered or settled; or
- *deductible temporary differences*, which result in amounts that are deductible in determining taxable profit (tax loss) of future periods when the carrying amount of the asset or liability is recovered or settled.

The *tax base* of an asset or liability is 'the amount attributed to that asset or liability for tax purposes'. *[IAS 12.5]*.

In consolidated financial statements, temporary differences are determined by comparing the carrying amounts of an asset or liability in the consolidated financial statements with the appropriate tax base. The appropriate tax base is determined:

- in those jurisdictions in which a consolidated tax return is filed, by reference to that return; and
- in other jurisdictions, by reference to the tax returns of each entity in the group. *[IAS 12.11]*.

As the definition of tax base is the one on which all the others relating to deferred tax ultimately depend, understanding it is key to a proper interpretation of IAS 12. A more detailed discussion follows at 6.1 and 6.2 below. However, the overall effect of IAS 12 can be summarised as follows:

A *taxable* temporary difference will arise when:

- *The carrying amount of an asset is higher than its tax base*

  For example, an item of PP&E is recorded in the financial statements at €8,000, but has a tax base of only €7,000. In future periods tax will be paid on €1,000 more profit than is recognised in the financial statements (since €1,000 of the remaining accounting depreciation is not tax-deductible).
- *The carrying amount of a liability is lower than its tax base*

  For example, a loan payable of €100,000 is recorded in the financial statements at €99,000, net of issue costs of €1,000 which have already been allowed for tax purposes (so that the loan is regarded as having a tax base of €100,000 – see 6.2.1.B below). In future periods tax will be paid on €1,000 more profit than is recognised in the financial statements (since the €1,000 issue costs will be charged to the income statement but not be eligible for further tax deductions).

Conversely, a *deductible* temporary difference will arise when:

- *The carrying amount of an asset is lower than its tax base*

  For example, an item of PP&E is recorded in the financial statements at €7,000, but has a tax base of €8,000. In future periods tax will be paid on €1,000 less profit than is recognised in the financial statements (since tax deductions will be claimed in respect of €1,000 more depreciation than is charged to the income statement in those future periods).

- *The carrying amount of a liability is higher than its tax base*

  For example, the financial statements record a liability for unfunded pension costs of €2 million. A tax deduction is available only as cash is paid to settle the liability (so that the liability is regarded as having a tax base of nil – see 6.2.2.A below). In future periods tax will be paid on €2 million less profit than is recognised in the financial statements (since tax deductions will be claimed in respect of €2 million more expense than is charged to the income statement in those future periods).

This may be summarised in the following table.

Asset/liability	Carrying amount higher or lower than tax base?	Nature of temporary difference	Resulting deferred tax (if recognised)
Asset	Higher	Taxable	Liability
Asset	Lower	Deductible	Asset
Liability	Higher	Deductible	Asset
Liability	Lower	Taxable	Liability

6.1 Tax base

6.1.1 Tax base of assets

The tax base of an asset is the amount that will be deductible for tax purposes against any taxable economic benefits that will flow to an entity when it recovers the carrying amount of the asset. If those economic benefits will not be taxable, the tax base of the asset is equal to its carrying amount. *[IAS 12.7].*

In some cases the 'tax base' of an asset is relatively obvious. In the case of a tax-deductible item of PP&E, it is the tax-deductible amount of the asset at acquisition less tax depreciation already claimed (see Example 29.1 at 1.2 above). Other items, however, require more careful analysis.

For example, an entity may have accrued interest receivable of €1,000 that will be taxed only on receipt. When the asset is recovered, all the cash received is subject to tax. In other words, the amount deductible for tax on recovery of the asset, and therefore its tax base, is nil. Another way of arriving at the same conclusion might be to consider the amount at which the tax authority would recognise the receivable in notional financial statements for the entity prepared under tax law. At the end of the reporting period the receivable would not be recognised in such notional financial statements, since the interest has not yet been recognised for tax purposes.

Conversely, an entity may have a receivable of €1,000 the recovery of which is not taxable. In this case, the tax base is €1,000 on the rule above that, where realisation of an asset will not be taxable, the tax base of the asset is equal to its carrying amount. This applies irrespective of whether the asset concerned arises from:

- a transaction already recognised in total comprehensive income and already subject to tax on initial recognition (e.g. in most jurisdictions, a sale);
- a transaction already recognised in total comprehensive income and exempt from tax (e.g. tax-free dividend income); or
- a transaction not affecting total comprehensive income at all (e.g. the principal of a loan receivable). *[IAS 12.7].*

The effect of deeming the tax base of the €1,000 receivable to be equal to its carrying amount will be that the temporary difference associated with it is nil, and that no deferred tax is recognised in respect of it. This is appropriate given that, in the first case, the debtor represents a sale that has already been taxed and, in the second and third cases, the debtors represent items that are outside the scope of tax.

6.1.2 *Tax base of liabilities*

The tax base of a liability is its carrying amount, less any amount that will be deductible for tax purposes in respect of that liability in future periods. In the case of revenue which is received in advance, the tax base of the resulting liability is its carrying amount, less any amount of the revenue that will not be taxable in future periods. *[IAS 12.8].*

As in the case of assets, the tax base of some items is relatively obvious. For example, an entity may have recognised a provision for environmental damage of CHF5 million, which will be deductible for tax purposes only on payment. The liability has a tax base of nil. Its carrying amount is CHF5 million, which is also the amount that will be deductible for tax purposes on settlement in future periods. The difference between these two (equal) amounts – the tax base – is nil. Another way of arriving at the same conclusion might be to consider the amount at which the tax authority would recognise the liability in notional financial statements for the entity prepared under tax law. At the end of the reporting period the liability would not be recognised in such notional financial statements, since the expense has not yet been recognised for tax purposes.

Likewise, if the entity records revenue of £1,000 received in advance that was taxed on receipt, its tax base is nil. Under the definition above, the carrying amount is £1,000, none of which is taxable in future periods. The tax base is the difference between the £1,000 carrying amount and the amount *not* taxed in future periods (£1,000) – i.e. nil.

Again, if we were to consider a notional statement of financial position of the entity drawn up by the tax authorities under tax law, this liability would not be included, since the relevant amount would, in the notional tax financial statements, have already been taken to income.

An entity may have a liability of (say) €1,000 that will attract no tax deduction when it is settled. In this case, the tax base is €1,000 (on the analogy with the rule in 6.1.1 above that where, realisation of an asset will not be taxable, the tax base of the asset is equal to its carrying amount). This applies irrespective of whether the liability concerned arises from:

- a transaction already recognised in total comprehensive income and already subject to a tax deduction on initial recognition (e.g. in most jurisdictions, the cost of goods sold or accrued expenses);
- a transaction already recognised in total comprehensive income and outside the scope of tax (e.g. non tax-deductible fines and penalties); or
- a transaction not affecting total comprehensive income at all (e.g. the principal of a loan payable). *[IAS 12.8]*.

This is appropriate given that, in the first case, the liability represents a cost that has already been deducted for tax purposes and, in the second and third cases, the liabilities represent items that are outside the scope of tax.

6.1.3 Assets and liabilities whose tax base is not immediately apparent

IAS 12 indicates that where the tax base of an asset or liability is not immediately apparent, it is helpful to consider the fundamental principle on which the standard is based: an entity should, with certain limited exceptions, recognise a deferred tax liability (asset) wherever recovery or settlement of the carrying amount of an asset or liability would make future tax payments larger (smaller) than they would be if such recovery or settlement were to have no tax consequences. *[IAS 12.10]*. In other words: provide for the tax that would be payable or receivable if the assets and liabilities in the statement of financial position were to be recovered or settled at book value.

The implication of this is that in the basic 'equation' of IAS 12, i.e.

carrying amount – tax base = temporary difference,

the true unknown is not in fact the temporary difference (as implied by the definitions of tax base and temporary difference) but the tax base (as implied by paragraph 10).

It will be apparent from the more detailed discussion at 6.2 below that this clarification is particularly relevant to determining the tax bases of certain financial liabilities, which often do not fit the general 'formula' of carrying amount less amount deductible on settlement.

6.1.4 Tax base of items not recognised as assets or liabilities in financial statements

Certain items are not recognised as assets or liabilities in financial statements, but may nevertheless have a tax base. Examples may include:

- research costs (which are required to be expensed immediately by IAS 38 – *Intangible Assets* – see Chapter 17);
- the cost of equity-settled share-based payment transactions (which under IFRS 2 – *Share-based Payment* – give rise to an increase in equity and not a liability – see Chapter 30); and
- goodwill deducted from equity under previous IFRS or national GAAP.

Where such items are tax-deductible, their tax base is the difference between their carrying amount (i.e. nil) and the amount deductible in future periods. *[IAS 12.9]*. This may seem somewhat contrary to the definition of tax base, in which it is inherent that, in order for an item to have a tax base, that item must be an asset or liability, whereas none of the items above was ever recognised as an asset.[9] The implicit argument is that all these items were initially (and very briefly!) recognised as assets before being immediately written off in full.

Local tax legislation sometimes gives rise to liabilities that have a tax base but no carrying amount. For example, a subsidiary of the reporting entity may receive a tax deduction for a provision that has been recognised in the individual financial statements of that subsidiary prepared under local accounting principles. For the purposes of the entity's consolidated financial statements, however, the provision does not currently satisfy the recognition requirements of IAS 37, but is likely to do so in the future. In such situations we consider it appropriate to regard the tax deduction received as giving rise to a deferred tax liability (by virtue of there being a provision with a tax base but no carrying amount) rather than current tax income.

Similar situations may arise where local tax legislation permits deductions for certain expenditure determined according to tax legislation without reference to any financial statements. Again, in those cases where an equivalent amount of expenditure is likely to be recognised in the financial statements at a later date, we would regard it as appropriate to regard the tax deduction received as giving rise to a deferred tax liability rather than current tax income.

6.1.5 Equity items with a tax base

The definition of 'tax base' refers to the tax base of an 'asset or liability'. This begs the question of whether IAS 12 regards equity items as having a tax base and therefore whether deferred tax can be recognised in respect of equity instruments (since deferred tax is the tax relating to temporary differences which, by definition, can only arise on items with a tax base – see above).

In February 2003 the Interpretations Committee considered this issue. It drew attention to the IASB's proposal at that time to amend the definition of 'tax base' so as to refer not only to assets and liabilities but also equity instruments as supporting the view that deferred tax should be recognised where appropriate on equity instruments. This was effectively the approach proposed in the exposure draft ED/2009/2 (see 1.3 above).[10]

An alternative analysis might be that equity items do not have a tax base, but that any tax effects of them are to be treated as items that are not recognised as assets or liabilities but nevertheless have a tax base (see 6.1.4 above).

Given the lack of explicit guidance in the current version of IAS 12 either analysis may be acceptable, provided that it is applied consistently. This is reflected in a number of the examples in the remainder of this Chapter.

6.1.6 *Items with more than one tax base*

Some assets and liabilities have more than one tax base, depending on the manner in which they are realised or settled. These are discussed further at 8.4 below.

6.1.7 *Tax bases disclaimed or with no economic value*

In some situations an entity may choose not to claim an available deduction for an item as part of an overall tax planning strategy. In other cases, a deduction available as a matter of tax law may have no real economic effect – for example because the deduction will increase a pool of brought forward tax losses which the entity does not expect to recover in the foreseeable future.

In our view, the fact that the entity chooses not to take advantage of a potential tax deduction, or that such a deduction would have no real economic effect in the foreseeable future, does not mean that the asset to which the deduction relates has no tax base. While such considerations will be relevant to determining whether a deductible temporary difference gives rise to a recoverable deferred tax asset (see 7.4 below), the tax base of an asset is determined by reference to the amount attributed to the item by tax law. *[IAS 12.5]*.

6.2 Examples of temporary differences

The following are examples of taxable temporary differences, deductible temporary differences and items where the tax base and carrying value are the same so that there is no temporary difference. They are mostly based on those given in IAS 12, *[IAS 12.17-20, 26, IE.A-C]*, but include several others that are encountered in practice. It will be seen that a number of categories of assets and liabilities may give rise to either taxable or deductible temporary differences.

A temporary difference will not always result in a deferred tax asset or liability being recorded under IAS 12, since the difference may be subject to other provisions of the standard restricting the recognition of deferred tax assets and liabilities, which are discussed at 7 below. Moreover, even where deferred tax is recognised, it does not necessarily create tax income or expense, but may instead give rise to additional goodwill or bargain purchase gain in a business combination, or to a movement in equity.

6.2.1 *Taxable temporary differences*

6.2.1.A *Transactions that affect profit or loss*

- *Interest received in arrears*

  An entity with a financial year ending on 31 December 2014 holds a medium-term cash deposit on which interest of €10,000 is received annually on 31 March. The interest is taxed in the year of receipt. At 31 December 2014, the entity recognises a receivable of €7,000 in respect of interest accrued but not yet received. The receivable has a tax base of nil, since its recovery has tax consequences and no tax deductions are available in respect of it. The temporary difference associated with the receivable is €7,000 (€7,000 carrying amount less nil tax base).

- *Sale of goods taxed on a cash basis*

  An entity has recorded revenue from the sale of goods of €40,000, together with a cost of the goods sold of €35,000, since the goods have been delivered. However, the transaction is taxed in the following financial year when the cash from the sale is collected.

  The entity will have recognised a receivable of €40,000 for the sale. The receivable has a tax base of nil, since its recovery has tax consequences and no tax deductions are available in respect of it. The temporary difference associated with the receivable is €40,000 (€40,000 carrying amount less nil tax base).

  There is also a deductible temporary difference of €35,000 associated with the (now derecognised) inventory, which has a carrying amount of zero but a tax base of €35,000 (since it will attract a tax deduction of €35,000 when the sale is taxed) – see 6.2.2.A below.

- *Depreciation of an asset accelerated for tax purposes*

  An entity with has an item of PP&E whose cost is fully tax deductible, but with deductions being given over a period shorter than the period over which the asset is being depreciated under IAS 16 – *Property, Plant and Equipment*. At the reporting date, the asset has been depreciated to £500,000 for financial reporting purposes but to £300,000 for tax purposes.

  Recovery of the PP&E has tax consequences since, although there is no deduction for accounting depreciation in the tax return, the PP&E is recovered through future taxable profits. There is a taxable temporary difference of £200,000 between the carrying value of the asset (£500,000) and its tax base (£300,000).

- *Capitalised development costs already deducted for tax*

  An entity incurred development costs of $1 million during the year ended 31 December 2014. The costs were fully deductible for tax purposes in the tax return for that period, but were recognised as an intangible asset under IAS 38 in the financial statements. The amount carried forward at 31 December 2014 is $800,000.

  Recovery of the intangible asset through use has tax consequences since, although there is no deduction for accounting amortisation in the tax return, the asset is recovered through future profits which will be taxed. There is a taxable temporary difference of $800,000 between the carrying value of the asset ($800,000) and its tax base (nil). Although the expenditure to create the asset is tax-deductible in the current period, its tax base is the amount deductible in *future* periods, which is nil, since all deductions were made in the tax return for 2014.

  A similar analysis would apply to prepaid expenses that have already been deducted on a cash basis in determining the taxable profit of the current or previous periods.

6.2.1.B *Transactions that affect the statement of financial position*

- *Non-deductible and partially deductible assets*

  An entity acquires a building for €1 million. Any accounting depreciation of the building is not deductible for tax purposes, and no deduction will be available for tax purposes when the asset is sold or scrapped.

  Recovery of the building, whether in use or on sale, nevertheless has tax consequences since the building is recovered through future taxable profits of €1 million. There is a taxable temporary difference of €1 million between the carrying value of the asset (€1 million) and its tax base of zero.

  A similar analysis applies to an asset which, when acquired, is deductible for tax purposes, but for an amount lower than its cost. The difference between the cost and the amount deductible for tax purposes is a taxable temporary difference.

- *Deductible loan transaction costs*

  A borrowing entity records a loan at £9.5 million, being the proceeds received of £10 million (which equal the amount due at maturity), less transaction costs of £500,000, which are deducted for tax purposes in the period when the loan was first recognised. For financial reporting purposes, IAS 39 requires the costs, together with interest and similar payments, to be accrued over the period to maturity using the effective interest method.

  Inception of the loan gives rise to a taxable temporary difference of £500,000, being the difference between the carrying amount of the loan (£9.5 million) and its tax base (£10 million). This tax base does not conform to the general definition of the tax base of a liability – i.e. the carrying amount, less any amount that will be deductible for tax purposes in respect of that liability in future periods (see 6.1.2 above).

  The easiest way to derive the correct tax base is to construct a notional statement of financial position prepared by the tax authorities according to tax law. This would show a liability for the full £10 million (since the amortisation of the issue costs that has yet to occur in the financial statements has already occurred in the notional tax authority financial statements). This indicates that the tax base of the loan is £10 million.

  A far simpler analysis for the purposes of IAS 12 might have been that the £9.5 million carrying amount comprises a loan of £10 million (with a tax base of £10 million, giving rise to temporary difference of zero) offset by prepaid transaction costs of £500,000 (with a tax base of zero, giving rise to a taxable temporary difference of £500,000). However, this is inconsistent with the analysis in IAS 39 that the issue costs are an integral part of the carrying value of the loan.

  The consequence of recognising a deferred tax liability in this case is that the tax deduction for the transaction costs is recognised in profit or loss, not on inception of the loan, but as the costs are recognised through the effective interest method in future periods.

- *Non-deductible loan transaction costs*

  As in the immediately preceding example, a borrowing entity records a loan at £9.5 million, being the proceeds received of £10 million (which equal the amount due at maturity), less transaction costs of £500,000. In this case, however, the transaction costs are not deductible in determining the taxable profit of future, current or prior periods. For financial reporting purposes, IAS 39 requires the costs to be accrued over the period to maturity using the effective interest method.

  Just as in the preceding example (and perhaps rather counter-intuitively, given that the costs are non-deductible) inception of the loan gives rise to a taxable temporary difference of £500,000, being the difference between the carrying amount of the loan (£9.5 million) and its tax base (£10 million). This is because a notional statement of financial position prepared by the tax authorities according to tax law would show a liability for the full £10 million, since the transaction costs would never have been recorded (as they never occurred for tax purposes).

- *Liability component of compound financial instrument*

  An entity issues a convertible bond for €5 million which, in accordance with the requirements of IAS 32 – *Financial Instruments: Presentation*, is analysed as comprising a liability component of €4.6 million and a residual equity component of €400,000. If the entity were to settle the liability for €4.6 million it would be liable to tax on €400,000 (€5 million less €4.6 million). Therefore the tax base of the liability is €5 million and there is a taxable temporary difference of €400,000 between this and the carrying amount of the liability component. This is discussed further at 7.2.8 below.

6.2.1.C Revaluations

- *Financial assets and property carried at valuation*

  An entity holds investments, accounted for at fair value through profit or loss, with a carrying amount of CHF2 million and an original cost (and tax base) of CHF1.3 million. There is a taxable temporary difference of CHF700,000 associated with the investments, being the amount on which the entity would pay tax if the investments were realised at their carrying value.

  A similar analysis would apply to investment property or PP&E carried at a value that exceeds cost, where no equivalent adjustment is made for tax purposes.

6.2.1.D Tax re-basing

- *Withdrawal of tax depreciation for classes of PP&E*

  An entity holds buildings with a carrying amount of £15 million and a tax base of £12 million, giving rise to a taxable temporary difference of £3 million. As part of a general fiscal reform package introduced by the government, future tax deductions for the buildings (their tax base) are reduced to £1 million. This increases the taxable temporary difference by £11 million to £14 million.

6.2.1.E Business combinations and consolidation

- *Fair value adjustments*

  Where the carrying amount of an asset is increased to fair value in a business combination, but no equivalent adjustment is made for tax purposes, a taxable temporary difference arises just as on the revaluation of an asset (see 6.2.1.C above).

- *Non-deductible or partially-deductible goodwill*

  Where goodwill is not deductible, or only partially deductible, in determining taxable profit there will be a taxable temporary difference between the carrying amount of the goodwill and its tax base, similar to that arising on a non-deductible or partially-deductible asset (see 6.2.1.B above).

- *Intragroup transactions*

  Although intragroup transactions are eliminated in consolidated financial statements, they may give rise to temporary differences. An entity in a group (A) might sell inventory with a cost and tax base of £1,000 to another group entity (B) for £900, which becomes the cost and tax base to B. If the carrying value in the consolidated financial statements remains £1,000 (i.e. the inventory is not actually impaired, notwithstanding the intragroup sale at a loss), a new taxable temporary difference of £100 emerges in the consolidated financial statements between the carrying value of £1,000 and the new tax base of £900.

- *Undistributed earnings of group investments*

  A parent entity P holds an investment in subsidiary S. Retained earnings of $1 million relating to S are included in the consolidated financial statements of P. S must pay a non-refundable withholding tax on any distribution of earnings to P. There is therefore a taxable temporary difference in the consolidated financial statements of $1 million associated with the net assets representing the retained earnings, since their recovery (in the form of distribution to the parent) has tax consequences, with no offsetting tax deductions.

  Similar temporary differences may arise on the retained earnings of branches, associates and joint arrangements.

6.2.1.F Foreign currency differences

- *Translation of foreign subsidiary to presentation currency*

  A UK entity acquires the equity of a French entity, which therefore becomes its subsidiary, for €10 million. For UK tax purposes, the tax base of the investment is £8 million (the spot-rate equivalent of €10 million at the date of acquisition). The presentation currency of the UK entity's consolidated financial statements is sterling.

  Between the date of acquisition and the first reporting date, the French entity makes no gains or losses, such that its net assets and goodwill as included in the consolidated financial statements, expressed in euros, remain €10 million.

However, the exchange rate has moved, so that the sterling equivalent of €10 million at the reporting date, included in the consolidated statement of financial position, is £9 million.

This gives rise to a £1 million taxable temporary difference between the £9 million carrying value of the investment and its £8 million tax base.

- *Functional currency different from currency used to compute tax*

  On 1 January 2014 an entity which, under IAS 21 – *The Effects of Changes in Foreign Exchange Rates*, has determined its functional currency as US dollars (see Chapter 15), purchases plant for $1 million, which will be depreciated to its estimated residual value of zero over 10 years. The entity is taxed in the local currency LC, and is entitled to receive tax deductions for the depreciation charged in the financial statements. The exchange rate is $1=LC2 at 1 January 2014 (so that the cost of the asset for local tax purposes is LC2 million). The exchange rate at 31 December 2014 is $1=LC2.5.

  At 31 December 2014 there is a taxable temporary difference of $180,000, being the difference between the net book value of the plant of $900,000 (cost $1,000,000 less depreciation $100,000) and its tax base of $720,000 (cost LC2,000,000 less depreciation LC200,000 = LC1,800,000 translated at year end rate of $1=LC2.5).

6.2.1.G Hyperinflation

A taxable temporary difference (similar to those in 6.2.1.F above) arises when non-monetary assets are restated in terms of the measuring unit current at the end of the reporting period under IAS 29 – *Financial Reporting in Hyperinflationary Economies* – but no equivalent adjustment is made for tax purposes.

6.2.2 Deductible temporary differences

6.2.2.A Transactions that affect profit of loss

- *Expenses deductible for tax on cash basis*

  An entity records a liability of €1 million for retirement benefit costs which are tax deductible only when paid. The tax base of the liability is zero, being its carrying amount (€1 million) less the amount deductible for tax purposes when the liability is settled (also €1 million). There is therefore a deductible temporary difference of €1 million (€1 million carrying amount less zero tax base) associated with the liability.

- *Depreciation of an asset delayed for tax purposes*

  An entity has an item of PP&E that originally cost £1 million. The cost is fully tax deductible, with deductions being given over a period longer than the period over which the asset is being depreciated under IAS 16. At the reporting date, the asset has been depreciated to £300,000 for financial reporting purposes but to only £500,000 for tax purposes.

  Recovery of the PP&E has tax consequences since, although there is no deduction for accounting depreciation in the tax return, the PP&E is recovered through future taxable profits of £300,000. There is a deductible temporary difference of £200,000 between the carrying value of the asset (£300,000) and its tax base (£500,000).

- *Sale of goods taxed on a cash basis*

  An entity has recorded revenue from the sale of goods of €40,000, together with a cost of the goods sold of €35,000, since the goods have been delivered. However, the transaction is taxed in the following financial year when the cash from the sale is collected.

  There is a deductible temporary difference of €35,000 associated with the (now derecognised) inventory, which has a carrying amount of zero but a tax base of €35,000 (since it will attract a tax deduction of €35,000 when the sale is taxed).

  There is also a taxable temporary difference of €40,000 associated with the receivable (see 6.2.1.A above).

- *Write-down of asset not deductible for tax purposes until realised*

  An entity purchases inventory for $1,000, which is also its tax base. The inventory is later written down to a net realisable value of $800. However, no loss is recognised for tax purposes until the inventory is sold. There is a deductible temporary difference of $200 between the $800 carrying amount of the inventory and its $1,000 tax base.

- *Deferred income taxed on receipt*

  In the year ended 31 December 2013, an entity received €2 million, being 5 years' rent of an investment property received in advance. In the statement of financial position as at 31 December, €1,800,000 is carried forward as deferred income. However, the whole €2 million is taxed in the tax return for the period.

  There is a deductible temporary difference of €1,800,000 associated with the deferred income, being its carrying amount (€1,800,000), less its tax base of zero, computed as the carrying amount (€1,800,000) less the amount not taxable in future periods (also €1,800,000 since the income has already been taxed).

- *Deferred non-taxable income*

  An entity receives a government grant of £1 million, of which £700,000 is carried forward in the statement of financial position as at the period end.

  There is a deductible temporary difference of £700,000 associated with the deferred income, being its carrying amount (£700,000), less its tax base of zero, computed as the carrying amount (£700,000) less the amount not taxable in future periods (also £700,000 since the income is tax free).

6.2.2.B *Transactions that affect the statement of financial position*

- *Asset deductible for more than cost*

  An entity invests NOK10 million in PP&E for which tax deductions of NOK13 million may be claimed. There is a deductible temporary difference of NOK3 million between the NOK10 million carrying value of the PP&E and its tax base of NOK13 million.

6.2.2.C Revaluations

- *Financial assets and property carried at valuation*

  An entity holds investments, accounted for at fair value through profit or loss, with a carrying amount of CHF2 million and an original cost (and tax base) of CHF2.5 million. There is a taxable temporary difference of CHF500,000 associated with the investments, being the amount for which the entity would receive a tax deduction if the investments were realised at their carrying value.

  A similar analysis would apply to investment property or PP&E carried at a value below cost, where no equivalent adjustment is made for tax purposes.

6.2.2.D Tax re-basing

- *Indexation of assets for tax purposes*

  An entity acquires land for $5 million, which is also its tax base at the date of purchase. A year later, as part of a general fiscal reform package introduced by the government, future tax deductions for the land (its tax base) are increased to $6 million. This creates a deductible temporary difference of $1 million in respect of the land.

6.2.2.E Business combinations and consolidation

- *Fair value adjustments*

  Where a liability is recognised at fair value in a business combination, but the liability is deductible for tax purposes only on settlement, a deductible temporary difference arises similar to that arising on the initial recognition of a liability for an expense deductible for tax on a cash basis (see 6.2.2.A above).

- *Intragroup transactions*

  Although intragroup transactions are eliminated in consolidated financial statements, they may give rise to deductible temporary differences. An entity in a group (A) might sell inventory with a cost and tax base of £1,000 to another group entity (B) for £1,200, which becomes the cost and tax base to B. Since the carrying value in the consolidated financial statements remains £1,000, a new deductible temporary difference of £200 emerges in the consolidated financial statements between the carrying value of £1,000 and the new tax base of £1,200.

6.2.2.F Foreign currency differences

- *Translation of foreign subsidiary to presentation currency*

  A UK entity acquires the equity of a French entity, which therefore becomes its subsidiary, for €10 million. For UK tax purposes, the tax base of the investment is £8 million (the spot-rate equivalent of €10 million at the date of acquisition). The presentation currency of the UK entity's consolidated financial statements is sterling.

  Between the date of acquisition and the first reporting date, the French entity makes no gains or losses, such that its net assets and goodwill as included in the consolidated financial statements, expressed in euros, remain €10 million.

However, the exchange rate has moved, so that the sterling equivalent of €10 million at the reporting date, included in the consolidated statement of financial position, is £7 million.

This gives rise to a £1 million deductible temporary difference between the £7 million carrying value of the investment and its £8 million tax base.

- *Functional currency different from currency used to compute tax*

  On 1 January 2014 an entity which, under IAS 21 – *The Effects of Changes in Foreign Exchange Rates*, has determined its functional currency as US dollars (see Chapter 15), purchases plant for $1 million, which will be depreciated to its estimated residual value of zero over 10 years. The entity is taxed in the local currency LC, and is entitled to receive tax deductions for the depreciation charged in the financial statements. The exchange rate is $1=LC2 at 1 January 2014 (so that the cost of the asset for local tax purposes is LC2 million). The exchange rate at 31 December 2014 is $1=LC1.8.

  At 31 December 2014 there is a deductible temporary difference of $100,000, being the difference between the net book value of the plant of $900,000 (cost $1,000,000 less depreciation $100,000) and its tax base of $1,000,000 (cost LC2,000,000 less depreciation LC200,000 = LC1,800,000 translated at year end rate of $1=LC1.8).

6.2.3 Assets and liabilities with no temporary difference (because tax base equals carrying amount)

- *Liability for expense already deducted for tax*

  An entity accrues £200,000 for electricity costs in the year ended 31 March 2013. The expense is deductible for tax in that period. The temporary difference associated with the liability is zero. This is calculated as the carrying amount of £200,000 less the tax base of £200,000, being the carrying amount (£200,000) less amount deductible for tax in future periods (zero).

- *Liability for expense never deductible for tax*

  An entity accrues €400,000 for a fine for environmental pollution, which is not deductible for tax. The temporary difference associated with the liability is zero. This is calculated as the carrying amount of €400,000 less the tax base of €400,000, being the carrying amount (€400,000) less amount deductible for tax in future periods (zero).

- *Loan repayable at carrying amount*

  An entity borrows $2 million. This is the carrying amount of the loan on initial recognition, which is the same as the amount repayable on final maturity of the loan. The temporary difference associated with the liability is zero. This is calculated as the carrying amount of $2 million less the tax base of $2 million, being the carrying amount ($2 million) less amount deductible for tax in future periods (zero).

- *Receivable for non-taxable income*

  In its separate financial statements an entity records a receivable for a £1 million dividend due from a subsidiary accounted for at cost. The dividend is not taxable. Accordingly it gives rise to a temporary difference of zero, since the tax base of any asset, the recovery of the carrying amount of which is not taxable, is taken to be the same as its carrying amount.

7 DEFERRED TAX – RECOGNITION

7.1 The basic principles

7.1.1 *Taxable temporary differences (deferred tax liabilities)*

IAS 12 requires a deferred tax liability to be recognised in respect of all taxable temporary differences except those arising from:

- the initial recognition of goodwill; or
- the initial recognition of an asset or liability in a transaction that:
  - is not a business combination; and
  - at the time of the transaction, affects neither accounting profit nor taxable profit (tax loss).

These exceptions to the recognition principles do not apply to taxable temporary differences associated with investments in subsidiaries, branches and associates, and interests in joint arrangements, which are subject to further detailed provisions of IAS 12 (see 7.5 below). *[IAS 12.15]*.

Examples of taxable temporary differences are given in 6.2.1 above.

7.1.2 *Deductible temporary differences (deferred tax assets)*

IAS 12 requires a deferred tax asset to be recognised in respect of all deductible temporary differences to the extent that it is probable that taxable profit will be available against which the deductible temporary difference will be utilised except those arising from the initial recognition of an asset or liability in a transaction that:

- is not a business combination; and
- at the time of the transaction, affects neither accounting profit nor taxable profit (tax loss). *[IAS 12.24]*.

IAS 12 does not define 'probable' in this context. However, it is generally understood that, as in other IFRSs, it should be taken to mean 'more likely than not'. The exposure draft ED/2009/2 (see 1.3 above) effectively clarified that this is the intended meaning.[11]

These exceptions to the recognition principles do not apply to deductible temporary differences associated with investments in subsidiaries, branches and associates, and interests in joint arrangements, which are subject to further detailed provisions of IAS 12 (see 7.5 below).

Examples of deductible temporary differences are given in 6.2.2 above.

7.1.3 Interpretation issues

7.1.3.A Accounting profit

The provisions of IAS 12 summarised above refer to a transaction that affects 'accounting profit'. In this context 'accounting profit' clearly means any item recognised in total comprehensive income, whether recognised in profit or loss or in other comprehensive income.

7.1.3.B Taxable profit 'at the time of the transaction'

The provisions of IAS 12 summarised above also refer to a transaction which affects taxable profit 'at the time of the transaction'. Strictly speaking, no transaction affects taxable profit 'at the time of the transaction', since the taxable profit is affected only when the relevant item is included (some time later) in the tax return for the period. It is clear, however, that the intended meaning is that the transaction that gives rise to the initial recognition of the relevant asset or liability affects the current tax liability for the accounting period in which the initial recognition occurs.

Suppose that, in the year ended 31 December 2013, an entity received €2 million, being 5 years' prepaid rent of an investment property. In the statement of financial position as at 31 December, €1,800,000 is carried forward as deferred income. The whole €2 million is taxed on receipt and will therefore be included in the tax return for the period, which is not filed until 2014.

It could be argued that, in a literal legal sense, the transaction 'affects taxable profit' only in 2014. For the purposes of IAS 12, however, the transaction is regarded as affecting taxable profit during 2013 (since it affects the current tax for that period). This gives rise to the recognition, subject to the restrictions discussed at 7.4 below, of a deferred tax asset based on a deductible temporary difference of €1,800,000 (see 6.2.2.A above).

7.2 The initial recognition exception

The exceptions (summarised in 7.1 above) from recognising the deferred tax effects of certain temporary differences arising on the initial recognition of some assets and liabilities are generally referred to as the 'initial recognition exception' or 'initial recognition exemption', sometimes abbreviated to 'IRE'. 'Exception' is the more accurate description, since a reporting entity is required to apply it, rather than having the option to do so implicit in the term 'exemption'.

The initial recognition exception has its origins in the now superseded 'income statement' approaches to accounting for deferred tax. Under these approaches, deferred tax was not recognised on so-called 'permanent differences' – items of income or expense that appeared in either the financial statements or the tax return, but not in both. The majority of transactions to which the initial recognition exception applies would have been regarded as permanent differences under income statement approaches of accounting for deferred tax.

The purpose of the initial recognition exception is most easily understood by considering the accounting consequences that would follow if it did not exist, as illustrated in Example 29.2 below.

Example 29.2: Rationale for initial recognition exception

An entity acquires an asset for €1,000 which it intends to use for five years and then scrap (i.e. the residual value is nil). The tax rate is 40%. Depreciation of the asset is not deductible for tax purposes. On disposal, any capital gain would not be taxable and any capital loss would not be deductible.

Although the asset is non-deductible, its recovery has tax consequences, since it will be recovered out of taxable income of €1,000 on which tax of €400 will be paid. The tax base of the asset it therefore zero, and a temporary difference of €1,000 arises on initial recognition of the asset.

Absent the initial recognition exception, the entity would recognise a deferred tax liability of €400 on initial recognition of the asset, being the taxable temporary difference of €1,000 multiplied by the tax rate of 40%. A debit entry would then be required to balance the credit for the liability.

One possibility might be to recognise tax expense of €400 in the statement of total comprehensive income. This would be meaningless, since the entity has clearly not suffered a loss simply by purchasing a non-deductible asset in an arm's length transaction for a price that (economically) must reflect the asset's non-deductibility.

A second possibility would be to gross up the asset by €400 to €1,400. However, IAS 12 states that to make such adjustments to the carrying value of the asset would make the financial statements 'less transparent'. *[IAS 12.22(c)].*

A third possibility (broadly the guidance provided under US GAAP) would be to gross up the asset to the amount that would rationally have been paid for it, had it been fully tax-deductible, and recognise a corresponding amount of deferred tax. As the asset is non-deductible, the €1,000 cost must theoretically represent the anticipated minimum *post*-tax return from the asset. In order to achieve a post-tax return of €1,000, an entity paying tax at 40% needs to earn pre-tax profits of €1,667 (€1,000/[1 – 0.4]). Therefore, the cost of an equivalent fully-deductible asset would, all else being equal, be €1,667. On this analysis, the entity would gross up the asset to €1,667 and recognise deferred tax of €667 (€1,667 @ 40%).

The fourth possibility, which is what is actually required by IAS 12, is not to provide for deferred tax at all, where to do so would lead to one of the three outcomes above. However, in cases where provision for the deferred tax on a temporary difference arising on initial recognition of an asset or liability would not lead to one of the outcomes above, the initial recognition exception does not apply. This is the case in a business combination or a transaction affecting taxable profit or accounting profit (or both).

- *Business combination*

  In a business combination, the corresponding accounting entry for a deferred tax asset or liability forms part of the goodwill arising or the bargain purchase gain recognised. No deferred tax income or expense is recorded.

- *Transaction affecting taxable profit or accounting profit*

  In a transaction affecting taxable profit or accounting profit (or both), the corresponding accounting entry for a deferred tax asset or liability is recorded as deferred tax income or expense.

  This ensures that the entity recognises all future tax consequences of recovering the assets, or settling the liabilities, recognised in the transaction. The effect of this on the statement of total comprehensive income is broadly to recognise items the tax effects of the various components of income and expenditure in the same period(s) in which those items are recognised for financial reporting purposes (as illustrated in 1.2.2 above).

In short, the initial recognition exception may simply be seen as the least bad of the four theoretically possible options for dealing with 'day one' temporary differences.

7.2.1 *Acquisition of tax losses*

The initial recognition exception applies only to deferred tax relating to temporary differences. It does not apply to tax assets, such as purchased tax losses, that do not arise from deductible temporary differences. The definition of 'deferred tax assets' (see 3 above) explicitly distinguishes between deductible temporary differences and unused losses and tax credits. *[IAS 12.5]*. There is therefore no restriction on the recognition of acquired tax losses other than the general criteria of IAS 12 for recognition of tax assets (see 7.4 below).

Under the general principles of IAS 12, acquired tax losses are initially recognised at the amount paid, subsequently re-assessed for recoverability (see 7.4.5 below) and re-measured accordingly (see 8 below). Changes in the recognised amount of acquired tax losses are generally recognised in profit or loss, on the basis that, as acquired losses, they do not relate to any pre-tax transaction previously accounted for by the entity (see 10 below). However, in some limited circumstances, changes to tax losses acquired as part of a business combination are required to be treated as an adjustment to goodwill (see 12.1.2 below).

7.2.2 *Initial recognition of goodwill*

7.2.2.A *Taxable temporary differences*

In many jurisdictions goodwill is not tax-deductible either as it is impaired or on ultimate disposal, such that it gives rise to a temporary difference equal to its carrying amount (representing its carrying amount less its tax base of zero).

It may well be that the shares in the acquired entity have a tax base equal to their cost so that, economically, an amount equal to the goodwill is deductible on disposal of those shares. However, accounting for the tax effects of the shares in an acquired subsidiary (or other significant group investment) is subject to separate provisions of IAS 12, which are discussed at 7.5 below.

The initial recognition exception for taxable temporary differences on goodwill prevents the grossing-up of goodwill that would otherwise occur. Goodwill is a function of all the net assets of the acquired business, including deferred tax. If deferred tax is provided for on goodwill, the goodwill itself is increased, which means that the deferred tax on the goodwill is increased further, which means that the goodwill increases again, and so on. Equilibrium is reached when the amount of goodwill originally recorded is grossed up by the fraction $1/(1 - t)$, where t is the entity's tax rate, expressed as a decimal fraction. For example, an entity that pays tax at 30% and recognises CU1,400 of goodwill before recognising deferred tax would (absent the initial recognition exception) increase the goodwill to CU2,000 and recognise a deferred tax liability of CU600 (which is 30% of the restated goodwill of CU2,000).

Chapter 29

IAS 12 takes the view that this would not be appropriate, since goodwill is intended to be a residual arising after fair values have been determined for the assets and liabilities acquired in a business combination, and recognition of deferred tax would increase that goodwill. *[IAS 12.21]*.

7.2.2.B Deductible temporary differences

Where the carrying amount of goodwill arising in a business combination is less than its tax base, a deductible temporary difference arises. IAS 12 requires a deferred tax asset to be recognised in respect of any deductible temporary difference, to the extent that it is probable that taxable profit will be available against which the temporary difference could be utilised. *[IAS 12.32A]*. This contrasts with the prohibition against recognising a deferred tax liability on any *taxable* temporary difference on initial recognition of goodwill (see 7.2.2.A above). A more general discussion of the criteria in IAS 12 for assessing the recoverability of deferred tax assets may be found at 7.4 below.

IAS 12 gives no guidance on the method to be used in calculating the resulting deferred tax asset, which is not entirely straightforward, as illustrated by the following example.

Example 29.3: Deferred tax asset on initial recognition of goodwill

An entity that pays tax at 40% recognises, in the initial accounting for a business combination, goodwill of €1,000. Tax deductions of €1,250 are given for the goodwill over a 5 year period.

One approach would be to adopt an iterative method similar to that described in 7.2.2.A above, whereby recognition of a deferred tax asset on goodwill leads to a reduction of the goodwill, which in turn will lead to a further increase in the deferred tax asset, and so on. Equilibrium is reached when the goodwill is adjusted to an amount equal to $(g - bt)/(1 - t)$, where:

- g is the amount of goodwill originally recorded (before recognising a deferred tax asset),
- b is the tax base of the goodwill, and
- t is the tax rate, expressed as a decimal fraction.

Under this method, the entity would record goodwill of €833 (being [€1,000 – 0.4 × €1,250] ÷ 0.6) and a deferred tax asset of €167. This represents a deductible temporary difference of €417 (comprising the tax base of €1,250 less the adjusted carrying amount of €833), multiplied by the tax rate of 40%. On any subsequent impairment or disposal of the goodwill, the entity would report an effective tax rate of 40% (the statutory rate), comprised of pre-tax expense of €833 and tax income of €333 (the real tax deduction of €500 (€1,250 @ 40%), less the write-off of the deferred tax asset of €167).

An alternative approach might be to record a deferred tax asset based on the carrying amount of goodwill before calculating the deferred tax asset, and adjust the goodwill only once, rather than undertaking the iterative reduction in the goodwill described in the previous paragraph. In the example above this would lead to the entity recording a deferred tax asset of €100 (representing 40% of the deductible temporary difference of €250 between the tax base of the goodwill of €1,250 and its original carrying amount of €1,000) and goodwill of €900. On any subsequent impairment or disposal of the goodwill the entity would report an effective tax rate of 44% (higher than the statutory rate), comprised of pre-tax expense of €900 and tax income of €400 (the real tax deduction of €500 (€1,250 @ 40%), less the write-off of the deferred tax asset of €100).

7.2.2.C Tax deductible goodwill

Where goodwill is tax-deductible, new temporary differences will arise after its initial recognition as a result of the interaction between tax deductions claimed and impairments (if any) of the goodwill in the financial statements. These temporary differences do not relate to the initial recognition of goodwill, and therefore deferred tax should be recognised on them, as illustrated by Example 29.14 at 7.2.4.C below. *[IAS 12.21B].*

7.2.3 Initial recognition of other assets and liabilities

Where a temporary difference arises on initial recognition of an asset or liability, its treatment depends on the circumstances which give rise to the recognition of the asset or liability.

If the temporary difference arises as the result of a business combination, deferred tax is recognised on the temporary difference with a corresponding adjustment to goodwill or any bargain purchase gain.

If the temporary difference arises in a transaction that gives rise to an accounting or taxable profit or loss, deferred tax is recognised on the temporary difference, giving rise to deferred tax expense or deferred tax income.

If the temporary difference arises in any other circumstances (i.e. neither in a business combination nor in a transaction that gives rise to an accounting or taxable profit or loss) no deferred tax is recognised. *[IAS 12.22].*

The application of the initial recognition exception to assets and liabilities is illustrated in Examples 29.4 to 29.7 below.

Example 29.4: Non-deductible PP&E

An entity acquires a building for €1 million. Any accounting depreciation of the building is not deductible for tax purposes, and no deduction will be available for tax purposes when the asset is sold or demolished.

Recovery of the building, whether in use or on sale, has tax consequences since the building is recovered through future taxable profits of €1 million. There is a taxable temporary difference of €1 million between the €1 million carrying value of the asset and its tax base of zero.

Under the initial recognition exception, no deferred tax liability is provided for. The non-deductibility of the asset is reflected in an effective tax rate higher than the statutory rate (assuming that all other components of pre-tax profit are taxed at the statutory rate) as the asset is depreciated in future periods.

If the asset had been acquired as part of a larger business combination, the initial recognition would not have applied. Deferred tax of would have been provided for, with a corresponding increase in goodwill. As the asset is depreciated, the deferred tax liability is released to deferred tax income in the income statement, as illustrated in Example 29.1 above. This results in an effective tax rate equal to the statutory rate (assuming that all other components of pre-tax profit are taxed at the statutory rate).

Example 29.5: Inception of loan with tax-deductible issue costs

A borrowing entity records a loan at £9.5 million, being the proceeds received of £10 million (which equal the amount due at maturity), less transaction costs of £500,000, which are deducted for tax purposes in the period when the loan is first recognised. For financial reporting purposes, IAS 39 requires the costs, together with interest and similar payments, to be accrued over the period to maturity using the effective interest method.

Inception of the loan gives rise to a taxable temporary difference of £500,000, being the difference between the carrying amount of the loan (£9.5 million) and its tax base (£10 million). This analysis is explained in more detail at 6.2.1.B above.

Initial recognition of the transaction costs gives rise to no accounting loss (because they are included in the carrying amount of the loan). However, there is a tax loss (since the costs are included in the tax return for the period of inception). Accordingly, the initial recognition exception does not apply and a deferred tax liability is recognised on the taxable temporary difference of £500,000.

Example 29.6: Inception of loan with non-deductible issue costs

A borrowing entity records a loan at £9.5 million, being the proceeds received of £10 million (which equal the amount due at maturity), less transaction costs of £500,000, which are not deductible for tax purposes either in the period when the loan is first recognised or subsequently. For financial reporting purposes, IAS 39 requires the costs, together with interest and similar payments, to be accrued over the period to maturity using the effective interest method.

Inception of the loan gives rise to a taxable temporary difference of £500,000, being the difference between the carrying amount of the loan (£9.5 million) and its tax base (£10 million). This analysis is explained in more detail at 6.2.1.B above.

Initial recognition of the transaction costs gives rise to no accounting loss (because they are included in the carrying amount of the loan) or tax loss (because in this case there is no deduction for the issue costs). Accordingly, the initial recognition exception applies and no deferred tax liability is recognised.

If the same loan (including the unamortised transaction costs) had been recognised as part of a larger business combination, the initial recognition exception would not have applied. Deferred tax of would have been provided for recognised on the taxable temporary difference of £500,000, with a corresponding increase in goodwill (or decrease in any bargain purchase gain).

Example 29.7: Purchase of PP&E subject to tax-free government grant

An entity acquires an item of PP&E for €1 million subject to a tax free government grant of €350,000. The asset is also fully-tax deductible (at €1 million). IAS 20 permits the grant to be accounted for either as deferred income or by deduction from the cost of the asset. Whichever treatment is followed, a deductible temporary difference arises:

- If the grant is accounted for as deferred income, there is a deductible temporary difference between the liability of €350,000 and its tax base of nil (carrying amount €350,000 less amount not taxed in future periods, also €350,000).
- If the grant is accounted for as a reduction in the cost of the PP&E, there is a deductible temporary difference between the carrying amount of the PP&E (€650,000) and its tax base (€1 million).

IAS 12 emphasises that the initial recognition exception applies, and no deferred tax asset should be recognised. *[IAS 12.33]*.

7.2.4 Changes to temporary differences after initial recognition

The initial recognition exception applies only to temporary differences arising on initial recognition of an asset or liability. It does not apply to new temporary differences that arise on the same asset or liability after initial recognition. When the exception has been applied to the temporary difference arising on initial recognition of an asset or liability, and there is a different temporary difference associated with that asset or liability at a subsequent date, it is necessary to analyse the temporary difference at that date between:

- any amount relating to the original temporary difference (on which no deferred tax is recognised); and
- the remainder, which has implicitly arisen after initial recognition of the asset or liability (on which deferred tax is recognised).

IAS 12 does not set out comprehensive guidance to be followed in making this analysis, but it does give a number of examples, from which the following general principles may be inferred:

- the new temporary difference is treated as part of the temporary difference arising on initial recognition to the extent that any change from the original temporary difference is due to:
  - the write-down (through depreciation, amortisation or impairment) of the original carrying amount of an asset with no corresponding change in the tax base (see 7.2.4.A below); or
  - the increase in the original carrying amount of a liability arising from the amortisation of any discount recognised at the time of initial recognition of that liability, with no corresponding change in the tax base (see 7.2.4.A below);
- the new temporary difference is regarded as arising after initial recognition to the extent that any change from the original temporary difference is due to:
  - a change in the carrying value of the asset or liability, other than for the reasons set out above (see 7.2.4.B below); or
  - a change in the tax base due to items being recorded on the tax return (see 7.2.4.C below); and
- where the change in the temporary difference results from a change in the tax base due to legislative change, IAS 12 provides no specific guidance, and more than one treatment may be possible (see 7.2.4.D below).

7.2.4.A Depreciation, amortisation or impairment of initial carrying value

The following are examples of transactions where the initial temporary difference changes as the result of the amortisation of the original carrying amount, so that the adjusted temporary difference is regarded as part of the temporary difference arising on initial recognition, rather than a new difference.

Example 29.8: Impairment of non-deductible goodwill

Goodwill of £10 million (not tax-deductible) arose on a business combination in 2007. In accordance with IAS 12 no deferred tax liability was recognised on the taxable temporary difference of £10 million that arose on initial recognition of the goodwill. During the year ended 31 December 2014, following an impairment test, the carrying amount of the goodwill is reduced to £6 million.

No deferred tax is recognised on the new temporary difference of £6 million, because it is part of the temporary difference arising on the initial recognition of the goodwill. *[IAS 12.21A].*

Example 29.9: Depreciation of non-deductible PP&E

During the year ended 31 March 2015 an entity acquires an item of PP&E for €1 million which it intends to use for 20 years, with no anticipated residual value. No tax deductions are available for the asset. In accordance with IAS 12 no deferred tax liability was recognised on the taxable temporary difference of €1 million that arises on initial recognition of the PP&E.

The entity's accounting policy is to charge a full year's depreciation in the year of purchase, so that the carrying amount of the asset at 31 March 2015 is €950,000. No deferred tax is recognised on the current temporary difference of €950,000, because it is part of the temporary difference arising on the initial recognition of the PP&E. *[IAS 12.22(c)]*.

Example 29.10: Amortisation of non-deductible loan issue costs

A borrowing entity records a loan at £9.5 million, being the proceeds received of £10 million (which equal the amount due at maturity), less transaction costs of £500,000, which are not deductible for tax purposes either in the period when the loan is first recognised or subsequently. For financial reporting purposes, IAS 39 requires the costs, together with interest and similar payments, to be accrued over the period to maturity using the effective interest method.

Inception of the loan gives rise to a taxable temporary difference of £500,000, being the difference between the carrying amount of the loan (£9.5 million) and its tax base (£10 million). This analysis is explained in more detail at 6.2.1.B above.

In accordance with IAS 12, no deferred tax liability was recognised on the taxable temporary difference of £10 million that arose on initial recognition of the loan.

One year later, the carrying amount of the loan is £9.7 million, comprising the proceeds received of £10 million (which equal the amount due at maturity), less unamortised transaction costs of £300,000. This gives rise to a new temporary difference of £300,000. No deferred tax is recognised on the current temporary difference, because it is part of the temporary difference arising on the initial recognition of the loan.

7.2.4.B Change in carrying value due to revaluation

As illustrated in Example 29.4 at 7.2.3 above, a temporary difference arises when a non tax-deductible asset is acquired. Where the asset is acquired separately (i.e. not as part of a larger business combination) in circumstances giving rise to neither an accounting nor a taxable profit or loss, no deferred tax liability is recognised for that temporary difference.

If such an asset is subsequently revalued, however, deferred tax is recognised on the new temporary difference arising as a result of the revaluation, since this does not arise on initial recognition of the asset, as illustrated in Examples 29.11 and 29.12.

Example 29.11: Revaluation of non-deductible asset (1)

On 1 January 2014 an entity paying tax at 30% acquires a non tax-deductible office building for €1,000,000 in circumstances in which IAS 12 prohibits recognition of the deferred tax liability associated with the temporary difference of €1,000,000.

Application of IAS 16 results in no depreciation being charged on the building.

On 1 January 2015 the entity revalues the building to €1,200,000. The temporary difference associated with the building is now €1,200,000, only €1,000,000 of which arose on initial recognition. Accordingly, the entity recognises a deferred tax liability based on the remaining temporary difference of €200,000 giving deferred tax expense at 30% of €60,000. This tax expense would be recognised in other comprehensive income (see 10 below).

Example 29.12: Revaluation of non-deductible asset (2)

On 1 January 2014 an entity paying tax at 30% acquires a non tax-deductible office building for €1,000,000 in circumstances in which IAS 12 prohibits recognition of the deferred tax liability associated with the temporary difference of €1,000,000. The building is depreciated over 20 years at €50,000 per year to a residual value of zero. The entity's financial year ends on 31 December.

At 1 January 2016, the carrying amount of the building is €900,000, and it is revalued upwards by €450,000 to its current market value of €1,350,000. As there is no change to the estimated residual value of zero, or to the life of the building, this will be depreciated over the next 18 years at €75,000 per year.

Following the revaluation, the temporary difference associated with the building is €1,350,000. Of this amount, only €900,000 arose on initial recognition, since €100,000 of the original temporary difference of €1,000,000 arising on initial recognition of the asset has been eliminated through depreciation of the asset (see 7.2.4.A above). The carrying amount (which equals the temporary difference, since the tax base is zero) and depreciation during the year ended 31 December 2016 may then be analysed as follows.

	Total carrying amount	*Arising on initial recognition*	*Arising on revaluation*
	€	€	€
1 January 2016	1,350,000	900,000	450,000
Depreciation[1]	75,000	50,000	25,000
31 December 2016	1,275,000	850,000	425,000

1 The depreciation is allocated pro-rata to the cost element and revalued element of the total carrying amount.

On 1 January 2016 the entity recognises a deferred tax liability based on the temporary difference of €450,000 arising on the revaluation (i.e. after initial recognition) giving a deferred tax expense of €135,000 (€450,000 @ 30%), recognised in other comprehensive income (see 10 below). This has the result that the effective tax rate shown in the financial statements for the revaluation is 30% (€450,000 gain with deferred tax expense of €135,000).

As can be seen from the table above, as at 31 December 2016, €425,000 of the total temporary difference arose after initial recognition. The entity therefore provides for deferred tax of €127,500 (€425,000 @ 30%), and deferred tax income of €7,500 (the reduction in the liability from €135,000 to €127,500) is recognised in profit or loss.

The deferred tax income can be explained as the tax effect at 30% of the €25,000 depreciation relating to the revalued element of the building (see table above).

7.2.4.C Change in tax base due to deductions in tax return

The following are examples of transactions where a new temporary difference emerges after initial recognition as the result of claiming tax deductions.

Example 29.13: Tax deduction for land

An entity that pays tax at 35% acquires land with a fair value of €5 million. Tax deductions of €100,000 per year may be claimed for the land for the next 30 years (i.e. the tax base of the land is €3 million). In accordance with IAS 12, no deferred tax liability is recognised on the taxable temporary difference of €2 million that arises on initial recognition of the land.

In the period in which the land is acquired, the entity claims the first €100,000 annual tax deduction, and the original cost of the land is not depreciated or impaired. The taxable temporary difference at the end of the period is therefore €2.1 million (cost €5.0 million less tax base €2.9 million). Of this, €2 million arose on initial recognition and no deferred tax is recognised on this. However, the remaining €100,000 of the gross temporary difference arose after initial recognition. Accordingly the entity recognises a deferred tax liability of €35,000 (€100,000 @ 35%).

The analysis if the land had been impaired would be rather more complicated. The general issue of the treatment of assets that are tax-deductible, but for less than their cost, is discussed at 7.2.6 below.

Example 29.14: Tax-deductible goodwill

On 1 January 2014 an entity with a tax rate of 35% acquires goodwill in a business combination with a cost of €1 million, which is deductible for tax purposes at a rate of 20% per year, starting in the year of acquisition.

During 2014 the entity claims the full 20% tax deduction and writes off €120,000 of the goodwill as the result of an impairment test. Thus at the end of 2014 the goodwill has a carrying amount of €880,000 and a tax base of €800,000. This gives rise to a taxable temporary difference of €80,000 that does not relate to the initial recognition of goodwill, and accordingly the entity recognises a deferred tax liability at 35% of €28,000.

If, during 2014, there had been no impairment of the goodwill, but the full tax deduction had nevertheless been claimed, at the end of the year the entity would have had goodwill with a carrying amount of €1 million and a tax base of €800,000. This would have given rise to a taxable temporary difference of €200,000 that does not relate to the initial recognition of goodwill, and accordingly the entity would have recognised a deferred tax liability at 35% of €70,000.

7.2.4.D Temporary difference altered by legislative change

Any change to the basis on which an item is treated for tax purposes alters the tax base of the item concerned. For example, if the government decides that an item of PP&E that was previously tax-deductible is no longer eligible for tax deductions, the tax base of the PP&E is reduced to zero. Under IAS 12, any change in tax base normally results in an immediate adjustment of any associated deferred tax asset or liability, and the recognition of a corresponding amount of deferred tax income or expense.

However, where such an adjustment to the tax base occurs in respect of an asset or liability in respect of which no deferred tax has previously been recognised because of the initial recognition exception, the treatment required by IAS 12 is not entirely clear. The issue is illustrated by Example 29.15 below.

Example 29.15: Asset non-deductible at date of acquisition later becomes deductible

During the year ended 31 March 2015 an entity acquired an item of PP&E for €1 million which it intends to use for 20 years, with no anticipated residual value. No tax deductions were available for the asset. In accordance with IAS 12 no deferred tax liability was recognised on the taxable temporary difference of €1 million that arose on initial recognition of the PP&E.

During the year ended 31 March 2016, the government announces that it will allow the cost of such assets to be deducted in arriving at taxable profit. The deductions will be allowed in equal annual instalments over a 10-year period. As at 31 March 2016, the carrying amount of the asset and its tax base are both €900,000. The carrying amount is the original cost of €1 million less two years' depreciation at €50,000 per year. The tax base is the original cost of €1 million less one year's tax deduction at €100,000 per year.

Prima facie, therefore, there is no temporary difference associated with the asset. However, the treatment required by IAS 12 in Examples 29.13 and 29.14 above would lead to the conclusion that this temporary difference of nil should in fact be analysed into:

- a taxable temporary difference of €900,000 arising on initial recognition of the asset (being the €1 million difference arising on initial recognition less the €100,000 depreciation charged), and
- a deductible temporary difference of €900,000 arising after initial recognition (representing the fact that, since initial recognition, the government increased the tax base by €1 million which has been reduced to €900,000 by the €100,000 tax deduction claimed in the current period).

This analysis indicates that no deferred tax liability should be recognised on the taxable temporary difference (since this arose on initial recognition), but a deferred tax asset should be recognised on the deductible temporary difference of €900,000 identified above. A contrary view would be that this is inappropriate, since it is effectively recognising a gain on the elimination of an income tax liability that was never previously recognised.

As far as the tax income and expense in profit or loss is concerned, the difference between the two approaches is one of timing. Under the analysis that the overall temporary difference of zero should be 'bifurcated' into an amount arising on initial recognition and an amount arising later, the change in legislation reduces income tax expense and the effective tax rate in the year of change. Under the analysis that the net temporary difference of zero is considered as a whole, the reduction in income tax expense and the effective tax rate is recognised prospectively over the remaining life of the asset.

In our view, the first approach ('bifurcation') is more consistent with the balance sheet approach of IAS 12, but, in the absence of specific guidance in the standard, the second approach is acceptable.

7.2.5 Intragroup transfers of assets with no change in tax base

In many tax jurisdictions the tax deductions for an asset are generally related to the cost of that asset to the legal entity that owns it. However, in some jurisdictions, where an asset is transferred between members of the same group within that jurisdiction, the tax base remains unchanged, irrespective of the consideration paid.

Therefore, where the consideration paid for an asset in such a case differs from its tax base, a temporary difference arises in the acquiring entity's separate financial statements on transfer of the asset. The initial recognition exception applies to any such temporary difference. A further complication is that the acquiring entity acquires an asset that, rather than conforming to the fiscal norms of being either deductible for its full cost or not deductible at all, is deductible, but for an amount different from its cost. The treatment of such assets in the context of the initial recognition exception is discussed more generally at 7.2.6 below.

In the consolidated financial statements of any parent of the buying entity, however, there is no change to the amount of deferred tax recognised provided that the tax rate of the buying and selling entity is the same. Where the tax rate differs, the deferred tax will be remeasured using the buying entity's tax rate.

Where an asset is transferred between group entities and the tax base of the asset changes as a result of the transaction, there will be deferred tax income or expense in the consolidated financial statements. This is discussed further at 8.7 below.

7.2.6 Partially deductible and super-deductible assets

In many tax jurisdictions the tax deductions for an asset are generally based on the cost of that asset to the legal entity that owns it. However, in some jurisdictions, certain categories of asset are deductible for tax but for an amount either less than the cost of the asset ('partially deductible') or more than the cost of the asset ('super-deductible').

IAS 12 provides no specific guidance on the treatment of partially deductible and super-deductible assets acquired in a transaction to which the initial recognition exception applies. The issues raised by such assets are illustrated in Examples 29.16 and 29.17 below.

Example 29.16: Partially deductible asset

An entity acquires an asset with a cost of €100,000 and a tax base of €60,000 in a transaction where IAS 12 prohibits recognition of deferred tax on the taxable temporary difference of €40,000 arising on initial recognition of the asset. The asset is depreciated to a residual value of zero over 10 years, and qualifies for tax deductions of 20% per year over 5 years. The temporary differences associated with the asset over its life will therefore be as follows.

Year	*Carrying amount* €	*Tax base* €	*Temporary difference* €
0	100,000	60,000	40,000
1	90,000	48,000	42,000
2	80,000	36,000	44,000
3	70,000	24,000	46,000
4	60,000	12,000	48,000
5	50,000	–	50,000
6	40,000	–	40,000
7	30,000	–	30,000
8	20,000	–	20,000
9	10,000	–	10,000
10	–	–	–

These differences are clearly a function both of:

- the €40,000 temporary difference arising on initial recognition relating to the non-deductible element of the asset; and
- the emergence of temporary differences arising from the claiming of tax deductions for the €60,000 deductible element in advance of its depreciation.

Whilst IAS 12 does not explicitly mandate the treatment to be followed here, the general requirement to distinguish between these elements of the gross temporary difference (see 7.2.4 above) suggests the following approach.

The total carrying amount of the asset is pro-rated into a 60% deductible element and a 40% non-deductible element, and deferred tax is recognised on the temporary difference between the 60% deductible element and its tax base. Under this approach, the temporary differences would be calculated as follows:

Year	*Carrying amount*	*40% non-deductible element*	*60% deductible element*	*Tax base*	*Temporary difference*
	a	b (40% of a)	c (60% of a)	d	c – d
0	100,000	40,000	60,000	60,000	–
1	90,000	36,000	54,000	48,000	6,000
2	80,000	32,000	48,000	36,000	12,000
3	70,000	28,000	42,000	24,000	18,000
4	60,000	24,000	36,000	12,000	24,000
5	50,000	20,000	30,000	–	30,000
6	40,000	16,000	24,000	–	24,000
7	30,000	12,000	18,000	–	18,000
8	20,000	8,000	12,000	–	12,000
9	10,000	4,000	6,000	–	6,000
10	–	–	–	–	–

If the entity pays tax at 30%, the amounts recorded for this transaction during year 1 (assuming that there are sufficient other taxable profits to absorb the tax loss created) would be as follows:

	€
Depreciation of asset	(10,000)
Current tax income[1]	3,600
Deferred tax charge[2]	(1,800)
Net tax credit	1,800
Post tax depreciation	(8,200)

1 €100,000 [cost of asset] × 60% [deductible element] × 20% [tax depreciation rate] × 30% [tax rate]

2 €6,000 [temporary difference] × 30% [tax rate] – brought forward balance [nil]

If this calculation is repeated for all 10 years, the following would be reported in the financial statements.

Year	*Depreciation*	*Current tax credit*	*Deferred tax (charge)/ credit*	*Total tax credit*	*Effective tax rate*
	a	b	c	d (=b+c)	e (=d/a)
1	(10,000)	3,600	(1,800)	1,800	18%
2	(10,000)	3,600	(1,800)	1,800	18%
3	(10,000)	3,600	(1,800)	1,800	18%
4	(10,000)	3,600	(1,800)	1,800	18%
5	(10,000)	3,600	(1,800)	1,800	18%
6	(10,000)	–	1,800	1,800	18%
7	(10,000)	–	1,800	1,800	18%
8	(10,000)	–	1,800	1,800	18%
9	(10,000)	–	1,800	1,800	18%
10	(10,000)	–	1,800	1,800	18%

This methodology has the result that, throughout the life of the asset, a consistent tax credit is reported in each period. The effective tax rate in each period corresponds to the effective tax rate for the transaction as a whole – i.e. cost of €100,000 attracting total tax deductions of €18,000 (€60,000 at 30%), an overall rate of 18%.

However, this approach cannot be said to be required by IAS 12 and other methodologies could well be appropriate, provided that they are applied consistently in similar circumstances.

Example 29.17: Super-deductible asset

The converse situation to that in Example 29.16 exists in some jurisdictions which seek to encourage certain types of investment by giving tax allowances for an amount in excess of the expenditure actually incurred. Suppose that an entity invests $1,000,000 in PP&E with a tax base of $1,200,000 in circumstances where IAS 12 prohibits recognition of deferred tax on the deductible temporary difference of $200,000 arising on initial recognition of the asset. The asset is depreciated to a residual value of zero over 10 years, and qualifies for five annual tax deductions of 20% of its deemed tax cost of $1,200,000.

The methodology we propose in Example 29.16 could be applied 'in reverse' – i.e. with the tax base, rather than the carrying amount, of the asset being apportioned in the ratio 10:2 into a 'cost' element and a 'super deduction' element, and the temporary difference calculated by reference to the 'cost' element as follows.

Year	*Book value* a	*Tax base* b	*'Super deduction' element* c (=2/12 of b)	*Cost element* d (=10/12 of b)	*Temporary difference* a – d
0	1,000,000	1,200,000	200,000	1,000,000	–
1	900,000	960,000	160,000	800,000	100,000
2	800,000	720,000	120,000	600,000	200,000
3	700,000	480,000	80,000	400,000	300,000
4	600,000	240,000	40,000	200,000	400,000
5	500,000	–	–	–	500,000
6	400,000	–	–	–	400,000
7	300,000	–	–	–	300,000
8	200,000	–	–	–	200,000
9	100,000	–	–	–	100,000
10	–	–	–	–	–

If the entity pays tax at 30%, the amounts recorded for this transaction during year 1 (assuming that there are sufficient other taxable profits to absorb the tax loss created) would be as follows:

	$
Depreciation of asset	(100,000)
Current tax income[1]	72,000
Deferred tax charge[2]	(30,000)
Net tax credit	42,000
Profit after tax	(58,000)

1 $1,200,000 [deemed tax cost of asset] × 20% [tax depreciation rate] × 30% [tax rate]

2 $100,000 [temporary difference] × 30% [tax rate] – brought forward balance [nil]

If this calculation is repeated for all 10 years, the following would be reported in the financial statements.

Year	*Depreciation*	*Current tax credit*	*Deferred tax (charge)/ credit*	*Total tax credit*	*Effective tax rate*
	a	b	c	d (=b+c)	e (=d/a)
1	(100,000)	72,000	(30,000)	42,000	42%
2	(100,000)	72,000	(30,000)	42,000	42%
3	(100,000)	72,000	(30,000)	42,000	42%
4	(100,000)	72,000	(30,000)	42,000	42%
5	(100,000)	72,000	(30,000)	42,000	42%
6	(100,000)	–	30,000	30,000	30%
7	(100,000)	–	30,000	30,000	30%
8	(100,000)	–	30,000	30,000	30%
9	(100,000)	–	30,000	30,000	30%
10	(100,000)	–	30,000	30,000	30%

This results in an effective 42% tax rate for this transaction being reported in years 1 to 5, and a rate of 30% in years 6 to 10, in contrast to the true effective rate of 36% for the transaction as a whole – i.e. cost of $1,000,000 attracting total tax deductions of $360,000 ($1,200,000 at 30%). This is because, whilst in the case of a partially deductible asset as in Example 29.16 above there is an accounting mechanism (i.e. depreciation) for allocating the non-deductible cost on a straight-line basis, in the present case of a super deductible asset there is no ready mechanism for spreading the additional $60,000 tax deductions on a straight-line basis.

In individual cases it might be possible to argue that the additional tax deductions had sufficient of the characteristics of a government grant (e.g. if it were subject to conditions more onerous that those normally associated with tax deductions in the jurisdiction concerned) to allow application of the principles of IAS 20 so as to allocate the additional tax deductions over the life of the asset (see 4.3 above). However, it would be difficult to sustain such an approach as a matter of routine. IAS 12 is fundamentally a balance sheet approach, and a volatile tax rate must sometimes be accepted as an inevitable consequence of that approach.

Again, as in Example 29.16 above, no single approach can be said to be required by IAS 12 and other methodologies could well be appropriate, provided that they are applied consistently in similar circumstances.

7.2.7 *Transactions involving the initial recognition of an asset and liability*

As noted at 7.2 above, the initial recognition exception is essentially a pragmatic remedy to avoid accounting problems that would arise without it, particularly in transactions where one asset is exchanged for another (such as the acquisition of PP&E for cash).

However, experience has shown that the exception creates new difficulties of its own. In particular, it does not deal adequately with transactions involving the initial recognition of an equal and opposite asset and liability which subsequently unwind on different bases. Examples of such transactions include:

- recording a liability for decommissioning costs, for which the corresponding debit entry is an increase in PP&E (see 7.2.7.A below); and
- the inception of a finance lease by a lessee, which involves the recording of an asset and a corresponding financial liability (see 7.2.7.B below).

7.2.7.A Decommissioning costs

The underlying issue is illustrated by the following example.

Example 29.18: Asset and liability giving rise to equal temporary differences on initial recognition

On 1 January 2014 an entity paying tax at 40% recognises a provision for the clean-up costs of a mine that will require expenditure of €10 million at the end of 2018. A tax deduction for the expenditure will be given when it is incurred (i.e. as a reduction in the current tax liability for 2018).

In accordance with IAS 37, this provision is discounted (at a rate of 6%) to €7.5m, giving rise to the following accounting entry (see Chapter 27 at 6.3):

	€m	€m
PP&E	7.5	
Provision for clean-up costs		7.5

On initial recognition, the tax base of the PP&E is nil, since no deductions are available and the €7.5 million carrying value of the asset is recovered through future taxable profits. The tax base of the provision is also nil (carrying amount of €7.5 million, less the amount deductible in future periods, also €7.5 million). Although deductions of €10 million are expected to be received in 2018 when the decommissioning costs are incurred, the tax base is determined by reference to the consequences of the liability being settled at its carrying amount of €7.5 million, which would result in a tax deduction of only €7.5 million (see 8.3.2.below).

There is therefore a taxable temporary difference of €7.5 million associated with the PP&E and a deductible temporary difference of the same amount associated with the provision. However, the initial recognition exception in IAS 12 prohibits recognition of deferred tax on either temporary difference.

Over the next five years an expense of €10 million (equivalent to the ultimate cash spend) will be recognised in profit or loss, comprising depreciation of the €7.5 million PP&E and accretion of €2.5 million finance costs on the provision. Given that this €10 million is fully tax-deductible, it would seem reasonable for the income statement to reflect €4 million of deferred tax credits over this period, giving rise to an effective tax rate of 40% in each period. However, the result is somewhat different.

Under the general approach of IAS 12 summarised in 7.2.4 above, the depreciation of the PP&E is regarded as reducing the temporary difference arising on initial recognition of the asset, and therefore gives rise to no tax effect. However, the accretion of €2.5 million finance costs on the provision gives rise to an additional temporary difference arising after initial recognition, requiring recognition of a deferred tax asset (assuming that the general recognition criteria for assets are met – see 7.5 below). This gives rise to the following overall accounting entries for the year ended 31 December 2014.

	€m	€m
2014		
Depreciation (€7.5m ÷ 5)	1.50	
PP&E		1.50
Finance cost (€7.5m × 6%)	0.45	
Provision for clean-up costs		0.45
Deferred tax (statement of financial position)	0.18	
Deferred tax (profit or loss) (40% × €0.45m)		0.18

If equivalent entries are made for the following periods, the following amounts will be included in subsequent income statements (all figures in € millions):

	2014	2015	2016	2017	2018	Total
Depreciation	1.50	1.50	1.50	1.50	1.50	7.50
Finance costs	0.45	0.47	0.50	0.53	0.55	2.50
Cost before tax	1.95	1.97	2.00	2.03	2.05	10.00
Current tax (income)					(4.00)	(4.00)
Deferred tax (income)/charge[1]	(0.18)	(0.19)	(0.20)	(0.21)	0.78	–
Cost after tax	1.77	1.78	1.80	1.82	(1.17)	6.00
Effective tax rate	9.2%	9.6%	10.0%	10.3%	157.1%	40.0%

1 In years 2014-2017 40% × finance cost for period. In 2018, reversal of cumulative deferred tax asset recognised in previous periods.

Absent the initial recognition exception, the entity would, on initial recognition of the provision and the addition to PP&E, establish a deferred tax asset of €3 million in respect of the provision (€7.5m @ 40%) and an equal liability in respect of the asset. This would result in the following amounts being included in subsequent income statements (all figures in € millions):

	2014	2015	2016	2017	2018	Total
Depreciation	1.50	1.50	1.50	1.50	1.50	7.50
Finance costs	0.45	0.47	0.50	0.53	0.55	2.50
Cost before tax	1.95	1.97	2.00	2.03	2.05	10.00
Current tax (income)					(4.00)	(4.00)
Deferred tax (income)/charge[1]	(0.78)	(0.79)	(0.80)	(0.81)	3.18	–
Cost after tax	1.17	1.18	1.20	1.22	1.23	6.00
Effective tax rate	40.0%	40.0%	40.0%	40.0%	40.0%	40.0%

1 In 2014, the net of the reduction in deferred tax liability in respect of PP&E €0.6m (€1.5m @ 40%) and increase in asset in respect of provision €0.18m (€0.45m @ 40%) – similarly for 2015-2017. The charge in 2018 represents the release of the remaining net deferred tax asset (equal to cumulative income statement credits in 2014-2017).

It is not clear that the accounting treatment strictly required by IAS 12, with its widely fluctuating effective tax rates – resulting in a post-tax profit in 2018 for what is in reality a post-tax loss-making transaction – appropriately reflects the economic reality that all expenditure is ultimately eligible for tax deductions at the standard rate of 40%. Indeed, it could be argued that the more realistic alternative treatment set out above is consistent with the underlying intention of the initial recognition exception (that the reporting entity should provide for deferred tax on initial recognition unless to do so would create an immediate net tax expense or credit in the statement of comprehensive income). That implied intention of the exception would not be breached by providing for deferred tax on initial recognition in such cases.

7.2.7.B Finance leases taxed as operating leases

In a number of jurisdictions, tax deductions are given for finance leases as if they were operating leases (i.e. on the basis of lease payments made). The total cost for both accounting and tax purposes is obviously the same over the period of the lease, but for accounting purposes the cost comprises depreciation of the asset together with finance costs on the lease liability, rather than the cash paid, which is treated as a movement in the statement of financial position. Strict application of the initial recognition exception will therefore lead to a result similar to that set out in the first table in Example 29.18 above.

That leads some to argue that, given that the asset and liability recognised at the inception of a finance lease (or on establishment of a decommissioning provision) are a single transaction, they should be regarded as effectively giving rise to a single (net) temporary difference of zero. This means that, as and when (net) temporary differences emerge after initial recognition, deferred tax may be recognised on those temporary differences, with the effect that the effective tax rate in the income statement reflects the statutory rate actually applicable to the transaction as a whole (as illustrated in the second table in Example 29.18 above).

Those who take this view might also argue that it is consistent with the implied, if not explicit, intention of the initial recognition exception that deferred tax should always be recognised unless it creates a 'day one' tax charge or credit in the statement of comprehensive income.

Others argue that this approach is not acceptable. The financial statements present a clearly separate asset and liability which do not meet any offset criteria. The initial recognition exception should therefore be applied to the asset and liability separately and not as if the two comprised some form of single net asset or liability.

The Interpretations Committee considered this issue on two occasions in 2005. *IFRIC Update* for April 2005 appeared to support the latter view:

> 'The [Interpretations Committee] noted that initial recognition exemption applies to each separate recognised element in the [statement of financial position], and no deferred tax asset or liability should be recognised on the temporary difference existing on the initial recognition of assets and liabilities arising from finance leases or subsequently.'[12]

However, only two months later, the Committee added:

> 'The [Interpretations Committee] considered the treatment of deferred tax relating to assets and liabilities arising from finance leases.
>
> 'While noting that there is diversity in practice in applying the requirements of IAS 12 to assets and liabilities arising from finance leases, the [Interpretations Committee] agreed not to develop any guidance because the issue falls directly within the scope of the Board's short-term convergence project on income taxes with the FASB.'[13]

This appears to indicate that, whilst the Interpretations Committee regards the analysis that the asset and lease liability must be considered separately as consistent with the letter of IAS 12 as drafted, it accepts the alternative approach.

7.2.8 Initial recognition of compound financial instruments by the issuer

IAS 32 requires 'compound' financial instruments (those with both a liability feature and an equity feature, such as convertible bonds) to be accounted for by the issuer using so-called split accounting. This is discussed in more detail in Chapter 43 at 6, but in essence an entity is required to split the proceeds of issue of such an instrument (say €1 million) into a liability component, measured at its fair value based on real market rates for non-convertible debt rather than the nominal rate on the bond (say €750,000), with the balance being treated as an equity component (in this case €250,000).

Over the life of the instrument, the €750,000 carrying value of the liability element will be accreted back up to €1,000,000 (or such lower or higher sum as might be potentially repayable), so that the cumulative income statement interest charge will comprise:

(a) any actual cash interest payments made (which are tax-deductible in most jurisdictions); and

(b) the €250,000 accretion of the liability from €750,000 to €1,000,000 (which is not tax-deductible in most jurisdictions).

Where such an instrument is issued, IAS 12 requires the treatment in Example 29.19 to be adopted. *[IAS 12 IE Example 4]*.

Example 29.19: Compound financial instrument

An entity issues a zero-coupon convertible loan of €1,000,000 on 1 January 2015 repayable at par on 1 January 2018. In accordance with IAS 32, the entity classifies the instrument's liability component as a liability and the equity component as equity. The entity assigns an initial carrying amount of €750,000 to the liability component of the convertible loan and €250,000 to the equity component. Subsequently, the entity recognises the imputed discount of €250,000 as interest expense at the effective annual rate of 10% on the carrying amount of the liability component at the beginning of the year. The tax authorities do not allow the entity to claim any deduction for the imputed discount on the liability component of the convertible loan. The tax rate is 40%.

Temporary differences arise on the liability element as follows (all figures in € thousands).

	1.1.15	*31.12.15*	*31.12.16*	*31.12.17*
Carrying value of liability component[1]	750	825	908	1,000
Tax base	1,000	1,000	1,000	1,000
Taxable temporary difference	250	175	92	–
Deferred tax liability @ 40%	100	70	37	–

1 Balance carried forward at end of previous period plus 10% accretion of notional interest less repayments.

The deferred tax arising at 1 January 2015 is deducted from equity. Subsequent reductions in the deferred tax balance are recognised in the income statement, resulting in an effective tax rate of 40%. For example, in 2015, the entity will accrete notional interest of €75,000 (closing loan liability €825,000 less opening balance €750,000) with deferred tax income of €30,000 (closing deferred tax liability €70,000 less opening liability €100,000).

Whilst this treatment is explicitly required by IAS 12, its conceptual basis is far from clear, and causes some confusion in practice. In the first instance, it appears to contravene the prohibition on recognition of deferred tax on temporary differences arising on the initial recognition of assets and liabilities (other than in a business combination) that do not give rise to accounting or taxable profit or loss. IAS 12 argues that this temporary difference does not arise on initial recognition of a liability but as a result of the initial recognition of the equity component as a result of split accounting. *[IAS 12.23]*.

Even if this analysis is accepted, it remains unclear why the deferred tax should be deducted from equity. It may have been seen as an application of the general allocation principle of IAS 12 that the tax effects of transactions accounted for in equity should also be accounted for in equity – see 10 below. However, this would have been correct only if the accounting entry giving rise to the liability had been:

DR	Equity	€750,000	
	CR Liability		€750,000

The actual entry was:

DR	Cash	€1,000,000	
	CR Liability		€750,000
	CR Equity		€250,000

Therefore, in fact the general allocation rule in IAS 12 would have required the deferred tax liability to be recognised as a charge to profit or loss. This would have resulted in a 'day one' tax expense, suggesting that that initial recognition exception ought, in principle, to have been applied here also.

The accounting treatment required by Example 29.19 above could be seen as no more than 'tax equalisation' accounting – i.e. the recognition of deferred tax of an amount that, when released to profit or loss, will yield an effective tax rate equivalent to the statutory rate. Some would question whether it is appropriate to represent as tax-deductible a charge to the income statement that in reality is not tax-deductible. Nevertheless, as noted above, this treatment is explicitly required by IAS 12.

7.2.9 Acquisition of subsidiary not accounted for as a business combination

Occasionally, an entity may acquire a subsidiary which is accounted for as the acquisition of an asset rather than as a business combination. This will most often be the case where the subsidiary concerned is a 'single asset entity' holding a single item of property, plant and equipment which is not considered to comprise a business. Where an asset is acquired in such circumstances, the initial recognition exception applies, but there is room for debate as to the extent to which it applies, as illustrated by the following example.

Example 29.20: Acquired subsidiary accounted for as asset purchase

An entity (P) acquires a subsidiary (S), whose only asset is a property, for \$10 million. The transaction is accounted for as the acquisition of a property rather than as a business combination. The tax base of the property is \$4 million and its carrying value in the financial statements of S (under IFRS) is \$6 million. The taxable temporary difference of \$2 million in the financial records of S arose after the initial recognition by S of the property, and accordingly a deferred tax liability of \$800,000 has been recognised by S at its tax rate of 40%.

The question then arises as to whether any deferred tax should be recognised for the property in the financial statements of P.

One view would be that the initial recognition exception applies to the entire \$6 million difference between the carrying value of the property of \$10 million and its tax base of \$4 million, in exactly the same way as if the property had been legally acquired as a separate asset rather than through acquisition of the shares of S. Under this approach, no deferred tax is recognised by P in respect of the property at the time of acquisition.

An alternative view might be that, although the acquisition of S is being treated as an asset acquisition rather than a business combination under IFRS 3 – *Business Combinations*, IFRS 10 – *Consolidated Financial Statements* – still requires P to consolidate S, and therefore to record the assets and liabilities (according to IFRS) of S in its consolidated financial statements. The deferred tax of $800,000 recognised by S should therefore be included in the financial statements of P. Under this approach, at the time of acquisition, the initial recognition exception applies only to the valuation uplift from $6 million to $10 million.

In our view, either analysis is acceptable, but should be applied consistently to similar transactions.

7.3 Assets carried at fair value or revalued amount

IAS 12 notes that certain IFRSs permit or require assets to be carried at fair value or to be revalued. These include:

- IAS 16 – *Property, Plant and Equipment*
- IAS 38 – *Intangible Assets*
- IAS 39 – *Financial Instruments: Recognition and Measurement*
- IAS 40 – *Investment Property*.

In most jurisdictions, the revaluation or restatement of an asset does not affect taxable profit in the period of the revaluation or restatement. Nevertheless, the future recovery of the carrying amount will result in a taxable flow of economic benefits to the entity and the amount that will be deductible for tax purposes (i.e. the original tax base) will differ from the amount of those economic benefits.

The difference between the carrying amount of a revalued asset and its tax base is a temporary difference and gives rise to a deferred tax liability or asset. IAS 12 clarifies that this is the case even if:

- the entity does not intend to dispose of the asset. In such cases, the revalued carrying amount of the asset will be recovered through use and this will generate taxable income which exceeds the depreciation that will be allowable for tax purposes in future periods; or
- tax on capital gains is deferred if the proceeds of the disposal of the asset are invested in similar assets. In such cases, the tax will ultimately become payable on sale or use of the similar assets. *[IAS 12.20]*. A discussion of the accounting for deferred taxable gains may be found at 7.7 below.

In some jurisdictions, the revaluation or other restatement of an asset to fair value affects taxable profit (tax loss) for the current period. In such cases, the tax base of the asset may be raised by an amount equivalent to the revaluation gain, so that no temporary difference arises.

7.4 Restrictions on recognition of deferred tax assets

There is an essential difference between deferred tax liabilities and deferred tax assets. An entity's deferred tax liabilities will crystallise if the entity recovers its existing net assets at their carrying amount. However, in order to realise its net deferred tax assets in full, an entity must earn profits in excess of those represented by the carrying amount of its net assets in order to generate sufficient taxable profits against which the deductions represented by deferred tax assets can be offset. Accordingly IAS 12 restricts the recognition of deferred tax assets to the extent that it is probable that taxable profit will be available against which the underlying deductible temporary differences can be utilised. *[IAS 12.27].*

7.4.1 Sources of 'probable' future taxable profit

It is 'probable' that there will be sufficient taxable profit if a deferred tax asset can be offset against a deferred tax liability relating to the same tax authority which will reverse in the same period as the asset, or in a period into which a loss arising from the asset may be carried back or forward. *[IAS 12.28].* Any deferred tax liability used as the basis for recognising a deferred tax asset must represent a future tax liability against which the future tax deduction represented by the deferred tax asset can actually be offset. For example, in a tax jurisdiction where revenue and capital items are treated separately for tax purposes, a deferred tax asset representing a capital loss cannot be recognised by reference to a deferred tax liability relating to PP&E against which the capital loss could never be offset in a tax return.

Where there are insufficient deferred tax liabilities relating to the same tax authority to offset a deferred tax asset, the asset should be recognised to the extent that:

- it is probable that in future periods there will be sufficient taxable profits:
  - relating to the same tax authority;
  - relating to the same taxable entity; and
  - arising in the same period as the reversal of the deductible temporary difference or in a period into which a loss arising from the deferred tax asset may be carried back or forward – see also 7.4.2 below; or
- tax planning opportunities are available that will create taxable profit in appropriate periods – see 7.4.3 below. *[IAS 12.29].*

Where an entity has a history of recent losses it should also consider the guidance in IAS 12 for recognition of such losses (see 7.4.4 below). *[IAS 12.31].*

7.4.2 Future deductible temporary differences ignored

In assessing the availability of future taxable profits, an entity must ignore taxable profits arising from deductible temporary differences expected to originate in future periods. This is because those new deductible differences will themselves require future taxable profit in order to be utilised. *[IAS 12.29].*

For example, suppose that in 2014 an entity charges £100 to profit or loss for which a tax deduction is not received until 2015. However, in 2015 a further £100 is charged to profit or loss, for which a deduction is made only in 2016, and so on for the foreseeable future. This will have the effect that, in 2014, the entity will pay tax on the £100 for which no deduction is made on the 2014 tax return. In the tax return for 2015, there will be a deduction for that £100, but this will be offset by the add-back in the same tax return for the equivalent £100 charged for accounting purposes in 2015. If this cycle of

'£100 deduction less £100 add-back' is perpetuated in each tax return for the foreseeable future, there is never any real recovery of the tax paid on the £100 in 2014.

7.4.3 Tax planning opportunities

'Tax planning opportunities' are actions that the entity would take in order to create or increase taxable income in a particular period before the expiry of a tax loss or tax credit carryforward. IAS 12 notes that, in some jurisdictions, taxable profit may be created or increased by:

- electing to have interest income taxed on either a received or receivable basis;
- deferring the claim for certain deductions from taxable profit;
- selling, and perhaps leasing back, assets that have appreciated but for which the tax base has not been adjusted to reflect such appreciation; and
- selling an asset that generates non-taxable income (such as, in some jurisdictions, a government bond) in order to purchase another investment that generates taxable income.

Where tax planning opportunities advance taxable profit from a later period to an earlier period, the utilisation of a tax loss or tax credit carryforward still depends on the existence of future taxable profit from sources other than future originating temporary differences. *[IAS 12.30].*

The requirement to have regard to future tax planning opportunities applies only to the measurement of deferred tax assets. It does not apply to the measurement of deferred tax liabilities. Thus, for example, it would not be open to an entity subject to tax at 30% to argue that it should provide for deferred tax liabilities at some lower rate on the grounds that it intends to invest in assets attracting investment tax credits that will allow it to pay tax at that lower rate (see 8.4.1 below).

IAS 12 describes tax planning opportunities as actions that the entity 'would' take – not those it 'could' take. In other words, they are restricted to future courses of action that the entity would actually undertake to realise such a deferred tax asset, and do not include actions that are theoretically possible but practically implausible, such as the sale of an asset essential to the ongoing operations of the entity.

Implementation of a tax planning opportunity may well entail significant direct costs or the loss of other tax benefits or both. Accordingly, any deferred tax asset recognised on the basis of a tax planning opportunity must be reduced by any cost of implementing that opportunity (measured, where applicable, on an after-tax basis).

Moreover, IAS 12 regards tax planning opportunities as a component of future net taxable profits. Thus, where a tax planning opportunity exists, but the entity is expected to remain loss-making (such that the opportunity effectively will simply reduce future tax losses), we believe that such an opportunity does not generally form the basis for recognising a deferred tax asset, except to the extent that it will create *net* future taxable profits (see also 7.4.4 below).

7.4.3.A Available-for-sale debt securities

At its meeting in May 2010 the Interpretations Committee considered a request for guidance on the recognition of a deferred tax asset relating to an unrealised loss on available-for-sale ('AFS') debt securities. The request asked:

- whether an entity's ability and intent to hold the AFS debt securities until the unrealised losses reverse is a tax planning opportunity; and, if so
- whether recognition of a deferred tax asset relating to the unrealised loss can be assessed separately from other deferred tax assets.

Both views were then accepted under US GAAP.

Following further discussion by the Interpretations Committee, the issue came onto the IASB's own agenda. The exposure draft *Annual Improvements to IFRSs 2010-2012 Cycle* (ED/2012/1), issued in 2012, proposed an amendment to IAS 12 to clarify that:

- an entity assesses whether to recognise a specific deferred tax asset in combination with other deferred tax assets of the 'appropriate type' – i.e. determined with regard to any legal restrictions on the utilisation of the type of tax loss represented by the asset (for example, if the tax law allows capital losses to be deducted only from capital gains);
- the taxable profit by reference to which an entity assesses whether a deferred tax asset is recoverable (see 7.4.1 above) is the amount of taxable profit before reversal of deductible temporary differences; and
- an action that results only in the reversal of existing deductible temporary differences is not a tax-planning opportunity that could justify recognition of a deferred tax asset. To qualify as a tax planning opportunity, the action must create or increase taxable profit.

The exposure draft noted that the proposed amendment to IAS 12 resulted from its tentative conclusions on the treatment of deferred tax assets arising from available-for-sale debt instruments, but might be relevant to other types of deferred tax asset.

Some respondents (including ourselves) observed that, as drafted, the proposals could be read as requiring more than one accounting treatment, depending on the reader's interpretation of some existing provisions of IAS 12. At its meeting in December 2012 the IASB appeared to accept this concern, since it decided to make only a limited scope amendment to IAS 12 dealing with unrealised losses on debt securities (i.e. the original focus of the question to the Interpretations Committee in 2010).[14] The IASB sought the views on the nature of the required amendment from the Interpretations Committee. At its meeting in May 2013, the Committee resolved to recommend the IASB to adopt an approach whereby a deferred tax asset on a debt instrument would be recognised 'unless recovering the debt instrument by holding it until an unrealised loss reverses does not reduce future tax payments and instead only avoids higher tax losses'. The Interpretations Committee noted that its proposals would result in an accounting treatment different from US GAAP and therefore decided to consult with the IASB before proceeding further.[15]

7.4.4 Unused tax losses and unused tax credits

A deferred tax asset should be recognised for the carryforward of unused tax losses and unused tax credits to the extent that it is probable that future taxable profit will be available against which the unused tax losses and unused tax credits can be utilised. *[IAS 12.34]*.

The criteria for recognition are essentially the same as those for deductible temporary differences, as set out in 7.4.1 to 7.4.3 above. However, IAS 12 emphasises that the existence of unused tax losses is strong evidence that taxable profits (other than those represented by deferred tax liabilities) may not be available. Therefore, an entity with a history of recent losses recognises a deferred tax asset arising from unused tax losses or tax credits only to the extent that:

- it has sufficient taxable temporary differences; or
- there is other convincing evidence that sufficient taxable profit will be available against which the unused tax losses or unused tax credits can be utilised by the entity.

IAS 12 requires disclosure in respect of losses recognised in the circumstances in the last bullet above (see 14.3 below). *[IAS 12.35]*.

Additionally, the entity should consider whether:

- the entity has sufficient taxable temporary differences relating to the same taxation authority and the same taxable entity, which will result in taxable amounts against which the unused tax losses or unused tax credits can be utilised before they expire;
- the entity will have taxable profits before the unused tax losses or unused tax credits expire;
- whether the unused tax losses result from identifiable causes which are unlikely to recur; and
- whether tax planning opportunities (see 7.4.3 above) are available to the entity that will create taxable profit in the period in which the unused tax losses or unused tax credits can be utilised.

To the extent that it is not probable that taxable profit will be available against which the unused tax losses or unused tax credits can be utilised, a deferred tax asset is not recognised. *[IAS 12.36]*.

IAS 12 does not provide more specific guidance on the assessment of the availability of future taxable profits, and the Interpretations Committee has resisted calls for such guidance.[16] However, it would clearly be appropriate to give more weight to (say) revenues from existing orders and contracts than to those from merely anticipated future trading.

Some have suggested that the IASB should set time limits on the foresight period used, as has been done by some national standard setters. We consider that such generalised guidance would be inappropriate, particularly in the context of an international standard, which must address the great variety of tax systems that exist worldwide, and which impose a wide range of restrictions on the carryforward of tax assets. In any event, it may well be the case that a deferred tax asset recoverable in twenty years from profits from a currently existing long-term supply contract with a creditworthy customer may be more robust than one recoverable in one year from expected future trading by a start-up company.

A deferred tax asset can be recovered only out of future *taxable* profit. Evidence of future accounting profit is not necessarily evidence of future taxable profit (for example, if significant tax deductions or credits not reflected in the accounting profit are likely to be claimed by the entity in the relevant future periods).

7.4.5 Re-assessment of deferred tax assets

An entity must review its deferred tax assets, both recognised and unrecognised, at each reporting date.

7.4.5.A Previously recognised assets

An entity should reduce the carrying amount of a deferred tax asset to the extent that it is no longer probable that sufficient taxable profit will be available to enable the asset to be recovered. Any such reduction should be reversed if it subsequently becomes probable that sufficient taxable profit will be available. *[IAS 12.56]*.

7.4.5.B Previously unrecognised assets

An entity recognises a previously unrecognised deferred tax asset to the extent that it has become probable that sufficient taxable profit will be available to enable the asset to be recovered. For example, an improvement in trading conditions may make it more probable that the entity will be able to generate sufficient taxable profit in the future for the deferred tax asset to meet the recognition criteria. Special considerations apply when an entity re-appraises deferred tax assets of an acquired business at the date of the business combination or subsequently (see 12.1.2 below). *[IAS 12.37]*.

7.4.6 Effect of disposals on recoverability of tax losses

In consolidated financial statements, the disposal of a subsidiary may lead to the derecognition of a deferred tax asset in respect of tax losses because either:

- the entity disposed of had incurred those tax losses itself; or
- the entity disposed of was the source of probable future taxable profits against which the tax losses of another member of the group could be offset, allowing the group to recognise a deferred tax asset.

It is clear that, once the disposal has been completed, those tax losses will no longer appear in the disposing entity's statement of financial position. What is less clear is whether those tax losses should be derecognised before the disposal itself is accounted for – and if so, when. IAS 12 does not give any explicit guidance on this point, beyond the general requirement to recognise tax losses only to the extent that their recoverability is probable (see 7.4 above).

In our view, three broad circumstances need to be considered:

- the entity has recognised a deferred tax asset in respect of tax losses of the subsidiary to be disposed of, the recoverability of which is dependent on future profits of that subsidiary (see 7.4.6.A below);
- the entity has recognised a deferred tax asset in respect of tax losses of a subsidiary that is to remain in the group, the recoverability of which is dependent on future profits of the subsidiary to be disposed of (see 7.4.6.B below); and
- the entity has recognised a deferred tax asset in respect of tax losses of the subsidiary to be disposed of, the recoverability of which is dependent on future profits of one or more entities that are to remain in the group (see 7.4.6.C below).

7.4.6.A Tax losses of subsidiary disposed of recoverable against profits of that subsidiary

In this situation, we consider that the deferred tax asset for the losses should remain recognised until the point of disposal, provided that the expected proceeds of the disposal are expected at least to be equal to the total consolidated net assets of the entity to be disposed of, including the deferred tax asset. Whilst the group will no longer recover the tax losses through a reduction in its future tax liabilities, it will effectively recover their value through the disposal. Moreover, it would be expected that the disposal price would reflect the availability of usable tax losses in the disposed of entity, albeit that any price paid would reflect the fair value of such tax losses, rather than the undiscounted value required to be recorded by IAS 12 (see 8.6 below).

7.4.6.B Tax losses of retained entity recoverable against profits of subsidiary disposed of

In this case, we believe that IAS 12 requires the deferred tax asset to be derecognised once the disposal of the profitable subsidiary is probable (effectively meaning that the recoverability of losses by the retained entity is no longer probable). This derecognition threshold may be reached before the subsidiary to be disposed of is classified as held for sale under IFRS 5 – *Non-current Assets Held for Sale and Discontinued Operations* (see Chapter 4). This is because the threshold for derecognising the deferred tax asset under IAS 12 (i.e. that the sale of the subsidiary is probable) is lower than the threshold for accounting for the net assets of subsidiary under IFRS 5 (i.e. that the subsidiary is ready for sale, and the sale is highly probable).

7.4.6.C Tax losses of subsidiary disposed of recoverable against profits of retained entity

In this situation, we believe that more than one analysis is possible. One view would be that – as in 7.4.6.A above – a deferred tax asset for the losses should remain recognised until the point of disposal, provided that the expected proceeds of the disposal are expected at least to be equal to the total consolidated net assets of the entity to be disposed of, including the deferred tax asset. Another view would be that the asset should be derecognised. In contrast to the situation in 7.4.6.A, it is not the case that the losses are of any benefit to the acquiring entity (since they are recognised by virtue of the expected profits of other entities in the group which are not being sold. Rather, as in 7.4.6.B above, the likely separation of the subsidiary from the profits available in one or more retained entities means that the utilisation of those losses by the retained subsidiary is no longer probable. A third view would be that it is necessary to determine whether or not the losses would be of value to the acquirer. If so, they should continue to be recognised to the extent that they are being recovered by the disposing entity through the sales proceeds (as in 7.4.6.A above). If not, they should be derecognised on the grounds that they will not be recovered either through a reduction in future taxable profits of the disposing entity, or through sale (as in 7.4.6.B above).

7.5 'Outside' temporary differences relating to subsidiaries, branches, associates and joint arrangements

Investments in subsidiaries, branches and associates or interests in joint arrangements can give rise to two types of temporary difference:

- Differences between the tax base of the investment or interest – typically the original cost of the equity held in that investment or interest – and its carrying amount. 'Carrying amount' in this context means:
  - in separate financial statements, the carrying amount of the relevant investment or interest, and
  - in financial statements other than separate financial statements, the carrying amount of the net assets (including goodwill) relating to the relevant investment or interest, whether accounted for by consolidation or equity accounting.

  These differences are generally referred to in practice as 'outside' temporary differences, and normally arise in the tax jurisdiction of the entity that holds the equity in the investment or interest.
- In financial statements other than separate financial statements, differences between the tax bases of the individual assets and liabilities of the investment or interest and the carrying amounts of those assets and liabilities (as included in those financial statements through consolidation or equity accounting).

  These differences are generally referred to in practice as 'inside' temporary differences, and normally arise in the tax jurisdiction of the investment or interest.

This section is concerned with 'outside' temporary differences, the most common source of which is the undistributed profits of the investee entities, where distribution to the investor would trigger a tax liability. 'Outside' temporary differences may also arise from a change in the carrying value of an investment due to exchange movements, provisions, or revaluations.

The reversal of most 'inside' temporary differences is essentially inevitable as assets are recovered or liabilities settled at their carrying amount in the normal course of business. However, an entity may be able to postpone the reversal of some or all of its 'outside' differences more or less permanently. For example, if a distribution of the retained profits of a subsidiary would be subject to withholding tax, the parent may effectively be able to avoid such a tax by making the subsidiary reinvest all its profits into the business. IAS 12 recognises this essential difference in the nature of 'outside' and 'inside' temporary differences by setting different criteria for the recognition of 'outside' temporary differences.

7.5.1 Calculation of 'outside' temporary differences

As noted above, 'outside' temporary differences arise in both consolidated and separate financial statements and may well be different, due to the different bases used to account for subsidiaries, branches and associates or interests in joint arrangements in consolidated and separate financial statements. *[IAS 12.38]*. This is illustrated by Example 29.21 below.

Example 29.21: Temporary differences associated with subsidiaries, branches, associates and joint arrangements

On 1 January 2014 entity H acquired 100% of the shares of entity S, whose functional currency is different from that of H, for €600m. The tax rate in H's tax jurisdiction is 30% and the tax rate in S's tax jurisdiction is 40%.

The fair value of the identifiable assets and liabilities (excluding deferred tax assets and liabilities) of S acquired by H is set out in the following table, together with their tax base in S's tax jurisdiction and the resulting temporary differences (all figures in € millions).

	Fair value	*Tax base*	*(Taxable)/ deductible temporary difference*
PP&E	270	155	(115)
Accounts receivable	210	210	–
Inventory	174	124	(50)
Retirement benefit obligations	(30)	–	30
Accounts payable	(120)	(120)	–
Fair value of net assets acquired excluding deferred tax	504	369	(135)
Deferred tax (135 @ 40%)	(54)		
Fair value of identifiable assets acquired and liabilities assumed	450		
Goodwill (balancing figure)	150		
Carrying amount	600		

No deferred tax is recognised on the goodwill, in accordance with the requirements of IAS 12 as discussed at 7.2.2.A above.

At the date of combination, the tax base, in H's tax jurisdiction, of H's investment in S is €600 million. Therefore, in H's jurisdiction, no temporary difference is associated with the investment, either in the consolidated financial statements of H (where the investment is represented by net assets and goodwill of €600 million), or in its separate financial statements, if prepared (where the investment is shown as an investment at cost of €600 million).

During 2014:

- S makes a profit after tax, as reported in H's consolidated financial statements, of €150 million, of which €80 million is paid as a dividend (after deduction of withholding tax) before 31 December 2014, leaving a net retained profit of €70 million.
- In accordance with IAS 21 – *The Effects of Changes in Foreign Exchange Rates*, H's consolidated financial statements record a loss of €15 million on retranslation to the closing exchange rate of S's opening net assets and profit for the period.
- In accordance with IAS 36 – *Impairment of Assets*, H's consolidated financial statements record an impairment loss of €10 million in respect of goodwill.

Thus in H's consolidated financial statements the carrying value of its investment in S is €645 million, comprising:

	€m
Carrying amount at 1.1.2014	600
Retained profit	70
Exchange loss	(15)
Impairment of goodwill	(10)
Carrying amount at 31.12.2014	645

7.5.1.A Consolidated financial statements

Assuming that the tax base in H's jurisdiction remains €600 million, there is a taxable temporary difference of €45 million (carrying amount €645m less tax base €600m) associated with S in H's consolidated financial statements. Whether or not any deferred tax is required to be provided for on this difference is determined in accordance with the principles discussed in 7.5.2 below. Any tax provided for would be allocated to profit or loss, other comprehensive income or equity in accordance with the general provisions of IAS 12 (see 10 below). In this case, the foreign exchange loss, as a presentational rather than a functional exchange difference, would be recognised in other comprehensive income (see Chapter 15 at 6.1), as would any associated tax effect. The other items, and their associated effects, would be recognised in profit or loss.

Irrespective of whether provision is made for deferred tax, H would be required to make disclosures in respect of this difference (see 14.2.2 below).

7.5.1.B Separate financial statements

The amount of any temporary difference in H's separate financial statements would depend on the accounting policy adopted in those statements. IAS 27 – *Separate Financial Statements* – allows entities the choice of accounting for investments in group companies at either cost (less impairment) or at fair value – see Chapter 8 at 2. Suppose that, notwithstanding the impairment of goodwill required to be recognised in the consolidated financial statements, the investment in S taken as a whole is not impaired, and indeed its fair value at 31 December 2014 is €660 million.

If, in its separate financial statements, H accounts for its investment at cost of €600 million, there would be no temporary difference associated with S in H's separate financial statements, since the carrying amount and tax base of S would both be €600 million.

If, however, in its separate financial statements, H accounts for its investment at its fair value of €660 million, there would be a taxable temporary difference of €60 million (carrying amount €660m less tax base €600m) associated with S in H's separate financial statements. Whether or not any deferred tax is required to be provided for on this difference is determined in accordance with the principles discussed in 7.5.2 below. Any tax provided for would be allocated to profit or loss, other comprehensive income or equity in accordance with the general provisions of IAS 12 (see 10 below). Irrespective of whether provision is made for deferred tax, H would be required to make disclosures in respect of this difference (see 14.2.2 below).

7.5.2 Taxable temporary differences

IAS 12 requires a deferred tax liability to be recognised for all taxable temporary differences associated with investments (both domestic and foreign) in subsidiaries, branches and associates or interests in joint arrangements, unless:

(a) the parent, investor joint venturer or joint operator is able to control the timing of the reversal of the temporary difference; and

(b) it is probable that the temporary difference will not reverse in the foreseeable future. *[IAS 12.39]*.

IAS 12 does not currently define the meaning of 'probable' in this context. However, we consider that, as in other IFRSs, it should be taken to mean 'more likely than not'. IAS 12 also does not elaborate on the meaning of 'foreseeable'. In our view, the period used will be a matter of judgement in individual circumstances.

What this means in practice is best illustrated by reference to its application to the retained earnings of subsidiaries, branches and joint arrangements on the one hand, and those of associates on the other.

In the case of a subsidiary or a branch, the parent is able to control when and whether the retained earnings are distributed. Therefore, no provision need be made for the tax consequences of distribution of profits that the parent has determined will not be distributed in the foreseeable future. *[IAS 12.40]*. In the case of a joint arrangement, provided that the joint venturer or joint operator can control the distribution policy, similar considerations apply. *[IAS 12.43]*.

In the case of an associate, however, the investor cannot control distribution policy. Therefore provision should be made for the tax consequences of the distribution of the retained earnings of an associate, except to the extent that there is a shareholders' agreement that those earnings will not be distributed.

Some might consider this a counter-intuitive result. In reality, it is extremely unusual for any entity (other than one set up for a specific project) to pursue a policy of full distribution. To the extent that it occurs at all, it is much more likely in a wholly-owned subsidiary than in an associate; and yet IAS 12 effectively treats full distribution by associates as the norm and that by subsidiaries as the exception. Moreover, it seems to ignore the fact that equity accounting was developed as a regulatory response to the perceived ability of investors in associates to exert some degree of control over the amount and timing of dividends from them.

In some jurisdictions, some or all of the temporary differences associated with such investments in subsidiaries, branches and associates or interests in joint arrangements are taxed on disposal of that investment or interest. Clearly, where the entity is contemplating such a disposal, it would no longer be able to assert that it is probable that the relevant temporary difference will not reverse in the foreseeable future.

The measurement of any deferred tax liability recognised is discussed at 8.4.9 below.

7.5.3 Deductible temporary differences

IAS 12 requires a deferred tax asset to be recognised for all deductible temporary differences associated with investments in subsidiaries, branches and associates or interests in joint arrangements, only to the extent that it is probable that:

(a) the temporary difference will reverse in the foreseeable future; and

(b) taxable profit will be available against which the temporary difference can be utilised. *[IAS 12.44]*.

IAS 12 does not currently define the meaning of 'probable' in this context. However, we consider that, as in other IFRS, it should be taken to mean 'more likely than not'.

The guidance discussed in 7.4 above is used to determine whether or not a deferred tax asset can be recognised for such deductible temporary differences. *[IAS 12.45]*.

Any analysis of whether a deductible temporary difference gives rise to an asset must presumably make the same distinction between controlled and non-controlled entities as is required when assessing whether a taxable temporary difference gives rise to a liability (see 7.5.2 above). This may mean, in practical terms, that it is never possible to recognise a deferred tax asset in respect of a non-controlled investment (such as an associate), unless either the investee entity is committed to a course of action that would realise the asset or, where the asset can be realised by disposal, that it is probable that the reporting entity will undertake such a disposal.

The measurement of any deferred tax asset recognised is discussed at 8.4.9 below.

7.5.4 Anticipated intragroup dividends in future periods

Under IAS 10 – *Events after the Reporting Period* – and IAS 18, a dividend may be recognised as a liability of the paying entity and revenue of the receiving entity only when it has been declared by the paying entity. This raises the question of when a reporting entity should account for the tax consequences of a dividend expected to be paid by a subsidiary out of its retained profits as at the reporting date.

7.5.4.A Consolidated financial statements of receiving entity

In our view, IAS 12 requires the group to make provision for the taxes payable on the retained profits of the group as at each reporting date based on the best evidence available to it at the reporting date. In other words, if in preparing its financial statements for 31 December 2014, an entity believes that, in order to meet the dividend expectations of its shareholders in 2015 and 2016, it will have to cause the retained earnings of certain overseas subsidiaries (as included in the group accounts at 31 December 2014) to be distributed, the group should provide for any tax consequences of such distributions in its consolidated financial statements for the period ended 31 December 2014.

It is not relevant that such dividends have not yet been recognised in the separate financial statements of the relevant members of the group. Indeed, such intragroup dividends will never be recognised in the group financial statements, as they will be eliminated on consolidation. What IAS 12 requires is a best estimate of the taxes ultimately payable on the net assets of the group as at 31 December 2014. However, for this reason it would not be appropriate to recognise any liability for the tax anticipated to be paid out of an intragroup dividend in a future period that is likely to be covered by profits made in *future* periods, since such profits do not form part of the net assets of the group as at 31 December 2014.

7.5.4.B Separate financial statements of paying entity

Irrespective of whether a provision is made in the consolidated financial statements for the tax effects of an expected future intragroup dividend of the retained earnings of a subsidiary, the paying subsidiary would not recognise a liability for the tax effects of any distribution in its individual or separate financial statements until the liability to pay the dividend was recognised in those individual or separate financial statements.

7.5.5 Unpaid intragroup interest, royalties, management charges etc.

It is common for groups of companies to access the earnings of subsidiaries not only through distribution by way of dividend, but also by levying charges on subsidiaries such as interest, royalties or general management charges for central corporate services. In practice, such charges are often not settled but left outstanding on the intercompany account between the subsidiary and the parent. In some jurisdictions such income is taxed only on receipt.

This has led some to argue that, where settlement of such balances is within the control of the reporting entity, and it can be demonstrated that there is no foreseeable intention or need to settle such balances, such balances are economically equivalent to unremitted earnings, so that there is no need to provide for the tax consequences of settlement.

In February 2003 the Interpretations Committee considered the issue and indicated that it believes that the exemption from provision for deferred taxes on 'outside' temporary differences arising from subsidiaries, branches, associates and interests in joint arrangements is intended to address the temporary differences arising from the undistributed earnings of such entities. The exception does not apply to the 'inside' temporary differences that exist between the carrying amount and the tax base of individual assets and liabilities within the subsidiary, branch, associate or interest in a joint arrangement. Accordingly, the Interpretations Committee concluded that a deferred tax liability should be provided for the tax consequences of settling unpaid intragroup charges.[17]

7.5.6 Other overseas income taxed only on remittance

In May 2007 the Interpretations Committee considered the more general issue of whether deferred taxes should be recognised in respect of temporary differences arising because foreign income is not taxable unless it is remitted to the entity's home jurisdiction.

The Interpretations Committee resolved not to add this issue to its agenda, but to draw it to the attention of the IASB. This decision reflected the status of the IASB's project on income taxes (see 15 below) at that time – particularly the Board's decision to eliminate the notion of a 'branch'.[18]

7.6 'Tax-transparent' ('flow-through') entities

In many tax jurisdictions certain entities are not taxed in their own right. Instead the income of such entities is taxed in the hands of their owners as if it were income of the owners. An example might be a partnership which does not itself pay tax, but whose partners each pay tax on their share of the partnership's profits. Such entities are sometimes referred to as 'tax-transparent' or 'flow-through' entities.

The tax status of such an entity is of no particular relevance to the accounting treatment, in the investor's financial statements, of the tax paid on the income of the entity. An investor in such an entity will determine whether the entity is a subsidiary, associate, joint arrangement, branch or a financial asset investment and account for it accordingly. The investor then accounts for its own current tax payable as it arises in the normal way.

The investor will also determine whether the basis on which the investment has been accounted for (e.g. through consolidation or equity accounting) has led to the recognition of assets or liabilities which give rise to temporary differences and recognise deferred tax on these in the normal way.

Finally, the investor will also determine whether there are 'outside' temporary differences associated with the investment as a whole and account for these as above.

Examples 29.22 and 29.23 illustrate the accounting treatment for, respectively, a consolidated and an equity-accounted tax-transparent entity.

Example 29.22: Tax-transparent entity (consolidated)

An entity (A) acquires 60% of a tax-transparent partnership (P) for $100 million in a transaction accounted for as a business combination. The aggregate fair value of the identifiable net assets of the partnership is $80 million and their tax base is $60m. A is directly liable to tax at 25% on 60% of the taxable profits of the partnership, in computing which it is entitled to offset 60% of the tax base of the assets. A elects to measure the non-controlling interest at its proportionate share of the net assets of the partnership.

The accounting entry to record the business combination is:

	$m	$m
Net assets	80	
Goodwill (balancing figure)	55	
Consideration paid		100
Deferred tax*		3
Non-controlling interest†		32

* In recovering the carrying value of the net assets ($80m), A will pay tax on 60% of $20m ($80m – $60m) = $12m at 25% = $3m.

† 40% of $80m.

By contrast, if the partnership were a tax-paying entity, the accounting entry would be:

	$m	$m
Net assets	80	
Goodwill (balancing figure)	55	
Consideration paid		100
Deferred tax*		5
Non-controlling interest†		30

* In recovering the carrying value of the net assets ($80m), P will pay tax on $20m ($80m – $60m) at 25% = $5m.

† 40% of $75m (net assets excluding deferred tax $80m less deferred tax (as above) $5m).

Example 29.23: Tax-transparent entity (equity-accounted)

The facts are the same as in Example 29.22 above, except that, due to an agreement between A and the other partners, P is a jointly-controlled entity, rather than a subsidiary, of A, which accounts for P using the equity method. In this case it is less clear how to account for the deferred tax liability, which, it must be remembered, is not a liability of P, but of A and therefore does not form part of the net assets and goodwill underlying A's investment in P.

One analysis might be that the deferred tax relates to a temporary difference arising on the initial recognition of the investment in P in a transaction that gives rise to no accounting or taxable profit, and therefore is not recognised under the initial recognition exception (see 7.2.3 above). On this view, the initial accounting entry is simply:

	$m	$m
Investment in P	100	
Consideration		100

Another analysis might be that the true cost of the investment in P comprises both the consideration paid to the vendor and the assumption by A of the deferred tax liability associated with its share of the underlying assets (other than goodwill) of the investment. On this view the initial accounting entry is:

	$m	$m
Investment in P	103	
Deferred tax (see Example 29.22 above)		3
Consideration		100

This second method has the merit that it results in the same implied underlying goodwill as arises on full consolidation in Example 29.22 above: $103m – $48m [60% of $80m] = $55m. However, it does raise the issue of an apparent 'day one' impairment, as discussed in more detail at 12.3 below.

In our view, either analysis is acceptable so long as it is applied consistently.

Any income tax relating to a tax-transparent entity accounted for using equity accounting forms part of the investor's tax charge. It is therefore included in the income tax line in profit or loss and not shown as part of the investor's share of the results of the tax-transparent entity.

7.7 Deferred taxable gains

Some tax regimes mitigate the tax impact of significant asset disposals by allowing some or all of the tax liability on such transactions to be deferred, typically subject to conditions, such as a requirement to reinvest the proceeds from the sale of the asset disposed of in a similar 'replacement' asset. The postponement of tax payments achieved in this way may either be for a fixed period (e.g. the liability must be paid in any event no later than ten years after the original disposal) or for an indefinite period (e.g. the liability crystallises when, and only when, the 'replacement' asset is subsequently disposed of).

As noted at 7.3 above, IAS 12 makes it clear that the ability to postpone payment of the tax liability arising on disposal of an asset – even for a considerable period – does not extinguish the liability. In many cases, the effect of such deferral provisions in tax legislation is to reduce the tax base of the 'replacement' asset. This will increase any taxable temporary difference, or reduce any deductible temporary difference, associated with the asset.

8 DEFERRED TAX – MEASUREMENT

8.1 Legislation at the end of the reporting period

Deferred tax should be measured by reference to the tax rates and laws, as enacted or substantively enacted by the end of the reporting period, that are expected to apply in the periods in which the assets and liabilities to which the deferred tax relates are realised or settled. *[IAS 12.47].*

When different tax rates apply to different levels of taxable income, deferred tax assets and liabilities are measured using the average rates that are expected to apply to the taxable profit (tax loss) of the periods in which the temporary differences are expected to reverse. *[IAS 12.49].*

IAS 12 comments that, in some jurisdictions, announcements of tax rates (and tax laws) by the government have the substantive effect of actual enactment, which may follow the announcement by a period of several months. In these circumstances, tax assets and liabilities are measured using the announced tax rate (and tax laws). *[IAS 12.48].*

IAS 12 gives no guidance as to how this requirement is to be interpreted in different jurisdictions and both the IASB and the Interpretations Committee have resisted various requests for it. In most jurisdictions, however, a consensus has emerged as to the meaning of 'substantive enactment' for that jurisdiction. Nevertheless, in practice apparently similar legislative processes in different jurisdictions may give rise to different treatments under IAS 12. For example, in most jurisdictions, tax legislation requires the formal approval of the head of state in order to become law. However, in some jurisdictions the head of state has real executive power (and could potentially not approve the legislation), whereas in others head of state has a more ceremonial role (and cannot practically fail to approve the legislation).

The view tends to be that, in those jurisdictions where the head of state has executive power, legislation is not substantively enacted until actually enacted by the head of state. Where, however, the head of state's powers are more ceremonial, substantive enactment is generally regarded as occurring at the stage of the legislative process where no further amendment is possible.

Some examples of the interpretation of 'substantive enactment' in particular jurisdictions are given at 5.1.1 above.

8.2 Uncertain tax positions

'Uncertain tax position' is not a defined term in IAS 12, but is generally understood in practice to refer to an item the tax treatment of which is unclear or is a matter subject to an unresolved dispute between the reporting entity and the relevant tax authority. An uncertain tax position generally occurs where there is an uncertainty as to the meaning of the tax law, or to the applicability of the law to a particular transaction, or both.

Accounting for uncertain tax positions is a particularly challenging aspect of accounting for tax, discussed further at 9 below.

8.3 'Prior year adjustments' of previously presented tax balances and expense (income)

This is discussed in the context of current tax at 5.3 above. The comments there apply equally to adjustments to deferred tax balances and expense (income). Accordingly, for accounting purposes, the normal provisions of IAS 8 apply, which require an entity to determine whether the revision represents a correction of a material prior period error or a refinement in the current period of an earlier estimate.

8.4 Expected manner of recovery of assets or settlement of liabilities

Deferred tax should be measured by reference to the tax consequences that would follow from the manner in which the entity expects, at the end of the reporting period, to recover or settle the carrying amount of the asset or liability to which it relates. *[IAS 12.51]*.

8.4.1 Tax planning strategies

As discussed at 7.5.2 above, IAS 12 allows tax planning strategies to be taken into account in determining whether a deferred tax asset may be recognised. This raises the question of the extent to which tax planning strategies may be taken into account more generally in applying IAS 12.

For example, some jurisdictions may offer incentives in the form of a significantly reduced basis tax rate for entities that undertake particular activities, or invest in particular plant, property and equipment, or create a certain level of employment.

Some argue that, where an entity has the ability and intention to undertake transactions that will lead to its being taxed at a lower rate, it may take this into account in measuring deferred tax liabilities relating to temporary differences that will reverse in future periods when the lower rate is expected to apply.

In our view, this is not appropriate. IAS 12's references to tax planning opportunities are purely in the context of determining whether a deferred tax asset should be recognised. Such opportunities do not impact on the measurement of deferred tax until the entity has undertaken them, or is at least irrevocably committed to doing so.

8.4.2 Carrying amount

IAS 12 requires an entity to account for the tax consequences of recovering an asset or settling a liability at its *carrying amount*, and not, for example, the tax that might arise on a disposal at the current estimated fair value of the asset. This is illustrated by the example below.

Example 29.24: Measurement of deferred tax based on carrying amount of asset

During 2009 an entity, which has an accounting date of 31 December and pays tax at 40%, purchased a business and assigned €3 million of the purchase consideration to goodwill. The goodwill originally had a tax base of €3 million, deductible only on disposal of the goodwill. Thus there was no temporary difference on initial recognition of the goodwill (and, even if there had been, no deferred tax would have been recognised under the initial recognition exception – see 7.2.2 above). During 2010 the entity disposed of another business giving rise to a taxable gain of €500,000. The tax law of the relevant jurisdiction allowed the gain to be deferred by deducting it from the tax base of the goodwill, which therefore became €2.5 million.

Since IFRS prohibits the amortisation of goodwill, but instead requires it to be measured at cost less impairment, in our view IAS 12 effectively requires any deferred tax to be measured at the amount that would arise if the goodwill were sold at its carrying amount. At the end of 2010, the goodwill was still carried at €3 million. The decrease in the tax base during the period through deferral of the taxable gain gave rise to a taxable temporary difference of €500,000 (€3 million carrying amount less €2.5 million tax base), which, since it arose *after* the initial recognition of the goodwill (see 7.2.4 above), gave rise to the recognition of a deferred tax liability of €200,000 (€500,000 @ 40%).

During 2011, the acquired business suffered a severe downturn in trading, such that the goodwill of €3 million was written off in its entirety. This gave rise to a deductible temporary difference of €2.5 million (carrying amount of zero less €2.5 million tax base). The deferred tax liability of €200,000 recognised at the end of 2010 was released. However, no deferred tax asset was recognised since it did not meet the criteria in IAS 12 for recognition of tax assets, since there was no expectation of suitable taxable profits sufficient to enable recovery of the asset (see 7.4 above).

During 2014, a new trading opportunity arises in the acquired business, with the result that, at the end of 2014, the value of the goodwill of that business is once more €3 million. However, in accordance with IAS 36, which prohibits the reinstatement of previously impaired goodwill (see Chapter 20 at 6.3), no accounting adjustment is made to the carrying value of goodwill.

If the goodwill were disposed of for its current fair value of €3 million, tax of €200,000 would arise. However, the entity recognises no deferred tax liability at the end of 2014, since IAS 12 requires the entity to recognise the tax (if any) that would arise on disposal of the goodwill for its *carrying amount* of zero. If the asset were sold for zero, a tax loss of €2.5 million would arise but, in accordance with the general provisions of IAS 12 discussed at 7.4 above, a deferred tax asset could be recognised in respect of this deductible temporary difference only if there were an expectation of suitable taxable profits sufficient to enable recovery of the asset.

This may mean that any deferred tax asset or liability recognised under IAS 12 will reflect the expected manner of recovery or settlement, but not the expected amount of recovery or settlement, where this differs from the current carrying amount.

8.4.3 *Assets and liabilities with more than one tax base*

IAS 12 notes that, in some jurisdictions, the manner in which an entity recovers (settles) the carrying amount of an asset (liability) may affect either or both of:

(a) the tax rate applicable when the entity recovers (settles) the carrying amount of the asset (or liability); and

(b) the tax base of the asset (or liability).

In such cases, an entity should measure deferred tax assets and liabilities using the tax rate and the tax base that are consistent with the expected manner of recovery or settlement. *[IAS 12.51A]*.

Assets which are treated differently for tax purposes depending on whether their value is recovered through use or sale are commonly referred to as 'dual-based assets'. The basic requirements of IAS 12 for dual-based assets can be illustrated with a simple example.

Example 29.25: Calculation of deferred tax depending on method of realisation of asset

A building, which is fully tax-deductible, originally cost €1 million. At the end of the reporting period it is carried at €1,750,000, but tax allowances of €400,000 have been claimed in respect of it. If the building were sold the tax base of the building would be €1.5 million due to inflation-linked increases in its tax base.

Any gain on sale (calculated as sale proceeds less tax base of €1.5 million) would be taxed at 40%. If the asset is consumed in the business, its depreciation will be charged to profits that are taxed at 30%.

If the intention is to retain the asset in the business, it will be recovered out of future income of €1.75 million, on which tax of €345,000 will be paid, calculated as:

	€000
Gross income	1,750
Future tax allowances for asset (£1m less £400,000 claimed to date)	(600)
	1,150
Tax at 30%	345

If, however, the intention is to sell the asset, the required deferred tax liability is only €100,000 calculated as:

	€000
Sales proceeds	1,750
Tax base	(1,500)
	250
Tax at 40%	100

8.4.4 *Determining the expected manner of recovery of assets*

Example 29.25 above, like the various similar examples in IAS 12, assumes that an asset will either be used in the business or sold. In practice, however, many assets are acquired, used for part of their life and then sold before the end of that life. This is particularly the case with long-lived assets such as property. We set out below the approach which we believe should be adopted in assessing the manner of recovery of:

- depreciable PP&E, investment properties and intangible assets (see 8.4.5 below);
- non-depreciable PP&E, investment properties and intangible assets (see 8.4.6 below); and
- other assets and liabilities (see 8.4.7 below).

8.4.5 Depreciable PP&E and intangible assets

Depreciable PP&E and investment properties are accounted for in accordance with IAS 16. Amortised intangibles are accounted for in accordance with IAS 38. IAS 16 and IAS 38, which are discussed in detail in Chapters 17 and 18, require the carrying amount of a depreciable asset to be separated into a 'residual value' and a 'depreciable amount'.

'Residual value' is defined as:

> '... the estimated amount that an entity would currently obtain from disposal of the asset, after deducting the estimated costs of disposal, if the asset were already of the age and condition expected at the end of its useful life'

and 'depreciable amount' as:

> '... the cost of an asset, or other amount substituted for cost, less its residual value'. *[IAS 16.6, IAS 38.8].*

It is inherent in the definitions of 'residual value' and 'depreciable amount' that, in determining residual value, an entity is effectively asserting that it expects to recover the depreciable amount of an asset through use and its residual value through sale. If the entity does not expect to sell an asset, but to use and scrap it, then the residual value (i.e. the amount that would be obtained from sale) must be nil.

Accordingly, we believe that, in determining the expected manner of recovery of an asset for the purposes of IAS 12, an entity should assume that, in the case of an asset accounted for under IAS 16 or IAS 38, it will recover the residual value of the asset through sale and the depreciable amount through use. This view is reinforced by the Basis for Conclusions on IAS 12 which notes that 'recognition of depreciation implies that the carrying amount of a depreciable asset is expected to be recovered through use to the extent of its depreciable amount, and through sale at its residual value'. *[IAS 12.BC6].*

Such an analysis is also consistent with the requirement of IAS 8 to account for similar transactions consistently (see Chapter 3 at 4.1.4). This suggests that consistent assumptions should be used in determining both the residual value of an asset for the purposes of IAS 16 and IAS 38 and the expected manner of its recovery for the purposes of IAS 12.

The effect of this treatment is as follows.

Example 29.26: Dual-based asset

As part of a business combination an entity purchases an opencast mine to which there is assigned a fair value of €10 million. The tax system of the jurisdiction where the mine is located provides that, if the site is sold (with or without the minerals *in situ*), €9 million will be allowed as a deduction in calculating the taxable profit on sale. The profit on sale of the land is taxed as a capital item. If the mine is exploited through excavation and sale of the minerals, no tax deduction is available.

The entity intends fully to exploit the mine and then to sell the site for retail development. Given the costs that any developer will need to incur in preparing the excavated site for development, the ultimate sales proceeds are likely to be nominal. Thus, for the purposes of IAS 16, the quarry is treated as having a depreciable amount of €10 million and a residual value of nil.

On the analysis above, there is a taxable temporary difference of €10 million associated with the depreciable amount of the asset (carrying amount of €10 million less tax base in use of nil), and a deductible temporary difference of €9 million associated with the residual value (carrying amount of nil less tax base on disposal of €9 million).

The entity will therefore provide for a deferred tax liability on the taxable temporary difference. Whether or not a deferred tax asset is recognised in respect of the deductible temporary difference will be determined in accordance with the criteria discussed in 7.4 above. In some tax regimes, capital profits and losses are treated more or less separately from revenue profits and losses to a greater or lesser degree, so that it may be difficult to recognise such an asset due to a lack of suitable taxable profits.

However, we acknowledge that this is not the only interpretation of IAS 12 adopted in practice. For example, BHP Billiton indicates that, where an asset has only a capital gains tax base deductible on sale, it computes deferred tax based on that tax base irrespective of the expected manner of recovery of the asset.

Extract 29.1: BHP Billiton Group (2012)

1 **Accounting policies** [extract]

Taxation [extract]

The amount of deferred tax recognised is based on the expected manner and timing of realisation or settlement of the carrying amount of assets and liabilities, with the exception of items that have a tax base solely derived under capital gains tax legislation, using tax rates enacted or substantively enacted at period end. To the extent that an item's tax base is solely derived from the amount deductible under capital gains tax legislation, deferred tax is determined as if such amounts are deductible in determining future assessable income.

If applied to the fact pattern in Example 29.26 above, this treatment would result in the recognition of a deferred tax liability on a taxable temporary difference of €1 million (i.e. the extent to which the capital gains tax base does not exceed the carrying amount). An argument for this treatment would be that disposal of the mine will attract a deduction of €9 million, and – at the time of initial acquisition – the entity could dispose of the asset in such a way as to recover the full potential tax deduction. If the mine were immediately disposed of for that amount, the deduction would be fully recovered. As the mine is depleted, its carrying amount will fall below its tax base, giving rise to a gradually increasing deductible temporary difference. It may well not be possible to recognise a deferred tax asset on this difference for all the reasons set out in Example 29.26.

In our view, the difficulty with this treatment is that, as BHP Billiton acknowledges in explaining its accounting policy, it effectively provides for the tax consequences of recovery of the asset in a single sale transaction, although it appears more likely that it will in fact be recovered through ongoing extraction over an extended period, with no current tax deductions for the depletion cost. This is difficult to reconcile to:

- the requirement of IAS 12 to have regard to the expected manner of recovery of the mine in determining its tax base, and
- the overall objective of IAS 12 to 'account for the current and future tax consequences of ... the future recovery (settlement) of the carrying amount of assets (liabilities) that are recognised in an entity's statement of financial position' (see 2.1 and 8.4.2 above).

8.4.6 Non-depreciable PP&E and intangible assets

During 2009 and 2010 the IASB received representations from various entities and bodies that it was often difficult and subjective to determine the manner of recovery of certain categories of asset for the purposes of IAS 12. This was particularly the case for investment properties accounted for at fair value under IAS 40 – *Investment Property*, which are often traded opportunistically, without a particularly specific business plan, but yield rental income until disposed of. In many jurisdictions rental income is taxed at the standard rate, while gains on asset sales are tax-free or taxed at a significantly lower rate. The principal difficulty was that the then extant guidance (SIC-21) effectively required entities to determine what the residual amount of the asset would be if it were depreciated under IAS 16 rather than accounted for at fair value,[19] which many regarded as an exercise divorced from commercial reality.

To deal with these concerns, in December 2010 the IASB amended IAS 12 so as to give more specific guidance on determining the expected manner of recovery for non-depreciable assets measured using the revaluation model in IAS 16 (see 8.4.6.A below) and for investment properties measured using the fair value model in IAS 40 (see 8.4.7 below)

8.4.6.A PP&E accounted for using the revaluation model

IAS 16 allows plant, property and equipment (PP&E) to be accounted for using a revaluation model under which PP&E is regularly revalued to fair value (see Chapter 18 at 6). IAS 12 clarifies that where a non-depreciable asset is revalued, any deferred tax on the revaluation should be calculated by reference to the tax consequences that would arise if the asset were sold at book value irrespective of the basis on which the carrying amount of the asset is measured. *[IAS 12.51B].* The rationale for this treatment is that, in accounting terms, the asset is never recovered through use, as it is not depreciated. *[IAS 12.BC6].*

IAS 12 clarifies that these requirements are subject to the general restrictions on the recognition of deferred tax assets (see 7.4 above). *[IAS 12.51E].*

An issue not explicitly addressed in IAS 12 is whether the term 'non-depreciable' asset refers to an asset that is not currently being depreciated or to one that does not have a limited useful life. This is explored further in the discussion of non-amortised intangible assets immediately below.

8.4.6.B Non-amortised intangible assets

Under IAS 38 an intangible asset with an indefinite life is not subject to amortisation.

The analysis in 8.4.5 and 8.4.6.A above would appear to lead to the conclusion that, where an intangible asset is not amortised, any deferred tax related to that asset should be measured on an 'on sale' basis. IAS 12 requires tax to be provided for based on the manner in which the entity expects to recover the 'carrying amount' of its assets. If the asset is not amortised under IAS 38, the financial statements are asserting that the carrying amount is never recovered through use.

However, an alternative analysis would be that the fact that an intangible asset is not being amortised does not of itself indicate that the expected manner of recovery is by sale. Rather, an intangible asset is regarded as having an indefinite life when it is determined that there is no foreseeable limit to the period over which the asset is expected to generate net cash inflows for the entity. *[IAS 38.88]*. This could still indicate an expectation of recovery through use.

An entity should consider which analysis is more appropriate in its particular circumstances. In many jurisdictions, however, either analysis may lead to an identical outcome, since many intangibles have no tax base either in use or on sale. This will typically be the case where an intangible asset is recognised in consolidated financial statements, but not in the financial statements of any individual entity included in the consolidation (for example, because the asset was internally generated by an entity which is later acquired).

8.4.7 Investment properties

IAS 40 allows investment properties to be accounted for at fair value (see Chapter 19 at 6). IAS 12 requires any deferred tax asset or liability associated with such a property to be measured using a rebuttable presumption that the carrying amount of the investment property will be recovered through sale. *[IAS 12.51C]*. The same rebuttable presumption is used when measuring any deferred tax asset or liability associated with an investment property acquired in a business combination if the entity intends to adopt the fair value model in accounting for the property subsequently. *[IAS 12.51D]*.

The presumption is rebutted if the investment property is depreciable and the entity's business model is to consume substantially all the economic benefits embodied in the investment property over time, rather than through sale. The Interpretations Committee has clarified that the presumption can be rebutted in other circumstances, provided that sufficient evidence is available to support that rebuttal. However, the Committee neither gave any indication of, nor placed any restriction on, what those other circumstances might be.[20] If the presumption is rebutted, the entity applies the normal requirements of IAS 12 for determining the manner of recovery of assets (see 8.4.1 to 8.4.5 above). *[IAS 12.51C]*.

IAS 12 clarifies that these requirements are subject to the general restrictions on the recognition of deferred tax assets (see 7.4 above). *[IAS 12.51E]*.

8.4.8 Other assets and liabilities

In a number of areas of accounting IFRS effectively requires a transaction to be accounted for in accordance with an assumption as to the ultimate settlement of that transaction that may not reflect the entity's expectation of the actual outcome.

For example, if the entity enters into a share-based payment transaction with an employee that gives the employee the right to require settlement in either shares or cash, IFRS 2 requires the transaction to be accounted for on the assumption that it will be settled in cash, however unlikely this may be. IAS 19 – *Employee Benefits* – may assert that an entity has a surplus on a defined benefit pension scheme on an accounting basis, when in reality it has a deficit on a funding basis. Similarly, if an entity issues a convertible bond that can also be settled in cash at the holder's option, IAS 32 requires the bond to be accounted for on the assumption that it will be repaid, however probable it is that the holders will actually elect for conversion. It may well be that such transactions have different tax consequences depending on the expected manner of settlement, as illustrated in Example 29.27 below.

Example 29.27: Convertible bond deductible if settled

An entity issues a convertible bond for €1 million. After three years, the holders can elect to receive €1.2 million or 100,000 shares of the entity. If the bond were settled in cash, the entity would receive a tax deduction for the €200,000 difference between its original issue proceeds and the amount payable on redemption. If the bond is converted, no tax deduction is available.

Under IAS 32, the bond would be accreted from €1 million to €1.2 million over the three year issue period. The tax base remains at €1 million throughout, so that a deductible temporary difference of €200,000 emerges over the issue period. It is assumed that the deferred tax asset relating to this difference would meet the recognition criteria in IAS 12 (see 7.4 above).

For various reasons, it is extremely unlikely that the bond will be redeemed in cash.

Example 29.27 raises the issue of whether any deferred tax asset should be recognised in respect of the €200,000 temporary difference.

One view would be that no deferred tax asset should be recognised on the basis that there is no real expectation that the transaction will be settled in cash, thus allowing the entity to claim a tax deduction. The contrary view would be that the underlying rationale of IAS 12 is that, in order for the financial statements to be internally consistent, the tax effects of recognised assets and liabilities must also be recognised (see 2.1 above). Accordingly, a deferred tax asset should be recognised.

8.4.9 'Outside' temporary differences relating to subsidiaries, branches, associates and joint arrangements

In this section, an 'outside' temporary difference means a difference between the tax base of an investment in a subsidiary, associate or branch or an interest in a joint arrangement and carrying amount of that investment or interest (or the net assets and goodwill relating to it) included in the financial statements. Such differences, and the special recognition criteria applied to them by IAS 12, are discussed in more detail at 7.5 above.

Where deferred tax is recognised on such a temporary difference, the question arises as to how it should be measured. Broadly speaking, investors can realise an investment in one of two ways – either indirectly (by remittance of retained earnings or capital) or directly (through sale of the investment). In many jurisdictions, the two means of realisation have very different tax consequences.

The entity should apply the general rule (discussed in more detail above) that, where there is more than one method of recovering an investment, the entity should measure any associated deferred tax asset or liability by reference to the expected manner of recovery of the investment. In other words, to the extent that the investment is expected to be realised through sale, the deferred tax is measured according to the tax rules applicable on sale, but to the extent that the temporary difference is expected to be realised through a distribution of earnings or capital, the deferred tax is measured according to the tax rules applicable on distribution.

Where the expected manner of recovery is through distribution, there may be tax consequences for more than one entity in the group. For example, the paying company may suffer a withholding tax on the dividend paid and the receiving company may suffer income tax on the dividend received. In such cases, provision should be made for the cumulative effect of all tax consequences. As discussed further at 10.3.3 below, a withholding tax on an intragroup dividend is not accounted for in the consolidated financial statements as a withholding tax (i.e. within equity), but as a tax expense in profit or loss, since the group is not making a distribution but transferring assets from a group entity to a parent of that entity.

8.4.10 'Single asset' entities

In many jurisdictions it is common for certain assets (particularly properties) to be bought and sold by transferring ownership of a separate legal entity formed to hold the asset (a 'single asset' entity) rather than the asset itself.

A 'single asset' entity may be formed for a number of reasons. For example, the insertion of a 'single asset' entity between that 'real' owner and the property may limit the 'real' owner's liability for obligations arising from ownership of the property. More pertinent to the current discussion, it may also provide shelter from tax liabilities arising on disposal of the property since, in many jurisdictions, the sale of shares is taxed at a lower rate than the sale of property.

This raises the question whether, in determining the expected manner of recovery of an asset for the purposes of IAS 12, an entity may have regard to the fact that an asset held by a 'single asset' entity can be disposed of by disposing of the shares of the entity rather than the asset itself.

One reading of IAS 12 might suggest that, where the reporting entity prepares consolidated financial statements (such that the asset held by the 'single asset' entity is included in those financial statements), it is not appropriate to have regard to the possible tax effects of disposing of the shares in the 'single asset' entity rather than the asset itself. This is because paragraph 51 of IAS 12 requires an entity to have regard to the expected manner of recovery or settlement of 'the carrying amount of its assets and liabilities'. Where consolidated financial statements are prepared, the asset recognised in the statement of financial position is the property held by, not the shares in, the 'single asset' entity (which are eliminated on consolidation).

However, we consider that there could be specific limited circumstances where the manner in which the entity expects, at the end of the reporting period, to recover or settle the carrying amount of its assets and liabilities may also include the sale of a 'single asset' entity. These circumstances will typically be confined to situations where a property that is clearly not a business is already held by such an entity. In such cases, we believe that an evaluation based on the sale of the entity holding the asset is consistent with the broader objective of IAS 12 to have regard to the expected manner of recovery of an asset.

8.4.10.A Possible future developments

The Interpretations Committee has discussed this matter on a number of occasions since September 2011. In its most recent deliberations, in May 2012, the Committee noted the following significant diversity in practice:

- some preparers recognise deferred tax on both the asset within, and the shares of, the 'single asset' entity;
- some preparers recognise tax on the shares only; and
- some preparers provide deferred tax on the difference between the asset within the entity and the tax base of its shares, using the tax rate applicable to a disposal of the shares.

The Interpretations Committee noted that current IAS 12 requires the parent to recognise deferred tax on both the asset within, and the shares of, the 'single asset' entity, if tax law considers the asset and the shares as two separate assets and if no specific exemptions in IAS 12 apply.

In the light of concerns raised by commentators, the Interpretations Committee asked its staff to undertake more research with the possible outcome of an amendment to IAS 12 addressing this specific type of transaction. Such an amendment would, in the Committee's view, be beyond the scope of the Annual Improvements project.[21]

Pending the final resolution of this issue, we believe that, in the appropriate circumstances (as discussed above), it remains appropriate to measure any deferred tax based on an assumption of sale of the shares in the single asset entity, rather than an assumption of sale of the asset by the single asset entity.

8.4.11 Change in expected manner of recovery of an asset or settlement of a liability

A change in the expected manner recovery of an asset or settlement of a liability should be dealt with as an item of deferred tax income or expense for the period in which the change of expectation occurs, and recognised in profit or loss or in other comprehensive income or movements in equity for that period as appropriate (see 10 below).

This may have the effect, in certain situations, that some tax consequences of a disposal transaction are recognised before the transaction itself. For example, an entity might own an item of PP&E which has previously been held for use but which the entity now expects to sell. In our view, any deferred tax relating to that item of

PP&E should be measured on a 'sale' rather than a 'use' basis from that point, even though the disposal itself, and any related current tax, will not be accounted for until the disposal occurs. As noted at 7.4.6 above, which discusses the effect of disposals on the recoverability of tax losses, the change in measurement will be required even if the asset does not yet meet the criteria for being classified as held for sale in IFRS 5 (see Chapter 4 at 2.1.2). This is because those criteria set a higher hurdle for reclassification ('highly probable') than the reference in IAS 12 to the entity's expected manner of recovery of an asset.

8.5 Different tax rates applicable to retained and distributed profits

In some jurisdictions, the rate at which tax is paid depends on whether profits are distributed or retained. In other jurisdictions, distribution may lead to an additional liability to tax, or a refund of tax already paid. IAS 12 requires current and deferred taxes to be measured using the rate applicable to undistributed profits until a liability to pay a dividend is recognised, at which point the tax consequences of that dividend should also be recognised, as illustrated in Example 29.28 below. *[IAS 12.52A, 52B]*.

Example 29.28: Different tax rates applicable to retained and distributed profits

An entity operates in a jurisdiction where income taxes are payable at a higher rate on undistributed profits (50%) with an amount being refundable when profits are distributed. The tax rate on distributed profits is 35%. At the end of the reporting period, 31 December 2014, the entity does not recognise a liability for dividends proposed or declared after the end of the reporting period. As a result, no dividends are recognised in the year 2014. Taxable income for 2014 is €100,000. Net taxable temporary differences have increased during the year ended 31 December 2014 by €40,000.

The entity recognises a current tax liability and a current income tax expense of €50,000 (€100,000 taxable profit @ 50%). No asset is recognised for the amount potentially recoverable as a result of future dividends. The entity also recognises a deferred tax liability and deferred tax expense of €20,000 (€40,000 @ 50%) representing the income taxes that the entity will pay when it recovers or settles the carrying amounts of its assets and liabilities based on the tax rate applicable to undistributed profits.

Subsequently, on 15 March 2015 the entity declares, and recognises as a liability, dividends of €10,000 from previous operating profits. At that point, the entity recognises the recovery of income taxes of €1,500 (€10,000 @ [50% – 35%]), representing the refund of tax due in respect of the dividends recognised as a liability, as a current tax asset and as a reduction of current income tax expense for the year ended 31 December 2015.

8.5.1 Effectively tax-free entities

In a number of jurisdictions certain types of entity, typically investment vehicles, are generally exempt from corporate income tax provided that they fulfil certain criteria, which generally include a requirement to distribute all, or a minimum percentage, of their annual income as a dividend to investors. This raises the question of how such entities should measure income taxes.

One view would be that, under the basic principle set out above, such an entity has a liability to tax at the normal rate until the dividend for a year becomes a liability. The liability for a dividend for an accounting period typically arises after the end of that period (as in Example 29.28 above). Under this analysis, therefore, such an entity would be required, at each period end, to record a liability for current tax at the standard corporate rate. That liability would be released in full when the dividend is recognised as a liability in the following period. This would mean that, on an ongoing basis, the income statement would show a current tax charge or credit comprising:

- a charge for a full liability for the current period, and
- a credit for the reversal of the corresponding liability for the prior period.

In addition, deferred tax would be recognised at the standard tax rate on all temporary differences.

A second view would be that the provisions of IAS 12 regarding different tax rates for distributed and undistributed tax rates are intended to apply where the only significant factor determining the differential tax rate is the retention or distribution of profit. By contrast, the tax status of an investment fund typically depends on many more factors than whether or not profits are distributed, such as restrictions on its activities, the nature of its investments and so forth. On this view, the analysis would be that such an entity can choose to operate within one of two tax regimes (a 'full tax' regime or a 'no tax' regime), rather than that it operates in a single tax regime with a dual tax rate depending on whether profits are retained or distributed.

The IASB previously appeared to regard IAS 12 as favouring the first analysis, while accepting that the resulting accounting treatment – a cycle of raising full tax provisions and then reversing them – does not reflect economic reality. Accordingly, the exposure draft ED/2009/2 proposed that the measurement of tax assets and liabilities should include the effect of expected future distributions, based on the entity's past practices and expectations of future distributions.[22] Following the withdrawal of the exposure draft, the IASB intends to consider this issue further. However, no formal decision has been taken, or proposals issued for comment.

8.5.2 Withholding tax or distribution tax?

In practice, it is sometimes difficult to determine whether a particular transaction should be accounted for under the provisions of IAS 12 relating to different tax rates for distributed and undistributed profits, or in accordance with the provisions of the standard relating to withholding taxes.

The classification can significantly affect tax expense, because IAS 12 requires a withholding tax to be accounted for as a deduction from equity, whereas a higher tax rate for distributed profits is typically accounted for as a charge to profit or loss.

This issue is discussed further at 10.3 below.

8.6 Discounting

IAS 12 prohibits discounting of deferred tax, on the basis that:

- it would be unreasonable to require discounting, given that it requires scheduling of the reversal of temporary differences, which can be impracticable or at least highly complex; and

- it would be inappropriate to permit discounting because of the lack of comparability between financial statements in which discounting was adopted and those in which it was not. *[IAS 12.53, 54].*

Moreover, IAS 12 notes that when deferred tax is recognised in relation to an item that is itself discounted (such as a liability for post-employment benefits or a finance lease liability), the deferred tax, being based on the carrying amount of that item, is also effectively discounted. *[IAS 12.55].*

8.7 Unrealised intragroup profits and losses in consolidated financial statements

As noted in 6.2.1 and 6.2.2 above, an unrealised intragroup profit or loss eliminated on consolidation will give rise to a temporary difference where the profit or loss arises on a transaction that alters the tax base of the item(s) subject to the transaction. Such an alteration in the tax base creates a temporary difference because there is no corresponding change in the carrying amount of the assets or liabilities in the consolidated financial statements, due to the intragroup eliminations.

IAS 12 does not specifically address the measurement of such items. However, IAS 12 generally requires an entity, in measuring deferred tax, to have regard to the expected manner of recovery or settlement of the tax. It would generally be consistent with this requirement to measure deferred tax on temporary differences arising from intragroup transfers at the tax rates and laws applicable to the 'transferee' company rather than those applicable to the 'transferor' company, since the 'transferee' company will be taxed when the asset or liability subject to the transfer is realised or sold.

This interpretation is reinforced by the fact that the measurement of deferred tax on intragroup transactions is an acknowledged difference between IAS 12 and US GAAP. Under US GAAP deferred tax on such intragroup temporary differences is measured using the 'transferor' company's tax rate and law as an explicit exception to the general application of the temporary difference approach. Under IAS 12 (which has no such exception), the 'transferee' company's tax rate and laws apply.

There are some jurisdictions where the tax history of an asset or liability subject to an intragroup transfer remains with the 'transferor' company. In such cases, the general principles of IAS 12 should be used to determine whether any deferred tax should be measured at the tax rate of the 'transferor' or the 'transferee' company.

The effect of the treatment required by IAS 12 is that tax income or expense may be recognised on transactions eliminated on consolidation, as illustrated by Examples 29.29 and 29.30.

Example 29.29: Elimination of intragroup profit (1)

H, an entity taxed at 30%, has a subsidiary S, which is taxed at 34%. On 15 December 2014 S sells inventory with a cost of €100,000 to H for €120,000, giving rise to a taxable profit of €20,000 and tax at 34% of €6,800. If H were preparing consolidated financial statements for the year ended 31 December 2014, the profit made by S on the sale to H would be eliminated.

Under IAS 12, a deferred tax asset would be recognised on the unrealised profit of €20,000, based on H's 30% tax rate, i.e. €6,000. The additional €800 tax actually paid by S would be recognised in profit or loss for the period ended 31 December 2014, the accounting entry being:

	DR	CR
	€	€
Current tax (profit or loss)	6,800	
Current tax (statement of financial position)		6,800
Deferred tax (statement of financial position)	6,000	
Deferred tax (profit or loss)		6,000

The net €800 tax charge to profit or loss (current tax charge €6,800 less deferred tax credit €6,000) reflects the fact that, by transferring the inventory from one tax jurisdiction to another with a lower tax rate, the group has effectively denied itself a tax deduction of €800 (i.e. €20,000 at the tax rate differential of 4%) for the inventory that would have been available had the inventory been sold by S, rather than H, to the ultimate third party customer.

Example 29.30: Elimination of intragroup profit (2)

H, an entity taxed at 34%, has a subsidiary S, which is taxed at 30%. On 15 December 2014 S sells inventory with a cost of €100,000 to H for €120,000, giving rise to a taxable profit of €20,000 and tax at 30% of €6,000. If H were preparing consolidated financial statements for the year ended 31 December 2014, the profit made by S on the sale to H would be eliminated.

In this case, the consolidated financial statements would record current tax paid by S of €6,000 and a deferred tax asset measured at H's effective tax rate of 34% of €6,800, giving rise to the following entry:

	DR	CR
	€	€
Current tax (profit or loss)	6,000	
Current tax (statement of financial position)		6,000
Deferred tax (statement of financial position)	6,800	
Deferred tax (profit or loss)		6,800

In this case there is a net €800 tax credit to profit or loss (current tax charge €6,000 less deferred tax credit €6,800). This reflects the fact that, by transferring the inventory from one tax jurisdiction to another with a higher tax rate, the group has put itself in the position of being able to claim a tax deduction for the inventory of €800 (i.e. €20,000 at the tax rate differential of 4%) in excess of that which would have been available had the inventory been sold by S, rather than H, to the ultimate third party customer.

8.7.1 Intragroup transfers of goodwill and intangible assets

It is common in some jurisdictions to sell goodwill and intangible assets from one entity in a group to another in the same group, very often in order either to increase tax deductions on an already recognised asset or to obtain deductions for a previously unrecognised asset. This raises the issue of how the tax effects of such transactions should be accounted for in the financial statements both of the individual entities concerned and in the consolidated financial statements, as illustrated by Example 29.31 below.

Example 29.31: Intragroup transfer of goodwill

A parent company P has two subsidiaries – A, which was acquired some years ago and B, which was acquired during the period ended 31 December 2013 at a cost of €10 million. For the purposes of this discussion, it is assumed that B had negligible identifiable assets and liabilities. Accordingly, P recorded goodwill of €10 million in its consolidated financial statements.

During 2014, B sells its business to A for its then current fair value of €12.5 million. As the goodwill inherent in B's business was internally generated, it was not recognised in the financial statements of B. Hence, the entire consideration of €12.5 million represents a profit to B, which is subject to current tax at 20% (i.e. €2.5 million). However, as a result of this transaction, A will be entitled to claim tax deductions (again at 20%) for its newly-acquired goodwill of €12.5 million. The deductions will be received in ten equal annual instalments from 2014 to 2023. For the purposes of this discussion, it is assumed that A will have sufficient suitable taxable profits to be able to recover these deductions in full.

8.7.1.A Individual financial statements of buyer

The buyer (A) accounts for the acquisition of B's business. As the business still has negligible identifiable assets and liabilities, this gives rise to goodwill of €12.5 million within A's own financial statements. A has acquired an asset for €12.5 million with a tax base of the same amount. There is therefore no temporary difference (and thus no deferred tax) to be accounted for in the financial statements of A.

8.7.1.B Individual financial statements of seller

As described above, the individual financial statements of the seller (B) reflect a profit of €12.5 million and current tax of €2.5 million.

8.7.1.C Consolidated financial statements

In the consolidated financial statements of P, the sale of the business from B to A will be eliminated on consolidation. However, the €2.5 million current tax suffered by B will be reflected in the consolidated financial statements, since this is a transaction with a third party (the tax authority), not an intragroup transaction. The question is what, if any, deferred tax arises as the result of this transaction.

One analysis would be that the tax base of consolidated goodwill has effectively been increased from nil to €12.5 million. Compared to its carrying amount of €10 million, this creates a deductible temporary difference of €2.5 million on which a deferred tax asset at 20% (€500,000) may be recognised. It could also be argued that there is an analogy here with the general treatment of deferred tax on intragroup profits and losses eliminated on consolidation (see Examples 29.29 and 29.30 above).

Under this analysis, the consolidated income statement would show a net tax charge of €2.0 million (€2.5 million current tax expense arising in B, less €0.5 million deferred tax income arising on consolidation). However, this is arguably inconsistent with the fact that the entity is not in an overall tax-paying position (since it has incurred a current tax loss of €2.5 million, but expects to receive tax deductions of the same amount over the next ten years). Clearly, there is an economic loss since the entity has effectively made an interest free loan equal to the current tax paid to the tax authority, but this is not relevant, since tax is not measured on a discounted basis under IAS 12 (see 8.6 above).

An alternative analysis might therefore be to argue that the goodwill reflected in the consolidated statement of financial position still has no tax base. Rather, the tax base attaches to the goodwill recognised in the separate financial statements of A, which is eliminated on consolidation, and therefore has no carrying amount in the consolidated financial statements. Thus, applying the general principle illustrated in Examples 29.29 and 29.30 above, there is a deductible temporary difference of €12.5 million, being the difference between the carrying value of the goodwill (zero in the *consolidated* statement of financial position) and its tax base (€12.5 million). Alternatively, as noted in 6.1.3 above, certain items may have a tax base, but no carrying amount, and thus give rise to deferred tax.

This analysis would allow recognition of a deferred tax asset of €2.5 million on a temporary difference of €12.5 million, subject to the recognition criteria for deferred tax assets. This would result in a net tax charge of nil (€2.5 million current tax expense arising in B less €2.5 million deferred tax income arising on consolidation).

In our view, there are arguments for either analysis and entities need to take a view on their accounting policy for such transactions and apply it consistently.

9 UNCERTAIN TAX POSITIONS

'Uncertain tax position' is a term widely used to refer to an item, the tax treatment of which is either unclear or is a matter of unresolved dispute between the reporting entity and the relevant tax authority. Uncertain tax positions generally occur where there is an uncertainty as to the meaning of the law, or to the applicability of the law to a particular transaction, or both. For example, the tax legislation may allow the deduction of research and development expenditure, but there may be disagreement as to whether a specific item of expenditure can be construed as relating to research and development.

Estimating the outcome of an uncertain tax position is often one of the most complex and subjective areas in accounting for tax. However, IAS 12 does not specifically address the measurement of uncertain tax positions, which are therefore implicitly subject to the general requirement of the standard to measure current tax at the amount expected to be paid or recovered *[IAS 12.46]* – see 5 above. This lack of specific guidance is seen by some as providing welcome flexibility and by others as a deficiency in the current standard.

Uncertain liabilities are generally accounted for under IAS 37. However, IAS 37 does not apply to income taxes (see Chapter 27 at 2.2.1.B). Therefore, whilst an entity might choose to apply IAS 37 to the measurement of uncertain tax positions by applying the 'GAAP hierarchy' in IAS 8 (see Chapter 3 at 4), it is not required to do so and, as a result, a number of methodologies for accounting for uncertain positions are seen in practice.

9.1 'One-step' and 'two-step' approaches to measurement

A key decision in developing any methodology is to decide whether to adopt what is often referred to as a 'one-step' approach or a 'two step' approach to the measurement of uncertain tax positions.

Under a 'one step' approach, each uncertain tax position is recognised, but the measurement of the position reflects the likelihood of the position crystallising. This was essentially the approach in the now superseded exposure draft ED/2009/2 published in March 2009 (see 1.3 above). Under a 'two-step' approach, a position is recognised only if there is a certain minimum probability – usually referred to as the 'recognition threshold' – that it will crystallise.

The use of a 'two-step' approach raises the linked issue of whether the uncertainty relating to a disputed deduction in a tax return should be considered in isolation as a potential asset, or as a component of the total liability to tax. This may affect the accounting outcome, since IFRS imposes a much higher recognition threshold for uncertain assets than for uncertain liabilities. In practice, most of the methods currently applied under IAS 12 implicitly regard the uncertainty as relating to the total liability for tax.

Where a 'two-step' approach is adopted, the recognition threshold selected for a liability is typically 'more likely than not' – i.e. more than 50%. This has doubtless been influenced by the 'more likely than not' recognition threshold for provisions in IAS 37 (see Chapter 27) and for uncertain tax positions under US GAAP (FASB ASC Topic 740 – *Income Taxes*).

The 'one-step' and 'two-step' methods both attract passionate support. Those who favour a 'two-step' approach argue that, until a minimum recognition threshold is reached, it is not possible to make an informed estimate of the likely outcome. Those who favour a 'one-step' approach argue that the determination of whether or not a recognition threshold has been reached is itself highly subjective. Also, a relatively small difference in view in the estimated probability of a liability crystallising (say from 51% to 49%) may result in a disproportionate impact on the amount of tax recognised.

It could be argued that, in practical terms, the real difference between the 'one-step' and 'two-step' approaches is less whether there is a recognition threshold than the level at which it is set. Even where a 'one-step' approach is adopted, it seems that in practice no liability is recognised where the probability of its crystallisation is very low.

9.2 Unit of account

Another key input to any methodology is to determine the unit of account for uncertain tax positions. In practice this might be an entire tax computation, individual uncertain positions, or a group of related uncertain positions (e.g. all positions in a particular tax jurisdiction, or all positions of a similar nature or relating to the same interpretation of tax legislation). This choice of unit of account is particularly important where a two-step approach is adopted, as illustrated by Example 29.32 below.

Example 29.32: Uncertain tax positions – unit of account[23]

An entity has submitted a tax return indicating a current tax liability of £2.5 million. This £2.5 million includes the tax effect of a deduction disputed by the tax authority, the tax effect of which is £500,000. In other words, if the tax authority's challenge is sustained the entity's tax liability will in fact be £3 million. The entity has received advice that the tax authority is extremely unlikely (say 10%) to sustain its challenge.

The entity's accounting policy for uncertain tax positions is that nothing is recognised for a position unless the position is considered more likely than not to occur. Where a position is considered more likely than not to occur, it is recognised and measured based on the probability of its occurrence.

If the entity regards the unit of account as the tax return as a whole, it is clearly more likely than not that the tax return will result in a payment of tax. Based on the advice the entity has received, there is a 90% probability that the liability will be £2.5 million and 10% probability that the liability will be £3 million. It would therefore record a current tax liability of 2.55 million (£2.5m × 0.9 + £3.0m × 0.1). This could equally have been calculated as £2.5m × 1 + £0.5m × 0.1 (i.e. the £2.5 million on the submitted return that is certain to be paid, with a 10% probability that an additional £500,000 will be paid).

If, however, the entity regards its unit of account as the disputed deduction, it would not recognise any liability for this at all, based on the advice received that the probability of the tax authority's challenge being sustained is only 10%. It would therefore recognise a current tax liability of only £2.5 million (i.e. the undisputed amount of the tax return).

9.3 Methodologies used in practice

A variety of acceptable methodologies for determining uncertain tax positions under IAS 12 are applied in practice. However, the chosen methodology should be applied consistently. The entity may also need to consider the relevance of the requirement of IAS 1 to disclose information about major sources of estimation uncertainty (see Chapter 3 at 5.2).

Methodologies seen in practice include both 'one-step' and 'two-step' approaches to recognition. Measurement bases may include a weighted average probability of outcomes, the most likely single outcome and an 'all or nothing approach' (i.e. no liability is recognised for an uncertain position with a probability of occurrence below the selected recognition threshold and a full liability for a position with a probability of occurrence.above the threshold).

9.4 Tax authority practice

IAS 12 requires tax to be recognised and measured based on enacted or substantively enacted tax legislation *[IAS 12.46, 47]* – see 5 to 8 above. In some tax jurisdictions, however, the tax authority may – with the general consent of taxpayers – collect tax other than in accordance with the strict letter of the law. One example might be where the law as drafted would lead to an inequitable or unintended outcome for either the state or the taxpayer. Another example might be that the law allows a deduction in general terms (e.g. for 'refurbishment'), but the tax authority applies the law by reference to more detailed criteria (e.g. by allowing deductions for repainting, but not for replacement of windows).

Whether or not such an application of the tax law represents an uncertain tax position will be a matter for judgement in individual cases. Where the tax authority publishes its interpretations of the law, and these interpretations are generally accepted by taxpayers and upheld in legal proceedings, it may be appropriate to treat such interpretations as equivalent to tax law. Where, however, a particular interpretation appears to be followed only by individual officers of the tax authority, or accepted only in a relatively small number of tax returns, it would generally be more appropriate to treat such an interpretation as an uncertain tax position.

9.5 Detection risk

'Detection risk' is a term used in practice to refer to the risk that the tax authority examines the amounts reported to it by the entity and has full knowledge of all relevant information. US GAAP requires an entity to assess its uncertain tax positions on the assumption that the tax authority will examine them with full knowledge of relevant information, even if the entity believes that the possibility of such examination is remote, or if there is a long history of the tax authority not performing an examination or overlooking an issue. A similar requirement was proposed in the now superseded exposure draft ED/2009/2 published in March 2009 (see 1.3 above).

IAS 12 in its current form makes no explicit reference to detection risk. However, in our view, that does not mean that it can be ignored. In many jurisdictions, the tax law imposes a legal obligation on an entity operating in that jurisdiction to disclose its full liability to tax, or to assess its own liability to tax, and to make all relevant information available to the tax authorities. In such a tax jurisdiction it might be difficult, as a matter of corporate governance, for an entity to record a tax provision calculated on the basis that the tax authority will not become aware of a particular position which the entity has a legal obligation to disclose to that authority.

9.6 Classification of uncertain tax positions

As noted above, uncertain tax positions generally relate to the provision for current tax. Any provision recognised for an uncertain current tax position should therefore normally be classified as current tax, and presented (or disclosed) as current or non-current in accordance with the general requirements of IAS 1 (see Chapter 3 at 3.1.1).

However, there are circumstances where an uncertain tax position affects the tax base of an asset or liability and therefore relates to deferred tax. For example, there might be doubt as to the amount of tax depreciation that can be deducted in respect of a particular asset, which in turn would lead to doubt as to the tax base of the asset. There may sometimes be an equal and opposite uncertainty relating to current and deferred tax. For example, there might be uncertainty as to whether a particular item of income is taxable, but – if it is – any tax payable will be reduced to zero by a loss carried forward from a prior period. As discussed at 13.1.1.C below, it is not appropriate to offset current and deferred tax items.

10 ALLOCATION OF TAX CHARGE OR CREDIT

Current and deferred tax is normally recognised as income or an expense in the profit or loss for the period, except to the extent that it arises from:

- an item that has been recognised directly outside profit or loss, whether in the same period or in a different period (see 10.1 to 10.7 below);
- a share-based payment transaction (see 10.8 below); or
- a business combination (see 12 below). *[IAS 12.57, 58, 68A-68C].*

Where a deferred tax asset or liability is remeasured subsequent to its initial recognition, the change should be accounted for in profit or loss, unless it relates to an item originally recognised outside profit or loss, in which case the change should also be accounted for outside profit or loss. Such remeasurement might result from:

- a change in tax law;
- a re-assessment of the recoverability of deferred tax assets (see 7.4 above); or
- a change in the expected manner of recovery of an asset or settlement of a liability (see 8.4.11 above). *[IAS 12.60].*

Whilst IAS 12 as drafted refers only to remeasurement of 'deferred' tax, it seems clear that these principles should also be applied to any remeasurement of current tax.

Any current tax or deferred tax on items recognised outside profit or loss, whether in the same period or a different period, is also recognised directly outside profit or loss. Such items include:

- revaluations of property, plant and equipment under IAS 16 (see 10.1 below);
- retrospective restatements or retrospective applications arising from corrections of errors and changes in accounting policy under IAS 8 – *Accounting Policies, Changes in Accounting Estimates and Errors* (see 10.2 below);
- exchange differences arising on translation of the financial statements of a foreign operation under IAS 21 – *The Effects of Changes in Foreign Exchange Rates* (see 7.5 above); and
- amounts taken to equity on initial recognition of a compound financial instrument by its issuer (so-called 'split accounting') under IAS 32 (see 7.2.8 above). *[IAS 12.61A, 62, 62A].*

IAS 12 acknowledges that, in exceptional circumstances, it may be difficult to determine the amount of tax that relates to items recognised in other comprehensive income and/or equity. In these cases a reasonable pro-rata method, or another method that achieves a more appropriate allocation in the circumstances, may be used. IAS 12 gives the following examples of situations where such an approach may be appropriate:

- there are graduated rates of income tax and it is impossible to determine the rate at which a specific component of taxable profit (tax loss) has been taxed;
- a change in the tax rate or other tax rules affects a deferred tax asset or liability relating (in whole or in part) to an item that was previously recognised outside profit or loss; or

- an entity determines that a deferred tax asset should be recognised, or should no longer be recognised in full, and the deferred tax asset relates (in whole or in part) to an item that was previously recognised outside profit or loss. *[IAS 12.63].*

IAS 12 requires tax relating to items not accounted for in profit or loss, whether in the same period or a different period, to be recognised:

- in other comprehensive income, if it relates to an item accounted for in other comprehensive income; and
- directly in equity, if it relates to an item accounted for directly in equity. *[IAS 12.61A].*

This requirement to have regard to the previous history of a transaction in accounting for its tax effects is commonly referred to as 'backward tracing'.

10.1 Revalued and rebased assets

Where an entity depreciates a revalued item of PP&E, it may choose to transfer the depreciation in excess of the amount that would have arisen on a historical cost basis from revaluation surplus to retained earnings. In such cases, the relevant portion of any deferred tax liability recognised on the revaluation should also be transferred to retained earnings. A similar treatment should be adopted by an entity which has a policy of transferring revaluation gains to retained earnings on disposal of a previously revalued asset. *[IAS 12.64].*

When an asset is revalued for tax purposes and that revaluation is related to an accounting revaluation of an earlier period, or to one that is expected to be carried out in a future period, the tax effects of both the asset revaluation and the adjustment of the tax base are credited or charged to equity in the periods in which they occur.

However, if the revaluation for tax purposes is not related to an accounting revaluation of an earlier period, or to one that is expected to be carried out in a future period, the tax effects of the adjustment of the tax base are recognised in profit or loss. *[IAS 12.65].*

10.2 Retrospective restatements or applications

IAS 8 requires retrospective restatements or retrospective applications arising from corrections of errors and changes in accounting policy to be accounted for by adjusting the amounts presented in the financial statements of comparative periods and restating the opening balances of assets, liabilities and equity for the earliest prior period presented.

Because IAS 12 requires tax relating to an item that has been recognised outside profit or loss to be treated in the same way, any tax effect of a retrospective restatement or retrospective application on the opening comparative statement of financial position is dealt with as an adjustment to equity also. *[IAS 12.58].*

However, the fact that IAS 12 states that tax arising in a different period, but relating to a transaction or event arising outside profit or loss should also be recognised in other comprehensive income or equity (as applicable) is taken by some to mean that any subsequent remeasurement of tax originally recognised in equity as part of a prior year adjustment should be accounted for in equity also. In our view, such an assertion fails to reflect the true nature of retrospective application, which is defined in IAS 8 as the application of a new accounting policy 'to transactions, other events or conditions *as if that policy had always been applied*' (our emphasis). *[IAS 8.5]*. This is illustrated by Example 29.33 below.

Example 29.33: Remeasurement of deferred tax liability recognised as the result of retrospective application

An entity's date of transition to IFRS was 1 January 2004. As a result of the adoption of IAS 37 – *Provisions, Contingent Liabilities and Contingent Assets*, its first IFRS financial statements (prepared for the year ended 31 December 2005) showed an additional liability for environmental rectification costs of €5 million as an adjustment to opening reserves, together with an associated deferred tax asset at 40% of €2 million.

The environmental liability does not change substantially over the next few accounting periods, but during the year ended 31 December 2014 the tax rate falls to 30%. This requires the deferred tax asset to be remeasured to €1.5 million giving rise to tax expense of €500,000. Should this expense be recognised in profit or loss for the period or in equity?

If read in isolation, IAS 12 could be construed as requiring this expense to be accounted for in equity, as being a remeasurement of an amount originally recognised in equity. However, as discussed above, IAS 8 defines retrospective application as the application of a new accounting policy 'to transactions, other events or conditions as if that policy had always been applied'. If the entity had presented comparative information for all periods since it first commenced business, rather than present a single 'catch up' adjustment at the start of the earliest period presented, the charge for environmental costs (and all the related deferred tax) would have been reflected in profit or loss in previous periods. It is therefore clear that the tax relates to a transaction which would have been recognised in profit or loss on a full retrospective application of IFRS, and that the tax expense arising from a change in tax rate should be treated in the same way.

10.3 Dividends and transaction costs of equity instruments

10.3.1 Dividend subject to differential tax rate

In some jurisdictions, the rate at which tax is paid depends on whether profits are distributed or retained. In other jurisdictions, distribution may lead to an additional liability to tax, or a refund of tax already paid. IAS 12 requires current and deferred taxes to be measured using the rate applicable to undistributed profits until a liability to pay a dividend is recognised, at which point the tax consequences of that dividend should also be recognised. This is discussed further at 8.5 above.

Where taxes are remeasured on recognition of a liability to pay a dividend, the difference should normally be recognised in profit or loss rather than directly in equity, even though the dividend itself is recognised directly in equity under IFRS. IAS 12 takes the view that any additional (or lower) tax liability relates to the original profit now being distributed rather than to the distribution itself. Where, however, the dividend is paid out of profit arising from a transaction that was originally recognised in other comprehensive income or equity, the adjustment to the tax liability should also be recognised in other comprehensive income or equity. *[IAS 12.52B].*

10.3.2 Dividend subject to withholding tax

Where dividends are paid by the reporting entity subject to withholding tax, the withholding tax should be included as part of the dividend charged to equity. *[IAS 12.65A].*

This provision of IAS 12 proves somewhat problematic in practice. There may be little economic difference, from the paying entity's perspective, between a requirement to pay a 5% 'withholding tax' on all dividends and a requirement to pay an additional 5% 'income tax' on distributed profit. Yet, the accounting treatment varies significantly depending on the analysis. If the tax is considered a withholding tax, it is treated as a deduction from equity in all circumstances. If, however, it is considered as an additional income tax, it will generally be treated as a charge to profit or loss (see 10.3.1 above). This distinction therefore relies on a clear definition of withholding tax, which IAS 12 unfortunately does not provide.

IAS 12 describes a withholding tax as a 'portion of the dividends [paid] to taxation authorities on behalf of shareholders'. *[IAS 12.65A].* However, this begs the question whether the determination of whether or not the tax is paid 'on behalf of shareholders' should be made by reference to the characterisation of the tax:

- in the paying entity's tax jurisdiction – in which case, there is the problem noted above that one jurisdiction's 'additional distribution tax' may be economically identical to another jurisdiction's 'withholding tax', or
- in the receiving entity's tax jurisdiction – in which case there would be the problem that the tax on a dividend paid to one shareholder is a 'withholding tax' (because credit is given for it on the shareholder's tax return) but the tax on a dividend paid to another shareholder the same time is not (because no credit is given for it on that shareholder's tax return).

10.3.3 Intragroup dividend subject to withholding tax

Where irrecoverable withholding tax is suffered on intragroup dividends, the withholding tax does not relate to an item recognised in equity in the consolidated financial statements (since the intragroup dividend to which it relates has been eliminated in those financial statements). The tax should therefore be accounted for in profit or loss for the period.

10.3.4 Incoming dividends

IAS 12 does not directly address the treatment of incoming dividends on which tax has been suffered (i.e. whether they should be shown at the amount received, or gross of withholding tax together with a corresponding tax charge).

However, in discussing the treatment prescribed for the paying company as summarised above, paragraph 65A of IAS 12 describes withholding tax as an amount 'paid to the tax authorities on behalf of shareholders'. It would therefore be most consistent with this treatment for the recipient to show dividends (and other income subject to withholding taxes) gross of withholding taxes, subject to the difficulties noted in 10.3.2 above in determining what exactly is a 'withholding tax'.

Some jurisdictions also give tax deductions for the 'underlying' tax suffered on dividends received. This is based on the concept that the dividend has been paid out of profits already subject to tax, so that to tax the full amount received again would amount to a punitive double taxation of the underlying profits. In our view, such underlying tax (which would form part of the tax charge, not the dividend, of the paying company) is not directly paid on behalf of the shareholder, and accordingly incoming dividends should not be grossed up for underlying tax.

10.3.5 Tax benefits of distributions and transaction costs of equity instruments

IAS 32 as originally issued required distributions to shareholders and transaction costs of equity instruments to be accounted for in equity net of any related income tax benefit (see Chapter 43 at 8.2).

Annual Improvements to IFRSs 2009-2011 Cycle, issued in May 2012, amended IAS 32 so as to remove the reference to income tax benefit. This means that all tax effects of equity transactions are allocated in accordance with the general principles of IAS 12. Unfortunately, it is not entirely clear how IAS 12 requires the tax effects of certain equity transactions to be dealt with, as illustrated by Example 29.34 below.

Example 29.34: Tax deductible distribution on equity instrument

An entity paying tax at 25% has issued a capital instrument that is treated as equity for accounting purposes (because distributions are discretionary), but as debt for tax purposes (i.e. all distributions are tax deductible). The entity makes a distribution of €1 million and is able to claim a tax deduction of €250,000. There no restrictions on the recoverability of that deduction for tax purposes.

Some take the view that the tax deduction clearly relates to the distribution, which was accounted for in equity, and that the deduction should therefore be credited to equity.

Others take the view that the provisions of IAS 12 regarding differential tax rates for retained and distributed profits (see 8.5 above) apply. They argue that, in most cases, the amount distributed is part of an accumulation of retained earnings originally accounted for in profit or loss. The tax deduction for the distribution means that those profits have effectively been taxed at a lower rate than would have been the case if the profits had been retained. Accordingly, under the general rule in IAS 12, the effect of that rate benefit should be accounted for in profit or loss.

Those who believe that the tax deduction should be accounted for in equity argue that the provisions of IAS 12 regarding differential tax rates for retained and distributed profits (see 8.5 above) do not apply, as there is no difference to the headline tax rate applied to the taxable profits of the entity as a whole. Instead, the treatment of the distribution as an expense for tax purposes simply reduces the amount of taxable profit to be taxed at the single headline rate.

Those who believe that the tax deduction should be credited to profit or loss counter that the reference in paragraph 52A of IAS 12 to taxes 'payable at a higher or lower rate', should be interpreted as including a higher or lower effective rate, as well as a higher or lower headline rate.

We believe that either view is acceptable, provided that it is applied consistently.

10.4 Gains and losses reclassified ('recycled') to profit or loss

Several IFRSs (notably IAS 21 and IAS 39) require certain gains and losses that have been accounted for outside profit or loss to be reclassified ('recycled') to profit or loss at a later date when the assets or liabilities to which they relate are realised or settled. Whilst IAS 12 requires any tax consequences of the original recognition of the gains or losses outside profit or loss also to be accounted for outside profit or loss, it is silent on the treatment to be adopted when the gains or losses are reclassified. In our view, any tax consequences of reclassified gains or losses originally recognised outside profit or loss should also be reclassified through profit or loss in the same period as the gains or losses to which they relate. Indeed, such reclassification is often an automatic consequence of the reversal of previously recognised deferred tax income or expense and its 're-recognition' as current tax income or expense, as illustrated in Example 29.35.

Example 29.35: Tax on reclassified ('recycled') items

On 1 January 2014 an entity purchases for €2,000 an equity security that it classifies as available-for-sale ('AFS'). At 31 December 2014 it restates the security to its fair value of €2,400, which was also its fair value on 1 May 2015. On 1 July 2015 it disposes of the investment for €2,100.

The entity's tax rate for 2014 is 40% and for 2015 35%. The change of rate was made in legislation enacted (without previous substantive enactment) on 1 May 2015. The entity is subject to tax on disposal of the investment (based on disposal proceeds less cost) in the period of disposal.

The accounting entries for this transaction would be as follows.

	€	€
1 January 2014		
AFS asset	2,000	
Cash		2,000
31 December 2014		
AFS asset [€2,400 – €2,000]	400	
Deferred tax (statement of financial position) [€400 @ 40%]		160
Other comprehensive income ('OCI')		240
Recognition of increase in value of asset, and related deferred tax		
1 May 2015		
Deferred tax (statement of financial position) [€400 @ (35% – 40%)]	20	
OCI		20
Remeasurement of deferred tax (no change in the fair value of the AFS asset since 31 December 2014)		
1 July 2015		
Cash	2,100	
OCI (reclassification of €400 (before tax) credited 31.12.14)	400	
AFS asset		2,400
Profit on disposal of AFS asset [cash €2,100 less original cost €2,000]		100
Deferred tax (statement of financial position)	140	
Deferred tax income (OCI)		140
Current tax (profit or loss)	35	
Current tax (statement of financial position) [35% of €100 pre-tax profit]		35

10.5 Gain/loss in profit or loss and loss/gain outside profit or loss offset for tax purposes

It often happens that a gain or loss accounted for in profit or loss can be offset for tax purposes against a gain or loss accounted for in other comprehensive income (or an increase or decrease in equity). This raises the question of how the tax effects of such transactions should be accounted for, as illustrated by Example 29.36 below.

Example 29.36: Loss in other comprehensive income and gain in profit or loss offset for tax purposes

During the year ended 31 December 2014, an entity that pays tax at 35% makes a taxable profit of €50,000 comprising:

- €80,000 trading profit less finance costs accounted for in profit or loss; and
- €30,000 foreign exchange losses accounted for in other comprehensive income ('OCI').

Should the total tax liability of €17,500 (35% of €50,000) be presented as either:

(a) a charge of €17,500 in profit or loss; or

(b) a charge of €28,000 (35% of €80,000) in profit or loss and a credit of €10,500 (35% of €30,000) in OCI?

In our view, (b) is the appropriate treatment, since the amount accounted for in OCI represents the difference between the tax that would have been paid absent the exchange loss accounted for in OCI and the amount actually payable. This indicates that this is the amount that, in the words of paragraph 61A of IAS 12, 'relates to' items that are recognised outside profit or loss.

Similar issues may arise where a transaction accounted for outside profit or loss generates a suitable taxable profit that allows recognition of a previously unrecognised tax asset relating to a transaction previously accounted for in profit or loss, as illustrated by Example 29.37 below.

Example 29.37: Recognition of deferred tax asset in profit or loss on the basis of tax liability accounted for outside profit or loss

An entity that pays tax at 30% has brought forward unrecognised deferred tax assets (with an indefinite life) totalling £1 million, relating to trading losses accounted for in profit or loss in prior periods. On 1 January 2014 it invests £100,000 in government bonds, which it holds until they are redeemed for the same amount on maturity on 31 December 2017. For tax purposes, any gain made by the entity on disposal of the bonds can be offset against the brought forward tax losses. The tax base of the bonds remains £100,000 at all times.

The entity elects to account for the bonds as available-for-sale and therefore carries them at fair value (see Chapter 46 at 4.4). Over the period to maturity the fair value of the bonds at the end of each reporting period (31 December) is as follows:

	£000
2014	110
2015	115
2016	120
2017	100

Under IAS 39 the movements in value would all be accounted for in other comprehensive income ('OCI') – see Chapter 46 at 4.4. Taken in isolation, the valuation gains in 2014 to 2016 would give rise to a deferred tax liability (at 30%) of £3,000 (2014), £4,500 (2015) and £6,000 (2016). However, these liabilities arise from taxable temporary differences that can be offset against the losses brought forward (see 7.4 above), and accordingly the (equal and opposite) deferred tax liability and deferred tax asset are offset in the statement of financial position (see 13.1.1 below). This raises the question as to whether there should be either:

(a) no tax charge or credit in either profit or loss or OCI in any of the periods affected; or

(b) in each period, a deferred tax charge in OCI (in respect of the taxable temporary difference arising from valuation gains on the bonds) and deferred tax income in profit or loss (representing the recognition of the previously unrecognised deferred tax asset).

In our view, the treatment in (b) should be followed. The fact that no deferred tax is presented in the statement of financial position arises from the offset of a deferred tax asset and deferred tax liability – it does not imply that there is no deferred tax. Moreover, although the recognition of the deferred tax asset is possible only as the result of the recognition of a deferred tax liability arising from a transaction accounted for in OCI, the asset itself relates to a trading loss previously accounted for in profit or loss. Accordingly, the deferred tax credit arising from the recognition of the asset is properly accounted for in profit or loss.

10.6 Discontinued operations

IAS 12 does not explicitly address the allocation of income tax charges and credits between continuing and discontinued operations. However, that some allocation is required is implicit in the requirement of paragraph 33(b)(ii) of IFRS 5 to disclose how much of the single figure post-tax profit or loss of discontinued operations disclosed in the statement of comprehensive income is comprised of 'the related income tax expense' (see Chapter 4). *[IFRS 5.33(b)(ii)]*. In our view, the provisions of IAS 12 for the allocation of tax income and expense between profit or loss, other comprehensive income and equity also form a basis for allocating tax income and expense between continuing and discontinued operations, as illustrated by Examples 29.38 to 29.40 below.

Example 29.38: Profit in continuing operations and loss in discontinued operations offset for tax purposes

Entity A, which pays tax at 25%, has identified an operation as discontinued for the purposes of IFRS 5. During the period the discontinued operation incurred a loss of £2 million and the continuing operations made a profit of £10 million. The net £8 million profit is fully taxable in the period, and there is no deferred tax income or expense. In our view, the tax expense should be allocated as follows:

	£m	£m
Current tax expense (continuing operations)[1]	2.5	
Current tax income (discontinued operation)[2]		0.5
Current tax liability[3]		2.0

1 Continuing operations profit £10m @ 25% = £2.5m

2 Discontinued operations loss £2m @ 25% = £0.5m.

3 Net taxable profit £8m @ 25% = £2.0m

The tax allocated to the discontinued operation represents the difference between the tax that would have been paid absent the loss accounted for in discontinued operations and the amount actually payable.

Example 29.39: Taxable profit on disposal of discontinued operation reduced by previously unrecognised tax losses

Entity B disposes of a discontinued operation during the current accounting period. The disposal gives rise to a charge to tax of €4 million. However, this is reduced to zero by offset against brought forward tax losses, which relate to the continuing operations of the entity, and for which no deferred tax asset has previously been recognised.

In our view, even though there is no overall tax expense, this should be reflected for financial reporting purposes as follows:

	€m	€m
Current tax expense (discontinued operation)	4.0	
Current tax income (continuing operations)		4.0

This allocation reflects that fact that, although the transaction that allows recognition of the brought forward tax losses is accounted for as a discontinued operation, the losses themselves arose from continuing operations. This is essentially the same analysis as is used in Example 29.37 above (where a deferred tax liability recognised in other comprehensive income gives rise to an equal deferred tax asset recognised in profit or loss).

Example 29.40: Taxable profit on disposal of discontinued operation reduced by previously recognised tax losses

Entity B disposes of a discontinued operation during the current accounting period. The disposal gives rise to a charge to tax of €4 million. However, this is reduced to zero by offset against brought forward tax losses, which relate to the entity's continuing operations, and for which a deferred tax asset has previously been recognised.

In our view, even though there is no overall tax expense, this should be reflected for financial reporting purposes as follows:

	€m	€m
Current tax expense (discontinued operation)	4.0	
Deferred tax expense (continuing operations)	4.0	
Current tax income (continuing operations)		4.0
Deferred tax asset (statement of financial position)		4.0

This allocation reflects that fact that, although the transaction that allows recognition of the brought forward tax losses is accounted for as a discontinued operation, the losses themselves arose from continuing operations. This is essentially the same analysis as is used in Example 29.39 above.

10.7 Defined benefit pension plans

IAS 19 requires an entity, in accounting for a defined benefit post-employment benefit plan, to recognise actuarial gains and losses relating to the plan in full in other comprehensive income ('OCI'). At the same time, a calculated current (and, where applicable, past) service cost and net interest on the net defined benefit liability or asset are recognised in profit or loss – see Chapter 31 at 5.5.

In many jurisdictions, tax deductions for post-employment benefits are given on the basis of cash contributions paid to the plan fund (or benefits paid when a plan is unfunded).

This significant difference between the way in which defined plans are treated for tax and financial reporting purposes can make the allocation of tax deductions for them between profit or loss and OCI somewhat arbitrary, as illustrated by Example 29.41 below.

Example 29.41: Tax deductions for defined benefit pension plans

At 1 January 2014 an entity that pays tax at 40% has a fully-funded defined benefit pension scheme. During the year ended 31 December 2014 it records a total cost of €1 million, of which €800,000 is allocated to profit or loss and €200,000 to other comprehensive income ('OCI'). In January 2015 it makes a funding payment of €400,000, a tax deduction for which is received through the current tax charge for the year ended 31 December 2015.

Assuming that the entity is able to recognise a deferred tax asset for the entire €1 million charged in 2014, it will record the following entry for income taxes in 2014.

	€	€
Deferred tax asset [€1,000,000 @ 40%]	400,000	
Deferred tax income (profit or loss) [€800,000 @ 40%]		320,000
Deferred tax income (OCI) [€200,000 @ 40%]		80,000

When the funding payment is made in January 2015, the accounting deficit on the fund is reduced by €400,000. This gives rise to deferred tax expense of €160,000 (€400,000 @ 40%), as some of the deferred tax asset as at 31 December 2014 is released, and current tax income of €160,000 is recorded. The difficulty is how to allocate this movement in the deferred tax asset between profit or loss and OCI, as it is ultimately a matter of arbitrary allocation as to whether the funding payment is regarded as making good (for example):

- €400,000 of the €800,000 deficit previously accounted for in profit or loss;
- the whole of the €200,000 of the deficit previously accounted for in OCI and €200,000 of the €800,000 deficit previously accounted for in profit or loss; or
- a pro-rata share of those parts of the total deficit accounted for in profit or loss and OCI.

Indeed, for an entity that has adopted the transitional provision of IFRS 1 – *First-time Adoption of International Financial Reporting Standards* – that allows all cumulative actuarial gains and losses to be recognised on transition to IFRS, it may be impossible to determine how much of the portion of those cumulative gains and losses that arose before transition to IFRS would have been accounted for in profit or loss, and how much in OCI.

In the example above, the split is of relatively minor significance, since the entity was able to recognise 100% of the potential deferred tax asset associated with the pension liability. This means that, as the scheme is funded, there will be an equal and opposite amount of current tax income and deferred tax expense. The only real issue is therefore one of presentation, namely whether the gross items comprising this net nil charge are disclosed within the tax charge in profit or loss or in OCI.

In other cases, however, there might be an amount of net tax income or expense that needs to be allocated. Suppose that, as above, the entity recorded a pension cost of €1 million in 2014 but determined that the related deferred tax asset did not meet the criteria for recognition under IAS 12. In 2015, the entity determines that an asset of €50,000 can be recognised in view of the funding payments and taxable profits anticipated in 2015 and later years. This results in a total tax credit of €210,000 (€160,000 current tax, €50,000 deferred tax) in 2015, raising the question of whether it should be allocated to profit or loss, to OCI, or allocated on a pro-rata basis. This question might also arise if, as the result of newly enacted tax rates, the existing deferred tax balance were required to be remeasured.

In our view, these are instances of the exceptional circumstances envisaged by IAS 12 when a strict allocation of tax between profit or loss and OCI is not possible (see 10 above). Accordingly, any reasonable method of allocation may be used, provided that it is applied on a consistent basis.

One approach might be to compare the funding payments made to the scheme in the previous few years with the charges made to profit or loss under IAS 19 in those periods. If, for example, it is found that the payments were equal to or greater than the charges to profit or loss, it might reasonably be concluded that the funding payments have 'covered' the charge recognised in profit or loss, so that any surplus or deficit on the statement of financial position is broadly represented by items that have been accounted for in OCI.

However, a surplus may also arise from funding the scheme to an amount greater than the liability recognised under IAS 19 (for example under a minimum funding requirement imposed by local legislation or agreed with the pension fund trustees). In this case, the asset does not result from previously recognised income but from a reduction in another asset (i.e. cash). The entity should assess the expected manner of recovery of any asset implied by the accounting treatment of the surplus – i.e. whether it has been recognised on the basis that it will be 'consumed' (resulting in an accounting expense) or refunded to the entity in due course. The accounting treatment of refunds is discussed further in Chapter 31, and at 10.7.1 below.

The entity will account for the tax consequences of the expected manner of recovery implied by the accounting treatment. Where it is concluded that the asset will be 'consumed' (resulting in accounting expense), the entity will need to determine whether such an expense is likely to be recognised in profit or loss or in OCI in a future period.

10.7.1 Tax on refund of pension surplus

In some jurisdictions, a pension fund may be permitted or required to make a refund to the sponsoring employee of any surplus in the fund not required to settle the known or anticipated liabilities of the fund. It may be that such a refund is subject to tax. IFRIC 14 – *IAS 19 – The Limit on a Defined Benefit Asset, Minimum Funding Requirements and their Interaction* – requires any asset recorded in respect of such a refund to be shown net of any tax other than an income tax (see Chapter 31). In determining whether such a tax is an income tax of the entity, the general principles in 4.1 above should be applied. Relevant factors may include:

- whether tax is levied on the pension fund or the sponsoring entity;
- whether tax is levied on the gross amount of the refund in all cases, or has regard to the sponsoring entity's other taxable income, or the amount of tax deductions received by the sponsoring entity in respect of contributions to the fund.

10.8 Share-based payment transactions

The accounting treatment of share-based payment transactions, some knowledge of which is required to understand the discussion below, is dealt with in Chapter 30.

In many tax jurisdictions, an entity receives a tax deduction in respect of remuneration paid in shares, share options or other equity instruments of the entity. The amount of any tax deduction may differ from the related remuneration expense, and may arise in a later accounting period. For example, in some jurisdictions, an entity may recognise an expense for employee services in accordance with IFRS 2 (based on the fair value of the award at the date of grant), but not receive a tax deduction until the share options are exercised (based on the intrinsic value of the award at the date of exercise).

As noted in 6.1.4 above, IAS 12 effectively considers the cumulative expense associated with share-based payment transactions as an asset that has been fully expensed in the financial statements in advance of being recognised for tax purposes, thus giving rise to a deductible temporary difference. *[IAS 12.68A, 68B].*

If the tax deduction available in future periods is not known at the end of the period, it should be estimated based on information available at the end of the period. For example, if the tax deduction will be dependent upon the entity's share price at a future date, the measurement of the deductible temporary difference should be based on the entity's share price at the end of the period. *[IAS 12.68B].*

10.8.1 Allocation of tax deduction between profit or loss and equity

Where the amount of any tax deduction (or estimated future tax deduction) exceeds the amount of the related cumulative remuneration expense, the current or deferred tax associated with the excess should be recognised directly in equity. *[IAS 12.68C].* This treatment is illustrated by Example 29.42 below.

Example 29.42: Tax deductions for share-based payment transactions – allocation to profit or loss and equity

At the start of year 1, an entity with a tax rate of 40% grants options, which vest at the end of year 3 and are exercised at the end of year 5. Tax deductions are received at the date of exercise of the options, based on their intrinsic value at the date of exercise. Details of the expense recognised for employee services received and consumed in each accounting period, the number of options expected to vest by the entity at each year-end during the vesting period and outstanding after the end of the vesting period, and the intrinsic value of the options at each year-end, are as follows:

Year	*IFRS 2 expense for period* £	*Cumulative IFRS 2 expense* £	*Number of options*	*Intrinsic value per option* £	*Total intrinsic value* £
1	188,000	188,000	50,000	5	250,000
2	185,000	373,000	45,000	8	360,000
3	190,000	563,000	40,000	13	520,000
4		563,000	40,000	17	680,000
5		563,000	40,000	20	800,000

The tax base of, and the temporary difference and deferred tax asset associated with, the employee services is calculated as follows. Since the book value of the employee services is in all cases zero, the temporary difference associated with the services is at all times equal to their tax base as set out below.

Chapter 29

Year	*Intrinsic value (see table above)*	*Expired portion of vesting period* [1]	*Tax base (and temporary difference)*	*Tax asset* [2]	*Tax income* [3]
	£		£	£	£
	a	b	c = a × b	40% of c	
1	250,000	1/3	83,333	33,333	33,333
2	360,000	2/3	240,000	96,000	62,667
3	520,000	3/3	520,000	208,000	112,000
4	680,000	3/3	680,000	272,000	64,000
5	800,000	3/3	800,000	320,000	48,000

1 The expired portion of the vesting period is consistent with that used to calculate the cumulative charge employee costs under IFRS 2 (see Chapter 30).

2 Deferred tax asset in years 1 to 4 and current tax asset in year 5.

3 Year-on-year increase in asset.

By comparing the 'Cumulative IFRS 2 expense' column in the first table with the 'Tax base (and temporary difference)' column in the second table it can be seen that in years 1 to 3 the expected tax deduction is lower than the cumulative expense charged, and is therefore dealt with entirely in profit or loss. However in years 4 and 5 the expected (and in year 5 the actual) tax deduction is higher than the cumulative expense charged. The tax relating to the cumulative expense charged is dealt with in profit or loss, and the tax relating to the excess of the tax-deductible amount over the amount charged in profit or loss is dealt with in equity as follows.

	DR	CR
Year 1		
Deferred tax (statement of financial position)	33,333	
Deferred tax (profit or loss)		33,333
Year 2		
Deferred tax (statement of financial position)	62,667	
Deferred tax (profit or loss)		62,667
Year 3		
Deferred tax (statement of financial position)	112,000	
Deferred tax (profit or loss)		112,000
Year 4		
Deferred tax (statement of financial position)	64,000	
Deferred tax (profit or loss)[1]		17,200
Equity		46,800
Year 5		
Deferred tax (profit or loss)	225,200	
Deferred tax (equity)	46,800	
Deferred tax (statement of financial position)		272,000
Current tax (statement of financial position)	320,000	
Current tax (profit or loss)[2]		225,200
Current tax (equity)		94,800

1 Cumulative tax credit to profit or loss restricted to 40% of cumulative expense of £563,000 = £225,200. Amount credited in years 1 to 3 is £(33,333 + 62,667 + 112,000) = £212,000. Therefore amount recognised in profit or loss is £(225,200 – 212,000) = £17,200.

2 Current tax credit in profit or loss is restricted to £225,200 as explained in note 1 above. The £48,000 net increase in total cumulative tax income since year 4 (£320,000 – £272,000) is dealt with entirely in equity (current tax income €94,800 less deferred tax charge €46,800).

Example 29.42 above is based on Example 5 in the illustrative examples accompanying IAS 12 (as inserted by IFRS 2). However, the example included in IAS 12 states that the cumulative tax income is based on the number of options 'outstanding' at each period end. This would be inconsistent with the methodology in IFRS 2 (see Chapter 30), which requires the share-based payment expense during the vesting period to be based on the number of options expected to vest (as that term is defined in IFRS 2), not the total number of options outstanding, at the period end. It would only be once the vesting period is complete that the number of options outstanding becomes relevant. We assume that this is simply a drafting slip by the IASB.

IAS 12 asserts that the allocation of the tax deduction between profit or loss and equity illustrated in Example 29.42 is appropriate on the basis that the fact that the tax deduction (or estimated future tax deduction) exceeds the amount of the related cumulative remuneration expense 'indicates that the tax deduction relates not only to remuneration expense but also to an equity item.' *[IAS 12.68C].*

However, some (including the IASB itself in the exposure draft that preceded IFRS 2) take the view that any tax deductions in excess of the amount charged to profit or loss relate to an increase in the fair value of the award from the date of grant to the date of exercise, which, under the 'grant date measurement' model in IFRS 2, is not recognised in equity, or indeed anywhere in the financial statements. The 'excess' tax deduction therefore does not meet the criteria for recognition in equity in IAS 12, and would (on application of the normal rules in IAS 12) be accounted for in profit or loss by default.

The treatment required by IFRS 2 seems to have been adopted for consistency with US GAAP. However, as the IASB acknowledges, while the final cumulative allocation of tax between profit or loss and equity is broadly consistent with that required by US GAAP, the basis on which it is measured and reported at reporting dates before exercise date is quite different. *[IFRS 2.BC311-BC329].*

10.8.2 Determining the tax base

IAS 12 does not specify exactly how the tax base of a share-based payment transaction is to be determined. However, Example 5 in the illustrative examples accompanying IAS 12 (the substance of which is reproduced at 10.8.1 above) calculates the tax base as:

- the amount that would be deductible for tax if the event triggering deduction occurred at the end of the reporting period; multiplied by
- the expired portion of the vesting period at the end of the reporting period.

IFRS 2 treats certain share-based payment awards as, in effect, a parcel of a number of discrete awards, each with a different vesting period. This may be the case where an award is subject to graded vesting, has been modified, or has separate equity and liability components (see Chapter 30). In order to determine the tax base for such an award, it is necessary to consider separately the part, or parts, of the award with the same vesting period, as illustrated in Example 29.43 below.

Example 29.43: Tax deductions for share-based payment transactions – 'multi-element' awards

An entity awards 550 free shares to an employee, with no conditions other than continuous service. 100 shares vest after one year, 150 shares after two years and 300 shares after three years. Any shares received at the end of years 1 and 2 have vested unconditionally.

At the date the award is granted, the fair value of a share delivered in one year's time is €3.00; in two years' time €2.80; and in three years' time €2.50.

Under IFRS 2, the analysis is that the employee has simultaneously received an award of 100 shares vesting over one year, an award of 150 shares vesting over two years and an award of 300 shares vesting over 3 years (see Chapter 30 at 6.2.2). This would be accounted for as follows (assuming that the award was expected to vest in full at each reporting date and did actually vest in full – see Chapter 30):

Year	Calculation of cumulative expense	Cumulative expense (€)	Expense for period (€)
1	[100 shares × €3.00] + [150 shares × €2.80 × 1/2] + [300 shares × €2.50 × 1/3]	760	760
2	[100 shares × €3.00] + [150 shares × €2.80 × 2/2] + [300 shares × €2.50 × 2/3]	1,220	460
3	[100 shares × €3.00] + [150 shares × €2.80 × 2/2] + [300 shares × €2.50 × 3/3]	1,470	250

The entity receives a tax deduction at 30% for the awards based on the fair value of the shares delivered. The fair value of a share at the end of years 1, 2 and 3 is, respectively, €3.60, €2.00 and €6.00.

At the end of year 1, a current tax deduction of €108 (100 shares × €3.60 @ 30%) is receivable in respect of the 100 shares that vest. The tax base of the shares expected to vest in years 2 and 3 is calculated by reference to the year-end share price of €3.60 as:

- in respect of the 150 shares expected to vest at the end of year 2, €270 (150 shares × €3.60 × 1/2). This will give rise to a deferred tax asset of €81 (€270 @ 30%); and
- in respect of the 300 shares expected to vest at the end of year 3, €360 (300 shares × €3.60 × 1/3). This will give rise to a deferred tax asset of €108 (€360 @ 30%).

The total deferred tax asset at the end of year is therefore €189 (€81 + €108).

At the end of year 2, a current tax deduction of €90 is receivable in respect of the 150 shares that vest (150 shares × €2.00 @ 30%). The tax base of the shares expected to vest in year 3 is calculated by reference to the year-end share price of €2.00 as €400 (300 shares × €2.00 × 2/3). This gives rise to a deferred tax asset of €120 (€400 @ 30%).

At the end of year 3, a current tax deduction of €540 (300 shares × €6.00 @ 30%) is receivable in respect of the 300 shares that vest.

When an award has multiple elements that vest at different times, the question arises as to whether the unit of account for applying the 'cap' on recognition of the tax benefit in profit or loss is the award as a whole or each element separately accounted for. In our view, the determination needs to be made for each element of the award separately. This is similar to our analysis in 10.7.3 below (multiple awards outstanding) and 10.7.4 below (awards for which a tax deduction is received on exercise which are exercised at different times).

Based on the information above, the total current and deferred tax income or expense (i.e. before allocation to profit or loss and equity) at the ends of years 1 to 3 would be as follows, assuming in each case that there is no restriction on the recognition of tax assets (see 7.4 above).

Year	*Current tax asset and income*	*Deferred tax asset*	*Deferred tax income/(expense)*
	€	€	€
1	108	189	189
2	90	120	(69)
3	540	–	(120)

The required accounting entries for income taxes are as follows:

	DR	CR
Year 1		
Current tax (statement of financial position)	108	
Current tax (profit or loss)		90
Current tax (equity)[1]		18
Deferred tax (statement of financial position)	189	
Deferred tax (profit or loss) (€63 + €75 – see below)		138
Deferred tax (equity)[2] (€18 + €33 – see below)		51

1 The current tax deduction relates to the 100 shares vesting in year 1, for which the charge to profit or loss is €300 (100 shares × €3.00). The tax deduction accounted for in profit or loss is therefore restricted to 30% of €300 = €90. The balance of €18 is credited to equity, and relates to the €0.60 difference between the grant date fair value of a 'Year 1' share at grant (€3.00) and at vesting (€3.60) – 100 shares × €0.60 = €60 @ 30% = €18.

2 The total deferred tax income of €189 represents:

- €81 (see above) in respect of the 150 shares expected to vest in year 2, for which the charge to profit or loss is €210 (150 shares × €2.80 × 1/2). The tax deduction accounted for in profit or loss is restricted to 30% of €210 = €63, with the balance of €18 credited to equity; and
- €108 (see above) in respect of the 300 shares expected to vest in year 3, for which the expected charge to profit or loss is €250 (300 shares × €2.50 × 1/3). The tax deduction accounted for in profit or loss is therefore restricted to 30% of €250 = €75, with the balance of €33 credited to equity.

	DR	CR
Year 2		
Current tax (statement of financial position)	90	
Current tax (profit or loss)[3]		90
Deferred tax (profit or loss)[4]	18	
Deferred tax (equity)[4]	51	
Deferred tax (statement of financial position)[4]		69

3 The current tax deduction relates to the 150 shares vesting in year 2, for which the cumulative charge to profit or loss is €420 (150 shares × €2.80). The cumulative tax deduction accounted for in profit or loss would therefore be restricted to 30% of €420 = €126. The entire amount of current tax deduction received (€90) is therefore credited to profit or loss.

4 At the end of year 2, the deferred tax relates to the 300 shares expected to vest at the end of year 3, which has been measured based on the year end share price of €2.00. This is lower than the share price on which the IFRS 2 charge has been based. Therefore there is no requirement to allocate any deferred tax to equity, and the balance of deferred tax in equity is reduced to nil. The balance of the total €69 movement in the deferred tax balance is allocated to profit or loss.

The net tax credit in profit or loss in year 2 of €72 (current tax credit €90, less deferred tax charge €18) can be seen as representing:

Credit relating to IFRS 2 expense recognised in the period[5]	105
Charge relating to remeasurement of prior year deferred tax[6]	(33)
Total	72

5 In this case the tax credit recognised in profit or loss is not the 'expected' credit of €138 (IFRS 2 charge of €460 @ 30%). This is because the current tax deduction for the shares vesting in year 2 and the deferred tax deduction for the shares expected to vest in year 3 are based on the year-end share price of €2.00, which is lower than the share values used to calculate the IFRS 2 charge (€2.80 and €2.50). During the year, an IFRS 2 expense has been recognised for 75 'whole share equivalents' in respect of the shares vesting in year 2 (150 shares × 1/2) and 100 'whole share equivalents' in respect of the shares expected to vest in year 3 (300 shares × 1/3), a total of 175 'whole share equivalents'. Accordingly the credit for the year is €105 (175 × €2.00 × 30%).

6 In year 1 the deferred tax credit (based on the year 1 year end share price of €3.60) recognised in profit of loss in respect of the shares expected to vest in years 2 and 3 was €138. If this had been based on the year 2 year end share price of €2.00 this would have been only €105. [150 × 1/2 × €2.00] + [300 × 1/3 × €2.00] = €350 × 30% = €105. €138 – €105 = €33.

	DR	CR
Year 3		
Current tax (statement of financial position)	540	
Current tax (profit or loss)		225
Current tax (equity)[7]		315
Deferred tax (profit or loss)	120	
Deferred tax (statement of financial position)[8]		120

7 The current tax deduction relates to the 300 shares vesting in year 1, for which the cumulative charge to profit or loss is €750 (300 shares × €2.50). The tax deduction accounted for in profit or loss is therefore restricted to 30% of €750 = €225.

8 The deferred tax asset, all of which was – on a cumulative basis – recognised in profit or loss, is derecognised in profit or loss.

The net tax credit in profit or loss in year 3 of €105 (current tax credit €225, less deferred tax charge €120) can be seen as representing:

Credit relating to IFRS 2 expense recognised in the period[9]	75
Credit relating to remeasurement of prior year deferred tax[10]	30
Total	105

9 €250 @ 30%.

10 The opening balance deferred tax asset of €120 is based on the year 2 share price of €2.00. If this had been based on the year 3 share price of €6.00 it would have been €360. However, the amount recognised in profit or loss would have been restricted to €150 – 30% of the cumulative expense at the end of year 2 of €500 (300 shares × €2.50 × 2/3). €150 – €120 = €30.

10.8.3 Allocation when more than one award is outstanding

As noted above, IAS 12 requires that, 'where the amount of any tax deduction ... exceeds the amount of the related cumulative remuneration expense, the current or deferred tax associated with the excess should be recognised directly in equity'.

Some have therefore argued that, as drafted, IAS 12 requires the cumulative expense for all outstanding share schemes to be compared in aggregate with the aggregate tax deduction for all share schemes. Others argue that the comparison should be made for each scheme separately. The effect of each treatment is illustrated in Example 29.44 below.

Example 29.44: Tax deductions for share-based payment transactions – more than one award

An entity that pays tax at 30% has two outstanding share schemes, Scheme A and Scheme B. The entity receives tax deductions for share-based payment transactions based on their intrinsic value at the date of exercise.

At the end of the reporting period, the cumulative expense charged for each scheme is £1 million. Scheme A has a negative intrinsic value at the end of the reporting period, and is not expected to recover its value to the extent that employees will exercise their options. Accordingly no deferred tax asset is recognised for Scheme A. Scheme B has an intrinsic value of £1.5 million. The entity will therefore record a deferred tax asset of £450,000 (30% of £1.5 million), subject to the recognition criteria for deferred tax assets being satisfied.

Those who argue that comparison of share-based payment expense to tax deduction should be made on an aggregated basis would conclude that, because the cumulative potential tax deduction of £1.5 million (which relates only to Scheme B) is lower than the cumulative aggregate expense for both Scheme A and Scheme B (£2 million), the deferred tax income should be recognised entirely in profit or loss.

However, those who argue that comparison of share-based payment expense to tax deduction should be made on a discrete basis for each scheme would conclude that, because the cumulative tax deduction for Scheme B (£1.5 million) is higher than the cumulative aggregate expense for Scheme B (£1 million), only £300,000 of the deferred tax income (30% of £1 million) should be recognised in profit or loss, with the remaining £150,000 recognised in equity.

In our view, the comparison must be made on a discrete scheme-by-scheme basis. As noted in 10.8.2 above, it is clear from IAS 12 and the Basis for Conclusions to IFRS 2 that the IASB's intention was to exclude from profit or loss any tax deduction that is effectively given for the growth in fair value of an award that accrues after grant date. *[IAS 12.68C, IFRS 2.BC311-BC329]*. This can be determined only on an award-by-award basis. Moreover, IAS 12 requires the amount of any tax deduction to be accounted for in equity when it 'exceeds the amount of the *related* cumulative remuneration expense'. In Example 29.44 above, the tax deduction on Scheme B cannot, in our view, be said to be 'related' to the remuneration expense for Scheme A. Accordingly, the expense relating to Scheme A is not relevant for determining the amount of tax income relating to Scheme B that is required to be accounted for in equity.

It may also be that what is regarded as a single scheme may need to be further sub-divided for the purposes of the comparison for reasons such as the following:

- where the same award is made to regular employees and also to top management, the fair value of the options granted to each population may nevertheless be different for the purposes of IFRS 2 given different exercise behaviours (see Chapter 30 at 8.5.2.A);
- an award is made to employees which attracts tax deductions in more than one tax jurisdiction;
- an award is made in the same tax jurisdiction to employees in different entities, not all of which are able to recognise a deferred tax asset.

10.8.4 Staggered exercise of awards

The example in IAS 12, the substance of which is included in Example 29.42 at 10.8.1 above, addresses a situation in which all vested awards are exercised simultaneously. In practice, however, vested awards are often exercised at different dates.

Once an award under a given scheme has vested, and different awards in that scheme are exercised at different times, the question arises as to whether the 'cap' on recognition of the tax benefit in profit or loss should be calculated by reference to the cumulative expense recognised in respect of the total number of awards vested, or in respect only of as yet unexercised vested awards. In our view, where a tax deduction is received on exercise, the calculation must be undertaken by reference to the cumulative expense recognised for outstanding unexercised options. This is illustrated by Example 29.45 below.

Example 29.45: Tax deductions for share-based payment transactions – staggered exercise of award

At the start of year 1, an entity with a tax rate of 40% grants 20 options each to 5 employees. The options have a fair value of €5 and vest at the end of year 2. The options vest in full. 25 are exercised at the end of year 3 and 75 at the end of year 6. The entity is able to support the view that any deferred tax asset arising before exercise will be recoverable, and may therefore be recognised in full.

Tax deductions are given in the year of exercise, based on the intrinsic value of the options at the date of exercise. The intrinsic value of options at the end of each reporting period is as follows:

Year	*Intrinsic value per option*
	€
1	3
2	8
3	8
4	1
5	7
6	6

On the basis of the information above:

- there would be an IFRS 2 charge of €250 in years 1 and 2 (20 options × 5 employees × €5 × 1/2 (portion of vesting period)
- current and deferred tax assets should be recognised at the end of each period as follows:

Current tax

Year	*Number of options exercised*	*Intrinsic value per option*	*Total intrinsic value*	*Tax effect at 40%*
		€	€	€
3	25	8	200	80
6	75	6	450	180

Deferred tax

Year	*Number of options outstanding*	*Temporary difference per option* €	*Total temporary difference* €	*Tax effect at 40%* €
1	100	1.5[1]	150	60
2	100	8	800	320
3	75	8	600	240
4	75	1	75	30
5	75	7	525	210
6	–	6	–	–

1 Intrinsic value €3 × 1/2 (expired portion of vesting period).

The required accounting entries for income taxes are as follows

	DR €	CR €
Year 1		
Deferred tax (statement of financial position)	60	
Deferred tax (profit or loss)[1]		60
Year 2		
Deferred tax (statement of financial position)[2]	260	
Deferred tax (profit or loss)[3]		140
Deferred tax (equity)		120
Year 3		
Deferred tax (profit or loss)[4]	50	
Deferred tax (equity)	30	
Deferred tax (statement of financial position)[5]		80
Current tax (statement of financial position)[6]	80	
Current tax (profit or loss)[4]		50
Current tax (equity)		30
Year 4		
Deferred tax (profit or loss)[7]	120	
Deferred tax (equity)	90	
Deferred tax (statement of financial position)[8]		210
Year 5		
Deferred tax (statement of financial position)[9]	180	
Deferred tax (profit or loss)[10]		120
Deferred tax (equity)		60
Year 6		
Deferred tax (profit or loss)[11]	150	
Deferred tax (equity)	60	
Deferred tax (statement of financial position)		210
Current tax (statement of financial position)[12]	180	
Current tax (profit or loss)[13]		150
Current tax (equity)		30

1 The cumulative tax income is based on expected deductions of €150, which is less than the cumulative IFRS 2 charge of €250 (see above).

2 Year 2 year-end balance of €320 (see table above), less €60 recognised at end of year 1 = €140.

3 Cumulative deferred tax recognised in profit or loss must not exceed 40% × €500 (cumulative IFRS 2 charge) = €200. This limits the credit for year 2 to €200 less the €60 credited in year 1 = €140.

4 Reversal of deferred tax income previously recognised in profit or loss for the 25 options exercised: 25 × €5 [IFRS 2 charge per option] × 40% = €50. This also represents the limit on the amount of current tax deduction that can be recognised in profit or loss.

5 Year 3 year-end balance of €240 (see table above), less €320 recognised at end of year 2 = €80.

6 25 options × €8 intrinsic value × 40% = €80

In years 4 to 6, the amount of tax recognised in profit or loss is restricted by the cumulative IFRS 2 expense of €375 for the 75 options left outstanding (75 options × €5).

7 Cumulative (maximum) tax deduction already recognised in profit or loss is €375 @ 40% = €150. This needs to be reduced to €30 (year end deferred tax balance), giving rise to a charge of €150 – €30 = €120. This can be seen as representing the fact that, at the start of the period a cumulative potential tax deduction of €5 per award had been recognised in profit or loss. At the end of the period it is expected that deductions of only €1 per award will be available. Therefore there is a loss to be recognised in profit or loss of 75 awards × (€5 – €1) × 40% = €120.

8 Year 4 year-end balance of €30 (see table above), less €240 recognised at end of year 3 = €(210).

9 Year 5 year end balance of €210 (see table above), less €30 recognised at end of year 4 = €180.

10 Cumulative maximum tax deduction that can be recognised in profit or loss is €150 (see note 7). €30 cumulative deduction is brought forward, so that credit for period is limited to €150 – €30 = €120.

11 Reversal of deferred tax previously recognised. The amount previously taken to profit or loss was limited to €150 (see notes 7 and 9).

12 75 options × €6 × 40% = €180.

13 Deduction restricted to €375 [IFRS 2 charge] × 40% = €150.

It will be noted that the cumulative effect of the above entries in profit or loss is as follows (tax income in brackets):

Year	*Deferred tax*	*Current tax*	*Total*
	€	€	€
1	(60)		(60)
2	(140)		(140)
3	50	(50)	–
4	120		120
5	(120)		(120)
6	150	(150)	–
		Total	(200)

The cumulative effect of the above entries in equity is as follows (tax income in brackets):

Year	*Deferred tax*	*Current tax*	*Total*
	€	€	€
1			–
2	(120)		(120)
3	30	(30)	–
4	90		90
5	(60)		(60)
6	60	(30)	30
		Total	(60)

The overall effect is to take credit in profit or loss for the lower of total tax deductions actually received of €260 (€80 in year 3 and €180 in year 6) and the tax deductions on the IFRS 2 expense of €200 (40% of €500). The excess tax deductions of €60 are recognised in equity.

10.8.5 Replacement awards in a business combination

IFRS 3 contains some detailed provisions on the treatment of share-based payment awards issued by an acquirer to replace awards made by the acquired entity before the business combination occurred. These are discussed in Chapter 30 at 11.

IFRS 3 amended IAS 12 to include an illustrative example for the treatment of tax deductions on such replacement awards, the substance of which is reproduced as Example 29.46 below. *[IAS 12 IE Example 6].*

Example 29.46: Deferred tax on replacement share-based awards in a business combination

On 1 January 2014 Entity A acquired Entity B. A paid cash consideration of €400 million to the former owners of B. At the acquisition date B had outstanding fully-vested employee share options with a fair value of €100 million. As part of the business combination B's outstanding share options are replaced by fully vested share options of A (replacement awards) with a market-based measure of €100 million and an intrinsic value of €80 million. In accordance with IFRS 3, the replacement awards are part of the consideration transferred for B (see Chapter 30 at 11).

A tax deduction will be given only when the options are exercised, based on the intrinsic value of the options at that date. A's tax rate is 40%.

A recognises a deferred tax asset of €32 million (intrinsic value of €80m × 40%) on the replacement awards at the acquisition date (see 10.8.1 above). IAS 12 does not indicate the calculation if only part of the fair value of the award were regarded as part of the consideration transferred. However, it would be consistent with the general approach indicated at 10.8.2 above to calculate the tax base of the award by adjusting the intrinsic value by the ratio of the expired vesting period at acquisition to the total vesting period of the award (as determined for the purposes of IFRS 3 – see Chapter 30 at 11).

A measures the identifiable net assets obtained in the business combination (excluding deferred tax assets and liabilities) at €450 million, with a combined tax base of €300 million, giving rise to a taxable temporary difference at the acquisition date of €150 million, on which deferred tax at 40% of €60 million is recognised. Goodwill is calculated as follows:

	€m
Cash consideration	400
Replacement options	100
Total consideration	500
Identifiable net assets (excluding deferred tax)	(450)
Deferred tax asset	(32)
Deferred tax liability	60
Goodwill	78

Reductions in the carrying amount of goodwill are not deductible for tax purposes. In accordance with the initial recognition exception in IAS 12 (see 7.2 above), A recognises no deferred tax liability for the taxable temporary difference associated with the goodwill recognised in the business combination. The accounting entry for the business combination is therefore as follows:

	DR €m	CR €m
Goodwill	78	
Identifiable net assets	450	
Deferred tax asset	32	
Cash		400
Equity		100
Deferred tax liability		60

On 31 December 2014 the intrinsic value of the replacement awards is €120 million, in respect of which A recognises a deferred tax asset of €48 million (€120 m at 40%). This gives rise to deferred tax income of €16 million (€48 million recognised at 31 December 2014 less €32 million arising on acquisition). IAS 12 notes, somewhat redundantly, that this amount is credited to 'deferred tax income', but with no indication as to whether the amount should be recognised in profit or loss or in equity. In our view, the general principles of IAS 12 regarding tax deductions on share-based payment transactions suggest that the entire amount is recognised in equity. This is because the consolidated financial statements of A have never recognised any expense for the award in profit or loss (since it is attributed fully to the consideration transferred). Therefore none of the tax deductions can be recognised in profit or loss either.

10.8.6 Share-based payment transactions subject to transitional provisions of IFRS 1 and IFRS 2

IFRS 1 and IFRS 2 provide, respectively, first-time adopters and existing IFRS preparers with some transitional exemptions from accounting for share-based payment transactions. The accounting treatment of the tax effects of transactions to which these exemptions have been applied is discussed in Chapter 5 at 7.4.2. Whilst that discussion specifically addresses the tax effects of transactions subject to the exemption for first-time adopters of IFRS, it is equally applicable to the tax effects of transactions subject to the exemptions in IFRS 2 for existing IFRS preparers.

10.9 Change in tax status of entity or shareholders

Sometimes there is a change in an entity's tax assets and liabilities as a result of a change in the tax status of the entity itself or that of its shareholders. SIC-25 clarifies that the effect of such a change should be recognised in profit or loss except to the extent that it involves a remeasurement of tax originally accounted for in other comprehensive income or in equity, in which case the change should also be dealt with in, respectively, other comprehensive income or equity. *[SIC-25.4]*.

10.10 Previous revaluation of PP&E treated as deemed cost on transition to IFRS

In some cases IFRS 1 allows an entity, on transition to IFRS, to treat the carrying amount of property, plant, and equipment (PP&E) revalued under its pre-transition GAAP as a deemed cost for the purposes of IFRS (see Chapter 5 at 5.5).

Where an asset is carried at deemed cost on transition to IFRS, but the tax base of the asset remains at original cost (or an amount based on original cost), the pre-transition revaluation will give rise to a temporary difference (typically, a taxable temporary difference) associated with the asset. IAS 12 requires deferred tax to be recognised on any such temporary difference at transition.

If, after transition, the deferred tax is required to be remeasured (e.g. because of a change in tax rate, or a re-basing of the asset for tax purposes), and the asset concerned was revalued outside profit or loss under pre-transition GAAP, the question arises as to whether the resulting deferred tax income or expense should be recognised in, or outside, profit or loss. This is discussed in Chapter 5 at 7.4.1.

11 CONSOLIDATED TAX RETURNS AND OFFSET OF TAXABLE PROFITS AND LOSSES WITHIN GROUPS

In some jurisdictions one member of a group of companies may file a single tax return on behalf of all, or some, members of the group. In other jurisdictions, it is possible for one member of a group to transfer tax losses to one or more other members of the group in order to reduce their tax liabilities. In some groups a company whose tax liability is reduced by such an arrangement may be required to make a payment to the member of the group that pays tax on its behalf, or transfers losses to it, as the case may be. In other groups no such charge is made.

Such transactions raise the question of the appropriate accounting treatment in the separate financial statements of the group entities involved – in particular, whether the company benefiting from such an arrangement should reflect income (or more likely a capital contribution) from another member of the group equal to the tax expense mitigated as a result of the arrangement.

Some argue that the effects of such transactions should be reflected in the separate financial statements of the entities involved, as is required by some national standards (e.g. those of the US and Australia). Others argue that, except to the extent that a management charge is actually made (see 11.1 below), there is no need to reflect such transactions in the separate financial statements of the entities involved. Those that take this view point out that it is inconsistent to require companies to show a capital contribution for tax losses ceded to them without charge, unless all other intragroup transactions are also restated on arm's-length terms – which would be somewhat radical. Moreover, IAS 24 – *Related Party Disclosures* – merely requires disclosure of the actual terms of such transactions, not that they be remeasured, either for financial reporting or disclosure purposes, on the same basis as a similar notional arm's length transaction (see Chapter 35).

At present, IAS 12 is silent on the issue and, in our view, neither approach can be said to either be prohibited or required. Accordingly, either approach may be adopted on a consistent basis.

The (now withdrawn) exposure draft of a standard to replace IAS 12 published in March 2009 (see 1.3 above) proposed that each entity within a group filing a consolidated tax return should recognise an appropriate share of the total tax liability shown in the return.

11.1 Payments for intragroup transfer of tax losses

Where one member of a group transfers tax losses to another member of the group, the entity whose tax liability is reduced may be required, as matter of group policy, to pay an amount of compensation to the member of the group that transfers the losses to it. Such payments are known by different terms in different jurisdictions, but are referred to in the discussion below as 'tax loss payments'.

Tax loss payments are generally made in an amount equal to the tax saved by the paying company. In some cases, however, payment may be made in an amount equal to the nominal amount of the tax loss, which will be greater than the amount of tax saved. This raises the question of how such payments should be accounted for.

The first issue is whether such payments should be recognised:

- in total comprehensive income, or
- as a distribution (in the case of a payment from a subsidiary to a parent) or a capital contribution (in the case of a payment from a parent to a subsidiary).

The second issue is, to the extent that the payments are accounted for in total comprehensive income, whether they should be classified as:

- income tax, allocated between profit or loss, other comprehensive income or equity (see 10 above). The argument for this treatment is that the payments made or received are amounts that would otherwise be paid to or received from (or offset against an amount paid to) a tax authority; or
- operating income or expense in profit or loss (on the grounds that, as a matter of fact, the payments are not made to or received from any tax authority).

IAS 12 is silent on these issues. However, there is a long-standing practice that such payments are treated as if they were income taxes. We believe that this practice is appropriate to the extent that the intragroup payment is for an amount up to the amount of tax that would otherwise have been paid by the paying company. Where a tax loss payment is made in excess of this amount, we consider that it is more appropriate to account for the excess not as an income tax but as either:

- a distribution or capital contribution (as applicable); or
- operating income or expense (as applicable).

The chosen treatment should be applied consistently.

12 BUSINESS COMBINATIONS

Additional deferred tax arises on business combinations as a result of items such as:

- the application of IAS 12 to the assets and liabilities of the acquired business in the consolidated financial statements, when it has not been applied in the separate financial statements of that business;
- where the acquired entity already applies IAS 12 in its own financial statements, the recognition in the fair value exercise of deferred tax in respect of assets and liabilities of the acquired entity where no deferred tax is provided in those financial statements. This may be the case where a temporary difference arose on initial recognition of an asset or liability in the acquired entity's own financial statements. Deferred tax would then be recognised in the acquirer's consolidated financial statements, because, in those statements, the difference arises on initial recognition in a business combination (see 7.2 above); and
- adjustments made to measure the assets and liabilities of the acquired business fair value, with consequential changes in the temporary differences associated with those assets and liabilities.

Any deferred tax assets or liabilities on temporary differences that arise on a business combination affect the amount of goodwill or bargain purchase gain. *[IAS 12.66].* Example 29.21 at 7.5.1 above illustrates the application of this principle.

12.1 Measurement and recognition of deferred tax in a business combination

IFRS 3 generally requires assets acquired and liabilities assumed in a business combination to be:

- recognised only to the extent that they were assets or liabilities of the acquired entity at the date of acquisition; *[IFRS 3.10]* and
- measured at fair value. *[IFRS 3.18]*.

These provisions of IFRS 3 are discussed in more detail in Chapter 9 at 5. As exceptions to this general principle, IFRS 3 requires an acquirer to:

- recognise and measure a deferred tax asset or liability arising from the assets acquired and liabilities assumed in a business combination 'in accordance with IAS 12'; *[IFRS 3.24]* and
- account for the potential tax effects of temporary differences and carryforwards of an acquiree that exist at the acquisition date or arise as a result of the acquisition 'in accordance with IAS 12'. *[IFRS 3.25]*.

There are essentially two reasons underlying these exceptions. The first is that IAS 12 does not purport to measure future tax at fair value, but at an amount based on a prescribed model that takes no account of the time value of money. Secondly, and more subtly, IAS 12 requires a number of questions of both recognition and measurement to be resolved by reference to management's plans and expectations – in particular, the expected manner of recovery of assets (see 8.4 above) or the likelihood of recovering deferred tax assets (see 7.4 above). The expectations and plans of the acquirer may well differ from those of the acquired entity. For example, the acquired entity might have assessed, for the purposes of IAS 12, that an asset would be recovered through use, whereas the acquirer assesses it as recoverable through sale. The exceptions made by IFRS 3 allow the deferred tax recognised in a business combination to reflect the expectations of the acquirer rather than those of the acquiree.

Areas that give rise to particular difficulties of interpretation are:

- determining the manner of recovery of assets and settlement of liabilities at the date of the business combination (see 12.1.1 below); and
- deferred tax assets (see 12.1.2 below).

12.1.1 Determining the manner of recovery of assets and settlement of liabilities

As discussed at 8.4 above, IAS 12 requires deferred tax to be measured at an amount that reflects the tax consequences that would follow from the manner in which the entity expects to recover its assets or settle its liabilities. The expected manner of recovery or settlement may affect both the tax base of an asset or liability and the tax rate to be applied to any temporary difference arising.

As further noted above, the acquirer's assessment of the manner of recovery for the purposes of IAS 12 may well differ from that of the acquired entity. For example, the acquired entity might have intended to recover an asset through use, whereas the acquirer intends to sell it. In such a case, in our view, the requirement of IFRS 3 to recognise and measure deferred tax in accordance with IAS 12 has the effect that the expectations of the acquirer are used to determine the tax base of an item and the measurement of any deferred tax associated with the item.

12.1.1.A Changes in tax base consequent on the business combination

In some jurisdictions, a business combination may provide the opportunity to revise the tax base of an asset to an amount equal to the fair value assigned to it in accounting for the business combination. Most significantly, this may include the ability to create a tax base for an intangible asset or goodwill which may have had no tax base at all for the acquiree.

In some cases, the increase (as it generally is) in tax base may be more or less automatic. In others, the taxpayer may be required to make a formal claim or election for the increase to the tax authority. Sometimes further restructuring may be required – for example, it may be necessary for the business of the acquired entity to be transferred to another entity in the acquirer's group in the same tax jurisdiction.

An increase in a tax base that requires action by the relevant entity after the acquisition (such as making a claim or election or undertaking a restructuring) occurs after the business combination. However, some hold the view that the ability to increase a tax base following a business combination is a benefit that is taken into account by an informed buyer in negotiating the purchase price. Accordingly, it is argued, the increase is most appropriately reflected by adjusting the tax base of assets acquired as at the date of the business combination as if the increase had occurred at that date. This reduces any deferred tax liability and, therefore, reduces any goodwill (or increases any 'bargain purchase' gain).

Those who support this view note that, if the increase in tax base is accounted for only when it legally occurs in the post-combination period, the net effect is to increase goodwill and reduce post-combination tax expense when in reality the entity may have done little more than fill in a form. It might also be difficult to sustain the higher carrying amount of goodwill arising from this treatment.

We believe that it is generally appropriate to anticipate an increase to a tax base that legally occurs following a business combination in accounting for the business combination where the increase:

- is automatic or requires only a notification to the tax authority;
- requires an application the tax authority that is not normally refused for transactions of a comparable nature; or
- is contingent on some post-acquisition restructuring, where this can be done without substantial difficulty.

Conversely, we believe that it would not generally be appropriate to account for an increase in a tax base until it occurs where the increase:

- relies on 'bespoke' tax planning that may be challenged by the tax authority;
- requires an application to the tax authority that in practice is frequently and successfully challenged for transactions of a comparable nature; or

- is contingent on some post-acquisition restructuring, where this will involve a substantial process, such as obtaining approval from regulators, unions, pension fund trustees etc.

12.1.2 *Deferred tax assets arising on a business combination*

12.1.2.A Assets of the acquirer

If, as a result of a business combination, the acquiring entity is able to recognise a previously unrecognised tax asset of its own (e.g. unused tax losses), the recognition of the asset is accounted for as income, and not as part of the accounting for the business combination. *[IAS 12.67].*

12.1.2.B Assets of the acquiree

It may be the case that deferred tax assets of an acquired entity do not meet the recognition criteria of IAS 12 from the perspective of the acquired entity, but do meet the criteria from the perspective of the acquirer. In such cases, the general principles of IAS 12 require the acquirer's perspective to be applied as at the date of the business combination.

The potential benefit of the acquiree's income tax loss carryforwards or other deferred tax assets may not satisfy the criteria for separate recognition when a business combination is initially accounted for but may be realised subsequently. Any changes in recognised deferred tax assets of an acquired entity are accounted for as follows:

- acquired deferred tax benefits recognised within the measurement period (see Chapter 9 at 5.6.2) that result from new information about facts and circumstances that existed at the acquisition date are applied to reduce the carrying amount of any goodwill related to that acquisition. If the carrying amount of that goodwill is zero, any remaining deferred tax benefits are recognised in profit or loss;
- all other acquired deferred tax benefits realised are recognised in profit or loss (or outside profit or loss if IAS 12 so requires – see 10 above). *[IAS 12.68].*

12.1.3 *Deferred tax liabilities of acquired entity*

IAS 12 contains no specific provisions regarding the recognition of a deferred tax liability of an acquired entity after the date of the original combination. The recognition of such liabilities should therefore be accounted for in accordance with the normal rules of IAS 12 (i.e. in the period in which the liability arises), unless either:

- the recognition of the liability occurs within the provisional measurement period for the business combination and reflects new information about facts and circumstances that existed at the acquisition date, in which case the acquisition date value of the liability is retrospectively adjusted – see Chapter 9 at 12; or
- the failure to recognise the liability at the time of the combination was an error, in which case the provisions of IAS 8 should be applied – see Chapter 3 at 4.6.

12.2 Tax deductions for replacement share-based payment awards in a business combination

IFRS 3 contains some guidance on the treatment of tax deductions for share-based payment transactions made by an acquirer as a replacement for awards made by the acquired entity before the business combination. This is discussed in more detail at 10.8.5 above.

12.3 Apparent immediate impairment of goodwill created by deferred tax

The requirement of IAS 12 to recognise deferred tax on all temporary differences arising on net assets acquired in a business combination leads to the creation of goodwill which, on a literal reading of IAS 36 – *Impairment of Assets*, may then be required to be immediately impaired, as illustrated by Example 29.47 below.

Example 29.47: Apparent 'day one' impairment arising from recognition of deferred tax in a business combination

Entity A, which is taxed at 40%, acquires Entity B for €100m in a transaction that is a business combination. The fair values and tax bases of the identifiable net assets of Entity B are as follows:

	Fair value (€m)	*Tax base* (€m)
Brand name	60	–
Other net assets	20	15

This will give rise to the following consolidation journal:

	€m	€m
Goodwill (balance)	46	
Brand name	60	
Other net assets	20	
Deferred tax[1]		26
Cost of investment		100

1 40% of (€[60m + 20m] – €15m)

The fair value of the consolidated assets of the subsidiary (excluding deferred tax) and goodwill is now €126m, but the cost of the subsidiary is only €100m. Clearly €26m of the goodwill arises solely from the recognition of deferred tax. However, IAS 36, paragraph 50, explicitly requires tax to be excluded from the estimate of future cash flows used to calculate any impairment. This raises the question of whether there should not be an immediate impairment write-down of the assets to €100m. In our view, this cannot have been the intention of IAS 36 (see the further discussion in Chapter 20 at 5.4).

12.4 Tax deductions for acquisition costs

12.4.1 Business combinations accounted for under 'old' IFRS 3

The discussion in this section is relevant to business combinations to which the current version of IFRS 3 (as revised in January 2008) is not applied. The current version of IFRS 3 generally requires transaction costs to be recognised as an expense, so that any tax deduction for those costs would be allocated to profit or loss, in accordance with the general principles discussed at 10 above. However, the previous version of IFRS 3 ('old IFRS 3') permitted certain acquisition costs to be treated as part of the consideration of the business.

In some jurisdictions, tax deductions are given for certain costs of an acquisition which, in the consolidated financial statements prepared under old IFRS 3, are effectively subsumed into the carrying amount of goodwill. This raises the question of how the effects of the tax deductions should be accounted for, as illustrated by Example 29.48 below.

Example 29.48: Tax deduction for acquisition costs under 'old' IFRS 3

Entity A, which pays tax at 40%, acquired 100% of Entity B for €1,000,000 on 1 January 2009. In addition A bore transaction costs, such as professional fees, of €50,000 so that the total purchase price recorded by A for B was €1,050,000. The transaction costs were deductible for tax purposes in the year ended 31 December 2009, so that A received a current tax credit of €20,000 as a result of the transaction costs.

The tax base of the investment in B is €1,000,000, and, if it were sold, any gain arising would be taxable.

In the separate financial statements of A, the carrying amount of the investment in B is €1,050,000. In the consolidated financial statements of A, the net assets of and goodwill of B are carried at €1,050,000 (i.e. the transaction costs represent €50,000 of the goodwill recognised).

A has received a tax deduction of €20,000 (€50,000 @ 40%) in the period and so must record current tax income of this amount.

The issue then arises as to how to deal with the taxable temporary difference of €50,000 associated with the carrying amount of the net assets and goodwill of the investment (cost €1,050,000 less tax base €1,000,000).

One view might be that, in financial reporting terms, this temporary difference relates to the goodwill into which the transaction costs have been subsumed. This temporary difference did not arise on the initial recognition of goodwill, since it resulted from the claiming of a tax deduction after the transaction costs had been recognised in the financial statements. It could also be argued that the difference arises from a transaction that gave rise to a tax loss on initial recognition (see 7.1.3.B above) Therefore, a deferred tax liability is required to be recognised (see 7.2 above).

An alternative analysis would be that as no deduction is received for an item described as 'goodwill' in the tax return, the temporary difference should not be regarded as relating specifically to the goodwill. Rather it is an example of the more general category of differences associated with the carrying amount of an investment in a subsidiary (see 7.5 above). Therefore, a deferred tax liability should be recognised, but subject to the exemptions from recognising such liabilities discussed in 7.5 above.

12.4.2 Business combinations accounted for under 'new' IFRS 3

The discussion in this section is relevant to business combinations to which the current version of IFRS 3 (as revised in January 2008) is applied. Under the current version of IFRS 3 transaction costs are required to be expensed. However, in a number of jurisdictions, transaction costs are regarded as forming part of the cost of the investment, with the effect that a tax deduction for them is given only when the investment is subsequently sold or otherwise disposed of, rather than at the time that the costs are charged to profit or loss.

In such jurisdictions, there will be a deductible 'outside' temporary difference (see 7.5 above) between the carrying value of the net assets and goodwill of the acquired entity in the consolidated financial statements (which will exclude transaction costs) and tax base of the investment in the entity (which will include transaction costs). Whether or not a deferred tax asset is recognised in respect of such a deductible temporary difference will be determined in accordance with the general provisions of IAS 12 for such differences (see 7.5.3 above).

In the separate financial statements of the acquirer, there may be no temporary difference where the transaction costs are, under IAS 27, included in the cost of the investment.

13 PRESENTATION

13.1 Statement of financial position

Tax assets and liabilities should be shown separately from other assets and liabilities and current tax should be shown separately from deferred tax on the face of the statement of financial position. Where an entity presents current and non-current assets and liabilities separately, deferred tax should not be shown as part of current assets or liabilities. *[IAS 1.54-56].*

13.1.1 Offset

13.1.1.A Current tax

Current tax assets and liabilities should be offset if, and only if, the entity:

- has a legally enforceable right to set off the recognised amounts; and
- intends either to settle them net or simultaneously. *[IAS 12.71].*

These restrictions are based on the offset criteria in IAS 32. Accordingly, while entities in many jurisdictions have a right to offset current tax assets and liabilities, and the tax authority permits the entity to make or receive a single net payment, IAS 12 permits offset in financial statements only where there is a positive intention for simultaneous net settlement. *[IAS 12.72].*

The offset restrictions also have the effect that, in consolidated financial statements, a current tax asset of one member of the group may be offset against a current tax liability of another only if the two group members have a legally enforceable right to make or receive a single net payment and a positive intention to recover the asset or settle the liability simultaneously. *[IAS 12.73].*

13.1.1.B Deferred tax

Deferred tax assets and liabilities should be offset if, and only if:

- the entity has a legally enforceable right to set off current tax assets and liabilities; and
- the deferred tax assets and liabilities concerned relate to income taxes raised by the same taxation authority on either:
  - the same taxable entity; or
  - different taxable entities which intend, in each future period in which significant amounts of deferred tax are expected to be settled or recovered, to settle their current tax assets and liabilities either on a net basis or simultaneously. *[IAS 12.74].*

The offset criteria for deferred tax are less clear than those for current tax. The position is broadly that, where in a particular jurisdiction current tax assets and liabilities relating to future periods will be offset, deferred tax assets and liabilities relating to that jurisdiction and those periods must be offset (even if the deferred tax balances actually recognised in the statement of financial position would not satisfy the criteria for the offset of current tax).

IAS 12 suggests that this slightly more pragmatic approach was adopted in order to avoid the detailed scheduling of the reversal of temporary differences that would be necessary to apply the same criteria as for current tax. *[IAS 12.75].*

However, IAS 12 notes that, in rare circumstances, an entity may have a legally enforceable right of set-off, and an intention to settle net, for some periods but not for others. In such circumstances, detailed scheduling may be required to establish reliably whether the deferred tax liability of one taxable entity in the group will result in increased tax payments in the same period in which a deferred tax asset of a second taxable entity in the group will result in decreased payments by that second taxable entity. *[IAS 12.76].*

13.1.1.C Offset of current and deferred tax

IAS 12 contains no provisions allowing or requiring the offset of current tax and deferred tax. Accordingly, in our view, current and deferred tax may not be offset against each other and should always be presented gross.

13.2 Statement of comprehensive income

The tax expense (or income) related to profit or loss from ordinary activities should be presented as a component of profit or loss in the statement of comprehensive income. *[IAS 12.77].*

The results of discontinued operations should be presented on a post-tax basis. *[IFRS 5.33].*

The results of equity-accounted entities should be presented on a post-tax basis. *[IAS 1.IG6].* Any income tax relating to a 'tax-transparent' equity-accounted entity (see 7.6 above) forms part of the investor's tax charge. It is therefore included in the income tax line in profit or loss and not shown as part of the investor's share of the results of the tax-transparent entity.

Components of other comprehensive income may be presented either:

- net of related tax effects; or
- before related tax effects with one amount shown for the total related income tax effects. *[IAS 1.91]*.

IAS 12 notes that, whilst IAS 21 requires certain exchange differences to be recognised within income or expense, it does not specify where exactly in the statement of comprehensive income they should be presented. Accordingly, exchange differences relating to deferred tax assets and liabilities may be classified as deferred tax expense (or income), if that presentation is considered to be the most useful to users of the financial statements. *[IAS 12.78]*. IAS 12 makes no reference to the treatment of exchange differences on current tax assets and liabilities but, presumably, the same considerations apply.

13.3 Statement of cash flows

Cash flows arising from taxes on income are separately disclosed and classified as cash flows from operating activities, unless they can be specifically identified with financing and investing activities. *[IAS 7.35]*.

IAS 7 – *Statement of Cash Flows* – notes that, whilst it is relatively easy to identify the expense relating to investing or financing activities, the related tax cash flows are often impracticable to identify. Therefore, taxes paid are usually classified as cash flows from operating activities. However, when it is practicable to identify the tax cash flow with an individual transaction that gives rise to cash flows that are classified as investing or financing activities, the tax cash flow is classified as an investing or financing activity as appropriate. When tax cash flows are allocated over more than one class of activity, the total amount of taxes paid is disclosed. *[IAS 7.36]*.

14 DISCLOSURE

IAS 1 notes that users would expect an entity subject to income taxes to disclose its accounting policies for income taxes, including those applicable to deferred tax liabilities and assets. *[IAS 1.120]*.

IAS 12 imposes extensive disclosure requirements as follows.

14.1 Components of tax expense

The major components of tax expense (or income) should be disclosed separately. These may include:

(a) current tax expense (or income);

(b) any adjustments recognised in the period for current tax of prior periods;

(c) the amount of deferred tax expense (or income) relating to the origination and reversal of temporary differences;

(d) the amount of deferred tax expense (or income) relating to changes in tax rates or the imposition of new taxes;

(e) the amount of the benefit arising from a previously unrecognised tax loss, tax credit or temporary difference of a prior period that is used to reduce current tax expense;

(f) the amount of the benefit from a previously unrecognised tax loss, tax credit or temporary difference of a prior period that is used to reduce deferred tax expense;

(g) deferred tax expense arising from the write-down, or reversal of a previous write-down, of a deferred tax asset; and

(h) the amount of tax expense (or income) relating to those changes in accounting policies and errors which are included in the profit or loss in accordance with IAS 8 because they cannot be accounted for retrospectively (see Chapter 3 at 4.7). *[IAS 12.79-80].*

14.2 Other disclosures

The following should also be disclosed separately: *[IAS 12.81]*

(a) the aggregate current and deferred tax relating to items that are charged or credited to equity; and

(b) the amount of income tax relating to each component of other comprehensive income;

(c) an explanation of the relationship between tax expense (or income) and accounting profit in either or both of the following forms:

  (i) a numerical reconciliation between tax expense (or income) and the product of accounting profit multiplied by the applicable tax rate(s), disclosing also the basis on which the applicable tax rate(s) is (are) computed; or

  (ii) a numerical reconciliation between the average effective tax rate (i.e. tax expense (or income) divided by accounting profit) *[IAS 12.86]* and the applicable tax rate, disclosing also the basis on which the applicable tax rate is computed;

  This requirement is discussed further at 14.2.1 below.

(d) an explanation of changes in the applicable tax rate(s) compared to the previous accounting period;

(e) the amount (and expiry date, if any) of deductible temporary differences, unused tax losses, and unused tax credits for which no deferred tax asset is recognised in the statement of financial position;

(f) the aggregate amount of temporary differences associated with investments in subsidiaries, branches and associates and interests in joint arrangements, for which deferred tax liabilities have not been recognised;

  This is discussed further at 14.2.2 below.

(g) in respect of each type of temporary difference, and in respect of each type of unused tax losses and unused tax credits:

   - (i) the amount of the deferred tax assets and liabilities recognised in the statement of financial position for each period presented;
   - (ii) the amount of the deferred tax income or expense recognised in profit or loss, if this is not apparent from the changes in the amounts recognised in the statement of financial position;

   The analysis in (ii) will be required, for example, by any entity with acquisitions and disposals, or deferred tax accounted for in other comprehensive income or equity, since this will have the effect that the year-on-year movement in the statement of financial position is not solely due to items recognised in profit or loss;

- (h) in respect of discontinued operations, the tax expense relating to:
   - (i) the gain or loss on discontinuance; and
   - (ii) the profit or loss from the ordinary activities of the discontinued operation for the period, together with the corresponding amounts for each prior period presented;
- (i) the amount of income tax consequences of dividends to shareholders of the entity that were proposed or declared before the financial statements were authorised for issue, but are not recognised as a liability in the financial statements.

   Further disclosures are required in respect of the tax consequences of distributing retained earnings, which are discussed at 14.4 below;
- (j) if a business combination in which the entity is the acquirer causes a change in the amount of a deferred tax asset of the entity (see 12.1.2 above), the amount of that change; and
- (k) if the deferred tax benefits acquired in a business combination are not recognised at the acquisition date, but are recognised after the acquisition date (see 12.1.2 above), a description of the event or change in circumstances that caused the deferred tax benefits to be recognised.

Tax-related contingent liabilities and contingent assets (such as those arising from unresolved disputes with taxation authorities) are disclosed in accordance with IAS 37 (see Chapter 27 at 7). *[IAS 12.88].*

Significant effects of changes in tax rates or tax laws enacted or announced after the reporting period on current and deferred tax assets and liabilities are disclosed in accordance with IAS 10 (see Chapter 34 at 2). *[IAS 12.88].*

14.2.1 Tax (or tax rate) reconciliation

IAS 12 explains that the purpose of the tax reconciliation required by (c) above is to enable users of financial statements to understand whether the relationship between tax expense (or income) and accounting profit is unusual and to understand the significant factors that could affect that relationship in the future. The relationship may be affected by the effects of such factors as:

- revenue and expenses that are outside the scope of taxation;
- tax losses; and
- foreign tax rates. *[IAS 12.84].*

Accordingly, in explaining the relationship between tax expense (or income) and accounting profit, an entity should use an applicable tax rate that provides the most meaningful information to the users of its financial statements.

Often, the most meaningful rate is the domestic rate of tax in the country in which the entity is domiciled. In this case, the tax rate applied for national taxes should be aggregated with the rates applied for any local taxes which are computed on a substantially similar level of taxable profit (tax loss). However, for an entity operating in several jurisdictions, it may be more meaningful to aggregate separate reconciliations prepared using the domestic rate in each individual jurisdiction. *[IAS 12.85]*. Where this latter approach is adopted, the entity may need to discuss the effect of significant changes in either tax rates, or the mix of profits earned in different jurisdictions, in order to satisfy the requirement of IAS 12 to give an explanation of changes in the applicable tax rate(s) compared to the previous accounting period – see item (d) at 14.2 above.

Example 29.49 illustrates how the selection of the applicable tax rate affects the presentation of the numerical reconciliation.

Example 29.49: Alternative presentations of tax reconciliation

In 2014 an entity has accounting profit of €3,000m (2013: €2,500m) comprising €1,500m (2013: €2,000m) in its own jurisdiction (country A) and €1,500m (2013: €500m) in country B. The tax rate is 30% in country A and 20% in country B. In country B, expenses of €200m (2013: €100m) are not deductible for tax purposes. There are no other differences between accounting profit and profit that is subject to current tax, or on which deferred tax has been provided for under IAS 12.

Thus the accounting tax charge in the financial statements for each period will be as follows:

	2014 €m	2013 €m
Country A		
€1,500m/€2,000m @ 30%	450	600
Country B		
€[1,500 + 200]m/€[500 + 100]m @ 20%	340	120
Total tax charge	790	720

Reconciliation based on A's domestic tax rate

If the entity presents a tax reconciliation based on its own (i.e. country A's) domestic tax rate, the following presentation would be adopted.

	2014 €m	2013 €m
Accounting profit	3,000	2,500
Tax at domestic rate of 30%	900	750
Effect of:		
Expenses not deductible for tax purposes[1]	60	30
Overseas tax rates[2]	(170)	(60)
Tax expense	790	720

1 €200m/€100m @ 30%

2 B's taxable profit €1,700m/€600m @ (20% – 30%)

Chapter 29

Reconciliation based on each jurisdiction's tax rate

If the entity presents a tax reconciliation based on each jurisdiction's domestic tax rate, the following presentation would be adopted.

	2014 €m	2013 €m
Accounting profit	3,000	2,500
Tax at domestic rates applicable to individual group entities[1]	750	700
Effect of:		
Expenses not deductible for tax purposes[2]	40	20
Tax expense	790	720

1 2014: A = €450m [€1,500m @ 30%], B = €300m [€1,500m @ 20%], total €750m
2013: A = €600m [€2,000m @ 30%], B = €100m [€500m @ 20%], total €700m

2 €200m/€100m @ 20%

14.2.2 Temporary differences relating to subsidiaries, associates, branches and joint arrangements

IAS 12 requires an entity to disclose the gross temporary differences associated with subsidiaries, associates, branches and joint arrangements, as opposed to the unrecognised deferred tax on those temporary differences – see (f) under 14.2 above.

IAS 12 clarifies that this approach is adopted because it would often be impracticable to compute the amount of unrecognised deferred tax. Nevertheless, where practicable, entities are encouraged to disclose the amounts of the unrecognised deferred tax liabilities because financial statement users may find such information useful. *[IAS 12.87]*.

14.3 Reason for recognition of certain tax assets

Separate disclosure is required of the amount of any deferred tax asset that is recognised, and the nature of the evidence supporting its recognition, when:

(a) utilisation of the deferred tax asset is dependent on future profits in excess of those arising from the reversal of deferred tax liabilities; and

(b) the entity has suffered a loss in the current or preceding period in the tax jurisdiction to which the asset relates. *[IAS 12.82]*.

In effect these disclosures are required when the entity has rebutted the presumption inherent in the recognition rules of IAS 12 that tax assets should not normally be recognised in these circumstances (see 7.4 above).

14.4 Dividends

As discussed at 8.5 above, where there are different tax consequences for an entity depending on whether profits are retained or distributed, tax should be measured at the rates applicable to retained profits except to the extent that there is a liability to pay dividends at the end of the reporting period, where the rate applicable to distributed profits should be used.

Where such differential tax rates apply, the entity should disclose the nature of the potential income tax consequences that would arise from a payment of dividends to shareholders. It should quantify the amount of potential income tax consequences that is practicably determinable and disclose whether there are any potential income tax consequences that are not practicably determinable. *[IAS 12.82A]*. This will include disclosure of the important features of the income tax systems and the factors that will affect the amount of the potential income tax consequences of dividends. *[IAS 12.87A]*.

The reason for this rather complicated requirement is that, as IAS 12 acknowledges, it can often be very difficult to quantify the tax consequences of a full distribution of profits (e.g. where there are a large number of overseas subsidiaries). Moreover, IAS 12 concedes that there is a tension between, on the one hand, the exemption from disclosing the deferred tax associated with temporary differences associated with subsidiaries and other investments (see 14.2.2 above) and, on the other hand, this requirement to disclose the tax effect of distributing undistributed profits – in some cases they could effectively be the same number.

However, to the extent that any liability can be quantified, it should be disclosed. This may mean that consolidated financial statements will disclose the potential tax effect of distributing the earnings of some, but not all, subsidiaries, associates, branches and joint arrangements.

IAS 12 emphasises that, in an entity's separate financial statements, this requirement applies only to the undistributed earnings of the entity itself and not those of any of its subsidiaries, associates, branches and joint arrangements. *[IAS 12.87A-87C]*.

14.5 Example of disclosures

Examples of many of the disclosures required under IAS 12 are given by BP.

Extract 29.2: BP p.l.c (2012)

Notes on financial statements [extract]

18. Taxation

Tax on profit

			$ million
	2012	2011	2010
Current tax			
Charge for the year	**6,632**	7,477	6,766
Adjustment in respect of prior years	**252**	111	(74)
	6.884	7,588	6,692
Deferred tax			
Origination and reversal of temporary differences in the current year	**212**	5,664	(8,157)
Adjustment in respect of prior years	**(103)**	(515)	(36)
	109	5,149	(8,193)
Tax charge (credit) on profit (loss)	**6,993**	12,737	(1,501)

Tax included in other comprehensive income[a]

			$ million
	2012	2011	2010
Current tax	**2**	(10)	(107)
Deferred tax	**(448)**	(1,649)	244
	(446)	(1,659)	137

a See Note 39 for further information.

Tax included directly in equity

			$ million
	2012	2011	2010
Current tax	**(10)**	–	(37)
Deferred tax	**4**	(7)	64
	(6)	(7)	27

Reconciliation of the effective tax rate

The following table provides a reconciliation of the UK statutory corporation tax rate to the effective tax rate of the group on profit or loss before taxation. With effect from 1 April 2012 the UK statutory corporation tax rate reduced from 26% to 24% on profits from activities outside the North Sea.

For 2010, the items presented in the reconciliation are distorted as a result of the overall tax credit for the year and the loss before taxation. In order to provide a more meaningful analysis of the effective tax rate for 2010, the table also presents separate reconciliations for the group excluding the impacts of the Gulf of Mexico oil spill, and for the impacts of the Gulf of Mexico oil spill in isolation.

					$ million
	2012	2011	2010 excluding impacts of Gulf of Mexico oil spill	2010 impacts of Gulf of Mexico oil spill	2010
Profit (loss) before taxation	**18,809**	38,834	36,110	(40,935)	(4,825)
Tax charge (credit) on profit (loss)	**6.993**	12,737	11,393	(12,894)	(1,501)
Effective tax rate	**37%**	33%	32%	31%	31%
			% of profit or loss before taxation		
UK statutory corporation tax rate	**24**	26	28	28	28
Increase (decrease) resulting from:					
UK supplementary and overseas taxes at higher or lower rates[a]	**11**	14	9	7	(4)
Tax reported in equity-accounted entities	**(5)**	(3)	(3)	–	23
Adjustments in respect of prior years	**1**	(1)	–	–	2
Movements in losses not recognized	**–**	–	–	–	1
Tax incentives for investment	**(2)**	(1)	(1)	–	9
Gulf of Mexico oil spill non-deductible costs	**8**	–	–	(4)	(30)
Permanent differences relating to disposals	**–**	(2)	(1)	–	5
Other	**–**	–	–	–	(3)
Effective tax rate	**37**	33	32	31	31

a For 2012, the jurisdictions which contributed significantly to this item were Angola, with an applicable statutory tax rate of 50%, the UK, with an applicable statutory tax rate of 62% for North Sea activities, and Trinidad & Tobago, with an applicable statutory tax rate of 55%.

Deferred tax

					$ million
		Income statement			Balance sheet
	2012	2011[a]	2010[a]	**2012**	2011[a]
Deferred tax liability					
Depreciation	**(121)**	4,738	1,304	**31,839**	32,119
Pension plan surpluses	**–**	–	38	**–**	–
Other taxable temporary differences	**(2,240)**	149	1,178	**3,681**	5,704
	(2,361)	4,887	2,520	**35,520**	37,823
Deferred tax asset					
Pension plan and other post-retirement benefit plan deficits	**160**	388	179	**(3,389)**	(2,872)
Decommissioning, environmental and other provisions	**1,872**	(1,443)	(8,210)	**(12,705)**	(14,743)
Derivative financial instruments	**(7)**	24	(56)	**(281)**	(274)
Tax credits	**1,802**	(401)	(1,088)	**(714)**	(2,549)
Loss carry forward	**(912)**	(218)	24	**(2,209)**	(1,295)
Other deductible temporary differences	**(445)**	1,912	(1,562)	**(2,032)**	(1,623)
	2,470	262	(10,713)	**(21,330)**	(23,356)
Net deferred tax charge (credit) and net deferred tax liability	**109**	5,149	(8,193)	**14,190**	14,467
Of which – deferred tax liabilities				**15,064**	15,078
– deferred tax assets				**874**	611

a Certain comparative amounts shown in the analysis of deferred tax by category of temporary difference have been reclassified. There is no change to the tax amounts reported in the income statement, balance sheet or cash flow statement.

		$ million
Analysis of movements during the year in the net deferred tax liability	**2012**	2011
At 1 January	**14,467**	10,380
Exchange adjustments	**(33)**	55
Charge for the year on profit	**109**	5,149
Credit for the year in other comprehensive income	**(448)**	(1,649)
Charge (credit) for the year in equity	**4**	(7)
Acquisitions	**11**	692
Reclassified as assets/liabilities held for sale	**48**	(140)
Deletions	**32**	(13)
At 31 December	**14,190**	14,467

Deferred tax assets are recognized to the extent that it is probable that taxable profit will be available against which the deductible temporary differences and the carry-forward of unused tax credits and unused tax losses can be utilized.

At 31 December 2012, the group had approximately $6.8 billion (2011 $4.6 billion) of carry-forward tax losses that would be available to offset against future taxable profit. A deferred tax asset has been recognized in respect of $6.0 billion of these losses (2011 $3.8 billion). No deferred tax asset has been recognized in respect of $0.8 billion of losses (2011 $0.8 billion). In 2012 no current tax benefit arose relating to losses utilized on which a deferred tax asset had not previously been recognized (2011 $0.1 billion). Substantially all the tax losses have no fixed expiry date.

At 31 December 2012, the group had approximately $19.0 billion of unused tax credits, predominantly in the UK and US (2011 $18.2 billion). At 31 December 2012, a deferred tax asset of $0.7 billion has been recognized in respect of unused tax credits (2011 $2.5 billion). No deferred tax asset has been recognized in respect of $18.3 billion of tax credits (2011 $15.7 billion). In 2012 a current tax benefit of $0.4 billion arose relating to tax credits utilized on which a deferred tax asset had not previously been recognized (2011 $0.1 billion). Also in 2012, a deferred tax benefit of $0.1 billion arose relating to the recognition of previously unrecognized tax credits (2011 nil). The UK tax credits, arising in overseas branches of UK entities, with no associated deferred tax asset, amount to $16.0 billion (2011 $13.0 billion) and have no fixed expiry date. These credits arise in branches predominantly based in high tax rate jurisdictions so are unlikely to have value in the future as UK taxes on these overseas branches are largely mitigated by the double tax relief on the overseas tax. The US tax credits with no associated deferred tax asset, amounting to $2.3 billion (2011 $2.7 billion) expire 10 years after generation and will all expire in the period 2014-2021.

The group had other unrecognized deferred tax assets at 31 December 2012 of $1.8 billion (2011 $1.1 billion), of which $1.3 billion arose in the UK (2011 $0.9 billion), which have not been recognized due to uncertainty over future recovery.

The group recognized significant costs in 2010 in relation to the Gulf of Mexico oil spill and in 2011 recognized certain recoveries relating to the incident as well as further costs. In 2012, the group has recognized further costs, including costs relating to the settlement of all criminal and securities claims with the US government which are not tax deductible. Tax has been calculated on the expenditures that are expected to qualify for tax relief, and on the recoveries, at the US statutory tax rate. A deferred tax asset has been recognized in respect of provisions for future expenditure that are expected to qualify for tax relief, included under the heading decommissioning, environmental and other provisions in the table above.

The other major components of temporary differences at the end of 2012 relate to tax depreciation, provisions, US inventory holding gains (classified as other taxable temporary differences) and pension and other post-retirement benefit plan deficits.

During 2012, our method of accounting, for tax purposes, for oil and gas inventory in the US has changed from the last-in first-out ("LIFO") basis to the first-in, first-out ("FIFO") basis. This has accelerated the taxation of inventory holding gains and reduced the taxable temporary difference in respect of this item.

At 31 December 2012, the group had $0.5 billion (2011 $0.1 billion) of taxable temporary differences associated with investments in subsidiaries and equity-accounted entities for which deferred tax liabilities have not been recognized on the basis that the group is able to control the timing of the reversal of the temporary differences and it is not probable that the temporary differences will reverse in the foreseeable future.

In 2012, legislation to restrict relief for UK decommissioning expenditure in the North Sea from 62% to 50% was enacted and increased the deferred tax charge in the income statement by $289 million, of which $256 million relates to the revaluation of the deferred tax balance at 1 January 2012. In 2011, the enactment of a 12% increase in the UK supplementary charge on oil and gas production activities in the North Sea raised the overall corporation tax rate applicable to North Sea activities to 62%. This rate change increased the deferred tax charge in the 2011 income statement by $713 million, of which $683 million related to the revaluation of the deferred tax balance at 1 January 2011.

Also in 2012, the enactment of a further 2% reduction in the rate of UK corporation tax to 23% with effect from 1 April 2013 on profits arising from activities outside the North Sea reduced the deferred tax charge in the income statement by $165 million. In 2011, the enactment of a 2% reduction in the rate of UK corporation tax to 25% with effect from 1 April 2011 similarly reduced the deferred tax charge in the income statement by $120 million.

14.6 Discontinued operations – interaction with IFRS 5

IFRS 5 requires the post-tax results of discontinued operations to be shown separately on the face of the statement of comprehensive income (and any separate income statement presenting the components of profit or loss). This may be done by giving the results of discontinued operations after those of continuing operations. This is discussed further in Chapter 4.

The definitions of income tax, tax expense and taxable profit in IAS 12 (see 3 above) do not distinguish between the results of continuing and discontinued operations, or the tax on those results. Thus, as drafted, IAS 12 applies not only to the tax income or expense on continuing operations (i.e. the amount shown in the 'tax line' in the income statement) but also to any tax income or expense relating to the results of discontinued operations separately disclosed after those of continuing operations.

However, IFRS 5 clarifies that items accounted for under that standard are not subject to the disclosure requirements of other standards, other than:

- specific disclosures in respect of non-current assets (or disposal groups) classified as held for sale or discontinued operations; or
- disclosures about the measurement of assets and liabilities within a disposal group that are not within the scope of the measurement requirements of IFRS 5, where such disclosures are not already provided in the other notes to the financial statements. *[IFRS 5.5B]*.

15 POSSIBLE FUTURE DEVELOPMENTS

The IASB's income taxes project had originally been one of the areas under discussion by the IASB and the FASB as part of the short-term convergence project of the two standard-setters aimed at eliminating differences between US GAAP and IFRS. This joint project had been expected to lead to the publication of exposure drafts of standards to replace IAS 12 and FASB ASC Topic 740. However, as the project progressed, it proved more difficult to reach agreement on a common approach than might have been expected, given the similarity of the two standards.

Since August 2008, the FASB has suspended its deliberations on the Income Taxes project.[24]

Notwithstanding the FASB's withdrawal from the project, in March 2009 the IASB published an exposure draft (ED/2009/2) of a standard proposed to replace IAS 12 (see 1.3 above). This exposure draft was not generally well received and was not proceeded with. As a result, the IASB's income taxes project has been restricted to the resolution of problems arising under IAS 12 in practice without changing the fundamental approach of the standard and preferably without increasing divergence from US GAAP.[25]

In its *Agenda Consultation 2011* issued in July 2011, the IASB recognised that IAS 12 is sometimes difficult to apply. An issue to be addressed within the current project is the accounting for uncertain tax positions (see 9 above). The *Agenda Consultation* also referred to a possible 'fundamental review' of accounting for income taxes. It is not clear what this might entail, but it might well take as its starting point the discussion paper *Improving the Financial Reporting of Income Tax* published by the EFRAG in December 2011. This paper noted a number of practical and conceptual problems with IAS 12 and suggested possible alternatives to the temporary difference approach. In responding to the discussion paper, we broadly agreed that there are a number of practical problems with IAS 12, but expressed the view that we would prefer to see these resolved by targeted amendments and improvements to IAS 12 rather than by a wholesale review of accounting for income taxes, particularly in view of the other priorities of the IASB and the constraints on its resources.

The IASB continues to consider a limited scope amendment to IAS 12 with respect to the recognition of deferred tax assets on losses on available-for-sale debt securities (see 7.4.3.A above).

The Interpretations Committee continues to consider the assessment, for the purposes of IAS 12, of the manner of recovery of assets held within a 'single asset' entity (see 8.4.10.A above).

References

1 This analysis is less relevant under the IASB's *Framework*, which would classify the state's 'participation' in an entity through taxation as a liability and expense, not an equity interest and distribution.

2 Throughout this Chapter, the tax treatment described in examples is purely illustrative, and does not necessarily relate to a specific provision of tax law in a jurisdiction using the currency in the example.

3 SIC-25, *Income Taxes – Changes in the Tax Status of an Entity or its Shareholders*, SIC, July 2000.

4 For transactions not accounted for under IFRS 3 – *Business Combinations* as revised in January 2008: 'the amount of any excess of the acquirer's interest in the net fair value of the acquiree's identifiable assets, liabilities and contingent liabilities over the cost of the combination'.

5 *IFRIC Update*, March 2006.

6 *IFRIC Update*, June 2004.

7 ED/2009/2 *Income Tax*, IASB, March 2009, para. 39.

8 Based on a summary in *IASB Update*, February 2005.

9 In some cases research and share-based payment costs may be included as part of the cost of other assets, such as inventories or PP&E.

10 ED/2009/2, Appendix A, definition of 'tax basis'.

11 ED/2009/2, paras. 20 and 23.

12 *IFRIC Update*, April 2005.

13 *IFRIC Update*, June 2005.

14 *IASB Update*, December 2012.

15 *IFRIC Update*, May 2013.

16 *IFRIC Update*, June 2005.

17 *IFRIC Update*, February 2003.

18 *IFRIC Update*, May 2007. The IFRIC made its decision based on the then current of IAS 12, which referred to 'joint ventures' rather than 'joint arrangements'

19 SIC-21, Income Taxes – *Recovery of Non-Depreciable Assets*, SIC, July 2000, para. 4.

20 *IFRIC Update*, November 2011.

21 *IFRIC Update*, May 2012.

22 ED/2009/2, paras. 27(d), B31-B32.

23 This example is illustrative only and does not imply any preference for the unit of account chosen by the entity in the example.

24 FASB website, September 2011.

25 IASB website, October 2012.

Chapter 30 Share-based payment

List of examples

Chapter 30 Share-based payment

1 INTRODUCTION

1.1 Background

Share-based payment is one of the most controversial projects so far tackled by the IASB, arousing as it does strong passions not only among the IASB's normal constituency but also at the highest political levels. The reason for this is that most share-based payment transactions undertaken by entities are awards of shares and options as remuneration to employees, in particular senior management and directors. In a number of countries, shares and options now comprise the greatest element of the total remuneration package of senior personnel, a trend encouraged by the current consensus that it is a matter of good corporate governance to promote significant long-term shareholdings by senior management, so as to align their economic interests with those of shareholders.

One advantage of shares and options as remuneration is that they need not entail any cash cost to the entity. If an executive is entitled under a bonus scheme to a free share, the entity can satisfy this award simply by printing another share certificate, which the executive can sell, so that the cash cost of the award is effectively borne by shareholders rather than by the entity itself. However, this very advantage was the source of the controversy surrounding share-based remuneration.

Investors became increasingly concerned that share-based remuneration was resulting in a significant cost to them, through dilution of their existing shareholdings. As a result, there emerged an increasing consensus among investors that awards of shares and share options should be recognised as a cost in the financial statements.

The opposing view, held by most entities, was that the financial statements were simply reflecting the economic reality that such awards are ultimately a cost to other shareholders and not to the entity. Another powerful argument for those opposed to expensing options was to point out that some patently successful companies, particularly in the new technology sector, would never have shown a profit if they had been required to book an accounting expense for options.

The strength of feeling amongst opponents of expensing share-based remuneration was graphically illustrated in the early 1990s when the FASB in the United States attempted to issue an accounting standard requiring options to be expensed, only to be forced into a partial climb-down by an unprecedented political campaign. As a result, the US standard issued by the FASB at that stage, FAS 123 – *Accounting for Stock-Based Compensation* – was a compromise which required the fair value of shares or options issued to employees to be disclosed, but merely recommended, without requiring, those fair values to be expensed in the financial statements. Eventually, however, in December 2004, following the issue of IFRS 2 – *Share-based Payment* – earlier that year (see 1.2 below), the FASB issued FASB ASC 718 – *Compensation – Stock Compensation* (formerly FAS 123(R) – *Share-Based Payment*) – which requires the fair value of share awards to be expensed.

1.2 Development of IFRS 2

In November 2002, the IASB issued an exposure draft ED 2 – *Share-based Payment* – proposing that share-based payments for goods and services should be expensed. The exposure draft proved highly controversial. Those who supported it in principle nevertheless had concerns on nearly every detail of the accounting treatment proposed, in particular the fact that it did not permit any 'truing up', i.e. reversing any expense previously charged for an award that never actually crystallises. More fundamentally, many questioned whether there yet existed a methodology sufficiently robust for valuing shares and share options subject to the restrictions and performance conditions typically associated with employee share awards. There also remained a significant minority who still questioned the whole principle of expensing options and other share awards.

Despite these comments, the IASB finalised its proposals with the publication of IFRS 2 – *Share-based Payment* – on 19 February 2004, although some significant changes had been necessary to the prohibition on 'truing up' in the ED. In particular, IFRS 2 requires an expense to be recognised only for awards that vest (or are considered by IFRS 2 to vest), but (in the case of awards settled in shares) based on their fair value at the date of grant. Nevertheless, IFRS 2 remains contentious: for example, there is still only limited provision for 'truing up', with the result that significant costs can potentially be recognised for awards that ultimately have no value to their recipients, and give rise to no dilution of the interests of other shareholders. Some commentators continue to question whether existing option valuation models can produce a reliable valuation of employee share awards.

The IASB has issued two amendments to the original version of IFRS 2:

- *Vesting Conditions and Cancellations*,[1] issued in January 2008 ('the January 2008 amendment'). Entities are required to apply IFRS 2 as modified by this amendment for periods beginning on or after 1 January 2009 *[IFRS 2.62]*; and
- *Group Cash-settled Share-based Payment Transactions*,[2] issued in June 2009 ('the June 2009 amendment'). Entities are required to apply IFRS 2 as modified by this amendment for periods beginning on or after 1 January 2010. *[IFRS 2.63]*.

Improvements to IFRSs issued in April 2009 made a minor amendment to the scope of IFRS 2 ('the April 2009 amendment'), discussed at 2.2.3.D below.

There have been two interpretations of IFRS 2 by the Interpretations Committee, IFRIC 8 – *Scope of IFRS 2* – and IFRIC 11 – *IFRS 2 – Group and Treasury Share Transactions*, but these were incorporated into IFRS 2 as part of the June 2009 amendment and the separate interpretations withdrawn. *[IFRS 2.64]*.

IFRS 3 – *Business Combinations* (as revised in 2008 and amended in 2010) amended IFRS 2 and provides guidance on the replacement of share-based payment awards in a business combination (see 11 below).

IFRS 10 – *Consolidated Financial Statements* – is relevant to accounting for employee benefit trusts and similar entities for accounting periods beginning on or after 1 January 2013 (see 12.3 below). For earlier periods SIC-12 – *Consolidation – Special Purpose Entities* – applied.

IFRS 2 is supplemented by implementation guidance. However, as noted above the first paragraph of the implementation guidance, this 'accompanies, but is not part of, IFRS 2'.

1.3 Scope of the Chapter and referencing convention

This Chapter generally discusses the requirements of IFRS 2 for accounting periods beginning on or after 1 January 2014 and reflects the amendments to the original version of IFRS 2 referred to at 1.2 above. This amended version of IFRS 2 is referred to as 'IFRS 2' throughout the Chapter.

1.4 Overall approach of IFRS 2

IFRS 2 is a complex standard, in part because its overall accounting approach is something of a hybrid. Essentially the total cost (i.e. measurement) of an award is calculated by determining whether the award is a liability or an equity instrument, using criteria somewhat different from those in IAS 32 – *Financial Instruments: Presentation* (see 1.4.1 below), but then applying the measurement principles generally applicable to liabilities or equity instruments under IAS 32 and IAS 39 – *Financial Instruments: Recognition and Measurement*. However the periodic allocation (i.e. recognition) of the cost[3] is determined using something closer to a straight-line accruals methodology, which would not generally be used for financial instruments.

This inevitably has the result that, depending on its legal form, a transaction of equal value to the recipient can result in several different potential charges in profit or loss, causing some to call into question the comparability of the information provided. Moreover, IFRS 2 is in many respects a rules-based 'anti-avoidance' standard, which often requires an expense to be recorded for transactions that either have no ultimate value to the counterparty or to which, in some cases, the counterparty actually has no entitlement at all. IFRS 2 has an unusually long Basis for Conclusions – longer in fact than the standard and implementation guidance combined, begging the question of whether a standard with clear conceptual foundations would have required such copious justification.

1.4.1 Classification differences between IFRS 2 and IAS 32/IAS 39

As noted above, not only are there differences between the accounting treatment of liabilities or equity under IFRS 2 as compared with that under IAS 32 and IAS 39, but the classification of a transaction as a liability or equity transaction under IFRS 2 may differ from that under IAS 32.

The most important difference between IAS 32 and IFRS 2 is that a transaction involving the delivery of equity instruments within the scope of IFRS 2 is always accounted for as an equity transaction, whereas a similar transaction within the scope of IAS 32 might well be classified as a liability if the number of shares to be delivered varies.

The IASB offers some (pragmatic rather than conceptual) explanation for these differences in the Basis for Conclusions to IFRS 2. First, it is argued that to apply IAS 32 to share option plans would mean that a variable share option plan (i.e. one where the number of shares varied according to performance) would give rise to a more volatile (and typically greater) cost than a fixed plan (i.e. one where the number of shares to be awarded is fixed from the start), even if the same number of shares was ultimately delivered under each plan, which would have 'undesirable consequences'. *[IFRS 2.BC109]*. Second, it is argued that this is just one of several inconsistencies between IAS 32 and IFRS 2 to be addressed in the round as part of the IASB's review of accounting for debt and equity (see below). *[IFRS 2.BC110]*.

1.4.1.A Fair value at grant date with no remeasurement: possible future developments

In July 2013 the IASB published the Discussion Paper 'A Review of the Conceptual Framework for Financial Reporting' (see Chapter 2 at 3).[4] Under the 'strict obligation' approach set out in the paper, remeasurement of all share-based payments would potentially be required, rather than just cash-settled awards as is currently the case (see paragraph 5.37 of the Discussion Paper). Under such an approach, it is likely that equity-settled awards would have to be remeasured through equity at each reporting date until exercise or settlement.

2 THE OBJECTIVE AND SCOPE OF IFRS 2

Section 2 sets out the objective of IFRS 2 (see 2.1 below) and then considers the scope of the standard in the following sub-sections:

- definitions in IFRS 2 relevant to the scope of the standard (see 2.2.1 below);
- transactions and arrangements within the scope of IFRS 2 (see 2.2.2 below) including arrangements within a group and with shareholders (see 2.2.2.A below);
- transactions outside the scope of IFRS 2 (see 2.2.3 below); and
- application of the scope requirements to a number of situations frequently encountered in practice (see 2.2.4 below).

Further details of the transactions and arrangements discussed are given at the start of each sub-section.

2.1 Objective

The stated objective of IFRS 2 is 'to specify the financial reporting by an entity when it undertakes a share-based payment transaction. In particular, it requires an entity to reflect in its profit or loss and financial position the effects of share-based payment transactions, including expenses associated with transactions in which share options are granted to employees'. *[IFRS 2.1].*

2.2 Scope

2.2.1 Definitions

The following definitions from Appendix A to IFRS 2 are relevant to the scope of IFRS 2.

A *share-based payment arrangement* is 'an agreement between the entity (or another group entity or any shareholder of any group entity) and another party (including an employee) that entitles the other party to receive

(a) cash or other assets of the entity for amounts that are based on the price (or value) of equity instruments (including shares or share options) of the entity or another group entity, or

(b) equity instruments (including shares or share options) of the entity or another group entity,

provided the specified vesting conditions, if any, are met.'

A *share-based payment transaction* is 'a transaction in which the entity

(a) receives goods or services from the supplier of those goods or services (including an employee) in a share-based payment arrangement, or

(b) incurs an obligation to settle the transaction with the supplier in a share-based payment arrangement when another group entity receives those goods or services.'

An *equity-settled share-based payment transaction* is 'a share-based payment transaction in which the entity

(a) receives goods or services as consideration for its own equity instruments (including shares or share options), or

(b) receives goods or services but has no obligation to settle the transaction with the supplier.'

A *cash-settled share-based payment transaction* is 'a share-based payment transaction in which the entity acquires goods or services by incurring a liability to transfer cash or other assets to the supplier of those goods or services for amounts that are based on the price (or value) of equity instruments (including shares or share options) of the entity or another group entity'.

A *group entity* in the four definitions above means any parent, subsidiary, or subsidiary of any parent, of the entity and is based on the definition of 'group' in Appendix A to IFRS 10 as 'a parent and its subsidiaries'. Prior to the application of IFRS 10 the definition is that in IAS 27 (2012) – *Consolidated and Separate Financial Statements* – but the change is not substantial. *[IFRS 2.63A, BC22E].*

An *equity instrument* is 'a contract that evidences a residual interest in the assets of an entity after deducting all of its liabilities'.

An *equity instrument granted* is 'the right (conditional or unconditional) to an equity instrument of the entity conferred by the entity on another party, under a share-based payment arrangement'.

A *share option* is 'a contract that gives the holder the right, but not the obligation, to subscribe to the entity's shares at a fixed or determinable price for a specified period of time'. *[IFRS 2 Appendix A].*

It will be seen from these definitions that IFRS 2 applies not only to awards of shares and share options but also to awards of cash (or other assets) of a value equivalent to the value, or a movement in the value, of a particular number of shares. Such cash awards may arise in a number of situations. For example:

- an entity may wish to extend its share scheme to the employees of overseas subsidiaries in jurisdictions where it may be difficult, or even illegal, to trade in the entity's shares, or where delivering shares would not give the same tax benefits to employees as would apply in the parent's own jurisdiction; or
- the entity may not wish to dilute existing shareholdings by significant share awards to employees.

In such cases, the employees may instead be offered cash equivalent to the value of the shares that they would otherwise have obtained.

2.2.2 *Transactions within the scope of IFRS 2*

Subject to the exceptions noted at 2.2.3 below, IFRS 2 must be applied to all share-based payment transactions, including:

(a) equity-settled share-based payment transactions (discussed at 4 to 8 below);

(b) cash-settled share-based payment transactions (discussed at 9 below); and

(c) transactions where either the entity or the supplier of goods or services can choose whether the transaction is to be equity-settled or cash-settled (discussed at 10 below). *[IFRS 2.2].*

Whilst the boundaries between these types of transaction are reasonably self-explanatory, there may – as discussed in more detail at 9 and 10 below – be transactions that an entity may intuitively regard as equity-settled which are in fact required to be treated as cash-settled under IFRS 2.

Although IFRS 2 was primarily a response to concerns over share-based remuneration, its scope is not restricted to transactions with employees. For example, if an external supplier of goods or services, including another group entity, is paid in shares or share options, or cash of equivalent value, IFRS 2 must be applied. Goods include:

- inventories;
- consumables;
- property, plant and equipment;
- intangibles; and
- other non-financial assets. *[IFRS 2.5].*

It will be seen that 'goods' do not include financial assets, which raises some further issues (see 2.2.3.F below).

The scope of IFRS 2 extends to:

- group share schemes and certain transactions with shareholders (see 2.2.2.A below);
- transactions with employee benefit trusts and similar vehicles (see 2.2.2.B below);
- transactions where the identifiable consideration received appears to be less than the consideration given (see 2.2.2.C below);
- 'all employee' share plans (see 2.2.2.D below); and
- vested transactions (see 2.2.2.E below).

2.2.2.A Group schemes and transactions with group shareholders: scope issues

The definitions of 'share-based payment arrangement' and 'share-based payment transaction' at 2.2.1 above have the effect that the scope of IFRS 2 is not restricted to transactions where the reporting entity acquires goods or services in exchange for its own equity instruments (or cash or other assets based on the cost or value of those equity instruments). Within a group of companies it is common for one member of the group (typically the parent) to settle a share-based payment transaction in which services are provided to another member of the group (typically a subsidiary). This transaction is within the scope of IFRS 2 for the entity receiving the services (even though it is not a direct party to the arrangement between its parent and its employee), the entity settling the transaction and the group as a whole.

Accordingly, IFRS 2 requires an entity to account for a transaction in which it either:

- receives goods or services when another entity in the same group (or a shareholder of any group entity) has the obligation to settle the share-based payment transaction, or
- has an obligation to settle a share-based payment transaction when another entity in the same group receives the goods or services

unless the transaction is clearly for a purpose other than payment for goods or services supplied to the entity receiving them. *[IFRS 2.3A].*

Moreover, the definitions of 'equity-settled share-based payment transaction' and 'cash-settled share-based payment transaction' have the effect that the analysis of the transaction as equity-settled or cash-settled (and its accounting treatment) may differ when viewed from the perspective of the entity receiving the goods or services, the entity settling the transaction and the group as a whole. *[IFRS 2.43A].*

We consider below seven scenarios, based on the simple structure in Figure 30.1 below. These scenarios are by no means exhaustive, but cover the situations most commonly seen in practice.

The accounting treatment of group share schemes is discussed in more detail at 12 below.

Figure 30.1: Scope of IFRS 2

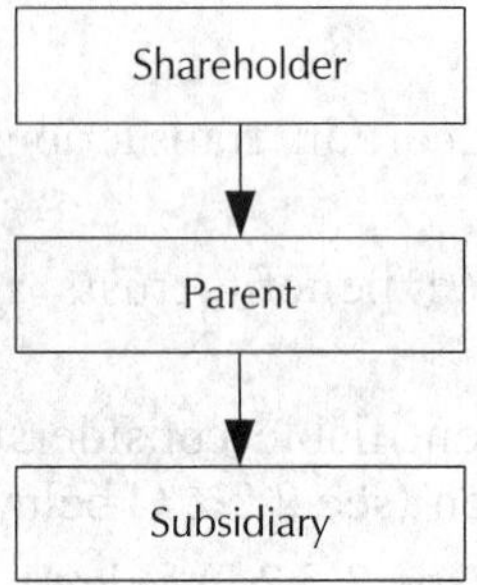

The scenarios assume that:

- the shareholder is not a group entity; and
- the subsidiary is directly owned by the parent company (see 12.2.1 below in relation to intermediate parent companies).

Scenario	Who grants the award?	Who receives the goods or services?	Who settles the award?	On whose shares is award based?	Settled in shares or cash?
1	Parent	Subsidiary	Parent	Parent	Shares
2	Shareholder	Subsidiary	Shareholder	Parent	Shares
3	Subsidiary	Subsidiary	Subsidiary	Parent	Shares
4	Subsidiary	Subsidiary	Subsidiary	Subsidiary	Shares
5	Parent	Subsidiary	Parent	Subsidiary	Shares
6	Parent	Subsidiary	Parent	Parent	Cash
7	Shareholder	Subsidiary	Shareholder	Parent	Cash

Scenario 1

Parent awards equity shares in Parent to employees of Subsidiary in exchange for services to Subsidiary. Parent settles the award with the employees of Subsidiary. *[IFRS 2.43B-43C, B52(a), B53-B54]*.

Consolidated financial statements of Parent

Under the definition of 'share-based payment transaction', 'the entity [i.e. the Parent group] ... receives goods or services ... in a share-based payment arrangement ...'. A share-based payment arrangement includes 'an agreement between the entity ... and another party (including an employee) that entitles the other party to receive ... equity instruments ... of the entity ...'.

The transaction is classified as an equity-settled transaction, because it is settled in an equity instrument of the group.

Separate financial statements of Parent

Under the definition of 'share-based payment transaction', the 'entity [i.e. the Parent as a single entity] ... incurs an obligation to settle the transaction with the supplier in a share-based payment arrangement when another group entity receives those goods or services'.

The transaction is classified as an equity-settled transaction, because it is settled in an equity instrument of Parent.

Subsidiary

Under the definition of 'share-based payment transaction', 'the entity [i.e. Subsidiary] ... receives goods or services ... in a share-based payment arrangement ...'. A 'share-based payment arrangement' includes 'an agreement between ... another group entity [i.e. Parent] ... and another party (including an employee) that entitles the other party to receive ... equity instruments of ... another group entity'.

The transaction is classified as an equity-settled transaction because Subsidiary 'has no obligation to settle the transaction with the supplier'.

Even if Subsidiary is not a party to the agreement with its employees, it nevertheless records a cost for this transaction. In effect, the accounting treatment is representing that Subsidiary has received a capital contribution from Parent, which Subsidiary has then 'spent' on employee remuneration. This treatment is often referred to as 'push-down' accounting – the idea being that a transaction undertaken by one group entity (in this case, Parent) for the benefit of another group entity (in this case, Subsidiary) is 'pushed down' into the financial statements of the beneficiary entity.

Scenario 2

Shareholder awards equity shares in Parent to employees of Subsidiary in exchange for services to Subsidiary. Shareholder settles the award with the employees of Subsidiary. *[IFRS 2.B48(b)]*.

Consolidated financial statements of Parent

Under the definition of 'share-based payment transaction', 'the entity [i.e. the Parent group] ... receives goods or services ... in a share-based payment arrangement'. A 'share-based payment arrangement' includes 'an agreement between ... any shareholder ... and another party (including an employee) that entitles the other party to receive ... equity instruments (including shares or share options) of the entity...'.

The transaction is classified as an equity-settled transaction, because the Parent group 'has no obligation to settle the transaction with the supplier'.

Separate financial statements of Parent

Scenario 2 is not within the scope of IFRS 2 for the separate financial statements of Parent, because Parent (as a separate entity) receives no goods or services, nor does it settle the transaction.

Subsidiary

Under the definition of 'share-based payment transaction', 'the entity [i.e. Subsidiary] ... receives goods or services ... in a share-based payment arrangement'. A 'share-based payment arrangement' includes 'an agreement between ... any shareholder of any group entity [i.e. Shareholder] ... and another party (including an employee) that entitles the other party to receive equity instruments of ... another group entity [i.e. Parent]'.

The transaction is classified as an equity-settled transaction, because Subsidiary 'has no obligation to settle the transaction with the supplier'.

IFRS 2 explicitly does not address the accounting treatment for such a transaction within the financial statements of a shareholder that is not a group entity. *[IFRS 2.BC22G].* We discuss at 12.9 below the accounting treatment of such transactions in the financial statements of a shareholder that is an investor in a joint venture or associate.

Scenario 3

Subsidiary awards equity shares in Parent to employees of Subsidiary in exchange for services to Subsidiary. Subsidiary settles the award with the employees of Subsidiary. *[IFRS 2.43B, B52(b), B55].*

Consolidated financial statements of Parent

Under the definition of 'share-based payment transaction', 'the entity [i.e. the Parent group] ... receives goods or services ... in a share-based payment arrangement'. A 'share-based payment arrangement' includes 'an agreement between the entity ... and another party (including an employee) that entitles the other party to receive ... equity instruments (including shares or share options) of the entity'.

The transaction is classified as an equity-settled transaction, because the Parent group 'receives goods or services as consideration for its own equity instruments (including shares or share options)...'.

Separate financial statements of Parent

Scenario 3 is not within the scope of IFRS 2 for the separate financial statements of Parent, because Parent (as a separate entity) receives no goods or services, nor does it settle the transaction.

Subsidiary

Under the definition of 'share-based payment transaction', 'the entity [i.e. Subsidiary] ... receives goods or services ... in a share-based payment arrangement'. A 'share-based payment arrangement' includes 'an agreement between ... [a] group entity [i.e. Subsidiary] ... and another party (including an employee) that entitles the other party to receive equity instruments of ... another group entity [i.e. Parent]'.

The transaction is classified as a cash-settled transaction because Subsidiary has the obligation to settle the award with equity instruments issued by Parent – i.e. a financial asset in Subsidiary's separate financial statements – rather than with Subsidiary's own equity instruments.

However, for the approach in this Scenario to apply, it must be the case that Subsidiary grants the award as a principal rather than as agent for Parent. If Subsidiary appears to be granting an award but is really doing so only on the instructions of Parent, as will generally be the case in certain jurisdictions, then the approach in Scenario 1 above is more likely to apply. This is discussed in more detail at 12.2.5.B below.

Scenario 4

Subsidiary awards equity shares in Subsidiary to employees of Subsidiary in exchange for services to Subsidiary. Subsidiary settles the award with the employees of Subsidiary. *[IFRS 2.43B, B49]*.

Consolidated financial statements of Parent

Under the definition of 'share-based payment transaction', 'the entity [i.e. the Parent group] ... receives goods or services ... in a share-based payment arrangement'. A share-based payment arrangement includes 'an agreement between the entity ... and another party (including an employee) that entitles the other party to receive ... equity instruments ... of the entity ...'.

The transaction is classified as an equity-settled transaction, because it is settled in an equity instrument of the group. In the consolidated financial statements of Parent, shares of Subsidiary not held by Parent are a non-controlling (minority) interest, classified as equity (see Chapter 7 at 4).

Subsidiary

Under the definition of 'share-based payment transaction', 'the entity [i.e. Subsidiary] ... receives goods or services ... in a share-based payment arrangement'.

The transaction is classified as an equity-settled transaction, because it is settled in an equity instrument of Subsidiary.

Scenario 5

Parent awards equity shares in Subsidiary to employees of Subsidiary in exchange for services to Subsidiary. Parent settles the award with the employees of Subsidiary. *[IFRS 2.43B-43C, B50]*.

Consolidated financial statements of Parent

Under the definition of 'share-based payment transaction', 'the entity [i.e. the Parent group] ... receives goods or services ... in a share-based payment arrangement'. A share-based payment arrangement includes 'an agreement between the entity ... and another party (including an employee) that entitles the other party to receive ... equity instruments of the entity ...'.

The transaction is classified as an equity-settled transaction, because it is settled in an equity instrument of the group. In the consolidated financial statements of Parent, shares of Subsidiary not held by Parent are a non-controlling (minority) interest, classified as equity (see Chapter 7 at 4).

Separate financial statements of Parent

Under the definition of 'share-based payment transaction', the 'entity [i.e. the Parent as a single entity] ... incurs an obligation to settle the transaction with the supplier in a share-based payment arrangement when another group entity [i.e. Subsidiary] receives those goods or services'. The transaction is a share-based payment arrangement for Subsidiary (see below) and the consolidated financial statements of Parent (see above).

For Parent, the transaction is classified as a cash-settled transaction, because it is settled not in an equity instrument issued by Parent, but in an equity instrument issued by a subsidiary and held by Parent – i.e. a financial asset in Parent's separate financial statements.

Subsidiary

Under the definition of 'share-based payment transaction', 'the entity [i.e. Subsidiary] ... receives goods or services ... in a share-based payment arrangement'. A 'share-based payment arrangement' includes 'an agreement between ... another group entity [i.e. Parent] ... and another party (including an employee) that entitles the other party to receive equity instruments of the entity...'.

The transaction is classified as an equity-settled transaction, because Subsidiary 'has no obligation to settle the transaction with the supplier'.

Scenario 6

Parent awards cash based on the value of shares in Parent to employees of Subsidiary in exchange for services to Subsidiary. Parent settles the award with the employees of Subsidiary. *[IFRS 2.43C, B56-B58].*

Consolidated financial statements of Parent

Under the definition of 'share-based payment transaction', 'the entity [i.e. the Parent group] ... receives goods or services ... in a share-based payment arrangement'. A 'share-based payment arrangement' includes 'an agreement between the entity ... and another party (including an employee) that entitles the other party to receive ... cash ... of the entity ... based on the price (or value) of equity instruments ... of the entity ...'.

The transaction is classified as a cash-settled transaction, because it is settled in cash of the group.

Separate financial statements of Parent

Under the definition of 'share-based payment transaction', the 'entity [i.e. the Parent as a single entity] ... incurs an obligation to settle the transaction with the supplier in a share-based payment arrangement when another group entity [i.e. Subsidiary] receives those goods or services'.

The transaction is classified as a cash-settled transaction, because it is settled in cash of Parent.

Subsidiary

IFRS 2 contains detailed guidance for the accounting treatment of such transactions by the employing subsidiary (see 12 below), from which it may reasonably be inferred that the IASB intended them to be in the scope of IFRS 2 for the subsidiary.

However, this is strictly not the case when the drafting of IFRS 2 is examined closely. In order to be a share-based payment *transaction* (and therefore in the scope of IFRS 2) for the reporting entity, a transaction must also be a share-based payment *arrangement*. A share-based payment arrangement is defined as one in which the counterparty receives (our emphasis added):

- equity of the entity *or any other group entity*, or
- cash or other assets *of the entity*.

As drafted, the definition has the effect that a transaction settled in equity is in the scope of IFRS 2 for a reporting entity, whether the equity used to settle is the entity's own equity or that of another group entity. Where a transaction is settled in cash, however, the definition has the effect that a transaction is in the scope of IFRS 2 for a reporting entity only when that entity's own cash (or other assets) is used in settlement, and not when another group entity settles the transaction.

However, given the guidance referred to above in IFRS 2 for the accounting treatment for the reporting entity of transactions settled in cash by another group entity, we believe that the exclusion of such transactions from the definition of 'share-based payment arrangement' should be disregarded as an unfortunate drafting slip.

The transaction is classified as an equity-settled transaction by Subsidiary, because Subsidiary 'has no obligation to settle the transaction with the supplier'.

Scenario 7

Shareholder awards cash based on the value of shares in Parent to employees of Subsidiary in exchange for services to Subsidiary. Shareholder settles the award with the employees of Subsidiary.

For the reasons set out in Scenario 6 above, this transaction is not strictly in the scope of IFRS 2 as drafted either for the consolidated financial statements of Parent or for the separate financial statements of Parent or Subsidiary. As noted in Scenario 6 above, the definition of 'share-based payment arrangement' as drafted excludes any arrangement that is settled in cash by a party other than the reporting entity. Moreover, whilst IFRS 2 gives detailed guidance that effectively appears to 'over-ride' the definition in respect of a transaction settled by another group entity (see Scenario 6 above), there is no such over-riding guidance in respect of a transaction settled in cash by a non-group shareholder.

Nevertheless, we believe that the transaction should be treated as within the scope of IFRS 2 for the consolidated financial statements of Parent and the separate financial statements of Subsidiary. One of the original objectives of the project that led to the issue of the June 2009 amendment to IFRS 2 was to address a concern that, as originally issued, IFRS 2 did not require an entity to account for a cash-settled share-based payment transaction settled by an external shareholder.

In addition to the accounting treatment under IFRS 2, the group entities in this Scenario would need to consider the requirements of IAS 24 – *Related Party Disclosures* – as any payments by a shareholder would potentially be disclosable (see Chapter 35).

2.2.2.B Transactions with employee benefit trusts and similar vehicles

In some jurisdictions, it is common for an entity to establish a trust to hold shares in the entity for the purpose of satisfying, or 'hedging' the cost of, share-based awards to employees. In such cases, it is often the trust, rather than any entity within the legal group, that actually makes share-based awards to employees.

A sponsoring employer (or its wider group) will need to assess whether it controls the trust in accordance with the requirements of IFRS 10 and therefore whether the trust should be consolidated. For entities not yet applying IFRS 10, such trusts are normally consolidated by the sponsoring employer in accordance with IAS 27 (2012) – *Consolidated and Separate Financial Statements* – as interpreted by SIC-12 (see 12.3 below and Chapter 6).

Awards by employee benefit trusts and similar vehicles are within the scope of IFRS 2, irrespective of whether or not the trust is consolidated, since:

- where the trust is consolidated, it is an award by a group entity; and
- where the trust is not consolidated, it is an award by a shareholder.

2.2.2.C Transactions where the identifiable consideration received appears to be less than the consideration given

A share-based payment transaction as defined (see 2.2.1 above) involves the receipt of goods or services by the reporting entity. Nevertheless, IFRS 2 also applies to share-based payment transactions where no specifically identifiable goods or services have been (or will be) received. *[IFRS 2.2]*.

IFRS 2 asserts that, if the identifiable consideration received (if any) appears to be less than the fair value of consideration given, the implication is that, in addition to the identifiable goods and services acquired, the entity must also have received some unidentifiable consideration equal to the difference between the fair value of the share-based payment and the fair value of any identifiable consideration received. Accordingly, the cost of the unidentified consideration must be accounted for in accordance with IFRS 2. *[IFRS 2.13A]*.

For example, if an entity agrees to pay a supplier of services with a clearly identifiable market value of £1,000 by issuing shares with a value of £1,500, IFRS 2 requires the entity to recognise an expense of £1,500. This is notwithstanding the normal requirement of IFRS 2 that an equity-settled share-based payment transaction with a non-employee be recognised at the fair value of the goods or services received (see 5.1 and 5.4 below).

This requirement was introduced by IFRIC 8 (since incorporated into IFRS 2). The reason for the change is alluded to in an illustrative example. *[IFRS 2.IG5D, IG Example 1]*. As part of general economic reforms in South Africa, under arrangements generally referred to as black economic empowerment or 'BEE' (discussed further at 15.5 below), various entities issued or transferred significant numbers of shares to bodies representing historically disadvantaged communities. Some held that these transactions did not fall within the scope of IFRS 2 as originally drafted because the entities concerned were not purchasing goods or services. Rather, BEE arrangements were simply meant to replicate a transfer of shares from one group of shareholders to another. Accordingly, it was argued, such transactions did not fall within the scope of IFRS 2, since it is intrinsic to the definition of a 'share-based payment transaction' (see 2.2.1 above) that goods or services are received.

IFRS 2 rejects this argument. It effectively takes the view that, since the directors of an entity would not issue valuable consideration for nothing, something must have been received. *[IFRS 2.BC18C]*. IFRS 2 suggests that a transfer of equity under BEE and similar schemes is made 'as a means of enhancing [the entity's] image as a good corporate citizen'. *[IFRS 2 IG Example 1]*.

There seems little doubt that this aspect of IFRS 2 is in part an 'anti-avoidance' measure. As discussed in 4 to 8 below, the general measurement rule in IFRS 2 is that share-based payment transactions with employees are measured by reference to the fair value of the consideration given and those with non-employees by reference to the fair value of the consideration received. We argue at 5.2.2 below that the requirement to measure transactions with employees by reference to the consideration given is essentially an anti-avoidance provision. It prevents entities from recognising a low cost for employee share options on the grounds that little incremental service is provided for them beyond that already provided for cash-based remuneration. The changes introduced by IFRIC 8 removed the potential for a similar abuse in accounting for transactions with non-employees.

Nevertheless, the IASB acknowledges that there may be rare circumstances in which a transaction may occur in which no goods or services are received by the entity. For example, a principal shareholder of an entity, for reasons of estate planning, may transfer shares to a relative. In the absence of indications that the relative has provided, or is expected to provide, goods or services to the entity in exchange for the shares, such a transfer would be outside the scope of IFRS 2. *[IFRS 2.BC18D]*.

2.2.2.D 'All employee' share plans

Many countries encourage wider share-ownership by allowing companies to award a limited number of free or discounted shares to employees without either the employee or the employer incurring tax liabilities which would apply if other benefits in kind to an equivalent value were given to employees.

Some existing national standards exempt some such plans from their scope, to some extent as the result of local political pressures. Prior to issuing IFRS 2, the IASB received some strong representations that IFRS should give a similar exemption, on the grounds that not to do so would discourage companies from continuing with such schemes.

The IASB concluded that such an exemption would be wrong in principle and difficult to draft in practice. By way of concession, the Basis for Conclusions hints that if the IFRS 2 charge for such schemes is (as asserted by some of the proponents of an exemption) *de minimis*, then there would be no charge under IFRS 2 anyway, since, like all IFRSs, it applies only to material items. *[IFRS 2.BC8-17]*. However, our experience is that, in many cases, the charge is material.

2.2.2.E Vested transactions

Once a transaction accounted for under IFRS 2 has vested in the counterparty (see 3 below), it does not necessarily cease to be in the scope of IFRS 2. This is made clear by the numerous provisions of IFRS 2 referring to the accounting treatment of vested awards.

Once shares have been delivered or beneficially transferred to the counterparty (e.g. as the result of the vesting of an award of shares, or the exercise of a vested option over shares), those shares should generally be accounted for under IAS 32 and IAS 39 rather than IFRS 2. If, however, the holder of such a share enjoys rights not applicable to all holders of that class of share, such as a right to put the share to the entity for cash, the share might still remain in the scope of IFRS 2. The significance of this is that issued equity instruments and financial liabilities not within the scope of IFRS 2 would typically fall within the scope of IAS 32 and IAS 39, which might require a significantly different accounting treatment from that required by IFRS 2. See, for example:

- the discussion at 2.2.4.B below of the treatment in consolidated financial statements of an award with a right to put the share to the parent entity;
- the discussion at 2.2.4.G below which highlights that a share option with a foreign currency strike price is accounted for as an equity instrument under IFRS 2, but as a liability under IAS 32 and IAS 39; and
- the discussion at 10.1.6 below of the treatment of convertible instruments issued in exchange for goods and services and accounted for under IFRS 2 rather than under IAS 32 and IAS 39.

2.2.3 Transactions not within the scope of IFRS 2

The following transactions are outside the scope of IFRS 2:

- transactions with shareholders as a whole and with shareholders in their capacity as such (see 2.2.3.A below);
- transfers of assets in certain group restructuring arrangements (see 2.2.3.B below);
- business combinations (see 2.2.3.C below);
- combinations of businesses under common control and the contribution of a business to form a joint venture (see 2.2.3.D below); and
- transactions in the scope of IAS 32 – *Financial Instruments: Presentation* – and IAS 39 – *Financial Instruments: Recognition and Measurement* (see 2.2.3.E below). The scope exemptions in IFRS 2 combined with those in IAS 32 and IAS 39 appear to have the effect that there is no specific guidance in IFRS for accounting for certain types of investment when acquired for shares (see 2.2.3.F below).

As noted at 2.2.2.D above, there is no exemption from IFRS 2 for share schemes aimed mainly at lower- and middle-ranking employees, referred to in different jurisdictions by terms such as 'all-employee share schemes', 'employee share purchase plans' and 'broad-based plans'.

2.2.3.A Transactions with shareholders in their capacity as such

IFRS 2 does not apply to transactions with employees (and others) purely in their capacity as shareholders. For example, an employee may already hold shares in the entity as a result of previous share-based payment transactions. If the entity then raises funds through a rights issue, whereby all shareholders (including the employee) can acquire additional shares for less than the current fair value of the shares, such a transaction is not a share-based payment transaction for the purposes of IFRS 2. *[IFRS 2.4].*

2.2.3.B Transfer of assets in group restructuring arrangements

In some group restructuring arrangements, one entity will transfer a group of net assets, which does not meet the definition of a business, to another entity in return for shares. Careful consideration of the precise facts and circumstances is needed in order to determine whether, for the separate or individual financial statements of any entity affected by the transfer, such a transfer falls within the scope of IFRS 2. If the transfer is considered primarily to be a transfer of goods by their owner in return for shares then, in our view, this should be accounted for under IFRS 2. However, if the transaction is for another purpose and is driven by the group shareholder in its capacity as such, the transaction may be outside the scope of IFRS 2 (see 2.2.3.A above). Accounting for intra-group asset transfers in return for shares is considered further in Chapter 8 at 4.4.1.

2.2.3.C Business combinations

IFRS 2 does not apply to share-based payments to acquire goods (such as inventories or property, plant and equipment) in the context of a business combination to which IFRS 3 – *Business Combinations* – applies.

However, the Interpretations Committee has clarified that in a reverse acquisition involving an entity that does not constitute a business (i.e. an asset acquisition), IFRS 2 rather than IFRS 3 is likely to apply (see Chapter 9 at 14.8).[5]

Transactions in which equity instruments are issued to acquire goods as part of the net assets in a business combination are outside the scope of IFRS 2 but equity instruments granted to the employees of the acquiree in their capacity as employees (e.g. in return for continued service) are within its scope, as are the cancellation, replacement or modification of a share-based payment transaction as the result of a business combination or other equity restructuring (see 11 and 12.8 below). *[IFRS 2.5].*

Thus, if a vendor of an acquired business remains as an employee of that business following the business combination and receives a share-based payment for transferring control of the entity and for remaining in continuing employment, it is necessary to determine how much of the share-based payment relates to the acquisition of control (which forms part of the cost of the combination, accounted for under IFRS 3) and how much relates to the provision of future services (which is a post-combination operating expense accounted for under IFRS 2). Guidance on this issue is given in IFRS 3 – see Chapter 9 at 11.2.

2.2.3.D Common control transactions and formation of joint arrangements

IFRS 2 also does not apply to a combination of entities or businesses under common control (see Chapter 10), or the contribution of a business on the formation of a joint venture as defined by IFRS 11 – *Joint Arrangements* (see Chapter 12). *[IFRS 2.5]*. For entities not yet applying IFRS 11, the exemption relates to the formation of a joint venture as defined by IAS 31 – *Interests in Joint Ventures*.

The exemptions for common control combinations and for joint ventures accounted for under IAS 31 took effect for annual periods beginning on or after 1 July 2009. *[IFRS 2.61]*. The amended exemption based on IFRS 11 takes effect when an entity applies that standard. *[IFRS 2.63A]*.

It should be noted that the contribution of assets (which do not constitute a business) to a joint venture in return for shares is within the scope of IFRS 2 (see 2.2.2 above).

IFRS 2 does not directly address other types of transactions involving joint ventures or transactions involving associates. These are discussed further at 12.9 below.

2.2.3.E Transactions in the scope of IAS 32 and IAS 39

IFRS 2 does not apply to transactions within the scope of IAS 32 or IAS 39 (see Chapter 41). Therefore, if an entity enters into a share-based payment transaction to purchase a commodity surplus to its production requirements or with a view to short-term profit taking, the contract is treated as a financial instrument under IAS 32 and IAS 39 rather than a share-based payment transaction under IFRS 2. *[IFRS 2.6]*.

Some practical examples of scope issues involving IFRS 2 and IAS 32 / IAS 39 are discussed at 2.2.4 below.

2.2.3.F Transactions in financial assets outside the scope of IAS 32 and IAS 39

As noted at 2.2.2 above, IFRS 2 applies to share-based payment transactions involving goods or services, with 'goods' defined so as to exclude financial assets, presumably on the basis that these fall within IAS 32 and IAS 39. However, investments in subsidiaries, associates and corporate joint ventures in the separate financial statements of the investing entity are financial assets as defined in IAS 32 (and hence outside the scope of IFRS 2), but are outside the scope of IAS 39 where the entity chooses to account for them at cost (see Chapter 8 at 2.1 and Chapter 41 at 3.1).

Moreover, IFRS has no general requirements for accounting for the issue of equity instruments. Rather, consistent with the position taken by the *Conceptual Framework* that equity is a residual rather than an item 'in its own right', the amount of an equity instrument is normally measured by reference to the item (expense or asset) in consideration for which the equity is issued, as determined in accordance with IFRS applicable to that other item.

This means that, when (as is commonly the case) an entity acquires an investment in a subsidiary, associate or joint venture for the issue of equity instruments, there is no explicit guidance in IFRS as to the required accounting in the separate financial statements of the investor, and in particular as to how the 'cost' of such an item is to be determined. This is discussed further in Chapter 8 at 2.1.1.A.

2.2.4 *Some practical applications of the scope requirements*

This section addresses the application of the scope requirements of IFRS 2 to a number of situations frequently encountered in practice:

- remuneration in non-equity shares and put rights over equity shares (see 2.2.4.A below);
- the treatment in the consolidated accounts of the parent of an equity-settled award of a subsidiary with a put option against the parent (see 2.2.4.B below);
- an increase in the counterparty's ownership interest with no change in the number of shares held (see 2.2.4.C below);
- awards for which the counterparty has paid 'fair value' (see 2.2.4.D below);
- a cash bonus which depends on share price performance (see 2.2.4.E below);
- cash-settled awards based on an entity's 'enterprise value' or other formula (see 2.2.4.F below);
- awards with a foreign currency strike price (see 2.2.4.G below);
- holding own shares to satisfy or 'hedge' awards (see 2.2.4.H below);
- shares or warrants issued in connection with a financial liability (see 2.2.4.I below);
- options over puttable instruments classified as equity under IAS 32 in the absence of other equity instruments (see 2.2.4.J below); and
- special discounts to certain categories of investor on a share issue (see 2.2.4.K below).

The following aspects of the scope requirements are covered elsewhere in this Chapter:

- employment taxes on share-based payment transactions (see 14 below); and
- instruments such as limited recourse loans and convertible bonds that sometimes fall within the scope of IFRS 2 rather than IAS 32/IAS 39 because of the link both to the entity's equity instruments and to goods or services received in exchange. Convertible bonds are discussed at 10.1.6 below and limited recourse loans at 15.2 below.

2.2.4.A *Remuneration in non-equity shares and put rights over equity shares*

A transaction is within the scope of IFRS 2 only where it involves the delivery of an equity instrument, or cash or other assets based on the price or value of an 'equity instrument' (see 2.2.1 above).

In some jurisdictions, there can be fiscal advantages in giving an employee, in lieu of a cash payment, a share that carries a right to a 'one-off' dividend, or is mandatorily redeemable, at an amount equivalent to the intended cash payment. Such a share would almost certainly be classified as a liability under IAS 32 (see Chapter 43). Accordingly, payment in such a share would not fall in the scope of IFRS 2 since the consideration paid by the entity for services received is a financial liability rather than an equity instrument (see the definitions in 2.2.1 above).

If, however, the amount of remuneration delivered in this way were equivalent to the value of a particular number of equity instruments issued by the entity, then the transaction would be in scope of IFRS 2 as a cash-settled share-based payment transaction, since the entity would have incurred a liability (i.e. by issuing the redeemable shares) for an amount based on the price of its equity instruments.

Similarly, if an entity grants an award of equity instruments to an employee together with a put right whereby the employee can require the entity to purchase those shares for fair value, both elements of that transaction are in the scope of IFRS 2 as a single cash-settled transaction (see 9 below). This is notwithstanding the fact that, under IAS 32, the share and the put right might well be analysed as a single synthetic instrument and classified as a liability with no equity component (see Chapter 43).

Differences in the classification of instruments between IFRS 2 and IAS 32 are discussed further at 1.4.1 above.

Put options over instruments that are only classified as equity in limited circumstances (in accordance with paragraphs 16A to 16B of IAS 32) are discussed at 2.2.4.J below.

2.2.4.B Equity-settled award of subsidiary with put option against the parent – treatment in consolidated accounts of parent

It is sometimes the case that a subsidiary entity grants an award over its own equity instruments and, either on the same date or later, the parent entity separately grants the same counterparty a put option to sell the equity instruments of the subsidiary to the parent for cash. Accounting for such an arrangement in the separate financial statements of the subsidiary and the parent will be determined in accordance with the general principles of IFRS 2 (see 2.2.2.A above). However, IFRS 2 does not explicitly address the accounting treatment of such arrangements in the parent's consolidated financial statements.

In our view, the analysis differs according to whether the put option is granted during or after the vesting period.

If the put option is granted during the vesting period (whether at the same time as the grant of the equity instruments or later), the two transactions should be treated as linked and accounted for in the consolidated financial statements as a single cash-settled transaction from the date the put option is granted. This reflects the fact that this situation is similar in group terms to a modification of an award to add a cash-settlement alternative – see 10.1.4 below.

If the put option is only granted once the equity instruments have vested, the accounting will depend on whether the equity instruments in the original share-based payment transaction are unexercised options or whether they are shares.

If they are unexercised options, the vested award remains within the scope of IFRS 2 (see 2.2.2.E above) and so the put option should be treated as a linked transaction. Its effect in group terms is to modify the original award from an equity- to a cash-settled transaction until final settlement date.

However, if the equity instruments are shares (free shares or exercised options), rather than unexercised options, they are no longer within the scope of IFRS 2. In such cases, the parent entity will need to evaluate whether or not the grant of the put option, as a separate transaction which modifies the terms of certain of the subsidiary's equity instruments, falls within the scope of IFRS 2.

2.2.4.C *Increase in ownership interest with no change in number of shares held*

An increasingly common arrangement, typically found in entities with venture capital investors, is one where an employee (typically part of the key management) subscribes initially for, say, 1% of the entity's equity with the venture capitalist holding the other 99%. The employee's equity interest will subsequently increase by a variable amount depending on the extent to which certain targets are met. This is achieved not by issuing new shares but by cancelling some of the venture capitalist's shares. In our view, such an arrangement falls within the scope of IFRS 2 as the employee is rewarded with an increased equity stake in the entity if certain targets are achieved. The increased equity stake is consistent with the definition in Appendix A of IFRS 2 of an equity instrument as 'a contract that evidences a residual interest...' notwithstanding the fact that no additional shares are issued.

In such arrangements, it is often asserted that the employee has subscribed for a share of the equity at fair value. However, the subscription price paid must represent a fair value using an IFRS 2 valuation basis in order for there to be no additional IFRS 2 expense to recognise (see 2.2.4.D below).

2.2.4.D *Awards for which the counterparty has paid 'fair value'*

In certain situations, such as where a special class of share is issued, the counterparty might be asked to subscribe a certain amount for the share which is agreed as being its 'fair value' for taxation or other purposes. This does not mean that such arrangements fall outside the scope of IFRS 2, either for measurement or disclosure purposes, if the arrangement meets the definition of a share-based payment transaction. In many cases, the agreed 'fair value' will be lower than a fair value measured in accordance with IFRS 2 because it will reflect the impact of non-market vesting conditions which are excluded from an IFRS 2 fair value. This is addressed in more detail at 15.4.5 below.

2.2.4.E *Cash bonus dependent on share price performance*

An entity might agree to pay its employees a €100 cash bonus if its share price remains at €10 or more over a given period. Intuitively, this does not appear to be in the scope of IFRS 2, since the employee is not being given cash of equivalent value to a particular number of shares. However, it could be argued that it does fall within the scope of IFRS 2 on the basis that the entity has incurred a liability, and the amount of that liability is 'based on' the share price – it is nil if the share price is below €10 and €100 if the share price is €10 or more. In our view, either interpretation is acceptable.

2.2.4.F Cash-settled awards based on an entity's 'enterprise value' or other formula

As noted at 2.2.1 above, IFRS 2 includes within its scope transactions in which the entity acquires goods or services by incurring a liability 'based on the price (or value) of equity instruments (including shares or share options) of the entity or another group entity'. Employees of an unquoted entity may receive a cash award based on the value of the equity of that entity. Such awards are typically, but not exclusively, made by venture capital investors to the management of entities in which they have invested and which they aim to sell in the medium term. Further discussion of the accounting implications of such awards may be found at 15.4 below.

Where employees of an unquoted entity receive a cash award based on the value of the equity, there is no quoted share price and an 'enterprise value' has therefore to be calculated as a surrogate for it. This begs the question of whether such awards are within the scope of IFRS 2 (because they are based on the value of the entity's equity) or that of IAS 19 – *Employee Benefits.*

In order for an award to be within the scope of IFRS 2, any calculated 'enterprise value' must represent the fair value of the entity's equity. Where the calculation uses techniques recognised by IFRS 2 as yielding a fair value for equity instruments (as discussed at 8 below), we believe that the award should be regarded as within the scope of IFRS 2.

Appendix B of IFRS 2 notes that an unquoted entity may have calculated the value of its equity based on net assets or earnings (see 8.5.3.B below). *[IFRS 2.B30]*. In our view, this is not intended to imply that it is always appropriate to do so, but simply to note that it may be appropriate in some cases.

Where, for example, the enterprise value is based on a constant formula, such as a fixed multiple of earnings before interest, tax, depreciation and amortisation ('EBITDA'), in our view it is unlikely that this will represent a good surrogate for the fair value of the equity on an ongoing basis, even if it did so at the inception of the transaction. It is not difficult to imagine scenarios in which the fair value of the equity of an entity could be affected with no significant change in EBITDA, for example as a result of changes in interest rates and effective tax rates, or a significant impairment of assets. Alternatively, there might be a significant shift in the multiple of EBITDA equivalent to fair value, for example if the entity were to create or acquire a significant item of intellectual property.

For an award by an individual entity, there is unlikely to be any significant difference in the cost ultimately recorded under IFRS 2 or IAS 19. However, the disclosure requirements of IFRS 2 are more onerous than those of IAS 19. In a group situation where the parent entity grants the award to the employees of a subsidiary, the two standards could result in different levels of expense in the books of the subsidiary because IAS 19, unlike IFRS 2, does not require the employing subsidiary to recognise an expense for a transaction which it has no obligation to settle.

The treatment of equity-settled awards based on the 'market price' of an unquoted entity raises similar issues to those discussed in this section, as discussed more fully at 6.3.8 below.

2.2.4.G Awards with a foreign currency strike price

Many entities award their employees options with a foreign currency strike price. This will arise most commonly in a multinational group where employees of overseas subsidiaries are granted options on terms that they can pay the option strike price in their local currency. They may also arise where an entity, which has a functional currency different from that of the country in which it operates (e.g. an oil company based in the United Kingdom with a functional currency of United States dollars), grants its UK-based employees options with a strike price in pounds sterling, which is a foreign currency from the perspective of the currency of the financial statements. Under IAS 32, as currently interpreted, such an award could not be regarded as an equity instrument because the strike price to be tendered is not, in terms of the reporting entity's own currency, a fixed amount (see Chapter 43 at 5.2.3). However, under IFRS 2, as discussed at 2.2.1 above, equity instruments include options, which are defined as the right to acquire shares for a 'fixed *or determinable* price'. Moreover, it is quite clear from the Basis for Conclusions in IFRS 2 that an award which ultimately results in an employee receiving equity is equity-settled under IFRS 2 whatever its status under IAS 32 might be (see 1.4.1 above). Thus an option over equity with a foreign currency strike price is an equity instrument if accounted for under IFRS 2.

The fair value of such an award should be assessed at grant date and, where the award is treated as equity-settled, not subsequently revised for foreign exchange movements (on the general rule that an entity should not reflect changes in the value of an equity instrument in its financial statements). This applies to the separate financial statements of a parent or subsidiary entity as well as to consolidated financial statements. Where the award is treated as cash-settled, however, the periodic reassessment of fair value required by IFRS 2 will take account, *inter alia*, of any movement in exchange rates.

2.2.4.H Holding own shares to satisfy or 'hedge' awards

Entities often seek to hedge the cost of share-based payment transactions, most commonly by buying their own equity instruments in the market. For example, an entity could grant an employee options over 10,000 shares and buy 10,000 of its own shares into treasury at the date that the award is made. If the award is share-settled, the entity will deliver the shares to the counterparty. If it is cash-settled, it can sell the shares to raise the cash it is required to deliver to the counterparty. In either case, the cash cost of the award is capped at the market price of the shares at the date the award is made, less any amount paid by the employee on exercise. It could of course be argued that such an arrangement is not a true hedge at all. If the share price goes down so that the option is never exercised, the entity is left holding 10,000 of its own shares that cost more than they are now worth.

Whilst these strategies may provide a hedge of the cash cost of share-based payment transactions that are eventually exercised, they will not have any effect in hedging the charge to profit or loss required by IFRS 2 for such transactions. This is because purchases and sales of own shares are accounted for as movements in equity and are therefore never included in profit or loss (see 4.1 below). In any event, IAS 39 does not recognise a hedge of, or using, own equity as a valid hedging relationship (see Chapter 48).

The illustrative examples of group share schemes at 12.4 and 12.5 below show the interaction of the accounting required for a holding of own shares and the requirements of IFRS 2.

2.2.4.I Shares or warrants issued in connection with a financial liability

As noted at 2.2.3.E above, IFRS 2 does not apply to transactions within the scope of IAS 32 and IAS 39. However, if shares or warrants are granted to the lender by the counterparty as part of a financing arrangement, the measurement of those shares or warrants might fall within the scope of IFRS 2. The determination of the relevant standard is likely to require significant judgement based on the precise terms of individual transactions. If the shares or warrants are considered to be in lieu of a cash fee for the lender's services then IFRS 2 is likely to be the appropriate standard, but if the shares or warrants are considered instead to be part of the overall return to the lender then IAS 32 and IAS 39 are more likely to apply.

2.2.4.J Options over puttable instruments classified as equity under IAS 32

Some entities, such as certain types of trust, issue tradeable puttable instruments that are classified as equity instruments when the entity has no other equity instruments. This classification is based on a specific exception and IAS 32 makes it clear that such instruments are not equity instruments for the purposes of IFRS 2. *[IAS 32.16A-16B, 96C]*. However, should options over such instruments granted to employees – and allowing them to obtain the instruments at a discount to the market price – be treated as cash-settled awards under IFRS 2 or are they outside the scope of IFRS 2 and within that of IAS 19?

The entity has no equity apart from the instruments classified as such under the narrow exception in IAS 32 and, in the absence of equity, the entity cannot logically issue equity instruments in satisfaction of an award to employees nor can it pay cash based on the price or value of its equity. In our view, paragraph 96C of IAS 32 should be interpreted as meaning that, for the purposes of IFRS 2, such options can be neither equity-settled nor cash-settled awards and the appropriate standard is IAS 19 rather than IFRS 2.

Others take the view that such options could be cash-settled share-based payments but this seems to rely more on the general IAS 32 definition of equity rather than on the more specific requirements of paragraph 96C of IAS 32.

2.2.4.K Special discounts to certain categories of investor on a share issue

In the context of a flotation or other equity fundraising, an entity might offer identical shares at different prices to institutional investors and to individual investors. Should the additional discount given to one class of investor be accounted for under IFRS 2 as representing unidentified goods or services received or receivable?

In our view, it will generally be the case that such dual pricing will not fall within the scope of IFRS 2 in a situation, such as a privatisation, where the relevant market rules dictate that the prices for institutional and individual investors are to be determined in different ways.

In other situations, where an entity voluntarily offers a discount to one class of investor, e.g. to an institution underwriting the share issue, then in our view an IFRS 2 expense will generally be required. IFRS 2 was specifically amended for situations where the identifiable consideration received by the entity appears to be less than the fair value of the equity instruments granted (see 2.2.2.C above). *[IFRS 2.2, 13A]*. An expense should therefore be recognised unless there is evidence that separate prices, and therefore different fair values, are required for each category of investor.

In some situations – such as the case above where an institution provides underwriting services – it might be possible to conclude that any additional expense under IFRS 2 is actually a cost of issuing the equity instruments and should therefore be debited to equity rather than profit or loss.

Similar considerations apply when, in advance of an IPO, a private company issues convertible instruments at a discount to their fair value in order both to attract key investors and to boost working capital. There is further discussion on convertible instruments at 10.1.6 below.

3 GENERAL RECOGNITION PRINCIPLES

The recognition rules in IFRS 2 are based on a so-called 'service date model'. In other words, IFRS 2 requires the goods or services received or acquired in a share-based payment transaction to be recognised when the goods are acquired or the services rendered. *[IFRS 2.7]*. For awards to employees (or others providing similar services), this contrasts with the measurement rules, which normally require a share-based payment transaction to be measured as at the date on which the transaction was entered into, which may be some time before or after the related services are received – see 4 to 7 below.

Where the goods or services received or acquired in exchange for a share-based payment transaction do not qualify for recognition as assets they should be expensed. *[IFRS 2.8]*. The standard notes that typically services will not qualify as assets and should therefore be expensed immediately, whereas goods will generally be recognised initially as assets and expensed later as they are consumed. However, some payments for services may be capitalised (e.g. as part of the cost of PP&E or inventories) and some payments for goods may be expensed immediately (e.g. where they are for items included within development costs written off as incurred). *[IFRS 2.9]*.

The corresponding credit entry is, in the case of an equity-settled transaction, an increase in equity and, in the case of a cash-settled transaction, a liability (or decrease in cash or other assets). *[IFRS 2.7]*.

The primary focus of the discussion in the remainder of this Chapter is the application of these rules to transactions with employees. The accounting treatment of transactions with non-employees is addressed further at 5.1 and 5.4 below.

3.1 Vesting conditions

Under IFRS 2, the point at which a cost is recognised for goods or services depends on the concept of 'vesting'.

A share-based payment to a counterparty is said to *vest* when it becomes an entitlement of the counterparty. Under IFRS 2, a share-based payment arrangement vests when the counterparty's entitlement is no longer conditional on the satisfaction of any vesting conditions. *[IFRS 2 Appendix A].*

Vesting conditions are the conditions that determine whether the entity receives the services that entitle the counterparty to receive cash, other assets or equity instruments of the entity, under a share-based payment arrangement. Vesting conditions are either service conditions or performance conditions. *[IFRS 2 Appendix A].*

Service conditions require the counterparty to complete a specified period of service. *[IFRS 2 Appendix A].* For example, if an employee is granted a share option with a service condition of remaining in employment for three years, the award vests three years after the date of grant if the employee is still employed at that date.

Performance conditions require the counterparty to complete a specified period of service and specified performance targets to be met (such as a specified increase in the entity's profit over a specified period of time). A performance condition might include a market condition (see 6.3 below). *[IFRS 2 Appendix A].* As discussed more fully at 3.2 below, performance conditions refer to performance by an employee (such as a personal sales target) or performance by the entity as a whole, rather than some external performance indicator, such as a general stock market index.

Thus a condition that an award vests if, in three years' time, earnings per share has increased by 10% and the employee is still in employment, is a performance condition. If, however, the award vests in three years' time if earnings per share has increased by 10%, irrespective of whether the employee is still in employment, that condition is not a performance condition, but a 'non-vesting' condition (see 3.2 below).

As part of the draft *Annual Improvements to IFRSs 2010-2012 Cycle*, the IASB has proposed some amendments to the definitions referred to above in order to clarify the distinction between the different types of condition (see 3.4 below).

In addition to the general discussion above and at 3.2 to 3.4 below, specific considerations relating to awards that vest on a flotation or change of control (or similar exit event) are addressed at 15.4 below.

3.2 Non-vesting conditions (conditions that are neither service conditions nor performance conditions)

Some share-based payment transactions, particularly those with employees, are dependent on the satisfaction of conditions that are neither service conditions nor performance conditions. For example, an employee might be given the right to 100 shares in three years, subject only to the employee not working in competition with the reporting entity during that time. An undertaking not to work for another entity does not 'determine whether the entity receives ... services' – the employee could sit on a beach for three years and still be entitled to collect the award. Accordingly, such a condition is not regarded as a vesting condition for the purposes of IFRS 2, but is instead referred to as a 'non-vesting condition'. The accounting impact of non-vesting conditions is discussed in detail at 6.4 below.

IFRS 2 does not explicitly define a 'non-vesting condition', but uses the term to describe a condition that is neither a service condition nor a performance condition. However, the identification of such conditions is not always straightforward.

As noted at 3.1 above, IFRS 2 defines vesting conditions as conditions that determine whether the entity receives the services that entitle the counterparty to receive payment in equity or cash. Performance conditions are those that require the counterparty to complete a specified period of service and specified performance targets to be met (such as a specified increase in the entity's profit over a specified period of time).

The Basis for Conclusions to IFRS 2 adds that the feature that distinguishes a performance condition from a non-vesting condition is that the former has an explicit or implicit service requirement and the latter does not. *[IFRS 2.BC171A].*

From this it appears to follow that:

- *A performance condition must be specific to the performance of the entity (or of the individual within the entity)*

  For example, a condition that requires the entity's profit before tax or its share price to reach a minimum level is a performance condition, provided that there is also a requirement for the employee to provide services (see below).

  However, a condition that does not relate directly to the performance of the entity or the individual is a non-vesting condition. Examples given by IFRS 2 include:

  - a requirement to make monthly savings during the vesting period;
  - a requirement for a commodity index to reach a minimum level;
  - restrictions on the transfer of vested equity instruments; or
  - an agreement not to work for a competitor after the award has vested – a 'non-compete' agreement (see 3.2.1 below). *[IFRS 2.BC171B, IG24].*

  The IASB and the Interpretations Committee have discussed some of the above conditions as part of their project on vesting and non-vesting conditions (see 3.4 below).

- *Any condition applicable to an award that does not also have a service condition (whether explicit or implied) is a non-vesting condition.*

  For a condition to be a performance condition, it is not sufficient that the condition is specific to the performance of the entity. There must also be an explicit or implied service condition. For example, a condition that requires the entity's profit before tax or its share price to reach a minimum level, but without any requirement for the employee to provide services, is not a performance condition, but a non-vesting condition.

  Thus, whilst conditions that are not related to the performance of the entity are always, by their nature, non-vesting conditions, conditions that relate to the performance of the entity may or may not be non-vesting conditions depending on whether there is also a requirement for the counterparty to render service.

  IFRS 2 currently defines a performance condition as one that requires the counterparty to complete a 'specified period of service' and 'specified performance targets' to be met. This raises the question of whether the 'specified period of service' must be the same as, or at least as long as, the period required to satisfy the performance target. An example might be an award granted on 1 January 2013 which vests if the employee remains in employment for the two years ended 31 December 2014 and the entity achieves a target cumulative profit for the three years ended 31 December 2015.

In our view, in order for the performance target to be treated as a performance condition, the terms of the award must require the employee to remain in service for substantially all of the period required to achieve the performance target. Thus, we believe that, in the example in the previous paragraph, the profit target is not a performance condition since it relates to a three-year period, while the terms of the award require the employee to provide service for only two of those years.

The Interpretations Committee discussed this issue as part of its project on vesting and non-vesting conditions and the IASB has proposed an amendment to the definitions in IFRS 2 to make it clear that the performance target period should not extend beyond the end of the service period (see 3.4 below).

Within these broad parameters, however, there remains considerable room for judgement under IFRS 2 as currently drafted. In 6.3.1 below we discuss an entity, engaged in investment management and listed only in London, which grants options to an employee responsible for the Far East equities portfolio. The options have a condition linked to movements in a general index of shares of entities listed in Hong Kong, so as to compare the performance of the portfolio of investments for which the employee is responsible with that of the overall market in which they are traded.

We conclude (see 6.3.1 below) that this condition is not a market condition but a non-vesting condition. This conclusion is based on the analysis that such a condition is directly analogous to a requirement for a commodity index to reach a particular level, which IFRS 2 gives as a specific example of a non-vesting condition (see above). On the other hand, in the absence of specific guidance to the contrary, it might be argued that it is a performance condition, if (as is likely to be the case) the entity's profits are based in whole or in part on a percentage of the performance of assets under management, so that increases in an index based on identical assets are in fact strongly and directly linked to the entity's performance.

Our conclusion above that this condition is not a market condition is consistent with the IASB's clarification as part of the draft *Annual Improvements to IFRSs 2010-2012 Cycle* that any share market index target, even if the index includes the entity's shares, is not a performance condition but a non-vesting condition (see 3.4 below).

The concept of a 'non-vesting condition', like much of IFRS 2 itself, had its origins as an anti-avoidance measure. It arose from a debate on how to account for employee share option schemes linked to a savings contract. In some jurisdictions, options are awarded to an employee on condition that the employee works for a fixed minimum period and, during that period, makes regular contributions to a savings account, which is then used to exercise the option. The employee is entitled to withdraw from the savings contract before vesting, in which case the right to the award lapses.

Entities applying IFRS 2 as originally issued almost invariably treated an employee's obligation to save as a vesting condition. Therefore, a cessation by the employee to save was treated as a failure to meet a vesting condition, and accordingly accounted for as a forfeiture, with the reversal of any expense so far recorded (see 6.1 and 6.2 below).

Some saw in this a scope for abuse of the general principle of IFRS 2 that, if a share-based payment transaction is cancelled, any amount not yet expensed for it is immediately recognised in full (see 7.4 below). The concern was that, if such a plan were 'out of the money', the employer, rather than cancel the plan (and thereby trigger an acceleration of expense) would 'encourage' the employee to stop saving (and thereby create a reversal of any expense already charged).

The broad effect of the January 2008 amendment to IFRS 2 (see 1.2 above) was to remove this perceived anomaly from the standard.

However, since the publication of the January 2008 amendment, it has become apparent that the concept of the 'non-vesting' condition is not clear. This has resulted in differing views on the appropriate classification of certain types of conditions. Examples of such ambiguous conditions include a vesting requirement that the entity opens a number of retail outlets or that the entity floats or is sold (see also 15.4.3 below). One view would be that these conditions are not direct measures of the entity's performance, and are therefore non-vesting conditions. A contrary view is that they are so strongly correlated to underlying business performance as to amount to performance conditions.

A secondary issue is the accounting treatment of awards with interactive vesting conditions and non-vesting conditions. For example, an award might vest if the entity floats or is sold and the holder of the award is in employment at that time. Should this be construed (or at least accounted for) as having:

- a single non-market vesting condition, or
- two distinct conditions – a non-market vesting condition (being in employment) and a non-vesting condition (the entity floating or being sold)?

This is discussed further at 15.4.3 below.

The Interpretations Committee has taken a number of the above issues onto its agenda and this project, together with the IASB's proposed amendments to IFRS 2, is discussed further at 3.4 below. However, both the Interpretations Committee and the IASB remain of the view that it is unnecessary to include a definition of a non-vesting condition in IFRS 2 rather than confining the discussion to the Basis for Conclusions.

3.2.1 Non-compete agreements

In some jurisdictions it is relatively common to have a non-compete clause in share-based payment arrangements so that if the counterparty starts to work for a competitor within a specified timescale, i.e. he breaches the non-compete provision, he is required to return the shares (or an equivalent amount of cash) to the entity. Generally, a non-compete provision is relevant once an individual has ceased employment with the entity and so no future service is expected to be provided to the entity. However, the non-compete provision is often found in share-based payment awards entered into while the individual is still an employee of the entity and when there is no current intention for employment to cease. There are divergent views on how such non-compete arrangements should be accounted for under IFRS 2.

The Basis for Conclusions to IFRS 2 states that 'a share-based payment vests when the counterparty's entitlement to it is no longer conditional on future service or performance conditions. Therefore, conditions such as non-compete provisions and transfer restrictions, which apply after the counterparty has become entitled to the share-based payment, are not vesting conditions.' *[IFRS 2.BC171B]*. In our view, under the current definitions in the standard, all non-compete agreements must therefore be non-vesting conditions (or post-vesting restrictions) with the condition reflected in the grant date fair value. Others disagree and take the view that in some situations such arrangements meet the definition of a vesting condition and this allows any IFRS 2 expense to be reversed should the condition not be met. The issue has been referred to the Interpretations Committee and to the IASB (see 3.4 below).

Those who take the view that a non-compete arrangement is not always a non-vesting condition read paragraph BC171B as distinguishing between non-compete clauses which apply after the counterparty has become entitled to an award (a non-vesting condition) and those that, by implication, apply before the counterparty has become entitled to an award (a vesting condition). Broadly, therefore, if an employee has been given shares at the start of a non-compete period he is entitled to them (a non-vesting condition), but if the shares are retained by the entity or held in escrow, the employee is not entitled to the shares until the end of the non-compete period (a vesting condition).

We believe that this view is difficult to reconcile with IFRS 2 as currently drafted because:

- it requires the reference to 'entitlement' to an award to be read as including a contingent obligation to forfeit the share, which is not in accordance with the general approach of IFRS 2; and
- it requires the words 'which apply after the counterparty has become entitled to the share-based payment' to be read with an implied emphasis on the word 'after', so as to distinguish it from an implied (unstated) alternative scenario in which the conditions apply *before* the counterparty becomes entitled to the share-based payment. We believe that a more natural reading is to consider these words as describing all non-compete agreements and transfer restrictions.

The classification of a non-compete provision remains a potential agenda item for the IASB (see 3.4 below).

3.3 Vesting period

The *vesting period* is the period during which all the specified vesting conditions of a share-based payment arrangement are to be satisfied. *[IFRS 2 Appendix A]*. This is not the same as the exercise period or the life of the option, as illustrated by Example 30.1 below.

Example 30.1: Meaning of 'vesting period' – award with vesting conditions only

An employee is awarded options that can be exercised, if the employee remains in service for at least three years from the date of the award, at any time between three and ten years from the date of the award. For this award, the vesting period is three years; the exercise period is seven years; and the life of the option is ten years. However, as discussed further in 8 below, for the purposes of calculating the cost of the award under IFRS 2, the life of the award is taken as the period ending with the date on which the counterparty is most likely actually to exercise the option, which may be some time before the full ten year life expires.

It is also important to distinguish between vesting conditions and other restrictions on the exercise of options and/or trading in shares, as illustrated by Example 30.2 below.

Example 30.2: Meaning of 'vesting period' – award with vesting conditions and other restrictions

An employee is awarded options that can be exercised, if the employee remains in service for at least three years from the date of the award, at any time between five and ten years from the date of the award. In this case, the vesting period remains three years as in Example 30.1 above, provided that the employee's entitlement to the award becomes absolute at the end of three years – in other words, the employee has to provide no services to the entity in years 4 and 5. The restriction on exercise of the award in the period after vesting is a non-vesting condition, which would be reflected in the original valuation of the award at the date of grant (see 4, 5 and 8 below).

The implications of vesting conditions, non-vesting conditions and vesting periods for equity-settled transactions are discussed in 4 to 7 below and for cash-settled transactions in 9 below.

3.4 Vesting and non-vesting conditions: future developments

In January 2010 the Interpretations Committee added to its agenda a request for clarification of the following:

- the basis on which vesting conditions, especially performance conditions, can be distinguished from non-vesting conditions, especially the distinction between a service condition, a performance condition and a non-vesting condition; and
- the interaction of multiple conditions.

As part of the request for clarification, the following two application issues were raised (see also the discussion at 3.2 above):

- whether there needs to be a direct link between a performance target and an individual employee's service in order for that target to be a performance condition; and
- when determining whether the target qualifies as a performance condition, does it matter whether the specified service period is shorter or longer than the period over which the performance target should be met?[6]

At its meetings in July and September 2010,[7] the Interpretations Committee made the following tentative decisions and decided to ask the IASB how to proceed:

- a performance condition should be defined by reference to the operations or activities of the entity rather than by reference to any attributes of performance conditions in general;
- there should be no change to the accounting for save as you earn ('SAYE') plans;
- IPO and change of control conditions should be deemed to constitute a performance condition;
- a non-compete provision should be presumed to be a 'contingent feature'[8]; and
- in order for a performance target to constitute a performance vesting condition, the performance target should fully coincide with an explicit or implicit service requirement for the entire period between the grant date and the performance target date.

The IASB subsequently asked the Interpretations Committee to consider whether any of the issues could be dealt with as annual improvements and to review other requests received in relation to IFRS 2 with a view to developing an agenda proposal.[9]

In November 2010 the Interpretations Committee proposed that the definitions of service and performance conditions be clarified through the annual improvements cycle and prioritised four issues from its earlier discussions. The IASB discussed the proposals in September 2011 and tentatively decided to include an amendment in the next exposure draft of *Annual Improvements to IFRSs* (discussed further below).[10]

The Interpretations Committee concluded that the questions relating to the classification of a non-compete provision and how to account for the interaction of multiple vesting conditions should be referred to the IASB for consideration as future agenda items.[11] This conclusion was reiterated in March 2011 when the Interpretations Committee reviewed the IFRS 2 issues submitted to it over the previous six years.[12]

The IASB's draft *Annual Improvements to IFRSs 2010-2012 Cycle,* issued in May 2012, included proposed amendments to the definitions of 'performance condition', 'service condition' and 'vesting conditions' designed to address the four issues identified by the Interpretations Committee in November 2010.[13] The IASB sought to make clear that:

- a performance target may relate either to the performance of the entity as a whole or to some part of the entity, such as a division or individual employee;
- the performance target in a performance condition should be defined by reference to 'the entity's own operations (or activities) or the price (or value) of its equity instruments'. Accordingly, a share market index target is a non-vesting condition rather than a performance condition – even if the entity's shares form part of the index;
- a performance condition needs to have an explicit or implicit service condition over a period at least as long as the period over which performance is being measured in order to for it to be a performance vesting condition rather than a non-vesting condition; and

- an employee's failure to meet a service condition should be treated as a forfeiture, and the IFRS 2 expense therefore reversed, whatever the reason for the failure (see 7.4.1.B below).

In January 2013, the Interpretations Committee considered comments received on the draft proposals and made the following recommendations to the IASB in order to address various concerns that had been raised about the draft definitions of 'performance condition' and 'service condition':

- a performance target can be set by reference to the price (or value) of another entity included within the group;
- a performance target that refers to a longer period than the required service period does not constitute a performance condition;
- the specified period of service that the counterparty is required to complete can be either implicit or explicit;
- management does not need to prove the employee's ability to influence the performance target;
- a share market index target is a non-vesting condition;
- the definition of 'performance condition' should indicate that it includes a 'market condition';
- a definition of 'non-vesting condition' is not needed; and
- the employee's failure to complete a required service period is considered to be a failure to satisfy a service condition.

The Interpretations Committee also recommended that, once finalised, the amendments be applied on a prospective basis.[14]

The IASB tentatively decided in February 2013[15] to finalise the draft amendments subject to some minor wording changes but in June 2013 discussed a further issue arising from the drafting of the amendments. The issue related to the length of the performance target period relative to the service period. The draft amendments made clear that the performance period could not end after the end of the service period but did not make clear whether a performance target period could start earlier than the service period and still be classified as a vesting condition rather than as a non-vesting condition.

The IASB tentatively decided to allow the start of the assessment period for the performance target to precede the service period provided that:

- the assessment period for the performance target substantially coincides with the service period; and
- the assessment period for the performance target does not extend beyond the end of the service period.

The IASB tentatively agreed to finalise the proposed amendments on this basis.[16]

This late adjustment will go some way towards removing an issue that is extremely common in practice, particularly with awards made to employees under a single scheme but at various times. However, there clearly remains an element of judgement in the interpretation of 'substantially coincides' where, for example, the starting point for the measurement of an earnings per share target precedes the granting of any awards.

The treatment of a non-compete provision and the question of how to account for the interaction of multiple vesting conditions have not yet been addressed and these issues continue to result in some diversity in practice (see also 3.2.1 above). At its September 2011 meeting the IASB agreed with the Interpretations Committee that these issues should be considered as future agenda items.[17]

4 EQUITY-SETTLED TRANSACTIONS – OVERVIEW

4.1 Summary of accounting treatment

The detailed provisions of IFRS 2 are complex, but their key points can be summarised as follows.

(a) All equity-settled transactions are measured at fair value. However, transactions with employees are normally measured using a 'grant date model' (i.e. the transaction is recorded at the fair value of the equity instrument at the date when it is originally granted), whereas transactions with non-employees are normally measured using a 'service date model' (i.e. the transaction is recorded at the fair value of the goods or services received at the date they are received). As noted in 3 above, all transactions, however *measured*, are *recognised* using a 'service date model' (see 5 below).

(b) Where an award is made subject to future fulfilment of conditions, a 'market condition' (i.e. one related to the market price of the entity's equity instruments) or a 'non-vesting condition' (i.e. one that is neither a service condition nor a performance condition) is taken into account in determining the fair value of the award. However, the effect of conditions other than market or non-vesting conditions is ignored in determining the fair value of the award (see 3 above and 6 below).

(c) Where an award is made subject to future fulfilment of vesting conditions, its cost is recognised over the period during which the conditions are fulfilled (see 3 above and 6 below). The corresponding credit entry is recorded within equity (see 4.2 below).

(d) Until an equity instrument has vested (i.e. the entitlement to it has become unconditional) any amounts recorded are in effect contingent and will be adjusted if more or fewer awards vest than were originally anticipated to do so. However, an equity instrument awarded subject to a market condition or a non-vesting condition is considered to vest irrespective of whether or not that market or non-vesting condition is fulfilled, provided that all other vesting conditions (if any) are satisfied (see 6 below).

(e) No adjustments are made, either before or after vesting, to reflect the fact that an award has no value to the person entitled to it e.g. in the case of a share option, because the option exercise price is above the current market price of the share (see 6.1.1 and 6.1.3 below).

(f) If an equity instrument is cancelled, whether by the entity or the counterparty (see (g) below) before vesting, any amount remaining to be expensed is charged in full at that point (see 7.4 below). If an equity instrument is modified before vesting (e.g. in the case of a share option, by changing the performance conditions or the exercise price), the financial statements must continue to show a cost for at least the fair value of the original instrument, as measured at the original grant date, together with any excess of the fair value of the modified instrument over that of the original instrument, as measured at the date of modification (see 7.3 below).

(g) Where an award lapses during the vesting period due to a failure by the counterparty to satisfy a non-vesting condition within the counterparty's control, or a failure by the entity to satisfy a non-vesting condition within the entity's control, the lapse of the award is accounted for as if it were a cancellation (see (f) above and 6.4.3 below).

(h) In determining the cost of an equity-settled transaction under IFRS 2, whether the entity satisfies its obligations under the transaction with a fresh issue of shares or by purchasing own shares in the financial markets is completely irrelevant to the charge in profit or loss, although there is clearly a difference in the cash flows. Where own shares are purchased, they are accounted for as treasury shares under IAS 32 (see 2.2.4.H above and Chapter 43 at 9). *[IFRS 2.BC330-333].*

The requirements summarised in (d) to (g) above can have the effect that IFRS 2 requires a cost to be recorded for an award that ultimately has no value to the counterparty, because the award either does not vest or vests but is not exercised. These rather counter-intuitive requirements of IFRS 2 are in part 'anti-abuse' provisions to prevent entities from applying a 'selective' grant date model, whereby awards that increase in value after grant date remain measured at grant date while awards that decrease in value are remeasured. This is discussed further in the detailed analysis at 5 to 7 below.

4.2 The credit entry

As noted at (c) in the summary in 4.1 above, the basic accounting entry for an equity-settled share-based payment transaction is:

DR Profit or loss for the period (employee costs)
    CR Equity.

IFRS 2 does not prescribe whether the credit should be to a separate component of equity, or, if the entity chooses to treat it as such, how it should be described.

The IASB presumably adopted this non-prescriptive approach so as to ensure there was no conflict between, on the one hand, the basic requirement of IFRS 2 that there should be a credit in equity and, on the other, the legal requirements of various jurisdictions as to exactly how that credit should be allocated within equity.

Occasionally there will be a credit to profit or loss (see for instance Example 30.11 at 6.2.4 below) and a corresponding reduction in equity.

A share-based payment transaction may be settled in equity instruments of a subsidiary of the reporting entity. This is most commonly the case where the subsidiary is partly-owned with traded shares held by external shareholders. In the consolidated financial statements, the question arises as to whether the credit entry for such transactions should be presented as a non-controlling interest (NCI) or as part of the equity attributable to the shareholders of the parent. In our view, classification within NCI is the preferable treatment but, for unvested shares and unexercised options, it is unlikely that the amounts recognised under IFRS 2 will align exactly with the measurement of NCI under IFRS 10 as the share of a present ownership interest. An adjustment between NCI and group equity might therefore be required at the point when shares are issued or when options lapse unexercised. For further discussion on the requirements of IFRS 10 in relation to changes in NCI see Chapter 7 at 4.5.

5 EQUITY-SETTLED TRANSACTIONS – COST OF AWARDS

5.1 Cost of awards – overview

The general measurement rule in IFRS 2 is that an entity must measure the goods or services received, and the corresponding increase in equity, directly, at the fair value of the goods or services received, unless that fair value cannot be estimated reliably. If the fair value of the goods or services received cannot be estimated reliably, the entity must measure their value, and the corresponding increase in equity, indirectly, by reference to the fair value of the equity instruments granted. *[IFRS 2.10]*. 'Fair value' is defined as the amount for which an asset could be exchanged, a liability settled, or an equity instrument granted could be exchanged, between knowledgeable, willing parties in an arm's length transaction. *[IFRS 2 Appendix A]*. IFRS 2 has its own specific rules in relation to determining the fair value of share-based payments which differ from the more general fair value measurement requirements in IFRS 13 – *Fair Value Measurement* (see 5.5 below). *[IFRS 2.6A]*.

On their own, the general measurement principles of IFRS 2 would suggest that the reporting entity must determine in each case whether the fair value of the equity instruments granted or that of the goods or services received is more reliably determinable. However, IFRS 2 goes on to clarify that:

- in the case of transactions with employees, the fair value of the equity instruments must be used (see 5.2 below), except in those extremely rare cases where it is not possible to measure this fair value reliably, when the intrinsic value of the equity instruments may be used instead (see 5.5 below); but
- in the case of transactions with non-employees, there is a rebuttable presumption that the fair value of the goods or services provided is more reliably determinable (see 5.4 below).

Moreover, transactions with employees are measured at the date of grant (see 5.2 below), whereas those with non-employees are measured at the date when goods or services are received (see 5.4 below).

The overall position can be summarised by the following matrix.

Counterparty	**Measurement basis**	**Measurement date**	**Recognition date**
Employee	Fair value of equity instruments awarded	Grant date	Service date
Non-employee	Fair value of goods or services received	Service date	Service date

The Basis for Conclusions addresses the issue of why the accounting treatment for apparently identical transactions should, in effect, depend on the identity of the counterparty.

The main argument put forward to justify the approach adopted for transactions with employees is essentially that, once an award has been agreed, the value of the services provided pursuant to the transaction does not change significantly with the value of the award. *[IFRS 2.BC88-96]*. However, some might question this proposition, on the grounds that employees are more likely to work harder when the value of their options is rising than when it has sunk irretrievably.

As regards transactions with non-employees, the IASB offers two main arguments for the use of measurement at service date.

The first is that, if the counterparty is not firmly committed to delivering the goods or services, the counterparty would consider whether the fair value of the equity instruments at the delivery date is sufficient payment for the goods or services when deciding whether to deliver the goods or services. This suggests that there is a high correlation between the fair value of the equity instruments at the date the goods or services are received and the fair value of those goods or services. *[IFRS 2.BC126]*. This argument is clearly vulnerable to the challenge that it has no relevance where (as would more likely be the case) the counterparty is firmly committed to delivering the goods or services.

The second is that non-employees generally provide services over a short period commencing some time after grant date, whereas employees generally provide services over an extended period beginning on the grant date. This leads to a concern that transactions with non-employees could be entered into well in advance of the due date for delivery of goods or services. If an entity were able to measure the expense of such a transaction at the grant date fair value, the result, assuming that the entity's share price rises, would be to understate the cost of goods and services delivered. *[IFRS 2.BC126-127]*.

The true reason for the IASB's approach may have been political as much as theoretical. One effect of a grant date measurement model is that, applied to a grant of share options that is eventually exercised, it 'freezes' the accounting cost at the (typically) lower fair value at the date of grant. This excludes from the post-grant financial statements the increased cost and volatility that would be associated with a model that constantly remeasured the award to fair value until exercise date. The IASB might well have perceived it as a marginally easier task to persuade the corporate sector of the merits of a 'lower cost, zero volatility' approach as opposed to a 'fair value at exercise date' model (such as is used for cash-settled awards – see 9 below).

The price to be paid in accounting terms for the grant date model is that, when an award falls in value after grant date, it continues to be recognised at its higher grant date value. It is therefore quite possible that, during a period of general economic downturn, financial statements will show significant costs for options granted in previous years, but which are currently worthless. This could well lead to (in fact, sometimes groundless) accusations of rewarding management for failure.

5.2 Transactions with employees

These will comprise the great majority of transactions accounted for under IFRS 2, and include all remuneration in the form of shares, share options and any other form of reward settled in equity instruments of the entity or a member of its group.

5.2.1 Who is an 'employee'?

Given the difference between the accounting treatment of equity-settled transactions with employees and that of those with non-employees, it is obviously important for IFRS 2 to define what is meant by employees. In fact IFRS 2 strictly refers to 'employees and others providing similar services' *[IFRS 2.11]*, who are defined as individuals who render personal services to the entity and either:

(a) the individuals are regarded as employees for legal or tax purposes;

(b) the individuals work for the entity under its direction in the same way as individuals who are regarded as employees for legal or tax purposes; or

(c) the services rendered are similar to those rendered by employees.

The term encompasses all management personnel, i.e. those persons having authority and responsibility for planning, directing and controlling the activities of the entity, including non-executive directors. *[IFRS 2 Appendix A]*.

The implication of (a) and (b) above is that it is not open to an entity to argue that an individual who is not an employee as a matter of law is therefore automatically a non-employee for the purposes of IFRS 2.

The implication of (b) and (c) above is that, where a third party provides services pursuant to a share-based payment transaction that could be provided by an employee (e.g. where an external IT consultant works alongside an in-house IT team), that third party is treated as an employee rather than a non-employee for the purposes of IFRS 2.

Conversely, however, where an entity engages a consultant to undertake work for which there is not an existing in-house function, the implication is that such an individual is not regarded as an employee. In other words, in our view, the reference in (c) to 'services ... similar to those rendered by employees' is to services rendered by employees that the entity actually has, rather than to employees that the entity might have if it were to recruit them. Otherwise, the distinction in IFRS 2 between employees and non-employees would have no effect, since it would always be open to an entity to argue that it could employ someone to undertake any task instead of engaging a contractor.

Exceptionally there might be cases where the same individual is engaged in both capacities. For example, a director of the entity might also be a partner in a firm of lawyers and be engaged in that latter capacity to advise the entity on a particular issue. It might be more appropriate to regard payment for the legal services as made to a non-employee rather than to an employee.

Related questions of interpretation arise where an award is made to an employee of an associate or a joint venture (see 12.9 below).

The effect of a change of status from employee to non-employee (or vice versa) is addressed at 5.4.1 below.

5.2.2 *Basis of measurement*

As noted above, IFRS 2 requires equity-settled transactions with employees to be measured by reference to the fair value of the equity instruments granted at 'grant date' (see 5.3 below). *[IFRS 2.11].* IFRS 2 asserts that this approach is necessary because shares, share options and other equity instruments are typically only part of a larger remuneration package, such that it would not be practicable to determine the value of the work performed in consideration for the cash element of the total package, the benefit-in-kind element, the share option element and so on. *[IFRS 2.12].*

In essence, this is really an anti-avoidance provision. The underlying concern is that, if an entity were able to value options by reference to the services provided for them, it might assert that the value of those services was zero, on the argument that its personnel are already so handsomely rewarded by the non-equity elements of their remuneration package (such as cash and health benefits), that no additional services are (or indeed could be) obtained by granting options.

5.3 Grant date

As noted above, IFRS 2 requires equity-settled transactions with employees to be accounted for at fair value at grant date, defined as 'the date at which the entity and another party (including an employee) agree to a share-based payment arrangement, being when the entity and the counterparty have a shared understanding of the terms and conditions of the arrangement'. *[IFRS 2 Appendix A].*

The determination of grant date is critical to the measurement of equity-settled share-based transactions with employees, since grant date is the date at which such transactions must be measured (see 5.2 above).

In practice, it is not always clear when a mutual understanding of the award (and, therefore, grant date) has occurred. Issues of interpretation can arise as to:

- how precise the shared understanding of the terms of the award must be; and
- exactly what level of communication between the reporting entity and the counterparty is sufficient to ensure the appropriate degree of 'shared understanding'.

As a consequence, the determination of the grant date is often difficult in practice. We discuss the following issues in more detail in the sections below:

- basic determination of grant date (see 5.3.1 below);
- the communication of awards to employees and cases where services are rendered in advance of grant date (see 5.3.2 below);
- awards where the exercise price depends on a formula or on a future share price (see 5.3.3 below);
- awards where the exercise price is paid in shares (see 5.3.4 below);
- an award of equity instruments to a fixed monetary value (see 5.3.5 below);
- awards over a fixed pool of shares (including 'last man standing' arrangements) (see 5.3.6 below);
- awards with multiple service periods (see 5.3.7 below);
- awards subject to modification or discretionary re-assessment by the entity after the original grant date (see 5.3.8 below);
- mandatory or discretionary awards to 'good leavers' (see 5.3.9 below); and
- special purpose acquisition companies (see 5.3.10 below).

The grant date for 'matching' awards (i.e. arrangements where an additional award of shares is granted to match an initial cash bonus or award of shares) is discussed at 15.1 below.

5.3.1 Determination of grant date

IFRS 2 and the accompanying implementation guidance emphasise that a grant occurs only when all the conditions are known and agreed. Thus, for example, if an entity makes an award 'in principle' to an employee of options whose terms are subject to review or approval by a remuneration committee or the shareholders, 'grant date' is the later date when the necessary formalities have been completed. *[IFRS 2 Appendix A, IG1-3].*

The implementation guidance to IFRS 2 notes that employees may begin rendering services in consideration for an award before it has been formally ratified. For example, a new employee might join the entity on 1 January 2014 and be granted options relating to performance for a period beginning on that date, but subject to formal approval by the remuneration committee at its quarterly meeting on 15 March 2014. In that case, the entity would typically begin expensing the award from 1 January 2014 based on a best estimate of its fair value, but would subsequently adjust that estimate so that the ultimate cost of the award was its actual fair value at 15 March 2014. *[IFRS 2.IG4].* This reference to formal approval could be construed as indicating that, in fact, IFRS 2 requires not merely that there is a mutual understanding of the award (which might well have been in existence since 1 January 2014), but also that the entity has completed all processes necessary to make the award a legally binding agreement.

In practice, many situations are much less clear-cut than the example given in the implementation guidance. For example, if a remuneration committee has discretion over some aspects of an award and whether it vests, does that mean that there is not a shared understanding until the vesting date? Similarly, does the counterparty need to have full quantification of every aspect of an award (performance targets, exercise price, etc.) or would an understanding of the formula for calculating performance or price be sufficient? Some of these practical interpretation issues are considered further below.

5.3.2 *Communication of awards to employees and services in advance of grant date*

As discussed at 5.3.1 above, the implementation guidance to IFRS 2 indicates that, in order for a grant to have been made, there must not merely be a mutual understanding of the terms, but there must also be a legally enforceable arrangement. Thus, if an award requires board or shareholder approval for it to be legally binding on the reporting entity, for the purposes of IFRS 2 it has not been granted until such approval has been given, even if the terms of the award are fully understood at an earlier date. However, if services are effectively being rendered for the award from a date earlier than the grant date as defined in IFRS 2, the cost of the award should be recognised over a period starting with that earlier date. *[IFRS 2.IG4]*.

The implications of this requirement are illustrated in Example 30.3 below. It is important, however, to retain a sense of proportion. In cases where the share price is not particularly volatile, whether the grant date is, say, 1 January or 1 April may not make a great difference to the valuation of the award, particularly when set beside the range of acceptable valuations resulting from the use of estimates in the valuation model.

Example 30.3: Determination of grant date

Scenario 1

On 1 January 2014 an entity advises employees of the terms of a share award designed to reward performance over the three years ended 31 December 2016. The award is subject to board approval, which is given on 1 March 2014. Grant date is 1 March 2014. However, the cost of the award would be recognised over the three year period beginning 1 January 2014, since the employees would have effectively been rendering service for the award from that date.

Scenario 2

On 1 January 2014 an entity's board resolves to implement a share scheme designed to reward performance over the three years ended 31 December 2016. The award is notified to employees on 1 March 2014. Grant date is again 1 March 2014. *Prima facie*, in this case, the cost of the award would be recognised over the two years and ten months period beginning 1 March 2014, since the employees could not be regarded as rendering service in January and February for an award of which they were not aware at that time.

However, if a similar award is made each year, and according to a similar timescale, there might be an argument that, during January and February 2014, employees are rendering service for an award of which there is high expectation, and that the cost should therefore, as in Scenario 1, be recognised over the full three year period. The broader issue of the accounting treatment for awards of which there is a high expectation is addressed in the discussion of matching share awards at 15.1 below.

Scenario 3

On 1 January 2014 an entity advises employees of the terms of a share award designed to reward performance over the three years ended 31 December 2016. The award is subject to board approval, which is given on 1 March 2014. However, in giving such approval, the Board makes some changes to the performance conditions as originally communicated to employees on 1 January. The revised terms of the award are communicated to employees on 1 April 2014. Grant date is 1 April 2014. However, the cost of the award would be recognised over the three year period beginning 1 January 2014, since the employees would have effectively been rendering service for the award from that date.

5.3.3 Exercise price or performance target dependent on a formula or future share price

Some share plans define the exercise price not in absolute terms, but as a factor of the share price. For example, the price might be expressed as:

- a percentage of the share price at exercise date; or
- a percentage of the lower of the share price at grant date and at exercise date.

The effect of this is that, although the actual exercise price is not known until the date of exercise, both the entity and the counterparty already have a shared understanding of how the price will be calculated.

A similar approach might be applied in the setting of performance targets i.e. they are set by reference to a formula rather than in absolute terms.

In order for there to be a shared understanding, the formula or method of determining the outcome needs to be sufficiently clear and objective to allow both the entity and the counterparty to make an estimate of the outcome of the award during the vesting period. Accordingly, in our view, grant date is the date on which the terms and conditions (including the formula for calculating the exercise price or performance target) are determined sufficiently clearly and agreed by the entity and the counterparty, subject to the matters discussed at 5.3.2 above.

5.3.4 Exercise price paid in shares (net settlement of award)

Some share awards allow the exercise price to be paid in shares. In practical terms, this means that the number of shares delivered to the counterparty will be the total 'gross' number of shares awarded less as many shares as have, at the date of exercise, a fair value equal to the strike price.

In our view, this situation is analogous to that in 5.3.3 above in that, whilst the absolute 'net' number of shares awarded will not be known until the date of exercise, the basis on which that 'net' number will be determined is established in advance. Accordingly, in our view, grant date is the date on which the terms and conditions (including the ability to surrender shares to a fair value equal to the exercise price) are determined and agreed by the entity and the counterparty, subject to the matters discussed at 5.3.2 above.

Such a scheme could also be analysed as a share-settled share appreciation right (whereby the employee receives shares to the value of the excess of the value of the shares given over the exercise price), which is treated as an equity-settled award under IFRS 2.

5.3.5 Award of equity instruments to a fixed monetary value

Some entities may grant awards to employees of shares to a fixed value. For example, an entity might award as many shares as are worth €100,000, with the number of shares being calculated by reference to the share price as at the vesting date. The number of shares ultimately received will not be known until the vesting date. This begs the question of whether such an award can be regarded as having been granted until that date, on the argument that it is only then that the number of shares to be delivered – a key term of the award – is known, and therefore there cannot be a 'shared understanding' of the terms of the award until that later date.

In our view, this situation is analogous to those in 5.3.3 and 5.3.4 above in that, whilst the absolute number of shares awarded will not be known until the vesting date, the basis on which that number will be determined is established in advance in a manner sufficiently clear and objective to allow an ongoing estimate by the entity and by the counterparty of the number of awards expected to vest. Accordingly, in our view, grant date is the date on which the terms and conditions are determined sufficiently clearly and agreed by the entity and the counterparty, subject to the matters discussed at 5.3.2 above.

However, the measurement of such awards raises further issues of interpretation, which we discuss at 8.10 below.

5.3.6 *Awards over a fixed pool of shares (including 'last man standing' arrangements)*

An award over a fixed pool of shares is sometimes granted to a small group of, typically senior, employees. Such awards might involve an initial allocation of shares to each individual but also provide for the redistribution of each employee's shares to the other participants should any individual leave employment before the end of the vesting period. This is often referred to as a 'last man standing' arrangement.

The accounting requirements of IFRS 2 for such an arrangement are unclear. In the absence of specific guidance, several interpretations are possible and we believe that an entity may make an accounting policy choice, provided that choice is applied consistently to all such arrangements.

The first approach is based on the view that the unit of account is all potential shares to be earned by the individual employee and that, from the outset, each employee has a full understanding of the terms and conditions of both the initial award and the reallocation arrangements. This means that there is a grant on day one with each individual's award being valued on the basis of:

- that employee's initial allocation of shares; plus
- an additional award with a non-vesting condition relating to the potential reallocation of other participants' shares.

Under this approach, the departure of an employee will be accounted for as a forfeiture (see 6.1.2 below) but the redistribution of that individual's shares to the other employees will have no accounting impact. This approach is likely to result in a total expense that is higher than the number of shares awarded multiplied by the grant date price per share.

The second approach, which we believe is consistent with US GAAP, also considers the individual employee's award to be the unit of account. Under this approach, there is an initial grant to all the employees and it is only these awards for which the fair value is measured at the date of the initial grant. Any subsequent reallocations of shares should be accounted for as a forfeiture of the original award and a completely new grant to the remaining employees. This approach accounts only for the specific number of shares that have been allocated to the individual employee as at the end of each reporting period. No account is taken in this approach of shares that might be allocated to the individual employee in the future due to another employee's forfeiture, even though the reallocation formula is known to the individual employees at the initial grant date.

A third view, which takes a pragmatic approach in the light of the issues arising from the two approaches outlined above, is to account for the award on the basis of the pool of shares granted rather than treating the individual employee as the unit of account. In our view this approach would be materially acceptable in many situations where there is a scheme with the same small number of participants from the outset. Under this approach, the fair value of the total pool of shares is measured at the grant date (day one) with the non-vesting condition effectively ignored for valuation purposes. Subsequent forfeitures and reallocations would have no effect on the accounting.

The 'last man standing' arrangement described above can be contrasted with a situation where an entity designates a fixed pool of shares to be used for awards to employees but where the allocation of leavers' shares is discretionary rather than pre-determined. In this situation, the valuation of the initial award would not take account of any potential future reallocations. If an employee left employment during the vesting period, that individual's award would be accounted for as a forfeiture and any reallocation of that individual's shares would be accounted for as a new grant with the fair value determined at the new grant date (i.e. a similar accounting treatment to that in approach two above).

A further type of award relating to a fixed pool of shares is one where an entity makes an award over a fixed number or percentage of its shares to a particular section of its workforce, the final allocation of the pool being made to those employed at the vesting date. In such an arrangement, some employees will typically join and leave the scheme during the original vesting period which will lead to changes in each employee's allocation of shares. Although employees are aware of the existence, and some of the terms, of the arrangement at the outset, the fact that there is no objective formula (see 5.3.3 to 5.3.5 above) for determining the number of shares that each individual will ultimately receive means that there is no grant under IFRS 2 until the date of final allocation. However, because the employees render service under the arrangement in advance of the grant date – either from day one or from a later joining date – the entity should estimate the fair value of the award to each individual from the date services commence and expense this over the full service period of the award with a final truing up of the expense to the fair value of the award at the eventual grant date (see 5.3.2 above).

This has the effect that, where an entity decides to set aside a bonus pool of a fixed amount of cash, say £1 million, with the allocation to individual employees to be made at a later date, there is a known fixed cost of £1 million. However, where an entity decides to set aside a bonus pool of a fixed number of shares, with the allocation to individual employees to be made at a later date, the final cost is not determined until the eventual grant date.

5.3.7 Awards with multiple service periods

Entities frequently make awards that cover more than one reporting period, but with different performance conditions for each period, rather than a single cumulative target for the whole vesting period. In such cases, the grant date may depend on the precision with which the terms of the award are communicated to employees, as illustrated by Example 30.4 below.

Example 30.4: Awards with multiple service periods

Scenario 1

On 1 January 2014, the entity enters into a share-based payment arrangement with an employee. The employee is informed that the maximum potential award is 40,000 shares, 10,000 of which will vest on 31 December 2014, and 10,000 more on each of 31 December 2015, 31 December 2016 and 31 December 2017. Vesting of each tranche of 10,000 shares is conditional on:

(a) the employee having been in continuous service until 31 December of the relevant year; and

(b) revenue targets for each of those four years, as communicated to the employee on 1 January 2014, having been attained.

In this case, the terms of the award are clearly understood by both parties at 1 January 2014, and this is therefore the grant date under IFRS 2 (subject to issues such as any requirement for later formal approval – see 5.3 to 5.3.2 above). The cost of the award would be recognised using a 'graded' vesting period – see 6.2.2 below.

Scenario 2

On 1 January 2014, the entity enters into a share-based payment arrangement with an employee. The employee is informed that the maximum potential award is 40,000 shares, 10,000 of which will vest on 31 December 2014, and 10,000 more on each of 31 December 2015, 31 December 2016 and 31 December 2017. Vesting of each tranche of 10,000 shares is conditional on:

(a) the employee having been in continuous service until 31 December of the relevant year; and

(b) revenue targets for each of those four years, to be communicated to the employee on 1 January of each year in respect of that year only, having been attained.

In this case, in our view, as at 1 January 2014, there is a clear shared understanding only of the terms of the first tranche of 10,000 shares that will potentially vest on 31 December 2014. There is no clear understanding of the terms of the tranches potentially vesting in 2015 to 2017 because their vesting depends on revenue targets for those years which have not yet been set.

Accordingly, each of the four tranches of 10,000 shares has a separate grant date – i.e. 1 January 2014, 1 January 2015, 1 January 2016 and 1 January 2017 – and a vesting period of one year from the relevant grant date.

A variation on the above two scenarios which is seen quite frequently in practice is an award where the target is quantified for the first year and the targets for subsequent years depend on a formula-based increase in the year 1 target. The formula is set at the same time as the year 1 target. Whether the accounting treatment for scenario 1 above or scenario 2 above is the more appropriate in such a situation is, in our view, a matter of judgement depending on the precise terms of the arrangement (see 5.3.3 above).

5.3.8 Awards subject to modification by entity after original grant date

As noted at 5.3.1 above, some employee share awards are drafted in terms that give the entity discretion to modify the detailed terms of the scheme after grant date. Some have questioned whether this effectively means that the date originally determined as the 'grant date' is not in fact the grant date as defined in IFRS 2, on the grounds that the entity's right to modify means that the terms are not in fact understood by both parties in advance.

In our view, this is very often not an appropriate analysis. If it were, it could also mean that, in some jurisdictions, nearly all share-based awards to employees would be required to be measured at vesting date, which clearly was not the IASB's intention.

However, there may well be room for debate as to the extent to which an intervention by the entity after grant date constitutes modification or not. Some situations commonly encountered in practice are considered in the sections below.

5.3.8.A Significant equity restructuring or transactions

Many schemes contain provisions designed to ensure that the value of awards is maintained following a major capital restructuring (such as a share split or share consolidation – see 7.8 below) or a major transaction with shareholders as a whole (such as the insertion of a new holding company over an existing group (see 12.8 below), a major share buyback or the payment of a special dividend). These provisions may allow the entity to make such adjustments as it sees fit to maintain the value of awards. In some cases the exercise of such powers may be relatively mechanistic (e.g. the adjustment of the number of shares subject to options following a share split). In some cases, more subjectivity will be involved (e.g. in determining whether a particular dividend is a 'special' dividend for the purposes of the scheme).

In our view, the presumption in such cases should be that the exercise of the entity's right to modify does not constitute a 'modification' as defined in IFRS 2. However, as the intention of such a provision is to preserve the value of the award before and after the restructuring, there would be no incremental value to account for even if the entity's exercise of such a discretion were regarded as a modification.

5.3.8.B Interpretation of general terms

More problematic might be the exercise of any discretion by the entity or its remuneration committee to interpret the more general terms of a scheme in deciding whether performance targets have been met and therefore whether, and to what extent, an award should vest. Suppose, for example, that an entity makes an award to its executives with a performance condition based on total shareholder return (TSR) with a maximum payout if the entity is in the top quartile of a peer group of 100 entities (i.e. it is ranked between 1 and 25 in the peer group).

It might be that the entity is ranked 26 until shortly before the end of the performance period, at which point the entity ranked 25 suddenly announces that it is in financial difficulties and ceases trading shortly afterwards. This then means that the reporting entity moves up from 26 to 25 in the rankings. However, the entity might take the view that, in the circumstances, it could not be considered as having truly been ranked 25 in the peer group, so that a maximum payout is not justified.

In this case, there might be more of an argument that the entity's intervention constitutes a modification. However, as the effect would be to reduce the fair value of the award, it would have no impact on the accounting treatment (see 7.3.2 below).

If such an intervention were not regarded as a modification, then the results might be different depending on the nature of the award. Where an award is subject to a market condition, as here, or to a non-vesting condition, an expense might well have to be recognised in any event, if all the non-market vesting conditions (e.g. service) were satisfied – see 6.3 and 6.4 below.

However, suppose that the award had been based on a non-market vesting condition, such as an EPS target, which was met, but only due to a gain of an unusual, non-recurring nature, such as the revaluation of PP&E for tax purposes, giving rise to a deferred tax credit. The remuneration committee concludes that this should be ignored, with the effect that the award does not vest. If this is regarded as the exercise of a pre-existing right to ensure that the award vests only if 'normal' EPS reaches a given level, then there has been no modification. On this analysis, the award has not vested, and any expense previously recognised would be reversed. If, however, the committee's intervention is regarded as a modification, it would have no impact on the accounting treatment in this case, as the effect would be to reduce the fair value of the award and this would be ignored under the general requirements of IFRS 2 relating to modifications (see 7.3.2 below).

5.3.8.C Discretion to make further awards

Some schemes may give the entity the power to increase an award in circumstances where the recipient is considered to have delivered exceptional performance, or some such similar wording. In our view, unless the criteria for judging such exceptional performance are so clear as to be, in effect, performance conditions under IFRS 2, the presumption should be that any award made pursuant to such a clause is granted, and therefore measured, when it is made. We note at 15.1 below that there may be circumstances where an award described as 'discretionary' may not truly be so, since the entity has created an expectation amounting to a constructive obligation to make the award. However, we believe that it would be somewhat contradictory to argue that such expectations had been created in the case of an award stated to be for (undefined) exceptional performance only.

5.3.9 'Good leaver' arrangements

In some jurisdictions it is common for awards to contain a so-called 'good leaver' clause. A 'good leaver' clause is one which makes provision for an employee who leaves employment before the end of the full vesting period of the award to receive some or all of the award on leaving (see 5.3.9.A below).

In other cases, the original terms of an award will either make no reference to 'good leavers' or will not be sufficiently specific to allow the accounting treatment to be based on the original terms of the scheme. In such cases, and where awards are made to leavers on a fully discretionary basis, the approach required by IFRS 2 differs from that required where the original terms are clear about 'good leaver' classification and entitlement (see 5.3.9.B below).

It is also increasingly common to see awards which allow the majority of participants, rather than just a few specified categories of 'good leaver', to retain all or part of an award if they leave employment during the vesting period (see 5.3.9.C below).

We refer throughout this section on 'good leavers' to an employee leaving employment, but similar considerations apply when an individual automatically becomes entitled to an award before the end of the original vesting period due to other reasons specified in the terms of the agreement, e.g. attaining a certain age or achieving a specified length of service, even if the individual remains in employment after the relevant date. In these situations, the date of full entitlement is the date on which any services – and therefore expense recognition – cease for IFRS 2 purposes.

Arrangements for a good leaver to receive all, or part, of an award on leaving employment should be distinguished from a situation where an employee leaves with no award and where forfeiture accounting is likely to apply (see 7.4.1.A and 7.4.1.B below).

5.3.9.A Provision for 'good leavers' made in original terms of award

In some cases the types of person who are 'good leavers' may be explicitly defined in the original terms of the arrangement (common examples being persons who die or reach normal retirement age before the end of the full vesting period, or who work for a business unit that is sold or closed during the vesting period). In other cases, the entity may have the discretion to determine on a case-by-case basis whether a person should be treated as a 'good leaver'.

In addition, some schemes may specify the entitlement of a 'good leaver' on leaving (e.g. that the leaver receive a portion of the award pro-rata to the extent that the performance conditions have been met), whereas others leave the determination of the award to the entity at the time that the employee leaves.

Whichever situation applies, any expense relating to an award to a good leaver must be fully recognised by the leaving date because, at that point, the good leaver ceases to provide any services to the entity and any remaining conditions attached to the award will be treated as non-vesting rather than vesting conditions (see 3.2 above).

In our view, an award which vests before the end of the original vesting period due to the operation of a 'good leaver' clause is measured at the original grant date only where – under the rules of the scheme as understood by both parties at the original grant date – the award is made:

- to a person clearly identified as a 'good leaver'; and
- in an amount clearly quantified or quantifiable.

Where, as outlined above, the rules of the scheme make clear the categories of 'good leaver' and their entitlement, the entity should assess at grant date how many good leavers there are likely to be and to what extent the service period for these particular individuals is expected to be shorter than the full vesting period. The grant date fair value of the estimated awards to good leavers should be separately determined, where significant, and the expense relating to good leavers recognised over the expected reduced vesting period between grant date and leaving employment. In this situation the entity would re-estimate the number of good leavers and adjust the cumulative expense at each reporting date. This would be a change of estimate rather than a modification of the award as it would all be in accordance with the original terms. We would not generally expect an entity to have significant numbers of good leavers under such an arrangement.

It is important that a clear distinction is drawn between the IFRS 2 accounting on a straight line basis over a reduced vesting period in the above case and that on a graded vesting basis in a situation of broader entitlement as outlined at 5.3.9.C below.

5.3.9.B Discretionary awards to 'good leavers'

Section 5.3.9.A above discusses awards where the arrangements for leavers are clear as at the original grant date of the award. However, where – as is more usually the case – the entity determines only at the time that the employee leaves either that the employee is a 'good leaver' or the amount of the award, grant date should be taken as the later of the date on which such determination is made, or the date on which the award is notified to the employee. This is because the employee had no clear understanding at the original grant date of an automatic entitlement to equity instruments other than through full vesting of the award and the award at the time of leaving is therefore considered to be a modification or new award on a discretionary basis (see 7.3 and 7.5 below).

In some cases, a good leaver will be allowed, on a discretionary basis, to keep existing awards subject to the fulfilment of the conditions (other than service) established at the original grant date. In this situation, any conditions that were previously treated as vesting conditions will become non-vesting conditions following the removal of the service requirement (see 3.1 and 3.2 above). This will be the case whether the discretionary arrangement is accounted for as a cancellation of the old award plus a new grant or as a modification of the original award.

The non-vesting conditions will need to be reflected in the measurement of the fair value of the award as at the date of modification or new grant (although the non-vesting conditions alone will not result in any incremental fair value). Any fair value that is unrecognised as at the date of the good leaver ceasing employment will need to be expensed immediately as there is no further service period over which to recognise the expense.

There is further discussion of modifications at 7.3 below and of replacement awards granted on termination of employment at 7.5 below.

5.3.9.C Automatic full or pro rata entitlement on leaving employment

In some jurisdictions it is becoming increasingly common for entities to establish schemes where a significant number of the participants will potentially leave employment before the end of the full vesting period and will be allowed to keep a pro rata share of the award. This gives rise to a much broader category of employee than the small number of good leavers that one would generally expect under a scheme where 'good leaver' refers only to employees who die, retire or work for a business unit that is sold or closed (see 5.3.9.A above).

In substance, this type of arrangement where significant numbers of employees are expected to leave with a pro rata entitlement indicates that the entire award to all participants vests on a graded basis over the vesting period as a whole. So, for example, an arrangement that gives employees 360 shares at the end of three years but, whether under the rules of the scheme or by precedent, allows the majority of leavers to take a pro rata share – based on the number of months that have elapsed – at their date of departure, should be treated as vesting at the rate of 10 shares per month for all employees. Such an arrangement should be accounted for using the graded vesting approach illustrated at 6.2.2 below.

Some take the view that the situation outlined in the previous paragraph does not require graded vesting and that a straight-line approach may be taken because the award only vests pro rata if an employee leaves. Supporters of this view argue that the requirement to leave employment in order to receive the award before the end of the full vesting period is itself a substantial condition over and above the requirement to provide ongoing service. If an employee remains in employment the award only vests on completion of three years' service and there is no earlier entitlement on a pro rata basis. Although this treatment has some appeal, in our view it is difficult to reconcile to the standard as currently drafted.

In other cases, rather than just a pro rata apportionment, any good leaver will be allowed to keep the entire award regardless of when they leave employment. If this is the case, and in substance there is no required minimum service period attached to the award, then the award should be treated as immediately vested in all employees and fully expensed at the grant date.

5.3.10 Special purpose acquisition companies ('SPACs')

An increasing number of IPOs and trade sales are being achieved through the medium of special purpose acquisition companies ('SPACs'). The detailed features of SPACs may vary, but common features tend to be:

- The SPAC is established by a small number of founders, typically with expertise in selecting attractive targets for flotation or sale. The founder shares contain a term to the effect that, if target is eventually identified and floated or sold, the holder of the founder shares will receive a greater proportion of any proceeds than other shareholders at the time of flotation.
- At a later date, other (non-founder) shareholders invest. This is typically achieved by an IPO of the SPAC. It is typically the case that, if a specific target is not identified, and agreed by a required majority of non-founder shareholders, within a finite timescale, the other (non-founder) shareholders will have their funds returned.
- The SPAC seeks a target which is then approved (or not, as the case may be) by the required majority of non-founder shareholders.

The three stages outlined above have given rise to three interpretations as to the grant date for IFRS 2 purposes.

Some take the view that there is no shared understanding until the specific target is identified and agreed (the third stage above). Those who take this view argue that the substance of the founder shareholders' interest is economically equivalent to an award of shares in any target finally approved. Therefore, until the target is finally approved, there is no clarity as to the nature and value of the award to the founder shareholders.

Others take the view that a shared understanding occurs at the point at which the non-founder shareholders invest (i.e. the second stage above). Those who take this view argue that a share-based payment can only occur when there has been a transfer of value from the non-founder shareholders to the founder shareholders and this cannot occur until there are some non-founder shareholders in place. However, once those non-founder shareholders are in place, there is a shared understanding that – if a transaction is subsequently approved – there will be a benefit for founder shareholders.

Others take the view that a shared understanding occurs on the issue of the founder shares (i.e. the first stage above). Those who take this view argue that at that point there is a shared understanding that – if non-founder shareholders are subsequently introduced and a transaction is subsequently approved – there will be a benefit for founder shareholders. The benefit for founder shareholders consists both in seeking further investors and in identifying a suitable target. The founder shareholders will be actively rendering service towards these goals from the outset.

The IFRS Interpretations Committee has conducted some initial outreach research into how SPACs are currently treated in practice, but the question has not been formally discussed to date. Until such time as additional guidance is given, it seems that the diversity in practice outlined above will remain and entities should determine an appropriate grant date based on the specific terms of the arrangement.

5.4 Transactions with non-employees

In accounting for equity-settled transactions with non-employees, the entity must adopt a rebuttable presumption that the value of the goods or services received provides the more reliable indication of the fair value of the transaction. The fair value to be used is that at the date on which the goods are obtained or the services rendered. *[IFRS 2.13]*. This implies that, where the goods or services are received on a number of dates over a period, the fair value at each date should be used, although in the case of a relatively short period there may be no great fluctuation in fair value.

If 'in rare cases' the presumption is rebutted, the entity may use as a surrogate measure the fair value of the equity instruments granted, but as at the date when the goods or services are received, not the original grant date. However, where the goods or services are received over a relatively short period where the share price does not change significantly, an average share price can be used in calculating the fair value of equity instruments granted. *[IFRS 2.13, IG5, IG6-7]*.

5.4.1 Effect of change of status from employee to non-employee (or vice versa)

IFRS 2 does not give specific guidance on how to account for an award when the status of the counterparty changes from employee to non-employee (or *vice versa*) but, in all other respects, the award remains unchanged. In our view, the accounting following the change of status will depend on the entity's assessment of whether or not the counterparty is performing the same or similar services before and after the change of status.

If it is concluded that the counterparty is providing the same or similar services before and after the change of status, the measurement approach remains unchanged.

However, if the services provided are substantially different, the accounting following the change of status will be determined by the counterparty's new status, as follows:

- For a change from non-employee to employee status, the expense for periods following the change should be measured as if the award had been granted at the date of change of status. This revised measurement only applies to the expense for the portion of the award that vests after the change of status and there is no effect on the expense recognised in prior periods.
- For a change from employee to non-employee status, the expense for periods following the change should be measured on the basis of the fair value of the counterparty's services as they are received – if this is reliably determinable. Otherwise, the fair value used is that of the equity instruments granted but measured at the date the services are received (see 5.4 above). There is no effect on the expense recognised in prior periods.

If the status of the counterparty changes and the terms of the award are modified in order to allow the award to continue to vest, the modification and change of status should be assessed in accordance with the general principles in IFRS 2 relating to the modification of awards (see 7.3 below).

5.5 Determining the fair value of equity instruments

As discussed in 5.2 to 5.4 above, IFRS 2 requires the following equity-settled transactions to be measured by reference to the fair value of the equity instruments issued rather than that of the goods or services received:

- all transactions with employees (except where it is impossible to determine fair value – see below); and
- transactions with non-employees where, exceptionally, the presumption that the fair value of goods or services provided is more reliably measurable is rebutted.

For all transactions measured by reference to the fair value of the equity instruments granted, IFRS 2 requires fair value to be measured at the 'measurement date' – i.e. grant date in the case of transactions with employees and service date in the case of transactions with non-employees. *[IFRS 2 Appendix A].* Fair value should be based on market prices if available. *[IFRS 2.16].* In the absence of market prices, a valuation technique should be used to estimate what the market price would have been on the measurement date in an arm's length transaction between informed and willing parties. The technique used should be a recognised technique and incorporate all factors that would be taken into account by knowledgeable and willing market participants. *[IFRS 2.17].*

Appendix B to IFRS 2 contains more detailed guidance on valuation, which is discussed at 8 below. *[IFRS 2.18].* IFRS 2 also deals with those 'rare' cases where it is not possible to value equity instruments reliably, where an intrinsic value approach may be used. This is more likely to apply in the case of awards of options rather than those of shares, and is discussed further at 8.8 below.

Paragraph 16 of IFRS 2 rather confusingly states that the fair value of equity instruments granted must take into account the terms and conditions on which they were granted, but this requirement is said to be 'subject to the requirements of paragraphs 19-22'. *[IFRS 2.16]*. When those paragraphs are consulted, however, a somewhat different picture emerges, since they draw a distinction between:

- non-vesting conditions (i.e. those that are neither service conditions nor performance conditions);
- vesting conditions which are market conditions (i.e. those related to the entity's share price); and
- other vesting conditions (i.e. service and non-market performance conditions).

These are discussed in more detail at 6.2 to 6.4 and at 8 below, but the essential difference is that, while non-vesting conditions and market conditions must be factored into any valuation, other vesting conditions must be ignored. *[IFRS 2.19-21A]*. As we explain in the more detailed discussion later, these essentially arbitrary distinctions originated in part as anti-avoidance measures.

The 'fair value' of equity instruments under IFRS 2 therefore takes account of some, but not all, conditions attached to an award rather than being a 'true' fair value.

The approach to determining the fair value of share-based payments continues to be that specified in IFRS 2 and share-based payments fall outside the scope of IFRS 13 which applies more generally to the measurement of fair value under IFRSs (see Chapter 14). *[IFRS 2.6A]*.

5.5.1 Reload features

A 'reload feature' is a feature in a share option that provides for an automatic grant of additional share options (reload options) whenever the option holder exercises previously granted options using the entity's shares, rather than cash, to satisfy the exercise price. *[IFRS 2 Appendix A]*. IFRS 2 requires reload features to be ignored in the initial valuation of options that contain them. Instead any reload option should be treated as if it were a newly granted option when the reload conditions are satisfied. *[IFRS 2.22]*. This is discussed further at 8.9 below.

6 EQUITY-SETTLED TRANSACTIONS – ALLOCATION OF EXPENSE

6.1 Overview

Equity-settled transactions, particularly those with employees, raise particular accounting problems since they are often subject to vesting conditions (see 3.1 above) that can be satisfied only over an extended vesting period. This raises the issue of whether a share-based payment transaction should be recognised:

- when the relevant equity instrument is first granted;
- when it vests;
- during the vesting period; or
- during the life of the option.

An award of equity instruments that vests immediately is presumed, in the absence of evidence to the contrary, to relate to services that have already been rendered, and is therefore expensed in full at grant date. *[IFRS 2.14]*. This may lead to the immediate recognition of an expense for an award to which the employee may not be legally entitled for some time, as illustrated in Example 30.5.

Example 30.5: Award with non-vesting condition only

An entity grants a director share options on condition that the director does not compete with the reporting entity for a period of at least three years. The 'non-compete' clause is considered to be a non-vesting condition (see 3.2 above and 6.4 below). As this is the only condition to which the award is subject, the award has no vesting conditions and therefore vests immediately. The fair value of the award at the date of grant, including the effect of the 'non-compete' clause, is determined to be €150,000. Accordingly, the entity immediately recognises a cost of €150,000.

This cost can never be reversed, even if the director goes to work for a competitor and loses the award. This is discussed more fully at 3.2.1 above and at 6.1.2 and 6.4 below.

Where equity instruments are granted subject to vesting conditions (as in many cases they will be, particularly where payments to employees are concerned), IFRS 2 creates a presumption that they are a payment for services to be received in the future, during the 'vesting period', with the transaction being recognised during that period, as illustrated in Example 30.6. *[IFRS 2.15]*.

Example 30.6: Award with service condition only

An entity grants a director share options on condition that the director remain in employment for three years. The requirement to remain in employment is a service condition, and therefore a vesting condition, which will take three years to fulfil. The fair value of the award at the date of grant, ignoring the effect of the vesting condition, is determined to be €300,000. The entity will record a cost of €100,000 a year in profit or loss for three years, with a corresponding increase in equity.

In practice, the calculations required by IFRS 2 are unlikely to be as simple as that in Example 30.6. In particular:

- the final number of awards that vest cannot be known until the vesting date (because employees may leave before the vesting date, or because relevant performance conditions may not be met); and/or
- the length of the vesting period may not be known in advance (since vesting may depend on satisfaction of a performance condition with no, or a variable, time-limit on its attainment).

In order to deal with such issues, IFRS 2 requires a continuous re-estimation process as summarised in 6.1.1 below.

6.1.1 The continuous estimation process of IFRS 2

The overall objective of IFRS 2 is that, at the end of the vesting period, the cumulative cost recognised in profit or loss (or, where applicable, included in the carrying amount of an asset), should represent the product of:

- the number of equity instruments that have vested, or would have vested, but for the failure to satisfy a market condition (see 6.3 below) or a non-vesting condition (see 6.4 below); and
- the fair value (excluding the effect of any non-market vesting conditions, but including the effect of any market conditions or non-vesting conditions) of those equity instruments at the date of grant.

It is essential to appreciate that the 'grant date' measurement model in IFRS 2 seeks to capture the value of the contingent right to shares promised at grant date, to the extent that that promise becomes (or is deemed by IFRS 2 to become – see 6.1.2 below) an entitlement of the counterparty, rather than the value of any shares finally delivered. Therefore, if an option vests, but is not exercised because it would not be in the counterparty's economic interest to do so, IFRS 2 still recognises a cost for the award.

In order to achieve this outcome, IFRS 2 requires the following process to be applied:

(a) at grant date, the fair value of the award (excluding the effect of any non-market vesting conditions, but including the effect of any market conditions or non-vesting conditions) is determined;

(b) at each subsequent reporting date until vesting, the entity calculates a best estimate of the cumulative charge to profit or loss at that date, being the product of:

  (i) the grant date fair value of the award determined in (a) above;

  (ii) the current best estimate of the number of awards that will vest (see 6.1.2 below); and

  (iii) the expired portion of the vesting period;

(c) the charge (or credit) to profit or loss for the period is the cumulative amount calculated in (b) above less the amounts already charged in previous periods. There is a corresponding credit (or debit) to equity *[IFRS 2.19-20]*;

(d) once the awards have vested, no further accounting adjustments are made to the cost of the award, except in respect of certain modifications to the award – see 7 below; and

(e) if a vested award is not exercised, an entity may (but need not) make a transfer between components of equity – see 6.1.3 below.

The overall effect of this process is that a cost is recognised for every award that is granted, except when it is forfeited, as that term is defined in IFRS 2 (see 6.1.2 below). *[IFRS 2.19]*.

6.1.2 *Vesting and forfeiture*

In normal English usage, and in many share scheme documents, an award is described as 'vested' when all the conditions needed to earn it have been met, and as 'forfeited' where it lapses before vesting because one or more of the conditions has not been met.

IFRS 2, however, uses the term 'forfeiture' in a much more restricted sense to mean an award that does not vest in IFRS 2 terms. This is a particularly complex aspect of IFRS 2, which is discussed in more detail at 6.2 to 6.4 below. Essentially:

- where an award is subject only to vesting conditions other than market conditions, failure to satisfy any one of the conditions is treated as a forfeiture by IFRS 2;
- where an award is subject to both
  - vesting conditions other than market conditions, and
  - market conditions and/or non-vesting conditions,

  failure to satisfy any one of the vesting conditions other than market conditions is treated as a forfeiture by IFRS 2. Otherwise (i.e. where all the vesting conditions other than market conditions are satisfied), the award is deemed to vest by IFRS 2 even if the market conditions and/or non-vesting conditions have not been satisfied; and
- where an award is subject only to non-vesting conditions, it is always deemed to vest by IFRS 2.

Where an award has been modified (see section 7.3 below) so that different vesting conditions apply to the original and modified elements of an award, forfeiture will not apply to the original award if the service and non-market performance conditions attached to that element have been met. This will be the case even if the service and non-market performance conditions attached to the modified award have not been met and so the modified award is considered to have been forfeited (resulting in the reversal of any incremental expense relating to the modification). Examples 30.22 and 30.23 at 7.3 below illustrate this point.

As a result of the interaction of the various types of condition, the reference in the summary at 6.1.1 above to the 'best estimate of the number of awards that will vest' really means the best estimate of the number of awards for which it is expected that all non-market vesting conditions will be met.

In practice, however, it is not always clear how that best estimate is to be determined, and in particular what future events may and may not be factored into the estimate. This is discussed further at 6.2 to 6.4 and 7.6 below.

6.1.3 Accounting after vesting

Once an equity-settled transaction has vested (or, in the case of a transaction subject to one or more market or non-vesting conditions, has been treated as vested under IFRS 2 – see 6.1.2 above), no further accounting entries are made to reverse the cost already charged, even if the instruments that are the subject of the transaction are subsequently forfeited or, in the case of options, are not exercised. However, the entity may make a transfer between different components of equity. *[IFRS 2.23].* For example, an entity's accounting policy might be to credit all amounts recorded for share-based transactions to a separate reserve such as 'Shares to be issued'. Where an award lapses after vesting, it would then be appropriate to transfer an amount equivalent to the cumulative cost for the lapsed award from 'Shares to be issued' to another component of equity.

This prohibition against 'truing up' (i.e. reversing the cost of vested awards that lapse) is controversial, since it has the effect that a cost is still recognised for options that are never exercised, typically because they are 'underwater' (i.e. the current share price is lower than the option exercise price), so that it is not in the holder's interest to exercise the option. Some commentators have observed that an accounting standard that can result in an accounting cost for non-dilutive options does not meet the needs of those shareholders whose concerns about dilution were the catalyst for the share-based payment project in the first place (see 1.1 above).

The IASB counters such objections by pointing out that the treatment in IFRS 2 is perfectly consistent with that for other 'contingent' equity instruments, such as warrants, that ultimately result in no share ownership. Where an entity issues warrants for valuable consideration such as cash and those warrants lapse unexercised, the entity recognises no gain under IFRS. *[IFRS 2.BC218-221]*.

6.2 Vesting conditions other than market conditions

6.2.1 *Awards with service conditions*

Most share-based payment transactions with employees are subject to explicit or implied service conditions. The application of the general periodic allocation principles discussed in 6.1 above to awards subject only to service conditions is illustrated by Examples 30.7 and 30.8 below. *[IFRS 2.IG11]*.

Example 30.7: Award with no re-estimation of number of awards vesting

An entity grants 100 share options to each of its 500 employees. Vesting is conditional upon the employees working for the entity over the next three years. The entity estimates that the fair value of each share option is €15. The entity estimates that 20% of the original 500 employees will leave during the three year period and therefore forfeit their rights to the share options.

If everything turns out exactly as expected, the entity will recognise the following amounts during the vesting period for services received as consideration for the share options.

Year	Calculation of cumulative expense	Cumulative expense (€)	Expense for period‡ (€)
1	50,000 options × 80%* × €15 × 1/3†	200,000	200,000
2	50,000 options × 80% × €15 × 2/3	400,000	200,000
3	50,000 options × 80% × €15 × 3/3	600,000	200,000

* The entity expects 20% of employees to leave and therefore only 80% of the options to vest.

† The vesting period is 3 years, and 1 year of it has expired.

‡ In each case the expense for the period is the difference between the calculated cumulative expense at the beginning and end of the period.

Example 30.8: Award with re-estimation of number of awards vesting due to staff turnover

As in Example 30.7 above, an entity grants 100 share options to each of its 500 employees. Vesting is conditional upon the employee working for the entity over the next three years. The entity estimates that the fair value of each share option is €15.

In this case, however, 20 employees leave during the first year, and the entity's best estimate at the end of year 1 is that 15% of the original 500 employees will have left before the end of the vesting period. During the second year, a further 22 employees leave, and the entity revises its estimate of total employee departures over the vesting period from 15% to 12% of the original 500 employees. During the third year, a further 15 employees leave. Hence, a total of 57 employees (20 + 22 + 15) forfeit their rights to the share options during the three year period, and a total of 44,300 share options (443 employees × 100 options per employee) finally vest.

The entity will recognise the following amounts during the vesting period for services received as consideration for the share options.

Year	Calculation of cumulative expense	Cumulative expense (€)	Expense for period (€)
1	50,000 options × 85% × €15 × 1/3	212,500	212,500
2	50,000 options × 88% × €15 × 2/3	440,000	227,500
3	44,300 options × €15 × 3/3	664,500	224,500

Note that in Example 30.8 above, the number of employees that leave during year 1 and year 2 is not directly relevant to the calculation of cumulative expense in those years, but would naturally be a factor taken into account by the entity in estimating the likely number of awards finally vesting.

6.2.2 *Equity instruments vesting in instalments ('graded' vesting)*

An entity may make share-based payments that vest in instalments (sometimes referred to as 'graded' vesting). For example, an entity might grant an employee 600 options, 100 of which vest if the employee remains in service for one year, a further 200 after two years and the final 300 after three years. In today's more mobile labour markets, such awards are increasingly favoured over awards which vest only on an 'all or nothing' basis after an extended period.

IFRS 2 requires such an award to be treated as three separate awards, of 100, 200 and 300 options, on the grounds that the different vesting periods will mean that the three tranches of the award have different fair values. *[IFRS 2.IG11]*. This may well have the effect that, compared to the expense for an award with a single 'cliff' vesting, the expense for an award vesting in instalments will be for a different amount in total and require accelerated recognition of the expense in earlier periods, as illustrated in Example 30.9 below.

Example 30.9: Award vesting in instalments ('graded' vesting)

An entity is considering the implementation of a scheme that awards 600 free shares to each of its employees, with no conditions other than continuous service. Two alternatives are being considered:

- All 600 shares vest in full only at the end of three years.
- 100 shares vest after one year, 200 shares after two years and 300 shares after three years. Any shares received at the end of years 1 and 2 would have vested unconditionally.

The fair value of a share delivered in one year's time is €3; in two years' time €2.80; and in three years' time €2.50.

For an employee that remains with the entity for the full three year period, the first alternative would be accounted for as follows:

Year	Calculation of cumulative expense	Cumulative expense (€)	Expense for period (€)
1	600 shares × €2.50 × 1/3	500	500
2	600 shares × €2.50 × 2/3	1,000	500
3	600 shares × €2.50 × 3/3	1,500	500

For the second alternative, the analysis is that the employee has simultaneously received an award of 100 shares vesting over one year, an award of 200 shares vesting over two years and an award of 300 shares vesting over 3 years. This would be accounted for as follows:

Year	Calculation of cumulative expense	Cumulative expense (€)	Expense for period (€)
1	[100 shares × €3.00] + [200 shares × €2.80 × 1/2] + [300 shares × €2.50 × 1/3]	830	830
2	[100 shares × €3.00] + [200 shares × €2.80 × 2/2] + [300 shares × €2.50 × 2/3]	1,360	530
3	[100 shares × €3.00] + [200 shares × €2.80 × 2/2] + [300 shares × €2.50 × 3/3]	1,610	250

At first sight, such an approach seems to be taking account of non-market vesting conditions in determining the fair value of an award, contrary to the basic principle of paragraph 19 of IFRS 2 (see 6.1.1 above). However, it is not the vesting conditions that are being taken into account *per se*, but the fact that the varying vesting periods will give rise to different lives for the award (which are required to be taken into account – see 7.2 and 8 below).

Provided all conditions are clearly understood at the outset, the accounting treatment illustrated in Example 30.9 would also apply even if the vesting of shares in each year also depended on a performance condition unique to that year (e.g. that profit in that year must reach a given minimum level), as opposed to a cumulative performance condition (e.g. that profit must have grown by a minimum amount by the end of year 1, 2 or 3). This is because there is an implied service condition covering a longer period. In other words, an award that vests at the end of year 3 conditional on profitability in year 3 is also implicitly conditional on the employee providing service for three years from the date of grant in order to be eligible to receive the award. This is discussed further at 5.3.7 above.

The accounting treatment illustrated in Example 30.9 is the only treatment for graded vesting permitted under IFRS 2. This contrasts with US GAAP[18] which permits, for awards with graded vesting where vesting depends solely on a service condition, a policy choice between the approach illustrated above and a straight-line recognition method.

6.2.3 Transactions with variable vesting periods due to non-market vesting conditions

An award may be made with a vesting period of variable length. For example, an award might be made contingent upon achievement of a particular target (such as achieving a given level of cumulative earnings) within a given period, but vesting immediately the target has been reached. Alternatively, an award might be contingent on levels of earnings growth over a period, but with vesting occurring more quickly if growth is achieved more quickly. Also some plans provide for 're-testing', whereby an original target is set for achievement within a given vesting period, but if that target is not met, a new target and/or a different vesting period are substituted.

In such cases, the entity needs to estimate the length of the vesting period at grant date, based on the most likely outcome of the performance condition. Subsequently, it is necessary continuously to re-estimate not only the number of awards that will finally vest, but also the date of vesting, as shown by

Example 30.10. *[IFRS 2.15(b), IG12]*. This contrasts with the treatment of awards with market conditions and variable vesting periods, where the initial estimate of the vesting period may not be revised (see 6.3.4 below).

Example 30.10: Award with non-market vesting condition and variable vesting period

At the beginning of year 1, the entity grants 100 shares each to 500 employees, conditional upon the employees remaining in the entity's employment during the vesting period. The shares will vest:

- at the end of year 1 if the entity's earnings increase by more than 18%;
- at the end of year 2 if the entity's earnings increase by more than an average of 13% per year over the two year period; or
- at the end of year 3 if the entity's earnings increase by more than an average of 10% per year over the three year period.

The award is estimated to have a fair value of $30 per share at grant date. It is expected that no dividends will be paid during the whole three year period.

By the end of the first year, the entity's earnings have increased by 14%, and 30 employees have left. The entity expects that earnings will continue to increase at a similar rate in year 2, and therefore expects that the shares will vest at the end of year 2. The entity expects, on the basis of a weighted average probability, that a further 30 employees will leave during year 2, and therefore expects that an award of 100 shares each will vest for 440 (500 – 30 – 30) employees at the end of year 2.

By the end of the second year, the entity's earnings have increased by only 10% and therefore the shares do not vest at the end of that year. 28 employees have left during the year. The entity expects that a further 25 employees will leave during year 3, and that the entity's earnings will increase by at least 6%, thereby achieving the average growth of 10% per year necessary for an award after 3 years, so that an award of 100 shares each will vest for 417 (500 – 30 – 28 – 25) employees at the end of year 3.

By the end of the third year, a further 23 employees have left and the entity's earnings have increased by 8%, resulting in an average increase of 10.67% per year. Therefore, 419 (500 – 30 – 28 – 23) employees receive 100 shares at the end of year 3.

The entity will recognise the following amounts during the vesting period for services received as consideration for the shares:

Year	Calculation of cumulative expense	Cumulative expense ($)	Expense for period ($)
1	440 employees × 100 shares × $30 × 1/2*	660,000	660,000
2	417 employees × 100 shares × $30 × 2/3*	834,000	174,000
3	419 employees × 100 shares × $30	1,257,000	423,000

* The entity's best estimate at the end of year 1 is that it is one year through a two year vesting period and at the end of year 2 that it is two years through a three year vesting period.

It will be noted that in Example 30.10, which is based on IG Example 2 in the implementation guidance to IFRS 2, it is assumed that the entity will pay no dividends (to any shareholders) throughout the maximum possible three year vesting period. This has the effect that the fair value of the shares to be awarded is (some might say, rather too conveniently) equivalent to their market value at the date of grant.

If dividends were expected to be paid during the vesting period, this would no longer be the case. Employees would be better off if they received shares after two years rather than three, since they would have a right to receive dividends from the end of year two. In practice, an entity is unlikely to suspend dividend payments in order to simplify the calculation of its share-based payment expense, and it is unfortunate that IG Example 2 is not more realistic. *[IFRS 2 IG Example 2]*.

One solution might be to use the approach in IG Example 4 in the implementation guidance to IFRS 2 (the substance of which is reproduced as Example 30.12 at 6.2.5 below). That Example deals with an award whose exercise price is either CHF12 or CHF16, dependent upon various performance conditions. Because vesting conditions other than market conditions must be ignored in determining the value of an award, the approach is in effect to treat the award as the simultaneous grant of two awards, whose value, in that case, varies by reference to the different exercise prices. *[IFRS 2 IG Example 4].*

The same principle could be applied to an award of shares that vests at different times according to the performance conditions, by determining different fair values for the shares (in this case depending on whether they vest after one, two or three years). The cumulative charge during the vesting period would be based on a best estimate of which outcome will occur, and the final cumulative charge would be based on the grant date fair value of the actual outcome (which will require some acceleration of expense if the actual vesting period is shorter than the previously estimated vesting period).

Such an approach appears to be taking account of non-market vesting conditions in determining the fair value of an award, contrary to the basic principle of paragraph 19 of IFRS 2 (see 6.1.1 above). However, it is not the vesting conditions that are being taken into account *per se*, but the fact that the varying vesting periods will give rise to different lives for the award (which are required to be taken into account – see 7.2 and 8 below). That said, the impact of the time value of the different lives on the fair value of the award will, in many cases, be insignificant and it will therefore be a matter of judgement as to how precisely an entity switches from one fair value to another.

Economically speaking, the entity in Example 30.10 has made a single award, the fair value of which must be a function of the weighted probabilities of the various outcomes occurring. However, under the accounting model for share-settled awards in IFRS 2, the probability of achieving non-market performance conditions is not taken into account in valuing an award. If this is required to be ignored, the only approach open is to proceed as above and treat the arrangement as if it consisted of the simultaneous grant of three awards.

Some might object that this methodology is not relevant to the award in Example 30.10 above, since it is an award of shares rather than, in the case of Example 30.12 (see 6.2.5 below), an award of options. However, an award of shares is no more than an award of options with an exercise price of zero. Moreover, the treatment in the previous paragraph is broadly consistent with the rationale given by IFRS 2 for the treatment of an award vesting in instalments (see 6.2.2 above).

In Example 30.10 above, the vesting period, although not known, is at least one of a finite number of known possibilities. The vesting period for some awards, however, may be more open-ended, such as an award that vests on a trade sale or flotation of the business. Such awards are discussed further at 15.4 below.

6.2.4 Transactions with variable number of equity instruments awarded depending on non-market vesting conditions

More common than awards with a variable vesting period are those where the number of equity instruments awarded varies, typically increasing to reflect the margin by which a particular minimum target is exceeded. In accounting for such awards, the entity must continuously revise its estimate of the number of shares to be awarded, as illustrated in Example 30.11 below (which is based on IG Example 3 in the implementation guidance to IFRS 2). *[IFRS 2 IG Example 3].*

Example 30.11: Award with non-market vesting condition and variable number of equity instruments

At the beginning of year 1, an entity grants an option over a variable number of shares (see below), estimated to have a fair value at grant date of £20 per share under option, to each of its 100 employees working in the sales department. The share options will vest at the end of year 3, provided that the employees remain in the entity's employment, and provided that the volume of sales of a particular product increases by at least an average of 5% per year. If the volume of sales of the product increases by an average of between 5% and 10% per year, each employee will be entitled to exercise 100 share options. If the volume of sales increases by an average of between 10% and 15% each year, each employee will be entitled to exercise 200 share options. If the volume of sales increases by an average of 15% or more, each employee will be entitled to exercise 300 share options.

By the end of the first year, seven employees have left and the entity expects that a total of 20 employees will leave by the end of year 3. Product sales have increased by 12% and the entity expects this rate of increase to continue over the next two years, so that 80 employees will be entitled to exercise 200 options each.

By the end of the second year, a further five employees have left. The entity now expects only three more employees to leave during year 3, and therefore expects a total of 15 employees to have left during the three year period. Product sales have increased by 18%, resulting in an average of 15% over the two years to date. The entity now expects that sales will average 15% or more over the three year period, so that 85 employees will be entitled to exercise 300 options each.

By the end of year 3, a further seven employees have left. Hence, 19 employees have left during the three year period, and 81 employees remain. However, due to trading conditions significantly poorer than expected, sales have increased by a 3 year average of only 12%, so that the 81 remaining employees are entitled to exercise only 200 share options.

The entity will recognise the following amounts during the vesting period for services received as consideration for the options.

Year	Calculation of cumulative expense	Cumulative expense (£)	Expense for period (£)
1	80 employees × 200 options × £20 × 1/3	106,667	106,667
2	85 employees × 300 options × £20 × 2/3	340,000	233,333
3	81 employees × 200 options × £20	324,000	(16,000)

This Example reinforces the point that, under the methodology in IFRS 2, it is quite possible for an equity-settled transaction to give rise to a credit to profit or loss for a particular period during the period to vesting.

6.2.5 Transactions with variable exercise price due to non-market vesting conditions

Another mechanism for delivering higher value to the recipient of a share award so as to reflect the margin by which a particular target is exceeded might be to vary the exercise price depending on performance. IFRS 2 requires such an award to be dealt with, in effect, as more than one award. The fair value of each award is determined, and the cost during the vesting period based on the best estimate of which award will actually vest, with the final cumulative charge being based on the actual outcome. *[IFRS 2.IG12, IG Example 4]*.

This is illustrated in Example 30.12 below.

Example 30.12: Award with non-market vesting condition and variable exercise price

An entity grants to a senior executive 10,000 share options, conditional upon the executive's remaining in the entity's employment for three years. The exercise price is CHF40. However, the exercise price drops to CHF30 if the entity's earnings increase by at least an average of 10% per year over the three year period.

On grant date, the entity estimates that the fair value of the share options, with an exercise price of CHF30, is CHF16 per option. If the exercise price is CHF40, the entity estimates that the share options have a fair value of CHF12 per option. During year 1, the entity's earnings increased by 12%, and the entity expects that earnings will continue to increase at this rate over the next two years. The entity therefore expects that the earnings target will be achieved, and hence the share options will have an exercise price of CHF30.

During year 2, the entity's earnings increased by 13%, and the entity continues to expect that the earnings target will be achieved. During year 3, the entity's earnings increased by only 3%, and therefore the earnings target was not achieved. The executive completes three years' service, and therefore satisfies the service condition. Because the earnings target was not achieved, the 10,000 vested share options have an exercise price of CHF40.

The entity will recognise the following amounts during the vesting period for services received as consideration for the options.

Year	Calculation of cumulative expense	Cumulative expense (CHF)	Expense for period (CHF)
1	10,000 options × CHF16 × 1/3	53,333	53,333
2	10,000 options × CHF16 × 2/3	106,667	53,334
3	10,000 options × CHF12	120,000	13,333

At first sight this may seem a rather surprising approach. In reality, is it not the case that the entity in Example 30.12 has made a single award, the fair value of which must lie between CHF12 and CHF16, as a function of the weighted probabilities of either outcome occurring? Economically speaking, this is indeed the case. However, under the accounting model for share-settled awards in IFRS 2, the probability of achieving non-market performance conditions is not taken into account in valuing an award. If this is required to be ignored, the only approach open is to proceed as above.

6.3 Market conditions

6.3.1 What is a 'market condition'?

IFRS 2 defines a market condition as 'a condition upon which the exercise price, vesting or exercisability of an equity instrument depends that is related to the market price of the entity's equity instruments, such as attaining a specified share price or a specified amount of intrinsic value of a share option, or achieving a specified target that is based on the market price of the entity's equity instruments relative to an index of market prices of equity instruments of other entities'. *[IFRS 2 Appendix A]*. In order for a market condition to be treated as a performance vesting condition rather than as non-vesting condition, there must also be an implicit or explicit service condition (see 3.2 above).

The 'intrinsic value' of a share option means 'the difference between the fair value of the shares to which the counterparty has the (conditional or unconditional) right to subscribe or which it has the right to receive, and the price (if any) the counterparty is (or will be) required to pay for those shares'. *[IFRS 2 Appendix A]*. In other words, an option to acquire for $8 a share with a fair value of $10 has an intrinsic value of $2. A performance condition based on the share price and one based on the intrinsic value of the option are effectively the same, since the values of each will obviously move in parallel.

An example of a market condition might be a condition based on total shareholder return (TSR). TSR is a measure of the increase or decrease in a given sum invested in an entity over a period on the assumption that all dividends received in the period had been used to purchase further shares in the entity. The market price of the entity's shares is an input to the calculation.

However, a condition linked to a purely internal financial performance measure such as profit or earnings per share is not a market condition. Such measures will affect the share price, but are not directly linked to it, and hence are not market conditions.

A condition linked to a general market index is not a market condition, but a non-vesting condition (see 6.4 below). For example, suppose that an entity engaged in investment management and listed only in London grants options to an employee responsible for the Far East equities portfolio. The options have a condition linked to movements in a general index of shares of entities listed in Hong Kong, so as to compare the performance of the portfolio of investments for which the employee is responsible with that of the overall market in which they are traded. That condition would not be regarded as a market condition under IFRS 2, because even though it relates to the performance of a market, the reporting entity's own share price is not relevant to the satisfaction of the condition.

However, if the condition were that the entity's own share price had to outperform a general index of shares of entities listed in Hong Kong, that condition would be a market condition because the reporting entity's own share price is then relevant to the satisfaction of the condition.

As discussed at 3.4 above, the IASB and the Interpretations Committee have an ongoing project to clarify the distinction between vesting and non-vesting conditions.

6.3.2 Summary of accounting treatment

The key feature of the accounting treatment of an equity-settled transaction subject to a market condition is that the market condition is taken into account in valuing the award at the date of grant, but then subsequently ignored, so that an award is treated as vesting irrespective of whether the market condition is satisfied, provided that all other non-market vesting conditions are satisfied. *[IFRS 2.21, IG13]*. This can have rather controversial consequences, as illustrated by Example 30.13.

Example 30.13: Award with market condition

An entity grants an employee an option to buy a share on condition of remaining in employment for three years and the share price at the end of that period being at least €7. At the end of the vesting period, the share price is €6.80. The share price condition is factored into the initial valuation of the option, and the option is considered to vest provided that the employee remains for three years, irrespective of whether the share price does in fact reach €7. Thus, IFRS 2 sometimes treats as vesting (and recognises a cost for) awards that do not actually vest in the natural sense of the word. See also Example 30.15 at 6.3.4 below.

This treatment is clearly significantly different from that for transactions involving a non-market vesting condition, where no cost would be recognised where the conditions were not met. The Basis for Conclusions indicates that the IASB accepted this difference for two main reasons:

(a) it was consistent with the approach in the US standard FAS 123; and

(b) in principle, the same approach should have been adopted for all performance conditions. However, whereas market conditions can be readily incorporated into the valuation of options, other conditions cannot. *[IFRS 2.BC183-184]*.

In our view, the over-riding reason for the IASB's approach was almost certainly harmonisation with US GAAP, since the second reason given does not really stand up to scrutiny. As discussed in 6.2 above, the methodology prescribed by IFRS 2 for transactions with a vesting condition other than a market condition is to determine the fair value of the option ignoring the condition and then essentially to multiply that fair value by the estimated (and ultimately the actual) probability of that non-market vesting condition occurring, which in broad terms is no different from incorporating those probabilities in the valuation in the first place. Moreover, the January 2008 amendment to IFRS 2 (see 1.2 above) had the effect that certain conditions previously regarded as non-market vesting conditions (and therefore 'impossible' to incorporate in the determination of fair value) became non-vesting conditions (and therefore required to be incorporated in the determination of fair value)!

One of the reasons for adoption of this approach under US GAAP (not referred to in the Basis for Conclusions in IFRS 2) was as an 'anti-avoidance' measure. The concern was that the introduction of certain market conditions could effectively allow for the reversal of the expense for 'underwater' options (i.e. those whose exercise price is higher than the share price such that it is not in the holder's interest to exercise the option) for which all significant vesting conditions had been satisfied, contrary to the general principle in US GAAP (and IFRS 2) that no revisions should be made to the expense for an already vested option.

For example, an entity could grant an employee an option, when the share price is £10, exercisable at £10, provided that a certain sales target had been met within one year. If the target were achieved, IFRS 2 would require an expense to be recognised even if the share price at the end of the year were only £8, so that the employee would not rationally exercise the option. If, however, the performance conditions were that (a) the sales target was achieved and (b) the share price was at least £10.01, the effect would be (absent specific provision for market conditions) that the entity could reverse any expense for 'underwater' options. Whilst this concern is easily understood, some might question whether an accounting methodology designed to thwart the use of a hypothetical artificial market condition necessarily produces appropriate results when applied to the real market conditions actually found in most awards.

In any event, it appears that it may be possible to soften the impact of IFRS 2's rules for market-based conditions relatively easily by introducing a non-market vesting condition closely correlated to the market condition. For instance, the option in Example 30.13 above could be modified so that exercise was dependent not only upon the €7 target share price and continuous employment, but also on a target growth in earnings per share. Whilst there would not be a perfect correlation between earnings per share and the share price, it would be expected that they would move roughly in parallel, particularly if the entity has historically had a fairly consistent price/earnings ratio. Thus, if the share price target were not met, it would be highly likely that the earnings per share target would not be met either. This would allow the entity to show no cumulative cost for the option, since only one (i.e. not *all*) of the non-market related vesting conditions would have been met.

Similarly, entities in sectors where the share price is closely related to net asset value (e.g. property companies and investment trusts) could incorporate a net asset value target as a non-market performance condition that would be highly likely to be satisfied only if the market condition was satisfied.

The matrices below illustrate the interaction of market conditions and vesting conditions other than market conditions. Matrix 1 summarises the possible outcomes for an award with the following two vesting conditions:

- the employee remaining in service for three years ('service condition'); and
- the entity's total shareholder return ('TSR') relative to that of a peer group being in the top 10% of its peer group at the end of the period ('TSR target').

Matrix 1

	Service condition met?	**TSR target met?**	**IFRS 2 expense?**
1	Yes	Yes	Yes
2	Yes	No	Yes
3	No	Yes	No
4	No	No	No

It will be seen that, to all intents and purposes, the 'TSR target met?' column is redundant, as this is not relevant to whether or not the award is treated as vesting by IFRS 2. The effect of this is that the entity would recognise an expense for outcome 2, even though no awards truly vest.

Matrix 2 summarises the possible outcomes for an award with the same conditions as in Matrix 1, plus a requirement for earnings per share to grow by a general inflation index plus 10% over the period ('EPS target').

Matrix 2

	Service condition met?	TSR target met?	EPS target met?	IFRS 2 expense?
1	Yes	Yes	Yes	Yes
2	Yes	No	Yes	Yes
3	Yes	Yes	No	No
4	Yes	No	No	No
5	No	Yes	Yes	No
6	No	No	Yes	No
7	No	Yes	No	No
8	No	No	No	No

Again it will be seen that, to all intents and purposes, the 'TSR target met?' column is redundant, as this is not relevant to whether or not the award is treated as vesting by IFRS 2. The effect of this is that the entity would recognise an expense for outcome 2, even though no awards truly vest. However, no expense would be recognised for outcome 4, which is, except for the introduction of the EPS target, equivalent to outcome 2 in Matrix 1, for which an expense is recognised. This illustrates that the introduction of a non-market vesting condition closely related to a market condition may mitigate the impact of IFRS 2.

Examples of the application of the accounting treatment for transactions involving market conditions are given in 6.3.3 to 6.3.5 below.

6.3.3 *Transactions with market conditions and known vesting periods*

The accounting for these is essentially the same as that for transactions with no market conditions and a known vesting period, except that adjustments are made to reflect the changing probability of the achievement of the non-market vesting conditions only, as illustrated by Example 30.14 below. *[IFRS 2.19-21, IG13, IG Example 5].*

Example 30.14: Award with market condition and fixed vesting period

At the beginning of year 1, an entity grants to 100 employees 1,000 share options each, conditional upon the employees remaining in the entity's employment until the end of year 3. However, the share options cannot be exercised unless the share price has increased from €50 at the beginning of year 1 to more than €65 at the end of year 3.

If the share price is above €65 at the end of year 3, the share options can be exercised at any time during the next seven years, i.e. by the end of year 10. The entity applies a binomial option pricing model (see 8 below), which takes into account the possibility that the share price will exceed €65 at the end of year 3 (and hence the share options become exercisable) and the possibility that the share price will not exceed €65 at the end of year 3 (and hence the options will be forfeited). It estimates the fair value of the share options with this market condition to be €24 per option.

IFRS 2 requires the entity to recognise the services received from a counterparty who satisfies all other vesting conditions (e.g. services received from an employee who remains in service for the specified service period), irrespective of whether that market condition is satisfied. It makes no difference whether the share price target is achieved, since the possibility that the share price target might not be achieved has already been taken into account when estimating the fair value of the share options at grant date. However, the options are subject to another condition (i.e. continuous employment) and the cost recognised should be adjusted to reflect the ongoing best estimate of employee retention.

By the end of the first year, seven employees have left and the entity expects that a total of 20 employees will leave by the end of year 3, so that 80 employees will have satisfied all conditions other than the market condition (i.e. continuous employment).

By the end of the second year, a further five employees have left. The entity now expects only three more employees will leave during year 3, and therefore expects that a total of 15 employees will have left during the three year period, so that 85 employees will have satisfied all conditions other than the market condition.

By the end of year 3, a further seven employees have left. Hence, 19 employees have left during the three year period, and 81 employees remain. However, the share price is only €60, so that the options cannot be exercised. Nevertheless, as all conditions other than the market condition have been satisfied, a cumulative cost is recorded as if the options had fully vested in 81 employees.

The entity will recognise the following amounts during the vesting period for services received as consideration for the options (which in economic reality do not vest).

Year	Calculation of cumulative expense	Cumulative expense (€)	Expense for period (€)
1	80 employees × 1,000 options × €24 × 1/3	640,000	640,000
2	85 employees × 1,000 options × €24 × 2/3	1,360,000	720,000
3	81 employees × 1,000 options × €24	1,944,000	584,000

6.3.4 Transactions with variable vesting periods due to market conditions

Where a transaction has a variable vesting period due to a market condition, a best estimate of the most likely vesting period will have been used in determining the fair value of the transaction at the date of grant. IFRS 2 requires the expense for that transaction to be recognised over an estimated expected vesting period consistent with the assumptions used in the valuation, without any subsequent revision. *[IFRS 2.15(b), IG14]*.

This may mean, for example, that, if the actual vesting period for an employee share option award turns out to be longer than that anticipated for the purposes of the initial valuation, a cost is nevertheless recorded in respect of all employees who reach the end of the *anticipated* vesting period, even if they do not reach the end of the *actual* vesting period, as shown by Example 30.15 below, which is based on Example 6 in the implementation guidance in IFRS 2. *[IFRS 2 IG Example 6]*.

Example 30.15: Award with market condition and variable vesting period

At the beginning of year 1, an entity grants 10,000 share options with a ten year life to each of ten senior executives. The share options will vest and become exercisable immediately if and when the entity's share price increases from £50 to £70, provided that the executive remains in service until the share price target is achieved.

The entity applies a binomial option pricing model, which takes into account the possibility that the share price target will be achieved during the ten year life of the options, and the possibility that the target will not be achieved. The entity estimates that the fair value of the share options at grant date is £25 per option. From the option pricing model, the entity determines that the most likely vesting period is five years. The entity also estimates that two executives will have left by the end of year 5, and therefore expects that 80,000 share options (10,000 share options × 8 executives) will vest at the end of year 5.

Throughout years 1 to 4, the entity continues to estimate that a total of two executives will leave by the end of year 5. However, in total three executives leave, one in each of years 3, 4 and 5. The share price target is achieved at the end of year 6. Another executive leaves during year 6, before the share price target is achieved.

Paragraph 15 of IFRS 2 requires the entity to recognise the services received over the expected vesting period, as estimated at grant date, and also requires the entity not to revise that estimate. Therefore, the entity recognises the services received from the executives over years 1-5. Hence, the transaction amount is ultimately based on 70,000 share options (10,000 share options × 7 executives who remain in service at the end of year 5). Although another executive left during year 6, no adjustment is made, because the executive had already completed the expected vesting period of 5 years.

The entity will recognise the following amounts during the initial expected five year vesting period for services received as consideration for the options.

Year	Calculation of cumulative expense	Cumulative expense (£)	Expense for period (£)
1	8 employees × 10,000 options × £25 × 1/5	400,000	400,000
2	8 employees × 10,000 options × £25 × 2/5	800,000	400,000
3	8 employees × 10,000 options × £25 × 3/5	1,200,000	400,000
4	8 employees × 10,000 options × £25 × 4/5	1,600,000	400,000
5	7 employees × 10,000 options × £25	1,750,000	150,000

IFRS 2 does not specifically address the converse situation, namely where the award actually vests before the end of the anticipated vesting period. In our view, where this occurs, any expense not yet recognised at the point of vesting should be immediately accelerated. We consider that this treatment is most consistent with the overall requirement of IFRS 2 to recognise an expense for share-based payment transactions 'as the services are received'. *[IFRS 2.7].* It is difficult to regard any services being received for an award after it has vested.

Moreover, the prohibition in IFRS 2 on adjusting the vesting period as originally determined refers to 'the estimate of the expected vesting period'. In our view, the acceleration of vesting that we propose is not the revision of an estimated period, but the substitution of a known vesting period for an estimate.

Suppose in Example 30.15 above, the award had in fact vested at the end of year 4. We believe that the expense for such an award should be allocated as follows:

Year	Calculation of cumulative expense	Cumulative expense (£)	Expense for period (£)
1	8 employees × 10,000 options × £25 × 1/5	400,000	400,000
2	8 employees × 10,000 options × £25 × 2/5	800,000	400,000
3	8 employees × 10,000 options × £25 × 3/5	1,200,000	400,000
4	8 employees × 10,000 options × £25 × 4/4	2,000,000	800,000

6.3.5 *Transactions with multiple outcomes depending on market conditions*

In practice, it is very common for an award subject to market conditions to give varying levels of reward that increase depending on the extent to which a 'base line' performance target has been met. Such an award is illustrated in Example 30.16 below.

Example 30.16: Award with market conditions and graded outcomes

On 1 January 2014, the reporting entity grants an employee shares if the employee is still in employment on the third anniversary of grant, subject to the share price. The employee will receive:

- no shares if the share price is below €10.00
- 100 shares if the share price is in the range €10.00 – €14.99
- 150 shares if the share price is in the range €15.00 – €19.99
- 180 shares if the share price is €20.00 or above.

In effect the entity has made three awards, which need to be valued as follows:

(a) 100 shares if the employee remains in service for three years and the share price is in the range €10.00 – €14.99

(b) 50 (150 – 100) shares if the employee remains in service for three years and the share price is in the range €15.00 – €19.99; and

(c) 30 (180 – 150) shares if the employee remains in service for three years and the share price is €20.00 or more.

Each award would be valued, ignoring the impact of the three-year service requirement (a non-market vesting condition) but taking account of the share price target. This would result in each tranche of the award being subject to an increasing level of discount to reflect the relative probability of the share price target for each tranche of the award being met. All three awards would then be expensed over the three-year service period, and forfeited only if the awards lapsed as a result of the employee leaving during that period.

It can be seen that the (perhaps somewhat counterintuitive) impact of this is that an equity-settled award that increases in line with increases in the entity's share price may nevertheless have a fixed grant date value irrespective of the number of shares finally awarded.

6.3.6 *Transactions with independent market conditions and non-market vesting conditions*

The discussion at 6.3.2 above addressed the accounting treatment of awards with multiple conditions that must all be satisfied, i.e. a market condition *and* a non-market vesting condition. However, it is increasingly common for entities to make awards with multiple conditions, only one of which need be satisfied, i.e. the awards vest on satisfaction of either a market condition *or* a non-market vesting condition. IFRS 2 provides no explicit guidance on the treatment of such awards, which is far from clear, as illustrated by Example 30.17 below.

Example 30.17: Award with independent market conditions and non-market vesting conditions

An entity grants an employee 100 share options that vest after three years if the employee is still in employment and the entity achieves either:

- cumulative total shareholder return (TSR) over three years of at least 15%, or
- cumulative profits over three years of at least £200 million.

The fair value of the award, ignoring vesting conditions, is £300,000. The fair value of the award, taking account of the TSR condition, but not the other conditions, is £210,000.

In our view, the entity has, in effect, simultaneously issued two awards – call them 'A' and 'B' – which vest as follows:

A on achievement of three years' service plus minimum TSR,

B on achievement of three years' service plus minimum earnings growth.

If the conditions for both awards are simultaneously satisfied, one or other effectively lapses.

It is clear that award A, if issued separately, would require the entity to recognise an expense of £210,000 if the employee were still in service at the end of the three year period. It therefore seems clear that, if the employee does remain in service, there should be a charge of £210,000 irrespective of whether the award actually vests. It would be anomalous for the entity to avoid recording a charge that would have been recognised if the entity had made award A in isolation simply by packaging it with award B.

If in fact the award vested because the earnings condition, but not the market condition, had been satisfied, it would then be appropriate to recognise a total expense of £300,000. This begs the question of whether the award should be accounted for:

(i) On the assumption in years 1 and 2 that it will vest because of the earnings condition, with an adjustment in the final year if the award vests by virtue of the TSR condition (or the award does not vest, but the employee remains in service). This would give rise to annual expense as follows:

Year	Calculation of cumulative expense	Cumulative expense (£)	Expense for period (£)
1	300,000 × 1/3	100,000	100,000
2	300,000 × 2/3	200,000	100,000
3	210,000 × 3/3	210,000	10,000

(ii) On the assumption in years 1 and 2 that it will vest by virtue of the TSR condition being met (or the employee remaining in service), with a 'catch-up' adjustment in the final period, if the award vests by virtue of the earnings condition, but not the TSR condition, being satisfied. This would give rise to annual expense as follows:

Year	Calculation of cumulative expense	Cumulative expense (£)	Expense for period (£)
1	210,000 × 1/3	70,000	70,000
2	210,000 × 2/3	140,000	70,000
3	300,000 × 3/3	300,000	160,000

(iii) At each reporting date, on the basis of the probability, as assessed at that date, of the award vesting by virtue of the earnings condition, but not the TSR condition, being satisfied. Assume (for example) that the entity assesses at the end of year 1 that the award is likely to vest by virtue of the TSR condition, and at the end of year 2 that it is likely to vest by virtue of the earnings condition, and that the award actually does not vest, but the employee remains in service. This would give rise to annual expense as follows:

Year	Calculation of cumulative expense	Cumulative expense (£)	Expense for period (£)
1	210,000 × 1/3	70,000	70,000
2	300,000 × 2/3	200,000	130,000
3	210,000 × 3/3	210,000	10,000

We believe that treatment (iii) is the most consistent with the general approach of IFRS 2 to awards with a number of possible outcomes.

Of course, as for other awards, the accounting treatment would also require an assessment of whether the employee was actually going to remain in service or not.

This begs the further question of how the award should be accounted for in a situation where both conditions are satisfied. It would clearly be inappropriate to recognise an expense of £510,000 (the sum of the separate fair values of the award) – this would be double-counting, because the employee receives only one package of 100 options. However, should the total expense be taken as £210,000 or £300,000? In our view, it is more appropriate to recognise a cost of £300,000 since the non-market vesting condition has been satisfied.

Ultimately, this is an issue which only the IASB can solve, since it arises from a problem of the IASB's own making – the fundamentally inconsistent treatment by IFRS 2 of awards with market conditions and those with non-market vesting conditions. In our experience, awards of this type are increasingly common, and, accordingly, there is an increasingly pressing need for a resolution of this issue. As noted at 3.4 above, following discussion of the subject by the Interpretations Committee, the IASB agreed in September 2011 to consider the interaction of multiple vesting conditions as a future agenda item.[19]

6.3.7 *Transactions with hybrid or interdependent market conditions and non-market vesting conditions*

Awards may sometimes have a performance benchmark which depends simultaneously on a market condition and a non-market vesting condition, sometimes known as 'hybrid' conditions. For example, some entities have made share-based payment awards to employees with conditions that require achievement of:

- a particular price-earnings (PE) ratio (calculated by reference to share price, a market condition, and earnings, a non-market vesting condition); or
- a maximum level of discount of market capitalisation (a market condition) below net asset value (a non-market vesting condition).

Such awards are rather curious, in the sense that these ratios may remain fairly constant irrespective of the underlying performance of the entity, so that a performance condition based on them is arguably of limited motivational value.

In our view, in contrast to our suggested treatment of awards with independent market and non-market vesting conditions discussed in 6.3.6 above, awards with interdependent market conditions and non-market vesting conditions must be accounted for entirely as awards with market conditions. An indicator such as the PE ratio, or discount of market capitalisation below net asset value, is a market condition as defined since it is 'related to the market price of the entity's equity instruments' (see 6.3.1 above).

6.3.8 *Awards based on the market value of a subsidiary or business unit*

Typically, awards with a market condition are based on the market value of the (typically quoted) equity of the parent entity. However, there is an increasingly held view that the parent's share price is a somewhat blunt instrument for measuring the performance of the employees of a particular subsidiary or business unit. Indeed, it is not difficult to imagine situations in which a particular subsidiary might perform well but the parent's share price be dragged down by other factors, or conversely where the parent's share price might rise notwithstanding lacklustre results for that subsidiary.

Accordingly, entities are increasingly implementing share-based remuneration schemes which aim to reward employees by reference to the market value of the equity of the business unit for which they work. The detail of such schemes varies, but the general effect is typically as follows:

- at grant date, the employee is allocated a (real or notional) holding in the equity of the employing subsidiary, the market value of which is measured at grant date; and
- the employee is granted an award of as many shares of the listed parent as have a value, at a specified future date (generally at or shortly after the end of the vesting period), equal to the increase in the market value of the holding in the equity of the employing subsidiary over the vesting period.

Some argue that such a scheme contains a market condition, since it is based on the fair value of the subsidiary's shares, with the result that the grant date fair value is:

- discounted to reflect this market condition (see 6.3.2 above); and
- fixed, irrespective of how many parent company shares are finally issued, since the entity has effectively issued a market-based award with multiple outcomes based on the market value of the equity of a subsidiary (see 6.3.5 above).

In our view, however, the treatment of such schemes under IFRS 2 is not as straightforward as suggested by this analysis. A fundamental issue is whether any award dependent on the change in value of the equity of an unquoted entity contains a market condition at all. IFRS 2 defines a market condition (see 6.3.1 above) as one dependent on the 'market price' of the entity's equity. *Prima facie*, if there is no market, there is no market price.

Some would argue that there are generally accepted valuation techniques for unquoted equities which can yield a fair value as a surrogate for market value. The difficulty with that argument, in our view, is that the IASB refers in the definition of 'market condition' to 'market price' and not to 'fair value'. The latter term is, of course, used extensively elsewhere in IFRS 2, which suggests that the IASB does not see the two terms as equivalent. This concern is reinforced by that fact that, even though it does not apply to the measurement of awards accounted for under IFRS 2, in the 'valuation hierarchy' in IFRS 13, a quoted market price is given as the preferred (but not the only) method of arriving at fair value (see Chapter 14 at 16). An entity implementing such an award must therefore consider whether the basis on which the subsidiary equity is valued truly yields a 'market price' or merely a fair value according to a hypothetical valuation model.

Awards based on the 'enterprise value' of an unquoted entity raise similar issues, as discussed more fully at 2.2.4.F above.

6.3.8.A Awards with a condition linked to flotation price

The situations discussed above and at 2.2.4.F relate to ongoing conditions linked to the calculated value of an unlisted entity and therefore differ from those where the condition is linked to the market price at which a previously unlisted entity floats. On flotation there is clearly a market and a market price for the entity's equity instruments and the achievement of a specific price on flotation would, in our view, be a market condition when accompanied by a corresponding service requirement (see 15.4 below).

6.4 Non-vesting conditions

The accounting treatment for awards with non-vesting conditions has some similarities to that for awards with market conditions in that:

- the fair value of the award at grant date is reduced to reflect the impact of the condition; and
- an expense is recognised for the award irrespective of whether the non-vesting condition is met, provided that all vesting conditions (other than market conditions) are met. *[IFRS 2.21A]*.

However, the accounting for non-vesting conditions differs from that for market conditions as regards the timing of the recognition of expense if the non-vesting condition is not satisfied (see 6.4.3 below).

As discussed at 3.4 above, the IASB and the Interpretations Committee have an ongoing project to clarify the distinction between vesting and non-vesting conditions.

6.4.1 Awards with no conditions other than non-vesting conditions

The effect of the treatment required by IFRS 2 is that any award that has only non-vesting conditions (e.g. an option award to an employee that may be exercised on a trade sale or IPO of the entity, irrespective of whether the employee is still in employment at that time) must be expensed in full at grant date. This is discussed further at 3.2 above and at 15.4 below, and illustrated in Example 30.5 at 6.1 above.

6.4.2 Awards with non-vesting conditions and variable vesting periods

IFRS 2 does not explicitly address the determination of the vesting period for an award with a non-vesting condition but a variable vesting period (e.g. an award which delivers 100 shares when the price of gold reaches a given level, but without limit as to when that level must be achieved, so long as the employee is still in employment when the target is reached). However, given the close similarity between the required treatment for awards with non-vesting conditions and that for awards with market conditions, we believe that entities should follow the guidance in the standard for awards with market conditions and variable vesting periods (see 6.3.4 above).

6.4.3 Failure to meet non-vesting conditions

As noted above, the accounting for non-vesting conditions differs from that for market conditions as regards the timing of the recognition of expense if the non-vesting condition is not satisfied. The treatment depends on the nature of the non-vesting condition, as follows:

- if a non-vesting condition within the control of the counterparty (e.g. making monthly savings in an SAYE scheme or holding a specified number of shares in a matching share arrangement) is not satisfied during the vesting period, the failure to satisfy the condition is treated as a cancellation (see 7.4 below), with immediate recognition of any expense for the award not previously recognised *[IFRS 2.28A, IG24]*;
- if a non-vesting condition within the control of the entity (e.g. continuing to operate the scheme) is not satisfied during the vesting period, the failure to satisfy the condition is treated as a cancellation (see 7.4 below), with immediate recognition of any expense for the award not previously recognised *[IFRS 2.28A, IG24]*; but
- if a non-vesting condition within the control of neither the counterparty nor the entity (e.g. a financial market index reaching a minimum level) is not satisfied, there is no change to the accounting and the expense continues to be recognised over the vesting period, unless the award is otherwise treated as forfeited by IFRS 2. *[IFRS 2.BC237A, IG24]*. In our view, the reference to the vesting period would include any deemed vesting period calculated as described in 6.4.2 above.

If an award is forfeited due to a failure to satisfy a non-vesting condition after the end of the vesting period (e.g. a requirement for an employee not to work for a competitor for a two year period after vesting), no adjustment is made to the expense previously recognised, consistent with the general provisions of IFRS 2 for accounting for awards in the post-vesting period (see 6.1.3 above). This would be the case even if shares previously issued to the employee were required to be returned to the entity on forfeiture (see 3.2.1 above for further discussion of non-compete arrangements).

7 EQUITY-SETTLED TRANSACTIONS – MODIFICATION, CANCELLATION AND SETTLEMENT

7.1 Background

It is quite common for equity instruments to be modified or cancelled before or after vesting. Typically this is done where the conditions for an award have become so onerous as to be virtually unachievable, or (in the case of an option) where the share price has fallen so far below the exercise price of an option that it is unlikely that the option will ever be 'in the money' to the holder during its life. In such cases, an entity may take the view that such equity awards are so unattainable as to have little or no motivational effect, and accordingly replace them with less onerous alternatives. Conversely, and more rarely, an entity may make the terms of a share award more onerous (possibly because of shareholder concern that targets are insufficiently demanding). In addition an entity may 'settle' an award, i.e. cancel it in return for cash or other consideration.

IFRS 2 contains detailed provisions for modification, cancellation and settlement. Whilst these provisions (like the summary of them below) are framed in terms of share-based payment transactions with employees, they apply to transactions with parties other than employees that are measured by reference to the fair value of the equity instruments granted (see 5.4 above). In that case, however, all references to 'grant date' should be taken as references to the date on which the third party supplied goods or rendered service. *[IFRS 2.26]*.

In the discussion below, any reference to a 'cancellation' is to any cancellation, whether instigated by the entity or the counterparty. Cancellations include:

- a failure by the entity to satisfy a non-vesting condition (see 6.4.3 above) within the control of the entity; and
- a failure by the counterparty to satisfy a non-vesting condition (see 6.4.3 above) within the control of the counterparty. *[IFRS 2.28A, IG24]*.

The discussion below is not relevant to cancellations and modifications of those equity-settled transactions that are (exceptionally) accounted for at intrinsic value (see 8.8 below).

The basic principles of the rules for modification, cancellation and settlement, which are discussed in more detail at 7.3 and 7.4 below, can be summarised as follows.

- As a minimum, the entity must recognise the amount that would have been recognised for the award if it remained in place on its original terms. *[IFRS 2.27]*.
- If the value of an award to an employee is reduced (e.g. by reducing the number of equity instruments subject to the award or, in the case of an option, by increasing the exercise price), there is no reduction in the cost recognised in profit or loss. *[IFRS 2.27, B42, B44]*.
- However, where the effect of the modification, cancellation or settlement is to increase the value of the award to an employee (e.g. by increasing the number of equity instruments subject to the award or, in the case of an option, by reducing the exercise price), the incremental fair value must be recognised as a cost. The incremental fair value is the difference between the fair value of the original award and that of the modified award, both measured at the date of modification. *[IFRS 2.27, B43]*.

Some argue that, when an award has been modified, and certainly when it has been cancelled altogether, it no longer exists, and that it is therefore not appropriate to recognise any cost for it. However, such a view is consistent with a vesting date measurement model rather than with the grant/service date measurement model of IFRS 2. The value of an award at grant date or service date cannot be changed by subsequent events.

Another reason given for the approach in IFRS 2 is that if entities were able not to recognise the cost of modified or cancelled options they would in effect be able to apply a selective form of 'truing up', whereby options that increased in value after grant would remain 'frozen' at their grant date valuation under the general principles of IFRS 2, whilst options that decreased in value could be modified or cancelled after grant date and credit taken for the fall in value. *[IFRS 2.BC222-237]*.

7.2 Valuation requirements when an award is modified, cancelled or settled

These provisions have the important practical consequence that, when an award is modified, cancelled or settled, the entity must obtain a fair value not only for the modified award, but also for the original award, updated to the date of modification. If the award had not been modified, there would have been no need to obtain a valuation for the original award after the date of grant.

Whilst any modification of a performance condition clearly has an impact on the 'real' value of an award, it may have no direct effect on the value of the award for the purposes of IFRS 2. This is because, as discussed at 6.2 to 6.4 above, whilst a market condition or a non-vesting condition is taken into account in valuing an award, a non-market vesting condition is not. Accordingly, by implication, a change to a non market-related performance condition will not necessarily affect the expense recognised for the award under IFRS 2.

For example, if an award is contingent upon sales of a given number of units and the number of units required to be sold is decreased, the value of the award is clearly increased. However, as the performance condition is a non-market vesting condition, and therefore not relevant to the original determination of the value of the award, there is no incremental fair value required to be accounted for by IFRS 2. However, if the change makes the award more, rather than less, likely than not to vest, this change of estimate will give rise to an accounting charge (see 6.1 to 6.4 above).

If an award is modified by changing the service period, the situation is somewhat more complex. Whilst a service condition does not of itself change the fair value of the award for the purposes of IFRS 2, a change in service period may well indirectly change the life of the award, which is relevant to its value (see 8 below). For example, if an award was previously subject to a three year service period (and exercisable during a two week period immediately thereafter) and its terms are changed such that it now has a two year vesting period (and again exercisable during a two week period thereafter), the value of the award will change, because its life has been reduced by one year. Similar considerations apply where performance conditions are modified in such a way as to alter the anticipated vesting date.

The valuation requirements relating to cancelled and settled awards are considered further at 7.4 below.

7.3 Modification

When an award is modified, the entity must as a minimum recognise the cost of the original award as if it had not been modified (i.e. at the original grant date fair value, spread over the original vesting period, and subject to the original vesting conditions). *[IFRS 2.27, B42-43]*.

In addition, a further cost must be recognised for any modifications that increase the fair value of the award. This additional cost is spread over the period from the date of modification until the vesting date of the modified award, which might not be the same as that of the original award. Where a modification is made after the original vesting period has expired, and is subject to no further vesting conditions, any incremental fair value should be recognised immediately. *[IFRS 2.27, B42-43]*.

Whether a modification increases or decreases the fair value of an award is determined as at the date of modification, as illustrated by Example 30.18. *[IFRS 2.27, B42-44]*.

Example 30.18: Does a modification increase or decrease the value of an award?

On 1 January 2013 an entity granted two executives, A and B, a number of options worth $100 each.

On 1 January 2014, A's options are modified such that they have a fair value of $85, their current fair value being $80. This is treated as an increase in fair value of $5 (even though the modified award is worth less than the original award when first granted). Therefore an additional $5 of expense would be recognised in respect of A's options.

On 1 January 2015, B's options are modified such that they have a fair value of $120, their current fair value being $125. This is treated as a reduction in fair value of $5 (even though the modified award is worth more than the original award when first granted). There is no change to the expense recognised for B's options.

This treatment ensures that movements in the fair value of the original award are not reflected in the entity's profit or loss, consistent with the treatment of other equity instruments under IFRS.

IFRS 2 provides further detailed guidance on this requirement as discussed below.

7.3.1 Modifications that increase the value of an award

7.3.1.A Increase in fair value of equity instruments granted

If the modification increases the fair value of the equity instruments granted, (e.g. by reducing the exercise price or changing the exercise period), the incremental fair value, measured at the date of modification, must be recognised over the period from the date of modification to the date of vesting for the modified instruments, as illustrated in Example 30.19 below. *[IFRS 2.B43(a), IG15, IG Example 7]*.

Example 30.19: Award modified by repricing

At the beginning of year 1, an entity grants 100 share options to each of its 500 employees. Each grant is conditional upon the employee remaining in service over the next three years. The entity estimates that the fair value of each option is €15.

By the end of year 1, the entity's share price has dropped, and the entity reprices its share options. The repriced share options vest at the end of year 3. The entity estimates that, at the date of repricing, the fair value of each of the original share options granted (i.e. before taking into account the repricing) is €5 and that the fair value of each repriced share option is €8.

40 employees leave during year 1. The entity estimates that a further 70 employees will leave during years 2 and 3, so that there will be 390 employees at the end of year 3 (500 – 40 – 70).

During year 2, a further 35 employees leave, and the entity estimates that a further 30 employees will leave during year 3, so that there will be 395 employees at the end of year 3 (500 – 40 – 35 – 30).

During year 3, 28 employees leave, and hence a total of 103 employees ceased employment during the original three year vesting period, so that, for the remaining 397 employees, the original share options vest at the end of year 3.

IFRS 2 requires the entity to recognise:

- the cost of the original award at grant date (€15 per option) over a three year vesting period beginning at the start of year 1, plus
- the incremental fair value of the repriced options at repricing date (€3 per option, being the €8 fair value of each repriced option less the €5 fair value of the original option) over a two year vesting period beginning at the date of repricing (end of year one).

This would be calculated as follows:

Year	Calculation of cumulative expense Original award (a)	 Modified award (b)	Cumulative expense (€) (a+b)	Expense for period (€)
1	390 employees × 100 options × €15 × 1/3		195,000	195,000
2	395 employees × 100 options × €15 × 2/3	395 employees × 100 options × €3 × 1/2	454,250	259,250
3	397 employees × 100 options × €15	397 employees × 100 options × €3	714,600	260,350

In effect, IFRS 2 treats the original award and the incremental value of the modified award as if they were two separate awards.

A similar treatment to that in Example 30.19 above is adopted where the fair value of an award subject to a market condition has its value increased by the removal or mitigation of the condition. *[IFRS 2.B43(c)]*. Where a vesting condition other than a market condition is changed, the treatment set out in 7.3.1.C below is adopted. IFRS 2 does not specifically address the treatment of an award, the fair value of which is increased by the removal or mitigation of a non-vesting condition. It seems appropriate, however, to account for it in the same way as a modification caused by the removal or mitigation of a market condition – i.e. as in Example 30.19 above.

7.3.1.B *Increase in number of equity instruments granted*

If the modification increases the number of equity instruments granted, the fair value of the additional instruments, measured at the date of modification, must be recognised over the period from the date of modification to the date of vesting for the modified instruments. If there is no further vesting period for the modified instruments, the incremental cost should be recognised immediately. *[IFRS 2.B43(b)]*.

7.3.1.C *Removal or mitigation of non-market related vesting conditions*

Where a vesting condition, other than a market condition, is modified, the modified vesting condition should be taken into account when applying the general requirements of IFRS 2 as discussed in 6.1 to 6.4 above – in other words, the entity would continuously estimate the number of awards likely to vest and/or the vesting period. *[IFRS 2.B43(c)]*. This is consistent with the general principle of IFRS 2 that vesting conditions, other than market conditions, are not factored into the valuation of awards, but are reflected by recognising a cost for those instruments that ultimately vest pursuant to those conditions. See also the discussion at 7.2 above.

IFRS 2 does not provide an example that addresses this point specifically, but we assume that something along the lines of Example 30.20 below is intended.

Example 30.20: Modification of non-market performance condition in employee's favour

At the beginning of year 1, the entity grants 1,000 share options to each member of its sales team, with exercise conditional upon the employee remaining in the entity's employment for three years, and the team selling more than 50,000 units of a particular product over the three year period. The fair value of the share options is £15 per option at the date of grant.

At the end of year 1, the entity estimates that a total of 48,000 units will be sold, and accordingly records no cost for the award in year 1.

During year 2, there is so severe a downturn in trading conditions that the entity believes that the sales target is too demanding to have any motivational effect, and reduces the target to 30,000 units, which it believes is achievable. It also expects 14 members of the sales team to remain in employment throughout the three year performance period. It therefore records an expense in year 2 of £140,000 (£15 × 14 employees × 1,000 options × 2/3). This cost is based on the originally assessed value of the award (i.e. £15) since the performance condition was never factored into the original valuation, such that any change in performance condition likewise has no effect on the valuation.

By the end of year 3, the entity has sold 35,000 units, and the share options vest. Twelve members of the sales team have remained in service for the three year period. The entity would therefore recognise a total cost of £180,000 (12 employees × 1,000 options × £15), giving an additional cost in year 3 of £40,000 (total charge £180,000, less £140,000 charged in year 2).

The difference between the accounting consequences for different methods of enhancing an award could cause confusion in some cases. For example, it may sometimes not be clear whether an award has been modified by increasing the number of equity instruments or by lowering the performance targets, as illustrated in Example 30.21.

Example 30.21: Increase in number of equity instruments or modification of vesting conditions?

An entity grants a performance-related award which provides for different numbers of options to vest after 3 years, depending on different performance targets as follows:

Profit growth	Number of options
5% – 10%	100
over 10% – 15%	200
over 15%	300

During the vesting period, the entity concludes that the criteria are too demanding and modifies them as follows:

Profit growth	Number of options
5% – 10%	200
over 10%	300

This raises the issue of whether the entity has changed:

(a) the performance conditions for the vesting of 200 or 300 options; or

(b) the number of equity instruments awarded for achieving 5%-10% or over 10% growth.

In our view, the reality is that the change is to the performance conditions for the vesting of 200 or 300 options, and should therefore be dealt with as in 7.3.1.C, rather than 7.3.1.B, above. Suppose, however, that the conditions had been modified as follows:

Profit growth	Number of options
5% – 10%	200
over 10% – 15%	300
over 15%	400

In that case, there has clearly been an increase in the number of equity instruments subject to an award for an increase of over 15% growth, which would have to be accounted for as such (i.e. under 7.3.1.B, rather than 7.3.1.C, above). In such a case, it might seem more appropriate to deal with the changes to the lower bands as changes to the number of shares awarded rather than changes to the performance conditions.

7.3.2 Modifications that decrease the value of an award

These do not occur very often, as their effect would be somewhat demotivating, although there have been occasional examples of an award being made more onerous – usually in response to criticism by shareholders that the original terms were insufficiently demanding. The general requirement of IFRS 2 is that, where an award is made more onerous (and therefore less valuable), the financial statements must still recognise the cost of the original award. This rule is in part an anti-avoidance measure since, without it, an entity could reverse the cost of an out-of-the-money award by modifying it so that it was unlikely to vest (for example, by adding unattainable performance conditions) rather than cancelling the award and triggering an acceleration of expense as in 7.1 above.

7.3.2.A Decrease in fair value of equity instruments granted

If the modification decreases the fair value of the equity instruments (e.g. by increasing the exercise price or reducing the exercise period), the decrease in value is effectively ignored and the entity continues to recognise a cost for services as if the awards had not been modified. *[IFRS 2.B44(a)]*. Reductions in the fair value of an award by the addition of a market condition or by making an existing market condition more onerous are similarly ignored *[IFRS 2.B44(c)]*, as, presumably, are reductions in the fair value resulting from the addition of a non-vesting condition.

7.3.2.B Decrease in number of equity instruments granted

If the modification reduces the number of equity instruments granted, IFRS 2 requires the reduction to be treated as a cancellation of that portion of the award (see 7.4 below). *[IFRS 2.B44(b)]*. Essentially this has the effect that any previously unrecognised cost of the cancelled instruments is immediately recognised in full, whereas the cost of an award whose value is reduced by other means continues to be spread in full over the remaining vesting period.

In situations where a decrease in the number of equity instruments is combined with other modifications so that the total fair value of the award remains the same or increases, it is unclear whether IFRS 2 requires an approach based on the value of the award as a whole or, as in the previous paragraph, one based on each equity instrument as the unit of account. This is considered further at 7.3.4 below.

7.3.2.C Additional or more onerous non-market related vesting conditions

Where a non-market vesting condition is modified in a manner not beneficial to the employee, again it is ignored and a cost recognised as if the original award had not been modified, as shown by Example 30.22. *[IFRS 2.B44(c), IG15, IG Example 8]*.

Example 30.22: Award modified by changing non-market performance conditions

At the beginning of year 1, the entity grants 1,000 share options to each member of its sales team, conditional upon the employee remaining in the entity's employment for three years, and the team selling more than 50,000 units of a particular product over the three year period. The fair value of the share options is £15 per option at the date of grant. During year 2, the entity believes that the sales target is insufficiently demanding and increases it to 100,000 units. By the end of year 3, the entity has sold 55,000 units, and the share options are forfeited. Twelve members of the sales team have remained in service for the three year period.

On the basis that the original target would have been met, and twelve employees would have been eligible for awards, the entity would recognise a total cost of £180,000 (12 employees × 1,000 options × £15). The cumulative cost in years 1 and 2 would, as in the Examples above, reflect the entity's best estimate of the *original* 50,000 unit sales target being achieved at the end of year 3. If, conversely, sales of only 49,000 units had been achieved, any cost booked for the award in years 1 and 2 would have been reversed in year 3, since the original target of 50,000 units would not have been met.

7.3.3 Modifications with altered vesting period

As noted at 7.3.1 above, where an award is modified so that its value increases, IFRS 2 requires the entity to continue to recognise an expense for the grant date fair value of the unmodified award over its *original* vesting period, even where the vesting period of the modified award is longer. This appears to have the effect that an expense may be recognised for awards that do not actually vest, as illustrated by Example 30.23 (which is based on Example 30.19 above).

Example 30.23: Award modified by reducing the exercise price and extending the vesting period

At the beginning of year 1, an entity grants 100 share options to each of its 500 employees, with vesting conditional upon the employee remaining in service over the next three years. The entity estimates that the fair value of each option is €15.

By the end of year 1, the entity's share price has dropped, and the entity reprices its share options. The repriced share options vest at the end of year 4. The entity estimates that, at the date of repricing, the fair value of each of the original share options granted (i.e. before taking into account the repricing) is €5 and that the fair value of each repriced share option is €7.

40 employees leave during year 1. The entity estimates that a further 70 employees will leave during years 2 and 3, and a further 25 employees during year 4, such that there will be 390 employees at the end of year 3 (500 – 40 – 70) and 365 (500 – 40 – 70 – 25) at the end of year 4.

During year 2, a further 35 employees leave, and the entity estimates that a further 30 employees will leave during year 3 and 30 more in year 4, such that there will be 395 employees at the end of year 3 (500 – 40 – 35 – 30) and 365 (500 – 40 – 35 – 30 – 30) at the end of year 4.

During year 3, 28 employees leave, and hence a total of 103 employees ceased employment during the original three year vesting period, so that, for the remaining 397 employees, the original share options would have vested at the end of year 3. The entity now estimates that only a further 20 employees will leave during year 4, leaving 377 at the end of year 4. In fact 25 employees leave, so that 372 satisfy the criteria for the modified options at the end of year 4.

In our view IFRS 2 requires the entity to recognise:

- the cost of the original award at grant date (€15 per option) over a three year vesting period beginning at the start of year 1, based on the ongoing best estimate of, and ultimately the actual, number of employees at the end of the *original three year* vesting period;
- the incremental fair value of the repriced options at repricing date (€2 per option, being the €7 fair value of each repriced option less the €5 fair value of the original option) over a three year vesting period beginning at the date of repricing (*end* of year one), but based on the ongoing best estimate of, and ultimately the actual, number of employees at the end of the *modified four year* vesting period.

This would be calculated as follows:

Year	Calculation of cumulative expense Original award	 Modified award	Cumulative expense (£)	Expense for period (£)
1	390 employees × 100 options × €15 × 1/3		195,000	195,000
2	395 employees × 100 options × €15 × 2/3	365 employees × 100 options × €2 × 1/3	419,333	224,333
3	397 employees × 100 options × €15	377 employees × 100 options × €2 × 2/3	645,767	226,434
4	397 employees × 100 options × €15	372 employees × 100 options × €2	669,900	24,133

It may seem strange that a cost is being recognised for the original award in respect of the 25 employees who leave during year 4, who are never entitled to anything. However, in our view, this is consistent with:

- the overall requirement of IFRS 2 that the minimum cost of a modified award should be the cost that would have recognised if the award had not been modified; and
- IG Example 8 in IFRS 2 (the substance of which is reproduced in Example 30.22 above) where an expense is clearly required to be recognised to the extent that the original performance conditions would have been met if the award had not been modified.

Moreover, as Examples 30.22 and 30.23 illustrate, the rule in IFRS 2 requiring recognition of a minimum expense for a modified award (i.e. as if the original award had remained in place) applies irrespective of whether the effect of the modification is that an award becomes less valuable to the employee (as in Example 30.22) or more valuable to the employee (as in Example 30.23).

Where a modified vesting period is shorter than the original vesting period, all of the expense relating to both the original and modified elements of the award should, in our view, be recognised by the end of the modified vesting period as no services will be rendered beyond that point. In this type of modification – as distinct from a change of estimate where there is a variable vesting period (see 6.2.3 above) – we believe that an entity has an accounting policy choice between retrospective and prospective adjustment of the vesting period as at the modification date. The overall expense recognised between grant date and vesting date will be the same in both cases, but there will be timing differences in the recognition of the expense, with retrospective accounting resulting in a higher expense as at the modification date itself.

7.3.4 Modifications that reduce the number of equity instruments granted but maintain or increase the value of an award

As discussed at 7.3.2.B above, cancellation accounting has to be applied to a reduction in the number of equity instruments when a modification reduces both the number of equity instruments granted and the total fair value of the award. *[IFRS 2.B44(b)]*. This approach is consistent with the fact that part of the award has been removed without compensation to the employee. However, because of the demotivating effect and, in some jurisdictions, a requirement to pay compensation in such situations, a modification of this kind is rarely seen in practice. An entity is more likely to modify an award so that the overall fair value remains the same, or increases, even if the number of equity instruments is reduced. These types of modification are considered below.

Where an entity reduces the number of equity instruments but also makes other changes so that the total fair value of the modified award either remains the same as that of the original award as at the modification date or exceeds it, it is unclear whether the accounting should be based on an individual equity instrument or on the award as a whole. Examples 30.24 and 30.25 below illustrate the two situations and the two approaches.

Example 30.24: Modification where number of equity instruments is reduced but total fair value is unchanged

An entity granted an employee 200 share options on 1 January 2013. On 31 December 2014 the exercise price of the options is significantly higher than the market price and the options have a fair value of £5 per option. On this date, the entity modifies the award and exchanges the 200 underwater options for 100 'at the money' options with a fair value of £10 each. The fair value of the new awards of £1,000 (100 × £10) equals the fair value of the awards exchanged (200 × £5) so that, for the award as a whole, there is no incremental fair value.

One view is that the unit of account is an individual option. Taking this approach, the decrease in the number of options from 200 to 100 will be accounted for as a cancellation with an acceleration at the modification date of any unexpensed element of the grant date fair value of 100 options. The grant date fair value of the remaining 100 options continues to be recognised over the remainder of the vesting period.

The alternative view is that the total number of options exchanged is the more appropriate unit of account. In this case, the cancellation of the original options and the grant of replacement options are accounted for as a modification. There would therefore be no acceleration of expense in respect of the reduction in the number of options from 200 to 100 and the grant date fair value of the original award would continue to be recognised over the vesting period.

Example 30.25: Modification where number of equity instruments is reduced but total fair value is increased

An entity has previously granted to its employees 1,000 share options with an exercise price equal to the market price of the shares at grant date. The grant date fair value is £10 per option. The entity's share price has declined significantly so that the share price is currently significantly less than the exercise price. The entity decides to reduce the exercise price of the options and, as part of the modification, it also reduces the number of options from 1,000 to 800. At the date of modification, the fair value of the original options is £7 per option and that of the modified options £11 per option.

One view is that the unit of account is an individual option. Taking this approach, the decrease in the number of options from 1,000 to 800 will be accounted for as a cancellation with an acceleration at the modification date of any remaining grant date fair value relating to those 200 options. The grant date fair value of the remaining 800 options continues to be recognised over the remainder of the vesting period together with the incremental fair value of those awards as measured at the modification date. In total the entity will recognise an expense of £13,200 (original grant date fair value of £10,000 (1,000 × £10) plus incremental fair value of £3,200 (800 × £(11 – 7)).

The alternative view is that the more appropriate unit of account is the total number of options as there are linked modifications forming one package. In this case, the incremental fair value is calculated as the difference between the total fair value before and after the modification. In total the entity will recognise an expense of £11,800 (original grant date fair value of £10,000 (1,000 × £10) plus incremental fair value on modification of £1,800 ((800 × £11) – (1,000 × £7)).

In both Examples above, the first view is based on paragraph B44(b) of IFRS 2 which states that 'if the modification reduces the number of equity instruments granted to an employee, that reduction shall be accounted for as a cancellation of that portion of the grant, in accordance with the requirements of paragraph 28'. This is perhaps further supported by paragraph B43(a) which, in providing guidance on accounting for a modification that increases the fair value of an equity instrument, appears only to refer to individual equity instruments when it states that 'the incremental fair value granted' in a modification is 'the difference between the fair value of the modified equity instrument and that of the original equity instrument, both estimated as at the date of modification'. *[IFRS 2.B43-44]*.

The alternative view is based on the overriding requirement in paragraph 27 of IFRS 2 for the grant date fair value of the equity instruments to be recognised unless the awards do not vest due to a failure to meet a vesting condition (other than a market condition). This requirement is applicable even if the award is modified after the grant date. The same paragraph also requires an entity to recognise the effect of modifications 'that increase the total fair value of the share-based payment arrangement or are otherwise beneficial to the employee'. This reference to 'total fair value' supports the view that the total award is the unit of account and is reiterated in paragraphs B42 and B44 which provide guidance, respectively, for situations where the total fair value decreases or increases as a consequence of the modification of an award. Supporters of the alternative view further consider that, in contrast to the cancellation accounting approach that is required in the very specific case where part of the award is, in effect, settled for no consideration (see 7.3.2.B above), a modification that reduces the number of equity instruments but maintains or increases the overall fair value of the award clearly provides the counterparty with a benefit. As a consequence, it is considered that no element of the grant date fair value should be accelerated as a cancellation expense. *[IFRS 2.27, B42, B44]*.

Given the lack of clarity in IFRS 2, we believe that an entity may make an accounting policy choice as to whether it considers the unit of account to be an individual equity instrument or an award as a whole. However, once made, that accounting policy choice should be applied consistently to all modifications that reduce the number of equity instruments but maintain or increase the overall fair value of an award. Whatever the policy choice, the general requirements of IFRS 2 will still need to be applied in order to determine whether or not it is appropriate to treat an award modified in this way as a modification (in IFRS 2 terms) rather than as a new award (see 7.4.2 and 7.4.4 below).

7.3.5 Modification of award from equity-settled to cash-settled (and vice versa)

Occasionally an award that was equity-settled when originally granted is modified so as to become cash-settled, or an originally cash-settled award is modified so as to become equity-settled. Such modifications are discussed at 9.4 below.

7.4 Cancellation and settlement

Where an award is cancelled or settled (i.e. cancelled with some form of compensation), other than by forfeiture for failure to satisfy the vesting conditions:

(a) if the cancellation or settlement occurs during the vesting period, it is treated as an acceleration of vesting, and the entity recognises immediately the amount that would otherwise have been recognised for services over the vesting period;

(b) where the entity pays compensation for a cancelled award:

  (i) any compensation paid up to the fair value of the award at cancellation or settlement date (whether before or after vesting) is accounted for as a deduction from equity, as being equivalent to the redemption of an equity instrument;

(ii) any compensation paid in excess of the fair value of the award at cancellation or settlement date (whether before or after vesting) is accounted for as an expense in profit or loss; and

(iii) if the share-based payment arrangement includes liability components, the fair value of the liability is remeasured at the date of cancellation or settlement. Any payment made to settle the liability component is accounted for as an extinguishment of the liability; and

(c) if the entity grants new equity instruments during the vesting period and, on the date that they are granted, identifies them as replacing the cancelled or settled instruments, the entity is required to account for the new equity instruments as if they were a modification of the cancelled or settled award. Otherwise it accounts for the new instruments as an entirely new award. *[IFRS 2.28, 29]*.

The treatment of the cancelled or settled award in (a) above is similar, in its effect on profit or loss, to the result that would have occurred if:

- the fair value of the equity instruments issued had been recorded in full at grant date with a corresponding debit to a prepayment for 'services to be rendered';
- the prepayment were written off on a periodic basis until cancellation or settlement; and
- any remaining prepayment at the date of cancellation or settlement were written off in full.

It should be noted that the calculation of any additional expense in (b) above depends on the fair value of the award at the date of cancellation or settlement, not on the cumulative expense already charged. This has the important practical consequence that, when an entity pays compensation on cancellation or settlement of an award, it must obtain a fair value for the original award, updated to the date of cancellation or settlement. If the award had not been cancelled or settled, there would have been no need to obtain a valuation for the original award after the date of grant.

These requirements raise some further detailed issues of interpretation on a number of areas, as follows:

- the distinction between 'cancellation' and 'forfeiture' (see 7.4.1 below);
- the distinction between 'cancellation' and 'modification' (see 7.4.2 below);
- the calculation of the expense on cancellation (see 7.4.3 below); and
- replacement awards (see 7.4.4 and 7.5 below).

7.4.1 Distinction between cancellation and forfeiture

The above provisions of IFRS 2 apply when an award of equity instruments is cancelled or settled 'other than a grant cancelled by forfeiture when the vesting conditions are not satisfied'. *[IFRS 2.28]*. The significance of this is that the terms of many share-based awards provide that they are, or can be, 'cancelled' on forfeiture. IFRS 2 is clarifying that, where an award is forfeited (within the meaning of that term in IFRS 2 – see 6.1.2 above), the entity should apply the accounting treatment for a forfeiture (i.e. reversal of expense previously recognised), even if the award is cancelled as a consequence of the forfeiture.

7.4.1.A Termination of employment by entity

In some cases, however, it is not clear whether cancellation or forfeiture has occurred, particularly where options lapse as the result of a termination of employment by the entity. For example, an entity might grant options to an employee on 1 January 2014 on condition of his remaining in employment until at least 31 December 2016. During 2015, however, economic conditions require the entity to make a number of its personnel, including that employee, redundant, as a result of which his options lapse. Is this lapse a forfeiture or a cancellation for the purposes of IFRS 2?

Some argue that, as a result of the redundancy, the employee will be unable to render the service required in order for the options to vest. On this analysis, the lapse of the award should be treated as a forfeiture. This view is supported by column 1 of the table included in paragraph IG24 of the implementation guidance in IFRS 2 which gives, as an example of a forfeiture, an award where a requirement to remain in service 'is not met' – implying that it does not matter whether the failure to meet the condition is due to the actions of the employee or those of the employer. *[IFRS 2.IG24]*.

Others argue that, since the options lapse as a direct result of the employer's actions, the effect is equivalent to a cancellation of the award by the employer. This view is, somewhat ironically, also supported by the table included in paragraph IG24 of the implementation guidance referred to above, column 6 of which gives, as an example of a non-vesting condition, the continuation of the plan by the entity. On this analysis, if the entity chooses to terminate the plan, it breaches a non-vesting condition within its control, requiring cancellation accounting to be applied (see 7.1 above). *[IFRS 2.IG24]*.

In our view, unlikely as it is that the IASB intended such an outcome, both analyses are supportable under IFRS 2 as currently drafted, and an entity may adopt either treatment as a choice of accounting policy. However, in making that choice, the IASB's proposed *Annual Improvements to IFRSs 2010-2012 Cycle* should be taken into consideration. Under these draft Annual Improvements, the IASB proposes to amend the definition of a service condition to clarify that any failure to meet such a condition, including a situation where the entity terminates the employment contract, is a forfeiture rather than a cancellation (see 3.4 above and 7.4.1.B below).

Another possible analysis under the current version of IFRS 2 might be that the lapse of an award on termination of employment for cause (such as gross misconduct) is a forfeiture, but a lapse on termination in other circumstances is a cancellation. The argument here would essentially be that refraining from gross misconduct is an implied term of any employment contract. An employee dismissed for such conduct has therefore not provided services of an appropriate nature, and the award is accordingly forfeited. We can see some theoretical merit in such an approach, but have the concern – from an auditor's perspective – that it is often difficult to determine the true reason for a termination of employment. There is the added complication that employees, particularly at senior levels of management, whose employment is in reality being terminated, will often agree to tender a letter of resignation for a number of reasons ranging from employment law to media relations.

At first sight, it might seem unlikely that an entity would not wish to treat the lapse of an award on a termination of employment as a forfeiture, given that this will give rise to a credit to profit or loss (as any cost previously recognised is reversed), whereas treatment as a cancellation will give rise to an additional expense (as any part of the grant date fair value not yet recognised as a cost is accelerated). However, where the employee is granted another award in compensation, the interaction between the rules in IFRS 2 for cancellation and those for replacement awards may make treatment as a cancellation less 'costly' in terms of the overall charge to profit or loss. This is discussed further at 7.5 below.

7.4.1.B Termination of employment by entity: future developments

In September 2010, the Interpretations Committee tentatively decided that if an employee is unable to satisfy a service condition for any reason, including the termination of employment by the entity, the entity should account for this as a forfeiture rather than as a cancellation.[20]

It identified this issue as one of the priorities during its project on vesting and non-vesting conditions (see 3.4 above) and referred the issue to the IASB[21] which proposed the following revised definition of a service condition in the draft *Annual Improvements to IFRSs 2010-2012 Cycle*:

'A vesting condition that requires the counterparty to complete a specified period of service. If the counterparty, regardless of the reason, ceases to provide service during the vesting period, the counterparty has failed to satisfy the condition...'.[22]

In its draft Basis for Conclusions, the IASB notes that IFRS 2 contains no specific guidance on how to account for a share-based payment award resulting from the entity's termination of an employee's employment and so it proposes to make clear through the above revised definition that 'if the employee fails to complete a specified service period, the employee fails to satisfy a service condition, regardless of what the reason for that failure is'.

7.4.1.C Surrender of award by employee

It is sometimes the case that an employee, often a member of senior management, will decide – or be encouraged by the entity – to surrender awards during the vesting period. The question arises as to whether this should be treated as a cancellation or forfeiture for accounting purposes. IFRS 2 allows forfeiture accounting, and the consequent reversal of any cumulative expense, only in situations where vesting conditions are not satisfied. A situation where the counterparty voluntarily surrenders an award and therefore the opportunity to meet the vesting conditions is similar, in our view, to a failure to exercise an award rather than a failure to satisfy a vesting condition and should therefore be accounted for as a cancellation rather than as a forfeiture.

As discussed at 7.4.1.B above, the IASB has proposed an amendment to IFRS 2 to clarify that if a counterparty ceases to provide service during the vesting period, he has failed to satisfy the condition (and hence the award is forfeited, regardless of the reason for the failure). We do not believe that the IASB's intention was to allow voluntary termination of a vesting condition by the counterparty to be treated as a forfeiture as a consequence of the proposed amendment and such an action should therefore continue to be treated as a cancellation.

7.4.2 Distinction between cancellation and modification

One general issue raised by IFRS 2 is where the boundary lies between 'modification' of an award in the entity's favour and outright cancellation of the award. As a matter of legal form, the difference is obvious. However, if an entity were to modify an award in such a way that there was no realistic chance of it ever vesting (for example, by introducing a requirement that the share price increase 1,000,000 times by vesting date), some might argue that this amounts to a *de facto* cancellation of the award. The significance of the distinction is that, whereas the cost of a 'modified' award continues to be recognised on a periodic basis (see 7.3 above), the remaining cost of a cancelled award is recognised immediately.

7.4.3 Calculation of the expense on cancellation

The basic accounting treatment for a cancellation and settlement is illustrated in Example 30.26 below.

Example 30.26: Cancellation and settlement – basic accounting treatment

At the start of year 1 an entity grants an executive 30,000 options on condition that she remain in employment for three years. Each option is determined to have a fair value of $10.

At the end of year 1, the executive is still in employment and the entity charges an IFRS 2 expense of $100,000 (30,000 × $10 × 1/3). At the end of year 2, the executive is still in employment. However, the entity's share price has suffered a decline which the entity does not expect to have reversed by the end of year 3, such that the options, while still 'in the money' now have a fair value of only $6. Moreover, the entity is under pressure from major shareholders to end option schemes with no performance criteria other than continuing employment.

Accordingly, the entity cancels the options and in compensation pays the executive $6.50 per option cancelled, a total payment of $195,000 (30,000 options × $6.50).

IFRS 2 first requires the entity to record a cost as if the options had vested immediately. The total cumulative cost for the award must be $300,000 (300 options × $10). $100,000 was recognised in year 1, so that an additional cost of $200,000 is recognised.

As regards the compensation payment, the fair value of the awards cancelled is $180,000 (30,000 options × $6.00). Accordingly, $180,000 of the payment is accounted for as a deduction from equity, with the remaining payment in excess of fair value, $15,000, charged to profit or loss.

The net effect of this is that an award that ultimately results in a cash payment to the executive of only $195,000 (i.e. $6.50 per option) has resulted in a total charge to profit or loss of $315,000 (i.e. $10.50 per option, representing $10 grant date fair value + $6.50 compensation payment – $6.00 cancellation date fair value).

Example 30.26 illustrates the basic calculation of the cancellation 'charge' required by IFRS 2. In more complex situations, however, the amount of the 'charge' may not be so clear-cut, due to an ambiguity in the drafting of paragraph 28(a) of the standard, which reads as follows:

> 'the entity shall account for the cancellation or settlement as an acceleration of vesting, and shall therefore recognise immediately the amount that would otherwise have been recognised for services received over the remainder of the vesting period.' *[IFRS 2.28(a)]*.

There is something of a contradiction within this requirement as illustrated by Example 30.27.

Example 30.27: Cancellation and settlement – best estimate of cancellation expense

On 1 January 2013, an entity (A) granted 150 employees an award of free shares, with a grant date fair value of £5, conditional upon continuous service and performance targets over the 3-year period ending 31 December 2015. The number of shares awarded varies according to the extent to which targets (all non-market vesting conditions) have been met, and could result in each employee still in service at 31 December 2015 receiving a minimum of 600, and a maximum of 1,000 shares.

On 1 July 2014, A is acquired by B, following which all of A's share awards are cancelled. At the time of the cancellation, 130 of the original 150 employees were still in employment. At that time, it was A's best estimate that, had the award run to its full term, 120 employees would have received 900 shares each. Accordingly the cumulative expense recognised by A for the award as at the date of takeover would, under the normal estimation processes of IFRS 2 discussed at 6.1 to 6.4 above, be £270,000 (900 shares × 120 employees × £5 × 18/36).

How should A account for the cancellation of this award?

The opening phrase of paragraph 28(a) – 'the entity shall account for the cancellation ...as an acceleration of vesting' – suggests that A should recognise a cost for all 130 employees in service at the date of cancellation. However, the following phrase – '[the entity] shall therefore recognise immediately the amount that would otherwise have been recognised for services received over the remainder of the vesting period' – suggests that the charge should be based on only 120 employees, the best estimate, as at the date of cancellation of the number of employees in whom shares will finally vest. In our view, either reading of paragraph 28(a) is possible.

There is then the issue of the number of shares per employee that should be taken into account in the cancellation charge. Should this be 1,000 shares per employee (the maximum amount that could vest) or 900 shares per employee (the amount expected by the entity at the date of cancellation actually to vest)?

In our view, the intention was probably that the cancellation charge should be based on the number of shares considered likely, at the date of cancellation, to vest for each employee (900 shares in this example). However, given the lack of clarity in the wording of the standard – as discussed above – an entity could also choose an accounting policy based on the maximum number of shares (1000 shares in this example).

In extreme cases, the entity might conclude, as at the date of cancellation, that no awards are likely to vest. In this situation, no cancellation expense would be recognised. However, there would need to be evidence that this was not just a rather convenient assessment made as at the date of cancellation. Typically, the previous accounting periods would also have reflected a cumulative IFRS 2 expense of zero on the assumption that the awards would not vest.

An effect of these requirements is that IFRS 2 creates an accounting arbitrage between an award that is 'out of the money' but not cancelled (which continues to be spread over the remaining period to vesting) and one which is formally cancelled (the cost of which is recognised immediately). Entities might well prefer to opt for cancellation so as to create a 'one-off' charge to earnings rather than continue to show, particularly during difficult trading periods, significant periodic costs for options that no longer have any real value. However, such early cancellation of an award precludes any chance of the cost of the award being reversed through forfeiture during, or at the end of, the vesting period.

7.4.4 Replacement awards

The required accounting treatment of replacement awards, whilst generally clear, nevertheless raises some issues of interpretation. Most of this sub-section addresses the replacement of unvested awards but the treatment of vested awards is specifically addressed at 7.4.4.C below.

7.4.4.A Designation of award as replacement award

Whether or not an award is a 'replacement' award (and therefore recognised at only its incremental, not its full, fair value) is determined by whether or not the entity designates it as such on the date that it is granted. In other words, the accounting treatment effectively hinges on declared management intent, notwithstanding the IASB's systematic exclusion of management intent from many other areas of financial reporting. The Basis for Conclusions does not really explain the reason for this approach, which is also hard to reconcile with the fact that the value of an award is unaffected by whether, or when, the entity declares it to be a 'replacement' award for the purposes of IFRS 2. Presumably, the underlying reason is to prevent a retrospective, and possibly opportunistic, assertion that an award that has been in issue for some time is a replacement for an earlier award.

Entities need to ensure that designation occurs on grant date as defined by IFRS 2 (see 5.3 above). For example, if an entity notifies an employee in writing on 15 March 2014 of its intention to ask the remuneration committee to grant replacement options at its meeting on 15 May 2014, such notification (although formal and in writing) may not strictly meet IFRS 2's requirement for designation on grant date (i.e. 15 May 2014).

As drafted, IFRS 2 gives entities an apparently free choice to designate any newly granted awards as replacement awards. In our view, however, such designation cannot credibly be made unless there is evidence of some connection between the cancelled and replacement awards. This might be that the cancelled and replacement awards involve the same counterparties, or that the cancellation and replacement are part of the same arrangement.

7.4.4.B Incremental fair value of replacement award

Where an award is designated as a replacement award, it must be recognised, over its vesting period, at its incremental fair value. This is the difference between the fair value of the replacement award and the 'net fair value' of the cancelled or settled award, both measured at the date on which the replacement awards are granted. The net fair value of the cancelled or settled award is the fair value of the award, immediately before cancellation, less any compensation payment that is accounted for as a deduction from equity. *[IFRS 2.28(c)]*. Thus the 'net fair value' of the original award can never be less than zero (since any compensation payment in excess of the fair value of the cancelled award would be accounted for in profit or loss, not in equity – see Example 30.26 at 7.4.3 above).

There is some confusion within IFRS 2 as to whether a different accounting treatment is intended to result from, on the one hand, modifying an award and, on the other hand, cancelling it and replacing it with a new award on the same terms as the modified award. This is explored in the discussion of Example 30.28 below, which is based on the same fact pattern as Example 30.19 at 7.3.1.A above.

Example 30.28: Is there an accounting arbitrage between modification and cancellation of an award?

At the beginning of year 1, an entity grants 100 share options to each of its 500 employees. Each grant is conditional upon the employee remaining in service over the next three years. The entity estimates that the fair value of each option is €15.

By the end of year 1, the entity's share price has dropped. The entity cancels the existing options and issues options which it identifies as replacement options, which also vest at the end of year 3. The entity estimates that, at the date of cancellation, the fair value of each of the original share options granted is €5 and that the fair value of each replacement share option is €8.

40 employees leave during year 1. The entity estimates that a further 70 employees will leave during years 2 and 3, so that there will be 390 employees at the end of year 3 (500 – 40 – 70).

During year 2, a further 35 employees leave, and the entity estimates that a further 30 employees will leave during year 3, so that there will be 395 employees at the end of year 3 (500 – 40 – 35 – 30).

During year 3, 28 employees leave, and hence a total of 103 employees ceased employment during the original three year vesting period, so that, for the remaining 397 employees, the replacement share options vest at the end of year 3.

The intention of the IASB appears to have been that the arrangement should be accounted for in exactly the same way as the modification in Example 30.19 above, since the Basis for Conclusions to IFRS 2 notes:

> '...the Board saw no difference between a repricing of share options and a cancellation of share options followed by the granting of replacement share options at a lower exercise price, and therefore concluded that the accounting treatment should be the same.' *[IFRS 2.BC233].*

However, it is not clear that this intention is actually reflected in the drafting of IFRS 2, paragraph 28 of which reads as follows:

> 'If a grant of equity instruments is cancelled or settled during the vesting period (other than a grant cancelled by forfeiture when the vesting conditions are not satisfied):
>
> (a) the entity shall account for the cancellation or settlement as an acceleration of vesting, and shall therefore recognise immediately the amount that otherwise would have been recognised for services received over the remainder of the vesting period.
>
> (b) any payment made to the employee on the cancellation or settlement of the grant shall be accounted for as the repurchase of an equity interest, i.e. as a deduction from equity, except to the extent that the payment exceeds the fair value of the equity instruments granted, measured at the repurchase date. Any such excess shall be recognised as an expense....
>
> (c) if new equity instruments are granted to the employee and, on the date when those new equity instruments are granted, the entity identifies the new equity instruments granted as replacement equity instruments for the cancelled equity instruments, the entity shall account for the granting of replacement equity instruments in the same way as a modification of the original grant of equity instruments ...'. *[IFRS 2.28].*

As a matter of natural construction, paragraph (a) requires the cancellation of the existing award to be treated as an acceleration of vesting – explicitly and without qualification. In particular there is no rider to the effect that the requirement of paragraph (a) is to be read as 'subject to paragraph (c) below'.

Paragraph (c) requires any 'new equity instruments' granted to be accounted for in the same way as a modification of the original grant of equity instruments. It does not require this treatment for the cancellation of the *original* instruments, because this has already been addressed in paragraph (a).

Moreover, in order to construe paragraphs (a) and (c) in a manner consistent with the Basis for Conclusions to the standard, it would be necessary to read paragraph (c) as effectively superseding paragraph (a). However, for this to be a valid reading, it would also be necessary to read paragraph (b) as also superseding paragraph (a), and this would produce a manifestly incorrect result, namely that, if an award is cancelled *and settled*, there is no need ever to expense any part of the cancelled award not yet expensed at the date of cancellation.

Therefore, the main text in IFRS 2 appears to require the entity in Example 30.28 to recognise:

- The entire cost of the original options at the end of year 1 (since cancellation has the effect that they are treated as vesting at that date), based on the 390 employees expected at that date to be in employment at the end of the vesting period. This is not the only possible interpretation of the requirement of paragraph 28(a) – see the broader discussion in Example 30.27 at 7.4.3 above.
- The incremental fair value of the replacement options at repricing date (€3 per option, being the €8 fair value of each replacement option less the €5 fair value of the cancelled option) over a two year vesting period beginning at the date of cancellation (end of year one), based on the (at first estimated and then actual) number of employees at the end of year 3.

This would be calculated as follows:

Year	Calculation of cumulative expense Original award	 Replacement award	Cumulative expense (€)	Expense for period (€)
1	390 employees × 100 options × €15	–	585,000	585,000
2	390 employees × 100 options × €15	395 employees × 100 options × €3 × 1/2	644,250	59,250
3	390 employees × 100 options × €15	397 employees × 100 options × €3	704,100	59,850

By contrast, the accounting treatment implied by the Basis for Conclusions is as follows (see Example 30.19 above):

Year	Calculation of cumulative expense Original award (a)	 Modified award (b)	Cumulative expense (€) (a+b)	Expense for period (€)
1	390 employees × 100 options × €15 × 1/3	–	195,000	195,000
2	395 employees × 100 options × €15 × 2/3	395 employees × 100 options × €3 × 1/2	454,250	259,250
3	397 employees × 100 options × €15	397 employees × 100 options × €3	714,600	260,350

It will be seen that both the periodic allocation of expense and the total expense differ under each interpretation. This is because, under the first interpretation, the cost of the original award is accelerated at the end of year 1 for all 390 employees expected at that date to be in employment at the end of the vesting period, whereas under the second interpretation a cost is recognised for the 397 employees whose awards finally vest. The difference between the two total charges of €10,500 (€714,600 – €704,100) represents 397 – 390 = 7 employees @ €1,500 [100 options × €15] each = €10,500.

We believe that either interpretation is valid, and an entity should adopt one or other consistently as a matter of accounting policy.

7.4.4.C Replacement of vested awards

The rules for replacement awards summarised in paragraph (c) at 7.4 above apply 'if a grant of equity instruments is cancelled or settled during the vesting period ...'. *[IFRS 2.28]*. This begs the question of the treatment required when a replacement award is granted after the original award has vested. There is of course no question of accelerating the cost of the cancelled award in such cases, as it has already been recognised during the vesting period. The issue is rather the treatment of the new award itself. Whilst IFRS 2 does not explicitly address this point, it appears that such a replacement award should be treated as if it were a completely new award. In other words, its full fair value should be recognised immediately or, if there are any vesting conditions for the replacement award, over its vesting period.

By contrast, the rules for modification of awards discussed in 7.3 above apply whether the award has vested or not. Paragraphs 26 and 27 of IFRS 2 (modifications) are not restricted to events 'during the vesting period' in contrast to paragraph 28 (cancellation and settlement, including replacement awards), which is restricted to events 'during the vesting period'. *[IFRS 2.26-28]*.

This has the effect that the accounting cost of modifying an already vested award (i.e. the incremental fair value of the modified award) may be lower than the cost of cancelling and replacing it, which requires the full fair value of the new award to be expensed. However, the fair value of the new award will be reduced by the fair value of the cancelled award that the employee has surrendered as part of the consideration for the new award. This analysis produces an accounting outcome similar to that of the modification of an unvested award.

7.5 Replacement award on termination of employment

When an employee's employment is terminated during the vesting period of an award of shares or options, the award will typically lapse in consequence. It is common in such situations, particularly where the employee was part of the senior management, for the entity to make an alternative award, or to allow the employee to retain existing awards, as part of the package of benefits agreed with the employee on termination of employment.

Generally, such an award is an *ex gratia* award – in other words, it is a voluntary award to which the outgoing employee had no legal entitlement. However, a number of plan rules set out, in a 'good leaver' clause (see 5.3.9 above), the terms on which any *ex gratia* award may be made, usually by applying a formula to determine, or limit, how much of the original award can be considered to have vested. In many cases the award will be made on a fully vested basis, i.e. the employee has full entitlement without further conditions needing to be fulfilled. In some cases, however, an employee will be allowed to retain awards that remain subject to the fulfilment of the original conditions (other than future service). Whichever form the award takes, in IFRS 2 terms it will be treated as vesting at the date of termination of employment because any remaining conditions will be accounted for as non-vesting conditions in the absence of an explicit or implied service condition (see 3.2 above).

Because IFRS 2, as currently drafted, is unclear about whether the termination of employment should be accounted for as a forfeiture or as a cancellation, there is more than one view as to the appropriate accounting for such awards, as illustrated in Example 30.29 below. As discussed at 7.4.1.B above, the IASB's proposed *Annual Improvements to IFRSs 2010-2012 Cycle* include a clarification that if an employee is unable to satisfy a service condition for any reason, including termination of employment, this should be accounted for as a forfeiture rather than as a cancellation.

However, these draft amendments, and the earlier discussions of the Interpretations Committee, do not specifically address the accounting for any replacement awards on termination of employment. The continued availability of an accounting policy choice, as illustrated in Example 30.29 below, should be considered in the light of the IASB's proposed amendments and any further discussions by the Interpretations Committee.

Example 30.29: Replacement award on termination of employment

On 1 January 2013, an executive is granted the right to 10,000 free shares on condition of remaining in service until 31 December 2015. The fair value of the award at grant date is £2.00 per share.

On 31 December 2014, the executive's employment is terminated and he therefore loses his right to any shares. However, as *ex gratia* (voluntary) compensation, the remuneration committee awards him 6,667 shares vesting immediately. At 31 December 2014, the share price was £4.00, and the fair value of the original award was £3.60 per share. (This is lower than the current share price because the holder of a share is entitled to receive any dividends paid during 2015, whereas the holder of an unvested right to a share is not – see 8.5.4 below).

This raises the question of how the *ex gratia* award of 6,667 shares should be accounted for. In our view, the starting point for any analysis is whether the entity, as a matter of accounting policy (pending application of the IASB's proposed clarification), accounts for the lapse of an award on termination of employment by the entity as a forfeiture or as a cancellation (see 7.4.1.A and 7.4.1.B above).

The factors to be considered in determining the grant date in such cases are discussed further at 5.3.9 above. For the purposes of this Example, it is assumed that the replacement award is treated as having been granted on 31 December 2014 rather than 1 January 2013.

If the lapse is treated as a forfeiture, the entity:

- reverses the cost already booked for the award of £13,333 (10,000 shares × £2 × 2/3); and
- recognises the cost of the *ex gratia* award (at the fair value at that award's grant date) of £26,668 (6,667 shares × £4)

This results in a net charge on termination of £13,335.

If the lapse is currently treated as a cancellation, the entity:

- accelerates the cost not yet booked for the original award of £6,667 (10,000 shares × £2 = £20,000, less £13,333 already recognised – see above); and
- treats the *ex gratia* award as a replacement award. The fair value of the replacement award of £26,668 (6,667 shares × £4 – see above) is compared to the fair value of the original award of £36,000 (10,000 shares × £3.60). Since the fair value of the replacement award is less than that of the original award, there is no incremental cost required to be recorded under IFRS 2.

This results in a net charge on termination of £6,667.

Some support a third analysis which argues that, of the original award of 10,000 shares:

- 3,333 are forfeited, giving rise to a reversal of expense previously charged of £4,444 (3,333 shares × £2 × 2/3); and
- 6,667 have their terms modified, by changing the vesting period from one year (as at 31 December 2014) to immediate vesting. A service period is a non-market vesting condition which is not factored into the fair value of the award. Thus, it is argued that although the modification clearly enhances the 'real' value of the award, it has no effect on its value for the purposes of IFRS 2 (see 7.3.1.C above). Therefore there is no incremental cost required to be recorded under IFRS 2, and the entity simply accelerates the cost (based on the original grant date fair value) not yet recognised for the awards of £4,444 (6,667 shares × £2 = £13,334, less the amount already recognised of £8,890 [6,667 shares × £2 × 2/3]).

This results in no profit or loss arising on the termination of employment. We do not believe that this approach is appropriate. Whilst the service period is not directly factored into the fair value of the award, the life of an award is one of the inputs to the fair value and a reduction in the life could therefore affect the fair value. The approach above relies on the change of vesting date having no effect on the fair value. In addition to this, in our view, the award must be considered as either forfeited and replaced as a whole, or as cancelled and replaced as a whole. An approach that treats part of the award as forfeited and part as modified effectively treats the original award as 10,000 awards of one share rather than what we regard as its true economic substance of one award of 10,000 shares.

7.6 Entity's plans for future modification or replacement of award – impact on estimation process at reporting date

As discussed at 6.1.1 and 6.1.2 above, IFRS 2 requires an entity to determine a cumulative IFRS 2 charge at each reporting date by reference to the 'best available estimate' of the number of awards that will vest (within the special meaning of that term in IFRS 2).

In addition to the normal difficulties inherent in any estimation process, IFRS 2 brings the further complication that it is not entirely clear as to which anticipated future events should be taken into account in the estimation process and which should not, as illustrated by Example 30.30 below.

Example 30.30: Estimation of number of awards expected to vest – treatment of anticipated future events

On 1 January 2014, an entity granted an award of 1,000 shares to each of its 600 employees at a particular manufacturing unit. The award vests on completion of three years' service at 31 December 2016. As at 31 December 2014, the entity firmly intends to close the unit, and terminate the employment of employees, as part of a rationalisation programme. This closure would occur on or around 1 July 2015. The entity has not, however, announced its intentions or taken any other steps so as to allow provision for the closure under IAS 37 – *Provisions, Contingent Liabilities and Contingent Assets* (see Chapter 27 at 6.1).

Under the original terms of the award, the award would lapse on termination of employment. However, the entity intends to compensate employees made redundant by changing the terms of their award so as to allow full vesting on termination of employment.

What is the 'best estimate', as at 31 December 2014, of the number of awards expected to vest? Specifically should the entity:

(a) ignore the intended closure altogether, on the grounds that there is no other recognition of it in the financial statements;

(b) take account of the impact of the intended closure on vesting of the current award, but ignore the intended modification to the terms of the award to allow vesting; or

(c) take account of both the intended closure and the intended modification of the award?

In our view, there is no basis in IFRS 2 for anticipating the modification of an award. The entity must account for awards in issue at the reporting date, not those that might be in issue in the future. Accordingly we do not consider approach (c) above to be appropriate.

Equally, we struggle to support approach (a) above. IFRS 2 requires the entity to use its 'best available estimate' and its best available estimate must be that the unit will be closed, and the employees' employment terminated, in 2015. This view is supported by the fact that, unlike IAS 36 – *Impairment of Assets* (see Chapter 20) and IAS 37 (see Chapter 27), IFRS 2 does not explicitly prohibit an entity from taking account of the consequences of reorganisations and similar transactions to which it is not yet committed.

Accordingly, we believe that approach (b) should be followed under IFRS 2 as currently drafted. The actual effect of doing so will depend on the view taken by the entity as to whether the loss of an award on termination of employment by the entity is a forfeiture or a cancellation – which will also need to take into account the IASB's proposed amendments to IFRS 2 (see 7.4.1.A and 7.4.1.B above).

If the entity takes the view that such a termination is a cancellation, we believe IFRS 2 requires a cancellation to be accounted for only when it happens (i.e. in 2015).

If the entity takes the view that such a termination is a forfeiture, the entity's best estimate, at 31 December 2014, must be that the award currently in place will vest in no employees (because they will be made redundant before the end of the vesting period). It therefore reverses any cost previously recorded for the award. When the award is modified at the time of the redundancy in 2015 to allow full vesting, the entity will recognise the full cost of the modified award. This will have what many may see as the less than ideal result that the entity will recognise a credit in profit or loss in 2014 and an expense in 2015, even though there has been no change in management's best estimate of the overall outcome. This follows from the analysis, discussed above, that we do not believe that the entity can, in 2014, account for the award on the basis of what its terms may be in 2015.

The best estimate is made as at each reporting date. A change in estimate made in a later period in response to subsequent events affects the accounting expense for that later period (i.e. there is no restatement of earlier periods presented).

7.7 Two awards running 'in parallel'

In some jurisdictions, it is not readily possible formally to cancel or modify an award. This may be because formal cancellation or modification may trigger either a legal requirement for the entity to pay compensation to the holder, or adverse tax consequences for the holder. In such cases, where an award has become unattractive (for example, because it is 'out-of-the-money'), the entity, rather than formally cancelling or modifying the award, may instead issue a second award. The second award cannot be designated as a replacement award, because the original award is still in place. Thus, the entity has two awards running 'in parallel'.

However, a mechanism is then put in place to ensure that the employee can effectively receive only one award. For instance, if the original award were 1,000 options, it might be replaced with a second award of 1,000 options, but with the proviso that, if options under one award are exercised, the number of options exercisable under the other award is correspondingly reduced, so that no more than 1,000 options can be exercised in total.

The accounting for such arrangements is discussed in Example 30.31 below.

Example 30.31: Two option awards running in parallel

On 1 January 2013, an entity granted 1,000 options (the 'A options') to an employee, subject to non-market vesting conditions. The grant date fair value of an A option was €50.

As at 1 January 2014, the share price is significantly below the exercise price of an A option, which had a fair value at that date of €5. Without modifying or cancelling the A options, the entity awards the employee 1,000 new options (the 'B options'). The B options are subject to non-market vesting conditions different in nature from, and more onerous than, those applicable to the A options, but have a lower exercise price. The terms of the B options include a provision that for every A option that is exercised, the number of B options that can be exercised is reduced by one, and *vice versa.* The fair value of a B option at 1 January 2014 is €15.

Clearly, the employee will exercise whichever series of options, A or B, has the higher intrinsic value. There are four possible outcomes:

1. Neither the A options nor the B options vest.
2. Only the A options vest.
3. Only the B options vest.
4. Both the A options and B options vest and the employee must choose which to exercise. Rationally, the employee would exercise the B options as they have the lower exercise price.

In our view, the B options are most appropriately accounted for as if they were a modification of the A options. As only one series of options can be exercised, we believe that the most appropriate treatment is to account for whichever award the entity believes, at each reporting date, is more likely to be exercised. This is analogous to the accounting treatment we suggest in Example 30.12 at 6.2.5 above and in Example 30.17 at 6.3.6 above.

If the entity believes that neither award will vest, any expense previously recorded would be reversed.

If the entity believes that only the A options will vest, it will recognise expense based on the grant date fair value of the A options (€50 each).

If the entity believes that only the B options will vest, or that both the A and B options will vest (so that, in either case, the B options will be exercised), it will recognise expense based on:

(a) the grant date fair value of the A options (€50 each) over the original vesting period of the A options, plus

(b) the incremental fair value of the B options, as at their grant date (€10 each, being their €15 fair value less the €5 fair value of an A option), over the vesting period of the B options.

A possible alternative analysis would have been that modification accounting is not applied, each award is accounted for separately, and the requirement that only one award can vest is treated as a non-vesting condition (i.e. it is a condition of exercising the A options that the B options are not exercised, and *vice versa*) – see 6.4 above. This treatment would result in a charge representing the total fair value of both awards at their respective grant dates. This is because the entity would recognise an expense for whichever series of options was exercised plus a charge for the cancellation of the second series (by reason of the employee's failure to satisfy a non-vesting condition in the employee's control, namely refraining from exercising the first series of options).

7.8 Share splits and consolidations

It is common for an entity to divide its existing equity share capital into a larger number of shares (share splits) or to consolidate its existing share capital into a smaller number of shares (share consolidations). The impact of such splits and consolidations is not specifically addressed in IFRS 2, and a literal application of IFRS 2 could lead to some rather anomalous results.

Suppose that an employee has options over 100 shares in the reporting entity, with an exercise price of £1. The entity undertakes a '1 for 2' share consolidation – i.e. the number of shares in issue is halved such that, all other things being equal, the value of one share in the entity after the consolidation is twice that of one share before the consolidation.

IFRS 2 is required to be applied to modifications to an award arising from equity restructurings. *[IFRS 2.BC24]*. However, in most cases, a share scheme will provide that, following the consolidation, the employee holds options over only 50 shares with an exercise price of £2. All things being equal, it would be expected that the modified award would have the same fair value as the original award and, therefore, there would be no incremental expense to be accounted for.

It may be that the scheme has no such provision for automatic adjustment, such that the employee still holds options over 100 shares. The clear economic effect is that the award has been modified, since its value has been doubled. However, it could be argued that, on a literal reading of IFRS 2, no modification has occurred, since the employee holds options over 100 shares at the same exercise price before and after the consolidation. The Interpretations Committee discussed this issue at its July and November 2006 meetings but decided not to take it onto its agenda because it 'was not a normal commercial occurrence and ... unlikely to have widespread significance'.[23] This decision was re-confirmed by the Interpretations Committee in March 2011.[24] In our view, whilst it seems appropriate to have regard to the substance of the transaction, and treat it as giving rise to a modification, it can be argued that IFRS 2 as drafted does not require such a treatment, particularly given the decision of the Interpretations Committee not to discuss the issue further.

Sometimes, the terms of an award give the entity discretion to make modifications at a future date in response to more complex changes to the share structure, such as those arising from bonus issues, share buybacks and rights issues where the effect on existing options may not be so clear-cut. These are discussed further at 5.3.8 above.

8 EQUITY-SETTLED TRANSACTIONS – VALUATION

8.1 Introduction

The IASB provides some guidance on valuation in Appendix B to the standard, which we summarise and elaborate upon below. The guidance is framed in terms of awards to employees which are valued at grant date, but many of the general principles are equally applicable to awards to non-employees valued at service date. *[IFRS 2.B1]*.

As discussed in more detail at 4 to 7 above, IFRS 2 requires a 'modified grant-date' approach, under which the fair value of an equity award is estimated on the grant date without regard to the possibility that any service conditions or non-market performance vesting conditions will not be met. Although the broad intention of IFRS 2 is to recognise the cost of the goods or services to be received, the IASB believes that, in the case of services from employees, the fair value of the share-based payment is more readily determinable than the fair value of the services received.

As noted at 5.1 above, IFRS 2 defines fair value as 'the amount for which an asset could be exchanged, a liability settled, or an equity instrument granted could be exchanged, between knowledgeable, willing parties in an arm's length transaction'.

IFRS 2 requires fair value to be determined based on the available information that ranks highest in the following hierarchy:

- Level 1 – observable market prices of identical instruments in active markets;
- Level 2 – observable market prices of similar instruments in active markets; and
- Level 3 – valuation techniques.

While fair value may be readily determinable for awards of shares, market quotations are not available for long-term, non-transferable share options because these instruments are not generally traded.

As discussed further at 8.2.2 below, the fair value of an option at any point in time is made up of two basic components – intrinsic value and time value. Intrinsic value is the greater of (a) the market value of the underlying share less the exercise price of the option and (b) zero.

Time value reflects the potential of the option for future gain to the holder, given the length of time during which the option will be outstanding, and possible changes in the share price during that period. Because the information described in Levels 1 and 2 of the fair value hierarchy is not normally available for an employee share option, the IASB believes that, in the absence of such information, the fair value of a share option awarded to an employee generally must be estimated using an option-pricing model. *[IFRS 2.BC130].* This is discussed further at 8.3 below.

The discussion below aims to provide guidance on the valuation of options and similar awards under IFRS 2. It is not intended to provide detailed instructions for constructing an option pricing model.[25]

The approach to determining the fair value of share-based payments continues to be that specified in IFRS 2 and share-based payments fall outside the scope of IFRS 13 which applies more generally to the measurement of fair value under IFRSs (see Chapter 14). *[IFRS 2.6A].*

8.2 Options

8.2.1 Call options – overview

Before considering the features of employee share options that make their valuation particularly difficult, a general overview of call options may be useful.

Call options give the holder the right, but not the obligation, to buy the underlying shares at a specified price (the 'exercise' or 'strike' price) on, or before, a specified date. Share-based payments take the form of call options over the underlying shares.

Options are often referred to as American or European. American options can be exercised at any time up to the expiry date, whereas European options can be exercised only on the expiry date itself.

The terms of employee options commonly have features of both American and European options, in that there is a period, generally two or three years, during which the option cannot be exercised (i.e. the vesting period). At the end of this period, if the options vest, they can be exercised at any time up until the expiry date. This type of option is known as a Window American option or Bermudan option.

A grant of shares is equivalent to an option with an exercise price of zero and will be exercised regardless of the share price on the vesting date. Throughout the discussion below, any reference to share options therefore includes share grants or zero strike price options. There is further discussion of grants of free shares at 8.7.1 below.

8.2.2 *Call options – valuation*

As noted in 8.1 above, option value consists of intrinsic value and time value. Intrinsic value, for a call option, is the greater of:

- the share price less the exercise price, and
- zero.

Figure 30.2 below sets out the intrinsic value (or payoff) for a call option with an exercise price of $5.00.

Figure 30.2: Intrinsic value of a call option

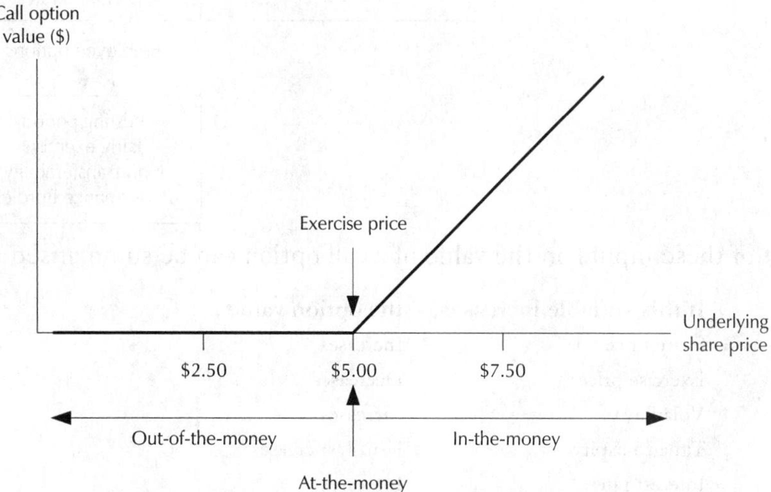

A call option is said to be 'in-the-money' when the share price is above the exercise price of the option and 'out-of-the-money' when the share price is less than the exercise price. An option is 'at-the-money' when the share price equals the exercise price of the option.

The time value of an option arises from the time remaining to expiry. As well as the share price and the exercise price, it is impacted by the volatility of the share price, time to expiry, dividend yield and the risk-free interest rate and the extent to which it is in- or out-of-the-money. For example, when the share price is significantly less than the exercise price, the option is said to be 'deeply' out-of-the-money. In this case, the fair value consists entirely of time value, which decreases the more the option is out-of-the-money.

The main inputs to the value of a simple option are:

- the exercise price of the option;
- the term of the option;
- the current market price of the underlying share;
- the expected future volatility of the price of the underlying share;
- the dividends expected to be paid on the shares during the life of the option (if any); and
- the risk-free interest rate(s) for the expected term of the option.

Their effect on each of the main components of the total value (intrinsic value and time value) is shown in Figure 30.3 below.

Figure 30.3: Determinants of the fair value of a call option

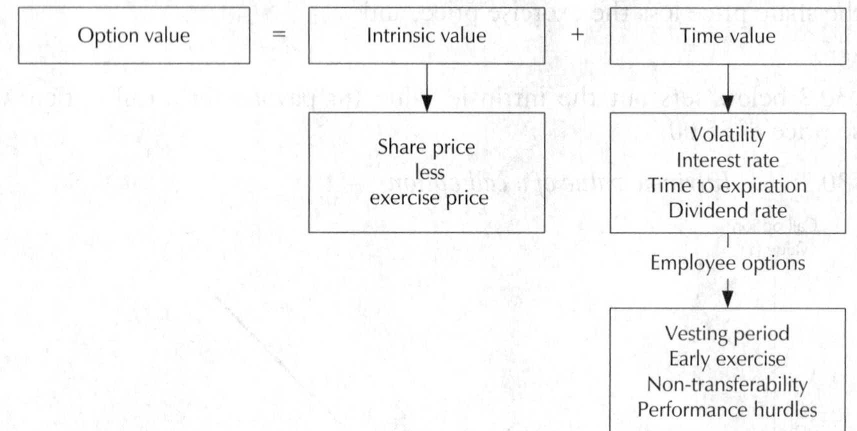

The effect of these inputs on the value of a call option can be summarised as follows:

If this variable increases,	**the option value ...**
Share price	Increases
Exercise price	Decreases
Volatility	Increases
Time to expiry	Usually increases*
Interest rate	Increases
Dividend yield/payout	Decreases

* When there is a dividend yield and the option is considerably in-the-money, an option may have a zero or negative time value. In this case, as the time to expiry increases, a European call option will reduce in value and an American call option will stay constant in value.

The factors to be considered in estimating the determinants of an option value in the context of IFRS 2 are considered in more detail at 8.5 below.

8.2.3 Factors specific to employee share options

In addition to the factors referred to in 8.2.2 above, employee share options are also affected by a number of specific factors that can affect their true economic value. These factors, not all of which are taken into account for IFRS 2 valuation purposes (see 8.4 and 8.5 below), include the following:

- non-transferability (see 8.2.3.A below);
- continued employment requirement (see 8.2.3.B below);
- vesting and non-vesting conditions (see 8.2.3.C below);
- periods during which holders cannot exercise their options – referred to in various jurisdictions as 'close', 'restricted' or 'blackout' periods (see 8.2.3.D below);
- limited ability to hedge option values (see 8.2.3.E below); and
- dilution effects (see 8.2.3.F below).

8.2.3.A Non-transferability

Holders of 'ordinary' traded share options can choose to 'sell' their options (typically by writing a call option on the same terms) rather than exercise them. By contrast, employee share options are generally non-transferable, leading to early (and sub-optimal) exercise of the option. This will lower the value of the options.

8.2.3.B Continued employment requirement

Holders of ordinary share options can maintain their positions until they wish to exercise, regardless of other circumstances. In contrast, employee share options cannot normally be held once employment is terminated. If the options have not vested, they will be lost. If the options have vested, the employee will be forced to exercise the options immediately or within a short timescale, or forfeit them altogether, losing all time value. This will lower the value of the options.

8.2.3.C Vesting and non-vesting conditions

Holders of ordinary share options have an unconditional right to exercise their options. In contrast, employee share options may have vesting and non-vesting conditions attached to them, which may not be met, reducing their value. This is discussed in more detail in 8.4 below.

Although a non-market vesting condition reduces the 'true' fair value of an award, it does not directly affect its valuation for the purposes of IFRS 2 (see 6.2 above). However, non-market vesting conditions may indirectly affect the value. For example, when an award vests on satisfaction of a particular target rather than at a specified time, its value may vary depending on the assessment of when that target will be met, since that may influence the expected life of the award, which is relevant to its fair value under IFRS 2 (see 8.2.2 above and 8.5.1 below).

8.2.3.D Periods during which exercise is restricted

Holders of ordinary American or Bermudan share options can exercise at any time during the exercisable window. In contrast, employees may be subject to 'blackout' periods in which they cannot exercise their options, for example to prevent insider trading. While this could conceivably make a significant impact if the shares were significantly mis-priced in the market, in an efficient market blackout periods will only marginally decrease the value.

8.2.3.E Limited ability to hedge option values

In the case of ordinary share options, it is reasonable to justify the theoretical valuation on the basis that, for any other value, arbitrage opportunities could arise through hedging. In contrast, employee share options are usually awarded only in relatively small amounts, and the employees are usually subject to restrictions on share trading (especially short selling the shares, as would be required to hedge an option). When considered in combination with the non-transferability of the options (see 8.2.3.A above), this means that exercising the options is the only way to remove exposure to fluctuations in value, which lowers the value of the options.

8.2.3.F Dilution effects

When third parties write traded share options, the writer delivers shares to the option holder when the options are exercised, so that the exercise of the traded share options has no dilutive effect. By contrast, if an entity writes share options to employees and, when those share options are exercised, issues new shares (or uses shares previously repurchased and held in treasury) to settle the awards, there is a dilutive effect. As the shares will be issued at the exercise price rather than the current market price at the date of exercise, this actual or potential dilution may reduce the share price, so that the option holder does not make as large a gain as would arise on the exercise of similar traded options which do not dilute the share price.

8.3 Selection of an option-pricing model

Where, as will almost invariably be the case, there are no traded options over the entity's equity instruments that mirror the terms of share options granted to employees, IFRS 2 requires the fair value of options granted to be estimated using an option-pricing model. The entity must consider all factors that would be considered by knowledgeable, willing market participants in selecting a model. *[IFRS 2.B4-5].*

The IASB decided that it was not necessary or appropriate to prescribe the precise formula or model to be used for option valuation. It notes that there is no particular option pricing model that is regarded as theoretically superior to the others, and there is the risk that any model specified might be superseded by improved methodologies in the future. *[IFRS 2.BC131].*

The three most common option-pricing methodologies for valuing employee options are:

- the Black-Scholes-Merton formula (see 8.3.1 below);
- the binomial model (see 8.3.2 below); and
- the Monte Carlo Simulation (see 8.3.3 below).

It is important to understand all the terms and conditions of a share-based payment arrangement, as this will influence the choice of the most appropriate option pricing model.

IFRS 2 names the Black-Scholes-Merton formula and the binomial model as examples of acceptable models to use when estimating fair value *[IFRS 2.BC152]*, while noting that there are certain circumstances in which the Black-Scholes-Merton formula may not be the most appropriate model (see 8.3.1 below). Moreover, there may be instances where, due to the particular terms and conditions of the share-based payment arrangement, neither of these models is appropriate, and another methodology is more appropriate to achieving the intentions of IFRS 2. A model commonly used for valuing more complex awards is Monte Carlo Simulation (often combined with the Black-Scholes-Merton formula or the binomial model). This can deal with the complexities of a plan such as one based on relative total shareholder return (TSR), which compares the return on a fixed sum invested in the entity to the return on the same amount invested in a peer group of entities.

8.3.1 *The Black-Scholes-Merton formula*

The Black-Scholes-Merton methodology is commonly used for assessing the value of a freely-traded put or call option. In recent years the formula has been further developed to allow the incorporation of static dividends on shares. The assumptions underlying the Black-Scholes-Merton formula are as follows:

- the option can be exercised only on the expiry date (i.e. it is a European option);
- there are no taxes or transaction costs and no margin requirements;
- the volatility of the underlying asset is constant and is defined as the standard deviation of the continuously compounded rates of return on the share over a specified period;
- the risk-free interest rate is constant over time;
- short selling is permitted;
- there are no risk-free arbitrage opportunities;
- there are log normal returns (i.e. the continuously compounded rate of return is normally distributed); and
- security trading is continuous.

The main limitation of the Black-Scholes-Merton methodology is that it only calculates the option price at one point in time. It does not consider the steps along the way when there could be a possibility of early exercise of an American option (although as discussed at 8.4 below this can be partially mitigated by using an assumed expected term as an input to the calculation).

The Black-Scholes-Merton formula is an example of a closed-form model, which is a valuation model that uses an equation to produce an estimated fair value. The formula is as shown in Figure 30.4 below.

Figure 30.4: The Black-Scholes-Merton formula

$$c = S_0 e^{-qT} N(d_1) - K e^{-rT} N(d_2)$$

Where :

$$d_1 = \frac{\ln(S_0 / K) + (r - q + \sigma^2 / 2)T}{\sigma\sqrt{T}}$$

$$d_2 = d_1 - \sigma\sqrt{T}$$

$c =$	price of a written call
$S_0 =$	price of the underlying share
$N =$	the cumulative probability distribution function for a standardised normal distribution
$q =$	dividend yield (continuously compounded)
$K =$	call option exercise price
$r =$	the continuously compounded risk-free rate
$\sigma =$	annualised volatility of the underlying share
$T =$	time to expiry (in years)

Note: 'e' represents the mathematical constant, the base of the natural logarithm (2.718282...), and 'ln' is the natural logarithm of the indicated value

Whilst the Black-Scholes-Merton formula is complex, its application in practice is relatively easy. It can be programmed into a spreadsheet, and numerous programs and calculators exist that use it to calculate the fair value of an option. As a result, the formula is used widely by finance professionals to value a large variety of options. However, a number of the assumptions underlying the formula may be better suited to valuing short-term, exchange-traded share options rather than employee share options.

The attributes of employee share options that render the Black-Scholes-Merton formula less effective as a valuation technique include:

- *Long term to expiry*

  The formula assumes that volatility, interest rates, dividends and share price are constant over the life of the option. While this may be appropriate when valuing short-term options, the assumption of constant values is less appropriate when valuing long-term options.
- *Non-transferability and early exercise*

  The formula assumes a fixed maturity/exercise date. While IFRS 2 provides for the use of an 'expected term' in place of the contractual life to reflect the possibility of early exercise resulting from the non-transferability of employee share options or other reasons (see 8.5 below), this may not adequately describe early exercise behaviour.
- *Vesting conditions and non-vesting conditions*

  The formula does not take into account any market-based vesting conditions or non-vesting conditions.
- *Blackout periods*

  As the formula assumes exercise on a fixed date, and does not allow earlier exercise, it does not take into consideration any blackout periods (see 8.2.3.D above).

In summary, application of the Black-Scholes-Merton formula is relatively simple, in part because many of the complicating factors associated with the valuation of employee share options cannot be incorporated into it directly and, therefore, must be derived outside of the formula (e.g. the input of an expected term).

IFRS 2 states that the Black-Scholes-Merton formula may not be appropriate for long-lived options which can be exercised before the end of their life and which are subject to variation in the various inputs to the model over the life of the option. However, IFRS 2 suggests that the Black-Scholes-Merton formula may give materially correct results for options with shorter lives and with a relatively short exercise period. *[IFRS 2.B5].*

The development of appropriate assumptions for use in the Black-Scholes-Merton formula is discussed at 8.5 below.

In certain circumstances it may be possible to use closed form solutions other than the Black-Scholes-Merton formula to value options where, for example, the share price has to reach a specified level for the options to vest. However, these other solutions are beyond the scope of this Chapter.

8.3.2 The binomial model

The binomial model is one of a subset of valuation models known as lattice models, which adopt a flexible, iterative approach to valuation that can capture the unique aspects of employee share options. A binomial model produces an estimated fair value based on the assumed changes in prices of a financial instrument over successive periods of time. In each time period, the model assumes that at least two price movements are possible. The lattice represents the evolution of the value of either a financial instrument or a market variable for the purpose of valuing a financial instrument.

The concepts that underpin lattice models and the Black-Scholes-Merton formula are the same, but the key difference between a lattice model and a closed-form model is that a lattice model is more flexible. The valuations obtained using the Black-Scholes-Merton formula and a lattice model will be very similar if the lattice model uses identical assumptions to the Black-Scholes-Merton calculation (e.g. constant volatility, constant dividend yields, constant risk-free rate, the same expected life). However, a lattice model can explicitly use dynamic assumptions regarding the term structure of volatility, dividend yields, and interest rates.

Further, a lattice model can incorporate assumptions about how the likelihood of early exercise of an employee share option may increase as the intrinsic value of that option increases, or how employees may have a high propensity to exercise options with significant intrinsic value shortly after vesting.

In addition, a lattice model can incorporate market conditions that may be part of the design of an option, such as a requirement that an option is only exercisable if the underlying share price achieves a certain level (sometimes referred to as 'target share price' awards). The Black-Scholes-Merton formula is not generally appropriate for awards that have a market-based performance condition because it cannot handle that additional complexity.

Most valuation specialists believe that lattice models, through their versatility, generally provide a more accurate estimate of the fair value of an employee share option with market performance conditions or with the possibility of early exercise than a value based on a closed-form Black-Scholes-Merton formula. As a general rule, the longer the term of the option and the higher the dividend yield, the larger the amount by which the binomial lattice model value may differ from the Black-Scholes-Merton formula value.

To implement the binomial model, a 'tree' is constructed the branches (or time steps) of which represent alternative future share price movements over the life of the option. In each time step over the life of the option, the share price has a certain probability of moving up or down by a certain percentage amount. It is important to emphasise the assumption, in these models, that the valuation occurs in a risk-neutral world, where investors are assumed to require no extra return on average for bearing risks and the expected return on all securities is the risk free interest rate.

To illustrate how the binomial model is used, Example 30.32 below constructs a simple binomial lattice model with a few time steps. The valuation assumptions and principles will not differ in essence from those in a Black-Scholes-Merton valuation except that it will allow for early exercise of the option. The relevant difference between the two models is the specification of a very small number of time steps, for illustrative purposes, in the binomial lattice model (see also 8.3.2.A below). We discuss below how the model can be augmented for a more complex set of assumptions.

Example 30.32: Binomial model

A share option is issued with an exercise price of $10, being the share price on the grant date. This Example assumes a constant volatility (50%) and risk-free rate (5% continuously compounded) although, as discussed later, those static assumptions may not be appropriate when valuing a long-term share option. It is also assumed that: the grantor pays dividends with a yield of 2% (continuously compounded) on its shares; the term of the option is five years; and each branch of the tree represents a length of time of one year.

At t = 0 (the grant date), the model is started at the grant date share price ($10 in this Example). At each node (the base of any price time step), two possible price changes (one increase and one decrease) are computed based on the volatility of the stock. The two new share prices are computed as follows:

The up-node price utilises the following formula:

$$u = e^{\sigma\sqrt{dt}} = e^{0.5*\sqrt{1}} = 1.6487$$

Where:

σ = annualised volatility of the underlying share

dt = period of time between nodes

The down-node is the inverse of the up-node:

$$d = \frac{1}{u} = \frac{1}{1.6487} = 0.6065$$

The probability of each upward and downward price movement occurring is calculated from:

- the probability of an upward movement in price:

$$p = \frac{e^{(r-q)dt} - d}{u-d} = \frac{e^{(.05-.02)*1} - 0.6065}{1.6487 - 0.6065} = 0.4068$$

  Where:

  r = continuously compounded risk free rate

  q = dividend yield (continuously compounded)

  dt = period of time between nodes

- the probability of a downward movement in price:

$$= 1 - p = 1 - 0.4068 = 0.5932$$

Using the above price multiples, the price tree can then be constructed as shown diagrammatically below – each rising node is built by multiplying the previous price by ‘u’ and each falling node is similarly calculated by multiplying the previous price by ‘d’.

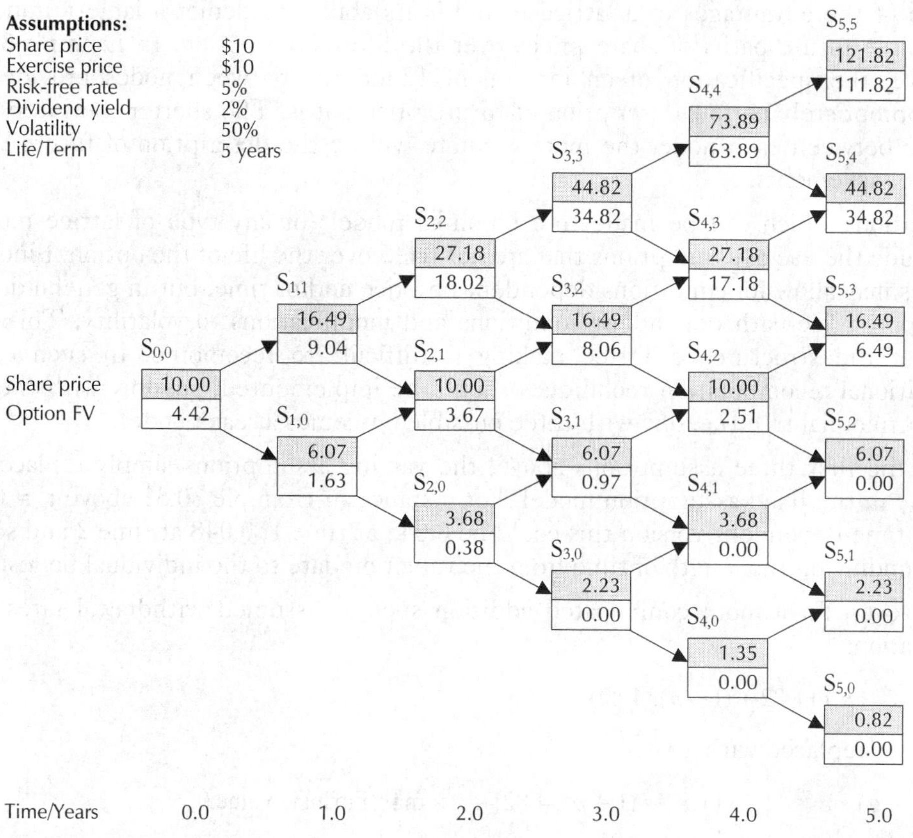

To calculate the option value:

- The option payoffs at the final time node (time 5 above) must be calculated. This is the share price less the exercise price, or zero if the payoff is negative.
- Then the option values must be calculated at the previous time point (time 4 above). This is done by calculating the expected value of the option for the branch paths available to the particular node being valued discounted at the risk-free rate. For example, for $S_{4,4}$ in the chart above the option value is the probability of going to node $S_{5,5}$ multiplied by the option value at that node plus the probability of going to node $S_{5,4}$ multiplied by the option value at that node, all discounted at the risk-free rate):

  $= e^{-r.dt}\{p.111.82 + (1 - p)34.82\} = 0.95\{0.4068 \times 111.82 + 0.5932 \times 34.82\} = 62.92$

  This would be the value at node $S_{4,4}$ if the option were European and could not be exercised earlier. As the binomial model can allow for early exercise, the option value at node $S_{4,4}$ is the greater of the option value just calculated and the intrinsic value of the option which is calculated the same way as the end option payoff. In this case, as the intrinsic value is $63.89 ($73.89 – $10.00), the node takes the value of $63.89.
- The previous steps are then repeated throughout the entire lattice (i.e. for all nodes at time 4, then all nodes at time 3, etc.) until finally the option value is determined at time 0 – this being the binomial option value of $4.42.
- Additionally, if there is a vesting period during which the options cannot be exercised, the model can be adjusted so as not to incorporate the early exercise condition stipulated in the previous point and allow for this only after the option has vested and has the ability to be exercised before expiry.

One of the advantages of a lattice model is its ability to depict a large number of possible future paths of share prices over the life of the option. In Example 30.32 above, the specification of an interval of 12 months between nodes provides an inappropriately narrow description of future price paths. The shorter the interval of time between each node, the more accurate will be the description of future share price movements.

Additions which can be made to a binomial model (or any type of lattice model) include the use of assumptions that are not fixed over the life of the option. Binomial trees may allow for conditions dependent on price and/or time, but in general do not support price-path dependent conditions and modifications to volatility. This may affect the structure of a tree making it difficult to recombine. In such cases, additional recombination techniques should be implemented, possibly with the use of a trinomial tree (i.e. one with three possible outcomes at each node).

For the first three assumptions above, the varying assumptions simply replace the value in the fixed assumption model. For instance in Example 30.32 above r = 0.05; in a time-dependent version this could be 0.045 at time 1, 0.048 at time 2 and so on, depending on the length of time from the valuation date to the individual nodes.

However, for a more complicated addition such as assumed withdrawal rates, the equation:

$$= e^{-r.dt}\{p.111.82 + (1 - p)34.82\}$$

may be replaced with

$$= (1 - g) \times e^{-r.dt}\{p.111.82 + (1 - p)34.82\} + \text{g} \times \max(\text{intrinsic value,0})$$

where 'g' is the rate of employee departure, on the assumption that, on departure, the option is either forfeited or exercised. As with the other time and price dependent assumptions, the rate of departure could also be made time or price dependent (i.e. the rate of departure could be assumed to increase as the share price increases, or increase as time passes, and so forth).

8.3.2.A Lattice models – number of time steps

When performing a lattice valuation, a decision must be taken as to how many time steps to use in the valuation (i.e. how much time passes between each node). Generally, the greater the number of time steps, the more accurate the final value. However, as more time steps are added, the incremental increase in accuracy declines. To illustrate the increases in accuracy, consider the diagram below, which values the option in Example 30.32 above as a European option. In this case, the binomial model has not been enhanced to allow for early exercise (i.e. the ability to exercise prior to expiry).

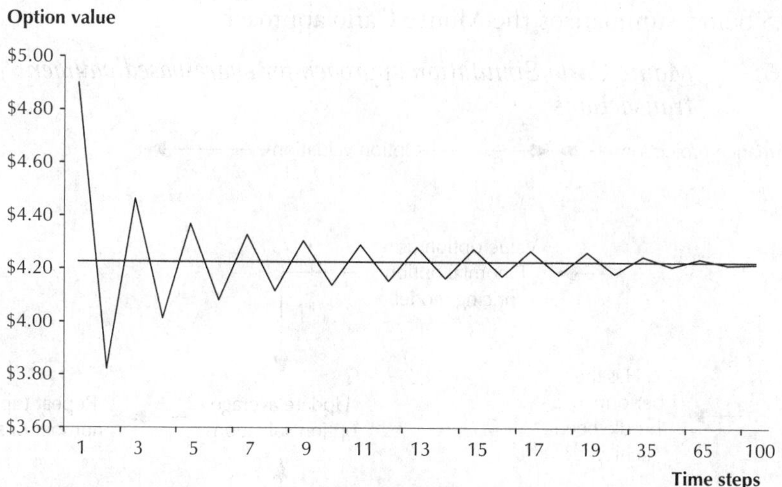

Whilst the binomial model is very flexible and can deal with much more complex assumptions than the Black-Scholes-Merton formula, there are certain complexities it cannot handle, which can best be accomplished by Monte Carlo Simulation – see 8.3.3 below.

The development of appropriate assumptions for use in a binomial model is discussed at 8.5 below.

In addition to the binomial model, other lattice models such as trinomial models or finite difference algorithms may be used. Discussion of these models is beyond the scope of this Chapter.

8.3.3 *Monte Carlo Simulation*

In order to value options with market-based performance targets where the market value of the entity's equity is an input to the determination of whether, or to what extent, an award has vested, the option methodology applied must be supplemented with techniques such as Monte Carlo Simulation.

TSR compares the return on a fixed sum invested in the entity to the return on the same amount invested in a peer group of entities. Typically, the entity is then ranked in the peer group and the number of share-based awards that vest depends on the ranking. For example, no award might vest for a low ranking, the full award might vest for a higher ranking, and a pro-rated level of award might vest for a median ranking.

The following table gives an example of a possible vesting pattern for such a scheme, with a peer group of 100 entities.

Ranking in peer group	Percentage vesting
Below 50	0%
50	50%
51 – 74	50% plus an additional 2% for each increase of 1 in the ranking
75 or higher	100%

Figure 30.5 below summarises the Monte Carlo approach.

Figure 30.5: Monte Carlo Simulation approach for share-based payment transactions

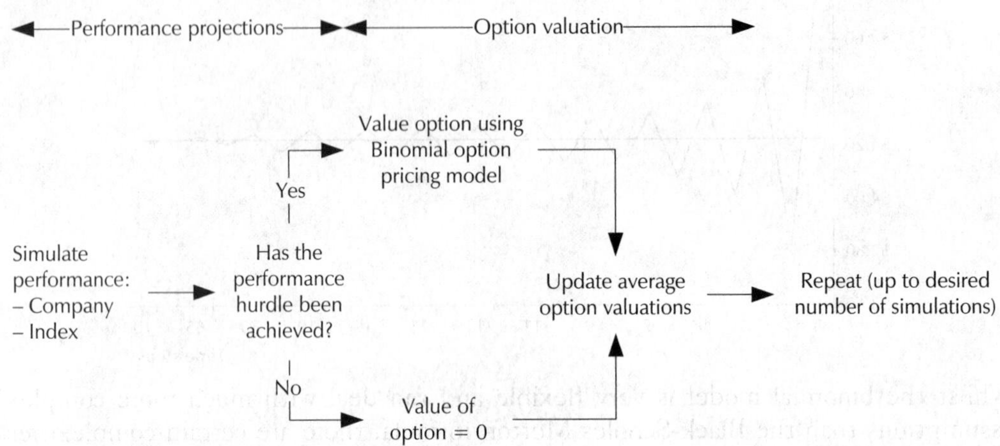

The valuation could be performed using either:

- a binomial valuation or the Black-Scholes-Merton formula, dependent on the results of the Monte Carlo Simulation; or
- the Monte Carlo Simulation on its own.

The framework for calculating future share prices uses essentially the same underlying assumptions as lie behind Black-Scholes-Merton and binomial models – namely a risk-neutral world and a log normal distribution of share prices.

For a given simulation, the risk-neutral returns of the entity and those of the peer group or index are projected until the performance target is achieved and the option vests. At this point, the option transforms into a 'vanilla' equity call option that may be valued using an option pricing model. This value is then discounted back to the grant date so as to give the value of the option for a single simulation.

When the performance target is not achieved and the option does not vest, a zero value is recorded. This process is repeated thousands or millions of times. The average option value obtained across all simulations provides an estimate of the value of the option, allowing for the impact of the performance target.

8.4 Adapting option-pricing models for share-based payment transactions

Since the option-pricing models discussed in 8.3 above were developed to value freely-traded options, a number of adjustments are required in order to account for the restrictions usually attached to share-based payment transactions, particularly those with employees. The restrictions not accounted for in these models include:

- non-transferability (see 8.4.1 below); and
- vesting conditions, including performance targets, and non-vesting conditions that affect the value for the purposes of IFRS 2 (see 8.4.2 below).

8.4.1 Non-transferability

As noted at 8.2.3.A above, employee options and other share-based awards are almost invariably non-transferable, except (in some cases) to the employee's estate in the event of death in service. Non-transferability often results in an option being exercised early (i.e. before the end of its contractual life), as this is the only way for the employee to realise its value in cash. Therefore, by imposing the restriction of non-transferability, the entity may cause the effective life of the option to be shorter than its contractual life, resulting in a loss of time value to the holder. *[IFRS 2.BC153-169]*.

One aspect of time value is the value of the right to defer payment of the exercise price until the end of the option term. When the option is exercised early because of non-transferability, the entity receives the exercise price much earlier than it otherwise would. Therefore, as noted by IFRS 2, the effective time value granted by the entity to the option holder is less than that indicated by the contractual life of the option.

IFRS 2 requires the effect of early exercise as a result of non-transferability and other factors to be reflected either by modelling early exercise in a binomial or similar model or by using expected life rather than contractual life as an input into the option-pricing model. This is discussed further at 8.5.1 below.

Reducing the time to expiry effectively reduces the value of the option. This is a simplified way of reducing the value of the employee stock option to reflect the fact that employees are unable to sell their vested options, rather than applying an arbitrary discount to take account of non-transferability.

8.4.2 Treatment of vesting and non-vesting conditions

Many share-based payment awards to employees have vesting and non-vesting conditions attached to them which must be satisfied before the award can be exercised. It must be remembered that a non-market vesting condition, while reducing the 'true' fair value of an award, does not directly affect its valuation for the purposes of IFRS 2 (see 6.2 above). However, non-market vesting conditions may indirectly affect the value. For example, when an award vests on satisfaction of a particular target rather than at a specified time, its value may vary depending on the assessment of when that target will be met, since that may influence the expected life of the award, which is relevant to its fair value under IFRS 2 (see 8.2.2 above and 8.5 below).

As discussed at 6.2 above, IFRS 2 requires a vesting condition, other than a market condition, to be taken into account by estimating the extent of forfeiture based on failure to vest (and making a corresponding adjustment to the number of equity instruments for which a cost is recognised), rather than by attempting to reflect the effect of the condition in the option-pricing model. If the actual numbers that vest differ from those originally estimated, adjustments are required so that the cumulative expense recognised over the vesting period reflects the number of instruments that actually vest (subject to the special provisions relating to awards subject to market conditions and/or non-vesting conditions – see 6.3 and 6.4 above).

8.4.2.A Market-based performance measures and non-vesting conditions

As discussed at 6.3 and 6.4 above, IFRS 2 requires market-based vesting conditions and non-vesting conditions to be taken into account in estimating the fair value of the options granted. Moreover, the entity is required to recognise a cost for an award with a market condition or non-vesting condition if all the non-market vesting conditions attaching to the award are satisfied regardless of whether the market condition or non-vesting condition is satisfied. This means that a more sophisticated option pricing model may be required.

8.4.2.B Non market-based vesting conditions

As discussed at 6.2 above, IFRS 2 requires non market-based vesting conditions to be ignored when estimating the fair value of share-based payment transactions. Instead, such vesting conditions are taken into account by adjusting the number of equity instruments included in the measurement of the transaction (by estimating the extent of forfeiture based on failure to vest) so that, ultimately, the amount recognised is based on the number of equity instruments that eventually vest.

8.5 Selecting appropriate assumptions for option-pricing models

IFRS 2 notes that, as discussed at 8.2.2 above, option pricing models take into account, as a minimum:

- the exercise price of the option;
- the life of the option (see 8.5.1 and 8.5.2 below);
- the current price of the underlying shares;
- the expected volatility of the share price (see 8.5.3 below);
- the dividends expected on the shares (if appropriate – see 8.5.4 below); and
- the risk-free interest rate for the life of the option (see 8.5.5 below). *[IFRS 2.B6].*

Of these inputs, only the exercise price and the current share price are objectively determinable. The others are subjective, and their development will generally require significant analysis. The discussion below addresses the development of assumptions for use both in a Black-Scholes-Merton formula and in a lattice model.

IFRS 2 requires other factors that knowledgeable, willing market participants would consider in setting the price to be taken into account, except for those vesting conditions and reload features that are excluded from the measurement of fair value – see 5 and 6 above and 8.9 below. Such factors include:

- restrictions on exercise during the vesting period or during periods where trading by those with inside knowledge is prohibited by securities regulators; or
- the possibility of the early exercise of options (see 8.5.1 below). *[IFRS 2.B7-9].*

However, the entity should not consider factors that are relevant only to an individual employee and not to the market as a whole (such as the effect of an award of options on the personal motivation of an individual). *[IFRS 2.B10].*

The objective of estimating the expected volatility of, and dividends on, the underlying shares is to approximate the expectations that would be reflected in a current market or negotiated exchange price for the option. Similarly, when estimating the effects of early exercise of employee share options, the objective is to approximate the expectations about employees' exercise behaviour that would be developed by an outside party with access to detailed information at grant date. Where (as is likely) there is a range of reasonable expectations about future volatility, dividends and exercise behaviour, an expected value should be calculated, by weighting each amount within the range by its associated probability of occurrence. *[IFRS 2.B11-12]*.

Such expectations are often based on past data. In some cases, however, such historical information may not be relevant (e.g. where the business of the entity has changed significantly) or even available (e.g. where the entity is unlisted or newly listed). An entity should not base estimates of future volatility, dividends or exercise behaviour on historical data without considering the extent to which they are likely to be reasonably predictive of future experience. *[IFRS 2.B13-15]*.

8.5.1 Expected term of the option

IFRS 2 allows the estimation of the fair value of an employee share award to be based on its expected life, rather than its maximum term, as this is a reasonable means of reducing the value of the award to reflect its non-transferability.

Option value is not a linear function of option term. Rather, value increases at a decreasing rate as the term lengthens. For example, a two year option is worth less than twice as much as a one year option, if all other assumptions are equal. This means that to calculate a value for an award of options with widely different individual lives based on a single weighted average life is likely to overstate the value of the entire award. Accordingly, assumptions need to be made as to what exercise or termination behaviour an option holder will exhibit. Considerations include:

- vesting period – the expected term of the option must be at least as long as its vesting period. The length of time employees hold options after they vest may vary inversely with the length of the vesting period;
- past history of employee exercise and termination patterns for similar grants (adjusted for current expectations) – see 8.5.2 below;
- expected volatility of the underlying share – on average, employees tend to exercise options on shares with higher volatility earlier;
- periods during which exercise may be precluded and related arrangements (e.g. agreements that allow for exercise to occur automatically during such periods if certain conditions are satisfied);
- employee demographics (age, tenure, sex, position etc.); and
- time from vesting date – the likelihood of exercise typically increases as time passes.

As discussed at 8.4 above, IFRS 2 notes that the effect of early exercise can be reflected:

- in a pricing model such as the Black-Scholes-Merton formula, by treating the expected, rather than the contractual, life of the option as an input to the model (see 8.5.1.A below); or
- by using a binomial or similar model. *[IFRS 2.B16-17]*.

8.5.1.A Expected term under the Black-Scholes-Merton formula

An estimate of expected term based on the types of inputs described above can be used in the Black-Scholes-Merton formula as well as a lattice model. However, the formula requires only a single expected term to be used. This is one of the reasons why the Black-Scholes-Merton formula may provide a higher valuation for the same options than a lattice model.

The difference in value that arises from using only a single expected term results, in part, from the convex shape of a typical option valuation curve, as illustrated below.

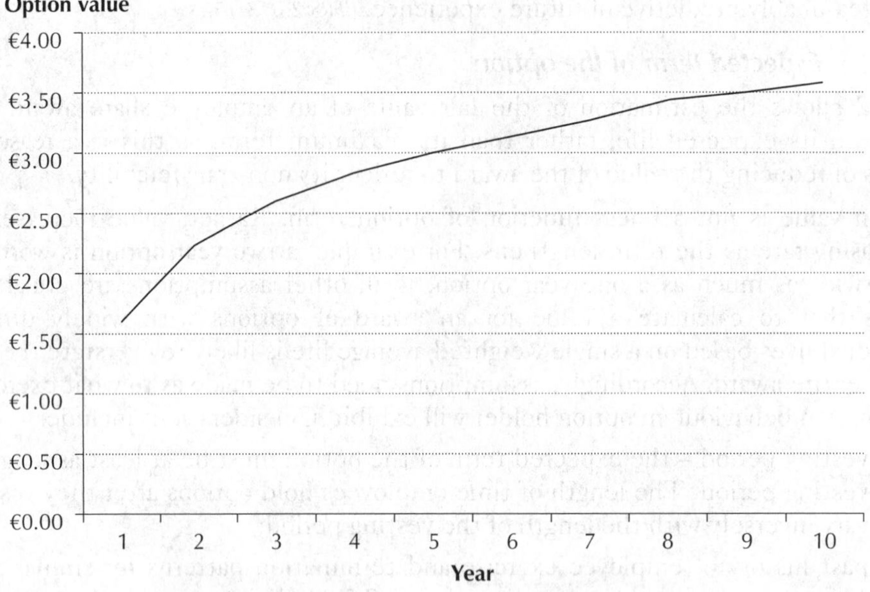

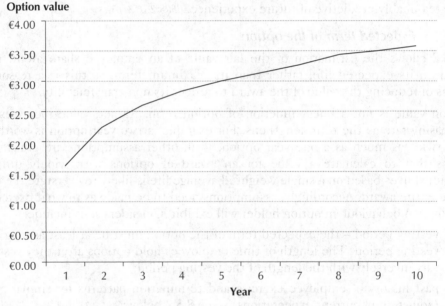

It is assumed, for the purposes of this illustration, that an at-the-money option on a €10 share with a 10-year contractual term is equally likely to be exercised at the end of each year beginning with year two. An average expected term of six years [(2+3+4+...9)/9] would be used in a Black-Scholes-Merton calculation giving a fair value of €3.10 for the option. If, instead, nine separate valuations were performed, each with a different expected term corresponding to each of the possible terms (from two to ten years), the average of those valuations (also calculated using the Black-Scholes-Merton formula) would be €2.9854. The latter amount is lower than €3.10 because of the convex shape of the valuation curve, reflecting the fact that the value increases at a decreasing rate as the term lengthens. Therefore, the value of the share option with an average expected term of six years will exceed the value derived from averaging the separate valuations for each potential term.

In a lattice model, exercise can occur at any time based on the rules specified in the model regarding exercise behaviour. The lattice model can therefore be thought of as analogous to the calculation in the above example in which the fair value was calculated as the average of the valuations from periods two to ten. In contrast, the Black-Scholes-Merton valuation allows only a single expected term to be specified. Therefore, it is analogous to the valuation described in the above example based on a single average expected term of six years.

Therefore, even if the expected term derived from a lattice model were used as an input in the Black-Scholes-Merton formula (and all other inputs were identical), the two models would give different values.

To mitigate the impact of the convex shape of the valuation curve, an entity with a broad-based share option plan might consider stratifying annual awards into different employee groups for the purposes of estimating the expected option lives (see 8.5.2 below).

Determining a single expected term can be quite challenging, particularly for an entity seeking to base its estimate on the periods for which previously granted options were outstanding, which would have been highly dependent on the circumstances during those periods. For example, if the entity's share price had increased significantly during the option period (as would be the case for share options granted by certain entities at the beginning of a bull market), it is likely that employees would have exercised options very soon after vesting. Alternatively, if options were granted at the end of a bull market and the share price declined significantly after the grant date, it is likely that the options would be exercised much later (if at all). These relationships would exist because, as discussed previously, the extent to which an option is in-the-money has a significant impact on exercise behaviour. Accordingly, deriving a single expected term in these situations involves considerable judgement.

8.5.2 Exercise and termination behaviour

IFRS 2 notes that employees often exercise options early for a number of reasons, most typically:

- restrictions on transferability mean that this is the only way of realising the value of the option in cash;
- aversion to the risk of not exercising 'in the money' options in the hope that they increase in value; or
- in the case of leavers, a requirement to exercise, or forfeit, all vested options on or shortly after leaving (see 8.5.2.B below).

Factors to consider in estimating early exercise include:

(a) the length of the vesting period, because the share option cannot be exercised until the end of the vesting period. Hence, determining the valuation implications of expected early exercise is based on the assumption that the options will vest;

(b) the average length of time similar options have remained outstanding in the past;

(c) the price of the underlying shares. Experience may indicate that employees tend to exercise options when the share price reaches a specified level above the exercise price;

(d) the employee's level within the organisation. For example, experience might indicate that higher-level employees tend to exercise options later than lower-level employees (see also 8.5.2.A below); and

(e) the expected volatility of the underlying shares. On average, employees might tend to exercise options on highly volatile shares earlier than on shares with low volatility. *[IFRS 2.B18]*.

In addition, the pattern of terminations of employment after vesting may be relevant (see 8.5.2.B below).

In our view, past exercise behaviour should generally serve as the starting point for determining expected exercise behaviour. That behaviour should be analysed, correlated to the factors above, and extrapolated into the future. However, significant changes in the underlying share price or in other salient characteristics of the entity, changes in option plans, tax laws, share price volatility and termination patterns may indicate that past exercise behaviour is not indicative of expected exercise behaviour. The expected life may also be estimated indirectly, by using a modified option pricing model to compute an option value, an input to which is an assumption that the options will be expected to be exercised when a particular share price is reached.

Some entities, including recently listed entities, or entities for which all outstanding grants have been out-of-the-money for a long period, may simply not be able to observe any exercise behaviour or may not possess enough history to perform a reasonable analysis of past exercise behaviour. In these cases, in our view, entities may have to look to the exercise history of employees of similar entities to develop expectations of employee exercise behaviour. At present there is only limited publicly-available information about employee exercise patterns, but valuation professionals and human resource consultants may have access to relevant data, which we expect to become more broadly available in the future.

In the absence of extensive information regarding exercise behaviour, another solution could be to use a midpoint assumption – i.e. selecting as the expected date of exercise the midpoint between the first available exercise date (the end of the vesting period) and the last available exercise date (the contracted expiry date). However, this should be undertaken only when the entity is satisfied that this does not lead to a material misstatement. It is also plausible to assume exercise at the earliest possible time or to undertake a reasonable analysis of past behaviour and set up the amount of intrinsic value which, when exceeded, will trigger exercise of the option.

8.5.2.A Grouping employees with homogeneous exercise behaviour

IFRS 2 emphasises that the estimated life of an option is critical to its valuation. Therefore, where options are granted to a group of employees, it will generally be necessary to ensure that either:

(a) all the employees are expected to exercise their options within a relatively narrow time-frame; or
(b) if not, that the group is divided into sub-groups of employees who are expected to exercise their options within a similar relatively narrow time-frame.

IFRS 2 suggests that it may become apparent that middle and senior management tend to exercise options later than lower-level employees, either because they choose to do so, or because they are encouraged or compelled to do so as a result of required minimum levels of ownership of equity instruments (including options) among more senior employees. *[IFRS 2.B19-21]*.

8.5.2.B Post-vesting termination behaviour

Most employee share options provide that, if employment is terminated, the former employee typically has only a short period (e.g. 90 days from the date of termination of employment) in which to exercise any vested options, the contractual expiry of which would otherwise be some years away. Accordingly, an entity should look at its prior termination patterns, adjust those patterns for future expectations and incorporate those expected terminations into a lattice model as expected early exercises.

Patterns of employee turnover are not necessarily linear and may be a non-linear function of a variety of factors, such as:

- employee demographics (age, sex, tenure, position, etc.);
- path of share price – for example, if options are deeply out-of-the-money, they may have little retention value and more employees may leave than if the options were at- or in-the-money; and
- economic conditions and other share prices.

8.5.3 Expected volatility of share price

Expected volatility is a measure of the amount by which a price is expected to fluctuate during a period. Share price volatility has a powerful influence on the estimation of the fair value of an option, much of the value of which is derived from its potential for appreciation. The more volatile the share price, the more valuable the option. It is therefore essential that the choice of volatility assumption can be properly supported.

IFRS 2 notes that the measure of volatility used in option pricing models is the annualised standard deviation of the continuously compounded rates of return on the share over a period of time. Volatility is typically expressed in annualised terms that are comparable regardless of the time period used in the calculation (for example, daily, weekly or monthly price observations).

The expected annualised volatility of a share is the range within which the continuously compounded annual rate of return is expected to fall approximately two-thirds of the time. For example, to say that a share with an expected continuously compounded rate of return of 12% has a volatility of 30% means that the probability that the rate of return on the share for one year will be between minus 18% (12% – 30%) and 42% (12% + 30%) is approximately two-thirds. If the share price is €100 at the beginning of the year, and no dividends are paid, the year-end share price would be expected to be between €83.53 (€100 × $e^{-0.18}$) and €152.20 (€100 × $e^{0.42}$) approximately two-thirds of the time.

The rate of return (which may be positive or negative) on a share for a period measures how much a shareholder has benefited from dividends and appreciation (or depreciation) of the share price. *[IFRS 2.B22-24]*.

IFRS 2 gives examples of factors to consider in estimating expected volatility including the following *[IFRS 2.B25]*:

- *Implied volatility from traded share options*

  Implied volatility is the volatility derived by using an option pricing model with the traded option price (if available) as an input and solving for the volatility as the unknown on the entity's shares. It may also be derived from other traded instruments of the entity that include option features (such as convertible debt).

  Implied volatilities are often calculated by analysts and reflect market expectations for future volatility as well as imperfections in the assumptions in the valuation model. For this reason, the implied volatility of a share may be a better measure of prospective volatility than historical volatility (see below). However, traded options are usually short-term, ranging in general from one month to two years. If the expected lives are much longer than this, both the implied and historical volatilities will need to be considered.

- *Historical volatility*

  It may be relevant to consider the historical volatility of the share price over the most recent period that is generally commensurate with the expected term of the option (taking into account the remaining contractual life of the option and the effects of expected early exercise). However, this assumes that past share price behaviour is likely to be representative of future share price behaviour. Upon any restructuring of an entity, the question of whether or not past volatility will be likely to predict future volatility would need to be reassessed.

  The historical volatilities of similar entities may be relevant for newly listed entities, unlisted entities or entities that have undergone substantial restructuring (see 8.5.3.A to 8.5.3.C below).

- *The length of time the entity's shares have been publicly traded*

  A newly listed entity might have a high historical volatility, compared with similar entities that have been listed longer. Further guidance for newly listed entities is given in 8.5.3.A below.

- *'Mean-reverting tendency'*

  This refers to the tendency of volatility to revert to its long-term average level, and other factors indicating that expected future volatility might differ from past volatility. For example, if an entity's share price was extraordinarily volatile for some identifiable period of time because of a failed takeover bid or a major restructuring, that period could be disregarded in computing historical average annual volatility. However, an entity should not exclude general economic factors such as the effect of an economic downturn on share price volatility.

- *Appropriate and regular intervals for price observations*

  The price observations should be consistent from period to period. For example, an entity might use the closing price for each week or the opening price for the week, but it should not use the closing price for some weeks and the opening price for other weeks. Also, the price observations should be expressed in the same currency as the exercise price. In our view, at least thirty observations are generally required to calculate a statistically valid standard deviation. Our experience has been that, in general, it is more appropriate to make such observations daily or weekly rather than monthly.

8.5.3.A Newly listed entities

As noted under 'Historical volatility' at 8.5.3 above, an entity should consider the historical volatility of the share price over the most recent period that is generally commensurate with the expected option term. If a newly listed entity does not have sufficient information on historical volatility, it should compute historical volatility for the longest period for which trading activity is available. It should also consider the historical volatility of similar entities. For example, an entity that has been listed for only one year and grants options with an average expected life of five years might consider the historical volatility of entities in the same industry, which are of a similar size and operate similar businesses, for the first six years in which the shares of those entities were publicly traded. *[IFRS 2.B26]*.

8.5.3.B Unlisted entities

An unlisted entity will have neither historical nor current market information to consider when estimating expected volatility. IFRS 2 suggests that, in some cases, an unlisted entity that regularly issues options or shares might have set up an internal market for its shares. The volatility of those share prices could be considered when estimating expected volatility. Alternatively, if the entity has based the value of its shares on the share prices of similar listed entities, the entity could consider the historical or implied volatility of the shares of those similar listed entities. *[IFRS 2.B27-29]*.

If the entity has not used a valuation methodology based on the share prices of similar listed entities, the entity could derive an estimate of expected volatility consistent with the valuation methodology used. For example, the entity might value its shares on a net asset or earnings basis, in which case it could consider the expected volatility of those net asset values or earnings. *[IFRS 2.B30]*.

8.5.3.C Listed entities that have undergone significant restructuring

An issue not specifically addressed by IFRS 2 is the approach required in the case of an entity that has been listed for some time but which has recently undergone significant restructuring or refocusing of the business (e.g. as a result of acquisitions, disposals or refinancing). In such cases, it may well be appropriate to adopt the approach advocated for newly listed entities in 8.5.3.A above.

8.5.3.D Expected volatility under the Black-Scholes-Merton formula

In calculating the fair value of a share option using the Black-Scholes-Merton formula, a single expected volatility assumption must be used. That amount should be based on the volatility expected over the expected term of the option. Frequently, expected volatility is based on observed historical share price volatility during the period of time equal to the expected term of the option and ending on the grant date. Implied volatilities (i.e. volatilities implied by actual option prices on the entity's shares observed in the market) also may be considered in determining the expected volatility assumption (see 8.5.3 above).

When developing an expected volatility assumption, current and historical implied volatilities for publicly traded options and historical realised share volatilities should be considered for:

- shares of the grantor;
- shares of other entities in the grantor's industry and comparable entities; and
- stock market indices.

8.5.3.E Expected volatility under lattice models

Expected volatility is more accurately taken into account by lattice models than by the Black-Scholes-Merton formula, because lattice models can accommodate dynamic assumptions regarding the term structure and path-dependence of volatility. For example, there is evidence that volatility during the life of an option depends on the term of the option and, in particular, that short-term options often exhibit higher volatility than similar options with longer terms. Additionally, volatility is path-dependent, in that it is often lower (higher) after an increase (decrease) in share price.

An entity that can observe sufficiently extensive trading of options over its shares may decide, when developing a term structure of expected volatility, to place greater weight on current implied volatilities than on historical observed and implied volatilities. It is likely that current implied volatilities are better indicators of the expectations of market participants about future volatility.

8.5.4 Expected dividends

The valuation of an award of options depends on whether or not the holder is entitled to dividends or dividend equivalents (whether in the form of cash payments or reductions in the exercise price) before the award is ultimately exercised. *[IFRS 2.B31-32, B34].* The accounting treatment of awards that entitle the holder to dividends before exercise is discussed further at 15.3 below.

Dividends paid on the underlying share will impact the share option value – the higher the expected dividend yield (i.e. dividend per share ÷ share price), the lower the option value. Option holders generally do not have dividend rights until they actually exercise the options and become shareholders. All other things being equal, a share option for a share yielding a high dividend is less valuable than one for a share yielding a low dividend.

Where employees are entitled to dividends or dividend equivalents, the options granted should be valued as if no dividends will be paid on the underlying shares, so that the input for expected dividends (which would otherwise reduce the valuation of an option) is zero. Conversely, where employees are not entitled to dividends or dividend equivalents, the expected dividends should be included in the application of the pricing model. *[IFRS 2.B31-32, B34].*

While option pricing models generally call for an expected dividend yield, they may be modified to use an expected dividend amount rather than a yield. Where an entity uses expected payments rather than expected yields, it should consider its historical pattern of increases in dividends. For example, if an entity's policy has generally been to increase dividends, its estimated option value should not assume a fixed dividend amount throughout the life of the option unless there is evidence to support that assumption. *[IFRS 2.B35].*

Determination of the expected dividends over the expected term of the option requires judgement. Generally, the expected dividend assumption should be based on current expectations about an entity's anticipated dividend policy. For example, an entity that has demonstrated a stable dividend yield in past years, and has indicated no foreseeable plans to change its dividend policy, may simply use its historical dividend yield to estimate the fair value of its options. If an entity has never paid a dividend, but has publicly announced that it will begin paying a dividend yielding 2% of the current share price, it is likely that an expected dividend yield of 2% would be assumed in estimating the fair value of its options.

Generally assumptions about expected dividends should be based on publicly available information. Thus, an entity that does not pay dividends and has no plans to do so should assume an expected dividend yield of zero. However, an emerging entity with no history of paying dividends might expect to begin paying dividends during the expected lives of its employee share options. Such entities could use an average of their past dividend yield (zero) and the mean dividend yield of a comparable peer group of entities. *[IFRS 2.B36].*

8.5.4.A Expected dividends under the Black-Scholes-Merton formula

Closed-form option-pricing models generally call for a single expected dividend yield as an input. That input should be determined based on the guidance at 8.5.4 above.

8.5.4.B Expected dividends under the binomial model and other lattice models

Lattice models can be adapted to use an expected dividend amount rather than a dividend yield, and therefore can also take into account the impact of anticipated dividend changes. Such approaches might better reflect expected future dividends, since dividends do not always move in a fixed fashion with changes in the entity's share price. This may be a time- or price-dependent assumption, similar to those described in the discussion of the binomial model at 8.3.2 above. Expected dividend estimates in a lattice model should be determined based on the general guidance above. Additionally, when the present value of dividends becomes significant in relation to the share price, standard lattice models may need to be amended.

8.5.5 *Risk-free interest rate*

Typically, the risk-free interest rate is the implied yield currently available on zero-coupon government issues of the country in whose currency the exercise price is expressed, with a remaining term equal to the expected term of the option being valued (based on the remaining contractual life of the option and taking into account the effects of expected early exercise). It may be necessary to use an appropriate substitute, if no such government issues exist, or where the implied yield on zero-coupon government issues may not be representative of the risk-free interest rate (for example, in high inflation economies). An appropriate substitute should also be used if market participants would typically determine the risk-free interest rate by using that substitute. *[IFRS 2.B37].*

The risk-free interest rate will not have an impact on most free share grants, since they have an exercise price of zero and therefore involve no cash outflow for the holder.

8.5.5.A *Risk-free interest rate under the Black-Scholes-Merton formula*

The Black-Scholes-Merton formula expressed at 8.3.1 above uses a continuously compounded interest rate, which means that any interest rate calculated or obtained needs to be in this format. The continuously compounded interest rate is given by the formula:

continuously compounding rate = ln(1 + annual rate),

where ln represents a natural logarithm. For example, a 7.79% annual effective rate results in a continuously compounded rate of 7.50%:

7.50% = ln(1 + 0.0779)

8.5.5.B *Risk-free interest rate under binomial and other lattice models*

At each node in the lattice, the option values in the lattice should be discounted using an appropriate forward rate as determined by a yield curve constructed from the implied yield on zero coupon government bond issues. In stable economies this will have minimal impact and it is therefore likely that a flat risk-free rate that is consistent with the expected life assumption will be a reasonable estimate for this input.

8.6 Capital structure effects and dilution

Typically, traded share options are written by third parties, not the entity issuing the shares that are the subject of the option. When these share options are exercised, the writer delivers to the option holder shares acquired from existing shareholders. Hence the exercise of traded share options has no dilutive effect. By contrast, when share options written by the entity are exercised, new shares may be issued (either in form or in substance, if shares previously repurchased and held in treasury are used), giving rise to dilution. This actual or potential dilution may reduce the share price, so that the option holder does not make as large a gain on exercise as on exercising an otherwise similar traded option that does not dilute the share price. *[IFRS 2.B38-39].*

Whether or not this has a significant effect on the value of the share options granted depends on various factors, such as the number of new shares that will be issued on exercise of the options compared with the number of shares already issued. Also, if the market already expects that the option grant will take place, the market may have already factored the potential dilution into the share price at the date of grant. However, the entity should consider whether the possible dilutive effect of the future exercise of the share options granted might have an impact on their estimated fair value at grant date. Option pricing models can be adapted to take into account this potential dilutive effect. *[IFRS 2.B40-41]*.

In practice, in our view, it is unlikely that a listed entity would be required to make such an adjustment unless it makes a very large, unanticipated grant of share options. Indeed, even in that case, if the potential dilution is material and is not already incorporated into the share price, it would be expected that the announcement of the grant would cause the share price to decline by a material amount. Unlisted entities should consider whether the dilutive impact of a very large option grant is already incorporated into the estimated share price used in their option-pricing model. If that is not the case, some adjustment to the fair value may be appropriate.

8.7 Other awards requiring the use of option valuation models

As noted at 8.1 above, the discussion in 8.3 to 8.5 above may well be relevant to share-based payments other than options. These include, but are not restricted to:

- awards of shares (see 8.7.1 below);
- non-recourse loans (see 8.7.2 below);
- share appreciation rights (SARs) (see 8.7.3 below); and
- performance rights (see 8.7.4 below).

8.7.1 Shares

IFRS 2 requires shares granted to employees to be valued at their market price (where one exists) or an estimated market value (where the shares are not publicly traded), in either case adjusted to take account of the terms and conditions on which the shares were granted, other than those vesting conditions that IFRS 2 requires to be excluded in determining the grant date fair value (see 6.2 above). *[IFRS 2.B2]*.

For example, the valuation should take account of restrictions on the employee's right:

- to receive dividends in the vesting period (see below); or
- to transfer shares after vesting, but only to the extent that such restrictions would affect the price that a knowledgeable and willing market participant would pay for the shares. Where the shares are traded in a deep and liquid market, the effect may be negligible.

The valuation should not, however, take account of restrictions that arise directly from the existence of the vesting conditions (such as the right to transfer shares during the vesting period). *[IFRS 2.B3]*.

Whether dividends should be taken into account in measuring the fair value of shares depends on whether the counterparty is entitled to dividends or dividend equivalents (which might be paid in cash) during the vesting period. When the grant date fair value of shares granted to employees is estimated, no adjustment is required if the employees are entitled to receive dividends during the vesting period (as they are in no different a position in this respect than if they already held shares). However, where employees are not entitled to receive dividends during the vesting period, the valuation should be reduced by the present value of dividends expected to be paid during the vesting period. *[IFRS 2.B31, B33-34]*. The basis on which expected dividends during the vesting period might be determined is discussed in the context of the impact of expected dividends on the fair value of share options at 8.5.4 above.

The accounting treatment of awards which give the right to receive dividends during the vesting period is discussed further at 15.3 below.

8.7.2 Non-recourse loans

Non-recourse loans are loans granted by an entity to the employee to allow the employee to buy shares, and are discussed in more detail at 15.2 below. Generally, however, the loan is interest-free, with the dividends received being used to repay the loan. The loan acts like an option, in that, at the point in time when the holder decides to sell the shares to repay the loan, if the shares are worth less than the loan, the remaining part of the loan is forgiven, with the effect that, just as in the case of an option, the holder bears no risk of ownership.

8.7.3 Share appreciation rights (SARs)

A share appreciation right (SAR) is a grant whereby the employee will become entitled either to shares or, more commonly, to a future cash payment based on the increase in the entity's share price from a specified level over a period of time (see further discussion at 9 below on cash-settled awards). This essentially has the same payoff as a call option, except the award is generally cash- rather than equity-settled.

8.7.4 Performance rights

A performance right is the right to acquire further shares after vesting, upon certain criteria being met. These criteria may include certain performance conditions which can usually be modelled with either a binomial lattice model or a Monte Carlo Simulation. Such awards may be structured as matching share awards, as discussed in more detail at 15.1 below.

8.8 Awards whose fair value cannot be measured reliably

IFRS 2 acknowledges that there may be rare cases where it is not possible to determine the fair value of equity instruments granted. In such cases, the entity is required to adopt a method of accounting based on the intrinsic value of the award (i.e. the price of the underlying share less the exercise price, if any, for the award). This is slightly puzzling in the sense that, for unlisted entities, a significant obstacle to determining a reliable fair value for equity instruments is the absence of a market share price, which is also a key input in determining intrinsic value. In fact, the intrinsic value model is arguably more onerous than the fair value model since, as discussed further in 8.8.1 and 8.8.2 below, it requires intrinsic value to be determined not just once, but at initial measurement date and each subsequent reporting date until exercise.

8.8.1 Intrinsic value method – the basic accounting treatment

Under the intrinsic value method:

(a) the entity measures the intrinsic value of the award at each reporting date between grant date and settlement (whether through exercise, forfeiture or lapse);

(b) at each reporting date during the vesting period the cumulative expense should be determined as the intrinsic value of the award at that date multiplied by the expired portion of the vesting period, with all changes in the cumulative expense recognised in profit or loss; and

(c) once options have vested, all changes in their intrinsic value until settlement should be recognised in profit or loss. *[IFRS 2.24(a)]*.

The cumulative expense during the vesting period, like that for awards measured at fair value, should always be based on the best estimate of the number of awards that will actually vest (see 6 above). However, the distinction between market vesting conditions, non-market vesting conditions and non-vesting conditions that would apply to equity-settled awards measured at fair value (see 6.1 to 6.4 above) does not apply in the case of awards measured at intrinsic value. *[IFRS 2.24(b)]*. In other words, where an award measured at intrinsic value is subject to a market condition or non-vesting condition that is not met, there is ultimately no accounting expense for that award. This is consistent with a model requiring constant remeasurement.

The cost of awards measured at intrinsic value is ultimately revised to reflect the number of awards that are actually exercised. However, during the vesting period the cost should be based on the number of awards estimated to vest and thereafter on the number of awards that have vested. In other words, any post-vesting forfeiture or lapse should not be anticipated, but should be accounted for as it occurs. *[IFRS 2.24(b)]*.

Example 30.33 illustrates the intrinsic value method.

Example 30.33: Intrinsic value method

At the beginning of year 1, an entity grants 1,000 share options to 50 employees.

The share options will vest at the end of year 3, provided the employees remain in service until then. The options can be exercised at the end of year 4, and then at the end of each subsequent year up to and including year 10. The exercise price, and the entity's grant date share price, is €60. At the date of grant, the entity concludes that it cannot estimate reliably the fair value of the share options granted.

At the end of year 1, the entity estimates that 80% of the share options will vest. At the end of year 2, the entity revises its estimate of the number of share options that it expects will vest to 86%.

During the vesting period, a total of seven employees leave, so that 43,000 share options vest.

The intrinsic value of the options, and the number of share options exercised during years 4-10, are as follows:

Year	Intrinsic value €	Number exercised
1	3	
2	5	
3	15	
4	28	6,000
5	40	8,000
6	30	5,000
7	36	9,000
8	45	8,000
9	48	5,000
10	55	2,000

The expense recognised under IFRS 2 will be as follows. In the period up to vesting the 'cumulative expense' methodology used in the examples in sections 6.1 to 6.4 above can be adopted to derive the expense for each period:

Year	Calculation of cumulative expense	Cumulative expense (€)	Expense for period (€)
1	50,000 options × €3 × 80% × 1/3	40,000	40,000
2	50,000 options × €5 × 86% × 2/3	143,333	103,333
3	43,000 options × €15	645,000	501,677

In years 4 to 10 it is more straightforward to calculate the expense directly. Since all options exercised during each year are exercised at the end of that year, the annual expense can be calculated as the change in intrinsic value during each year of the options outstanding at the *start* of the year.

Year		Expense for period (€)
4	43,000 options × €(28 – 15)	559,000
5	43,000 – 6,000 = 37,000 options × €(40 – 28)	444,000
6	37,000 – 8,000 = 29,000 options × €(30 – 40)	(290,000)
7	29,000 – 5,000 = 24,000 options × €(36 – 30)	144,000
8	24,000 – 9,000 = 15,000 options × €(45 – 36)	135,000
9	15,000 – 8,000 = 7,000 options × €(48 – 45)	21,000
10	7,000 – 5,000 = 2,000 options × €(55 – 48)	14,000

If, more realistically, the options had been exercisable, and were exercised, at other dates, it would have been necessary to record as an expense for those options the movement in intrinsic value from the start of the year until exercise date. For example, if the 6,000 options in year 4 had been exercised during the year when the intrinsic value was €20, the expense for that period would have been €511,000 comprising €481,000 change in value for the options outstanding at the end of year [37,000 options × €(28 – 15)] and €30,000 change in value of options exercised during the period [6,000 options × €(20 – 15)].

8.8.2 Modification, cancellation and settlement

The methodology of the intrinsic value method has the effect that modification or cancellation is dealt with automatically, and the rules for modification and cancellation of awards measured at fair value (see 7 above) therefore do not apply. *[IFRS 2.25]*.

Where an award accounted for at intrinsic value is settled in cash, the following provisions apply, which are broadly similar to the rules for settlement of awards accounted for at fair value.

If settlement occurs before vesting, the entity must 'recognise immediately the amount that would otherwise have been recognised for services received over the remainder of the vesting period'. *[IFRS 2.25(a)]*. The wording here is the same as that applicable to settlement of awards accounted for at fair value, which we discuss in more detail at 7.4.3 above.

Any payment made on settlement must be deducted from equity, except to the extent that it is greater than the intrinsic value of the award at settlement date. Any such excess is accounted for as an expense. *[IFRS 2.25(b)]*.

8.9 Awards with reload features

Some share options contain a reload feature (see 5.5.1 above). Reloads commonly provide that, where an exercise price is satisfied in shares of the issuing entity rather than cash, there is a new grant of at-the-money options over as many shares as are equal to the exercise price of the exercised option. For example, if there were 100 options with an exercise price of $10, and the new share price were $15, 67 options (€1,000 ÷ €15) would be re-issued.

Even though the reload feature (i.e. the possibility that additional options would be issued in the future) is a feature of the original option, and can be readily incorporated into the valuation of the original option using a lattice model, the IASB concluded that the fair value of a reload feature should not be incorporated into the estimate of the fair value of the award at grant date. As a result, subsequent grants of reload awards under the reload feature would be accounted for as new awards and measured on their respective grant dates. *[IFRS 2.BC188-192]*.

On the assumption that the exercise price of an award is at least the share price at grant date, the grant-date fair value of the reload award will generally be greater than the incremental value of the reload feature as at the date the original award was granted. This is because the reload award will only be granted if the original option is in-the-money and is exercised. As a result, the award would have increased in the period between the original grant date and the reload grant date, and the higher share price would be used to value the reload grant. However, from the perspective of the aggregate compensation cost, this result is mitigated by the fact that, as the value of the underlying share increases, fewer shares must be tendered to satisfy the exercise price requirement of the exercised option and, therefore, fewer reload options will be granted (as above when only 67 options are re-issued for the 100 originally issued).

If the reload feature were incorporated into the valuation of the original grant, then not only would a lower price be used, but the valuation would consider the possibility that the original option would never be exercised and, therefore, that the reload options would not be granted. Under the approach in IFRS 2, if the original award expires unexercised, no compensation cost results from the reload feature, so that the compensation cost is lower than would be the case if the value of the reload feature were incorporated into the measurement of the original award. Effectively, the approach in IFRS 2 incorporates subsequent share price changes into the valuation of a reload award.

8.10 Awards of equity instruments to a fixed monetary value

Entities may make an award of shares to a fixed monetary value (see 5.3.5 above). This is commonly found as part of a matching share award where an employee may be offered the choice of receiving cash or shares of an equivalent value, or a multiple of that value (see 15.1 below).

IFRS 2 does not address the valuation of such awards directly. Intuitively, it might seem obvious that an award which promises (subject to vesting conditions) shares to the value of €10,000 must have a grant date fair value of €10,000, adjusted for the time value of money, together with market conditions and non-vesting conditions. However, matters are not so clear-cut, as Example 30.34 illustrates:

Example 30.34: Award of shares to a fixed monetary value

On 1 January 2014, the reporting entity grants:

- to Employee A an award of 1,000 shares subject to remaining in employment until 31 December 2016; and
- to Employee B €10,000 subject to remaining in employment until 31 December 2016, to be paid in as many shares as are (on 31 December 2016) worth €10,000.

Both awards vest, and the share price on 31 December 2016 is €10, so that both employees receive 1,000 shares.

The IFRS 2 charge for A's award is clearly 1000 × the fair value as at 1 January 2014 of a share deliverable in three years' time. What is the charge for B's award – the same as for A's or €10,000, adjusted for the time value of money?

The Basis for Conclusions to IFRS 2 creates some confusion over this point. Paragraphs BC106 to BC118 discuss in general terms why IFRS 2 adopts a definition of equity instrument different from that in IAS 32. Paragraphs BC107 to BC109 particularly note that the IASB did not believe it appropriate that a fixed-cost award and a variable-cost award ultimately delivered in shares should be classified, and measured, (as would be the case under IAS 32) as, respectively, equity and a liability. *[IFRS 2.BC106-118]*.

Whilst the primary focus of the discussion in the Basis for Conclusions is whether variable equity-settled awards should be liabilities (as they would be under IAS 32) or equity (as they are under IFRS 2), the reference to measurement as well as classification of awards can be read as meaning that the IASB believed that two awards that ultimately deliver 1,000 shares (as in Example 30.34 above) should have the same grant date fair value.

If the same grant date fair value per share were used for both employees' awards, Employee B's award would have to be valued as the number of shares that actually vest (which would need to be continually re-estimated until vesting) multiplied by the fair value of a share at grant date. This would have the somewhat counter-intuitive outcome that, if the value of the entity's equity falls, the IFRS 2 charge increases (since more shares are needed to deliver €10,000 of value), whereas if the value of the entity's equity rises, the IFRS 2 charge falls (since fewer shares are needed to deliver €10,000 of value).

For this reason, many take the view that this not an appropriate analysis, since an award of 1,000 shares (where the recipient bears share price risk) is fundamentally different in nature to an award of shares to a given value (where the entity bears share price risk) which happens to translate into 1,000 shares at vesting.

Some argue that an award of shares to a given monetary amount contains a market condition, since the number of shares ultimately delivered (and therefore vesting) depends on the market price of the shares on the date of delivery. This allows the award to be valued at a fixed amount at grant date. We acknowledge that a literal reading of the definition of 'market condition' in IFRS 2 supports this view, but question whether this can really have been intended. In our view, the essential feature of a share-based payment transaction subject to a market condition must be that the employee's ultimate entitlement to the award depends on the share price.

In our view, in the absence of clear guidance in IFRS 2, entities may take a number of views on how to value awards of shares to a given value, but should adopt a consistent approach for all such awards.

9 CASH-SETTLED TRANSACTIONS

Throughout the discussion in this section, 'cash' should be read as including 'other assets' in accordance with the definition of a cash-settled share-based payment transaction (see 2.2.1 above).

9.1 Scope of requirements

Cash-settled share-based payment transactions include transactions such as:

- share appreciation rights (SARs), where employees are entitled to a cash payment equivalent to the gain that would have arisen from a holding of a particular number of shares from the date of grant to the date of exercise; or
- phantom options, where employees are entitled to a cash payment equivalent to the gain that would have been made by exercising options at a notional price over a notional number of shares and then selling the shares at the date of exercise. *[IFRS 2.31]*.

However, IFRS 2 looks beyond the simple issue of whether an award entitles an employee to receive instruments that are in form shares or options to the terms of those instruments. For example, an award of shares or options over shares whose terms provide for their redemption either mandatorily according to their terms (e.g. on cessation of employment) or at the employee's option would be treated as a cash-settled, not an equity-settled, award under IFRS 2. *[IFRS 2.31]*. This is consistent with the fact that IAS 32 would regard a share with these terms as a financial liability rather than an equity instrument of the issuer (see Chapter 43 at 4).

In some cases the boundary between equity-settled and cash-settled schemes may appear somewhat blurred, so that further analysis may be required to determine whether a particular arrangement is equity-settled or cash-settled. Some examples of such arrangements are discussed at 9.2 below.

9.2 What constitutes a cash-settled award?

There are a number of possible circumstances in which, on, or shortly after, settlement of an equity-settled award either:

- the entity incurs a cash outflow equivalent to that that would arise on cash-settlement (e.g. because it purchases shares in the market at fair value to deliver to counterparties); or
- the counterparty receives a cash inflow equivalent to that that would arise on cash-settlement (e.g. because the shares are sold in the market for cash on behalf of the counterparty).

Such situations raise the question of whether such schemes are in fact truly equity-settled or cash-settled.

Examples of relatively common mechanisms for delivering the cash-equivalent of an equity-settled award to employees are discussed below. It emerges from the analysis below that, in reality, IFRS 2 is driven by questions of form rather than substance. To put it rather crudely, what matters is often not so much whether the entity has written a cheque for the fair value of the award, but rather the name of the payee on the cheque.

The significance of this is that the analysis affects the profit or loss charge for the award, as illustrated by Example 30.35 below.

Example 30.35: Equity-settled award satisfied with market purchase of treasury shares

An entity awards an employee a free share with a fair value at grant date of £5 which has a fair value of £8 at vesting. At vesting the entity purchases a share in the market for £8 for delivery to the employee. If the scheme were treated as cash-settled, there would be a charge to profit or loss of £8 (the fair value at vesting date – see 9.3 below). If it were treated as equity-settled (as required in this case by IFRS 2), profit or loss would show a charge of only £5 (the fair value at grant date), with a further net charge of £3 in equity, comprising the £8 paid for the share accounted for as a treasury share (see Chapter 43 at 9) less the £5 credit to equity (being the credit entry corresponding to the £5 charge to profit or loss – see 4.2 above).

The analyses below all rely on a precise construction of the definition of a cash-settled share-based payment transaction, i.e. one 'in which the entity acquires goods or services *by incurring a liability to transfer cash or other assets to the supplier of those goods or services* for amounts that are based on the price (or value) of the entity's shares or other equity instruments of the entity' (emphasis added). *[IFRS 2 Appendix A]*. Thus, if the entity is not actually required – legally or constructively – to pay cash to the *counterparty*, there is no cash-settled transaction under IFRS 2, even though the arrangement may give rise to an external cash flow and, possibly, a liability under another standard.

9.2.1 Market purchases of own equity used to satisfy awards

It is common for an entity to choose to settle equity-settled transactions using shares previously purchased in the market rather than by issuing new shares. This does not mean that the transaction is cash-settled, since there is no obligation to deliver cash to the counterparty. *[IFRS 2.B48-49]*.

The purchase of own shares is accounted for in accordance with the provisions of IAS 32 relating to treasury shares and other transactions over own equity (see Chapter 43 at 9).

Some have raised the question of whether the entity should recognise some form of liability to repurchase own equity in situations where the entity has a stated policy of settling equity-settled transactions using previously purchased treasury shares. In our view, the normal provisions of IAS 32 apply. For example, a public commitment to settle equity-settled transactions by purchasing treasury shares is no different in substance to a commitment to a share buyback programme. There would be no question under IAS 32 of recognising a liability to repurchase own equity on the basis merely of a declared intention. It is only when the entity enters into a forward contract or a call option with a third party that some accounting recognition of a future share purchase may be required.

9.2.2 Market purchases of own equity following equity-settlement of award

It sometimes happens that an entity, having issued shares in settlement of an equity-settled transaction, will shortly thereafter purchase a similar number of its own shares in the market. This raises the question of whether such a scheme would be considered as in substance cash-settled.

In our view, further enquiry into the detailed circumstances of the market purchase is required in order to determine the appropriate analysis under IFRS 2.

Broadly speaking, so long as there is no obligation (explicit or implicit) for the entity to settle in cash with the counterparty, such arrangements will not require a scheme to be treated as cash-settled under IFRS 2. This will be the case even where the entity, as a means of managing the dilutive impact on earnings per share of equity-settlement, routinely buys back shares broadly equivalent to the number issued in settlement.

However, in our view, there might be situations in which post-settlement market share purchases are indicative of an obligation to the counterparty, such that treatment as a cash-settled scheme would be appropriate.

For example, the shares might be quoted in a market which is not very deep, or in which the entity itself is a major participant. If the entity were to create an expectation by employees that any shares awarded can always be liquidated immediately, because the entity will ensure that there is sufficient depth in the market to do so, it could well be appropriate to account for such a scheme as cash-settled. The treatment of schemes in which the entity has a choice of settlement, but has created an expectation of cash-settlement, provides a relevant analogy (see 10.2.1 below).

A more extreme example of such a situation would be where the entity has arranged for the shares delivered to the counterparty to be sold on the counterparty's behalf by a broker (see 9.2.3 below), but has at the same time entered into a contract to purchase those shares from the broker. In that situation, in our view, the substance is that:

- the entity has created an expectation by the counterparty of a right to receive cash; and
- the broker is no more than an agent paying that cash to the counterparty on behalf of the entity.

Accordingly, it would be appropriate to account for such an arrangement as a cash-settled award.

In a situation where the entity had pre-arranged to purchase some, but not all, the shares from the broker, in our view it would generally be appropriate to treat the award as cash-settled only to the extent of the shares subject to the purchase agreement.

9.2.3 Arrangements to sell employees' shares including 'broker settlement'

Many recipients of share awards, particularly employees in lower and middle ranking positions within an entity, do not wish to become long-term investors in the entity and prefer instead to realise any equity-settled awards in cash soon after receipt. In order to facilitate this, the entity may either sell the shares in the market on the employees' behalf or, more likely, arrange for a third party broker to do so.

Such an arrangement (sometimes referred to as 'broker settlement') does not of itself create a cash-settled award, provided that the entity has not created any obligation to the employees. If, however, the entity has either created an expectation among employees that it will step in to make good any lack of depth in the market, or has indeed itself contracted to repurchase the shares in question, that may well mean that analysis as a cash-settled scheme is more appropriate (see also 9.2.2 above).

Broker settlement arrangements raise a general concern – at least for regulators and auditors – that an entity may be masking what are really issues of shares to raise cash to pay its employees as sales of shares on behalf of employees. If an entity were simply to issue shares (or reissue treasury shares) for cash, and then use that cash to pay an employee's salary, the normal accounting treatment for such a transaction would be to credit equity with the proceeds of issue or reissue of shares, and to charge the payment to the employee to profit or loss.

By contrast, a sale of shares on behalf of an employee is undertaken by the entity as agent and does not give rise to an increase in equity and an expense, although an expense will be recognised for the award of shares under IFRS 2. However, the entity may enter into much the same transaction with a broker whether it is selling shares on its own behalf or on behalf of its employees. The challenge is therefore for the entity to be able to demonstrate the true economic nature of the transaction.

For this reason, some take the view that a sale of shares can be regarded as part of a broker settlement arrangement only if the shares are first legally registered in the name of the employee. Whilst we understand the concerns that lie behind this view, we nevertheless question whether legal registration is necessary to demonstrate a broker settlement arrangement. For example, suppose that 100 shares vest in each of

10 employees who all express a wish that the entity sell the shares on their behalf, and the entity then sells 1,000 treasury shares on behalf of the employees, but without first re-registering title to the shares to the employees. We do not believe that the entity should automatically be precluded from regarding this as a broker settlement arrangement, particularly where the treasury shares are held not by the entity directly but through an employee benefit trust or similar entity (see 12.3 below) that is permitted to hold or sell shares only for the benefit of employees.

By contrast, the entity might regularly purchase and sell treasury shares, but identify some of the sales as being undertaken on behalf of employees only after they have occurred. Such an arrangement, in our view, is more difficult to construe as a true broker-settlement arrangement.

Where shares are sold on behalf of an employee, they will typically attract transaction costs, such as brokerage fees or taxes. If such costs are borne by the entity, they should, in our view, be included within profit or loss as an additional component of employment costs, rather than deducted from equity as a cost of a transaction in own shares.

This highlights a commercial disadvantage of broker settlement arrangements. The entity may have to:

- purchase shares in the market (incurring transaction costs) on behalf of an employee who does not want them and then sell them back into the market on the employee's behalf (incurring more transaction costs); or
- sell shares in the market (incurring transaction costs) on behalf of an employee who does not want them and then buy them back in the market on behalf of another employee who does want them (incurring more transaction costs).

In order to avoid this, entities may try to structure arrangements with their brokers involving back-to-back sale and purchase contracts, under which shares are never physically delivered, but the entity makes a cash payment to the broker in purported settlement of the purchase of shares on behalf of the entity and the broker passes it on to the employee in purported settlement of the sale of the shares on behalf of the employee.

In our view, such arrangements cannot be seen as equity-settled transactions with broker settlement, but must be regarded as cash-settled share-based payment transactions, using the broker as paying agent.

Related issues are raised by the 'drag along' and 'tag along' rights that are often a feature of awards designed to reward employees for a successful flotation or other exit event (see 15.4.6 below).

9.2.4 *Economic compulsion for cash settlement (including unlisted company schemes)*

Some share-based payment awards by unlisted entities might appear to be equity-settled in form but, in our view, it is likely that a substantial number of such arrangements should be accounted for as cash-settled. This reflects either specific arrangements put in place for the employees to sell their shares or, more generally, the illiquid market in the shares which, in the absence of compelling evidence to the contrary, is likely to result in a cash payment at some stage.

This is similar to the assessment for awards where the agreement states that entities have a choice of settlement in equity or cash (see 10.2.1.A below).

9.3 Required accounting

9.3.1 Basic accounting treatment

It is clear that the ultimate cost of a cash-settled transaction must be the actual cash paid to the counterparty, which will be the fair value at settlement date. Moreover, the cumulative cost recognised until settlement is clearly a liability, not a component of equity.

The periodic determination of this liability is as follows:

- at each reporting date between grant and settlement the fair value of the award is determined in accordance with the specific requirements of IFRS 2;
- during the vesting period, the liability recognised at each reporting date is the IFRS 2 fair value of the award at that date multiplied by the expired portion of the vesting period;
- from the end of the vesting period until settlement, the liability recognised is the full fair value of the liability at the reporting date.

All changes in the liability are recognised in profit or loss for the period. *[IFRS 2.30-33, IG Example 12].* Where the cost of services received in a cash-settled transaction is recognised in the carrying amount of an asset (e.g. inventory) in the entity's statement of financial position, the carrying amount of the asset is not adjusted for changes in the fair value of the liability. *[IFRS 2.IG19].*

The fair value of the liability should be determined, initially and at each reporting date until it is settled, by applying an option pricing model, taking into account the terms and conditions on which the cash-settled transaction was granted, and the extent to which the employees have rendered service to date. It should be noted that IFRS 2 uses the term 'share appreciation rights' when referring to measurement of the liability but this should clearly be read as including any cash-settled share-based payment transaction. *[IFRS 2.33].*

This has the effect that, although the liability will ultimately be settled at its then intrinsic value, its measurement at reporting dates before settlement is based on its fair value. During the exposure period of ED 2, a number of respondents suggested that, for reasons of consistency and simplicity of calculation, cash-settled transactions should be measured at intrinsic value throughout their entire life. The IASB, while accepting these merits of the intrinsic value approach (together with the fact that it is also required under US GAAP), rejected it on the basis that, since it does not include a time value, it is not an adequate measure of either the liability or the cost of services consumed. *[IFRS 2.BC246-251].*

As noted at 5.5 above, the approach to determining the fair value of share-based payments continues to be that specified in IFRS 2 and share-based payments fall outside the scope of IFRS 13 which applies more generally to the measurement of fair value under IFRSs (see Chapter 14). *[IFRS 2.6A].*

9.3.2 Application of the accounting treatment

The treatment required by IFRS 2 for cash-settled transactions is illustrated by Example 30.36 (which is based on Example 12 in the implementation guidance accompanying IFRS 2). *[IFRS 2 IG Example 12]*.

Example 30.36: Cash-settled transaction

An entity grants 100 cash share appreciation rights (SARs) to each of its 500 employees, on condition that the employees remain in its employment for the next three years. The SARs can be exercised on the third, fourth and fifth anniversary of the grant date.

During year 1, 35 employees leave. The entity estimates that a further 60 will leave during years 2 and 3 (i.e. the award will vest in 405 employees).

During year 2, 40 employees leave and the entity estimates that a further 25 will leave during year 3 (i.e. the award will vest in 400 employees).

During year 3, 22 employees leave, so that the award vests in 403 employees. At the end of year 3, 150 employees exercise their SARs (leaving 253 employees still to exercise).

Another 140 employees exercise their SARs at the end of year 4, leaving 113 employees still to exercise, who do so at the end of year 5.

The entity estimates the fair value of the SARs at the end of each year in which a liability exists as shown below. The intrinsic values of the SARs at the date of exercise (which equal the cash paid out) at the end of years 3, 4 and 5 are also shown below.

Year	Fair value	Intrinsic value
	£	£
1	14.40	
2	15.50	
3	18.20	15.00
4	21.40	20.00
5		25.00

The entity will recognise the cost of this award as follows:

Year	Calculation of liability	Calculation of cash paid	Liability (£)	Cash paid (£)	Expense for period (£)*
1	405 employees × 100 SARs × £14.40 × 1/3		194,400	–	194,400
2	400 employees × 100 SARs × £15.50 × 2/3		413,333	–	218,933
3	253 employees × 100 SARs × £18.20	150 employees × 100 SARs × £15.00	460,460	225,000	272,127
4	113 employees × 100 SARs × £21.40	140 employees × 100 SARs × £20.00	241,820	280,000	61,360
5	–	113 employees × 100 SARs × £25.00	–	282,500	40,680

* Liability at end of period + cash paid in period – liability at start of period

The accounting treatment for cash-settled transactions is therefore (despite some similarities in the methodology) significantly different from that for equity-settled transactions. An important practical issue is that, for a cash-settled transaction, the entity must determine the fair value at each reporting date and not merely at grant date (and at the date of any subsequent modification or settlement) as would be the case for equity-settled transactions. However, as Example 30.36 shows, it is not actually necessary, although arguably required by IFRS 2, to determine the fair value of a cash-settled transaction at grant date, at least to determine the expense under IFRS 2. However, for entities subject to IAS 33 – *Earnings per Share* – the grant date fair value may be required in order to make the disclosures required by that standard – see Chapter 33 at 6.4.2.

IFRS 2 raises some issues of interpretation on detailed aspects of the methodology such as:

- determining the vesting period (see 9.3.2.A below);
- periodic allocation of cost (see 9.3.2.B below);
- treatment of non-market vesting conditions (see 9.3.2.C below);
- treatment of market conditions and non-vesting conditions (see 9.3.2.D below); and
- treatment of modification, cancellation and settlement (see 9.3.2.E below).

9.3.2.A Determining the vesting period

The rules for determining vesting periods are the same as those applicable to equity-settled transactions, as discussed in 6.1 to 6.4 above. Where an award vests immediately, IFRS 2 creates a presumption that, in the absence of evidence to the contrary, the award is in respect of services that have already been rendered, and should therefore be expensed in full at grant date. *[IFRS 2.32].*

Where cash-settled awards are made subject to vesting conditions (as in many cases they will be, particularly where payments to employees are concerned), IFRS 2 creates a presumption that they are a payment for services to be received in the future, during the 'vesting period', with the transaction being recognised during that period, as illustrated in Example 30.36 above. *[IFRS 2.32].*

9.3.2.B Periodic allocation of cost

IFRS 2 states that the required treatment for cash-settled transactions is simply to measure the fair value of the liability at each reporting date *[IFRS 2.30]*, which might suggest that the *full* fair value, and not just a time-apportioned part of it, should be recognised at each reporting date – as would be the case for any liability that is a financial instrument and measured at fair value under IAS 39.

However, the standard goes on to clarify that the liability is to be measured at an amount that reflects 'the extent to which employees have rendered service to date', and the cost is to be recognised 'as the employees render service'. *[IFRS 2.32-33].* This, together with IG Example 12 in IFRS 2 (the substance of which is reproduced as Example 30.36 above), indicates that a spreading approach is to be adopted.

9.3.2.C Non-market vesting conditions

As drafted, IFRS 2 does not specifically address the impact of vesting conditions in the context of cash-settled transactions – the provisions of IFRS 2 relating to vesting conditions are to be found in paragraphs 19 to 21 of IFRS 2, all of which fall under the main heading 'Equity-settled share-based payment transactions' immediately before paragraph 10.

Where a vesting condition is a minimum service period, IG Example 12 in IFRS 2 (broadly reproduced as Example 30.36 above) clearly indicates that, during the period to vesting, the liability should be estimated on the basis of the current best estimate of the number of awards that will vest, this estimate being made exactly as for an equity-settled transaction. Therefore, it appears that IFRS 2 does not require the probability of achieving a service condition to be directly reflected in the fair value of a cash-settled award but, instead, requires this to be taken into account in estimating the expense, as for an equity-settled award.

As regards other non-market performance conditions, in the absence of clear guidance in IFRS 2, we believe that an entity may adopt either of the following approaches:

- analogise to the treatment of service periods in IG Example 12 (see Example 30.36 above), basing the liability until vesting date on the current best estimate of the outcome of those conditions; or
- reflect the estimated outcome of the conditions as part of the fair value calculation.

As at the time of writing, a staff paper on this subject was to be discussed by the IFRS Interpretations Committee.

9.3.2.D Market conditions and non-vesting conditions

There is no specific guidance in IFRS 2 as to whether, in the case of a cash-settled transaction, a distinction is to be drawn between non-vesting conditions or vesting conditions that are market conditions and other non-market vesting conditions, as would be the case for an equity-settled transaction (see 6.2 to 6.4 above). In our view, no such distinction need be drawn, since a cash-settled transaction must ultimately reflect the amount of cash paid. A cash-settled award is required to be valued at each reporting date, so that there will be no cost for an award subject to a market condition or non-vesting condition that is not satisfied. This is different from the accounting model for equity-settled transactions with market conditions or non-vesting conditions, which can result in a cost being recognised for awards subject to a market or non-vesting condition that is not satisfied (see 6.3 and 6.4 above).

9.3.2.E Modification, cancellation and settlement

IFRS 2 provides no specific guidance on modification, cancellation and settlement of cash-settled awards. However, as cash-settled awards are accounted for using a full fair value model no such guidance is needed. It is clear that:

- where an award is modified, the liability recognised at and after the point of modification will be based on its new fair value, with the effect of any movement in the liability recognised immediately;
- where an award is cancelled the liability will be derecognised, with a credit immediately recognised in profit or loss; and
- where an award is settled, the liability will be derecognised, and any gain or loss on settlement immediately recognised in profit or loss.

9.4 Modification of award from equity-settled to cash-settled or from cash-settled to equity-settled

An entity will sometimes modify the terms of an award in order to change the manner of settlement. In other words, an award that at grant date was equity-settled is modified so as to become cash-settled, or *vice versa.*

IFRS 2 provides no explicit guidance on such modifications. However, we believe that it is possible to arrive at a reasonable approach by analogy to the provisions of IFRS 2 in respect of:

- the modification of equity-settled awards during the vesting period (see 7.3 above);
- the addition of a cash-settlement alternative to an equity-settled award after grant date (see 10.1.4 below);
- the settlement of equity-settled awards in cash (see 7.4 above); and
- the settlement in equity of awards where the entity has a choice of settlement, but where the awards have been accounted for as cash-settled during the vesting period (see 10.2 below).

9.4.1 *Equity-settled award modified to cash-settled*

This section focuses solely on a change of settlement method rather than on any other modifications to an equity-settled award. If other modifications are made to an award (see 7.3 above) at the same time as a change from equity- to cash-settlement there is no clear guidance in IFRS 2 as to the sequence in which the accounting for the other modifications and for the change of settlement method should be applied. In the absence of clear guidance, we believe that either sequence is acceptable.

Drawing on the principles within the guidance referred to at 9.4 above, in our view there are two alternative approaches to accounting for the modification of an award from equity-settled to cash-settled during the vesting period. The first approach is based more closely on the IFRS 2 treatment for the modification of an equity-settled award (see 7.3 above) and the second on that for the repurchase or settlement in cash of an equity instrument (see 7.4 above).

Both approaches take into account IG Example 9 in the implementation guidance to IFRS 2 (see 10.1.4 below) which shows the recognition of an expense for the post-modification remeasurement of the cash-settlement alternative in addition to an expense for the full grant date fair value of the equity-settled arrangement. Although this Example reflects a choice of settlement by the counterparty, rather than the elimination of a method of settlement (as is the case in a modification from equity-settlement to cash-settlement), we believe that an analogy may be drawn between the two situations because the addition of a cash alternative for the counterparty effectively results in the award being treated as cash-settled from the date of modification.

The two approaches are discussed in more detail below and illustrated in Example 30.37. In our view, either approach is acceptable in the absence of clear guidance in IFRS 2 but the choice of approach should be applied consistently to all such modifications.

Both approaches require the recognition, as a minimum, of an IFRS 2 expense which comprises the following elements:

- the grant date fair value of the original equity-settled award (see 7.3 above); plus
- any incremental fair value arising from the modification of that award (see 7.1 above); plus
- any remeasurement of the liability between its fair value at the modification date and the amount finally settled (see 10.1.4 below).

Over the vesting period as a whole, both approaches result in the same total IFRS 2 expense and liability/cash settlement amount with the net overall difference between the two being an adjustment to equity. However, the timing of recognition of any incremental fair value arising on modification will differ under the two approaches, as explained below.

Approach 1

- At the date of modification a liability is recognised based on the fair value of the cash-settled award as at that date and the extent to which the vesting period has expired.
- The entire corresponding debit is taken to equity. Any incremental fair value of the cash-settled award over that of the equity-settled award as at the modification date will be expensed over the period from the date of modification to the date of settlement of the cash-settled award (i.e. no expense is recognised at the date of modification).
- The total fair value of the cash-settled award is remeasured through profit or loss on an ongoing basis between the date of modification and the date of settlement.

As Approach 1 is based on the accounting treatment for a modification of an equity-settled award, no incremental fair value is recognised as an expense at the modification date. This means that, in cases where the fair value of the modified award is higher at the date of modification than that of the original award, the reduction in equity at the date of modification will be higher than the proportionate fair value at that date of the original equity-settled award. This situation reverses over the remainder of the vesting period when an expense (and corresponding credit to equity) will be recognised for the incremental fair value of the modified award.

Approach 2

- As for Approach 1, at the date of modification a liability is recognised based on the fair value of the cash-settled award as at that date and the extent to which the vesting period has expired.
- Unlike Approach 1, the corresponding debit is taken to equity only to the extent of the fair value of the original equity-settled award as at the date of modification. Any incremental fair value of the cash-settled award over the equity-settled award as at the modification date is expensed immediately on modification to the extent that the vesting period has expired. The remainder of any incremental value is expensed over the period from the date of modification to the date of settlement.
- As for Approach 1, the total fair value of the cash-settled award is remeasured through profit or loss on an ongoing basis between the date of modification and the date of settlement.

Approach 2 is based on the accounting treatment for the repurchase of an equity instrument where a reduction in equity up to the fair value of the equity instrument is recognised as at the date of repurchase with any incremental fair value of the repurchase arrangement being treated as an expense. Whilst Approach 2 avoids the potential problem of an immediate reduction in equity in excess of the fair value of the equity-settled award, its settlement approach could be seen as diverging from the basic IFRS 2 treatment for the modification of an equity-settled award where none of the incremental fair value arising on a modification is expensed at the date of modification.

As noted at the start of this section, the Approaches outlined above are based on the specific principles referred to at 9.4 above. In the absence of clear guidance in the standard, other interpretations of the appropriate expense and equity adjustment are also possible. For example, in relation to the cash-settled award, the Approaches outlined above expense only the difference between the final settlement amount and the full fair value of the liability at the modification date, with the remainder adjusted through equity. Some, however, take the view that it is more appropriate to follow the accounting treatment for cash-settled awards and to expense the entire remeasurement of the liability from the amount recognised for a part-vested award at modification date to the amount finally settled.

Example 30.37: Modification of equity-settled award to cash-settled award

A Modified award with same fair value as original award

On 1 January 2014 an entity granted an equity-settled award, with a fair value at that date of €500, and vesting if the employee is still in service on 31 December 2017. On 1 January 2016, the award is modified so as to become cash-settled, but its terms are otherwise unchanged. The fair value at that date of both alternatives is €150. The liability is actually settled for €180 on 31 December 2017.

	Approach 1			Approach 2		
	Expense	Equity	Liability	Expense	Equity	Liability
	€	€	€	€	€	€
Two years ended 31.12.2015	250	(250)	–	250	(250)	–
1.1.2016 – modification	–	75	(75)	–	75	(75)
Two years ended 31.12.2017	280	(175)	(105)	280	(175)	(105)
Totals	530	(350)	(180)	530	(350)	(180)

During 2014 and 2015 the entity recognises a cumulative expense of €250, being the proportion of the grant date fair value of the equity-settled award of €500 attributable to 2/4 of the vesting period.

At 1 January 2016, it is necessary to recognise a liability of €75 (€150 × 2/4 – see 9.3.2 above). The full amount of this liability is recognised as a reduction in equity under both Approaches as there is no difference between the fair value of the original and modified awards as at the modification date.

As the award is continuing, there is no acceleration at the modification date of the as yet unrecognised amount of the grant date fair value of the original award (€250, being €500 × 2/4), as would occur in an immediate settlement (see 7.4 above).

During 2016 and 2017 (the period from modification to settlement date), the entity recognises an increase of €105 in the fair value of the liability (€180 – €75). During this period it also recognises employee costs totalling €280, being the remaining grant date fair value of €250 (€500 total less €250 expensed prior to modification) plus the post-modification remeasurement of the liability of €30 (€180-€150). The balance of €175 is credited to equity.

In total the entity recognises an expense of €530, being the original grant date fair value of the equity-settled award of €500 plus the post-modification remeasurement of the liability of €30. This adjustment of €30 is consistent with the approach taken in IG Example 9 in the implementation guidance to IFRS 2 (see 10.1.4 and Example 30.40 below).

B Modified award with greater fair value than original award

On 1 January 2014 an entity granted an equity-settled award, with a fair value at that date of €500, and vesting if the employee is still in service on 31 December 2017. On 1 January 2016, the award is modified so as to become cash-settled, with the new award having a higher fair value than the original award. At that date, the fair value of the original award is €150, but that of the cash-settled replacement award is €170. The liability is actually settled for €200 on 31 December 2017.

	Approach 1			Approach 2		
	Expense	Equity	Liability	Expense	Equity	Liability
	€	€	€	€	€	€
Two years ended 31.12.2015	250	(250)	–	250	(250)	–
1.1.2016 – modification	–	85	(85)	10	75	(85)
Two years ended 31.12.2017	300	(185)	(115)	290	(175)	(115)
Totals	550	(350)	(200)	550	(350)	(200)

During 2014 and 2015 the entity recognises a cumulative expense of €250, being the proportion of the grant date fair value of the equity-settled award of €500 attributable to 2/4 of the vesting period.

At 1 January 2016, it is necessary to recognise a liability of €85 (€170 × 2/4 – see 9.3.2 above). Under Approach 1 the difference between the fair value of the original equity-settled award and the modified award (€20 in total) is not recognised immediately as an expense but is spread over the remainder of the vesting period (i.e. starting from the date of modification). The liability of €85 is therefore recognised as a reduction in equity. Under Approach 2, the difference between the fair value of the original equity-settled award and the modified award is expensed immediately to the extent that the vesting period has already expired (€20 × 2/4) with the remainder being expensed in the post-modification period.

As the award is continuing, there is no acceleration at the modification date of the as yet unrecognised amount of the grant date fair value of the original award (€250, being €500 × 2/4) as would occur in an immediate settlement (see 7.4 above).

During 2016 and 2017 (the period from modification to settlement date), the entity recognises an increase of €115 in the fair value of the liability (€200 – €85). During this period, under Approach 1 it also recognises employee costs totalling €300, being the remaining grant date fair value of €250 (€500 total less €250 expensed prior to modification) plus the incremental modification fair value of €20 (€170-€150) plus the remeasurement of the liability of €30 (€200-€170) between modification date and settlement date. The balance of €185 is credited to equity. For Approach 2, the expense and the credit to equity during this period are €10 less than under Approach 1 because a proportionate amount of the incremental fair value was expensed immediately at the modification date.

In total the entity recognises an expense of €550, being the original grant date fair value of the equity-settled award of €500 plus the incremental fair value of €20 arising on modification of the award plus the post-modification remeasurement of the liability of €30. This remeasurement adjustment of €30 is consistent with the approach taken in IG Example 9 in the implementation guidance to IFRS 2 (see 10.1.4 and Example 30.40 below).

C Modified award with lower fair value than original award

On 1 January 2014 an entity granted an equity-settled award, with a fair value at that date of €500, and vesting if the employee is still in service on 31 December 2017. On 1 January 2016, the award is modified so as to become cash-settled, with the new award having a lower fair value than the original award. At that date, the fair value of the original award is €150, but that of the cash-settled replacement award is €130. The liability is actually settled for €180 on 31 December 2017.

	Approach 1			Approach 2		
	Expense	Equity	Liability	Expense	Equity	Liability
	€	€	€	€	€	€
Two years ended 31.12.2015	250	(250)	–	250	(250)	–
1.1.2016 – modification	–	65	(65)	–	65	(65)
Two years ended 31.12.2017	300	(185)	(115)	300	(185)	(115)
Totals	550	(370)	(180)	550	(370)	(180)

During 2014 and 2015 the entity recognises a cumulative expense of €250, being the proportion of the grant date fair value of the equity-settled award of €500 attributable to 2/4 of the vesting period.

At 1 January 2016, it is necessary to recognise a liability of €65 (€130 × 2/4 – see 9.3.2 above). The full amount of this liability is recognised as a reduction in equity under both Approaches as the fair value of the modified award is lower than that of the original award. No gain is recognised for the reduction in fair value consistent with the general principle in IFRS 2 that the cost recognised for an equity-settled award must be at least the grant date fair value of the award.

As the award is continuing, there is no acceleration at the modification date of the as yet unrecognised amount of the grant date fair value of the original award (€250, being €500 × 2/4) as would occur in an immediate settlement (see 7.4 above).

During 2016 and 2017 (the period from modification to settlement date), the entity recognises an increase of €115 in the fair value of the liability (€180 – €65). During this period it also recognises employee costs totalling €300, being the remaining grant date fair value of €250 (€500 total less €250 expensed prior to modification) plus the remeasurement of the liability of €50 (€180-€130) between modification date and settlement date. The balance of €185 is credited to equity.

In total the entity recognises an expense of €550, being the original grant date fair value of the equity-settled award of €500 plus the post-modification remeasurement of the liability of €50. This adjustment of €50 is consistent with the approach taken in IG Example 9 in the implementation guidance to IFRS 2 (see 10.1.4 and Example 30.40 below).

Whilst the overall liability in Scenario C is the same as that in Scenario A above, the total expense and overall net credit to equity are higher even though the cash-settled award had a lower fair value at the modification date than that in Scenario A. This might appear illogical but is consistent with the approach in IG Example 9 and the requirement to recognise, as a minimum, the grant date fair value of the original equity-settled award together with any post-modification change in the fair value of the liability.

D Modified award with greater fair value than original award but settled for less than modification date fair value

On 1 January 2014 an entity granted an equity-settled award, with a fair value at that date of €500, and vesting if the employee is still in service on 31 December 2017. On 1 January 2016, the award is modified so as to become cash-settled, with the new award having a higher fair value than the original award. At that date, the fair value of the original award is €150, but that of the cash-settled replacement award is €170. The liability is actually settled for €125 on 31 December 2017.

	Approach 1			Approach 2		
	Expense	Equity	Liability	Expense	Equity	Liability
	€	€	€	€	€	€
Two years ended 31.12.2015	250	(250)	–	250	(250)	–
1.1.2016 – modification	–	85	(85)	10	75	(85)
Two years ended 31.12.2017	225	(185)	(40)	215	(175)	(40)
Totals	475	(350)	(125)	475	(350)	(125)

During 2014 and 2015 the entity recognises a cumulative expense of €250, being the proportion of the grant date fair value of the equity-settled award of €500 attributable to 2/4 of the vesting period.

At 1 January 2016, it is necessary to recognise a liability of €85 (€170 × 2/4 – see 9.3.2 above). Under Approach 1 the difference between the fair value of the original equity-settled award and the modified award (€20 in total) is not recognised immediately as an expense but is spread over the remainder of the vesting period (i.e. starting from the date of modification). The liability of €85 is therefore recognised as a reduction in equity. Under Approach 2, the difference between the fair value of the original equity-settled award and the modified award is expensed immediately to the extent that the vesting period has already expired (€20 × 2/4) with the remainder being expensed in the post-modification period.

As the award is continuing, there is no acceleration at the modification date of the as yet unrecognised amount of the grant date fair value of the original award (€250, being €500 × 2/4) as would occur in an immediate settlement (see 7.4 above).

During 2016 and 2017 (the period from modification to settlement date), the entity recognises an increase of €40 in the fair value of the liability (€125 – €85). During this period, under Approach 1 it also recognises employee costs totalling €225, being the remaining grant date fair value of €250 (€500 total less €250 expensed prior to modification) plus the incremental modification fair value of €20 less a reduction of €45 (€170-€125) in the fair value of the liability since modification date. The balance of €185 is credited to equity. For Approach 2, the expense and the credit to equity during this period are €10 less than under Approach 1 because a proportionate amount of the incremental fair value was expensed immediately at the modification date.

In total the entity recognises an expense of €475, being the original grant date fair value of the equity-settled award of €500 plus the incremental fair value of €20 arising on modification of the award less the post-modification remeasurement of the liability of €45. This remeasurement adjustment of €45 is consistent with the approach taken in IG Example 9 in the implementation guidance to IFRS 2 (see 10.1.4 and Example 30.40 below).

9.4.2 *Cash-settled award modified to equity-settled*

In the absence of specific guidance for modifications from cash-settlement to equity-settlement, we believe that it is appropriate to draw on the guidance in IFRS 2 for the settlement in equity of awards where there is a choice of settlement, but which have been accounted for as cash-settled during the vesting period (see 10.1.3.B and 10.2 below). Essentially, IFRS 2 requires the liability to be remeasured to fair value at the date of settlement and transferred to equity. Any excess of the fair value of the equity instruments used to settle the award over the fair value of the liability is recognised in profit or loss. This principle can be adapted to the modification of an award from cash- to equity-settlement so that, in effect, the original cash-settled award is treated as having been cancelled and replaced with an equity-settled award.

Within this overall approach, we believe that there are two alternative methodologies for the recognition of any incremental fair value of the equity-settled award as measured at the date of modification and an accounting policy choice may be made to recognise the excess either:

- immediately in profit or loss for the vested portion of the award (an approach that follows more closely the requirements of settlement accounting); or
- over the remaining vesting period (an approach that combines settlement accounting with the spreading approach applied when an equity-settled award is modified – see 7.3 above).

The two methodologies result in the same total expense and credit to equity by the end of the vesting period and differ only in the timing of recognition of part of the expense. Example 30.38 below illustrates the two approaches.

The Interpretations Committee has discussed the situation set out in Scenario B of Example 30.38 and a summary of the discussions is included below.

Example 30.38: Modification of cash-settled award to equity-settled award

A Modified award with same fair value as original award

In this situation there is no difference between accounting alternatives 1 and 2.

On 1 January 2014 an entity granted a cash-settled award, vesting over four years. On 1 January 2016, the award is modified so as to become equity-settled, but its terms are otherwise unchanged. The fair value of both alternatives at that date is €150.

As at 1 January 2016, the entity will have recognised a liability of €75 (€150 × 2/4 – see 9.3.2 above). This is transferred to equity. As there is no difference between the fair value of the original cash-settled award and the modified award, no further expense is recognised:

		€	€
1.1.2016	Liability	75	
	Equity		75

The remainder of the fair value of the equity-settled award, measured as at the date of modification, of €75 (€150 – €75) is recognised in profit or loss over the remaining vesting period, with a corresponding credit to equity:

		€	€
Two years ended 31.12.2017	Employee costs	75	
	Equity		75

B Modified award with greater fair value than original award

On 1 January 2014 an entity granted a cash-settled award, vesting over four years. On 1 January 2016, the award is modified so as to become equity-settled. At that date, the fair value of the original award is €150, but that of the equity-settled replacement award is €190.

Accounting alternative 1: immediate recognition of increase in fair value as an expense

As at 1 January 2016, the entity will have recognised a liability of €75 (€150 × 2/4 – see 9.3.2 above). This is transferred to equity. The fair values of the original and modified awards, to the extent that they have vested, must be compared. These are respectively €75 (€150 × 2/4) and €95 (€190 × 2/4). The increase in value of €20 is recognised immediately as an expense at the date of modification, with a corresponding credit to equity:

		€	€
1.1.2016	Employee costs	20	
	Liability	75	
	Equity		95

The remainder of the fair value of the equity award, measured as at the date of modification, of €95 (€190 – €95) is recognised in profit or loss over the remaining two year vesting period from the date of modification (as in A above):

		€	€
Two years ended 31.12.2017	Employee costs	95	
	Equity		95

Accounting alternative 2: recognition of increase in fair value as an expense over the remainder of the vesting period

As at 1 January 2016, the entity will have recognised a liability of €75 (€150 × 2/4 – see 9.3.2 above). This is transferred to equity. The fair values of the original and modified awards, to the extent that they have vested, must be compared. These are respectively €75 (€150 × 2/4) and €95 (€190 × 2/4). The liability of €75 is transferred to equity at the date of modification and the increase in value of €20, is recognised as an expense over the two years to 31 December 2017, with a corresponding credit to equity (together with the remainder of the cost of the equity-settled award of €95 (€190 × 2/4)):

		€	€
1.1.2016	Liability	75	
	Equity		75
Two years ended 31.12.2017	Employee costs	115	
	Equity		115

C ***Modified award with lower fair value than original award***

In this situation there is no difference between accounting alternatives 1 and 2.

On 1 January 2014 an entity granted a cash-settled award, vesting over four years. On 1 January 2016, the award is modified so as to become equity-settled. At that date, the fair value of the original award is €150, but that of the equity-settled replacement award is only €130.

As at 1 January 2016, the entity will have recognised a liability and employee costs of €75 (€150 × 2/4 – see 9.3.2 above). The fair values of the original and modified awards, to the extent that they have vested, are compared. These are respectively €75 (€150 × 2/4) and €65 (€130 × 2/4). Although the fair value of the modified award is lower than that of the original award, no gain is recognised. This is considered to be consistent with the requirements of IFRS 2 (see 10.1.3.B below) for an award that has been accounted for as cash-settled during the vesting period but which is settled with equity instruments (See also Chapter 43 at 7):

		€	€
1.1.2016	Liability	75	
	Equity		75

The remainder of the fair value of the equity award, measured as at the date of modification, of €65 (€130 × 2/4) is recognised in profit or loss over the remaining two year vesting period from the date of modification:

		€	€
Two years ended 31.12.2017	Employee costs	65	
	Equity		65

The Interpretations Committee discussed modification from cash- to equity-settlement in May 2011 but its discussions were limited to consideration of an arrangement where a cash-settled award is cancelled and replaced with an equity-settled award with a higher fair value (similar to Scenario B in Example 30.38 above).

In addition to an approach based on settlement accounting (as discussed above and illustrated in Example 30.38), the Interpretations Committee considered whether the requirements in IFRS 2 for the modification of equity-settled awards could be fully applied by analogy to cash-settled awards that become equity-settled. It did not comment on the relative merits or shortcomings of the two approaches and simply observed that the amendments needed to IFRS 2 to provide specific guidance on this matter would be beyond the scope of the *Annual Improvements* process and better suited to a separate IASB project.[26]

Having asked its staff to update the analysis of the issue,[27] the Interpretations Committee considered the matter again in March 2013. It noted that research indicated that the issue is widespread with significant diversity of accounting treatment, primarily because IFRS 2 lacks guidance on a modification that changes the classification of a share-based payment award. The Interpretations Committee tentatively decided to recommend that the IASB make narrow-scope amendments to IFRS 2 based on the following summary (which takes the settlement accounting approach):

- the cancellation of a cash-settled award followed by a replacement equity-settled award should be viewed as a modification of the award 'because the economic substance of cancellation followed by replacement is the same as the modification of the terms of the original share-based award. This is consistent with the requirements in paragraph 28(c) of IFRS 2, which requires replacement of an equity-settled award to be accounted for in the same manner as a modification of the original grant of equity instruments';
- the new equity-settled award should be measured by reference to its modification date fair value, because the modification date should be viewed as the grant date of the new award;
- the liability for the original cash-settled award should be derecognised upon the modification and the equity-settled replacement award should be recognised to the extent that service has been rendered up to the modification date;
- the unrecognised portion of the modification date fair value of the new equity-settled award should be recognised as an expense over the remaining vesting period as the services are rendered; and
- the difference between the carrying amount of the liability and the amount recognised in equity as at the modification date should be recorded in profit or loss immediately in order to show that the liability has been remeasured to its fair value at the settlement date in accordance with paragraph 30 of IFRS 2.[28]

The accounting treatment recommended by the Interpretations Committee is consistent with Alternative 1 in scenario B of Example 30.38 above.

It is worth noting that the Interpretations Committee has not specifically addressed the reverse situation, i.e. where the replacement award has a lower fair value than the original award as at the modification date (Scenario C in Example 30.38 above), and it is therefore unclear whether there would be a credit to profit or loss for the difference between the carrying amount of the liability and the value of the replacement award. The timing of any future discussions by the IASB on changes of classification of share-based payment arrangements is not yet known.

10 TRANSACTIONS WITH EQUITY AND CASH ALTERNATIVES

It is common for share-based payment transactions (particularly those with employees) to provide either the entity or the counterparty with the choice of settling the transaction either in shares (or other equity instruments) or in cash (or other assets). The general principle of IFRS 2 is that a transaction with a cash alternative, or the components of that transaction, should be accounted for:

(a) as a cash-settled transaction if, and to the extent that, the entity has incurred a liability to settle in cash or other assets; or

(b) as an equity-settled transaction if, and to the extent that, no such liability has been incurred. *[IFRS 2.34].*

More detailed guidance is provided as to how that general principle should be applied to transactions:

- where the counterparty has choice of settlement (see 10.1 below); and
- where the entity has choice of settlement (see 10.2 below).

10.1 Transactions where the counterparty has choice of settlement

Where the counterparty has the right to elect for settlement in either shares or cash, IFRS 2 regards the transaction as a compound transaction to which split accounting must be applied. The general principle is that the transaction must be analysed into a liability component (the counterparty's right to demand settlement in cash) and an equity component (the counterparty's right to demand settlement in shares). *[IFRS 2.35]*. Once split, the two components are accounted for separately. Confusingly, the methodology of split accounting required by IFRS 2 is somewhat different from that required by IAS 32 for issuers of other compound instruments (see Chapter 43 at 6).

A practical issue is that, where a transaction gives the counterparty a choice of settlement, it will be necessary to establish a fair value for the liability component both at grant date and at each subsequent reporting date until settlement. By contrast, in the case of transactions that can be settled in cash only, no fair value is required at grant date, but a fair value is required at each subsequent reporting date until settlement (see 9 above). However, for entities subject to IAS 33, the grant date fair value is required in order to make the disclosures required by that standard – see Chapter 33 at 6.4.2.

10.1.1 Transactions in which the fair value is measured directly

Transactions with non-employees are normally measured by reference to the fair value of goods and services supplied at service date (i.e. the date at which the goods or services are supplied) – see 4 and 5 above.

Accordingly where an entity enters into such a transaction where the counterparty has choice of settlement, it determines the fair value of the liability component at service date. The equity component is the difference between the fair value (at service date) of the goods or services received and the fair value of the liability component. *[IFRS 2.35]*.

10.1.2 Other transactions

All other transactions, including those with employees, are measured by reference to the fair value of the instruments issued at 'measurement date', being grant date in the case of transactions with employees and service date in the case of transactions with non-employees *[IFRS 2 Appendix A]* – see 4.1 and 5.1 above.

The fair value should take into account the terms and conditions on which the rights to cash or equity instruments were issued. *[IFRS 2.36]*. IFRS 2 does not elaborate further on this, but we assume that the IASB intends a reporting entity to apply:

- as regards the equity component of the transaction, the provisions of IFRS 2 relating to the impact of terms and conditions on the valuation of equity-settled transactions (see 4 to 6 above); and

- as regards the liability component of the transaction, the provisions of IFRS 2 relating to the impact of terms and conditions on the valuation of cash-settled transactions (see 9.3 above).

The entity should first measure the fair value of the liability component and then that of the equity component. The fair value of the equity component must be reduced to take into account the fact that the counterparty must forfeit the right to receive cash in order to receive shares. In practice, IG Example 13 in IFRS 2 (the substance of which is reproduced as Example 30.39 below) suggests that this will be done by establishing the fair value of the equity alternative and subtracting from it the fair value of the liability component. The sum of the two components is the fair value of the whole compound instrument. *[IFRS 2.37]*.

In many share-based payment transactions with a choice of settlement, the value of the share and cash alternatives is equal. The counterparty will have the choice between (say) 1,000 shares or the cash value of 1,000 shares. This will mean that the fair value of the liability component is equal to that of the transaction as a whole, so that the fair value of the equity component is zero. In other words, the transaction is accounted for as if it were a cash-settled transaction.

However, in some jurisdictions it is not uncommon, particularly in transactions with employees, for the equity-settlement alternative to have more value. For example, an employee might be able to choose at vesting between the cash value of 1,000 shares immediately or 2,000 shares (often subject to further conditions such as a minimum holding period, or a further service period). In such cases the equity component will have an independent value. *[IFRS 2.37]*. Such schemes are discussed in more detail at 15.1 below.

10.1.3 Accounting treatment

10.1.3.A During vesting period

Having established a fair value for the liability and equity components as set out in 10.1.1 and 10.1.2 above, the entity accounts for the liability component according to the rules for cash-settled transactions (see 9 above) and for the equity component according to the rules for equity-settled transactions (see 4 to 8 above). *[IFRS 2.38]*.

Example 30.39 below illustrates the accounting treatment for a transaction with an employee (as summarised in 10.1.2 above) where the equity component has a fair value independent of the liability component.

Example 30.39: Award with employee choice of settlement with different fair values for cash-settlement and equity-settlement

An entity grants to an employee an award with the right to choose settlement in either:

- 1,000 phantom shares, i.e. a right to a cash payment equal to the value of 1,000 shares, or
- 1,200 shares.

Vesting is conditional upon the completion of three years' service. If the employee chooses the share alternative, the shares must be held for three years after vesting date.

At grant date, the entity estimates that the fair value of the share alternative, after taking into account the effects of the post-vesting transfer restrictions, is €48 per share. The fair value of the cash alternative is estimated as:

	€
Grant date	50
Year 1	52
Year 2	55
Year 3	60

The grant date fair value of the equity alternative is €57,600 (1,200 shares × €48). The grant date fair value of the cash alternative is €50,000 (1,000 phantom shares × €50). Therefore the fair value of the equity component excluding the right to receive cash is €7,600 (€57,600 – €50,000). The entity recognises a cost based on the following amounts.

	Equity component			Liability component		
Year	Calculation of cumulative expense	Cumulative expense (€)	Expense for year (€)	Calculation of cumulative expense	Cumulative expense (€)	Expense for year (€)
1	€7,600 × 1/3	2,533	2,533	1,000 phantoms × €52 × 1/3	17,333	17,333
2	€7,600 × 2/3	5,066	2,533	1,000 phantoms × €55 × 2/3	36,667	19,334
3	€7,600	7,600	2,534	1,000 phantoms × €60	60,000	23,333

This generates the following accounting entries.

	€	€
Year 1		
Profit or loss (employment costs)	19,866	
Liability		17,333
Equity		2,533
Year 2		
Profit or loss (employment costs)	21,867	
Liability		19,334
Equity		2,533
Year 3		
Profit or loss (employment costs)	25,867	
Liability		23,333
Equity		2,534

The above Example is based on IG Example 13 in IFRS 2, in which the fair value of the cash alternative is treated as being the share price at each reporting date. This is clearly an error of principle in the Example in IFRS 2 since, as discussed more fully at 9 above, the fair value of a cash award is not the same as the share price, a point reinforced by IG Example 12 in IFRS 2 (the basis for Example 30.36 at 9.3.2 above). Accordingly, in adapting IG Example 13 as Example 30.39 above, we have deliberately described the numbers used in respect of the liability component as 'fair value' and not as the 'share price'. *[IFRS 2 IG Example 13].*

Example 30.39 also ignores the fact that transactions of this type often have different vesting periods for the two settlement alternatives. For instance, the employee might have been offered:

(a) the cash equivalent of 1,000 shares in three years' time subject to performance conditions; or

(b) subject to the performance criteria in (a) above being met over three years, 3,000 shares after a further two years' service.

IFRS 2 offers no guidance as to how such transactions are to be accounted for. Presumably, however, the equity component would be recognised over a five year period and the liability component over a three year period. This is considered further in the discussion of 'matching' share awards at 15.1 below.

10.1.3.B Settlement

At the date of settlement, the liability component is restated to fair value. If the counterparty elects for settlement in equity, the liability is transferred to equity as consideration for the equity instruments issued. If the liability is settled in cash, the cash is obviously applied to reduce the liability. *[IFRS 2.39-40].* In other words, if the transaction in Example 30.39 above had been settled in shares the accounting entry would have been:

	€	€
Liability*	60,000	
Equity†		60,000

* There is no need to remeasure the liability in this case as it has already been stated at fair value at vesting date, which is the same as settlement date.

† The precise allocation of this amount within equity, and its impact on distributable reserves, will depend on a number of factors, including jurisdictional legal requirements, which are not discussed here.

If the transaction had been settled in cash the entry would simply have been:

	€	€
Liability	60,000	
Cash		60,000

If the transaction is settled in cash, any amount taken to equity during the vesting period (€7,600 in Example 30.39 above) is not adjusted. However, the entity may transfer it from one component of equity to another (see 4.2 above). *[IFRS 2.40].*

10.1.4 Transactions with cash-settlement alternative for employee introduced after grant date

Such transactions are not specifically addressed in the main body of IFRS 2. However, IG Example 9 in the implementation guidance does address this issue, in the context of the rules for the modification of awards discussed in 7 above. The substance of this example is reproduced as Example 30.40 below. *[IFRS 2 IG Example 9].*

Example 30.40: Award with employee cash-settlement alternative introduced after grant

At the beginning of year 1, the entity grants 10,000 shares with a fair value of $33 per share to a senior executive, conditional upon the completion of three years' service. By the end of year 2, the fair value of the award has dropped to $25 per share. At that date, the entity adds a cash alternative to the grant, whereby the executive can choose whether to receive 10,000 shares or cash equal to the value of 10,000 shares on vesting date. The share price is $20 on vesting. The implementation guidance to IFRS 2 proposes the following approach.

For the first two years, the entity would recognise an expense of $110,000 per year, (representing 10,000 shares × $33 × 1/3), giving rise to the cumulative accounting entry by the end of year 2:

	$	$
Profit or loss (employee costs)	220,000	
Equity		220,000

The addition of a cash alternative at the end of year 2 constitutes a modification of the award, but does not increase the fair value of the award at the date of modification, which under either settlement alternative is $250,000 (10,000 shares × $25), excluding the effect of the non-market vesting condition as required by IFRS 2.

The fact that the employee now has the right to be paid in cash requires the 'split accounting' treatment set out in 10.1 above. Because of the requirement, under the rules for modification of awards (see 7.3 above), to recognise at least the fair value of the original award, the total fair value of the equity alternative of the award is deemed to remain $330,000. This is then reduced (in accordance with the rules in 10.1 above) to reflect the fact that the equity-settlement option would entail the sacrifice of the cash-settled option (modification date fair value $250,000), giving an implied value for the equity-settlement option of $80,000 ($330,000 – $250,000).

The award is now 2/3 through its vesting period, implying that the cumulative amount accounted for in equity should be only $53,333 ($80,000 × 2/3), as opposed to the $220,000 that has actually been accounted for in equity. Accordingly, the difference of $166,667 is transferred from equity to liabilities, the entry being:

	$	$
Equity	166,667	
Liability		166,667

The $166,667 carrying amount of the liability can be seen as representing 2/3 of the $250,000 fair value of the liability component at modification date.

From now on, the accounting for the equity component will be based on this implied value of $80,000. This results in the following accounting entry for the expense in year 3.

	$	$
Profit or loss	60,000*	
Liability		33,333†
Equity		26,667‡

* Balancing figure.

† Carried forward liability $200,000 (10,000 shares × year 3 fair value $20) less the brought forward liability $166,667.

‡ $80,000 equity component (as determined above) × 1/3.

This results in a total cumulative expense for the award of $280,000 ($220,000 for years 1 and 2 and $60,000 for year 3), which represents the actual cash liability at the end of year 3 of $200,000 plus the $80,000 deemed excess of the fair value of the equity component over the liability component at the end of year 2.

The $280,000 expense could also be analysed (as is done by the implementation guidance to IFRS 2 itself), as representing the grant date fair value of the award ($330,000) less the movement in the fair value of the liability alternative ($50,000, representing the fair value of $250,000 at the end of year 2 less the fair value of $200,000 at vesting). The implementation guidance may have adopted this approach to support an argument that, despite all appearances to the contrary, this methodology does not breach the fundamental principle of the modification rules for equity-settled transactions that the minimum expense recognised for a modified award should be the expense that would have been recognised had the award not been modified (see 7.3 above).

10.1.5 'Backstop' cash settlement rights

Some schemes may provide cash settlement rights to the holder so as to cover more or less remote contingencies. For example, an employee whose nationality and/or country of permanent residence is different from the jurisdiction of the reporting entity may be offered the option of cash settlement in case unforeseen future events make the transfer of equity from the entity's jurisdiction, or the holding or trading of it in the employee's country, inconvenient or impossible.

If the terms of the award provide the employee with a general right of cash-settlement, IFRS 2 requires the award to be treated as cash-settled. This is the case even if the right of cash settlement is unlikely to be exercised except in the most extreme circumstances (e.g. because it would give rise to adverse tax consequences for the employee as compared with equity settlement). If, however, the right to cash-settlement is exercisable only in specific circumstances, a more detailed analysis may be required (see 10.3 below).

10.1.6 Convertible bonds issued to acquire goods or services

In some jurisdictions entities issue convertible bonds to employees or other counterparties in exchange for goods or services. When this occurs, the bond will generally be accounted for under IFRS 2 rather than IAS 32 since it falls within the scope of IFRS 2 as a transaction 'in which the entity receives or acquires goods or services and the terms of the arrangement provide either the entity or the supplier of those goods or services with a choice of whether the entity settles the transaction in cash (or other assets) or by issuing equity instruments' (see 2.2.1 and 2.2.2 above). *[IFRS 2.2(c)].*

As noted at 10.1 above, the methodology for splitting such an instrument into its liability and equity components under IFRS 2 differs from that under IAS 32. Moreover, under IAS 32 a convertible is (broadly) recognised at fair value on the date of issue, whereas under IFRS 2 the fair value is accrued over time if the arrangement includes the rendering of services.

It is therefore possible that, if an entity has issued to employees convertible bonds that have also been issued in the market, the accounting treatment for the bonds issued to employees will differ significantly from that of those issued in the market.

Where a convertible instrument is issued to an employee, the IFRS 2 expense will be based on the fair value of the instrument. If an entity issues a convertible instrument in return for an asset, for example a property, the entity would initially recognise a liability component at fair value and an equity component based on the difference between the fair value of the asset and the fair value of the liability component. *[IFRS 2.35].* If the fair value of the asset were lower than the fair value of the instrument as a whole then, in our view, the entity should also recognise the shortfall in accordance with the requirements of IFRS 2 for unidentified goods or services. *[IFRS 2.13A]*. In the case of the acquisition of an asset, it is possible that this additional debit could be capitalised as part of the cost of the asset under IAS 16 – *Property, Plant and Equipment* – but in other cases it would be expensed.

After the initial accounting outlined above, the question arises as to whether the subsequent accounting for the convertible instrument should be in accordance with IFRS 2 or IAS 39. In our view, the instrument should continue to be accounted for under IFRS 2 until shares or cash are delivered to the counterparty. However, if the instrument were transferable then a switch to IAS 39 might be appropriate following transfer to a different counterparty (if considered practical to apply).

10.2 Transactions where the entity has choice of settlement

The accounting treatment for transactions where the entity has choice of settlement is quite different from transactions where the counterparty has choice of settlement, in that:

- where the counterparty has choice of settlement, a liability component and an equity component are identified (see 10.1 above); whereas
- where the entity has choice of settlement, the accounting treatment is binary – in other words the whole transaction is treated either as cash-settled or as equity-settled, depending on whether or not the entity has a present obligation to settle in cash, *[IFRS 2.41]*, determined according to the criteria discussed in 10.2.1 below.

10.2.1 Transactions treated as cash-settled

IFRS 2 requires a transaction to be treated as a liability (and accounted for using the rules for cash-settled transactions discussed in 9 above) if:

(a) the choice of settlement has no commercial substance (for example, because the entity is legally prohibited from issuing shares);

(b) the entity has a past practice or stated policy of settling in cash; or

(c) the entity generally settles in cash whenever the counterparty asks for cash settlement. *[IFRS 2.41-42]*.

These criteria are fundamentally different from those in IAS 32 for derivatives over own shares (which is what cash-settled share-based payment transactions are) not within the scope of IFRS 2. IAS 32 rejects an approach based on past practice or intention and broadly requires all derivatives over own equity that could result in the reporting entity being compelled to settle in cash as giving rise to a financial liability (see Chapter 43 at 4).

An important practical effect of these criteria is that some schemes that may appear at first sight to be equity-settled may in fact have to be treated as cash-settled. For example, if an entity has consistently adopted a policy of granting *ex gratia* cash compensation to all 'good' leavers (or all 'good' leavers of certain seniority) in respect of partially vested options, such a scheme may well be treated as cash-settled for the purposes of IFRS 2. 'Good leavers' are also discussed at 5.3.9 above.

Another common example is that an entity may have a global share scheme with an entity option for cash settlement which it always exercises in respect of awards to employees in jurisdictions where it is difficult or illegal to hold shares in the parent. Such a scheme should be treated as a cash-settled scheme in respect of those jurisdictions. It would, however, in our view, be appropriate to account for the scheme in other jurisdictions as equity-settled (provided of course that none of the criteria in (a) to (c) above applied in those jurisdictions).

IFRS 2 gives no specific guidance as to the accounting treatment on settlement, but it is clear from other provisions of IFRS 2 that the liability should be remeasured to fair value at settlement date and:

- if cash-settlement occurs, the cash paid is applied to reduce the liability; and
- if equity-settlement occurs, the liability is transferred into equity (see 10.1.3.B above).

10.2.1.A Economic compulsion for cash settlement (including unlisted entity awards with a presumption of cash settlement)

Some awards may nominally give the reporting entity the choice of settling in cash or equity, while in practice giving rise to an economic compulsion to settle only in cash. An example might be where an entity that is a subsidiary or owned by a small number of individuals, such as members of the same family, grants options to employees. In such cases there will normally be a very strong presumption that the entity will settle in cash in order to avoid diluting the existing owners' interests. Similarly, where the entity is not listed, there is little real benefit for an employee in receiving a share that cannot be realised except when another shareholder wishes to buy it or there is a change in ownership of the business as a whole.

In our view, such schemes are generally most appropriately accounted for as cash-settled schemes at inception. In any event, once the scheme has been operating for a while, it is likely that there will be a past practice of cash settlement such that the scheme is required to be treated as a liability under the general provisions of IFRS 2 summarised above.

A similar conclusion is often reached even where the terms of the agreement do not appear to offer the entity a choice of settling the award in cash (see 9.2.4 above).

10.2.2 Transactions treated as equity-settled

A transaction not meeting the criteria in 10.2.1 above should be accounted for as an equity-settled transaction using the rules for such transactions discussed in 4 to 8 above. *[IFRS 2.43].*

However, when the transaction is settled the following approach is adopted:

(a) subject to (b) below:

  (i) if the transaction is cash-settled, the cash is accounted for as a deduction from equity; or

  (ii) if the transaction is equity-settled, there is a transfer from one component of equity to another (if necessary); and

(b) if the two methods of settlement are of different fair value at the date of settlement, and the entity chooses the method with the higher fair value, the entity recognises an additional expense for the excess fair value of the chosen method. *[IFRS 2.43]*.

This is illustrated in Examples 30.41 and 30.42 below.

Example 30.41: Settlement of transaction treated as equity-settled where fair value of cash settlement exceeds fair value of equity settlement

An entity has accounted for a share-based payment transaction where it has the choice of settlement as an equity-settled transaction, and has recognised a cumulative expense of £1,000 based on the fair value at grant date.

At settlement date the fair value of the equity-settlement option is £1,700 and that of the cash-settlement option £2,000. If the entity settles in equity, no further accounting entry is required by IFRS 2. However, either at the entity's discretion or in compliance with local legal requirements, there may be a transfer within equity of the £1,000 credited to equity during the vesting period.

If the entity settles in cash, the entity must recognise an additional expense of £300, being the difference between the fair value of the equity-settlement option (£1,700) and that of the cash-settlement option (£2,000). The accounting entry is:

	£	£
Profit or loss (employee costs)	300	
Equity	1,700	
Cash		2,000

Example 30.42: Settlement of transaction treated as equity-settled where fair value of equity settlement exceeds fair value of cash settlement

As in Example 30.41, an entity has accounted for a share-based payment transaction where it has the choice of settlement as an equity-settled transaction, and has recognised a cumulative expense of £1,000 based on the fair value at grant date.

In this case, however, at settlement date the fair value of the equity-settlement option is £2,000 and that of the cash-settlement option £1,700. If the entity chooses to settle in equity, it must recognise an additional expense of £300, being the difference between fair value of the equity-settlement option (£2,000) and that of the cash-settlement option (£1,700). The accounting entry is:

	£	£
Profit or loss (employee costs)	300	
Equity		300

No further accounting entry is required by IFRS 2. However, either at the entity's discretion or in compliance with local legal requirements, there may be a transfer within equity of the £1,300 credited during the vesting period and on settlement.

If the entity settles in cash, no extra expense is recognised, and the accounting entry is:

	£	£
Equity	1,700	
Cash		1,700

It can be seen in this case that, if the transaction is settled in equity, an additional expense is recognised. If, however, the transaction had simply been an equity-settled transaction (i.e. with no cash alternative), there would have been no additional expense on settlement and the cumulative expense would have been only £1,000 based on the fair value at grant date.

10.2.3 Change in classification of award after grant date

IFRS 2 does not specify whether a transaction where the entity has a choice of settlement in equity or cash should be assessed as equity-settled or cash-settled only at the inception of the transaction or also at each reporting date until it is settled.

However, in describing the accounting treatment IFRS 2 states several times that the accounting depends on whether the entity '*has a present obligation* to settle in cash'. In our view, this suggests that IFRS 2 intends the position to be reviewed at each reporting date and not just considered at the inception of the transaction.

IFRS 2 does not specify the accounting treatment to be followed if such a change in classification is considered appropriate following a change in the entity's policy or intention. In our view, however, the most appropriate treatment is to account for such a change as if it were a modification of the manner of settlement of the award (see 9.4 above). In this situation, the entity is able to choose the manner of settlement which, in substance, is the same as choosing to modify the manner of settlement of an award which does not already give the entity a choice. These situations are distinct from those where the manner of settlement depends on the outcome of a contingency outside the entity's control (see 10.3 below).

10.3 Awards requiring cash settlement in specific circumstances (awards with contingent cash settlement)

Some awards, rather than giving a general right to cash settlement to either the entity or the counterparty, require cash settlement in certain specific and limited circumstances – what IAS 32 refers to as contingent settlement provisions (see Chapter 43 at 4.3). In the absence of specific guidance, questions then arise as to whether such an award should be accounted for as equity-settled or cash-settled and whether this should be re-assessed on an ongoing basis during the vesting period.

10.3.1 Analysis 1 – Treat as cash-settled if contingency is outside entity's control

One approach might be to observe that the underlying principle that determines whether an award is accounted for as an equity instrument or liability under IFRS 2 appears to be whether the reporting entity can unilaterally avoid cash-settlement (see 10.1 and 10.2 above). Thus, any award where the counterparty has a right to cash-settlement is treated as a liability in any event, irrespective of the probability of cash-settlement, since there is nothing that the entity could do to prevent cash-settlement. However, an award where the choice of settlement rests with the entity is accounted for as a liability only where the entity's own actions have effectively put it in a position where it has no real choice but to settle in cash.

This analysis would lead to the conclusion that it is first necessary to consider whether the event that requires cash-settlement is one over which the entity has control. If the event, however improbable, is outside the entity's control, the award should be treated as cash-settled. However, if the event is within the entity's control, the award should be treated as cash-settled only if the entity has a liability by reference to the criteria summarised in 10.1 and 10.2 above.

This analysis does not seem entirely satisfactory. For example, in a number of jurisdictions, it is common for an equity-settled share-based payment award to contain a provision to the effect that, if the employee dies in service, the entity will pay to the employee's estate the fair value of the award in cash. The analysis above would lead to the conclusion that the award must be classified as cash-settled, on the basis that it is beyond the entity's control whether or not an employee dies in service. This seems a somewhat far-fetched conclusion, and is moreover inconsistent with the accounting treatment that the entity would apply to any other death-in-service benefit under IAS 19. IAS 19 would generally require the entity to recognise a liability for such a benefit based on an actuarial estimate (see Chapter 31 at 3.6), rather than on a presumption that the entire workforce will die in service.

10.3.2 Analysis 2 – Treat as cash-settled if contingency is outside entity's control and probable

It was presumably considerations such as these that led the FASB staff to provide an interpretation[29] of the equivalent provisions of FASB ASC 718 – *Compensation – Stock Compensation* (formerly FAS 123(R) – *Share-Based Payment*) regarding awards that are cash-settled in certain circumstances. This interpretation states that a cash settlement feature that can be exercised only upon the occurrence of a contingent event that is outside the employee's control (such as an initial public offering) does not give rise to a liability until it becomes probable that that event will occur.[30]

In our view, this approach based on the probability of a contingent event that is outside the control of both the counterparty and the entity is also acceptable. The implied rationale (by reference to IFRS literature) is that:

- it is not necessary to have regard to the principles of IAS 32, given that IFRS 2 clearly notes a number of inconsistencies between IFRS 2 and IAS 32 (see 1.4.1 above); and
- it is therefore appropriate to have regard to the principles of IAS 37 in determining whether an uncertain future event gives rise to a liability. IAS 37 currently requires a liability to be recognised only when it is probable (i.e. more likely than not) to occur (see Chapter 27).

The impact of these two analyses can be illustrated by reference to an award that requires cash-settlement in the event of a change of control of the entity (see 10.3.3 below).

10.3.3 Awards requiring cash settlement on a change of control

It is not uncommon for an award to be compulsorily cash-settled if there is a change of control of the reporting entity. Such a provision ensures that there is no need for any separate negotiations to buy out all employee options, so as to avoid non-controlling (minority) interests arising in the acquired entity as equity-settled awards are settled after the change of control.

The question of whether or not a change of control is within the control of the entity is a matter that has become the subject of much recent discussion in the context of determining the classification of certain financial instruments by their issuer, and is considered more fully in Chapter 43 at 4.3.

If the view is taken, in a particular case, that a change of control is within the entity's control, the conclusion under either Analysis 1 or Analysis 2 above would be that the award should be treated as cash-settled only if the entity has a liability by reference to the criteria summarised in 10.2.1 above.

If, however, the view is taken, in a particular case, that a change of control is not within the control of the reporting entity, the conclusion will vary depending on whether Analysis 1 or Analysis 2 is followed. Under Analysis 1, an award requiring settlement in cash on a change of control outside the control of the entity would be treated as cash-settled, however unlikely the change of control may be. Under Analysis 2 however, an award requiring settlement in cash on a change of control outside the control of the entity would be treated as cash-settled only if a change of control were probable.

A difficulty with Analysis 2 is that it introduces rather bizarre inconsistencies in the accounting treatment for awards when the relative probability of their outcome is considered. As noted at 10.1.5 above, an award that gives the counterparty an absolute right to cash-settlement is accounted for as a liability, however unlikely it is that the counterparty will exercise that right. Thus, under this approach, the entity could find itself in the situation where it treats:

- as a liability: an award with a unrestricted right to cash-settlement for the counterparty, where the probability of the counterparty exercising that right is less than 1%; but
- as equity: an award that requires cash settlement in the event of a change of control which is assessed as having a 49% probability of occurring.

In our view, an entity may adopt either approach, but should do so consistently and state its policy for accounting for such transactions if material.

There is further discussion at 15.4 below of awards that vest or are exercisable on a flotation or change of control.

10.3.4 Accounting for change in manner of settlement where award is contingent on future events

When, under Analysis 2 above, the manner of settlement of an award changes as a consequence of a re-assessment of the probability of a contingent event, there is no settlement of the award or modification of its original terms. The award is such that there have been two potential outcomes, one equity-settled and one cash-settled, running in parallel since grant date. At each reporting date the entity should assess which outcome is more likely and account for the award on an equity- or cash-settled basis accordingly. In our view, any adjustments to switch between the cumulative cash-settled award and the cumulative equity-settled award should be taken to profit or loss in the current period. This is similar to the approach for an award with multiple independent vesting conditions (see 6.3.6 above).

Taking the approach that the two outcomes have both been part of the arrangement from grant date, the fair value of the equity-settled award would be measured only at the original grant date and would not be remeasured at the date of change in settlement method. As the cash-settled award would be remeasured on an ongoing basis, a switch in the manner of settlement during the vesting period could give rise to significant volatility in the cumulative expense. At the end of the vesting period, however, the cumulative expense will equate to either the grant date fair value of the equity-settled approach or the settlement value of the cash-settled approach depending on whether or not the contingent event has happened.

An alternative approach is to treat the arrangement as two mutually exclusive awards, one equity-settled and one cash-settled. Under this alternative approach:

- the cash-settled award always has a fair value and a corresponding liability is recognised over the vesting period. The fair value of the liability depends on the likelihood of cash-settlement and will reduce to nil at the end of the vesting period if the award is finally settled in equity; and
- the equity-settled alternative is only recognised if it is considered to be probable and no amount is recognised for an award finally settled in cash.

In effect, this alternative approach treats the settlement method as a vesting condition. During the vesting period, this approach is likely to result in an expense that exceeds the total value of the award because a fair value is recognised for the cash-settled award until such time as an award is finally settled in equity. If the award is finally settled in equity there will be a credit to profit or loss on the release of any liability for cash-settlement.

The situation discussed above (i.e. an arrangement with two potential outcomes from grant date) contrasts with an award where the manner of settlement is entirely within the entity's control. Where such a choice of settlement exists, a change in the manner of settlement would be treated as a modification with a potential catch-up through equity (see 9.4 and 10.2.3 above).

10.3.5 Manner of settlement contingent on future events: possible future developments

During 2009 the Interpretations Committee was asked to clarify how share-based payment transactions should be classified and measured if the manner of settlement is contingent on either:

- a future event that is outside the control of both the entity and the counterparty; or
- a future event that is within the control of the counterparty.

The Interpretations Committee noted that IFRS 2 does not provide guidance on share-based payment transactions for which the manner of settlement is contingent on a future event that is outside the control of both the entity and the counterparty. At its January 2010 meeting, the Interpretations Committee recommended that this issue be dealt with by the IASB, in conjunction with a number of other IFRS 2 classification issues, in a post-implementation review of IFRS 2.[31] This view was reiterated by the Interpretations Committee in March 2011.[32]

In September 2011 the IASB agreed that transactions in which the manner of settlement is contingent on future events should be considered in a future agenda proposal together with other issues relating to IFRS 2 (see 3.4 above).[33] However, in July 2012 the Interpretations Committee asked its staff to update the analysis of this issue so that the Committee could discuss once again whether to add it to its agenda.[34]

The Interpretations Committee discussed the matter again in May 2013, noting that paragraph 34 of IFRS 2 requires an entity to account on a cash-settled basis if, and to the extent that, the entity has incurred a liability to settle in cash or other assets. However, it was further noted that IFRS 2 only provides guidance where the entity or the counterparty has a choice of settlement and not where the manner of settlement is contingent on a future event that is outside the control of both parties. The Interpretations Committee also observed that is was unclear which other guidance within IFRS and the Conceptual Framework would provide the best analogy to this situation.

Having noted significant diversity in practice, the Interpretations Committee asked its staff 'to explore approaches to providing guidance for the classification of the share-based payment transaction in which the manner of settlement is contingent on a future event that is outside the control of both parties.' The Interpretations Committee will discuss whether guidance can be developed on the basis of additional analysis at a future meeting.[35]

10.4 Cash settlement alternative not based on share price

Some awards may provide a cash-settlement alternative not based on the share price. For example, an employee might be offered a choice between 500 shares or €1,000,000 on the vesting of an award. Whilst an award of €1,000,000, if considered in isolation, would obviously not be a share-based payment transaction, it nevertheless falls within the scope of IFRS 2, rather than – say – IAS 19, if it is offered as an alternative to a transaction that is within the scope of IFRS 2. The Basis for Conclusions to IFRS 2 states that the cash alternative may be fixed or variable and, if variable, may be determinable in a manner that is related, or unrelated, to the price of the entity's shares. *[IFRS 2.BC256].*

10.5 Matching awards with cash and equity alternatives

Section 15.1 below addresses in detail the accounting treatment in situations where, at the end of an initial period, an employee is offered a share award or a cash alternative to 'match' a share award or cash bonus earned during that initial period.

11 REPLACEMENT SHARE-BASED PAYMENT AWARDS ISSUED IN A BUSINESS COMBINATION

11.1 Background

It frequently occurs that an entity (A) acquires another (B) which, at the time of the business combination, has outstanding employee share options or other share-based awards. If no action were taken by A, employees of B would be entitled, once any vesting conditions had been satisfied, to shares in B. This is not a very satisfactory outcome for either party: A now has non-controlling (minority) shareholders in its hitherto wholly-owned subsidiary B, and the employees of B are the proud owners of unmarketable shares in an effectively wholly-owned subsidiary.

The obvious solution, adopted in the majority of cases, is for some mechanism to be put in place such that the employees of B end up holding shares in the new parent A. This can be achieved, for example, by:

- A granting the employees of B options over the shares of A in exchange for the surrender of their options over the shares of B; or
- changing the terms of the options so that they are over a special class of shares in B which are mandatorily convertible into shares of A.

This raises the question of how such a substitution transaction should be accounted for in the consolidated financial statements of A (the treatment in the single entity financial statements of B is discussed at 11.4 below).

IFRS 3 (as revised in 2008 and amended in May 2010) addresses the accounting treatment required in a business combination where an acquirer:

- replaces acquiree awards on a mandatory basis (see 11.2.1 below);
- replaces acquiree awards on a voluntary basis, even if the acquiree awards would not expire as a consequence of the business combination (see 11.2.2 below); or
- does not replace acquiree awards (see 11.3 below).

Section 11 relates only to business combinations. Share-based payment arrangements in the context of group reorganisations are addressed at 12.8 below.

11.2 Replacement awards in business combinations accounted for under IFRS 3

A more comprehensive discussion of the requirements of IFRS 3 may be found in Chapter 9.

IFRS 3 requires an acquirer to measure a liability or an equity instrument related to the replacement of an acquiree's share-based payment awards in accordance with IFRS 2, rather than in accordance with the general principles of IFRS 3. References to the 'fair value' of an award in the following discussion therefore mean the fair value determined under IFRS 2, for which IFRS 3 uses the term 'market-based measure'. The fair value measurement is to be made as at the acquisition date. *[IFRS 3.30].*

IFRS 3 notes that a transaction entered into by or on behalf of the acquirer or primarily for the benefit of the acquirer or the combined entity, rather than that of the acquiree (or its former owners) before the combination, is likely to be a transaction separate from the business combination itself. This includes a transaction that remunerates employees or former owners of the acquiree for future services. *[IFRS 3.52].*

The Application Guidance in Appendix B to IFRS 3 and the illustrative examples accompanying the standard explain how this general principle is to be applied to replacement share-based payment transactions. Essentially, however, IFRS 3 appears to view an exchange of share options or other share-based payment awards in conjunction with a business combination as a form of modification (see 7.3 above). *[IFRS 3.B56].*

11.2.1 Awards that the acquirer is 'obliged' to replace

Where the acquirer is 'obliged' to replace the acquiree awards (see below), either all or a portion of the fair value of the acquirer's replacement awards forms part of the consideration transferred in the business combination. *[IFRS 3.B56].*

IFRS 3 regards the acquirer as 'obliged' to replace the acquiree awards if the acquiree or its employees have the ability to enforce replacement, for example if replacement is required by:

- the terms of the acquisition agreement;
- the terms of the acquiree's awards; or
- applicable laws or regulations.

The required treatment of replacement awards may be summarised as follows:

(a) at the date of acquisition, the fair values of the replacement award and the original award are determined in accordance with IFRS 2;

(b) the amount of the replacement award attributable to pre-combination service (and therefore included as part of the consideration transferred for the business) is determined by multiplying the fair value of the original award by the ratio of the vesting period completed, as at the date of the business combination, to the greater of:

  - the total vesting period, as determined at the date of the business combination (being the period required to satisfy all vesting conditions, including conditions added to, or removed from, the original award by the replacement award); and
  - the original vesting period; and

(c) any excess of the fair value of the replacement award over the amount determined in (b) above is recognised as a post-combination remuneration expense, in accordance with the normal principles of IFRS 2 (see 3 to 7 above). *[IFRS 3.B57-59]*.

The requirements summarised in (a) to (c) above have the effect that any excess of the fair value of the replacement award over the original award is recognised as a post-combination remuneration expense. The requirement in (b) above has the effect that, if the replacement award requires service in the period after the business combination, an IFRS 2 cost is recognised in the post-combination period, even if the acquiree award being replaced had fully vested at the date of acquisition. It also has the effect that if a replacement award requires no service in the post-combination period, but the acquiree award being replaced would have done so, a cost must be recognised in the post-combination period. *[IFRS 3.B59]*.

There is no specific guidance in IFRS 3 on how and when to recognise the post-combination remuneration expense in the consolidated financial statements of the acquirer. In our view, the expense should be recognised over the post-combination vesting period of the replacement award in accordance with the general principles of IFRS 2 (see 6.2 to 6.4 above).

The portions of the replacement award attributable to pre- and post-combination service calculated in (b) and (c) above are calculated, under the normal principles of IFRS 2, based on the best estimate of the number of awards expected to vest (or to be treated as vesting by IFRS 2). Rather than being treated as adjustments to the consideration for the business combination, any changes in estimates or forfeitures occurring after the acquisition date are reflected in remuneration cost for the period in which the changes occur in accordance with the normal principles of IFRS 2. Similarly, the effects of other post-acquisition events, such as modifications or the outcome of performance conditions, are accounted for in accordance with IFRS 2 as part of the determination of the remuneration expense for the period in which such events occur. *[IFRS 3.B60]*. The application of these requirements is discussed in more detail at 11.2.3 below.

The requirements above to split an award into pre-combination and post-combination portions apply equally to equity-settled and cash-settled replacement awards. All changes after the acquisition date in the fair value of cash-settled replacements awards and their tax effects (recognised in accordance with IAS 12 – *Income Taxes*) are recognised in the post-combination financial statements when the changes occur. *[IFRS 3.B61-62]*. IFRS 3 does not specify where in the income statement any changes in the pre-combination element of a cash-settled award should be reflected and, in the absence of clear guidance, this will depend on an analysis of whether this is considered to be remuneration expense or whether it is actually closer to a change in a liability for contingent consideration.

The treatment of the income tax effects of replacement share-based payment transactions in a business combination is discussed further in Chapter 29 at 10.8.5.

11.2.1.A Illustrative examples of awards that the acquirer is 'obliged' to replace

IFRS 3 provides some examples in support of the written guidance summarised above, the substance of which is reproduced as Examples 30.43 to 30.46 below. *[IFRS 3.IE61-71]*. These deal with the following scenarios.

Is post-combination service required for the replacement award?	Has the acquiree award being replaced vested before the combination?	Example
Not required	Vested	30.43
Not required	Not vested	30.44
Required	Vested	30.45
Required	Not vested	30.46

In all the examples, it is assumed that the replacement award is equity-settled.

Example 30.43: Replacement award requiring no post-combination service replacing vested acquiree award

Entity A acquires Entity B and issues replacement awards with a fair value at the acquisition date of €1.1 million for awards of Entity B with a fair value at the acquisition date of €1.0 million. No post-combination services are required for the replacement awards and Entity B's employees had rendered all of the required service for the acquiree awards as of the acquisition date.

The amount attributable to pre-combination service, and therefore included in the consideration transferred in the business combination, is the fair value of Entity B's awards at the acquisition date (€1.0 million). The amount attributable to post-combination service is €0.1 million, the difference between the total value of the replacement awards (€1.1 million) and the portion attributable to pre-combination service (€1.0 million). Because no post-combination service is required for the replacement awards, Entity A immediately recognises €0.1 million as remuneration cost in its post-combination financial statements.

Example 30.44: Replacement award requiring no post-combination service replacing unvested acquiree award

Entity A acquires Entity B and issues replacement awards with a fair value at the acquisition date of €1.0 million for awards of Entity B also with a fair value at the acquisition date of €1.0 million. When originally granted, the awards of Entity B had a vesting period of four years and, as of the acquisition date, the employees of Entity B had rendered two years' service. The replacement award vests in full immediately.

The portion of the fair value of the replacement awards attributable to pre-combination services is the fair value of the award of Entity B being replaced (€1 million) multiplied by the ratio of the pre-combination vesting period (two years) to the greater of the total vesting period (now two years) and the original vesting period of Entity B's award (four years). Thus, €0.5 million (€1.0 million × 2/4 years) is attributable to pre-combination service and therefore included in the consideration transferred for the acquiree. The remaining €0.5 million is attributable to post-combination service, but, because no post-combination service is required for the replacement award to vest, Entity A recognises the entire €0.5 million immediately as remuneration cost in the post-combination financial statements.

Example 30.45: Replacement award requiring post-combination service replacing vested acquiree award

Entity A acquires Entity B and issues replacement awards with a fair value at the acquisition date of €1.0 million for awards of Entity B also with a fair value at the acquisition date of €1.0 million. The replacement awards require one year of post-combination service. The awards of Entity B being replaced had a vesting period of four years. As of the acquisition date, employees of Entity B holding unexercised vested awards had rendered a total of seven years of service since the grant date.

Even though the Entity B employees have already rendered all of the service for their original awards, Entity A attributes a portion of the replacement award to post-combination remuneration cost, because the replacement awards require one year of post-combination service. The total vesting period is five years – the vesting period for the original Entity B award completed before the acquisition date (four years) plus the vesting period for the replacement award (one year). The fact that the employees have rendered seven years of service in total in the pre-combination period is not relevant to the calculation because only four years of that service were necessary in order to earn the original award.

The portion attributable to pre-combination services equals the fair value of the award of Entity B being replaced (€1 million) multiplied by the ratio of the pre-combination vesting period (four years) to the total vesting period (five years). Thus, €0.8 million (€1.0 million × 4/5 years) is attributed to the pre-combination vesting period and therefore included in the consideration transferred in the business combination. The remaining €0.2 million is attributed to the post-combination vesting period and is recognised as remuneration cost in Entity A's post-combination financial statements in accordance with IFRS 2, over the remaining one year vesting period.

Example 30.46: Replacement award requiring post-combination service replacing unvested acquiree award

Entity A acquires Entity B and issues replacement awards with a fair value at the acquisition date of €1.0 million for awards of Entity B also with a fair value at the acquisition date of €1.0 million. The replacement awards require one year of post-combination service. When originally granted, the awards of Entity B being replaced had a vesting period of four years and, as of the acquisition date, the employees had rendered two years' service.

The replacement awards require one year of post-combination service. Because employees have already rendered two years of service, the total vesting period is three years. The portion attributable to pre-combination services equals the fair value of the award of Entity B being replaced (€1 million) multiplied by the ratio of the pre-combination vesting period (two years) to the greater of the total vesting period (three years) or the original vesting period of Entity B's award (four years). Thus, €0.5 million (€1.0 million × 2/4 years) is attributable to pre-combination service and therefore included in the consideration transferred for the acquiree. The remaining €0.5 million is attributable to post-combination service and therefore recognised as remuneration cost in Entity A's post-combination financial statements, over the remaining one year vesting period.

11.2.2 Acquiree awards that the acquirer is not 'obliged' to replace

IFRS 3 notes that, in some situations, acquiree awards may expire as a consequence of a business combination. In such a situation, the acquirer might decide to replace those awards even though it is not obliged to do so. It might also be the case that the acquirer decides voluntarily to replace awards that would not expire and which it is not otherwise obliged to replace.

Following the May 2010 amendment to IFRS 3 there is no difference in the basic approach to accounting for a replacement award that the acquirer is obliged to make and one that it makes on a voluntary basis (i.e. the approach is as set out at 11.2.1 above). In other words, the accounting is based on the fair value of the replacement award at the date of acquisition, with an apportionment of that amount between the cost of acquisition and post-acquisition employment expense.

However, in situations where the acquiree awards would expire as a consequence of the business combination if they were not voluntarily replaced by the acquirer, none of the fair value of the replacement awards is treated as part of the consideration transferred for the business (and therefore included in the computation of goodwill), but the full amount is instead recognised as a remuneration cost in the post-combination financial statements. The IASB explains that this is because the new award by the acquirer can only be for future services to be provided by the employee as the acquirer has no obligation to the employee in respect of past services. *[IFRS 3.B56, BC311B]*.

11.2.3 Accounting for changes in vesting assumptions after the acquisition date

Whilst the requirements outlined at 11.2.1 above to reflect changes in assumptions relating to the post-acquisition portion of an award through post-combination remuneration appear consistent with the general principles of IFRS 2 and IFRS 3, the application of the requirements to the pre-combination portion is less straightforward.

Paragraph B60 of IFRS 3 appears to require all changes to both the pre- and post-combination portions of the award to be reflected in post-combination remuneration expense. *[IFRS 3.B60]*. This could lead to significant volatility in post-combination profit or loss as a consequence of forfeitures, or other changes in estimates, relating to awards accounted for as part of the consideration for the business combination. It is also noteworthy that this approach appears to require the ongoing reassessment of an estimate of an equity-based transaction made as at the date of the business combination whereas, more generally, IFRS 3 does not permit the remeasurement of equity-settled contingent consideration.

An alternative approach relies on a combination of paragraphs B60 and B63(d). Whilst paragraph B60 is clear that no adjustment can be made to the purchase consideration, paragraph B63(d) refers to IFRS 2 providing 'guidance on subsequent measurement and accounting for *the portion of replacement share-based payment awards ... that is attributable to employees' future services'* (emphasis added). *[IFRS 3.B60, B63(d)].* Supporters of this view therefore argue that the remeasurement requirements of paragraph B60 apply only to the portion of the replacement award that is attributed to future service and that the award should be split into two parts:

- a pre-combination element that is treated as if it were vested at the acquisition date and then accounted for in the same way as other contingent consideration settled in equity; and
- a post-combination portion that is treated as a new award and reflects only the employees' post-combination service.

A further alternative approach is based on the guidance in paragraph B59 of IFRS 3 which states that 'the acquirer attributes any excess of the market-based measure of the replacement award over the market-based measure of the acquiree award to post-combination service and recognises that excess as remuneration cost in the post-combination financial statements'. *[IFRS 3.B59].* As for the second approach above, the pre-combination element is considered to be fixed and cannot be reversed. However, any subsequent changes in assumptions that give rise to an incremental expense over the amount recognised as pre-combination service should be recognised as part of the post-combination remuneration expense.

Whilst the second and third approaches above are more consistent with the general requirement under IFRS 2 that vested awards should not be adjusted, the first approach, based on paragraph B60, is arguably the most obvious reading of IFRS 3 as currently drafted. In the absence of clear guidance in the standard, we believe that an entity may make an accounting policy choice between the three approaches but, once chosen, the policy should be applied consistently.

The three approaches are illustrated in Example 30.47 below.

Example 30.47: Accounting for post-acquisition changes in estimates relating to replacement awards

Entity A grants an award of 1,000 shares to each of two employees. The award will vest after three years provided the employees remain in service. At the end of year 2, Entity A is acquired by Entity B which replaces the award with one over its own shares but otherwise on the same terms. The fair value of each share at the date of acquisition is €1. At this date, Entity B estimates that one of the two employees will leave employment before the end of the remaining one year service period.

At the date of acquisition, Entity B recognises €667 (1 employee × 1,000 shares × €1 × 2/3) as part of the consideration for the business combination and expects to recognise a further €333 as an expense through post-acquisition profit or loss (1 × 1,000 × €1 × 1/3).

However, if the estimates made as at the date of the acquisition prove to be inaccurate and either both employees leave employment during year 3, or both remain in employment until the vesting date, there are three alternative approaches to the accounting as explained above:

- Approach 1 – all changes in estimates are reflected in post-acquisition profit or loss (drawing on paragraph B60 of IFRS 3);
- Approach 2 – changes to the estimates that affect the amount recognised as part of the purchase consideration are not adjusted for and changes affecting the post-acquisition assumptions are adjusted through post-acquisition profit or loss (drawing on paragraph B63(d) of IFRS 3); or

- Approach 3 – the amount attributable to pre-combination service, and treated as part of the business combination, is fixed and cannot be reversed. However, any changes in assumptions that give rise to an additional cumulative expense are reflected through post-acquisition profit or loss (drawing on paragraph B59 of IFRS 3).

Using the fact pattern above, and assuming that both employees leave employment in the post-acquisition period, the three alternative approaches would give rise to the following entries in accounting for the forfeitures:

- Approach 1 – a credit of €667 to post-acquisition profit or loss to reflect the reversal of the amount charged to the business combination. In addition to this, any additional expense that had been recognised in the post-acquisition period would be reversed.
- Approaches 2 and 3 – the reversal through post-acquisition profit or loss of any additional expense that had been recognised in the post-acquisition period.

If, instead, both employees remained in employment in the post-acquisition period and both awards vested, the three alternative approaches would give rise to the following entries:

- Approach 1 – an expense of €1,333 through post-acquisition profit or loss to reflect the remaining €333 fair value of the award to the employee who was expected to remain in service plus €1,000 for the award to the employee who was not expected to remain in service.
- Approach 2 – an expense of €666 (2 × €333) through post-acquisition profit or loss for the remaining 1/3 of the acquisition date fair value of the two awards. There is no adjustment to the business combination or to post-acquisition profit or loss for the €667 pre-acquisition element of the award that, as at the acquisition date, was not expected to vest.
- Approach 3 – an expense of €1,333 through post-acquisition profit or loss to reflect the remaining €333 fair value of the award to the employee who was expected to remain in service plus €1,000 for the award to the employee who was not expected to remain in service.

11.3 Acquiree award not replaced by acquirer

It may occasionally happen that the acquirer does not replace awards of the acquiree at the time of the acquisition. This might be the case where the acquired subsidiary is only partly-owned and is itself listed.

IFRS 3 distinguishes between vested and unvested share-based payment transactions of the acquiree that are outstanding at the date of the business combination but which the acquirer chooses not to replace.

If vested, the outstanding acquiree share-based payment transactions are treated by the acquirer as part of the non-controlling interest in the acquiree and measured at their IFRS 2 fair value at the date of acquisition.

If unvested, the outstanding share-based payment transactions are fair valued in accordance with IFRS 2 as if the acquisition date were the grant date. The fair value should be allocated to the non-controlling interest in the acquiree on the basis of the ratio of the portion of the vesting period completed to the greater of:

- the total vesting period; and
- the original vesting period of the share-based payment transactions.

The balance is treated as a post-combination remuneration expense in accordance with the general principles of IFRS 2. *[IFRS 3.B62A-B62B]*.

11.4 Financial statements of the acquired entity

A replacement of an award based on the acquiree's equity with one based on the acquirer's equity is, from the perspective of the acquired entity, a cancellation and replacement, to be accounted for in accordance with the general principles of IFRS 2 for such transactions (see 7.4 above). However, in addition to considerations about whether this is accounted for as a separate cancellation and new grant or as a modification of the original terms, the acquiree needs to take into account its new status as a subsidiary of the acquirer.

If the acquirer is responsible for settling the award in its own equity with the acquiree's employees, the acquiree will continue to account for the award on an equity-settled basis. If, however, the acquiree is responsible for settling the award with shares of the acquirer, then the acquiree would have to switch from an equity-settled basis of accounting to a cash-settled basis of accounting (see 2.2.2.A and 9.4.1 above).

Even if the acquiree continues to account for the award on an equity-settled basis, the share-based payment expense recorded in the consolidated financial statements (based on fair value at the date of the business combination) will generally not be the same as that in the financial statements of the acquired entity (based on fair value at the date of original grant plus any incremental value granted at the date of acquisition, if modification accounting is applied). The exact timing of the recognition of the expense in the financial statements of the acquired entity after the date of cancellation and replacement will depend on its interpretation of the requirements of IFRS 2 for the cancellation and replacement of options (see Example 30.28 at 7.4.4.B above).

12 GROUP SHARE SCHEMES

In this section we consider various aspects of share-based payment arrangements operated within a group of companies and involving several legal entities. The focus of the section is on the accounting by the various parties involved and includes several comprehensive illustrative examples. The main areas covered are as follows:

- typical features of a group share scheme (see 12.1 below);
- a summary of the accounting treatment of group share schemes (see 12.2 below);
- employee benefit trusts ('EBTs') and similar entities (see 12.3 below);
- an example of a group share scheme (based on an equity-settled award satisfied by a market purchase of shares) illustrating the accounting by the different entities involved (see 12.4 below);
- an example of a group share scheme (based on an equity-settled award satisfied by a fresh issue of shares) illustrating the accounting by the different entities involved (see 12.5 below);
- an example of a group cash-settled transaction where the award is settled by an entity other than the one receiving goods or services (see 12.6 below);
- the accounting treatment when an employee transfers between group entities (see 12.7 below); and
- group reorganisations (see 12.8 below).

Whilst associates and joint arrangements do not meet the definition of group entities, there will sometimes be share-based payment arrangements that involve the investor or venturer and the employees of its associate or joint venture. These arrangements are discussed at 12.9 below.

12.1 Typical features of a group share scheme

In this section we use the term 'share scheme' to encompass any transaction falling within the scope of IFRS 2, whether accounted for as equity-settled or cash-settled.

It is common practice for a group to operate a single share scheme covering several subsidiaries. Depending on the commercial needs of the entity, the scheme might cover all group entities, all group entities in a particular country or all employees of a particular grade throughout a number of subsidiaries.

The precise terms and structures of group share schemes are so varied that it is rare to find two completely identical arrangements. From an accounting perspective, however, group share schemes can generally be reduced to a basic prototype, as described below, which will serve as the basis of the discussion.

A group scheme typically involves transactions by several legal entities:

- the trust that administers the scheme. Such trusts are known by various names in different jurisdictions, but, for the sake of convenience, in this section we will use the term 'EBT' ('employee benefit trust') to cover all such vehicles by whatever name they are actually known. The accounting treatment of transactions with EBTs is discussed at 12.3 below;
- the subsidiary employing an employee who has been granted an award ('the employing subsidiary'); and
- the parent, over whose shares awards are granted.

In some cases the scheme may be directed by a group employee services entity. Where an employee services company is involved it will be necessary to evaluate the precise group arrangements in order to determine which entity is receiving an employee's services and which entity is responsible for settling the award. It will often be the case that the services company is simply administering the arrangements on behalf of the parent entity.

A share-based award is often granted to an employee by the parent, or a group employee services entity, which will in turn have an option exercisable against the EBT for the shares that it may be required to deliver to the employee. Less commonly, the trustees of the EBT make awards to the employees and enter into reciprocal arrangements with the parent.

If the parent takes the view that it will satisfy any awards using existing shares it will often seek to fix the cash cost of the award by arranging for the EBT to purchase in the market, on the day that the award is made, sufficient shares to satisfy all or part of the award. This purchase will be funded by external borrowings, a loan from the parent, a contribution from the employing subsidiary, or some combination. The cash received from the employee on exercise of the option can be used by the EBT to repay any borrowings.

If the parent takes the view that it will satisfy the options with a fresh issue of shares, these will be issued to the EBT, either:

(a) at the date on which the employee exercises his option (in which case the EBT will subscribe for the new shares using the cash received from the employee together with any non-refundable contribution made by the employing subsidiary – see below). Such arrangements are generally referred to as 'simultaneous funding';

(b) at some earlier date (in which case the EBT will subscribe for the new shares using external borrowings, a loan from the parent or a contribution from the employing subsidiary, or some combination. The cash received from the employee on exercise of the option may then be used by the EBT to repay any borrowings). Such arrangements are generally referred to as 'pre-funding'; or

(c) some shares will be issued before the exercise date as in (b) above, and the balance on the exercise date as in (a) above.

As noted in (a) above, the employing subsidiary often makes a non-refundable contribution to the EBT in connection with the scheme, so as to ensure that employing subsidiaries bear an appropriate share of the overall cost of a group-wide share scheme.

12.2 Accounting treatment of group share schemes – summary

12.2.1 Background

From a financial reporting perspective, it is generally necessary to consider the accounting treatment in:

- the group's consolidated financial statements;
- the parent's separate financial statements; and
- the employing subsidiary's financial statements.

We make the assumption throughout Section 12 that the subsidiary is directly owned by the parent company. In practice, there will often be one or more intermediate holding companies between the ultimate parent and the subsidiary. The intermediate parent company generally will not be the entity granting the award, receiving the goods or services or responsible for settling the award. Therefore, under IFRS 2, we believe that there is no requirement for the intermediate company to account for the award in its separate financial statements (although it might choose to recognise an increase in its investment in the subsidiary and a corresponding capital contribution from the ultimate parent in order for the transaction to be reflected throughout the chain of companies).

The accounting entries to be made will broadly vary according to:

- whether the award is satisfied using shares purchased in the market or a fresh issue of shares;
- whether any charge is made to the employing subsidiary for the cost of awards to its employees;

- whether an employee benefit trust (EBT) is involved. The accounting treatment of transactions undertaken with and by EBTs is discussed in more detail at 12.3 below; and
- the tax consequences of the award. However, for the purposes of the discussion and illustrative examples below, tax effects are ignored, since these will vary significantly by jurisdiction. A more general discussion of the tax effects of share-based payment transactions may be found at 14 below and in Chapter 29 at 10.8.

12.2.2 Scope of IFRS 2 for group share schemes

By virtue of the definition of 'share-based payment transaction' (see 2.2.1 and 2.2.2.A above), a group share-based payment transaction is in the scope of IFRS 2 for:

- the consolidated financial statements of the group (the accounting for which follows the general principles set out in 3 to 10 above);
- the separate or individual financial statements of the entity in the group that receives goods or services (see 12.2.3 below); and
- the separate or individual financial statements of the entity in the group (if different from that receiving the goods or services) that settles the transaction with the counterparty. This entity will typically, but not necessarily, be the parent (see 12.2.4 below).

IFRS 2 provides further guidance on the implication of its general principles to:

- transactions settled in the equity of the entity, or in the equity of its parent (see 12.2.5 below); and
- cash-settled transactions settled by a group entity other than the entity receiving the goods or services (see 12.2.6 below).

Section 2.2.2.A above considers seven scenarios commonly found in practice and outlines the approach required by IFRS 2 in the consolidated and separate or individual financial statements of group entities depending on whether the award is settled in cash or shares and which entity grants the award, settles the award and receives the goods or services.

It is common practice in a group share scheme to require each participating entity in the group to pay a charge, either to the parent or to an EBT, in respect of the cost of awards made under the scheme to employees of that entity. This is generally done either as part of the group's cash-management strategy, or in order to obtain tax relief under applicable local legislation. The amount charged could in principle be at the discretion of the group, but is often based on either the fair value of the award at grant date or the fair value at vesting, in the case of an award of free shares, or exercise, in the case of an award of options.

IFRS 2 does not directly address the accounting treatment of such intragroup management charges and other recharge arrangements, which is discussed further at 12.2.7 below. *[IFRS 2.B45-46]*.

Worked examples illustrating how these various principles translate into accounting entries are given at 12.4 to 12.6 below.

12.2.3 *Entity receiving goods or services*

The entity in a group receiving goods or services in a share-based payment transaction determines whether the transaction should be accounted for, in its separate or individual financial statements, as equity-settled or cash-settled. It does this by assessing the nature of the awards granted and its own rights and obligations. *[IFRS 2.43A].*

The entity accounts for the transaction as equity-settled when either the awards granted are the entity's own equity instruments, or the entity has no obligation to settle the share-based payment transaction. Otherwise, the entity accounts for the transaction as cash-settled. Where the transaction is accounted for as equity-settled it is remeasured after grant date only to the extent permitted or required by IFRS 2 for equity transactions generally, as discussed at 3 to 6 above. *[IFRS 2.43B].*

IFRS 2 notes that a possible consequence of these requirements is that the amount recognised by the entity may differ from the amount recognised by the consolidated group or by another group entity settling the share-based payment transaction. *[IFRS 2.43A].* This is discussed further at 12.6 below.

The cost recognised by the entity receiving goods or services is always calculated according to the principles set out above, regardless of any intragroup recharging arrangement. *[IFRS 2.43D, B45].* The accounting for such arrangements is discussed at 12.2.7 below.

12.2.4 *Entity settling the transaction*

A group entity which settles a share-based payment transaction in which another group entity receives goods or services accounts for the transaction as an equity-settled share-based payment transaction only if it is settled in the settling entity's own equity instruments. Otherwise, the transaction is accounted for as cash-settled. *[IFRS 2.43C].*

IFRS 2 specifies only the credit entry – the classification of the transaction as equity- or cash-settled, and its measurement. IFRS 2 does not specify the debit entry, which is therefore subject to the general requirement of IFRS 2 that a share-based payment transaction should normally be treated as an expense, unless there is the basis for another treatment under other IFRS (see 3 above).

In our view, the settling entity should not normally treat the transaction as an expense. Instead:

- Where the settling entity is a parent (direct or indirect) of the entity receiving the goods or services, it accounts for the settlement under IAS 27 – *Separate Financial Statements* – as an addition to the cost of its investment in the employing subsidiary (or of that holding company of the employing subsidiary which is the settling entity's directly-held subsidiary). *[IFRS 2.B45].* It may then be necessary to review the carrying value of that investment to ensure that it is not impaired.
- In other cases (i.e. where the settling entity is a subsidiary (direct or indirect) or fellow subsidiary of the entity receiving the goods or services), it should treat the settlement as a distribution, and charge it directly to equity. Whether or not such a settlement is a legal distribution is a matter of law in the jurisdiction concerned.

We adopt this approach in the worked examples set out in 12.4 to 12.6 below.

12.2.5 Transactions settled in equity of the entity or its parent

12.2.5.A Awards settled in equity of subsidiary

Where a subsidiary grants an award to its employees and settles it in its own equity, the subsidiary accounts for the award as equity-settled.

The parent accounts for the award as equity-settled in its consolidated financial statements. In its separate financial statements, the parent is not required by IFRS 2 to account for the award. In both cases, the transaction may have implications for other aspects of the financial statements, since its settlement results in the partial disposal of the subsidiary (see Chapter 7).

Where the parent settles the award, it accounts for the transaction as equity-settled in its consolidated financial statements. In its separate financial statements, however, it accounts for the award as cash-settled, since it is settled not in its own equity, but in the equity of the subsidiary. From the perspective of the parent's separate financial statements, the equity of a subsidiary is a financial asset. *[IFRS 2.B50]*.

12.2.5.B Awards settled in equity of the parent

Where the parent grants an award directly to the employees of a subsidiary and settles it in its own equity, the subsidiary accounts for the award as equity-settled, with a corresponding increase in equity as a contribution from the parent. *[IFRS 2.B53]*.

The parent accounts for the award as equity-settled in both its consolidated and separate financial statements. *[IFRS 2.B54]*.

Where a subsidiary grants an award of equity in its parent to its employees and settles the award itself, it accounts for the award as cash-settled, since it is settled not in its own equity, but in the equity of its parent. From the perspective of the subsidiary's separate or individual financial statements, the equity of the parent is a financial asset. *[IFRS 2.B55]*.

This requirement potentially represents something of a compliance burden. For the purposes of the parent's consolidated financial statements the fair value of the award needs to be calculated once, at grant date. For the purposes of the subsidiary's financial statements, however, IFRS 2 requires the award to be accounted for as cash-settled, with the fair value recalculated at each reporting date.

It is, however, important to note that IFRS 2 requires this accounting treatment only for a subsidiary that 'grants' such an award. *[IFRS 2.B52, headings to B53 & B55]*. In some jurisdictions it is normal for grants of share awards to be made by the parent, or an employee service company or EBT, rather than by the subsidiary, although the subsidiary may well make recommendations to the grantor of the award as to which of its employees should benefit.

In those cases, the fact that the subsidiary may communicate the award to the employee does not necessarily mean that the subsidiary itself has granted the award. It may simply be notifying the employee of an award granted by another group entity. In that case the subsidiary should apply the normal requirement of IFRS 2 to account for the award as equity-settled.

12.2.6 Cash-settled transactions not settled by the entity receiving goods or services

IFRS 2 considers arrangements in which the parent has an obligation to make cash payments to the employees of a subsidiary linked to the price of either:

- the subsidiary's equity instruments, or
- the parent's equity instruments.

In both cases, the subsidiary has no obligation to settle the transaction and therefore accounts for the transaction as equity-settled, recognising a corresponding credit in equity as a contribution from its parent.

The subsidiary then subsequently remeasures the cost of the transaction only for any changes resulting from non-market vesting conditions not being met in accordance with the normal provisions of IFRS 2 discussed at 3 to 6 above. IFRS 2 points out that this will differ from the measurement of the transaction as cash-settled in the consolidated financial statements of the group. *[IFRS 2.B56-57].*

In both cases, the parent has an obligation to settle the transaction in cash. Accordingly, the parent accounts for the transaction as cash-settled in both its consolidated and separate financial statements. *[IFRS 2.B58].*

The requirement for the subsidiary to measure the transaction as equity-settled is somewhat controversial. The essential rationale for requiring the subsidiary to record the cost of a share-based payment transaction settled by its parent is to reflect that the subsidiary is effectively receiving a capital contribution from its parent. Many commentators, including ourselves, consider it more appropriate to measure that contribution by reference to the cash actually paid by the parent, rather than to use a notional accounting cost derived from a valuation model.

The IASB specifically considered this issue, but concluded that the approach adopted in IFRS 2 better reflects the perspective of the subsidiary as a separate reporting entity. An accounting treatment based on the cash paid by the parent would, in the IASB's view, reflect the perspective of the parent rather than that of the subsidiary. *[IFRS 2.BC268H-268K].*

12.2.7 Intragroup recharges and management charges

As noted at 12.2.2 above, IFRS 2 does not deal with the accounting treatment of intragroup recharges and management charges that may be levied on the subsidiary that receives goods or services, the consideration for which is equity or cash of another group entity. The timing of the recognition of intercompany recharges was considered by the Interpretations Committee in 2013 as noted at 12.2.7.A below.

The accounting requirements of IFRS 2 for group share schemes derive from IFRIC 11 (now incorporated within IFRS 2 – see 1.2 above), which was based on an exposure draft (D17) published in 2005.

D17 proposed that any such payment made by a subsidiary should be charged directly to equity, on the basis that it represents a return of the capital contribution recorded as the credit to equity required by IFRS 2 (see 12.2.3 and 12.2.6 above) up to the amount of that contribution, and a distribution thereafter.[36]

In our view, whilst IFRS 2 clearly does not require this treatment, this is the preferable analysis. Indeed, the only alternative, 'mechanically' speaking, would be to charge the relevant amount to profit or loss. This would result in a double charge (once for the IFRS 2 charge, and again for the management charge or recharge) which we consider inappropriate in cases where the recharge is directly related to the value of the share-based payment transaction. Accordingly, in the examples at 12.4 to 12.6 below, we apply the treatment originally proposed in D17 to any payments made by the subsidiary for participation in the group scheme.

Many intragroup recharge arrangements are based directly on the value of the underlying share-based payment – typically at grant date, vesting date or exercise date. In other cases, a more general management charge might be levied that reflects not just share-based payments but also a number of other arrangements or services provided to the subsidiary by the parent. Where there is a more general management charge of this kind, we believe that it is more appropriate for the subsidiary to recognise a double charge to profit or loss rather than debiting the management charge to equity as would be the case for a direct recharge.

Before the June 2009 amendment to IFRS 2 (see 1.2 above), some took the view that, whilst any recharge up to the amount of the IFRS 2 charge should be charged to equity, any excess should be charged to profit or loss. The objective of this treatment is to ensure that profit or loss bears the full cash cost of the award where this is greater than the IFRS 2 charge. It is difficult to reconcile this approach to the clear requirement of IFRS 2 (as amended) that the receiving entity should measure the goods or services received by reference to IFRS 2 'regardless' of any intragroup charging arrangements (see 12.2.3 above). Moreover, we struggle to see a satisfactory conceptual basis for this 'split' treatment, and, in particular, for why one part of a payment made under the same intragroup charging arrangement should be accounted for as a distribution and the remainder as an expense.

IFRS 2 also does not address how the parent should account for a recharge or management charge received. In our view, to the extent that the receipt represents a return of a capital contribution made to the subsidiary, the parent may choose whether to credit:

- the carrying amount of its investment in the subsidiary; or
- profit or loss (with a corresponding impairment review of the investment).

Any amount received in excess of the capital contribution previously debited to the investment in subsidiary should be accounted for as a distribution from the subsidiary and credited to the income statement of the parent. Where applicable, the illustrative examples at 12.4 to 12.6 below show the entire amount as a credit to the income statement rather than part of the recharge being treated as a credit to the investment in subsidiary.

The treatment of a distribution from a subsidiary in the separate financial statements of a parent is more generally discussed in Chapter 8 at 2.3.

A further issue that arises in practice is the timing of recognition of the recharge by the parties to the arrangement. The treatment adopted might depend to some extent on the precise terms of the arrangement but two approaches are seen in practice:

- to account for the recharge when it is actually levied or paid (which is consistent with accounting for a distribution); or
- to accrue the recharge over the life of the award or the recharge agreement even if, as is commonly the case, the actual recharge is only made at vesting or exercise date.

In our view, the first approach is often the more appropriate in a group context where recharge arrangements might not be binding until such time as payment is required to be made. It is also consistent with the overall recognition of the arrangement through equity and with a situation where uncertainties are likely to exist during the vesting period about the existence of a present obligation and the estimated cash outflow. The alternative approach treats the recharge more like a provision or financial liability but, unlike the requirements of IAS 37 or IAS 39, reflects changes in the recognised amount through equity rather than profit or loss and builds up the recharge liability over the life of the award rather than recognising the liability in full when a present obligation has been identified.

Where applicable, the examples at 12.4 to 12.6 below illustrate the first of the two treatments outlined above and recognise the recharge only when it becomes payable at the date of exercise.

Whichever accounting treatment is adopted, any adjustments to the amount to be recognised as a recharge, whether arising from a change in the IFRS 2 expense or other changes, should be recognised in the current period and previous periods should not be restated.

12.2.7.A Timing of recognition of intercompany recharges: discussion by the IFRS Interpretations Committee

The Interpretations Committee received a request for clarification of the treatment of intragroup recharges for share-based payments. In the example considered by the Interpretations Committee at its January 2013 meeting, a parent entity responsible for settling an award with the employees of a subsidiary enters into a recharge agreement that requires the subsidiary to pay to the parent the value of the share-based payments on settlement of the awards by the parent. The Interpretations Committee was asked whether the liability to the parent should be recognised by the subsidiary from the grant date of the award or only at the date of settlement of the award.

Outreach conducted by the Interpretations Committee suggested that there is diversity in practice (as indicated at 12.2.7 above). On this basis, and following discussion, the Interpretations Committee concluded in May 2013 that the topic could not be restricted to recharges relating to share-based payments and therefore decided not to add this issue to its agenda.[37]

12.3 Employee benefit trusts ('EBTs') and similar entities

12.3.1 Background

For some time entities have established trusts and similar entities for the benefit of employees. These are known by various names in different jurisdictions, but, for the sake of convenience, in this section we will use the term 'EBT' ('employee benefit trust') to cover all such vehicles by whatever name they are actually known.

The commercial purposes of using such entities vary from employer to employer, and from jurisdiction to jurisdiction, but may include the following:

- An EBT, in order to achieve its purpose, needs to hold shares that have either been issued to it by the company or been bought by the EBT on the open market. In some jurisdictions, the direct holding of shares in an entity by the entity itself is unlawful.
- In the case of longer-term benefits the use of an EBT may 'ring fence' the assets set aside for the benefit of employees in case of the insolvency of the company.
- The use of an EBT may be necessary in order to achieve a favourable tax treatment for the company or the employees, or both.

The detailed features of an EBT will again vary from entity to entity, and from jurisdiction to jurisdiction, but typical features often include the following:

- The EBT provides a warehouse for the sponsoring entity's shares, for example by acquiring and holding shares that are to be sold or transferred to employees in the future. The trustees may purchase the shares with finance provided by the sponsoring entity (by way of cash contributions or loans), or by a third-party bank loan, or by a combination of the two. Loans from the entity are usually interest-free. In other cases, the EBT may subscribe directly for shares issued by the sponsoring company or acquire shares in the market.
- Where the EBT borrows from a third party, the sponsoring entity will usually guarantee the loan, i.e. it will be responsible for any shortfall if the EBT's assets are insufficient to meet its debt repayment obligations. The entity will also generally make regular contributions to the EBT to enable the EBT to meet its interest payments, i.e. to make good any shortfall between the dividend income of the EBT (if any) and the interest payable. As part of this arrangement the trustees may waive their right to dividends on the shares held by the EBT.
- Shares held by the EBT are distributed to employees through an employee share scheme. There are many different arrangements – these may include:
  - the purchase of shares by employees when exercising their share options under a share option scheme;
  - the purchase of shares by the trustees of an approved profit-sharing scheme for allocation to employees under the rules of the scheme; or
  - the transfer of shares to employees under some other incentive scheme.
- The trustees of an EBT may have a legal duty to act at all times in accordance with the interests of the beneficiaries under the EBT. However, most EBTs (particularly those established as a means of remunerating employees) are

specifically designed so as to serve the purposes of the sponsoring entity, and to ensure that there will be minimal risk of any conflict arising between the duties of the trustees and the interest of the entity.

12.3.2 Accounting for EBTs

Historically, transactions involving EBTs were accounted for according to their legal form. In other words, any cash gifted or lent to the EBT was simply treated as, respectively, an expense or a loan in the financial statements of the employing entity.

However, this treatment gradually came to be challenged, not least by some tax authorities who began to question whether it was appropriate to allow a corporate tax deduction for the 'expense' of putting money into an EBT which in some cases might remain in the EBT for some considerable time (or even be lent back to the company) before being actually passed on to employees. Thus, the issue came onto the agenda of the national standard setters.

The accounting solution proposed by some national standard setters, such as in the United States and the United Kingdom, was to require a reporting entity to account for an EBT as an extension of the entity. The basis for this treatment was essentially that, as noted at 12.3.1 above, EBTs are specifically designed to serve the purposes of the sponsoring entity, and to ensure that there will be minimal risk of any conflict arising between the duties of the trustees and the interest of the entity, suggesting that they are under the de facto control of the entity.

For accounting periods beginning on or after 1 January 2013, unless a later adoption date applies in an entity's jurisdiction, an entity has to assess whether it is required to consolidate an EBT based on the control criteria set out in IFRS 10 – *Consolidated Financial Statements:*

- it has power over the EBT;
- it has exposure, or rights, to variable returns from its involvement with the EBT; and
- it has the ability to use its power over the EBT to affect the amount of the sponsoring entity's returns.

The requirements of IFRS 10 are discussed in more detail in Chapter 6.

The required treatment of EBTs in an employer's separate financial statements is somewhat less clear, and is discussed at 12.3.4 below.

Paragraphs BC70 to BC74 of the Basis for Conclusions to IFRS 2 are clearly written on the assumption that the trust referred to in paragraph BC70 is being included in the financial statements of the reporting entity. This further suggests that the IASB regards the consolidation of such entities as normal practice. *[IFRS 2.BC70-74]*.

Consolidation of an EBT will have the following broad consequences for the consolidated financial statements of the reporting entity:

- Until such time as the entity's own shares held by the EBT vest unconditionally in employees:
  - any consideration paid for the shares should be deducted in arriving at shareholders' equity in accordance with IAS 32 (see Chapter 43 at 9); and
  - the shares should be treated as if they were treasury shares when calculating earnings per share under IAS 33 (see Chapter 33 at 3.2).
- Other assets and liabilities (including borrowings) of the EBT should be recognised as assets and liabilities in the consolidated financial statements of the sponsoring entity.
- No gain or loss should be recognised in profit or loss on the purchase, sale, issue or cancellation of the entity's own shares, as required by IAS 32. Although not explicitly required by IFRS, we suggest that entities show consideration paid or received for the purchase or sale of the entity's own shares in an EBT separately from other purchases and sales of the entity's own shares in the reconciliation of movements in shareholders' equity. This may be particularly relevant for entities in jurisdictions that distinguish between 'true' treasury shares (i.e. those legally held by the issuing entity) and those accounted for as such under IFRS (such as those held by an EBT).
- Any dividend income arising on own shares should be excluded in arriving at profit before tax and deducted from the aggregate of dividends paid and proposed. In our view, the deduction should be disclosed if material.
- Finance costs and any administration expenses should be charged as they accrue and not as funding payments are made to the EBT.

In some cases, an EBT will reach the stage where, or be designed so that, it only holds employees' fully vested shares (the shares often remaining in trust for tax purposes once they have vested). Where this is the case, and the EBT is no longer holding any unvested shares, consolidation of the EBT will cease. Within Section 12, however, our focus is on arrangements where the EBT holds unallocated shares of the entity and/or shares that have been allocated to employees but which have not yet vested.

12.3.3 Illustrative Examples – awards satisfied by shares purchased by, or issued to, an EBT

The following Examples assume that the EBT is consolidated in accordance with IFRS 10, and show the interaction of the requirements of IFRS 10 with those of IFRS 2. Example 30.48 illustrates the treatment where an award is satisfied using shares previously purchased in the market. Example 30.49 illustrates the treatment where freshly issued shares are used.

Example 30.48: Interaction of IFRS 10, IAS 32 and IFRS 2 (market purchase)

On 1 January 2014, the EBT of ABC plc made a market purchase of 100,000 shares of ABC plc at £2.50 per share. These were the only ABC shares held by the EBT at that date.

On 1 May 2014, ABC granted executives options over between 300,000 and 500,000 shares at £2.70 per share, which will vest on 31 December 2014, the number vesting depending on various performance criteria. It is determined that the cost to be recognised in respect of this award under IFRS 2 is 15p per share.

On 1 September 2014, the EBT made a further market purchase of 300,000 shares at £2.65 per share.

On 31 December 2014, options vested over 350,000 shares and were exercised immediately.

The accounting entries for the above transaction required by IFRS 10, IAS 32 and IFRS 2 in the consolidated financial statements of ABC would be as follows. It should be noted that all these pronouncements require various entries to be recorded in 'equity'. Thus, some variation may be found in practice as to the precise characterisation of the reserves, in deference to local legal requirements and other 'traditions' in national GAAP which are retained to the extent that they do not conflict with IFRS.

	£	£
1 January 2014		
Own shares (equity)	250,000	
Cash		250,000
To record purchase of 100,000 £1 shares at £2.50/share		
1 May 2014 – 31 December 2014		
Profit or loss	52,500	
Equity†		52,500
To record cost of vested 350,000 options at 15p/option		
1 September 2014		
Own shares (equity)	795,000	
Cash		795,000
To record purchase of 300,000 £1 shares at £2.65/share		
31 December 2014		
Cash	945,000	
Equity†[1]		945,000
Receipt of proceeds on exercise of 350,000 options at £2.70/share		
Equity†	914,375	
Own shares (equity)[2]		914,375
Release of shares from EBT to employees		

1 This reflects the fact that the entity has had an increase in resources as a result of a transaction with an owner, which gives rise to no gain or loss and is therefore credited direct to equity.

2 It is necessary to transfer the cost of the shares 'reissued' by the EBT out of own shares, as the deduction for own shares would otherwise be overstated. The total cost of the pool of 400,000 shares immediately before vesting was £1,045,000 (£250,000 purchased on 1 January 2014 and £795,000 purchased on 1 September 2014), representing an average cost per share of £2.6125. £2.6125 × 350,000 shares = £914,375.

† We recommend that, subject to any local legal restrictions, these amounts should all be accounted for in the same component of equity.

Example 30.48 illustrates the importance of keeping the accounting treatment required by IAS 32 for the cost of the shares completely separate from that for the cost of the award required by IFRS 2. In cash terms, ABC has made a 'profit' of £30,625, since it purchased 350,000 shares with a weighted average cost of £914,375 and issued them to the executives for £945,000. However, this 'profit' is accounted for entirely within equity, whereas a calculated IFRS 2 cost of £52,500 is recognised in profit or loss.

Example 30.49: Interaction of IFRS 10, IAS 32 and IFRS 2 (fresh issue of shares)

On 1 January 2014, the EBT of ABC plc subscribed for 100,000 £1 shares of ABC plc at £2.50 per share, paid for in cash provided by ABC by way of loan to the EBT. Under local law, these proceeds must be credited to the share capital account up to the par value of the shares issued, with any excess taken to a share premium account (additional paid-in capital). These were the only ABC shares held by the EBT at that date.

On 1 May 2014, ABC granted executives options over between 300,000 and 500,000 shares at £2.70 per share, which will vest on 31 December 2014, the number vesting depending on various performance criteria. It is determined that the cost to be recognised in respect of this award is 15p per share.

On 1 September 2014, the EBT subscribed for a further 300,000 shares at £2.65 per share, again paid for in cash provided by ABC by way of loan to the EBT.

On 31 December 2014, options vested over 350,000 shares and were exercised immediately.

The accounting entries for the above transaction required by IFRS 10, IAS 32 and IFRS 2 in the consolidated financial statements of ABC would be as follows. It should be noted that all these pronouncements require various entries to be recorded in 'equity'. Thus, some variation may be found in practice as to the precise characterisation of the reserves, in deference to local legal requirements and other 'traditions' in national GAAP which are retained to the extent that they do not conflict with IFRS.

	£	£
1 January 2014		
Equity†1	250,000	
Share capital		100,000
Share premium		150,000
To record issue of 100,000 £1 shares to EBT at £2.50/share		
1 May 2014 – 31 December 2014		
Profit or loss	52,500	
Equity†		52,500
To record cost of vested 350,000 options at 15p/option		
1 September 2014		
Equity†1	795,000	
Share capital		300,000
Share premium		495,000
To record issue of 300,000 £1 shares at £2.65/share		
31 December 2014		
Cash	945,000	
Equity2†		945,000
Receipt of proceeds on exercise of 350,000 options at £2.70/share		

1 This entry is required to reconcile the requirement of local law to record an issue of shares with the fact that, in reality, there has been no increase in the resources of the reporting entity. All that has happened is that one member of the reporting group (the EBT) has transferred cash to another (the parent entity). In our view, this amount should not be accounted for within any 'Own shares reserve' in equity, which should be restricted to shares acquired from third parties.

2 This reflects the fact that the entity has had an increase in resources as a result of a transaction with an owner, which gives rise to no gain or loss and is therefore credited direct to equity.

† We recommend that, subject to any local legal restrictions, these amounts should all be accounted for in the same component of equity.

12.3.4 Separate financial statements

In contrast to some national GAAPs, where an EBT is treated as a direct extension of the parent entity, such that the assets and liabilities of the EBT are included in both the separate and consolidated financial statements of the parent, under IFRS the accounting model is *prima facie* to treat the EBT as a separate group entity.

This means that the separate financial statements of the employing entity must show transactions and balances with, rather than the transactions, assets and liabilities of, the EBT. This raises some accounting problems, for some of which IFRS currently provides no real solution, as illustrated by Example 30.50 below. This has led the Interpretations Committee and others to discuss whether the 'separate entity' approach to accounting for EBTs is appropriate.

Example 30.50: EBTs in separate financial statements of sponsoring entity

An entity lends its EBT €1 million which the EBT uses to make a market purchase of 200,000 shares in the entity. In the separate financial statements of the EBT the shares will be shown as an asset. In the consolidated financial statements, the shares will be accounted for as treasury shares, by deduction from equity.

In the separate financial statements of the entity, on the basis that the EBT is a separate entity, like any other subsidiary, the normal accounting entry would be:

	€	€
Loan to EBT	1,000,000	
Cash		1,000,000

The obvious issue with this approach is that it is, in economic substance, treating the shares held by the EBT (represented by the loan to the EBT) as an asset of the entity, whereas, if they were held directly by the entity, they would have to be accounted for as treasury shares, by deduction from equity. If the share price falls such that the EBT has no means of repaying the full €1,000,000, *prima facie* this gives rise to an impairment of the €1,000,000 loan. Again, however, this seems in effect to be recognising a loss on own equity.

Suppose now that employees are granted options over the shares with an exercise price of zero, which have a value under IFRS 2 of €1,200,000. The entity will therefore book an expense of €1,200,000 under IFRS 2. When the options are exercised, the shares are delivered to employees. At that point the €1,000,000 loan to the EBT clearly becomes irrecoverable (as it has no assets), and must be written off. Normally, the write-off of an investment or loan is an expense required to be recognised in profit or loss. However, to recognise the €1,000,000 investment write-off as an expense as well as the €1,200,000 IFRS 2 charge would clearly be a form of double counting.

Some suggest that a solution to this problem is to say that the entity has effectively bought a gross-settled call option over its own shares from the EBT, whereby it can require the EBT to deliver 200,000 shares in return for a waiver of its €1,000,000 loan. Thus the accounting for the settlement of the call over the shares is as for any other gross-settled purchased call option over own equity under IAS 32 – see Chapter 43 at 11.2.1.

	€	€
Own shares (deduction from equity)	1,000,000	
Loan to EBT		1,000,000

When the shares are delivered to employees (some milliseconds later), the entry is:

	€	€
Other component of equity	1,000,000	
Own shares (deduction from equity)		1,000,000

At its meetings in May and July 2006, the Interpretations Committee discussed whether the EBT should be treated as an extension of the sponsoring entity, such as a branch, or as a separate entity. The Interpretations Committee decided to explore how specific transactions between the sponsor and the EBT should be treated in the sponsor's separate or individual financial statements and whether transactions between the EBT and the sponsor's employees should be attributed to the sponsor.

Interestingly, the Interpretations Committee fell short of dismissing the 'extension of the parent company' approach and has not since revisited this topic other than to re-confirm in March 2011 that it had not become aware of additional concerns or of diversity in practice and hence it did not think it necessary for this to be considered for the IASB's agenda. In our view, whilst any requirement to consolidate EBTs under IFRS 10 could be argued to give a clear steer towards treating the EBT as a separate entity, until there is any final clarification of this issue, it appears acceptable to treat an EBT as an extension of, or agent for, the sponsoring entity in that entity's separate financial statements. This treatment would result in outcomes essentially the same as those in Examples 30.48 and 30.49 above, while avoiding the problems highlighted in Example 30.50 above.

12.3.5 *Financial statements of the EBT*

The EBT may be required to prepare financial statements in accordance with requirements imposed by local law or by its own trust deed. The form and content of such financial statements are beyond the scope of this Chapter.

12.4 Illustrative example of group share scheme – equity-settled award satisfied by market purchase of shares

The discussion in 12.4.1 to 12.4.3 below is based on Example 30.51 and addresses the accounting treatment for three distinct aspects of a group share scheme – a share-based payment arrangement involving group entities (see 12.2 above), the use of an EBT (see 12.3 above) and a group recharge arrangement (see 12.2.7 above).

This illustrative example treats the recharge by the parent to the subsidiary as an income statement credit in the individual accounts of the parent and recognises the recharge when it is paid. In some situations, entities might consider it appropriate to apply alternative accounting treatments (see 12.2.7 above).

Example 30.51: Group share scheme (market purchase of shares)

On 1 July 2014 an employee of S Limited, a subsidiary of the H plc group, is awarded options under the H group share scheme over 3,000 shares in H plc at £1.50 each, exercisable between 1 July 2017 and 1 July 2020, subject to certain performance criteria being met in the three years ending 30 June 2017.

H plc is the grantor of the award, and has the obligation to settle it. On 1 January 2015, in connection with the award, the H plc group EBT purchases 3,000 shares at the then prevailing market price of £2.00 each, funded by a loan from H plc. On exercise of the option, S Limited is required to pay the differential between the purchase price of the shares and the exercise price of the option (50p per share) to the EBT.

For the purposes of IFRS 2, the options are considered to have a fair value at grant date of £1 per option. Throughout the vesting period of the option, H takes the view that the award will vest in full.

The option is exercised on 1 September 2019, at which point the EBT uses the option proceeds, together with the payment by S Limited, to repay the loan from H plc.

H plc and its subsidiaries have a 31 December year end.

12.4.1 Consolidated financial statements

So far as the consolidated financial statements are concerned, the transactions to be accounted for are:

- the purchase of the shares by the EBT and their eventual transfer to the employee; and
- the cost of the award.

Transactions between H plc or S Limited and the EBT are ignored since, in this Example, the EBT is consolidated (see 12.3 above). The accounting entries required are set out below. As in other examples in this Chapter, where an entry is shown as being made to equity the precise allocation to a particular component of equity will be a matter for local legislation and, possibly, local accounting 'tradition', to the extent that this is not incompatible with IFRS.

		£	£
y/e 31.12.2014	Profit or loss (employee costs)*	500	
	Equity		500
1.1.2015	Own shares (equity)	6,000	
	Cash		6,000
y/e 31.12.2015	Profit or loss (employee costs)*	1,000	
	Equity		1,000
y/e 31.12.2016	Profit or loss (employee costs)*	1,000	
	Equity		1,000
y/e 31.12.2017	Profit or loss (employee costs)*	500	
	Equity		500
1.9.2019	Cash (option proceeds)†	4,500	
	Equity‡	1,500	
	Own shares (equity)**		6,000

* Total cost £3,000 (3000 options × £1) spread over 36 months. Charge for period to December 2014 is 6/36 × £3,000 = £500, and so on. In practice, where options are granted to a group of individuals, or with variable performance criteria, the annual charge will be based on a continually revised cumulative charge (see further discussion at 6.1 to 6.4 above).

† 3,000 options at £1.50 each.

‡ This reflects the fact that the overall effect of the transaction for the group *in cash terms* has been a 'loss' of £1,500 (£6,000 original cost of shares less £4,500 option proceeds received). However, under IFRS this is an equity transaction, not an expense.

** £6,000 cost of own shares purchased on 1 January 2015 now transferred to the employee. In practice, it is more likely that the appropriate amount to be transferred would be based on the weighted average price of shares held by the EBT at the date of exercise, as in Example 30.48 at 12.3.3 above. In such a case there would be a corresponding adjustment to the debit to equity marked with ‡ above.

12.4.2 Parent

The parent has to consider the accounting treatment of the EBT (i.e. whether it is accounted for as a separate entity or an extension of the parent – see 12.3 above). This gives two possible accounting treatments:

- EBT treated as separate entity (see 12.4.2.A below); and
- EBT treated as extension of parent (see 12.4.2.B below).

We also discuss, at 12.4.2.C below, the accounting implications if the parent, rather than – as in Example 30.51 – a subsidiary, is the employing entity.

12.4.2.A EBT treated as separate entity

The parent accounts for the share-based payment transaction under IFRS 2 as an equity-settled transaction, since the parent settles the award by delivering its own equity instruments to the employees of the subsidiary (see 12.2.4 above). However, as discussed at 12.2.4 above, instead of recording a cost, as in its consolidated financial statements, the parent records an increase in the carrying value of its investment in subsidiary. It might then be necessary to consider whether the ever-increasing investment in subsidiary is supportable or is in fact impaired. As this is a matter to be determined in the light of specific facts and circumstances, it is not considered in this example. Any impairment charge would be recorded in profit or loss.

In addition to accounting for the share-based payment transaction, the parent records its transactions with the EBT and the purchase of shares.

This gives rise to the following entries:

		£	£
y/e 31.12.2014	Investment in subsidiary*	500	
	Equity		500
1.1.2015	Loan to EBT	6,000	
	Cash		6,000
y/e 31.12.2015	Investment in subsidiary*	1,000	
	Equity		1,000
y/e 31.12.2016	Investment in subsidiary*	1,000	
	Equity		1,000
y/e 31.12.2017	Investment in subsidiary*	500	
	Equity		500
1.9.2019	Cash	6,000	
	Loan to EBT		6,000

* Total increase in investment £3,000 (3000 shares × £1 fair value of each option) recognised over 36 months. Increase during period to December 2014 is 6/36 × £3,000 = £500, and so on. In practice, where options were granted to a group of individuals, or with variable performance criteria, the annual adjustment would be based on a continually revised cumulative adjustment (see further discussion at 6.1 to 6.4 above).

12.4.2.B EBT treated as extension of the parent

The parent accounts for the share-based payment transaction under IFRS 2 as an equity-settled transaction, since the parent settles the award by delivering its own equity instruments to the employees of the subsidiary (see 12.2.4 above). However, as discussed at 12.2.4 above, instead of recording a cost, as in its consolidated financial statements, the parent records an increase in the carrying value of its investment in subsidiary. It might then be necessary to consider whether the ever-increasing investment in subsidiary is supportable or is in fact impaired. As this is a matter to be determined in the light of specific facts and circumstances, it is not considered in this example. Any impairment charge would be recorded in profit or loss.

In addition to accounting for the share-based payment transaction, the parent records the transactions of the EBT and the purchase of shares.

This gives rise to the following entries:

		£	£
y/e 31.12.2014	Investment in subsidiary*	500	
	Equity		500
1.1.2015	Own shares (equity)	6,000	
	Cash		6,000
y/e 31.12.2015	Investment in subsidiary*	1,000	
	Equity		1,000
y/e 31.12.2016	Investment in subsidiary*	1,000	
	Equity		1,000
y/e 31.12.2017	Investment in subsidiary*	500	
	Equity		500
1.9.2019	Cash†	6,000	
	Equity‡	1,500	
	Profit or loss§		1,500
	Own shares** (equity)		6,000

* Total increase in investment £3,000 (3000 shares × £1 fair value of each option) spread over 36 months. Increase during period to December 2014 is 6/36 × £3,000 = £500, and so on. In practice, where options were granted to a group of individuals, or with variable performance criteria, the annual adjustment would be based on a continually revised cumulative adjustment (see further discussion at 6.1 to 6.4 above).

† £4,500 option exercise proceeds from employee plus £1,500 contribution from S Limited.

‡ This is essentially a balancing figure representing the fact that the entity is distributing own shares with an original cost of £6,000, but has treated £1,500 of the £6,000 of the cash it has received as income (see § below) rather than as payment for the shares.

§ The £1,500 contribution by the subsidiary to the EBT has been treated as a distribution from the subsidiary (see 12.2.7 above) and recorded in profit or loss. It might then be necessary to consider whether, as a result of this payment, the investment in the subsidiary had become impaired (see Chapter 8 at 2.3). As this is a matter to be determined in the light of specific facts and circumstances, it is not considered in this example. Any impairment charge would be recorded in profit or loss.

** £6,000 cost of own shares purchased on 1 January 2015 now transferred to employee. In practice, it is more likely that the appropriate amount to be transferred would be based on the weighted average price of shares held by the EBT at the date of exercise, as in Example 30.48 at 12.3.3 above.

12.4.2.C Parent company as employing company

If, in Example 30.51, the employing entity were the parent, it would record an expense under IFRS 2. It would also normally waive £1,500 of its £6,000 loan to the EBT (i.e. the shortfall between the original loan and the £4,500 option proceeds received from the employee).

If the EBT is treated as an extension of the parent, the accounting entries for the parent would be the same as those for the group, as set out in 12.4.1 above.

If the EBT is treated as a separate entity, the accounting entries might be as follows:

		£	£
y/e 31.12.2014	Profit or loss*	500	
	Equity		500
1.1.2015	Loan to EBT	6,000	
	Cash		6,000
y/e 31.12.2015	Profit or loss*	1,000	
	Equity		1,000
y/e 31.12.2016	Profit or loss*	1,000	
	Equity		1,000
y/e 31.12.2017	Profit or loss*	500	
	Equity		500
1.9.2019	Own shares (Equity)†	1,500	
	Cash	4,500	
	Loan to EBT		6,000
	Equity	1,500	
	Own shares (Equity)		1,500

* Total cost £3,000 (3000 options × £1) spread over 36 months. Charge for period to December 2014 is 6/36 × £3,000 = £500, and so on. In practice, where options were granted to a group of individuals, or with variable performance criteria, the annual charge would be based on a continually revised cumulative charge (see further discussion at 6.1 to 6.4 above).

† This takes the approach of treating the parent as having a gross-settled purchased call option over its own equity (see Example 30.50 at 12.3.4 above), under which it can acquire 3,000 own shares from the EBT for the consideration of the waiver of £1,500 of the original £6,000 loan. The £4,500 cash inflow represents the £4,500 option exercise proceeds received by the EBT from the employee, which is then used to pay the balance of the original £6,000 loan.

12.4.3 Employing subsidiary

The employing subsidiary is required to account for the IFRS 2 expense and the contribution to the EBT on exercise of the award. This gives rise to the accounting entries set out below. The entries to reflect the IFRS 2 expense are required by IFRS 2 (see 12.2.3 above). The treatment of the contribution to the EBT as a distribution is based on the proposal in D17 (see 12.2.7 above).

		£	£
y/e 31.12.2014	Profit or loss*	500	
	Equity		500
y/e 31.12.2015	Profit or loss*	1,000	
	Equity		1,000
y/e 31.12.2016	Profit or loss*	1,000	
	Equity		1,000
y/e 31.12.2017	Profit or loss*	500	
	Equity		500
1.9.2019	Equity†	1,500	
	Cash		1,500

* Total cost £3,000 (3000 options × £1) spread over 36 months. Charge for period to December 2014 is 6/36 × £3,000 = £500, and so on. In practice, where options were granted to a group of individuals, or with variable performance criteria, the annual charge would be based on a continually revised cumulative charge (see further discussion at 6.1 to 6.4 above).

† This should be treated as a reduction of whatever component of equity was credited with the £3,000 quasi-contribution from the parent in the accounting entries above.

12.5 Illustrative example of group share scheme – equity-settled award satisfied by fresh issue of shares

Such schemes raise slightly different accounting issues. Again, these are most easily illustrated by way of an example. The discussion in 12.5.1 to 12.5.3 below is based on Example 30.52. As with Example 30.51 at 12.4 above, this section addresses the accounting treatment for three distinct aspects of a group share scheme – a share-based payment arrangement involving group entities (see 12.2 above), the use of an EBT (see 12.3 above) and a group recharge arrangement (see 12.2.7 above).

This illustrative example treats the recharge by the parent to the subsidiary as an income statement credit in the individual accounts of the parent and recognises the recharge when it is paid. In some situations, entities might consider it appropriate to apply alternative accounting treatments (see 12.2.7 above).

Example 30.52: Group share scheme (fresh issue of shares)

On 1 July 2014 an employee of S Limited, a subsidiary of the H plc group, is awarded options under the H group share scheme over 3,000 shares in H plc at £1.50 each, exercisable between 1 July 2017 and 1 July 2020, subject to certain performance criteria being met in the three years ending 30 June 2017. The fair value of the options on 1 July 2014 is £1 each.

H plc grants the award and has the obligation to settle it.

When preparing accounts during the vesting period H plc and its subsidiaries assume that the award will vest in full. The options are finally exercised on 1 September 2019, at which point H plc issues 3,000 new shares to the EBT at the then current market price of £3.50 for £10,500. The EBT funds the purchase using the £4,500 option proceeds received from the employee together with £6,000 contributed by S Limited, effectively representing the fair value of the options at exercise date (3,000 × [£3.50 – £1.50]). H plc and its subsidiaries have a 31 December year end.

12.5.1 Consolidated financial statements

The consolidated financial statements need to deal with:

- the charge required by IFRS 2 in respect of the award; and
- the issue of shares.

Transactions between H plc or S Limited and the EBT are ignored since, in this Example, the EBT is consolidated (see 12.3 above). The accounting entries required are set out below. As in other examples in this Chapter, where an entry is shown as being made to equity, the precise allocation to a particular component of equity will be a matter for local legislation and, possibly, local accounting 'tradition', to the extent that this is not incompatible with IFRS.

		£	£
y/e 31.12.2014	Profit or loss*	500	
	Equity		500
y/e 31.12.2015	Profit or loss*	1,000	
	Equity		1,000
y/e 31.12.2016	Profit or loss*	1,000	
	Equity		1,000
y/e 31.12.2017	Profit or loss*	500	
	Equity		500
1.9.2019	Cash	4,500	
	Equity†		4,500

* Total cost £3,000 (3000 options × £1) spread over 36 months. Charge for period to December 2014 is 6/36 × £3,000 = £500, and so on. In practice, where options were granted to a group of individuals, or with variable performance criteria, the annual charge would be based on a continually revised cumulative charge (see further discussion at 6.1 to 6.4 above).

† From the point of view of the consolidated group, the issue of shares results in an increase in net assets of only £4,500 (i.e. the exercise price received from the employee), since the £6,000 contribution from the employing subsidiary to the EBT is an intragroup transaction. However, it may be that, in certain jurisdictions, the entity is required to increase its share capital and share premium (additional paid in capital) accounts by the £10,500 legal consideration for the issue of shares. In that case, this entry would be expanded as below, which effectively treats the £6,000 consideration provided from within the group as a bonus issue.

		£	£
1.9.2019	Cash	4,500	
	Other equity	6,000	
	Share capital/premium		10,500

12.5.2 Parent

The parent has to consider the accounting treatment of the EBT (i.e. whether it is accounted for as a separate entity or an extension of the parent – see 12.3 above). This gives two possible accounting treatments:

- EBT treated as separate entity (see 12.5.2.A below); and
- EBT treated as extension of parent (see 12.5.2.B below).

We also discuss, at 12.5.2.C below, the accounting implications if the parent, rather than – as in Example 30.52 – a subsidiary, is the employing entity.

12.5.2.A EBT treated as separate entity

The parent accounts for the share-based payment transaction under IFRS 2 as an equity-settled transaction, since the parent settles the award by delivering its own equity instruments to the employees of the subsidiary (see 12.2.4 above). However, as discussed at 12.2.4 above, instead of recording a cost, as in its consolidated financial statements, the parent records an increase in the carrying value of its investment in subsidiary. It might then be necessary to consider whether the ever-increasing investment in subsidiary is supportable or is in fact impaired. As this is a matter to be determined in the light of specific facts and circumstances, it is not considered in this example. Any impairment charge would be recorded in profit or loss.

In addition to accounting for the share-based payment transaction, the parent records its transactions with the EBT and the issue of shares.

		£	£
y/e 31.12.2014	Investment in subsidiary*	500	
	Equity		500
y/e 31.12.2015	Investment in subsidiary*	1,000	
	Equity		1,000
y/e 31.12.2016	Investment in subsidiary*	1,000	
	Equity		1,000
y/e 31.12.2017	Investment in subsidiary*	500	
	Equity		500
1.9.2019	Cash†	10,500	
	Share capital/premium		10,500

* Total increase in investment £3,000 (3000 shares × £1 fair value of each option), recognised over 36 months. Increase in period to December 2014 is 6/36 × £3,000 = £500, and so on. In practice, where options were granted to a group of individuals, or with variable performance criteria, the annual adjustment would be based on a continually revised cumulative adjustment (see further discussion at 6.1 to 6.4 above).

† £4,500 option exercise proceeds from employee plus £6,000 contribution from the subsidiary.

12.5.2.B EBT treated as extension of parent

The parent accounts for the share-based payment transaction under IFRS 2 as an equity-settled transaction, since the parent settles the award by delivering its own equity instruments to the employees of the subsidiary (see 12.2.4 above). However, as discussed at 12.2.4 above, instead of recording a cost, as in its consolidated financial statements, the parent records an increase in the carrying value of its investment in subsidiary. It might then be necessary to consider whether the ever-increasing investment in subsidiary is supportable or is in fact impaired. As this is a matter to be determined in the light of specific facts and circumstances, it is not considered in this example. Any impairment charge would be recorded in profit or loss.

In addition to accounting for the share-based payment transaction, the parent records the transactions of the EBT and the issue of shares.

		£	£
y/e 31.12.2014	Investment in subsidiary*	500	
	Equity		500
y/e 31.12.2015	Investment in subsidiary*	1,000	
	Equity		1,000
y/e 31.12.2016	Investment in subsidiary*	1,000	
	Equity		1,000
y/e 31.12.2017	Investment in subsidiary*	500	
	Equity†		500
1.9.2019	Cash†	10,500	
	Equity‡	6,000	
	Profit or loss**		6,000
	Share capital/premium		10,500

* Total increase in investment £3,000 (3000 shares × £1 fair value of each option) spread over 36 months. Increase during period to December 2014 is 6/36 × £3,000 = £500, and so on. In practice, where options were granted to a group of individuals, or with variable performance criteria, the annual adjustment would be based on a continually revised cumulative adjustment (see further discussion at 6.1 to 6.4 above).

† £4,500 option exercise proceeds from employee plus £6,000 contribution from the subsidiary.

‡ This assumes that local law requires the entity to record share capital and share premium (additional paid-in capital) of £10,500, as in 12.5.2.A above. However, IFRS *prima facie* requires the £6,000 cash received by the EBT from the subsidiary to be treated as income (see ** below) rather than as part of the proceeds of the issue of shares. In order, in effect, to reconcile these conflicting analyses, £6,000 of the £10,500 required by law to be capitalised as share capital and share premium has been treated as an appropriation out of other equity.

** The £6,000 contribution by the subsidiary to the EBT has been treated as a distribution from the subsidiary (see 12.2.7 above) and recorded in profit or loss. It might then be necessary to consider whether, as a result of this payment, the investment in the subsidiary had become impaired (see Chapter 8 at 2.3). As this is a matter to be determined in the light of specific facts and circumstances, it is not considered in this Example. Any impairment charge would be recorded in profit or loss.

12.5.2.C Parent company as employing company

If, in Example 30.52, the employing entity were the parent rather than the subsidiary, it would clearly have to record an expense under IFRS 2. It would also have to fund the £6,000 shortfall between the option exercise proceeds of £4,500 and the £10,500 issue proceeds of the shares.

If the EBT is treated as an extension of the parent, the accounting entries for the parent would be the same as those for the group, as set out in 12.5.1 above.

In our view, the treatment in 12.5.1 above may also be appropriate for this specific transaction, even where the EBT is treated as a separate entity. The issue of shares requires the parent company to fund the EBT with £6,000 which immediately returns it to the parent, along with the £4,500 received from the employee, in exchange for an issue of shares. Whilst this 'circulation' of the £6,000 might have some significance for legal purposes it is, economically speaking, a non-transaction that could be ignored for accounting purposes under IFRS. It might, however, be relevant, under local law, to the amount of equity shown as share capital and share premium (additional paid-in capital), in which case the expanded entry in 12.5.1 above would be appropriate.

Where, however, the EBT is treated as a separate entity, and the cash used to subscribe for the shares arises from a prior transaction, such as an earlier loan to the EBT, matters are more complicated. Suppose that, during the life of the award under discussion, the company were to advance £50,000 to the EBT for general funding purposes. At that point it would clearly record the entry:

	£	£
Loan to EBT	50,000	
Cash		50,000

Suppose that, on exercise of the option, the EBT were to use some of that cash to fund the parent's 'top up' for the share issue. This effectively impairs the loan by £6,000 and leaves a 'missing debit' indicated by '?' in the journal below:

	£	£
Cash	10,500	
?	6,000	
Loan to EBT		6,000
Share capital/premium		10,500

This looks very much like an impairment loss on the loan required to be reported in profit or loss. On the other hand, it does not resemble a loss in any conventional sense. This suggests that another analysis may be possible.

Example 30.50 at 12.3.4 above addresses the situation where an EBT is pre-funded to enable it to buy the reporting entity's own shares in the market, and those shares are finally delivered to the entity for distribution to employees. Example 30.50 suggests that this could be construed as the execution of a gross-settled purchased call option by the entity.

If that analogy is extended, the present situation could be construed as comprising a back-to-back:

- gross-settled purchased call option (whereby the entity can require the EBT to provide 3,000 shares in return for waiver of £6,000 of its outstanding loan to the EBT), which triggers the exercise of
- a gross-settled written call option (whereby the EBT can require the entity to issue 3,000 fresh shares for £10,500 to the EBT, so that it can satisfy its obligations to the entity under the purchased call).

If these two call options are accounted for under IAS 32 (see Chapter 43 at 11.2), the write-off of the loan to the EBT can be effectively charged to equity, as follows:

	£	£
Cash	10,500	
Share capital/premium		10,500
Exercise by EBT of written call		
Own shares (Equity)	6,000	
Loan to EBT		6,000
Exercise by entity of purchased call		
Equity (other)	6,000	
Own shares (Equity)		6,000
Issue of shares to employee		

12.5.3 Employing subsidiary

The employing subsidiary is required to account for the IFRS 2 expense and the contribution to the EBT on exercise of the award. This gives rise to the accounting entries set out below. The entries to reflect the IFRS 2 expense are required by IFRS 2 (see 12.2.3 above). The treatment of the contribution to the EBT as a distribution is based on the proposal in D17 (see 12.2.7 above).

		£	£
y/e 31.12.2014	Profit or loss*	500	
	Equity		500
y/e 31.12.2015	Profit or loss*	1,000	
	Equity		1,000
y/e 31.12.2016	Profit or loss*	1,000	
	Equity		1,000
y/e 31.12.2017	Profit or loss*	500	
	Equity		500
1.9.2019	Equity†	6,000	
	Cash		6,000

* Total cost £3,000 (3000 options × £1) spread over 36 months. Charge for period to December 2014 6/36 × £3,000 = £500, and so on. In practice, where options were granted to a group of individuals, or with variable performance criteria, the annual charge would be based on a continually revised cumulative charge (see further discussion at 6.1 to 6.4 above).

† £3,000 of this payment should be treated as a reduction of whatever component of equity was credited with the £3,000 quasi-contribution from the parent in the accounting entries above. The remaining £3,000 would be treated as a distribution and charged to any appropriate component of equity.

12.6 Illustrative example – cash-settled transaction not settled by the entity receiving goods or services

The discussion in 12.6.1 to 12.6.3 below is based on Example 30.53.

Example 30.53: Cash-settled scheme not settled by receiving entity

On 1 July 2014 an employee of S Limited, a subsidiary of the H plc group, is awarded a right, exercisable between 1 July 2017 and 1 July 2020, to receive cash equivalent to the value of 3,000 shares in H plc at the date on which the right is exercised. Exercise of the right is subject to certain performance criteria being met in the three years ending 30 June 2017. The cash will be paid to the employee not by S, but by H. Throughout the vesting period of the award, H and S take the view that it will vest in full.

The award does in fact vest, and the right is exercised on 1 September 2019.

The fair value of the award (per share-equivalent) at various relevant dates is as follows:

Date	Fair value
	£
1.7.2014	1.50
31.12.2014	1.80
31.12.2015	2.70
31.12.2016	2.40
31.12.2017	2.90
31.12.2018	3.30
1.9.2019	3.50

If the award had been equity-settled (i.e. the employee had instead been granted a right to 3,000 free shares), the grant date fair value of the award would have been £1.50 per share.

H plc and its subsidiaries have a 31 December year end.

12.6.1 Consolidated financial statements

The group has entered into a cash-settled transaction which is accounted for using the methodology discussed at 9.3 above. This gives rise to the following accounting entries:

		£	£
y/e 31.12.2014	Profit or loss*	900	
	Liability		900
y/e 31.12.2015	Profit or loss*	3,150	
	Liability		3,150
y/e 31.12.2016	Profit or loss*	1,950	
	Liability		1,950
y/e 31.12.2017	Profit or loss*	2,700	
	Liability		2,700
y/e 31.12.2018	Profit or loss*	1,200	
	Liability		1,200
y/e 31.12.2019	Profit or loss*	600	
	Liability		600
1.9.2019	Liability	10,500	
	Cash		10,500

* Charge for period to 31 December 2014 is 6/36 × 3000 × £1.80 [reporting date fair value] = £900. Charge for year ended 31 December 2015 is 18/36 × 3000 × £2.70 = £4,050 less £900 charged in 2014 = £3,150 and so on (refer to Example 30.36 at 9.3.2 above). In practice, where options were granted to a group of individuals, or with variable performance criteria, the annual charge would be based on a continually revised cumulative charge (see further discussion at 9 above).

12.6.2 Parent company

The parent accounts for the share-based payment transaction under IFRS 2 as a cash-settled transaction, since the parent settles the award by delivering cash to the employees of the subsidiary (see 12.2.4 above). However, as discussed at 12.2.4 above, instead of recording a cost, as in its consolidated financial statements, the parent records an increase in the carrying value of its investment in subsidiary. It might then be necessary to consider whether the ever-increasing investment in subsidiary is supportable or is in fact impaired. As this is a matter to be determined in the light of specific facts and circumstances, it is not considered in this example. Any impairment charge would be recorded in profit or loss.

This would result in the following accounting entries.

		£	£
y/e 31.12.2014	Investment in subsidiary*	900	
	Liability		900
y/e 31.12.2015	Investment in subsidiary*	3,150	
	Liability		3,150
y/e 31.12.2016	Investment in subsidiary*	1,950	
	Liability		1,950
y/e 31.12.2017	Investment in subsidiary*	2,700	
	Liability		2,700
y/e 31.12.2018	Investment in subsidiary*	1,200	
	Liability		1,200
y/e 31.12.2019	Investment in subsidiary*	600	
	Liability		600
1.9.2019	Liability	10,500	
	Cash		10,500

* Increase in investment to 31 December 2014 is 6/36 × 3000 × £1.80 [reporting date fair value] = £900. Increase for year ended 31 December 2015 is 18/36 × 3000 × £2.70 = £4,050 less £900 charged in 2014 = £3,150 and so on (refer to Example 30.36 at 9.3.2 above). In practice, where options were granted to a group of individuals, or with variable performance criteria, the annual charge would be based on a continually revised cumulative charge (see further discussion at 9 above).

Where the parent entity was also the employing entity (and therefore receiving goods or services), it would apply the same accounting treatment in its separate financial statements as in its consolidated financial statements (see 12.6.1 above).

12.6.3 Employing subsidiary

The employing subsidiary accounts for the transaction as equity-settled, since it receives services, but incurs no obligation to its employees (see 12.2.3 and 12.2.6 above). This gives rise to the following accounting entries.

		£	£
y/e 31.12.2014	Profit or loss*	750	
	Equity		750
y/e 31.12.2015	Profit or loss*	1,500	
	Equity		1,500
y/e 31.12.2016	Profit or loss*	1,500	
	Equity		1,500
y/e 31.12.2017	Profit or loss*	750	
	Equity		750

* Charge for period to 31 December 2014 is 6/36 × 3000 × £1.50 [grant date fair value] = £750, and so on. In practice, where options were granted to a group of individuals, or with variable performance criteria, the annual charge would be based on a continually revised cumulative charge (see further discussion at 6.1 to 6.4 above).

The effect of this treatment is that, while the group ultimately records a cost of £10,500, the subsidiary records a cost of only £4,500.

However, there may be cases where the subsidiary records a higher cost than the group. This would happen if, for example:

- the award vests, but the share price has fallen since grant date, so that the value of the award at vesting (as reflected in the consolidated financial statements) is lower than the value at grant (as reflected in the subsidiary's financial statements); or
- the award does not actually vest because of a failure to meet a market condition and/or a non-vesting condition (so that the cost is nil in the consolidated financial statements) but is treated by IFRS 2 as vesting in the subsidiary's financial statements, because it is accounted for as equity-settled (see 6.3 and 6.4 above).

12.7 Employee transferring between group entities

It is not uncommon for an employee to be granted an equity-settled share-based payment award while in the employment of one subsidiary in the group, but to transfer to another subsidiary in the group before the award is vested, but with the entitlement to the award being unchanged.

In such cases, each subsidiary measures the services received from the employee by reference to the fair value of the equity instruments at the date those rights to equity instruments were originally granted, and the proportion of the vesting period served by the employee with each subsidiary. *[IFRS 2.B59].* In other words, for an award with a three-year vesting period granted to an employee of subsidiary A, who transfers to subsidiary B at the end of year 2, subsidiary A will (cumulatively) record an expense of 2/3, and subsidiary B 1/3, of the fair value at grant date. However, any subsidiary required to account for the transaction as cash-settled in accordance with the general principles discussed at 12.2 above accounts for its portion of the grant date fair value and also for any changes in the fair value of the award during the period of employment with that subsidiary. *[IFRS 2.B60].*

After transferring between group entities, an employee may fail to satisfy a vesting condition other than a market condition, for example by leaving the employment of the group. In this situation each subsidiary adjusts the amount previously recognised in respect of the services received from the employee in accordance with the general principles of IFRS 2 (see 6.1 to 6.4 above). *[IFRS 2.B61].* This imposes upon the original employing entity the rather curious burden of tracking the service record of its former employee.

12.8 Group reorganisations

Following a group reorganisation, such as the insertion of a new parent company above an existing group of companies, share-based payment arrangements with employees are often amended or replaced so that they relate to the shares of the new parent company. Group reorganisations of entities under common control are not within the scope of IFRS 3 and so the requirements set out at 11 above are not directly applicable.

In some cases, the terms and conditions of a share-based payment arrangement will contain provisions relating to restructuring transactions (see 5.3.8.A above) so that the application of any changes is not necessarily considered to be a modification in IFRS 2 terms. Where no such provision is made, the situation is less clear-cut.

In our view, in the consolidated financial statements, such changes to share-based payments would generally be construed as a cancellation and replacement to which modification accounting could be applied (see 7.4.4 above). However, in most cases, the changes made to the share awards following a group reorganisation are likely to be such that there is no incremental fair value, the intention being simply to replace like with like.

A subsidiary receiving the services of employees but with no obligation to settle the amended award would continue to apply equity-settled accounting in its own financial statements and, as for the consolidated financial statements, would strictly account for the changes as a cancellation and replacement of the original award. The accounting consequences would be more complicated if the subsidiary had an obligation to settle the award in the shares of its new parent, when previously it had had to settle in its own shares, as this would mean a change from equity-settled to cash-settled accounting (see 9.4 above). However, we would expect this to be a rare occurrence in practice (see 12.2.5.B above in relation to the grantor of an award in a situation involving parent and subsidiary entities).

The new parent entity becomes a party to the share-based payment arrangements for the first time and, assuming it has no employees of its own but is considered to have granted the awards, needs to account for the awards to the employees of its subsidiaries (see 12.2.4 and 12.2.5 above). The requirements of IFRS 2 in this situation are unclear and one could argue:

- either that this is a new award by the parent and so should be valued as at the date of the new award; or
- in accordance with the general principle that there is no overall change as a consequence of a reorganisation of entities under common control, that the parent should use the same (original grant date) fair value as the subsidiary.

In our view, either approach is acceptable provided it is applied consistently.

12.9 Share-based payments to employees of joint ventures or associates

The majority of share-based payment transactions with employees involve payments to employees of the reporting entity or of another entity in the same group. Occasionally, however, share-based payments may be made to employees of significant investees of the reporting entity such as joint ventures or associates. For example, if one party to a joint venture is a quoted entity and the other not, it might be commercially appropriate for the quoted venturer to offer payments based on its quoted shares to employees of the joint venture, while the unquoted party contributes to the venture in other ways.

Such arrangements raise some questions of interpretation of IFRS 2, as illustrated by Example 30.54 below.

Example 30.54: Share-based payment to employees of associate

On 1 January 2014, an entity grants an award of free shares with a fair value at that date of €600,000 to employees of its 40% associate. The shares vest over the three-year period ended 31 December 2016. It is assumed throughout the vesting period of the award that it will vest in full, which is in fact the case. The associate and the investor both have a financial reporting date of 31 December.

12.9.1 Financial statements of the associate

For the financial statements of the associate, the transaction does not strictly fall within the scope of IFRS 2. In order for a transaction to be in the scope of IFRS 2 for a reporting entity, it must be settled in the equity of the entity itself, or that of another member of the same group. A group comprises a parent and its subsidiaries (see Chapter 6 at 2.3), and does not include associates.

Nevertheless, we believe that it would be appropriate for the associate to account for the transaction as if it did fall within the scope of IFRS 2 by applying the 'GAAP hierarchy' in IAS 8 – *Accounting Policies, Changes in Accounting Estimates and Errors* (see Chapter 3 at 4.3). The investor has effectively made a capital contribution to the associate (in the form of the investor's own equity), no less than if it made a capital contribution in cash which was then used to pay employees of the associate.

If the investor in the associate had instead granted an award settled in the equity of the associate, the transaction would have been in the scope of IFRS 2 for the associate, as being the grant of an award over the equity of the reporting entity by a shareholder of that entity (see 2.2.2.A above).

If the award is, or is treated as being, within the scope of IFRS 2 for the associate, the following entries are recorded:

		€000	€000
y/e 31.12.14	Employee costs†	200	
	Equity		200
y/e 31.12.15	Employee costs	200	
	Equity		200
y/e 31.12.16	Employee costs	200	
	Equity		200

† Grant date fair value of award €600,000 × 1/3. The credit to equity represents a capital contribution from the investor

12.9.2 Consolidated financial statements of the investor

The investor has entered into a share-based payment transaction since it has granted an award over its equity to third parties (the employees of the associates) in exchange for their services to a significant investee entity. However, employees of an associate are not employees of a group entity and are therefore not employees of the investor's group.

The issue for IFRS 2 purposes is, therefore, whether the award should be regarded as being made to persons providing similar services to employees (and therefore measured at grant date) or to persons other than employees or those providing similar services to employees (and therefore measured at service date) – see 5.2 to 5.4 above.

In our view, it is more appropriate to regard such awards as made to persons providing similar services to employees and therefore measured at grant date.

There are then, we believe, two possible approaches to the accounting. In any event, the investor's consolidated financial statements must show a credit to equity of €200,000 a year over the vesting period. The accounting issue is the analysis of the corresponding debit.

It seems clear that the investor must as a minimum recognise an annual cost of €80,000 (40% of €200,000), as part of its 'one-line' share of the result of the associate. The issue then is whether it should account for the remaining €120,000 as a further cost or as an increase in the cost of its investment in its associate.

The argument for treating the €120,000 as an expense is that the associate will either have recorded nothing or, as set out in 12.9.1 above, an entry that results in no net increase in the equity of the associate. Therefore there has been no increase in the investor's share of the net assets of the associate, and there is therefore no basis for the investor to record an increase in its investment. This is broadly the approach required under US GAAP.

However, there may be cases where another shareholder has made, or undertaken to make, contributions to the associate that are not reflected in its recognised net assets (for example, an undertaking to provide knowhow or undertake mineral exploration). In such circumstances, it may be possible to conclude that the €120,000 is an increase in the cost of the investment in associate. IAS 28 – *Investments in Associates and Joint Ventures* – defines the equity method of accounting as (emphasis added):

> 'a method of accounting whereby the investment is *initially recognised at cost and adjusted thereafter* for the post-acquisition change in the investor's share of the investee's net assets'. *[IAS 28.3].*

Where an entity takes the view that the €120,000 is an increase in the cost of its investment, it is essential to ensure that the resulting carrying value of the investment is sustainable. This may be the case if, for example:

- the fair value of the investment in the associate exceeds its carrying amount; or
- the investor has agreed to enter into the transaction while another major shareholder has agreed to bear equivalent costs.

In other circumstances, the carrying amount of the investment may not be sustainable, and the investor may need to recognise an impairment of its investment in accordance with IAS 36 (see Chapter 20).

12.9.3 Separate financial statements of the investor

The discussion below assumes that the investor accounts for its investment in the associate at cost in its separate financial statements (see Chapter 8).

The issues here are much the same as in 12.9.2 above. The investor has clearly entered into a share-based payment transaction since it has granted an award over its equity to third parties (the employees of the associates) in exchange for their services to a significant investee entity. As in 12.9.2 above, we believe that this is most appropriately characterised as a transaction with persons providing similar services to employees and therefore measured at its grant date fair value.

In any event, the investor's separate financial statements must show a credit to equity of €200,000 a year over the vesting period. However, as in 12.9.2 above, the analysis of the debit entry is more complex.

13 DISCLOSURES

IFRS 2 requires three main groups of disclosures, explaining:

- the nature and extent of share-based payment arrangements (see 13.1 below);
- the valuation of share-based payment arrangements (see 13.2 below); and
- the impact on the financial statements of share-based payment transactions (see 13.3 below).

All of the disclosure requirements of IFRS 2 are subject to the overriding materiality considerations of IAS 1 – *Presentation of Financial Statements* (see Chapter 3 at 4.1.5). However, depending on the identity of the counterparty and whether, for example, the individual is a member of key management, it will be necessary to assess whether an arrangement is material by nature even if it is immaterial in monetary terms.

13.1 Nature and extent of share-based payment arrangements

IFRS 2 requires an entity to 'disclose information that enables users of the financial statements to understand the nature and extent of share-based payment arrangements that existed during the period'. *[IFRS 2.44].*

In order to satisfy this general principle, the entity must disclose at least:

(a) a description of each type of share-based payment arrangement that existed at any time during the period, including the general terms and conditions of each arrangement, such as vesting requirements, the maximum term of options granted, and the method of settlement (e.g. whether in cash or equity). An entity with substantially similar types of share-based payment arrangements may aggregate this information, unless separate disclosure of each arrangement is necessary to satisfy the general principle above;

(b) the number and weighted average exercise prices of share options for each of the following groups of options:
  (i) outstanding at the beginning of the period;
  (ii) granted during the period;
  (iii) forfeited during the period;
  (iv) exercised during the period;
  (v) expired during the period;
  (vi) outstanding at the end of the period; and
  (vii) exercisable at the end of the period;

(c) for share options exercised during the period, the weighted average share price at the date of exercise. If options were exercised on a regular basis throughout the period, the entity may instead disclose the weighted average share price during the period; and

(d) for share options outstanding at the end of the period, the range of exercise prices and weighted average remaining contractual life. If the range of exercise prices is wide, the outstanding options must be divided into ranges that are meaningful for assessing the number and timing of additional shares that may be issued and the cash that may be received upon exercise of those options. *[IFRS 2.45].*

The reconciliation in (b) above should, in our view, reflect all changes in the number of equity instruments outstanding. In addition to awards with a grant date during the period, the reconciliation should include subsequent additions to earlier grants e.g. options or shares added to the award in recognition of dividends declared during the period (where this is part of the original terms of the award), and changes to the number of equity instruments as a result of demergers, share splits or consolidations and other similar changes.

The following extract from the financial statements of Dairy Crest Group plc shows additional awards from the reinvestment of dividends within the reconciliation of outstanding awards.

Extract 30.1: Dairy Crest Group plc (2012)

Notes to the financial statements [extract]
26 Share based payment plans [extract]
[...]

The number of share options and weighted average exercise price for each of the schemes is set out as follows:

	LTISP*	Sharesave scheme	
	Number	Number	Weighted average exercise price (pence)
Options outstanding at 1 April 2011	1,957,774	3,855,782	237.8
Options granted during the year	995,183	1,445,978	265.0
Reinvested dividends	158,226		–
Options exercised during the year	(3,252)	(45,195)	227.0
Options forfeited during the year	(1,247,523)	(488,155)	313.4
Options outstanding at 31 March 2012	**1,860,408**	**4,768,410**	**238.4**
Exercisable at 31 March 2012	**25,563**	**–**	**–**

[...]
*The weighted average exercise price for LTISP options is nil.

As drafted, the requirements in (b) to (d) above appear to apply only to share options. However, since there is little distinction in IFRS 2 between the treatment of an option with a zero exercise price and the award of a free share, in our view the disclosures should not be restricted to awards of options.

13.2 Valuation of share-based payment arrangements

IFRS 2 requires an entity to 'disclose information that enables users of the financial statements to understand how the fair value of the goods or services received, or the fair value of the equity instruments granted, during the period was determined'. *[IFRS 2.46].*

As drafted, this requirement, and some of the detailed disclosures below, appears to apply only to equity-settled transactions. However, it would be anomalous if detailed disclosures were required about the valuation of an award to be settled in shares, but not one to be settled in cash. In our view, therefore, the disclosures apply both to equity-settled and to cash-settled transactions.

If the entity has measured the fair value of goods or services received as consideration for equity instruments of the entity indirectly, by reference to the fair value of the equity instruments granted (i.e. transactions with employees and, in exceptional cases only, with non-employees), the entity must disclose at least the following:

(a) for share options granted during the period, the weighted average fair value of those options at the measurement date and information on how that fair value was measured, including:
  (i) the option pricing model used and the inputs to that model, including the weighted average share price, exercise price, expected volatility, option life, expected dividends, the risk-free interest rate and any other inputs to the model, including the method used and the assumptions made to incorporate the effects of expected early exercise;
  (ii) how expected volatility was determined, including an explanation of the extent to which expected volatility was based on historical volatility; and
  (iii) whether and how any other features of the option grant were incorporated into the measurement of fair value, such as a market condition;

(b) for other equity instruments granted during the period (i.e. other than share options), the number and weighted average fair value of those equity instruments at the measurement date, and information on how that fair value was measured, including:
  (i) if fair value was not measured on the basis of an observable market price, how it was determined;
  (ii) whether and how expected dividends were incorporated into the measurement of fair value; and
  (iii) whether and how any other features of the equity instruments granted were incorporated into the measurement of fair value;

(c) for share-based payment arrangements that were modified during the period:
  (i) an explanation of those modifications;
  (ii) the incremental fair value granted (as a result of those modifications); and
  (iii) information on how the incremental fair value granted was measured, consistently with the requirements set out in (a) and (b) above, where applicable. *[IFRS 2.47]*.

These requirements can be seen to some extent as an anti-avoidance measure. It would not be surprising if the IASB had concerns that entities might seek to minimise the impact of IFRS 2 by using unduly pessimistic assumptions that result in a low fair value for share-based payment transactions, and the disclosures above seem designed to deter entities from doing so. However, these disclosures give information about other commercially sensitive matters. For example, (a)(i) above effectively requires disclosure of future dividend policy for a longer period than is generally covered by such forecasts. Entities may need to consider the impact on investors and analysts of dividend yield assumptions disclosed under IFRS 2.

In our view, it is important for entities, in making these disclosures, to ensure that any assumptions disclosed, particularly those relating to future performance, are consistent with those used in other areas of financial reporting that rely on estimates of future events, such as the impairment of property, plant and equipment, intangible assets and goodwill, income taxes (recovery of deferred tax assets out of future profits) and pensions and other post-retirement benefits.

If the entity has measured a share-based payment transaction directly by reference to the fair value of goods or services received during the period, the entity must disclose how that fair value was determined (e.g. whether fair value was measured at a market price for those goods or services). *[IFRS 2.48].*

As discussed in 5.4 above, IFRS 2 creates a rebuttable presumption that, for an equity-settled transaction with a counterparty other than an employee, the fair value of goods and services received provides the more reliable basis for assessing the fair value of the transaction. Where the entity has rebutted this presumption, and has valued the transaction by reference to the fair value of equity instruments issued, it must disclose this fact, and give an explanation of why the presumption was rebutted. *[IFRS 2.49].*

13.3 Impact of share-based payment transactions on financial statements

IFRS 2 requires an entity to 'disclose information that enables users of the financial statements to understand the effect of share-based payment transactions on the entity's profit or loss for the period and on its financial position.' *[IFRS 2.50].*

In order to do this, it must disclose at least:

(a) the total expense recognised for the period arising from share-based payment transactions in which the goods or services received did not qualify for recognition as assets and hence were recognised immediately as an expense, including separate disclosure of that portion of the total expense that arises from transactions accounted for as equity-settled share-based payment transactions;

(b) for liabilities arising from share-based payment transactions:

   (i) the total carrying amount at the end of the period; and

   (ii) the total intrinsic value at the end of the period of liabilities for which the counterparty's right to cash or other assets had vested by the end of the period (e.g. vested share appreciation rights). *[IFRS 2.51].*

The requirement in (b)(ii) above is slightly curious, in the sense that the IASB specifically rejected the suggestion that cash-settled transactions should be accounted for using an intrinsic value methodology, rather than the fair value methodology required by IFRS 2, stating that the intrinsic value method '... is not an adequate measure of either the ... liability or the cost of services consumed'. *[IFRS 2.BC250].* This rather begs the question of why the IASB requires disclosure of what is, in its eyes, a defective measure.

The disclosures section of IFRS 2 has a final paragraph requiring an entity to disclose additional information about its share-based payments should the information requirements set out above and in sections 13.1 and 13.2 be insufficient to meet the general disclosure principles of the standard. *[IFRS 2.52]*.

13.4 Example of IFRS 2 disclosures

An example of many of the disclosures required by IFRS 2 may be found in the financial statements of Aviva plc for the year ended 31 December 2012.

Extract 30.2: Aviva plc (2012)

Notes to the consolidated financial statements [extract]

30 – Group's share plans

This note describes the Group's various equity compensation plans, and shows how the Group values the options and awards of shares in the Company.

(a) Description of the plans

The Group maintains a number of active share option and award plans and schemes (the Group's Share Plans). These are as follows:

(i) Savings-related options

These are options granted under the HMRC-approved Save As You Earn (SAYE) share option schemes in the UK and Irish Revenue-approved SAYE share option scheme in Ireland. Options are normally exercisable during the six-month period following either the third, fifth or seventh anniversary of the start of the relevant savings contract. Options granted in 2012 are normally exercisable following the third or fifth anniversary.

(ii) Executive share options

These are options granted on various dates until 2004 under the Aviva Executive Share Option Plan and in 2010, under the Aviva Executive Share Option Plan 2005. Options granted between 2001 and 2004 were subject to the satisfaction of conditions relating to both the Company's Return on Equity (ROE) and its relative Total Shareholder Return (TSR). The performance was measured over a three-year performance period and the options are normally exercisable between the third and tenth anniversary of their grant. The options granted in 2010 are described in the Directors' Remuneration Report.

(iii) Long-term incentive plan awards

These awards have been made under the Aviva Long Term Incentive Plan 2005 and Aviva Long Term Incentive Plan 2011, and are described in section (b) below and in the Directors' Remuneration Report.

(iv) Annual bonus plan awards

These awards have been made under the Aviva Annual Bonus Plan 2005 and Aviva Annual Bonus Plan 2011, and are described in section (b) below and in the Directors' Remuneration Report.

(v) One Aviva, twice the value bonus plan awards

These are conditional awards granted under the Aviva Annual Bonus Plan 2005 between 2008 and 2010, and are described in section (b) below and in the Directors' Remuneration Report.

(vi) Recruitment and retention share award plan awards

These are conditional awards granted under the Aviva Recruitment and Retention Share Award Plan in relation to the recruitment or retention of senior managers excluding Executive Directors. The awards vest in tranches on various dates and vesting is conditional upon the participant being employed by the Group on the vesting date and not having served notice of resignation. If a participant's employment is terminated due to resignation or dismissal, any tranche of the award which has vested within the 12 months prior to the termination date will be subject to clawback and any unvested tranches of the award will lapse in full. No new Aviva plc ordinary shares will be issued or transferred from treasury to satisfy vested awards under this plan.

(vii) CFO recruitment share awards plan awards

The following awards were granted to Patrick Regan under the CFO Recruitment Share Awards Plan following his recruitment in 2010: the Replacement Restricted Share Award (RRSA), the Bonus Replacement Deferred Share Award (BRDSA) and the One Aviva Twice the Value (OATTV) Award. The RRSA was awarded to compensate Mr Regan for the loss of share awards granted by his previous employer and the BRDSA was awarded to compensate Mr Regan for the loss of bonus from his previous employer. The awards are described in section (b) below and in the Directors' Remuneration Report. No further awards will be made under this plan.

(viii) Conditional share award granted to Trevor Matthews

A conditional share award was awarded to Trevor Matthews as compensation for the loss of share awards granted by his previous employer. The awards are described in section (b) below and in the Directors' Remuneration Report.

(b) Outstanding options and awards

(i) Share options

At 31 December 2012, options to subscribe for ordinary shares of 25 pence each in the Company were outstanding as follows:

Aviva Savings Related Share Option Scheme	Option price p	Number of shares	Normally exercisable	Option price p	Number of shares	Normally exercisable
	491	13,228	2012	316	2,337,854	2012, 2014 or 2016
	593	39,615	2013	310	2,421,083	2013, 2015 or 2017
	563	139,960	2012 or 2014	268	10,302,920	2014, 2016 or 2018
	410	502,299	2013 or 2015	266	5,892,828	2015 or 2017

Aviva Ireland Savings Related Share Option Scheme (in euros)	Option price c	Number of shares	Normally exercisable	Option price c	Number of shares	Normally exercisable
	830	32,130	2012	374	140,085	2013 or 2015
	509	49,387	2013	304	507,254	2014 or 2016
	360	362,066	2012 or 2014	336	268,003	2015 or 2017

Aviva Executive Share Option Plan	Option price p	Number of shares	Normally exercisable
	512	533,707	2006 to 2013
	526	361,010	2007 to 2014
	386	1,308,781	2013

The following table summarises information about options outstanding at 31 December 2012:

Range of exercise prices	Outstanding options Number	Weighted average remaining contractual life Years	Weighted average exercise price p
£2.66 – £4.29	24,092,560	3	287.77
£4.30 – £5.89	1,080,035	1	524.55
£5.90 – £10.35	39,615	1	593.00

The comparative figures as at 31 December 2011 were:

Range of exercise prices	Outstanding options Number	Weighted average remaining contractual life Years	Weighted average exercise price p
£2.68 – £4.29	27,743,093	3	303.84
£4.30 – £5.89	2,052,537	2	524.03
£5.90 – £10.35	278,354	1	593.00

(ii) Share awards

At 31 December 2012, awards issued under the Company's executive incentive plans over ordinary shares of 25 pence each in the Company were outstanding as follows:

Aviva Long Term Incentive Plan 2005	Number of shares	Vesting period
	5,458,500	2010 to 2012

Aviva Long Term Incentive Plan 2011	Number of shares	Vesting period
	7,391,026	2011 to 2013
	11,321,800	2012 to 2014

One Aviva, twice the value bonus plan	Number of shares	Vesting period
	1,422,544	2010 to 2012

Aviva Annual Bonus Plan 2005	Number of shares	Vesting period
	2,762,731	2010 to 2012

Aviva Annual Bonus Plan 2011	Number of shares	Vesting period
	2,496,279	2011 to 2013
	4,476,090	2012 to 2014

CFO Recruitment Share Awards Plan	Award type	Number of shares	Vesting period
	RRSA	85,197	2013
	BRDSA	43,231	2010 to 2012
	OATTV	55,051	2010 to 2012

Conditional Share Award granted to Trevor Matthews	Number of shares	Vesting period
	435,814	2013 and 2014

Recruitment and Retention Share Award Plan	Number of shares	Vesting period
	19,481	2013
	166,921	2013 and 2014
	39,122	2013, 2014 and 2015
	78,167	2015

The vesting of awards under the Aviva Long Term Incentive Plan 2005, the Aviva Long Term Incentive Plan 2011, the OATTV bonus plan and the OATTV Award under the CFO Recruitment Share Awards Plan is subject to the attainment of performance conditions as described in the Directors' Remuneration Report. Shares which do not vest will lapse.

(iii) Shares to satisfy awards and options

Since July 2008, it has been the Company's practice to satisfy all awards and options using shares purchased in the market and held by employee trusts except where local regulations make it necessary to issue new shares. Further details are given in note 31.

(c) Movements in the year

A summary of the status of the option plans as at 31 December 2011 and 2012, and changes during the years ended on those dates, is shown below.

	2012		2011	
	Number of options	Weighted average exercise price p	Number of options	Weighted average exercise price p
Outstanding at 1 January	30,073,984	321.55	27,256,640	367.51
Granted during the year	6,236,944	269.02	13,486,990	268.00
Exercised during the year	(2,862,952)	315.24	(182,907)	353.26
Forfeited during the year	(2,187,371)	337.96	(1,089,738)	347.58
Cancelled during the year	(3,282,095)	300.34	(7,142,132)	320.36
Expired during the year	(2,766,300)	432.85	(2,254,869)	539.48
Outstanding at 31 December	25,212,210	298.40	30,073,984	321.55
Exercisable at 31 December	1,943,130	424.99	3,460,979	471.26

(d) Expense charged to the income statement

The total expense recognised for the year arising from equity compensation plans was as follows:

	2012 £m	2011 £m
Equity-settled expense	42	48
Cash-settled expense	5	10
Total (note 10b)	47	58

(e) Fair value of options and awards granted after 7 November 2002

The weighted average fair values of options and awards granted during the year, estimated by using the Binomial option pricing model, were £0.70 and £2.61 (*2011*: £0.99 and £4.20) respectively.

(i) Share options

The fair value of the options was estimated on the date of grant, based on the following weighted average assumptions:

Weighted average assumption	2012	2011
Share price	326p	312p
Exercise price	266p	268p
Expected volatility	41%	58%
Expected life	3.71 years	3.64 years
Expected dividend yield	7.98%	6.40%
Risk-free interest rate	0.37%	0.89%

The expected volatility used was based on the historical volatility of the share price over a period equivalent to the expected life of the option prior to its date of grant. The risk-free interest rate was based on the yields available on UK government bonds as at the date of grant. The bonds chosen were those with a similar remaining term to the expected life of the options. 2,862,952 options granted after 7 November 2002 were exercised during the year (*2011:* 182,907).

(ii) Share awards

The fair value of the awards was estimated on the date of grant based on the following weighted average assumptions:

Weighted average assumption	2012	2011
Share price	331.54p	435.70p
Expected volatility[1]	37%	66%
Expected volatility of comparator companies' share price[1]	38%	65%
Correlation between Aviva and competitors' share price[1]	63%	57%
Expected life	3.00 years	3.00 years
Expected dividend yield[2]	n/a	n/a
Risk-free interest rate[1]	0.42%	1.79%

[1] For awards with market-based performance conditions.

[2] The long term incentive plan awards granted in 2011 and 2012 include additional shares being provided to employees equal to dividend rights before vesting. As a result, no dividend yield assumption is required for these awards.

The expected volatility used was based on the historical volatility of the share price over a period equivalent to the expected life of the share award prior to its date of grant. The risk-free interest rate was based on the yields available on UK government bonds as at the date of grant. The bonds chosen were those with a similar remaining term to the expected life of the share awards.

In certain jurisdictions, some of the IFRS 2 disclosure requirements are similar to the disclosures required by local law or other regulations and it might therefore be possible to meet some of the IFRS 2 requirements by means of a cross-reference to other parts of the Annual Report (as in the case of Aviva plc above). However, care needs to be taken to ensure that all the relevant IFRS 2 requirements have been addressed as the requirements vary depending on when an award was granted. For example, detailed fair value information for an equity-settled award is generally required only in the year of grant (and as comparative information in the following period(s)), whereas the conditions attached to an award are required to be disclosed in every period in which that award is outstanding.

14 TAXES RELATED TO SHARE-BASED PAYMENT TRANSACTIONS

14.1 Income tax deductions for the entity

In many jurisdictions entities are entitled to receive tax deductions for share-based payment transactions. In many, if not most, cases the tax deduction is given for a cost different to that recorded under IFRS 2. For example, some jurisdictions give a tax deduction for the fair or intrinsic value of the award at the date of exercise; others may give a tax deduction for amounts charged to a subsidiary by its parent or a trust controlled by the parent in respect of the cost of group awards to the employees of that subsidiary. In either case, both the amount and timing of the expense for tax purposes will be different from the amount and timing of the expense required by IFRS 2.

The particular issues raised by share-based payment transactions are addressed in IAS 12, and discussed further in Chapter 29 at 10.8.

14.2 Employment taxes of the employer

In many jurisdictions, an employing entity is required to pay employment taxes or social security contributions on share options and other share-based payment transactions with employees, just as if the employees had received cash remuneration. This raises the question of how such taxes should be accounted for.

14.2.1 Applicable standard

The choice of accounting method does not affect the total expense ultimately recognised (which must always be the tax actually paid), but rather its allocation to different accounting periods. Some consider that such taxes are most appropriately accounted for under IAS 37 – *Provisions, Contingent Liabilities and Contingent Assets* (see 14.2.1.A below). However, others favour the alternatives set out in 14.2.1.B and 14.2.1.C below (IFRS 2 and IAS 19 – *Employee Benefits*). A reporting entity must therefore choose what it considers an appropriate policy in its particular circumstances.

Such taxes do not fall within the scope of IAS 39 since, like income taxes, they are not contractual liabilities (see Chapter 41 at 2.2.1).

14.2.1.A IAS 37

Some consider that, for the reasons set out in 14.2.1.B and 14.2.1.C below, employment taxes are in the scope neither of IFRS 2 nor of IAS 19. Accordingly, since the amount ultimately payable is uncertain, the most appropriate standard to apply is IAS 37 – *Provisions, Contingent Liabilities and Contingent Assets.*

Where IAS 37 is applied, the entity will recognise a provision for the employment tax when it has a present obligation to pay it as the result of a past event, it is probable (i.e. more likely than not) that it will be paid, and a reliable estimate can be made of the amount of the obligation (see Chapter 27 at 3.1).

Where IAS 37 is applied, however, there is some room for discussion as to what constitutes the critical past event that gives rise to the liability. Is it:

- the granting of the award;
- the event (typically exercise) that gives rise to a real tax liability; or
- the vesting of the award?

In our view, where IAS 37 is used to account for employment taxes, the critical event that gives rise to the liability for tax is the granting of the award and therefore, a liability for the tax should be recognised as soon as it becomes more likely than not that it will become payable. However, other analyses may be possible. It is of interest that:

- United States GAAP takes the view that the critical event is the event (typically exercise) that gives rise to a real tax liability. This is the case even for employment taxes relating to cash-settled awards, even though a liability is recognised for the awards themselves before exercise; while
- United Kingdom GAAP, where the national standard FRS 12 – *Provisions, Contingent Liabilities and Contingent Assets* – is essentially identical to IAS 37, regards the critical event as the granting of the award. However an interpretation of FRS 12[38] takes the view that the liability gradually accrues in line with the vesting of the award to which it relates. UK GAAP therefore recognises a liability for such taxes based on the intrinsic value of the award, and the expired portion of the vesting period, as at each reporting date. This is not unlike the methodology required by IAS 12 – *Income Taxes* – for measuring any deferred tax asset associated with a share-based payment transaction (see Chapter 29 at 10.8).

14.2.1.B IFRS 2

Some argue that, since the taxes are a payment of an amount of cash typically directly linked to the share price, they should be accounted for as a cash-settled share-based payment transaction under IFRS 2. This would require the taxes to be measured at each reporting date at fair value, multiplied by the expired vesting period of the award to which they relate (see 9.3.1 above).

A difficulty with this analysis is that IFRS 2 defines a cash-settled share-based payment transaction as one in which the entity incurs a liability to the 'supplier of ... goods or services'. The liability for such employment taxes is clearly due to the tax authorities, not to the supplier of goods and services (i.e. the employee). This leads some who support the application of IFRS 2 to accept that IFRS 2 is not directly applicable, but to argue that it is nevertheless the most appropriate standard to apply under the 'GAAP hierarchy' in IAS 8 (see Chapter 3 at 4.3). The objective of IFRS 2 (see 2.1 above) states that the standard is intended to apply to 'expenses associated with transactions in which share options are granted to employees'. However, the standard contains no explicit provisions relevant to this objective.

14.2.1.C IAS 19

Some argue that such payments are more appropriately accounted for under IAS 19 – *Employee Benefits* (see Chapter 31). Again the difficulty is that IAS 19 defines employee benefits as 'all forms of consideration given by an entity in exchange for service rendered by employees or for the termination of employment' *[IAS 19.8]*, which would appear to rule out payments to the tax authority, but for the fact that IAS 19 refers to social security contributions as a component part of short-term employee benefits. *[IAS 19.9(a)]*. However, many share-based payment transactions would, if they were within the scope of IAS 19, be classified as long-term benefits. That brings the added complication that IAS 19 would require the employment taxes due on long-term benefits to be accounted for, like the benefits themselves, using the projected unit credit method, which seems an unduly complex, and not altogether appropriate, approach in the circumstances.

In some situations the entity may require employees to discharge any liability for employment taxes. The accounting issues raised by such arrangements are discussed at 14.2.2 and 14.3 below.

14.2.2 Recovery of taxes from employees

In some jurisdictions, employers are required to pay employment taxes on share-based payment transactions. This detracts from one of the key attractions for an employer of a share-based payment transaction, namely that it entails no cash cost. This is particularly the case where the tax payable is based on the fair value of the award at vesting, where the employer's liability is potentially unlimited.

Accordingly, employers liable to such taxes are increasingly making it a condition of receiving a share-based award that the employee bear all or some of the cash cost of any related employment taxes. This may be done in a number of ways, including:

- direct payment to the entity;
- authorising the entity to deduct the relevant amount from the employee's salary; or
- surrendering as many shares to the entity as have a fair value equal to the tax liability.

The accounting treatment of schemes where the recovery of the cost from the employee is made through surrendering of a number of shares with an equivalent value is discussed at 14.3 below.

Where the scheme requires direct cash reimbursement of the cost, different considerations apply, as illustrated by Example 30.55 below.

Example 30.55: Recovery of employment tax on share-based payment from employee

On 1 January 2014, an entity granted an executive an award of free shares with a fair value of €100,000 on condition that the executive remain in employment for three years ending on 31 December 2016. In the jurisdiction concerned, an employment tax at the rate of 12% is payable when the shares vest, based on their fair value at the date of vesting. As a condition of obtaining the shares on vesting, the executive is required to pay cash equal to the tax liability to the employer.

When the shares vest on 31 December 2016, their fair value is €300,000, on which employment taxes of €36,000 are due. The executive pays this amount to the entity.

In our view, this arrangement can be construed in one of two ways, with somewhat different accounting outcomes:

- View 1: The executive's obligation to make whole the employer's tax liability means that this is, economically, not an award of free shares, but an option to acquire the shares for an exercise price equivalent to 12% of their market value at the date of exercise. The employer's tax liability is a separate transaction.
- View 2: The executive's obligation to make whole the employer's tax liability should be accounted for as such, separately from the share-based payment transaction.

In our view, either approach may be adopted, so long as it is applied consistently as a matter of accounting policy. The essential differences between View 1 and View 2, as illustrated below, are that:

- under View 1 the reimbursement received from the employee is credited to equity, whereas under View 2 it is credited to profit or loss; and
- under View 1, the IFRS 2 charge is lower than under View 2 reflecting the fact that under View 1 the award is construed as an option, not an award of free shares.

View 1 Reimbursement treated as exercise price

On this analysis, the award is construed as an option to acquire shares with an exercise price of 12% of the fair value, at vesting, of the shares. The grant date fair value of the award construed as an option is €88,000. The entity would process the following accounting entries (on a cumulative basis).

	€000	€000
Employee costs*	88	
Equity		88
Employee costs†	36	
Cash		36
Cash§	36	
Equity		36

* IFRS 2 charge.

† Employment taxes (12% of €300,000).

§ The receipt of cash from the employee to reimburse the tax is treated as the receipt of the exercise price for an option and credited to equity.

View 2 Reimbursement treated separately from the IFRS 2 charge

On this analysis, the award is construed as an award of free shares, with a grant date fair value of €100,000. The reimbursement is accounted for as such, giving rise to a credit to profit or loss. The entity would process the following accounting entries (on a cumulative basis).

	€000	€000
Employee costs*	100	
Equity		100
Employee costs†	36	
Cash		36
Cash§	36	
Employee costs		36

* IFRS 2 charge.

† Employment taxes (12% of €300,000).

§ The receipt of cash from the employee to reimburse the tax is treated as a reduction in employee costs.

It will be seen that View 1 results in a total employee expense of €124,000, while View 2 results in a total employee expense of €100,000.

14.2.3 Holding of own shares to 'hedge' tax liabilities

In many jurisdictions, an award of shares or options to an employee also gives rise to an employment tax liability for the employer, often related to the fair value of the award when it vests or, in the case of an option, is exercised. Employers may hold their own shares in order to hedge this liability (in an economic sense, if not under the criteria in IAS 39 – see 2.2.4.H above), and later sell as many shares as are needed to raise proceeds equal to the tax liability.

These are two separate transactions. The purchase and sale of own shares are treasury share transactions accounted for in accordance with IAS 32 (see Chapter 43 at 9). The accounting treatment of the employment tax liability is discussed at 14.2.1 above.

14.3 Sale of shares by employee to meet employee's tax liability ('sell to cover')

In some jurisdictions, an award of shares or options to an employee gives rise to a personal tax liability for the employee, often related to the fair value of the award when it vests or, in the case of an option, is exercised. In order to meet this tax liability, employees may wish to sell as many shares as are needed to raise proceeds equal to the tax liability (sometimes described as 'sell to cover').

This *in itself* does not, in our view, require the scheme to be considered as cash-settled, any more than if the employee wished to liquidate the shares in order to buy a car or undertake home improvements. However, if the manner in which the cash is passed to the employee gives rise to a legal or constructive obligation for the employer, then the scheme might well be cash-settled (see 9.2.1 to 9.2.3 above), to the extent of any such obligation.

In some jurisdictions where employees must pay income tax on share awards, the tax is initially collected from (and is a legal liability of) the employer, but with eventual recourse by the tax authorities to the employee for tax not collected from the employer. Such tax collection arrangements mean that even an equity-settled award results in a cash cost for the employer for the income tax.

In such a situation, the employer may require the employee, as a condition of taking delivery of any shares earned, to indemnify the entity against the tax liability, for example by:

- direct payment to the entity;
- authorising the entity to deduct the relevant amount from the employee's salary; or
- surrendering as many shares to the entity as have a fair value equal to the tax liability.

If the entity requires the employee to surrender the relevant number of shares, in our view it is more appropriate to treat the scheme as cash-settled to the extent of the indemnified amount, as explained in Example 30.56 below. However, the tentative conclusions of the Interpretations Committee in March 2013 on certain aspects of this issue should be taken into consideration pending any amendment to IFRS 2 (see below).

Example 30.56: Surrendering of vested shares by employee to indemnify liability of entity to pay employee's tax liability

An entity operates in a jurisdiction where the personal tax rate is 40%, and free shares are taxed at their fair value on vesting. The entity grants an award of 100 free shares with a grant date fair value of £3 each. The fair value at vesting date is £5, so that the employee's tax liability (required to be discharged in the first instance by the employer) is £200 (40% of £500). The award is to be satisfied using treasury shares with an original cost of £2.50 per share.

If the employee were required to surrender the 40 shares needed to settle the tax liability, in our view the substance of the transaction is that, at grant date, the entity is making an award of only 60 shares (with a grant date fair value of £3 each) and is bearing the cost of the employment tax itself. On this analysis, the entity will have recorded the following entries by the end of the vesting period:

	£	£
Employee costs	180	
Equity		180
Employee costs	200	
Employment tax liability		200

The award is then satisfied by delivery of 60 treasury shares (with a cost of £2.50 each) to the employee:

	£	£
Equity	150	
Treasury shares		150

The entity might well then sell the 40 shares 'surrendered' by the employee in order to raise the cash to pay the tax, but this would be accounted for as an increase in equity on the reissue of treasury shares, not as income (see 14.2.3 above).

If, however, the employee has a free choice as to how to indemnify the employer, the employer will have recorded the following entries by the end of the vesting period:

	£	£
Employee costs	300	
Equity		300
Receivable from employee	200	
Employment tax liability		200

The award is then satisfied by delivery of shares to the employee, and the employee indicates that he wishes to surrender 40 shares to discharge his obligation to the employer under the indemnity arrangement. The entity then receives 40 shares from the employee in settlement of the £200 receivable from him.

In practice, this would almost certainly be effected as a net delivery of 60 shares, but in principle there are two transactions, a release of 100 treasury shares, with a cost of £2.50 each, to the employee:

	£	£
Equity	250	
Treasury shares		250

and the re-acquisition of 40 of those shares at £5 each from the employee:

	£	£
Treasury shares	200	
Receivable from employee		200

The entity then settles the tax liability:

	£	£
Employment tax liability	200	
Cash		200

Even in this case, however, some might take the view that the substance of the arrangement is that the employee has the right to put 40 shares to the employer, and accordingly 40% of the award should be accounted for as cash-settled, resulting in essentially the same accounting as when the employee is required to surrender 40 shares, as set out above.

The Interpretations Committee was asked to consider the classification of a share-based payment transaction in which an entity withholds a specified portion of shares that would otherwise be issued to the counterparty at the date of exercise or vesting.

The shares are withheld in return for the entity settling the counterparty's tax liability relating to the share-based payment. Should the portion of the share-based payment that is withheld be classified as cash-settled or equity-settled in a situation where, in the absence of the net settlement feature, the award would be treated in its entirety as equity-settled?

In summarising the request following its September 2010 meeting, the Interpretations Committee noted, somewhat unusually in a request to interpret IFRSs, that liability classification would not be required for any portion of the award under US GAAP as an exemption is available to entities allowing them to treat the entire award as equity-settled in a situation where shares are withheld to meet a statutory tax liability. It is noteworthy however that the summary by the Interpretations Committee does not make clear that, under US GAAP, withholding an amount for tax in excess of a prescribed minimum level would trigger the classification of the entire award as a liability.

At its September 2010 meeting, the Interpretations Committee also noted that 'the definitions in Appendix A [to IFRS 2] ... provide that an award is classified as cash-settled if the entity incurs a liability to transfer cash or other assets as a result of acquiring goods or services. In the circumstances considered by the Committee, cash is transferred to the tax authority, in settlement of the counterparty's tax obligation, in respect of the shares withheld'.[39]

The Interpretations Committee further noted at this stage that IFRS 2 provides sufficient guidance to address the issue and that it did not expect diversity in practice. Therefore, a tentative decision was reached not to add the issue to the Committee's agenda. However, it was recommended that the issue should be reconsidered by the IASB as part of a post-implementation review of IFRS 2 in order to determine whether it would be appropriate to amend IFRS 2 to permit the portion of the award withheld to be classified as equity-settled.[40]

As a result of comments received in relation to the tentative decision, the Interpretations Committee discussed the issue again in November 2010 and asked for some illustrative examples to be prepared before considering the matter further.[41] The question was discussed again in March 2011 and the Interpretations Committee identified 'a number of issues arising from the submission for which the application of the requirements of IFRS 2 caused concern, such as separately classifying components of a single award'. To address these concerns would require an amendment to IFRS 2.[42] In July 2012 the Interpretations Committee asked its staff to update the analysis of this issue, as one of a number of issues previously referred to the IASB, so that the Interpretations Committee could discuss at a future meeting whether to take the issue back onto its agenda.[43]

In a shift from its earlier position, the Interpretations Committee observed at its March 2013 meeting that the issue is widespread and that there appears to be significant diversity in practice. As a consequence, the Committee tentatively decided to recommend to the IASB that IFRS 2 be amended to clarify the accounting for this type of arrangement. The Interpretations Committee observed that under the existing requirements of IFRS 2 'it is difficult to reach a consensus on whether the portion withheld by the entity ... should be classified as cash-settled or equity-settled ...'. It also noted that requiring a different classification for the withheld portion and the remainder of the award could cause an undue burden for entities.

The Interpretations Committee decided to recommend a narrow-scope amendment to IFRS 2 to add specific guidance for certain types of share-based payment transaction with a net settlement feature. The guidance would be to clarify that a share-based payment which the entity settles net 'by withholding a specified portion of the equity instruments to meet its minimum statutory tax withholding requirements would be classified as equity-settled in its entirety, if the entire award would otherwise be classified as equity-settled without the net settlement feature'. These recommendations are to be taken to a future meeting of the IASB.[44]

It should be noted that the discussions by the Interpretations Committee only addressed the narrow situation where the entity is required by law to withhold shares to meet the counterparty's tax liability. The submission did not address other types of arrangement that exist in practice, such as where either the entity or the counterparty is able to choose whether or not shares are withheld and/or directly sold in order to raise cash to settle the tax liability. In our view, a careful analysis of the arrangement is a necessary starting point in determining whether part of it should be treated as a separate cash-settled award under IFRS 2 as currently drafted.

15 OTHER PRACTICAL ISSUES

We discuss below the following aspects of the practical application of IFRS 2 that do not fit easily into any one of the sections above:

- matching share awards (see 15.1 below);
- limited recourse and full recourse loans (see 15.2 below);
- awards entitled to dividends during the vesting period (see 15.3 below);
- awards vesting or exercisable on a flotation (or trade sale or other change of control etc.) (see 15.4 below); and
- arrangements under South African black economic empowerment ('BEE') legislation and similar arrangements (see 15.5 below).

15.1 Matching share awards

As noted in the discussion at 10.1.2 above, the rules in IFRS 2 for awards where there is a choice of equity- or cash-settlement do not deal adequately, in our view, with awards where the equity and cash alternatives may have significantly different fair values and vesting periods. In some jurisdictions, an increasingly popular type of scheme giving rise to such issues is a matching share award.

Under a matching share award, the starting point is usually that an employee is awarded a bonus for a one year performance period. At the end of that period, the employee may then be either required or permitted to take all or part of that bonus in shares rather than cash. To the extent that the employee takes shares rather than cash, the employing entity may then be required or permitted to make a 'matching' award of an equal number of shares (or a multiple or fraction of that number). The matching award will typically vest over a longer period.

Whilst such schemes can appear superficially similar, the accounting analysis under IFRS 2 may vary significantly, according to whether:

- the employee has a choice, or is required, to take some of the 'base' bonus in shares; and/or
- the employer has a choice, or is required, to match any shares taken by the employee.

Examples 30.57 to 30.61 below set out an analysis of the five basic variants of such schemes, as summarised in the following matrix.

Employee's taking shares required or discretionary?	**Employer's matching required or discretionary?**	**Example**
Required	Required	30.57
Required	Discretionary	30.58
Discretionary	No provision for matching award	30.59
Discretionary	Required	30.60
Discretionary	Discretionary	30.61

Example 30.57: Mandatory investment by employee of cash bonus into shares with mandatory matching award by employer

On 1 January 2014 an employee is told that he is to participate in a bonus scheme which will pay £1,000 if certain performance criteria are met for the year ended 31 December 2014 and he remains in service. The bonus will be paid on 1 January 2015. 50% will be paid in cash and the employee will be required to invest the remaining 50% in as many shares as are worth £500 at 1 January 2015. Thus, if the share price were £2.50, the employee would receive £500 cash and 200 shares. These shares are fully vested.

If this first award is achieved, the entity is required to award an equal number of additional shares ('matching shares') – in this example 200 shares – conditional upon the employee remaining in service until 31 December 2016. The award of any matching shares will be made on 1 January 2015.

Annual bonus

The 50% of the bonus paid in cash is outside the scope of IFRS 2 and within that of IAS 19 (see Chapter 31). The 50% of the annual bonus settled in shares is an equity-settled share-based payment transaction within the scope of IFRS 2, since there is no discretion over the manner of settlement. The measurement date for this element of the bonus is 1 January 2014 and the vesting period is the year ended 31 December 2014, since all vesting conditions have been met as at that date. Notwithstanding that the two legs of the award strictly fall within the scope of two different standards, the practical effect will be to charge an expense over the year ended 31 December 2014.

Matching shares

The terms of the award of 200 matching shares have the effect that the entity has committed, as at 1 January 2014, to award shares with a value of £500 as at 1 January 2015, subject to satisfaction of:

- a performance condition relating to the year ended 31 December 2014; and
- a service condition relating to the three years ended 31 December 2016.

Those terms are understood by all parties at 1 January 2014, which is therefore the measurement date. The fact that the matching award is not formally made until 1 January 2015 is not relevant, since there has been a binding commitment to make the award, on terms understood both by the entity and the employee, since 1 January 2014 (see 5.3 above).

The vesting period is the three years ended 31 December 2016. As at 31 December 2014 only one of the vesting conditions (i.e. the performance condition) has been met. The further vesting condition (i.e. the service condition) is not met until 31 December 2016.

The discussion in 8.10 above is relevant to the valuation of the equity elements of the award.

Example 30.58: Mandatory investment by employee of cash bonus into shares with discretionary matching award by employer

On 1 January 2014 an employee is told that he is to participate in a bonus scheme which will pay £1,000 if certain performance criteria are met for the year ended 31 December 2014. The bonus will be paid on 1 January 2015. 50% will be paid in cash and the employee will be required to invest the remaining 50% in as many shares as are worth £500 at 1 January 2015. Thus, if the share price were £2.50, the employee would receive £500 cash and 200 shares. These shares are fully vested.

If this first award is achieved, the entity has the discretion, but not the obligation, to award an equal number of additional shares ('matching shares') – in this case 200 shares – conditional upon the employee remaining in service until 31 December 2016. The award of any matching shares will be made on 1 January 2015.

Annual bonus

The 50% of the bonus paid in cash is outside the scope of IFRS 2 and within that of IAS 19 (see Chapter 31). The 50% of the annual bonus settled in shares is an equity-settled share-based payment transaction within the scope of IFRS 2, since there is no discretion over the manner of settlement. The measurement date for this element of the bonus is 1 January 2014 and the vesting period is the year ended 31 December 2014, since all vesting conditions have been met as at that date. Notwithstanding that the two legs of the award strictly fall within the scope of two different standards, the practical effect will be to charge an expense over the year ended 31 December 2014.

Matching shares

In our view, it is necessary to consider whether the entity's discretion is real or not, this being a matter for judgement in the light of individual facts and circumstances.

In some cases the entity's discretion to make awards may be more apparent than real. For example, the awards may simply be documented as 'discretionary' for tax and other reasons. It may also be that the entity has consistently made matching awards to all eligible employees (or all members of a particular class of eligible employees), so that it has no realistic alternative but to make matching awards if it wants to maintain good staff relations. In such cases, it may be helpful to consider what the accounting for the 'matching' award would be if it were a pure cash award falling within the scope of IAS 19:

> 'An entity may have no legal obligation to pay a bonus. Nevertheless, in some cases, an entity has a practice of paying bonuses. In such cases, the entity has a constructive obligation because the entity has no realistic alternative but to pay the bonus. The measurement of the constructive obligation reflects the possibility that some employees may leave without receiving a bonus.' *[IAS 19.21].*

This is discussed further in Chapter 31 at 6.1.3.

In making the determination of whether a constructive obligation would exist under IAS 19, it would be necessary to consider past data (e.g. the percentage of employees who have received matching awards having received the original award).

If it is concluded that the entity does not have a constructive obligation to make a matching award, the accounting treatment would follow the legal form of the transaction. On this view, the grant date (and therefore measurement date) would be 1 January 2015, and the vesting period two years from 1 January 2015 to 31 December 2016.

If it is concluded that the entity does have a constructive obligation to make a matching award, the effect is that the matching award of shares is equivalent to the mandatory matching award in Example 30.57 above, and should therefore be accounted for in the same way – i.e. the measurement date is 1 January 2014 and the vesting period is the three years ended 31 December 2016.

The discussion in 8.10 above is relevant to the valuation of the matching equity award.

Example 30.59: Discretionary investment by employee of cash bonus into shares with no matching award

On 1 January 2014 an employee is told that he is to participate in a bonus scheme which will pay £1,000 if certain performance criteria are met for the year ended 31 December 2014. The bonus will be paid on 1 January 2015. 50% will be paid in cash and the employee will be permitted, but not required, to invest the remaining 50% in as many shares as are worth £500 at 1 January 2015. Thus, if the share price were £2.50, the employee could choose to receive either (a) £1,000 or (b) £500 cash and 200 shares. Any shares received are fully vested.

The 50% of the bonus automatically paid in cash is outside the scope of IFRS 2 and within that of IAS 19 (see Chapter 31).

The 50% of the bonus that may be invested in shares falls within the scope of IFRS 2 as a share-based payment transaction in which the terms of the arrangement provide the counterparty with the choice of settlement. This is the case even though the value of the alternative award is always £500 and does not depend on the share price (see 10.4 above).

The measurement date of the award is 1 January 2014 and the vesting period is the year ended 31 December 2014. The methodology set out in IFRS 2 for awards where the counterparty has a choice of settlement would lead to recognition over the vesting period of a liability component of £500 and an equity component of zero (see 10.1.2 above). If in fact the employee took shares at vesting, the £500 liability would be transferred to equity.

Example 30.60: Discretionary investment by employee of cash bonus into shares with mandatory matching award by employer

On 1 January 2014 an employee is told that he is to participate in a bonus scheme which will pay £1,000 if certain performance criteria are met for the year ended 31 December 2014. The bonus will be paid on 1 January 2015. 50% will be paid in cash and the employee will be permitted, but not required, to invest the remaining 50% in as many shares as are worth £500 at 1 January 2015. Thus, if the share price were £2.50, the employee could choose to receive either (a) £1,000 or (b) £500 cash and 200 shares.

If the employee elects to reinvest the bonus in shares, the shares are not fully vested unless the employee remains in service until 31 December 2016. However, if the employee elects to receive 50% of the bonus in shares, the entity is required to award an equal number of additional shares ('matching shares'), in this case 200 shares, also conditional upon the employee remaining in service until 31 December 2016. The award of any matching shares will be made on 1 January 2015.

The 50% of the bonus automatically paid in cash is outside the scope of IFRS 2 and within that of IAS 19 (see Chapter 31).

The 50% of the bonus that may be invested in shares falls within the scope of IFRS 2 as a share-based payment transaction in which the terms of the arrangement provide the counterparty with the choice of settlement. This is the case even though the value of the alternative award is always £500 and does not depend on the share price (see 10.4 above).

The mandatory nature of the matching shares means that the award is a share-based payment transaction, entered into on (and therefore measured as at) 1 January 2014, in which the terms of the arrangement provide the counterparty with a choice of settlement between:

- at 1 January 2015: cash of £500, subject to performance in the year ended 31 December 2014; or
- at 31 December 2016: shares with a value of £1,000 as at 1 January 2015, subject to:
  - (i) performance in the year ended 31 December 2014; and
  - (ii) service during the three years ended 31 December 2016.

The equity component as calculated in accordance with IFRS 2 will have a value in excess of zero (see 10.1.2 above). The measurement date of the equity component is 1 January 2014. However, as discussed at 10.1.3.A above, IFRS 2 does not specify how to deal with a transaction where the counterparty has the choice of equity- or cash-settlement but the liability and equity components have different vesting periods. In our view it is appropriate to recognise the liability and equity components independently over their different vesting periods, i.e. in this case:

- for the liability component (i.e. the fair value of the cash alternative), the year ended 31 December 2014;
- for the equity component (i.e. the excess of the total fair value of the award over the fair value of the cash alternative), the three years ended 31 December 2016.

Thus, at the end of the year ended 31 December 2014, the entity will have recorded:

- as a liability, the cost of the portion of the annual award that the employee may take in cash or equity;
- in equity, one-third of the cost of the matching award.

If the employee decides to take shares, the entity would simply transfer the amount recorded as a liability to equity and recognise the remaining cost of the matching shares over the following two years.

If, however, the employee elects to take cash, the position is more complicated. Clearly, the main accounting entry is to reduce the liability, with a corresponding reduction in cash, when the liability is settled. However, this raises the question of what is to be done with the one-third cost for the matching award already recognised in equity.

In our view, by electing to receive cash, the employee has effectively failed to exercise his option to receive additional equity at the end of 2016. This should therefore be accounted for as a failure to exercise (see 6.1.3 and 10.1.3 above), so that the amount already recognised in equity would not be reversed, but no further cost would be recognised. *[IFRS 2.40]*.

Some take the view that IFRS 2 could be read as requiring an election by the employee for cash at the end of 2014 to be treated as a cancellation of the matching award, due to the employee's failure to fulfil a non-vesting condition (i.e. not taking the cash alternative) for the matching award – see 3.2 and 6.4 above. This would require the remaining two-thirds of the matching award not yet recognised to be recognised immediately, resulting in an expense for an award that does not actually crystallise. The alternative view is that the requirement of IFRS 2 to 'account separately' for the liability and equity components of a transaction offering the employee alternative methods of settlement (see 10.1.3 above) suggests that not taking the cash alternative should not be considered as a non-vesting condition for the equity alternative. *[IFRS 2.38]*. As IFRS 2 is unclear, in our view, an entity may make a choice between the two accounting treatments provided a consistent approach is adopted.

Example 30.61: Discretionary investment by employee of cash bonus into shares with discretionary matching award by employer

On 1 January 2014 an employee is told that he is to participate in a bonus scheme which will pay £1,000 if certain performance criteria are met for the year ended 31 December 2014. The bonus will be paid on 1 January 2015. 50% will be paid in cash and the employee will be permitted, but not required, to invest the remaining 50% in as many shares as are worth £500. Thus, if the share price were £2.50, the employee could choose to receive either (a) £1,000 or (b) £500 cash and 200 shares. Any shares received under this part of the arrangement are fully vested.

If the employee elects to receive shares, the entity has the discretion, but not the obligation, to award additional shares ('matching shares') – in this case 200 shares – conditional upon the employee remaining in service until 31 December 2016. The award of any matching shares will be made on 1 January 2015.

The 50% of the bonus automatically paid in cash is outside the scope of IFRS 2 and within that of IAS 19 (see Chapter 31).

The 50% of the bonus that may be invested in shares falls within the scope of IFRS 2 as a share-based payment transaction in which the terms of the arrangement provide the counterparty with the choice of settlement. This is the case even though the value of the alternative award is always £500 and does not depend on the share price (see 10.4 above).

It is in our view necessary, as discussed in Example 30.58 above, to consider whether the entity's discretion to make an award of matching shares is real or not, this being a matter for judgement in the light of individual facts and circumstances.

If it is determined that the entity is effectively obliged to match any share award taken by the employee, then the award should be analysed as giving the employee the choice of settlement between:

- at 1 January 2015: cash of £500, subject to performance in the year ended 31 December 2014; or
- at 1 January 2015 shares with a value of £500 at 1 January 2014 subject to performance in the year ended 31 December 2014; and, at 31 December 2016: the same number of shares again subject to (i) performance in the year ended 31 December 2014 and (ii) service during the three years ended 31 December 2016.

In this case the grant date (and therefore measurement date) of all the equity awards would be taken as 1 January 2014. As regards the award due on 1 January 2015, this would be split into its equity and liability components, and in this case the equity component would have a value of zero (since the two components are essentially worth the same). Thus the entity would accrue a liability over the year to 31 December 2014. The matching share award would be expensed over the three years ending on 31 December 2016.

Thus, at the end of the year ended 31 December 2014, the entity will have recorded:

- as a liability, the cost of the portion of the annual award that the employee may take in cash or equity;
- in equity, one-third of the cost of the matching award.

If the employee decides to take shares, the entity would simply transfer the amount recorded as a liability to equity and recognise the remaining cost of the matching shares over the following two years.

If, however, the employee elects to take cash, the position is more complicated. Clearly, the main accounting entry is to reduce the liability, with a corresponding reduction in cash, when the liability is settled. However, what is to be done with the one-third cost for the matching award already recognised in equity?

In our view, by electing to receive cash, the employee has effectively failed to exercise his option to receive additional equity at the end of 2016. This should therefore be accounted for as a failure to exercise (see 6.1.3 and 10.1.3 above), so that the amount already recognised in equity would not be reversed, but no further cost would be recognised. *[IFRS 2.40]*.

As in Example 30.60 above, there is an argument that IFRS 2 could be read as requiring an election by the employee for cash at the end of 2014 to be treated as a cancellation of the matching award, due to the employee's failure to fulfil a non-vesting condition (i.e. not taking the cash alternative) for the matching award – see 3.2 and 6.4 above This would require the remaining two-thirds of the matching award not yet recognised to be recognised immediately, resulting in an expense for an award that does not actually crystallise. The alternative view is that the requirement of IFRS 2 to 'account separately' for the liability and equity components of a transaction offering the employee alternative methods of settlement (see 10.1.3 above) suggests that not taking the cash alternative should not be considered as a non-vesting condition for the equity alternative. *[IFRS 2.38]*. As IFRS 2 is unclear, in our view, an entity may make a choice between the two accounting treatments provided a consistent approach is adopted.

If it is concluded that the entity has genuine discretion to make a matching award, the analysis is somewhat different.

The portion of the annual award that may be taken in shares should be analysed as giving the employee the choice, at 1 January 2015, between cash of £500 and shares worth £500 (the number of shares being determined by reference to the share price at that date). This would be split into its equity and liability components, and in this case the equity component would have a value of zero (since the two components are essentially worth the same). Thus the entity would accrue a liability over the year to 31 December 2014. If the employee elected to receive shares, this would be transferred to equity.

Any matching share award would be treated as being made on, and measured as at, 1 January 2015. The cost would be recognised over the two years ended 31 December 2016.

The discussion in 8.10 above is relevant to the valuation of the matching equity award.

If, in Examples 30.57 to 30.61 above, the employee had to retain his original holding of shares in addition to completing a further period of service in order for the matching award to vest, the requirement to retain the original shares would be treated as a non-vesting condition and taken into account in the grant date fair value of the matching award (see 6.4 above).

15.2 Limited recourse and full recourse loans

In some jurisdictions, share awards to employees are made by means of so-called 'limited recourse loan' schemes. The detailed terms of such schemes vary, but typical features include the following:

- the entity makes an interest-free loan to the employee which is immediately used to acquire shares to the value of the loan on behalf of the employee;
- the shares may be held by the entity, or a trust controlled by it (see 12.3 above), until the loan is repaid;
- the employee is entitled to dividends, except that these are treated as paying off some of the outstanding loan;
- within a given period (say, five years) the employee must either have paid off the outstanding balance of the loan, at which point the shares are delivered to the employee, or surrendered the shares. Surrender of the shares by the employee is treated as discharging any outstanding amount on the loan, irrespective of the value of the shares.

The effect of such an arrangement is clearly equivalent to an option exercisable within five years with a strike price per share equal to the share price at grant date less total dividends since grant date – a view reinforced by the Interpretations Committee.[45] There is no real loan at the initial stage. The entity has no right to receive cash or anther financial asset, since the loan can be settled by the employee returning the (fixed) amount of equity 'purchased' at grant date.

Indeed, the only true cash flow in the entire transaction is any amount paid at the final stage if the employee chooses to acquire the shares at that point. The fact that the strike price is a factor of the share price at grant date and dividends paid between grant date and the date of repayment of the 'loan' is simply an issue for the valuation of the option.

Where, as is generally the case, such an award is subject to no future service or performance condition, IFRS 2 requires the cost to be recognised in full at grant date (see 6.1 above).

More recently, some more complex arrangements have begun to appear where the loan to the employee to acquire the shares is a full recourse loan (i.e. it cannot be discharged simply by surrendering the shares). However, the amount repayable on the loan is reduced not only by dividends paid on the shares, but also by the achievement of performance targets, such as the achievement of a given level of earnings.

The appropriate analysis of such awards is more difficult, as they could be viewed in two ways. One view would be that the employer has made a loan (which the employee has chosen to use to buy a share), accounted for under IAS 39, and has then entered into a performance-related cash bonus arrangement with the employee, accounted for under IAS 19. An alternative analysis would be that the transaction is a share option where the strike price varies according to the satisfaction of performance conditions and the amount of dividends on the shares, accounted for under IFRS 2. The different analyses give rise to potentially significantly different expenses. This will particularly be the case where one of the conditions for mitigation of the amount repayable on the loan is linked to the price of the employer's equity. As this is a market condition, the effect of accounting for the arrangement under IFRS 2 may be that an expense is recognised in circumstances where no expense would be recognised under IAS 19.

Such awards need to be carefully analysed, in the light of their particular facts and circumstances, in order to determine the appropriate treatment. Factors that could suggest that IFRS 2 is the more relevant standard would, in our view, include:

- the employee can use the loan only to acquire shares;
- the employee cannot trade the shares until the loan is discharged; or
- the entity has a practice of accepting (e.g. from leavers) surrender of the shares as full discharge for the amount outstanding on the loan and does not pursue any shortfall between the fair value of the shares and the amount owed by the employee. This would tend to indicate that, in substance, the loan is not truly full recourse.

15.3 Awards entitled to dividends during the vesting period

Some awards entitle the holder to receive dividends on unvested shares during the vesting period.

For example, in some jurisdictions, entities make awards of shares that are regarded as fully vested for the purposes of tax legislation (typically because the employee enjoys the full voting and dividend rights of the shares), but not for accounting purposes (typically because the shares are subject to forfeiture if a certain minimum service period is not achieved). In practice, the shares concerned are usually held by an EBT until the potential forfeiture period has expired.

Another variant of such an award that is sometimes seen is where an entity grants an employee an option to acquire shares in the entity which can be exercised immediately. However, if the employee exercises the option but leaves within a certain minimum period from the grant date, he is required to sell back the share to the entity (typically either at the original exercise price, or the lower of that price or the market value of the share at the time of the buy-back).

Such awards do not fully vest for the purposes of IFRS 2 until the potential forfeiture or buy-back period has expired. The cost of such awards should therefore be recognised over this period.

This raises the question of the accounting treatment of any dividends paid to employees during the vesting period. Conceptually, it could be argued that such dividends cannot be dividends for financial reporting purposes since the equity instruments to which they relate are not yet regarded as issued for financial reporting purposes (and would be excluded from the number of shares in issue for the purposes of IAS 33). This would lead to the conclusion that dividends paid in the vesting period should be charged to profit or loss as an employment cost.

However, the charge to be made for the award under IFRS 2 will already have been increased to take account of the fact that the recipient is entitled to receive dividends during the vesting period (see 8.5.4 above). Thus, it could be argued that also to charge profit or loss with the dividends paid is a form of double counting. Moreover, whilst the relevant shares may not have been fully issued for financial reporting purposes, the basic IFRS 2 accounting does build up an amount in equity over the vesting period. It could therefore be argued that – conceptually, if not legally – any dividend paid relates not to an issued share, but rather to the equity instrument represented by the cumulative amount that has been recorded for the award as a credit to equity, and can therefore appropriately be shown as a deduction from equity.

However, this argument is valid only to the extent that the credit to equity represents awards that are expected to vest. It cannot apply to dividends paid to employees whose awards are either known not to have vested or treated as expected not to vest when applying IFRS 2 (since there is no credit to equity for these awards). Accordingly, we believe that the most appropriate approach is to analyse the dividends paid so that, by the date of vesting, cumulative dividends paid on awards treated by IFRS 2 as vested are deducted from equity and those paid on awards treated by IFRS 2 as unvested are charged to profit or loss. The allocation for periods before that in which vesting occurs should be based on a best estimate of the final outcome, as illustrated by Example 30.62 below.

Example 30.62: Award with rights to receive (and retain) dividends during vesting period

An entity grants 100 free shares to each of its 500 employees. The shares are treated as fully vested for legal and tax purposes, so that the employees are eligible to receive any dividends paid. However, the shares will be forfeited if the employee leaves within three years of the award being made. Accordingly, for the purposes of IFRS 2, vesting is conditional upon the employee working for the entity over the next three years. The entity estimates that the fair value of each share (including the right to receive dividends during the IFRS 2 vesting period) is €15. Employees are entitled to retain any dividend received even if the award does not vest.

20 employees leave during the first year, and the entity's best estimate at the end of year 1 is that 75 employees will have left before the end of the vesting period. During the second year, a further 22 employees leave, and the entity revises its estimate of total employee departures over the vesting period from 75 to 60. During the third year, a further 15 employees leave. Hence, a total of 57 employees (20 + 22 + 15) forfeit their rights to the shares during the three year period, and a total of 44,300 shares (443 employees × 100 shares per employee) finally vest.

The entity pays dividends of €1 per share in year 1, €1.20 per share in year 2, and €1.50 in year 3.

Under IFRS 2, the entity will recognise the following amounts during the vesting period for services received as consideration for the shares.

Year	Calculation of cumulative expense	Cumulative expense (€)	Expense for period (€)
1	100 shares × 425 employees × €15 × 1/3	212,500	212,500
2	100 shares × 440 employees × €15 × 2/3	440,000	227,500
3	100 shares × 443 × €15 × 3/3	664,500	224,500

On the assumption that all employees who leave during a period do so on the last day of that period (and thus receive dividends paid in that period), in our view the dividends paid on the shares should be accounted for as follows:

		€	€
Year 1	Profit or loss (employee costs)[1]	7,500	
	Equity[1]	42,500	
	Cash[2]		50,000
Year 2	Profit or loss (employee costs)[3]	3,300	
	Equity[3]	54,300	
	Cash[4]		57,600
Year 3	Profit or loss (employee costs)[5]	1,590	
	Equity[5]	67,110	
	Cash[6]		68,700

1 20 employees have left and a further 55 are anticipated to leave. Dividends paid to those employees (100 shares × 75 employees × €1 = €7,500) are therefore recognised as an expense. Dividends paid to other employees are recognised as a reduction in equity.

2 100 shares × 500 employees × €1.

3 22 further employees have left and a further 18 are anticipated to leave. The cumulative expense for dividends paid to leavers and anticipated leavers should therefore be €10,800 (100 shares × 20 employees × €1 = €2,000 for leavers in year 1 + 100 shares × 40 employees × [€1 + €1.20] for leavers and anticipated leavers in year 2 = €8,800). €7,500 was charged in year 1, so the charge for year 2 should be €10,800 – €7,500 = €3,300. This could also have been calculated as charge for leavers and expected leavers in current year €4,800 (100 shares × 40 [22 + 18] employees × €1.20) less reversal of expense in year 1 for reduction in anticipated final number of leavers €1,500 (100 shares × 15 [75 – 60] employees × €1.00). Dividends paid to other employees are recognised as a reduction in equity.

4 100 shares × 480 employees in employment at start of year × €1.20.

5 15 further employees have left. The cumulative expense for dividends paid to leavers should therefore be €12,390 (€2,000 for leavers in year 1 (see 3 above) + 100 shares × 22 employees × [€1 + €1.20] = €4,840 for leavers in year 2 + 100 shares × 15 employees × [€1 + €1.20 + €1.50] = €5,550 for leavers in year 3). A cumulative expense of €10,800 (see 3 above) was recognised by the end of year 2, so the charge for year 3 should be €12,390 – €10,800 = €1,590. This could also have been calculated as charge for leavers in current year €2,250 (100 shares × 15 employees × €1.50) less reversal of expense in years 1 and 2 for reduction in final number of leavers as against estimate at end of year 2 €660 (100 shares × 3 [60 – 57] employees × [€1.00 + €1.20]). Dividends paid to other employees are recognised as a reduction in equity.

6 100 shares × 458 employees in employment at start of year × €1.50.

15.4 Awards vesting or exercisable on flotation (or trade sale, change of control, etc.)

Entities frequently issue awards connected to a significant event such as a flotation, change of control or a trade sale of the business. It may be, as discussed at 10.3 above, that an award that would normally be only equity-settled becomes cash-settled on such an event.

However, it may also be that an award vests only on such an event, which raises various issues of interpretation, as discussed below.

The sections below should be read together with the more general discussions elsewhere in this Chapter (as referred to in the narrative below) on grant date, vesting period and vesting and non-vesting conditions.

15.4.1 Grant date

Sometimes such awards are structured so that they will vest on flotation, or that they will vest on flotation subject to further approval at that time. For awards in the first category, grant date as defined in IFRS 2 will be the date on which the award is first communicated to employees. For awards in the second category, grant date will be at or around the date of flotation, when the required further approval is given.

This means that the IFRS 2 cost of awards subject to final approval at flotation will generally be significantly higher than that of awards that do not require such approval. Moreover, as discussed further at 5.3 above, it may well be the case that employees begin rendering service for such awards before grant date (e.g. from the date on which the entity communicates its intention to make the award in principle). In that case, the entity would need to make an initial estimate of the value of the award for the purpose of recognising an expense from the date services have been provided, and continually re-assess that value up until the actual grant date. As with any award dependent on a non-market vesting condition (although it should be noted that the classification of a requirement to float as a non-market vesting condition is the matter of some discussion – see 15.4.3 below), an expense would be recognised only to the extent that the award is considered likely to vest.

15.4.2 Vesting period

Many awards that vest on flotation (or another similar event) have a time limit – in other words, the award lapses if flotation (or another similar event) has not occurred on or before a given future date. In principle, as discussed at 6.2.3 above, when an award has a variable vesting period, the reporting entity should make a best estimate of the likely vesting period at each reporting date and calculate the IFRS 2 charge on the basis of that best estimate.

In practice, the likely timing of a future flotation is notoriously difficult to assess months, let alone years, in advance. In such cases, it would generally be acceptable simply to recognise the cost over the full potential vesting period until there is real clarity that a shorter period may be more appropriate. However, in making the assessment of the likelihood of vesting, it is important to take the company's circumstances into account. The likelihood of an exit event in the short- to medium-term is perhaps greater for a company owned by private equity investors seeking a return on their investment than for a long-established family-owned company considering a flotation.

It is worth noting that, under IFRS, once an exit event becomes likely, the IFRS 2 expense will in some cases need to be recognised over a shorter vesting period than was originally envisaged as the probability of the exit event occurring will form the basis at the reporting date of the estimate of the number of awards expected to vest (see also the discussion at 6.2.3 and 7.6 above). This contrasts with the US GAAP approach where, in practice, an exit event that is a change in control or an initial public offering is only recognised when it occurs. It is therefore possible that, in a situation where a change in control or an initial public offering occurs shortly after the reporting date, the expense will need to be recognised in an earlier period under IFRS than under US GAAP.

15.4.3 Is flotation or sale a vesting condition?

As discussed at 3.2 above, it is unclear whether a requirement for a flotation or sale to occur in order for an award to vest is a vesting condition, as defined by IFRS 2, or a non-vesting condition. The argument as to why flotation or sale is not a vesting condition would be that flotation or sale may occur irrespective of the performance of the entity and is, in any event, outside the control of the entity. The counter-argument is essentially that the price achieved on flotation or sale, which typically affects the ultimate value of the award (see 15.4.4 below), does reflect performance. Moreover, flotation or sale, although not wholly within the control of the entity, is not wholly outside the control of the entity.

The view taken will clearly have a significant impact on the expense recorded. If the view is that flotation or sale is a non-vesting condition, an expense will always be recognised for such an award, provided that all non-market vesting conditions, such as a service condition, have been met, irrespective of whether the award truly vests or not.

Even if it is concluded that a requirement for a flotation or sale, together with a service condition, is a performance vesting condition, the conclusion could differ if the service period is shorter than the period during which flotation or a sale must be achieved. The issue of non-coterminous service and performance targets is considered further at 3.2 and 3.4 above.

The classification of flotation or sale as a vesting or non-vesting condition and the required treatment when a performance target is measured over a period exceeding the service period are part of the Interpretations Committee's wider project on vesting and non-vesting conditions. The Interpretations Committee reached a tentative decision in July 2010 that a requirement to float or be sold is a performance vesting condition rather than a non-vesting condition but no specific amendment has been made to IFRS 2 to clarify this point.

However, the IASB's more general proposed amendments to the definition of a performance condition as part of the *Annual Improvements to IFRSs 2010-2012 Cycle* are intended, inter alia, to make clear the view that flotation or sale is a vesting condition rather than a non-vesting condition – on the basis that the flotation or sale condition is by reference to the entity's own operations. The proposed amendments also make it clear that a performance target period cannot extend beyond the end of the associated service period in order to meet the definition of a vesting condition (see 3.4 above).

15.4.4 Awards requiring achievement of a minimum price

Some awards contingent on flotation (or another similar event) vest only if a minimum price per share is achieved. For example, an entity might grant all its employees options over its shares, the vesting of which is contingent upon a flotation or sale of the shares at a price of at least €5 per share within five years, and the employee being in employment at that time.

Even if it is concluded that the requirement for a flotation or sale to occur is a vesting condition (see 15.4.3 above), there remains the question of whether such an award comprises:

- *two* conditions:
  - a market performance condition (i.e. float or sell within five years at a share price of at least €5); and
  - a service condition (i.e. being in employment at the time of flotation or sale);

or

- *three* conditions:
  - a market performance condition (share price at time of flotation or sale of at least €5); and
  - two non-market vesting conditions:
    - flotation or sale achieved within five years; and
    - a service condition (i.e. being in employment at the time of flotation or sale).

The significance of this is the issue discussed at 6.3 above, namely that an expense must always be recognised for all awards with a market condition, if *all* the non-market vesting conditions are satisfied, even if the market condition is not. In either case, however, there is a market condition which needs to be factored into the valuation of the award.

If the view is that 'flotation or sale at €5 within five years' is a single condition, the entity will recognise an expense for the award for all employees still in service at the end of the five year period, since the sole non-market vesting condition (i.e. service) will have been met.

If, on the other hand, the view is that 'flotation or sale within five years' and 'flotation or sale share price €5' are two separate conditions, and no flotation or sale occurs, no expense will be recognised since, of the two non-market vesting conditions (i.e. 'service' and 'flotation or sale within five years'), only one has been satisfied. However, even on this second analysis, if a sale or flotation is achieved at a price less than €5, an expense must be recognised, even though the award does not truly vest, since both non-market vesting conditions (i.e. 'service' and 'flotation or sale within five years') will have been met.

In our view, the appropriate analysis is to regard 'flotation or sale within five years' and 'flotation/sale share price €5' as two separate conditions.

There is, however, a third possible analysis (see 15.4.3 above) which is that there are *three* conditions:

- a market condition (share price at time of flotation or sale at least €5);
- a non-vesting condition (flotation or sale achieved within five years); and
- a non-market vesting condition (being in employment at the time of flotation or sale).

On this analysis, an expense would always be recognised for all employees still in service at the end of the five year period, since the sole non-market vesting condition (i.e. service) will have been met.

This third analysis ignores the view expressed by the Interpretations Committee that a requirement for flotation or sale is a performance condition when there is a corresponding service requirement. Finalisation of the proposed *Annual Improvements to IFRSs 2010-2012 Cycle* would mean that the above analysis is no longer appropriate (see 3.4 and 15.4.3 above).

The example of an award requiring flotation at a minimum price provides a useful illustration of some of the practical difficulties created by the concept of the non-vesting condition (see 3.2 and 3.4 above).

15.4.5 Awards 'purchased for fair value'

As noted at 2.2.4.D above, entities that are contemplating a flotation or trade sale may invite employees to subscribe for a special class of shares for a relatively nominal amount, which, in the event of a flotation or trade sale occurring, will be redeemable at a substantial premium. It may be argued that the initial subscription price paid represents the fair value of the share at the time, given the inherent high uncertainty as to whether a flotation or trade sale will in fact occur.

The premium paid on a flotation or trade sale will typically be calculated in part by reference to the price achieved. The question therefore arises as to whether such awards fall within the scope of IFRS 2. It might be argued for example that, as the employee paid full fair value for the award at issue, there has been no share-based payment and, accordingly, the instrument should be accounted for under IAS 32 and IAS 39.

In our view, it is necessary to consider whether the award has features that would not be expected in 'normal' equity – specifically a requirement for the holder of the shares to remain in employment until flotation. If this is the case, regardless of the amount subscribed, the terms suggest that the shares are being awarded in return for employee services and hence that the award is within the scope of IFRS 2. This may mean that, even if the award has no material fair value (and therefore gives rise to no expense), it may be necessary to make the disclosures required by IFRS 2.

Moreover, even if the amount paid by the employees can be demonstrated to be fair value, that amount would not necessarily constitute fair value under IFRS 2. Specifically, a 'true' fair value would take into account non-market vesting conditions (such as a requirement for the employee to remain in employment until flotation or a trade sale occurs). However, a valuation for IFRS 2 purposes would not take such conditions into account (see 5.5 and 6.2.1 above) and would therefore typically be higher than the 'true' fair value.

A non-equity share such as that described above might well be classified as a liability under IAS 32. However, if the redemption amount is linked to the flotation price of the 'real' equity, it is a cash-settled share-based payment transaction under IFRS 2 (see 2.2.4.A above).

It is common in such situations for the cost of satisfying any obligations to the special shareholders to be borne by shareholders rather than the entity itself. This raises a number of further issues, which are discussed at 2.2.2.A above.

15.4.6 'Drag along' and 'tag along' rights

An increasingly common form of award is for the management of an entity to be allowed to acquire a special class of equity at fair value (as in 15.4.5 above), but (in contrast to 15.4.5 above) with no redemption right on an exit event. However, rights are given:

- to any buyer of the 'normal' equity also to buy the special shares (sometimes called a 'drag along' right);
- to a holder of the special shares to require any buyer of the 'normal' equity also to buy the special shares (sometimes called a 'tag along' right).

Such schemes are particularly found in entities where the 'normal' equity is held by a provider of venture capital, which will generally be looking for an exit in the medium term.

It may well be that, under the scheme, the entity itself is required to facilitate the operation of the drag along or tag along rights, which may involve the entity collecting the proceeds from the buyer and passing them on to the holder of the special shares.

This raises the issue of whether such an arrangement is equity-settled or cash-settled. The fact that, in certain circumstances the entity is required to deliver cash to the holder of a share suggests that the arrangement is an award requiring cash settlement in specific circumstances, the treatment of which is discussed at 10.3 above.

However, if the terms of the award are such that the entity is obliged to pass on cash to the holder of the share only if, and to the extent that, proceeds are received from an external buyer, in our view, the arrangement may be economically no different to the broker settlement arrangements typically entered into by listed entities, as discussed at 9.2.3 above. This could allow the arrangement to be regarded as equity-settled because the entity's only involvement as a principal is in the initial delivery of shares to employees, provided that consideration is given to all the factors (discussed at 9.2.3 above) that could suggest that the scheme is more appropriately regarded as cash-settled.

In making such an assessment, care needs to be taken to ensure that the precise facts of the arrangement are considered. For example, a transaction where the entity has some discretion over the amount of proceeds attributable to each class of shareholder might indicate that it is inappropriate to treat the entity simply as an agent in the cash payment arrangement. It might also be relevant to consider the extent to which, under relevant local law, the proceeds received can be 'ring fenced' so as not to be available to settle other liabilities of the entity.

It is also the case that arrangements that result in employees obtaining similar amounts of cash can be interpreted very differently under IFRS 2 depending on how the arrangement is structured and whether, for example:

- the entity is required to pay its employees cash on an exit (having perhaps held shares itself via a trust and those shares having been subject to 'drag along' rights); or
- the employees themselves have held the right to equity shares on a restricted basis with vesting – and 'drag along' rights – taking effect on a change of control and the employees receiving cash for their shares.

The appropriate accounting treatment in such cases requires a significant amount of judgement based on the precise facts and circumstances.

15.5 South African black economic empowerment ('BEE') and similar arrangements

As part of general economic reforms in South Africa, arrangements – commonly referred to as black economic empowerment or 'BEE' deals – have been put in place to encourage the transfer of equity, or economic interests in equity, to historically disadvantaged individuals. Similar arrangements have also been put in place in other jurisdictions.

An entity can enhance its BEE status in a number of ways (through employment equity, skills development or preferential procurement policies to name but a few). This section focuses on BEE deals involving transfers of equity instruments, or interests in equity instruments, to historically disadvantaged individuals.

Such transfers have generally been concluded at a discount to the fair value of the equity instruments concerned. As a result of having empowered shareholders, the reporting entity is able to claim its 'BEE credentials', thus allowing the reporting entity greater business opportunities in the South African economy. These arrangements raise a number of practical issues of interpretation, and indeed led to the scope of IFRS 2 being extended to include transactions where the consideration received appears less than the consideration given, as discussed further at 2.2.2.C above.

BEE deals are typically complex and their specific structures and terms may vary considerably. However, they do exhibit certain features with some regularity, as discussed below.

Typically BEE arrangements have involved the transfer of equity instruments to:

- empowerment companies controlled by prominent BEE qualifying individuals;
- BEE qualifying employees of the reporting entity; or
- beneficiaries in the BEE qualifying communities in which the entity operates.

The arrangements generally lock the parties in for a minimum specified period and if they want to withdraw they are able to sell their interest only to others with qualifying BEE credentials.

Generally these individuals have not been able to raise sufficient finance in order to purchase the equity instruments. Accordingly, the reporting entity often facilitates the transaction and assists the BEE party in securing the necessary financing.

A BEE arrangement often involves the creation of a trust or corporate entity, with the BEE party holding beneficial rights in the trust which in turn holds equity instruments of the reporting entity (or a member of its group).

The awards made by the trust may be in the form of:

- the equity instruments originally transferred to the trust;
- units in the trust itself, usually with a value linked in some way to the value of the equity instruments of the reporting entity originally transferred to the trust; or
- payments made from the proceeds (dividends received, sale of equity instruments etc. that the trust generates.

The accounting issues arising from such schemes include:

- the nature of the trust (specifically, whether it meets the criteria for consolidation by the reporting entity);
- whether any charge arises under IFRS 2 and, if so, the grant date and therefore, under a grant date model, the amount of the charge; and
- whether awards are equity-settled or cash-settled.

15.5.1 Nature of the trust

The first issue to consider in any accounting analysis is whether any trust to which the equity instruments of the reporting entity have been transferred meets the requirements for consolidation under IFRS 10 (see Chapter 6). Factors that may indicate that the trust should be consolidated include:

- the reporting entity is involved in the design of the trust and the trust deed at inception, the intention being that the design is such that the desired BEE credentials are obtained;
- the potential beneficiaries of the trust are restricted to persons in the employment of, or otherwise providing services to, the reporting entity;
- the reporting entity has a commitment to ensure that the trust operates as designed in order to maintain its BEE credentials;
- the reporting entity has the right to control (on 'autopilot' or otherwise), or does in practice control, the management of the trust;
- the reporting entity assumes the residual risk associated with the trust;
- the relevant activities of the trust are to service the loan and to make distributions to the beneficiaries in line with the trust deed; or
- the servicing of the loan depends on variable dividends received by the trust

but all the IFRS 10 control criteria will need to be assessed.

The generic form of a BEE arrangement normally requires the reporting entity either to finance the acquisition of the shares by the trust or to provide cross guarantees to the financiers of the trust. Alternative methodologies that have been employed include capital enhancements created in the trust by the sale of equity instruments at a severely discounted amount.

When the reporting entity finances the arrangement, the finance is generally interest-free or at a lower than market interest rate. The debt is serviced with the dividends received and, at the end of the repayment period, any outstanding balance can be treated in various ways; refinanced or waived by the reporting entity, or settled by the return of a number of shares equal to the outstanding value.

In summary, the BEE party generally injects only a notional amount of capital into the trust, which obtains financing to acquire the shares in the reporting entity and uses the dividend cash flows to service the debt it has raised. In such generic schemes, the BEE party faces a typical option return profile: the maximum amount of capital at risk is notional and the potential upside increase in value of the shares of the reporting entity accrues to the BEE party through the party's beneficial rights in the trust.

15.5.2 Measurement and timing of the accounting cost

If the analysis under 15.5.1 above is that the trust should be consolidated, the transfer of equity instruments to that entity is essentially the same as a transfer of own equity to an employee benefit trust, as discussed at 12.3 above. Such a transfer, considered alone, is an intra-entity transaction and therefore does not give rise to a charge under IFRS 2. The equity instruments held by the trust are therefore treated as treasury shares, and no non-controlling (minority) interests are recognised.

It is only when the trust itself makes an award to a third party that a charge arises, which will be measured at the time at which the transfer to the third party occurs. In a rising stock market this will lead to a higher charge than would have occurred had there been a grant, as defined in IFRS 2, on the date that the equity instruments were originally transferred to the trust. Generally, the value of the award is based on an option model and the BEE party is treated as the holder of an option.

Where the trust is not consolidated, the presumption will be that the transfer of equity instruments to the trust crystallises an IFRS 2 charge at the date of transfer. However, it is important to consider the terms of the transaction in their totality. For example, if the entity has the right to buy back the equity instruments at some future date, the benefit transferred may in fact be an economic interest in the equity instruments for a limited period. This may, depending on the method used to determine the buy-back price, influence the measurement of any IFRS 2 charge (which would normally be based on the presumption that the benefits of a vested share had been passed in perpetuity).

Some have sought to argue that BEE credentials result in the recognition of an intangible asset rather than an expense. However, we concur with the conclusion of interpretive guidance issued in South Africa that BEE credentials do not qualify for recognition of intangible assets in terms of IAS 38 – *Intangible Assets* – and the difference between the fair value of the award and the consideration received should therefore be expensed.[46]

An issue to be considered in determining the timing of the IFRS 2 expense is that many BEE transactions require the BEE party to be 'locked into' the transaction for a pre-determined period. During this period the BEE party or trust is generally prohibited from selling or transferring the equity instruments. As no specific performance is generally required during this period, it is not considered part of the vesting period (see 3.3 and 6.1 above). Rather, the restrictions would be considered to be post-vesting restrictions, and taken into account in calculating the fair value of the equity instruments (see 8.4.1 above).

15.5.3 Classification of awards as equity- or cash-settled

Certain schemes, particularly where the reporting entity is not listed, give the BEE party the right to put the shares back to the entity (or another group entity) after a certain date. This is often done to create liquidity for the BEE parties, should they decide to exit the scheme. Such a feature would require the scheme to be classified as cash-settled (see 9.1 above).

Similarly, where the BEE transaction is facilitated through a trust, the trust may have granted awards to beneficiaries in the form of units in the trust. The trustees may have the power to reacquire units from beneficiaries in certain circumstances (e.g. where the beneficiaries are employees, when they leave the employment of the entity). Where the trust does not have sufficient cash with which to make such payments, the reporting entity may be obliged, legally or constructively, to fund them.

Such arrangements may – in their totality – create a cash-settled scheme from the perspective of the reporting entity. In analysing a particular scheme, it should be remembered that, under IFRS 2, cash-settled schemes arise not only from legal liabilities, but also from constructive or commercial liabilities (e.g. to prevent a former employee having rights against what is essentially an employee trust) – see 10.2 above.

Finally, a transaction may be structured in such a way that the trust holds equity instruments of the reporting entity for an indefinite period. Dividends received by the trust may be used to fund certain expenses in a particular community in which the reporting entity operates (e.g. tuition fees for children of the reporting entity's employees or the costs of certain community projects). The scheme may even make provision for the shares to be sold after a certain period with the eventual proceeds being distributed amongst members of the community.

In such a case it is necessary to consider the nature of the distribution requirement and whether or not the reporting entity (through the trust) has a legal or constructive obligation under the scheme to make cash payments based on the price or value of the shares held by the trust. Where there is such an obligation, the arrangement would be classified as a cash-settled scheme. If however the trust merely acts as a conduit through which:

- dividend receipts by the trust are paid out to beneficiaries with the shares never leaving the trust; or
- proceeds from the sale of shares are distributed to beneficiaries,

the precise terms of the arrangement should be assessed to determine whether or not the arrangement meets the definition of a cash-settled share-based payment (see section 15.4.6 above for a discussion of similar considerations in the context of 'drag along' and 'tag along' rights).

Any dividend payments by the Group for the period that the trust is consolidated should be treated as an equity distribution or as an expense, as appropriate, in accordance with the principles discussed at 15.3 above.

16 FIRST-TIME ADOPTION AND TRANSITIONAL PROVISIONS

16.1 First-time adoption provisions

These are discussed in Chapter 5 at 5.3. However, one provision may remain relevant for entities that have already adopted IFRS and would no longer generally be considered 'first-time adopters'.

IFRS 1 – *First-time Adoption of International Financial Reporting Standards* – does not require an entity to account for equity-settled transactions:

- granted on or before 7 November 2002; or
- granted after 7 November 2002 but vested before the later of the date of transition to IFRS and 1 January 2005.

However, where such an award is modified, cancelled or settled, the rules regarding modification, cancellation and settlement (see 7 above) apply in full unless the modification occurred before the date of transition to IFRS. *[IFRS 1.D2].* The intention of this provision is to prevent an entity from avoiding the recognition of a cost for a new award by structuring it as a modification to an earlier award not in the scope of IFRS 2.

There is slight ambiguity on this point in the wording of IFRS 1, paragraph D2 of which refers only to the *modification* of such awards. This could allow a literalistic argument that IFRS 1 does not prescribe any specific treatment when an entity cancels or settles (as opposed to modifying) an equity-settled award subject to the first-time adoption exception. However, paragraph D2 also requires an entity to apply 'paragraphs 26-29' of IFRS 2 to 'modified' awards. Paragraphs 26-29 deal not only with modification but also with cancellation and settlement, and indeed paragraphs 28 and 29 are not relevant to *modification* at all. This makes it clear, in our view, that the IASB intended IFRS 1 to be applied not only to the modification but also to the cancellation and settlement of such awards.

16.2 Transitional provisions

The original version of IFRS 2 published in February 2004 contained a number of transitional provisions that are now of limited application. The principal transitional provision likely to remain of relevance is that IFRS 2 as originally published did not require an entity to account for equity-settled transactions:

- granted on or before 7 November 2002; or
- granted after 7 November 2002 but vested before the effective date of IFRS 2 (the first day of the accounting period in which IFRS 2 first applied). *[IFRS 2.53, 60].*

However, where such an award is modified, cancelled or settled after the effective date, the rules regarding modification, cancellation and settlement (see 7 above) apply in full. *[IFRS 2.57, 60].* The intention of this provision is to prevent an entity from avoiding the recognition of a cost for a new award by structuring it as a modification of an earlier award not in the scope of IFRS 2 although, as in paragraph D2 of IFRS 1 (see 16.1 above), there is slight ambiguity in IFRS 2 as currently drafted.

References

1 *Amendment to International Financial Reporting Standards: IFRS 2 Share-based Payment – Vesting Conditions and Cancellations*, IASB, January 2008 ('January 2008 amendment').

2 *Group Cash-settled Share-based Payment Transactions, Amendments to IFRS 2*, IASB, June 2009 ('June 2009 amendment').

3 For convenience, throughout this Chapter we refer to the recognition of a cost for share-based payments. In some cases, however, a share-based payment transaction may initially give rise to an asset (e.g. where employee costs are capitalised as part of the cost of PP&E or inventories).

4 Discussion Paper DP/2013/1 – *A Review of the Conceptual Framework for Financial Reporting*, IASB, July 2013.

5 *IFRIC Update*, November 2012.

6 *IFRIC Update*, January 2010.

7 *IFRIC Update*, July 2010 and September 2010.

8 'Contingent feature' is not a defined term in IFRS 2 but is used in the September 2011 IASB Agenda Paper 7D (para. 49) to refer to a condition not currently defined in IFRS 2.

9 *IASB Update*, September 2010.

10 *IASB Update*, September 2011.

11 *IFRIC Update*, November 2010.

12 *IFRIC Update*, March 2011.

13 Exposure Draft – *Annual Improvements to IFRSs 2010-2012 Cycle*, IASB, May 2012.

14 *IFRIC Update*, January 2013.

15 *IASB Update*, February 2013.

16 *IASB Update*, June 2013.

17 *IASB Update*, September 2011.

18 FASB ASC 718 – Compensation – Stock Compensation (formerly FAS123(R), *Share-Based Payment*), FASB, December 2004, [20-55-25].

19 *IASB Update*, September 2011 and IASB Agenda Paper 7D September 2011 para. 57 et seq.

20 *IFRIC Update*, September 2010.

21 *IFRIC Update*, November 2010.

22 Exposure Draft – *Annual Improvements to IFRSs 2010-2012 Cycle*, IASB, May 2012.

23 *IFRIC Update*, July 2006.

24 *IFRIC Update*, March 2011.

25 More detailed guidance on this may be found in a publication such as Options, Futures, and Other Derivatives, John C. Hull.

26 *IFRIC Update*, May 2011.

27 *IFRIC Update*, July 2012.

28 *IFRIC Update*, March 2013.

29 FASB Staff Position 123(R)-4, *Classification of Options and Similar Instruments Issued as Employee Compensation That Allow for Cash Settlement upon the Occurrence of a Contingent Event.*

30 FASB ASC 718 – Compensation – Stock Compensation (formerly FAS123(R), *Share-Based Payment*), FASB, December 2004, para. 32, footnote 18a.

31 *IFRIC Update*, January 2010.

32 *IFRIC Update*, March 2011.

33 *IASB Update*, September 2011.

34 *IFRIC Update*, July 2012.

35 *IFRIC Update*, May 2013.

36 D17 – *IFRS 2 – Group and Treasury Share Transactions*, IASB, 2005, para. IE5.

37 *IFRIC Update*, May 2013.

38 UITF 25 – *National Insurance contributions on share option gains*, Urgent Issues Task Force of United Kingdom Accounting Standards Board, July 2000.

39 *IFRIC Update*, September 2010.

40 *IFRIC Update*, September 2010.

41 *IFRIC Update*, November 2010.

42 *IFRIC Update*, March 2011.

43 *IFRIC Update*, July 2012.

44 *IFRIC Update*, March 2013.

45 *IFRIC Update*, November 2005.

46 AC 503, Accounting Practices Committee (South Africa), January 2010.

Chapter 31 Employee benefits

List of examples

Chapter 31 Employee benefits

1 INTRODUCTION

This chapter deals with IAS 19 – *Employee Benefits* – as published in June 2011 which comes into mandatory force for periods beginning on or after 1 January 2013, with earlier adoption permitted. *[IAS 19.172]*. Predecessors of this standard are discussed in earlier editions of International GAAP. The revised standard differs in many ways from its predecessor. The principal differences, including the removal of the so-called 'corridor' approach to the recognition of actuarial gains and losses, are discussed at 10 below.

Employee benefits typically form a very significant part of any entity's costs, and can take many and varied forms. Accordingly, IFRS devotes considerable attention to them in two separate standards. IFRS 2 – *Share-based Payment* – which was issued primarily in response to concerns over share-based remuneration and is discussed in Chapter 30. All other employee benefits are dealt with in IAS 19 which is discussed in this Chapter.

Many issues raised in accounting for employee benefits can be straightforward, such as the allocation of wages paid to an accounting period, and are generally dealt with by IAS 19 accordingly. In contrast, accounting for the costs of retirement benefits in the financial statements of employers presents one of the most difficult challenges in the whole field of financial reporting. The amounts involved are large, the timescale is long, the estimation process is complex and involves many areas of uncertainty which have to be made the subject of assumptions. Furthermore, the complexities for an International Standard are multiplied by the wide variety of arrangements found in different jurisdictions.

2 OBJECTIVE AND SCOPE OF IAS 19

2.1 Objective

IAS 19 sets out its objective as follows:

'The objective of this Standard is to prescribe the accounting and disclosure for employee benefits. The Standard requires an entity to recognise:

(a) a liability when an employee has provided service in exchange for employee benefits to be paid in the future; and

(b) an expense when the entity consumes the economic benefit arising from service provided by an employee in exchange for employee benefits.' *[IAS 19.1]*.

This provides the first glimpse of the direction taken by the standard. Driven by the focus on assets and liabilities in the IASB's *Conceptual Framework* it approaches the issues from the perspective of the statement of financial position.

2.2 Scope

Section 2.2.1 below deals with the general scope of the standard. The issue of employee benefits settled not by the employing entity but by a shareholder or other member of a group is discussed at 2.2.2 below.

2.2.1 *General scope requirements of IAS 19*

As its name suggests, IAS 19 is not confined to pensions and other post-retirement benefits, but rather addresses all forms of consideration (aside of share based payments which are dealt with by IFRS 2 and discussed in Chapter 30) given by an employer in exchange for service rendered by employees or for the termination of employment. *[IAS 19.2, 8]*. In particular, in addition to post-retirement benefits employee benefits include: *[IAS 19.5]*

(a) short-term benefits, including wages and salaries, paid annual leave, bonuses, benefits in kind, etc. The accounting treatment of these is discussed at 6.1 below;

(b) long-term benefits, such as long-service leave, long-term disability benefits, long-term bonuses, etc. These are to be accounted for in a similar way to post-retirement benefits by using actuarial techniques and are discussed at 6.2 below; and

(c) termination benefits. These are to be provided for and expensed when the employer becomes committed to the redundancy plan, on a similar basis to that required by IAS 37 – *Provisions, Contingent Liabilities and Contingent Assets* – for provisions generally, and are discussed at 6.3 below.

The standard addresses only the accounting by employers, and excludes from its scope reporting by employee benefit plans themselves. These are dealt with in IAS 26 – *Accounting and Reporting by Retirement Benefit Plans*. *[IAS 19.3]*. The specialist nature of these requirements puts them beyond the scope of this book.

The standard makes clear it applies widely and in particular to benefits:

(a) provided to all employees (whether full-time, part-time, permanent, temporary or casual staff and specifically including directors and other management personnel); *[IAS 19.7]*

(b) however settled – including payments in cash or goods or services, whether paid directly to employees, their spouses, children or other dependants or any other party (such as insurance companies); *[IAS 19.6]* and

(c) however provided, including:

 (i) under formal plans or other formal agreements between an entity and individual employees, groups of employees or their representatives;

 (ii) under legislative requirements, or through industry arrangements, whereby entities are required to contribute to national, state, industry or other multi-employer plans; or

 (iii) by those informal practices that give rise to a constructive obligation, that is where the entity has no realistic alternative but to pay employee benefits. An example of a constructive obligation is where a change in the entity's informal practices would cause unacceptable damage to its relationship with employees. *[IAS 19.4].*

The standard does not define the term 'employee'. However, it is clear from the reference in (a) above to 'full-time, part-time, permanent, casual or temporary staff' and specifically including directors and other management personnel that the term is intended to apply widely. In particular, it is not necessary for there to be a contract of employment in order for an individual to be considered an employee for IAS 19 purposes. In our view the standard applies to anyone who is in substance an employee, and that will be a matter of judgement in light of all the facts and circumstances.

2.2.2 *Employee benefits settled by a shareholder or another group entity*

In some circumstances, employee benefits may be settled by a party other than the entity to which services were rendered by employees. Examples would include a shareholder or another entity in a group of entities under common control.

IAS 19 is silent on whether, and if so how, an entity receiving employee services in this way should account for them. IFRS 2, on the other hand, devotes quite some detail to this topic for employee services within its scope. Despite a certain infelicity in the drafting of IFRS 2, it generally requires the entity receiving employee services in this way to account for the cost of them.

An entity could make reference to the hierarchy in IAS 8 – *Accounting Policies, Changes in Accounting Estimates and Errors* (discussed in Chapter 3 at 4.3) when deciding on an accounting policy under IAS 19. Accordingly, these provisions of IFRS 2 could be applied by analogy to transactions within the scope of IAS 19.

The relevant requirements of IFRS 2 are discussed in Chapter 30 at 2.2.2.A.

3 PENSIONS AND OTHER POST-EMPLOYMENT BENEFITS – DEFINED CONTRIBUTION AND DEFINED BENEFIT PLANS

3.1 The distinction between defined contribution plans and defined benefit plans

IAS 19 draws the natural, but important, distinction between defined contribution plans and defined benefit plans. The determination is made based on the economic substance of the plan as derived from its principal terms and conditions. *[IAS 19.27].* The approach it takes is to define defined contribution plans, with the defined benefit plans being the default category. The relevant terms defined by the standard are as follows:

'*Post-employment benefits* are employee benefits (other than termination benefits and short-term employee benefits – discussed at 6.1 and 6.3 below) that are payable after the completion of employment'.

'*Post-employment benefit plans* are formal or informal arrangements under which an entity provides post-employment benefits for one or more employees'.

'*Defined contribution plans* are post-employment benefit plans under which an entity pays fixed contributions into a separate entity (a fund) and will have no legal or constructive obligation to pay further contributions if the fund does not hold sufficient assets to pay all employee benefits relating to employee service in the current and prior periods'.

'*Defined benefit plans* are post-employment benefit plans other than defined contribution plans'. *[IAS 19.8].*

IAS 19 applies to all post-employment benefits (whether or not they involve the establishment of a separate entity to receive contributions and pay benefits) which include, for example, retirement benefits such as pensions; and post-employment life assurance or medical care. *[IAS 19.26].* A less common benefit is the provision of services.

Under defined benefit plans the employer's obligation is not limited to the amount that it agrees to contribute to the fund. Rather, the employer is obliged (legally or constructively) to provide the agreed benefits to current and former employees. Examples of defined benefit schemes given by IAS 19 are:

(a) plans where the benefit formula is not linked solely to the amount of contributions and requires the entity to provide further contributions if assets are insufficient to meet the benefits in the plan formula;

(b) guarantees, either directly or indirectly through a plan, of a specified return on contributions; and

(c) those informal practices that give rise to a constructive obligation, such as a history of increasing benefits for former employees to keep pace with inflation even where there is no legal obligation to do so. *[IAS 19.29].*

The most significant difference between defined contribution and defined benefit plans is that, under defined benefit plans, some actuarial risk or investment risk fall in substance on the employer. This means that if actuarial or investment experience is worse than expected, the employer's obligation may be increased. *[IAS 19.30].* Consequently, because the employer is in substance underwriting the actuarial and investment risks associated with the plan, the expense recognised for a defined benefit plan is not necessarily the amount of the contribution due for the period. *[IAS 19.56].* Conversely, under defined contribution plans the benefits received by the employee are determined by the amount of contributions paid (either by the employer, the employer or both) to benefit plan or insurance company, together with investment returns, and hence actuarial and investment risk fall in substance on the employee. *[IAS 19.28].*

3.2 Insured benefits

One factor that can complicate making the distinction between defined benefit and defined contribution plans is the use of external insurers. IAS 19 recognises that some employers may fund their post-employment benefit plans by paying insurance premiums and observes that the benefits insured need not have a direct or automatic relationship with the entity's obligation for employee benefits. However it makes clear that post-employment benefit plans involving insurance contracts are subject to the same distinction between accounting and funding as other funded plans. *[IAS 19.47]*.

Where insurance premiums are paid to fund post-employment benefits, the employer should treat the plan as a defined contribution plan unless it has (either directly or indirectly through the plan) a legal or constructive obligation to:

(a) pay the employee benefits directly when they fall due; or

(b) pay further amounts if the insurer does not pay all future employee benefits relating to employee service in the current and prior periods.

If the employer has retained such a legal or constructive obligation it should treat the plan as a defined benefit plan. *[IAS 19.46]*. In setting out this requirement, the standard does not use quite the same wording as when discussing the situation when such obligations are not retained. In the defined benefit scenario the description of the retention of the obligation is supplemented with the following underlined text. '... (either directly, indirectly through the plan, through the mechanism for setting future premiums or through a related party relationship with the insurer) retains a legal or constructive obligation ...' *[IAS 19.48]*. In our view, this asymmetry is most likely a drafting error and the additional text applies in both instances.

In cases where such obligations are retained by the employer, it recognises its rights under a 'qualifying insurance policy' as a plan asset and recognises other insurance policies as reimbursement rights. *[IAS 19.48]*. Plan assets are discussed at 5.2.1 below.

By way of final clarification, the standard notes that where an insurance policy is in the name of a specified plan participant or a group of plan participants and the employer does not have any legal or constructive obligation to cover any loss on the policy, the employer has no obligation to pay benefits to the employees and the insurer has sole responsibility for paying the benefits. In that case, the payment of fixed premiums under such contracts is, in substance, the settlement of the employee benefit obligation, rather than an investment to meet the obligation. Consequently, the employer no longer has an asset or a liability. Accordingly, it should treat the payments as contributions to a defined contribution plan. *[IAS 19.49]*. The important point here is that employee entitlements will be of a defined benefit nature unless the employer has no obligation whatsoever to pay them should the insurance fail or otherwise be insufficient.

The standard's analysis of insured plans described above, along with the definition of defined benefit and defined contribution plans seems comprehensive at first glance. However, there will be circumstances where the distinction may not be so apparent and careful analysis may be required. For example, it is possible that an employer buys insurance on a regular basis (say annually), retaining no further obligation in respect of the benefits insured, but has an obligation (legal or constructive) to keep doing so in the future. In such a scenario the employer may be exposed to future actuarial variances reflected in a variable cost of purchasing the required insurance in future years (for example, due to changing mortality estimates by the insurer). An example would be where each year the employee earns an entitlement to a pension of (say) 2% of that year's (i.e. current as opposed to final) salary and the employer purchases each year an annuity contract to commence on the date of retirement.

In our view the standard is not entirely clear as to the nature of such an arrangement. On the one hand, it could be argued that it is a defined contribution plan because the definition of defined contribution plans is met when:

- 'fixed' payments are paid to a separate fund; and
- the employer is not obliged to pay further amounts if the fund has insufficient assets to pay the benefits relating to employee service in the *current and prior periods*.

Further, as noted above the standard considers the payment of 'fixed' premiums to purchase insurance specific to an employee (or group thereof) with no retention of risk in respect of the insured benefits to be a defined contribution arrangement.

On the other hand, it could be argued that this is a defined benefit plan on the grounds that:

- the premiums of future years are not 'fixed' in any meaningful sense (certainly not in the same way as an intention simply to pay a one-off contribution of a given % of salary);
- the standard acknowledges that one factor that can mean insured arrangements are defined benefit in nature is when the employer retains an obligation indirectly through the mechanism for setting future premiums *[IAS 19.48]*; and
- the standard observes that under defined benefit plans '...actuarial risk (that benefits will cost more than expected) and investment risk fall, in substance, on the entity. If actuarial or investment experience are worse than expected, the entity's obligation may be increased'. *[IAS 19.30]*.

Much would seem to depend on just what 'fixed' means in such circumstances. Although not expressly addressed by the standard, in our view such arrangements will very likely be defined benefit in nature, albeit with regular (and perhaps only partial) settlement and, if so, should be accounted for as such. This is because the employer has retained actuarial risks by committing to pay whatever it takes in future years to secure the requisite insurance. Naturally, for any schemes that are determined to be defined benefit plans, the next step would be to see whether the frequent settlement renders the output of the two accounting models materially the same. That would depend, inter alia, on the attribution of the benefit to years of service and the impact of an unwinding discount. The wide variety of possible arrangements in practice mean that careful consideration of individual circumstances will be required to determine the true substance of such arrangements.

3.3 Multi-employer plans

3.3.1 Multi-employer plans other than those sharing risks between entities under common control

3.3.1.A The treatment of multi-employer plans

Multi-employer plans, other than state plans (see 3.4 below), under IAS 19 are defined contribution plans or defined benefit plans that:

(a) pool assets contributed by various entities that are not under common control; and

(b) use those assets to provide benefits to employees of more than one entity, on the basis that contribution and benefit levels are determined without regard to the identity of the entity that employs the employees. *[IAS 19.8].*

Accordingly, they exclude group administration plans, which simply pool the assets of more than one employer, for investment purposes and the reduction of administrative and investment costs, but keep the claims of different employers segregated for the sole benefit of their own employees. The standard observes that group administration plans pose no particular accounting problems because information is readily available to treat them in the same way as any other single employer plan and because they do not expose the participating employers to actuarial risks associated with the current and former employees of other entities. Accordingly, the standard requires group administration plans to be classified as defined contribution plans or defined benefit plans in accordance with the terms of the plan (including any constructive obligation that goes beyond the formal terms). *[IAS 19.38].*

The standard gives a description of one example of a multi-employer scheme as follows:

(a) the plan is financed on a pay-as-you-go basis: contributions are set at a level that is expected to be sufficient to pay the benefits falling due in the same period; and future benefits earned during the current period will be paid out of future contributions; and

(b) employees' benefits are determined by the length of their service and the participating entities have no realistic means of withdrawing from the plan without paying a contribution for the benefits earned by employees up to the date of withdrawal. Such a plan creates actuarial risk for the entity: if the ultimate cost of benefits already earned at the end of the reporting period is more than expected, it will be necessary for the entity either to increase its contributions or persuade employees to accept a reduction in benefits. Therefore, such a plan is a defined benefit plan. *[IAS 19.35].*

A multi-employer plan should be classified as either a defined contribution plan or a defined benefit plan in accordance with its terms in the normal way (see 3.1 above) *[IAS 19.32].* If a multi-employer plan is classified as a defined benefit plan, IAS 19 requires that the employer should account for its proportionate share of the defined benefit obligation, plan assets and costs associated with the plan in the same way as for any other defined benefit plan (see 5 below). *[IAS 19.33, 36].*

The standard does, however, contain a practical exemption if insufficient information is available to use defined benefit accounting. This could be the case, for example, where:

(a) the entity does not have access to information about the plan that satisfies the requirements of the standard; or

(b) the plan exposes the participating entities to actuarial risks associated with the current and former employees of other entities, with the result that there is no consistent and reliable basis for allocating the obligation, plan assets and cost to individual entities participating in the plan. *[IAS 19.36]*.

In such circumstances, an entity should account for the plan as if it were a defined contribution plan and make the disclosures set out at 7.2.4 below. *[IAS 19.36]*.

The standard notes that there may be a contractual agreement between the multi-employer plan and its participants that determines how the surplus in the plan will be distributed to the participants (or the deficit funded). In these circumstances, an entity participating in such a plan, and accounting for it as a defined contribution plan (as described above), should recognise the asset or liability arising from the contractual agreement and the resulting profit or loss. *[IAS 19.37]*. The standard illustrates this with an example of an entity participating in a multi-employer defined benefit plan which it accounts for as a defined contribution plan because no IAS 19 valuations are prepared. A non-IAS 19 funding valuation shows a deficit of CU100 million in the plan. The plan has agreed under contract a schedule of contributions with the participating employers in the plan that will eliminate the deficit over the next five years. The entity's total contributions to eliminate the deficit under the contract are CU8 million. IAS 19 requires the entity to recognise immediately a liability for the contributions adjusted for the time value of money and an equal expense in profit or loss. The important point here is that the standard makes clear that 'defined contribution accounting' is not the same as cash accounting. Extra payments to make good a deficit should be provided for immediately that they are contracted for.

3.3.1.B What to do when 'sufficient information' becomes available

As discussed above, IAS 19 requires a multi-employer defined benefit plan to be treated for accounting purposes as a defined contribution plan when insufficient information is available to use defined benefit accounting. The standard does not address the accounting treatment required when that situation changes because sufficient information becomes available in a period. Two possible approaches present themselves:

(a) an immediate charge/credit to profit or loss equal to the deficit/surplus; or

(b) an actuarial gain or loss.

Arguments in favour of (a) would be that *for accounting purposes* the scheme was a defined contribution scheme. Accordingly, starting defined benefit accounting is akin to introducing a new scheme. The defined benefit obligation recognised is essentially a past service cost. In addition, as discussed at 3.3.1.A above, the standard makes clear that while defined contribution accounting is being applied an asset or liability should be recognised where there is a contractual arrangement to share a surplus or fund a deficit. The receipt of full information could be considered to represent such an arrangement and hence require full recognition in the statement of financial position with an equivalent item in profit or loss.

Arguments for (b) would be that the scheme has not changed and that defined contribution accounting was a proxy (and best available estimate) for what the defined benefit accounting should have been. Accordingly, any change to that estimate due to the emergence of new information is an actuarial variance.

Given the ambiguity of the standard either approach is acceptable if applied consistently.

3.3.1.C Withdrawal from or winding-up of a multi-employer scheme

IAS 19 requires the application of IAS 37 – *Provisions, Contingent Liabilities and Contingent Assets* – to determine when to recognise and how to measure a liability to a multi-employer scheme relating to the withdrawal from or winding-up of it. *[IAS 19.39]*.

3.3.2 Multi-employer plans sharing risks between entities under common control

IAS 19 provides that defined benefit plans that share risks between various entities under common control, for example a parent and its subsidiaries, are not multi-employer plans. *[IAS 19.40]*.

The test, described earlier, for allowing a defined benefit multi-employer plan to be accounted for as a defined contribution plan is that insufficient information is available. By completely excluding entities that are under common control from the definition of multi-employer plans the standard is essentially saying that for these employers sufficient information is deemed always to be available – at least for the plan as a whole. The standard requires an entity participating in such a plan to obtain information about the plan as a whole measured in accordance with IAS 19 on the basis of assumptions that apply to the plan as a whole. *[IAS 19.41]*. Whilst a subsidiary may not be in a position to demand such information (any more than participants in schemes described at 3.3.1 above), the standard is essentially saying that the parent must make the information available if it wants the subsidiary to be able to comply with IAS 19.

The standard then goes on to specify the accounting treatment to be applied in the individual financial statements of the participating entities. The requirements are somewhat opaque, and it is useful to set them out in full. What the standard says is this. 'If there is a contractual agreement or stated policy for charging to individual group entities the net defined benefit cost for the plan as a whole measured in accordance with this Standard, the entity shall, in its separate or individual financial statements, recognise the net defined benefit cost so charged. If there is no such agreement or policy, the net defined benefit cost shall be recognised in the separate or individual financial statements of the group entity that is legally the sponsoring employer for the plan. The other group entities shall, in their separate or individual financial statements, recognise a cost equal to their contribution payable for the period.' *[IAS 19.41]*. This seems to raise more questions than it answers. For example it provides no clarity on what is meant by:

- the 'net defined benefit cost ... measured in accordance with IAS 19' actually means. In particular, are actuarial gains and losses part of this 'net cost'?
- an entity that 'is legally the sponsoring employer for the plan'. The pan-jurisdictional scope of IFRS makes such a determination particularly difficult. Furthermore, it suggests that there is only one such legal sponsor – which may not be the case in practice.

A further difficulty with these provisions of the standard is whether it is ever likely in practice that entities would be charged an amount based on the 'defined benefit cost measured in accordance with [IAS 19]'. Naturally situations vary not just across, but also within, individual jurisdictions. However, it is typically the case that funding valuations will not be on an IAS 19 basis, so that any amounts 'charged' will not be measured in accordance with IAS 19. Indeed, as discussed at 3.3.1 above, the standard gives non-IAS 19 funding valuations in a multi-employer plan as a reason why sufficient information to allow defined benefit accounting is not available.

Some further insight as to the IASB's intentions can be found in the Basis for Conclusions to the standard. Again, it is worth reproducing this in full.

'The Board noted that, if there were a contractual agreement or stated policy on charging the net defined benefit cost to group entities, that agreement or policy would determine the cost for each entity. If there is no such contractual agreement or stated policy, the entity that is the sponsoring employer bears the risk relating to the plan by default. The Board therefore concluded that a group plan should be allocated to the individual entities within a group in accordance with any contractual agreement or stated policy. If there is no such agreement or policy, the net defined benefit cost is allocated to the sponsoring employer. The other group entities recognise a cost equal to any contribution collected by the sponsoring employer. This approach has the advantages of (a) all group entities recognising the cost they have to bear for the defined benefit promise and (b) being simple to apply'. *[IAS 19.BC48-49]*.

This analysis is particularly noteworthy in these respects:

(a) there is no mention of amounts charged being measured in accordance with IAS 19. Indeed, the third sentence refers to *any* such agreement or stated policy;

(b) the focus is not on 'amounts charged' but rather an 'allocation' of the scheme across entities;

(c) references are to a 'sponsoring employer' crucially not a *legally* sponsoring employer. The term is slightly clarified by the explanation that a sponsoring employer is one that by default bears the 'risks relating to the plan'; and

(d) the discussion of employers other than the sponsoring employer is explicitly to 'amounts collected'.

Given the ambiguities in the standard we expect that, for entities applying IFRS at an individual company level, there may well be divergent treatments in practice.

The standard makes clear that, for each individual group entity, participation in such a plan is a related party transaction. Accordingly, the disclosures set out at 7.2.5 below are required. *[IAS 19.42]*.

3.4 State plans

IAS 19 observes that state plans are established by legislation to cover all entities (or all entities in a particular category, for example a specific industry) and are operated by national or local government or by another body (for example an autonomous agency created specifically for this purpose) which is not subject to control or influence by the reporting entity. *[IAS 19.44]*. The standard requires that state plans be accounted for in the same way as for a multi-employer plan (see 3.3.1 above). *[IAS 19.43]*. It goes on to note that it is characteristic of many state plans that:

- they are funded on a pay-as-you-go basis with contributions set at a level that is expected to be sufficient to pay the required benefits falling due in the same period; and
- future benefits earned during the current period will be paid out of future contributions.

Nevertheless, in most state plans, the entity has no legal or constructive obligation to pay those future benefits: its only obligation is to pay the contributions as they fall due and if the entity ceases to employ members of the state plan, it will have no obligation to pay the benefits earned by its own employees in previous years. For this reason, the standard considers that state plans are normally defined contribution plans. However, in cases when a state plan is a defined benefit plan, IAS 19 requires it to be treated as such as a multi-employer plan. *[IAS 19.45]*.

Some plans established by an entity provide both compulsory benefits which substitute for benefits that would otherwise be covered under a state plan and additional voluntary benefits. IAS 19 clarifies that such plans are not state plans. *[IAS 19.44]*.

3.5 Plans that would be defined contribution plans but for the existence of a minimum return guarantee

It is common in some jurisdictions for the employer to make contributions to a defined contribution post-employment benefit plan and to guarantee a minimum level of return on the assets in which the contributions are invested. In other words the employee enjoys upside risk on the investments but has some level of protection from downside risk.

The existence of such a guarantee means the arrangement fails to meet the definition of a defined contribution plan (see 3.1 above) and accordingly is a defined benefit plan. Indeed, the standard is explicit as it uses plans which guarantee a specified return on contributions as an example of a defined benefit arrangement. *[IAS 19.29(b)]*. The somewhat thornier issue is how exactly to apply defined benefit accounting to such an arrangement, as this would require projecting forward future salary increases and investment returns, and discounting these amounts at corporate bond rates. Although this approach is clearly required by the standard, some would consider it inappropriate in such circumstances. This issue was debated by the Interpretations Committee, which published a draft interpretation on 8 July 2004 entitled D9 – *Employee Benefit Plans with a Promised Return on Contributions or Notional Contributions.* The approach taken in D9 was to distinguish two different types of benefits:

(a) a benefit of contributions or notional contributions plus a guarantee of a fixed return (in other words, benefits which can be estimated without having to make an estimate of future asset returns); and

(b) a benefit that depends on future asset returns.

For benefits under (a) above, it was proposed that IAS 19's defined benefit methodology be applied as normal. In summary, that means:

- calculating the benefit to be paid in the future by projecting forward the contributions or notional contributions at the guaranteed fixed rate of return;
- allocating the benefit to periods of service;
- discounting the benefits allocated to the current and prior periods at the rate specified in IAS 19 to arrive at the plan liability, current service cost and interest cost; and
- recognising any actuarial gains and losses in accordance with the entity's accounting policy.

For benefits covered by (b) above, it was proposed that the plan liability should be measured at the fair value, at the end of the reporting period, of the assets upon which the benefit is specified (whether plan assets or notional assets). No projection forward of the benefits would be made, and discounting of the benefit would not therefore be required.

D9 suggested that plans with a combination of a guaranteed fixed return and a benefit that depends on future asset returns should be accounted for by analysing the benefits into a fixed component and a variable component. The defined benefit asset or liability that would arise from the fixed component alone would be measured and recognised as described above. The defined benefit asset (or liability) that would arise from the variable component alone would then be calculated as described above and compared to the fixed component. An additional plan liability would be recognised to the extent that the asset (or liability) calculated for the variable component is smaller (or greater) than the asset (or liability) recognised in respect of the fixed component.

The great complexity of these provisions was not wholeheartedly supported by respondents to the document. Also, many commentators pointed out that the proposals effectively re-wrote, rather than interpreted, the standard. In August 2005 the Interpretations Committee announced the withdrawal of D9, observing the following: 'The staff found the fixed/variable and modified fixed/variable approaches inadequate to give a faithful representation of the entity's obligation for more complex benefit structures. They believed that some aspects of the fixed/variable approach in D9 were not fully consistent with

IAS 19. ... The staff ... recommended that the correct treatment for D9 plans should be determined as part of an IASB project.'

What this means is that the current text of IAS 19 applies. Accordingly the projected unit credit method will need to be applied to such benefits as it is to other defined benefit arrangements.

This issue was one of the topics the Board was seeking to address in its (relatively) short-term amendments to IAS 19. In March 2008 the Board published a discussion paper called Preliminary Views on Amendments to IAS 19 Employee Benefits. In this the Board observes that 'IAS 19 does not result in a faithful representation of the liability for some benefit promises that are based on contributions and a promised return on assets.' The discussion paper outlines an approach that the Board believed would overcome this measurement defect that is based on defining a new category of promises – 'contribution-based promises' – and measuring them at fair value. However, as discussed at 9 below, it now seems the Board is no longer actively pursuing this project.

The Interpretations Committee has subsequently been asked whether the revisions to IAS 19 in 2011 affect the accounting for these types of employee benefits and concluded they do not.[1]

Perhaps as a result of the IASB's decision, the Interpretations Committee has re-opened its examination of the subject. It is currently considering 'limited-scope proposals' on accounting for contribution-based promises. At its November 2012 meeting, the Committee considered proposals by the staff but reached no conclusions. The Interpretations Committee asked the staff to prepare examples illustrating how the proposed measurement approach would apply to different employee benefit plan designs. The staff will bring these examples for discussion to a future Interpretations Committee meeting.[2]

3.6 Death-in-service benefits

The provision of death-in-service benefits is a common part of employment packages (either as part of a defined benefit plan or on a standalone basis). We think it is regrettable that IAS 19 provides no guidance on how to account for such benefits, particularly as E54 (the exposure draft preceding an earlier version of IAS 19) devoted considerable attention to the issue.[3] IAS 19 explains the removal of the guidance as follows: 'E54 proposed guidance on cases where death-in-service benefits are not insured externally and are not provided through a post-employment benefit plan. IASC concluded that such cases will be rare. Accordingly, IASC deleted the guidance on death-in-service benefits.' *[IAS 19.BC253]*.

In our view this misses the point – E54 also gave guidance on cases where the benefits *are* externally insured and where they are provided through a post-employment benefit plan. In our view the proposals in E54 were had merit, and it is worth reproducing them here.

'An enterprise should recognise the cost of death-in-service benefits ... as follows:

(a) in the case of benefits insured or re-insured with third parties, in the period in respect of which the related insurance premiums are payable; and

(b) in the case of benefits not insured or re-insured with third parties, to the extent that deaths have occurred before the end of the reporting period.

'However, in the case of death-in-service benefits provided through a post-employment benefit plan, an enterprise should recognise the cost of those benefits by including their present value in the post-employment benefit obligation.

'If an enterprise re-insures a commitment to provide death-in-service benefits, it acquires a right (to receive payments if an employee dies in service) in exchange for an obligation to pay the premiums.

'Where an enterprise provides death-in-service benefits directly, rather than through a post-employment benefit plan, the enterprise has a future commitment to provide death-in-service coverage in exchange for employee service in those same future periods (in the same way that the enterprise has a future commitment to pay salaries if the employee renders service in those periods). That future commitment is not a present obligation and does not justify recognition of a liability. Therefore, an obligation arises only to the extent that a death has already occurred by the end of the reporting period.

'If death-in-service benefits are provided through a pension plan (or other post-employment plan) which also provides post-employment benefits to the same employee(s), the measurement of the obligation reflects both the probability of a reduction in future pension payments through death in service and the present value of the death-in-service benefits (see [E-54's discussion of mutual compatibility of actuarial assumptions]).

'Death-in-service benefits differ from post-employment life insurance because post-employment life insurance creates an obligation as the employee renders services in exchange for that benefit; an enterprise accounts for that obligation in accordance with [the requirements for defined benefit plans]. Life insurance benefits that are payable regardless of whether the employee remains in service comprise two components: a death-in-service benefit and a post-employment benefit. An enterprise accounts for the two components separately.'

We suggest that the above may continue to represent valid guidance to the extent it does not conflict with extant IFRS. In particular, an appropriate approach could be that:

- death-in-service benefits provided as part of a defined benefit post-employment plan are factored into the actuarial valuation. In this case any insurance cover should be accounted for in accordance with the normal rules of IAS 19 (see 5.2.1 below). An important point here is that insurance policies for death-in-service benefits typically cover only one year, and hence will have a low or negligible fair value. As a result, it will not be the case that the insurance asset is equal and opposite to the defined benefit obligation;

- other death-in-service benefits which are externally insured are accounted for by expensing the premiums as they become payable; and
- other death-in-service benefits which are not externally insured are provided for as deaths in service occur.

The first bullet is particularly important. The measure of the post-employment benefit (like a pension) will be reduced to take account of expected deaths in service. Accordingly it would be inappropriate to ignore the death in service payments that would be made. The question that arises is how exactly to include those expected payments. This raises the same issue as disability benefits (discussed at 6.2.2.B below) – i.e. what to do with the debit entry. However, IAS 19 has no explicit special treatment for death-in-service benefits comparable to that for disability benefits. Given the absence of specific guidance, the requirement is to apply the projected unit credit method to death in service benefits. As the benefit is fully vested, an argument could be made that the expected benefit should be accrued fully (on a discounted basis). Another approach would be to build up the credit entry in the statement of financial position over the period to the expected date of death.

An alternative approach could be to view death-in-service benefits as being similar to disability benefits (perhaps the ultimate disability). Proponents of this view would argue that the recognition requirements for disability benefits (discussed at 6.2.2.B below) could also be applied to death-in-service.

In January 2008, the Interpretations Committee published its agenda decision explaining why it decided not to put death-in-service benefits onto its agenda.[4] In the view of the Interpretations Committee, 'divergence in this area was unlikely to be significant. In addition, any further guidance that it could issue would be application guidance on the use of the Projected Unit Credit Method'. In our view the second reason seems more credible that the first.

As part of its analysis, the 'rejection notice' sets out some of the Interpretation Committee's views on the subject. It observes the following:

(a) in some situations, IAS 19 requires these benefits to be attributed to periods of service using the Projected Unit Credit Method;

(b) IAS 19 requires attribution of the cost of the benefits until the date when further service by the employee will lead to no material amount of further benefits under the plan, other than from further salary increases;

(c) the anticipated date of death would be the date at which no material amount of further benefit would arise from the plan; and

(d) using different mortality assumptions for a defined benefit pension plan and an associated death in service benefit would not comply with the requirement in paragraph 72 of IAS 19 to use actuarial assumptions that are mutually compatible.

Points (a) to (c) above support the analysis that a provision should be built up gradually from the commencement of employment to the expected date of death. They also suggest that making an analogy to the standard's specific rules on disability may not be appropriate. Point (c) is simply re-iterating a clear requirement of the standard. In our view, the above agenda decision of the Interpretations Committee is not as helpful as we would have liked. Aside of concerns over the status of rejection notices, the use of the phrase 'in some situations' in (a) above seems deliberate obfuscation. In September 2007, the Interpretations Committee published a tentative agenda decision which said 'If these benefits are provided as part of a defined benefit plan, IAS 19 requires them to be attributed to periods of service using the Projected Unit Credit Method.'[5] At the following meeting the Interpretations Committee discussed the comment letter received which noted that it could be argued that such attribution would be required only if the benefits were dependent on the period of service. No decision was reached on the final wording of the rejection notice because 'IFRIC ... was unable to agree on wording for its agenda decision.'[6] This leaves us with the impression that the final 'authoritative' version is written deliberately to avoid addressing the point.

Given the lack of explicit guidance on death-in-service benefits in IAS 19 itself, and given the Interpretations Committee's decision not to address the matter, it seems likely that practice will be mixed.

4 DEFINED CONTRIBUTION PLANS

4.1 Accounting requirements

4.1.1 General

Accounting for defined contribution plans (see 3 above) is straightforward under IAS 19 because, as the standard observes, the reporting entity's obligation for each period is determined by the amounts to be contributed for that period. Consequently, no actuarial assumptions are required to be made to measure the obligation or the expense and there is no possibility of any actuarial gain or loss to the reporting entity. Moreover, the obligations are measured on an undiscounted basis, except where they are not expected to be settled wholly before twelve months after the end of the period in which the employees render the related service. *[IAS 19.50].* Where discounting is required, the discount rate should be determined in the same way as for defined benefit plans, which is discussed at 5.2.2.F below. *[IAS 19.52].* In general, though, it would seem unlikely for a defined contribution scheme to be structured with such a long delay between the employee service and the employer contribution.

IAS 19 requires that, when an employee has rendered service during a period, the employer should recognise the contribution payable to a defined contribution plan in exchange for that service:

(a) as a liability (accrued expense), after deducting any contribution already paid. If the contribution already paid exceeds the contribution due for service before the end of the reporting period, the excess should be recognised as an asset (prepaid expense) to the extent that the prepayment will lead to, for example, a reduction in future payments or a cash refund; and

(b) as an expense, unless another IFRS requires or permits capitalisation of such expense. *[IAS 19.51].*

As discussed at 3.3.1.A above, IAS 19 requires multi-employer defined benefit plans to be accounted for as defined contribution plans in certain circumstances. The standard makes clear that contractual arrangements to make contributions to fund a deficit should be fully provided for (on a discounted basis) even if they are to be paid over an extended period. *[IAS 19.37].*

4.1.2 Defined contribution plans with vesting conditions

The Interpretations Committee received a request seeking clarification on the effect that vesting conditions have on the accounting for defined contribution plans. The Committee was asked whether contributions to such plans should be recognised as an expense in the period for which they are paid or over the vesting period. In the examples given in the submission, the employee's failure to meet a vesting condition could result in the refund of contributions to, or reductions in future contributions by, the employer.

The Committee decided not to add the issue to its agenda, noting that there is no significant diversity in practice in respect of the effect that vesting conditions have on the accounting for defined contribution post-employment benefit plans, nor does it expect significant diversity in practice to emerge in the future.

Explaining its decision, the Committee observed that each contribution to a defined contribution plan is to be recognised as an expense or recognised as a liability (accrued expense) over the period of service that obliges the employer to *pay* this contribution to the defined contribution plan. This period of service is distinguished from the period of service that entitles an employee to *receive* the benefit from the defined contribution plan (i.e. the vesting period). Refunds are recognised as an asset and as income when the entity/employer becomes entitled to the refunds, e.g. when the employee fails to meet the vesting condition.[7]

5 DEFINED BENEFIT PLANS

5.1 General

The standard notes that accounting for defined benefit plans is complex because actuarial assumptions are required to measure both the obligation and the expense, and there is a possibility of actuarial gains and losses. Moreover, the obligations are measured on a discounted basis because they may be settled many years after the employees render the related service. *[IAS 19.55].* Also, IAS 19 makes clear that it applies not just to unfunded obligations of employers but also to funded plans. The details of pension scheme arrangements vary widely from jurisdiction to jurisdiction and, indeed, within them. Frequently though, they involve some entity or fund, separate from the employer, to which contributions are made by the employer (and sometimes employees) and from which benefits are paid. Typically, the employer (through either legal or constructive obligations) essentially underwrites the fund in the event that the assets in the fund are insufficient to pay the required benefits. This is the key feature which means such an arrangement is a defined benefit plan (see 3 above). *[IAS 19.56].*

In addition to specifying accounting and disclosure requirements, IAS 19 summarises the steps necessary to apply its rules, to be applied separately to each separate plan, as follows:

(a) determining the deficit or surplus by:
   (i) using an actuarial technique, the projected unit credit method, to make a reliable estimate of the ultimate cost to the entity of the benefit that employees have earned in return for their service in the current and prior periods. This requires an entity to determine how much benefit is attributable to the current and prior periods and to make estimates (actuarial assumptions) about demographic variables (such as employee turnover and mortality) and financial variables (such as future increases in salaries and medical costs) that will affect the cost of the benefit; and
   (ii) discounting that benefit in order to determine the present value of the defined benefit obligation and the current service cost;
   (iii) deducting the fair value of any plan assets from the present value of the defined benefit obligation.
(b) determining the amount of the net defined benefit liability (asset) as the amount of the deficit or surplus determined in (a), adjusted for any effect of limiting a net defined benefit asset to the asset ceiling;
(c) determining amounts to be recognised in profit or loss:
   (i) current service cost;
   (ii) any past service cost and gain or loss on settlement, and;
   (iii) net interest on the net defined benefit liability (asset); and
(d) determining the remeasurements of the net defined benefit liability (asset), to be recognised in other comprehensive income, comprising:
   (i) actuarial gains and losses;
   (ii) return on plan assets, excluding amounts included in net interest on the net defined benefit liability (asset); and
   (iii) any change in the effect of the asset ceiling, excluding amounts included in net interest on the net defined benefit liability (asset). *[IAS 19.57]*.

Retirement benefits will often be very significant in the context of an employer's financial statements. However, the standard acknowledges that in some circumstances estimates, averages and computational shortcuts may provide a reliable approximation. *[IAS 19.60]*.

5.2 Valuation of the plan surplus or deficit

5.2.1 Plan assets

5.2.1.A Definition of plan assets

IAS 19 provides a definition of plan assets as follows:

'*Plan assets* comprise:

(a) assets held by a long-term employee benefit fund; and

(b) qualifying insurance policies. *[IAS 19.8]*.

'Plan assets exclude unpaid contributions due from the employer to the fund, and any non-transferable financial instruments issued by the employer and are to be reduced by any liabilities of the fund not related to employee benefits such as trade and other payables and derivative financial instruments. *[IAS 19.114]*.

'*Assets held by a long-term employee benefit fund* are assets (other than non-transferable financial instruments issued by the reporting entity) that:

(a) are held by an entity (a fund) that is legally separate from the reporting entity and exists solely to pay or fund employee benefits; and

(b) are available to be used only to pay or fund employee benefits, are not available to the reporting entity's own creditors (even in bankruptcy), and cannot be returned to the reporting entity, unless either:
    (i) the remaining assets of the fund are sufficient to meet all the related employee benefit obligations of the plan or the reporting entity; or
    (ii) the assets are returned to the reporting entity to reimburse it for employee benefits already paid.

'A *qualifying insurance policy* is an insurance policy issued by an insurer that is not a related party (as defined in IAS 24 – *Related Party Disclosures*) of the reporting entity, if the proceeds of the policy:

(a) can be used only to pay or fund employee benefits under a defined benefit plan; and

(b) are not available to the reporting entity's own creditors (even in bankruptcy) and cannot be paid to the reporting entity, unless either:
    (i) the proceeds represent surplus assets that are not needed for the policy to meet all the related employee benefit obligations; or
    (ii) the proceeds are returned to the reporting entity to reimburse it for employee benefits already paid'. *[IAS 19.8]*.

A footnote to this definition clarifies that a qualifying insurance policy is not necessarily an insurance contract as defined in IFRS 4 – *Insurance Contracts*.

Whilst non-transferable financial instruments issued by the employer are excluded from the definition of plan assets, it is not uncommon for plans to own shares in the employer as plan assets.

5.2.1.B Measurement of plan assets

IAS 19 requires plan assets to be measured at their fair value, *[IAS 19.8, 63]*, which is defined as the price that would be received to sell an asset or paid to transfer a liability in an orderly transaction between market participants at the measurement date. *[IAS 19.8]*. This is the same definition as is used in IFRS 13 – *Fair Value Measurement* (see Chapter 14).

The fair value of any plan assets is deducted from the present value of the defined benefit obligation in determining the deficit or surplus – see 5.3 below. *[IAS 19.113]*.

Where plan assets include qualifying insurance policies that exactly match the amount and timing of some or all of the benefits payable under the plan, the fair value of those insurance policies is deemed to be the present value of the related obligations, subject to any reductions required if the amounts receivable under the insurance policies are not recoverable in full. *[IAS 19.115]*.

Some employers may have in place arrangements to fund defined benefit obligations which do not meet the definition of qualifying insurance policies above but which do provide for another party to reimburse some or all of the expenditure required to settle a defined benefit obligation. In such a case, the expected receipts under the arrangement are not *classified* as plan assets under IAS 19 (and hence they are not presented as part of a net pension asset/liability – see 5.3 below). Instead, the employer should recognise its right to reimbursement as a separate asset, but only when it is virtually certain that another party will reimburse some or all of the expenditure required to settle a defined benefit obligation. The asset should be measured at fair value and, in all other respects, it should be treated in the same way as a plan asset. In profit or loss, the expense relating to a defined benefit plan may be presented net of the amount recognised for a reimbursement. *[IAS 19.116-118]*. In particular, changes in fair value are disaggregated and accounted for in the same way as plan assets – see 5.5.2 below.

As is the case for qualifying insurance policies, for reimbursement rights that exactly match the amount and timing of some or all of the benefits payable fair value is determined as the present value of the related obligation, subject to any reduction required if the reimbursement is not recoverable in full. *[IAS 19.119]*.

5.2.1.C Contributions to defined benefit funds

Contributions to defined benefit plans under IAS 19 are a movement between line items in the statement of financial position – the reduction in cash for the employer being reflected by an increase in the plan assets. Perhaps because of this straightforward accounting, the standard provides no guidance on contributions, which it implicitly deals with as always being in the form of cash.

Although contributions are very commonly in cash, there is no reason why an employer could not contribute any other assets to a defined benefit plan and that raises the question of how to account for the disposal – particularly so, since from the point of transfer the assets will be measured at fair value under IAS 19. In our view, such a transfer of a non-cash asset should be treated as a disposal, with proceeds equal to the fair value of the asset. That would give rise to gains and losses in profit or loss (unless the asset in question was already carried at fair value) and, for certain assets (such as available for sale securities), the reclassification into profit or loss of amounts previously recognised in other comprehensive income.

5.2.2 Plan liabilities

5.2.2.A Legal and constructive obligations

IAS 19 refers to the liabilities of defined benefit plans as the present value of defined benefit obligations, which it defines as '... the present value, without deducting any plan assets, of expected future payments required to settle the obligation resulting from employee service in the current and prior periods'. *[IAS 19.8]*.

The obligations should include not only the benefits set out in the plan, but also any constructive obligations that arise from the employer's informal practices which go beyond the formal plan terms, and should where relevant include an estimate of expected future salary increases (taking into account inflation, seniority, promotion and other relevant factors, such as supply and demand in the employment market). *[IAS 19.61, 87-90]*.

A constructive obligation exists where a change in the employer's informal practices would cause unacceptable damage to its relationship with employees and which therefore leaves the employer with no realistic alternative but to pay those employee benefits. *[IAS 19.61]*. The term constructive obligation is not defined by IAS 19; however as can be seen from the above it is very similar to the meaning of the term as used in IAS 37 where it is defined as follows:

'A constructive obligation is an obligation that derives from an entity's actions where:

(a) by an established pattern of past practice, published policies or a sufficiently specific current statement, the entity has indicated to other parties that it will accept certain responsibilities; and

(b) as a result, the entity has created a valid expectation on the part of those other parties that it will discharge those responsibilities'. *[IAS 37.10]*.

However, IAS 19 goes on to add a subtly different nuance. The standard observes that it is usually difficult to cancel a retirement benefit plan (without payment) whilst still retaining staff, and in light of this it requires that reporting entities assume (in the absence of evidence to the contrary) any currently promised benefits will continue for the remaining working lives of employees. *[IAS 19.62]*. In our view this is a somewhat lower hurdle, and could bring into the scope of defined benefit accounting promises which are (strictly) legally unenforceable and which would not necessarily be considered constructive obligations under IAS 37.

An employer's obligations (legal or constructive) may also extend to making changes to benefits in the future. The standard requires all such effects to be built into the computation of the obligation and gives the following examples of what they might comprise:

(a) a past history of increasing benefits, for example, to mitigate the effects of inflation, and no indication that this practice will change in the future;

(b) the entity is obliged, either by the formal terms of the plan (or a further constructive obligation) or by legislation to use any surplus in the plan for the benefit of plan participants; or

(c) benefits vary in response to a performance target or other criteria. For example, the terms of the plan may state that it will pay reduced benefits or require additional contributions from employees if the plan assets are insufficient. The measurement of the obligation reflects the best estimate of the effect of target or other criteria. *[IAS 19.88]*.

By contrast, any other future changes in the obligation (i.e. where no legal or constructive obligation previously existed) will be reflected in future current service costs, future past service costs or both (discussed at 5.5.1 below). *[IAS 19.89]*.

IAS 19 also deals with the situation where the level of defined benefits payable by a scheme varies with the level of state benefits. When this is the case a best estimate of any changes in state benefit should be factored into the actuarial computations only if they are enacted by the end of the reporting period or are predictable based on past history or other evidence. *[IAS 19.87, 95].*

Some defined benefit plans limit the contributions that an entity is required to pay. The ultimate cost of the benefits takes account of the effect of a limit on contributions. The effect of a limit on contributions is determined over the shorter of the estimated life of the entity and the estimated life of the plan. *[IAS 19.91].*

5.2.2.B Contributions by employees and third parties

The standard notes that some defined benefit plans require employees or third parties to contribute to the cost of the plan. Contributions by employees reduce the cost of the benefits to the entity. The standard requires an entity to 'consider' whether third-party contributions reduce the cost of the benefits to the entity, or are a reimbursement right (discussed at 5.2.1.B above). Contributions by employees or third parties are either set out in the formal terms of the plan (or arise from a constructive obligation that goes beyond those terms), or are discretionary. IAS 19 requires discretionary contributions by employees or third parties to be accounted for as a reduction in service cost when they are paid to the plan. *[IAS 19.92].*

The standard draws a distinction between contributions from employees or third parties set out in the formal terms of the plan which are 'linked to service' and those which are not. Such contributions linked to service are accounted for as a reduction in service cost and should be attributed to periods of service in the same way as the defined benefit obligation is attributed (see 5.2.2.C below). *[IAS 19.93].* The basis for conclusions to the standard describes this as 'attribution ... based on the net benefit'. *[IAS 19.BC150].*

Regrettably, the standard does not explain the 'mechanics' of such an attribution. In the case of employee contributions made at the date a benefit is delivered (for example, the employee paying a proportion of post-retirement medical costs) it is clearly straight forward; the entity will estimate the defined benefit obligation based on its net commitment.

What is less clear is the treatment of employee contributions made over the service period. As shown in Example 31.2 at 5.2.2.C below, the projected unit method requires the net benefit to be expressed as a single net sum as at the date of retirement. Example 31.2 illustrates post employment benefit payments being discounted to their present value as at the retirement date using the IAS 19 discount rate (discussed at 5.2.2.F below). On the same principle, therefore, employee contributions made over the period of employment would logically need to be inflated to be expressed in the 'time value' as at retirement. However, IAS 19 does not indicate what rate should be used for this purpose.

This issue was referred to the Interpretations Committee. At their meeting in September 2012, the committee referred the matter to the IASB which published an expose draft – *Defined Benefit Plans: Employee Contributions,* Proposed amendments to IAS 19 – in March 2013.

The draft proposes a limited-scope amendment to the standard. The proposal is to amend paragraph 93 IAS 19 as follows (new text underlined and deleted text struck through):

'Contributions from employees or third parties set out in the formal terms of the plan either reduce service cost (if they are linked to service), or reduce remeasurements of the net defined benefit liability (asset) (e.g. if the contributions are required to reduce a deficit arising from losses on plan assets or actuarial losses). Contributions from employees or third parties that are linked to service ~~in respect of service~~ are attributed to periods of service as a negative benefit in the same way that the gross benefit is attributed in accordance with paragraph 70 ~~(i.e. the net benefit is attributed in accordance with that paragraph)~~.

However, if, and only if, contributions from employees or third parties are linked solely to the employee's service rendered in the same period in which they are payable, the contributions may be recognised as a reduction in the service cost in that period. An example would be contributions that are a fixed percentage of the employee's salary, so the percentage of the employee's salary does not depend on the employee's number of years of service to the employer.'

The exposure draft does not deal with situations where the above relaxation does not apply and leaves unanswered the key question: how to express the sum of in-service contributions as at the retirement date.

We note, in this regard, that when the Interpretations Committee discussed the matter in November 2012, it considered a Staff Paper which touched on the matter. The numerical examples appended to the paper expressed the 'future value' of in-service employee contributions as at the date of retirement using the IAS 19 discount rate.[8] The content of the third example is reflected in the example set out below.

Example 31.1: Defined benefit plan with employee contributions, where the discount rate is higher than the salary growth rate

A lump sum benefit is payable on termination of service and equal to 1 per cent of final salary for each year of service.
The salary in year 1 is CU10,000 and is assumed to increase at 7 per cent (compound) each year. The discount rate used is 10 per cent per year.
Employees are required to contribute 0.5% of salary each year, on the last day of the year.

Year	**1** **CU**	**2** **CU**	**3** **CU**	**4** **CU**	**5** **CU**	**Total**
Salary	10,000	10,700	11,449	12,250	13,108	
Benefit attributed to:						
– Prior years	–	131	262	393	524	
– Current year (1% of final salary) (a)	131	131	131	131	131	
	131	262	393	524	655	
Gross benefit						
Opening obligation	–	90	197	325	476	
Interest at 10%	–	9	20	32	48	109
Current service cost	90	98	108	119	131	546
Closing obligation	90	197	325	476	655	

Year	1 CU	2 CU	3 CU	4 CU	5 CU	Total
Employee contributions						
Actual contributions	(50)	(54)	(57)	(61)	(66)	(288)
Projected total contributions ('gross') (b)	(73)	(71)	(69)	(67)	(66)	(346)
Attributed contributions ('gross') (c)	(69)	(69)	(69)	(69)	(70)	(346)
Attributed contributions ('discounted')						
Opening	–	(47)	(104)	(172)	(251)	
Interest at 10%	–	(5)	(11)	(17)	(25)	(58)
Negative benefit (d)	(47)	(52)	(57)	(62)	(70)	(288)
Closing	(47)	(104)	(172)	(251)	(346)	
Benefit including effect of contributions						
Opening obligation	–	93	202	330	480	
Interest at 10% (e)	–	9	20	32	48	109
Net current service cost – current service cost less negative benefit (f)	43	46	51	57	61	258
Actual Contributions	50	54	57	61	66	288
Closing	93	202	330	480	655	

Net benefit (gross benefit minus projected total contribution) is attributed to each year using the discount rate

Current service cost (f)	43	46	51	57	61	258

(a) Straight-lined per paragraph 70
(b) Future-valued contributions (e.g. for Year 1, value of contribution paid at end of year 1 at end of year 5 using discount rate of 10% will be CU50 × 1.1^4 = CU73)
(c) Straight-lined to be on the same basis with the attributed benefit
(d) Present value of attributed contributions
(e) Includes rounding difference of (1) in Year 4
(f) Present value of gross benefit minus present value of projected total contributions

Journal entries (for Year 1)
To recognise net service cost
Dr Service cost 43
Cr Defined obligation 43
To reflect employee contributions
Dr plan asset 50
Cr Defined benefit obligation 50

The standard notes that changes in employee or third-party contributions in respect of service result in:

(a) current and past service cost if the changes are not set out in the formal or constructive obligations of the arrangement; or

(b) actuarial gains and losses if the changes in contributions are set out in the formal terms of the plan or arise from a constructive obligation. *[IAS 19.94]*.

Such contributions not linked to service should 'reduce remeasurements of the net defined benefit liability (asset)'. An example given by the standard is if the contributions are required to reduce a deficit arising from losses on plan assets or actuarial losses. *[IAS 19.93]*.

5.2.2.C Actuarial methodology

IAS 19 notes that the ultimate cost of a defined benefit plan may be influenced by many variables, such as final salaries, employee turnover and mortality, employee contributions and medical cost trends. The ultimate cost of the plan is uncertain and this uncertainty is likely to persist over a long period of time. In order to measure the present value of the post-employment benefit obligations and the related current service cost, it is necessary:

- to apply an actuarial valuation method;
- to attribute benefit to periods of service; and
- to make actuarial assumptions. *[IAS 19.66].*

These steps are discussed in the following sections.

Plan obligations are to be measured using the projected unit credit method, *[IAS 19.67]*, (sometimes known as the accrued benefit method pro-rated on service or as the benefit/years of service method). This method sees each period of service as giving rise to an additional unit of benefit entitlement and measures each unit separately to build up the final obligation. *[IAS 19.68].* This actuarial method also determines the current service cost and any past service cost. *[IAS 19.67].* IAS 19 provides a simple example of what this entails as follows: *[IAS 19.68]*

Example 31.2: The projected unit credit method

A lump sum benefit is payable on termination of service and equal to 1% of final salary for each year of service. The salary in year 1 is 10,000 and is assumed to increase at 7% (compound) each year. The discount rate used is 10% per year. The following table shows how the obligation builds up for an employee who is expected to leave at the end of year 5, assuming that there are no changes in actuarial assumptions. For simplicity, this example ignores the additional adjustment needed to reflect the probability that the employee may leave the entity at an earlier or later date.

Year	*1*	*2*	*3*	*4*	*5*
Benefit attributed to:					
– prior years	0	131	262	393	524
– current year (1% of final salary)	131	131	131	131	131
– current and prior years	131	262	393	524	655
Opening Obligation	–	89	196	324	476
Interest at 10%	–	9	20	33	48
Current Service Cost	89	98	108	119	131
Closing Obligation	89	196	324	476	655

Note:

– The Opening Obligation is the present value of benefit attributed to prior years.

– The Current Service Cost is the present value of benefit attributed to the current year.

– The Closing Obligation is the present value of benefit attributed to current and prior years.

As can be seen in this simple example, the projected unit credit method also produces a figure for current service cost and interest cost (and, although not illustrated here, would where appropriate produce a figure for past service cost). These cost components are discussed at 5.5 below.

This example from the standard contains no underlying workings or proofs. The most useful would be as follows:

Final salary at year 5 (10,000 compounded at 7%)	$10{,}000 \times (1 + 0.07)^4 = 13{,}100$
1% of final salary attributed to each year	131
Expected final benefit	5 years × 1% × 131,000 = 655

Current service cost, being present value of 131 discounted at 10%: e.g.

Year 1	$131 \times (1 + 0.1)^{-4} = 89$
Year 2	$131 \times (1 + 0.1)^{-3} = 98$

Closing obligation, being years served multiplied by present value of 131: e.g.

Year 3	$3 \text{ years} \times 131 \times (1 + 0.1)^{-2} = 324$

5.2.2.D Attributing benefit to years of service

The projected unit credit method requires benefits to be attributed to the current period (in order to determine current service cost) and the current and prior periods (in order to determine the present value of defined benefit obligations). IAS 19 requires benefits to be attributed to the periods in which the obligation to provide post-employment benefits arises. That is taken to be when employees render services in return for post-employment benefits which an entity expects to pay in future reporting periods. The standard takes the view that actuarial techniques allow an entity to measure that obligation with sufficient reliability to justify recognition of a liability. *[IAS 19.71]*.

In applying the projected unit credit method, IAS 19 normally requires benefits to be attributed to periods of service under the plan's benefit formula (as is the case in Example 31.2 above). If, however, an employee's service in later years will lead to a materially higher level of benefit, the benefit should be attributed on a straight-line basis from:

(a) the date when service by the employee first leads to benefits under the plan; until

(b) the date when further service by the employee will lead to no material amount of further benefits under the plan, other than from further salary increases. *[IAS 19.70]*.

The standard considers that this requirement is necessary because the employee's service throughout the entire period will ultimately lead to benefit at that higher level. *[IAS 19.73]*.

The standard explains that employee service gives rise to an obligation under a defined benefit plan even if the benefits are conditional on future employment (in other words they are not vested). *[IAS 19.70]*. Employee service before the vesting date is considered to give rise to a constructive obligation because, at each successive period end, the amount of future service that an employee will have to render before becoming entitled to the benefit is reduced. In measuring its defined benefit obligation, an entity should consider the probability that some employees may not satisfy any vesting requirements. Similarly, although certain post-employment benefits, such as post-employment medical benefits, become payable only if a specified event occurs when an employee is no longer employed, an obligation is considered to be created when the employee renders service that will provide entitlement to the benefit if the specified event occurs. The probability that the specified event will occur affects the measurement of the obligation, but does not determine whether for accounting purposes the obligation exists. *[IAS 19.72]*.

The obligation is considered to increase until the date when further service by the employee will lead to no material amount of further benefits, and accordingly all benefit should be attributed to periods ending on or before that date. *[IAS 19.73]*.

IAS 19 illustrates the attribution of benefits to service periods with a number of worked examples as follows: *[IAS 19.71-74]*

Example 31.3: Attributing benefits to years of service

1. *A defined benefit plan provides a lump-sum benefit of 100 payable on retirement for each year of service.*

   A benefit of 100 is attributed to each year. The current service cost is the present value of 100. The present value of the defined benefit obligation is the present value of 100, multiplied by the number of years of service up to the end of the reporting period.

   If the benefit is payable immediately when the employee leaves the entity, the current service cost and the present value of the defined benefit obligation reflect the date at which the employee is expected to leave. Thus, because of the effect of discounting, they are less than the amounts that would be determined if the employee left at the end of the reporting period.

2. *A plan provides a monthly pension of 0.2% of final salary for each year of service. The pension is payable from the age of 65.*

   Benefit equal to the present value, at the expected retirement date, of a monthly pension of 0.2% of the estimated final salary payable from the expected retirement date until the expected date of death is attributed to each year of service. The current service cost is the present value of that benefit. The present value of the defined benefit obligation is the present value of monthly pension payments of 0.2% of final salary, multiplied by the number of years of service up to the end of the reporting period. The current service cost and the present value of the defined benefit obligation are discounted because pension payments begin at the age of 65.

3. *A plan pays a benefit of 100 for each year of service. The benefits vest after ten years of service.*

   A benefit of 100 is attributed to each year. In each of the first ten years, the current service cost and the present value of the obligation reflect the probability that the employee may not complete ten years of service.

4. *A plan pays a benefit of 100 for each year of service, excluding service before the age of 25. The benefits vest immediately.*

   No benefit is attributed to service before the age of 25 because service before that date does not lead to benefits (conditional or unconditional). A benefit of 100 is attributed to each subsequent year.

5. *A plan pays a lump-sum benefit of 1,000 that vests after ten years of service. The plan provides no further benefit for subsequent service.*

   A benefit of 100 (1,000 divided by ten) is attributed to each of the first ten years. The current service cost in each of the first ten years reflects the probability that the employee may not complete ten years of service. No benefit is attributed to subsequent years.

6. *A plan pays a lump-sum retirement benefit of 2,000 to all employees who are still employed at the age of 55 after twenty years of service, or who are still employed at the age of 65, regardless of their length of service.*

For employees who join before the age of 35, service first leads to benefits under the plan at the age of 35 (an employee could leave at the age of 30 and return at the age of 33, with no effect on the amount or timing of benefits). Those benefits are conditional on further service. Also, service beyond the age of 55 will lead to no material amount of further benefits. For these employees, the entity attributes benefit of 100 (2,000 divided by 20) to each year from the age of 35 to the age of 55.

For employees who join between the ages of 35 and 45, service beyond twenty years will lead to no material amount of further benefits. For these employees, the entity attributes benefit of 100 (2,000 divided by 20) to each of the first twenty years.

For an employee who joins at the age of 55, service beyond ten years will lead to no material amount of further benefits. For this employee, the entity attributes benefit of 200 (2,000 divided by 10) to each of the first ten years.

For all employees, the current service cost and the present value of the obligation reflect the probability that the employee may not complete the necessary period of service.

7. *A post-employment medical plan reimburses 40% of an employee's post-employment medical costs if the employee leaves after more than ten and less than twenty years of service and 50% of those costs if the employee leaves after twenty or more years of service.*

   Under the plan's benefit formula, the entity attributes 4% of the present value of the expected medical costs (40% divided by ten) to each of the first ten years and 1% (10% divided by ten) to each of the second ten years. The current service cost in each year reflects the probability that the employee may not complete the necessary period of service to earn part or all of the benefits. For employees expected to leave within ten years, no benefit is attributed.

8. *A post-employment medical plan reimburses 10% of an employee's post-employment medical costs if the employee leaves after more than ten and less than twenty years of service and 50% of those costs if the employee leaves after twenty or more years of service.*

   Service in later years will lead to a materially higher level of benefit than in earlier years. Therefore, for employees expected to leave after twenty or more years, the entity attributes benefit on a straight-line basis under paragraph 68 of the standard. Service beyond twenty years will lead to no material amount of further benefits. Therefore, the benefit attributed to each of the first twenty years is 2.5% of the present value of the expected medical costs (50% divided by twenty).

   For employees expected to leave between ten and twenty years, the benefit attributed to each of the first ten years is 1% of the present value of the expected medical costs. For these employees, no benefit is attributed to service between the end of the tenth year and the estimated date of leaving.

   For employees expected to leave within ten years, no benefit is attributed.

9. *Employees are entitled to a benefit of 3% of final salary for each year of service before the age of 55.*

   Benefit of 3% of estimated final salary is attributed to each year up to the age of 55. This is the date when further service by the employee will lead to no material amount of further benefits under the plan. No benefit is attributed to service after that age.

None of the illustrations above is controversial. The following points of note are brought out in the above:

- the scenarios in 3 and 5 are economically identical, and are attributed to years of service accordingly. In each case benefits only vest after ten years, however an obligation is to be built up over that period rather than at the end; and
- example 8 illustrates that accruing a 10% benefit over a period of 20 years of service which jumps to 50% once 20 years has been completed is an example of service in later years leading to a materially higher level of benefit. Accordingly the obligation is to be built-up on a straight-line basis over 20 years.

As regards example 9, the standard explains that where the amount of a benefit is a constant proportion of final salary for each year of service, future salary increases will affect the amount required to settle the obligation that exists for service before the end of the reporting period, but do not create an additional obligation. Therefore:

(a) for the purpose of allocating benefits to years of service, salary increases are not considered to lead to further benefits, even though the amount of the benefits is dependent on final salary; and

(b) the amount of benefit attributed to each period should be a constant proportion of the salary to which the benefit is linked. *[IAS 19.74]*.

5.2.2.E Actuarial assumptions

The long timescales and numerous uncertainties involved in estimating obligations for post-employment benefits require many assumptions to be made when applying the projected unit credit method. These are termed actuarial assumptions and comprise:

(a) demographic assumptions about the future characteristics of current and former employees (and their dependants) who are eligible for benefits and deal with matters such as:
   (i) mortality, both during and after employment;
   (ii) rates of employee turnover, disability and early retirement;
   (iii) the proportion of plan members with dependants who will be eligible for benefits; and
   (iv) claim rates under medical plans; and

(b) financial assumptions, dealing with items such as:
   (i) the discount rate;
   (ii) future salary and benefit levels, excluding the cost of benefits that will be met by the employees;
   (iii) in the case of medical benefits, future medical costs, including claim handling costs, which the standard describes as costs that will be incurred in processing and resolving claims, including legal and adjuster's fees; and
   (iv) taxes payable by the plan on contributions relating to service before the reporting date or on benefits resulting from that service. *[IAS 19.76]*.

The requirements of IAS 19 in this regard are set out below, with the exception of the discount rate which is discussed at 5.2.2.F below.

The standard requires that actuarial assumptions be unbiased (that is, neither imprudent nor excessively conservative), mutually compatible and represent the employer's best estimates of the variables that will determine the ultimate cost of providing post-employment benefits. *[IAS 19.75-77]*.

The financial assumptions must be based on market expectations at the end of the reporting period, for the period over which the obligations are to be settled. *[IAS 19.80]*. Actuarial assumptions are mutually compatible if they reflect the economic relationships between factors such as inflation, rates of salary increase and discount rates. For example, all assumptions which depend on a particular inflation level (such as assumptions about interest rates and salary and benefit increases) in any given future period should assume the same inflation level in that period. *[IAS 19.78]*.

The standard requires that a defined benefit obligation be measured on a basis that reflects:

(a) the benefits set out in the terms of the plan (or resulting from any constructive obligation that goes beyond those terms) at the end of the reporting period;

(b) any estimated future salary increases that affect the benefits payable;

(c) the effect of any limit on the employer's share of the cost of the future benefits; and

(d) contributions from employees or third parties that reduce the ultimate cost to the entity of those benefits. *[IAS 19.87]*.

Regarding mortality, the standard requires assumptions to be a best estimate of the mortality of plan members both during and after employment. *[IAS 19.81]*. In particular, expected changes in mortality should be considered, for example by modifying standard mortality tables with estimates of mortality improvements. *[IAS 19.82]*.

Assumptions about medical costs should take account of inflation as well as specific changes in medical costs (including technological advances, changes in health care utilisation or delivery patterns, and changes in the health status of plan participants). *[IAS 19.96-97]*. The standard provides a quite detailed discussion of the factors that should be taken into account in making actuarial assumptions about medical costs, in particular:

(a) measuring post-employment medical benefits requires assumptions about the level and frequency of future claims, and the cost of meeting them. An employer should make such estimates based on its own experience, supplemented where necessary by historical data from other sources (such as other entities, insurance companies and medical providers); *[IAS 19.97]*

(b) the level and frequency of claims is particularly sensitive to the age, health status and sex of the claimants, and may also be sensitive to their geographical location. This means that any historical data used for estimating future claims need to be adjusted to the extent that the demographic mix of the plan participants differs from that of the population used as the basis for the historical data. Historical data should also be adjusted if there is reliable evidence that historical trends will not continue; *[IAS 19.98]* and

(c) estimates of future medical costs should take account of any contributions that claimants are required to make based on the terms (whether formal or constructive) of the plan at the end of the reporting period. The treatment of contributions by employees and third parties is discussed at 5.2.2.B.

Clearly, the application of actuarial techniques to compute plan obligations is a complex task, and it seems likely that few entities would seek to prepare valuations without the advice of qualified actuaries. However, IAS 19 only encourages, but does not require that an entity take actuarial advice. *[IAS 19.59]*.

However sophisticated actuarial projections may be, reality will (aside of the most simple scenarios) always diverge from assumptions. This means that when a surplus or deficit is estimated, it will almost certainly be different from the predicted value based on the last valuation. These differences are termed actuarial gains and losses. The standard observes that actuarial gains and losses result from increases or decreases in the present value of a defined benefit obligation because of changes in actuarial assumptions and experience adjustments. Causes of actuarial gains and losses could include, for example:

(a) unexpectedly high or low rates of employee turnover, early retirement or mortality or of increases in salaries, benefits (if the formal or constructive terms of a plan provide for inflationary benefit increases) or medical costs;

(b) differences between the actual return on plan assets and amounts included as net interest in profit or loss;

(c) the effect of changes to assumptions concerning benefit payment options;

(d) the effect of changes in estimates of future employee turnover, early retirement or mortality or of increases in salaries, benefits (if the formal or constructive terms of a plan provide for inflationary benefit increases) or medical costs; and

(e) the effect of changes in the discount rate.

Actuarial gains and losses are discussed further at 5.5.3 below.

5.2.2.F Discount rate

Due to the long timescales involved, post-employment benefit obligations are discounted. Also, the whole obligation should be discounted, even if part of it is expected to be settled within twelve months of the end of the reporting period. *[IAS 19.69].* The standard requires that the discount rate reflect the time value of money but not the actuarial or investment risk. Furthermore, the discount rate should not reflect the entity-specific credit risk borne by the entity's creditors, nor should it reflect the risk that future experience may differ from actuarial assumptions. *[IAS 19.84].* The discount rate should reflect the estimated timing of benefit payments. For example, an appropriate rate may be quite different for a payment due in, say, ten years as opposed to one due in twenty. The standard observes that in practice, an acceptable answer can be obtained by applying a single weighted average discount rate that reflects the estimated timing and amount of benefit payments and the currency in which the benefits are to be paid. *[IAS 19.85].*

The rate used should be determined 'by reference to' the yield (at the end of the reporting period) on high quality corporate bonds of currency and term consistent with the liabilities. In countries where there is no deep market in such bonds, the yields on government bonds should be used instead. *[IAS 19.83].*

IAS 19 does not explain what is meant by the term 'high quality'. In practice it is considered, rightly in our view, to mean either: bonds rated AA, bonds rated AA or higher by Standard and Poor's, or an equivalent rating from another rating agency.

The requirement that the rate be determined 'by reference to' high quality bond rates adds an important nuance.

The standard gives an example of this in the context of the availability of bonds with sufficiently long maturities. It notes that in some cases, there may be no deep market in bonds with a sufficiently long maturity to match the estimated maturity of all the benefit payments. In such cases, the standard requires the use of current market rates of the appropriate term to discount shorter-term payments, and estimation of the rate for longer maturities by extrapolating current market rates along the yield curve. It goes on to observe that the total present value of a defined benefit obligation is unlikely to be particularly sensitive to the discount rate applied to the portion of benefits that is payable beyond the final maturity of the available corporate or government bonds. *[IAS 19.86]*.

Of the three characteristics of corporate bonds stipulated by the standard (quality, currency and term) the above example of extrapolation is making an adjustment to observed yields with respect to term.

The Interpretations Committee is currently discussing two matters relating to discount rates.

The first is whether the rate should be pre- or post-tax. It observed that the discount rate used to calculate a defined benefit obligation should be a pre-tax discount rate and decided not to add this issue to its agenda.[9]

The second relates to the meaning of 'high quality corporate bonds'. The committee was asked whether corporate bonds with a rating lower than 'AA' can be considered to be high quality.

The Committee observed the following and tentatively decided not to add the item to its agenda as issuing additional guidance or changing the requirements would be too broad for it to achieve in an efficient manner.[10]

The key observations of the committee were as follows.

- IAS 19 does not specify how to determine the market yields on high quality corporate bonds, and in particular what grade of bonds should be designated as high quality.
- The term 'high quality' reflects an absolute concept of credit quality and not a concept of credit quality that is relative to a given population of corporate bonds, which would be the case, for example, if the paragraph used the term 'the highest quality'.
- An entity's policy for determining the discount rate should be applied consistently over time. The Interpretations Committee does not expect that an entity's method for determining the discount rate so as to reflect the yields on high quality corporate bonds will change significantly from period to period. Similarly, because high quality refers to an absolute notion, the Committee does not expect that there would be changes in the method for identifying the population of such bonds that serves as a basis for determining the discount rate. Accordingly, a reduction in the number of high quality bonds should not result in a change to an entity's policy for determining the discount rate, provided that the relevant market remains deep.

- Typically the discount rate will be a material assumption to be disclosed with sensitivity analyses under IAS 19.
- As required by IAS 1 – *Presentation of Financial Statements* (see Chapter 3 at 5.1.1.B), disclosure is required of the judgements that management has made in the process of applying the entity's accounting policies and that have the most significant effect on the amounts recognised in the financial statements

In June 2005 the Interpretations Committee discussed another form of extrapolation from observed inputs and published an explanation as to why it decided not to take the issue onto its agenda. The question considered was, when there is no deep market in high quality corporate bonds in a country, whether the discount rate could be determined by reference to a synthetically constructed equivalent instead of using the yield on government bonds? The Interpretations Committee concluded that the standard 'is clear that a synthetically constructed equivalent to a high quality corporate bond by reference to the bond market in another country may not be used to determine the discount rate.' The Interpretations Committee further observed that the reference to 'in a country' could reasonably be read as including high quality corporate bonds that are available in a regional market to which the entity has access, provided that the currency of the regional market and the country were the same (e.g. the euro). This would not apply if the country currency differed from that of the regional market.[11]

It is more than a little difficult to know what to make of those observations. First, without a proper and detailed fact pattern one cannot know the details of the question being addressed and quite what a 'synthetically constructed equivalent' actually means. Second, as the observation is not a formal interpretation its status is questionable at best. Furthermore, the wording of the standard itself and of the Interpretations Committee's 'non-interpretation' implies that the defined benefit obligation is denominated in the same currency as government bonds in the country concerned. Whilst that may well be the case, there is no reason why employee benefits could not be denominated in another currency. In our view it would have been more helpful if the Interpretations Committee had progressed a formal interpretation to explore how and to what extent observed bond yields could form a starting point to extrapolate a discount rate. Whilst it would be wrong to understate the liabilities of the plan by using an inappropriately high rate (say, because the only relevant bonds in issue are not 'high quality') it would be equally wrong, in our view, to overstate them by using the default rate of government debt when a reliable rate could be estimated by reference to market yields. Indeed, the standard suggests this in its discussion of actuarial assumptions in general, requiring that they be unbiased, that is neither imprudent nor excessively conservative. *[IAS 19.75, 77].*

IAS 19 also stipulates that the discount rate (and other financial assumptions) should be determined in nominal (stated) terms, unless estimates in real (inflation-adjusted) terms are more reliable, for example, in a hyper-inflationary economy (see Chapter 16 for a discussion of IAS 29 – *Financial Reporting in Hyperinflationary Economies*), or where the benefit is index-linked and there is a deep market in index-linked bonds of the same currency and term. *[IAS 19.79].*

The basic part of this requirement – that a nominal rate be used – is consistent with the definition of the present value of a defined benefit obligation in that it should be '... the present value ... of expected future payments required to settle the obligation ...' (see 5.2.2.A above). In other words, as the future cash flows are stated at the actual amounts expected to be paid, the rate used to discount them should reflect that and not be adjusted to remove the effects of expected inflation. In contrast, the reference to the use of index-linked bonds seems to allow taking account of inflation through the discount rate (which would require expressing cash flows in current prices). This approach seems to be in conflict with the definition of the obligation, although in practice few index-linked corporate bonds exist (so it may be quite rare to have a deep market in them) so a more reliable approach may often be to take account of inflation via the projected cash flows.

5.2.2.G Frequency of valuations

When it addresses the frequency of valuations, IAS 19 does not give particularly prescriptive guidance. Rather, its starting point is simply to require that the present value of defined benefit obligations, and the fair value of plan assets, should be determined frequently enough to ensure that the amounts recognised in the financial statements do not differ materially from the amounts that would be determined at the end of the reporting period. *[IAS 19.58]*. An argument could be launched that without a full valuation as at the end of the reporting period to compare with, it cannot be possible to know whether any less precise approach is materially different. However, it is reasonably clear that the intention of the standard is not necessarily to require full actuarial updates as at the year-end. This is because the standard goes on to observe that for practical reasons a detailed valuation may be carried out before the end of the reporting period and that if such amounts determined before the end of the reporting period are used, they should be updated to take account of any material transactions or changes in circumstances up to the end of the reporting period. *[IAS 19.59]*. Much may turn on what is considered to be a 'material change', however it is expressly to include changes in market prices (hence requiring asset values to be those at the end of the reporting period) and interest rates, as well as financial actuarial assumptions. *[IAS 19.59, 80]*.

In this regard, it is also worth noting the observation in the standard that 'In some cases, estimates, averages and computational shortcuts may provide a reliable approximation of the detailed computations illustrated in this Standard.' *[IAS 19.60]*. It should be remembered, though, that it is the amounts in the financial statements which must not differ materially from what they would be based on a valuation at the end of the reporting period. For funded schemes, the net surplus or deficit is usually the difference between two very large figures – plan assets and plan liabilities. Such a net item is inevitably highly sensitive, in percentage terms, to a given percentage change in the gross amounts.

In summary, these rules will require a detailed valuation on an annual basis, but not necessarily as at the end of the reporting period. A valuation undertaken other than as at the end of the reporting period will then need to be updated as at the end of the reporting period to reflect *at least* changes in financial assumptions, asset values and discount rates. The need for updates in respect of other elements of the valuation will depend on individual circumstances.

5.3 Treatment of the plan surplus or deficit in the statement of financial position

5.3.1 Net defined benefit liability (asset)

IAS 19 defines the net defined benefit liability or asset as the deficit or surplus in the plan adjusted for any effect of the asset ceiling (see 5.3.2 below).

The deficit or surplus is the present value of the defined benefit obligation (see 5.2.2 above) less the fair value of the plan assets (if any) (see 5.2.1 above).

The standard requires that the net defined benefit liability (asset) be recognised in the statement of financial position at each reporting period. *[IAS 19.63].*

5.3.2 Restriction of assets to their recoverable amounts

The net defined benefit balance determined under IAS 19 may be an asset. The standard asserts that an asset may arise (that is, an asset measured on the basis of IAS 19) where a defined benefit plan has been 'over-funded' or when actuarial gains have arisen. The standard justifies the recognition of an asset in such cases because:

(a) the entity controls a resource, which is the ability to use the surplus to generate future benefits;

(b) that control is a result of past events (contributions paid by the entity and service rendered by the employee); and

(c) future economic benefits are available to the entity in the form of a reduction in future contributions or a cash refund, either directly to the entity or indirectly to another plan in deficit; the present value of those benefits is described as the asset ceiling. *[IAS 19.8, 65].*

In practice, pension plans tend to be funded on a significantly more prudent basis than would be the case if a surplus or deficit was measured in accordance with IAS 19. In particular, the discount rate used for funding purposes is typically lower than the rate specified in the standard. For this reason, IAS 19 may produce an asset, when for funding purposes there is a deficit.

When there is a surplus in a defined benefit plan, the standard requires it to be restricted to the lower of the surplus in the plan and the asset ceiling discounted using the same discount rate used for determining the defined benefit obligation (see 5.2.2.F above). *[IAS 19.8, 64].*

Any adjustment required by the ceiling test is accounted for in other comprehensive income (see 5.5.3 below).

This limitation has proved quite problematic in practice and as a result was considered by the Interpretations Committee, initially in the context of statutory minimum funding requirements ('MFR'). This resulted in the publication, in July 2007, of IFRIC 14 – *IAS 19 – The Limit on a Defined Benefit Asset, Minimum Funding Requirements and their Interaction.* Whilst dealing with the interaction of the asset ceiling with MFR, IFRIC 14 also deals more generally with the restriction of an asset on recoverability grounds. With effect for periods beginning on or after 1 January 2011, IFRIC 14 was amended to deal with pre-paid MFR – see 5.3.2.C below. These issues are discussed in the following sections.

5.3.2.A IFRIC Interpretation 14 – general requirements concerning the limit on a defined benefit asset

IFRIC 14 clarifies that economic benefits, in the form of refunds or reduced future contributions, are available if they can be realised at some point during the life of the plan or when the plan liabilities are settled. In particular, such economic benefits may be available even if they are not realisable immediately at the end of the reporting period. *[IFRIC 14.8].* Furthermore, the benefit available does not depend on how the entity intends to use the surplus. The entity should determine the maximum economic benefit that is available from refunds, reductions in future contributions or a combination of both. However, economic benefits should not be recognised from a combination of refunds and reductions in future contributions based on assumptions that are mutually exclusive. *[IFRIC 14.9].* Perhaps unnecessarily, the interpretation requires the availability of a refund or a reduction in future contributions to be determined in accordance with the terms and conditions of the plan and any statutory requirements in the jurisdiction of the plan. *[IFRIC 14.7].*

The interpretation observes that an unconditional right to a refund can exist whatever the funding level of a plan at the end of the reporting period. However, if the right to a refund of a surplus depends on the occurrence or non-occurrence of one or more uncertain future events not wholly within an entity's control, the entity does not have an unconditional right and should not recognise an asset. *[IFRIC 14.12].* The interpretation further states that benefits are available as a refund only if the entity has an unconditional right to a refund: *[IFRIC 14.11-12]*

(a) during the life of the plan, without assuming that the plan liabilities must be settled in order to obtain the refund; or

(b) assuming the gradual settlement of the plan liabilities over time until all members have left the plan; or

(c) assuming the full settlement of the plan liabilities in a single event (i.e. as a plan wind-up).

The economic benefit available as a refund should be measured as the amount of the surplus at the end of the reporting period (being the fair value of the plan assets less the present value of the defined benefit obligation) that the entity has a right to receive as a refund, less any associated costs. For example, if a refund would be subject to a tax other than income tax of the reporting entity, it should be measured net of the tax. *[IFRIC 14.13].*

In measuring the amount of a refund available when the plan is wound up (point (c) above), the costs to the plan of settling the plan liabilities and making the refund should be included. For example, a deduction should be made for professional fees if these are paid by the plan rather than the entity, and the costs of any insurance premiums that may be required to secure the liability on wind-up. *[IFRIC 14.14].*

Commonly, the trustees of a pension fund will be independent and have absolute discretion to set investment strategy, asset allocation and also the ability to buy annuities to settle liabilities.

These powers would allow the trustees to 'spend' any current or future surplus. Investing plan assets in ultra-cautious investments (yielding less that the unwinding discount on the obligation) could unwind any surplus over time. Settlements by way of buying annuities would absorb surpluses because the cost of settlement typically exceeds the IAS 19 measure of the obligation.

These trustee powers raise the following questions:

- whether the exercise of such powers by the trustees are 'uncertain future events not wholly within [the entity's] control'; and
- if so, whether 'the entity's right to a refund of a surplus depends on the occurrence or non-occurrence of' them and accordingly no surplus could be recognised in any scenario where trustees have such powers.

Our view is that such a trustee powers should not, of themselves, preclude the recognition of a surplus (or, indeed, require the accrual of a liability for future MFR payments – discussed at 5.3.2.D below).

The reason for this is that the test in IFRIC 14 is whether the entity has an unconditional right to any surplus which may happen to exist at any future date. It is not concerned with whether such a surplus will exist, or with the powers of others to influence that. Put another way, the question is whether any surplus existing in any of the three scenarios in (a) to (c) above would revert unconditionally to the employer. The fact that any surplus could be extinguished by uncertain future events not controlled by the employer is not relevant – it is the right to a surplus, not its existence, which is relevant. IFRIC 14 makes this clear for future actuarial losses and benefit improvements made by the employer. *[IFRIC 14.BC10]*. Our view is that the same applies to asset allocation decisions (including settlements) whether decided by the employer or the trustees. Naturally, there will be different rules in different jurisdictions. The above arguments are predicated on clear reversion of any surplus should one exist following final settlement of obligations.

This view is further supported by the general requirements in IAS 19 surrounding settlements. Settlements are accounted for only when they happen, and this is so whether the decision to settle is taken by the employer or by trustees (see 5.5.1.B below). Put simply, the test in (b) above is: if the scheme were to be run-off as reflected in the statement of financial position, would the employer have an unconditional right to whatever is left? If the answer is 'Yes' (for example, because that is what the trust deed provides for), then measurement of a surplus follows the 'normal' IAS 19 methodology.

If the amount of a refund is determined as the full amount or a proportion of the surplus, rather than a fixed amount, an entity should make no adjustment for the time value of money, even if the refund is realisable only at a future date. *[IFRIC 14.15]*.

5.3.2.B Economic benefits available as reduced future contributions when there are no minimum funding requirements for future service

IFRIC 14 addresses separately cases where there are minimum funding requirements relating to benefits to be awarded in future periods in exchange for services to be rendered in those periods, and cases where there are no such funding requirements.

This section deals with the situation where there are no such funding requirements. The implications of future service minimum funding requirements are discussed at 5.3.2.C below.

IFRIC 14 requires that the economic benefit available by way of reduced future contributions be determined as the future service cost to the entity for each period over the shorter of the expected life of the plan and the expected life of the entity. The future service cost to the entity excludes amounts that will be borne by employees. *[IFRIC 14.16].*

Future service costs should be determined using assumptions consistent with those used to determine the defined benefit obligation and with the situation that exists at the end of the reporting period as determined by IAS 19. Accordingly, no future changes to the benefits to be provided by a plan should be assumed until the plan is amended, and a stable workforce in the future should be assumed unless the entity makes a reduction in the number of employees covered by the plan. In the latter case, the assumption about the future workforce should include the reduction. The present value of the future service cost should be determined using the same discount rate as that used in the calculation of the defined benefit obligation (discount rates are discussed at 5.2.2.F above). *[IFRIC 14.17].*

5.3.2.C IFRIC Interpretation 14 – the effect of a minimum funding requirement on the economic benefit available as a reduction in future contributions

IFRIC 14 defines minimum funding requirements as 'any requirements to fund a post-employment or other long-term defined benefit plan'. *[IFRIC 14.5].* This is clearly quite a wide definition encompassing more than just statutory regimes.

The interpretation requires any minimum funding requirement at a given date to be analysed into contributions that are required to cover: *[IFRIC 14.18]*

(a) any existing shortfall for past service on the minimum funding basis. These contributions do not affect future contributions for future service. However, they may give rise to a liability under IFRIC 14 (see 5.3.2.D below); *[IFRIC 14.19]* and

(b) future service.

If there is a minimum funding requirement for contributions relating to future service, the economic benefit available as a reduction in future contributions is the sum of: *[IFRIC 14.20]*

(a) any amount that reduces future minimum funding requirement contributions for future service because the entity made a pre-payment (that is, it paid the amount before being required to do so); and

(b) the estimated net future service cost in each period (as discussed at 5.3.2.B above) less the estimated minimum funding requirement contributions that would be required for future service in those periods if there were no pre-payment as described in (a).

The future minimum funding contributions required in respect of future service should be calculated taking into account the effect of any existing surplus on the minimum funding requirement basis but excluding the pre-payment discussed in

(a) immediately above. The assumptions used for this calculation should be consistent with the minimum funding requirement basis. For any factors not specified by the minimum funding requirement, the assumptions used should be consistent with those used to determine the defined benefit obligation and with the situation that exists at the end of the reporting period as determined by IAS 19. The estimate should include any changes expected as a result of the entity paying the minimum contributions when they are due. However, the estimate should not include the effect of expected changes in the terms and conditions of the minimum funding basis that are not substantively enacted or contractually agreed at the end of the reporting period. *[IFRIC 14.21]*.

If the future minimum funding contribution required in respect of future service exceeds the future IAS 19 service cost in any given period, the present value of that excess reduces the amount of the asset available as a reduction in future contributions. However, the amount of the asset available as a reduction in future contributions can never be less than zero. *[IFRIC 14.22]*.

The mechanics of the above requirements are illustrated in the following two examples based the illustrative examples accompanying IFRIC 14. Example 31.4 also illustrates the requirement in certain circumstances to recognise an additional liability for future MFR payments in respect of past service (discussed at 5.3.2.D below).

Example 31.4: Deficit-clearing future minimum funding requirements when refunds are not available [IFRIC 14.IE9-IE21]

An entity has a funding level on the minimum funding requirement basis (which is measured on a different basis from that required under IAS 19) of 95% in Plan C. Under the minimum funding requirements, the entity is required to pay contributions to increase the funding level to 100% over the next three years. The contributions are required to make good the deficit on the minimum funding requirement basis (shortfall) and to cover future service.

Plan C also has an IAS 19 surplus at the end of the reporting period of €50m, which cannot be refunded to the entity under any circumstances. There are no unrecognised amounts.

The nominal amounts of the minimum funding contribution requirements in respect of the shortfall and the future IAS 19 service cost for the next three years are set out below.

Year	Total minimum funding contribution requirement	Minimum contributions required to make good the shortfall	Minimum contributions required to cover future accrual
	€m	€m	€m
1	135	120	15
2	125	112	13
3	115	104	11

The entity's present obligation in respect of services already received includes the contributions required to make good the shortfall but does not include the minimum contributions required to cover future accrual.

The present value of the entity's obligation, assuming a discount rate of 6% per year, is approximately 300, calculated as follows:

$€120m/(1.06) + €112m /(1.06)^2 + €104m/(1.06)^3$

When these contributions are paid into the plan, the IAS 19 surplus (i.e. the fair value of assets less the present value of the defined benefit obligation) would, other things being equal, increase from €50m to €350m. However, the surplus is not refundable although an asset may be available as a future contribution reduction.

As noted above, the economic benefit available as a reduction in future contributions is the present value of:

- the future service cost in each year to the entity; less
- any minimum funding contribution requirements in respect of the future accrual of benefits in that year

over the expected life of the plan.

The amounts available as a future contribution reduction are set out below.

Year	IAS 19 service cost €m	Minimum contributions required to cover future accrual €m	Amount available as contribution reduction €m
1	13	15	(2)
2	13	13	0
3	13	11	2
4+	13	9	4

Assuming a discount rate of 6%, the economic benefit available as a future contribution reduction is therefore equal to:

$€(2)m/(1.06) + €0m/(1.06)^2 + €2m/(1.06)^3 + €4m/(1.06)^4 + €4m/(1.06)^5 + €4m/(1.06)^6 .... = €56m.$

The asset available from future contribution reductions is accordingly limited to €56m.

As discussed at 5.3.2.D below, IFRIC 14 requires the entity to recognise a liability to the extent that the additional contributions payable will not be fully available. Therefore, the entity reduces the defined benefit asset by €294m (€50m + €300m – €56m).

As discussed at 5.5.3 below, the effect of the asset ceiling is part of remeasurements and the €294m is recognised immediately in other comprehensive income and the entity recognises a net liability of €244m. No other liability is recognised in respect of the obligation to make contributions to fund the minimum funding shortfall.

When the contributions of €300m are paid into the plan, the net asset will become €56m (€300m – €244m).

Example 31.5: Effect of a prepayment when a minimum funding requirement exceeds the expected future service charge [IFRIC 14.IE22-27]

An entity is required to fund Plan D so that no deficit arises on the minimum funding basis. The entity is required to pay minimum funding requirement contributions to cover the service cost in each period determined on the minimum funding basis.

Plan D has an IAS 19 surplus of 35 at the beginning of 2014. This example assumes that the discount rate is 0%, and that the plan cannot refund the surplus to the entity under any circumstances but can use the surplus for reductions of future contributions.

The minimum contributions required to cover future service are €15 for each of the next five years. The expected IAS 19 service cost is €10 in each year.

The entity makes a pre-payment of €30 at the beginning of 2014 in respect of years 2014 and 2015, increasing its surplus at the beginning of 2014 to €65. That prepayment reduces the future contributions it expects to make in the following two years, as follows:

Year	IAS 19 service cost (€)	Minimum funding requirement: Before pre-payment (€)	After pre-payment (€)
2014	10	15	0
2015	10	15	0
2016	10	15	15
2017	10	15	15
2018	10	15	15
Total	50	75	45

At the beginning of 2014, the economic benefit available as a reduction in future contributions is the sum of:

- 30, being the prepayment of the minimum funding requirement contributions; and
- nil. The estimated minimum funding requirement contributions required for future service would be 75 if there was no prepayment. Those contributions exceed the estimated future service cost (50); therefore the entity cannot use any part of the surplus of 35.

Assuming a discount rate of 0%, the present value of the economic benefit available as a reduction in future contributions is equal to 30. Accordingly, the entity recognises an asset of 30 (because this is lower than the IAS 19 surplus of 65).

Two points worth noting in the above are as follows. The first is that, if IFRIC 14 did not allow the recognition of such prepayments, the full surplus of 60 would have been written off. The second is that, in the fact pattern of the question, it is unnecessary to know that the surplus before the prepayment was 35. This is because any surplus (other than the prepayment of MFR) would not be recognised because refunds are not available and future MFR exceed future service costs.

5.3.2.D *IFRIC Interpretation 14 – when a minimum funding requirement may give rise to a liability*

If there is an obligation under a minimum funding requirement to pay contributions to cover an existing shortfall on the minimum funding basis in respect of services already received, the entity should determine whether the contributions payable will be available as a refund or reduction in future contributions after they are paid into the plan. *[IFRIC 14.23].* Recovery through reduced future contributions is discussed at 5.3.2.B and 5.3.2.C above.

If a surplus is recoverable by way of a refund (see 5.3.2.A above), a minimum funding requirement to cover a shortfall in respect of past services will neither restrict an IAS 19 asset nor trigger the recognition of a liability. IFRIC 14 illustrates this by way of an example upon which the following is based.

Example 31.6: Effect of the minimum funding requirement when there is an IAS 19 surplus and the minimum funding contributions payable are fully refundable to the entity [IFRIC 14.IE1-2]

An entity has a funding level on the minimum funding requirement basis (which is measured on a different basis from that required under IAS 19) of 82% in Plan A. Under the minimum funding requirements, the entity is required to increase the funding level to 95% immediately. As a result, the entity has a statutory obligation at the end of the reporting period to contribute €200m to Plan A immediately. The plan rules permit a full refund of any surplus to the entity at the end of the life of the plan. The year-end valuations for Plan A are set out below.

Chapter 31

	€million
Market value of assets	1,200
Present value of defined benefit obligation under IAS 19	(1,100)
Surplus	100
Defined benefit asset (before consideration of the minimum funding requirement)*	100

*For simplicity, it is assumed that there are no unrecognised amounts.

Payment of the contributions of €200m will increase the IAS 19 surplus from €100m to €300m. Under the rules of the plan this amount will be fully refundable to the entity with no associated costs. Therefore, no liability is recognised for the obligation to pay the contributions. To the extent that the contributions payable would not be fully available IFRIC 14 requires the entity to recognise a liability and the net defined benefit asset will be recognised at €100m. This is discussed below.

To the extent that the contributions payable will not be available after they are paid into the plan, a liability should be recognised when the obligation arises. The liability should reduce the net defined benefit asset or increase the net defined benefit liability so that no gain or loss is expected to result from the effect of the asset ceiling when the contributions are paid. *[IFRIC 14.24]*.

IFRIC 14 illustrates this by way of an example upon which the following is based.

Example 31.7: Effect of a minimum funding requirement when there is an IAS 19 deficit and the minimum funding contributions payable would not be fully available [IFRIC 14.IE3-8]

An entity has a funding level on the minimum funding requirement basis (which is measured on a different basis from that required under IAS 19) of 77% in Plan B. Under the minimum funding requirements, the entity is required to increase the funding level to 100% immediately. As a result, the entity has a statutory obligation at the end of the reporting period to pay additional contributions of €300m to Plan B. The plan rules permit a maximum refund of 60% of the IAS 19 surplus to the entity and the entity is not permitted to reduce its contributions below a specified level which happens to equal the IAS 19 service cost. The year-end valuations for Plan B are set out below.

	€million
Market value of assets	1,000
Present value of defined benefit obligation under IAS 19	(1,100)
Deficit	(100)

The payment of €300m would change the IAS 19 deficit of €100m to a surplus of €200m. Of this €200m, 60% (€120m) is refundable. Therefore, of the contributions of €300m, €100m eliminates the IAS 19 deficit and €120m (60% of €200m) is available as an economic benefit. The remaining €80m (40% of €200m) of the contributions paid is not available to the entity. As discussed above, IFRIC 14 requires the entity to recognise a liability to the extent that the additional contributions payable are not available to it. Accordingly, the net defined benefit liability is €180m, comprising the deficit of €100m plus the additional liability of €80m. No other liability is recognised in respect of the statutory obligation to pay contributions of €300m. When the contributions of €300m are paid, the net asset will be €120m.

5.3.2.E IFRIC Interpretation 14 – disclosure requirements

IFRIC 14 does not introduce any new disclosure requirements. However, it suggests that any restrictions on the current realisability of the surplus or a description of the basis used to determine the amount of the economic benefit available, may require disclosure under the provisions in IAS 1 about key sources of estimation uncertainty. *[IFRIC 14.10].* These requirements are discussed in Chapter 3 at 5.2.1.

5.4 Presentation of the net defined benefit liability (asset)

Neither IAS 19 nor IAS 1 specifies where in the statement of financial position an asset or liability in respect of a defined benefit plan should be presented, nor whether such balances should be shown separately on the face of the statement of financial position or only in the notes – this is left to the discretion of the reporting entity subject to the general requirements of IAS 1 discussed in Chapter 3 at 3.1. If the format of the statement of financial position distinguishes current assets and liabilities from non-current ones, the question arises as to whether this split needs also to be made for pension balances. IAS 19 does not specify whether such a split should be made, on the grounds that it may sometimes be arbitrary. *[IAS 19.133, BC200].*

Employers with more than one plan may find that some are in surplus while others are in deficit. IAS 19 contains offset criteria closely modelled on those in IAS 32 – *Financial Instruments: Presentation. [IAS 19.132].* An asset relating to one plan may only be offset against a liability relating to another plan when there is a legally enforceable right to use a surplus in one plan to settle obligations under the other plan, and the employer intends to settle the obligations on a net basis or realise the surplus and settle the obligation simultaneously. *[IAS 19.131].* In our view these offset criteria are unlikely to be met in practice.

5.5 Treatment of defined benefit plans in profit or loss and other comprehensive income

IAS 19 identifies three components of annual pension cost as follows:

(a) service cost (see 5.5.1 below);

(b) net interest on the net defined benefit liability (asset) (see 5.5.2 below); and

(c) remeasurements of the net defined benefit liability (see 5.5.3 below). *[IAS 19.120].*

Of these, (a) and (b) are recognised in profit or loss and (c) is recognised in other comprehensive income. This is unless another standard requires or permits the costs to be included in the cost of an asset, for example IAS 2 – *Inventories* – and IAS 16 – *Property, Plant and Equipment.* Where the post-employment benefit costs are included in the cost of an asset the appropriate proportion of *all* the above items must be included. *[IAS 19.121].* There is no guidance in the standard as to what an 'appropriate' proportion of these items might be, although both IAS 2 and IAS 16 are clear that only those costs which are directly attributable to the asset qualify for capitalisation. In our view, it is not necessarily the case that the appropriate proportion will be the same for all of the components and judgement will be required in deciding how much of each item can meaningfully be said to relate to the production of an asset.

Remeasurements recognised in other comprehensive income should not be reclassified to profit and loss in a subsequent period. The standard notes that those amounts may be transferred within equity. *[IAS 19.122]*.

In terms of income statement 'geography' the standard states that it does not specify how an entity should present service cost and net interest on the net defined benefit liability. These components are accounted for in accordance with IAS 1 (see Chapter 3 at 3.2). *[IAS 19.134]*.

5.5.1 Service cost

Service cost comprises:

(a) current service cost – the increase in the present value of the defined benefit obligation resulting from employee service in the current period;

(b) past service cost – which is the change in the present value of the defined benefit obligation for employee service in prior periods, resulting from a plan amendment (the introduction or withdrawal of, or changes to, a defined benefit plan) or a curtailment (a significant reduction by the entity in the number of employees covered by a plan); and

(c) any gain or loss on settlement – being the difference, at the date of settlement, between the present value of the defined benefit obligation being settled and the settlement price, including any plan assets transferred and any payments made directly by the entity in connection with the settlement. *[IAS 19.8, 109]*.

The current service cost should be determined using the projected unit credit method. *[IAS 19.67]*. The basic computation is illustrated in Example 31.2 at 5.2.2.C above.

Past service costs and settlements are discussed in sections 5.5.1.A and 5.5.1.B below.

Before determining past service cost, or a gain or loss on settlement, the net defined benefit liability (asset) should be remeasured using the current fair value of plan assets and current actuarial assumptions (including current market interest rates and other current market prices) reflecting the benefits offered under the plan before the plan amendment, curtailment or settlement. *[IAS 19.99]*.

There is no need to distinguish between past service cost resulting from a plan amendment, past service cost resulting from a curtailment and a gain or loss on settlement if these transactions occur together. In some cases, a plan amendment occurs before a settlement, such as when an entity changes the benefits under the plan and settles the amended benefits later. In those cases an entity recognises past service cost before any gain or loss on settlement. *[IAS 19.8, 100]*.

A settlement occurs together with a plan amendment and curtailment if a plan is terminated with the result that the obligation is settled and the plan ceases to exist. However, the termination of a plan is not a settlement if the plan is replaced by a new plan that offers benefits that are, in substance, the same. *[IAS 19.101]*.

5.5.1.A Past service cost

Past service cost is the change in the present value of the defined benefit obligation resulting from a plan amendment or curtailment. *[IAS 19.8, 102]*.

Past service costs should be recognised at the earlier of the date when:

(a) the plan amendment or curtailment occurs; and

(b) the entity recognises related restructuring costs in accordance with IAS 37 (discussed in Chapter 27 at 6.1). *[IAS 19.8, 103].*

A plan amendment occurs when an entity introduces, or withdraws, a defined benefit plan or changes the benefits payable under an existing defined benefit plan. *[IAS 19.8, 104].*

A curtailment occurs when an entity significantly reduces the number of employees covered by a plan. A curtailment may arise from an isolated event, such as the closing of a plant, discontinuance of an operation or termination or suspension of a plan. *[IAS 19.8, 105].*

Past service cost may be either positive (when benefits are introduced or changed so that the present value of the defined benefit obligation increases) or negative (when benefits are withdrawn or changed so that the present value of the defined benefit obligation decreases). *[IAS 19.8, 106].*

Where an entity reduces benefits payable under an existing defined benefit plan and, at the same time, increases other benefits payable under the plan for the same employees, the entity treats the change as a single net change. *[IAS 19.8, 107].*

Past service cost excludes:

(a) the effect of differences between actual and previously assumed salary increases on the obligation to pay benefits for service in prior years (there is no past service cost because actuarial assumptions allow for projected salaries, accordingly the effect of any such difference is an actuarial gain or loss – see 5.2.2 above);

(b) under- and over-estimates of discretionary pension increases when an entity has a constructive obligation to grant such increases (there is no past service cost because actuarial assumptions allow for such increases, accordingly the effect of any such under- or over-estimate is an actuarial gain or loss – see 5.2.2 above);

(c) estimates of benefit improvements that result from actuarial gains or from the return on plan assets that have been recognised in the financial statements if the entity is obliged, by either the formal terms of a plan (or a constructive obligation that goes beyond those terms) or legislation, to use any surplus in the plan for the benefit of plan participants, even if the benefit increase has not yet been formally awarded (the resulting increase in the obligation is an actuarial loss and not past service cost, see 5.2.2 above); and

(d) the increase in vested benefits (that is, those not conditional on future employment) when, in the absence of new or improved benefits, employees complete vesting requirements (there is no past service cost because the estimated cost of benefits was recognised as current service cost as the service was rendered, accordingly the effect of any such increase is an actuarial gain or loss, see 5.2.2 above). *[IAS 19.108].*

5.5.1.B Settlements

IAS 19 defines a settlement as a transaction that eliminates all further legal or constructive obligations for part or all of the benefits provided under a defined benefit plan, other than a payment of benefits to, or on behalf of, employees that is set out in the terms of the plan and included in the actuarial assumptions. *[IAS 19.8]*.

A settlement occurs when an employer enters into a transaction that eliminates all further legal or constructive obligations for part or all of the benefits provided under a defined benefit plan (other than a payment of benefits to, or on behalf of, employees in accordance with the terms of the plan and included in the actuarial assumptions). For example, a one-off transfer of significant employer obligations under the plan to an insurance company through the purchase of an insurance policy is a settlement; a lump sum cash payment, under the terms of the plan, to plan participants in exchange for their rights to receive specified post-employment benefits is not. *[IAS 19.111]*.

A gain or loss on settlement should be recognised when it occurs. *[IAS 19.110]*.

IAS 19 observes that an employer may acquire an insurance policy to fund some or all of the employee benefits relating to employee service in the current and prior periods. The acquisition of such a policy is not a settlement if the employer retains a legal or constructive obligation to pay further amounts if the insurer does not pay the employee benefits specified in the insurance policy. *[IAS 19.112]*. However, the acquisition of an insurance policy will mean an entity has an asset which needs to be measured at fair value. As discussed at 5.2.1.B above, certain insurance policies are valued at an amount equal to the present value of the defined benefit obligation which they match. The cost of buying such a policy will typically greatly exceed its subsequent carrying amount. That raises the question of how to treat the resultant debit entry. One view might be that the loss is, in substance, very similar to a settlement loss and should be recognised in profit or loss. This treatment may be appropriate, for example, if the purchase of the insurance is in anticipation of full settlement with the insurer at a later date. Another view is that because the loss results from exchanging one plan asset for another it is an actuarial loss. The typical bid-offer spread in quoted investments results in the same type of actuarial loss, albeit typically less significant. In our view, either approach is acceptable if applied consistently and, where material, disclosed.

5.5.2 Net interest on the net defined benefit liability (asset)

Net interest on the net defined benefit liability (asset) is the change during the period in the net defined benefit liability (asset) that arises from the passage of time. *[IAS 19.8]*. It is determined by multiplying the net defined benefit liability (asset) by the discount rate (see 5.2.2.F above), both as determined at the start of the annual reporting period, taking account of any changes in the net defined benefit liability (asset) during the period as a result of contribution and benefit payments. *[IAS 19.123]*.

In our view, the requirement to take account of payments to and from the fund implies that an entity should also take account of other significant changes in the net defined benefit liability, for example settlements and curtailments.

As the net item in the statement of financial position is comprised of two or three separate components (the defined benefit obligation, plan assets and the asset ceiling), the net interest is made up of interest unwinding on each of these components in the manner described above. *[IAS 19.124]*. Although, computationally, the net interest is so composed, for the purposes of presentation in profit or loss it is a single net amount.

Interest on plan assets calculated as described above will not, other than by coincidence, be the same as the actual return on plan assets. The difference is a remeasurement recognised in other comprehensive income. *[IAS 19.125]*.

Similarly, the difference in the asset ceiling between the start and end of the period is unlikely to equal the interest described above. Any difference is accounted for as a remeasurement in other comprehensive income. *[IAS 19.126]*.

5.5.3 Remeasurements

Remeasurements of the net defined benefit liability (asset) comprise:

(a) actuarial gains and losses;

(b) the return on plan assets, excluding amounts included in net interest on the net defined benefit liability (asset); and

(c) any change in the effect of the asset ceiling, excluding amounts included in net interest on the net defined benefit liability (asset). *[IAS 19.8, 127]*.

5.5.3.A Actuarial gains and losses

Actuarial gains and losses are changes in the present value of the defined benefit obligation resulting from: experience adjustments (the effects of differences between the previous actuarial assumptions and what has actually occurred); and the effects of changes in actuarial assumptions. *[IAS 19.8]*. These can result, for example, from:

(a) unexpectedly high or low rates of: employee turnover, early retirement, mortality, increases in salaries or benefits, or medical costs (if the formal or constructive terms of the plan provide for inflationary benefits);

(b) the effect of changes to assumptions concerning benefit payment options;

(c) the effect of changes in estimates of: future employee turnover, early retirement or mortality or of increases in salaries, benefits (if the formal or constructive terms of the plan provide for inflationary benefit increases) or medical costs; and

(d) the effect of changes in the discount rate. *[IAS 19.128]*.

Actuarial gains and losses do not include changes in the present value of the defined benefit obligation because of the introduction, amendment, curtailment or settlement of the defined benefit plan, or changes to the benefits payable under the defined benefit plan. Such changes result in past service cost or gains or losses on settlement. *[IAS 19.129]*.

5.5.3.B The return on plan assets, excluding amounts included in net interest on the net defined benefit liability (asset)

The return on plan assets is interest, dividends and other income derived from the plan assets, together with realised and unrealised gains on the assets, less

- any costs of managing plan assets; and
- any tax payable by the plan itself, other than tax included in the actuarial assumptions used to measure the present value of the defined benefit obligation.

Other administration costs are not deducted from the return on plan assets. *[IAS 19.130].*

5.6 Costs of administering employee benefit plans

Some employee benefit plans incur costs as part of delivering employee benefits. The costs are generally more significant for post-retirement benefits such as pensions. Examples of costs would include actuarial valuations, audits and the costs of managing any plan assets.

IAS 19 deals with some costs but is silent on others.

The following costs are required to be factored into the measurement of the defined benefit obligation:

- in the case of medical benefits, future medical costs, including claim handling costs (i.e. the costs that will be incurred in processing and resolving claims, including legal and adjuster's fees); and
- taxes payable by the plan on contributions relating to service before the reporting date or on benefits resulting from that service. *[IAS 19.76(b)].*

The following costs (and no others) are deducted from the return on plan assets:

- the costs of managing the plan assets; and
- any tax payable by the plan itself, other than tax included in the actuarial assumptions used to measure the defined benefit obligation. *[IAS 19.130].*

As discussed at 5.2.2 above, net interest on the net liability or asset is reported in the income statement. This is wholly computed amount which is uninfluenced by actual asset returns; the difference between actual asset returns and the credit element of the net interest amount forms part of remeasurements reported in other comprehensive income.

So, although not couched in these terms, costs of administering plan assets and the tax mentioned above are reported in other comprehensive income.

The standard is silent on the treatment of any other costs of administering employee benefit plans. However, the Basis for Conclusions on IAS 19 contains the following: 'the Board decided that an entity should recognise administration costs when the administration services are provided. This practical expedient avoids the need to attribute costs between current and past service and future service.' *[IAS 19.127].* The Board may well have taken that decision, however it did not include such a requirement in the standard.

In our view, such an approach is certainly an acceptable way to account for costs not dealt with in the standard; however other approaches could be acceptable, for example, in relation to closed schemes discussed below. Entities need, in compliance with IAS 8, to develop an accounting policy in light of the standard not dealing with these costs. However, IAS 1 is clear that such costs would not be reported in other comprehensive income. *[IAS 1.88]*.

One alternative to simple accruals-accounting as costs are incurred could be relevant to closed plans, where employees are no longer exchanging services for defined benefits. In this situation, it is clear that any and all future costs of administering the plan relate to past periods and no attribution is necessary. An entity with such an arrangement may select a policy of full provision of all costs of 'running-off' the plan (aside of those specifically dealt with by the standard).

One point is noteworthy regarding a change from the previous version of the standard. That version allowed costs of administering a plan to be deducted from the expected return on plan assets in the income statement. That exception to the requirements on aggregation and offsetting in IAS 1 was not retained in the current standard. Accordingly, such costs will be presented in the statement of comprehensive income according to an entity's normal policy for such costs (audit fees, professional valuations etc.).

6 OTHER EMPLOYEE BENEFITS

6.1 Short-term employee benefits

Short-term employee benefits are employee benefits (other than termination benefits) that are expected to be settled wholly before twelve months after the end of the annual reporting period in which the employees render the related service. *[IAS 19.8]*.

The standard states that reclassification is not necessary if an entity's expectation of the timing of settlement changes temporarily. However, if the characteristics of the benefit change (such as a change from a non-accumulating benefit to an accumulating benefit) or if a change in expectations of the timing of settlement is not temporary, then the entity considers whether the benefit still meets the definition of short-term employee benefits. *[IAS 19.10]*.

They can include:

- wages, salaries and social security contributions;
- paid annual leave and paid sick leave;
- profit-sharing and bonuses; and
- non-monetary benefits (such as medical care, housing, cars and free or subsidised goods or services) for current employees. *[IAS 19.9]*.

6.1.1 General recognition criteria for short-term employee benefits

An entity should recognise the undiscounted amount of short-term benefits attributable to services that have been rendered in the period as an expense, unless another IFRS requires or permits the benefits to be included in the cost of an asset. This may particularly be the case under IAS 2 (see Chapter 22 at 3) and IAS 16 (see Chapter 18 at 4). Any difference between the amount of cost recognised and cash payments made should be treated as a liability or prepayment as appropriate. *[IAS 19.11]*. There are further requirements in respect of short-term paid absences and profit-sharing and bonus plans.

6.1.2 Short-term paid absences

These include absences for vacation (holiday), sickness and short-term disability, maternity or paternity leave, jury service and military service. These can either be accumulating or non-accumulating absences. *[IAS 19.14]*. Accumulating absences are those that can be carried forward and used in future periods if the entitlement in the current period is not used in full. They can be either vesting entitlements (which entitle employees to a cash payment in lieu of absences not taken on leaving the entity) or non-vesting entitlements (where no cash compensation is payable). Non-accumulating absences are those where there is no entitlement to carry forward unused days. An obligation arises as employees render service that increases their entitlement to future paid absences. *[IAS 19.15]*.

6.1.2.A Accumulating absences

The cost of accumulating paid absences should be recognised when employees render the service that increases their entitlement to future paid absences. No distinction should be made between the recognition of vesting and non-vesting entitlements (see above), on the basis that the liability arises as services are rendered in both cases. However, the measurement of non-vesting entitlements should take into account the possibility of employees leaving before receiving them. *[IAS 19.15]*.

The cost of accumulating paid absences should be measured as the additional amount that the entity expects to pay as a result of the unused entitlement that has accumulated at the end of the reporting period. *[IAS 19.16]*. In the case of unused paid sick leave, provision should be made only to the extent that it is expected that employees will use the sick leave in subsequent periods. The standard observes that in many cases, it may not be necessary to make detailed computations to estimate that there is no material obligation for unused paid absences. For example, IAS 19 considers it unlikely that a sick leave obligation will be material unless if there is a formal or informal understanding that unused paid sick leave may be taken as paid vacation. *[IAS 19.17]*.

The standard provides an example to illustrate the requirements for accumulating paid absences upon which the following is based: *[IAS 19.17]*

Example 31.8: Accumulating paid absences

An entity has 100 employees, who are each entitled to five working days of paid sick leave for each year. Unused sick leave may be carried forward for one calendar year. Sick leave is taken first out of the current year's entitlement and then out of any balance brought forward from the previous year (a LIFO basis). At 31 December 2014, the average unused entitlement is two days per employee. The entity expects, based on past experience which is expected to continue, that 92 employees will take no more than five days of paid sick leave in 2015 and that the remaining eight employees will take an average of six and a half days each.

The entity expects that it will pay an additional 12 days of sick pay as a result of the unused entitlement that has accumulated at 31 December 2014 (one and a half days each, for eight employees). Therefore, the entity recognises a liability equal to 12 days of sick pay.

6.1.2.B Non-accumulating paid absences

The cost of non-accumulating absences should be recognised as and when they arise, on the basis that the entitlement is not directly linked to the service rendered by employees in the period. This is commonly the case for sick pay (to the extent that unused past entitlement cannot be carried forward), maternity or paternity leave and paid absences for jury service or military service. *[IAS 19.13(b), 18].*

6.1.3 Profit-sharing and bonus plans

An entity should recognise the expected cost of profit-sharing and bonus payments when, and only when:

- the entity has a present legal or constructive obligation to make such payments as a result of past events; and
- a reliable estimate of the obligation can be made. *[IAS 19.19].*

The above are discussed in turn at 6.1.3.A and 6.1.3.B below. Statutory profit sharing arrangements based on taxable profit are discussed at 6.1.3.C.

6.1.3.A Present legal or constructive obligation

A present obligation exists when, and only when, the entity has no realistic alternative but to make the payments. *[IAS 19.19].* IAS 19 clarifies that where a profit-sharing plan is subject to a loyalty period (i.e. a period during which employees must remain with the entity in order to receive their share), a constructive obligation is created as employees render service that increases the amount to be paid if they remain in service until the end of the specified period. However, the possibility of employees leaving during the loyalty period should be taken into account in measuring the cost of the plan. *[IAS 19.20].* The standard illustrates the approach as follows:

Example 31.9: Profit sharing and bonus plans

A profit-sharing plan requires an entity to pay a specified proportion of its net profit for the year to employees who serve throughout the year. If no employees leave during the year, the total profit-sharing payments for the year will be 3% of profit. The entity estimates that staff turnover will reduce the payments to 2.5% of profit.

The entity recognises a liability and an expense of 2.5% of net profit.

It is worth noting that in the scenario above, when an entity prepares its accounts for the year it will no longer be uncertain whether all eligible employees become entitled to the bonus, as that is determined at the year-end. That means the reduction in the accrual from 3% to 2.5% should be an observable fact not an 'estimate'.

In our view the standard is ambiguous regarding the period over which the expense of profit sharing arrangements should be recognised where the amount paid is calculated by reference to the profit for a period, but payment is conditional upon the employee remaining in service beyond the end of that period. In particular, the requirement to recognise a cost over the period during which '... employees render service that increases the amount to be paid if they remain in service until the end of the specified period' could be read in two ways depending on the view taken as to what is the reference point in relation to which the amount paid increases.

One interpretation would be that the employee would receive nothing if he were to leave before the end of the additional service period. On this view, the cost would be recognised over not just the year in which it is 'earned', but over the longer period to when the employee has an unconditional right.

An alternative interpretation would be that, as the profit share is determined by reference to profit for a particular financial year, the amount of the bonus to be received stops increasing once the profit for the financial year stops increasing. Under this view, the cost of the bonus would all be recognised during that financial year.

In our opinion, either view is acceptable if applied consistently.

The standard also states that where an entity has a practice of paying bonuses, it has a constructive obligation to pay a bonus, even though there may be no legal obligation for it to do so. Again, however, in measuring the cost, the possibility of employees leaving before receiving a bonus should be taken into account. *[IAS 19.21]*.

6.1.3.B Reliable estimate of provision

A reliable estimate of a legal or constructive obligation under a profit-sharing or bonus plan can be made when, and only when:

- the formal terms of the plan contain a formula for determining the amount of the benefit;
- the entity determines the amounts to be paid before the financial statements are authorised for issue; or
- past practice gives clear evidence of the amount of the entity's constructive obligation. *[IAS 19.22]*.

IAS 19 states that an obligation under a profit-sharing or bonus plan must be accounted for as expense and not a distribution of profit, since it results from employee service and not from a transaction with owners. *[IAS 19.23]*. Where profit-sharing and bonus payments are not expected to be settled wholly within twelve months after the end of the annual reporting period in which the employees render the related service, they should be accounted for as other long-term employee benefits (see 6.2 below). *[IAS 19.24]*.

6.1.3.C Statutory profit sharing based on taxable profit.

The Interpretations Committee was asked to clarify how to account for a particular statutory employee benefit whereby 10% of taxable profit is shared with employees. In particular, the request sought clarification as to whether analogy could be made to IAS 12 – *Income Taxes* – to account for temporary differences between accounting and taxable profit which would reverse in the future.

The Committee thought that such an approach was not acceptable. It decided not to add the item to its agenda saying 'The Committee noted that the statutory employee profit-sharing arrangement described in the request should be accounted for in accordance with IAS 19, and that IAS 19 provides sufficient guidance on amounts that should be recognised and measured, with the result that significantly divergent interpretations are not expected in practice. Consequently, the Committee decided not to add this issue to its agenda.'[12]

6.2 Long-term employee benefits other than post-employment benefits

6.2.1 Meaning of other long-term employee benefits

These are all employee benefits other than post-employment benefits and termination benefits. *[IAS 19.8]*. They include the following if not expected to be settled wholly before twelve months after the end of the annual reporting period in which the employees rendered the related service:

- long-term paid absences such as long-service or sabbatical leave;
- jubilee or other long-service benefits;
- long-term disability benefits;
- profit sharing and bonuses; and
- deferred remuneration. *[IAS 19.153]*.

6.2.2 Recognition and measurement

For such benefits IAS 19 requires a simplified version of the accounting treatment required in respect of defined benefit plans (which is discussed in detail at 5 above). The amount recognised as a liability for other long-term employee benefits should be the net total, at the end of the reporting period, of the present value of the defined benefit obligation and the fair value of plan assets (if any) out of which the obligations are to be settled directly. The net total of the following amounts should be recognised in profit or loss, except to the extent that another IFRS requires or permits their inclusion in the cost of an asset:

(a) service cost;

(b) net interest on the net defined benefit liability (asset); and

(c) remeasurements of the net defined benefit liability (asset).

In other words, all assets, liabilities, income and expenditure relating to such benefits should be accounted for in the same way, and subject to the same restrictions on the recognition of assets and income, as those relating to a defined benefit pension plan (see 5.3.1 and 5.3.2 above), except that remeasurements are recognised in profit or loss. *[IAS 19.155-156]*.

The standard explains the use of this simplified approach by asserting that the measurement of other long-employee benefits is not subject to the same degree of uncertainty as that of post-employment benefits. *[IAS 19.154]*.

6.2.2.A Attribution to years of service

In our view, IAS 19 is unclear on the attribution of long-term remuneration to the years of service over which they are earned.

Consider an award made at the start of the year for a fixed cash payment a third of which vests on each of the first second and third anniversary of the grant for employees still employed at each vesting date.

One interpretation would be that the 'benefit formula' attributes a third of the award to each year and that each of the three income statements will bear one third of the expense.

An alternative view is that there are three distinct awards with the same grant date, but with durations of one two and three years. This pattern of vesting is sometimes described as 'graded vesting' and is discussed, in relation to share-based payments, in Chapter 30 at 6.2.2 and illustrated in Example 30.9.

In our view, either approach is acceptable if applied consistently.

6.2.2.B Long-term disability benefit

Where long-term disability benefit depends on the length of service of the employee, an obligation arises as the employee renders service, which is to be measured according to the probability that payment will be required and the length of time for which payment is expected to be made. If, however, the level of benefit is the same for all disabled employees regardless of years of service, the expected cost is recognised only when an event causing disability occurs. *[IAS 19.157]*.

It is not clear why this distinction is made, since in principle both types of benefit are equally susceptible to actuarial measurement. If anything the cost of benefits applicable to all employees regardless of service is probably easier to quantify actuarially. Given that an exposure to disability benefits which grows with years of service is fully provided for (actuarially) as it grows over time, it would seem logical for full provision to be made immediately for an exposure which comes into being (in full) on the day the employee commences employment. The problem with such an approach would be what to do with the debit entry. It would not represent an asset as envisaged in the *Conceptual Framework*, which would tend to imply an instant charge to profit or loss. This may have been the reason for the Board to make the exception and link the recognition to the actual disability event. These issues are similar to those surrounding death-in-service benefits discussed at 3.6 above.

6.3 Termination benefits

Termination benefits are employee benefits payable as a result of either:

- an entity's decision to terminate an employee's employment before the normal retirement date; or
- an employee's decision to accept an offer of benefits in exchange for the termination of employment. *[IAS 19.8]*.

They are accounted for differently from other employee benefits because the event that gives rise to an obligation for them is the termination of employment rather than the rendering of service by the employee. *[IAS 19.159]*.

Termination benefits do not include employee benefits resulting from termination of employment at the request of the employee without an entity's offer, or as a result of mandatory retirement requirements, because those benefits are post-employment benefits. Some entities provide a lower level of benefit for termination of employment at the request of the employee (in substance, a post-employment benefit) than for termination of employment at the request of the entity. The difference between the benefit provided for termination of employment at the request of the employee and a higher benefit provided at the request of the entity is a termination benefit. *[IAS 19.160].*

The form of the employee benefit does not determine whether it is provided in exchange for service or in exchange for termination of the employee's employment. Termination benefits are typically lump sum payments, but sometimes also include:

- enhancement of post-employment benefits, either indirectly through an employee benefit plan or directly; and
- salary until the end of a specified notice period if the employee renders no further service that provides economic benefits to the entity. *[IAS 19.161].*

Indicators that an employee benefit is provided in exchange for services include the following:

- the benefit is conditional on future service being provided (including benefits that increase if further service is provided); and
- the benefit is provided in accordance with the terms of an employee benefit plan. *[IAS 19.162].*

Some termination benefits are provided in accordance with the terms of an existing employee benefit plan. For example, they may be specified by statute, employment contract or union agreement, or may be implied as a result of the employer's past practice of providing similar benefits. As another example, if an entity makes an offer of benefits available for more than a short period, or there is more than a short period between the offer and the expected date of actual termination, an entity should consider whether it has established a new employee benefit plan and hence whether the benefits offered under that plan are termination benefits or post-employment benefits. Employee benefits provided in accordance with the terms of an employee benefit plan are termination benefits if they both result from an entity's decision to terminate an employee's employment and are not conditional on future service being provided. *[IAS 19.163].*

Some employee benefits are provided regardless of the reason for the employee's departure. The payment of such benefits is certain (subject to any vesting or minimum service requirements) but the timing of their payment is uncertain. Although such benefits are described in some jurisdictions as termination indemnities or termination gratuities, they are post-employment benefits rather than termination benefits, and an entity accounts for them as post-employment benefits. *[IAS 19.164].*

6.3.1 Recognition

An entity should recognise termination benefits as a liability and an expense at the earlier of the following dates:

- when it can no longer withdraw the offer of those benefits; and
- when it recognises costs for a restructuring that is within the scope of IAS 37 and involves the payment of termination benefits (discussed in Chapter 27 at 6.1). *[IAS 19.165].*

For termination benefits payable as a result of an employee's decision to accept an offer of benefits in exchange for the termination of employment, the time when an entity can no longer withdraw the offer of termination benefits is the earlier of:

- when the employee accepts the offer; and
- when a restriction (e.g. a legal, regulatory or contractual requirement or other restriction) on the entity's ability to withdraw the offer takes effect. This would be when the offer is made, if the restriction existed at the time of the offer. *[IAS 19.166]*.

For termination benefits payable as a result of an entity's decision to terminate an employee's employment, the entity can no longer withdraw the offer when the entity has communicated to the affected employees a plan of termination meeting all of the following criteria:

- actions required to complete the plan indicate that it is unlikely that significant changes to the plan will be made;
- the plan identifies the number of employees whose employment is to be terminated, their job classifications or functions and their locations (but the plan need not identify each individual employee) and the expected completion date; and
- the plan establishes the termination benefits that employees will receive in sufficient detail that employees can determine the type and amount of benefits they will receive were their employment to be terminated. *[IAS 19.167]*.

The standard notes that when an entity recognises termination benefits, it may also have to account for a plan amendment or a curtailment of other employee benefits (discussed at 5.5.1.A above). *[IAS 19.168]*.

6.3.2 Measurement

IAS 19 requires that on initial recognition and subsequent remeasurement, termination benefits should be measured in accordance with the nature of the employee benefit. If the termination benefits are an enhancement to post-employment benefits, the entity applies the requirements for post-employment benefits. Otherwise:

- if the termination benefits are expected to be settled wholly before twelve months after the end of the annual reporting period in which the termination benefit is recognised, the requirements for short-term employee benefits should be applied (discussed at 6.1 above); and
- if the termination benefits are not expected to be settled wholly before twelve months after the end of the annual reporting period, the requirements for other long-term employee benefits should be applied (discussed at 6.2 above). *[IAS 19.169]*.

Because termination benefits are not provided in exchange for service, the standard notes that its rules relating to the attribution of the benefit to periods of service are not relevant (discussed at 5.2.2.D above). *[IAS 19.170]*.

IAS 19 illustrates the accounting for termination benefits with an example.

Example 31.10: Termination benefits

Background

As a result of a recent acquisition, an entity plans to close a factory in ten months and, at that time, terminate the employment of all of the remaining employees at the factory. Because the entity needs the expertise of the employees at the factory to complete some contracts, it announces a plan of termination as follows.

Each employee who stays and renders service until the closure of the factory will receive on the termination date a cash payment of \$30,000. Employees leaving before closure of the factory will receive \$10,000.

There are 120 employees at the factory. At the time of announcing the plan, the entity expects 20 of them to leave before closure. Therefore, the total expected cash outflows under the plan are \$3,200,000 (i.e. 20 × \$10,000 + 100 × \$30,000). As required by the standard, the entity accounts for benefits provided in exchange for termination of employment as termination benefits and accounts for benefits provided in exchange for services as short-term employee benefits.

Termination benefits

The benefit provided in exchange for termination of employment is \$10,000. This is the amount that an entity would have to pay for terminating the employment regardless of whether the employees stay and render service until closure of the factory or they leave before closure. Even though the employees can leave before closure, the termination of all employees' employment is a result of the entity's decision to close the factory and terminate their employment (i.e. all employees will leave employment when the factory closes). Therefore the entity recognises a liability of \$1,200,000 (i.e. 120 × \$10,000) for the termination benefits provided in accordance with the employee benefit plan at the earlier of when the plan of termination is announced and when the entity recognises the restructuring costs associated with the closure of the factory.

Benefits provided in exchange for service

The incremental benefits that employees will receive if they provide services for the full ten-month period are in exchange for services provided over that period. The entity accounts for them as short-term employee benefits because the entity expects to settle them before twelve months after the end of the annual reporting period. In this example, discounting is not required, so an expense of \$200,000 (i.e. \$2,000,000 ÷ 10) is recognised in each month during the service period of ten months, with a corresponding increase in the carrying amount of the liability.

7 DISCLOSURE REQUIREMENTS

7.1 Defined contribution plans

IAS 19 requires the disclosure of the expense recognised for defined contribution plans. It also notes that IAS 24 requires disclosure of the contributions in respect of key management personnel. *[IAS 19.53, 54].*

7.2 Defined benefit plans

IAS 19 requires extensive disclosure in relation to defined benefit plans, which are set out below.

Chapter 31

The standard requires disclosure of information that:

(a) explains the characteristics of its defined benefit plans and risks associated with them;

(b) identifies and explains the amounts in its financial statements arising from its defined benefit plans; and

(c) describes how its defined benefit plans may affect the amount, timing and uncertainty of the entity's future cash flows. *[IAS 19.135]*.

To achieve the above, the standard sets out a long and detailed list of narrative and numerical disclosure (considered further below).

The Board also noted that entities must comply with the general materiality requirements of IAS 1 (discussed in Chapter 3 at 4.1.5), including the requirement to disclose additional information if necessary, and that the financial statements need not contain disclosures that are not material. *[IAS 19.BC209]*.

One of the Board's objectives in regard to disclosure was to ensure that financial statements provide relevant information that is not obscured by excessive detail. *[IAS 19.BC207]*.

These references to excessive detail and non-disclosure of immaterial items suggest the Board is expecting entities to apply judgement regarding the level of detail to be provided rather than giving everything set out in the standard.

In our view this is a worthy aim and would, perhaps, have been better set out in the standard itself. It remains to be seen what entities will do in practice.

To meet the objectives above, the standard requires consideration of all the following:

(a) the level of detail necessary to satisfy the disclosure requirements;

(b) how much emphasis to place on each of the various requirements;

(c) how much aggregation or disaggregation to undertake; and

(d) whether users of financial statements need additional information to evaluate the quantitative information disclosed. *[IAS 19.136]*.

If the disclosures provided in accordance with the requirements of IAS 19 and other IFRSs are insufficient to meet the objectives above, an entity should disclose additional information necessary to meet those objectives. For example, an entity may present an analysis of the present value of the defined benefit obligation that distinguishes the nature, characteristics and risks of the obligation. Such a disclosure could distinguish:

(a) between amounts owing to active members, deferred members, and pensioners;

(b) between vested benefits and accrued but not vested benefits; and

(c) between conditional benefits, amounts attributable to future salary increases and other benefits. *[IAS 19.137]*.

An assessment should be made as to whether all or some disclosures should be disaggregated to distinguish plans or groups of plans with materially different risks.

For example, an entity may disaggregate disclosure about plans showing one or more of the following features:

(a) different geographical locations;

(b) different characteristics such as flat salary pension plans, final salary pension plans or post-employment medical plans;

(c) different regulatory environments;

(d) different reporting segments; and

(e) different funding arrangements (e.g. wholly unfunded, wholly funded or partly funded). *[IAS 19.138]*.

7.2.1 Characteristics of defined benefit plans and risks associated with them

IAS 19 requires disclosure of:

(a) information about the characteristics of its defined benefit plans, including:

  (i) the nature of the benefits provided by the plan (e.g. final salary defined benefit plan or contribution-based plan with guarantee);

  (ii) a description of the regulatory framework in which the plan operates, for example the level of any minimum funding requirements, and any effect of the regulatory framework on the plan, such as the asset ceiling;

  (iii) a description of any other entity's responsibilities for the governance of the plan, for example responsibilities of trustees or of board members of the plan; and

(b) a description of the risks to which the plan exposes the entity, focused on any unusual, entity-specific or plan-specific risks, and of any significant concentrations of risk. For example, if plan assets are invested primarily in one class of investments, e.g. property, the plan may expose the entity to a concentration of property market risk; and

(c) a description of any plan amendments, curtailments and settlements. *[IAS 19.139]*.

7.2.2 Explanation of amounts in the financial statements

The disclosures should provide a reconciliation from the opening balance to the closing balance for each of the following, if applicable:

(a) the net defined benefit liability (asset), showing separate reconciliations for:

  (i) plan assets;

  (ii) the present value of the defined benefit obligation; and

  (iii) the effect of the asset ceiling; and

(b) any reimbursement rights. If there are reimbursement rights a description of the relationship between them and the related obligation should be given. *[IAS 19.140]*.

Each reconciliation listed in (a) and (b) above should show each of the following, if applicable:

(a) current service cost;

(b) interest income or expense;

(c) remeasurements of the net defined benefit liability (asset), showing separately:

  (i) the return on plan assets, excluding amounts included in interest in (b) above;

  (ii) actuarial gains and losses arising from changes in demographic assumptions;

  (iii) actuarial gains and losses arising from changes in financial assumptions; and

  (iv) changes in the effect of limiting a net defined benefit asset to the asset ceiling, excluding amounts included in interest in (b). There should also be disclosure of how the maximum economic benefit available was determined, i.e. whether those benefits would be in the form of refunds, reductions in future contributions or a combination of both;

(d) past service cost and gains and losses arising from settlements. Past service cost and gains and losses arising from settlements need not be distinguished if they occur together (see 5.5.1 above);

(e) the effect of changes in foreign exchange rates;

(f) contributions to the plan, showing separately those by the employer and by plan participants;

(g) payments from the plan, showing separately the amount paid in respect of any settlements; and

(h) the effects of business combinations and disposals. *[IAS 19.141].*

The fair value of the plan assets should be disaggregated into classes that distinguish the nature and risks of those assets, subdividing each class of plan asset into those that have a quoted market price in an active market (as defined in IFRS 13 – *Fair Value Measurement,* see Chapter 14) and those that do not. For example, and considering the level of detail of disclosure, aggregation and emphasis discussed at 7.2 above, an entity could distinguish between:

(a) cash and cash equivalents;

(b) equity instruments (segregated by industry type, company size, geography etc.);

(c) debt instruments (segregated by type of issuer, credit quality, geography etc.);

(d) real estate (segregated by geography etc.);

(e) derivatives (segregated by type of underlying risk in the contract, for example, interest rate contracts, foreign exchange contracts, equity contracts, credit contracts, longevity swaps etc.);

(f) investment funds (segregated by type of fund);

(g) asset-backed securities; and

(h) structured debt. *[IAS 19.142].*

The fair value of an entity's own transferable financial instruments held as plan assets, and the fair value of plan assets that are property occupied by, or other assets used by, the entity should be disclosed. *[IAS 19.143]*.

An entity should disclose the significant actuarial assumptions used to determine the present value of the defined benefit obligation. Such disclosure should be in absolute terms (e.g. as an absolute percentage, and not just as a margin between different percentages and other variables). When an entity provides disclosures in total for a grouping of plans, it should provide such disclosures in the form of weighted averages or relatively narrow ranges. *[IAS 19.144]*.

7.2.3 Amount, timing and uncertainty of future cash flows

An entity should disclose:

(a) a sensitivity analysis for each significant actuarial assumption as of the end of the reporting period, showing how the defined benefit obligation would have been affected by changes in the relevant actuarial assumption that were reasonably possible at that date;

(b) the methods and assumptions used in preparing the sensitivity analyses required by (a) and the limitations of those methods; and

(c) changes from the previous period in the methods and assumptions used in preparing the sensitivity analyses, and the reasons for such changes. *[IAS 19.145]*.

A description should be given of any asset-liability matching strategies used by the plan or the entity, including the use of annuities and other techniques, such as longevity swaps, to manage risk. *[IAS 19.146]*.

To provide an indication of the effect of the defined benefit plan on the entity's future cash flows, an entity should disclose:

(a) a description of any funding arrangements and funding policies that affect future contributions;

(b) the expected contributions to the plan for the next annual reporting period; and

(c) information about the maturity profile of the defined benefit obligation. This will include the weighted average duration of the defined benefit obligation and may include other information about the distribution of the timing of benefit payments, such as a maturity analysis of the benefit payments. *[IAS 19.147]*.

7.2.4 Multi-employer plans

If an entity participates in a multi-employer defined benefit plan, different disclosures are required depending upon how the arrangement is accounted for. These are discussed below.

7.2.4.A Plans accounted for as defined benefit plans

If an entity participates in a multi-employer defined benefit plan and accounts for it as such, it should make all the required disclosures discussed above. In addition it should disclose:

(a) a description of the funding arrangements, including the method used to determine the entity's rate of contributions and any minimum funding requirements;

(b) a description of the extent to which the entity can be liable to the plan for other entities' obligations under the terms and conditions of the multi-employer plan;

(c) a description of any agreed allocation of a deficit or surplus on:

 (i) wind-up of the plan; or

 (ii) the entity's withdrawal from the plan. *[IAS 19.148]*.

7.2.4.B Plans accounted for as defined contribution plans

If an entity accounts for a multi-employer defined benefit plan as if it were a defined contribution plan, it should disclose the following, in addition to the information required by 7.2.4.A above and instead of the disclosures normally required for defined benefits and discussed in 7.2 to 7.2.3 above:

(a) the fact that the plan is a defined benefit plan;

(b) the reason why sufficient information is not available to enable the entity to account for the plan as a defined benefit plan;

(c) the expected contributions to the plan for the next annual reporting period;

(d) information about any deficit or surplus in the plan that may affect the amount of future contributions, including the basis used to determine that deficit or surplus and the implications, if any, for the entity; and

(e) an indication of the level of participation of the entity in the plan compared with other participating entities. Examples of measures that might provide such an indication include the entity's proportion of the total contributions to the plan or the entity's proportion of the total number of active members, retired members, and former members entitled to benefits, if that information is available. *[IAS 19.148]*.

7.2.5 Defined benefit plans that share risks between entities under common control

If an entity participates in a defined benefit plan that shares risks between entities under common control, the entity should disclose:

(a) the contractual agreement or stated policy for charging the net defined benefit cost or the fact that there is no such policy; and

(b) the policy for determining the contribution to be paid by the entity. *[IAS 19.149]*.

Further disclosures are required depending upon how the arrangement is accounted for. These are discussed below.

7.2.5.A Plans accounted for as defined benefit plans

If an entity participates in a defined benefit plan that shares risks between entities under common control and accounts for an allocation of the net defined benefit cost, it should also disclose all the information about the plan as a whole set out in 7.2 to 7.2.3 above. *[IAS 19.149]*.

7.2.5.B Plans accounted for as defined contribution plans

If an entity participates in a defined benefit plan that shares risks between entities under common control and accounts for the net contribution payable for the period, it should also disclose the information set out below. *[IAS 19.149]*.

The standard requires disclosure of information that:

(a) explains the characteristics of its defined benefit plans and risks associated with them;

(b) identifies and explains the amounts in its financial statements arising from its defined benefit plans; and

(c) describes how its defined benefit plans may affect the amount, timing and uncertainty of the entity's future cash flows.

To meet the objectives above, the standard requires consideration of all the following:

(a) the level of detail necessary to satisfy the disclosure requirements;

(b) how much emphasis to place on each of the various requirements;

(c) how much aggregation or disaggregation to undertake; and

(d) whether users of financial statements need additional information to evaluate the quantitative information disclosed. *[IAS 19.136]*.

If the disclosures provided in accordance with the requirements in IAS 19 and other IFRSs are insufficient to meet the objectives above, an entity should disclose additional information necessary to meet those objectives. For example, an entity may present an analysis of the present value of the defined benefit obligation that distinguishes the nature, characteristics and risks of the obligation. Such a disclosure could distinguish:

(a) between amounts owing to active members, deferred members, and pensioners;

(b) between vested benefits and accrued but not vested benefits; and

(c) between conditional benefits, amounts attributable to future salary increases and other benefits. *[IAS 19.137]*.

IAS 19 requires disclosure of:

(a) information about the characteristics of its defined benefit plans, including:

    (i) the nature of the benefits provided by the plan (e.g. final salary defined benefit plan or contribution-based plan with guarantee);

   (ii) a description of the regulatory framework in which the plan operates, for example the level of any minimum funding requirements, and any effect of the regulatory framework on the plan, such as the asset ceiling; and
   (iii) a description of any other entity's responsibilities for the governance of the plan, for example responsibilities of trustees or of board members of the plan;

(b) a description of the risks to which the plan exposes the entity, focused on any unusual, entity-specific or plan-specific risks, and of any significant concentrations of risk. For example, if plan assets are invested primarily in one class of investments, e.g. property, the plan may expose the entity to a concentration of property market risk; and

(c) a description of any plan amendments, curtailments and settlements.

The fair value of the plan assets should be disaggregated into classes that distinguish the nature and risks of those assets, subdividing each class of plan asset into those that have a quoted market price in an active market (as defined in IFRS 13 – *Fair Value Measurement* – discussed in Chapter 14) and those that do not. For example, and considering the level of detail of disclosure, aggregation and emphasis discussed at 7.2 above, an entity could distinguish between:

(a) cash and cash equivalents;
(b) equity instruments (segregated by industry type, company size, geography etc.);
(c) debt instruments (segregated by type of issuer, credit quality, geography etc.);
(d) real estate (segregated by geography etc.);
(e) derivatives (segregated by type of underlying risk in the contract, for example, interest rate contracts, foreign exchange contracts, equity contracts, credit contracts, longevity swaps etc.);
(f) investment funds (segregated by type of fund);
(g) asset-backed securities; and
(h) structured debt. *[IAS 19.142]*.

The fair value of the entity's own transferable financial instruments held as plan assets, and the fair value of plan assets that are property occupied by, or other assets used by, the entity should be disclosed. *[IAS 19.143]*.

An entity should disclose the significant actuarial assumptions used to determine the present value of the defined benefit obligation. Such disclosure should be in absolute terms (e.g. as an absolute percentage, and not just as a margin between different percentages and other variables). When an entity provides disclosures in total for a grouping of plans, it shall provide such disclosures in the form of weighted averages or relatively narrow ranges.

To provide an indication of the effect of the defined benefit plan on the entity's future cash flows, an entity should disclose:

(a) a description of any funding arrangements and funding policy that affect future contributions;
(b) the expected contributions to the plan for the next annual reporting period.

The information described in 7.2.5 (a) and (b) must be presented in the entity's own accounts. The rest of the information discussed in this section may be disclosed by cross-reference to disclosures in another group entity's financial statements if:

(a) that group entity's financial statements separately identify and disclose the information required about the plan; and

(b) that group entity's financial statements are available to users of the financial statements on the same terms as the financial statements of the entity and at the same time as, or earlier than, the financial statements of the entity. *[IAS 19.150].*

7.2.6 Disclosure requirements in other IFRSs

Where required by IAS 24 an entity discloses information about:

(a) related party transactions with post-employment benefit plans; and

(b) post-employment benefits for key management personnel. *[IAS 19.151].*

Where required by IAS 37 an entity discloses information about contingent liabilities arising from post-employment benefit obligations. *[IAS 19.152].*

7.3 Other employee benefits

IAS 19 has no specific disclosure requirements in respect of other types of employee benefits within its scope (i.e. short-term employee benefits, long-term employee benefits other than post-employment benefits and termination benefits) but contains reminders that:

- IAS 24 requires disclosure of employee benefits for key management personnel (see Chapter 35); and
- IAS 1 requires disclosure of employee benefits expense. *[IAS 19.25, 158, 171].*

8 EFFECTIVE DATE AND TRANSITIONAL PROVISIONS

The standard applies to periods beginning on or after 1 January 2013. Early application is permitted if disclosed. *[IAS 19.172].*

The standard applies retrospectively, in accordance with IAS 8 – *Accounting Policies, Changes in Accounting Estimates and Errors*, except that:

(a) an entity need not adjust the carrying amount of assets outside the scope of IAS 19 for changes in employee benefit costs that were included in the carrying amount before the date of initial application. The date of initial application is the beginning of the earliest prior period presented in the first financial statements in which the entity adopts this Standard.

(b) in financial statements for periods beginning before 1 January 2014, an entity need not present comparative information for the disclosures required by paragraph 145 of the standard about the sensitivity of the defined benefit obligation (see 7.2.3 above). *[IAS 19.173].*

9 POSSIBLE FUTURE DEVELOPMENTS

As discussed at 1 above, the IASB published the current version of IAS 19 in June 2011. This represented the first phase in what was originally to be a two phase project. The second phase was to be a comprehensive review of all aspects of the standard. The IASB's website is now entirely silent on the matter of a second phase and the revised standard contains the following: 'The discussion paper included proposals on contribution-based promises. The Board will consider whether to develop those proposals further if it undertakes a comprehensive review of employee benefit accounting.' *[IAS 19.BC13]*. The use of 'if' and the removal of the discussion of the project from the website seem to suggest the Board has lost appetite for a second phase.

However, in 2011 the IASB launched a consultation on its future agenda which resulted, in December 2012 in the publication of Feedback Statement: *Agenda Consultation* 2011. That document includes the following. 'When the IASB completed the revisions to IAS 19 Employee Benefits it indicated that there were matters that needed to be considered as part of a more fundamental review of pensions and related benefits. The French standard-setter, the Autorité des Normes Comptables, has undertaken some preliminary work for the IASB.' This suggests that the standard may be re-visited at some future point.

The IASB has exposed for comment a limited-scope amendment to the standard relating to the attribution to years of service of employee contributions, this is discussed at 5.2.2.B above.

The Interpretations Committee is currently discussing two IAS 19 matters:

- employee benefits plans with a guaranteed return on contributions or notional contributions (discussed at 3.5 above); and
- discount rates and the meaning of 'high quality' corporate bonds (discussed at 5.2.2.F above).

10 PRINCIPAL DIFFERENCES BETWEEN THE CURRENT STANDARD AND ITS PREDECESSOR

As noted at 1 above, earlier versions of IAS 19 are discussed in earlier editions of *International GAAP.*

The principal differences between the old and the new requirements are as follows:

- the option to delay the recognition of actuarial variances (the so-called 'corridor' approach) has been removed. This means that actuarial variances are recognised as they occur with the result that the surplus or deficit computed under the standard is recognised in the balance sheet (subject to any restriction of an asset);
- unvested past-service costs are recognised immediately they occur, rather than being spread over the vesting period;
- the concept of an expected return on plan assets has been removed. Income is now credited with the product of the IAS 19 discount rate and the fair value of plan assets at the start of the period. Differences between this computed figure and actual asset returns are reported in other comprehensive income;

- employee contributions towards post-employment benefits are now to be attributed to service-periods in the same way as the defined benefit obligation;
- the distinction between a long-term and a short-term employee benefit is now based on the expected timing of settlement rather than the date of vesting of the benefit;
- earlier versions of the standard contained an ambiguity about how to account for the costs of administering a post employment benefit plan. The standard now distinguishes three types of cost and prescribes a single treatment for each of them; and
- new disclosure requirements apply.

References

1 *IFRIC Update,* IFRS Interpretations Committee, September 2012.
2 *IFRIC Update,* IFRS Interpretations Committee, November 2012.
3 E54 *Employee Benefits*, IASC, October 1996, paras. 17-21.
4 *IFRIC Update*, January 2008.
5 *IASB Update*, September 2007.
6 *IASB Update*, November 2007.
7 *IFRIC Update,* July 2011.
8 Staff paper for the February 2013 IASB meeting, Agenda ref 9B, Appendix C-Staff paper for the November 2012 IFRS IC meeting, Appendix A, Examples 3-5.
9 *IFRIC Update*, July 2013.
10 *IFRIC Update*, July 2013.
11 *IFRIC Update*, June 2005.
12 *IFRIC Update*, November 2010.

Chapter 32 Operating segments

List of examples

Chapter 32 Operating segments

1 INTRODUCTION

1.1 Background

IFRS 8 – *Operating Segments* – was published in November 2006. The Standard became mandatory for accounting periods beginning on or after 1 January 2009. *[IFRS 8.35]*.

In Europe, the introduction of IFRS 8 was controversial. Opponents shared concerns expressed in the dissenting opinions of two IASB members that the lack of a defined measure of segment profit or loss and the absence of any requirement for that measure to be consistent with the attribution of assets to reportable segments would encourage the proliferation of non-GAAP measures that could mislead users.[1] These concerns were raised in the European Parliament together with questions about the governance of the IASB, as a result of which the process to endorse IFRS 8 in the European Union was not completed until November 2007, a year after the Standard had been published.

During this period, the IFRS Foundation announced enhancements to oversight and due process to include a requirement for the IASB to conduct 'a review of issues identified as contentious as part of the consultation process related to all new IFRSs (including IFRS 8), major amendments to IFRSs and major IFRIC interpretations'. Such a review would be performed after at least two full years of implementation and be completed within three years of the pronouncement's effective date.[2] IFRS 8 is the first standard subject to a post-implementation review, which was completed in 2013 and is further discussed at 7 below.

1.2 The main features of IFRS 8

IFRS 8 is a disclosure standard. It specifies the way an entity should report information about its operating segments in annual financial statements and, as a consequential amendment to IAS 34 – *Interim Financial Reporting*, requires an entity to report selected information about its operating segments in interim financial reports (see Chapter 37 at 4.4). It also sets out requirements for related disclosures about an entity's products and services, geographical areas and major customers. *[IFRS 8.IN4]*. The disclosures required include:

- financial and descriptive information about the entity's reportable segments, which are operating segments or aggregations of operating segments that meet the criteria in the Standard for separate disclosure; *[IFRS 8.IN5]*
- segment revenues and a measure of profit or loss for each reportable segment, reconciled to the amounts disclosed in the entity's financial statements; *[IFRS 8.IN6]*
- a measure of segment assets, segment liabilities and particular income and expense items to the extent that such information is regularly provided to the chief operating decision maker of the entity, reconciled to the amounts disclosed in the entity's financial statements; *[IFRS 8.IN6]*
- unless the information is not available and the cost of its development would be excessive, information about the revenues derived from the entity's products and services (or groups of similar products and services), about the countries in which it earns revenues and holds assets, and about major customers, regardless of whether this information is used by management in making operating decisions; and *[IFRS 8.IN7]*
- descriptive information about the way that operating segments were determined, the products and services provided by the segments, differences between the measurements used in reporting segment information and those used in the entity's financial statements, and changes in the measurement of segment amounts from period to period. *[IFRS 8.IN8]*.

The process of identifying operating segments for external reporting purposes begins with the information used by the entity's chief operating decision maker to assess performance and to make decisions about future allocations of resources. *[IFRS 8.5]*. Entities applying IFRS 8 report on a single set of components according to the way that the business is sub-divided for management reporting purposes. *[IFRS 8.10]*.

If a component of an entity is managed as a separate segment, IFRS 8 requires it to be treated as such even if it sells exclusively or primarily to internal customers. *[IFRS 8.IN12]*.

IFRS 8 does not go so far as to require an entity to report all the information that is reviewed by the chief operating decision maker, recognising that such detail may not be useful to users of financial statements and could be cumbersome in its presentation. Instead it allows entities to aggregate components and to disclose information only for those segments that exceed certain quantitative criteria. *[IFRS 8.BC Appendix A 72]*.

Under IFRS 8, the amounts reported about identified segments are prepared according to the manner in which information is presented to the entity's chief operating decision maker. This can be different to the way that the entity applies its accounting policies used in the preparation of the financial statements under IFRSs. *[IFRS 8.IN13]*.

IFRS 8 requires an entity to describe the factors used to identify the entity's operating segments, including a description of the basis of organisation. This description would explain whether the organisation is structured according to products and services, geographical areas, regulatory environments or other factors and state whether operating segments have been aggregated for reporting purposes. In addition, the entity must describe the types of products and services from which each reportable segment derives its revenues. *[IFRS 8.IN15]*.

IFRS 8 specifies amounts which should be disclosed about each reportable segment, but only if those measures are included in the measure of profit or loss used by, or otherwise regularly provided to, the chief operating decision maker (see 5.2 below). *[IFRS 8.IN16]*. These specified amounts include a requirement to report separately interest revenue and interest expense by segment (but only if those measures are included in the measure of profit or loss used, or otherwise regularly provided to the by the chief operating decision maker) unless a majority of the segment's revenues is derived from interest and performance is assessed primarily on the basis of net interest revenue. *[IFRS 8.IN17]*.

Certain 'entity-wide disclosures' are also required to be provided under IFRS 8, even if the entity has only one reportable segment (see 6 below). Entity-wide information is disclosed for the entity as a whole about its products and services, geographical areas and major customers, regardless of the way the entity is organised and the information presented to the chief operating decision maker. *[IFRS 8.IN18]*. The amounts reported for this entity-wide information is based on the financial information used to produce the entity's financial statements. *[IFRS 8.32-33]*.

There is no 'competitive harm' exemption in IFRS 8 from the requirement to disclose segment information, or components of such information, for example on the grounds of commercial sensitivity, confidentiality or being otherwise detrimental to the entity's competitive position. *[IFRS 8.BC43-45]*.

1.3 Terms used in IFRS 8

The following terms are used in IFRS 8 with the meanings specified:

Term	Meaning
Operating segment	A component of an entity: (a) that engages in business activities from which it may earn revenues and incur expenses (including revenues and expenses relating to transactions with other components of the same entity); (b) whose operating results are regularly reviewed by the entity's chief operating decision maker to make decisions about resources to be allocated to the segment and assess its performance; and (c) for which discrete financial information is available. *[IFRS 8.5, Appendix A]*.

Chief operating decision maker	The function of allocating resources to and assessing the performance of the operating segments of an entity. This is not necessarily a manager with a specific title, but can be an entity's chief executive officer, chief operating officer, a group of executive directors or others. *[IFRS 8.7]*.
Segment manager	The function of being directly accountable to and maintaining regular contact with the chief operating decision maker to discuss operating activities, financial results, forecasts, or plans for the segment. *[IFRS 8.9]*.
Reportable segment	An operating segment or a group of two or more operating segments determined to be eligible for aggregation in accordance with IFRS 8.12; and which exceeds the quantitative thresholds in IFRS 8.13. *[IFRS 8.11]*.
Aggregation criteria	Two or more operating segments may be aggregated into a single operating segment if aggregation is consistent with the core principle of IFRS 8, they have similar economic characteristics, such as long-term average gross margins, and are similar in each of the following respects: (a) the nature of the products and services; (b) the nature of the production processes; (c) the type or class of customer for their products and services; (d) the methods used to distribute their products or provide their services; (e) if applicable, the nature of the regulatory environment, for example, banking, insurance or public utilities. *[IFRS 8.12]*.
Quantitative thresholds	Information about an operating segment that meets any of the following criteria: (a) its reported revenue, including both sales to external customers and intersegment sales or transfers, is 10% or more of combined revenue, internal and external, of all operating segments; or (b) its reported profit or loss is, in absolute terms, 10% or more of the greater of, in absolute amount: (i) the combined profit of all operating segments that did not report a loss; and (ii) the combined reported loss of all operating segments that reported a loss; or (c) its assets are 10% or more of the combined assets of all operating segments. *[IFRS 8.13]*.

1.4 Transitional provisions

There are no special arrangements for entities applying IFRS 8 for the first time, with the Standard requiring comparative information to be restated. Only where the necessary information is both unavailable and incapable of being developed without excessive cost is an entity exempt from full restatement. *[IFRS 8.36]*. Accordingly, an entity should ensure that internal reporting systems can provide the information needed to meet the disclosure requirements of IFRS 8 for all periods presented in its financial statements.

2 OBJECTIVE AND SCOPE OF IFRS 8

2.1 Objective

The objective of IFRS 8 is expressed as a 'core principle', being that an entity shall disclose information to enable users of its financial statements to evaluate the nature and financial effects of the business activities in which it engages and the economic environments in which it operates. *[IFRS 8.1]*.

2.2 Scope of IFRS 8

IFRS 8 applies to both the separate or individual financial statements of an entity and the consolidated financial statements of a group with a parent:

(a) whose debt or equity instruments are traded in a public market (a domestic or foreign stock exchange or an over-the-counter market, including local and regional markets), or

(b) that files, or is in the process of filing, its financial statements with a securities commission or other regulatory organisation for the purpose of issuing any class of instruments in a public market. *[IFRS 8.2]*

The Board has confirmed that for consolidated financial statements, the above test is applied to the parent entity alone. *[IFRS 8.BC23]*. Therefore, IFRS 8 does not apply to a group headed by a parent that has no listed financial instruments, even if the group includes a subsidiary that has any of its equity or debt instruments traded in a public market. The scope of IAS 33 – *Earnings per Share* – is similarly defined. *[IFRS 8.BC23]*. Of course, a subsidiary with publicly traded debt or equity instruments would be required to provide segment information under IFRS 8 in its own financial statements from its perspective as a reporting entity.

2.2.1 *The meaning of 'traded in a public market'*

The Standard describes a 'public market' as including a domestic or foreign stock exchange or an over-the-counter market, including local and regional markets, *[IFRS 8.2]*, but does not define what would make some markets 'public' and others not.

In our view, a market is 'public' where buyers and sellers (market participants) can transact with one another (directly; through agents; and in a secondary market) at a price determined in that market. A public market does not exist where the buyers and sellers can transact only with the entity itself (or an agent acting on its behalf). The requirement for an entity to list its securities on a stock exchange is not the sole factor determining whether the entity is in the scope of IFRS 8. Its securities must be *traded* in a public market meeting the criteria noted above.

Example 32.1: The meaning of 'public market' in the context of a fund

Many investment funds are listed on a public stock exchange for informational purposes, in particular to facilitate the valuation of portfolios by investors or because it is a requirement for the fund to be listed on a public stock exchange to make it eligible for investment by entities that are required to invest only in listed securities. However, in spite of such a listing, subscriptions and redemptions are handled by a fund administrator or a transfer agent (acting on behalf of the fund) and no transactions are undertaken on the public stock exchange. In addition, the prices for those transactions are

Chapter 32

determined by the fund agreement, such as on the basis of the fund's Net Asset Value, rather than the price quoted on the public stock exchange and determined by supply and demand.

In our view the debt or equity instruments of such entities are not traded in a public market and so the entity would not fall within the scope of IFRS 8.

Such 'public markets' would include exchange markets, dealer markets, brokered markets, and principal-to-principal markets as described in IFRS 13 – *Fair Value Measurement* – and listed in that Standard as examples of markets in which fair value inputs might be observable (see Chapter 14 at 15.1). *[IFRS 13.B34].*

2.2.2 Consolidated financial statements presented with those of the parent

Where both the consolidated financial statements and the parent's separate or individual financial statements are contained in the same financial report, segment information is only required in the consolidated financial statements. *[IFRS 8.4].*

2.2.3 Extending the scope of IFRS 8 to 'publicly accountable entities'

It had been proposed in the exposure draft that preceded IFRS 8 (ED 8 – *Operating Segments*) that the scope of the Standard be extended to require entities which hold assets in a fiduciary capacity for a broad group of outsiders to provide segment information, even if those entities do not issue securities that are publicly traded. Examples included a non-listed bank, insurance company, securities broker/dealer, mutual fund or investment banking entity.[3] The IASB removed this requirement following concerns raised by respondents to the exposure draft that terms like 'fiduciary capacity' or wider concepts of public accountability would not be adequately defined until the Board had completed its project on small and medium-sized entities. When it issued IFRS 8, the IASB indicated that an amendment to the Standard would be issued together with the IFRS for Small and Medium-sized Entities, to bring publicly accountable entities within the scope of IFRS 8. *[IFRS 8.BC18-20].* Whilst no amendment was made to IFRS 8 when the IFRS for Small and Medium-sized Entities was issued in July 2009, the definition of a publicly accountable entity in the latter uses similar wording to the intended scope of ED 8.[4] This, and the fact that the Post-implementation Review of IFRS 8 did not identify any demand for the scope of the Standard to be extended, would indicate that this proposal is unlikely to be implemented.

2.2.4 Entities providing segment information on a voluntary basis

Entities for which IFRS 8 is not mandatory might still want to provide information about their business activities, for example about sales by segment, without triggering the need to comply fully with the Standard. The Board concluded that this would be acceptable, provided that such disclosure is not referred to as 'segment information'. *[IFRS 8.BC22].* Consequently, entities giving information about segments on a voluntary basis cannot describe that information as 'segment information' unless it has been prepared in compliance with IFRS 8. *[IFRS 8.3].*

3 IDENTIFYING A SINGLE SET OF OPERATING SEGMENTS

IFRS 8 adopts a 'bottom up' approach to determining the level of detail required for segment reporting in the notes to the financial statements. It requires the entity's revenue earning activities to be divided into operating segments (based on the same components used by management to run the business) and only allows that information to be aggregated for reporting purposes if specific criteria are met. This process can involve considerable judgement, as it may not always be immediately clear what activities are operating segments for the purposes of the Standard or which layer of the entity's organisational structure represents the level at which those activities are managed. This is particularly the case when management information is presented in a number of different ways (for example by product, by geographical market and by legal entity) or where management structures distinguish operational, strategic and oversight responsibilities.

Notwithstanding such difficulties, the requirement is to identify a single set of components as constituting the entity's operating segments. *[IFRS 8.8]*.

The process for determining operating segments is important not only to entities applying IFRS 8 for external reporting purposes, but also to entities implementing the requirements of IAS 36 – *Impairment of Assets* – for testing indefinite-lived intangible assets and goodwill for impairment. As such, the way that operating segments are defined and determined under IFRS 8 can affect the financial statements of entities to which the disclosure requirements in IFRS 8 do not apply, such as those without traded equity or debt. This is because the Standard on impairment, applicable to all entities, states that a group of cash-generating units (CGUs) for impairment testing purposes cannot be larger than an operating segment before aggregation (as determined below). *[IAS 36.80b]*. See Chapter 20 at 4.2.

3.1 Definition of an operating segment

An operating segment is defined as a component of an entity:

(a) that engages in business activities from which it may earn revenues and incur expenses (including revenues and expenses relating to transactions with other components of the same entity);

(b) whose operating results are regularly reviewed by the entity's chief operating decision maker to make decisions about resources to be allocated to the segment and assess its performance; and

(c) for which discrete financial information is available. *[IFRS 8.5]*.

This means that the determination of an entity's operating segments starts with the smallest components of the business for which information about profit is presented for use by the entity's chief operating decision maker (sometimes referred to as 'CODM').

3.1.1 Revenue earning business activities

A significant feature of an operating segment is the potential for revenue generation rather than actually earning revenues in the reporting period. Accordingly, a start-up operation can be treated as an operating segment while it has yet to earn revenues. *[IFRS 8.5]*.

However, not every part of an entity is necessarily an operating segment. For example, a corporate headquarters or a functional department (such as a centralised data processing centre) that either does not earn revenues or for which revenues are only incidental to the activities of the entity would not be an operating segment for the purposes of IFRS 8. Similarly, an entity's post-employment benefit plans would not be regarded as operating segments. *[IFRS 8.6]*.

3.1.2 'Chief operating decision maker' and 'segment manager'

Arguably the most important judgements made in implementing IFRS 8 relate to the identification of the entity's chief operating decision maker. The nature of what is ultimately disclosed in the financial statements about operating segments and the level of detail (or segmentation) required is directly related to the information regularly provided to the chief operating decision maker.

References in the standard to 'chief operating decision maker' are to the function of allocating resources and assessing performance of the operating segments and not to a manager with a specific title. Often the chief operating decision maker of an entity is its chief executive officer or chief operating officer (i.e. an individual), but the term could refer equally to a group of executive directors or others charged with that role. *[IFRS 8.7]*.

In Extract 32.1 below, the Go-Ahead Group identifies its Group Chief Executive as the chief operating decision maker:

Extract 32.1: The Go-Ahead Group plc (2013)

Notes to the consolidated financial statements [extract]

3. Segmental analysis [extract]

The information reported to the Group Chief Executive in his capacity as Chief Operating Decision Maker does not include an analysis of assets and liabilities and accordingly IFRS 8 does not require this information to be presented. Segment performance is evaluated based on operating profit or loss excluding amortisation of goodwill and intangible assets and exceptional items.

The determination of chief operating decision maker will not be the same for all entities applying IFRS 8 and will depend upon the particular facts and circumstances applying to each entity. However, in stating that the term could apply to a group of executive directors or others, *[IFRS 8.7]*, the Standard is clear that the function of CODM is an executive role. The IFRS Interpretations Committee confirmed this view in 2011. While it observed that in practice the functions of CODM are sometimes carried out by multiple persons and that all such persons involved in those activities would be part of the CODM group, the Committee noted that the CODM would not normally include non-executive directors.[5] For example, an entity may have a single board of executive and non-executive directors which reviews the performance of individual business units, makes decisions about the operating budgets for those businesses and reviews significant applications for investment. In that case, the full board could be identified as the chief operating decision maker. However, if the entity also has a sub-committee of executive directors or another grouping of key management personnel (sometimes referred to as an 'operational board'), this smaller group of executives would be identified as the chief operating decision maker.

Essentially, the chief operating decision maker is found at the most senior executive decision-making level of an organisation and as such should be distinguished from higher levels of management fulfilling primarily an oversight or approval role and who, to reflect their non-executive function, are provided information at a more aggregated level as a matter of course. For example, in some jurisdictions, supervisory bodies may be part of an entity's governance structure and be entrusted with significant oversight responsibilities. This role may give the supervisory body significant veto rights and rights of approval. However, that supervision will not typically represent the level of decision-making implicit in the notion of the CODM.

In the extract below, ABB Ltd identifies as the CODM its Executive Committee, a group of senior executives which is headed by the Chief Executive Officer and is appointed by and reports to the Board of Directors.

Extract 32.2: ABB Ltd. (2012)

NOTES TO THE CONSOLIDATED FINANCIAL STATEMENTS [extract]

Note 23 Operating segment and geographic data [extract]

The Chief Operating Decision Maker (CODM) is the Company's Executive Committee. The CODM allocates resources to and assesses the performance of each operating segment using the information outlined below. The Company's operating segments consist of Power Products, Power Systems, Discrete Automation and Motion, Low Voltage Products and Process Automation. The remaining operations of the Company are included in Corporate and Other.

Another important distinction to be made is between chief operating decision maker and the function of 'segment manager'. The segment manager is accountable to and maintains regular contact with the chief operating decision maker to discuss operating activities, financial results, forecasts or plans for the segment. The chief operating decision maker may also fulfil the role of segment manager for some operating segments and a single segment manager may be responsible for more than one operating segment. *[IFRS 8.9].* For example, if the CODM is a group of executives, members of that group may fulfil the role of segment manager for certain components of the entity.

These considerations are relevant to the identification of an entity's operating segments and not to how they might be reported in the financial statements. Accordingly, separate operating segments which otherwise meet the definition at 3.1 above are not combined simply because they have a common segment manager. The Standard is clear that such segments are only combined if they exhibit similar long-term economic characteristics and are similar in respect of the qualitative criteria set out at 3.2.1 below. *[IFRS 8.12].* In addition, because the oversight role of the CODM is separate from the operational role of the segment manager, it is possible that an entity could regard an investee accounted for by the equity method as an operating segment (see 3.1.5 below).

In practice, judgement is required to determine whether the component(s) for which a segment manager is held responsible represents one or more operating segments. For example, if targets are set by the CODM for the entire area of one segment manager's responsibility and the remuneration of that segment manager is based on the achievement of those targets, on an aggregated basis, this could support a determination that the area of responsibility is one operating segment in the absence of other evidence indicating that the CODM reviews the results of these components separately. Equally, whilst IFRS 8 states that segment managers will generally exist, their existence is an important indicator for identifying operating segments, but not a necessary condition. The key determinant is based on the activity of the CODM with respect to the internally reported results of that component.

A common situation in practice is that detailed financial information is provided or available to the chief operating decision maker on a regular basis about various levels of management and operational activity within an entity. In these circumstances, the interplay between the three criteria at 3.1 above becomes very important, as the existence of more detailed internal reporting could otherwise lead to a determination that there are more operating segments. If the three criteria apply to more than one set of components of an entity, but there is only one set that has segment managers, generally the set of components with segment managers constitutes the operating segments. *[IFRS 8.8]*.

Example 32.2: Identifying operating segments – CODM and segment manager

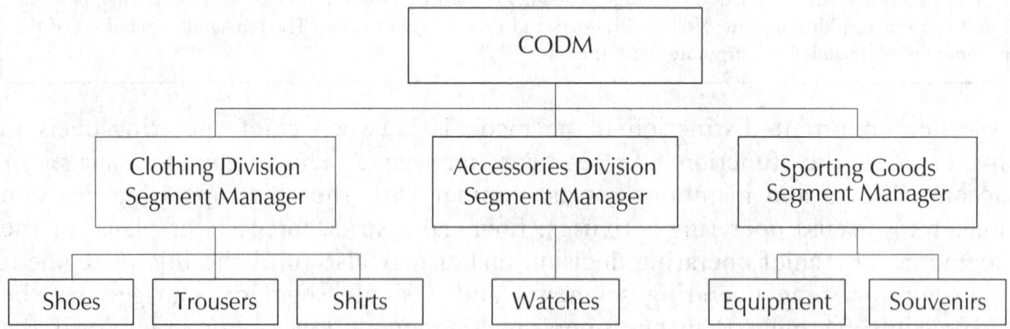

The diagram above sets out the internal reporting structure of Entity A. The CODM receives financial information about the entity's operations, the most detailed of which (including revenue and operating profit) relates to the six business units (Shoes, Trousers, Shirts, Watches, Equipment and Souvenirs). However, these units do not have their own segment manager. Instead, the six business units are grouped into three divisions (Clothing, Accessories and Sporting Goods), each of which has a segment manager who reports directly to the CODM. The three divisions report financial information to the CODM who uses it to assess performance and allocate resources.

In this case, the entity decides that the operating segments as defined in IFRS 8 comprise the three divisions as opposed to the six business units, because only the divisions have segment managers.

Proper application of the requirements of IFRS 8 requires a clear understanding of what information is given to the chief operating decision maker and how the CODM uses that information, in conjunction with the segment managers. In the above example, the fact that the CODM receives detailed financial information about activities below the divisional level could raise doubts about the determination that the divisions represent the entity's operating segments, rather than the business units. In these circumstances, entities would be required to demonstrate that:

- the more detailed information is not used by the CODM to assess performance and allocate resources.
- segment managers operate only at the divisional level and are not, in effect, managers for each of the business units in their division. As noted above, components otherwise meeting the characteristics of an operating segment under IFRS 8 are not combined simply because they share a segment manager.

It might be evident from the records of the discussions between segment managers and the CODM that results are monitored at divisional rather than at business unit level. It might equally be clear from the records of board meetings that more detailed information is not referred to by the CODM in its deliberations. However, there is evidence that when regulators and other enforcement agencies assess the quality of an entity's compliance with IFRS 8, they adopt the presumption that the CODM uses whatever detailed information is provided to him/her on a regular basis for decision-making and assessment purposes.

3.1.3 Availability of discrete financial information

As noted above, a component of an entity can only be regarded as an operating segment if discrete financial information is available about that component. *[IFRS 8.5(c)]*. This requirement relates solely to the existence of discrete information that allows the chief operating decision maker to make decisions about the allocation of resources and to assess the performance of that component.

Accordingly, a component of an entity is still regarded as an operating segment if the only information available relates to the profitability of that component. Such information would be sufficient for the chief operating decision maker to review its operating results, assess performance and make decisions about resource allocation. *[IFRS 8.5(b)]*. The financial information is not rendered useless by the lack of, for example, a separate statement of financial position or a separate statement of cash flows for that component.

However, it would be unlikely that a component of an entity could be regarded as an operating segment solely because the chief operating decision maker receives information about revenue from that component. Without a measure of the component's operating results it would be difficult to make meaningful assessments of the effect of allocating more or less resource to that activity. As such, information on revenue alone would have limited value in decision making. Therefore, the search for an entity's operating segments starts with the smallest components of the business for which a measure of profitability is provided to the entity's chief operating decision maker.

3.1.4 When a single set of components is not immediately apparent

For many entities, the search for operating segments is concluded after applying the three criteria listed at 3.1 above.

However, in cases where a single set of operating segments cannot be identified clearly by applying the above criteria, for example in an entity where its business activities are reported internally and assessed in a variety of ways, IFRS 8 states that other factors should be considered, including the nature of the business activities of each component, the existence of a manager responsible for it, and the information presented to the board of directors. *[IFRS 8.8]*. Therefore, if an entity's activities are reported internally in a number of different ways, each with their own set of business components as defined above, but there is only one set to which segment managers are assigned, then that will comprise the operating segments to report in the financial statements for IFRS 8 purposes. *[IFRS 8.9]*. For example, if an entity's board of directors manages its business using information on revenues and costs analysed both by product grouping as well as by geographical market, but the management structure operates only on geographical lines, then the financial statements would include segmental information on a geographical basis.

A single set of operating segments must be identified, even where two or more sets of components of an entity are managed in a matrix structure, for example where financial information is available and performance is assessed and segment managers assigned not only on the basis of product and service lines worldwide but also by geographical area irrespective of products and service lines. In that situation the choice of a single set of components is a matter of judgement, made by reference to the core principle of the Standard as set out at 2.1 above. *[IFRS 8.10]*. This requirement is different to FASB ASC Topic 280 and ED 8, which proposed that in such circumstances operating segments be drawn up on product and service lines.[6] The IASB agreed with respondents to the exposure draft that a default position mandating the use of components based on products and services was inconsistent with a management approach founded on what is important to the chief operating decision maker. *[IFRS 8.BC27]*.

3.1.5 An equity accounted investment can be an operating segment

The definition of an operating segment focuses on the review of its operating results by the entity's chief operating decision maker and the assessment of its performance and the allocation of resources to it by the CODM. *[IFRS 8.5(b)]*. This raises the question of whether the reporting entity needs to have control over the activities conducted in what otherwise would meet the definition of an operating segment, or whether it is sufficient that the CODM reviews its results and this review influences decisions about investment in those activities. In our view, control over the activities in which the entity is investing is not a requirement. The core principle of IFRS 8 requires the disclosure of information relating to the business activities in which an entity engages and the economic environments in which it operates. *[IFRS 8.1]*. No restriction is imposed according to the manner of that engagement, just the way in which the CODM makes decisions about allocating resources and assesses its performance.

For example, an equity method investee (i.e. associate or joint venture) could be considered an operating segment, if it meets the criteria in IFRS 8. The CODM may regularly review the operating results and performance of an equity method investee for the purposes of making additional investments or advances, evaluating financial performance or evaluating whether to retain its investment. The CODM is not required to be responsible for making decisions at the investee operating level that affect the investee's operations and performance in order for it to be identified as an operating segment. Further, the definition of an operating segment does not require that the revenue generating activities of the investee are included in the entity's revenue as reported in the IFRS financial statements. Segment performance could be measured by reference to the amounts included in the entity's IFRS financial statements or equally by reference to the financial information prepared by the investee itself. Any difference between the measures used by the CODM and the accounting treatment under IFRS would be reported as a reconciling item in the entity's disclosures under IFRS 8 (see 5.6 below).

This view is consistent with the disclosure requirements of IFRS 8, which require the entity's share of the profits and losses of equity accounted associates and joint ventures and the amount of investment in equity accounted investees to be presented, if those amounts are included in the measures reviewed by the chief operating decision maker of segment profit or loss and segment assets respectively (see 5.4 below). *[IFRS 8.23]*.

3.2 Identifying externally reportable segments

Having identified a single set of internal operating segments, the Standard describes how reportable segments are determined. As a minimum an entity must separately disclose information on reportable segments above a certain size (see 3.2.2 below). In addition, a previously identified reportable segment continues to be disclosed separately in the current period if management judges it to be of continuing significance, even if it no longer satisfies the quantitative thresholds. *[IFRS 8.17]*.

Thereafter, an entity is only compelled to give information on other segments (either individually or in certain circumstances on a combined basis) if the unallocated element is too large (see 3.2.4 below).

The implementation guidance to IFRS 8 includes a diagram illustrating how to apply the main provisions of the Standard for identifying reportable segments, which is reproduced below:

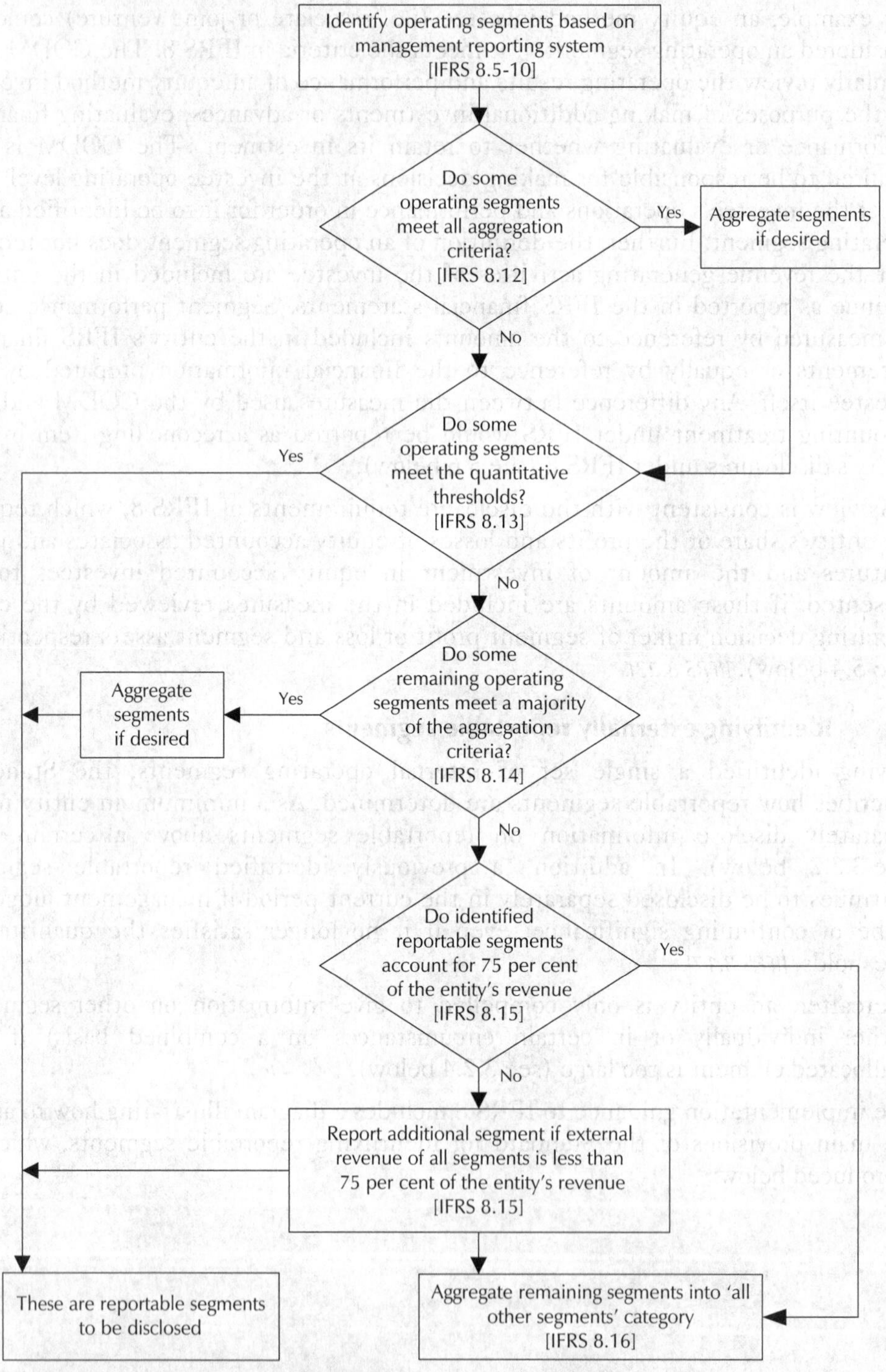

As indicated in the implementation guidance, the diagram is a visual supplement to the IFRS. It should not be interpreted as altering or adding to any requirements of the IFRS nor should it be regarded as a substitute for its requirements. *[IFRS 8.IG7]*.

IFRS 8 does not permit the omission of segment information when management believe that its disclosure is commercially sensitive or potentially detrimental to the entity's competitive position. If the criteria for separate disclosure described at 3.2.2 and 3.2.4 below are met, an entity is compelled to give information on that operating segment in the financial statements. The IASB considered both a general 'competitive harm' exemption and a 'comply or explain' basis for disclosure and rejected both. *[IFRS 8.BC43-45].*

3.2.1 Aggregation criteria – combining internally reported operating segments

Regardless of their size, two or more operating segments can be combined if they have similar economic characteristics (demonstrated, for example, by similar long-term average gross margins) and are similar in each of the following respects:

(a) the nature of the products and services;

(b) the nature of the production processes;

(c) the type or class of customer for the products and services;

(d) the methods used to distribute the products or provide the services; and

(e) if applicable, the nature of the regulatory environment. *[IFRS 8.12].*

At this stage in the process only segments which are similar in *all* the above respects can be combined. Further aggregation can only be achieved for segments which do not merit separate disclosure by virtue of their size (see 3.2.2 below).

Example 32.3: Combining internally reported operating segments with similar characteristics

In the information presented to the executive directors, a single-product company has six internally reported operating segments, Australia, France, Germany, Italy, UK and USA. The company dominates its markets in Australia and Germany and consequently enjoys superior operating profits. Its other markets are fragmented, competition is greater and therefore margins are lower. Can any segments be combined for external reporting purposes?

It would not be possible to combine operating segments with different underlying currency risks, as this is indicative of different economic characteristics. That would leave only France, Germany and Italy as candidates for combination, since they all operate within the Euro zone. However, Germany could not be included in a larger reportable segment because, whilst similar in all other ways, its long-term financial performance is not comparable to France and Italy, as evidenced by its superior operating profits. On this basis the company could only combine at this stage its operations in France and Italy for external segment reporting purposes.

It is important that entities do not overlook the requirement for operating segments to exhibit similar economic characteristics before considering the other factors allowing aggregation. The fact that certain operating segments have been selected by management as a separately reportable component of activities in the business would suggest that there are good commercial reasons why their performance is monitored separately by the chief operating decision maker and, therefore, might usefully be reported separately to users of the financial statements. Only if those components exhibit similar economic characteristics does their aggregation not compromise the entity's ability to achieve the core principle of IFRS 8, to disclose information that is useful to users of its financial statements. *[IFRS 8.BC32].*

As can be seen in the above example, operating segments trading in clearly different economic environments (for example with unrelated functional currencies) should not be combined for segment reporting purposes (unless they are so small as to fall within the 'all other segments' category discussed at 3.2.4 below). The Standard states that the existence of similar long-term average gross margins would be a positive indicator. *[IFRS 8.12]*. This implies that operating segments should not be combined if their long-term average gross margins are significantly different, even if they are similar in all the other respects noted above. While IFRS 8 refers to the long-term average gross margin as an example, other measures of operating performance may be more relevant to determining economic similarity if that measure is used by the CODM.

It follows that operating segments that have been profitable over the longer term should not be combined with segments that over the longer term have been consistently loss-making.

In a response to a submission, the Interpretations Committee has acknowledged that IFRS 8 could usefully include further guidance on the meaning of 'similar economic characteristics' and the criteria for identifying similar segments listed in (a) to (e) above.[7] In a move to improve the Standard in this area, the IASB proposed to enhance the disclosures on the aggregation of segments (see 5.1.1 below).

3.2.2 Quantitative thresholds – operating segments which are reportable because of their size

IFRS 8 includes a number of quantitative measures for determining whether information on the identified operating segments should be reported separately. Accordingly, an operating segment (or combination of segments meeting the qualitative criteria for aggregation described at 3.2.1 above) merits separate disclosure if it meets any of the following thresholds:

(a) its reported revenue (including both sales to external customers and intersegment sales or transfers) is 10% or more of the combined revenue (internal and external) of all operating segments; or

(b) its reported profit or loss is, in absolute terms, 10% or more of the greater of:

  (i) the combined profit of all operating segments that did not report a loss; or

  (ii) the combined loss of all operating segments that reported a loss; or

(c) its assets are 10% or more of the combined assets of all operating segments. *[IFRS 8.13]*.

The definition of an operating segment includes a component of an entity earning revenues and incurring expenses relating to transactions with other components of the same entity. *[IFRS 8.5]*. Therefore an entity would have to report separately information on an operating segment that exceeds the above criteria, even if that segment earns a majority of its revenues from transactions with other components of the same entity.

Example 32.4: Identifying reportable segments using the quantitative thresholds

An entity divides its business into 9 operating units for internal reporting purposes and presents information to the Chief Operating Decision Maker as follows:

	Unit 1	Unit 2	Unit 3	Unit 4	Unit 5	Unit 6	Unit 7	Unit 8	Unit 9	Total
	£000	£000	£000	£000	£000	£000	£000	£000	£000	£000
Revenue:										
External	34,000	3,000	15,000	30,000	35,000	35,000	77,500	55,500	25,000	310,000
Internal	35,000	34,000	12,500	2,200	0	1,500	7,800	2,300	0	95,300
Total	69,000	37,000	27,500	32,200	35,000	36,500	85,300	57,800	25,000	405,300
Profit/(loss)	21,500	24,500	(4,500)	2,300	10,000	7,500	3,500	35,000	(21,250)	78,550
Assets	12,250	77,800	25,000	24,000	40,000	7,730	145,000	55,000	4,300	391,080

Assuming that none are eligible for aggregation under the qualitative aggregation criteria set out at 3.2.1 above, which units are required to be reported as operating segments in the entity's financial statements?

Applying the above quantitative thresholds, Units 1, 2, 5, 7, 8 and 9 should be identified as reportable segments, as follows:

- A Unit whose internal and external revenue is 10% or more of the total revenue of all segments is a reportable segment. On this criterion Unit 1 (17%), Unit 7 (21%) and Unit 8 (14%) are reportable segments.
- A Unit is a reportable segment if its profit or loss, in absolute terms, is 10% or more of the greater of the combined profits of all profitable segments or the combined losses of all segments in loss. The combined profit of all profitable segments is £104.3m, which is greater than the total of £25.75m for segments in loss. On this basis, Unit 1 (21%), Unit 2 (23%), Unit 8 (34%) and the loss-making Unit 9 (20%) are reportable segments.
- A Unit is also a reportable segment if the measure of assets reported to the chief operating decision maker is 10% or more of the total reported measure of assets of all segments. On this test, Unit 5 (10%) joins the list of reportable segments, with Unit 2 (20%), Unit 7 (37%) and Unit 8 (14%) having been already identified under other criteria.

Only those segments that have similar economic characteristics (demonstrated, for example, by similar long-term average gross margins) and are similar in all of the qualitative criteria set out at 3.2.1 above could be combined into a larger segment for reporting purposes.

Even if an internally reported operating segment falls below all of the quantitative thresholds, it may still be considered as reportable, and separately disclosed, if management believes information about the segment would be useful to users of the financial statements. *[IFRS 8.13]*. Where information about segment assets is not disclosed under IFRS 8 because it is not provided regularly to the CODM, *[IFRS 8.23]*, it would be appropriate to ignore criterion (c) above for determining the reportable segments.

3.2.3 Combining small operating segments into a larger reportable segment

Operating segments which individually fall below the size criteria may be combined with other small operating segments into a single larger reporting segment provided that:

(a) the operating segments being combined have similar economic characteristics; and

(b) they share a majority (rather than all) of the criteria listed at 3.2.1 above. *[IFRS 8.14]*.

For the avoidance of doubt, if an entity proposes to combine a small operating segment with one that exceeds any of the quantitative thresholds, they must share all of the criteria described at 3.2.1 above. The requirement that combining segments must demonstrate similar economic characteristics applies to combinations of both larger and smaller operating segments into reportable segments, without exception. Therefore, irrespective of their size, operating segments cannot be combined if they do not meet the criteria in 3.2.1.

3.2.4 'All other segments'

At this stage the entity has been divided into a single set of components, based on the elements reported to the chief operating decision maker. Components (operating segments) have been combined where permitted by the Standard and the entity has identified a number of individual operating segments or groups of operating segments that are required to be disclosed separately in the financial statements because each exceeds the quantitative thresholds for a reportable segment. The entity may then be left with a number of operating segments which have not been identified as being reportable, as well as other business activities that are not an operating segment or part of an operating segment.

Information about other business activities and operating segments that are not reportable should be combined and disclosed in a separate category for 'all other segments'. *[IFRS 8.16]*. However, this residual category cannot be too large. If total external revenue for the operating segments already reported separately is less than 75% of the entity's revenue, the entity should identify additional operating segments for external reporting until the 75% target is reached. In this situation segments would have to be reported separately even if they fall below the quantitative thresholds described at 3.2.2 above and are not otherwise regarded as being significant. *[IFRS 8.15]*.

There is no requirement to identify as a reportable segment the next largest internally reported operating segment. The choice of additional reporting segments is aimed simply to reach the 75% threshold, as illustrated below.

Example 32.5: Reaching the threshold of 75% of external revenue

In Example 32.4 above, Units 1, 2, 5, 7, 8 and 9 were identified as reportable segments. The total external revenue attributable to these reportable segments is £230m. This is only 74.2% of total external revenues and therefore less than the required 75% of total external revenue of £310m.

The entity is therefore required to identify additional segments as reportable segments, even if they do not meet the quantitative thresholds at 3.2.2 above. Unit 3, with external revenue of £15m (4.8%), Unit 4's external revenue of £30m (9.7%) and Unit 6's external revenue of £35m (11.3%) would each take the total above the required 75%. The entity can choose to present any of these as a reportable segment, leaving the others to be combined to form the item for 'all other segments'.

The 'all other segments' category must be presented separately from other reconciling items. *[IFRS 8.16]*. This raises the question whether headquarters, treasury and similar central functions (sometimes referred to as 'corporate items') should be included in 'all other segments' or in the reconciliation. In practice, the headquarters activities and its related accounting effects will not always be allocated to the operating segments for internal reporting purposes. The description of 'all other segments' refers to 'other business activities and operating segments'. *[IFRS 8.16]*. It could be argued that central functions are not business activities, but support functions which should be part of the reconciliation. On the other hand, they could be regarded as incidental business activities. There is no guidance to suggest that either presentation is ruled out by the Standard.

3.2.5 *A 'practical limit' for the number of reported operating segments*

IFRS 8 states that there may be a practical limit to the number of separately reportable segments beyond which segment information may become too detailed. Without prescribing such a limit, it suggests that an entity expecting to disclose more than 10 separate reportable segments should consider whether the practical limit has been reached. *[IFRS 8.19]*.

3.2.6 *Restatement of segments reported in comparative periods*

When an operating segment is identified for the first time as a reportable segment in accordance with the thresholds at 3.2.2 above, the prior period segment data that is presented for comparative purposes should be restated to reflect the newly reportable segment regardless of whether it would have satisfied the quantitative thresholds in the prior period. Only if the necessary information is not available and the cost to develop it would be excessive would prior periods not be restated. *[IFRS 8.18]*.

4 MEASUREMENT

For an entity that does not present IFRS-compliant financial information to its chief operating decision maker, the measurement regime in IFRS 8 means that the values disclosed for segment revenue, profit or loss, and (when reported) assets or liabilities could be very different to those reported elsewhere in the financial statements. For example, management might include gains on sale of property, plant and equipment in its measure of segment revenue but not be permitted to do so in its financial statements. *[IAS 16.68]*.

There is no requirement in IFRS 8 for segment information to be prepared in conformity with the accounting policies used to present the financial statements of the consolidated group or entity. IFRS 8 requires amounts reported to be the same as those measures used by the chief operating decision maker for determining resource allocation and for assessing performance. *[IFRS 8.25]*. This requirement is interpreted strictly. For example, unless adjustments and eliminations made in preparing the financial statements are reflected in the information used by the chief operating decision maker, an entity is prohibited from restating reported segment profit or loss for those adjustments and eliminations. In addition, the Standard prohibits any further allocation of revenues, expenses and gains and losses in determining segment profit or loss unless that measure is used by the chief operating decision maker. *[IFRS 8.25]*. IFRS 8 does not require symmetry between the revenues and expenses included in segment result and the assets and liabilities allocated to segments; it simply requires disclosure of the nature and effect of any asymmetrical allocations to reportable segments, for example when depreciation expense is reflected in segment profit or loss, but the related depreciable assets are not allocated to that segment. *[IFRS 8.27(f)]*. Only those assets and liabilities taken into account by the chief operating decision maker will be included in assets and liabilities reported for that segment. *[IFRS 8.25]*.

The amounts presented for segment revenue, profit or loss, assets and liabilities need bear no relationship to the values reported elsewhere in the financial statements, if the *only* measure of each that is used by the chief operating decision maker is not prepared in accordance with the entity's accounting policies or even under IFRS. *[IFRS 8.26].* However, there is a constraint on this otherwise 'free-for-all', since in those cases where a number of measures of segment profit or loss, assets or liabilities are used by the chief operating decision maker, an entity is required to select for its segment disclosures the measurements that are most consistent with those used in preparing the financial statements. *[IFRS 8.26].* A key judgement that can significantly affect the segment disclosures reported in the financial statements arises when an entity seeks to distinguish information used by the chief operating decision maker for determining resource allocation and for assessing performance from other information and supporting detail which is regularly provided. Whether, for example, it is appropriate to ignore IFRS-compliant measures provided to the chief operating decision maker on the basis that they are not used for determining resource allocation and for assessing performance depends on the facts and circumstances supporting that assertion. Nevertheless, it might be appropriate to apply a rebuttable presumption that management effort is not normally wasted in providing the chief operating decision maker with information that is not used.

Instead of defining the elements of segment information to be disclosed and requiring that they be prepared under the same policies and principles applied in producing the financial statements, IFRS 8 requires an entity to explain how it has measured segment profit or loss and segment assets and liabilities for each reportable segment and to reconcile this to the information reported under IFRS. *[IFRS 8.27].* These requirements are discussed at 5.5 and 5.6 below.

5 INFORMATION TO BE DISCLOSED ABOUT REPORTABLE SEGMENTS

IFRS 8 establishes a general principle for an entity to disclose information to enable users of its financial statements to evaluate the nature and financial effects of the types of business activities in which the entity engages and the economic environments in which it operates. *[IFRS 8.20].* This principle is met by disclosing the following information for each period for which a statement of comprehensive income or separate income statement is presented:

(a) general information on segments identified for reporting;

(b) reported segment profit or loss, including information about specified revenues and expenses included in reported segment profit or loss, segment assets and segment liabilities (if reported to the CODM) and the basis of measurement; and

(c) reconciliations of the totals of segment revenues, reported segment profit or loss, segment assets, segment liabilities and other material segment items to the corresponding entity amounts in the financial statements. *[IFRS 8.21].*

Reconciliations of amounts reported in the statement of financial position for reportable segments are required as at each date for which a statement of financial position is presented. *[IFRS 8.21]*.

These requirements are addressed in more detail below and the information described therein should be given separately for each segment determined to be reportable using the process set out at 3.2 above. *[IFRS 8.11]*.

As discussed at 3.1.2 above, the identification of the chief operating decision maker can be a critical judgment in applying IFRS 8 because of its potential impact on what information is considered for disclosure. However, there is no explicit requirement in the Standard to identify the CODM. When in 2011, the Interpretations Committee and the IASB considered a request to amend the Standard to require disclosure, they decided to defer this issue until the completion of the Post-implementation Review of IFRS 8 rather than through an interpretation or annual improvement.[8] The results of the Post-implementation Review are discussed at 7 below. In our view, it would be good practice to disclose the individual or group identified as CODM.

5.1 General information about reportable segments

The factors used to identify reportable segments should be described. This would include an explanation of the entity's basis of organisation, for example whether management has chosen to organise the entity by different products and services, by geographical area, by regulatory environment or by applying a combination of factors. The description would also indicate whether operating segments have been aggregated. The general information on reportable segments would include a description of the types of products and services from which each reportable segment derives its revenues. *[IFRS 8.22]*. The disclosures should also include a description of the sources of the revenue classified in the 'all other segments' category. *[IFRS 8.16]*.

In Extract 32.3 below, Daimler describes how its activities have been segmented into its principal business activities and specific product lines.

Extract 32.3: Daimler AG (2011)

Notes to the Consolidated Financial Statements [extract]

32. Segment reporting [extract]

Reportable segments. The reportable segments of the Group are Mercedes-Benz Cars, Daimler Trucks, Mercedes-Benz Vans, Daimler Buses and Daimler Financial Services. The segments are largely organized and managed separately according to nature of products and services provided, brands, distribution channels and profile of customers.

The vehicle segments develop and manufacture passenger cars and off-road vehicles, trucks, vans and buses. Mercedes-Benz Cars sells its passenger cars and off-road vehicles under the brand names Mercedes-Benz, smart and Maybach. Daimler Trucks distributes its trucks under the brand names Mercedes-Benz, Freightliner, Western Star and Fuso. The vans of the Mercedes-Benz Vans segment are primarily sold under the brand name Mercedes-Benz. Daimler Buses sells completely built-up buses under the brand names Mercedes-Benz, Setra and Orion. In addition, Daimler Buses produces and sells bus chassis. The vehicle segments also sell related spare parts and accessories.

The Daimler Financial Services segment supports the sales of the Group's vehicle segments worldwide. Its product portfolio mainly comprises tailored financing and leasing packages for customers and dealers. The segment also provides services such as insurance, fleet management, investment products and credit cards.

5.1.1 Proposed improvements to IFRS 8 in relation to disclosure of how operating segments are aggregated

As discussed at 3.2.1 above, the aggregation of operating segments is a significant judgement by an entity, since IFRS 8 does not elaborate on the economic characteristics that should be considered and how similarity is determined, except for reference to similar long-term financial performance. *[IFRS 8.12].* This matter was referred to the Interpretations Committee by the European Securities and Markets Authority (ESMA). In its exposure draft, *Annual Improvements to IFRSs 2010-2012 Cycle* (ED/2012/1), the IASB (based on IFRIC's recommendation) proposed that additional disclosures be provided in this respect. In February 2013, the IASB tentatively agreed to finalise this proposal.[9] Accordingly, it is expected that IFRS 8 will be amended to require disclosure of the judgements made by management in applying the aggregation criteria in the Standard. In particular, entities should identify the operating segments that have been combined and the economic indicators that were considered in determining that they share similar economic characteristics.[10]

The proposals in the Exposure Draft had cited profit margin spreads and sales growth rates as examples of economic indicators to consider in addition to the existing reference in the Standard to the long-term average gross margin.[11] In response to comments from respondents to the Exposure Draft, it was agreed that the application of the aggregation criteria requires significant judgement and it is management who should specify the economic indicators that have been evaluated (whether qualitative or quantitative). Therefore, it was decided that examples would not be given in the final amendment.[12]

In our view, other economic measures of operating performance, such as sales metrics, return on investment, or other standard industry measures, including earnings before interest, taxes, depreciation and amortisation (EBITDA), may be equally relevant to determining economic similarity if such measures are used by the CODM. Qualitative indicators would take into account the economic risks involved. In addition to currency risks, this might include operating risks and the economic and political circumstances relevant to the activities of the operating segment.

Another aspect of the analysis is whether to consider future prospects and developments. Entities should look to past and present performance as indicators that segments are expected to have the same future prospects. Also companies should consider any additional information or knowledge regarding relevant trends (e.g. sales or growth trends) that may have an effect on future operating performance. In other words, if operating segments do not currently have similar gross margins and sales trends but the operating segments are expected again to have similar long-term average gross margins and sales trends, it may be appropriate to aggregate the two operating segments (provided all other criteria are met). Conversely, if operating segments happen to have similar gross margins or sales trends in a given year but it is not expected that the similar gross margins or sales trends will continue in the future, the operating segments should be not aggregated for the current-year segment disclosures just because current economic measures happen to be similar.

Under the current Standard, Bayer includes the following disclosure in its report on the first quarter 2012 about the combination of various activities:

Extract 32.4: Bayer AG (2012)

CONDENSED CONSOLIDATED INTERIM FINANCIAL STATEMENTS AS OF MARCH 31, 2012 [extract]

Explanatory Notes [extract]

SEGMENT REPORTING [extract]

Since the second quarter of 2011, the CropScience subgroup has been presented as a single reportable segment. This resulted from organizational changes undertaken to more closely align Crop Protection and BioScience and integrate the steering of these businesses. The Crop Protection/BioScience and Environmental Science operating segments are combined into a single reportable segment because they show a similar long-term economic performance, have comparable products, production processes, customer industries and distribution channels, operate in the same regulatory environment, and are steered and monitored together. The strategic business entity "Diagnostic Imaging," comprising contrast agents for imaging applications such as X-ray and MRI, was transferred at the end of 2011 from the Specialty Medicine business unit (Pharmaceuticals segment) to the Medical Care Division (Consumer Health segment) for organizational reasons and combined with the related injection systems into a single business unit. The prior-year figures have been restated accordingly.

It remains to be seen how disclosure practice will evolve once IFRS 8 is amended.

5.2 A measure of segment profit or loss, total assets and total liabilities

For each reportable segment, an entity is required to disclose a measure of profit or loss for each segment. An entity is also required to disclose a measure of total assets and total liabilities for each reportable segment, but only if such amounts are regularly provided to the chief operating decision maker. *[IFRS 8.23]*. This 'measure' means segment profit or loss and segment assets and liabilities as defined in the information used by the chief operating decision maker.

5.2.1 Other measures of segment performance

Entities typically use not only a measure of profit or loss, but also a combination of different financial and non-financial key performance indicators to assess performance of their operating segments and allocate resources to them. Examples include key measures based on capital invested like return on capital employed (ROCE), free cash flow or orders on hand. Since these are not measures of profit or loss, they would not need to be disclosed. However, the Standard does not prohibit their disclosure.

Siemens includes measures of new orders and free cash flow in its segment information as shown in Extract 32.5 below.

Chapter 32

Extract 32.5: Siemens AG (2011)

D.6 Notes to Consolidated Financial Statements [extract]

Segment information (continuing operations) [extract]

As of and for the fiscal years ended September 30, 2011 and 2010 [extract]

(in millions of €)	*New orders[1]*		Free cash flow[4]	
	2011	*2010*	2011	2010
Sectors				
Industry	*37,594*	*30,243*	3,475	3,208
Energy	*34,765*	*30,122*	2,937	4,322
Healthcare	*13,116*	*12,872*	1,887	2,296
Total Sectors	***85,476***	***73,237***	**8,299**	**9,826**
Equity Investments	–	–	116	402
Financial Services (SFS)	*961*	*787*	344	330
Reconciliation to Consolidated Financial Statements				
Centrally managed portfolio activities	*473*	*760*	(86)	(155)
Siemens Real Estate (SRE)	*2,204*	*1,941*	(240)	9
Corporate items and pensions	*449*	*606*	(1,168)	(1,069)
Eliminations, Corporate Treasury and other reconciling items	*(3,982)*	*(3,275)*	(1,381)	(2,300)
Siemens	***85,582***	***74,055***	**5,885**	**7,043**

1 This supplementary information on New Orders is provided on a voluntary basis. It is not part of the Consolidated Financial Statements subject to the audit opinion.

4 Free cash flow represents net cash provided by (used in) operating activities less additions to intangible assets and property, plant and equipment. Free cash flow of the Sectors, Equity Investments and Centrally managed portfolio activities primarily exclude income tax, financing interest and certain pension related payments and proceeds. Free cash flow of SFS, a financial services business, and of SRE includes related financing interest payments and proceeds; income tax payments and proceeds of SFS and SRE are excluded.

Due to rounding, numbers presented may not add up precisely to totals provided.

5.3 Disclosure of other elements of revenue, income and expense

The following items should also be disclosed about each reportable segment if the specified amounts are included in the measure of segment profit or loss reviewed by the chief operating decision maker or are otherwise regularly provided in respect of those segments to the chief operating decision maker (even if not included in that measure of segment profit or loss):

(a) revenues from external customers;

(b) revenues from transactions with other operating segments of the same entity;

(c) interest revenue;

(d) interest expense;

(e) depreciation and amortisation;

(f) material items of income and expense disclosed in accordance with paragraph 97 of IAS 1 – *Presentation of Financial Statements*;

(g) the entity's interest in the profit or loss of associates and joint ventures accounted for by the equity method;

(h) income tax expense or income; and

(i) material non-cash items other than depreciation and amortisation. *[IFRS 8.23].*

Interest revenue should be reported separately from interest expense for each reportable segment unless a majority of the segment's revenues are from interest and the chief operating decision maker relies primarily on net interest revenue to assess the performance of the segment and make decisions on the allocation of resources to it. In that case, the entity can report net interest revenue or expense for the segment provided that it discloses it has done so. *[IFRS 8.23]*.

Where the measure of segment profit or loss is determined after deducting depreciation and amortisation, these amounts will have to be disclosed separately for purposes of segment reporting, even if they are not separately reported to the CODM.

It can be seen that whilst IFRS 8 indicates the line items of income or expense or other information that might merit disclosure by segment, what an entity actually reports in its financial statements is determined by the line items used by the chief operating decision maker to define segment profit or loss and segment assets or liabilities, together with the other information otherwise regularly provided to the chief operating decision maker. *[IFRS 8.23-24]*. This means that different entities (even those with very similar activities) will make different disclosures, depending on what information is provided to the chief operating decision maker. Indeed, what is disclosed by one entity for each of its reportable segments might vary because, for example, the result of one segment is determined after deducting interest whilst that of other segments is drawn before interest; or because the information provided to the chief operating decision maker about one segment includes equity-accounted associates but for other segments does not. As such the disclosures made by an entity are tailored according to exactly what appears in the information presented to the chief operating decision maker.

Statoil provides segment disclosures based on its internal management reporting, with reportable segments determined based on differences in the nature of their operations, products and services, as follows:

Extract 32.6: Statoil ASA (2011)

Notes to the Consolidated Financial Statements [extract]

8.1.4 Segments [extract]

Segment data for the years 31 December 2011, 2010 and 2009 is presented below: [extract]

(in NOK million)	Development and Production Norway	Development and Production International	Marketing, Processing and Renewable Energy	Fuel and Retail	Other	Eliminations	Total
Year ended 31 December 2011							
Revenues third party and Other income	7,861	25,158	564,139	70,779	1,004	0	668,941
Revenues inter-segment	204,181	44,810	45,674	2,904	1	(297,570)	0
Net income (loss) from associated companies	60	953	163	3	85	0	1,264
Total revenues and other income	212,102	70,921	609,976	73,686	1,090	(297,570)	670,205
Net operating income	152,713	32,821	24,743	1,869	(256)	(106)	211,784

Chapter 32

Significant non-cash items recognised in segment profit or loss							
– Depreciation and amortisation	29,577	15,933	2,762	1,169	759	0	50,200
– Net impairment losses (reversals)	0	(2,098)	3,248	0	0	0	1,150
– Unrealised (gain) loss on commodity derivatives	(5,580)	(12)	(3,629)	0	0	0	(9,221)
– Exploration expenditure written off	1,064	467	0	0	0	0	1,531
Investments in associated companies	153	5,529	2,684	49	802	0	9,217
Other segment non-current assets*	211,632	239,378	34,443	10,814	3,992	0	500,259
Assets classified as held for sale	0	0	0	0	0	0	0
Non-current assets, not allocated to segments*							61,043
Total non-current assets and assets classified as held for sale							570,519
Additions to PP&E and intangible assets**	41,490	84,339	4,716	1,479	1,590	0	133,614

* Deferred tax assets, post employment benefit assets and non-current financial instruments are not allocated to segments.

** Excluding movements due to changes in asset retirement obligations.

5.4 Additional disclosures relating to segment assets

If any of the following items are either included in the measure of segment assets reviewed by the chief operating decision maker or otherwise regularly provided in respect of those segments (whether included in segment assets or not), an entity should also disclose for each segment:

(a) the investment in equity-accounted associates and joint ventures; and

(b) total expenditures for additions to non-current assets other than financial instruments, deferred tax assets, post-employment benefit assets and rights arising under insurance contracts. *[IFRS 8.24].*

5.5 Explanation of the measurements used in segment reporting

As noted at 4 above, instead of prescribing how an entity should calculate the amounts reported in its segmental disclosures, IFRS 8 requires an entity to explain how its measures of segment profit or loss, segment assets and segment liabilities have been determined. As a minimum, the following information is required:

(a) the basis of accounting for any transactions between reportable segments;

(b) if not apparent from the required reconciliations (see 5.6 below), the nature of any differences between the measurement of total reported segment profit or loss and the entity's profit or loss before income taxes and discontinued operations;

(c) the nature of any differences between the measurements of total reported segment assets and the entity's assets, if not apparent from the required reconciliations;

(d) the nature of any differences between the measurements of total reported segment liabilities and the entity's liabilities, if not apparent from the required reconciliations;

(e) the nature of any changes from prior periods in the measurement methods used to determine segment profit or loss, including the financial effect, if any, of those changes; and

(f) the nature and effect of any asymmetrical allocations to reportable segments, such as where depreciation is included in segment profit but the related property, plant and equipment is not included in segment assets. *[IFRS 8.27].*

The kind of disclosures in (b), (c) and (d) above that are necessary for an understanding of the reported segment information could relate to the accounting policies used, including policies for the allocation of centrally incurred costs in arriving at segment profit or loss and for the allocation of jointly used assets and liabilities in determining segment assets and segment liabilities. *[IFRS 8.27].* Other examples might include the use of previous local GAAP numbers, where internal reporting does not reflect the entity's move to IFRS, or the use of budgeted figures, for example when applying budgeted or constant foreign currency rates.

In Extract 32.7 below, Daimler confirms that segment information is prepared using the same accounting policies as the IFRS financial statements, describes how 'EBIT' is the measure of segment profit or loss and explains how segment assets and liabilities are determined.

Extract 32.7: Daimler AG (2011)

Notes to the Consolidated Financial Statements [extract]

32. Segment reporting [extract]

Management reporting and controlling systems. The Group's management reporting and controlling systems principally use accounting policies that are the same as those described in Note 1 in the summary of significant accounting policies under IFRS.

The Group measures the performance of its operating segments through a measure of segment profit or loss which is referred to as "EBIT" in our management and reporting system.

EBIT is the measure of segment profit/loss used in segment reporting and comprises gross profit, selling and general administrative expenses, research and non-capitalized development costs, other operating income and expense, and our share of profit/loss from investments accounted for using the equity method, net, as well as other financial income/expense, net.

Intersegment revenue is generally recorded at values that approximate third-party selling prices.

Segment assets principally comprise all assets. The industrial business segments' assets exclude income tax assets, assets from defined pension benefit plans and other post-employment benefit plans and certain financial assets (including liquidity).

Segment liabilities principally comprise all liabilities. The industrial business segments' liabilities exclude income tax liabilities, liabilities from defined pension benefit plans and other post-employment benefit plans and certain financial liabilities (including financing liabilities).

Pursuant to risk sharing agreements between Daimler Financial Services and the respective vehicle segments the residual value risks associated with the Group's operating leases and its finance lease receivables are primarily borne by the vehicle segments that manufactured the leased equipment. The terms of the risk sharing arrangement vary by segment and geographic region.

Non-current assets comprise of intangible assets, property plant and equipment and equipment on operating leases.

Capital expenditures for property, plant and equipment and intangible assets reflect the cash effective additions to these property, plant and equipment and intangible assets as far as they do not relate to capitalized borrowing costs or goodwill and finance leases.

The effects of certain legal proceedings are excluded from the operative results and liabilities of the segments, if such items are not indicative of the segments' performance, since their related results of operations may be distorted by the amount and the irregular nature of such events. This may also be the case for items that refer to more than one reportable segment.

If the Group hedges investments in associated companies for strategic reasons, the related financial assets and earnings effects are generally not allocated to the segments. They are included in the reconciliation to Group figures as corporate items.

With respect to information about geographical regions, revenue is allocated to countries based on the location of the customer; non-current assets are disclosed according to the physical location of these assets.

In its 2008 financial statements, Roche provided a detailed explanation of the basis of accounting for transactions between reportable segments.

Extract 32.8: Roche Holding Limited (2008)

Notes to the Roche Group Consolidated Financial Statements [extract]

1. **Summary of significant accounting policies** [extract]

Segment reporting

Within the Group's consolidated financial statements, transactions and balances between consolidated subsidiaries, such as between Genentech, Chugai and other Roche Group subsidiaries, are eliminated on consolidation.

Genentech and Chugai are considered separately reportable operating segments for the purposes of the Group's operating segment disclosures in Note 2. Additional information relating to Genentech and Chugai results is given in Notes 3 and 4, respectively.

Profits on product sales between the Roche Pharmaceuticals, Genentech and Chugai operating segments are recorded as part of the segment results of the operating segment making the sale. Unrealised internal profits on inventories that have been sold by one operating segment to another but which have not yet been sold on to external customers as at the balance sheet date are eliminated as a consolidation entry at a Pharmaceuticals Division level.

Additionally the results of each operating segment may include income received from another operating segment in respect of:

- Royalties
- Licensing, milestone and other upfront payments
- Transfers in respect of research collaborations

These are recognised as income in the segment results of the operating segment receiving the income consistently with the accounting policies applied to third-party transactions and set out in these financial statements. Corresponding expenses are recorded in the other operating segment so that these eliminate at a Pharmaceuticals Division level.

5.6 Reconciliations

Reconciliations are required of all the following:

(a) the total of revenue from reportable segments to the entity's revenue;

(b) the total profit or loss for reportable segments to the entity's profit or loss before income taxes and discontinued operations. Where items such as income taxes have been allocated to arrive at segment profit or loss, the reconciliation can be made to the entity's profit or loss after those items;

(c) if segment assets are reported (see 5.2 above), the total of the reportable segments' assets to the entity's assets;

(d) if segment liabilities are reported (see 5.2 above), the total of reportable segments' liabilities to the entity's liabilities; and

(e) for every other material item of information the entity chooses to give in its segment information, the total of each item from all reportable segments to the corresponding amount for the entity. *[IFRS 8.28]*.

In each of the above reconciliations an entity must separately identify and describe all material reconciling items. For example, when reconciling segment profit or loss to the entity's profit or loss before income taxes and discontinued operations, each material adjustment arising from differences in accounting policies would have to be separately identified and described. *[IFRS 8.28]*. In addition, IFRS 8 requires information about the 'all other segments' category to be shown separately from other reconciling items. *[IFRS 8.16]*.

National Australia Bank evaluates the performance of operating segments on the basis of cash earnings. This post-tax measure of the profit or loss of reportable segments is reconciled to the consolidated financial statements as follows:

Extract 32.9: National Australia Bank Limited (2012)

Notes to the financial statements [extract]

2 **Segment information** [extract]

Reconciliations between reportable segment information and statutory results are as follows [extract]

The tables below reconcile the information in the segment tables presented above, which have been prepared on a cash earnings basis, to the relevant statutory information presented in the Financial Report. In addition to the sum of the reportable segments, the cash earnings basis includes the segments that do not meet the threshold to be reportable segments and intra group eliminations. The NAB Wealth net adjustment represents a reallocation of the income statement of the NAB Wealth business prepared on a cash earnings basis into the appropriate statutory income statement lines.

[...]

	Group	
	2012	2011
	$m	$m
Cash earnings		
Group cash earnings[1]	**5,433**	5,460
Non-cash earnings items (after tax)		
Distributions	**207**	225
Treasury shares	**(155)**	39
Fair value and hedge ineffectiveness	**(265)**	(181)
IoRE discount rate variation	**16**	26
Hedging costs on SCDO assets	**(99)**	(127)
Property revaluation	**(5)**	–
Litigation expense	**(101)**	(4)
Amortisation of acquired intangible assets	**(99)**	(82)
Customer redress provision	**(239)**	(117)
Impairment of goodwill and software	**(349)**	–
Restructure Costs	**(174)**	–
Due diligence, acquisition and integration costs	**(88)**	(162)
Refund of tax on exchangeable capital units (ExCaps) settlement	**–**	142
Net profit attributable to owners of the Company	**4,082**	5,219

[1] *Includes eliminations and distributions*

Chapter 32

5.7 Restatement of previously reported information

Entities may need to change their organisation to respond to their business needs. This may have an impact on the entity's segment reporting. IFRS 8 provides explicit guidance if such a change in the organisation changes the composition of its reportable segments. However, it does not explicitly address any changes that impact reportable segments, such as a change in segment measures. This is discussed further below.

5.7.1 Changes in organisation structure

When an entity changes its organisational structure in a manner that causes a change in the composition of its reportable segments, corresponding amounts for earlier periods should be restated unless the information is not available and the cost to develop it would be excessive. This requirement also applies to the presentation of segment information in respect of interim periods. *[IFRS 8.29].*

The exemption from restatement on grounds of excessive cost is applied to each individual item of disclosure. *[IFRS 8.29].* This means that an entity should restate its comparative information for all the items it can, even if this results in some comparative information not being presented or restated, such as inter-segment revenues. When the composition of reportable segments has changed, an entity should disclose whether the corresponding items of segment information have been restated. *[IFRS 8.29].*

Where corresponding information is not restated to reflect the new composition of reportable segments, the segment information for the current period should be presented on both the old and the new bases of segmentation. Only if the necessary information were unavailable and the cost of developing it excessive would an entity not have to show current information on the old basis of segmentation. *[IFRS 8.30].*

If an entity decides to change its organisational structure during the reporting period, the fact that this requirement applies equally to interim periods *[IFRS 8.29]* indicates that information presented at the reporting date is also restated to reflect the new basis of segmentation, even though for part of the annual reporting period the entity was managed and monitored on the old basis.

One example for a disclosure about a change in segment reporting was presented above in Extract 32.4. A further example is the change described by SAP AG in Extract 32.10. This Extract illustrates that changes in the composition of operating segments will often be combined with a review of other aspects of segment reporting, such as a review of performance measures:

Extract 32.10: SAP AG (2012)

Notes to the consolidated financial statements [extract]

(28) SEGMENT AND GEOGRAPHIC INFORMATION [extract]

General Information [extract]

Following SAP's increased focus on the cloud business, in the 3rd quarter of 2012 we changed both the structure of the components that SAP management uses to make decisions about operating matters, and the main profit measure used for the purposes of allocating resources to these components and measuring their performance. The segment information for earlier periods has been restated to conform with these changes. As part of this realignment, the previous Consulting and Training segments have been aggregated into the On-Premise Services segment. Certain activities of the previous Consulting and Training segments were shifted to the On-Premise Product segment. Discrete financial information for the previous Consulting and Training segments is no longer used by SAP management.

Segment information may also change as a result of the disposal of an entire reportable segment or a component of it which qualifies under IFRS 5 – *Non-current Assets Held for Sale and Discontinued Operations* – as a discontinued operation. The presentation of discontinued operations is governed by IFRS 5. The requirements of other standards do not apply to discontinued operations, unless they specify disclosures applicable to them. *[IFRS 5.5B]*. Since IFRS 8 does not refer to discontinued operations, entities are not required to include them in their segment disclosures. This would be the case even if the CODM continued to monitor the discontinued operation until disposal. Nevertheless, an entity would not be prohibited from disclosing such information if it wished, on the basis that the requirements of IFRS 8 relate to the measures reported to the CODM without any adjustments being made in preparing the entity's IFRS financial statements. *[IFRS 8.25]*.

5.7.2 Changes in segment measures

When an entity changes any of its segment measures, including the definition of segment profit, or changes the allocation of income, expenses, assets or liabilities to segments, without a change to the composition of its reportable segments, the general principles of IAS 1 for changes in presentation or classification of items apply. Therefore, comparative information would be restated, unless this is impracticable. *[IAS 1.41]*.

Daimler changed the allocation of one of its equity interests as a result of a transaction:

Extract 32.11: Daimler AG (2011)

Notes to the Consolidated Financial Statements [extract]

7.29. Summarized IFRS financial information on investments accounted for using the equity method [extract]

Engine Holding/Tognum [extract]

With the completion of the public tender offer, the management of the Daimler Trucks segment assumed control of Daimler's equity interest in Engine Holding. Engine Holding was therefore allocated to the Daimler Trucks segment as of September 30, 2011. As a result, our equity interest in Tognum and our proportionate share of Tognum's profit or loss, which were previously presented in segment reporting in the reconciliation from the segments to the Group, are now also allocated to the Daimler Trucks segment. The prior-year figures have been adjusted accordingly.

5.8 Disclosure of commercially sensitive information

The criteria for determining the externally reportable segments, as discussed at 3.2 above, attempt to define which internally reported operating units can be combined, which must be reported separately and which are included in an unallocated reconciling item. The interaction between these criteria, in particular with the requirement that segments cannot be combined if they exhibit different long-term financial performance, leaves entities open to the risk of having to disclose information that management would be concerned about sharing with competitors, customers, suppliers or employees.

However, IFRS 8 does not permit the omission of segment information when management believes that its disclosure is commercially sensitive or potentially detrimental to the entity's competitive position. Indeed, IAS 1 requires an entity not only to present information in a manner that provides relevant, reliable, comparable and understandable information, but also to provide *additional* disclosures if compliance with an individual standard is insufficient to enable users to understand the entity's financial position and financial performance. *[IAS 1.17]*. The only justification for failing to meet these requirements is if disclosure would be so misleading that it would conflict with the objective of financial statements set out in the IASB's *Conceptual Framework*. *[IAS 1.19]*.

Given that the objective of IFRS 8 is to disclose information to help users of financial statements evaluate the nature and financial effects of the entity's business activities and the economic environments in which it operates, *[IFRS 8.1]*, this possibility would seem to be remote. The IASB rejected similar concerns raised by respondents to ED 8, noting that entities would be unlikely to suffer competitive harm from the required disclosures since most competitors have sources of detailed information about an entity other than its financial statements. *[IFRS 8.BC44]*.

6 ENTITY-WIDE DISCLOSURES FOR ALL ENTITIES

In addition to disclosing segment information derived from the formats and measurements presented to the chief operating decision maker, IFRS 8 requires certain entity-wide disclosures about products and services, geographical areas and major customers. The information described below is required even if the entity has only a single reportable segment, but need not be repeated if already provided as part of the disclosures on reportable segments set out above. *[IFRS 8.31]*. The amounts reported about products and services and about geographical areas in these entity-wide disclosures are measured using the same accounting policies and estimates as the entity's financial statements (i.e. IFRS amounts). *[IFRS 8.32-33]*. As such, the amounts disclosed in this part of the segment disclosures might well be different to the information already provided in other segment information, which might not be measured in accordance with IFRS (see 4 above).

Exemption from the requirements set out at 6.1 and 6.2 below is offered if the necessary information is unavailable and the cost to develop it would be excessive. If disclosure is not made on these grounds, that fact should be stated. *[IFRS 8.32-33]*. Some respondents to ED 8 expressed concern that the basis of this exemption was inconsistent with the test of impracticability in IAS 1, which makes no allowance for the cost of compliance. *[IAS 1.7]*. However, the IASB did not see any merit in divergence from FASB ASC Topic 280 in this respect and therefore retained the exemption from disclosure if the necessary information were unavailable and the cost of developing it excessive. *[IFRS 8.BC46-47]*.

This exemption is not available in respect of the disclosures about major customers set out at 6.3 below.

6.1 Information about products and services

An entity should report revenues from external customers for each product and service or for each group of similar products and services, measuring revenues on the same basis as the entity's financial statements. *[IFRS 8.32]*.

In Extract 32.6 at 5.3 above, Statoil provides segment disclosures based on its internal management reporting, with reportable segments relating to domestic and international exploration and production, natural gas and manufacturing activities. Accordingly, it also discloses external revenues by product group (and combines it with a geographical analysis of revenue), as follows:

Extract 32.12: Statoil ASA (2011)

Notes to the Consolidated Financial Statements [extract]

8.1.4 Segments [extract]

Geographical data for the year ended 31 December 2011, 2010 and 2009 is presented below: [extract]

(in NOK million)	**Crude oil**	**Gas**	**NGL**	**Refined Products**	**Other**	**Total Sale**
Year ended 31 December 2011						
Norway	269,457	87,713	58,757	62,368	38,089	516,384
USA	34,101	7,305	1,904	17,237	5,127	65,674
Sweden	0	0	0	17,699	4,953	23,652
Denmark	0	0	0	17,448	1,642	19,090
Other	11,586	3,946	1,606	14,036	13,967	45,141
Total revenues (excluding net income (loss) from associated companies)	315,144	98,964	62,267	128,788	63,778	668,941

6.2 Information about geographical areas

IFRS 8 requires disclosure of the following geographical information:

(a) revenues from external customers, analysed between amounts attributed to the entity's country of domicile and the total of those attributed to all foreign countries; and

(b) non-current assets other than financial instruments, deferred tax assets, post-employment benefit assets and rights arising under insurance contracts, analysed between assets located in the entity's country of domicile and the total of those located in all foreign countries. *[IFRS 8.33]*.

In addition, if revenues from external customers or assets attributed to an individual foreign country are material, separate disclosure of that country's revenues or assets is required. *[IFRS 8.33]*. The Standard does not indicate what might be regarded as 'material', but given the criteria for a reportable segment and a major customer for reporting purposes (see 3.2.2 above and 6.3 below respectively) it would seem appropriate to consider the need for separate disclosure in respect of a foreign country accounting for more than 10% of total external revenues or more than 10% of total non-current assets.

Disclosure of the above information would be required even if the entity's segment reporting is already based on geography and it is determined that individual operating segments include a number of countries. Thus, an entity may need to provide additional information on revenue or non-current assets by country that is not disclosed in the segment information used by the chief operating decision maker.

The basis on which revenues from external customers are attributed to individual countries should be disclosed. An entity can elect to provide, in addition to the information required above, subtotals of geographical information about groups of countries. *[IFRS 8.33]*. In Extract 32.13 below, BAE Systems provides this more detailed level of disclosure and goes on to reconcile the measure of total segment assets to the amounts shown on the statement of financial position, even though such a reconciliation is not required for this entity-wide disclosure.

Extract 32.13: BAE Systems plc (2012)

NOTES TO THE GROUP ACCOUNTS – BALANCE SHEET [extract]

20. Geographical analysis of assets

Analysis of non-current assets by geographical location

Asset location	**2012 £m**	2011 £m
United Kingdom	**2,402**	2,515
Rest of Europe	**707**	1,274
Saudi Arabia	**615**	703
United States	**9,464**	10,000
Australia	**599**	617
Rest of Asia and Pacific	**4**	7
Africa, Central and South America	**21**	24
Non-current reporting segment assets	**13,812**	15,140
Financial instruments	**104**	139
Inventories	**655**	716
Trade and other receivables	**2,873**	3,369
Total reporting segment assets	**17,444**	19,364
Tax	**1,386**	1,469
Pension prepayments	**47**	53
Assets held for sale	**20**	18
Cash (as defined by the Group)	**3,377**	2,197
Consolidated total assets	**22,274**	23,101

6.3 Information about major customers

IFRS 8 also requires an entity to give disclosures indicating the extent of its reliance on its major customers. If revenues from a single external customer account for 10% or more of the entity's total revenues, the entity should disclose:

(a) that fact;

(b) the total amount of revenues from each such customer; and

(c) the identity of the reportable segment or segments reporting the revenues. *[IFRS 8.34].*

Disclosure is not required of the name of each major customer, nor the amounts of revenue reported in each segment for that customer. However, the disclosure must be provided if it relates only to one segment.

Roche elects to provide the customers' names in the following extract.

Extract 32.14: Roche Holding Limited (2011)

Notes to the Roche Group Consolidated Financial Statements [extract]

2. Operating segment information [extract]

Major customers

The US national wholesale distributor, AmerisourceBergen Corp., represented approximately 5 billion Swiss francs (2010: 6 billion Swiss francs) of the Group's revenues. Approximately 99% of these revenues were in the Pharmaceuticals operating segment, with the residual in the Diagnostics segment. The Group also reported substantial revenues from the US national wholesale distributors, Cardinal Health, Inc. and McKesson Corp., and in total these three customers represented approximately a quarter of the Group's revenues.

6.3.1 *Customers known to be under common control*

For the purposes of the above disclosures, a group of entities known to a reporting entity to be under common control are to be considered a single customer. *[IFRS 8.34].*

However, judgement is required to assess whether a government (including government agencies and similar bodies whether local, national or international), and entities known to the reporting entity to be under the control of that government are considered a single customer. The assessment of whether entities should be regarded as a single customer for these purposes should take into account the extent of economic integration between those entities. *[IFRS 8.34].*

The requirement to exercise judgement to assess whether a government and entities controlled by that government should be regarded as a single customer was introduced as part of the revision of IAS 24 – *Related Party Disclosures* – which became effective for annual periods beginning on or after 1 January 2011. *[IFRS 8.36B].* Previously the Standard made no distinction between government-controlled and privately controlled entities, despite the fact that respondents to ED 8 had noted the difficulty presented by this requirement for an entity with a number of customers under common state control. *[IFRS 8.BC58].* The IASB's Project Summary on the revision of IAS 24 had stated that IASB staff had been asked to develop guidance on the factors relevant to determining the extent of economic integration,[13] but the final amendment was issued without it.

BAE Systems identifies revenues from three principal governments.

Extract 32.15: BAE Systems plc (2012)

NOTES TO THE GROUP ACCOUNTS – INCOME STATEMENT [extract]

1. **Segmental analysis** [extract]

Revenue by major customer

Revenue from the Group's three principal customers, which individually represent over 10% of total revenue, is as follows:

	2012 £m	2011 £m
UK Ministry of Defence[1]	**4,475**	4,802
US Department of Defense	**4,986**	5,675
Kingdom of Saudi Arabia Ministry of Defence and Aviation	**2,302**	2,276

Revenue from the UK Ministry of Defence and the US Department of Defense was generated by the five principal reporting segments. Revenue from the Kingdom of Saudi Arabia Ministry of Defence and Aviation was generated by the Platforms & Services (UK) and Platforms & Services (International) reporting segments.

[1]Includes £1.3bn (2011 £1.3bn) generated under the Typhoon work share agreement with Eurofighter Jagdflugzeug GmbH.

In its segment disclosures made under FASB ASC Topic 280, Lockheed Martin provides more detailed information about customer revenues by segment as well as total revenues for foreign governments and commercial customers.

Extract 32.16: Lockheed Martin Corporation (2012)

Notes to the consolidated financial statements [extract]

Note 3 Selected Financial Data by Business Segment [extract]

Net Sales by Customer Category

Net sales by customer category were as follows (in millions)

	2012	2011	2010
U.S. Government			
Aeronautics	**$ 11,587**	$10,749	$10,623
Information Systems & Global Solutions	**8,340**	8,769	9,488
Missiles and Fire Control	**5,224**	5,455	5,422
Mission Systems and Training	**5,685**	5,180	5,301
Space Systems	**7,952**	7,848	8,026
Total U.S. Government net sales	**$38,788**	$38,001	$38,860
International [(a)]			
Aeronautics	**$ 3,323**	$ 3,577	$ 2,458
Information Systems & Global Solutions	**380**	464	320
Missiles and Fire Control	**2,208**	1,977	1,480
Mission Systems and Training	**1,826**	1,906	2,082
Space Systems	**319**	144	97
Total international net sales	**$ 8,056**	$ 8,068	$ 6,437

U.S. Commercial and Other			
Aeronautics	**$ 43**	$ 36	$ 28
Information Systems & Global Solutions	**126**	148	113
Missiles and Fire Control	**25**	31	28
Mission Systems and Training	**68**	46	60
Space Systems	**76**	169	145
Total U.S. commercial and other net sales	**$ 338**	$ 430	$ 374
Total net sales	**$47,182**	$46,499	$45,671

(a) Sales made to other governments through the U.S. Government (i.e. foreign military sales) are included in the "International" category.

7 FUTURE DEVELOPMENTS

As discussed at 5.1.1 above, the exposure draft *Annual Improvements to IFRSs 2010-2012 Cycle* (ED/2012/1) proposes limited amendments to disclosures about the aggregation of operating segments. The finalisation of the amendments is planned for the last quarter of 2013.[14]

Further developments may result from the post-implementation review discussed at 7.1 below.

7.1 Post-implementation review

As noted at 1.1 above, IFRS 8 is the first standard to be subject to a post-implementation review (PIR), which was added to the IASB's due process by the Trustees in 2007. The first phase of the PIR consisted of an initial assessment of the issues related to IFRS 8 and consultation with interested parties about these issues. That initial phase identified the areas of focus to be considered. As a second step of the PIR, the IASB issued in July 2012 its first due process document, *Request for Information – Post-implementation Review: IFRS 8 Operating Segments*, which was intended to formally gather information from the various groups of IASB's constituents about their experience with implementing IFRS 8.[15]

The Request for Information included open questions which focused not only on those aspects of IFRS 8 which had been considered to be the benefits of the new segment approach but also on the aspects of the Standard that were considered to be controversial when it was issued, including the effects of:

- using the management perspective;
- using non-IFRS measurements in segment reporting;
- using internally-reported line items;
- the IFRS 8 disclosures on the role of preparers and investors; and
- the implementation of IFRS 8 on preparers and investors.

In July 2013, the IASB issued its *Report and Feedback Statement – Post-implementation Review: IFRS 8 Operating Segments*, which summarised the PIR process, the feedback received and conclusions reached by IASB.[16] The IASB found that preparers, auditors, accounting firms, standard-setters and regulators were generally supportive of the Standard, although some improvements were suggested for its application. However, feedback from investor groups was mixed, with investors being more positive about the benefits of the Standard when segment information is aligned to the measures used by management elsewhere in the financial statements, in the management commentary and in presentations to analysts. In some cases, investors expressed some concern about the application of the segmentation process by entities, in particular where they suspect that segments have been presented in a way that obscures the entity's true management structure (often as a result of concerns about commercial sensitivity) or to mask loss-making activities within individual segments.[17]

Based on all of the feedback, the IASB concluded that the benefits of applying the Standard were largely as expected and that overall the Standard achieved its objectives and has improved financial reporting. The IASB noted the concerns raised by some investors but concluded that they do not suggest significant failings in the Standard and therefore do not warrant a revision of the principles underlying IFRS 8.[18]

However, the IASB acknowledged that some issues could be considered for improvement and warrant further investigation. The areas identified for potential improvement and amendment comprise requests for implementation guidance and requests for improved disclosures.

Requests for implementation guidance include:[19]

- further clarification of the concept of the chief operating decision maker; and
- guidance on how reconciliations should be presented, including illustrative examples.

Requests for improved disclosures include:[20]

- the provision of additional periods of comparative information when entities change the basis of segmentation, to give revised trend information for investors;
- the introduction of defined line items of segmental disclosure to provide some degree of comparability between entities;
- measures to prevent inappropriate aggregation of segments, including guidance on the nature of 'similar economic characteristics'; and
- reconciliations being prepared on a segment-by-segment basis, where reconciling items can be allocated on a systematic basis.

The IASB confirmed that any proposed changes to IFRS 8 would be assessed within the context of its more general review of disclosure requirements and would also take into account concerns about disclosure overload. Since IFRS 8 is substantially converged with US GAAP, this assessment will also involve active liaison with the FASB.[21]

At the time of writing, no specific projects are included in the project plan of the IASB.

References

1 IFRS 8 D01-D04.
2 Press Release, *Summary of the IASC Foundation Trustees meeting 2 and 3 July 2007, Madrid,* IFRS Foundation, 18 July 2007.
3 ED 8, *Operating Segments*, IASB, January 2006, 2.
4 *IFRS for Small and Medium-sized Entities*, IASB, July 2009, 1.3.
5 *IFRIC Update*, July 2011, p. 5.
6 ED 8, *Operating Segments*, IASB, January 2006, 9.
7 *IFRIC Update*, September 2011, p. 5.
8 *IASB Update*, September 2011, p. 15.
9 *IASB Update*, February 2013, p. 7.
10 IASB Agenda Paper 8B: *Annual Improvements to IFRSs 2010-2012 Cycle – IFRS 8 Operating Segments – aggregation of operating segments*, IASB, February 2013, Appendix A.
11 Exposure Draft ED/2012/1: *Annual Improvements to IFRSs 2010-2012 Cycle*, IASB, May 2012, p. 25.
12 IASB Agenda Paper 8B, paragraphs 17-18, p. 5.
13 Project Summary, *Related Party Disclosures, Update on the Other Amendments Proposed in the 2007 Exposure Draft*, IASB, July 2009.
14 *IASB Work Plan – projected timetable as at 29 July 2013*, IASB
15 Request for Information *Post-implementation Review: IFRS 8 Operating Segments*, Introduction, p. 4.
16 Report and Feedback Statement *Post-implementation Review: IFRS 8 Operating Segments*, July 2013.
17 Report and Feedback Statement, p. 5.
18 Report and Feedback Statement, p. 6.
19 Report and Feedback Statement, p. 7.
20 Report and Feedback Statement, p. 7.
21 Report and Feedback Statement, p. 8.

Chapter 33 Earnings per share

List of examples

Chapter 33 Earnings per share

1 INTRODUCTION

Earnings per share (EPS) is one of the most widely quoted statistics in financial analysis. It came into great prominence in the US during the late 1950s and early 1960s due to the widespread use of the price earnings ratio (PE) as a yardstick for investment decisions. As a result, standard setters in some jurisdictions (notably the USA and the UK) have had rules on EPS for many years. However, it was not until 1997 that an international accounting standard on the subject was published.

IAS 33 – *Earnings per Share* – was introduced for accounting periods beginning on or after 1 January 1998. In December 2003, as part of the improvements project, the IASB updated IAS 33 to provide more detailed guidance in some complex areas. The requirements of IAS 33 are discussed at 2 to 7 below, and the standard's illustrative examples of particular issues are included in the text of the chapter, whilst its comprehensive worked example is included as an Appendix.

1.1 Definitions

IAS 33 defines a number of its terms and these are dealt with in the text of this chapter where appropriate. One term which is particularly pervasive is 'fair value'. This term is defined and explained in IFRS 13 – *Fair Value Measurement* – and is discussed in Chapter 14. *[IAS 33.8]*. However, in the context of share-based payments the term fair value has the meaning used in IFRS 2 – *Share-based Payment.* The relevance of share-based payment to EPS is discussed at 6.4.5 below; IFRS 2 is discussed in Chapter 30. *[IAS 33.47A]*.

2 OBJECTIVE AND SCOPE OF IAS 33

2.1 Objective

IAS 33 sets out its objective as follows: 'to prescribe principles for the determination and presentation of earnings per share, so as to improve performance comparisons between different entities in the same reporting period and between different reporting periods for the same entity. Even though earnings per share data have limitations because of the different accounting policies that may be used for determining "earnings", a consistently determined denominator enhances financial reporting. The focus of this Standard is on the denominator of the earnings per share calculation.' *[IAS 33.1]*.

The standard requires the computation of both basic and diluted EPS, explaining the objective of each as follows:

- the objective of basic earnings per share information is to provide a measure of the interests of each ordinary share of a parent entity in the performance of the entity over the reporting period; *[IAS 33.11]* and
- the objective of diluted earnings per share is consistent with that of basic earnings per share – to provide a measure of the interest of each ordinary share in the performance of an entity – while giving effect to all dilutive potential ordinary shares outstanding during the period. *[IAS 33.32]*.

The underlying logic here is that EPS, including diluted EPS, should be an historical performance measure. This impacts particularly on the reporting of diluted EPS, in steering it away from an alternative purpose: to warn of potential future dilution. Indeed the tension between these differing objectives is evident in the standard. As discussed more fully at 6.4.6 below, IAS 33 sets out a very restrictive regime for including certain potentially dilutive shares in the diluted EPS calculation. Yet diluted EPS is only to take account of those potential shares that would dilute earnings from *continuing* operations which seems to have more of a forward looking 'warning signal' flavour.

2.2 Scope

IAS 33 applies to:

(a) the separate or individual financial statements of an entity:
   (i) whose ordinary shares or potential ordinary shares are traded in a public market (a domestic or foreign stock exchange or an over-the-counter market, including local and regional markets); or
   (ii) that files, or is in the process of filing, its financial statements with a securities commission or other regulatory information for the purpose of issuing ordinary shares in a public market; and

(b) the consolidated financial statements of a group with a parent:
   (i) whose ordinary shares or potential ordinary shares are traded in a public market (a domestic or foreign stock exchange or an over-the-counter market, including local and regional markets); or
   (ii) that files, or is in the process of filing, its financial statements with a securities commission or other regulatory information for the purpose of issuing ordinary shares in a public market. *[IAS 33.2]*.

IAS 33 also applies to any other entity that discloses earnings per share. *[IAS 33.3]*. Where both the parent's and consolidated financial statements are presented, the standard only requires consolidated earnings per share to be given. If the parent chooses to present EPS data based on its separate financial statements the standard requires that the disclosures be restricted to the face of the parent-only statement of comprehensive income (or separate income statement) and not be included in the consolidated financial statements. *[IAS 33.4]*.

3 THE BASIC EPS

IAS 33 requires the computation of basic EPS for the profit or loss (and, if presented, the profit or loss from continuing operations) attributable to ordinary equity holders. *[IAS 33.9]*. It defines, or rather describes, basic earnings per share in the following manner: 'Basic earnings per share shall be calculated by dividing profit or loss attributable to ordinary equity holders of the parent entity (the numerator) by the weighted average number of ordinary shares outstanding (the denominator) during the period.' *[IAS 33.10]*.

3.1 Earnings

The starting point for determining the earnings figure to be used in the basic EPS calculation (both for total earnings and, if appropriate, earnings from continuing operations) is the net profit or loss for the period attributable to ordinary equity holders. *[IAS 33.12]*. This will, in accordance with IAS 1 – *Presentation of Financial Statements* – include all items of income and expense, including, dividends on preference shares classified as liabilities and tax and is stated after the deduction of non-controlling interests *[IAS 33.13, A1]*. This is then adjusted for the after-tax amounts of preference dividends, differences arising on the settlement of preference shares, and other similar effects of preference shares classified as equity. *[IAS 33.12]*. These adjustments are discussed at 5.2 below.

3.2 Number of shares

An ordinary share is defined as 'an equity instrument that is subordinate to all other classes of equity instruments'. *[IAS 33.5]*. 'Equity instrument' has the same meaning as in IAS 32 – *Financial Instruments: Presentation* – that is 'any contract that evidences a residual interest in the assets of an entity after deducting all of its liabilities' *[IAS 33.8, IAS 32.11]*. IAS 33 goes on to observe that ordinary shares participate in profit for the period only after other types of share such as preference shares have participated. *[IAS 33.6]*. The standard also clarifies that there may be more than one class of ordinary share and requires the computation and presentation of EPS for each class that has a different right to share in profit for the period. *[IAS 33.6, 66]*. In practice, it is usually straightforward to determine which instruments are ordinary shares for EPS purposes. The treatment of different classes of shares is discussed at 5.4 below.

The basic rule in IAS 33 is that all outstanding ordinary shares are brought into the basic EPS computation – time-weighted for changes in the period (changes in ordinary shares is discussed at 4 below). *[IAS 33.19]*. There are three exceptions to this:

- ordinary shares that are issued as partly paid are included in the weighted average as a fraction of a share based on their dividend participation relative to fully paid shares (so, if although only partly paid they ranked equally for dividends they would be included in full); *[IAS 33.A15]*

- treasury shares, which are presented in the financial statements as a deduction from equity, are not considered outstanding for EPS purposes for the period they are held in treasury. Although not stated explicitly in the standard itself, this requirement is clearly logical (as although the shares are still in issue, they are accounted for as if redeemed) and is illustrated in one of the examples appended to the standard (see Example 33.1 at 4.1 below); *[IAS 33.IE2]* and
- shares that are contingently returnable (that is, subject to recall) are not treated as outstanding until they cease to be subject to recall, and hence are excluded from basic EPS until that time. *[IAS 33.24].*

The standard contains some specific guidance on when newly issued ordinary shares should be considered outstanding. In general, shares are to be included from the date consideration is receivable (considered by the standard generally to be the date of their issue), for example: *[IAS 33.21]*

- shares issued in exchange for cash are included when cash is receivable;
- shares issued on the voluntary reinvestment of dividends on ordinary or preference shares are included when the dividends are reinvested;
- shares issued as a result of the conversion of a debt instrument to ordinary shares are included as of the date interest ceases accruing;
- shares issued in place of interest or principal on other financial instruments are included as of the date interest ceases accruing;
- shares issued in exchange for the settlement of a liability of the entity are included as of the settlement date;
- shares issued as consideration for the acquisition of an asset other than cash are included as of the date on which the acquisition is recognised;
- shares issued in exchange for the rendering of services to the entity are included as the services are rendered; and
- shares that will be issued upon the conversion of a mandatorily convertible instrument are included in the calculation of basic earnings per share from the date the contract is entered into. *[IAS 33.23].*

Most of these provisions are straightforward, however some are worthy of note.

Shares issued in exchange for services will be accounted for in accordance with IFRS 2 – *Share-based Payment*, with a charge to income matched by a credit to equity. IAS 33 has some guidance on the inclusion of such potential shares in *diluted* EPS (see 6.4.5 below); however there is no further elaboration of the meaning of 'included as the services are rendered'. What seems to be implicit in the phrase is that the shares concerned vest unconditionally as services are rendered. On that basis, clearly it would be appropriate to include shares in basic EPS as entitlement to them vests, notwithstanding that the actual issue of shares may be at a different time. However, a very common form of share-based remuneration involves entitlement to shares vesting at the end of an extended period conditional on future events (typically continued employment and sometimes specific future performance). In our view, such arrangements are clearly conditionally issuable shares and should be excluded from basic EPS until vesting. Indeed, when discussing employee share schemes in the context of diluted EPS the standard is explicit, as follows. 'Employee share options with fixed or determinable terms and non-vested ordinary shares are treated as options in the calculation of diluted earnings per share, even though they may be contingent on vesting. They are treated as outstanding on the grant date. Performance-based employee share options are treated as contingently issuable shares because their issue is contingent upon satisfying specified conditions in addition to the passage of time.' *[IAS 33.48].* Contingently issuable shares are discussed at 6.4.6 below.

In respect of the final bullet point, the standard does not define what a mandatorily convertible instrument is. One view would be that the requirement to account for the shares in EPS from inception must mean it refers to instruments where the proceeds also are received at inception. On that basis, it would exclude a forward contract for the issue of shares which (as required by the first bullet above) would increase the denominator of basic EPS only from the time the cash is receivable. Similarly, in the reverse situation of a forward contract to redeem ordinary shares the shares would only be removed from basic EPS when the consideration becomes payable. Another view would be that all binding agreements to issue or redeem ordinary shares should be reflected in basic EPS when the entity becomes party to the arrangement. A further possible complexity is the question of whether or not a symmetrical treatment for the issue and redemption of shares should be applied for EPS purposes. Whilst that certainly seems logical, it is not beyond question in all circumstances particularly given the asymmetrical accounting treatment for certain derivatives over own shares required by IAS 32 (discussed in Chapter 43 at 5).

More generally, the standard goes on to say the timing of inclusion is determined by the attaching terms and conditions, and also that due consideration should be given to the substance of any contract associated with the issue. *[IAS 33.21].* Ordinary shares that are issuable on the satisfaction of certain conditions (contingently issuable shares) are to be included in the calculation of basic EPS only from the date when all necessary conditions have been satisfied; in effect when they are no longer contingent. *[IAS 33.24].* This provision is interpreted strictly, as illustrated in Example 7 appended to the standard (see Example 33.14 at 6.4.6.A below). In that example earnings in a year, by meeting certain thresholds, would trigger the issue of shares. Because it is not certain that the condition is met until the last day of the year (when earnings become known with certainty) the new shares are excluded from basic EPS until the following year. Where shares will be issued at some future date (that is, solely after the passage of time) they are not considered contingently issuable by IAS 33, as the passage of time is a certainty. *[IAS 33.24].* In principle, this would seem to mean that they should be included in basic EPS from the agreement date. However, careful consideration of the individual facts and circumstances would be necessary.

The calculation of the basic EPS is often simple but a number of complications can arise; these may be considered under the following two headings:

(a) changes in ordinary shares outstanding; and

(b) matters affecting the numerator.

These are discussed in the next two sections.

4 CHANGES IN OUTSTANDING ORDINARY SHARES

Changes in ordinary share outstanding can occur under a variety of circumstances, the most common of which are dealt with below. Whenever such a change occurs during the accounting period, an adjustment is required to the number of shares in the EPS calculation for that period; furthermore, in certain situations the EPS for previous periods will also have to be recalculated.

4.1 Weighted average number of shares

Implicit in the methodology of IAS 33 is a correlation between the capital of an entity (or rather the income generating assets it reflects) and earnings. Accordingly, to compute EPS as a performance measure requires adjusting the number of shares in the denominator to reflect any variations in the period to the capital available to generate that period's earnings. The standard observes that using the weighted average number of ordinary shares outstanding during the period reflects the possibility that the amount of shareholders' capital varied during the period as a result of a larger or smaller number of shares being outstanding at any time. The weighted average number of ordinary shares outstanding during the period is the number of ordinary shares outstanding at the beginning of the period, adjusted by the number of ordinary shares bought back or issued during the period multiplied by a time-weighting factor. The time-weighting factor is the number of days that the shares are outstanding as a proportion of the total number of days in the period; IAS 33 notes that a reasonable approximation of the weighted average is adequate in many circumstances. *[IAS 33.20]*. Computation of a weighted average number of shares is illustrated in the following example:

Example 33.1: Calculation of weighted average number of shares [IAS 33.IE2]

		Shares issued	*Treasury shares**	*Shares outstanding*
1 January 2014	Balance at beginning of year	2,000	300	1,700
31 May 2014	Issue of new shares for cash	800	–	2,500
1 December 2014	Purchase of treasury shares for cash	–	250	2,250
31 December 2014	Balance at year end	2,800	550	2,250

Calculation of weighted average:
(1,700 × 5/12) + (2,500 × 6/12) + (2,250 × 1/12) = 2,146 shares *or*
(1,700 × 12/12) + (800 × 7/12) – (250 × 1/12) = 2,146 shares

* Treasury shares are equity instruments reacquired and held by the issuing entity itself or by its subsidiaries.

The use of a weighted average number of shares is necessary because the increase in the share capital would have affected earnings only for that portion of the year during which the issue proceeds were available to management for use in the business.

4.2 Purchase and redemption of own shares

An entity may, if it is authorised to do so by its constitution and it complies with any relevant legislation, purchase or otherwise redeem its own shares. Assuming this is done at fair value, then the earnings should be apportioned over the weighted average share capital in issue for the year. This was illustrated in Example 33.1 above in relation to the purchase of treasury shares. If, on the other hand, the repurchase is at significantly more than market value then IAS 33 requires adjustments to be made to EPS for periods before buy-back. This is discussed at 4.3.5 below.

4.3 Changes in ordinary shares without corresponding changes in resources

IAS 33 requires the number of shares used in the calculation to be adjusted (for all periods presented) for any transaction (other than the conversion of potential ordinary shares) that changes the number of shares outstanding without a corresponding change in resources. *[IAS 33.26]*. This is also to apply where some, but curiously not all, such changes have happened after the year-end but before the approval of the financial statements.

The standard gives the following as examples of changes in the number of ordinary shares without a corresponding change in resources:

(a) a capitalisation or bonus issue (sometimes referred to as a stock dividend);

(b) a bonus element in any other issue, for example a bonus element in a rights issue to existing shareholders;

(c) a share split; and

(d) a reverse share split (share consolidation). *[IAS 33.27]*.

Another example not mentioned by the standard would be any bonus element in a buy-back, such as a put warrant involving the repurchase of shares at significantly more than their fair value.[1] The adjustments required to EPS for each of these is discussed below.

As noted above, IAS 33 requires retrospective adjustment for all such events that happen in the reporting period. However, it only requires restatement for those in (a), (c) and (d) if they happen after the year-end but before the financial statements are authorised for issue. *[IAS 33.64]*. We are not convinced that this was the intention of the board, and suspect that it may be the result of less than precise drafting (particularly as the paragraph requiring restatement for these post-balance sheet changes also applies to events that have happened during the reporting period, but refers only to the same items) – however it is what the standard literally requires.

4.3.1 Capitalisation, bonus issue, share split and share consolidation

4.3.1.A Capitalisation, bonus issues and share splits

A capitalisation or bonus issue or share split has the effect of increasing the number of shares in issue without any inflow of resources, as further ordinary shares are issued to existing shareholders for no consideration. Consequently, no additional earnings will be expected to accrue as a result of the issue. The additional shares should be treated as having been in issue for the whole period and also included in the EPS calculation of all earlier periods presented so as to give a comparable result. For example, on a two-for-one bonus issue, the number of ordinary shares outstanding before the issue is multiplied by three to obtain the new total number of ordinary shares, or by two to obtain the number of additional ordinary shares. *[IAS 33.28]*.

The EPS calculation involving a bonus issue is illustrated in the following example.

Example 33.2: A bonus issue [IAS 33.IE3]

Profit attributable to ordinary equity holders of the parent entity 2013	€180
Profit attributable to ordinary equity holders of the parent entity 2014	€600
Ordinary shares outstanding until 30 September 2014	200
Bonus issue 1 October 2014	2 ordinary shares for each ordinary share outstanding at 30 September 2014 200×2=400
Basic earnings per share 2014	$\frac{€\,600}{(200+400)} = €1.00$
Basic earnings per share 2013	$\frac{€180}{(200+400)} = €0.30$

Because the bonus issue was without consideration, it is treated as if it had occurred before the beginning of 2013, the earliest period presented.

Again, although the standard is silent on the matter, we believe that any financial ratios disclosed for earlier periods, which are based on the number of equity shares at a year-end (e.g. dividend per share) should also be adjusted by in a similar manner.

4.3.1.B Stock dividends

Stock or scrip dividends refer to the case where an entity offers its shareholders the choice of receiving further fully paid up shares in the company as an alternative to receiving a cash dividend. It could be argued that the dividend foregone represents payment for the shares, usually at fair value, and hence no restatement is appropriate. Alternatively, the shares could be viewed as being, in substance, bonus issues which require the EPS for the earlier period to be adjusted. IAS 33 seems to suggest the latter view, as it notes that capitalisation or bonus issues are sometimes referred to as stock dividends. However, entities often refer to these arrangements as dividend reinvestment plans which suggests the acquisition of new shares for valuable consideration.

In our view, this distinction should be a factual one. If an entity (say, through proposal and subsequent approval by shareholders) has a legal obligation to pay a dividend in cash or, at the shareholder's option, shares then the cash payment avoided if the scrip dividend is taken up is consideration for the shares. This may be equivalent to an issue at fair value or it may contain some bonus element requiring retrospective adjustment of EPS. In practice the fair value of shares received as a scrip alternative may exceed the cash alternative; this is often referred to as an enhanced scrip dividend. In these cases IAS 33 will require a bonus element to be identified, and prior EPS figures restated accordingly. This is essentially the same as adjustments for the bonus element in a rights issue, discussed at 4.3.3 below. Furthermore, in this scenario, during the period between the obligation coming into existence and its settlement (in cash or shares) it could be argued to represent a written call option and hence potentially affect diluted EPS (see 6.4.2.B below). Given that the standard is silent on this aspect of some stock dividends we doubt that such an approach was intended. In any event it strikes us as unlikely in most cases that the effect would be significant. Conversely, if the entity issues fresh shares *instead of* a dividend it is a bonus issue requiring full retrospective adjustment to EPS.

4.3.1.C Share consolidations

Occasionally, entities will consolidate their equity share capital into a smaller number of shares. Such a consolidation generally reduces the number of shares outstanding without a corresponding outflow of resources, and this would require an adjustment to the denominator for periods before the consolidation. *[IAS 33.29]*.

4.3.2 Share consolidation with a special dividend

Share consolidations as discussed above normally do not involve any outflow of funds from the entity. However, entities may return surplus cash to their shareholders by paying special dividends accompanied by a share consolidation, the purpose of which is to maintain the value of each share following the payment of the dividend. This issue is specifically addressed by IAS 33 as revised in 2003 (the original standard being silent on the issue), perhaps because such schemes had been quite common when it was being revised. The normal rule of restating the outstanding number of shares for all periods for a share consolidation is not applied when the overall effect is a share repurchase at fair value because in such cases the reduction of shares *is* the result of a corresponding reduction in resources. In such cases the weighted average number of shares is adjusted for the consolidation from the date the special dividend is recognised. *[IAS 33.29]*.

There is undoubtedly a conceptual attraction in trying to standardise adjustments made to prior years' EPS figures. However, in our view the approach taken by the standard is rather piecemeal, in that restatement is only ever triggered by a change in the number of shares, and it will not necessarily achieve the objective of standardising the restatement of EPS. Capital may be returned to shareholders in various different ways, including demergers and group reconstructions, as well as share buybacks and special dividends. In many such cases the number of shares in issue is only reduced if the entity opts to consolidate its shares. The natural consequence of returning capital is that earnings will fall, so it is debatable whether a fall in EPS in these circumstances should be regarded as a distortion that needs to be corrected at all. Of course, if an entity buys back its shares, the number of shares will automatically be reduced and therefore affect the EPS calculation in a way that other returns of capital do not, but this does not necessarily mean that a special dividend should be treated as if it were a share buyback. However, the standard is now clear, so entities must apply these provisions so that this specific type of return of capital will fall to be treated as a share repurchase, but only when the entity also chooses to consolidate its shares.

4.3.3 Rights issue

A rights issue is a popular method through which entities are able to access the capital markets for further capital. Under the terms of such an issue, existing shareholders are given the opportunity to acquire further shares in the entity on a pro-rata basis to their existing shareholdings.

The 'rights' shares will usually be offered either at the current market price or at a price below that. In the former case, the treatment of the issue for EPS purposes is as discussed in 4.1 above. However, where the rights price is at a discount to market it is not quite as straightforward, since the issue is equivalent to a bonus issue (see 4.3.1 above) combined with an issue at full market price. In such cases, IAS 33 requires an adjustment to the number of shares outstanding before the rights issue to reflect the bonus element inherent in it. *[IAS 33.26-27]*.

The bonus element of the rights issue available to all existing shareholders is given by the following adjustment factor, sometimes referred to as the bonus fraction: *[IAS 33.A2]*

$$\frac{\text{Fair value per share immediately before the exercise of rights}}{\text{Theoretical ex-rights fair value per share}}$$

The fair value per share immediately before the exercise of rights is the *actual* price at which the shares are quoted inclusive of the right to take up the future shares under the rights issue. Where the rights are to be traded separately from the shares the fair value used is the closing price on the last day on which the shares are traded inclusive of the right. *[IAS 33.A2]*.

The 'ex-rights fair value' is the *theoretical* price at which the shares would be expected to be quoted, other stock market factors apart, after the rights issue shares have been issued. It is calculated by adding the aggregate fair value of the shares immediately before the exercise of the rights to the proceeds from the exercise, and dividing by the number of shares outstanding after the exercise. *[IAS 33.A2]*. The EPS calculation involving a rights issue is illustrated in the following example.

Example 33.3: Rights issue at less than full market price [IAS 33.IE4]

	2012	*2013*	*2014*
Profit attributable to ordinary equity holders of the parent entity	€1,100	€1,500	€1,800

Shares outstanding before rights issue	500 shares
Rights issue	One new share for each five outstanding shares (100 new shares total) Exercise price: €5.00 Date of rights issue: 1 January 2013 Last date to exercise rights: 1 March 2013
Market price of one ordinary share immediately before exercise on 1 March 2013	€11.00
Reporting date	31 December

Calculation of theoretical ex-rights value per share

$$\frac{\text{Fair value of all outstanding shares before the exercise of rights} + \text{Total amount received from exercise of rights}}{\text{Number of shares outstanding before exercise} + \text{Number of shares issued in the exercise}} =$$

$$\frac{(€11.00 \times 500 \text{ shares}) + (€5.00 \times 100 \text{ shares})}{500 \text{ shares} + 100 \text{ shares}}$$

Theoretical ex-rights value per share = €10.00

Calculation of adjustment factor

$$\frac{\text{Fair value per share before exercise of rights}}{\text{Theoretical ex-rights value per share}} = \frac{€11.00}{€10.00} = 1.10$$

Calculation of basic earnings per share

	2012	*2013*	*2014*
2012 basic EPS as originally reported:			
€1,100 ÷ 500 shares =	€2.20		
2012 basic EPS restated for rights issue:			
€1,100 ÷ (500 shares × 1.1) =	€2.00		
2013 basic EPS including effects of rights issue:			
$\frac{€1,500}{(500 \times 1.1 \times 2/12) + (600 \times 10/12)} =$		€2.54	
2014 basic EPS:			
€1,800 ÷ 600 shares =			€3.00

Rather than multiplying the denominator by 11/10ths, the previous year's EPS (and any EPS disclosures in a historical summary) could alternatively be arrived at by multiplying the original EPS by 10/11ths.

Whilst the rights are outstanding they represent, strictly speaking, a written call option over the entity's shares which could have implications for diluted EPS (see 6.4.2 below).

It is possible that shares could be issued as a result of open offers, placings and other offerings of equity shares not made to existing shareholders, at a discount to the market price. In such cases it would be necessary to consider whether the issue contained a bonus element, or rather simply reflected differing views on the fair value of the shares. In our opinion the latter seems a far more realistic alternative. Accordingly the shares should be dealt with on a weighted average basis without calculating any bonus element when computing the EPS.

4.3.4 *B share schemes*

One method by which some entities have returned capital to shareholders is the so-called 'B share scheme'. These schemes involve issuing 'B shares' (usually undated preference shares with low or zero coupons) to existing shareholders, either as a bonus issue or via a share split. These are then repurchased for cash and cancelled, following which the ordinary shares are consolidated. The overall effect is intended to be the same as a repurchase of ordinary shares at fair value, and accordingly no retrospective adjustment to EPS is necessary, assuming that the intention is achieved. *[IAS 33.29]*.

4.3.5 Put warrants priced above market value

As noted at 4.3 above, an example of a change in the number of shares outstanding without a corresponding change in resources not mentioned by the standard would be any bonus element in a buy-back, such as a put warrant involving the repurchase of shares at significantly more than their fair value. The accounting requirements for such instruments are discussed in Chapter 43 at 5.

Unfortunately IAS 33 does not give an illustrative calculation for a put warrant at significantly more than fair value, but it does for the familiar rights issue (rights issues are discussed at 4.3.3 above). In a rights issue new shares are issued at a discount to market value, whereas with put warrants shares are bought back at a premium to market value. In both cases the remaining shares are viewed as being devalued for the purposes of comparing EPS over time. Applying the logic of adjusting EPS when there is a change in the number of shares without a corresponding change in resources seems to require that put warrants are treated as a reverse rights issue. This would mean calculating a similar 'adjustment factor', and applying it to the number of shares outstanding before the transaction. The difference in the calculation would be that the number of shares issued and the consideration received for them would be replaced by negative amounts representing the number of shares put back to the entity and the amount paid for them.

An illustration of what this might entail is as follows:

Example 33.4: Put warrants priced above market value

The following example takes the same scenario as Example 33.3 above (a rights issue), altered to illustrate a put warrant scheme. In that example the shares are issued at a discount of €6.00 to the €11.00 market price on a one for five basis two months into the year. Reversing this would give a put warrant to sell shares back to the company at a €6 premium, again on a one for five basis. All other details have been left the same for comparability, although in reality the rising earnings following a rights issue may well become falling earnings after a buy-back. The calculation would then become:

Calculation of theoretical ex-warrant value per share

$$\frac{\text{fair value of all outstanding shares before the exercise of warrants} - \text{total amount paid on exercise of warrants}}{\text{shares outstanding before exercise} - \text{shares cancelled in the exercise}} =$$

$$\frac{(€11 \times 500) - (€17 \times 100)}{500 - 100} = €9.50$$

Calculation of adjustment factor

$$\frac{\text{Fair value per share before exercise of warrants}}{\text{Theoretical ex-warrant value per share}} = \frac{€11}{€9.5} = 1.16$$

Calculation of basic earnings per share

	2012	*2013*	*2014*
	€	€	€
2012 EPS as originally reported:			
€1,100 ÷ 500 shares =	2.20		
2012 EPS restated for warrants:			
€1,100 ÷ (500 shares × 1.16) =	1.90		
2013 EPS including effects of warrants:			
$\frac{€1,500}{(500 \times 1.16 \times 2/12) + (400 \times 10/12)} =$		3.49	
2014 basic EPS:			
€1,800 ÷ 400 shares =			3.49

Whilst the above seems a sensible interpretation of the requirements, as the procedure is not specified there may be scope for other interpretations.

4.4 Options exercised during the year

Shares issued as a result of options being exercised should be dealt with on a weighted average basis in the basic EPS. *[IAS 33.38]*. Furthermore, options that have been exercised during the year will also affect diluted EPS calculations. If the options in question would have had a diluting effect on the basic EPS had they been exercised at the beginning of the year, then they should be considered in the diluted EPS calculation as explained in 6.4.2 below, but on a weighted average basis for the period up to the date of exercise. The exercise of options is a 'conversion of potential ordinary shares'. The standard excludes such conversions from the general requirement (see 4.3 above) to adjust prior periods' EPS when a change in the number of shares happens without a corresponding change in resources. *[IAS 33.26]*.

4.5 Post balance sheet changes in capital

The EPS figure should not reflect any changes in the capital structure occurring after the reporting period, but before the financial statements are approved, which was effected for fair value. This is because any proceeds received from the issue were not available for use during the period. However, EPS for all periods presented should be adjusted for any bonus element in certain post year-end changes in the number of shares, as discussed at 4.3 above. When this is done that fact should be stated. *[IAS 33.64]*.

4.6 Issue to acquire another business

4.6.1 Acquisitions

As a result of a share issue to acquire another business, funds or other assets will flow into the business and extra profits will be expected to be generated. When calculating EPS, it should be assumed that the shares were issued on the acquisition date (even if the actual date of issue is later), since this will be the date from which the results of the newly acquired business are recognised. *[IAS 33.21(f), 22]*.

4.6.2 Reverse acquisitions

Reverse acquisition is the term used to describe a business combination whereby the legal parent entity after the combination is in substance the acquired and not the acquiring entity (discussed in Chapter 9 at 14). IAS 33 is silent on the subject; however, an appendix to IFRS 3 – *Business Combinations* – contains a discussion of the implications for EPS of such transactions. Following a reverse acquisition the equity structure appearing in the consolidated financial statements will reflect the equity of the legal parent, including the equity instruments issued by it to effect the business combination. *[IFRS 3.B25]*.

For the purposes of calculating the weighted average number of ordinary shares outstanding during the period in which the reverse acquisition occurs:

(a) the number of ordinary shares outstanding from the beginning of that period to the acquisition date shall be computed on the basis of the weighted average number of ordinary shares of the legal acquiree (accounting acquirer) outstanding during the period multiplied by the exchange ratio established in the merger agreement; and

(b) the number of ordinary shares outstanding from the acquisition date to the end of that period shall be the actual number of ordinary shares of the legal acquirer (the accounting acquiree) outstanding during that period. *[IFRS 3.B26]*.

The basic EPS disclosed for each comparative period before the acquisition date is calculated by dividing the profit or loss of the legal subsidiary attributable to ordinary shareholders in each of those periods by the legal acquiree's historical weighted average number of ordinary shares outstanding multiplied by the exchange ratio established in the acquisition agreement *[IFRS 3.B27]*.

IFRS 3 presents an illustrative example of a reverse acquisition, including the EPS calculation, see Chapter 9 at 14.5.

4.6.3 Establishment of a new parent undertaking

Where a new parent entity is established by means of a share for share exchange and the pooling of interest method has been adopted (discussed in Chapter 10 at 3.3), the number of shares taken as being in issue for both the current and preceding periods would be the number of shares issued by the new parent entity. However, EPS calculations for previous periods in the new parent entity's financial statements would have to reflect any changes in the number of outstanding ordinary shares of the former parent entity that may have occurred in those periods, as illustrated in the example below:

Example 33.5: Calculation of EPS where a new holding company is established

Entity A has been established as the newly formed parent entity of Entity B in a one for one share exchange on 30 June 2014. At that date, Entity B has 1,000,000 €1 ordinary shares in issue. Previously, on 30 June 2013 Entity B had issued 200,000 €1 ordinary shares for cash at full market price. Both entities have a 31 December year-end and the trading results of Entity B are as follows:

	2014 €	*2013* €
Profit for equity shareholders after taxation	500,000	300,000

The earnings per share calculation of Entity A is shown below:

	2014	*2013*
Number of equity shares	$800,000 \times \frac{6}{12} =$	400,000
	$1,000,000 \times \frac{6}{12} =$	500,000
	1,000,000	900,000
EPS	$\frac{500,000}{1,000,000} = €0.50$	$\frac{300,000}{900,000} = €0.33$

If, in the above example, the share exchange did not take place on a one for one basis, but Entity A issued three shares for every one share held in Entity B, then the number of shares issued by Entity B in 2013 would have to be apportioned accordingly before carrying out the weighted average calculation. The earnings per share calculation would, therefore, have been as follows:

	2014	*2013*
Number of equity shares	$2,400,000 \times \frac{6}{12} =$	1,200,000
	$3,000,000 \times \frac{6}{12} =$	1,500,000
	3,000,000	2,700,000
EPS	$\frac{500,000}{3,000,000} = €0.17$	$\frac{300,000}{2,700,000} = €0.11$

4.7 Adjustments to EPS in historical summaries

In order to ensure comparability of EPS figures, the previously published EPS figures for all periods presented in IFRS financial statements should be adjusted for subsequent changes in capital not involving full consideration at fair value (apart from the conversion of potential ordinary shares) in the manner described in 4.3 above; they should also be adjusted, in our view, for certain group reconstructions. Often entities will include EPS figures in historical summaries (typically five years) in the analyses and discussions accompanying (but not part of) the financial statements. We suggest that all such analyses need similar adjustments in order to be meaningful. We would also suggest that the resultant figures should be described as restated.

5 MATTERS AFFECTING THE NUMERATOR

5.1 Earnings

The earnings figure on which the basic EPS calculation is based should be the consolidated net profit or loss for the year after tax, non-controlling interests and after adjusting for returns to preference shareholders that are not already included in net profit (as will be the case for preference shares classified as liabilities under IAS 32).

5.2 Preference dividends

The adjustments to net profit attributable to ordinary shareholders in relation to returns to preference shareholders should include:

- the after-tax amount of any preference dividends on non-cumulative preference shares declared in respect of the period; *[IAS 33.14(a)]*
- the after-tax amount of the preference dividends for cumulative preference shares required for the period, whether or not the dividends have been declared. This does not include the amount of any preference dividends for cumulative preference shares paid or declared during the current period in respect of previous periods; *[IAS 33.14(b)]*
- any original issue discount or premium on increasing rate preference shares which is amortised to retained earnings using the effective interest method. Increasing rate preference shares are those that provide: a low initial dividend to compensate an entity for selling them at a discount; or an above-market dividend in later periods to compensate investors for purchasing them at a premium (see Example 33.6 below); *[IAS 33.15]*
- the excess of the fair value of the consideration paid to shareholders over the carrying amount of the preference shares when the shares are repurchased under an entity's tender offer to the holders. As this represents a return to the holders of the shares (and a charge to retained earnings for the entity) it is deducted in calculating profit or loss attributable to ordinary equity holders of the parent entity; *[IAS 33.16]*
- the excess of the fair value of the ordinary shares or other consideration paid over the fair value of the ordinary shares issuable under the original conversion terms when early conversion of convertible preference shares is induced through favourable changes to the original conversion terms or the payment of additional consideration. This is a return to the preference shareholders, and accordingly is deducted in calculating profit or loss attributable to ordinary equity holders of the parent entity; *[IAS 33.17]* and
- any excess of the carrying amount of preference shares over the fair value of the consideration paid to settle them. This reflects a gain to the entity and is added in calculating profit or loss attributable to ordinary equity holders. *[IAS 33.18]*.

The computation of EPS involving increasing rate preference shares is illustrated in the following example.

Example 33.6: Increasing rate preference shares *[IAS 33.IE1]*

Entity D issued non-convertible, non-redeemable class A cumulative preference shares of €100 par value on 1 January 2014. The class A preference shares are entitled to a cumulative annual dividend of €7 per share starting in 2017. At the time of issue, the market rate dividend yield on the class A preference shares was 7 per cent a year. Thus, Entity D could have expected to receive proceeds of approximately €100 per class A preference share if the dividend rate of €7 per share had been in effect at the date of issue.

In consideration of the dividend payment terms, however, the class A preference shares were issued at €81.63 per share, i.e. at a discount of €18.37 per share. The issue price can be calculated by taking the present value of €100, discounted at 7 per cent over a three-year period. Because the shares are classified as equity, the original issue discount is amortised to retained earnings using the effective interest method and treated as a preference dividend for earnings per share purposes. To calculate basic earnings per share, the following imputed dividend per class A preference share is deducted to determine the profit or loss attributable to ordinary equity holders of the parent entity:

Year paid	Carrying amount of class A preference shares 1 January	Imputed dividend [1]	Carrying amount of class A preference shares 31 December [2]	Dividend
	€	€	€	€
2014	81.63	5.71	87.34	–
2015	87.34	6.12	93.46	–
2016	93.46	6.54	100.00	–
Thereafter:	100.00	7.00	107.00	(7.00)

[1] at 7%

[2] This is before dividend payment.

5.3 Retrospective adjustments

Where comparative figures have been restated (for example, to correct a material error or as a result of a change in accounting policy), earnings per share for all periods presented should also be restated. *[IAS 33.64]*.

5.4 Participating equity instruments and two class shares

As noted at 3.2 above, IAS 33 envisages entities having more than one class of ordinary shares and requires the calculation and presentation of EPS for each such class. *[IAS 33.66]*. Although perhaps not exactly obvious from the definition, some instruments that have a right to participate in profits are viewed by the standard as ordinary shares. The standard observes that the equity of some entities includes:

(a) instruments that participate in dividends with ordinary shares according to a predetermined formula (for example, two for one) with, at times, an upper limit on the extent of participation (for example, up to, but not beyond, a specified amount per share); and

(b) a class of ordinary shares with a different dividend rate from that of another class of ordinary shares but without prior or senior rights. *[IAS 33.A13]*.

In our view whilst category (a) could encompass some participating preference shares (as illustrated in Example 33.7 below), not all participating preference shares would necessarily fall to be treated as ordinary shares for EPS purposes. This is because the participation features of some instruments could mean that they are not subordinate to all other classes of equity instrument. The meaning of ordinary shares for EPS purposes is discussed at 3.2 above.

To calculate basic (and diluted) earnings per share:

(a) profit or loss attributable to ordinary equity holders of the parent entity is adjusted (a profit reduced and a loss increased) by the amount of dividends declared in the period for each class of shares and by the contractual amount of dividends (or interest on participating bonds) that must be paid for the period (for example, unpaid cumulative dividends);

(b) the remaining profit or loss is allocated to ordinary shares and participating equity instruments to the extent that each instrument shares in earnings as if all of the profit or loss for the period had been distributed. The total profit or loss allocated to each class of equity instrument is determined by adding together the amount allocated for dividends and the amount allocated for a participation feature; and

(c) the total amount of profit or loss allocated to each class of equity instrument is divided by the number of outstanding instruments to which the earnings are allocated to determine the earnings per share for the instrument.

For the calculation of diluted earnings per share, all potential ordinary shares assumed to have been issued are included in outstanding ordinary shares. *[IAS 33.A14].* This is discussed at 6.4 below.

Participating equity instruments and two-class ordinary shares are illustrated with the following example.

Example 33.7: Participating equity instruments and two-class ordinary shares [IAS 33.IE11]

Profit attributable to equity holders of the parent entity	€100,000
Ordinary shares outstanding	10,000
Non-convertible preference shares	6,000
Non-cumulative annual dividend on preference shares (before any dividend is paid on ordinary shares)	€5.50 per share

After ordinary shares have been paid a dividend of €2.10 per share, the preference shares participate in any additional dividends on a 20:80 ratio with ordinary shares (i.e. after preference and ordinary shares have been paid dividends of €5.50 and €2.10 per share, respectively, preference shares participate in any additional dividends at a rate of one-fourth of the amount paid to ordinary shares on a per-share basis).

Dividends on preference shares paid	€33,000	(€5.50 per share)
Dividends on ordinary shares paid	€21,000	(€2.10 per share)

Basic earnings per share is calculated as follows:

	€	€
Profit attributable to equity holders of the parent entity		100,000
Less dividends paid:		
Preference	33,000	
Ordinary	21,000	
		(54,000)
Undistributed earnings		46,000

Allocation of undistributed earnings:
Allocation per ordinary share = A
Allocation per preference share = B; B = 1/4 A

(A 10,000) + (1/4 A 6,000) = €46,000
A = €46,000 ÷ (10,000 + 1,500)
A = €4.00
B = 1/4 A
B = €1.00

Basic per share amounts:

	Preference shares	*Ordinary shares*
Distributed earnings	€5.50	€2.10
Undistributed earnings	€1.00	€4.00
Totals	€6.50	€6.10

NB. This example does not illustrate the classification of the components of convertible financial instruments as liabilities and equity or the classification of related interest and dividends as expenses and equity as required by IAS 32.

It is worth noting that this calculation provided by the standard does not actually follow the procedure specified by IAS 33. As noted above, the method outlined by the standard is to allocate dividends and then all remaining profits to the different classes of share then divide this by the number of shares in each class. The above example computes dividends and then remaining profit on a per-share basis and then combines them.

5.5 Other bases

It is not uncommon for entities to supplement the EPS figures required by IAS 33 by voluntarily presenting additional amounts per share. For additional *earnings* per share amounts, the standard requires that:

(a) the denominator used should be that required by IAS 33;

(b) basic and diluted amounts be disclosed with equal prominence and presented in the notes;

(c) an indication of the basis on which the numerator is determined, including whether amounts per share are before or after tax; and

(d) if the numerator is not reported as a line item in the statement of comprehensive income or separate statement of profit or loss, a reconciliation between it and a line item that is reported in the statement of comprehensive income. *[IAS 33.73, 73A].*

The requirement in (b) is a curious one – or at least curiously phrased. The wording of the standard requires that additional EPS figures be 'presented in the notes'. Some commentators have asserted that this amounts to banning the presentation of such figures on the face of the statement of comprehensive income (or separate income statement if one is presented). In our view, however, it is clear that a requirement to put a disclosure in the notes does not amount to a prohibition on also presenting it elsewhere as well.

In September 2007 the IASB indicated that it intended to modify IAS 33 to prohibit the presentation of alternative EPS figures on the face of the income statement as part of the annual improvements project. *[IAS 1.BC103]*. However, that project was ultimately finalised without addressing this issue.

In August 2008 the IASB published an exposure draft proposing changes to IAS 33 (see 8 below). One of the proposals in the exposure draft was to amend the standard so as to prohibit the presentation of alternative EPS in the statement of comprehensive income (or separate income statement) and allow it only in the notes.[2] At the time of writing, the project is paused. Likely future developments of IAS 33 are discussed at 8 below.

The requirements discussed above apply to voluntarily presented *earnings* per share figures. The standard does not mention the presentation of other 'per share' figures. We believe that if the per share disclosure is of some measure of performance over time (say, cash flow per share) then it would be necessary to use the same denominator as required by the standard for EPS. Other measures may relate to a point in time (say, net assets per share). In such cases the quantity of shares as at the measurement date would be a more appropriate denominator.

6 DILUTED EARNINGS PER SHARE

6.1 The need for diluted EPS

The presentation of basic EPS seeks to show a performance measure, by computing how much profit an entity has earned for each of the shares in issue for the period. Entities often enter into commitments to issue shares in the future which would result in a change in basic EPS. IAS 33 refers to such commitments as potential ordinary shares, which it defines as 'a financial instrument or other contract that may entitle its holder to ordinary shares'. *[IAS 33.5]*.

Examples of potential ordinary shares given by IAS 33 are:

(a) financial liabilities or equity instruments, including preference shares, that are convertible into ordinary shares;

(b) options and warrants (whether accounted for under IAS 32 or IFRS 2);

(c) shares that would be issued upon the satisfaction of conditions resulting from contractual arrangements, such as the purchase of a business or other assets. *[IAS 33.7]*.

When potential shares are actually issued, the impact on basic EPS will be two-fold. First, the number of shares in issue will change; second, profits could be affected, for example by lower interest charges or the return made on cash inflows. Scenarios whereby such an adjustment to basic EPS is unfavourable are described by the standard as dilution, defined as 'a reduction in earnings per share or an increase in loss per share resulting from the assumption that convertible instruments are converted, that options or warrants are exercised, or that ordinary shares are issued upon the satisfaction of specified conditions'. *[IAS 33.5]*. This potential fall in EPS is quantified by computing diluted EPS, and as a result:

(a) profit or loss attributable to equity holders is increased by the after-tax amount of dividends and interest recognised in the period in respect of the dilutive potential ordinary shares and is adjusted for any other changes in income or expense that would result from the conversion of the dilutive potential ordinary shares; and
(b) the weighted average number of ordinary shares outstanding is increased by the weighted average number of additional ordinary shares that would have been outstanding assuming the conversion of all dilutive potential ordinary shares. *[IAS 33.32]*.

6.2 Calculation of diluted EPS

IAS 33 requires a diluted EPS figure to be calculated for the profit or loss attributable to ordinary equity holders of the parent and, if presented, profit or loss from continuing operations attributable to them. *[IAS 33.30]*. For these purposes, the profit or loss attributable to ordinary equity holders and the weighted average number of shares outstanding should be adjusted for the effects of all potential ordinary shares. *[IAS 33.31]*. In calculating diluted EPS, the number of shares should be that used in calculating basic EPS, plus the weighted average number of shares that would be issued on the conversion of all the dilutive potential ordinary shares into ordinary shares. As is the case for outstanding shares in the basic EPS calculation, potential ordinary shares should be weighted for the period they are outstanding. *[IAS 33.36, 38]*. Accordingly, potential ordinary shares:

- should be deemed to have been converted into ordinary shares at the beginning of the period or, if not in existence at the beginning of the period, the date of their issue; *[IAS 33.36]*
- which are cancelled or allowed to lapse should be included only for the period they are outstanding; and
- which convert into ordinary shares during the period are included up until the date of conversion (from which point they will be included in the basic EPS). *[IAS 33.38]*.

The number of dilutive potential ordinary shares should be determined independently for each period presented, and not subsequently revisited. In particular, prior periods' EPS are not restated for changes in assumptions about the conversion of potential shares into shares. IAS 33 also stresses, unnecessarily in our view, that the number of dilutive potential ordinary shares included in the year-to-date period is not a weighted average of the dilutive potential ordinary shares included in each interim computation. *[IAS 33.37, 65]* The reason the standard stresses this point is probably that it represents a change from the proposal in the draft 'improved' standard.[3]

6.2.1 *Diluted earnings*

The earnings figure should be that used for basic EPS adjusted to reflect any changes that would arise if the potential shares outstanding in the period were actually issued. Adjustment is to be made for the post-tax effects of:

(a) any dividends or other items related to dilutive potential ordinary shares deducted in arriving at the earnings figure used for basic EPS;

(b) any interest recognised in the period related to dilutive potential ordinary shares; and

(c) any other changes in income or expense that would result from the conversion of the dilutive potential ordinary shares. *[IAS 33.33]*.

These adjustments will also include any amounts charged in accordance with the effective interest method prescribed by IAS 39 – *Financial Instruments: Recognition and Measurement* – as a result of allocating transaction costs, premiums or discounts over the term of the instrument. *[IAS 33.34]*. Instruments with a choice of settlement method may also require adjustments to the numerator as discussed at 6.2.2 below.

The standard notes that certain earnings adjustments directly attributable to the instrument could have a knock-on impact on other items of income or expense which will need to be accounted for. For example, the lower interest charge following conversion of convertible debt could lead to higher charges under profit sharing schemes. *[IAS 33.35]*.

No imputed earnings are taken into account in respect of the proceeds to be received on exercise of share options or warrants. The effect of such potential ordinary shares on the diluted EPS is reflected in the computation of the denominator. This is discussed at 6.4.2 below.

6.2.2 Diluted number of shares

IAS 33 discusses a number of specific types of potential ordinary shares and how they should be brought into the calculation, which are discussed at 6.4 below.

More generally, the standard also discusses scenarios where the method of conversion or settlement of potential ordinary shares is at the discretion of one of the parties, as follows:

(a) The number of shares that would be issued on conversion should be determined from the terms of the potential ordinary shares. When more than one basis of conversion exists, the calculation should assume the most advantageous conversion rate or exercise price from the standpoint of the holder of the potential ordinary shares; *[IAS 33.39]*

(b) When an entity has issued a contract that may be settled in shares or cash at its option, it should presume that the contract will be settled in shares. The resulting potential ordinary shares would be included in diluted earnings per share if the effect is dilutive. *[IAS 33.58]*. When such a contract is presented for accounting purposes as an asset or a liability, or has an equity component and a liability component, the numerator should be adjusted for any changes in profit or loss that would have resulted during the period if the contract had been classified wholly as an equity instrument. That adjustment is similar to the adjustments discussed at 6.2.1 above; *[IAS 33.59]* and

(c) For contracts that may be settled in ordinary shares or cash at the holder's option, the more dilutive of cash settlement and share settlement should be used in calculating diluted earnings per share. *[IAS 33.60]*.

An example of an instrument covered by (b) above is a debt instrument that, on maturity, gives the issuer the unrestricted right to settle the principal amount in cash or in its own ordinary shares (see Example 33.10 at 6.4.1.A below). An example of an instrument covered by (c) is a written put option that gives the holder a choice of settling in ordinary shares or cash. *[IAS 33.61]*.

In our view, the requirements of the standard in (b) and (c) above relating to settlement options are somewhat confused. In particular they seem to envisage a binary accounting model based on the strict legal form of settlement (cash or shares). However, IAS 32 sets out rules for *three* different settlement methods – net cash, net shares and gross physical settlement (discussed in Chapter 43 at 5). One consequence of the above is that, if taken literally, the numerator is only required to be adjusted to remove items of income or expense arising from a liability when there is a choice of settlement method. However, mandatory net share settlement also gives rise to a liability and income/expense under IAS 32. In our view any such income statement items should be removed for diluted EPS purposes.

6.3 Dilutive potential ordinary shares

Only those potential shares whose issue would have a dilutive effect on EPS are brought into the calculation. Potential ordinary shares are 'antidilutive' when their conversion to ordinary shares would increase earnings per share or decrease loss per share. *[IAS 33.5, 43]*. The calculation of diluted earnings per share should not assume conversion, exercise, or other issue of potential ordinary shares that would have an antidilutive effect on earnings per share. *[IAS 33.43]*. The standard gives detailed guidance for determining which potential shares are deemed to be dilutive, and hence brought into the diluted EPS calculation. This guidance covers the element of profit which needs to be diluted to trigger inclusion, and the sequence in which potential shares are tested to establish cumulative dilution. Each is discussed below.

6.3.1 Dilution judged by effect on profits from continuing operations

Potential ordinary shares are only to be treated as dilutive if their conversion to ordinary shares would decrease earnings per share or increase loss per share from *continuing* operations. The 'control number' that this focuses on is therefore the net result from continuing operations, which is the net profit or loss attributable to the parent entity, after deducting items relating to preference shares (see 5.2 above) and after excluding items relating to discontinuing operations. *[IAS 33.42]*. The same denominator is required to be used to compute diluted EPS from continuing operations and total diluted EPS. By determining which potential shares are to be included by reference to their impact on continuing EPS can produce some slightly curious results for total EPS. For example, it is possible to exclude instruments which would dilute basic EPS (but not continuing EPS), and include items which are anti-dilutive as regards total profit. This latter point is acknowledged by the standard as follows.

> 'To illustrate the application of the control number notion ... assume that an entity has profit from continuing operations attributable to the parent entity of CU 4,800, a loss from discontinuing operations attributable to the parent entity of (CU 7,200), a loss attributable to the parent entity of (CU 2,400),

and 2,000 ordinary shares and 400 potential ordinary shares outstanding. The entity's basic earnings per share is CU 2.40 for continuing operations, (CU 3.60) for discontinuing operations and (CU 1.20) for the loss. The 400 potential ordinary shares are included in the diluted earnings per share calculation because the resulting CU 2.00 earnings per share for continuing operations is dilutive, assuming no profit or loss impact of those 400 potential ordinary shares. Because profit from continuing operations attributable to the parent entity is the control number, the entity also includes those 400 potential ordinary shares in the calculation of the other earnings per share amounts, even though the resulting earnings per share amounts are antidilutive to their comparable basic earnings per share amounts, i.e. the loss per share is less [(CU 3.00) per share for the loss from discontinuing operations and (CU 1.00) per share for the loss].' *[IAS 33.A3].*

6.3.2 *Dilution judged by the cumulative impact of potential shares*

Where a entity has a number of different potential ordinary shares, in deciding whether they are dilutive (and hence reflected in the calculation), each issue or series of potential ordinary shares is to be considered in sequence from the most to the least dilutive. Only those potential shares which produce a cumulative dilution are to be included. This means that some potential shares which would dilute basic EPS if viewed on their own may need to be excluded. This results in a diluted EPS showing the maximum overall dilution of basic EPS. The standard observes that options and warrants should generally be included first as they do not affect the numerator in the diluted EPS calculation (but see the discussion at 6.4.2 below). *[IAS 33.44].* The way this is to be done is illustrated in the following example.

Example 33.8: Calculation of weighted average number of shares: determining the order in which to include dilutive instruments [IAS 33.IE9]

Earnings	€
Profit from continuing operations attributable to the parent entity	16,400,000
Less dividends on preference shares	(6,400,000)
Profit from continuing operations attributable to ordinary equity holders of the parent entity	10,000,000
Loss from discontinuing operations attributable to the parent entity	(4,000,000)
Profit attributable to ordinary equity holders of the parent entity	6,000,000
Ordinary shares outstanding	2,000,000
Average market price of one ordinary share during year	€75.00

Potential Ordinary Shares

Options	100,000 with exercise price of €60
Convertible preference shares	800,000 shares with a par value of €100 entitled to a cumulative dividend of €8 per share. Each preference share is convertible to two ordinary shares.
5% convertible bonds	Nominal amount €100,000,000. Each €1,000 bond is convertible to 20 ordinary shares. There is no amortisation of premium or discount affecting the determination of interest expense.
Tax rate	40%

Increase in Earnings Attributable to Ordinary Equity Holders on Conversion of Potential Ordinary Shares

	Increase in earnings €	Increase in number of ordinary shares	Earnings per incremental share €
Options			
Increase in earnings	Nil		
Incremental shares issued for no consideration			
100,000 × (€75 – €60) ÷ €75 =		20,000	Nil
Convertible preference shares			
Increase in earnings			
€800,000 × 100 × 0.08 =	6,400,000		
Incremental shares			
2 × 800,000 =		1,600,000	4.00
5% convertible bonds			
Increase in earnings			
€100,000,000 × 0.05 × (1 – 0.40) =	3,000,000		
Incremental shares			
100,000 × 20 =		2,000,000	1.50

The order in which to include the dilutive instruments is therefore:

(1) Options
(2) 5% convertible bonds
(3) Convertible preference shares

Calculation of Diluted Earnings per Share

	Profit from continuing operations attributable to ordinary equity holders of the parent entity (control number)	Ordinary shares	Per share	
	€		€	
As reported	10,000,000	2,000,000	5.00	
Options	–	20,000		
	10,000,000	2,020,000	4.95	Dilutive
5% convertible bonds	3,000,000	2,000,000		
	13,000,000	4,020,000	3.23	Dilutive
Convertible preference shares	6,400,000	1,600,000		
	19,400,000	5,620,000	3.45	Antidilutive

Because diluted earnings per share is increased when taking the convertible preference shares into account (from €3.23 to €3.45), the convertible preference shares are antidilutive and are ignored in the calculation of diluted earnings per share. Therefore, diluted earnings per share for profit from continuing operations is €3.23:

	Basic EPS		Diluted EPS	
	€		€	
Profit from continuing operations attributable to ordinary equity holders of the parent entity	5.00		3.23	
Loss from discontinuing operations attributable to ordinary equity holders of the parent entity	(2.00)	(a)	(0.99)	(b)
Profit attributable to ordinary equity holders of the parent entity	3.00	(c)	2.24	(d)

(a) (€4,000,000) ÷ 2,000,000 = (€2.00)
(b) (€4,000,000) ÷ 4,020,000 = (€0.99)
(c) €6,000,000 ÷ 2,000,000 = €3.00
(d) (€6,000,000 + €3,000,000) ÷ 4,020,000 = €2.24

This example does not illustrate the classification of the components of convertible financial instruments as liabilities and equity or the classification of related interest and dividends as expenses and equity as required by IAS 32.

6.4 Particular types of dilutive instruments

6.4.1 *Convertible instruments*

In order to secure a lower rate of interest, entities sometimes attach benefits to loan stock, debentures or preference shares in the form of conversion rights. These permit the holder to convert his holding in whole or part into equity capital. The right is normally exercisable between specified dates. The ultimate conversion of the instrument will have the following effects:

(a) there will be an increase in earnings by the amount of the interest (or items relating to preference shares) no longer payable. As interest is normally allowable for tax purposes, the effect on earnings may be net of a tax deduction relating to some or all of the items; and

(b) the number of ordinary shares in issue will increase. The diluted EPS should be calculated assuming that the instrument is converted into the maximum possible number of shares. *[IAS 33.49]*.

Convertible preference shares will be antidilutive whenever the amount of the dividend on such shares declared in or accumulated for the current period per ordinary share obtainable on conversion exceeds basic earnings per share. Similarly, convertible debt will be antidilutive whenever its interest (net of tax and other changes in income or expense) per ordinary share obtainable on conversion exceeds basic earnings per share. *[IAS 33.50]*.

A curious feature of the standard is the different treatment applied to the conversion feature in a convertible instrument to that applied to a standalone option or warrant (see 6.4.2 below). IAS 32 requires split accounting for embedded conversion rights in a host convertible instrument (see Chapter 43 at 6). The effect of that is that for accounting purposes convertible instruments are treated in the same way as an equivalent non-convertible instrument accompanied by a standalone warrant. It is somewhat illogical, therefore, that IAS 33 requires a different treatment to assess the dilution arising from separate and embedded warrants and options. In January 2006 the IASB indicated that it intended to address this, and proposed extending the so called treasury stock method to convertible instruments.[4] In March 2007, the IASB indicated that its earlier deliberations on the subject had been superseded by revised proposals. The revised proposals themselves were suspended as discussed at 8.1 below.

6.4.1.A *Convertible debt*

The EPS calculation for convertible bonds is illustrated in the following example:

Example 33.9: Treatment of convertible bonds in diluted EPS calculations *[IAS 33.IE6]*

Profit attributable to ordinary equity holders of the parent entity	€1,004
Ordinary shares outstanding	1,000
Basic earnings per share	€1.00
Convertible bonds	100
Each block of 10 bonds is convertible into three ordinary shares	
Interest expense for the current year relating to the liability component of the convertible bonds	€10
Current and deferred tax relating to that interest expense	€4

Note: the interest expense includes amortisation of the discount arising on initial recognition of the liability component (see IAS 32 – *Financial Instruments: Presentation*).

Adjusted profit attributable to ordinary equity holders of the parent entity	€1,004 + €10 – €4 = €1,010
Number of ordinary shares resulting from conversion of bonds	30
Number of ordinary shares used to calculate diluted earnings per share	1,000 + 30 = 1,030
Diluted earnings per share	€1,010 ÷ 1,030 = €0.98

This example does not illustrate the classification of the components of convertible financial instruments as liabilities and equity or the classification of related interest and dividends as expenses and equity as required by IAS 32.

As discussed at 6.2.2 above, the standard also discusses the impact on diluted EPS of different settlement options. As discussed earlier, we believe this should be taken to mean that for diluted EPS purposes earnings should be adjusted to remove any items that arose from an instrument being classified as an asset or liability rather than equity. The standard claims to illustrate settlement options with the following example.

Example 33.10: Convertible bonds settled in shares or cash at the issuer's option [IAS 33.IE8]

An entity issues 2,000 convertible bonds at the beginning of Year 1. The bonds have a three-year term, and are issued at par with a face value of €1,000 per bond, giving total proceeds of €2,000,000. Interest is payable annually in arrears at a nominal annual interest rate of 6 per cent. Each bond is convertible at any time up to maturity into 250 common shares. The entity has an option to settle the principal amount of the convertible bonds in ordinary shares or in cash.

When the bonds are issued, the prevailing market interest rate for similar debt without a conversion option is 9 per cent. At the issue date, the market price of one common share is €3. Income tax is ignored.

Profit attributable to ordinary equity holders of the parent entity Year 1	€1,000,000
Ordinary shares outstanding	1,200,000
Convertible bonds outstanding	2,000
Allocation of proceeds of the bond issue:	
Liability component	* €1,848,122
Equity component	€151,878
	€2,000,000

The liability and equity components would be determined in accordance with IAS 32. These amounts are recognised as the initial carrying amounts of the liability and equity components. The amount assigned to the issuer conversion option equity element is an addition to equity and is not adjusted.

* This represents the present value of the principal and interest discounted at 9% – €2,000,000 payable at the end of three years; €120,000 payable annually in arrears for three years.

Basic earnings per share Year 1:

$$\frac{€1,000,000}{1,200,000} = €0.83 \text{ per ordinary share}$$

Diluted earnings per share Year 1:

It is presumed that the issuer will settle the contract by the issue of ordinary shares. The dilutive effect is therefore calculated in accordance with paragraph 59 of the Standard.

$$\frac{€1,000,000 + €166,331^{(a)}}{1,200,000 + 500,000^{(b)}} = €0.69 \text{ per ordinary share}$$

(a) Profit is adjusted for the accretion of €166,331 (€1,848,122 × 9%) of the liability because of the passage of time.

(b) 500,000 ordinary shares = 250 ordinary shares × 2,000 convertible bonds

It is a little hard to know what to make of this example, which seems to raise more questions than it answers without actually illustrating any impact on the calculation. As regards settlement options, it really adds nothing to the text of the standard and the basic approach to convertibles shown in Example 33.9 above – aside of saying that, because the issuer can choose to settle in shares or cash, share settlement is assumed and a diluted EPS calculated at all. Furthermore, the description of the terms that the entity 'has an option to settle the principal in shares or cash' is far from precise, and its meaning far from clear. Given that a component of the instrument is classified as a liability, we presume that the settlement option means that if the holder does not convert, the issuer could choose to deliver a *variable* quantity of shares having a value equal to the principal (€2,000,000). This is because all of the instrument would be equity if the quantity of shares was fixed (discussed in Chapter 43 at 5). That would then mean that the number of shares to be issued would either be:

- 500,000 assuming the holder converts; or
- such a quantity that has a value at the repayment date of €2,000,000.

Regrettably, neither the text of the standard nor the example appended to it gives any indication of which of these should be used, or how the latter should be calculated. One possible approach would be to compare the principal of the convertible debt at the end of the reporting period with the market value of the entity's shares at that date. This would then enable the more dilutive of the two options to be used.

6.4.1.B *Convertible preference shares*

The rules for convertible preference shares are very similar to those detailed above in the case of convertible debt, i.e. dividends and other returns to preference shareholders are added back to earnings used for basic EPS and the maximum number of ordinary shares that could be issued on conversion should be used in the calculation.

As discussed at 5.2 above, one possible return to preference shareholders is a premium payable on redemption or induced early conversion in excess of the original terms. IAS 33 notes that the redemption or induced conversion of convertible preference shares may affect only a portion of the previously outstanding convertible preference shares. In such cases, the standard makes clear that any excess consideration is attributed to those shares that are redeemed or converted for the purpose of determining whether the remaining outstanding preference shares are dilutive. In other words, the shares redeemed or converted are considered separately from those shares that are not redeemed or converted. *[IAS 33.51]*.

6.4.1.C *Participating equity instruments and two class shares with conversion rights*

The treatment for basic EPS of participating equity instruments and two class shares is discussed at 5.4 above. When discussing these instruments the standard observes that when calculating diluted EPS;

- conversion is assumed for those instruments that are convertible into ordinary shares if the effect is dilutive;
- for those that are not convertible into a class of ordinary shares, profit or loss for the period is allocated to the different classes of shares and participating equity instruments in accordance with their dividend rights or other rights to participate in undistributed earnings. *[IAS 33.A14]*.

What the standard seems to be hinting at here, without directly addressing, is how to present EPS for two or more classes of ordinary shares (say, class A and class B) when one class can convert into another (say, class B can convert into class A). It this scenario, in our view the basic EPS for each class should be calculated based on profit entitlement (see 5.4 above). For diluted EPS it would be necessary to attribute to class A the profits attributed to class B in the basic EPS – if the overall effect were dilutive to class A, conversion should be assumed.

6.4.2 *Options, warrants and their equivalents*

6.4.2.A *The numerator*

IAS 33 contains a fair quantity of detailed guidance on the treatment for diluted EPS purposes of options, warrants and their equivalents which it defines as 'financial instruments that give the holder the right to purchase ordinary shares'. *[IAS 33.5]*. However, it was largely written before the significant developments in accounting for such instruments (IFRS 2 and IAS 32). Although the standard was updated as part of the 'improvements' project in 2003 and further amended as a consequence of IFRS 2, in our view the result is a somewhat unclear patchwork.

IAS 33 clearly states that 'Options and warrants ... do not affect the numerator of the calculation' *[IAS 33.44]* and this text was added in 2003 as part of the improvements project, so clearly drafted against the back drop of the impending move to expensing share-based payments and also the (then) recent changes to IAS 32 regarding accounting for derivatives over an entity's own shares. As regards employee share options in particular, neither IAS 33 (as updated by IFRS 2) nor the worked example appended to it (see Example 33.13 at 6.4.5 below) make reference to removing either some or all the charge when computing diluted EPS. However, this seems to sit somewhat awkwardly (particularly for options outside the scope of IFRS 2) with the general requirement for calculating diluted EPS that earnings be adjusted for the effects of 'any other changes in income or expense that would result from the conversion of the dilutive potential ordinary shares.' *[IAS 33.33]*. Furthermore, IAS 33 explicitly requires an adjustment to the numerator in some circumstances:

(a) as discussed at 6.2.2 above, adjustment to the numerator may be required for a contract (which could include options and warrants) that may be settled in ordinary shares or cash at the entity's option when such a contract is presented for accounting purposes as an asset or a liability, or has an equity component and a liability component. In such a case, the standard requires that 'the entity shall adjust the numerator for any changes in profit or loss that would have resulted during the period if the contract had been classified wholly as an equity instrument'. For contracts that may be settled in ordinary shares or cash at the holder's option, 'the more dilutive of cash settlement and share settlement shall be used in calculating diluted earnings per share'; *[IAS 33.59-60]*

(b) where an option agreement requires or permits the tendering of debt in payment of the exercise price (and, if the holder could choose to pay cash, that tendering debt is more advantageous to him) the numerator should be adjusted for the after tax amount of any such debt assumed to be tendered (see 6.4.2.E below); and *[IAS 33.A7]*

(c) where option proceeds are required to be applied to redeem debt or other instruments of the entity (see 6.4.2.F below). *[IAS 33.A9]*.

For situations covered by (b) and (c) above the specific requirements of the standard for adjusting the numerator should be followed. In other circumstances, the interaction of these complex and conflicting requirements with each other and with IFRS 2 and IAS 32 seem to lead to the following requirements when computing the numerator for diluted EPS:

(a) for instruments accounted for under IAS 32:
   (i) for a contract classified wholly as an equity instrument, no adjustment to the numerator will be necessary; and
   (ii) for a contract not classified wholly as an equity instrument, the numerator should be adjusted for any changes in profit or loss that would have resulted if it had been classified wholly as an equity instrument; and

(b) for instruments accounted for under IFRS 2:
   (i) for those treated as equity settled, the IFRS 2 charge should *not* be adjusted for; and
   (ii) for those treated as cash settled, the numerator should be adjusted for any changes in profit or loss that would have resulted if the instrument had been classified wholly as an equity instrument.

In respect of (b), part (i) is supported by the IASB's view regarding share-based payments as follows. 'Some argue that any cost arising from share-based payment transactions is already recognised in the dilution of earnings per share (EPS). If an expense were recognised in the income statement, EPS would be "hit twice". However, the Board noted that this result is appropriate. For example, if the entity paid the employees in cash for their services and the cash was then returned to the entity, as consideration for the issue of share options, the effect on EPS would be the same as issuing those options direct to the employees. The dual effect on EPS simply reflects the two economic events that have occurred: the entity has issued shares or share options, thereby increasing the number of shares included in the EPS calculation – although, in the case of options, only to the extent that the options are regarded as dilutive – and it has also consumed the resources it received for those options, thereby decreasing earnings. ... In summary, the Board concluded that the dual effect on diluted EPS is not double-counting the effects of a share or share option grant – the same effect is not counted twice. Rather, two different effects are each counted once.'[5]

As for part (ii) of (b) above, this is the explicit requirement of IAS 33 when the entity can choose cash or share settlement. It is, in our view, also implicit in the requirement of the standard that for contracts that may be settled in ordinary shares or cash at the holder's option, the more dilutive of cash settlement and share settlement should be used in calculating diluted earnings per share. This would also explain why IFRS 2 requires the computation of grant date fair values for cash settled share based payments when that information is not actually required for accounting purposes (see Chapter 30 at 9.3.2).

6.4.2.B Written call options

Entities may issue options or warrants which give holders the right to subscribe for shares at fixed prices on specified future dates. If the options or warrants are exercised then:

(a) the number of shares in issue will be increased; and

(b) funds will flow into the company and these will produce income.

For calculating diluted EPS, IAS 33 requires the exercise of all dilutive options and warrants to be assumed. *[IAS 33.45]*. Options and warrants are considered dilutive when they would result in the issue of ordinary shares for less than the average market price of ordinary shares during the period. The amount of the dilution is taken to be the average market price of ordinary shares during the period minus the issue price. *[IAS 33.46]*.

Under IAS 33 the effects of such potential ordinary shares on the diluted EPS are reflected in the computation of the denominator using a method sometimes called the 'treasury stock method'.

For this purpose, the weighted average number of shares used in calculating the basic EPS is increased, but not by the full number of shares that would be issued on exercise of the instruments. To work out how many additional shares to include in the denominator, the assumed proceeds from these issues are to be treated as having been received in exchange for:

- a certain number of shares at their average market price for the period (i.e. no EPS impact); and
- the remainder for no consideration (i.e. full dilution with no earnings enhancement). *[IAS 33.45-46]*.

This means that the excess of the total number of potential shares over the number that could be issued at their average market price for the period out of the issue proceeds is included within the denominator; the calculation is illustrated as follows:

Example 33.11: Effects of share options on diluted earnings per share [IAS 33.IE5]

Profit attributable to ordinary equity holders of the parent entity for year	€1,200,000
Weighted average number of ordinary shares outstanding during year	500,000 shares
Average market price of one ordinary share during year	€20.00
Weighted average number of shares under option during year	100,000 shares
Exercise price for shares under option during year	€15.00

Calculation of earnings per share

	Earnings		*Shares*	*Per share*
Profit attributable to ordinary equity holders of the parent entity for year	€1,200,000			
Weighted average shares outstanding during year			500,000	
Basic earnings per share				€2.40
Weighted average number of shares under option			100,000	
Weighted average number of shares that would have been issued at average market price: (100,000 × €15.00) ÷ €20.00		*	(75,000)	
Diluted earnings per share	€1,200,000		525,000	€2.29

* Earnings have not increased because the total number of shares has increased only by the number of shares (25,000) deemed to have been issued for no consideration.

The number of shares viewed as fairly priced (and hence neither dilutive nor antidilutive) for this purpose is calculated on the basis of the average price of the ordinary shares during the reporting period. *[IAS 33.46].* The standard observes that, in theory, calculating an average share price for the period could include every market transaction in the shares. However, it notes that as a practical matter an average (weekly or monthly) will usually be adequate. *[IAS 33.A4].* The individual prices used should generally be the closing market price unless prices fluctuate widely, in which case the average of high and low prices may be more representative. Whatever method is adopted, it should be used consistently unless it ceases to yield a representative price. For example, closing prices may have been used consistently in a series of relatively stable periods then a change to high/low average could be appropriate when prices begin to fluctuate more widely. *[IAS 33.A5].*

The shares would be deemed to have been issued at the beginning of the period or, if later, the date of issue of the warrants or options. Options which are exercised or lapse in the period are included for the portion of the period during which they were outstanding. *[IAS 33.36, 38]*

Although the standard seems to require that the fair value used should be the average for the reporting period for all outstanding options or warrants, in our view, for instruments issued, lapsed or exercised during the period a credible case could be made for using an average price for that part of the reporting period that the instrument was outstanding. Indeed, this view is supported by the comprehensive example included in the standard (see the appendix to this chapter), where in computing the number of warrants to be included in calculating the diluted EPS for the full year, the average price used was not that for the full year, but only for the period that the warrants were outstanding.

One practical problem with this requirement is that the average market price of ordinary shares for the reporting period may not be available. Examples would include an entity only listed for part of the period, or an unlisted entity giving voluntary disclosures. In such cases estimates of the market price would need to be made.

6.4.2.C *Written put options and forward purchase agreements*

Contracts that require the entity to repurchase its own shares, such as written put options and forward purchase contracts, should be reflected in the calculation of diluted earnings per share if the effect is dilutive. If these contracts are 'in the money' during the period (i.e. the exercise or settlement price is above the average market price for that period), IAS 33 requires the potential dilutive effect on EPS to be calculated as follows:

- it should be assumed that at the beginning of the period sufficient ordinary shares are issued (at the average market price during the period) to raise proceeds to satisfy the contract;
- the proceeds from the issue are then assumed to be used to satisfy the contract (i.e. to buy back ordinary shares); and
- the incremental ordinary shares (the difference between the number of ordinary shares assumed issued and the number of ordinary shares received from satisfying the contract) should be included in the calculation of diluted earnings per share. *[IAS 33.63].*

The standard illustrates this methodology as follows: '... assume that an entity has outstanding 120 written put options on its ordinary shares with an exercise price of CU 35. The average market price of its ordinary shares for the period is CU 28. In calculating diluted earnings per share, the entity assumes that it issued 150 shares at CU 28 per share at the beginning of the period to satisfy its put obligation of CU 4,200. The difference between the 150 ordinary shares issued and the 120 ordinary shares received from satisfying the put option (30 incremental ordinary shares) is added to the denominator in calculating diluted earnings per share.' *[IAS 33.A10]*.

6.4.2.D Options over convertible instruments

Although not common, it is possible that an entity grants options or warrants to acquire not ordinary shares directly but other instruments convertible into them (such as convertible preference shares or debt). In this scenario, IAS 33 sets a dual test:

- exercise is assumed whenever the average prices of both the convertible instrument and the ordinary shares obtainable upon conversion are above the exercise price of the options or warrants; but
- exercise is not assumed unless conversion of similar outstanding convertible instruments, if any, is also assumed. *[IAS 33.A6]*.

6.4.2.E Settlement of option exercise price with debt or other instruments of the entity

The standard notes that options or warrants may permit or require the tendering of debt or other instruments of the entity (or its parent or a subsidiary) in payment of all or a portion of the exercise price. In the calculation of diluted earnings per share, those options or warrants have a dilutive effect if (a) the average market price of the related ordinary shares for the period exceeds the exercise price or (b) the selling price of the instrument to be tendered is below that at which the instrument may be tendered under the option or warrant agreement and the resulting discount establishes an effective exercise price below the market price of the ordinary shares obtainable upon exercise. In the calculation of diluted EPS, those options or warrants should be assumed to be exercised and the debt or other instruments assumed to be tendered. If tendering cash is more advantageous to the option or warrant holder and the contract permits it, tendering of cash should be assumed. Interest (net of tax) on any debt assumed to be tendered is added back as an adjustment to the numerator. *[IAS 33.A7]*.

Similar treatment is given to preference shares that have similar provisions or to other instruments that have conversion options that permit the investor to pay cash for a more favourable conversion rate. *[IAS 33.A8]*.

6.4.2.F Specified application of option proceeds

IAS 33 observes that the underlying terms of certain options or warrants may require the proceeds received from the exercise of those instruments to be applied to redeem debt or other instruments of the entity (or its parent or a subsidiary). In which case it requires that in 'the calculation of diluted earnings per share, those options or warrants are assumed to be exercised and the proceeds applied to purchase the debt at its average market price rather than to purchase ordinary shares. However, the excess proceeds received from the assumed exercise over the amount used for the assumed purchase of debt are considered (i.e. assumed to be used to buy back ordinary shares) in the diluted earnings per share calculation. Interest (net of tax) on any debt assumed to be purchased is added back as an adjustment to the numerator.' *[IAS 33.A9].*

In our view this drafting is far from clear and with it the intentions of the IASB. However, it seems to have in mind what one might call an 'in substance convertible bond' made up of a straight option and a requirement that the proceeds be used to redeem debt. On that basis, the phrase 'rather than purchase ordinary shares' presumably means that the 'normal' treasury stock rules for options are not applied, but rather more shares are brought into the denominator and interest is added back to the numerator. Put another way, we believe this provision is trying to achieve consistency with the requirements for convertible debt.

6.4.3 Purchased options and warrants

IAS 33 states that a holding by an entity of options over its own shares will always be antidilutive because:

- put options would only be exercised if the exercise price were higher than the market price; and
- call options would only be exercised if the exercise price were lower than the market price.

Accordingly, the standard requires that such instruments are not included in the calculation of diluted EPS. *[IAS 33.62].*

This ostensibly rather neat dismissal of the issue strikes us as another example of IAS 33 failing to recognise the accounting requirements of IAS 32. It is true that the application of the treasury stock method to an option which is in-the-money from the entity's perspective (by reference to the average share price for the period) would *reduce* the number of shares in the denominator, and hence be anti-dilutive. However, dependent upon the settlement mechanism and the share price at the beginning and end of the period, the option could have resulted in a gain being reported (see Chapter 43 at 5). It is possible that the removal of the gain from the numerator could have a greater dilutive effect than the reduction in the denominator and hence render the option dilutive. If that is the case, we believe the option should be included in the diluted EPS calculation.

6.4.4 Partly paid shares

As noted at 3 above, shares issued in partly paid form are to be included in the basic EPS as a fraction of a share, based on dividend participation. As regards diluted EPS they are to be treated, to the extent that they are not entitled to participate in dividends, as the equivalent of options or warrants. The unpaid balance is assumed to represent proceeds used to purchase ordinary shares. The number of shares included in diluted earnings per share is the difference between the number of shares subscribed and the number of shares assumed to be purchased. *[IAS 33.A16].*

The mechanics of this treatment are not further spelt out in the standard, but curiously the phrase 'treated as a fraction of an ordinary share' is not repeated. Instead, it is 'the number of shares subscribed' which the standard says should be compared to the number assumed purchased to measure dilution. Unfortunately 'the number of shares subscribed' is not defined. Whilst this could be read to mean that the remaining unpaid consideration is to be treated as the exercise price for options over *all* of the shares issued in partly paid form, the results would make little sense. In our view, the more sensible interpretation is that the unpaid capital should be viewed as the exercise price for options over the proportion of the shares not reflected in the basic EPS. This would mean that if the average share price for the period were the same as the total issue price, then no dilution would be reported. Furthermore, an issue of partly paid shares, say 50% paid with 50% dividend entitlement is, economically identical to an issue of half the quantity as fully paid (with full dividend entitlement) and a forward contract for the remaining half. In that scenario, the issued shares would be incorporated into the basic and diluted EPS in full from the date of issue. The forward contract would be included in diluted EPS calculation by comparing the contracted number of shares with the number of shares that could be bought out of proceeds based on the average share price for the period. In our view, these economically identical transactions should produce the same diluted EPS – that would be achieved by interpreting 'the number of shares subscribed' as the number *economically* subscribed, i.e. the proportion of part-paid shares not already included in basic EPS.

An illustration of what the calculation would look like is as follows:

Example 33.12: Partly paid shares

Capital structure

Issued share capital as at 31 December 2013:
2,000,000 ordinary shares of 10c each

Issued on 1 January 2014:
500,000 part paid ordinary shares of 10c each. Full consideration of 50c per share (being fair value at 1 January 2012) paid up 50% on issue. Dividend participation 50% until fully paid. New shares remain part paid at 31 December 2014.

Average fair value of one ordinary share for the period 60c.

Trading results

Net profit attributable to ordinary shareholders for the year ended 31 December 2014: €100,000.

Computation of basic and diluted EPS

	Net profit attributable to ordinary shareholders €	*Ordinary shares* No.	*Per share*
Fully paid shares	100,000	2,000,000	
Partly paid shares (1)		250,000	
Basic EPS	100,000	2,250,000	4.44c
Dilutive effect of partly paid shares (2)		41,667	
Diluted EPS	100,000	2,291,667	4.36c

(1) 50% dividend rights for 500,000 shares.

(2) Outstanding consideration of €125,000 (500,000 × 25c), using fair value of 60c this equates to 208,333 shares, hence the number of dilutive shares deemed issued for free is 41,667 (250,000 – 208,333).

The example assumes the fair value of the shares over the year is higher than the issue price, which explains why some extra shares fall to be included in the diluted EPS. If the average fair value remained at the issue price of 50c then no additional shares would be included for diluted EPS.

6.4.5 Share based payments

Share options and other incentive schemes are an increasingly common feature of employee remuneration, and can come in many forms. For diluted EPS purposes, IAS 33 identifies two categories and specifies the diluted EPS treatment for each. The categories are:

(a) performance-based employee share options; and

(b) employee share options with fixed or determinable terms and non-vested ordinary shares. *[IAS 33.48].*

Before moving on to the diluted EPS treatment, it is worth noting an issue that arises from the way IAS 33 phrases this categorisation and subsequent guidance. The drafting does not make clear whether the two categories cover all possible schemes. In our view all schemes should fall to be treated as either category (a) or category (b). Any arrangements where entitlement is subject to future performance would fall into category (a) with category (b) being the default for all other arrangements.

Schemes in the first category are to be treated as contingently issuable shares (see 6.4.6 below) because their issue is contingent upon satisfying specified conditions in addition to the passage of time. *[IAS 33.48].* This gives rise to an apparent paradox relating to shares held in treasury (and shown as a deduction from equity). Frequently employee share schemes will be arranged in this way, with shares released from treasury to satisfy the exercise of options. The rules for, and indeed the title, 'contingently issuable shares' seems to refer to shares which do not exist at the end of the reporting period, but may be issued subsequently. Shares held in treasury to satisfy employee options are obviously already 'in issue', so a literal reading of the standard would seem to imply that these have no dilutive impact. In our view this makes little sense, and does not seem to be what the standard setters intended. A sensible interpretation would be to consider the vesting of treasury shares, and hence ceasing to be treated as cancelled for EPS purposes (see 3.2 above), as an issue for calculating diluted EPS.

Those in the second category are to be treated as options (see 6.4.2 above). They should be regarded as outstanding from the grant date, even if they vest, and hence can be realised by the employees, at some later date. *[IAS 33.48].* An example would be an unexpired loyalty period. This means that some shares may be included in diluted EPS which never, in fact, get issued to employees because they fail to remain with the company for this period. Whilst this requirement is clear, it sits rather awkwardly with the rules for contingently issuable shares which, as discussed at 6.4.6 below, tend to restrict the number of potential shares accounted for. Furthermore, for share options and other share-based payment arrangements to which IFRS 2 applies, the proceeds figure to be used in calculating the dilution under such schemes should include the fair value (as determined in accordance with IFRS 2) of any goods or services to be supplied to the entity in the future under the arrangement. *[IAS 33.47A].* An example illustrating the latter point is as follows:

Example 33.13: Determining the exercise price of employee share options [IAS 33.IE5A]

Weighted average number of unvested share options per employee	1,000
Weighted average amount per employee to be recognised over the remainder of the vesting period for employee services to be rendered as consideration for the share options, determined in accordance with IFRS 2	€1,200.00
Cash exercise price of unvested share options	€15.00
Calculation of adjusted exercise price	
Fair value of services yet to be rendered per employee:	€1,200.00
Fair value of services yet to be rendered per option: (€1,200 ÷ 1,000)	€1.20
Total exercise price of share options: (€15.00 + €1.20)	€16.20

Whilst the standard requires that the additional deemed proceeds is the *fair value* of goods or services yet to be received (which could, in theory, vary over time), the example seems to clarify that it is the IFRS 2 expense yet to be charged to income.

What this requirement seeks to reflect is that for such options the issuer will receive not just the cash proceeds (if any) under the option when it is exercised but also valuable goods and services over its life. This will result in the dilutive effect of the options increasing over time as the deemed proceeds on exercise of the options reduces.

6.4.6 Contingently issuable shares

As part of the improvements project, IAS 33 was updated to contain considerable detailed guidance, including a numerical worked example, on contingently issuable shares. Contingently issuable ordinary shares are defined as 'ordinary shares issuable for little or no cash or other consideration upon satisfaction of specified conditions in a contingent share agreement.' A contingent share agreement is, perhaps unnecessarily, also defined by the standard as 'an agreement to issue shares that is dependent on the satisfaction of specified conditions.' *[IAS 33.5].* The basic rule is that the number of contingently issuable shares to be included in the diluted EPS calculation is 'based on the number of shares that would be issuable if the end of the period were the end of the contingency period'. *[IAS 33.52].* This requirement to look at the status of the contingency at the end of the reporting period, rather than to consider the most likely outcome, seems to have the overall result of *reducing* the amount of dilution disclosed. Furthermore, these detailed rules on contingently issuable shares are arguably at odds with the more general requirement of 'giving effect to *all* dilutive potential ordinary shares outstanding during the period'. *[IAS 33.32].* (Emphasis added).

The discussions in the standard cover three broad categories: earnings-based contingencies, share-price-based contingencies, and other contingencies. These are discussed in turn below.

The number of shares contingently issuable may depend on future earnings and future prices of the ordinary shares. In such cases, the standard makes clear that the number of shares included in the diluted EPS calculation is based on both conditions (i.e. earnings to date and the current market price at the end of the reporting period). In other words, contingently issuable shares are not included in the diluted EPS calculation unless both conditions are met. *[IAS 33.55].*

6.4.6.A Earnings-based contingencies

The standard discusses the scenario where shares would be issued contingent upon the attainment or maintenance of a specified amount of earnings for a period. In such a case the standard requires that 'if that amount has been attained at the end of the reporting period but must be maintained beyond the end of the reporting period for an additional period, then the additional ordinary shares are treated as outstanding, if the effect is dilutive, when calculating diluted earnings per share. In that case, the calculation of diluted earnings per share is based on the number of ordinary shares that would be issued if the amount of earnings at the end of the reporting period were the amount of earnings at the end of the contingency period'. *[IAS 33.53].* Although perhaps not the clearest of drafting, this seems to be saying that earnings-based contingencies need to be viewed as an absolute cumulative hurdle which either is met or not met at the reporting date. Often, such contingencies may be contractually expressed in terms of *annual* performance over a number of years, say an average of €1million profit per year for three years. In our view, 'the attainment or maintenance of a specified amount of earnings for a period' in this scenario would mean generating a total of €3million of profits. If that is achieved by the end of a reporting period, the shares are outstanding for diluted EPS purposes and included in the computation if the effect is dilutive. It could, perhaps, be argued that the potential shares should be considered outstanding if profits of €1million were generated at the end of the first year. However, the requirement that the calculation be 'based on the number of ordinary shares that would be issued if the amount of earnings at the end of the reporting period were the amount of earnings at the end of the contingency period' means that the test must be: would shares be issued if the current earnings of €1million were all the profits earned by the end of the three year contingency period? In this example the answer is no, as that amount of earnings would fall short of averaging €1million per year. The standard then notes that, because earnings may change in a future period, the calculation of basic EPS does not include such contingently issuable shares until the end of the contingency period because not all necessary conditions have been satisfied. *[IAS 33.53].*

An earnings-based contingency is illustrated in the following example:

Example 33.14: Contingently issuable shares [IAS 33.IE7]

Ordinary shares outstanding during 2014:	1,000,000 (there were no options, warrants or convertible instruments outstanding during the period)

An agreement related to a recent business combination provides for the issue of additional ordinary shares based on the following conditions:

	5,000 additional ordinary shares for each new retail site opened during 2014
	1,000 additional ordinary shares for each €1,000 of consolidated profit in excess of €2,000,000 for the year ended 31 December 2014
Retail sites opened during the year:	one on 1 May 2014 one on 1 September 2014
Consolidated year-to-date profit attributable to ordinary equity holders of the parent entity:	€1,100,000 as of 31 March 2014 €2,300,000 as of 30 June 2014 €1,900,000 as of 30 September 2014 (including a €450,000 loss from a discontinuing operation) €2,900,000 as of 31 December 2014

Basic earnings per share

	First quarter	*Second quarter*		*Third quarter*		*Fourth quarter*	*Full year*	
Numerator (€)	1,100,000	1,200,000		(400,000)		1,000,000	2,900,000	
Denominator:								
Ordinary shares outstanding	1,000,000	1,000,000		1,000,000		1,000,000	1,000,000	
Retail site contingency	–	3,333	(a)	6,667	(b)	10,000	5,000	(c)
Earnings contingency (d)	–	–		–		–	–	
Total shares	1,000,000	1,003,333		1,006,667		1,010,000	1,005,000	
Basic earnings per share (€)	1.10	1.20		(0.40)		0.99	2.89	

(a) 5,000 shares × 2/3
(b) 5,000 shares + (5,000 shares × 1/3)
(c) (5,000 shares × 8/12) + (5,000 shares × 4/12)
(d) The earnings contingency has no effect on basic earnings per share because it is not certain that the condition is satisfied until the end of the contingency period. The effect is negligible for the fourth-quarter and full-year calculations because it is not certain that the condition is met until the last day of the period.

Diluted earnings per share

	First quarter		*Second quarter*		*Third quarter*		*Fourth quarter*		*Full year*	
Numerator (€)	1,100,000		1,200,000		(400,000)		1,000,000		2,900,000	
Denominator:										
Ordinary shares outstanding	1,000,000		1,000,000		1,000,000		1,000,000		1,000,000	
Retail site contingency	–		5,000		10,000		10,000		10,000	
Earnings contingency	–	(e)	300,000	(f)		(g)	900,000	(h)	900,000	(h)
Total shares	1,000,000		1,305,000		1,010,000		1,910,000		1,910,000	
Diluted earnings per share (€)	1.10		0.92		(0.40)	(i)	0.52		1.52	

(e) Year-to-date profits do not exceed €2,000,000 at 31 March 2014. The Standard does not permit projecting future earnings levels and including the related contingent shares.
(f) [(€2,300,000 – €2,000,000) ÷ 1,000] × 1,000 shares = 300,000 shares.
(g) Year-to-date profit is less than €2,000,000.
(h) [(€2,900,000 – €2,000,000) ÷ 1,000] × 1,000 shares = 900,000 shares.
(i) Because the loss during the third quarter is attributable to a loss from a discontinuing operation, the antidilution rules do not apply. The control number (i.e. profit or loss from continuing operations attributable to the equity holders of the parent entity) is positive. Accordingly, the effect of potential ordinary shares is included in the calculation of diluted earnings per share.

Curiously, this example from IAS 33 illustrates *quarterly* financial reporting. However, the principles are the same whether the reporting period is illustrated as three months or one year. The example does illustrate that the earnings target is a cumulative hurdle over the entire contingency period (four reporting periods in the example) rather than including potential shares based on the assumption that the level of quarterly profit would be maintained for the four quarters.

The standard only discusses earnings criteria based on *absolute* measures; in the example above a cumulative profit of in excess of €2,000,000. In our experience such criteria are rare. In practice criteria are often phrased in terms of *relative* performance against an external benchmark. Examples would be earnings growth targets of inflation plus 2% or EPS growth being in the top quartile of a group of competitors. For contingencies such as these it is impossible to establish an absolute target in order to ask whether it is met at the period end. For example, consider the earnings contingency in IAS 33, discussed above, to achieve profits in excess of €2,000,000 over four quarters. If this instead required the profits to be €2,000,000 adjusted in line with inflation, it would be impossible to know how many shares would be issued if the cumulative profit at the end of the second quarter of €2,300,000 were the amount of earnings at the end of the contingency period. Until the end of the year the absolute level of profit required would be unknown; it would be more or less than €2,000,000 depending on the level of inflation or deflation over the period.

There would seem to be (at least) two different ways of interpreting the requirements of IAS 33 in such a scenario, each resulting in a different diluted EPS figure. One approach would be to consider such criteria as being based on 'a condition other than earnings or market price'. That would mean (as discussed under C below) that the number of shares brought into diluted EPS would be based on the status of the condition at the end of the reporting period. *[IAS 33.56]*. So, if the target was earnings for the year in excess of €2,000,000 adjusted in line with inflation and at the end of the second quarter inflation had been 4%, then the target would become €2,080,000 and hence 220,000 shares would be included for diluted EPS for the second quarter. An alternative approach would be to regard it as an earnings-based contingency and make an assumption as to future inflation over the contingency period. This would allow a cumulative hurdle to be calculated and compared with actual earnings to date. So if at the end of the second quarter it was estimated that the annual inflation for the year was 5%, then the target would become €2,100,000 and hence 200,000 shares would be included for diluted EPS for the second quarter. Given the lack of clarity in the standard, it seems likely that either of the above approaches may be selected in practice.

6.4.6.B Share-price-based contingencies

The provisions here are more straightforward. In these cases, if the effect is dilutive, the calculation of diluted EPS is based on the number of shares that would be issued if the market price at the end of the reporting period were the market price at the end of the contingency period. If the condition is based on an average of market prices over a period of time that extends beyond the end of the reporting period, the average for the period of time that has lapsed should be used. Again the standard explains that, because the market price may change in a future period, the calculation of basic earnings per share does not include such contingently issuable ordinary shares until the end of the contingency period because not all necessary conditions have been satisfied. *[IAS 33.54]*.

6.4.6.C Other contingencies

The requirement regarding contingencies not driven by earnings or share price is as follows: 'assuming that the present status of the condition remains unchanged until the end of the contingency period, the contingently issuable ordinary shares are included in the calculation of diluted earnings per share according to the status at the end of the reporting period.' *[IAS 33.56]*.

The standard illustrates the 'other contingency' rules by the example of shares being issued depending upon the opening of a specified number of retail sites, and such a contingency is included in the numerical example in the standard (see Example 33.14 above). As is the case for earnings-based contingencies discussed above, it would seem that such conditions are always deemed to be expressed as a cumulative hurdle which may or may not be met by the end of the reporting period. Accordingly, the required treatment would be the same if the condition had been expressed in terms of achieving a certain average annual level of shop openings.

6.4.7 Potential ordinary shares of investees

A subsidiary, joint venture or associate may issue to parties other than the parent or investors with joint control of, or significant influence over the investee potential ordinary shares that are convertible into either ordinary shares of the subsidiary, joint venture or associate, or ordinary shares of the parent or investors with joint control of, or significant influence over the investee (the reporting entity). If these potential ordinary shares of the subsidiary, joint venture or associate have a dilutive effect on the basic EPS of the reporting entity, they should be included in the calculation of diluted earnings per share. *[IAS 33.40]*.

The standard requires that such potential ordinary shares should be included in the calculation of diluted EPS as follows:

(a) instruments issued by a subsidiary, joint venture or associate that enable their holders to obtain ordinary shares of the subsidiary, joint venture or associate should be included in calculating the diluted EPS data of the subsidiary, joint venture or associate. Those EPS are then included in the reporting entity's EPS calculations based on the reporting entity's holding of the instruments of the subsidiary, joint venture or associate; and

(b) instruments of a subsidiary, joint venture or associate that are convertible into the reporting entity's ordinary shares should be considered among the potential ordinary shares of the reporting entity for the purpose of calculating diluted EPS. Similarly, options or warrants issued by a subsidiary, joint venture or associate to purchase ordinary shares of the reporting entity should be considered among the potential ordinary shares of the reporting entity in the calculation of consolidated diluted EPS. *[IAS 33.A11]*.

For the purpose of determining the EPS effect of instruments issued by a reporting entity that are convertible into ordinary shares of a subsidiary, joint venture or associate, the standard requires that the instruments are assumed to be converted and the numerator (profit or loss attributable to ordinary equity holders of the parent entity) adjusted as necessary in accordance with the normal rules (see 6.2.1 above). In addition to those adjustments, the numerator is adjusted for any change in the profit or loss recorded by the reporting entity (such as dividend income or equity method income) that is attributable to the increase in the number of ordinary shares of the subsidiary, joint venture or associate outstanding as a result of the assumed conversion. The denominator of the diluted EPS calculation is not affected because the number of ordinary shares of the reporting entity outstanding would not change upon assumed conversion. *[IAS 33.A12]*.

The computation under (a) above is illustrated in the following example.

Example 33.15: Warrants issued by a subsidiary [IAS 33.IE10]

Parent:

Profit attributable to ordinary equity holders of the parent entity	€12,000 (excluding any earnings of, or dividends paid by, the subsidiary)
Ordinary shares outstanding	10,000
Instruments of subsidiary owned by the parent	800 ordinary shares 30 warrants exercisable to purchase ordinary shares of subsidiary 300 convertible preference shares

Subsidiary:

Profit	€5,400
Ordinary shares outstanding	1,000
Warrants	150, exercisable to purchase ordinary shares of the subsidiary
Exercise price	€10
Average market price of one ordinary share	€20
Convertible preference shares	400, each convertible into one ordinary share
Dividends on preference shares	€1 per share

No inter-company eliminations or adjustments were necessary except for dividends.
For the purposes of this illustration, income taxes have been ignored.

Chapter 33

Subsidiary's earnings per share

Basic EPS €5.00 calculated: $\dfrac{€5{,}400^{(a)} - €400^{(b)}}{1{,}000^{(c)}}$

Diluted EPS €3.66 calculated: $\dfrac{€5{,}400^{(d)}}{1{,}000 + 75^{(e)} + 400^{(f)}}$

(a) Subsidiary's profit.
(b) Dividends paid by subsidiary on convertible preference shares.
(c) Subsidiary's ordinary shares outstanding.
(d) Subsidiary's profit attributable to ordinary equity holders (€5,000) increased by €400 preference dividends for the purpose of calculating diluted earnings per share.
(e) Incremental shares from warrants, calculated: [(€20 – €10) ÷ €20] × 150.
(f) Subsidiary's ordinary shares assumed outstanding from conversion of convertible preference shares, calculated: 400 convertible preference shares × conversion factor of 1.

Consolidated earnings per share

Basic EPS €1.63 calculated: $\dfrac{€12{,}000^{(g)} + €4{,}300^{(h)}}{10{,}000^{(i)}}$

Diluted EPS €1.61 calculated: $\dfrac{€12{,}000 + €2{,}928^{(j)} + €55^{(k)} + €1{,}098^{(l)}}{10{,}000}$

(g) Parent's profit attributable to ordinary equity holders of the parent entity.
(h) Portion of subsidiary's profit to be included in consolidated basic earnings per share, calculated: (800 × CU 5.00) + (300 × €1.00)
(i) Parent's ordinary shares outstanding.
(j) Parent's proportionate interest in subsidiary's earnings attributable to ordinary shares, calculated: (800 ÷ 1,000) × (1,000 shares × €3.66 per share)
(k) Parent's proportionate interest in subsidiary's earnings attributable to warrants, calculated: (30 ÷ 150) × (75 incremental shares × €3.66 per share)
(l) Parent's proportionate interest in subsidiary's earnings attributable to convertible preference shares, calculated: (300 ÷ 400) × (400 shares from conversion × €3.66 per share)

This example does not illustrate the classification of the components of convertible financial instruments as liabilities and equity or the classification of related interest and dividends as expenses and equity as required by IAS 32.

6.4.8 Contingently issuable potential ordinary shares

The standard requires that contingently issuable potential ordinary shares (other than those covered by a contingent share agreement, such as contingently issuable convertible instruments) to be included in the diluted EPS calculation as follows:

(a) determine whether the potential ordinary shares may be assumed to be issuable on the basis of the conditions specified for their issue in accordance with the provisions of the standard for contingent ordinary shares (see 6.4.6 above); and

(b) if those potential ordinary shares should be reflected in diluted EPS, determine their impact on the calculation of diluted earnings per share by following the provisions of the standard for that type of potential ordinary share.

However, exercise or conversion is not to be assumed for the purpose of calculating diluted earnings per share unless exercise or conversion of similar outstanding potential ordinary shares that are not contingently issuable is assumed. *[IAS 33.57]*.

This two-stage test (essentially, are the contingencies met and are the resulting potential shares dilutive?) is a perfectly logical stance for the standard to take. However, we are mystified by the somewhat cryptic scope of these provisions in that they apply to 'contingently issuable potential ordinary shares (other than those covered by a contingent share agreement, such as contingently issuable convertible instruments)'. A contingent share agreement is defined as 'an agreement to issue shares that is dependent on the satisfaction of specified conditions'. *[IAS 33.5]*. We fail to see how a contingent agreement to issue *potential* ordinary shares could be 'covered' by an agreement 'to issue shares'. In our view the methodology described above seems appropriate for a contingently issuable convertible bond.

7 PRESENTATION, RESTATEMENT AND DISCLOSURE

7.1 Presentation

As discussed in Chapter 3 at 3.2.1, IAS 1 requires that all items of income and expense be presented either:

(a) in a single statement of profit or loss and comprehensive income; or

(b) in two separate statements:

 (i) a statement of profit or loss; and

 (ii) a statement, beginning with profit or loss, presenting items of other comprehensive income. *[IAS 1.10A]*.

If the approach in (b) is followed, the separate statement of profit or loss must be displayed immediately before the statement of comprehensive income. *[IAS 1.10A]*.

If (a) is adopted, the EPS presentational requirements below apply to that single statement. If (b) is chosen, the requirements apply to the separate statement of profit or loss only and not the separate statement of comprehensive income. *[IAS 33.4A, 67A, 68A]*.

IAS 33 requires the presentation of basic and diluted EPS (with equal prominence and even if the amounts are negative – i.e. a loss per share) for each period for which a statement of comprehensive income (or separate income statement) is presented. *[IAS 33.66, 69]*. This is required for the profit or loss attributable to ordinary equity holders for:

(a) overall profit;

(b) profit or loss from continuing operations; and

(c) profit or loss from discontinued operations, if any. *[IAS 33.66, 68]*.

In the case of (a) and (b), separate figures are required for each class of ordinary shares with a different right to share in profits for the period. The figures for (a) and (b) must be displayed on the face of the statement. *[IAS 33.66]*. Those for (c) may be either on the face or in the notes. *[IAS 33.68]*. The standard (somewhat unnecessarily given the requirement to show basic and diluted EPS for all periods) states that if diluted EPS is given for at least one period it must be given for all periods presented. In what some might view as a further statement of the obvious, IAS 33 notes that if basic and diluted EPS are equal, dual presentation can be accomplished in one line in the statement. *[IAS 33.67]*. It stops short, however, of explaining that this is only true if the caption is amended to address both.

Regarding (c), the wording of the standard is not very clear. In particular, if an entity has more than one discontinued operation it does not clarify whether separate EPS disclosures are required for each or whether one aggregate figure is needed. The wording leans to the former, as it uses the singular – 'An entity that reports a discontinued operation shall disclose the basic and diluted amounts per share for the discontinued operation ...'. However, IFRS 5 – *Non-current Assets Held for Sale and Discontinued Operations* – only requires the statement of comprehensive income (or separate income statement) to identify the total result from all discontinued operations. *[IFRS 5.33]*. In light of this, we believe aggregate figures are acceptable.

7.2 Restatement

IAS 33 contains requirements to restate prior periods' EPS for events that change the number of shares outstanding without a corresponding change in resources. Additionally it specifies circumstances when EPS should not be restated.

Basic and diluted EPS for all periods presented should be adjusted for:

- events (other than the conversion of potential ordinary shares) which change the number of ordinary shares without a corresponding change in resources (discussed at 4.3 above); *[IAS 33.26, 64]*
- the effects of errors and adjustments resulting from changes in accounting policies accounted for retrospectively (see 5.3 above); *[IAS 33.64]* and
- in our opinion, the effects of business combinations that are accounted for as a uniting of interests (discussed at 4.6 above).

No adjustment should be made:

- to basic or diluted EPS when a share consolidation is combined with a special dividend where the overall commercial effect is that of a share repurchase at fair value (discussed at 4.3.2 above); *[IAS 33.29]*
- to previously reported diluted EPS due to changes in the prices of ordinary shares which would have given a different dilutive effect for options and warrants; *[IAS 33.47]*
- to prior period diluted EPS as a result of a contingency period coming to an end without the conditions attaching to contingently issuable shares being met; *[IAS 33.52]* or

- to prior period diluted EPS for changes in the assumptions used in the calculations or for the conversion of potential ordinary shares into ordinary shares. *[IAS 33.65]*.

7.3 Disclosure

IAS 33 requires disclosure of the following:

(a) the amounts used as the numerators in calculating basic and diluted EPS, and a reconciliation of those amounts to profit or loss attributable to the parent entity for the period. The reconciliation should include the individual effect of each class of instruments that affects EPS;

(b) the weighted average number of ordinary shares used as the denominator in calculating basic and diluted earnings per share, and a reconciliation of these denominators to each other. The reconciliation should include the individual effect of each class of instruments that affects EPS;

(c) instruments (including contingently issuable shares) that could potentially dilute basic EPS in the future, but were not included in the calculation because they were antidilutive for the period(s) presented; and

(d) a description of ordinary share transactions or potential ordinary share transactions (other than those accounted for in EPS for the year – see 4.3 above – in which case that fact should be stated), that occur after the end of the reporting period and that would have changed significantly the number of ordinary shares or potential ordinary shares outstanding at the end of the period if those transactions had occurred before the end of the reporting period. *[IAS 33.70]*.

Examples of transactions in (d) include:

(a) an issue of shares for cash;

(b) an issue of shares when the proceeds are used to repay debt or preference shares outstanding at the end of the reporting period;

(c) the redemption of ordinary shares outstanding;

(d) the conversion or exercise of potential ordinary shares outstanding at the end of the reporting period into ordinary shares;

(e) an issue of options, warrants, or convertible instruments; and

(f) the achievement of conditions that would result in the issue of contingently issuable shares.

The standard observes that EPS amounts are not adjusted for such transactions occurring after the reporting period because such transactions do not affect the amount of capital used to produce profit or loss for the period. *[IAS 33.71]*. Changes in ordinary shares are discussed at 4 above.

The standard observes that financial instruments and other contracts generating potential ordinary shares may incorporate terms and conditions that affect the measurement of basic and diluted earnings per share. These terms and conditions may determine whether any potential ordinary shares are dilutive and, if so, the effect on the weighted average number of shares outstanding and any consequent adjustments to profit or loss attributable to ordinary equity holders. The disclosure of the terms and conditions of such financial instruments and other contracts is encouraged by IAS 33, if not otherwise required by IFRS 7 – *Financial Instruments: Disclosures* (discussed in Chapter 50). *[IAS 33.72].*

8 FUTURE DEVELOPMENTS

8.1 General

In August 2008 the IASB published an exposure draft of proposed amendments to IAS 33 as part of its convergence project with the FASB.[6] The proposals aimed to achieve convergence of the denominator of the EPS calculation and to clarify and simplify the calculation of EPS.

The proposals aimed to achieve convergence by:[7]

- establishing a principle to determine which instruments are included in the calculation of basic EPS. According to this principle, the weighted average number of ordinary shares includes only those instruments that give (or are deemed to give) their holder the right to share currently in profit or loss of the period. As a consequence, if ordinary shares issuable for little or no cash or other consideration or mandatorily convertible instruments do not meet this condition, they will not be included in basic EPS.
- clarifying the treatment of contracts for the purchase of own ordinary shares for cash or other financial assets. Such contracts include gross physically settled written put options, forward purchase contracts and mandatorily redeemable ordinary shares. The exposure draft treats those contracts as if the entity had already repurchased the shares.
- amending the calculation of diluted EPS for participating instruments and two-class ordinary shares. The proposed amendment introduces a test to determine whether a convertible financial instrument would have a more dilutive effect if conversion is assumed. The diluted EPS calculation should assume the more dilutive treatment.

The proposals aimed to clarify and simplify the calculation of EPS as follows.[8]

- Instruments measured at fair value through profit or loss to be ignored for diluted EPS purposes. This is because the Boards believe changes in fair value reflect the economic effect of such instruments on current equity holders for the period. In other words, the changes in fair value reflect the benefits received, or detriments incurred, by the current equity holders during the period.
- Using the year-end share price, rather than the average for the period, to calculate the dilutive effect of options, warrants and their equivalents.
- Providing explicit requirements for the diluted EPS calculation of forward contracts to sell an entity's own shares. The proposal is to clarify that for the calculation of diluted EPS an entity assumes that ordinary shares relating to such a contract are sold and the effect is dilutive.
- Contracts to repurchase an entity's own shares and contracts that may be settled in ordinary shares or cash would either be measured at fair value

through profit or loss or the liability for the present value of the redemption amount would meet the definition of a participating instrument. Accordingly, either no adjustments would be required in calculating diluted EPS or the application guidance on participating instruments and two-class ordinary shares would apply. Therefore, the Board proposes to delete the current requirements for contracts that may be settled in ordinary shares or cash in and for contracts to repurchase an entity's own shares.

The Board reviewed a summary of responses to the ED in its meeting in April 2009. In the light of other priorities, the Board directed the staff to consider towards the end of 2009 when would be the best time for the Board to start reviewing the responses in more detail.[9]

In 2011 the IASB launched a consultation on its future agenda which resulted, in December 2012, in the publication of Feedback Statement: *Agenda Consultation 2011*. That document includes the following: 'The IASB is aware that it still has several projects on which work has stopped, including Earnings per Share, Government Grants, and Discontinued Operations. The IASB has asked its staff to review these projects and report on them with recommended courses of action.'

8.2 Rate-regulated activities

In April 2013, the IASB published an Exposure Draft called *Regulatory Deferral Accounts*. This draft proposes that when EPS amounts are presented by entities within its scope they should present additional basic and diluted earnings per share amounts that are calculated in the same way, except that they should exclude the net movement in the regulatory deferral account balances (which, absent the proposals in the ED, would not be recognised under IFRSs). It also stipulates, at paragraph B8, that all earnings per share amounts should be presented with equal prominence for all periods presented.

9 APPENDIX

Reproduced below is the comprehensive worked example in IAS 33 of the computation and presentation of EPS. *[IAS 33.IE12]*. It illustrates four quarters and then the full year, but the principles and calculations would be the same whatever the length of the periods considered.

CALCULATION AND PRESENTATION OF BASIC AND DILUTED EARNINGS PER SHARE (COMPREHENSIVE EXAMPLE)

This example illustrates the quarterly and annual calculations of basic and diluted earnings per share in the year 20X1 for Company A, which has a complex capital structure. The control number is profit or loss from continuing operations attributable to the parent entity. Other facts assumed are as follows:

Average market price of ordinary shares: The average market prices of ordinary shares for the calendar year 20X1 were as follows:

First quarter	CU 49
Second quarter	CU 60
Third quarter	CU 67
Fourth quarter	CU 67

The average market price of ordinary shares from 1 July to 1 September 20X1 was CU 65.

Ordinary shares: The number of ordinary shares outstanding at the beginning of 20X1 was 5,000,000. On 1 March 20X1, 200,000 ordinary shares were issued for cash.

Convertible bonds: In the last quarter of 20X0, 5 per cent convertible bonds with a principal amount of CU 12,000,000 due in 20 years were sold for cash at CU 1,000 (par). Interest is payable twice a year, on 1 November and 1 May. Each CU 1,000 bond is convertible into 40 ordinary shares. No bonds were converted in 20X0. The entire issue was converted on 1 April 20X1 because the issue was called by Company A.

Convertible preference shares: In the second quarter of 20X0, 800,000 convertible preference shares were issued for assets in a purchase transaction. The quarterly dividend on each convertible preference share is CU 0.05, payable at the end of the quarter for shares outstanding at that date. Each share is convertible into one ordinary share. Holders of 600,000 convertible preference shares converted their preference shares into ordinary shares on 1 June 20X1.

Warrants: Warrants to buy 600,000 ordinary shares at CU 55 per share for a period of five years were issued on 1 January 20X1. All outstanding warrants were exercised on 1 September 20X1.

Options: Options to buy 1,500,000 ordinary shares at CU 75 per share for a period of 10 years were issued on 1 July 20X1. No options were exercised during 20X1 because the exercise price of the options exceeded the market price of the ordinary shares.

Tax rate: The tax rate was 40 per cent for 20X1.

20X1	*Profit (loss) from continuing operations attributable to the parent entity* (a) *CU*	*Profit (loss) attributable to the parent entity* *CU*	
First quarter	5,000,000	5,000,000	
Second quarter	6,500,000	6,500,000	
Third quarter	1,000,000	(1,000,000)	(b)
Fourth quarter	(700,000)	(700,000)	
Full year	11,800,000	9,800,000	

(a) This is the control number (before adjusting for preference dividends).

(b) Company A had a CU 2,000,000 loss (net of tax) from discontinuing operations in the third quarter.

First Quarter 20X1

Basic EPS calculation			*CU*	
Profit from continuing operations attributable to the parent entity			5,000,000	
Less: preference shares dividends			(40,000)	(c)
Profit attributable to ordinary equity holders of the parent entity			4,960,000	

Dates	*Shares Outstanding*	*Fraction of period*	*Weighted-average shares*
1 January 28 February	5,000,000	2/3	3,333,333
Issue of ordinary shares on 1 March	200,000		
1 March 31 March	5,200,000	1/3	1,733,333
Weighted-average shares			5,066,666
Basic EPS			**CU 0.98**

(c) 800,000 shares × CU 0.05

Diluted EPS calculation			
Profit attributable to ordinary equity holders of the parent entity			CU 4,960,000
Plus: profit impact of assumed conversions			
Preference share dividends	CU 40,000	(d)	
Interest on 5% convertible bonds	CU 90,000	(e)	
Effect of assumed conversions			CU 130,000
Profit attributable to ordinary equity holders of the parent entity including assumed conversions			CU 5,090,000
Weighted-average shares			5,066,666
Plus: incremental shares from assumed conversions			
Warrants	0	(f)	
Convertible preference shares	800,000		
5% convertible bonds	480,000		
Dilutive potential ordinary shares			1,280,000
Adjusted weighted-average shares			6,346,666
Diluted EPS			**CU 0.80**

(d) 800,000 shares × CU 0.05

(e) (CU 12,000,000 × 5%) ÷ 4; less taxes at 40%

(f) The warrants were not assumed to be exercised because they were antidilutive in the period (CU 55 [exercise price] > CU 49 [average price]).

Second Quarter 20X1

Basic EPS calculation	*CU*	
Profit from continuing operations attributable to the parent entity	6,500,000	
Less: preference shares dividends	(10,000)	(g)
Profit attributable to ordinary equity holders of the parent entity	6,490,000	

Dates	*Shares outstanding*	*Fraction of period*	*Weighted-average shares*
1 April	5,200,000		
Conversion of 5% bonds on 1April	480,000		
1 April – 31 May	5,680,000	2/3	3,786,666
Conversion of preference shares on 1June	600,000		
1 June – 30 June	6,280,000	1/3	2,093,333
Weighted-average shares			5,880,000
Basic EPS			**CU 1.10**

(g) 200,000 shares × CU 0.05

Diluted EPS calculation			
Profit attributable to ordinary equity holders of the parent entity			CU 6,490,000
Plus: profit impact of assumed conversions			
Preference share dividends	CU 10,000	(h)	
Effect of assumed conversions			CU 10,000
Profit attributable to ordinary equity holders of the parent entity including assumed conversions			CU 6,500,000
Weighted-average shares			5,880,000
Plus: incremental shares from assumed conversions			
Warrants	50,000	(i)	
Convertible preference shares	600,000	(j)	
Dilutive potential ordinary shares			650,000
Adjusted weighted-average shares			6,530,000
Diluted EPS			**CU 1.00**

(h) 200,000 shares × CU 0.05

(i) CU 55 × 600,000 = CU 33,000,000; CU 33,000,000 ÷ CU 60 = 550,000; 600,000 – 550,000 = 50,000 shares *or* [(CU 60 – CU 55) ÷ CU 60] × 600,000 shares = 50,000 shares

(j) (800,000 shares × 2/3) + (200,000 shares × 1/3)

Third Quarter 20X1

Basic EPS calculation			*CU*
Profit from continuing operations attributable to the parent entity			1,000,000
Less: preference shares dividends			(10,000)
Profit from continuing operations attributable to ordinary equity holders of the parent entity			990,000
Loss from discontinuing operations attributable to the parent entity			(2,000,000)
Loss attributable to ordinary equity holders of the parent entity			(1,010,000)

Dates	*Shares outstanding*	*Fraction of period*	*Weighted-average shares*
1 July – 31 August	6,280,000	2/3	4,186,666
Exercise of warrants on 1 September	600,000		
1 September – 30 September	6,880,000	1/3	2,293,333
Weighted-average shares			6,480,000
Basic EPS			
Profit from continuing operations			**CU 0.15**
Loss from discontinuing operations			**(CU 0.31)**
Loss			**(CU 0.16)**

Diluted EPS calculation			
Profit from continuing operations attributable to ordinary equity holders of the parent entity			CU 990,000
Plus: profit impact of assumed conversions			
Preference shares dividends	CU 10,000		
Effect of assumed conversions			CU 10,000
Profit from continuing operations attributable to ordinary equity holders of the parent entity including assumed conversions			CU 1,000,000
Loss from discontinuing operations attributable to the parent entity			(CU 2,000,000)
Loss attributable to ordinary equity holders of the parent entity including assumed conversions			(CU 1,000,000)
Weighted-average shares			6,480,000
Plus: incremental shares from assumed conversions			
Warrants	61,538	(k)	
Convertible preference shares	200,000		
Dilutive potential ordinary shares			261,538
Adjusted weighted-average shares			6,741,538
Diluted EPS			
Profit from continuing operations			**CU 0.15**
Loss from discontinuing operations			**(CU 0.30)**
Loss			**(CU 0.15)**

(k) [(CU 65 – CU 55) ÷ CU 65] × 600,000 = 92,308 shares; 92,308 × 2/3 = 61,538 shares

Note: The incremental shares from assumed conversions are included in calculating the diluted per-share amounts for the loss from discontinuing operations and loss even though they are antidilutive. This is because the control number (profit from continuing operations attributable to ordinary equity holders of the parent entity, adjusted for preference dividends) was positive (i.e. profit, rather than loss).

Fourth Quarter 20X1

Basic and diluted EPS calculation	*CU*
Loss from continuing operations attributable to the parent entity	(700,000)
Add: preference shares dividends	(10,000)
Loss attributable to ordinary equity holders of the parent entity	(710,000)

Dates	*Shares outstanding*	*Fraction of period*	*Weighted-average shares*
1October – 31 December	6,880,000	3/3	6,880,000
Weighted-average shares			6,880,000
Basic and diluted EPS			
Loss attributable to ordinary equity holders of the parent entity			**(CU 0.10)**

Note: The incremental shares from assumed conversions are not included in calculating the diluted per-share amounts because the control number (loss from continuing operations attributable to ordinary equity holders of the parent entity adjusted for preference dividends) was negative (i.e. a loss, rather than profit).

Full Year 20X1

Basic EPS calculation	*CU*
Profit from continuing operations attributable to the parent entity	11,800,000
Less: preference shares dividends	(70,000)
Profit from continuing operations attributable to ordinary equity holders of the parent entity	11,730,000
Loss from discontinuing operations attributable to the parent entity	(2,000,000)
Profit attributable to ordinary equity holders of the parent entity	9,730,000

Dates	*Shares Outstanding*	*Fraction of period*	*Weighted-average shares*
1 January – 28 February	5,000,000	2/12	833,333
Issue of ordinary shares on 1March	200,000		
1 March – 31 March	5,200,000	1/12	433,333
Conversion of 5% bonds on 1April	480,000		
1 April – 31 May	5,680,000	2/12	946,667
Conversion of preference shares on 1June	600,000		
1 June – 31 August	6,280,000	3/12	1,570,000
Exercise of warrants on 1September	600,000		
1 September – 31 December	6,880,000	4/12	2,293,333
Weighted-average shares			6,076,667

Basic EPS	
Profit from continuing operations	**CU 1.93**
Loss from discontinuing operations	**(CU 0.33)**
Profit	**CU 1.60**

Diluted EPS calculation

Profit from continuing operations attributable to ordinary equity holders of the parent entity			CU 11,730,000
Plus: profit impact of assumed conversions			
Preference share dividends	CU 70,000		
Interest on 5% convertible bonds	CU 90,000	(l)	
Effect of assumed conversions			CU 160,000
Profit from continuing operations attributable to ordinary equity holders of the parent entity including assumed conversions			CU 11,890,000
Loss from discontinuing operations attributable to the parent entity			(CU 2,000,000)
Profit attributable to ordinary equity holders of the parent entity including assumed conversions			CU 9,890,000
Weighted-average shares			6,076,667
Plus: incremental shares from assumed conversions			
Warrants	14,880	(m)	
Convertible preference shares	450,000	(n)	
5% convertible bonds	120,000	(o)	
Dilutive potential ordinary shares			584,880
Adjusted weighted-average shares			6,661,547
Diluted EPS			
Profit from continuing operations			**CU 1.78**
Loss from discontinuing operations			**(CU 0.30)**
Profit			**CU 1.48**

(l) (CU 12,000,000 × 5%) ÷ 4; less taxes at 40%

(m) [(CU 57.125* – CU 55) ÷ CU 57.125] × 600,000 = 22,320 shares; 22,320 × 8/12 = 14,880 shares

* The average market price from 1 January 20X1 to 1 September 20X1

(n) (800,000 shares × 5/12) + (200,000 shares × 7/12)

(o) 480,000 shares × 3/12

The following illustrates how Company A might present its earnings per share data in its statement of comprehensive income. Note that the amounts per share for the loss from discontinuing operations are not required to be presented on the face of the statement of comprehensive income.

	For the year ended 20X1
	CU
Earnings per ordinary share	
Profit from continuing operations	1.93
Loss from discontinuing operations	(0.33)
Profit	1.60
Diluted earnings per ordinary share	
Profit from continuing operations	1.78
Loss from discontinuing operations	(0.30)
Profit	1.48

Chapter 33

The following table includes the quarterly and annual earnings per share data for Company A. The purpose of this table is to illustrate that the sum of the four quarters' earnings per share data will not necessarily equal the annual earnings per share data. The Standard does not require disclosure of this information.

	First quarter CU	*Second quarter CU*	*Third quarter CU*	*Fourth quarter CU*	*Full year CU*
Basic EPS					
Profit (loss) from continuing operations	0.98	1.10	0.15	(0.10)	1.93
Loss from discontinuing operations	–	–	(0.31)	–	(0.33)
Profit (loss)	0.98	1.10	(0.16)	(0.10)	1.60
Diluted EPS					
Profit (loss) from continuing operations	0.80	1.00	0.15	(0.10)	1.78
Loss from discontinuing operations	–	–	(0.30)	–	(0.30)
Profit (loss)	0.80	1.00	(0.15)	(0.10)	1.48

This example does not illustrate the classification of the components of convertible financial instruments as liabilities and equity or the classification of related interest and dividends as expenses and equity as required by IAS 32.

References

1 A put warrant, involving the repurchase of shares at significantly more than their fair value was included as an example in the equivalent standard in the UK (FRS 14 – *Earnings per Share*, The Accounting Standards Board Limited, October 1998) which was developed at the same time as, and was very similar to, IAS 33. FRS 14 has subsequently been replaced with a standard identical to IAS 33).

2 *Exposure Draft, Simplifying Earnings per Share: Proposed amendments to IAS 33*, IASB, August 2008, para. 67.

3 Proposed Improvements to International Accounting Standard IAS 33, IASB, December 2003, Invitation to Comment Question 2 and Appendix B, examples 7 and 12.

4 *IASB Update*, January 2006, page 2.

5 IFRS 2, paras. BC54-BC57.

6 *Exposure Draft, Simplifying Earnings per Share: Proposed amendments to IAS 33*, IASB, August 2008.

7 *Exposure Draft, Simplifying Earnings per Share: Proposed amendments to IAS 33*, para. IN2.

8 *Exposure Draft, Simplifying Earnings per Share: Proposed amendments to IAS 33*, paras. IN5-IN8.

9 *IASB Update*, April 2009.

Chapter 34 Events after the reporting period

List of examples

Chapter 34 Events after the reporting period

1 INTRODUCTION

IAS 10 – *Events after the Reporting Period* – deals with accounting for, and disclosure of, events after the reporting period, which are defined as 'those events, favourable and unfavourable, that occur between the end of the reporting period and the date when the financial statements are authorised for issue'. *[IAS 10.2, 3]*. Therefore, the definition includes all events occurring between those dates – irrespective of whether they relate to conditions that existed at the end of the reporting period. The principal issue is determining which events after the reporting period to reflect in the financial statements.

The following timeline of an entity with a 31 December year-end illustrates events after the end of the reporting period that are within the scope of IAS 10:

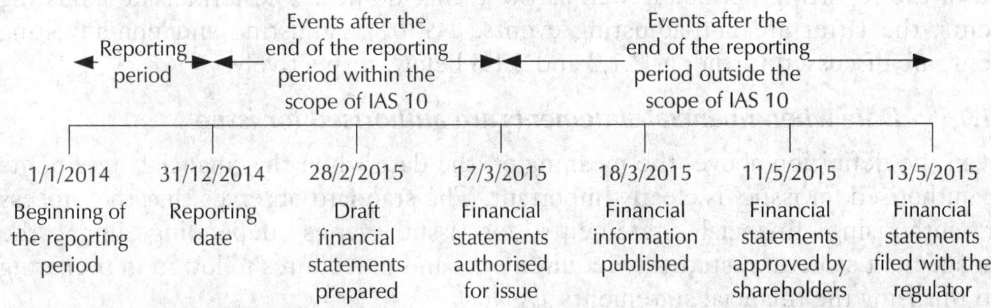

The financial statements of an entity present, among other things, an entity's financial position at the end of the reporting period. Therefore, it is appropriate to adjust the financial statements for all events that offer greater clarity concerning the conditions that existed at the end of the reporting period, that occur prior to the date the financial statements are authorised for issue. The standard requires entities to adjust the amounts recognised in the financial statements for 'adjusting events' that provide evidence of conditions that existed at the end of the reporting period. *[IAS 10.3(a), 8]*. An entity does not recognise in the financial statements those events that relate to conditions that arose after the reporting period ('non-adjusting events'). However, if non-adjusting events are material, the standard requires certain disclosures about them. *[IAS 10.3(b), 10, 21]*.

One exception to the general rule of the standard for non-adjusting events is when the going concern basis becomes inappropriate. This is treated as an adjusting event. *[IAS 10.1, 14]*.

The requirements of IAS 10 and practical issues resulting from these requirements are dealt with at 2 and 3 below.

2 REQUIREMENTS OF IAS 10

2.1 Objective, scope and definitions

The objective of IAS 10 is to prescribe:

- when an entity should adjust its financial statements for events after the reporting period; and
- the required disclosures about the date when the financial statements were authorised for issue and about events after the reporting period.

The standard does not permit an entity to prepare its financial statements on a going concern basis if events after the reporting period indicate that the going concern assumption is not appropriate. *[IAS 10.1]*. This requirement is discussed further at 2.2.2 below. The going concern basis is discussed in Chapter 3 at 4.1.2.

IAS 10 defines events after the reporting period as 'those events, favourable and unfavourable, that occur between the end of the reporting period and the date when the financial statements are authorised for issue'. *[IAS 10.3]*. This definition therefore includes events that provide additional evidence about conditions that existed at the end of the reporting period, as well as those that do not. The former are adjusting events, the latter are non-adjusting events. *[IAS 10.3]*. Adjusting and non-adjusting events are discussed further at 2.1.2 and 2.1.3 below, respectively.

2.1.1 Date when financial statements are authorised for issue

Given the definition above, the meaning of 'the date when the financial statements are authorised for issue' is clearly important. The standard observes that the process for authorising financial statements for issue varies depending upon the management structure, statutory requirements and procedures followed in preparing and finalising the financial statements. *[IAS 10.4]*.

The standard identifies two particular instances of the different meaning of 'authorised for issue' as follows:

(a) An entity may be required to submit its financial statements to its shareholders for approval (as in France, for example) after the financial statements have been issued. In such cases, the financial statements are authorised for issue on the date of issue, not the date when shareholders approve them. *[IAS 10.5]*.

(b) The management of an entity may be required to issue its financial statements to a supervisory board (made up solely of non-executives) for approval. Such financial statements are authorised for issue when management authorises them for issue to the supervisory board. *[IAS 10.6]*.

These two meanings are illustrated by the following two examples, which are based on the illustrative examples contained in IAS 10.

Example 34.1: Financial statements required to be approved by shareholders [IAS 10.5]

The management of an entity completes draft financial statements for the year to 31 December 2014 on 28 February 2015. On 17 March 2015, the board of directors reviews the financial statements and authorises them for issue. The entity announces its profit and certain other financial information on 18 March 2015. The financial statements are made available to shareholders and others on 1 April 2015. The shareholders approve the financial statements at their annual meeting on 11 May 2015 and the approved financial statements are then filed with a regulatory body on 13 May 2015.

The financial statements are authorised for issue on 17 March 2015 (date of board authorisation for issue).

Example 34.2: Financial statements required to be approved by supervisory board [IAS 10.6]

On 17 March 2015, the management of an entity authorises for issue to its supervisory board financial statements for the year to 31 December 2014. The supervisory board consists solely of non-executives and may include representatives of employees and other outside interests. The supervisory board approves the financial statements on 25 March 2015. The financial statements are made available to shareholders and others on 1 April 2015. The shareholders approve the financial statements at their annual meeting on 11 May 2015 and the financial statements are filed with a regulatory body on 13 May 2015.

The financial statements are authorised for issue on 17 March 2015 (date of management authorisation for issue to the supervisory board).

An uncommon, but possible, situation that may occur is that the financial statements are changed after they are authorised for issue to the supervisory board. The following example illustrates such a situation.

Example 34.3: Financial statements required to be approved by supervisory board – changes are made by supervisory board

Same facts as in Example 34.2 above, except that the supervisory board reviews the financial statements on 25 March 2015 and proposes changes to certain note disclosures. The management of the entity incorporates the suggested changes and re-authorises those financial statements for issue to the supervisory board on 27 March 2015. The supervisory board then approves the financial statements on 30 March 2015.

The financial statements are authorised for issue on 27 March 2015 (date of management re-authorisation for issue to the supervisory board).

A fourth example illustrates when the entity releases preliminary information, but not complete financial statements, before the date of the authorisation for issue.

Example 34.4: Release of financial information before date of authorisation for issue

The management of an entity completes the primary financial statements (e.g. statement of financial position, statement of comprehensive income, cash flow statement) for the year to 31 December 2014 on 21 January 2015, but has not yet completed the explanatory notes. On 26 January 2015, the board of directors (which includes management and non-executives) reviews the primary financial statements and authorises them for public media release. The entity announces its profit and certain other financial information on 28 January 2015. On 11 February 2015, management issues the financial statements (with full explanatory notes) to the board of directors, which approves the financial statements for filing on 18 February 2015. The entity files the financial statements with a regulatory body on 21 February 2015.

The financial statements are authorised for issue on 18 February 2015 (date the board of directors, approves the financial statements for filing).

Example 34.4 illustrates that events after the reporting period include all events up to the date when the financial statements are authorised for issue, even if those events occur after the public announcement of profit or of other selected financial information. *[IAS 10.7]*. Accordingly, the information in the financial statements might differ from the equivalent information in a preliminary announcement. As governance structures vary by jurisdiction, entities may be allowed to organise their procedures differently and adjust the financial reporting process accordingly.

An example of a company which is required to submit its financial statements to its shareholders for approval is Holcim Ltd, as illustrated in the following extract:

Extract 34.1: Holcim Ltd (2012)

Notes to the consolidated financial statements [extract]

42 Authorization of the financial statements for issuance

The consolidated financial statements were authorized for issuance by the Board of Directors of Holcim Ltd on February 25, 2013, and are subject to shareholder approval at the annual general meeting of shareholders scheduled for April 17, 2013.

As discussed above, an entity may be required to issue its financial statements to a supervisory board (made up solely of non-executives) for approval. For such instances, the phrase 'made up solely of non-executives' is not defined by the standard, although it contemplates that a supervisory board may include representatives of employees and other outside interests. However, it seems to draw a distinction between those responsible for the executive management of an entity (and the preparation of its financial statements) and those in a position of high-level oversight (including reviewing and approving the financial statements). This situation seems to describe the typical two-tier board system seen in some jurisdictions (for example, Germany). An example of a company with this structure is Bayer AG, as illustrated in the following extract.

Extract 34.2: Bayer Group and Bayer AG (2012)

Combined Management Report [extract]

13. Corporate Governance Report [extract]

13.1 Declaration on Corporate Governance [extract]

SUPERVISORY BOARD: OVERSIGHT AND CONTROL FUNCTIONS

The role of the 20-member Supervisory Board is to oversee and advise the Board of Management. Under the German Codetermination Act, half the members of the Supervisory Board are elected by the stockholders, and half by the company's employees. The Supervisory Board is directly involved in decisions on matters of fundamental importance to the company, regularly conferring with the Board of Management on the company's strategic alignment and the implementation status of the business strategy.

> The Chairman of the Supervisory Board coordinates its work and presides over the meetings. Through regular discussions with the Board of Management, the Supervisory Board is kept constantly informed of business policy, corporate planning and strategy. The Supervisory Board approves the annual budget and financial framework. It also approves the financial statements of Bayer AG and the consolidated financial statements of the Bayer Group, along with the combined management report, taking into account the reports by the auditor.

2.1.1.A Re-issuing financial statements

IFRSs do not address whether and how an entity may amend its financial statements after they have been authorised for issue. Generally, such matters are dealt with in local laws or regulations.

If an entity re-issues financial statements (whether to correct an error or to include events that occurred after the financial statements were originally authorised for issue), there is a new date of authorisation for issue. The financial statements should then appropriately reflect all adjusting and non-adjusting events (including those that occurred in the interim period between the original and new date of authorisation for issue). This means an entity cannot 'dual date' its financial statements. That is, an entity cannot retain the original date of authorisation of the financial statements with a second authorisation date for specific events occurring between the two dates. The re-issued financial statements must reflect all adjusting and non-adjusting events occurring up to the new date of authorisation.

In certain circumstances, the re-issuing of previously issued financial statements is required by local regulators particularly for inclusion in public offering and similar documents. Consequently, in November 2012, the Interpretations Committee was asked to clarify the accounting implications of applying IAS 10 when previously issued financial statements are re-issued in connection with an offering document.[1]

The issue arose in jurisdictions in which securities laws and regulatory practices require an entity to re-issue its previously issued annual financial statements in connection with an offering document, when the most recently filed interim financial statements reflect matters that are accounted for retrospectively under the applicable accounting standards. In these jurisdictions, securities law and regulatory practices do not require or permit the entity, in its re-issued financial statements, to recognise events or transactions that occur between the time the financial statements were first authorised for issuance and the time the financial statements are re-issued, unless the adjustment is required by national regulation. Instead, security and regulatory practices require the entity to recognise in its re-issued financial statements only those adjustments that would ordinarily be made to the comparatives in the following year's financial statements. These adjustments would include, for example, adjustments for changes in accounting policy that are applied retrospectively, but would not include changes in accounting estimates. As alluded to above, this approach is called 'dual dating'.

Accordingly, in January 2013, the Interpretations Committee was asked to clarify whether IAS 10 permits only one date of authorisation for issue (i.e. 'dual dating' is not permitted) when considered within the context of re-issuing previously issued financial statements in connection with an offering document.[2]

In May 2013, the Interpretations Committee responded that:

- the scope of IAS 10 is the accounting for, and disclosure of, events after the reporting period and that the objective of this Standard is to prescribe:
  - (a) when an entity should adjust its financial statements for events after the reporting period; and
  - (b) the disclosures that an entity should give about the date when the financial statements were authorised for issue and about events after the reporting period;
- financial statements prepared in accordance with IAS 10 should reflect all adjusting and non-adjusting events up to the date that the financial statements were authorised for issue; and
- IAS 10 does not address the presentation of re-issued financial statements in an offering document when the originally issued financial statements have not been withdrawn, but the re-issued financial statements are provided either as supplementary information or a re-presentation of the original financial statements in an offering document in accordance with regulatory requirements.

The Interpretations Committee decided not to add this issue to its agenda on the basis of the above and because the issue arises in multiple jurisdictions, each with particular securities laws and regulations which may dictate the form for re-presentations of financial statements.[3]

2.1.2 Adjusting events

Adjusting events are 'those that provide evidence of conditions that existed at the end of the reporting period.' *[IAS 10.3(a)].*

Examples of adjusting events are as follows:

(a) the settlement after the reporting period of a court case that confirms that the entity had a present obligation at the end of the reporting period. In this situation, an entity adjusts any previously recognised provision related to this court case under IAS 37 – *Provisions, Contingent Liabilities and Contingent Assets*, or recognises a new provision. Mere disclosure of a contingent liability is not sufficient because the settlement provides additional evidence of conditions that existed at the end of the reporting period that would be considered in accordance with IAS 37 (see Chapter 27 at 3.1.1 and 3.2.1);

(b) the receipt of information after the reporting period indicating that an asset was impaired at the end of the reporting period, or that the amount of a previously recognised impairment loss for that asset needs to be adjusted. For example:

  (i) the bankruptcy of a customer that occurs after the reporting period usually confirms that a loss existed at the end of the reporting period on a trade receivable and that the entity needs to adjust the carrying amount of the trade receivable; and

  (ii) the sale of inventories after the reporting period may give evidence about their net realisable value at the end of the reporting period;

(c) the determination after the reporting period of the cost of assets purchased, or the proceeds from assets sold, before the end of the reporting period;

(d) the determination after the reporting period of the amount of profit-sharing or bonus payments, if the entity had a present legal or constructive obligation at the end of the reporting period to make such payments as a result of events before that date; and

(e) the discovery of fraud or errors that show that the financial statements are incorrect (see 3.5 below). *[IAS 10.9]*.

In addition, IAS 33 – *Earnings per Share* – requires an adjustment to earnings per share for certain share transactions after the reporting period (such as bonus issues, share splits or share consolidations as discussed in Chapter 33 at 4.5) even though the transactions themselves are non-adjusting events (see 2.1.3 below). *[IAS 10.22]*.

2.1.3 Non-adjusting events

The standard states that non-adjusting events are 'those that are indicative of conditions that arose after the reporting period'. *[IAS 10.3(b)]*.

As examples of non-adjusting events, the standard gives the following events after the reporting period:

(a) a major business combination (IFRS 3 – *Business Combinations* – requires specific disclosures in such cases, see Chapter 9 at 16.1.2) or disposing of a major subsidiary;

(b) announcing a plan to discontinue an operation;

(c) major purchases of assets, classification of assets as held for sale in accordance with IFRS 5 – *Non-current Assets Held for Sale and Discontinued Operations*, other disposals of assets, or expropriation of major assets by government (see Chapter 4 at 5 for certain disclosures required to be made);

(d) the destruction of a major production plant by a fire;

(e) announcing, or commencing the implementation of, a major restructuring (discussed in Chapter 27 at 6.1);

(f) major ordinary share transactions and potential ordinary share transactions (although as noted at 2.1.2 above, some transactions in ordinary shares are adjusting events for the purposes of computing earnings per share);

(g) abnormally large changes in asset prices or foreign exchange rates;

(h) changes in tax rates or the enactment or announcement of tax laws that significantly affect current and deferred tax assets and liabilities (discussed in Chapter 29 at 8.1);

(i) entry into significant commitments or contingent liabilities, for example, by issuing significant guarantees;

(j) start of major litigation arising solely out of events that occurred after the reporting period;

(k) a decline in fair value of investments; and

(l) a declaration of dividends to holders of equity instruments (as defined in IAS 32 – *Financial Instruments: Presentation* – discussed in Chapter 43 at 8). *[IAS 10.11, 12, 22]*.

The reference in (a) and (c) above to asset disposals as examples of non-adjusting events is not quite the whole story as they may indicate an impairment of assets, which may be an adjusting event. In addition, (b) and (e) above regarding announcements of plans to discontinue an operation or to restructure a business, respectively, may also lead to an impairment charge (see Chapter 20 at 2.3.1).

For declines in fair value of investments, as in (k) above, the standard notes that the decline in fair value does not *normally* relate to the condition of the investments at the end of the reporting period, but reflects circumstances that arose subsequently. Therefore, in those circumstances the amounts recognised in financial statements for the investments are not adjusted. Similarly, the standard states that an entity does not update the amounts disclosed for the investments as at the end of the reporting period, although it may need to give additional disclosure, if material, as discussed at 2.3 below. *[IAS 10.11]*.

However, the assertion that a decline in fair value of investments does not *normally* relate to conditions at the end of the reporting period is similar wording to that used for bankruptcy and the sale of inventories (see 2.1.2(b) above). Therefore, it requires an assessment of the circumstances in order to determine which conditions actually existed at the end of the reporting period – although this can be difficult in practice, particularly when fraud is involved (see 3.5 below).

In respect of dividend declarations, as in (l) above, IAS 10 takes a strict balance sheet approach. Dividends are only recognised as a liability if declared on or by the end of the reporting period. If an entity declares dividends to holders of equity instruments (as defined in IAS 32) after the reporting period, the entity shall not recognise those dividends as a liability at the end of the reporting period. *[IAS 10.13]*. While an entity may have a past practice of paying dividends, such dividends are not declared and, therefore, not recognised as an obligation. *[IAS 10.BC4]*.

As a consequential amendment to IAS 10, the definition of 'declared' in this context was moved to IFRIC 17 – *Distributions of Non-cash Assets to Owners*. IFRIC 17 did not change the principle regarding the appropriate timing for the recognition of dividends payable. *[IFRIC 17.BC18-20]*. It states that an entity recognises a liability to pay a dividend when the dividend is appropriately authorised and is no longer at the discretion of the entity, which is the date:

- when declaration of the dividend, e.g. by management or the board of directors, is approved by the relevant authority, e.g. the shareholders, if the jurisdiction requires such approval; or
- when the dividend is declared, e.g. by management or the board of directors, if the jurisdiction does not require further approval. *[IFRIC 17.10]*.

In many jurisdictions, the directors may keep discretion to cancel an interim dividend until such time as it is paid. In this case, the interim dividend is not declared (within the meaning described above), and is, therefore, not recognised until paid. Final dividends proposed by directors, in many jurisdictions, are binding when approved by shareholders in general meeting or by the members passing a written resolution. Therefore, such a final dividend is only recognised as a liability when declared i.e. approved by the shareholders at the annual general meeting or through the passing of a resolution by the members of an entity.

IAS 10 contains a reminder that an entity discloses dividends, both proposed and declared after the reporting period but before the financial statements are authorised for issue, in the notes to the financial statements in accordance with IAS 1 – *Presentation of Financial Statements* (see Chapter 3 at 5.5). *[IAS 10.13]*.

Similar issues arise regarding the declaration of dividends by subsidiaries and associates. Although IAS 10 does not specifically address such items, IAS 18 – *Revenue* – requires that a shareholder recognise dividends when its right to receive payment is established. *[IAS 18.30(c)]*. Similarly, IAS 27 – *Separate Financial Statements* – contains this general principle in recognising in an entity's separate financial statements those dividends received from subsidiaries, joint ventures or associates when its right to receive the dividend is established (see Chapter 8 at 2.3.1). *[IAS 27.12]*. Accordingly, a shareholder does not recognise such dividend income until the period in which the dividend is declared.

2.2 The treatment of adjusting events

2.2.1 Events requiring adjustment to the amounts recognised, or disclosures, in the financial statements

IAS 10 requires that the amounts recognised in the financial statements be adjusted to take account of an adjusting event. *[IAS 10.8]*.

The standard also notes that an entity may receive information after the reporting period about conditions existing at the end of the reporting period relating to disclosures made in the financial statements but not affecting the amounts recognised in them. *[IAS 10.20]*. In such cases, the standard requires the entity to update the disclosures that relate to those conditions for the new information. *[IAS 10.19]*.

For example, evidence may become available after the reporting period about a contingent liability that existed at the end of the reporting period. In addition to considering whether to recognise or change a provision under IAS 37, IAS 10 requires an entity to update its disclosures about the contingent liability for that evidence. *[IAS 10.20]*.

2.2.2 Events indicating that the going concern basis is not appropriate

If management determines after the reporting period either that it intends to liquidate the entity or to cease trading, or that it has no realistic alternative but to do so, the financial statements should not be prepared on the going concern basis. *[IAS 10.14]*.

Deterioration in operating results and financial position after the reporting period may indicate a need to consider whether the going concern assumption is still appropriate. If the going concern assumption is no longer appropriate, the standard states that the effect is so pervasive that it results in a fundamental change in the basis of accounting, rather than an adjustment to the amounts recognised within the original basis of accounting. *[IAS 10.15]*. As discussed in Chapter 3 at 4.1.2, IFRS contains no guidance on this 'fundamental change in the basis of accounting'. Accordingly, entities will need to consider carefully their individual circumstances to arrive at an appropriate basis.

The standard also contains a reminder of the specific disclosure requirements under IAS 1:

(a) when the financial statements are not prepared on a going concern basis, that fact should be disclosed, together with the basis on which the financial statements have been prepared and the reason why the entity is not regarded as a going concern; or

(b) when management is aware of material uncertainties related to events or conditions that may cast significant doubt upon the entity's ability to continue as a going concern, disclosure of those uncertainties should be made. *[IAS 10.16, IAS 1.25]*.

While IFRSs are generally written from the perspective that an entity is a going concern, they are also applicable when another basis of accounting is used to prepare financial statements. Various IFRSs acknowledge that financial statements may be prepared on either a going concern basis or an alternative basis of accounting. *[IAS 1.25, IAS 10.14, Framework 4.1]*. Such IFRSs do not specifically exclude the application of IFRS when an alternative basis of accounting, for example, the liquidation basis of accounting issued by the FASB,[4] is used. Therefore, in our view, in preparing financial statements on a basis of accounting other than going concern, the above-mentioned FASB guidance may be relevant to consider under IFRSs, depending on facts and circumstances.

When an entity prepares financial statements on a basis other than a going concern basis, certain deviations from specific sections or paragraphs of IFRSs may be appropriate. Significant judgement may be involved in determining the appropriate degree of deviation from IFRSs based on the facts and circumstances that is acceptable whilst still meeting the requirement to 'present fairly' the financial statements using the stated basis of preparation. Adequate disclosure as required under (a) above, including disclosure of individual accounting policies used, is important in such circumstances to allow users of financial statements to understand how the financial statements have been prepared. *[IAS 1.117(b)]*. Further considerations on disclosures relating to accounting policies are discussed in Chapter 3 at 5.1.

Regarding the requirement in (b) above, the events or conditions requiring disclosure may arise after the reporting period. *[IAS 10.16(b)]*.

2.3 The treatment of non-adjusting events

IAS 10 prohibits the adjustment of amounts recognised in financial statements to reflect non-adjusting events. *[IAS 10.10]*. It indicates that if non-adjusting events are material, non-disclosure could influence the economic decisions of users of the financial statements. Accordingly, an entity should disclose the following for each material category of non-adjusting event: *[IAS 10.21]*

(a) the nature of the event; and

(b) an estimate of its financial effect, or a statement that such an estimate cannot be made.

To illustrate how these requirements have been applied in practice, example disclosures for certain types of non-adjusting events are given below.

Possibly the non-adjusting events that appear most regularly in financial statements are the acquisition/disposal of a non-current asset, such as an investment in a subsidiary or a business, subsequent to the end of the reporting period. Extract 34.3 contains examples of the disclosures required for 2.1.3(a) and (l) above related to business combinations and disposals, and the declaration of dividends, respectively:

Extract 34.3: Reed Elsevier PLC (2007)

Notes to the combined financial statements [extract]

36. Post balance sheet events

On 18 January 2008, Reed Elsevier PLC paid a special distribution of 82.0p per ordinary share and Reed Elsevier NV paid a special distribution of €1.767 per ordinary share, from the net proceeds of the disposal of Harcourt Education. The aggregate special distribution, announced on 12 December 2007, of £2,013m was recognised when paid in January 2008.

The special distributions were accompanied by a consolidation of the ordinary share capital of Reed Elsevier PLC and Reed Elsevier NV on the basis of 58 new ordinary shares for every 67 existing ordinary shares, being the ratio of the aggregate special distribution to the combined market capitalisation of Reed Elsevier PLC and Reed Elsevier NV (excluding the 5.8% indirect equity interest in Reed Elsevier NV held by Reed Elsevier PLC) as at the date of the announcement of the special distributions.

On 30 January 2008 the sale of Harcourt Assessment and the remaining Harcourt International businesses, first announced in May 2007, completed following receipt of regulatory clearance in the United States. Proceeds received on disposal were £330m.

On 20 February 2008, Reed Elsevier approved a plan to divest Reed Business Information. In the year to 31 December 2007, Reed Business Information reported revenues of £906m, operating profits of £89m and adjusted operating profits of £119m.

On 20 February 2008, Reed Elsevier entered into a definitive merger agreement with ChoicePoint, Inc to acquire the company for cash. Taking into account ChoicePoint's estimated net debt of $0.6bn, the total value of the transaction is $4.1bn. The ChoicePoint board will convene a meeting of ChoicePoint shareholders to approve the merger and is unanimous in its recommendation of the merger. The merger is subject to customary regulatory approvals and is expected to be completed later in the year. The transaction will be financed initially through committed new bank facilities, to be later refinanced through the issuance of term debt.

ChoicePoint provides unique information and analytics to support underwriting decisions within the property and casualty insurance sector; screening and authentication services for employment, real estate leasing and customer enrolment; and public information solutions primarily to banking, professional services and government customers. In 2007 ChoicePoint reported revenues of £491m, operating income (before goodwill and asset write downs) of £112m and earnings before interest, tax, depreciation and amortisation of £144m.

Extract 34.4 contains examples of the disclosures required for ordinary share transactions as described at 2.1.3(f) above:

Extract 34.4: Northern Rock plc (2007)

Notes to the accounts [extract]

45. Events after the balance sheet date

On 10 January 2008, the Company sold its Lifetime mortgage portfolio to JP Morgan at a premium of 2.25% to the balance sheet value. Proceeds of the sale amounted to approximately £2.2bn and were used to reduce the level of the Bank of England facility.

On 22 February 2008 the entire share capital of the Company was transferred to the Treasury Solicitor in accordance with The Northern Rock plc Transfer Order 2008 taking Northern Rock into a period of temporary public ownership. Details of the impact of temporary public ownership are given throughout the Annual Report and Accounts as it affects the Company's operations and financial disclosures.

On 29 March 2008 the Bank of England and HM Treasury agreed to extend the existing on demand loan facilities as set out in note 28 above to 30 April 2008.

On 29 March 2008 the Bank of England and HM Treasury confirmed that they intend to make arrangements to provide an additional committed secured revolving loan reserve facility to the Company in addition to the existing facilities as set out in note 28 above.

Extract 34.5 shows an example of the disclosures required for changes in tax laws as described at 2.1.3(h) above:

Extract 34.5: British Energy Group plc (2008)

Notes to the Financial Statements [extract]

38. Non-adjusting Post Balance Sheet Events

On 21 March 2007, the Government announced its intention to phase out industrial buildings allowances with effect from 1 April 2008. The phasing out of industrial buildings allowances was not included in the 2007 Finance Act and so is not considered to be substantively enacted at the balance sheet date. An estimate of the financial effect of this change, calculated at 28%, is that it would increase the net deferred tax liability by £37m to £82m.

Extract 34.6 contains an example of the disclosures required for a decline in fair value of investments as described in 2.1.3(k) above:

Extract 34.6: Imperial Innovations Group plc (2008)

Notes to the Consolidated Financial Statements [extract]

31. Post balance sheet events

Since the year end and as at 7 October 2008, the latest practical date prior to the approval of the accounts, the value of the Group's most significant asset Ceres Power Holdings plc (CWR.L) has reduced by £2.9 million (32%). This has had the effects of reducing investments by £2.9 million and of reducing the provision for liabilities and charges by £1.4m million since the year end. This is a non-adjusted post balance sheet event since it does not relate to conditions existing at the balance sheet date.

The list of examples of non-adjusting events in IAS 10, and summarised at 2.1.3 above, is not all-inclusive. IAS 10 requires disclosure of any material non-adjusting event. Extract 34.7 contains examples of the disclosures required for other non-adjusting events, which are not specifically listed by IAS 10:

> *Extract 34.7: GlaxoSmithKline plc (2007)*
>
> **Notes to the financial statements** [extract]
>
> **40. Post balance sheet events**
>
> On 25th January 2008, the FDA issued a not approvable letter in respect of Merck's NDA seeking approval for over-the-counter Mevacor. This triggered repayment to GSK of the upfront fee GSK had paid to Merck in 2007 for the US OTC rights.
>
> On 18th February 2008, GSK's long-term Standard and Poor's debt rating was revised from AA with negative outlook to A+ stable. Standard and Poor's also revised GSK's short-term rating for paper issued under the Group's commercial paper programme from A-1+ to A-1.

2.3.1 Declaration to distribute non-cash assets to owners

There are specific disclosure requirements when an entity declares a dividend to distribute a *non-cash asset* to owners after the end of a reporting period but before the financial statements are authorised for issue. IFRIC 17 requires an entity in such cases to disclose:

(a) the nature of the asset to be distributed;

(b) the carrying amount of the asset to be distributed as of the end of the reporting period; and

(c) the fair value of the asset to be distributed as of the end of the reporting period, if it is different from its carrying amount, and the following information about the method(s) used to measure that fair value: *[IFRIC 17.17]*

 (i) the level of the fair value hierarchy within which the fair value measurement is categorised (Level 1, 2 or 3); *[IFRS 13.93(b)]*;

 (ii) for fair value measurement categorised within Level 2 and Level 3 of the fair value hierarchy, a description of the valuation technique(s) and the inputs used in the fair value measurement. If there has been a change in valuation technique (e.g. changing from a market approach to an income approach or the use of an additional valuation technique), the entity should disclose that change and the reason(s) for making it. For fair value measurement categorised within Level 3 of the fair value hierarchy, quantitative information about the significant unobservable inputs used in the fair value measurement should be provided. An entity is not required to create quantitative information to comply with this disclosure requirement if quantitative unobservable inputs are not developed by the entity when measuring fair value (e.g. when an entity uses prices from prior transactions or third-party pricing information without adjustment). However, when providing this disclosure the quantitative unobservable inputs that are significant to the fair value measurement and are reasonably available to the entity should not be ignored; *[IFRS 13.93(d)]*;

(iii) for fair value measurement categorised within Level 3 of the fair value hierarchy, a description of the valuation processes used by the entity (including, for example, how an entity decides its valuation policies and procedures and analyses changes in fair value measurements from period to period); *[IFRS 13.93(g)]*; and

(iv) if the highest and best use of the non-financial asset differs from its current use, an entity should disclose that fact and why the non-financial asset is being used in a manner that differs from its highest and best use. *[IFRS 13.93(i)]*.

In the case of (c) above, any quantitative disclosures are required to be presented in a tabular format, unless another format is more appropriate. *[IFRS 13.99]*. Fair value measurement is further discussed in Chapter 14.

2.3.2 Breach of a long-term loan covenant and its subsequent rectification

When an entity breaches a provision of a long-term loan arrangement on or before the end of the reporting period with the effect that the liability becomes payable on demand, it classifies the liability as current in its statement of financial position. *[IAS 1.74]*. This may also give rise to going concern uncertainties (see 2.2.2 above).

It is not uncommon that such covenant breaches are subsequently rectified; however, a subsequent rectification is not an adjusting event and therefore does not change the classification of the liability in the statement of financial position from current to non-current.

IAS 1 requires disclosure of the following remedial arrangements if such events occur between the end of the reporting period and the date the financial statements are authorised for issue:

- refinancing on a long-term basis;
- rectification of a breach of a long-term loan arrangement; and
- the granting by the lender of a period of grace to rectify a breach of a long-term loan arrangement ending at least twelve months after the reporting period (see Chapter 3 at 5.5). *[IAS 1.76]*.

2.4 Other disclosure requirements

The disclosures required in respect of non-adjusting events are discussed at 2.3 above. As IAS 10 only requires consideration to be given to events that occur up to the date when the financial statements are authorised for issue, it is important for users to know that date, since the financial statements do not reflect events after that date. *[IAS 10.18]*. Accordingly, it requires disclosure of the date the financial statements were authorised for issue. Furthermore, it requires disclosure of who authorised the financial statements for issue and, if the owners of the entity or others have the power to amend them after issue, disclosure of that fact is needed. *[IAS 10.17]*. In practice, this information can be presented in a number of ways:

(a) on the face of a primary statement (for example, entities that are required to have the statement of financial position signed could include the information at that point);

(b) in the note dealing with other IAS 10 disclosures or another note (such as the summary of significant accounting policies); or

(c) in a separate statement such as a statement of directors' responsibilities for the financial statements (that is, outside of the financial statements as permitted in certain jurisdictions).

Strictly speaking, this information is required to be presented within the financial statements. So, if (c) were chosen, either the whole report would need to be part of the financial statements or the information could be incorporated into them by way of a cross-reference.

The financial statements should also disclose new standards that are issued but are not yet effective for the entity (see Chapter 3 at 5.1.2.C).

3 PRACTICAL ISSUES

The standard alludes to practical issues such as those discussed below. It states that a decline in fair value of investments after the reporting period *does not normally* relate to conditions at the end of the reporting period (see 2.1.3 above). At the same time, the standard asserts that the bankruptcy of a customer that occurs after the reporting period *usually* confirms that a loss on a trade receivable existed at the end of the reporting period (see 2.1.2(b)(i) above). Judgement of the facts and circumstances is required to determine whether an event that occurs after the reporting period provides evidence about a condition that existed at the end of the reporting period, or whether the condition arose subsequent to the reporting period.

3.1 Valuation of inventory

The sale of inventories after the reporting period is normally a good indicator of their net realisable value (NRV) at that date. IAS 10 states that such sales 'may give evidence about their net realisable value at the end of the reporting period'. *[IAS 10.9(b)(ii)]*. However, in some cases, NRV decreases because of conditions that did not exist at the end of the reporting period.

Therefore, the problem is determining why NRV decreased. Did it decrease because of circumstances that existed at the end of the reporting period, which subsequently became known, or did it decrease because of circumstances that arose subsequently? A decrease in price is merely a response to changing conditions so it is important to assess the reasons for these changes.

Some examples of changing conditions are as follows:

(a) Price reductions caused by a sudden increase in cheap imports

Whilst it is arguable that the 'dumping' of cheap imports after the reporting period is a condition that arises subsequent to that date, it is more likely that this is a reaction to a condition that already existed such as overproduction in other parts of the world. Thus, it might be more appropriate in such a situation to adjust the value of inventories based on its subsequent NRV.

(b) Price reductions caused by increased competition

The reasons for price reductions and increased competition do not generally arise overnight but normally occur over a period. For example, a competitor may have built up a competitive advantage by investing in machinery that is more efficient. In these circumstances, it is appropriate for an entity to adjust the valuation of its inventories because its own investment in production machinery is inferior to its competitor's and this situation existed at the end of the reporting period.

(c) Price reductions caused by the introduction of an improved competitive product

It is unlikely that a competitor developed and introduced an improved product overnight. Therefore, it is correct to adjust the valuation of inventories to their NRV after that introduction because the entity's failure to maintain its competitive position in relation to product improvements existed at the end of the reporting period.

Competitive pressures that caused a decrease in NRV after the reporting period are generally additional evidence of conditions that developed over a period and existed at the end of the reporting period. Consequently, their effects normally require adjustment in the financial statements.

However, for certain types of inventory, there is clear evidence of a price at the end of the reporting period and it is inappropriate to adjust the price of that inventory to reflect a subsequent decline. An example is inventories for which there is a price on an appropriate commodities market. In addition, inventory may be physically damaged or destroyed after the reporting period (e.g. by fire, flood, or other disaster). In these cases, the entity does not adjust the financial statements. However, the entity may be required to disclose the subsequent decline in NRV of the inventories if the impact is material (see 2.3 above).

3.2 Percentage of completion estimates

Events after the reporting period frequently give evidence about the profitability of construction contracts (or other contracts for which revenue is recognised using percentage of completion) that are in progress at the end of the reporting period.

IAS 11 – *Construction Contracts* – requires an assessment to be made of the *outcome* of a contract, as of the end of the reporting period, to recognise revenue and expenses under the percentage of completion method (see Chapter 23 at 3). *[IAS 11.22]*. In such an assessment, consideration should be given to events that occur after the reporting period and a determination should be made as to whether they are adjusting or non-adjusting events for which the financial effect is included in the percentage of completion calculation.

3.3 Insolvency of a debtor

The insolvency of a debtor or inability to pay debts usually builds up over a period. Consequently, if a debtor has an amount outstanding at the end of the reporting period and this amount is written off because of information received after the reporting period, the event is normally adjusting. IAS 10 states that the bankruptcy of a customer that occurs after the reporting period usually confirms that a loss existed at the end of the reporting period. *[IAS 10.9(b)(i)]*. If, however, there is evidence to show that the insolvency of the debtor resulted solely from an event occurring after the reporting period, then the event is a non-adjusting event. However, if the impact is material, the entity may be required to disclose the impact of the debtor's default (see 2.3 above).

3.4 Valuation of investment property at fair value and tenant insolvency

The fair value of investment property reflects, among other things, the quality of tenants' covenants and the future rental income from the property. If a tenant ceases to be able to meet its lease obligations due to insolvency after the reporting period, an entity considers how this event is reflected in the valuation at the end of the reporting period.

IAS 40 – *Investment Property* – requires the fair value of investment property, when measured in accordance with IFRS 13 – *Fair Value Measurement*, to reflect, among other things, rental income from current leases and other assumptions that market participants would use when pricing investment property under current market conditions. *[IAS 40.40]*. In addition, professional valuations generally reference the state of the market at the date of valuation without the use of hindsight. Consequently, the insolvency of a tenant is not *normally* an adjusting event to the fair value of the investment property because the investment property still holds value in the market. It is, however, an adjusting event for any amounts due from the tenant at the end of the reporting period.

This conclusion is consistent with the treatment of investment property measured using the alternative cost model. IAS 10 states that a decline in fair value of investments after the reporting period and before the date the financial statements are authorised for issue is a non-adjusting event, as the decline does not *normally* relate to a condition at the end of the reporting period (see 2.1.3 above). This decline in fair value, however, may be required to be disclosed if material (see 2.3 above).

3.5 Valuation of investments and fraud

The fair value of an investment may be based on its trading price in an active market. If no active market exists, the fair value may be derived from a model, such as in a cash flow forecast, and is based on the conditions that existed at the end of the reporting period.

In practice, such forecasts are prepared after the reporting period when some of the actual results of the subsequent period are available. However, it is often difficult to determine whether a difference between an actual and forecast cash flow after the reporting period resulted from conditions that existed at the end of the reporting period or relate to an event after the reporting period. Therefore, it requires judgement and careful consideration of the facts and circumstances.

The valuation for investments carried at fair value that are traded in an active market is easier because that market price records the conditions at the end of the reporting period. The standard states that a decline in fair value of investments after the reporting period *does not normally* relate to conditions that existed at the end of the reporting period (see 2.1.3 above). If the impact is material, however, the entity may be required to disclose this decline in fair value (see 2.3 above).

However, when fraud is discovered after the reporting period, the determination of whether a condition existed at the end of the reporting period becomes even more difficult. In some cases, an investment has a significantly lower value than previously believed. Is this an adjusting or non-adjusting event?

Consideration should be given to all facts and circumstances related to the investment. Generally, if a fraud is discovered after the reporting period but before the financial statements are authorised for issue and the security is found never to have existed, this is an adjusting event because the discovery of fraud provides new information about the conditions that existed as of the end of the reporting period.

However, if fraud is discovered after the reporting period but before the financial statements are authorised for issue and the fair value of the security (subsequent to the reporting period) is much lower than the original (fraudulent) amount, this is generally a non-adjusting event. This is because a decline in the value of an investment, whether based on a market price or a valuation model, after the reporting period is a change in estimate that resulted from new information or developments. *[IAS 8.5]*. For traded securities, the fact that the entity could have sold the security at the end of the reporting period and received the original (fraudulent) amount is a further support that the decline in fair value after the reporting period does not provide evidence about a condition that existed as of the end of the reporting period. However, if the impact is material, the entity may be required to disclose the subsequent decline in fair value (see 2.3 above).

Determining whether the discovery of fraud is an adjusting event is a complex task and requires judgement and careful consideration of the facts and circumstances.

References

---

1 *IFRIC Update*, November 2012.
2 *IFRIC Update*, January 2013.
3 *IFRIC Update*, May 2013.
4 US FASB Accounting Standards Update No. 2013-07, *Presentation of Financial Statements (Topic 205): The Liquidation Basis of Accounting*. 22 April 2013.

Chapter 35 Related party disclosures

List of examples

Chapter 35 Related party disclosures

1 INTRODUCTION

Related party relationships and transactions between related parties are a normal feature of business. Many entities carry on their business activities through subsidiaries, joint ventures, and associates and there are inevitably transactions between these parties. It is also common for entities under common control, which are not a group for financial reporting purposes, to transact with each other. These are matters addressed by IAS 24 – *Related Party Disclosures.*

1.1 The related party issue

The problems posed by related party relationships and transactions are described in IAS 24 as follows:

> 'A related party relationship could have an effect on the profit or loss and financial position of an entity. Related parties may enter into transactions that unrelated parties would not. For example, an entity that sells goods to its parent at cost might not sell on those terms to another customer. Also, transactions between related parties may not be made at the same amounts as between unrelated parties.
>
> The profit or loss and financial position of an entity may be affected by a related party relationship even if related party transactions do not occur. The mere existence of the relationship may be sufficient to affect the transactions of the entity with other parties. For example, a subsidiary may terminate relations with a trading partner on acquisition by the parent of a fellow subsidiary engaged in the same activity as the former trading partner. Alternatively, one party may refrain from acting because of the significant influence of another – for example, a subsidiary may be instructed by its parent not to engage in research and development.' *[IAS 24.6-7].*

1.2 Possible solutions

1.2.1 Remeasurement of related party transactions at fair values

One solution to the problems posed by related party relationships and transactions is to adjust the financial statements to value related party transactions as if they occurred with an independent third party and recognise any such transactions at an arm's length price. However, the consensus for over thirty years is that it is often impossible to establish what would have been the terms of any non-arm's length transaction had it been negotiated on an arm's length basis. This is because no comparable transactions may have taken place and, in any event, the transaction might never have taken place at all if it had been negotiated using different values.

1.2.2 Disclosure of transactions

Because of this problem, accounting standards internationally require disclosure of related party transactions and relationships, rather than adjustment of the financial statements. This approach is adopted by the IASB in IAS 24 which is a disclosure standard. IAS 24 does not establish any recognition or measurement requirements. Related party transactions are accounted for in accordance with the requirements of the IFRS applicable to the transaction. The disclosures required by IAS 24 are in addition to those required by other IFRSs. For example, a loan to a related party will also be subject to the disclosure requirements of IFRS 7 – *Financial Instruments: Disclosures.*

The purpose of presenting the disclosures required by IAS 24 is to give users of the financial statements information about transactions, outstanding balances, including commitments, and relationships with related parties that may affect their assessment of an entity's operations, including assessments of the risks and opportunities facing an entity. *[IAS 24.8]*.

2 REQUIREMENTS OF IAS 24

2.1 Objective and scope

2.1.1 Objective

IAS 24 states that its objective 'is to ensure that an entity's financial statements contain the disclosures necessary to draw attention to the possibility that its financial position and profit or loss may have been affected by the existence of related parties and by transactions and outstanding balances, including commitments, with such parties'. *[IAS 24.1]*.

Accordingly, IAS 24 requires disclosure of related party transactions and outstanding balances, including commitments, together with the names of any parties who control the reporting entity.

2.1.2 Scope

IAS 24 applies in:

(a) identifying related party relationships and transactions;

(b) identifying outstanding balances, including commitments, between an entity and its related parties;

(c) identifying the circumstances in which disclosure of the items in (a) and (b) is required; and

(d) determining the disclosures to be made about those items. *[IAS 24.2]*.

The standard explicitly requires disclosure of related party relationships, transactions and outstanding balances, including commitments, in both the consolidated and separate financial statements of a parent or investors with joint control of, or significant influence over, an investee presented in accordance with IFRS 10 – *Consolidated Financial Statements* – or IAS 27 – *Separate Financial Statements*. *[IAS 24.3]*.

All entities within a group that prepare their financial statements under IFRS must disclose related party transactions and outstanding balances with other entities in the group in the entity's own financial statements. *[IAS 24.4]*. There are no disclosure exemptions for subsidiaries, or for parent companies that produce separate financial statements even where those separate financial statements are issued with the consolidated financial statements of the group of which they are a part. The IASB considers that the financial statements of an entity that is part of a consolidated group may include the effects of extensive intragroup transactions. Therefore, it concluded that the disclosures required by IAS 24 are essential to understanding the financial position and financial performance of such an entity and should be required for separate financial statements presented in accordance with IAS 27. The IASB also believes that disclosure of intragroup transactions is essential because external users of the financial statements need to be aware of the interrelationships between related parties, including the level of support provided by related parties, to assist in their economic decisions. *[IAS 24.BC16-17]*.

The standard notes that 'intragroup related party transactions and outstanding balances are eliminated in the preparation of consolidated financial statements of the group'. *[IAS 24.4]*. This implies that disclosure of such transactions and balances is not required in the group's consolidated financial statements since, so far as those financial statements are concerned, such items do not exist.

IFRS 10 was amended in October 2012 to exempt an 'investment entity' from consolidating subsidiaries held as part of its investment portfolio. Such subsidiaries are instead required to be measured at fair value through profit or loss (see Chapter 6). In consequence, IAS 24 was amended to indicate that transactions and balances between an investment entity and those of its subsidiaries that are measured at fair value through profit or loss are required to be disclosed in line with the requirements of IAS 24.

This amendment (together with the amendment to IFRS 10) is effective for annual periods beginning on or after 1 January 2014, and early adoption is permitted.

2.2 Identification of a related party and related party transactions

A related party is defined as 'a person or entity that is related to the entity that is preparing its financial statements (the "reporting entity")'. *[IAS 24.9]*.

The standard contains a multi-part definition of 'related party', which is discussed in sections 2.2.1 to 2.2.9 below. The standard emphasises that attention should be directed to the substance of the relationship and not merely the legal form. *[IAS 24.10]*.

A related party transaction is a transfer of resources, services or obligations between a reporting entity and a related party, regardless of whether a price is charged. *[IAS 24.9]*.

2.2.1 Persons or close family members that are related parties

A person or close member of that person's family is related to a reporting entity if that person:

(i) has control or joint control over the reporting entity;

(ii) has significant influence over the reporting entity; or

(iii) is a member of the key management personnel of the reporting entity or of a parent of the reporting entity. *[IAS 24.9].*

Close members of a family of a person are defined as 'those family members who may be expected to influence, or be influenced by, that person in their dealings with the entity' and include:

(a) that person's children and spouse or domestic partner;

(b) children of that person's spouse or domestic partner; and

(c) dependants of that person or that person's spouse or domestic partner. *[IAS 24.9].*

The definition appears to provide no scope to argue that there are circumstances in which the specific family members described in (a) to (c) above are not related parties. Dependants are not limited to children and may include elderly or infirm parents.

IAS 24 does not, however, elaborate on the meaning of 'may be expected to influence, or be influenced by, that person'. A narrow interpretation is that the standard explicitly mentions only those instances where such influence is expected without doubt. Thus, a relationship with, for example, parents, siblings or relatives that are even more distant would need to be assessed to determine whether there is evidence of sufficient influence. A broader interpretation would support the fact that the mere existence of the family relationship is sufficient to trigger the disclosure requirements included in IAS 24.

We believe that the definition is broad, and most likely intentionally so, in order to cover, among other things, many diverse cultural backgrounds. Furthermore, the list of close family members in paragraph 9 of IAS 24 is not exhaustive, and therefore does not preclude other types of relationship from being considered related party relationships. The facts and circumstances would need to be considered in each case.

Relationships involving a person or close family members as investors are illustrated in the following examples, which are based on illustrative examples published by the IASB, which accompany, but are not part of IAS 24.

Example 35.1: Person as investor

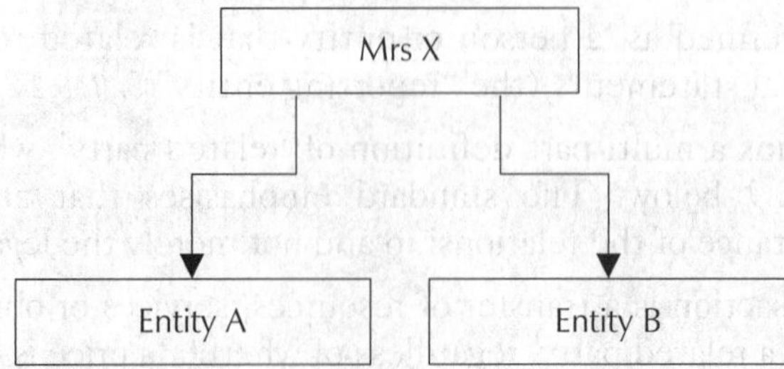

Mrs X has an investment in Entity A and Entity B.

For Entity A's financial statements, if Mrs X controls or jointly controls Entity A, Entity B is related to Entity A when Mrs X has control, joint control or significant influence over Entity B.

For Entity B's financial statements, if Mrs X controls or jointly controls Entity A, Entity A is related to Entity B when Mrs X has control, joint control or significant influence over Entity B. If Mrs X has significant influence over both Entity A and Entity B, Entities A and B are not related to each other.

If Mrs X is a member of the key management personnel of both Entity A and Entity B, Entities A and B are not, in the absence of any other indicator of a related party relationship, related to each other (see 2.3 below).

Example 35.2: Close members of the family holding investments

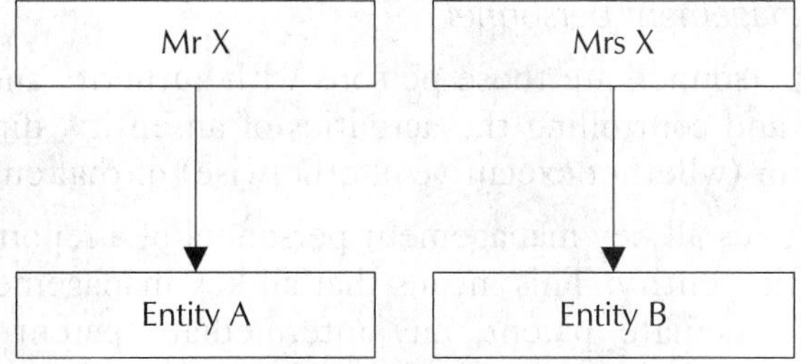

Mr X is the spouse of Mrs X. Mr X has an investment in Entity A and Mrs X has an investment in Entity B.

For Entity A's financial statements, if Mr X controls or jointly controls Entity A, Entity B is related to Entity A when Mrs X has control, joint control or significant influence over Entity B.

For Entity B's financial statements, if Mr X controls or jointly controls Entity A, Entity A is related to Entity B when Mrs X has control, joint control or significant influence over Entity B.

If Mr X has significant influence (but not control or joint control) over Entity A and Mrs X has significant influence (but not control or joint control) over Entity B, Entities A and B are not related to each other (see 2.3 below).

If Mr X is a member of the key management personnel of Entity A and Mrs X is a member of the key management personnel of Entity B, Entities A and B are not related to each other (see 2.3 below).

2.2.1.A Control

The definition of 'control' in IAS 24 is a cross-reference to the definition in IFRS 10. IFRS 10 states that 'an investor controls an investee when the investor is exposed, or has rights, to variable returns from its involvement with the investee and has the ability to affect those returns through its power over the investee'. *[IFRS 10 Appendix A].*

2.2.1.B Joint control

The definition of 'joint control' in IAS 24 is a cross-reference to the definition in IFRS 11 – *Joint Arrangements.* IFRS 11 defines joint control as 'the contractually agreed sharing of control of an arrangement, which exists only when decisions about the relevant activities require the unanimous consent of the parties sharing control'. *[IFRS 11 Appendix A].*

In the definition of a related party, a joint venture includes subsidiaries of the joint venture. *[IAS 24.12].* Therefore, for example, the subsidiary of a joint venture and the investor who has joint control are related to each other.

2.2.1.C Significant influence

The definition of 'significant influence' in IAS 24 is a cross-reference to the definition in IAS 28 – *Investments in Associates and Joint Ventures.* IAS 28 defines significant influence as 'the power to participate in the financial and operating policy decisions of the investee but is not control or joint control of those policies'. *[IAS 28.3]*.

In the definition of a related party, an associate includes subsidiaries of the associate. Therefore, for example, the subsidiary of an associate and the investor who has significant influence over the associate are related to each other. *[IAS 24.12]*.

2.2.1.D Key management personnel

'Key management personnel' are those persons with authority and responsibility for planning, directing and controlling the activities of an entity, directly or indirectly, including any director (whether executive or otherwise) of that entity. *[IAS 24.9]*.

A related party includes all key management personnel of a reporting entity and of a parent of the reporting entity. This means that all key management personnel of all parents (i.e. the immediate parent, any intermediate parent and the ultimate parent) of a reporting entity are related parties of the reporting entity.

Some entities may have more than one level of key management. For example, some entities may have a supervisory board, whose members have responsibilities similar to those of non-executive directors, as well as a board of directors that sets the overall operating strategy. All members of either board will be considered to be key management personnel.

The definition of key management personnel is not restricted to directors. It also includes other individuals with authority and responsibility for planning, directing and controlling the activities of an entity. The main intention of the definition is presumably to ensure that transactions with persons with responsibilities similar to those of directors, and the compensation paid to such persons, do not escape disclosure simply because they are not directors. Otherwise, there would be an obvious loophole in the standard. For example, in some jurisdictions, a chief financial officer or a chief operating officer may not be directors but could meet the definition of key management personnel. Other examples of the type of persons who are not directors but may meet the definition of key management personnel include a divisional chief executive or a director of a major trading subsidiary of the entity, but not of the entity itself, who nevertheless participates in the management of the reporting entity. A reference to individuals who are not directors in a reporting entity's business review or management discussion and analysis might indicate that those persons are considered to be key management personnel. One might argue that, if the individual is truly part of the 'key management' of the group, he or she would be on the parent entity's board. However, this view is inconsistent with the view of the IASB that 'key management' may be found outside the boardroom.

'Key management personnel' are normally employees of the reporting entity (or of another entity in the same group). However, the definition does not restrict itself to employees. Therefore, seconded staff and persons engaged under management or outsourcing contracts may also have a level of authority or responsibility such that they are 'key management personnel'.

The definition of key management personnel refers to 'persons'. In some jurisdictions, the term 'person' includes both a 'corporate person' and a 'natural person'. Additionally, in some jurisdictions, a corporate entity must by law have the authority and responsibility for planning, directing and controlling the activities of an investment fund for the benefit of the fund's investors in accordance with the fund's constitution and relevant statutes (i.e. the corporate entity is the body acting as key management personnel). We therefore believe that, although the definition of 'key management personnel' appears to restrict its application to natural persons, the definition can include a corporate entity.

A further issue is whether staff acting for the corporate entity having responsibility for planning, directing and controlling the activities of the reporting entity could be considered to be key management personnel of the reporting entity. In our view, it is not necessary to look through the corporate entity to determine natural persons as key management personnel of the investment fund unless the corporate entity is a sole practitioner or there is a sole person in the corporate entity who has been specifically contracted to undertake the role of key management personnel of the investment fund. This determination is important for complying with the disclosure requirements for key management personnel (see 2.6 below).

The issue of the identification of and disclosure requirements for related party transactions that take place when key management personnel services are provided by a management entity that is not otherwise a related party of the reporting entity is the subject of a proposed amendment to IAS 24 in an *Exposure Draft – Annual Improvements to IFRSs 2010-2012 Cycle (ED/2012/1)* issued by the IASB in May 2012. See 3 below for further details.

2.2.2 Entities that are members of the same group

'An entity is related to a reporting entity if:

(i) The entity and the reporting entity are members of the same group (which means that each parent, subsidiary and fellow subsidiary is related to the others).' *[IAS 24.9(b)].*

IAS 24 does not define group, parent and subsidiary. However, these terms are defined in IFRS 10 as follows:

- a group is 'a parent and its subsidiaries';
- a parent is 'an entity that controls one or more entities'; and
- a subsidiary as 'an entity that is controlled by another entity'. *[IFRS 10 Appendix A].*

Therefore, all entities controlled by the same ultimate parent are related parties. This would include entities where the reporting entity holds less than a majority of the voting rights but which are subsidiaries as defined in IFRS 10. There are no exceptions to this rule.

Example 35.3: Entities that are members of the same group

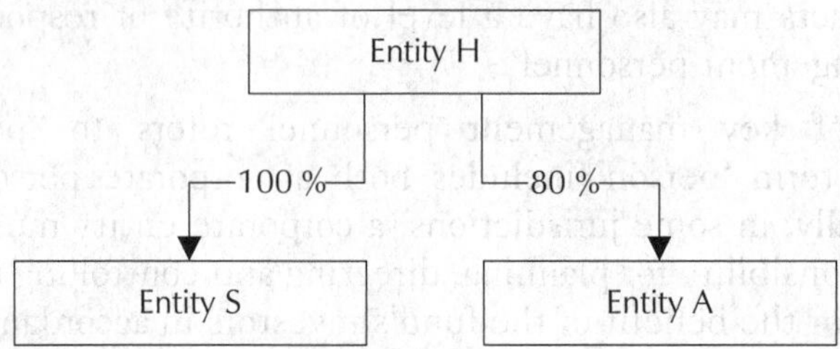

Entities H, S and A are all related parties to each other as they are members of the same group. Both Entity S and Entity A are subsidiaries of Entity H.

Related party disclosures will be required in the financial statements of Entity S in respect of transactions with Entities H and A, in the financial statements of Entity A in respect of transactions with Entities H and S and in the separate financial statements of Entity H in respect of transactions with Entities S and A.

2.2.3 Entities that are associates or joint ventures

'An entity is related to a reporting entity if:

...

(ii) One entity is an associate or joint venture of the other entity (or an associate or joint venture of a member of a group of which the other entity is a member).' *[IAS 24.9(b)]*.

IAS 24 does not define associate or joint venture. However, these terms are defined in IAS 28 and IFRS 11.

IAS 28 defines an associate as 'an entity over which the investor has significant influence'. *[IAS 28.2]*.

IFRS 11 defines a joint venture as 'a joint arrangement whereby the parties that have joint control of the arrangement have rights to the net assets of the arrangement'. *[IFRS 11 Appendix A]*.

Any entity that a reporting entity determines is an associate under IAS 28 or a joint venture under IFRS 11 is a related party. This requirement further applies to investments in associates or joint ventures held by a venture capital organisation, mutual fund, unit trust or similar entity, even where the investment is accounted for at fair value through profit or loss or held for trading under IAS 39 – *Financial Instruments: Recognition and Measurement* – rather than under the equity method. Likewise, any reporting entity that is an associate or joint venture of another entity must treat that investor entity as a related party.

As noted above, in the definition of a related party, an associate includes subsidiaries of the associate and a joint venture includes subsidiaries of the joint venture. Therefore, for example, an associate's subsidiary and the investor that has significant influence over the associate are related to one another. *[IAS 24.12]*.

The definition also means that an associate of a reporting entity's parent is also a related party of the reporting entity.

However, the definition does not cause investors in a joint venture or an associate to be related to each other (see 2.3 below). Investors in joint operations (as defined in IFRS 11) are also not related to each other.

The application of these requirements is illustrated in the example below, which is based on an illustrative example accompanying IAS 24.

Example 35.4: Associates of the reporting entity's group that are related parties

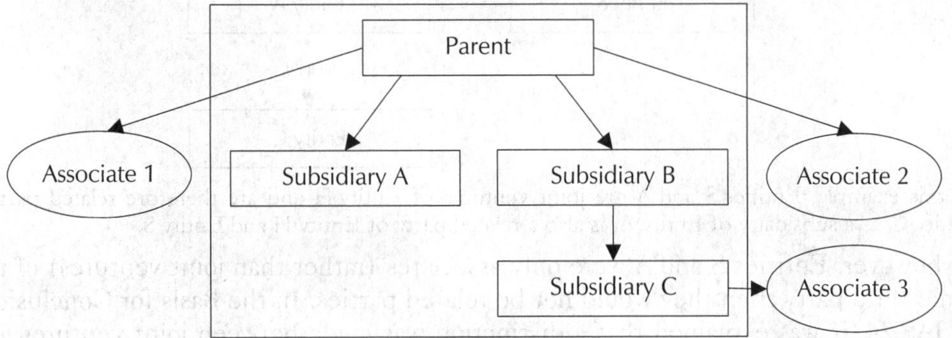

In Parent's separate financial statements, Associates 1, 2 and 3 are related parties. For Parent's consolidated financial statements, Associates 1, 2 and 3 are related to the group.

For Subsidiary A's financial statements, Associates 1, 2 and 3 are related parties. For Subsidiary B's consolidated or separate financial statements, Associates 1, 2 and 3 are related parties. For Subsidiary C's financial statements, Associates 1, 2 and 3 are related parties.

For the financial statements of Associates 1, 2 and 3, Parent and Subsidiaries A, B and C are related parties. Associates 1, 2 and 3 are not related to each other.

2.2.3.A Joint operations

IAS 24 defines 'joint ventures' of the reporting entity as related parties. The definition of a joint venture in IFRS 11 excludes joint operations, so that an investment in a joint operation is not a related party.

A share in a joint operation can be seen as being part of the entity itself, since IFRS 11 refers to the recognition by a joint operator of its assets, revenue, liabilities and expenses. *[IFRS 11.20]*. Thus, a transaction with a joint operation is either a transaction by the reporting entity with itself or a transaction with the other joint operator which would not be a related party unless it otherwise met the related party definition in IAS 24 for some other reason (e.g. because it was an entity controlled by a member of key management personnel).

2.2.4 Entities that are joint ventures of the same third party

'An entity is related to a reporting entity if:

...

(iii) Both entities are joint ventures of the same third party.' *[IAS 24.9(b)]*.

This is illustrated by the following example:

Chapter 35

Example 35.5: Entities that are joint ventures of the same third party

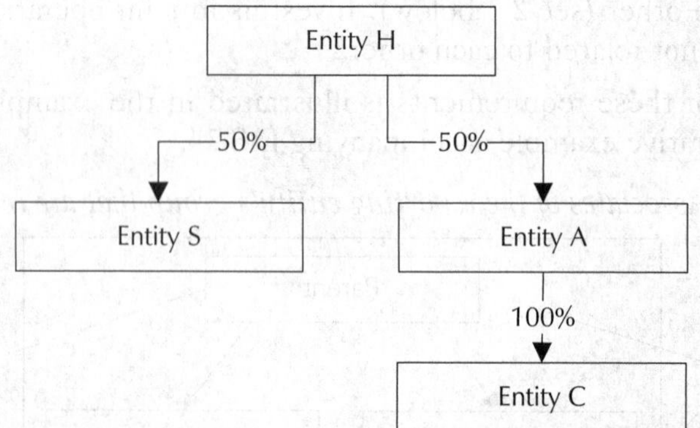

In this example, Entities S and A are joint ventures of Entity H and are therefore related parties. Entity C, as a subsidiary of Entity A, is also a related party of Entity H and Entity S.

If, however, Entities S and A were only associates (rather than joint ventures) of the same third party then they would not be related parties. In the Basis for Conclusions to IAS 24, it was explained that a distinction was made between joint ventures and associates because the IASB considered that 'significant influence' was not as close a relationship as control or joint control. *[IAS 24.BC19(a)]*.

As noted above, in the definition of a related party, a joint venture includes subsidiaries of the joint venture. Therefore, for example, a joint venture's subsidiary and the investor that has joint control over the joint venture are related to each other. *[IAS 24.12]*.

2.2.5 *Entities that are joint ventures and associates of the same third entity*

'An entity is related to a reporting entity if:

...

(iv) One entity is a joint venture of a third entity and the other entity is an associate of the third entity.' *[IAS 24.9(b)]*.

This definition treats joint ventures in a similar manner to subsidiaries as illustrated in Examples 35.3 and 35.5 above and therefore an associate and a joint venture are related parties where they share the same investor. This is illustrated in the example below:

Example 35.6: Entities that are joint ventures and associates of the same third entity

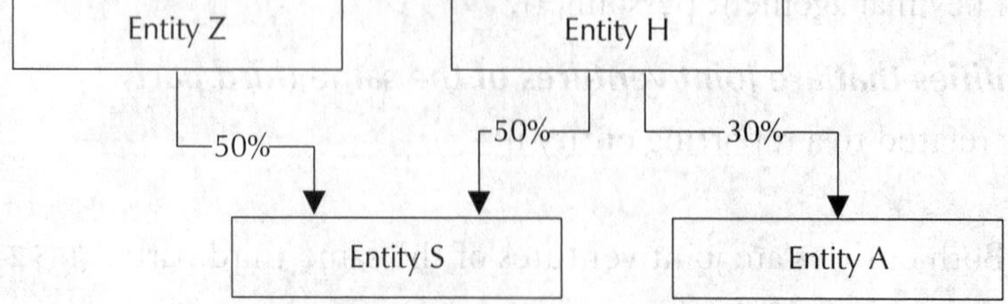

Entity S is a joint venture of Entity H and Entity A is an associate of Entity H. Therefore, Entities S and A are related parties.

However, Entities Z and H are not related parties (see 2.3 below).

2.2.6 Post-employment benefit plans

'An entity is related to a reporting entity if:

...

(v) The entity is a post-employment benefit plan for the benefit of employees of either the reporting entity or an entity related to the reporting entity. If the reporting entity is itself such a plan, the sponsoring employers are also related to the reporting entity.' *[IAS 24.9(b)].*

The standard does not indicate why a post-employment benefit plan is a related party of the entity. Presumably, the reason for including this category is that an entity sponsoring a post-employment benefit plan generally has at least significant influence over the plan.

The definition is quite wide-ranging and includes post-employment benefit plans of any entity related to the reporting entity. This includes, for example, post-employment benefit plans of an associate or joint venture of the reporting entity or a post-employment benefit plan of an associate of the reporting entity's parent.

Sponsoring employers are also related parties of a post-employment benefit plan.

2.2.7 Entities under control or joint control of certain persons or close members of their family

'An entity is related to a reporting entity if:

...

(vi) The entity is controlled or jointly controlled by a person or close member of that person's family who has control or joint control over the reporting entity, has significant influence over the reporting entity or is a member of key management personnel of the reporting entity.' *[IAS 24.9].*

This is intended to cover situations in which an entity is controlled or jointly controlled by a person or close family member of that person and that person or close family member also controls, jointly controls, has significant influence over, or is a member of key management personnel of, the reporting entity. The situation whereby one company owns another is covered by Example 35.3 above.

This is illustrated below:

Example 35.7: Persons who control an entity and are a member of the key management personnel of another entity

Mrs X has a 100% investment in Entity A and is a member of the key management personnel of Entity S. Entity M has a 100% investment in Entity S.

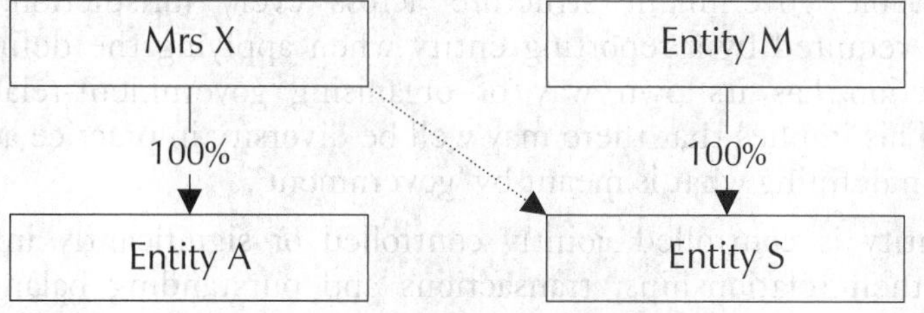

For Entity S's financial statements, Entity A is related to Entity S because Mrs X controls Entity A and is a member of the key management personnel of Entity S.

For Entity S's financial statements, Entity A is also related to Entity S if Mrs X is a member of the key management personnel of Entity M and not of Entity S.

This outcome would be the same if Mrs X has joint control over Entity A (if Mrs X only had significant influence over Entity A and not control or joint control then Entities A and S would not be related parties).

For Entity A's financial statements, Entity S is related to Entity A because Mrs X controls Entity A and is a member of Entity S's key management personnel. This outcome would be the same if Mrs X has joint control over Entity A and would further be the same if Mrs X is a member of the key management personnel of Entity M rather than Entity S (see 2.2.8 below). Note that Entity A and Entity M would also be related parties in this instance.

For Entity M's consolidated financial statements, Entity A is a related party of the Group if Mrs X is a member of the key management personnel of the Group.

2.2.8 Entities under significant influence of certain persons or close members of their family

'An entity is related to a reporting entity if:

...

> (vii) A person or a close family member of that person who has control or joint control over the reporting entity has significant influence over the entity or is a member of the key management personnel of the entity (or of a parent of the entity).' *[IAS 24.9(b)].*

This is the reciprocal of 2.2.7 and is illustrated in Example 35.7 above.

Entities that are significantly influenced by the same person or close member of that person's family or who simply share the same key management personnel are not related parties in the absence of any control or joint control by those persons (see 2.3 below).

2.2.9 Government-related entities

A 'government-related entity' is an entity that is controlled, jointly controlled or significantly influenced by a government. *[IAS 24.9].*

'Government' in this context refers to government, government agencies and similar bodies whether local, national or international. *[IAS 24.9].* This is the same as the definition used in IAS 20 – *Accounting for Government Grants and Disclosure of Government Assistance.* The Board decided that it would not provide a more comprehensive definition or additional guidance on how to determine what is meant by 'government'. In the Board's view, a more detailed definition could not capture every conceivable government structure across every jurisdiction. In addition, judgement is required by a reporting entity when applying the definition because every jurisdiction has its own way of organising government-related activities. *[IAS 24.BC41].* This implies that there may well be diversity in practice across different jurisdictions in defining what is meant by 'government'.

Where an entity is controlled, jointly controlled or significantly influenced by a government then relationships, transactions and outstanding balances, including commitments, with that government are related party transactions. Similarly, transactions and outstanding balances, including commitments, with other entities controlled, jointly controlled or significantly influenced by that government are related party transactions.

Related party transactions with government-related entities are subject to certain disclosure exemptions. These are discussed at 2.8 below.

2.3 Parties that are not related parties

Having included such a detailed definition of related parties, the standard clarifies that the following are not related parties:

- two entities simply because they have a director or other member of key management personnel in common or because a member of key management personnel of one entity has significant influence over the other entity;
- two venturers simply because they share joint control over a joint venture;
- providers of finance, trade unions, public utilities and departments and agencies of, a government that does not control, jointly control or significantly influence the reporting entity, simply by virtue of their normal dealings with the entity (even though they may affect the freedom of action of an entity or participate in its decision-making process); and
- a customer, supplier, franchisor, distributor or general agent with whom an entity transacts a significant volume of business, simply by virtue of the resulting economic dependence. *[IAS 24.11].*

The reason for these exclusions is that, without them, many entities that are not normally regarded as related parties could fall within the definition of related party. For example, a small clothing manufacturer selling 90% of its output to a single customer could be under the effective economic control of that customer.

These exclusions are effective only where these parties are 'related' to the reporting entity simply because of the relationship noted above. If there are other reasons why a party is a related party, the exclusions do not apply. Consider the following examples:

- A water company that supplies the reporting entity is not a related party if the only link between the two is the supply of water. If, however, the water company is also an associate of the reporting entity, the exclusion does not apply; the two are related parties, and the transactions relating to the supply of water are disclosed if material.
- Two investors in the same entity are not related parties simply because one holds a controlling interest and the other shareholder (not in the group) holds a non-controlling interest in a subsidiary of the group. Even if the investor holding the non-controlling interest exercises significant influence over the subsidiary, provided it is not otherwise related to the controlling investor, it is not normally a related party of the controlling investor. However, the non-controlling investor might have significant influence over the group if the subsidiary was significant to the group in which case the group, including the controlling investor, and the non-controlling investor are related parties.

- Two entities are not related parties simply because they share common key management personnel. However, if the common member of key management personnel exerts control or joint control over one or more of the entities then they are related parties. See 2.2.7 or 2.2.8 above.
- An administrator, custodian, broker and fund manager of the same fund are not related parties, to each other or to the fund to which they provide services simply because they each provide services to the fund, even if any of the parties are economically dependent upon the income from such services. However, any such party could meet the definition of 'key management personnel' of the fund if it provides key management personnel services. In addition, any shared ownership (e.g. control, joint control, or significant influence) between such parties should be evaluated to determine if the parties are related. As discussed at 3 below, the IASB has issued an Exposure Draft (ED/2012/1) proposing to amend IAS 24 so that the definition of a related party is extended to include an entity, or a member of its group, which provides key management personnel services to a reporting entity.

In addition, an interest in an unconsolidated structured entity as defined by IFRS 12 – *Disclosure of Interests in Other Entities* – held by a reporting entity does not make the structured entity a related party to the reporting entity unless it would otherwise meet the definition of a related party (e.g. because the structured entity is an associate of the reporting entity).

2.4 Disclosure of controlling relationships

IAS 24 asserts that, in order to enable users of financial statements to form a view about the effects of related party relationships on an entity, it is appropriate to disclose the related party relationship when control exists, irrespective of whether there have been transactions between the related parties. *[IAS 24.14]*. Accordingly, the standard requires an entity to disclose:

- the name of its parent and, if different;
- the ultimate controlling party.

If neither the entity's parent nor the ultimate controlling party produces consolidated financial statements available for public use, the name of the next most senior parent that does so must also be disclosed. *[IAS 24.13]*.

The 'next most senior parent' is the first parent in the group above the immediate parent that produces consolidated financial statements available for public use. *[IAS 24.16]*. Consequently, in some circumstances, an entity may need to disclose the names of three parents.

The use of the word 'party' means that the disclosure applies to both individuals and to entities. Disclosure must be made even if the parent or ultimate controlling party does not prepare financial statements. In the situation when the ultimate controlling party is an individual, rather than an entity, the reporting entity is likely to have to disclose the name of the next most senior parent in addition since the individual undoubtedly does not produce financial statements for public use. IAS 1 – *Presentation of Financial Statements* – also requires disclosure of the 'ultimate parent' of the group. *[IAS 1.138(c)]*. This is not necessarily synonymous with the 'ultimate controlling party' where that party is an individual. This is illustrated in the example below.

Example 35.8: Disclosure of parent, ultimate parent and ultimate controlling party

Entity S is controlled by Entity P which in turn is controlled by Entity H which in turn is controlled by Entity Y. The ultimate controlling party of Entity Y is Mr A. Entities P and Y do not produce consolidated financial statements available for public use.

The group structure is illustrated as follows:

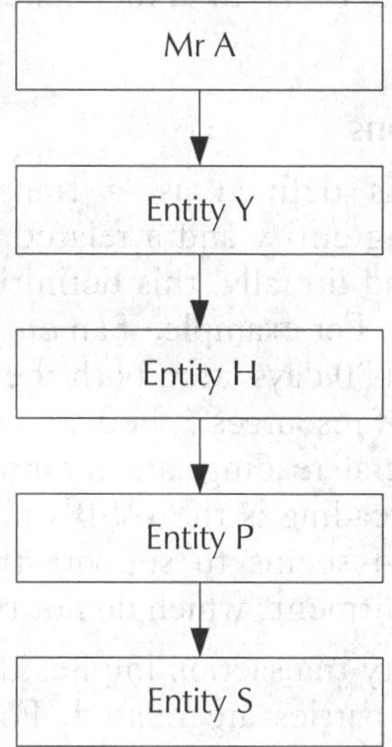

For Entity S's financial statements, IAS 24 requires disclosure of Entity P (the parent), Entity H (the next most senior parent that produces consolidated financial statements available for public use) and Mr A (the ultimate controlling party). In addition, IAS 1 requires disclosure of Entity Y (the ultimate parent of the group).

For Entity P's financial statements, IAS 24 requires disclosure of Entity H (the parent) and Mr A (the ultimate controlling party). In addition, IAS 1 requires disclosure of Entity Y (the ultimate parent of the group).

For Entity H's financial statements, IAS 24 requires disclosure of Entity Y (the parent) and Mr A (the ultimate controlling party). IAS 1 does not require any additional disclosure.

For Entity Y, IAS 24 requires disclosure of Mr A (ultimate controlling party). IAS 1 does not require any additional disclosure.

The ultimate controlling party could be a group of individuals or entities acting together. IAS 24 is silent on the issue of individuals or entities acting together to exercise joint control. However, IFRS 3 – *Business Combinations* – states that a group of individuals can be regarded as a controlling party when, as a result of contractual arrangements, they collectively have the power to govern that entity's financial and operating policies so as to obtain benefits from its activities. *[IFRS 3.B2]*. In such circumstances, these entities or individuals should be identified as the controlling party. Where there is no such contractual arrangement, IFRS is silent on whether a group of individuals acting in an informal way could be considered to be the ultimate controlling party of an entity. However, as discussed at 2.2 above,

IAS 24 emphasises that attention should be directed to the substance of any related party relationship and not merely the legal form. It is likely that such an informal arrangement would at least give such individuals acting collectively significant influence over the reporting entity and as such, those individuals would be related parties to the reporting entity under IAS 24.

The standard also clarifies that the requirement to disclose related party relationships between a parent and its subsidiaries is in addition to the disclosure requirements of IAS 27 and IFRS 12. *[IAS 24.15]*. IFRS 12 requires an entity to disclose information to enable users to understand the composition of a group *[IFRS 12.10(a)(i)]*.

2.5 Disclosable transactions

A related party transaction is defined as 'a transfer of resources, services or obligations between a reporting entity and a related party, regardless of whether a price is charged.' *[IAS 24.9]*. Read literally, this definition requires many transactions to be disclosed more than once. For example, if an entity buys goods on credit from a related party and pays for them 30 days later, both the original purchase and the final payment represent a 'transfer of resources ... between a reporting entity and a related party' and, therefore on a literal reading, are required to be separately disclosed. However, we doubt that this reading is the IASB's intention, and the nature of the disclosures required by IAS 24 seems to support this view. This definition also appears to exclude those commitments which do not transfer resources.

The definition of a related party transaction implies that transactions are disclosable only for the period in which parties are related. For example, where a reporting entity has disposed of a subsidiary during the reporting period, only transactions with the subsidiary up to the date of disposal are related party transactions in the financial statements of the reporting entity. Similarly, if a person became a member of key management personnel of a reporting entity during a reporting period, no disclosure is required of any remuneration paid to that person before that person's appointment as key management personnel.

There is no requirement in IAS 24 to disclose information about related party transactions in one comprehensive note. However, it may be more useful to users of the financial statements to present information this way.

IAS 1 requires that, except where a standard permits otherwise (which IAS 24 does not), comparative information in respect of the previous period must be disclosed for all amounts reported in the current period's financial statements. *[IAS 1.38]*.

2.5.1 Materiality

In determining whether an entity discloses related party transactions in financial statements, the general concept of materiality is applied. IAS 24 does not refer specifically to materiality since this requirement is in IAS 1, which states that 'an entity need not provide a specific disclosure required by an IFRS if the information is not material.' *[IAS 1.31]*. Omissions or misstatements of items are material within IAS 1 'if they could, individually or collectively, influence the economic decisions that users make on the basis of the financial statements. Materiality depends on the size and nature of the omission or misstatement judged in the surrounding circumstances. The size or nature of the item, or a combination of both, could be the determining factor.' *[IAS 1.7]*.

This may have the effect that any related party transaction whose disclosure is considered sensitive (for tax reasons perhaps) is by definition material because it is expected by the reporting entity to influence a user of the financial statements. Therefore, it may not be possible to avoid disclosing such items on the grounds that they are quantitatively immaterial. In addition, a transaction conducted at advantageous terms to either the related party or the reporting entity is more likely to be material than one conducted at arm's length. Since IAS 24 requires disclosure of related party transactions irrespective of whether consideration is received, disclosure cannot be avoided on the argument that, since there is no consideration, the transaction must be immaterial.

2.6 Disclosure of key management personnel compensation

IAS 24 requires disclosure of key management personnel compensation.

There is no requirement in IAS 24 to disclose individual key management personnel compensation. Instead, the standard requires an entity to disclose key management personnel compensation in total and for each of the following categories:

- short-term employee benefits;
- post-employment benefits;
- other long-term benefits;
- termination benefits; and
- share-based payment. *[IAS 24.17]*.

In certain jurisdictions, some of the key management personnel compensation disclosures are similar to the disclosures required by local law or other regulations and it might therefore be possible to give some of the disclosures by means of a cross-reference to other parts of the Annual Report, such as a directors' remuneration report. However, care should be taken that all of the IAS 24 requirements have been addressed. If the remuneration report does not give the information required by IAS 24 because, for example, it requires disclosure of the number of shares granted rather than the share-based payment compensation, additional disclosures must be made to comply with IAS 24.

2.6.1 Compensation

'Compensation' includes all employee benefits (as defined in IAS 19 – *Employee Benefits*) including employee benefits to which IFRS 2 – *Share-based Payment* – applies. Employee benefits are all forms of consideration given by an entity, or on behalf of the entity, in exchange for services rendered to the entity. Employee benefits also include such consideration paid on behalf of the entity in respect of the entity. *[IAS 24.9]*. Therefore, the compensation disclosed by an entity in its financial statements is that which is for services to that entity, irrespective of whether it is paid by the reporting entity or by another entity or individual on behalf of the reporting entity.

Under IAS 24, compensation includes:

(a) short-term employee benefits, such as wages, salaries and social security contributions, paid annual leave and paid sick leave, profit-sharing and bonuses (if payable within twelve months of the end of the period) and non-monetary benefits (such as medical care, housing, cars and free or subsidised goods or services) for current employees;

(b) post-employment benefits such as pensions, other retirement benefits, post-employment life insurance and post-employment medical care;

(c) other long-term employee benefits, including long-service leave or sabbatical leave, jubilee or other long-service benefits, long-term disability benefits and, if they are not payable wholly within twelve months after the end of the reporting period, profit-sharing, bonuses and deferred compensation;

(d) termination benefits; and

(e) share-based payment. *[IAS 24.9]*.

It is unclear from the standard the basis on which the amount for each of the categories above is determined. There are alternative views that the disclosure is the amount:

- paid or payable by the entity (or on its behalf);
- recognised as an expense under the relevant standard by the entity (or on its behalf);
- attributed to the benefit for tax purposes;
- due under contract by the entity (or due on its behalf); or
- determined on some other basis.

In the Basis for Conclusions accompanying the standard, the IASB noted that the guidance on compensation in IAS 19 is sufficient to enable an entity to disclose the relevant information which suggests that the IASB is expecting the amounts to be based on the expense recognised under the relevant standards. *[IAS 24.BC10]*. It is helpful to remember that the definition of compensation states that 'employee benefits are all forms of consideration paid, payable or provided by the entity, or on behalf of the entity in exchange for services rendered...'. *[IAS 24.9]*.

Issues relating to each of the categories are discussed below.

For an illustrative example of the disclosure of key management personnel compensation, see Extract 35.1 at 2.6.9 below.

2.6.2 *Short-term employee benefits*

As indicated at 2.6.1 above, these include wages, salaries and social security contributions, paid annual leave and paid sick leave, profit-sharing and bonuses (if expected to be settled wholly before twelve months after the end of the reporting period). Most of these should not cause difficulty, since the expense for such items under IAS 19 is generally equivalent to the amount payable for the period. However, there are instances when adjustments are necessary. For example, if the total expense under IAS 19 for a profit-sharing plan includes a deduction for anticipated staff turnover, this deduction may need to be adjusted in determining the amount disclosed for key management personnel. That is, the turnover rate for staff as a whole is likely different from the turnover rate for key management personnel, and the deduction should be adjusted accordingly for disclosure purposes.

Non-monetary benefits (such as medical care, housing, cars and free or subsidised goods or services) must also be included within the amount disclosed for short-term employee benefits. *[IAS 24.9].* In some cases, these might have been provided at no direct cost to the entity. In such circumstances it would appear reasonable to either attribute a value for non-monetary benefits (for example, the attributable tax benefit), so as to describe them quantitatively, or to describe such benefits qualitatively.

2.6.3 Post-employment benefits

As indicated at 2.6.1 above, these include pensions, other retirement benefits, post-employment life insurance and post-employment medical care. The inclusion of this category suggests that amounts are disclosed while members of key management are providing services. If amounts were only disclosed when the benefits are payable, then in many cases there would be no disclosure since the individuals would no longer be members of key management.

For defined contribution plans, it seems appropriate that the amount included is based on the total expense recognised under IAS 19, which is the equivalent of the contributions payable to the plan for service rendered in the period.

The main issue related to defined benefit plans is to determine an appropriate calculation for the disclosable cost for the period. Normally, for defined benefit plans, the expense recognised under IAS 19 differs from the contributions payable to the plan. Disclosing the contributions payable is generally not appropriate, particularly where the entity is benefiting from a contribution holiday, since the amount payable does not reflect the benefits provided by the entity in exchange for the services rendered. One approach is to include an amount based on the expense recognised. However, this approach requires an apportionment of the total expense, for example, based on the proportion of the pensionable salaries of key management to that of all employees within the plan. The total amounts recognised under IAS 19 for defined benefit plans includes items such as interest, recognised actuarial gains and losses and the effects of curtailments and settlements. One view is that these are included to the extent that they relate to the individuals concerned. An alternative view is that, since these items relate more to the overall plan, they are not included, and the amount included is the current service cost and, where applicable, past service cost related to those individuals. An entity might obtain an actuarial valuation of such amounts, or apportion these elements appropriately.

2.6.4 Other long-term benefits

As indicated at 2.6.1 above, these include long-service leave or sabbatical leave, jubilee or other long-service benefits, long-term disability benefits and, if they are not expected to be settled wholly before twelve months after the end of the reporting period, profit-sharing, bonuses and deferred compensation. Since the accounting for such items under IAS 19 is on a similar basis to that for post-employment benefits similar issues to those discussed at 2.6.3 above are applicable.

2.6.5 *Termination benefits*

These should not cause difficulty, since an entity generally recognises such items, particularly for key management personnel, in line with the recognition criteria included in IAS 19.

2.6.6 *Share-based payment transactions*

This category includes share options, share awards or cash-settled awards granted in return for service by the members of key management. Such compensation is accounted for under IFRS 2. For equity-settled share based payment transactions, such as share options or share awards, IFRS 2 broadly requires measurement of their fair value at grant date, and that expense is recognised over the period that employees render services. For cash-settled share-based payment transactions, IFRS 2 requires measurement and recognition based on the cash ultimately paid.

One approach is to disclose an amount based on the expense under IFRS 2. An alternative approach is to disclose amounts based on the fair value that the individual received (based on the value of the shares at date of vesting, or at date of exercise of share options or the cash that is ultimately payable) at those later dates, rather than over the period of the service. An entity should adopt a consistent accounting policy for determining the amounts disclosed.

2.6.7 *Reporting entity part of a group*

One additional practical difficulty for an entity in a group is that the disclosure of its key management personnel compensation is for the services rendered to the reporting entity. Accordingly, where key management personnel of the reporting entity also provide services to other entities within the group, an apportionment of the compensation is necessary. Likewise, where the reporting entity receives services from key management personnel that are also key management personnel of other entities within the group, the reporting entity may have to impute the compensation received. Such apportionments and allocations required judgment and an assessment of the time commitment involved.

2.6.8 *Key management personnel compensated by other entities*

A reporting entity also applies the principles set out in 2.6.7 above to situations in which the other entity is a third party, outside of the group, but is a related party.

As discussed at 3 below, the IASB has issued an Exposure Draft (ED/2012/1) proposing to amend IAS 24 so that the definition of a related party is extended to include an entity, or a member of its group, which provides key management personnel services to a reporting entity. The conclusion of this amendment may have an impact on the types of situations envisaged here, as well as in 2.6.7 above.

2.6.9 *Illustrative disclosure of key management personnel compensation*

An example of the disclosure of key management personnel compensation can be found in the financial statements of BP p.l.c.

Extract 35.1: BP p.l.c. (2012)

Notes on financial statements [extract]

42. Remuneration of directors and senior management [extract]

Remuneration of directors and senior management

			$ million
	2012	2011	2010
Total for all senior management			
Short-term employee benefits	**27**	34	25
Pensions and other post-retirement benefits	**3**	3	3
Share-based payments	**34**	27	29
Total	**64**	64	57

Senior management, in addition to executive and non-executive directors, includes other senior managers who are members of the executive management team.

Short-term employee benefits

In addition to fees paid to the non-executive chairman and non-executive directors, these amounts comprise, for executive directors and senior managers, salary and benefits earned during the year, plus cash bonuses awarded for the year. Deferred annual bonus awards, to be settled in shares, are included in share-based payments. There was no compensation for loss of office paid in 2012 (2011 $9 million and 2010 $3 million).

Pensions and other post-retirement benefits

The amounts represent the estimated cost to the group of providing defined benefit pensions and other post-retirement benefits to senior management in respect of the current year of service measured in accordance with IAS 19 'Employee Benefits'.

Share-based payments

This is the cost to the group of senior management's participation in share-based payment plans, as measured by the fair value of options and shares granted accounted for in accordance with IFRS 2 'Share-based Payments'. The main plans in which senior management have participated are the EDIP, DAB, SVP and RSP. For details of these plans refer to Note 40.

2.7 Disclosure of other related party transactions, including commitments

IAS 24 requires an entity that has had related party transactions during the periods covered by its financial statements to disclose the nature of the related party relationship as well as information about those transactions and outstanding balances, including commitments, necessary for users to understand the potential effect of the relationship on the financial statements. *[IAS 24.18]*.

2.7.1 Related party transactions requiring disclosure

IAS 24 gives the following as examples of transactions to be disclosed, if they are with a related party. The list is not intended to be exhaustive:

- purchases or sales of goods (finished or unfinished);
- purchases or sales of property and other assets;
- rendering or receiving of services;
- leases;
- transfers of research and development;
- transfers under licence agreements;
- transfers under finance arrangements (including loans and equity contributions in cash or in kind);

- provisions of guarantees or collateral;
- commitments to do something if a particular event occurs or does not occur in the future, including executory contracts (recognised and unrecognised); and
- settlement of liabilities on behalf of the entity or by the entity on behalf of that related party. *[IAS 24.21]*.

The standard does not contain any exemptions based on the nature of the transaction. Consequently, related party transactions include transactions such as dividend payments and the issue of shares under rights issues to major shareholders or key management personnel (i.e. those that fall within the definition of related parties), even where they participate on the same basis as other shareholders. However, for dividend payments, a preparer might conclude that no additional disclosures are necessary beyond those required by IAS 1, to explain the potential effect of the relationship on the financial statements. *[IAS 1.137]*.

The standard also includes transactions with those individuals identified as related parties where their dealings with the entity are in a private capacity, rather than in a business capacity.

As indicated at 2.5 above, disclosure is required irrespective of whether or not consideration is received, which means that the standard applies to gifts of assets or services and to asset swaps. Common examples of such transactions which may occur within a group include:

- administration by an entity of another entity within a group (or of its post-employment benefit plan) free of charge;
- transfer of tax assets from one member of a group to another without payment;
- rent-free accommodation or the loan of assets at no charge; or
- guarantees by directors of bank loans to the entity.

2.7.1.A Aggregation of items of a similar nature

Presumably in order to minimise the volume of disclosures, IAS 24 permits aggregation of items of a similar nature, except when separate disclosure is necessary for an understanding of the effects of the related party transactions on the financial statements of the entity. *[IAS 24.24]*. The standard does not expand on this requirement, but it seems appropriate that, for example, purchases or sales of goods with other subsidiaries within a group can be aggregated, but any purchases or sales of property, plant, and equipment or of intangible assets with such entities are shown as a separate category. However, the level of aggregation is limited by the separate disclosure of transactions with particular categories of related parties (see 2.7.2 below).

2.7.1.B Commitments

'Commitments' are not defined in IFRS. However, IAS 39 describes a firm commitment as 'a binding agreement for the exchange of a specified quantity of resources at a specified price on a specified future date or dates'. *[IAS 39.9]*. IFRS 12 states that the commitments relating to joint ventures are those that may give rise to a future outflow of cash or other resources. *[IFRS 12.B18]*.

IAS 24 specifically mentions executory contracts (recognised and unrecognised) as commitments requiring disclosure. Executory contracts are excluded from the scope of IAS 37 – *Provisions, Contingent Liabilities and Contingent Assets* – unless they are onerous to the reporting entity. An executory contract is a contract under which neither party has performed any of its obligations or both parties have partially performed their obligations to an equal extent. *[IAS 37.3]*. An example of an executory contract would be a contract to buy an asset at a future date where neither the transfer of the asset nor the payment of consideration has occurred.

The words 'commitments to do something if a particular event occurs or does not occur in the future' can potentially have a wide application. One obvious type of arrangement to which this applies would be some form of commitment by a subsidiary to its parent to undertake certain trading or research and development activities.

With respect to the type of transaction that the IASB is expecting to be disclosed, IFRS 12 provides a list of illustrative but not exhaustive examples of the type of unrecognised commitments that could relate to joint ventures. Some of these examples could apply equally to other related party arrangements. IFRS 12 clarifies that the commitments required to be disclosed under IAS 24 in respect of joint ventures include an entity's share of commitments made jointly with other investors with joint control of a joint venture. *[IFRS 12.B18]*.

IFRS 12 provides the following illustrations of commitments relating to joint ventures that would typically be disclosable under paragraph 18 of IAS 24 and could apply equally to other related party arrangements:

- unrecognised commitments to contribute funding or resources as a result of, for example:
  - the constitution or acquisition agreements of a joint venture (that, for example, require an entity to contribute funds over a specific period);
  - capital intensive projects undertaken by a joint venture;
  - unconditional purchase obligations, comprising procurement of equipment, inventory or services that an entity is committed to purchasing from, or on behalf of, a joint venture;
  - unrecognised commitments to provide loans or other financial support to a joint venture;
  - unrecognised commitments to contribute resources to a joint venture, such as assets or services; and
  - other non-cancellable unrecognised commitments relating to a joint venture.
- unrecognised commitments to acquire another party's ownership interest (or a portion of that ownership interest) in a joint venture if a particular event occurs or does not occur in the future. *[IFRS 12.B19-20]*.

Provisions of guarantees, which are a form of commitment, require separate disclosure. Disclosure of commitments to purchase property, plant and equipment and intangible assets in aggregate is required separately by IAS 16 – *Property, Plant and Equipment* – and IAS 38 – *Intangible Assets* – respectively. *[IAS 16.74(c), IAS 38.122(e)]*.

2.7.2 Disclosures required for related party transactions, including commitments

The standard states that, at a minimum, the disclosures must include:

(a) the amount of the transactions;

(b) the amount of outstanding balances, including commitments, and:

  (i) their terms and conditions, including whether they are secured, and the nature of the consideration to be provided in settlement; and

  (ii) details of any guarantees given or received;

(c) provisions for doubtful debts related to the amount of outstanding balances; and

(d) the expense recognised during the period in respect of bad or doubtful debts due from related parties. *[IAS 24.18].*

The standard gives no exemption from disclosure on the grounds of sensitivity or confidentiality. However, since there is no requirement to disclose the name of a related party, this lack of exemption is likely to be less of a concern.

The requirement in (b) above could be read literally as requiring outstanding balances and commitments to be amalgamated into a single balance. However, commitments such as executory contracts do not give rise to outstanding balances. In practice, narrative disclosure of the terms and conditions of material commitments will be necessary.

There is no requirement to disclose individually significant transactions. However, as discussed at 2.8 below, there is such a requirement for transactions with government-related entities where a reporting entity has decided to apply the disclosure exemption. One IASB member dissented from the decision not to require all entities to provide information about each individually significant transaction for all related parties. *[IAS 24.DO1].*

The disclosures are made separately for each of the following categories:

(a) the parent;

(b) entities with joint control of, or significant influence over, the entity;

(c) subsidiaries;

(d) associates;

(e) joint ventures in which the entity is a joint venturer;

(f) key management personnel of the entity or its parent; and

(g) other related parties. *[IAS 24.19].*

In our view the references in (a) and (f) above to 'the parent' should be read as including all parents of the entity, i.e. its immediate parent, any intermediate parent, and the ultimate parent. In the context of the financial statements of an entity within a group, it is insufficient to disclose related party transactions for a single category of 'group companies'. Separate categories are required for parent(s), subsidiaries and 'other related parties'.

IAS 24 does not identify fellow subsidiaries as a separate category of related party, and they are therefore included within the category 'other related parties'. However, a preparer might wish to consider separate disclosure of transactions with fellow subsidiaries if this would provide useful information to users of the subsidiary's financial statements.

The classification of amounts payable to, and receivable from, related parties in the different categories is an extension of the disclosure requirement in IAS 1 for an entity to present information either in the statement of financial position or in the notes. *[IAS 1.78(b)]*. The categories are extended to provide a more comprehensive analysis of related party balances and apply to related party transactions. *[IAS 24.20]*.

Outstanding balances with key management personnel would include unpaid bonuses or liabilities under cash-settled share-based payment transactions.

IAS 24 discourages an entity from disclosing that transactions are on normal commercial terms or on an arm's length basis, by stating that such disclosures 'are made only if such terms can be substantiated.' *[IAS 24.23]*. This wording implies a rebuttable presumption that related party transactions are not on an arm's length basis unless the reporting entity can demonstrate otherwise. To substantiate that related party transactions are on an arm's length basis an entity would need to be satisfied that a transaction with similar terms and conditions could be obtained from an independent third party.

The company financial statements of J Sainsbury plc provide the following disclosures of related party relationships with subsidiaries and joint ventures.

Extract 35.2: J Sainsbury plc (2013)

Notes to the financial statements [extract]

32 Related party transactions [extract]

Company [extract]

a) Subsidiaries

The company enters into loans with its subsidiaries at both fixed and floating rates of interest on a commercial basis. Hence, the Company incurs interest expense and earns interest income on these loans and advances. The Company also received dividend income from its subsidiaries during the financial year.

Transactions with subsidiaries

	2013 £m	2012 £m
Loans and advances given to, and dividend income received from subsidiaries		
Loans and advances given	**402**	341
Loans and advances repaid by subsidiaries	**(330)**	(281)
Interest income received in respect of interest bearing loans and advances	**161**	146
Dividend income received	**250**	276
Loans and advances received from subsidiaries		
Loans and advances received	**(318)**	(339)
Loans and advances repaid	**3**	61
Interest expense paid in respect of interest bearing loans and advances	**(104)**	(108)

Year-end balances arising from transactions with subsidiaries

	2013 £m	2012 £m
Receivables		
Loans and advances due from subsidiaries	**2,461**	2,352
Payables		
Loans and advances due to subsidiaries	**(5,390)**	(5,316)

b) Joint ventures

Transactions with joint ventures

For the 52 weeks to 16 March 2013, the Company entered into transactions with joint ventures as set out below.

	2013 £m	2012 £m
Services and loans provided to joint ventures		
Interest income received in respect of interest bearing loans	**1**	1

Year-end balances arising from transactions with joint ventures

	2013 £m	2012 £m
Receivables		
Loans due from joint ventures		
Floating rate subordinated undated loan capital [1]	**25**	25
Floating rate subordinated dated loan capital [2]	**30**	30
Payables		
Loans due to joint ventures	**(5)**	(5)

1 The undated subordinated loan capital shall be repaid on such date as the Financial Services Authority shall agree in writing for such repayment and in any event not less than five years and one day from the dates of drawdown. In the event of a winding up of Sainsbury's Bank, the loan is subordinated to ordinary unsecured liabilities. Interest is payable three months in arrears at LIBOR plus a margin of 1.0 per cent per annum for the duration of the loan.

2 No repayment of dated subordinated debt prior to its stated maturity may be made without the consent of the Financial Services Authority. In the event of a winding up of Sainsbury's Bank, the loan is subordinated to ordinary unsecured liabilities. Interest is payable three months in arrears at LIBOR plus a margin of 0.6 per cent per annum for the duration of the loan.

The financial statements of British Sky Broadcasting Group plc illustrate the disclosure of transactions with a party controlled by a close family member of key management.

Extract 35.3: British Sky Broadcasting Group plc (2012)

Notes to the consolidated financial statements [extract]

30. Transactions with related parties and major shareholders [extract]

c) Other transactions with related parties [extract]

A close family member of one Director of the Company runs Freud Entertainment Limited ('Freud'), which has provided external support to the press and publicity activities of the Group. During the year the Group incurred expenditure amounting to £1 million (2011: £2 million) with Freud. At 30 June 2012 there was £1 million (2011:£1 million) due to Freud.

The financial statements of BP p.l.c illustrate the disclosure of commitments to related parties:

> *Extract 35.4: BP p.l.c. (2012)*
>
> **Notes on financial statements** [extract]
> **24. Investments in jointly controlled entities** [extract]
>
> BP has commitments amounting to $4,391 million (2011 $4,155 million) in relation to contracts with jointly controlled entities for the purchase of LNG, crude oil and oil products, refinery operating costs and storage and handling services. See Note 44 for further information on capital commitments relating to BP's investments in jointly controlled entities.
>
> **44 Capital commitments**
>
> Authorized future capital expenditure for property, plant and equipment by group companies for which contracts had been signed at 31 December 2012 amounted to $14,068 million (2011 $12,517 million). In addition, at 31 December 2012, the group had contracts in place for future capital expenditure relating to investments in jointly controlled entities of $275 million (2011 $296 million) and investments in associates of nil (2011 $36 million). BP's share of capital commitments of jointly controlled entities amounted to $825 million (2011 $1,244 million). The group has also signed definitive and binding sale and purchase agreements for the sale of BP's 50% interest in TNK-BP to Rosneft and for BP's further investment in Rosneft, as described in Note 4.

2.8 Disclosures with government-related entities

IAS 24 provides an exemption from the disclosure requirements of paragraph 18, discussed at 2.7.2 above, in relation to related party transactions and outstanding balances, including commitments, with:

(a) a government that has control or joint control of, or significant influence over, the reporting entity; and

(b) another entity that is a related party because the same government has control or joint control of, or significant influence over, both the reporting entity and the other entity. *[IAS 24.25]*.

This wording implies that a reporting entity is related to an entity that is significantly influenced by a government that also has significant influence over the reporting entity. However, the definition of a related party does not include entities that are subject to significant influence from the same entity, but are not otherwise related parties as defined in IAS 24 (see 2.2.3 above).

The application of the disclosure exemption is illustrated in the example below, which is based on an illustrative example accompanying IAS 24.

Example 35.9: Application of the disclosure exemption for government-related entities

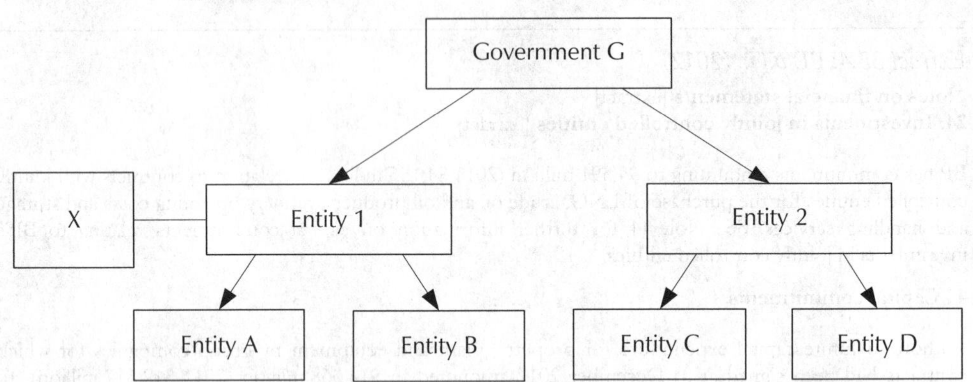

Government G directly or indirectly controls Entities 1 and 2 and Entities A, B, C and D. Person X is a member of the key management personnel of Entity 1.

For Entity A's financial statements the exemption applies to: (a) transactions with Government G which is the government that ultimately controls Entity A; and (b) transactions with Entities 1, 2, B, C and D which are related entities because they are controlled by the same government as A, i.e.: Government G.

The exemption does not apply to transactions with Person X because Person X is not controlled by Government G.

The use of the disclosure exemption is conditional on the reporting entity making the following disclosures about the transactions and related outstanding balances with the government-related entities:

(a) the name of the government and the nature of its relationship with the reporting entity (i.e. control, joint control or significant influence);

(b) the following information in sufficient detail to enable users of the entity's financial statements to understand the effect of related party transactions on its financial statements:

  (i) the nature and amount of each individually significant transaction; and

  (ii) for other transactions that are collectively, but not individually, significant, a qualitative or quantitative indication of their extent. Types of transactions include those discussed at 2.7.1 above. *[IAS 24.26].*

The wording above does not explicitly mention 'commitments' when referring to transactions. However, given that IAS 24 describes a commitment as a form of transaction (see 2.7.1 above), disclosure of individually and collectively significant commitments with government-related entities is required.

In using its judgement to determine the level of detail to be disclosed in accordance with the requirements in (b) above, a reporting entity considers the closeness of the related party relationship and other factors relevant in establishing the level of significance of the transaction such as whether it is:

(a) significant in terms of size;
(b) carried out on non-market terms;
(c) outside normal day-to-day business operations, such as the purchase and sale of businesses;
(d) disclosed to regulatory or supervisory authorities;
(e) reported to senior management; and
(f) subject to shareholder approval. *[IAS 24.27]*.

Disclosure of the nature and amount of each individually significant transaction is not a requirement for other related party transactions (see 2.7.2 above). The Board considered that this requirement should not be too onerous for a reporting entity because:

(a) individually significant transactions should be a small subset, by number, of total related party transactions;
(b) the reporting entity should know what these transactions are; and
(c) reporting such items on an exceptional basis takes into account cost-benefit considerations. *[IAS 24.BC45]*.

The Board also considered that more disclosure of individually significant transactions would better meet the objective of IAS 24 because this approach focuses on transactions that, through their nature or size, are of more interest to users and are more likely to be affected by the related party relationship. *[IAS 24.BC46]*. In response to concerns about whether a reporting entity would be able to identify whether the counterparty to such transactions was a government-related entity, the Board concluded that 'management will know, or will apply more effort in establishing, who the counterparty to an individually significant transaction is and will have, or be able to obtain, background information on the counterparty'. *[IAS 24.BC47-48]*.

One Board member disagreed with the decision to give a disclosure exemption for government-related parties in IAS 24. That same member also disagreed with the decision not to require all entities to provide information about individually significant transactions with a related party. *[IAS 24.DO1]*.

Extract 35.5 below from the financial statements of The Royal Bank of Scotland Group plc illustrates disclosure summarising the types of transactions with government-controlled entities that are related parties and details of an individually material transaction.

Extract 35.5: The Royal Bank of Scotland Group plc (2012)

Notes on the consolidated accounts [extract]

41 Related parties [extract]

UK Government

On 1 December 2008, the UK Government through HM Treasury became the ultimate controlling party of The Royal Bank of Scotland Group plc. The UK Government's shareholding is managed by UK Financial Investments Limited, a company wholly owned by the UK Government. As a result, the UK Government and UK Government controlled bodies became related parties of the Group.

The Group enters into transactions with many of these bodies on an arm's length basis. The principal transactions during 2012, 2011 and 2010 were: the Asset Protection Scheme, Bank of England facilities and the issue of debt guaranteed by the UK Government discussed below. In addition, the redemption of non-cumulative sterling preference shares and the placing and open offer in April 2009 was underwritten by HM Treasury and, in December 2009, B shares were issued to HM Treasury and a contingent capital agreement concluded with HM Treasury (see Note 26). Other transactions include the payment of: taxes principally UK corporation tax (page 386) and value added tax; national insurance contributions; local authority rates; and regulatory fees and levies (including the bank levy (page 375) and FSCS levies (page 454)); together with banking transactions such as loans and deposits undertaken in the normal course of banker-customer relationships.

....

Government credit and asset-backed securities guarantee schemes

These schemes guarantee eligible debt issued by qualifying institutions for a fee. The fee, payable to HM Treasury is based on a per annum rate of 25 (asset-backed securities guarantee scheme) and 50 (credit guarantee scheme) basis points plus 100% of the institution's median five-year credit default swap spread during the twelve months to 1 July 2008. The asset-backed securities scheme closed to new issuance on 31 December 2009 and the credit guarantee scheme on 28 February 2010.

At 31 December 2012, the Group had no debt outstanding guaranteed by the Government (2011 – £21.3 billion; 2010 – £41.5 billion).

The following are other illustrations of the type of disclosures required for transactions with government-related entities based on examples in the standard:

Example 35.10: Individually significant transaction carried out on non-market terms

On 15 January 2013 the company sold a 10 hectare piece of land to an entity controlled by Government G for €5,000,000. On 31 December 2013 a plot of land in a similar location, of similar size and with similar characteristics, was sold for €3,000,000. There had not been any appreciation or depreciation of the land in the intervening period. See Note X for disclosure of government assistance as required by IAS 20.

Example 35.11: Individually significant transaction because of size of transaction

In the year ended 31 December 2013 Government G provided the company with a loan equivalent to 50% of its funding requirement, repayable in quarterly instalments over the next five years. Interest is charged on the loan at a rate of 5% which is comparable to that charged on the company's external bank loans.

Example 35.12: Collectively significant transactions

The company's significant transactions with Government G and other entities controlled, jointly controlled or significantly influenced by Government G are a large portion of its sales of goods and purchases of raw materials [alternatively – about 50% of its sales of goods and services and about 35% of its purchases of raw materials].

The company also benefits from guarantees by Government G of the company's bank borrowing. See Note X of the financial statements for disclosure of government assistance as required by IAS 20.

In Example 35.12 above, either a qualitative or a quantitative disclosure is permitted for transactions that are collectively but not individually significant.

3 FUTURE DEVELOPMENTS

As discussed at 2.2.1.D above, the IASB issued an Exposure Draft – *Annual Improvements to IFRSs 2010-2012 Cycle* in May 2012. The ED proposes that:

- the definition of a related party is extended to include an entity, or a member of its group, which provides key management personnel services to the reporting entity;
- amounts recognised as an expense by the reporting entity for the provision of key management personnel services provided by a separate management entity should be separately disclosed; and
- the key management personnel compensation provided by a management entity to its own employees is excluded from the disclosure requirements of paragraph 17 to prevent duplication.

Comments on the ED were requested by 5 September 2012. The amendments would apply for annual periods beginning on or after 1 January 2014.

Chapter 36 Statement of cash flows

List of examples

Chapter 36 Statement of cash flows

1 INTRODUCTION

A statement of cash flows provides useful information about an entity's activities in generating cash to repay debt, distribute dividends, or reinvest to maintain or expand operating capacity; about its financing activities, both debt and equity; and about its investing or spending of cash. This information, when combined with information in the rest of the financial statements, is useful in assessing factors that may affect the entity's liquidity, financial flexibility, profitability, and risk.

IAS 7 – *Statement of Cash Flows* – specifies how entities report information about the historical changes in cash and cash equivalents and has a relatively flexible approach, which allows it to be applied by all entities regardless of their business activities, including financial institutions. This flexibility can be seen, for example, in the way entities can determine their own policy for the classification of interest and dividend cash flows, provided they are separately disclosed and this is applied consistently from period to period (see 4.4.1 below). It can also accommodate the need of entities to provide additional information specific to their circumstances and indeed encourages additional disclosures. In addition, IAS 7 is based on a relatively straightforward principle, that only transactions which require the use of cash or cash equivalents should be included in the statement of cash flows (see 4.8 below).

1.1 Terms used in IAS 7

The following terms are used in IAS 7 with the meanings specified: [IAS 7.6]

Cash comprises cash on hand and demand deposits.

Cash equivalents are short-term, highly liquid investments that are readily convertible to known amounts of cash and which are subject to an insignificant risk of changes in value.

Cash flows are inflows and outflows of cash and cash equivalents.

Operating activities are the principal revenue-producing activities of the entity and other activities that are not investing or financing activities.

Investing activities are the acquisition and disposal of long-term assets and other investments not included in cash equivalents.

Financing activities are activities that result in changes in the size and composition of the contributed equity and borrowings of the entity.

2 OBJECTIVE AND SCOPE OF IAS 7

2.1 Objective

The objective of IAS 7 is to require entities to provide information about historical changes in cash and cash equivalents in a statement which classifies cash flows during the period from operating, investing and financing activities. The standard aims to give users of financial statements a basis to evaluate the entity's ability to generate cash and cash equivalents and its needs to utilise those cash flows. *[IAS 7 Objective].* The historical cash flow information is often used as an indicator of the amount, timing and certainty of future cash flows. It is also useful in examining the relationship between profitability and net cash flow and the impact of changing prices. *[IAS 7.5].*

2.2 Scope

IAS 7 applies to all entities, regardless of size, operations, ownership structure or industry, and therefore includes wholly owned subsidiaries and banks, insurance entities and other financial institutions. There are no exemptions from the standard. Users of an entity's financial statements are interested in how the entity generates and uses cash and cash equivalents regardless of the nature of the entity's activities and irrespective of whether cash can be viewed as the product of the entity, as may be the case with a financial institution. All entities need cash to conduct their operations, to pay their obligations, and to provide returns to their investors. Accordingly, all entities are required to present a statement of cash flows. *[IAS 7.3].* In particular, a parent entity preparing its separate financial statements in accordance with IFRS is required to publish a statement of cash flows, even if the separate financial statements are presented together with consolidated financial statements which include a statement of cash flows.

3 CASH AND CASH EQUIVALENTS

Since the objective of a statement of cash flows is to provide an analysis of changes in cash and cash equivalents, the definitions of cash and cash equivalents at 1.1 above are essential to its presentation. It is also important to understand the reporting entity's cash management policies, especially when considering whether balances that are not obviously cash on hand and demand deposits should be classified as cash equivalents, as the standard states that cash equivalents are held for the purpose of meeting short-term cash commitments rather than for investment or other purposes. *[IAS 7.7].* Cash management includes the investment of cash in excess of immediate needs into cash equivalents, *[IAS 7.9]*, such as short-term investments. For short term investments to qualify as a cash equivalent, they must be:

- highly liquid;
- readily convertible into known amounts of cash; and
- subject to insignificant risk of changes in value. *[IAS 7.6].*

Having determined that such highly liquid investments are equivalent to cash, a statement of cash flows under IAS 7 excludes movements between cash on hand and cash equivalents because these are components of an entity's cash management, rather than part of its operating, investing and financing activities. *[IAS 7.9].* However, as shown below, the definition of cash equivalents can cause some difficulty in practice.

3.1 Policy for determining components of cash equivalents

Because an entity's cash management policies are an important factor, not all investments that appear to satisfy the definition at 1.1 and the criteria at 3 above are required to be classified as cash equivalents. However, regardless of an entity's policies and practices, an investment can only be classified within cash equivalents if all of the criteria in the definition are satisfied (see 3.2 below).

In view of the variety of cash management practices and banking arrangements around the world, entities are required to disclose the policy adopted in determining the composition of cash and cash equivalents. *[IAS 7.46].* Changes in that policy, such as a reclassification of financial instruments previously considered as being part of an entity's investment portfolio, should be reported under IAS 8 – *Accounting Policies, Changes in Accounting Estimates and Errors. [IAS 7.47].* This would require comparatives to be restated and additional disclosures given, including the reasons for the change in policy.

The inclusion or exclusion of a certain type of investment in cash equivalents gives rise to a change in policy, if an entity reclassified investments already held at the beginning of the current period or if it makes a different classification of new investments held for the same purposes as those in the prior period. On the contrary, a new investment in the current period (even in a type of investment previously classified otherwise) which is included in or excluded from cash equivalents according to the reason for holding that investment under the entity's cash management practices, is not considered a change in policy.

VTech Holdings disclosed its policy to include short-term investments and bank overdrafts as components of cash equivalents.

Extract 36.1: VTech Holdings Limited (2012)

Principal Accounting Policies [extract]

O Cash And Cash Equivalents

Cash and cash equivalents comprise cash on hand, demand deposits with banks and other financial institutions, short-term highly liquid investments that are readily convertible into known amounts of cash and which are subject to an insignificant risk of changes in value and which have a maturity of three months or less at acquisition. Bank overdrafts that are repayable on demand and form an integral part of the Group's cash management are also included as a component of cash and cash equivalents for the purpose of statement of cash flows.

Lufthansa reconciled the requirement to report cash and cash equivalents (as defined in IAS 7) with the wish to include all the assets used by the entity to manage its liquidity, by adding lines of analysis to the foot of the statement of cash flows.

Extract 36.2: Deutsche Lufthansa AG (2011)

Consolidated cash flow statement [extract]

The cash flow statement shows how cash and cash equivalents have changed over the reporting period at the Lufthansa Group. In accordance with IAS 7 cash flows are divided into cash flows from operating activities, from investing activities and from financing activities. The cash and cash equivalents shown in the cash flow statement correspond to the balance sheet item cash and cash equivalents. The amount of liquidity in the broader sense is reached by adding short-term securities.

3.2 Components of cash and cash equivalents

3.2.1 Demand deposits and short-term investments

In defining 'cash', IAS 7 does not explain what is meant by 'demand deposits', perhaps because the term is commonly understood as amounts that can be withdrawn on demand, without prior notice being required or a penalty being charged (for example, by an additional fee or forfeiture of interest). In any event, the distinction is largely irrelevant because amounts not classified as demand deposits may qualify as cash equivalents and end up being treated in the same way. Thus, whether or not an amount meets the definition of a cash equivalent may become the more important determination.

Cash equivalents are held for the purpose of meeting short-term cash commitments rather than for investment or other purposes. For an investment to qualify as a cash equivalent it must be readily convertible to a known amount of cash and be subject to an insignificant risk of changes in value. Normally only an investment with a short maturity of, say, three months or less from the date of acquisition qualifies as a cash equivalent. Equity investments are excluded unless they are cash equivalents in substance. IAS 7 provides an example, being redeemable preference shares acquired within a short period of their maturity and with a specified redemption date. *[IAS 7.7]*.

When the standard refers to a 'known amount of cash' it means that the amount should be known or determinable at the date on which the investment is acquired. Accordingly, traded commodities, such as gold bullion, would not be eligible for inclusion in cash equivalents because the proceeds to be realised from such an investment is determined at the date of disposal rather than being known or determinable when the investment is made.

3.2.2 Money market funds

Entities commonly invest in money market funds (MMF) such as an open-ended mutual fund that invests in certificates of deposit, commercial paper, treasury bills, bankers' acceptances and repurchase agreements and other money market instruments. An investment in a MMF aims to provide investors with low-risk, low-return investment while preserving the value of the assets and maintaining a high level of liquidity. The question then arises as to whether investments in such funds can be classified as cash equivalents.

In most cases, a MMF investment is quoted in an active market and, as such, could be regarded as highly liquid. However, this is not enough to meet the definition of a cash equivalent. The short-term and highly liquid investment must be readily convertible into known amounts of cash which are subject to an insignificant risk of changes in value. *[IAS 7.6].* The Interpretations Committee considered the issue in July 2009 and confirmed that the amount of cash that will be received must be known at the time of the initial investment. Accordingly, investments in shares or units of money market funds cannot be considered as cash equivalents simply because they are convertible at any time at the then market price in an active market. The Interpretations Committee also confirmed that an entity would have to satisfy itself that any investment was subject to an insignificant risk of change in value for it to be classified as a cash equivalent.[1]

Therefore in assessing whether the change in value of an investment in a money market fund can be regarded as insignificant, an entity has to conclude that the range of possible returns is very small. This evaluation is made at the time of acquiring the investment and will involve consideration of factors such as the maturity of the investment (for example a maturity of less than 90 days); the credit rating of the fund (for example AAA or an equivalent highest rating); the nature of the investments held by the fund (i.e. not subject to volatility); the extent of diversification in the portfolio (which is expected to be very high); and any mechanisms by the fund to guarantee returns (for example by reference to short-term money market interest rates).

Investments are often held for purposes other than to act as a ready store of value that can be quickly converted into cash when needed to meet short-term cash commitments. It is therefore important to understand why the entity invested in a particular money market fund when determining whether classification as a cash equivalent is appropriate. This approach is illustrated by Henkel AG in Extract 36.3 below.

Extract 36.3: Henkel AG &Co. KGaA (2012)

Notes to the consolidated financial statements [extract]

(8) Cash and cash equivalents

Recognized under cash and cash equivalents are liquid funds, sight deposits and other financial assets with an original term of not more than three months. In accordance with IAS 7, also recognized under cash equivalents are shares in money market funds which, due to their first-class credit rating and investments in extremely short-term money market securities, undergo only minor value fluctuations and can be readily converted within one day into known amounts of cash. Utilized bank overdrafts are recognized in the statement of financial position as liabilities to banks.

The volume of cash and cash equivalents decreased compared to the previous year, from 1,980 million euros to 1,238 million euros. Of this figure, 913 million euros (previous year: 829 million euros) relate to cash and 325 million euros (previous year: 1,151 million euros) to cash equivalents. The change is shown in the consolidated statement of cash flows.

3.2.3 Investments with maturities greater than three months

The longer the term of the investment, the greater the risk that a change in market conditions (such as interest rates) can have an effect on its value that is other than insignificant. For this reason, IAS 7 excludes most equity investments from cash equivalents and restricts the inclusion of other investments to those with a short maturity of, say, three months or less from the date of their acquisition by the entity. *[IAS 7.7].*

Similarly, an investment with a term on acquisition of, say, nine months is not reclassified as a cash equivalent from the date on which there is less than three months remaining to its maturity. If such reclassifications were permitted, the statement of cash flows would have to reflect movements between investments and cash equivalents. This would be misleading because no actual cash flows would have occurred.

The criteria explained above are guidelines, not rules, and a degree of common sense should be used in their application. In the final analysis, cash equivalents are held for the purpose of meeting short-term cash commitments and amounts should be included in cash equivalents only if they can be regarded as being nearly as accessible as cash and essentially as free from exposure to changes in value as cash.

For example, an entity might justify including in cash equivalents a fixed deposit with an original term longer than three months if it effectively functions like a demand deposit. Typically, a fixed deposit will carry a penalty charge for withdrawal prior to maturity. A penalty will usually indicate that the investment is held for investment purposes rather than the purpose of meeting short-term cash needs. However, some fixed deposits still offer interest at a prevailing demand deposit rate in the event of early withdrawal, with any penalty limited to the entity being required to forego the incremental higher interest that it would have received if the deposit were held to maturity. In this case, it may be arguable that there is effectively no significant penalty for early withdrawal, as the entity receives at least the same return that it otherwise would have in a demand deposit arrangement. Where an entity does assert that this type of investment is held for meeting short-term cash needs and classifies the investment as a cash equivalent, the accrual of interest receivable should be on a consistent basis. In this example, the entity should consider accruing interest receivable at the demand deposit rate.

3.2.4 Bank overdrafts

Although bank borrowings are generally considered to be financing activities, there are circumstances in which bank overdrafts repayable on demand are included as a component of cash and cash equivalents. This is in cases where the use of short-term overdrafts forms an integral part of an entity's cash management practices. Evidence supporting such an assertion would be that the bank balance often fluctuates from being positive to overdrawn. *[IAS 7.8].*

3.3 Reconciliation with items in the statement of financial position

The amount shown alongside the caption in the statement of financial position for 'cash and cash equivalents' will not always be a reliable guide for IAS 7 purposes. Many entities present the components of cash and cash equivalents separately on the face of the statement of financial position, such as 'cash and bank balances' and 'short-term bank deposits'. Additionally, some entities may include bank overdrafts in cash and cash equivalents for cash flow purposes, but, if no legal right of set-off exists, will present bank overdrafts separate from cash in the statement of financial position as financial liabilities. *[IAS 32.42]*.

The standard requires an entity to disclose the components of cash and cash equivalents and to present a reconciliation to the statement of financial position, *[IAS 7.45]*, which means that any difference between 'cash and cash equivalents' for IAS 7 purposes and presentation in the statement of financial position will be evident in the notes to the financial statements.

Rio Tinto plc provides a reconciliation of the components of cash and cash equivalents, which includes overdrafts.

Extract 36.4: Rio Tinto plc (2012)

Notes to the 2012 financial statements [extract]

22 Cash and cash equivalents [extract]

	2012 US$ m	2011 US$ m
Cash at bank and in hand	1,267	2,167
Other short term deposits	5,815	7,503
Balance per Group statement of financial position	7,082	9,670
Bank overdrafts repayable on demand (unsecured)	(94)	(16)
Cash and cash equivalents included in Assets held for sale	234	–
Balance per Group cash flow statement	7,222	9,654

Cash and cash equivalents include US$108 million (2011: US$305 million) for which there are restrictions on remittances. Other short term borrowings principally earn interest at a floating rate based on Libor plus a fixed spread.

3.4 Restrictions on the use of cash and cash equivalents

The amount of significant cash and cash equivalent balances that is not available for use by the group should be disclosed, together with a commentary by management to explain the circumstances of the restriction. *[IAS 7.48]*. Examples include cash and cash equivalents held by a subsidiary operating under exchange controls or other legal restrictions that prevent their general use by the parent or other subsidiaries. *[IAS 7.49]*.

Lloyds Banking Group discloses balances held by its life fund subsidiaries as restricted cash.

Extract 36.5: Lloyds Banking Group plc (2012)

Notes to the consolidated financial statements [extract]

Note 56: Consolidated cash flow statement [extract]

(D) Analysis of cash and cash equivalents as shown in the balance sheet

	2012	2011	2010
	£m	£m	£m
Cash and balances at central banks	**80,298**	60,722	38,115
Less: mandatory reserve deposits[1]	**(580)**	(1,070)	(1,089)
	79,718	59,652	37,026
Loans and advances to banks	**29,417**	32,606	30,272
Less: amounts with a maturity of three months or more	**(8,077)**	(6,369)	(4,998)
	21,340	26,237	25,274
Total cash and cash equivalents	**101,058**	85,889	62,300

[1] Mandatory reserve deposits are held with local central banks in accordance with statutory requirements; these deposits are not available to finance the Group's day-to-day operations.

Included within cash and cash equivalents at 31 December 2012 is £17,889 million (2011: £21,601 million; 2010: £14,694 million) held within the Group's life funds, which is not immediately available for use in the business.

The nature of the restriction must be assessed to determine if the balance is ineligible for inclusion in cash equivalents because the restriction results in the investment ceasing to be highly liquid or readily convertible. For example, where an entity covenants to maintain a minimum level of cash or deposits as security for certain short-term obligations and provided that no amounts are required to be designated for that specific purpose, such balances could still be regarded as cash equivalents, albeit subject to restrictions, as part of a policy of managing resources to meet short-term commitments.

However, an entity may be required formally to set aside cash, for example by way of a deposit into an escrow account, as part of a specific project or transaction, such as the acquisition or construction of a property. In such circumstances, it is necessary to consider the terms and conditions relating to the account and the conditions relating to both the entity's and the counterparty's access to the funds within it to determine whether it is appropriate for the deposit to be classified in cash equivalents.

In Extract 36.5 above, Lloyds Banking Group excludes from cash and cash equivalents the mandatory reserve deposits held with local central banks, because these amounts are not available to finance the entity's day-to-day operations. Similarly, in the following extract, InterContinental Hotels Group includes certain amounts of restricted cash, which are pledged as collateral to insurance companies for risks retained by the group, in loans and receivables within 'Other financial assets' on the statement of financial position rather than in cash and cash equivalents.

Extract 36.6: InterContinental Hotels Group PLC (2012)

Notes to the Group Financial Statements [extract]

15. Other financial assets [extract]

Loans and receivables consist of trade deposits and restricted cash which are held at amortised cost. A deposit of $37m was made in 2011 to a hotel owner in connection with the renegotiation of a management contract. The deposit is non-interest-bearing and repayable at the end of the management contract, and is therefore held at its discounted value of $11m (2011 $10m); the discount will unwind to the income statement within financial income over the period to repayment. Restricted cash of $29m (2011 $27m) relates to cash held in bank accounts which is pledged as collateral to insurance companies for risks retained by the Group.

4 PRESENTATION OF THE STATEMENT OF CASH FLOWS

The statement of cash flows reports inflows and outflows of cash and cash equivalents during the period classified under:

- operating activities;
- investing activities; and
- financing activities. *[IAS 7.10]*.

This classification is intended to allow users to assess the impact of these three types of activity on the financial position of the entity and the amount of its cash and cash equivalents. Whilst not stated explicitly in the standard, the presentation of operating, investing and financing cash flows usually follows this sequence in practice, and a total net cash flow for each standard heading should be shown. Comparative figures are required for all items in the statement of cash flows and the related notes. *[IAS 1.38]*.

The components of cash flows are classified as operating, investing or financing activities in a manner which is most appropriate to the business of the entity. *[IAS 7.11]*. For example, the purchase of investments is likely to be classified as an operating cash flow for a financial institution, but as an investing cash flow for a manufacturer. Additionally, a single transaction may comprise elements of differently classified cash flows. For example, when repayments on a loan include both interest and capital, the interest element may be included in either operating activities or financing activities (see 4.4.1 below) whereas the capital repayment must be classified as a financing cash flow. *[IAS 7.12]*.

The format of the statement of cash flows is illustrated in Extract 36.7. As permitted by the standard, AstraZeneca has included interest paid under operating activities, interest received under investing activities and dividends paid under financing activities.

Extract 36.7: AstraZeneca PLC (2012)

Consolidated Statement Of Cash Flows For The Year Ended 31 December

	2012 $m	2011 $m	2010 $m
Cash flows from operating activities			
Profit before tax	**7,718**	12,367	10,977
Finance income and expense	**430**	428	517
Depreciation, amortisation and impairment	**2,518**	2,550	2,741
Decrease/(increase) in trade and other receivables	**755**	(1,108)	10
(Increase)/decrease in inventories	**(150)**	(256)	88
(Decrease)/increase in trade and other payables and provisions	**(1,311)**	467	(16)
Profit on disposal of subsidiary	**–**	(1,483)	–
Non-cash and other movements	**(424)**	(597)	(463)
Cash generated from operations	**9,536**	12,368	13,854
Interest paid	**(545)**	(548)	(641)
Tax paid	**(2,043)**	(3,999)	(2,533)
Net cash inflow from operating activities	**6,948**	7,821	10,680
Cash flows from investing activities			
Acquisitions of business operations	**(1,187)**	–	(348)
Movement in short-term investments and fixed deposits	**3,619**	(2,743)	(125)
Purchase of property, plant and equipment	**(672)**	(839)	(791)
Disposal of property, plant and equipment	**199**	102	83
Purchase of intangible assets	**(3,947)**	(458)	(1,390)
Disposal of intangible assets	**–**	–	210
Purchase of non-current asset investments	**(46)**	(11)	(34)
Disposal of non-current asset investments	**43**	–	5
Net cash received on disposal of subsidiary	**–**	1,772	–
Dividends received	**7**	–	–
Interest received	**145**	171	174
Payments made by subsidiaries to non-controlling interests	**(20)**	(16)	(10)
Net cash outflow from investing activities	**(1,859)**	(2,022)	(2,226)
Net cash inflow before financing activities	**5,089**	5,799	8,454
Cash flows from financing activities			
Proceeds from issue of share capital	**429**	409	494
Repurchase of shares	**(2,635)**	(6,015)	(2,604)
Repayment of obligations under finance leases	**(17)**	–	–
Issue of loans	**1,980**	–	–
Repayment of loans	**(1,750)**	–	(1,741)
Dividends paid	**(3,665)**	(3,764)	(3,361)
Hedge contracts relating to dividend payments	**48**	3	(114)
Movement in short-term borrowings	**687**	46	(8)
Net cash outflow from financing activities	**(4,923)**	(9,321)	(7,334)
Net increase/(decrease) in cash and cash equivalents in the period	**166**	(3,522)	1,120
Cash and cash equivalents at beginning of the period	**7,434**	10,981	9,828
Exchange rate effects	**(4)**	(25)	33
Cash and cash equivalents at the end of the period	**7,596**	7,434	10,981

Having reviewed requests received from constituents over recent years for further guidance on the classification of cash flows, the Interpretations Committee and the IASB have observed that the primary principle for classification of cash flows should be in accordance with the nature of the activity in a manner that is most appropriate to the business of the entity (see 4.4.7 below).[2]

4.1 Cash flows from operating activities

Operating activities are defined as 'the principal revenue-producing activities of the entity and other activities that are not investing or financing activities'. *[IAS 7.6]*. This means that operating is the 'default category', with all cash flows that do not fall within either the investing or financing classifications being automatically deemed to be of an operating nature. The standard states that the value of information on operating cash flows is twofold. It provides a key indicator of the extent to which the entity has generated sufficient cash flows from its operations to repay debt, pay dividends and make investments to maintain and increase its operating capability, without recourse to external sources of financing. Also, information about the components of historical operating cash flows may assist in the process of forecasting future operating cash flows, when used in conjunction with other financial statement information. *[IAS 7.13]*.

Cash flows from operating activities generally result from transactions and other events that enter into the determination of profit or loss. Examples include:

(a) cash receipts from the sale of goods and the rendering of services;

(b) cash receipts from royalties, fees, commissions and other revenue;

(c) cash payments to suppliers for goods and services;

(d) cash payments to and on behalf of employees;

(e) cash receipts and cash payments of an insurance entity for premiums and claims, annuities and other policy benefits;

(f) cash payments or refunds of income taxes unless they can be specifically identified with financing and investing activities; and

(g) cash receipts and payments from contracts held for dealing or trading purposes (see 4.4.6 below regarding the allocation of cash flows on derivative contracts). *[IAS 7.14]*.

As discussed at 5.2.1 below, acquisition-related costs in a business combination that have to be recognised as an expense *[IFRS 3.53]* would also be classified as operating cash flows because there is no related asset that would justify classification as an investing cash flow. *[IAS 7.16]*.

When an entity holds securities and loans for dealing or trading purposes they are similar to inventory acquired specifically for resale. Therefore, any related cash flows are classified as operating activities. Similarly, cash advances and loans made by financial institutions are usually classified as operating activities, since they relate to the main revenue-generating activity of that entity (see 6.1 below). *[IAS 7.15]*.

The proceeds from the sale of property, plant and equipment, which are usually included in cash flows from investing activities, are an example of an item that enters into the determination of profit or loss that is *not* usually an operating cash flow. *[IAS 7.14]*. However, the proceeds from sales of assets previously held for rental purposes are classified as cash flows from operating activities, if the entity routinely sells such assets in its ordinary course of business. Similarly, cash payments to manufacture or acquire property, plant and equipment held for rental to others, and that are routinely sold in the ordinary course of business after rental, are also classified as cash flows from operating activities (see 4.2.1 below). *[IAS 7.14]*.

Cash flows from operating activities may be reported on a gross or net basis, also known as the direct and indirect methods. *[IAS 7.18]*.

4.1.1 The direct method

Under the direct method, major classes of gross cash receipts and gross cash payments are disclosed. *[IAS 7.18]*. IAS 7 encourages entities to use the direct method, on the grounds that it provides information which may be useful in estimating future cash flows and which is not available under the indirect method. *[IAS 7.19]*.

Under the direct method, information about major classes of gross cash receipts and payments may be obtained either:

(a) from the accounting records of the entity (essentially based on an analysis of the cash book); or

(b) by adjusting sales, cost of sales (interest and similar income and interest expenses and similar charges for a financial institution) and other items recognised in profit or loss for:

   (i) changes during the period in inventories and operating receivables and payables;

   (ii) other non-cash items; and

   (iii) other items for which the cash effects are investing or financing cash flows. *[IAS 7.19]*.

The direct method statement of cash flows should include the same disclosures of gross cash receipts and gross cash payments irrespective of which approach has been used to determine their value. In particular, there is no requirement for entities using the approach described in (b) above to present a reconciliation showing the adjustments made between, for example, revenue in the statement of comprehensive income and cash receipts from customers.

The IASB has contemplated for some time whether it should mandate reporting under the direct method or the indirect method. As part of its joint project with the FASB, the IASB issued a staff draft of an exposure draft *Financial Statement Presentation* in July 2010. The staff draft proposed a requirement for the statement of cash flows to be prepared using the direct method and to be structured based on the following:[3]

(a) business activities, analysed between
 (i) operating cash flows; and
 (ii) investing cash flows;
(b) financing activities;
(c) multi-category transactions;
(d) income taxes; and
(e) discontinued operations.

However, this project has been put on hold after the IASB's review of its strategy for developing its technical programme based on feedback received from its 2011 agenda consultation process.[4]

Portugal Telecom is an example of an entity using the direct method for presenting its cash flows from operating activities, as illustrated in Extract 36.8 below.

Extract 36.8: Portugal Telecom, SGPS, S.A. (2012)

Consolidated Statement of Cash Flows [extract]
Years ended 31 December 2012 and 2011

		(Euro)
	2012	**2011**
OPERATING ACTIVITIES		
Collections from clients	8,346,301,510	7,653,745,672
Payments to suppliers	(3,579,536,743)	(3,071,030,520)
Payments to employees	(1,111,039,110)	(1,052,530,685)
Payments relating to income taxes	(155,766,302)	(164,560,300)
Payments relating to post retirement benefits, net	(197,666,333)	(198,223,997)
Payments relating to indirect taxes and other	(1,728,169,403)	(1,392,247,645)
Cash flows from operating activities	**1,574,123,619**	**1,775,152,525**

4.1.2 *The indirect method*

The indirect method arrives at the same value for net cash flow from operating activities, but does so by working back from amounts reported in the statement of comprehensive income. There are two approaches for presenting the net cash flow from operating activities when using the indirect method. The most common approach adjusts reported profit or loss for the effects of:

(a) changes during the period in inventories and operating receivables and payables;
(b) non-cash items such as depreciation, provisions, deferred taxes, unrealised foreign currency gains and losses, and undistributed profits of associates; and
(c) all other items for which the cash effects are investing or financing cash flows.

[IAS 7.20].

Anheuser-Busch InBev (AB InBev) has used this adjusted profit approach to present its indirect method statement of cash flows, as illustrated in Extract 36.9 below.

Extract 36.9: Anheuser-Busch InBev NV (2012)

Consolidated Cash Flow Statement [extract]
For the year ended 31 December

Million US dollar	**2012**	**2011**
Operating activities		
Profit	9 434	7 959
Depreciation, amortization and impairment	2 747	2 783
Impairment losses on receivables, inventories and other assets	106	47
Additions/(reversals) in provisions and employee benefits	146	441
Net finance cost	2 206	3137
Loss/(gain) on sale of property, plant and equipment and intangible assets	(68)	(39)
Loss/(gain) on sale of subsidiaries, associates and assets held for sale	(19)	(71)
Equity-settled share-based payment expense	201	203
Income tax expense	1 717	1 856
Other non-cash items included in the profit	(118)	(314)
Share of result of associates	(624)	(623)
Cash flow from operating activities before changes in working capital and use of provisions	**15 728**	**15 379**
Decrease/(increase) in trade and other receivables	(102)	174
Decrease/(increase) in inventories	(130)	(157)
Increase/(decrease) in trade and other payables	1 331	1 392
Pension contributions and use of provisions	(621)	(710)
Cash generated from operations	**16 206**	**16 078**
Interest paid	(1 978)	(2 612)
Interest received	112	308
Dividends received	720	406
Income tax paid	(1 792)	(1 694)
Cash flow from operating activities	**13 268**	**12 486**

Alternatively, the indirect method of presentation can show reported revenues and expenses in the statement of cash flows, with the changes during the period in inventories and operating receivables and payables. *[IAS 7.20]*. An example of this rarely used alternative is given at the end of Appendix A to IAS 7.

When an entity adopts the adjusted profit approach to presenting net cash flows from operating activities under the indirect method, the reconciliation should start either with profit or loss before tax (as in Extract 36.7 above) or profit or loss after tax (as in Extract 36.9 above). Any other basis, such as EBITDA, EBIT, or profit or loss excluding non-controlling interests, does not meet the requirement in IAS 7 for 'adjusting profit or loss', *[IAS 7.20]*, which includes 'all items of income and expense in a period'. *[IAS 1.88]*.

To obtain the information on working capital movements for the indirect method, the figures in the statement of financial position have to be analysed according to the three standard headings of the statement of cash flows. Thus, the reconciliation of profit or loss to cash flow from operating activities will include, not the increase or decrease in all receivables or payables, but only in respect of those elements which relate to operating activities. For example, amounts owed in respect of the acquisition of property, plant and equipment (other than assets held for rental and subsequent sale), intangible assets, or investments will be excluded from the movement in payables included in this reconciliation. Although this may not present practical difficulties in the preparation of a single-entity statement of cash flows, it is important that sufficient information is collected from subsidiaries for preparing the group statement of cash flows.

Furthermore, when a group has made an acquisition of a subsidiary during the year, the change in working capital items will have to be split between the increase due to the acquisition (to the extent that the purchase consideration was settled in cash, this will be shown under investing activities) and the element related to post-acquisition operating activities which will be shown in the reconciliation.

4.2 Cash flows from investing activities

Investing activities are defined as 'the acquisition and disposal of long-term assets and other investments not included in cash equivalents'. *[IAS 7.6]*. This separate category of cash flows allows users of the financial statements to understand the extent to which expenditures have been made for resources intended to generate future income and cash flows. Cash flows arising from investing activities include:

(a) payments to acquire, and receipts from the sale of, property, plant and equipment, intangibles and other long-term assets (including payments and receipts relating to capitalised development costs and self-constructed property, plant and equipment);
(b) payments to acquire, and receipts from the sale of, equity or debt instruments of other entities and interests in jointly controlled entities (other than payments and receipts for those instruments considered to be cash equivalents or those held for dealing or trading purposes);
(c) advances and loans made to, and repaid by, other parties (other than advances and loans made by a financial institution); and
(d) payments for, and receipts from, futures contracts, forward contracts, option contracts and swap contracts, except when the contracts are held for dealing or trading purposes, or the cash flows are classified as financing activities (see 4.4.6 regarding allocation of cash flows on derivative contracts). *[IAS 7.16]*.

Only expenditures that result in a recognised asset in the statement of financial position are eligible for classification as investing activities (see 4.2.2 below). *[IAS 7.16]*. Major classes of gross receipts and gross payments arising from investing activities are reported separately, except for those items that IAS 7 permits to be reported on a net basis, as discussed at 4.6 below. *[IAS 7.21]*.

4.2.1 *Property, plant and equipment held for rental*

Payments to acquire and receipts from the sale of, property, plant and equipment are usually included in investing cash flows; however, this is not always the case.

A number of entities sell assets that were previously held for rental, for example, car rental companies that may acquire vehicles with the intention of holding them as rental cars for a limited period and then selling them. IAS 16 – *Property, Plant and Equipment* – requires an entity, that, in its ordinary course of business, routinely sells items of property, plant and equipment that it has held for rental to others, to classify gains on the sale of such property, plant and equipment as revenue. *[IAS 16.68A].* Accordingly, the proceeds from the sale of such assets are classified as cash flows from operating activities, as are cash payments to manufacture or acquire property, plant and equipment held for rental to others and routinely sold in the ordinary course of business. *[IAS 7.14].*

The requirement to classify payments for such property, plant and equipment held for rental under operating cash flows is intended to avoid initial expenditure on purchases of assets being classified as investing activities, while inflows from sales are recorded within operating activities. However, this means that management will need to determine, at the time of acquisition or manufacture, which of the assets that it intends to rent out will be ultimately held for sale in the ordinary course of business.

4.2.2 Cash flows relating to costs intended to generate future income

As part of its annual improvements process, the IASB amended the definition of investing activities in IAS 7, effective for annual periods beginning on or after 1 January 2010, *[IAS 7.56]*, whereby 'only expenditures that result in a recognised asset in the statement of financial position are eligible for classification as investing activities'. *[IAS 7.16].* Cash flows relating to costs recognised as an expense can no longer be classified within investing activities. As a result, payments including those for exploration and evaluation activities and for research and development that are recognised as an asset are classified as investing cash flows, while entities that recognise such expenditures as an expense would classify the related payments as operating cash flows.

The IASB believes that this requirement better aligns the classification of investing cash flows with the presentation in the statement of financial position; reduces divergence in practice and, therefore, results in financial statements that are easier for users to understand. *[IAS 7.BC7].* It does not seem unreasonable that recurrent expenditure on the items noted above should be classified as operating cash flows. However, as discussed at 5.2 below, application to other items that do not give rise to an asset in the statement of financial position, such as acquisition-related costs and the settlement of contingent consideration in a business combination may prove to be more complicated.

4.2.2.A Cash flows for service concession arrangements

Because a cash flow is only classified in investing activities if it results in a recognised asset in the statement of financial position, a question arises regarding the classification of the cash inflows and outflows of the operator of a service concession arrangement that is within the scope of IFRIC 12 – *Service Concession Arrangements.*

IFRIC 12 features two possible accounting models – the intangible asset model or the financial asset model. Under both models, the service element relating to the construction of the infrastructure asset is accounted for in accordance with IAS 11 – *Construction Contracts.* In the intangible asset model, the revenue recognised gives rise to an intangible asset. Under the financial asset model, a receivable is recognised. Amounts recognised as revenue give rise to a financial asset.

It is unclear whether the cash flows incurred in the construction phase should always be regarded as operating cash flows, because they relate to the provision of construction services; or whether, in the case of an arrangement under the intangible asset model, the related cash flows could be classified in investing activities as relating to the acquisition of an intangible asset. Similarly, when considering the classification of the cash inflows received during the operating phase of the arrangement, there can be divergence in practice. It would seem appropriate to classify in operating activities the cash inflows for arrangements that are accounted for under the intangible asset model. On the other hand, when the financial asset model applies, cash inflows may be reported as inflows from a debt instrument requiring a split to be made between the redemption component, an investing cash inflow, and an interest element that will be an operating or investing cash flow according to the accounting policy of the entity. Since there is no specific guidance relating to the classification of cash flows for service concession arrangements, current practice is mixed. IFRIC 12 is discussed in more detail in Chapter 26.

4.3 Cash flows from financing activities

Financing activities are defined as those 'activities that result in changes in the size and composition of the contributed equity and borrowings of the entity'. *[IAS 7.6].* The standard states that this information is useful in predicting claims on future cash flows by providers of capital to the entity. *[IAS 7.17].* However, it would seem more likely that information on financing cash flows would indicate the extent to which the entity has had recourse to external financing to meet its operating and investing needs in the period. The disclosure of the value and maturity of the entity's financial liabilities would contribute more to predicting future claims on cash flows.

Cash flows arising from financing activities include:

(a) proceeds from issuing shares or other equity instruments;

(b) payments to owners to acquire or redeem the entity's shares;

(c) proceeds from issuing, and outflows to repay, debentures, loans, notes, bonds, mortgages and other short or long-term borrowings; and

(d) payments by a lessee for the reduction of the outstanding liability relating to a finance lease. *[IAS 7.17].*

In consolidated financial statements, financing cash flows will include those arising from changes in ownership interests in a subsidiary that do not result in a loss of control (see 5.3.2 below). *[IAS 7.42A].*

Major classes of gross receipts and gross payments arising from financing activities should be reported separately, except for those items that can be reported on a net basis, as discussed at 4.6 below. *[IAS 7.21].*

4.4 Allocating items to operating, investing and financing activities

Sometimes it is not clear how cash flows should be classified between operating, investing and financing activities. IAS 7 provides additional guidance on the classification of interest, dividends and income taxes. Other questions are not addressed explicitly in the standard, such as the classification of cash flows for:

- purchase and sales taxes, such as value added tax (VAT) in the European Union;
- receipts and payments arising from the factoring of trade receivables;
- the purchase and sale of treasury shares; and
- certain derivative contracts.

These areas are discussed below.

4.4.1 Interest and dividends

An entity is required to disclose separately cash flows from interest and dividends received and paid, and their classification as either operating, investing or financing activities should be applied in a consistent manner from period to period. *[IAS 7.31].* For a financial institution, interest paid and interest and dividends received are usually classified as operating cash flows. However, IAS 7 notes that there is no consensus on the classification of these cash flows for other entities and suggests that:

- interest paid may be classified under either operating or financing activities; and
- interest received and dividends received may be included in either operating or investing cash flows. *[IAS 7.33].*

The standard allows dividends paid to be classified as a financing cash flow (because they are a cost of obtaining financial resources) or as a component of cash flows from operating activities. *[IAS 7.34].*

In Extract 36.7 at 4 above, AstraZeneca has included interest paid under operating activities, interest received under investing activities and dividends paid under financing activities, as permitted by the standard. A different treatment is adopted by AB InBev in Extract 36.9 at 4.1.2 above, where interest paid, interest received and dividends received are all disclosed as operating cash flows.

All of these treatments are equally acceptable. Nevertheless, it could be argued that entities which do not include interest or dividends received within revenue should not include interest or dividends in operating cash flows, because cash flows from operating activities are primarily derived from the principal revenue-producing activities of the entity, *[IAS 7.14]*, and the amount of cash flows arising from operating activities is intended to be a key indicator of the extent to which the operations of the entity have generated sufficient cash flows to repay loans, pay dividends and make new investments without recourse to external sources of financing. *[IAS 7.13].* On this basis, interest paid would be a financing cash flow and interest and dividends received classified as investing cash flows. *[IAS 7.33].* Such entities would also treat dividends paid as a financing cash flow, because they are a cost of obtaining financial resources. *[IAS 7.34].* This approach is taken by AstraZeneca (see Extract 36.7 at 4 above).

In addition, the standard requires the total amount of interest paid during the period to be disclosed in the statement of cash flows, whether it has been recognised as an expense or capitalised as part of the cost of an asset in accordance with IAS 23 – *Borrowing Costs. [IAS 7.32].* Total interest paid could be disclosed either on the face of the statement of cash flows or in the notes.

A literal reading of this requirement might suggest that interest paid should be presented as a single figure under operating or financing activities. However, it would also seem appropriate to include the cash outflow relating to capitalised borrowing costs under investing activities, provided that when this is done, the total amount of interest paid is also disclosed. The Interpretations Committee tried to address this apparent inconsistency between paragraph 16 of IAS 7 and paragraphs 32 to 33 of IAS 7 in May 2011. They had initially recommended that the IASB amend IAS 7 through the annual improvements process to clarify that interest payments capitalised under IAS 23 should be classified in a manner consistent with the classification of the underlying asset to which those payments were capitalised.[5] This proposed amendment was issued for public consultation under the exposure draft *Annual Improvements to IFRSs 2010-2012 Cycle*.[6]

However, in response to concerns raised by respondents to the proposed amendments about the difficulty of implementation, the Committee recommended that the IASB refrain from making the proposed changes. The IASB agreed and decided in April 2013 not to finalise the proposed amendment.[7]

4.4.2 Taxes on income

Cash flows arising from taxes on income should be separately disclosed within operating cash flows unless they can be specifically identified with investing or financing activities. *[IAS 7.35]*.

Whilst it is possible to match elements of tax expense to transactions for which the cash flows are classified under investing or financing activities; taxes paid are usually classified as cash flows from operating activities, because it is often impracticable to match tax cash flows with specific elements of tax expense. Also, those tax cash flows may arise in a different period from the underlying transaction. *[IAS 7.36]*. This is the presentation adopted by AB InBev in Extract 36.9 at 4.1.2 above. However, when it is practicable to make this determination, the tax cash flow is identified as an investing or financing activity in accordance with the individual transaction that gives rise to such cash flows. In cases where tax cash flows are allocated over more than one class of activity, the entity should disclose the total amount for taxes paid. *[IAS 7.36]*.

4.4.3 Sales taxes and other non-income tax cash flows

Although it provides guidance on the treatment of taxes on income, IAS 7 does not specifically address the treatment of cash flows relating to other taxes, such as value added tax (VAT) or other sales taxes and duty. The Interpretations Committee has considered whether it should add the question about VAT to its agenda and decided that it was not appropriate to develop an interpretation. Instead, it suggested that the issue of cash flows relating to VAT be considered by the IASB in its review of IAS 7 as part of the project on Financial Statement Presentation.

In explaining why it would not add this question to its agenda, the Interpretations Committee noted that 'IAS 7 does not explicitly address the treatment of VAT' and added that 'while different practices may emerge, they are not expected to be widespread'.[8]

Therefore, it seems that entities can choose to disclose VAT receipts and VAT payments separately in the statement of cash flows or as part of the related cash inflows and outflows. Given the availability of alternative treatments, the Interpretations Committee noted that it would be appropriate in complying with IAS 1 – *Presentation of Financial Statements* – for entities to disclose whether cash flows are presented inclusive or exclusive of related VAT.[9] We believe that the same principles should be applied for other non-income taxes.

4.4.4 Cash flows from factoring of trade receivables

Another question not explicitly addressed in the standard is the classification of cash receipts from the factoring of trade receivables. In these circumstances, an entity uses a factoring structure to provide cash flow from trade receivables more quickly than would arise from normal collection from customers, generally by transferring rights over those receivables to a financial institution. In our view, the classification of the cash receipt from the financial institution depends on whether the transfer gives rise to the derecognition of the trade receivable, or to the continued recognition of the trade receivable and the recognition of a financial liability for the funding received from the factoring entity. The characteristics determining which of these accounting treatments would be appropriate are discussed in Chapter 47 at 4.5 and 5.

Only to the extent that the factoring arrangement results in the derecognition of the original trade receivable would it be appropriate to regard the cash receipt in the same way as any other receipt from the sale of goods and rendering of services and classify it in operating activities. *[IAS 7.14(a)]*. In cases where the trade receivable is not derecognised and a liability is recorded, the nature of the arrangement is a borrowing secured against trade receivables and accordingly we believe that the cash receipt from factoring should be treated in the same way as any short-term borrowing and included in financing activities. *[IAS 7.17(c)]*. The later cash inflow from the customer for settlement of the trade receivable would be included in operating cash flows and the reduction in the liability to the financial institution would be a financing outflow. Following the same principle in IAS 39 – *Financial Instruments: Recognition and Measurement* – for the disclosure of income and expenditure relating to a transferred asset that continues to be recognised, *[IAS 39.36]*, these two amounts would not be netted off in the statement of cash flows. However, it would be acceptable for the entity to disclose the net borrowing receipts from, and repayments to, the financial institution, if it was determined that these relate to advances made for and the repayment of short-term borrowings such as those which have a maturity period of three months or less. *[IAS 7.23]*.

In some cases, the factoring arrangement requires customers to remit cash directly to the financial institution. When the transfer does not give rise to derecognition of the trade receivable by the reporting entity, we believe that the later satisfaction of the debt by the customer can be depicted either:

(a) as a non-cash transaction. No cash flows would be reported at the time of the ultimate derecognition of the trade receivable and the related factoring liability; or

(b) as a transaction in which the factoring entity collects the receivable as agent of the entity and then draws down amounts received in settlement of the entity's liability to the financial institution. In this case the entity would report an operating cash inflow from the customer and a financing cash outflow to the financial institution.

4.4.5 *Treasury shares*

Treasury shares are an entity's own equity instruments that are acquired and held by the entity, a subsidiary or other members of the consolidated group. The consideration paid or received for treasury shares is recognised directly in equity and not as a movement in investments. *[IAS 32.33].* As such, it should be clear that payments and receipts to acquire or issue treasury shares should be classified within financing activities. *[IAS 7.17].* Even where such treasury shares are acquired by the entity as part of an equity-settled share-based payment transaction, the cash outflow should be classified under financing activities. Whilst cash payments to and on behalf of employees are classified under operating activities, *[IAS 7.14]*, the acquisition of treasury shares does not settle a transaction between the entity and its employees. An equity-settled share-based payment transaction is completed when the entity transfers its equity instruments to employees in consideration for the services received.

When a cash payment is made by a subsidiary to its parent or a trust that holds treasury shares as part of an equity-settled share-based payment arrangement, the payment should be accounted for as a deduction from equity, on the grounds that the payment does not settle the transaction with the employees, but is effectively a distribution to the parent or the trust (see Chapter 30 at 12.4.3 and 12.5.3). Having regarded this as a distribution, it follows that the cash flow should be classified as either operating or financing, according to the entity's policy on dividends as discussed at 4.4.1 above.

4.4.6 *Cash flows on derivative contracts*

Payments and receipts relating to derivative contracts can be classified within operating, investing or financing in different circumstances. Where the contract is held for dealing or trading purposes, the cash flows are classified under operating activities. *[IAS 7.14].* IAS 7 requires that payments for, and receipts from, futures contracts, forward contracts, option contracts and swap contracts are classified as cash flows from investing activities, except when the contracts are held for dealing or trading purposes, or the cash flows are classified as financing activities. *[IAS 7.16].*

The standard adds that when a contract is accounted for as a hedge of an identifiable position, the cash flows of the contract are classified under the same heading as the cash flows of the position being hedged. *[IAS 7.16].* An example is an interest rate swap. An entity wishing to convert an existing fixed rate borrowing into a floating rate equivalent could enter into an interest rate swap under which it receives interest at fixed rates and pays at floating rates. All the cash flows under the swap should be reported under the same cash flow heading as interest paid (i.e. as financing activities or operating activities, in accordance with the entity's determined policy, as discussed at 4.4.1 above), because they are equivalent to interest or are hedges of interest payments.

The standard suggests that receipts and payments on contracts might be included in financing cash flows; but, except for the text on contracts accounted for as hedges of an identifiable position, gives no indication of the circumstances under which such a classification would be appropriate. *[IAS 7.16]*.

So how should an entity classify the cash flows from a derivative contract that is considered by management as part of a hedging relationship, but for which the entity elects not to apply hedge accounting (taking all movements to profit or loss) or for which hedge accounting is not permitted under IAS 39? Consider the following example.

Example 36.1: Cash flows from derivatives not qualifying for hedge accounting

Company A has the euro as its functional currency. On 1 January 2014, it sells goods to a US customer for which it charges US$1,000,000. The spot exchange rate on this date is 1:1 and it recognises revenue of €1,000,000. Payment is due to be received on 30 June 2014. A enters into a forward contract to exchange US$1,000,000 for €1,095,000 on 30 June 2014. It does not designate it as a hedge because the effects of movements on the contract and those of retranslating the receivable will already offset in profit or loss. On 30 June 2014 the exchange rate is such that A receives the equivalent of €1,200,000 from its customer and pays €105,000 on the forward contract.

Taken literally, IAS 7 would suggest that the receipt from the customer of €1,200,000 is classified as an operating cash inflow; but, because the forward contract is not held for dealing or trading purposes and is not accounted for as a hedge of an identifiable position, the €105,000 cash outflow on the forward contract cannot be classified under operating activities. As such, the €105,000 would have to appear in investing or possibly financing cash flows. However, had the entity elected to apply hedge accounting, the standard would require the €105,000 to be included in operating cash flows.

This example highlights a current deficiency in IAS 7; its terminology was never updated or refined when IAS 39 was issued. This deficiency is acknowledged by the IASB when it discusses, in the implementation guidance to IAS 39, the classification of cash flows from hedging instruments. *[IAS 39.IG.G.2]*. Therefore, in our opinion, since the IASB has not reflected the requirements of IAS 39 in the text of IAS 7, it does not require the treatment of cash flows 'when a contract is accounted for as a hedge of an identifiable position' *[IAS 7.16]* to be restricted only to those hedging relationships that either are designated as hedges under IAS 39 or would otherwise qualify for hedge accounting had they been so designated. Accordingly, in Example 36.1 above, entity A would include the payment on the forward contract in cash flows from operating activities.

4.4.7 Classification of cash flows – current developments

The Interpretations Committee has received several requests from constituents for guidance on the classification of cash flows for a variety of transactions, including the classification of cash payments for deferred and contingent consideration arising from a business combination; and cash flows for an operator in a service concession arrangement. In deliberating whether to address these two issues through the annual improvements process, the IASB asked the Interpretations Committee to consider them together with all of the previous issues that the Committee has discussed on the classification of cash flows and determine whether they can be dealt with collectively, by applying an appropriate guiding principle under IAS 7.[10]

In March 2012 the Committee noted that two alternative classification principles had been applied in the past to support its conclusions whether to issue an agenda decision or to propose an improvement:

(a) classification according to the nature of the activity to which the cash flows relate; and

(b) consistency with the classification of the related or underlying item in the statement of financial position (otherwise referred to as the cohesiveness principle).

The Committee observed that in some circumstances the application of the cohesiveness principle could lead to transactions being divided into operating, investing or financing components.

The Committee decided that the primary principle behind the classification of cash flows in IAS 7 should be in accordance with the nature of the activity that is most appropriate to the business of the entity, according to the IAS 7 definitions of operating, investing and financing activities. This would be used as a guiding principle in addressing future questions on classification.[11]

At its July 2012 meeting the Committee discussed some fact patterns to test the application of this primary principle in an attempt to consider how appropriate guidance could be developed. These included cash received as compensation for an insured loss; payment to purchase assets on deferred terms; and cash received from a government grant. Those discussions revealed that the existing guidance did not lead to consistent application of the principle. Consequently, the Committee directed the staff to consider how the descriptions of operating, investing and financing cash flows could be clarified to promote more consistent application and to consider the relevance of other factors such as the identity of the counterparty or the timing of cash flows to their classification.[12]

At its March 2013 meeting, the Committee considered a number of staff recommendations for clarifying the definitions of operating, investing and financing activities, as well as amendments to the related guidance in the Standard. The Committee concluded that the issue of clarifying the application of the primary principle by modifying the current definitions in IAS 7 would be too broad for the Committee to address. The IASB agreed.

In addition, the Committee determined that since it could not take a holistic approach in clarifying the classification of cash flows, amendments to IAS 7 should not be made on a piecemeal basis, for example in response to specific requests made by submitters on classification of cash flows for particular transactions. The IASB agreed.

However, the IASB did not agree with the Committee's recommendation to remove the guidance in paragraph 16 of IAS 7 which states that only expenditures that result in a recognised asset in the statement of financial position are eligible for classification as investing activities. The Interpretations Committee had observed that this guidance seems to give precedence to the application of the cohesiveness principle over the nature of the activity giving rise to the cash flow. Whilst the IASB agreed with the Committee's observation that the primary principle for the classification of cash flows should be in accordance with the nature of the activity, it disagreed with the removal of this guidance as it has potentially reduced diversity in practice for the classification of cash flows relating to exploration and evaluation activities. Instead it was suggested that the guidance should be read as a constraint on the application of the primary principle, rather than as a competing principle to the classification of cash flows according to the nature of the activity.[13]

4.5 Exceptional and other material cash flows

IAS 1 prohibits the presentation of extraordinary items either on the face of the statement of comprehensive income, the separate income statement (if presented) or in the notes. *[IAS 1.87]*. Consequently, IAS 7 does not refer to extraordinary items.

As regards exceptional and other material cash flows, IAS 1 requires the nature and amount of material items of income and expense to be disclosed separately, *[IAS 1.97]*. It also requires additional line items, headings and sub-totals to be presented on the face of the statement of financial position when this is relevant to an understanding of the entity's financial position. *[IAS 1.55]*. Therefore, although IAS 7 is silent on the matter, it would be appropriate for material cash flows or cash flows relating to material items in the statement of comprehensive income to be presented as separate line items on the face of the statement of cash flows, provided that they remain classified according to their nature as either operating, investing or financing cash flows.

If items are described as 'exceptional' cash flows, the entity's statement of accounting policies should explain the circumstances under which an item would be classified as exceptional and the notes to the financial statements should include an appropriate description of the nature of the amounts so treated.

4.6 Gross or net presentation of cash flows

In general, major classes of gross receipts and gross payments should be reported separately. *[IAS 7.21]*. Operating, investing or financing cash flows can be reported on a net basis if they arise from:

(a) cash flows that reflect the activities of customers rather than those of the entity and are thereby made on behalf of customers; or

(b) cash flows that relate to items in which the turnover is quick, the amounts are large, and the maturities are short. *[IAS 7.22]*.

Examples of cash receipts and payments that reflect the activities of customers rather than those of the entity include the acceptance and repayment of demand deposits by a bank, funds held for customers by an investment entity and rents collected on behalf of, and paid over to, the owners of properties. *[IAS 7.23]*. Other transactions where the entity is acting as an agent or collector for another party would be included in this category, such as the treatment of cash receipts and payments relating to concession sales.

Examples of cash receipts and payments in which turnover is quick, the amounts are large and the maturities are short include advances made for and the repayment of:

(a) principal amounts relating to credit card customers;

(b) the purchase and sale of investments; and

(c) other short-term borrowings, such as those with a maturity on draw down of three months or less. *[IAS 7.23A]*.

An example noted in IAS 20 – *Accounting for Government Grants and Disclosure of Government Assistance* – where separate presentation is deemed appropriate for major classes of cash flows is the receipt of government grants, which 'are often disclosed as separate items in the statement of cash flows regardless of whether or not the grant is deducted from the related asset for presentation purposes in the statement of financial position'. *[IAS 20.28]*.

4.7 Foreign currency cash flows

IAS 21 – *The Effects of Changes in Foreign Exchange Rates* – excludes from its scope the translation of cash flows of a foreign operation and the presentation of foreign currency cash flows in a statement of cash flows. *[IAS 21.7]*. Nevertheless, IAS 7 requires foreign currency cash flows to be reported in a manner consistent with IAS 21. *[IAS 7.27]*.

Accordingly, cash flows arising from transactions in a foreign currency should be reported in an entity's functional currency in the statement of cash flows by applying the exchange rate in effect at the date of the cash flow. *[IAS 7.25]*. Similarly, the cash flows of a foreign subsidiary should be translated using the exchange rates prevailing at the dates of the cash flows. *[IAS 7.26]*.

For practical reasons, an entity can apply a rate that approximates the actual rate on the date of the cash flow (such as a weighted average for a period) but, like IAS 21, translation using the exchange rate as at the end of the reporting period is not permitted. *[IAS 7.27]*. The requirements for entities falling within the scope of IAS 29 – *Financial Reporting in Hyperinflationary Economies* – are discussed in Chapter 16.

Unrealised gains and losses arising from exchange rate movements on foreign currency cash and cash equivalents are not cash flows. However, it is necessary to include these exchange differences in the statement of cash flows in order to reconcile the movement in cash and cash equivalents to the corresponding amounts shown in the statement of financial position at the beginning and end of the period. The effect of exchange rate movements on cash and cash equivalents is presented as a single amount at the foot of the statement of cash flows, separately from operating, investing and financing cash flows and includes the differences, if any, had those cash flows been reported at end of period exchange rates. *[IAS 7.28]*. This is illustrated in Extract 36.7 at 4 above.

4.7.1 Entities applying the direct method

When an entity enters into a transaction denominated in a foreign currency, there are no consequences for the statement of cash flows until payments are received or made. The receipts and payments will be recorded in the entity's accounting records at the exchange rate prevailing at the date of payment and these amounts should be reflected in the statement of cash flows. *[IAS 7.25]*.

The consolidated statement of cash flows prepared under the direct method uses the foreign currency financial statements of each foreign subsidiary as the starting point. This means that cash flows are measured first in the functional currency of the subsidiary and then retranslated into the currency in which the consolidated financial statements are presented.

4.7.2 Entities applying the indirect method

Under the indirect method, profit or loss is adjusted for the effects of transactions of a non-cash nature, any deferrals of operating cash receipts or payments and income or expenses associated with investing or financing cash flows. *[IAS 7.18]*. Exchange differences will appear in the statement of comprehensive income when the settled amount differs from the amount recorded at the date of the transaction. Alternatively, if the transaction remains unsettled at the reporting date, exchange differences will also be taken to the statement of comprehensive income on the retranslation of the unsettled monetary items at closing rates. Entities must determine what adjustments should be made to ensure that foreign currency items are shown in the statement of cash flows at the value as translated on the date of settlement.

4.7.2.A Foreign currency operating transactions settled in the period

Where the exchange differences relate to operating items such as sales or purchases of inventory by an entity, no further adjustments need to be made when the indirect method of calculating the cash flow from operating activities is used. For example, if a sale transaction and cash settlement take place in the same period, the operating profit will include both the amount recorded at the date of sale and the amount of the exchange difference on settlement, the combination of which gives the amount of the actual cash flow.

4.7.2.B Unsettled foreign currency operating transactions

Similarly, where an exchange difference has been recognised on an unsettled balance no reconciling item is needed. This is because the movement in the related receivable or payable included in the reconciliation to operating profit will incorporate the exchange gain or loss. Adjusting profit for the movement on the receivable or payable will eliminate the effect of movements in exchange rates since the date of the transaction.

4.7.2.C Determining the value of non-operating cash flows

Any exchange difference arising on a settled transaction relating to non-operating cash flows will give rise to an adjustment between reported profit and the cash flow from operating activities.

For example, the foreign currency purchase of property, plant and equipment would be recorded initially at the rate prevailing on the date of the transaction. The difference on payment of the foreign currency payable would be taken to the statement of comprehensive income as an exchange gain or loss. If left unadjusted in the statement of cash flows, the investing cash flow for the asset purchase would be recorded at the historical rate, rather than at the exchange rate prevailing at the date of settlement. This difference needs to be taken into account in calculating the cash flow to be shown under the relevant classification, in this case investing cash flows, which would otherwise be recorded at the amount shown in the note of the movements in the reporting date value of property, plant and equipment.

4.7.2.D The indirect method and foreign subsidiaries

Entities should take care when applying the indirect method at the 'more consolidated level' as described at 5.1 below when there are foreign subsidiaries. If the translated financial statements are used, exchange differences will be included in the movements between the opening and closing group balance sheets. For example, an increase in inventories held by a US subsidiary from $240 to $270 during the year will be reported as an unchanged amount of £150 if the opening exchange rate of £1=$1.60 becomes £1=$1.80 by the year-end. In these circumstances an entity should take the functional currency financial statements of the foreign subsidiary as the starting point. The $30 increase in inventories can then be translated at the average exchange rate.

4.8 Non-cash transactions and transactions on deferred terms

Non-cash transactions only ever appear in a statement of cash flows as adjustments to profit or loss for the period when using the indirect method of presenting cash flows from operating activities as discussed at 4.1.2 above. Investing and financing transactions that do not involve cash or cash equivalents are always excluded from the statement of cash flows. Disclosure is required elsewhere in the financial statements in order to provide all relevant information about these investing and financing activities. *[IAS 7.43]*. Examples of such non-cash transactions include the conversion of debt to equity; acquiring assets by assuming directly related liabilities or by means of a finance lease; and issuing equity as consideration for the acquisition of another entity. *[IAS 7.44]*. Similarly, asset exchange transactions and the issue of bonus shares out of retained earnings are disclosed as non-cash transactions. Extract 36.10 below shows the disclosures made by Independent News & Media plc.

Extract 36.10: Independent News & Media plc (2010)

29 CASH AND CASH EQUIVALENTS [extract]

Significant non-cash transactions

(i) As part of the Group's refinancing in 2009, 723,200,000 new shares were issued to the Group's Bondholders in settlement of €122.9 m principal and interest outstanding on the Bonds. The remaining principal and interest, of €92.2 m due to the Bondholders was satisfied by a Rights Issue, of which €52.0 m was raised in cash with the remainder being an exchange of shares. The Bondholders received 92,204,958 shares in the Company for underwriting the Rights Issue.

(ii) During 2009, as part of the Group's refinancing, €673 m due under the Group's previous loan facilities was rolled into the Group's new loan facility, which was drawn down in December.

4.8.1 Asset purchases on deferred terms

The purchase of assets on deferred terms can be a complicated area because it may not be clear whether the associated cash flows should be classified under investing activities, as capital expenditure, or within financing activities, as the repayment of borrowings. In the US, FASB ASC Topic 230 – *Statement of Cash Flows* – takes the line that only advance payments, the down payment or other amounts paid at or near to the time of purchase of property, plant and equipment and other productive assets are investing cash flows; and, incurring directly related debt to the seller is a financing transaction with subsequent payments of principal on that debt classified as financing cash flows.[14] This treatment also appears to be implicit in IAS 7.

Where an entity acquires an asset under a finance lease, the acquisition of the asset is clearly a non-cash transaction, *[IAS 7.44]*, and the payments to reduce the outstanding liability relating to a finance lease are clearly financing cash flows. *[IAS 7.17]*. The 2010 amendment to the IAS 7 definition of investing activities resulting from the annual improvements project, discussed at 4.2.2 above, would suggest that entities also consider whether the payments should be classified as investing cash flows if they did not result in a recognised asset. *[IAS 7.16]*. On this basis, because payments of deferred amounts do not result in recognition of an asset, but rather a reduction of a liability, they would not be treated as investing cash flows. However, as discussed at 4.4.7 above, the Interpretations Committee and the IASB have affirmed in 2013 their position that in determining the classification of cash flows, the nature of the activity is still the primary principle to be considered.[15] Accordingly, the classification of the payment comes down to a judgement as to whether its nature relates to the acquisition of an asset or the repayment of a liability.

In our view, in cases where financing is provided by the seller of the asset, the acquisition and financing should be treated as a non-cash transaction and disclosed accordingly. Subsequent payments to the seller are then included in financing cash flows. Nevertheless, if the period between acquisition and payment is not significant, the existence of credit terms should not be interpreted as changing the nature of the cash payment from investing to financing. The period between acquisition and payment would be regarded as significant if it gave rise to the seller recognising imputed interest under IAS 18 – *Revenue* (see Chapter 28 at 3.5). *[IAS 18.11]*. Therefore, the settlement of a short-term payable for the purchase of an asset is an investing cash flow, whereas payments to reduce the liability relating to a finance lease or other finance provided by the seller for the purchase of an asset should be included in financing cash flows.

4.8.2 *Asset disposals on deferred terms*

It follows that the disposal of property, plant and equipment under a finance lease or other arrangement determined to be the provision of finance by the vendor would be disclosed as a non-cash transaction. Receipts to reduce the receivable from the purchaser would still be investing cash flows, but described as the repayment of advances and loans rather than the proceeds on sale of property, plant and equipment. *[IAS 7.16]*.

It should be noted that, just as in the case of the factoring of trade receivables (see 4.4.4 above), the proceeds received on disposal of an asset in a sale and leaseback transaction is classified as a financing cash flow if the related asset is not derecognised.

4.9 Voluntary disclosures

IAS 7 encourages the disclosure of additional cash flow related information that may help users better understand the financial position of the entity, including a commentary by management, as follows:

(a) the amount of undrawn borrowing facilities that may be available for future operating activities and to settle capital commitments, indicating any restrictions on the use of these facilities;

(b) the aggregate amounts of the cash flows from each of operating, investing and financing activities related to interests in joint ventures reported using proportionate consolidation;

(c) the aggregate amount of cash flows that represent increases in operating capacity separately from those cash flows that are required to maintain operating capacity (see 4.9.1 below); and

(d) the amount of the cash flows arising from the operating, investing and financing activities of each reportable segment (as defined in IFRS 8 – *Operating Segments*) (see 4.9.2 below). *[IAS 7.50]*.

4.9.1 *Cash flows to increase and maintain operating capacity*

IAS 7 does not contain any guidance as to how to distinguish cash flows for expansion from cash flows for maintenance in relation to the voluntary disclosure referred to under (c) above. The standard merely states that this information is useful in helping the user to determine whether the entity is investing adequately in the maintenance of its operating capacity or whether it may be sacrificing future profitability for the sake of current liquidity and distributions to owners. *[IAS 7.51]*.

Hongkong Land Holdings distinguishes renovations expenditure from developments capital expenditure in its analysis of investing cash flows.

Extract 36.11: Hongkong Land Holdings Ltd (2012)

Consolidated Cash Flow Statement [extract]
for the year ended 31st December 2012

	2012	2011
	US$m	US$m
Investing activities		
Major renovations expenditure	**(47.8)**	(50.8)
Developments capital expenditure	**(515.0)**	(38.3)
Investments in and loans to associates and joint ventures	**(179.0)**	(146.2)
Deposit for a joint venture	**(112.1)**	–
Disposal of an investment property	**8.3**	–
Cash flows from investing activities	**(845.6)**	(235.3)

4.9.2 *Segment cash flow disclosures*

Disclosure is encouraged of segmental cash flows because it reveals the availability and variability of cash flows in each segment and allows users to better understand the relationship between the cash flows of the business as a whole and those of its component parts. *[IAS 7.52]*.

IAS 7 contains an example of the segmental disclosure advocated under (d) at 4.9 above.[16] However, this example simply reports the operating, investing and financing cash flows of its two segments with no reconciliation of the total to the statement of cash flows. In practice it might be difficult to allocate financing cash flows across the entity's reportable segments, given that this is not how treasury functions tend to operate.

A.P. Møller – Mærsk provides an analysis of operating cash flows and capital expenditure (part of its investing cash flows) by reportable segment. The entity does not disclose financing cash flows by reportable segment (comparative information is provided in the financial statements but is not reproduced here).

Extract 36.12: A.P. Møller – Mærsk A/S (2012)

Notes to the consolidated financial statements [extract]

Amounts in DKK million

3 Segment information [extract]

2012	Maersk Line	Maersk Oil	APM Terminals	Maersk Drilling	Maersk Supply Service	Maersk Tankers
Cash flow from operating activities	10,422	22,347	5,653	3,776	1,767	824
Cash flow used for capital expenditure	–20,566	–11,352	–7,823	–3,414	–1,242	–2,672

	Damco	SVITZER	Dansk Supermarked	Maersk FPSOs and Maersk LNG	Total reportable segments
Cash flow from operating activities	–562	1,489	2,316	600	48,632
Cash flow used for capital expenditure	–126	–590	–2,055	15,176	–34,664

5 ADDITIONAL IAS 7 CONSIDERATIONS FOR GROUPS

IAS 7 does not distinguish between single entities and groups, and there are no specific requirements as to how an entity should prepare a consolidated statement of cash flows. In the absence of specific requirements, cash inflows and outflows would be treated in the same way as income and expenses under IFRS 10 – *Consolidated Financial Statements* – or, where IFRS 10 is not yet applicable, IAS 27 – *Consolidated and Separate Financial Statements* (referred to as 'IAS 27 (2012)' in the remainder of this Chapter). Applying these principles, the statement of cash flows presented in consolidated financial statements should reflect only the flows of cash and cash equivalents into and out of the group, i.e. consolidated cash flows are presented as those of a single economic entity. *[IFRS 10 Appendix A]*. Cash flows that are internal to the group (such as payments and receipts for intra-group sales, management charges, dividends, interest and financing arrangements) should be eliminated. *[IFRS 10.B86]*. However, dividends paid to non-controlling shareholders in subsidiaries represent an outflow of cash from the perspective of the shareholders in the parent entity. They should, accordingly, be included under cash flows from financing activities or operating activities, in accordance with the entity's determined policy for classification of dividend cash flows (see 4.4.1 above). Payments arising from other transactions with non-controlling interests are discussed at 5.3.2 below.

5.1 Preparing a consolidated statement of cash flows

In principle, the group statement of cash flows should be built up from those prepared by individual subsidiaries with intra-group cash flows being eliminated as part of the aggregation process. This would generally be the case for entities presenting operating cash flows under the direct method, where information on gross cash receipts and payments has been obtained from each group entity's accounting records.

In practice, however, it may be possible to prepare a statement of cash flows at a more consolidated level, by starting with the disclosures in the consolidated statement of comprehensive income and statement of financial position and then applying the adjustments reflected as part of the financial statements consolidation process, together with information provided on external cash flows by individual subsidiaries. Thus, an entity adopting the direct method could use this information to derive the value of the major classes of gross cash receipts and gross cash payments. *[IAS 7.19].* An entity presenting operating cash flows under the indirect method would use this information to calculate the values for movements in inventories, operating receivables and payables and other non-cash items that appear in the reconciliation of consolidated profit or loss to the group's cash flow from operating activities. *[IAS 7.20].*

Cash flows from investing and financing activities could similarly be derived from a reconciliation of the relevant headings in the consolidated statement of comprehensive income to balance sheet movements. However, for this to be possible, subsidiaries would have to provide supplementary information (as part of internal group reporting) to prevent gross cash flows from being netted off and to ensure that the cash flows are shown under the correct classifications. In particular, detailed information about receivables and payables would be essential to ensure that the movements in operating, investing and financing receivables and payables are identified.

5.2 Acquisitions and disposals

When a subsidiary joins or leaves the group, it should be included in the consolidated statement of cash flows for the same period as its results are reported in the consolidated statement of comprehensive income.

An entity should present separately within investing activities the aggregate cash flows arising from obtaining or losing control of subsidiaries or other businesses. *[IAS 7.39].* For transactions involving obtaining or losing control of subsidiaries or other businesses during the period, disclosure is also required, in aggregate, of each of the following:

(a) the total consideration paid or received;

(b) the portion of the consideration consisting of cash and cash equivalents;

(c) the amount of cash and cash equivalents in the subsidiaries or other businesses over which control is obtained or lost; and

(d) the amount of the assets and liabilities, other than cash or cash equivalents, in the subsidiaries or other businesses over which control is obtained or lost, summarised by each major category. *[IAS 7.40].*

Cash flows arising from changes in ownership interests in a subsidiary that do not result in a loss of control are classified as financing cash flows (see 5.3.2 below). *[IAS 7.42A].*

The aggregate amount of cash paid or received as consideration is reported in the statement of cash flows net of cash and cash equivalents acquired or disposed of. *[IAS 7.42]*. The cash flow effects of losing control are not deducted from those of gaining control. *[IAS 7.41]*. This implies that entities should present one analysis for all acquisitions and another for all disposals, such as that presented by Nestlé, shown in Extract 36.13 below.

Extract 36.13: Nestlé S.A. (2010)

Consolidated cash flow statement [extract]
for the year ended 31 December 2010

	2010	**2009**
Investing activities		
Capital expenditure	(4,576)	(4,641)
Expenditure on intangible assets	(408)	(400)
Sale of property, plant and equipment	113	111
Acquisition of businesses	(5,582)	(796)
Disposal of businesses	27,715	242
Cash flows with associates	254	195
Other investing cash flows	(2,967)	(110)
Cash flow from investing activities[(a)]	**14,549**	**(5,399)**

[(a)] Detailed information related to Alcon discontinued operations is disclosed in Note 2. In 2010, even if Alcon's assets and liabilities were classified as held for sale, included lines of the cash flow statement comprise Alcon's movement until disposal.

NOTES [extract]

2 **Acquisitions, disposals and discontinued operations** [extract]

2.2 **Acquisitions of businesses** [extract]

In millions of CHF	**2010**	**2009**
Property, plant and equipment	342	54
Intangible assets	2 134	385
Inventories and other assets	292	150
Assets held for sale	845	–
Non-controlling interests	(6)	–
Purchase of non-controlling interests in existing participations	–	3
Financial debt	(18)	(5)
Employee benefits, deferred taxes and provisions	(35)	(90)
Other liabilities	(74)	(48)
Liabilities directly associated with assets held for sale	(177)	–
Fair value of net assets acquired	**3 303**	**449**
Goodwill	2 437	407
Fair value of consideration transferred	**5 740**	**856**
Cash and cash equivalents acquired	(41)	(5)
Consideration payable	(135)	(214)
Payment of consideration payable on prior years acquisition	18	159
Cash outflow on acquisitions	**5 582**	**796**

2.3 Disposal of businesses [extract]: In millions of CHF	**2010**	**2009**
Property, plant and equipment	4	71
Goodwill and intangible assets	1	64
Other assets	8	52
Non-controlling interests	(4 352)	(12)
Financial debt	–	–
Employee benefits, deferred taxes and provisions	–	(7)
Other liabilities	(31)	(55)
Alcon net assets held for sale disposed of	8 936	–
Net assets and non-controlling interests disposed of	**4 566**	**137**
Cumulative other comprehensive income items, net, reclassified to income statement	899	–
Profit/(loss) on current year disposals	24 472	105
Total disposal consideration	**29 937**	**242**
Cash and cash equivalents disposed of	(2 242)	(2)
Consideration receivable	(2)	(27)
Receipt of consideration receivable on prior years disposals	22	29
Cash inflow on disposals	**27 715**	**242**

5.2.1 Acquisition-related costs

IFRS 3 – *Business Combinations* – requires acquisition-related costs (other than those costs relating to the issue of equity or debt securities) to be recognised as an expense in the period in which the costs are incurred and the services are received. *[IFRS 3.53]*. Considering that acquisition costs can no longer be included in the measure of the cost of a business combination, is it no longer appropriate to classify the related payments in investing activities?

As discussed at 4.2.2 above, the IASB amended the definition of investing activities in IAS 7, whereby 'only expenditures that result in a recognised asset in the statement of financial position' give rise to investing cash flows. *[IAS 7.16]*. As a result, cash flows relating to acquisition costs recognised as an expense would have to be classified within operating activities.

5.2.2 Deferred and other non-cash consideration

Not all acquisitions or disposals of businesses are satisfied in full by the exchange of cash. The amount to be disclosed on the face of the statement of cash flows for obtaining or losing control of subsidiaries or other business is the aggregate amount of cash paid or received in the transaction, net of cash and cash equivalents acquired or disposed of. *[IAS 7.42]*. Any non-cash consideration, such as shares issued by either party or amounts to be paid or received by the entity at a later date, is not included in the amount presented under investing activities. *[IAS 7.43]*. Instead, the non-cash element of the acquisition or disposal is disclosed; and in acquisitions where the deferred element of the consideration is regarded as the provision of finance by the vendor, its settlement is classified as a financing cash flow. This is explained in more detail at 4.8 above.

5.2.3 Contingent consideration

5.2.3.A Business combinations

When a business combination agreement allows for adjustments to the cost of the combination that are contingent on one or more future events, IFRS 3 requires the acquirer to recognise the acquisition-date fair value of contingent consideration *[IFRS 3.39]* and classify an obligation to pay contingent consideration as a liability or as equity in accordance with the provisions of IAS 32 – *Financial Instruments: Presentation*. *[IFRS 3.40]*. Changes resulting from events after the acquisition date, such as meeting a performance target, are *not* reflected by adjusting the recorded cost of the business combination. Instead, any payment or receipt in excess of the carrying amount of the related liability or asset is recognised in profit or loss or in other comprehensive income. *[IFRS 3.58]*.

The primary principle for the classification of cash flows should be the nature of the activity giving rise to the cash flow, according to the definitions of operating, investing and financing activities in the Standard (see 4.4.7 above). This might imply that all payments relating to a business combination should be classified as investing cash flows. However, as discussed at 4.2.2 above, the definition of investing activities states that only expenditures that result in a recognised asset are eligible for classification as investing activities. *[IAS 7.16]*. This raises the question of how an entity should classify cash payments for any contingent consideration in excess of the amount that was recorded on the acquisition date (and thereby included in the carrying value of the acquired assets including goodwill). When the final value of the contingent consideration is dependent upon meeting performance targets after the acquisition date, it could be considered that the nature of activity giving rise to the incremental payment is the earning of revenues and profits in the period after the business combination. Accordingly, cash payments in excess of the acquisition-date fair value of the contingent consideration would be classified as cash flows from operating activities.

In most circumstances, cash payments up to the amount recognised for the acquisition-date fair value of the contingent consideration would be classified in investing activities, on the basis that these are cash flows arising from obtaining or losing control of subsidiaries. *[IAS 7.39]*. However, to the extent that an element of the contingent consideration payment represents a provision of finance by the seller, it may qualify to be included in financing activities (see 4.8.1 above). Judgment is required to determine whether the terms of the arrangement indicate that any of the amount attributed to the acquisition date fair value of the contingent consideration represents the provision of finance by the vendor.

In our view, if the period between acquisition and payment is not significant, it would not be appropriate to regard any of the payment as a financing cash flow. On the other hand, if the period of deferral is significant (to the extent that it would give rise to the vendor recognising imputed interest under IAS 18, *[IAS 18.11]*), payments to reduce this liability could be regarded as financing cash flows. However, the greater the extent to which the actual value of the contingent consideration payable depends on factors other than the time value of money, such as future business performance, the more difficult it would be to identify a financing element.

5.2.3.B Asset acquisitions outside of business combinations

The purchase price of intangible assets or tangible assets acquired outside of a business combination often includes contingent consideration as well. The appropriate disclosure of the cash payment of that contingent consideration will depend on the facts and circumstances of the transaction. The classification in the statement of cash flow should follow the accounting treatment adopted in the statement of financial position and statement of comprehensive income with regard to changes in the fair value of that contingent consideration.

5.2.4 Settlement of amounts owed by the acquired entity

A question that sometimes arises is how to treat a payment made by the acquirer to settle amounts owed by a new subsidiary, either to take over a loan that is owed to the vendor by that subsidiary or to extinguish an external borrowing.

Payments made to acquire debt instruments of other entities are normally included under investing activities. *[IAS 7.16]*. Therefore, the payment to the vendor is classified under the same cash flow heading irrespective of whether it is regarded as being part of the purchase consideration or the acquisition of a debt. This presentation can be contrasted with the repayment of external debt by the new subsidiary, using funds provided by the parent, which is a cash outflow from financing activities. *[IAS 7.17]*.

5.2.5 Settlement of intra-group balances on a demerger

A similarly fine distinction might apply on the demerger of subsidiaries. These sometimes involve the repayment of intra-group indebtedness out of the proceeds from external finance raised by the demerged subsidiary. If the external funding is raised immediately prior to the subsidiary leaving the group, it is strictly a financing inflow in the consolidated statement of cash flows, being cash proceeds from issuing short or long-term borrowings. *[IAS 7.17]*. If the subsidiary both raises the external funding and repays the intra-group debt after the demerger, the inflow is shown in the consolidated statement of cash flows under investing activities, being a cash receipt from the repayment of advances and loans made to other parties. *[IAS 7.16]*.

5.3 Cash flows in subsidiaries, associates and joint ventures

5.3.1 Investments in subsidiaries, associates and joint ventures

Changes in cash and cash equivalents relating to associates, joint ventures or subsidiaries accounted for under the equity or cost method will impact the entity's statement of cash flows only to the extent of the cash flows between the group and the investee. Examples include cash dividends received and loans advanced or repaid. *[IAS 7.37]*. Cash flows in respect of an entity's investments in an equity accounted associate or joint venture would also be presented. *[IAS 7.38]*.

Cash dividends received from equity accounted associates and joint ventures would be classified as operating or investing activities in accordance with the entity's determined policy for other dividends received (see 4.4.1 above). Where the net cash inflow from operating activities is determined using the indirect method, the group's share of profits or losses from equity-accounted investments will appear as a non-cash reconciling item in the cash flow statement (see 4.1.2 above).

5.3.2 Transactions with non-controlling interests

Dividends paid to non-controlling interest holders in subsidiaries are included under cash flows from financing activities or operating activities, in accordance with the entity's determined policy for dividends paid (see 4.4.1 above).

IFRS 10 (or, where IFRS 10 is not yet applied, IAS 27 (2012) – see 5 above) requires entities to distinguish between transactions that give rise to a change in control and those that do not, because this is consistent with the requirement that non-controlling interests are a separate component of equity. *[IFRS 10.BCZ169]*. Since changes in ownership interests in a subsidiary that do not result in a loss of control are accounted for as equity transactions, the resulting cash flows are classified in the same way as other transactions with owners. *[IAS 7.42B]*. Accordingly, IAS 7 requires that cash flows arising from changes in ownership interests in a subsidiary that occur after control is obtained, but do not give rise to a loss of control are classified as cash flows from financing activities. *[IAS 7.42A]*. In cases where there is a loss of control, the proceeds would be disclosed as a cash flow arising from disposals and classified as investing activities. *[IAS 7.16]*.

5.3.3 Group treasury arrangements

Some groups adopt treasury arrangements under which cash resources are held centrally, either by the parent company or by a designated subsidiary company. Any excess cash is transferred to the designated group entity. In some cases a subsidiary might not even have its own bank account, with all receipts and payments being made directly from centrally controlled funds. Subsidiaries record an intercompany receivable when otherwise they would have held cash and bank deposits at each period end. A question that arises is whether or not a statement of cash flows should be presented when preparing the separate financial statements of such a subsidiary given that there is no cash or cash equivalents balance held at each period end. In our view, the preparation of the statement of cash flows should be based upon the actual cash flows during the period regardless of cash and cash equivalents balance held at each period end. The cash and cash equivalents may fluctuate from being positive to overdrawn or nil as the subsidiary needs cash to conduct its operations, to pay its obligations and to provide returns to its investors, or sweeps up excess cash to the designated group entity. This approach is consistent with the requirements in IAS 7 that all entities should prepare a statement of cash flows which forms an integral part of the financial statements. *[IAS 7.1]*.

Where the subsidiary makes net deposits of funds to, or net withdrawals of funds from the designated group entity during the reporting period, a further question arises as to how movements should be presented in the subsidiary's statement of cash flows. Normally these transactions give rise to intercompany balances. Therefore, the net deposits or net withdrawals should be shown as investing activities or financing activities, respectively.

In extremely rare cases the intercompany balances may meet the definition of cash equivalents and be regarded as short-term highly liquid investments that are readily convertible into known amounts of cash and are subject to insignificant risk of changes in value. *[IAS 7.1].* However, in most cases such funds are transferred to the designated group entity for an indeterminate term and the fact that both the subsidiary and designated group entity are controlled by the parent company makes it difficult to conclude that the subsidiary could demand repayment of amounts deposited independently of the wishes of the parent company.

6 ADDITIONAL IAS 7 CONSIDERATIONS FOR FINANCIAL INSTITUTIONS

IAS 7 applies to banks, insurance entities and other financial institutions. Nevertheless, there are some differences in its application as compared to entities that are not financial institutions. For example, in considering the components of cash and cash equivalents, banks would not usually have borrowings with the characteristics of an overdraft, and cash for their purposes should normally include cash and balances at central banks, together with loans and advances to other banks repayable on demand. Allianz discloses such items as components of its cash and cash equivalents, as shown in Extract 36.14 below.

Extract 36.14: Allianz Group (2012)

NOTES TO THE CONSOLIDATED BALANCE SHEETS [extract]

7 - Cash and cash equivalents

€ MN As of 31 December	2012	2011
Balances with banks payable on demand	7,295	7,498
Balances with central banks	2,277	389
Cash on hand	223	263
Treasury bills, discounted treasury notes, similar treasury securities, bills of exchange and checks	2,642	2,342
Total	**12,437**	**10,492**

As of 31 December 2012, compulsory deposits on accounts with national central banks under restrictions due to required reserves from the European Central Bank totaled €305 MN (2011: €389 MN).

IAS 7 contains a number of additional provisions affecting the preparation of statements of cash flow by financial institutions. These are covered in broad outline below.

6.1 Operating cash flows

Cash advances and loans made by financial institutions are usually classified as operating activities (and not as investing activities, as they are for other entities) since they relate to a financial institution's main revenue-producing activity.

Chapter 36

[IAS 7.15, 16(e)]. Similarly, receipts from the repayment of loans and advances would be included in operating cash flows. *[IAS 7.16(f)]*.

Interest paid and interest and dividends received are usually classified as operating cash flows for a financial institution. *[IAS 7.33]*.

For an insurance entity, cash receipts and cash payments for premiums and claims, annuities and other policy benefits would be included in its operating cash flows. *[IAS 7.14(e)]*.

Under the direct method of reporting operating cash flows, a financial institution that does not obtain information from its accounting records can derive the disclosures for major classes of gross cash receipts and payments by adjusting interest and similar income and interest expense and similar charges and other items recognised in profit or loss for:

(a) changes during the period in operating receivables and payables;

(b) other non-cash items; and

(c) other items for which the cash effects are investing or financing cash flows. *[IAS 7.19]*.

Where an insurance entity presents its operating cash flows using the direct method, it should separately disclose cash flows arising from insurance contracts. *[IFRS 4.37(b)]*. Comparative information is required. *[IFRS 4.42]*.

6.2 Reporting cash flows on a net basis

Cash flows from each of the following activities of a financial institution may be reported on a net basis:

(a) cash receipts and payments for the acceptance and repayment of deposits with a fixed maturity date;

(b) the placement of deposits with and withdrawal of deposits from other financial institutions; and

(c) cash advances and loans made to customers and the repayment of those advances and loans. *[IAS 7.24]*.

6.3 Reporting operating cash flows using the indirect method

Subject to the differences noted at 6.1 above, the principles for a financial institution presenting operating cash flows under the indirect method are the same as those discussed at 4.1.2 above for other entities. An example of presentation by a financial institution using the indirect method is that of UBS AG.

Extract 36.15: UBS AG (2012)

Statement of cash flows [extract]

CHF million	For the year ended 31.12.12	31.12.11	31.12.10
Cash flow from/(used in) operating activities			
Net profit/(loss)	**(2,235)**	4,406	7,756
Adjustments to reconcile net profit to cash flow from/(used in) operating activities			
Non-cash items included in net profit and other adjustments:			
Depreciation and impairment of property and equipment	**689**	761	918
Impairment of goodwill	**3,030**	0	0
Amortization and impairment of intangible assets	**106**	127	117
Credit loss expense/(recovery)	**118**	84	66
Share of net profits of associates	**(88)**	(42)	(81)
Deferred tax expense/(benefit)	**294**	795	(634)
Net loss/(gain) from investing activities	**(507)**	(996)	(531)
Net loss/(gain) from financing activities	**3,717**	(5,856)	1,125
Other net adjustments	**6,081**	3,703	15,298
Net (increase)/decrease in operating assets and liabilities:			
Net due from/to banks	**(7,686)**	(14,569)	10,046
Reverse repurchase agreements and cash collateral on securities borrowed	**102,436**	(67,262)	(47,207)
Trading portfolio, net replacement values and financial assets designated at fair value	**8,740**	17,225	6,635
Loans/due to customers	**16,011**	6,068	(1,703)
Accrued income, prepaid expenses and other assets	**(889)**	9,648	(1,994)
Repurchase agreements, cash collateral on securities lent	**(66,111)**	27,116	17,588
Net cash collateral on derivative instruments	**4,399**	6,330	5,239
Accrued expenses, deferred income and other liabilities	**(794)**	(1,430)	1,246
Income taxes paid, net of refunds	**(261)**	(349)	(498)
Net cash flow from/(used in) operating activities	**67,050**	(14,241)	13,385
Cash flow from/(used in) investing activities			
Purchase of subsidiaries, associates and intangible assets	**(11)**	(58)	(75)
Disposal of subsidiaries, associates and intangible assets[2]	**41**	50	307
Purchase of property and equipment	**(1,118)**	(1,129)	(541)
Disposal of property and equipment	**202**	233	242
Net (investment in)/divestment of financial investments available-for-sale	**(13,946)[3]**	20,281	4,164
Net cash flow from/(used in) investing activities	**(14,831)**	19,377	4,097
Cash flow from/(used in) financing activities			
Net short-term debt issued/(repaid)	**(37,967)**	15,338	4,459
Net movements in treasury shares and own equity derivative activity	**(1,159)**	(1,885)	(1,456)
Capital issuance	**0**	0	(113)
Dividends paid	**(379)**	0	0
Issuance of long-term debt, including financial liabilities designated at fair value	**55,747**	52,590	78,418
Repayment of long-term debt, including financial liabilities designated at fair value	**(53,996)**	(62,626)	(77,497)
Increase in non-controlling interests	**0**	1	6
Dividends paid to/decrease in non-controlling interests	**(288)**	(749)	(2,053)
Net cash flow from/(used in) financing activities	**(38,041)**	2,670	1,764

[...]

CHF Million	For the year ended 31.12.12	31.12.11	31.12.10
Effects of exchange rate differences	**(673)**	(2,129)	(12,181)
Net increase/(decrease) in cash and cash equivalents	**13,506**	5,678	7,066
Cash and cash equivalents at the beginning of the year	**85,612**	79,934	72,868
Cash and cash equivalents at the end of the year	**99,118**	85,612	79,934
Cash and cash equivalents comprise:			
Cash and balances with central banks	**66,383**	40,638	26,939
Money market paper[1]	**4,382**	3,900	17,110
Due from banks[2]	**28,354**	41,074	35,885
Total	**99,118**	85,612	79,934
Additional information			
Net cash flow from/(used in) operating activities include:			
Cash received as interest	14,551	16,669	17,344
Cash paid as interest	9,153	9,845	12,606
Cash received as dividends on equity investments, investment funds and associates	1,430	1,343	1,395

[...]

Significant non-cash investing and financing activities

No significant items for 2012, 2011 and 2010.

7 REQUIREMENTS OF OTHER STANDARDS

7.1 Cash flows of discontinued operations

IFRS 5 – *Non-current Assets Held for Sale and Discontinued Operations* – requires an entity to disclose the net cash flows attributable to the operating, investing and financing activities of discontinued operations. These disclosures can be presented either on the face of the statement of cash flows or in the notes. Disclosure is not required for disposal groups that are newly acquired subsidiaries which are classified as held for sale on acquisition in accordance with IFRS 5. *[IFRS 5.33(c)]*. The general presentation requirements of IFRS 5 are dealt with in Chapter 4 at 3.2.

In 2007, Bayer AG disclosed the net operating cash flows from discontinued operations on the face of the statement of cash flows as part of its indirect method reconciliation from reported profit to cash flows from operating activities. Investing and financing cash flows are shown inclusive of discontinued operations on the face of the statement of cash flows, with the analysis required by IFRS 5 given in the notes. Bayer AG further analysed these cash flows by business segment, as shown below.

Extract 36.16: Bayer AG (2007)

Bayer Group Consolidated Statements of Cash Flows [extract]

€ million	Note	2006	2007
Net cash provided by (used in) operating activities (net cash flow), continuing operations		3.928	4,281
Net cash provided by (used in) operating activities (net cash flow), discontinued operations	[6.3]	275	2
Net cash provided by (used in) operating activities (net cash flow) (total)		**4,203**	**4,283**

Notes to the Consolidated Financial Statements of the Bayer Group [extract]

6.3 Divestitures and discontinued operations [extract]

Discontinued operations affected the Group cash flow statements as follows:

	Diagnostics		H.C.Stark		Wolff Walsrode		Total	
€ million	2006	**2007**	2006	**2007**	2006	**2007**	2006	**2007**
Net cash provided by (used in) operating activities	154	(34)	78	23	43	13	275	2
Net cash provided by (used in) investing activities	(107)	3,292	(55)	927	(17)	429	(179)	4,648
Net cash provided by (used in) financing activities	(47)	(3,258)	(23)	(950)	(26)	(442)	(96)	(4,650)
Change in cash and cash equivalents	**0**	**0**	**0**	**0**	**0**	**0**	**0**	**0**

7.2 Cash flows arising from insurance contracts

IFRS 4 – *Insurance Contracts* – requires that where an insurance entity presents its operating cash flows using the direct method, it should separately disclose cash flows arising from insurance contracts. *[IFRS 4.37(b)]*. Comparative information is required. *[IFRS 4.42]*.

7.3 Cash flows arising from the exploration of mineral resources

In a similar vein, IFRS 6 – *Exploration for and Evaluation of Mineral Resources* – requires that an entity discloses the amounts of operating and investing cash flows arising from the exploration for and evaluation of mineral resources. *[IFRS 6.24(b)]*. The requirements of IFRS 6 are discussed in Chapter 39. The amendment to IAS 7 in respect of investing cash flows, discussed at 4.2.2 above, is also relevant to entities applying IFRS 6.

7.4 Cash flows arising from interests in subsidiaries, joint ventures and associates

IFRS 12 – *Disclosure of Interests in Other Entities* – which is effective for accounting periods beginning on or after 1 January 2013, requires an entity to disclose in its consolidated financial statements summarised financial information about the cash flows for each subsidiary that has non-controlling interests that are material to the entity. *[IFRS 12.B10(b)]*. These amounts are stated before inter-company eliminations. *[IFRS 12.B11]*.

In addition, for each material joint venture and associate an entity is also required to disclose dividends received from the joint venture or associate *[IFRS 12.B12(a)]* and the amount of cash and cash equivalents for the joint venture or associate. *[IFRS 12.B13(a)]*. IFRS 12 is discussed in more detail in Chapter 13.

References

1 *IFRIC Update*, July 2009, p.3.
2 *IASB Update*, April 2013, p.13
3 Staff Draft of an Exposure Draft, *Financial Statement Presentation,* IASB and FASB, July 2010.
4 *Feedback Statement: Agenda Consultation 2011,* December 2012.
5 *IFRIC Update*, May 2011, p.4.
6 ED 2012/1, *Annual Improvements to IFRSs 2010-2012 Cycle,* IASB, May 2012, p. 36.
7 *IASB Update*, April 2013, p.12.
8 *IFRIC Update*, August 2005, p.5.
9 *IFRIC Update*, August 2005, p.5.
10 *IASB Update*, January 2012, p.6.
11 *IFRIC Update,* March 2012, p.7.
12 *IFRIC Update,* July 2012, p.6.
13 *IASB Update*, April 2013, p.13.
14 FASB Accounting Standards Codification (ASC) Topic *Statement of Cash Flows,* 230-10-45-13, (Formerly SFAS 95, *Statement of Cash Flows, FASB, November 1987,* para. 17, footnote.)
15 *IASB Update*, April 2013, p.13.
16 IAS 7, *Statement of Cash Flows,* IASB, Appendix A, part D. *Segment Information.*

Chapter 37 Interim financial reporting

List of examples

Chapter 37 Interim financial reporting

1 INTRODUCTION

The biggest issue in interim financial reporting is whether the interim period is a discrete period, or whether an interim period is an instalment of the full year. Under the first approach, an entity uses the same accounting policies and principles for annual financial statements as for interim periods. Under the second approach, the purpose of the interim report is to give investors, analysts and other users a better guide to the outcome of the full year, which requires modifications to the policies and principles used in annual financial reporting. The former approach is generally referred to as the 'discrete' approach, and the latter as the 'integral' approach.

The integral approach is not clearly defined, but implies deferring or accruing items of income or expense in order to present measures of performance for that interim period that are more indicative of the expected outcome for the year as a whole. Critics say that this approach obscures the results of the interim period. Proponents say that such modifications prevent distortion; an interim period is a more artificial interval than a financial year, and that to report transactions outside of the context of the annual operating cycle for which they are incurred does not make sense.

In practice, the distinction between discrete and integral approaches is less clear-cut than the description above suggests. IAS 34 – *Interim Financial Reporting* – requires an entity to use a 'year-to-date' approach, *[IAS 34.28]*, which is largely based on the requirement to report the entity's financial position as at the interim reporting date, but for which certain estimates and measurements are based on the expected financial position of the entity at year-end. However, the standard does not allow such estimates and measurements to amount to smoothing. For example, the estimate of tax expense for an interim period is based on actual profits earned as at the interim reporting date and not the expected tax expense for the year divided by the number of interim reporting periods, as discussed at 9.5 below.

The extent of disclosures in interim reports raises similar questions as to the purpose. If interim reporting is simply a more frequently published version of annual reporting, then the form and content of the interim reporting should be the same.

However, if interim reporting is only an instalment of a longer period, then a reporting package that highlights changes in circumstances during an interim period makes more sense than an update of all the disclosures in an entity's annual financial statements. IAS 34 allows an entity to include either a complete set of financial statements or a condensed version in the interim report. *[IAS 34.4].* While some jurisdictions require the complete form and even an audit of the interim report, present practice under IFRS favours the condensed version, although probably more as a practical compromise than as the result of meeting a carefully researched need. The differences between full and condensed interim financial statements are discussed at 3 below.

IAS 34 is not mandatory for entities that prepare annual financial statements that contain an explicit and unreserved statement of compliance with IFRS. *[IAS 34.2].* Historically, interim reporting was the prerogative of capital markets and regulators and IAS 34 leaves governments, securities regulators, stock exchanges and others to determine which entities report interim information, how often and how soon after the reporting period. *[IAS 34.1].* Accordingly, adherence to local regulatory or legal requirements in interim financial reports is required.

However, governments and regulators are increasingly referring to IFRS as they establish or revise their own requirements for interim financial reporting. For example, the European Union's Council of Economics and Finance Ministers (ECOFIN) issued *Directive 2004/109/EC of the European Parliament and of the Council on the harmonisation of transparency requirements in relation to information about issuers whose securities are admitted to trading on a regulated market and amending Directive 2001/34/EC* (the Transparency Directive) in December 2004. Article 5.3 of that Directive requires half-yearly financial reports that 'where the issuer is required to prepare consolidated accounts, the condensed set of financial statements shall be prepared in accordance with the international accounting standard applicable to the interim financial reporting adopted pursuant to the procedure provided for under Article 6 of Regulation (EC) No. 1606/2002.' Therefore, the half-yearly reports of entities subject to the Transparency Directive in the European Union comply with IAS 34. However, the timing and manner of adoption in member states varies based on local regulations. Other variations arise in interim reports for other periods (e.g. quarterly reporting) because the requirement in the Transparency Directive to apply IAS 34 is limited to half-yearly reports.

1.1 Definitions

The standard defines an interim period as 'a financial reporting period shorter than a full financial year.' *[IAS 34.4].*

The term 'interim financial report' means a financial report for an interim period that contains either a complete set of financial statements (as described in IAS 1 – *Presentation of Financial Statements*) or a set of condensed financial statements as described in IAS 34 (see 3.2 below). *[IAS 34.4].*

2 OBJECTIVE AND SCOPE OF IAS 34

2.1 Objective

The stated objective of the standard is 'to prescribe the minimum content of an interim financial report and to prescribe the principles for recognition and measurement in complete or condensed financial statements for an interim period. Timely and reliable interim financial reporting improves the ability of investors, creditors, and others to understand an entity's capacity to generate earnings and cash flows and its financial condition and liquidity.' *[IAS 34 Objective].*

2.2 Scope

IAS 34 does not prescribe which entities are required to publish interim financial reports, how often, or how soon after the end of an interim period. The standard notes that governments, securities regulators, stock exchanges, and accountancy bodies often require entities whose debt or equity securities are publicly traded to publish interim financial reports. Therefore, in the absence of any specific regulatory requirement (or obligation of the entity, for example, by covenant), entities are not required to publish interim financial information in a form that complies with IAS 34. Instead, IAS 34 only applies if an entity either elects or is required to publish an interim financial report in accordance with IFRS. *[IAS 34.1].* Accordingly, if an entity's interim financial report states that it complies with IFRS, then the requirements of IAS 34 must be met in full. *[IAS 34.3].*

The decision to present interim financial reports in accordance with IFRS operates independently of the annual financial statements. Hence, entities may still prepare annual financial statements conforming to IFRS even if their interim financial statements do not comply with IAS 34. *[IAS 34.2].*

Nevertheless, the IASB encourages publicly traded entities to issue interim financial reports that conform to the recognition, measurement and disclosure principles set out in IAS 34. Those entities are specifically encouraged: *[IAS 34.1]*

(a) to provide interim financial reports at least as of the end of the first half of their financial year; and

(b) to make their interim financial reports available not later than 60 days after the end of the interim period.

However, since an entity can only describe an interim financial report as complying with IFRS if it meets all of the requirements of IAS 34, *[IAS 34.3]*, an entity that applies all IFRS recognition and measurement requirements in its interim financial report, but does not include all the required disclosures may not describe the interim financial report as complying with IFRS.

As shown in the Extract below, before the issuance of the Transparency Directive, British Energy disclosed that its interim financial statements for the period ended 31 December 2006 were not prepared in accordance with IAS 34.

> *Extract 37.1: British Energy Group plc (Q3, 2006)*
>
> **Notes to the financial statements** [extract]
>
> **1. Basis of Preparation** [extract]
>
> In preparing the interim financial statements for the period ended 31 December 2006, the Board of Directors have used the principal accounting policies as set out in the Group's Annual Report and Accounts for the year ended 31 March 2006. The Group has chosen not to adopt IAS 34 – Interim Financial Statements, in preparing these interim financial statements, and therefore this information is not wholly compliant with International Financial Reporting Standards. The preparation of interim financial statements requires management to make judgements, estimates and assumptions that affect the application of policies and reported amounts of assets, liabilities, income and expenses.

3 COMPONENTS, FORM AND CONTENT OF AN INTERIM FINANCIAL REPORT UNDER IAS 34

The standard does not prohibit or discourage an entity from: *[IAS 34.7]*

- publishing a complete set of financial statements (as described in IAS 1) in its interim financial report, rather than condensed financial statements and selected explanatory notes; or
- including in condensed interim financial statements more than the minimum line items or selected explanatory notes as set out in IAS 34.

The recognition and measurement guidance in the standard, together with the note disclosures required by the standard, apply to both complete and condensed financial statements presented for an interim period. *[IAS 34.7].*

3.1 Complete set of interim financial statements

An entity that publishes a complete set of financial statements in its interim financial report should include the following components, as required in IAS 1: *[IAS 34.5]*

(a) a statement of financial position as at the end of the interim period;

(b) a statement of profit or loss and other comprehensive income for the period;

(c) a statement of changes in equity for the period;

(d) a statement of cash flows for the period;

(e) notes, comprising a summary of significant accounting policies and other explanatory information;

(f) comparative information in respect of the preceding period for all amounts reported in the current period's financial statements (unless specifically exempted by another IFRS); as well as (if relevant to understanding the current period's financial statements) comparative information for narrative and descriptive information; *[IAS 1.38, 38A]*; and

(g) a statement of financial position as at the beginning of the preceding period (without a requirement for related notes) when: *[IAS 1.40A, 40D]*:

  (i) an accounting policy has been applied retrospectively; or

(ii) a retrospective restatement has been made; or

(iii) items have been reclassified,

and the effect of such retrospective application on the information presented in that statement of financial position is material.

Entities may use titles for the above statements other than those used above. For example, an entity may use the title 'statement of comprehensive income' instead of 'statement of profit or loss and other comprehensive income'. *[IAS 34.5]*. Also an entity can refer to the 'statement of financial position' as 'balance sheet'.

If an entity publishes a complete set of financial statements in its interim financial report, the form and content of those statements should conform to the requirements of IAS 1. *[IAS 34.9]*. These requirements are discussed in Chapter 3 at 3. In addition, the entity should disclose the information specifically required by IAS 34 for interim financial reports as well as those required by other IFRSs (particularly those discussed at 4 below). *[IAS 34.7]*.

3.2 Condensed interim financial statements

In the interest of timeliness, cost, and avoiding repetition of previously reported information, an entity might be required or elect to give less information at interim dates as compared with its annual financial statements. *[IAS 34.6]*. The standard defines the minimum content of an interim report, as including condensed financial statements and selected notes, as follows: *[IAS 34.6, 8]*

(a) a condensed statement of financial position;

(b) a condensed statement or condensed statements of profit or loss and other comprehensive income;

(c) a condensed statement of changes in equity;

(d) a condensed statement of cash flows; and

(e) selected explanatory notes.

Consistent with the standard's requirements for accounting policies (see 8.1 below), an entity would only depart from using the same presentation as in its most recent annual financial statements if it had determined that the format will change in its next annual financial statements. *[IAS 34.28]*.

The condensed statement of profit or loss and other comprehensive income referred to at (b) above should be presented using the same format as the entity's annual financial statements. Accordingly, if an entity presents a separate statement of profit or loss in its annual financial statements, then it should present a separate statement in the interim financial report as well. Similarly, if a combined statement of profit or loss and other comprehensive income is presented in the annual financial statements, the same format is adopted in the interim financial report. *[IAS 34.8A]*.

As a minimum, the condensed financial statements should include each of the headings and subtotals that were included in the entity's last annual financial statements. *[IAS 34.10]*. However, the primary financial statements do not need to look exactly like the year-end financial statements. This is because the 'headings and subtotals' referred to in IAS 34 are not the same as 'line items' referred to in IAS 1. This is illustrated by the fact that IAS 1 uses all three terms to describe separate components of the statement of financial position, statement of comprehensive income and income statement (if presented separately). *[IAS 1.55, 85].* Therefore, a strict interpretation means that an entity is only required to present non-current assets, current assets, etc., on an interim statement of financial position.

On the other hand, one of the purposes of an interim report is to help the users of the financial statements to understand the changes in financial position and performance of the entity since the previous annual reporting period. *[IAS 34.15].* To that end, IAS 34 also states that additional line items or notes should be included if their omission makes the condensed financial statements misleading. *[IAS 34.10].* Therefore, judgement is required to determine which line items provide useful information for decision-makers, and are presented, accordingly.

Inclusion of most of the line items in the annual financial statements has the benefit of providing the most information to help users of the financial statements understand the changes since the previous year-end. Nonetheless, entities may aggregate line items used in the annual financial statements, if doing so does not make the information misleading or prevent users of the financial statements from performing meaningful trend analysis.

Consideration should also be given to regulatory requirements, for example, where a regulator requires an entity to present certain line items using some form of materiality criteria (e.g. in terms of amount, percentage relative to headings, or percentage change from prior periods). Entities may apply similar measures of materiality as a guide for determining which line items to present separately, even where this is not a regulatory requirement.

The following example illustrates one possible way in which an entity might choose to combine line items presented separately in the annual financial statements when preparing a condensed set of interim financial statements. However, such presentation is at the discretion of management, based on facts and circumstances, including materiality (as noted above), regulatory environment, etc. Accordingly, other presentations may be appropriate.

Example 37.1: Presenting the same headings and sub-totals in condensed interim financial statements

Statement of financial position	*Annual financial statements*	*Condensed interim financial statements*
Assets		
Non-current assets		
Intangible assets	●	●
Property, plant and equipment	●	●
Deferred tax assets	●	●
Investments in associates	○	
Available-for-sale financial assets	○	
Other non-current assets	○	○
Total non-current assets	●	●
Current assets		
Inventories	○	
Trade and other receivables	●	●
Current income tax assets	○	
Other current assets	○	○
Cash and cash equivalents	●	●
Total current assets	●	●
Total assets	●	●
Liabilities		
Current liabilities		
Trade and other payables	●	●
Current income tax liabilities	○	
Borrowings	●	●
Provisions for other liabilities	○	
Other current liabilities	○	○
Total current liabilities	●	●
Non-current liabilities		
Borrowings	●	●
Pension obligations	●	●
Deferred tax liabilities	●	●
Other non-current liabilities	○	○
Provisions for other liabilities	○	
Total non-current liabilities	●	●
Total liabilities	●	●

	Annual financial statements	*Condensed interim financial statements*
Equity		
Share capital	●	●
Other reserves	●	●
Retained earnings	●	●
Total equity	●	●

● Included same line item in annual and interim financial statements
○ This line item is condensed from the annual to the interim financial statements

Statement of profit or loss and other comprehensive income	*Annual financial statements*	*Condensed interim financial statements*
Sale of goods	○	
Rendering of services	○	
Total revenue	○	○
Cost of goods	●	●
Cost of services	●	●
Gross profit	●	●
Selling costs	○	
General and administrative costs	○	
Other operating expenses	○	
Total operating expenses	○	○
Operating profit	●	●
Finance costs	●	●
Share of profit of associates	●	●
Profit before tax	●	●
Income tax expense	●	●
Profit for the period	●	●
Other comprehensive income to be reclassified to profit or loss in subsequent periods		
Translation of foreign operations	○	
Net gain on hedge of net investment	○	
Related income tax expense	○	
Net other comprehensive income to be reclassified to profit or loss in subsequent periods	○	○
Other comprehensive income that will not be reclassified subsequently to profit or loss		
Actuarial losses on defined benefit plans	○	
Related income tax credit	○	
Net other comprehensive income that will not be reclassified subsequently to profit or loss	○	○
Total other comprehensive income	●	●
Comprehensive income for the period	●	●

● Included same line item in annual and interim financial statements
○ This line item is condensed from the annual to the interim financial statements

Statement of cash flows	*Annual financial statements*	*Condensed interim financial statements*
Operating activities		
Profit before tax	●	●
Non-cash adjustments:		
Depreciation and amortisation	○	
Gain on disposal of property	○	
Finance cost	○	
Share of net profit of associate	○	
Movements in pensions	○	
Total non-cash adjustments	●	○
Working capital adjustments:		
Trade and other receivables	○	
Inventories	○	
Trade and other payables	○	
Total working capital adjustments	●	○
Net cash flows generated from operations	●	●
Income taxes paid	●	●
Acquisition expenses paid	●	●
Net cash flows from operating activities	●	●
Investing activities		
Interest received	●	●
Proceeds from sale of property	●	●
Purchases of property	●	●
Purchase of intangible assets	●	●
Proceeds from sale of available-for-sale financial assets	●	●
Net cash flows from investing activities	●	●
Financing activities		
Proceeds from borrowings	●	●
Repayment of borrowings	●	●
Interest paid	●	●
Dividends paid	●	●
Net cash flows from financing activities	●	●
Net increase in cash and cash equivalents	●	●
Net foreign exchange difference	●	●
Cash and cash equivalents at beginning of year	●	●
Cash and cash equivalents at end of year	●	●

● Included same line item in annual and interim financial statements
○ This line item is condensed from the annual to the interim financial statements

Note that a statement of changes in equity is not presented in this example.

3.3 Requirements for both complete and condensed interim financial information

The general principles for preparing annual financial statements are equally applicable to condensed interim financial statements. These principles include fair presentation, going concern, the accrual basis of accounting, materiality and aggregation, and offsetting. *[IAS 1.4, 15-35].* (See Chapter 3 at 4.1).

Furthermore, the following requirements apply irrespective of whether an entity provides complete or condensed financial statements for an interim period:

- if applicable, basic and diluted earnings per share should be presented on the face of the statement that presents items of profit or loss for an interim period. *[IAS 34.11].* If the entity presents items of profit or loss in a separate statement in its annual financial statements, it should present basic and diluted earnings per share on the face of that separate statement in the interim financial report; *[IAS 34.11A]* and
- if the last annual financial statements were consolidated financial statements, the interim financial report should also be prepared on a consolidated basis. *[IAS 34.14].*

If the entity's last annual financial report included the parent's separate financial statements and consolidated financial statements, IAS 34 neither requires nor prohibits the inclusion of the parent's separate financial statements in the interim financial report. *[IAS 34.14].*

3.4 Management commentary

A management commentary is not explicitly required by IAS 34, but frequently included by entities in their interim financial reports along with the interim financial statements. In most cases the requirement for a narrative review comes from local stock market regulations and the entities should, therefore, follow the relevant guidance issued by those regulators.

IAS 34 allows information required under the standard to be presented outside the interim financial statements, i.e. in other parts of interim financial report. Thus some of the required disclosures may be included in a management commentary (see 4.2.1 below). The standard itself does not elaborate further on what information entities might give in other parts of the interim financial report.

4 DISCLOSURES IN CONDENSED FINANCIAL STATEMENTS

IAS 34 combines a number of disclosure principles:

- Entities should provide information about events and transactions in the interim period that are significant to an understanding of the changes in financial position and performance since the last annual reporting period. In this context it is not necessary to provide relatively insignificant updates to information reported in the last annual financial statements (see 4.1 below). *[IAS 34.15, 15A].*

- In addition to information to explain significant changes since the last annual reporting period, certain 'minimum' disclosures are required to be given, if not disclosed elsewhere in the interim financial report. *[IAS 34.16A]*. In this case the decision to disclose is subject to a materiality assessment (see 4.2 below).
- The materiality assessment for disclosure is based on the interim period to ensure all information is provided that is relevant to understanding the developments of the interim period (further discussed at 6 below). *[IAS 34.25]*.

Overall, applying those disclosure principles requires a significant amount of judgement by the entity – in the first case above on the basis of relevance and in the second case materiality. The practice of interim reporting confirms that entities take advantage of that room for judgement, both for disclosures provided in the notes to the financial statements and outside.

4.1 Significant events and transactions

IAS 34 presumes that users of an entity's interim financial report also have access to its most recent annual financial report. *[IAS 34.15A]*. On that basis, an interim financial report should explain events and transactions that are significant to an understanding of the changes in financial position and performance of the entity since the previous annual reporting period and provide an update to the relevant information included in the financial statements of the previous year. *[IAS 34.15, 15C]*. The inclusion of only selected explanatory notes is consistent with the purpose of an interim financial report, to update the latest complete set of annual financial statements. Accordingly, condensed financial statements avoid duplicating previously reported information and focus on new activities, events, and circumstances. *[IAS 34.6]*.

The standard requires disclosure of following events and transactions in interim financial reports, if they are significant: *[IAS 34.15B]*

(a) write-down of inventories to net realisable value and the reversal of such a write-down;

(b) recognition of a loss from the impairment of financial assets, property, plant, and equipment, intangible assets, or other assets, and the reversal of such an impairment loss;

(c) reversal of any provisions for the costs of restructuring;

(d) acquisitions and disposals of items of property, plant, and equipment;

(e) commitments for the purchase of property, plant, and equipment;

(f) litigation settlements;

(g) corrections of prior period errors;

(h) changes in the business or economic circumstances that affect the fair value of the entity's financial assets and financial liabilities, whether those assets or liabilities are recognised at fair value or amortised cost;

(i) any loan default or breach of a loan agreement that is not remedied on or before the end of the reporting period;

(j) related party transactions;

(k) transfers between levels of the fair value hierarchy used in measuring the fair value of financial instruments;

(l) changes in the classification of financial assets as a result of a change in the purpose or use of those assets; and

(m) changes in contingent liabilities or contingent assets.

The standard specifies that the above list of events and transactions is not exhaustive and the interim financial report should explain any additional events and transactions that are significant to an understanding of changes in the entity's financial position and performance. *[IAS 34.15, 15B].* Therefore, when information changes significantly, (for example, the values of assets and liabilities that are marked to market) an entity should provide disclosure regarding such change, in addition to the requirements listed above; the disclosure should be sufficiently detailed to explain the nature of the change and any changes in estimates. However, the notes to an interim financial report do not need to include insignificant updates to the information presented in the most recent annual report. *[IAS 34.15A].*

As discussed at 4.2.1 below, the Interpretations Committee and the IASB are currently considering questions around the delineation of the interim financial statements within an interim financial report and have tentatively agreed to amend paragraph 16A of the standard to require a cross-reference from the interim financial statements when information required by the Standard is presented elsewhere in the interim financial report. In our view, users of the interim financial report would also benefit from the provision of such a cross-reference where the information required above about significant events and transactions is given outside the interim financial statements.

4.1.1 Relevance of other standards in condensed financial statements

Whilst other standards specify disclosures required in a complete set of financial statements, if an entity's interim financial report includes only condensed financial statements as described in IAS 34, then the disclosures required by those other standards are not mandatory. However, if disclosure is considered to be necessary in the context of an interim report, those other standards provide guidance on the appropriate disclosures for many of these items. *[IAS 34.15C].*

Thus, there is some tension in determining what disclosures are required when a new accounting pronouncement is issued, and effective for the entity's next annual financial statements, but does not include specific disclosure requirements under IAS 34. The new disclosures are not specifically required under IAS 34, but may be material to an understanding of the entity. Therefore, judgement is required to determine whether including the disclosures in the interim report will provide the most useful information to users of the financial statements (see 6 below).

Another complication arises when a new standard or interpretation refers to interim financial reporting without a corresponding change to IAS 34. In December 2011, the IASB issued Amendments to IFRS 7 – *Disclosures –*

Offsetting Financial Assets and Financial Liabilities – which introduced disclosures to facilitate evaluation of the effect of netting arrangements on an entity's financial position. These new requirements became applicable for 'annual periods beginning on or after 1 January 2013 and interim periods within those annual periods'. *[IFRS 7.44R]*. However, no corresponding requirement has been added to IAS 34. In April 2013, the IASB clarified that the additional disclosure required by IFRS 7 is not specifically required in all interim periods after the first year of application of the Amendments. In future periods the inclusion or not of these disclosures is subject to an assessment of its relevance in the context of the interim period, as discussed above.[1] In July 2013 the Interpretations Committee recommended that IFRS 7 is amended to this effect.[2] The IFRS 7 requirements are discussed further in Chapter 50 at 7.4.2.

4.2 Other disclosures required by IAS 34

In addition to disclosing significant events and transactions as discussed at 4.1 above, IAS 34 requires an entity to include the following information in the notes to its interim financial statements if not disclosed elsewhere in the interim financial report: *[IAS 34.16A]*

(a) a statement that the same accounting policies and methods of computation are followed in the interim financial statements as in the most recent annual financial statements or, if those policies or methods have changed, a description of the nature and effect of the change;

(b) explanatory comments about the seasonality or cyclicality of interim operations;

(c) the nature and amount of items affecting assets, liabilities, equity, net income, or cash flows that are unusual because of their nature, size, or incidence;

(d) the nature and amount of changes in estimates of amounts reported in prior interim periods of the current year or changes in estimates of amounts reported in prior years;

(e) issues, repurchases, and repayments of debt and equity securities;

(f) dividends paid (aggregate or per share) separately for ordinary shares and other shares;

(g) certain segment disclosures required by IFRS 8 – *Operating Segments* – as discussed at 4.4 below;

(h) events after the interim period that are not reflected in the financial statements for the interim period;

(i) the effect of changes in the composition of the entity during the interim period, including business combinations, obtaining or losing control of subsidiaries and long-term investments, restructurings, and discontinued operations. For business combinations, the entity should disclose the information required under IFRS 3 – *Business Combinations* (see Chapter 9 at 16); and

(j) for financial instruments, certain fair value disclosures required by IFRS 7 – *Financial Instruments: Disclosures* – and IFRS 13 – *Fair Value Measurement* – as discussed at 4.5 below.

This information is normally reported on a financial year-to-date basis (see 8 below). *[IAS 34.16A]*. However, the requirement in item (i) above for disclosures of business combinations applies not only for those effected during the current interim period, but also to business combinations after the reporting period but before the interim financial report is authorised for issue. *[IFRS 3.59(b), IFRS 3.B66]*. An entity is not required to provide all of the disclosures for business combinations after the reporting period, if the accounting for the business combination is incomplete as at the date on which the financial statements are authorised for issue. In this case, the entity should state which disclosures cannot be made and the reasons why they cannot be made. *[IFRS 3.B66]*.

IFRS 3 requires disclosures in aggregate for business combinations effected during the reporting period that are individually immaterial. *[IFRS 3.B65]*. However, materiality is assessed for the interim period, which implies that IFRS 3 may require more detailed disclosures on business combinations that are material to an interim period even if they could be aggregated for disclosure purposes in the annual financial statements.

If an entity has operations that are discontinued or disposed of during an interim period, these operations should be presented separately in the condensed interim statement of comprehensive income following the principles set out in IFRS 5 – *Non-current Assets Held for Sale and Discontinued Operations*. In addition if an entity has non-current assets or a disposal group classified as held for sale or distribution at the end of the interim reporting period, then these should be measured in accordance with the requirements of IFRS 5 and presented separately from other assets and liabilities in the condensed interim statement of financial position.

An entity contemplating a significant restructuring that will have an impact on its composition should follow the guidance in IAS 37 – *Provisions, Contingent Liabilities and Contingent Assets* – for the recognition of any restructuring cost, *[IAS 37.71]*, and IAS 19 – *Employee Benefits* – for termination benefits. *[IAS 19.165(b)]*. In subsequent interim periods any significant changes to provisions will require disclosure. *[IAS 34.15B(c)]*.

In summary, the 'minimum' disclosures required under IFRSs for interim financial reporting are extensive and more onerous than the minimum requirements of many securities markets and regulators. For example, the disclosures are significant for business combinations, segments, and the recognition and reversal of impairments of assets.

4.2.1 Location of the specified disclosures in an interim financial report

IAS 34 defines an 'interim financial report' as 'a financial report containing either a complete set of financial statements... or a set of condensed financial statements... for an interim period.' *[IAS 34.4]*. Therefore, since an interim financial report *contains* the interim financial statements, it is clear that these are two different concepts. Accordingly, an entity is not required to disclose the information listed at 4.2 above in the interim financial statements themselves (but rather, might include the disclosures in the management commentary), as long as the information is included in another part of the interim financial report. *[IAS 34.16A]*.

This begs the question about the delineation of the interim financial statements within the interim financial report. This is an issue currently being considered by the Interpretations Committee and the IASB. While at the time of writing there is no intention to revise the definition of an interim financial report, the need has been recognised for users of the interim financial report to be made aware when information required by the Standard is presented outside the perimeter of the condensed financial statements. In May 2013, the IASB tentatively agreed with the Interpretation Committee's recommendation that paragraph 16A is amended to clarify the meaning of disclosure 'elsewhere in the interim financial report' and to require the inclusion of a cross-reference from the interim financial statements to the location of this information.[3]

In our view, such cross-referencing is beneficial in that it assists users in confirming that the information given in the condensed financial statements is complete. We therefore believe that under the current Standard cross-referencing represents a good practice. An entity should also consider whether cross-referencing may be appropriate or required under local regulations governing the publication of interim financial information.

As discussed at 4.1 above, notwithstanding the fact that the Standard only specifies that the information required about significant events and transactions is given in the entity's interim financial report, *[IAS 34.15A]*, we believe that a similar practice of cross-referencing would be beneficial when the required information is given outside the interim financial statements.

4.3 Illustrative examples of disclosures

The extracts below show examples of disclosures required by IAS 34.

4.3.1 Inventory write-down and reversals

In the extract below, BP discloses write downs of its inventories and reversals in the current and corresponding periods. *[IAS 34.15B(a)]*.

Extract 37.2: BP p.l.c. (Group results; Second quarter and half year 2012)

Notes [extract]

8. Inventory valuation

A provision of $152 million was held at 31 December 2011 to write inventories down to their net realizable value. The net movement in the provision during the second quarter 2012 was an increase of $398 million (first quarter 2012 was a decrease of $38 million and second quarter 2011 was an increase of $381 million). The net movement in the provision in the half year 2012 was an increase of $360 million, compared with an increase of $397 million for the half year 2011.

4.3.2 Impairment

In Extract 37.3 below, as part of its note on intangible assets, Roche discloses the impairment charges on its intangible assets during the reporting period and provides a breakdown by division and further background to those impairments. *[IAS 34.15B(b)].*

Extract 37.3: Roche Group (Half-Year Report, 2013)

Notes to the Roche Group Interim Consolidated Financial Statements [extract]

10. Intangible assets [extract]

Intangible asset impairment charges – 2013 [extract]

Pharmaceuticals Division. Impairment charges totalling 268 million Swiss francs were recorded which related to:

- A portfolio reassessment within the hepatitis C virus (HCV) franchise (235 million Swiss francs). The assets concerned, which were not yet being amortised, were written down to their recoverable value of 222 million Swiss francs;
- A decision to stop two collaboration projects with alliance partners (26 million Swiss francs). The assets concerned, which were being amortised, were fully written down; and
- A decision to stop development of one compound with an alliance partner (7 million Swiss francs). The asset concerned, which was not yet being amortised, was fully written down.

Diagnostic Division. [...].

4.3.3 Reversal of restructuring provisions

Included in various items, in the below extract, that have impacted net operating income of Continental AG, are reversals of restructuring costs. *[IAS 34.15B(c)].*

Extract 37.4: Continental AG (Half-Year Financial Report as of June 30, 2012)

Corporate Management Report [extract]

Earnings Position [extract]

Special effects in the first half of 2012 [extract]

In the Interior division, special effects from the reversal of restructuring provisions no longer required had a positive impact totaling €6.5 million in the first half of 2012.

4.3.4 *Acquisition and disposal of property, plant and equipment*

In Extract 37.5 below, Wilmington meets the requirement to disclose additions and disposals of items of property, plant and equipment in the interim period *[IAS 34.15B(d)]* in a note reconciling the movements, in aggregate, in property, plant and equipment; intangible assets; and goodwill. In addition, Wilmington provides information about movements in the comparative periods (not reproduced here).

Extract 37.5: Wilmington Group plc (Interim results for the six months ended 31 December 2012)

Notes to the Financial Information [extract]

14. Property, plant and equipment, intangible assets and goodwill [extract]

	Property, plant and equipment £'000	Intangible assets £'000	Goodwill £'000
At 1 July 2011 (audited)	7,776	36,216	74,681
[...]			
Closing net book amount as at 30 June 2012 (audited)	6,772	31,522	74,593
Additions	506	506	–
Acquisitions	–	–	–
Disposals	(12)	(22)	–
Exchange translation differences	4	–	–
Depreciation of property, plant and equipment	(515)	–	–
Amortisation of publishing rights, titles and benefits	–	(2,803)	–
Amortisation of computer software	–	(317)	–
Amortisation of freehold property	(325)	–	–
Change in provisions for the future purchase of non-controlling interests	–	–	(101)
Movement in offset of provisions for future purchase of non-controlling interests	–	–	13
Closing net book amount as at 31 December 2012 (unaudited)	6,430	28,886	74,505

4.3.5 *Capital commitments*

In a brief descriptive note, Lufthansa discloses its commitments for capital expenditure. *[IAS 34.15B(e)]*.

Extract 37.6: Lufthansa AG (2nd Interim report January - June 2013)

Interim financial statements [extract]

Notes [extract]

4 Contingencies and events after the balance sheet date [extract]

[...] At the end of June 2013, there were order commitments of EUR 9.4bn for capital expenditure on property, plant and equipment and intangible assets. As of 31 December 2012, the order commitments came to EUR 5.7bn. [...]

4.3.6 Litigation settlements

UBS provides details about significant litigation in its interim report. The extract below illustrates its disclosure about related settlements. *[IAS 34.15B(f)]*.

Extract 37.7: UBS AG (Second quarter 2013 report)

Notes to the Financial Statements [extract]
Note 17 Provisions and contingent liabilities [extract]
b) Litigation, regulatory and similar matters [extract]

10. LIBOR and other benchmark rates

Numerous government agencies, including the SEC, the US Commodity Futures Trading Commission (CFTC), the US Department of Justice (DOJ), the UK Financial Conduct Authority (FCA) [...] have conducted or are continuing to conduct investigations regarding submissions with respect to British Bankers' Association LIBOR (London Interbank Offered Rate) and other benchmark rates, including HIBOR (Hong Kong Interbank Offered Rate) and ISDAFIX. These investigations focus on whether there were improper attempts by UBS (among others), either acting on our own or together with others, to manipulate LIBOR and other benchmark rates at certain times. [...]

In 2012, UBS reached settlements with the FSA, the CFTC and the Criminal Division of the DOJ in connection with their investigations of benchmark interest rates. At the same time FINMA issued an order concluding its formal proceedings with respect to UBS relating to benchmark interest rates. UBS will pay a total of approximately CHF 1.4 billion in fines and disgorgement - including GBP 160 million in fines to the FSA, USD 700 million in fines to the CFTC, and CHF 59 million in disgorgement to FINMA. Under a non-prosecution agreement (NPA) that UBS entered into with the DOJ, UBS has agreed to pay a fine of USD 500 million. [...]

4.3.7 Correction of prior period errors

In Extract 37.8 below, Zurich Insurance provides disclosures around restatement of prior period financial statements due to errors, which they believe are material to the half-year interim financial statements of 2012. *[IAS 34.15B(g)]*.

Extract 37.8: Zurich Insurance Group Limited (Half Year Report 2012)

Consolidated financial statements (unaudited) [extract]

1. Basis of presentation [extract]

Restatements [extract]

In the Group's General Insurance business in Germany, prior year results were misstated for a period of time due to some errors in adjustments between local GAAP and IFRS. This resulted in incorrect reserves for losses, unearned premium reserves and deferred acquisition costs for some specific products. The errors identified by management have been restated and resulted in an increase in net income after taxes of USD 6 million and in business operating profit of USD 8 million for the six months ended June 30, 2011. The impact on various line items for the six months ended June 30, 2011 in the consolidated financial statements is set out in table 1.4. Consolidated income statements, consolidated balance sheets, consolidated statements of cash flows, consolidated statements of changes in equity and notes 4, 6, 7, 10, 12 and 15 have been restated accordingly. [...]

4.3.8 Changes in circumstances affecting fair values

In their half yearly interim report for 2010, HSBC provides a brief update on the market turmoil and then describes its impact, quantifying financial effect, on fair value of their financial instruments. *[IAS 34.15B(h)].*

Extract 37.9: HSBC Holdings plc (Interim Report 2010)

Interim Management Report: Impact of Market Turmoil [extract]

Background and disclosure policy [extract]

Following the market turmoil which began in 2007, there was a modest recovery in the risk appetite of investors in 2009. The first quarter of 2010 saw renewed uncertainty regarding the future growth prospects of the global economy, however, and concerns over sovereign credit risk that began in Greece and extended to other obligors, particularly in Southern Europe. As a result, the second quarter of 2010 saw significant falls in the prices of many assets perceived to be of higher risk, although some stability was regained with the announcement of a package of measures by the EU and the International Monetary Fund.

Widespread downgrading of securitised assets continued in the first half of 2010 as rating agencies changed their rating methodologies in response to the new circumstances. Although these downgrades were largely expected and did not affect management's loss estimates, for those institutions subject to the Basel II framework, which ties capital requirements to external credit ratings, the appetite for securitised assets remained limited regardless of the actual level of expected loss on the securities...

...Financial instruments which were most affected by the market turmoil include exposures to direct lending which are held at fair value through profit or loss, or are classified as available for sale and are also held at fair value. Financial instruments included in these categories comprise asset-backed securities ('ABS's), including mortgage-backed securities ('MBS's) and collateralised debt obligations ('CDO's), exposures to and contingent claims on monoline insurers ('monolines') in respect of structured credit activities and leveraged finance transactions originated for distribution...

Financial effect of market turmoil

The write-downs incurred by the Group for the last three half-year periods on ABSs, trading loans held for securitisation, leveraged finance transactions and the movement in fair values on available-for-sale ABSs taken to equity, plus impairment losses on specific exposures to banks, are summarised in the following table. Virtually all of these effects were recorded in Global Banking and Markets. Further analyses of the write-downs taken to the income statement by Global Banking and Markets and the net carrying amounts of the positions that generated these write-downs are shown in the succeeding table:

Financial effect of market turmoil on HSBC

	Half-year to		
	30 June 2010	30 June 2009	31 December 2009
	US$bn	US$bn	US$bn
(Write-downs)/write-backs taken to income statement	0.1	(1.3)	(0.6)
Net movement on available-for-sale reserve on ABSs in the period	4.1	1.2	5.3
Closing balance of available-for-sale reserve relating to ABSs	(8.1)	(17.5)	(12.2)

Global Banking and Markets write-downs/(write-backs) taken to the income statement and carrying amounts

	Write-downs/(write-backs) during half-year to			Carrying amount at		
	30 June 2010	30 June 2009	31 December 2009	**30 June 2010**	30 June 2009	31 December 2009
	US$m	US$m	US$m	**US$m**	US$m	US$m
Sub-prime mortgage-related assets						
– loan securitisation	**(49)**	156	80	**478**	943	758
– credit trading	**(32)**	83	17	**146**	303	282
Other ABSs	**(125)**	103	(196)	**959**	1,376	990
Impairments on reclassified assets	**(25)**	160	3	**11,774**	16,308	15,612
Derivative exposure to monoclines						
– investment grade counterparts	**(6)**	25	(78)	**828**	1,593	897
– Non-investment grade counterparts	**(117)**	241	45	**276**	510	408
Leveraged finance loans[4]	**(30)**	(11)	(120)	**154**	285	196
Other credit related items	**(3)**	5	(19)	**25**	116	61
Available-for-sale impairments and other non-trading related items	**256**	564	833			
	(131)	1,326	565			

4 The carrying amount includes funded loans plus the net exposure to unfunded leveraged finance commitments, held within fair value through profit or loss.

4.3.9 Default or breach of loan covenants not remedied before the end of interim period

In Extract 37.10 below, Develica discusses breaches of certain loan covenants. *[IAS 34.15B(i)]*. In view of such defaults that have not been remedied by the end of the reporting period, Develica goes on to explain why the interim financial statements have been prepared on a going concern basis.

Extract 37.10: Develica Deutschland Limited (Interim Report 2009)

Notes to the Consolidated Financial Statements for the period 1 April 2009 to 30 September 2009 [extract]

2 Basis of preparation [extract]

(c) Fundamental accounting concept [extract]

The current economic climate has resulted in a global trend of declining property values, which results in the Group being exposed to increased risks against covenant breaches set out in the Group's debt facilities.

The 30 September 2009 portfolio valuation indicates that the Loan-to-Value ("LTV") ratio of the loans classified as current liabilities in the consolidated balance sheet would, if tested by the debt providers as set out in the facilities agreement, exceed their respective LTV covenants.

Loan interest and amortisation continues to be well serviced through strong rental income. Due to tenant related difficulties, there is one loan facility of €51.5m in which the Interest Cover Ratio ("ICR") covenant is not being met. The Group is currently in ongoing discussions with the relevant debt provider to remedy the breach. ICR covenants continue to be met on the remaining facilities.

Excluding the amended Citibank International PLC ("Citi") facilities, the Group's borrowing arrangements include covenants that require maintenance of LTV ratios ranging between 85% and 95% with a weighted average of 90.9%.

As reported in the Annual Report, the Group has been notified of two LTV breaches during the six month period relating to €116.1m of the Group's loan facilities. In each case, the lender has requested a valuation entitled under the rights of the respective loan facility agreements. The Group continues to have positive discussions with the lender to seek to remedy these breaches. No further notifications of breach have been served on the Company by its other lenders although we continue in discussion with these lenders regarding the remaining loan facilities.

The strong cash flow generated from a diverse range of quality tenants enables the Group to service these financing obligations. The Group has entered into hedging instruments across the entire portfolio which fix the ongoing interest obligations and also reduce the ongoing debt exposure.

In all cases where an actual or potential breach of any loan has/could arise, the Company has engaged in discussions with the Company's debt providers to work together in reaching a satisfactory conclusion for all parties. The Company has already reached a successful agreement on amending five facilities through Citi and the Directors are hopeful that, through maintaining close links and dialogue with the remaining debt providers, it will be able to implement similar arrangements across the entire portfolio. In the event that a breach occurs resulting in an event of default, and the Group is unable to reach a resolution with the relevant debt provider, then the only recourse available to the debt provider are the assets secured against the given loan at the subsidiary level and not the Group's assets.

As the debt facilities and related interest swaps are ring-fenced and the Company has sufficient cash and other resources, the Directors do not consider that the risk of breaching LTV covenants will impact the ability of the Group to continue to trade as a going concern. Accordingly the financial statements have been prepared on a going concern basis.

4.3.10 Related party transactions

In Extract 37.11 below, Deutsche Bank discloses related party transactions. *[IAS 34.15B(j)]*.

Extract 37.11: Deutsche Bank AG (Interim Report as of June 30, 2013)

Other Financial Information (unaudited) [extract]

Related Party Transactions [extract]

Transactions with related parties are made in the ordinary course of business and on substantially the same terms, including interest rates and collateral, as those prevailing for comparable transactions with other parties.

Transactions with Key Management Personnel

Key management personnel are those persons having authority and responsibility for planning, directing and controlling the activities of Deutsche Bank Group, directly or indirectly. The Group considers the members of the Management Board as currently mandated and the Supervisory Board of the parent company to constitute key management personnel for purposes of IAS 24. Among the Group's transactions with key management personnel as of June 30, 2013, were loans and commitments of €4 million and deposits of €13 million. As of December 31, 2012, there were loans and commitments of €7 million and deposits of €13 million among the Group's transactions with key management personnel. In addition, the Group provides banking services, such as payment and account services as well as investment advice, to key management personnel and their close family members.

For further details about key management changes in the current quarter, please refer to the section Supervisory Board in the Management Report.

Transactions with Subsidiaries, Associates and Joint Ventures

Transactions between Deutsche Bank AG and its subsidiaries meet the definition of related party transactions. If these transactions are eliminated on consolidation, they are not disclosed as related party transactions. Transactions between the Group and its associated companies and joint ventures and their respective subsidiaries also qualify as related party transactions.

Loans issued and guarantees granted

in € m.	Associated companies and other related parties Jun 30, 2013	Dec 31, 2012
Loans outstanding, beginning of period	**918**	**5,151**
Loans issued during the period	460	436
Loan repayments during the period	643	4,610[1]
Changes in the group of consolidated companies	(386)[2]	0
Exchange rate changes/other	4	(58)
Loans outstanding, end of period[3]	**353**	**918**
Other credit risk related transactions:		
Allowance for loan losses	4	47
Provision for loan losses	0	47
Guarantees and commitments	55	55

1 The increase in repayments during 2012 is mainly related to the sale of a restructured loan transaction in Europe.

2 In the second quarter of 2013, some entities were fully consolidated for the first time, which were formerly classified as equity method investments. Therefore loans made to these investments were eliminated on consolidation. Consequently related provisions and allowance for loan losses reduced at the same time.

3 Loans past due were €9 million as of June 30, 2013, and €3 million as of December 31, 2012.

Deposits received

in € m.	Associated companies and other related parties Jun 30, 2013	Dec 31, 2012
Deposits, beginning of period	**245**	**247**
Deposits received during the period	46	284
Deposits repaid during the period	127	284
Changes in the group of consolidated companies	(10)	(3)
Exchange rate changes/other	0	1
Deposits, end of period	**154**	**245**

Other transactions

Trading assets and positive market values from derivative financial transactions with associated companies amounted to €390 million as of June 30, 2013, and €110 million as of December 31, 2012. Trading liabilities and negative market values from derivative financial transactions with associated companies amounted to €2 million as of June 30, 2013, and €4 million as of December 31, 2012.

Transactions with Pension Plans

The Group has business relationships with a number of its pension plans pursuant to which it provides financial services to these plans, including investment management. Pension funds may hold or trade Deutsche Bank AG shares or securities. As of June 30, 2013, transactions with these plans were not material for the Group.

4.3.11 Transfers between different levels of fair value hierarchy

Detailed reconciliation is provided by HSBC in the below extract relating to fair value measurements in level 3 of the fair value hierarchy. The reconciliation, among other items, includes transfer of items in and out of level 3. *[IAS 34.15B(k)]*. The same level of detail is provided for the comparative period from 1 July 2012 to December 2012.

Extract 37.12: HSBC Holdings plc (Interim Report 2013)

Notes on the Financial Statements (unaudited) (continued) [extract]

8 – Fair values of financial instruments carried at fair value [extract]

The basis for determining the fair value of the financial instruments in the table above is explained on page 442 of the *Annual Report and Accounts 2012.*

Movement in Level 3 financial instruments

	Assets				Liabilities		
	Available for sale US$m	Held for trading US$m	Designated at fair value through profit or loss US$m	Derivatives US$m	Held for trading US$m	Designated at fair value through profit or loss US$m	Derivatives US$m
At 1 January 2013	8,511	4,378	413	3,059	7,470	–	3,005
Total gains/(losses) recognised in profit or loss	37	48	23	(25)	(844)	–	875
– trading income excluding net interest income	–	48	–	(25)	(844)	–	875
– net income/(expense) from other financial instruments designated at fair value	–	–	23	–	–	–	–
– gains less losses from financial investments	23	–	–	–	–	–	–
– loan impairment charges and other credit risk provisions	14	–	–	–	–	–	–
Total gains/(losses) recognised in other comprehensive income[1]	60	(26)	–	(105)	(157)	–	(109)
– available for sale investments: fair value gains/(losses)	295	–	–	–	–	–	–
– exchange differences	(235)	(26)	–	(105)	(157)	–	(109)
Purchases	1,112	486	21	–	–	–	–
New issuances	–	–	–	–	2,017	–	–
Sales	(345)	(1,689)	(4)	–	(497)	–	–
Settlements	(266)	(177)	(4)	(283)	(559)	–	(1,114)
Transfers out	(1,009)	(80)	(30)	(43)	(565)	–	(49)
Transfers in	860	104	52	57	169	–	35
At 30 June 2013	8,960	3,044	471	2,660	7,034	–	2,643

[...]

1 Included in 'Available-for-sale investments: fair value gains/(losses)' and 'Exchange differences' in the consolidated statement of comprehensive income.

Transfers between levels of the fair value hierarchy are deemed to occur at the end of the reporting period.

Purchases of Level 3 available-for-sale assets reflect acquisition of certain less liquid emerging market government and corporate debt. Transfers out of Level 3 available-for-sale securities increased confidence in the pricing of certain ABS assets. Sales of Level 3 trading assets reflect the unwind of certain legacy monocline and structured credit exposures. New issuances of trading liabilities reflect structured note issuances, predominantly equity-linked notes. [...]

4.3.12 Changes in classification of financial assets arising from changes in use

In the Extract below, Deutsche Bank discloses changes in classification of certain financial assets due to a change in purpose or use. *[IAS 34.15B(l)].*

Extract 37.13: Deutsche Bank AG (Interim Report as of June 30, 2009)

Information on the Balance Sheet (unaudited) [extract]

Amendments to IAS 39 and IFRS 7, "Reclassification of Financial Assets" [extract]

During the second half of 2008 and the first quarter of 2009 the Group reclassified certain trading assets and financial assets available for sale to loans and receivables. No reclassifications were made during the second quarter of 2009.

The Group identified assets, eligible under the amendments, for which at the reclassification date it had a clear change of intent and ability to hold for the foreseeable future rather than to exit or trade in the short term. The reclassifications were made at the fair value of the assets at the reclassification date. The disclosures below detail the impact of the reclassifications to the Group.

The following table shows the carrying values and fair values of assets reclassified in 2008 and 2009.

	Carrying value at	June 30, 2009	
in €m.	reclassification date	Carrying value	Fair value
Assets reclassified in 2008:			
Trading assets reclassified to loans	23,633	22,501	18,914
Financial assets available for sale reclassified to loans	11,354	10,335	8,245
Total financial assets reclassified to loans[1]	**34,987**	**32,836**	**27,159**
Assets reclassified in 2009:			
Trading assets reclassified to loans	2,961	3,001	2,724
Trading assets reclassified to loans	**2,961**	**3,001**	**2,724**

1 The decline of the carrying value since reclassification was mainly attributable to repayments, credit loss provisions and foreign exchange movements.

4.3.13 Contingent liabilities

In the Extract below, Skanska discloses changes in its contingent liabilities during the interim period as a footnote to its statement of financial position. *[IAS 34.15B(m)].*

Extract 37.14: Arkema S.A. (Half-Year Report, 2013)

Condensed consolidated interim financial statements at 30 June 2013 [extract]

12 Liabilities and contingent liabilities

Liabilities and contingent liabilities are described in note C21 of the consolidated financial statements at 31 December 2012. This note describes the liabilities and contingent liabilities with an actual or potential significant effect on the Group's consolidated financial statements.

- Kem One

ARKEMA sold its vinyls activities, grouped into the Kem One Group, to the Klesch Group which specializes in development of industrial commodity businesses, with effect from 1 July 2012.

On 27 March 2013, the Lyon commercial court began insolvency proceedings concerning Kem One, with continuation of its business for a six-month observation period. ARKEMA's contribution to finances for the observation period amounts to €68.7 million. Part of this amount corresponds to the payment of contractual sale price adjustments for which provisions were booked in the financial statements at 31 December 2012. The rest corresponds to the provision by ARKEMA to Kem One of certain warranties for third parties throughout the observation period. ARKEMA's exposure in relation to Kem One is estimated at a total €125 million, and ARKEMA has booked an exceptional expense of an equivalent amount in its financial statements.

Klesch has initiated arbitration proceedings against ARKEMA. The Company does not consider it necessary to establish a provision.

4.3.14 Accounting policies and methods of computation

In the Extract below, Roche explains how the accounting polices used in the interim report compare to the most recent annual financial statements, and discloses changes in the current period. Using the guidance in IAS 8 – *Accounting Policies, Changes in Accounting Estimates and Errors,* Roche provides comprehensive quantitative information for the most significant change. In addition to the table illustrated below on the effect of the application of IAS 19 (2011) on the consolidated income statement for the year ended 31 December 2012, similar tables, not included here, are provided for the effects on:

- the consolidated income statement for the six months ended 30 June 2012;
- the statement of comprehensive income for the year ended December 31, 2012 and the six months ended June 2013; and
- selected items in the balance sheet as of December 31, 2012 and as of June 30, 2013. *[IAS 34.16A(a)].*

Extract 37.15: Roche Holding Ltd (Half-Year Report 2013)

Notes to the Roche Group Interim Consolidated Financial Statements [extract]

1. Accounting policies [extract]

Significant accounting policies [extract]

Except as described below, the accounting policies applied in these Interim Financial Statements are the same as those applied in the Annual Financial Statements. The following changes in accounting policies will be reflected in the Group's Consolidated Financial Statements for the year ended 31 December 2013.

Changes in accounting policies [extract]

The Group has adopted the following new standards and amendments to standards, including any consequential amendments to other standards, with a date of initial application of 1 January 2013.

- IAS 19 (revised) 'Employee Benefits'
- IFRS 10 'Consolidated Financial Statements'
- IFRS 11 'Joint Arrangements' [...]

With the exception of the revisions to IAS 19, these do not have a material impact on the Group's overall results and financial position. The nature and the effects of the changes most relevant to the Group's financial statements are explained below.

Pensions and other post-employment benefits

As a result of IAS 19 (revised) the Group amended its accounting policy with respect to the basis for determining the income or expense related to defined benefit plans and restated the 2012 results retrospectively. The main changes are as follows:

- The revised standard eliminated the option to defer the recognition of actuarial gains and losses from defined benefit plans, known as the 'corridor method'. The Group did not apply this option, but rather uses the option to recognise such gains and losses directly in other comprehensive income. The option currently applied by the Group is the requirement under the revised standard and therefore this change had no impact on the Group's financial statements.

- Net interest on the net defined benefit liability comprises of interest income on plan assets, interest cost on the defined benefit obligation and interest on the effect of the limit on the recognition of pension assets. The net interest is calculated using the same discount rate that is used in calculating the defined benefit obligation, applied to the net defined liability at the start of the period, taking account of any changes from contribution or benefit payments. Previously, expected income on plan assets was based on the estimated long-term rate of the underlying assets in the various plans. The impact on the restated 2012 result was a reduction in net financial income of 164 million Swiss francs for the year ended 31 December 2012 and a reduction of 81 million Swiss francs for the six months ended 30 June 2012. The ongoing impact for 2013 and beyond is expected to be of a similar magnitude. There was no impact on the Group's operating income or net assets from this change.
- Past service costs are now recognised immediately in the income statement in the period of a plan amendment. [...] The impact of this change was an increase in the Group's net assets by 22 million Swiss francs at 31 December 2012 and an increase of 24 million Swiss francs at 30 June 2012.

Following the revision to IAS 19 disclosed above the Group has also made a presentational change to the income statement, which has renamed 'Financial income' to 'Other financial income (expense)' and moved this caption below 'Financing costs'.

The reconciliations between the results published previously in 2012 (using the previous accounting policy) and the restated amounts which are reported as comparatives in 2013 (using the revised accounting policy) are presented below.

Restated Roche Group consolidated income statement in millions of CHF [extract]

	Year ended 31 December 2012		
	As originally published	Application of IAS 19(revised)	Restated
Operating profit	**14,125**	–	**14,125**
Associates	–	–	–
Financing costs	(2,273)	350	(1,923)
Other financial income (expense)	471	(514)	(43)
Profit before taxes	**12,323**	**(164)**	**12,159**
Income taxes	(2,550)	51	(2,499)
Net income	**9,773**	**(113)**	**9,660**
Attributable to			
– Roche shareholders	9,539	(112)	9.427
– Non-controlling interests	234	(1)	233
Earnings per share and non-voting equity security			
Basic (CHF)	11.25	(0.13)	11.12
Diluted (CHF)	11.16	(0.13)	11.03

[...]

4.3.15 Seasonality or cyclicality of operations

Extract 37.16 below shows how Lancashire Holdings discloses the effects of seasonality in its interim report. *[IAS 34.16A(b)].*

Extract 37.16: Lancashire Holdings Limited (six months ended 30 June 2012)

Risk and other disclosures [extract]

Seasonality of interim operations [extract]

The Group underwrites worldwide short-tail insurance and reinsurance contracts that transfer insurance risk, including risks exposed to both natural and man-made catastrophes. The Group's exposure in connection with insurance contracts is, in the event of insured losses, whether premiums will be sufficient to cover the loss payments and expenses. Insurance and reinsurance markets are cyclical and premium rates and terms and conditions vary by line of business depending on market conditions and the stage of the cycle. Market conditions are impacted by capacity and recent loss events, amongst other factors. The Group's underwriters assess likely losses using their experience and knowledge of past loss experience, industry trends and current circumstances. This allows them to estimate the premium sufficient to meet likely losses and expenses.

The Group bears exposure to large losses arising from non-seasonal natural catastrophes, such as earthquakes, and also from risk losses throughout the year and from war, terrorism and political risk losses. On certain lines of business the Group's most significant exposures to catastrophe losses is greater during the second half of the fiscal year. There is therefore potential for significantly greater volatility in earnings during that period. This is broadly in line with the most active period of the North American windstorm season which is typically June to November. The Group is also exposed to Japanese and European windstorm seasons which are typically June to November and November to March, respectively. The majority of the premiums for these lines of business are written during the first half of the fiscal year.

4.3.16 *Amounts that are unusual because of their nature, size or incidence*

Tomkins discloses the nature and effects of unusual items in Extract 37.17 below by identifying 'restructuring costs' and a 'gain on disposals and on the exit of businesses' not identified as discontinued operations. *[IAS 34.16A(c)].*

Extract 37.17: Tomkins plc (six months ended 28 June 2008)

CONSOLIDATED INCOME STATEMENT UNAUDITED [extract]

	6 months ended 28 June 2008 US$ million	6 months ended 30 June 2007 US$ million	Year ended 29 December 2007 US$ million
Continuing operations			
Sales	**2,927.0**	2,967.9	5,886.1
Cost of sales	**(2,118.4)**	(2,159.1)	(4,284.6)
Gross profit	**808.6**	808.8	1,601.5
Distribution costs	**(313.2)**	(290.3)	(578.4)
Administrative expenses	**(432.1)**	(255.2)	(501.4)
Restructuring costs	**(17.0)**	(3.2)	(27.6)
Gain on disposals and on the exit of businesses	**42.4**	64.3	91.4
Restructuring initiatives	**25.4**	61.1	63.8
Share of profit of associates	**0.5**	0.6	0.8
Operating profit	**89.2**	325.0	586.3

> **NOTES TO THE CONDENSED FINANCIAL STATEMENTS (UNAUDITED)** [extract]
>
> **4. RESTRUCTURING INITIATIVES** [extract]
>
> Restructuring costs recognised during the six months ended 28 June 2008 principally related to the rationalisation of production facilities in the Building Products businesses in the United States, the closure of Power Transmission's facility at Moncks Corner, South Carolina and the outsourcing of information technology services.
>
> During the six months ended 28 June 2008, the Group recognised a gain of US$42.4 million on the disposal of Stant Manufacturing, Inc. and Standard-Thomson Corporation.

4.3.17 Changes in estimates

In the Extract below, Telekom Austria Group discloses the nature and amounts of changes in estimates of amounts that resulted in a material effect on the current interim period. *[IAS 34.16A(d)]*.

> *Extract 37.18: Telekom Austria Group (Q1, 2009)*
>
> **Selected Explanatory Notes to the Consolidated Interim Financial Statement (unaudited)** [extract]
> **Segment Reporting** [extract]
>
> In 2009, the Company reduced estimated useful lives of certain technical and office equipment due to the rapid development of technological environment in the relevant areas. The change in estimate resulted in an increase of depreciation by EUR 0.9million in the Mobile Communication segment.

4.3.18 Issues, repurchases and repayments of debt and equity securities

Extract 37.19 below illustrates the disclosure of material changes in borrowings. *[IAS 34.16A(e)]*.

> *Extract 37.19: Electrolux (Q2, 2009)*
>
> **Interim report January – June 2009** [extract]
> **Financial Position** [extract]
> **Net borrowings** [extract]
>
> Net borrowings amounted to SEK 2,197m (5,217). The net debt/equity ratio was 0.13 (0.36). The equity/assets ratio was 27.1% (23.8).
>
> During the first half of 2009, SEK 1,632 of new long-term borrowings were raised. Long-term borrowings as of June 30, 2009, excluding long-term borrowings with maturities within 12 months, amounted to SEK 10,702m with average maturities of 4.3 years, compared to SEK 9,963m and 4.7 years by the end of 2008.
>
> During 2009 and 2010, long-term borrowings in the amount of approximately SEK 1,500m will mature. Liquid funds as of June 30, 2009, excluding a committed unused revolving credit facility of EUR 500m, amounted to SEK 12,886m.

4.3.19 Dividends paid for each class of share

In the Extract below, Roche discloses dividends paid during the interim period. *[IAS 34.16A(f)]*. In many cases this information may be evident from the disclosure of these amounts in the statement of cash flows.

Extract 37.20: Roche Group Limited (Half-year Report, 2010)

Notes to the Roche Group Interim Consolidated Financial Statements [extract]
Note 13 Equity [extract]
Dividends

On 2 March 2010 the shareholders approved the distribution of a dividend of 6.00 Swiss francs per share and non-voting equity security (2009: 5.00 Swiss francs) in respect of the 2009 business year. The distribution to holders of outstanding shares and non-voting equity securities totalled 5,144 million Swiss francs (2009: 4,300 million Swiss francs) and has been recorded against retained earnings in 2010.

4.3.20 Events after the interim reporting date

In the Extract below, Allianz Group reports a significant acquisition made after the interim period and determines that not all information required by IFRS 3 is available at the interim date. *[IAS 34.16A(h)]*.

Extract 37.21: Allianz Group (Half-Year Report, 2013)

Notes to the Condensed Consolidated Interim Financial Statements [extract]
3 – Consolidation [extract]
SIGNIFICANT ACQUISITIONS [extract]

Yapi Kredi Sigorta A.Ş. and Yapi Kredi Emeklilik A.Ş.

On 12 July 2013, the Allianz Group acquired Yapi Kredi Bank's 93.94% shareholding in the Turkish property-casualty insurance company Yapi Kredi Sigorta, including its life and pension insurance subsidiary Yapi Kredi Emeklilik. The transaction includes a 15 year exclusive distribution agreement with Yapi Kredi Bank. Yapi Kredi Bank retains a 20% stake in Yapi Kredi Emeklilik to support the long-term strategic partnership with Allianz. This transaction is consistent with the Allianz strategy to access growth through strategic relationships in high-growth insurance markets. The transaction was approved by the Turkish Competition Authority on 26 June 2013 and by the Republic of Turkey Prime Ministry Undersecretariat of Treasury on 5 July 2013.

The total gross consideration paid in cash to Yapi Kredi Bank amounted to €714 MN (TYL 1,791 MN), while net of proceeds received from the sale of the Yapi Kredi Emeklilik stake to Yapi Kredi Bank, the consideration to Yapi Kredi Bank amounted to €639 MN (TYL 1,603 MN).

At the time the condensed consolidated interim financial statements were authorized for issue, the reconciliation from local GAAP to IFRS, including the change in accounting for insurance and investment contracts, was not complete and as a result the purchase accounting for the business combination was not fully completed. Therefore, information about the total assets acquired and liabilities assumed as well as total revenues, net income and the impact on the respective consolidated figures for the Allianz Group were not available.

Effective 1 July 2013, the entities will be included in the condensed consolidated interim financial statements for the third quarter and first nine months of 2013. [...]

41 – Subsequent Events [extract]
ALLIANZ CLOSES YAPI KREDI TRANSACTION IN TURKEY

On 12 July 2013, Allianz completed the acquisition of Yapi Kredi Sigorta. For further information on the acquisition and the related mandatory tender offer, please refer to note 3 – Consolidation.

Although not a requirement under IAS 34, it is useful to disclose the date on which the interim financial statements are authorised for issue as it would help the users to better understand the context of any disclosure of events after the interim reporting date. *[IAS 10.17]*.

4.3.21 Changes in the composition of the entity

In the Extract below, Rolls-Royce discloses a change in the composition of its group during the interim period. This disclosure about the change in the nature of their interest in Tognum AG is accompanied by other disclosures required by IFRS 3 for business combinations, which are not included here. *[IAS 34.16A(i)].*

> *Extract 37.22: Rolls-Royce plc (Half-year Results 2013)*
>
> **Condensed consolidated financial statements** [extract]
> **12 Acquisitions and disposals** [extract]
>
> **Tognum**
>
> On 1 January 2013, conditions were fulfilled which gave the Group certain rights that result in Tognum AG being classified as a subsidiary and consolidated. Rolls-Royce and Daimler AG each hold 50% of the shares of Rolls-Royce Power Systems Holding GmbH (RRPSH), which itself held over 99% of the shares of Tognum AG. From 25 August 2011 to 31 December 2012 the Group's interest in Tognum was classified as a joint venture and equity accounted. Tognum is a premium supplier of engines, propulsion systems and components for Marine, Energy, Defence, and other industrial applications (often described as "off-highway" applications).
>
> Accordingly, Rolls-Royce's current joint venture interest in RRPSH has been reclassified as a subsidiary. The fair values of the identifiable assets and liabilities assumed are £1,339 million, giving rise to goodwill of £773 million, as set out in the table below. [...]

4.4 Segment information

If an entity is required to disclose segment information in its annual financial statements, certain segment disclosures are required in its interim financial report. IFRS 8 is discussed in more detail in Chapter 32.

An entity applying IFRS 8 in its annual financial statements should include the following information in its interim financial report about its reportable segments: *[IAS 34.16A(g)]*

(a) segment revenues from external customers (if included in the measure of segment profit or loss reviewed by or otherwise regularly provided to the chief operating decision maker);

(b) intersegment revenues (if included in the measure of segment profit or loss reviewed by or otherwise regularly provided to the chief operating decision maker);

(c) a measure of segment profit or loss;

(d) a measure of total assets and liabilities for a particular reportable segment if such amounts are regularly provided to the chief operating decision maker and if there has been a material change from the amount disclosed in the last annual financial statements for that reportable segment;

(e) a description of differences in the basis of segmentation or in the basis of measurement of segment profit or loss from the last annual financial statements;

(f) a reconciliation of the total profit or loss for reportable segments to the entity's profit or loss before income taxes and discontinued operations. However, if an entity allocates such items as income taxes to arrive at segment profit or loss, the reconciliation can be to the entity's profit or loss after those items. The entity should separately identify and describe all material reconciling items.

In extract 37.23 below, Daimler AG discloses segment revenues and segment profit or loss in its interim financial report for the second quarter of 2009. Presumably, information required by (d) above is not included because it is not applicable for the periods presented.

Extract 37.23: Daimler AG (Q2, 2009)

Notes to the Unaudited Interim Consolidated Financial Statements [extract]

11. Segment reporting

Segment information. At the beginning of 2009, the Group adjusted the presentation of its segment reporting. The business activities of Mercedes-Benz Vans and Daimler Buses, which were previously reported as part of Vans, Buses, Other, are presented separately. The other business activities of the Group which previously also formed part of Vans, Buses, Other and which primarily include the equity method investment in EADS are included in the column "Reconciliation" together with corporate items and eliminations of intersegment transactions. Prior-year figures have been adjusted accordingly. The Group's proportionate share in the results of Chrysler Holding as well as other Chrysler-related gains and losses (see Notes 2 and 4) are included in the reconciliation of total segments' EBIT to Group EBIT.

Segment information for the three-month periods ended June 30, 2009 and 2008 is as follows:

Amounts in millions of €	Mercedes -Benz Cars	Daimler Trucks	Mercedes -Benz Vans	Daimler Buses	Daimler Financial Services	Total segments	Reconc -iliation	Consol- idated
Three months ended June 30, 2009								
Revenue	**10,274**	**3,772**	**1,394**	**1,098**	**2,933**	**19,471**	**141**	**19,612**
Intersegment revenue	**294**	**445**	**87**	**5**	**175**	**1,006**	**(1,006)**	**–**
Total revenue	**10,568**	**4,217**	**1,481**	**1,103**	**3,108**	**20,477**	**(865)**	**19,612**
Segment profit (loss) (EBIT)	**(340)**	**(508)**	**(10)**	**49**	**79**	**(730)**	**(275)**	**(1,005)**

Amounts in millions of €	Mercedes -Benz Cars	Daimler Trucks	Mercedes -Benz Vans	Daimler Buses	Daimler Financial Services	Total segments	Reconc -iliation	Consol- idated
Three months ended June 30, 2008								
Revenue	12,470	6,848	2,412	1,319	2,754	25,803	202	26,005
Intersegment revenue	451	537	145	2	123	1,258	(1,258)	–
Total revenue	12,921	7,385	2,557	1,321	2,877	27,061	(1,056)	26,005
Segment profit (loss) (EBIT)	1,212	608	262	170	183	2,435	(382)	2,053

Segment information for the six-month periods ended June 30, 2009 and 2008 is as follows:

Amounts in millions of €	Mercedes -Benz Cars	Daimler Trucks	Mercedes -Benz Vans	Daimler Buses	Daimler Financial Services	Total segments	Reconc -iliation	Consol- idated
Six months ended June 30, 2009								
Revenue	**19,095**	**8,361**	**2,633**	**1,992**	**5,932**	**38,013**	**278**	**38,291**
Intersegment revenue	**540**	**774**	**139**	**15**	**326**	**1,794**	**(1,794)**	**–**
Total revenue	**19,635**	**9,135**	**2,772**	**2,007**	**6,258**	**39,807**	**(1,516)**	**38,291**
Segment profit (loss) (EBIT)	**(1,463)**	**(650)**	**(101)**	**114**	**(88)**	**(2,188)**	**(243)**	**(2,431)**

Amounts in millions of €	Mercedes -Benz Cars	Daimler Trucks	Mercedes -Benz Vans	Daimler Buses	Daimler Financial Services	Total segments	Reconc -iliation	Consol- idated
Six months ended June 30, 2008								
Revenue	24,727	12,539	4,654	2,229	5,448	49,597	406	50,003
Intersegment revenue	691	1,173	238	11	243	2,356	(2,356)	–
Total revenue	25,418	13,712	4,892	2,240	5,691	51,953	(1,950)	50,003
Segment profit (loss) (EBIT)	2,364	1,011	448	245	351	4,419	(390)	4,029

Reconciliation. Reconciliation of the total segments' profit (loss) (EBIT) to profit (loss) before income taxes is as follows:

The line item "Corporate items / Other" includes corporate items for which headquarters is responsible. Transactions between the segments are eliminated in the reconciliation.

Amounts in millions of €	Three months ended June 30, 2009	2008	Six months ended June 30, 2009	2008
Total segments' profit (loss) (EBIT)	**(730)**	2,435	**(2,188)**	4,419
Equity method result EADS[1]	**15**	67	**98**	191
Equity method result Chrysler	**–**	(356)	**–**	(696)
Corporate items/Other	**(408)**	(76)	**(480)**	131
Eliminations	**118**	(17)	**139**	(16)
Group EBIT	**(1,005)**	2,053	**(2,431)**	4,029
Interest income (expense), net	**(207)**	24	**(412)**	57
Profit (loss) before income taxes	**(1,212)**	2,077	**(2,843)**	4,086

1 The amounts for 2008 also include gains in connection with the transfer of equity interests in EADS.

4.5 Fair value disclosures for financial instruments

IAS 34 requires that an entity should include the following in its interim financial report in relation to financial instruments: *[IAS 34.16A(j)]*:

(a) disclosures to help users of the financial statements assess the valuation techniques and inputs used to develop the fair value measurements used for financial instruments in the statement of financial position and, for financial instruments measured using unobservable inputs, the effect of those measurements on profit or loss or other comprehensive income in the period *[IFRS 13.91]* (see Chapter 14 at 20.1);

(b) certain disclosures for fair value measurements that are *recognised* in the statement of financial position after initial recognition, including the carrying amount, categorisation within the fair value hierarchy and additional disclosures for those not classified as level 1 *[IFRS 13.93]* (see Chapter 14 at 20.3);

(c) accounting policy disclosures relating to how the entity has determined appropriate classes of financial assets and liabilities for which information about fair value measurement is given; how it determined when transfers between levels of the fair value hierarchy have occurred; and how the entity has measured any groups of financial assets and liabilities managed on the basis of its net exposure *[IFRS 13.94-96]* (see Chapter 14 at 20.1.2.A and 2);

(d) disclosures regarding liabilities measured at fair value and issued with an inseparable third-party credit enhancement *[IFRS 13.98]* (see Chapter 14 at 20.5); and

(e) disclosures about fair value required by IFRS 7, including for each class of financial asset and financial liability a comparison between fair value and carrying amount, unless the carrying amount is a reasonable approximation of the fair value; *[IFRS 7.25, 26, 29a]*; and disclosures relating to the deferral and subsequent recognition of gains and losses arising when fair value is determined using unobservable inputs or when the fair value cannot be determined reliably *[IFRS 7.28, 7.29b, 30]* (see Chapter 50 at 4.5).

Quantitative disclosures would normally be given in a tabular format unless another format is more appropriate. *[IFRS 13.99]*. In respect of (a) above, the entity should assess whether the disclosures are sufficient to meet the disclosure objectives of IFRS 13. This requires judgements to be made about the level of detail; how much emphasis to place on each of the various requirements; and level of aggregation or disaggregation. If necessary, additional information should be given in order to meet those objectives *[IFRS 13.92]* (see Chapter 16 at 20.1).

In our view, the inclusion of this disclosure requirement among the items required by the Standard to be given 'in addition to disclosing significant events and transactions' *[IAS 34.16A]* distinguishes it from the items listed at 4.1 above, which are disclosed to update information presented in the most recent annual financial report. *[IAS 34.15]*. Therefore, disclosure of the above information is required for each interim reporting period, subject only to a materiality assessment in relation to that interim report, i.e. an entity could consider it unnecessary to disclose the above information on the grounds that it is not relevant to an understanding of its financial position and performance in that specific interim period. *[IAS 34.25]*. In making that judgement care would need to be taken to ensure any omitted information would not make the interim financial report incomplete and therefore misleading.

4.6 Disclosure of compliance with IFRS

If an interim financial report complies with the requirements of IAS 34, this fact should be disclosed. Furthermore, an interim financial report should not be described as complying with IFRS unless it complies with all the requirements of International Financial Reporting Standards, *[IAS 34.19]*, a requirement similar to that found in IAS 1. *[IAS 1.16]*. Therefore, an entity would only provide a statement of compliance with IFRS (as opposed to IAS 34 alone) in its interim report if it prepared a complete set of interim financial statements.

Extract 37.24: BMW AG (Q1, 2012)

Notes to the Group Financial Statement to 31 March 2012 [extract]
Accounting Principles and Policies [extract]
1 Basis of preparation [extract]

The Group Financial Statements of BMW AG at 31 December 2011 were drawn up in accordance with International Financial Reporting Standards (IFRSs), as applicable in the EU. The Interim Group Financial Statements (Interim Report) at 31 March 2012, which have been prepared in accordance with International Accounting Standard (IAS) 34 (Interim Financial Reporting), have been drawn up using, in all material respects, the same accounting methods as those utilised in the 2011 Group Financial Statements. The BMW Group applies the option, available under IAS 34.8, of publishing condensed group financial statements. All Interpretations issued by the International Financial Reporting Interpretations Committee (IFRIC) which are mandatory at 31 March 2012, have also been applied. The Interim Report also complies with German Accounting Standard No. 16 (GAS 16) – Interim Financial Reporting – issued by the German Accounting Standards Committee e.V. (GASC).

When entities either choose or are required by local regulations to meet other requirements in addition to IAS 34, the statement of compliance can be more complicated. In the extract above, BMW simply adds a statement confirming its compliance with the specific German Accounting Standard on interim reporting. Additional complexity can arise when the entity seeks to meet the requirements of its (IFRS-based) local GAAP as well as IFRS as issued by the IASB. Extract 37.25 below shows how the dual listed BHP Billiton Group disclosed compliance with IFRS, Australian Accounting Standards and the requirements of the Financial Conduct Authority in the UK (formerly known as the Financial Services Authority).

Extract 37.25: BHP Billiton Group (six months ended 31 December 2011)

Notes to the Half-Year Financial Statements [extract]
1 Accounting policies [extract]

This general purpose financial report for the half year ended 31 December 2011 is unaudited and has been prepared in accordance with IAS 34 'Interim Financial Reporting' as issued by the International Accounting Standards Board ("IASB"), IAS 34 'Interim Financial Reporting' as adopted by the EU, AASB 134 'Interim Financial Reporting' as issued by the Australian Accounting Standards Board ("AASB") and the Disclosure and Transparency Rules of the Financial Services Authority in the United Kingdom and the Australian Corporations Act 2001 as applicable to interim financial reporting.

The extract above also highlights a compliance issue for adopters of IFRS-based standards, such as entities in Australia and the European Union. Because of the time taken to secure local endorsement of IFRS issued by the IASB, an entity may not be able to state at a particular reporting date that the financial statements comply with both IFRS as issued by the IASB and IFRS as endorsed locally.

For example, when the Interpretations Committee issues an interpretation that is effective before the end of the interim reporting period, entities may choose not to comply with IAS 34 in their interim financial statements rather than risk applying an interpretation in their full year financial statements that is not yet locally endorsed. Extract 37.1 above shows a disclosure by an entity choosing not to comply with the requirements of IAS 34. Alternatively, an entity may publish interim financial information prepared under locally endorsed IFRS, for example, IFRS as adopted by the European Union. In such cases, the basis of preparation should state that IAS 34 is being applied in this context.

5 PERIODS FOR WHICH INTERIM FINANCIAL STATEMENTS ARE REQUIRED TO BE PRESENTED

Irrespective of whether an entity presents condensed or complete interim financial statements, its interim reports include the following components: *[IAS 34.20]*

(a) statements of financial position as of the end of the current interim period and a comparative statement of financial position as of the end of the immediately preceding year;

(b) statements of profit or loss and other comprehensive income for the current interim period and cumulatively for the current year-to-date, with comparative statements of profit or loss and other comprehensive income for the comparable interim periods (current and year-to-date) of the immediately preceding year;

(c) statements of changes in equity cumulatively for the current year-to-date period, with a comparative statement for the comparable year-to-date period of the immediately preceding year; and

(d) statements of cash flows cumulatively for the current year-to-date, with a comparative statement for the comparable year-to-date period of the immediately preceding year.

An interim report may present for each period either a single statement of 'profit or loss and other comprehensive income', or separate statements of 'profit or loss' and 'comprehensive income'. *[IAS 1.10A, IAS 34.20(b)]*. The condensed statement of comprehensive income referred to at (b) above should be presented in a manner consistent with the entity's annual financial statements. Accordingly, if the entity presents a separate statement for items of profit or loss in its annual financial statements, it should present a separate condensed statement of profit or loss in the interim financial report. *[IAS 34.8A]*.

If an entity's business is highly seasonal, then the standard encourages reporting additional financial information for the twelve months up to the end of the interim period, and comparative information for the prior twelve-month period, in addition to the financial statements for the periods set out above. *[IAS 34.21]*.

The standard does not require an entity to present a statement of financial position as at the end of the comparable interim period. However, in practice many entities reporting under IFRS disclose this information, either on a voluntary basis, or due to local regulations. Similarly, many entities also present the income statement for the immediately preceding full year. Such presentation is allowed under IAS 34, but any additional information included in the interim report should be prepared and presented in compliance with the standard.

The examples below illustrate the periods that an entity is required and encouraged to disclose under IAS 34. *[IAS 34.22, Illustrative examples, part A].* In addition to the requirements set out in these examples and as noted at 3.1 above, an entity presenting a complete set of interim financial statements is required to include a statement of financial position as at the beginning of the preceding period if the entity restated prior periods (for example, to change an accounting policy). *[IAS 34.5(f)].*

Example 37.2: Entity publishes interim financial reports half-yearly

If an entity's financial year ends on 31 December (calendar year), it should present the following financial statements (condensed or complete) in its half-yearly interim financial report as of 30 June 2014:

Half-yearly interim report	*End of the current interim period*	*End of the comparative interim period*	*Immediately preceding year-end*
	30/6/2014	30/6/2013	31/12/2013
Statement of financial position	●		●
Statement(s) of profit or loss and other comprehensive income			
– Current period and year-to-date (6 months) ending	●	●	
– 12 months ending	○	○	
Statement of changes in equity			
– Year-to date (6 months) ending	●	●	
– 12 months ending	○	○	
Statement of cash flows			
– Year-to-date (6 months) ending	●	●	
– 12 months ending	○	○	

● Required ○ Disclosure encouraged if the entity's business is highly seasonal

If an entity publishes a separate interim financial report for the final interim period (i.e. second half of its financial year), it presents the following financial statements (condensed or complete) in its second half-yearly interim financial report as of 31 December 2014:

Second half-yearly interim report	*End of the current interim period*	*End of the comparative interim period*
	31/12/2014	31/12/2013
Statement of financial position	●	●
Statement(s) of profit or loss and other comprehensive income		
– Current period (6 months) ending	●	●
– Year-to-date (12 months) ending	●	●

Statement of changes in equity			
– Year-to-date (12 months) ending	●	●	
Statement of cash flows			
– Year-to-date (12 months) ending	●	●	

● Required

Example 37.3: Entity publishes interim financial reports quarterly

If an entity's financial year ends on 31 December (calendar year), it should present the following financial statements (condensed or complete) in its quarterly interim financial reports for 2014:

First quarter interim report	*End of the current interim period*	*End of the comparative interim period*	*Immediately preceding year-end*
	31/3/2014	31/3/2013	31/12/2013
Statement of financial position	●		●
Statement(s) of profit or loss and other comprehensive income			
– Current period and year-to-date (3 months) ending	●	●	
– 12 months ending	○	○	
Statement of changes in equity			
– Year-to-date (3 months) ending	●	●	
– 12 months ending	○	○	
Statement of cash flows			
– Year-to-date (3 months) ending	●	●	
– 12 months ending	○	○	

● Required ○ Disclosure encouraged if the entity's business is highly seasonal

Second quarter interim report	*End of the current interim period*	*End of the comparative interim period*	*Immediately preceding year-end*
	30/6/2014	30/6/2013	31/12/2013
Statement of financial position	●		●
Statement(s) of profit or loss and other comprehensive income			
– Current period (3 months) ending	●	●	
– Year-to-date (6 months) ending	●	●	
– 12 months ending	○	○	
Statement of changes in equity			
– Year-to-date (6 months) ending	●	●	
– 12 months ending	○	○	
Statement of cash flows			
– Year-to-date (6 months) ending	●	●	
– 12 months ending	○	○	

● Required ○ Disclosure encouraged if the entity's business is highly seasonal

Third quarter interim report	*End of the current interim period*	*End of the comparative interim period*	*Immediately preceding year-end*
	30/9/2014	30/9/2013	31/12/2013
Statement of financial position	●		●
Statement(s) of profit or loss and other comprehensive income			
– Current period (3 months) ending	●	●	
– Year-to-date (9 months) ending	●	●	
– 12 months ending	○	○	
Statement of changes in equity			
– Year-to-date (9 months) ending	●	●	
– 12 months ending	○	○	
Statement of cash flows			
– Year-to-date (9 months) ending	●	●	
– 12 months ending	○	○	

● Required ○ Disclosure encouraged if the entity's business is highly seasonal

If an entity publishes a separate interim financial report for the final interim period (i.e. fourth quarter of its financial year), it presents the following financial statements (condensed or complete) in its fourth quarter interim financial report as of 31 December 2014:

Fourth quarter interim report	*End of the current interim period*	*End of the comparative interim period*
	31/12/2014	31/12/2013
Statement of financial position	●	●
Statement(s) of profit or loss and other comprehensive income		
– Current period (3 months) ending	●	●
– Year-to-date (12 months) ending	●	●
Statement of changes in equity		
– Year-to-date (12 months) ending	●	●
Statement of cash flows		
– Year-to-date (12 months) ending	●	●

● Required

5.1 Other comparative information

For entities presenting condensed financial statements under IAS 34, there is no explicit requirement that comparative information be presented in the explanatory notes. Nevertheless, where an explanatory note is required by the standard (such as for inventory write-downs, impairment provisions, segment revenues etc.) or otherwise determined to be needed to provide useful information about changes in the financial position and performance of the entity since the end of the last annual reporting period, *[IAS 34.15]*, it would be appropriate to provide information for each period presented. However, in certain cases it would be unnecessary to provide comparative information where this repeats information that was reported in the notes to the most recent annual financial statements. *[IAS 34.15A]*. For example it would only be necessary to provide information about business combinations in a comparative period when there is a revision of previously disclosed fair values.

For entities presenting complete financial statements, whilst IAS 34 sets out the periods for which components of the interim report are included, it is less clear how these rules interact with IAS 1's requirement to report comparative information for all amounts in the financial statements. *[IAS 1.38]*. In our view, a complete set of interim financial statements that contains a statement of compliance under IAS 1 should meet the requirements of IAS 1 in full, irrespective of any apparent contradiction with IAS 34, as shown in the example below.

Example 37.4: Disclosing movements on non-current assets in a complete set of interim financial statements

An entity preparing complete IFRS financial statements is required to reconcile the carrying amount at the beginning and end of the period showing movements during that period for both intangible assets and property, plant and equipment. *[IAS 38.118, IAS 16.73]*. Therefore, an entity presenting complete IFRS financial statements for the six months ended 30 June 2014 would disclose the movements in intangible assets and in property, plant and equipment between 1 January 2014 and 30 June 2014. In our view, the requirement for comparatives in IAS 1 requires the entity to reconcile movements during the comparative interim period, between 1 January 2013 and 30 June 2013, even though the entity is not required to present a statement of financial position as at 30 June 2013 (as shown in Example 37.2 above).

In addition to presenting comparative information for the corresponding interim period, it is suggested that entities preparing a complete set of interim financial statements also include information for the previous full year, such as the required comparative information for the current interim period and reconciliations to the previous year-end statement of financial position. In Example 37.4 above, this requirement could be achieved by reconciling movements in non-current assets during the second six months of the previous year (between 1 July 2013 and 31 December 2013). This approach is adopted in Extract 37.5 at 4.3.4 above.

If an entity presents complete financial statements and restates comparative information (e.g. following a change in accounting policy, correction of an error, or reclassification) and this restatement is material, then the entity should present a third statement of financial position at the beginning of the earliest comparative period in its interim financial reporting accordance with IAS 1. *[IAS 1.10(f)]*. No such requirement applies in the case of an entity preparing a condensed set of interim financial statements, *[IAS 1.BC33]*, however, additional disclosures are required in the case of correction of prior period errors, *[IAS 34.15B(g)]* (see 4.3.7 above), or when accounting policies are changed, *[IAS 34.16A(a)]* (see 4.3.14 above).

5.2 Length of interim reporting period

IAS 34 does not limit interim reporting to quarterly or half-yearly periods; an interim period may be any period shorter than a full year. *[IAS 34.4]*. In the extract below Bossard AG presented its interim reports for four-month and eight-month interim periods under IAS 34. This was acceptable under local regulation, but not a common practice. Since then the company has changed to the local minimum requirement of half-year interim reporting.

> *Extract 37.26: Bossard Holding AG (First four months 2008)*
>
> **Notes to the Consolidated Financial Statements** [extract]
>
> **Basis for the Preparation of the Consolidated Financial Statements (2)** [extract]
>
> The unaudited, consolidated interim financial statements for the first four months of 2008 were prepared in accordance with the International Financial Reporting Standards (IFRS) "Interim Financial Reporting IAS 34".
>
> The consolidated financial statements of the Bossard Group are based on the financial statements of the individual Group companies at April 30, 2008 prepared in accordance with uniform accounting policies. The consolidated financial statements have been prepared under the historical cost convention except for the revaluation of certain financial assets and liabilities at market value, in accordance with International Financial Reporting Standards (IFRS), including International Accounting Standards (IAS) and interpretations issued by the International Accounting Standards Board (IASB). They are prepared in accordance with Swiss law and the listing rules of the Swiss Exchange SWX.

5.3 Change in financial year-end

A change in an entity's annual financial reporting period-end impacts the periods presented for interim reporting. For example, an entity changing its reporting date from 31 December to 31 March would have to change its half-year reporting date from 30 June to 30 September. As IAS 34 requires comparative information for 'the *comparable* interim periods (current and year-to-date) of the immediately preceding financial year,' the entity would also have to change the comparative interim periods presented. *[IAS 34.20]*.

Example 37.5: Entity changes financial year-end

If an entity changes its financial year-end from 31 December (calendar year) to 31 March, and first reflects the change in its annual financial statements for the period ended 31 March 2014, it should present the following financial statements (condensed or complete) in its half-yearly interim financial reports for 2014:

Half-yearly interim report	*End of the current interim period*	*End of the comparative interim period*	*Immediately preceding year-end*
	30/9/2014	30/9/2013	31/03/2014
Statement of financial position	●		●
Statement(s) of profit or loss and other comprehensive income			
– Current period and year-to-date (6 months) ending	●	●	
– 12 months ending	○	○	
Statement of changes in equity			
– Year-to date (6 months) ending	●	●	
– 12 months ending	○	○	
Statement of cash flows			
– Year-to-date (6 months) ending	●	●	
– 12 months ending	○	○	

● Required ○ Disclosure encouraged if the entity's business is highly seasonal

The entity in the example above should not show information for half-year ended 30 June 2013 as the comparative period, notwithstanding the fact that this period was the reporting date for the last published half-yearly report.

5.4 Comparatives following a financial period longer than a year

The discussion at 5.3 above demonstrates that when an entity changes is annual reporting date, the determination of comparative periods in the interim financial statements is made by reference to the new annual reporting date.

Another situation where confusion may be caused by the requirement to present comparative information for 'the *comparable* interim periods (current and year-to-date) of the immediately preceding financial year' *[IAS 34.20]* arises when the previous annual financial statements related to a period other than twelve months. This situation is not uncommon for a newly incorporated entity, which might have either a shorter or a longer reporting period in its first financial year.

Consider an entity that has a long initial accounting period of eighteen months and that is required to prepare interim financial reports on a quarterly basis. Accordingly, it would have *six* 'quarters' in its first financial reporting period and in line with the requirements of IAS 34, the entity would present statements of profit or loss and other comprehensive income, changes in equity and cash flows for each three month period and cumulatively for the year-to-date. In the next financial year, however, the previously published year-to-date amounts would no longer be comparable. The following example illustrates this situation.

Example 37.6: Disclosing comparatives in interim financial statements when the preceding financial year covers a longer period

An entity's financial year-end is 31 December and it issues quarterly interim financial statements. It was incorporated on 1 July 2012 and prepared its first set of financial statements for a period of eighteen months to 31 December 2013. In this period, the entity prepared interim financial statements under IAS 34 for each of the three month periods ended 30 September 2012, 31 December 2012, 31 March 2013, 30 June 2013, 30 September 2013 and 31 December 2013. Each interim report contained information for the three month period and the year-to-date, which started on 1 July 2012.

In the next year, a twelve month annual reporting period, the entity is preparing its interim financial report for the three months ending 30 June 2014. Accordingly, it presents statements of profit or loss and other comprehensive income, changes in equity and cash flows for the three month period from 1 April 2014 to 30 June 2014 and for the year-to-date (from 1 January 2014 to 30 June 2014). Under IAS 34, the entity is also required to present comparative statements of profit or loss and other comprehensive income, cash flows, and changes in equity for the comparable interim periods in the preceding financial year. However, in its interim report for the three months ended 30 June 2013, the entity presented information for the three month period from 1 April 2013 to 30 June 2013 as well as for the year-to-date, from 1 July 2012 to 30 June 2013, a period of twelve months.

To be *comparable* to the current period, the year-to-date comparative statements should cover the same period in the preceding year as the current year, which in this case would be from 1 January 2013 to 30 June 2013.

The reason for not using previously reported year-to-date information as comparatives should be disclosed.

It should be noted in the above example that none of the interim financial statements issued in the entity's first (eighteen month) reporting period would contain comparative information. In particular, no comparatives would be required for the three month periods ended 30 September 2013 and 31 December 2013 because the corresponding periods in the preceding *calendar* year (i.e. 30 September 2012 and 31 December 2012) actually form part of the same (eighteen month) financial period and therefore comparatives from a preceding financial reporting period did not exist.

5.5 When the comparative period is shorter than the current period

The same considerations apply when determining the comparable comparative period in the following circumstances.

Example 37.7: Disclosing comparatives in interim financial statements when the preceding financial year covers a shorter period

An entity was incorporated on 17 December 2013 and its equity shares were admitted to trading on a recognised stock market in April 2014. It determined that its annual reporting date will be 30 June each year and issues its first set of annual financial statements for the period ended 30 June 2014.

In compliance with the rules of the stock market, the entity issues its first half-yearly report for the six months ended 31 December 2014. This begs the question whether the comparative period for this interim would be the short period from 17 December 2013 (i.e. the date of incorporation) to 31 December 2013 or the first six months following the entity's incorporation, from 17 December 2013 to 16 June 2014.

As in Example 37.6 above, to be comparable to the current interim reporting period, the period-to-date comparative statements should cover the same period in the preceding annual reporting period as the current year, which in this case would be from 17 December 2013 to 31 December 2013. The entity would need to provide sufficient disclosure to explain the particular circumstances and the limited comparability with the current period.

6 MATERIALITY

In making judgements on recognition, measurement, classification, or disclosures in interim financial reports, the overriding goal in IAS 34 is to ensure that an interim financial report includes all information relevant to understanding an entity's financial position and performance during the interim period. *[IAS 34.25].* The standard draws from IAS 1 and IAS 8, which define an item as material if its omission or misstatement could influence the economic decisions of users of the financial statements but do not contain quantitative guidance on materiality. *[IAS 34.24].* IAS 34 requires materiality to be assessed based on the interim period financial data. *[IAS 34.23].*

Therefore, decisions on the recognition and disclosure of unusual items, changes in accounting policies or estimates, and errors are based on materiality in relation to the interim period figures to determine whether non-disclosure is misleading. *[IAS 34.25].*

Neither the previous year's financial statements nor any expectations of the financial position at the current year-end are relevant in assessing materiality for interim reporting. However, the standard adds that interim measurements may rely on estimates to a greater extent than measurements of annual financial data. *[IAS 34.23].*

7 DISCLOSURE IN ANNUAL FINANCIAL STATEMENTS

An estimate of an amount reported in an interim period can change significantly during the remainder of the year. An entity that does not present a separate interim financial report for its final interim period should disclose the nature and amount of significant changes in estimates in a note to the annual financial statements for that year. *[IAS 34.26]*. This disclosure requirement is intended to be narrow in scope, relating only to the change in estimate, and does not create a requirement to include additional interim period financial information in the annual financial statements. *[IAS 34.27]*.

The requirement to disclose significant changes in estimates since the previous interim reporting date is consistent with IAS 8 and paragraph 16A(d) of IAS 34. These standards require disclosure of the nature and the amount of a change in estimate that has a material effect in the current reporting period or is expected to have a material effect in subsequent periods. IAS 34 cites changes in estimate in the final interim period relating to inventory write-downs, restructurings, or impairment losses recognised in an earlier interim period as examples of items that are required to be disclosed. *[IAS 34.27]*.

8 RECOGNITION AND MEASUREMENT

The recognition and measurement requirements in IAS 34 arise mainly from the requirement to report the entity's financial position as at the interim reporting date, but also requires certain estimates and measurements to take into account the expected financial position of the entity at year-end, where those measures are determined on an annual basis (as in the case of income taxes). Many preparers misinterpret this approach as representing some form of hybrid of the discrete and integral methods to interim financial reporting. This can cause confusion in application and can lead to the accusation that IAS 34 seems internally inconsistent.

In requiring the year-to-date to be treated as a discrete period, IAS 34 prohibits the recognition or deferral of revenues and costs for interim reporting purposes unless such recognition or deferral is appropriate at year-end. As with a set of annual financial statements complying with IAS 8, IAS 34 requires changes in estimates and judgements reported in previous interim periods to be revised prospectively, whereas changes in accounting policies and errors are required to be recognised by prior period adjustment. However, IAS 34 allows looking beyond the interim reporting period, for example in estimating the tax rate to be applied on earnings for the period, when a year-to-date approach does not.

The recognition and measurement requirements of IAS 34 are discussed below.

8.1 Same accounting policies as in annual financial statements

The principles for recognising assets, liabilities, income and expenses for interim periods are the same as in the annual financial statements. *[IAS 34.29]*. Accordingly, an entity uses the same accounting policies in its interim financial statements as in its most recent annual financial statements, adjusted for accounting policy changes that will be reflected in the next annual financial statements. However, IAS 34 also states that the frequency of an entity's reporting (annual, half-yearly or quarterly) do not affect the measurement of its annual results. To achieve that objective, measurements for interim reporting purposes are on a year-to-date basis. *[IAS 34.28]*.

8.1.1 Measurement on a year-to-date basis

Measurement on a year-to-date basis acknowledges that an interim period is a part of a full year and allows adjustments to estimates of amounts reported in prior interim periods of the current year. *[IAS 34.29]*.

Still, the principles for recognition and the definitions of assets, liabilities, income, and expenses for interim periods are the same as in annual financial statements. *[IAS 34.29, 31]*. Therefore, for assets, the same tests of future economic benefits apply at interim dates as at year-end. Costs that, by their nature, do not qualify as assets at year-end, do not qualify for recognition at interim dates either. Similarly, a liability at the end of an interim reporting period must represent an existing obligation at that date, just as it must at the end of an annual reporting period. *[IAS 34.32]*. Under IAS 34, as under the IASB's *Conceptual Framework*, an essential characteristic of income and expenses is that the related inflows and outflows of assets and liabilities have already occurred. If those inflows or outflows have occurred, the related income and expense are recognised; otherwise they are not recognised. *[IAS 34.33]*.

The standard lists several circumstances that illustrate these principles:

- inventory write-downs, impairments, or provisions for restructurings are recognised and measured on the same basis as at a year-end. Except for reversals of certain impairments (see 9.2 below), later changes in the original estimate are recognised in the subsequent interim period, either by recognising additional accruals or reversals of the previously recognised amount; *[IAS 34.30(a)]*
- costs that do not meet the definition of an asset at the end of an interim period are not deferred in the statement of financial position, either to await information on whether it meets the definition of an asset, or to smooth earnings over interim periods within a year. *[IAS 34.30(b)]*. For example, costs incurred in acquiring an intangible asset before the recognition criteria are met are expensed under IAS 38 – *Intangible Assets*. Only those costs incurred after the recognition criteria are met can be recognised as an asset; there is no reinstatement as an asset in a later period of costs previously expensed because the recognition criteria were not met at that time; *[IAS 38.71]* and
- income tax expense is 'recognised in each interim period based on the best estimate of the weighted-average annual income tax rate expected for the full financial year. Amounts accrued for income tax expense in one interim period may have to be adjusted in a subsequent interim period of that financial year if the estimate of the annual income tax rate changes'. *[IAS 34.30(c)]*.

Another example would be acquisition costs incurred in relation to a business combination, even if that business combination had not been completed as at the interim reporting date.

The year-to-date approach differs from the discrete approach in that the financial position and performance at each reporting date are evaluated not as an isolated period but as part of a cumulative period that builds up to a full year, whose results should not be influenced by interim reporting practices. Amounts reported for previous interim periods are not retrospectively adjusted, and therefore year-to-date measurements may involve changes in estimates of amounts reported in previous interim periods of the current year. As discussed at 4.2 and 7 above, IAS 34 requires disclosure of the nature and amount of material changes in previously reported estimates in the interim financial report and when separate interim financial report is not presented for the final interim period, in the full year financial statements. *[IAS 34.16A(d), 26, 34-36]*. However, the principle that the results of the full year should not be influenced by interim reporting practices, has been challenged, as the IASB and Interpretations Committee have identified and tried to resolve certain conflicts between IAS 34 and other standards, as discussed at 9.2 below.

8.1.2 New accounting standards and other changes in accounting policies

As noted above, under IAS 34, an entity uses the same accounting policies in its interim financial statements as in its most recent annual financial statements, adjusted for accounting policy changes that will be in the next annual financial statements, and to determine measurements for interim reporting purposes on a year-to-date basis. *[IAS 34.28]*.

Unless transition rules are specified by a new standard or interpretation, IAS 34 requires a change in accounting policy to be reflected by: *[IAS 34.43]*

(a) restating the financial statements of prior interim periods of the current year and the comparable interim periods of any prior financial years that will be restated in the annual financial statements under IAS 8; or

(b) when it is impracticable to determine the cumulative effect at the beginning of the year of applying a new accounting policy to all prior periods, adjusting the financial statements of prior interim periods of the current year and comparable interim periods of prior years to apply the new accounting policy prospectively from the earliest date practicable.

Therefore, regardless of when in a financial year an entity decides to adopt a new accounting policy, it has to be applied from the beginning of the current year. *[IAS 34.44]*. For example, if an entity that reports on a quarterly basis decides in its third quarter to change an accounting policy, it must restate the information presented in earlier quarterly financial reports to reflect the new policy as if it had been applied from the start of the annual reporting period.

It should be noted that entities preparing condensed interim financial statements in accordance with IAS 34 are not required to include a third statement of financial position when retrospectively applying a change in accounting policy or changing the presentation. *[IAS 1.4, BC33]*. However, the requirement to include a third statement of financial position does apply in such cases to entities preparing a complete set of interim financial statements. *[IAS 34.5(f)]*.

8.1.2.A New standards becoming mandatory during the current year

One objective of the year-to-date approach is to ensure that a single accounting policy is applied to a particular class of transactions throughout a year. *[IAS 34.44]*. To allow accounting policy changes as of an interim date would mean applying different accounting policies to a particular class of transactions within a single year. This would make interim allocation difficult, obscure operating results, and complicate analysis and understandability of the interim period information. *[IAS 34.45]*.

Accordingly, when preparing interim financial information, consideration is given to which new standards and interpretations are mandatory in the next (current year) annual financial statements. The entity generally adopts these standards in all interim periods during that year.

For example, an entity with a 31 December year-end should apply IFRS 11 – *Joint Arrangements* – in its half-yearly report for the six months ending 30 June 2014 because this standard applies for annual periods beginning on or after 1 January 2014. *[IFRS 11.C1]*.

While IAS 34 generally prohibits an entity from adopting a new accounting policy during an interim period, it makes an exception for standards that specifically require or permit transition during the financial year. *[IAS 34.43]*. For example, IFRIC 18 – *Transfers of Assets from Customers* – was applied prospectively to transfers of assets received from customers *on or after* 1 July 2009, which was a departure from the Interpretations Committee's and IASB's normal practice of issuing standards to be applied for annual periods beginning on or after a certain date. Thus, in this circumstance, an entity could have used two different accounting policies during a financial year.

The disclosure requirements with respect to new standards that are effective for the entity's next annual financial statements, but which do not contain specific disclosure requirements under IAS 34, are not clear. In some cases, it might be determined that an understanding of a new standard is material to an understanding of the entity, in which case the entity discloses this fact, as well as information relevant to assessing the possible impact of the new standard on the entity's financial statements. *[IAS 8.28]*. In other cases, an entity might conclude that the issuance of a new standard is not material to an understanding of its interim financial report, and thus not disclose information about the issuance of the new standard, or its possible impact on the entity.

8.1.2.B Voluntary changes of accounting policy

An entity can also elect at any time during a year to apply a new standard or interpretation before it becomes mandatory, or otherwise decide to change an accounting policy voluntarily. However, before voluntarily changing an accounting policy, consideration should be given to the interaction of the requirements of IAS 1 and IAS 8, which only permit an entity to change an accounting policy if the information results in information that is 'more reliable and more relevant' to the users of the financial statements. *[IAS 8.14(b)]*.

When it is concluded that a voluntary change in accounting policy is permitted and appropriate, its effect is generally reflected in the first interim report the entity presents after the date on which the entity changed its policy. The entity generally restates amounts reported in earlier interim periods, from a date no later than the beginning of the current year. *[IAS 34.44]*. An entity is generally not permitted to reflect the effect of a change an accounting policy from a later date in the year, such as at the start of the most recent interim period in which the decision was made to change the policy. To allow two different accounting policies to be applied to a particular class of transactions within a single year would make interim allocations difficult, obscure operating results, and complicate analysis and understandability of the interim period information. *[IAS 34.45]*. The restatement of information reported in previous interim periods is also discussed at 11 below.

An added complication arises for entities incorporated in the European Union, when the IASB issues a new standard or interpretation that is not yet endorsed as at the end of the interim reporting period. For example, as noted at 4.4 above, an entity applying IFRS 8 should disclose the specified segment information in its interim financial reports. In its interim report for the six months ended 30 June 2007, Deutsche Bank stated its intention to apply IFRS 8 in its first IFRS annual financial statements. However, because the European Union had not yet endorsed the standard as at the end of the interim reporting period, it included the disclosures required by both IFRS 8 and IAS 14 – *Segment Reporting* – as explained in the Extract below.

Extract 37.27: Deutsche Bank AG (H1, 2007)

Basis of Preparation [extract]

The consolidated interim financial statements were prepared in accordance with IFRS issued and effective at December 31, 2006, which were unchanged at 30 June 2007. The segment information presented in this Report is based on IFRS 8, "Operating Segments," with a reconciliation to IAS 14, "Segment Reporting". IFRS 8, whilst approved by the IASB, has yet to be endorsed by the EU. On this basis, the Group presents the accounting policies that are expected to be adopted when the Group prepares its first annual financial statements under IFRS.

One exception to this principle of retrospective adjustment of earlier interim periods is when an entity changes from the cost model to the revaluation model under IAS 16 – *Property, Plant and Equipment* – or IAS 38 – *Intangible Assets*. These are not changes in accounting policy that are covered by IAS 8 in the usual manner, but instead required to be treated as a revaluation in the period. *[IAS 8.17]*. Therefore, the general requirements of IAS 34 do not over-ride the specific requirements of IAS 8 to treat such changes prospectively.

However, to avoid using two differing accounting policies for a particular class of assets in a single financial year, consideration should be given to changing from the cost model to the revaluation model at the beginning of the financial year. Otherwise, an entity will end up depreciating based on cost for some interim periods and based on the revalued amounts for later interim periods.

8.1.3 Change in going concern assumption

Another situation in which an entity applies different accounting policies in its interim financial statements as compared to its most recent annual financial statements is when the going concern assumption is no longer appropriate.

Although IAS 34 does not specifically address the issue of going concern, the general requirements of IAS 1 apply to both a complete set and to condensed interim financial statements. *[IAS 1.4]*. IAS 1 states that when preparing financial statements, management assesses an entity's ability to continue as a going concern, and that the financial statements are prepared on a going concern basis unless management either intends to liquidate the entity or cease trading, or has no realistic alternative but to do so. *[IAS 1.25]*. The going concern assessment is discussed in more detail in Chapter 3 at 4.1.2.

Under IAS 1, the assessment is made based on all available information about the future, which at a minimum is twelve months from the *end of the reporting period*. *[IAS 1.26]*. Therefore, with respect to interim reporting under IAS 34, the minimum period for management's assessment is also at least twelve months from the interim reporting date; it is not limited, for example, to one year from the date of the most recent annual financial statements.

Example 37.8: Going concern assessment

An entity's financial year-end is 31 December (calendar year) and its annual financial statements as of 31 December 2013 are prepared on a going concern basis. In assessing the going concern assumption as at 31 December 2013, management considered all future available information through to 31 December 2014.

In preparing its quarterly interim financial statements (condensed or complete) as at 31 March 2014, management should evaluate all future available information to at least 31 March 2015.

If management becomes aware, in making its assessment, of material uncertainties related to events or conditions that may cast significant doubt upon the entity's ability to continue as a going concern, the entity should disclose those uncertainties. If the entity does not prepare financial statements on a going concern basis, it should disclose that fact, together with the basis on which it prepared the financial statements and the reason why the entity is not regarded as a going concern. *[IAS 1.25]*.

In Extract 37.28 below, Agennix, a biotech company, discloses various issues around its financial position, including material uncertainties related to events and conditions that cast significant doubt upon its ability to continue as a going concern and critical judgements supporting the going concern assessment.

Extract 37.28: Agennix AG (H1, 2012)

Notes to the unaudited interim condensed consolidated financial statements [extract]

1. Basis of Presentation and Accounting Policies [extract]

Going Concern

These interim condensed consolidated financial statements have been prepared on a going concern basis, which assumes that the Company will continue in operation for the foreseeable future and will be able to realize its assets and discharge its liabilities in the normal course of operations.

During the six month period ended June 30, 2012, the Company incurred a net loss of €23.3 million and used cash in its operations of €21.3 million. At June 30, 2012, the Company had cash, cash equivalents, other current financial assets and restricted cash of €22.7 million and current liabilities of €6.6 million. The Company has incurred recurring operating losses and has generated negative cash flows from operations since its inception and expects such results to continue for the foreseeable future.

Based on the Company's current financial position and base-case estimates of future cash burn, management believes that Agennix will have sufficient cash to fund its current level of operations into the first quarter of 2013. This should enable the Company to obtain top-line data from the FORTIS-M Phase III trial, now expected in August 2012. Base-case estimates of future cash burn assume reduction of cash spending in the second half of 2012 due to the wind down of the FORTIS-M trial but do not include projected changes in spending related to the outcome of the FORTIS-M Phase III trial.

If the top-line data from the FORTIS-M trial are positive, the Company anticipates significantly increasing its spending related to talactoferrin production, as well as regulatory and pre-commercialization activities, in anticipation of a Biologics License Application ("BLA") submission with the U.S. Food and Drug Administration ("FDA") and potential commercial launch. In this positive scenario, Agennix believes that it will have sufficient cash to fund operations into the middle of the fourth quarter of 2012. In such a positive data scenario the Company anticipates raising additional funds through issuance of equity or debt in the near term to fund increased spending into 2013 and continue as a going concern and would then expect to raise additional funds through licensing agreements and/or issuance of equity during 2013.

If the FORTIS-M trial were to have negative results, the Company's ability to continue as a going concern would be at immediate risk, as the Company's ability to obtain additional funding would be limited. In this situation, the Company would quickly reduce costs through restructuring activities in order to preserve cash. Furthermore, the Company would evaluate other business opportunities, including mergers and acquisitions and/or partnering and/or advancing other internal development programs.

Agennix cannot accurately predict when or whether it will successfully complete the development of its product candidates or obtain additional funding.

These interim condensed consolidated financial statements do not reflect adjustments in the carrying values of the Company's assets and liabilities, the reported income and expenses, and the current/non-current classifications in the statement of financial position that would be necessary if the going concern assumption was not appropriate. The potential adjustments, if any, could be material and would be recorded when events and circumstances occurred or when they could be estimated reliably.

8.1.4 *Voluntary changes in presentation*

In some cases, the presentation of the interim financial statements might be changed from that used in prior interim reporting periods. However, before changing the presentation used in its interim report from that of previous periods, management should consider the interaction of the requirements of IAS 34 to include in a set of condensed financial statements the same headings and sub-totals as the most recent annual financial statements *[IAS 34.10]* and to apply the same accounting policies as the most recent or the next annual financial report *[IAS 34.28]* and the requirements of IAS 1 as they will relate to those next annual financial statements. IAS 1 states that an entity should retain the presentation and classification of items in the financial statements, unless it is apparent following a significant change in the nature of operations or a review of the financial statements that another presentation is more appropriate, or unless the change is required by IFRS. *[IAS 1.45]*.

If a presentation is changed, the entity should also reclassify comparative amounts for both earlier interim periods of the current financial year and comparable periods in prior years. *[IAS 34.43(a)]*. In such cases, an entity should disclose the nature of the reclassifications, the amount of each item (or class of items) that is reclassified, and the reason for the reclassification. *[IAS 8.29]*.

8.2 Seasonal businesses

Some entities do not earn revenues or incur expenses evenly throughout the year, for example, agricultural businesses, holiday companies, domestic fuel suppliers, or retailers who experience peak demand at Christmas. The financial year-end is often chosen to fit their annual operating cycle, which means that an individual interim period would give little indication of annual performance and financial position.

An extreme application of the integral approach would suggest that they should predict their annual results and contrive to report half of that in the half-year interim financial statements. However, this approach does not portray the reality of their business in individual interim periods, and is, therefore, not permitted under the year-to-date approach adopted in IAS 34. *[IAS 34.28]*.

8.2.1 Revenues received seasonally, cyclically, or occasionally

The standard prohibits the recognition or deferral of revenues that are received seasonally, cyclically, or occasionally at an interim date, if recognition or deferral would not be appropriate at year-end. *[IAS 34.37]*. Examples of such revenues include dividend revenue, royalties, government grants, and seasonal revenues of retailers; such revenues are recognised when they occur. *[IAS 34.38]*.

IAS 34 also requires an entity to explain the seasonality or cyclicality of its business and the effect on interim reporting (see 4.3.15 above). *[IAS 34.16A(b)]*. If businesses are highly seasonal, IAS 34 encourages reporting of additional information for the twelve months up to the end of the interim period and comparatives for the prior twelve-month period (see 5.1 above). *[IAS 34.21]*.

8.2.2 Costs incurred unevenly during the year

IAS 34 prohibits the recognition or deferral of costs for interim reporting purposes if recognition or deferral of that type of cost is inappropriate at year-end, *[IAS 34.39]*, which is based on the principle that assets and liabilities are recognised and measured using the same criteria as at year-end. *[IAS 34.29, 31]*. This principle prevents smoothing of costs in seasonal businesses, and the recognition of assets or liabilities at the interim date that would not qualify for recognition at the end of an annual reporting period.

For direct costs, this approach has limited consequences, as the timing of recognising these costs and the related revenues is usually similar. However, for indirect costs, the consequences are greater, and depend on which standard an entity follows, as an entity may not recognise or defer such costs under IAS 34 in an interim period if such a policy is not appropriate at year-end.

For example, manufacturing entities that use fixed production overhead absorption rates should recognise variances and unallocated overheads in the interim period in which they are incurred. *[IAS 2.13]*. In contrast, construction contractors that use the percentage of completion method may recognise as an asset indirect contract costs that are attributable to contract activity in general, if it is probable that they will be recovered. *[IAS 11.27]*. IAS 11 – *Construction Contracts* – does not provide any guidance on how to determine if it is probable that a cost will be recovered when it relates to contract activity in general.

The implications are unclear for professional service companies that recognise revenue under IAS 18 – *Revenue* – using the percentage of completion method. On one hand, IAS 18 refers to IAS 11, *[IAS 18.21]*, implying that such entities can defer costs and the related variances at the end of an interim reporting period, even though they may not be constructing an asset and are therefore not technically within the scope of IAS 11. On the other hand, service providers might also follow the guidance in IAS 2 – *Inventories*, which also gives guidance for the cost of inventories of a service provider, and which results in expensing such costs and variances at the end of the reporting period. *[IAS 2.19]*. However, these are issues that an entity would also face at the end of an annual reporting period. What is clear is that an entity should not diverge from these requirements just because information is being prepared for an interim period.

This application of the discrete approach reflects the reality of that interim period's performance, but also emphasises the limited usefulness of the interim report for a seasonal business, because it shows that the results of that period mean little in isolation. Conversely, allocating costs to interim periods in proportion to the expected levels for the year, which IAS 34 does not allow, might show the results in context, but is subjective and requires forecasting, rather than reporting on the results of the interim period. Probably for this reason, IAS 34 recommends that entities wishing to give the results in context include additional year-to-date disclosures for seasonal businesses, as discussed at 5 above.

9 EXAMPLES OF THE RECOGNITION AND MEASUREMENT PRINCIPLES

Part B of the illustrative examples accompanying the standard provides several examples that illustrate the recognition and measurement principles in interim financial reports. *[IAS 34.40]*. In addition, the Interpretations Committee addressed one particular conflict between IAS 34 and other standards, in the reversal of impairment losses for goodwill, investments in an equity instruments classified as available-for-sale and financial assets carried at cost. These examples are discussed below.

9.1 Property, plant and equipment and intangible assets

9.1.1 Depreciation and amortisation

Depreciation and amortisation for an interim period is based only on assets owned during that interim period and does not consider asset acquisitions or disposals planned for later in the year. *[IAS 34.B24]*.

An entity applying a straight-line method of depreciation (amortisation) does not allocate the depreciation (amortisation) charge between interim periods based on the level of activity. However, under IAS 16 and IAS 38 an entity may use a 'unit of production' method of depreciation, which results in a charge based on the expected use or output (see Chapter 18 at 5.6.2). An entity can only apply this method if it most closely reflects the expected pattern of consumption of the future economic benefits embodied in the asset. The chosen method should be applied consistently from period to period unless there is a change in the expected pattern of consumption of those future economic benefits. *[IAS 16.62, IAS 38.98]*. Therefore, an entity cannot apply a straight-line method of depreciation in its annual financial statements, while allocating the depreciation charge to interim periods using a 'unit of production' based approach.

9.1.2 Impairment of assets

IAS 36 – *Impairment of Assets* – requires an entity to recognise an impairment loss if the recoverable amount of an asset declines below its carrying amount. *[IAS 34.B35]*. An entity should apply the same impairment testing, recognition, and reversal criteria at an interim date as it would at year-end. *[IAS 34.B36]*.

However, IAS 34 states that an entity is not required to perform a detailed impairment calculation at the end of each interim period. Rather, an entity should perform a review for indications of significant impairment since the most recent year-end to determine whether such a calculation is needed. *[IAS 34.B36]*. Nevertheless, the standard does not exempt an entity from performing impairment tests at the end of its interim periods. For example, an entity that recognised an impairment charge in the immediately preceding year, may find that it needs to update its impairment calculations at the end of subsequent interim periods because impairment indicators remain. There is also no exemption under IFRIC 10 – *Interim Financial Reporting and Impairment* – for the assessment of goodwill impairment (see 9.2 below).

9.1.3 Recognition of intangible assets

An entity should apply the same IAS 38 definitions and recognition criteria for intangible assets in an interim period as in an annual period. Therefore, costs incurred before the recognition criteria are met should be recognised as an expense. *[IAS 34.B8]*. Expenditures on intangibles that are initially expensed under IAS 38 cannot be reinstated and recognised as part of the cost of an intangible asset subsequently (e.g. in a later interim period). *[IAS 38.71]*. Furthermore, 'deferring' costs as assets in an interim period in the hope that the recognition criteria will be met later in the year is not permitted. Only costs incurred after the specific point in time at which the criteria are met should be recognised as part of the cost of an intangible asset. *[IAS 34.B8]*. Therefore, in practice, the frequency of interim reporting may impact the amount of costs being recognised as expenses and the amount of costs being capitalised as assets.

9.1.4 Capitalisation of borrowing costs

An entity that recognises finance expenses in the cost of a qualifying asset under IAS 23 – *Borrowing Costs* – should determine the amount to be capitalised from the actual finance cost during the period (when funds are specifically borrowed) *[IAS 23.12]* or, when the asset is funded out of general borrowings, by applying a capitalisation rate equal to the weighted-average of the finance costs attributable to actual borrowings outstanding during the period *[IAS 23.14]* (see Chapter 21 at 5.2 and 5.3). For interim financial reporting, measurement should be made on a year-to-date basis, *[IAS 34.28]*, even if the entity reports on a quarterly basis. Therefore, the estimated capitalisation rate should be revised in successive quarters during the same year for changes in actual year-to-date borrowings and finance costs. As required in IAS 34, the cumulative effect of changes in the estimated capitalisation rate should be recognised in the current quarter and not retrospectively. *[IAS 34.36]*.

9.2 Reversal of impairment losses recognised in a previous interim period (IFRIC 10)

The two requirements in IAS 34, to apply the same accounting policies in interim financial reports as are applied for the annual financial statements, and to use year-to-date measurements for interim reporting purposes, do not sit easily together when considering the reversal of certain impairments.

As discussed at 9.1.2 above, the requirement to use the same accounting policies means that an entity should apply the same impairment testing, recognition, and reversal criteria at the end of an interim period as it would at year-end. *[IAS 34.B36]*. In applying the same reversal criteria at the end of an interim period, the following requirements are significant: *[IFRIC 10.4-6]*

- IAS 36 prohibits the reversal in a subsequent period of an impairment loss recognised for goodwill; *[IAS 36.124]*
- an impairment loss recognised in profit or loss for an investment in an equity instrument classified under IAS 39 – *Financial Instruments: Recognition and Measurement* – as available for sale cannot be reversed through profit or loss; *[IAS 39.69]* and
- IAS 39 also prohibits the reversal of an impairment loss relating to an unquoted equity instrument carried at cost because its fair value cannot be reliably measured, or to a derivative asset that is linked to and must be settled by such an unquoted equity instrument. *[IAS 39.66]*.

However, the use of year-to-date measurements implies that the calculation of impairments as at interim reporting dates in the same annual reporting period should be based on conditions as at the end of each interim period and determined independently of assessments at earlier interim dates. Applying this requirement of

IAS 34 would lead to reversals of previously reported impairments if conditions change and justify a higher carrying value for the related asset.

Whilst it may be unlikely for the conditions causing an impairment of goodwill at an interim date to reverse before year-end, IFRIC 10 states that the specific requirements of the standards noted above take precedence over the more general statement in IAS 34. *[IFRIC 10.BC9]*. As such, IFRIC 10 prohibits the reversal of an impairment loss recognised in a previous interim period for goodwill or an investment in either an equity instrument or a financial asset carried at cost. *[IFRIC 10.8]*.

Thus, in the albeit unlikely event that the conditions mentioned above do reverse in successive interim periods, there can be situations where two entities facing an identical set of circumstances, yet with different frequency of interim reporting, could end up reporting different annual results. Consider the following example:

Example 37.9: Impact of IFRIC 10 on results due to differences in frequency of interim financial reporting

Entity A, reporting quarterly and entity B, reporting six-monthly, are otherwise identical, having financial years ending on 31 December and holding an investment in equity instruments of Company X. As at 31 March, the fair value of the investment in X has declined significantly below cost. However, the decline has reversed in full before the end of June. In its interim financial statements for the 1st Quarter, entity A recognises an impairment loss on its investment in X based on the significant decline in its fair value below cost. At the end of 2nd Quarter, following the guidance in IFRIC 10, entity A cannot reverse the impairment that it recognised in 1st Quarter to reflect the recovery in the value of the investment.

By contrast, entity B does not recognise any impairment in its investment in entity X in its interim financial statements for half year ended 30 June. Consequently, the entities would report different annual results for the year ended 31 December due to an impairment recognised in an interim period by entity A but not by entity B.

In November 2009, IASB issued IFRS 9 – *Financial Instruments* – (subsequently amended in October 2010), which inter alia amends IFRIC 10 (see 12.2 below). This amendment should be applied in tandem with the adoption of IFRS 9 and deletes references to equity instruments and financial assets carried at cost. With the adoption of IFRS 9, no financial assets would be carried at cost and therefore, determination of impairment and its reversal would not be relevant for such instruments in this context.

IFRIC 10 should not be applied by analogy to derive a general principle that the specific requirements of a standard take precedence over the year-to-date approach in IAS 34. *[IFRIC 10.9]*. It is unfortunate that the Interpretations Committee did not initiate a wider project to address other similar conflicts.

9.3 Employee benefits

9.3.1 Employer payroll taxes and insurance contributions

If employer payroll taxes or contributions to government-sponsored insurance funds are assessed on an annual basis, the employer's related expense should be recognised in interim periods using an estimated average annual effective rate, even if it does not reflect the timing of payments. A common example contained in Appendix B to

IAS 34 is employer payroll tax or insurance contribution subject to a certain maximum level of earnings per employee. Higher income employees would reach the maximum income before year-end, and the employer would make no further payments for the remainder of the year. *[IAS 34.B1]*.

9.3.2 *Year-end bonuses*

The nature of year-end bonuses varies widely. Some bonus schemes only require continued employment whereas others require certain performance criteria to be attained on a monthly, quarterly, or annual basis. Payment of bonuses may be purely discretionary, contractual or based on years of historical precedent. *[IAS 34.B5]*. A bonus is recognised for interim reporting only if: *[IAS 34.B6]*

(a) the entity has a present legal or constructive obligation to make such payments as a result of past events; and

(b) a reliable estimate of the obligation can be made.

A present obligation exists only when an entity has no realistic alternative but to make the payments. *[IAS 19.13]*. IAS 19 gives guidance on accounting for profit sharing and bonus plans (see Chapter 31 at 6.1.3).

In recognising a bonus at an interim reporting date, an entity should consider the facts and circumstances under which the bonus is payable, and determine an accounting policy that recognises an expense reflecting the obligation on the basis of the services received to date. Several possible accounting policies are illustrated in Example 37.10 below.

Example 37.10: Measuring interim bonus expense

An entity pays an annual performance bonus if earnings exceed £10 million, under which 5% of any earnings in excess over £10 million will be paid up to a maximum of £500,000. Earnings for the six months ended 30 June 2014 are £7 million, and the entity expects earnings for the full year ended 31 December 2014 to be £16 million.

The following table shows various accounting policies and the expense recognised thereunder in the interim financial statements for the six months ended 30 June 2014.

	Expense (£)
Method 1 – constructive obligation exists when earnings target is met	Nil
Method 2 – assume earnings for remainder of year will be same	200,000
Method 3 – proportionate recognition based on full-year estimate	131,250
Method 4 – one-half recognition based on full-year estimate	150,000

Method 1 is generally not appropriate, as this method attributes the entire bonus to the latter portion of the year, whereas employees provided service during the first six months to towards earning the bonus.

Likewise, Method 2 is generally not appropriate, as the expense of £200,000 [(£14 million – £10 million) × 5%] assumes that the employees will continue to provide service in the latter half of the year to achieve the bonus target, but does not attribute any service to that period.

In contrast to Methods 1 and 2, Method 3 illustrates an accounting policy whereby an estimate is made of the full-year expense and attributed to the period based on the proportion of that bonus for which employees have provided service at 30 June 2014. The amount recognised is calculated as (£7 million ÷ £16 million) × [5% × (£16 million – £10 million)].

Chapter 37

Similar to Method 3, Method 4 also takes the approach of recognising an expense based on the full year estimate, but allocates that full-year estimate equally to each period (which is similar to the approach used for share-based payment transactions). The amount recognised is calculated as [50% × 5% × (£16 million – £10 million)].

In addition to Methods 3 and 4, which might be appropriate, depending on the facts and circumstances, an entity might determine another basis on which to recognise bonus that considers both the constructive obligation that exists as of 30 June 2014, and the services performed to date, which is also appropriate.

9.3.3 Pensions

Pension costs for an interim period are calculated on a year-to-date basis using the actuarially determined pension cost rate at the end of the prior year, adjusted for significant market fluctuations and for significant one-off events, such as plan amendments, curtailments and settlements. *[IAS 34.B9]*.

In the absence of such significant market fluctuations and one-off events, the estimate of the actuarial liabilities is rolled forward in the scheme based on assumptions as at the beginning of the year and adjusted for significant changes in the membership of the scheme. If there are significant changes to pension arrangements during the interim period (such as changes resulting from a material business combination or from a major redundancy programme) consideration should be given to obtaining a new actuarial valuation of scheme liabilities. Similarly, if there are significant market fluctuations, such as those arising from changes in corporate bond markets, the validity of the assumptions in the last actuarial estimate, such as the discount rate applied to scheme liabilities, should be reviewed and revised as appropriate. Since the revised version of IAS 19 became effective on 1 January 2013, entities are required to recognise the full defined benefit obligation as liability. With this approach it is more likely than under the previous corridor approach that changes in market conditions may have a significant effect on the pension liability.

In Extract 37.29 Bayer discloses changes in the discount rates used for pension obligations. In normal circumstances, companies would not necessarily go through the full process of measuring pension liabilities at interim reporting dates, but rather would look to establish a process to assess the impact of any changes in underlying parameters (e.g. through extrapolation). If, for example, the discount rate estimated based on circumstances prevalent at the half-year interim reporting date has changed, the following 'rule of thumb' may help assess the impact on the pension obligation:

- Estimated change in DBO (%) = [Change in the discount rate (basis points) × duration of the pension obligation (in years)]/100

(Note: Basis points = 0.01%)

As with all approximations, the appropriateness in the circumstances should be considered.

Extract 37.29: Bayer AG (H1, 2013)

Management Report [extract]

ASSET AND CAPITAL STRUCTURE [extract]

[...] The net amount recognized for post-employment benefits decreased from €9.4 billion to €8.2 billion in the second quarter of 2013, due especially to higher long-term capital market rates.

Notes to the Condensed Consolidated Interim Financial Statements of the Bayer Group [extract]

Explanatory Notes [extract]

CHANGES IN UNDERLYING PARAMETERS [extract]

Changes in the underlying parameters relate primarily to currency exchange rates and the interest rates used to calculate pension obligations [...]

The most important interest rates used to calculate the present value of pension obligations are given below:

Discount Rate for Pension Obligations [Table 38]

	Dec. 31, 2012	**March 31, 2013**	**June 30, 2013**
	%	**%**	**%**
Germany	3.20	3.10	3.50
United Kingdom	4.40	4.35	4.75
United States	3.60	3.80	4.40

9.3.4 *Vacations, holidays, and other short-term paid absences*

IAS 19 distinguishes between accumulating and non-accumulating paid absences. *[IAS 19.13].* Accumulating paid absences are those that are carried forward and can be used in future periods if the current period's entitlement is not used in full. IAS 19 requires an entity to measure the expected cost of and obligation for accumulating paid absences at the amount the entity expects to pay as a result of the unused entitlement that has accumulated at the end of the reporting period (see Chapter 31 at 6.1.2). IAS 34 requires the same principle to be applied at the end of interim reporting periods. Conversely, an entity should not recognise an expense or liability for non-accumulating paid absences at the end of an interim reporting period, just as it would not recognise any at the end of an annual reporting period. *[IAS 34.B10].*

9.4 Inventories and cost of sales

9.4.1 *Inventories*

An entity should apply the recognition and measurement requirements of IAS 2 for interim financial reporting in the same way as it does for annual reporting purposes, despite the problems of determining inventory quantities, costs, and net realisable values. However, IAS 34 does comment that to save cost and time, entities often use estimates to measure inventories at interim dates to a greater extent than at annual reporting dates. *[IAS 34.B25].*

Net realisable values are determined using selling prices and costs to complete and dispose at the end of the interim period. A write-down should be reversed in a subsequent interim period only if it would be appropriate to do so at year-end (see Chapter 22 at 3.4). *[IAS 34.B26].*

9.4.2 Contractual or anticipated purchase price changes

Both the payer and the recipient of volume rebates, or discounts and other contractual changes in the prices of raw materials, labour, or other purchased goods and services should anticipate these items in interim periods if it is probable that these have been earned or will take effect. However, discretionary rebates and discounts should not be recognised because the resulting asset or liability would not meet the recognition criteria in the IASB's *Conceptual Framework*. *[IAS 34.B23].*

9.4.3 Interim period manufacturing cost variances

Price, efficiency, spending, and volume variances of a manufacturing entity should be recognised in profit or loss at interim reporting dates to the same extent that those variances are recognised at year-end. It is not appropriate to defer variances expected to be absorbed by year-end, which could result in reporting inventory at the interim date at more or less than its actual cost. *[IAS 34.B28].* See 8.2.2 above for a discussion on this topic as it applies to costs incurred by service providers.

9.5 Taxation

Taxation is one of the most difficult areas of interim financial reporting, primarily because IAS 34 does not adequately distinguish between current income tax and deferred tax, referring only to 'income tax expense.' This causes tension between the approach for determining the expense and the asset or liability in the statement of financial position. In addition, the standard's provisions combine terminology, suggesting an integral approach with guidance requiring a year-to-date basis to be applied. The integral method is used in determining the effective income tax rate for the whole year, but that rate is applied to year-to-date profit in the interim financial statements. In addition, under a year-to-date basis, the estimated rate is based on tax rates and laws that are enacted or substantively enacted by the end of the interim period. Changes in legislation expected to occur before the end of the current year are not recognised in preparing the interim financial report. The assets and liabilities in the statement of financial position, at least for deferred taxes, are derived solely from a year-to-date approach, but sometimes the requirements of the standard are unclear, as discussed below.

9.5.1 Measuring interim income tax expense

IAS 34 states that income tax expense should be accrued using the tax rate applicable to expected total annual earnings, by applying the estimated weighted-average annual effective income tax rate to pre-tax income for the interim period. *[IAS 34.30(c), B12].* However, this is not the same as estimating the total tax expense for the year and allocating a proportion of that to the interim period (even though it might sometimes appear that way), as demonstrated in the discussion below.

Because taxes are assessed on an annual basis, using the integral approach to determine the annual effective income tax rate and applying it to year-to-date actual earnings, it is consistent with the basic concept in IAS 34, that the same recognition and measurement principles apply in interim financial reports as in annual financial statements. *[IAS 34.B13].*

In estimating the weighted-average annual income tax rate, an entity should consider the progressive tax rate structure expected for the full year's earnings, including changes in income tax rates scheduled to take effect later in the year that are enacted or substantively enacted as at the end of the interim period. *[IAS 34.B13]*. This situation is illustrated in Example 37.11 below.

Example 37.11: Measuring interim income tax expense [IAS 34.B15]

An entity reporting quarterly expects to earn 10,000 pre-tax each quarter and operates in a jurisdiction with a tax rate of 20% on the first 20,000 of annual earnings and 30% on all additional earnings. Actual earnings match expectations. The following table shows the income tax expense reported each quarter:

	Pre-tax earnings	Effective tax rate	Tax expense
First quarter	10,000	25%	2,500
Second quarter	10,000	25%	2,500
Third quarter	10,000	25%	2,500
Fourth quarter	10,000	25%	2,500
Annual	40,000		10,000

10,000 of tax is expected to be payable for the full year on 40,000 of pre-tax income (20,000 @ 20% + 20,000 @ 30%), implying an average annual effective income tax rate of 25% (10,000 / 40,000).

In the above example, it might look as if the interim income tax expense is calculated by dividing the total expected tax expense for the year (10,000) by the number of interim reporting periods (4). However, this is only the case in this example because profits are earned evenly over each quarter. The expense is actually calculated by determining the effective annual income tax rate and multiplying that rate to year-to-date earnings, as illustrated in Example 37.12 below.

Example 37.12: Measuring interim income tax expense – quarterly losses [IAS 34.B16]

An entity reports quarterly, earns 15,000 pre-tax profit in the first quarter but expects to incur losses of 5,000 in each of the three remaining quarters (thus having zero income for the year), and operates in a jurisdiction in which its estimated average annual income tax rate is 20%. The following table shows the income tax expense reported each quarter:

	Pre-tax earnings	Effective tax rate	Tax expense
First quarter	15,000	20%	3,000
Second quarter	(5,000)	20%	(1,000)
Third quarter	(5,000)	20%	(1,000)
Fourth quarter	(5,000)	20%	(1,000)
Annual	0		0

The above example shows how an expense is recognised in periods reporting a profit and a credit is recognised when a loss is incurred. This result is very different from allocating a proportion of the expected total income tax expense for the year, which in this case is zero.

If an entity operates in a number of tax jurisdictions, or where different income tax rates apply to different categories of income (such as capital gains or income earned in particular industries), the standard requires that to the extent practicable, an entity: *[IAS 34.B14]*

- estimates the average annual effective income tax rate for each taxing jurisdiction separately and apply it individually to the interim period pre-tax income of each jurisdiction; and
- applies different income tax rates to each individual category of interim period pre-tax income.

This means that the entity should perform the analysis illustrated in Example 37.12 above for each tax jurisdiction and arrive at an interim tax charge by applying the tax rate for each jurisdiction to actual earnings from each jurisdiction in the interim period. However, the standard recognises that, whilst desirable, such a degree of precision may not be achievable in all cases and allows using a weighted-average rate across jurisdictions or across categories of income, if such rate approximates the effect of using rates that are more specific. *[IAS 34.B14]*.

Example 37.13: Measuring interim tax expense – many jurisdictions [IAS 34.B14]

An entity operates in 3 countries, each with its own tax rates and laws. In order to determine the interim tax expense, the entity determines the effective annual income tax rate for each jurisdiction and applies those rates to the actual earnings in each jurisdiction, as follows:

(All values in €)	Country A	Country B	Country C	Total
Expected annual tax rate	25%	40%	20%	
Expected annual earnings	300,000	250,000	200,000	750,000
Expected annual tax expense	75,000	100,000	40,000	215,000
Actual half-year earnings	140,000	80,000	150,000	370,000
Interim tax expense	35,000	32,000	60,000	127,000

By performing a separate analysis for each jurisdiction, the entity determines an interim tax expense of €127,000, giving an effective average tax rate of 34.3% (€127,000 ÷ €370,000). Had the entity used a weighted-average rate across jurisdictions, using the expected annual earnings, it would have determined an effective tax rate of 28.7% (€215,000 ÷ €750,000), resulting in a tax expense for the interim period of €106,190 (370,000 @ 28.7%). Whether the difference of nearly €21,000 is significant is a matter of judgement.

9.5.2 Changes in the effective tax rate during the year

9.5.2.A Enacted changes for the current year that apply after the interim reporting date

As noted above, the estimated income tax rate applied in the interim financial report should reflect changes that are enacted or substantively enacted as at the end of the interim reporting period, but scheduled to take effect later in the year. *[IAS 34.B13]*. IAS 12 – *Income Taxes* – acknowledges that in some jurisdictions, announcements by government have substantively the same effect as enactment. *[IAS 12.48]*.

Accordingly, an entity should determine the date on which a change in tax rate or tax law is substantively enacted based on the specific constitutional arrangements of the jurisdiction.

For example, assume that the 30% tax rate (on earnings above 20,000) in Example 37.11 was substantively enacted as at the second quarter reporting date and applicable before year-end. In that case, the estimated income tax rate for interim reporting would be the same as the estimated average annual effective income tax rate computed in that example (i.e. 25%) after considering the higher rate, even though the entity's earnings are not above the required threshold at the half-year.

If legislation is enacted only after the end of the interim reporting period but before the date of authorisation for issue of the interim financial report, its effect is disclosed as a non-adjusting event. *[IAS 10.22(h)]*. Under IAS 10 – *Events after the Reporting Period* – estimates of tax rates and related assets or liabilities are not revised. *[IAS 10.10]*.

9.5.2.B *Changes to previously reported estimated income tax rates for the current year*

IAS 34 requires an entity to re-estimate at the end of each interim reporting period the estimated average annual income tax rate on a year-to-date basis. *[IAS 34.B13]*. Accordingly, the amounts accrued for income tax expense in one interim period may have to be adjusted in a subsequent interim period if that estimate changes. *[IAS 34.30(c)]*. IAS 34 requires disclosure in interim financial statements of material changes in estimates of amounts reported in an earlier period or, in the annual financial statements, of material changes in estimates of amounts reported in the latest interim financial statements. *[IAS 34.16A(d), 26]*.

Accordingly, just as the integral approach does not necessarily result in a constant tax charge in each interim reporting period, it also does not result in a constant effective tax rate when circumstances change. In 2008, Coca-Cola HBC described how its tax rate is estimated in the following interim report.

Extract 37.30: Coca-Cola Hellenic Bottling Company S.A. (Q2, 2008)

Condensed notes to the consolidated financial statements [extract]

5. Tax

The effective tax rate for the Company differs from the 2008 Greek statutory rate of 25% as a consequence of a number of factors, the most significant of which are the non-deductibility of certain expenses and the fact that the tax rates in the countries in which the Company operates differ materially from the Greek statutory tax rate. The statutory tax rates applicable to the country operations of the Company range from 0%-31%.

The effective tax rate for the Company varies on a quarterly basis as a result of the mix of taxable profits and deductible expenses across territories and as a consequence of tax adjustments arising during the year, which do not necessarily refer to the current period's operations.

The effective tax rate (excluding the adjustments to intangible assets) is approximately 17% for the first half of 2008 (2007: 22%). This rate is quoted before any tax credit is recognised for the current recognition of acquired and previously unrecognised accumulated tax benefits.

Example 37.14: Changes in the effective tax rate during the year

Taking the fact pattern in Example 37.11 above, an entity reporting quarterly expects to earn 10,000 pre-tax each quarter; from the start of the third quarter the higher rate of tax on earnings over 20,000 increases from 30% to 40%. Actual earnings continue to match expectations. The following table shows the income tax expense reported in each quarter:

	Period pre-tax earnings	Pre-tax earnings: year to date	Effective tax rate	Tax expense: year to date	Period tax expense
First quarter †	10,000	10,000	25%	2,500	2,500
Second quarter †	10,000	20,000	25%	5,000	2,500
Third quarter	10,000	30,000	30%	9,000	4,000
Fourth quarter	10,000	40,000	30%	12,000	3,000
Annual	40,000				12,000

† As previously reported from Example 37.11 using an effective tax rate of 25%.

The increase in the tax rate means that 12,000 of tax is expected to be payable for the full year on 40,000 of pre-tax income (20,000 @ 20% + 20,000 @ 40%), implying an average annual effective income tax rate of 30% (12,000 / 40,000). With cumulative pre-tax earnings of 30,000 as at the end of the third quarter, the estimated tax liability is 9,000, requiring a tax expense of 4,000 (9,000 – 2,500 – 2,500) to be recognised during that quarter. In the final quarter, earnings of 10,000 results in a tax charge of 3,000, using the revised effective rate of 30%.

9.5.2.C *Enacted changes applying only to subsequent years*

In many jurisdictions, tax legislation is enacted that takes effect not only after the interim reporting date but also after year-end. Such circumstances are not addressed explicitly in the standard. Indeed, the failure of IAS 34 to adequately distinguish between current income tax and deferred tax, combined with the different approaches taken in determining the expense recognised in profit or loss compared to the statement of financial position, can lead to confusion in this situation.

On the one hand, the standard states that the estimated income tax rate for the interim period includes enacted or substantively enacted changes scheduled to take effect later in the year. *[IAS 34.B13]*. Accordingly, the effect of changes that do not take effect in the current year is ignored. On the other hand, IAS 34 also requires that the principles for recognising assets, liabilities, income, and expenses for interim periods are the same as in the annual financial statements. *[IAS 34.29]*. In annual financial statements, deferred tax is measured at the tax rates expected to apply to the period when the asset is realised or the liability is settled, based on tax rates (and tax laws) enacted or substantively enacted by the end of the reporting period, as required by IAS 12. *[IAS 12.47]*. Therefore, an entity should recognise the effect of a change applying to future periods if enacted by the end of the interim reporting period.

These two requirements seem to be mutually incompatible. IAS 34 makes sense only in the context of calculating the effective *current* tax rate on income earned in the period. Once a deferred tax asset or liability is recognised, it should be measured under IAS 12. Therefore, an entity should recognise an enacted change applying to future years in measuring deferred tax assets and liabilities as at the end of the interim reporting period. In our view, one way to treat the cumulative effect to date of this remeasurement is to recognise it in full, by a credit to profit or loss or to other comprehensive income, depending on the nature of the temporary difference being remeasured, in the period during which the tax legislation is enacted, in a similar way to the treatment shown in Example 37.14 above, and as illustrated in Example 37.15 below.

Example 37.15: Enacted changes to tax rates applying after the current year

An entity reporting half-yearly operates in a jurisdiction subject to a tax rate of 30%. Legislation is enacted during the first half of the current year, which reduces the tax rate to 28% on income earned from the beginning of the entity's next financial year. Based on a gross temporary difference of 1,000, the entity reported a deferred tax liability in its most recent annual financial statements of 300 (1,000 @ 30%). Of this temporary difference, 200 is expected to reverse in the second half of the current year and 800 in the next financial year. Assuming that no new temporary differences arise in the current period, what is the deferred tax balance at the interim reporting date?

Whilst the entity uses an effective tax rate of 30% to determine the tax expense relating to income earned in the period, it should use a rate of 28% to measure those temporary differences expected to reverse in the next financial year. Accordingly, the deferred tax liability at the half-year reporting date is 284 (200 @ 30% + 800 @ 28%).

Alternatively, if the effective *current* tax rate is not distinguished from the measurement of deferred tax, it could be argued that IAS 34 allows the reduction in the deferred tax liability of 16 (300 – 284) to be included in the estimate of the effective income tax rate for the year. Approach 2 in Example 37.18 below applies this argument.

9.5.3 Difference in financial year and tax year

If an entity's financial year and the income tax year differ, the income tax expense for the interim periods of that financial year should be measured using separate weighted-average estimated effective tax rates for each of the income tax years applied to the portion of pre-tax income earned in each of those income tax years. *[IAS 34.B17]*. In other words, an entity should compute a weighted-average estimated effective tax rate for each income tax year, rather than for its financial year.

Example 37.16: Difference in financial year and tax year [IAS 34.B18]

An entity's financial year ends 30 June and it reports quarterly. Its taxable year ends 31 December. For the financial year that begins 1 July 2013 and ends 30 June 2014, the entity earns 10,000 pre-tax each quarter.

The estimated average annual income tax rate is 30% in the income tax year to 31 December 2013 and 40% in the year to 31 December 2014.

Quarter ending	Pre-tax earnings	Effective tax rate	Tax expense
30 September 2013	10,000	30%	3,000
31 December 2013	10,000	30%	3,000
31 March 2014	10,000	40%	4,000
30 June 2014	10,000	40%	4,000
Annual	40,000		14,000

9.5.4 Tax loss and tax credit carrybacks and carryforwards

Appendix B to IAS 34 repeats the requirement in IAS 12 that for carryforwards of unused tax losses and tax credits, a deferred tax asset should be recognised to the extent that it is probable that future taxable profit will be available against which the unused tax losses and unused tax credits can be utilised. In assessing whether future taxable profit is available, the criteria in IAS 12 are applied at the interim date. If these criteria are met as at the end of the interim period, the effect of the tax loss carryforwards is included in the estimated average annual effective income tax rate. *[IAS 34.B21]*.

Example 37.17: Tax loss carryforwards expected to be recovered in the current year [IAS 34.B22]

An entity that reports quarterly has unutilised operating losses of 10,000 for income tax purposes at the start of the current financial year for which a deferred tax asset has not been recognised. The entity earns 10,000 in the first quarter of the current year and expects to earn 10,000 in each of the three remaining quarters. Excluding the effect of utilising losses carried forward, the estimated average annual income tax rate is 40%. Including the carryforward, the estimated average annual income tax rate is 30%. Accordingly, tax expense is determined by applying the 30% rate to earnings each quarter as follows:

	Pre-tax earnings	Effective tax rate	Tax expense
First quarter	10,000	30%	3,000
Second quarter	10,000	30%	3,000
Third quarter	10,000	30%	3,000
Fourth quarter	10,000	30%	3,000
Annual	40,000		12,000

This result is consistent with the general approach for measuring income tax expense in the interim report, in that any entitlement for relief from current tax due to carried forward losses is determined on an annual basis. Accordingly, its effect is included in the estimate of the average annual income tax rate and not, for example, by allocating all of the unutilised losses against the earnings of the first quarter to give an income tax expense of zero in the first quarter and 4,000 thereafter.

In contrast, the year-to-date approach of IAS 34 means that the benefits of a tax loss carryback are recognised in the interim period in which the related tax loss occurs, *[IAS 34.B20]*, and are not included in the assessment of the estimated average annual tax rate, as shown in Example 37.12 above. This approach is consistent with IAS 12, which requires the benefit of a tax loss that can be carried back to recover current tax already incurred in a previous period to be recognised as an asset. *[IAS 12.13]*. Therefore, a corresponding reduction of tax expense or increase of tax income is also recognised. *[IAS 34.B20]*.

Where previously unrecognised tax losses are expected to be utilised in full in the current year, it seems intuitive to recognise the recovery of those carried forward losses in the estimate of the average annual tax rate, as shown in Example 37.16 above. However, where the level of previously unrecognised tax losses exceeds expected taxable profits for the current year, a deferred tax asset should be recognised for the carried forward losses that are now expected to be utilised, albeit in future years.

The examples in IAS 34 do not show how such a deferred tax asset is created in the interim financial report. In our view, two approaches are acceptable, as shown in Example 37.18 below.

Example 37.18: Tax loss carryforwards in excess of current year expected profits

An entity that reports half-yearly has unutilised operating losses of 75,000 for income tax purposes at the start of the current financial year for which no deferred tax asset has been recognised. At the end of its first interim period, the entity reports a profit before tax of 25,000 and expects to earn a profit of 20,000 before tax in the second half of the year. The entity reassesses the likelihood of generating sufficient profits to utilise its carried forward tax losses and determines that the IAS 12 recognition criteria for a deferred tax asset are satisfied for the full amount of 75,000. Excluding the effect of utilising losses carried forward, the estimated average annual income tax rate is the same as the enacted or substantially enacted rate of 40%.

As at the end of the current financial year the entity expects to have unutilised losses of 30,000 (75,000 carried forward less current year pre-tax profits of 45,000). Using the enacted rate of 40%, a deferred tax asset of 12,000 is recognised at year-end. How is this deferred tax asset recognised in the interim reporting periods?

Approach 1

Under the first approach, the estimate of the average annual effective tax rate includes only those carried forward losses expected to be utilised in the current financial year and a separate deferred tax asset is recognised for those carried forward losses now expected to be utilised in future annual reporting periods.

In the fact pattern above, using 45,000 of the carried forward tax losses gives an average effective annual tax rate of nil, as follows:

Estimation of the annual effective tax rate – Approach 1	
Expected annual tax expense before utilising losses carried forward (45,000 @ 40%)	18,000
Tax benefit of utilising carried forward tax losses (45,000 @ 40%)	(18,000)
Expected annual tax expense before the effect of losses carried forward to future annual periods	0
Expected annual effective tax rate	0%
Effect of tax losses carried forward to future periods (75,000 – 45,000 @ 40%)	(12,000)
Tax income to be recognised in the interim period	(12,000)

The remaining tax losses give rise to a deferred tax asset of 12,000, which is recognised in full at the half-year, to give reported profits after tax as follows:

	First half-year	*Second half-year*	*Annual*
Profit before income tax	25,000	20,000	45,000
Income tax (expense)/credit			
– at expected annual effective rate	0	0	0
– recognition of deferred tax asset	12,000	0	12,000
Net profit after tax	37,000	20,000	57,000

Approach 2

Under the second approach, the estimate of the average annual effective tax rate reflects the expected recovery of all the previously unutilised tax losses from the beginning of the period in which the assessment of recoverability changed. In the fact pattern above, recognition of the unutilised tax losses gives an average effective annual tax rate of –26.67%, as follows:

Estimation of the annual effective tax rate – Approach 2

Expected annual tax expense before utilising losses carried forward (45,000 @ 40%)	18,000
Tax benefit of recognising unutilised tax losses (75,000 @ 40%)	(30,000)
Expected annual tax credit after recognising unutilised tax losses	(12,000)
Expected annual effective tax rate (–12,000 ÷ 45,000)	–26.67%

This approach results in reported profits after tax as follows:

	First half-year	*Second half-year*	*Annual*
Profit before income tax	25,000	20,000	45,000
Income tax (expense)/credit – at expected annual effective rate	6,667	5,333	12,000
Net profit after tax	31,667	25,333	57,000

Approach 1 is consistent with the requirements of IAS 12 as it results in recognising the full expected deferred tax asset as soon as it becomes 'probable that taxable profit will be available against which the deductible temporary difference can be utilised'. *[IAS 12.24]*. However, given that IAS 34 does not specifically address this situation, and is unclear about whether the effective tax rate reflects changes in the assessment of the recoverability of carried forward tax losses, we also believe that Approach 2 is acceptable.

9.5.5 *Tax credits*

IAS 34 also discusses in more detail the treatment of tax credits, which may for example be based on amounts of capital expenditures, exports, or research and development expenditures. Such benefits are usually granted and calculated on an annual basis under tax laws and regulations and therefore are reflected in the estimated annual effective income tax rate used in the interim report. However, if tax benefits relate to a one-time event, they should be excluded from the estimate of the annual rate and deducted separately from income tax expense in that interim period. Occasionally, some tax credits are more akin to a government grant, which are recognised in the interim period in which they arise. *[IAS 34.B19]*.

In Extract 37.31 below, Inmarsat explains the reasons for a decrease in the effective tax rate in the interim period and the effect of related one-off tax credits.

Extract 37.31: Inmarsat plc (H1, 2011)

Interim Management Report [extract]
Operating and Financial Review [extract]
Total Group Results [extract]

Income tax expense

The tax charge for the half year ended 30 June 2011 was US$63.5m, an increase of US$18.7m, or 42%, compared with the half year ended 30 June 2010. The increase in the tax charge is largely driven by the underlying increase in profits for the half year ended 30 June 2011. The change in the UK main rate of corporation tax from 28% in 2010 to 26% with effect from 1 April 2011 has given rise to a one-off tax credit of US$0.9m on the revaluation of UK deferred tax liabilities at 31 March 2011. There was also a prior year adjustment which resulted in a one off tax credit of US$2.9m.

The effective tax rate for the half year ended 30 June 2011 was 24.9% compared to 29.5% for the half year ended 30 June 2010. If the effect of the prior year adjustment is removed, the effective rate for the half year ended 30 June 2011 is 26.1% compared to 27.6% for the half year ended 30 June 2010. The decrease in the adjusted effective tax rate is predominately due to the reduction of the UK main rate of corporation tax from 28% in 2010 to 26% with effect from 1 April 2011. Although the change in tax rate became effective on 1 April 2011, this has the effect of lowering the average UK statutory tax rate for 2011, and therefore the rate upon which the half year's tax charge is based, to 26.5%.

9.6 Foreign currency translation

9.6.1 *Foreign currency translation gains and losses*

An entity measures foreign currency translation gains and losses for interim financial reporting using the same principles that IAS 21 – *The Effects of Changes in Foreign Exchange Rates* – requires at year-end (see Chapter 15). *[IAS 34.B29]*. An entity should use the actual average and closing foreign exchange rates for the interim period (i.e. it may not anticipate changes in foreign exchange rates for the remainder of the current year in translating at an interim date). *[IAS 34.B30]*. Where IAS 21 requires translation adjustments to be recognised as income or expense in the period in which they arise, the same approach should be used in the interim report. An entity should not defer some foreign currency translation adjustments at an interim date, even if it expects the adjustment to reverse before year-end. *[IAS 34.B31]*.

9.6.2 *Interim financial reporting in hyperinflationary economies*

Interim financial reports in hyperinflationary economies are prepared using the same principles as at year-end. *[IAS 34.B32]*. IAS 29 – *Financial Reporting in Hyperinflationary Economies* – requires that the financial statements of an entity that reports in the currency of a hyperinflationary economy be stated in terms of the measuring unit current at the end of the reporting period, and the gain or loss on the net monetary position be included in net income. In addition, comparative financial data reported for prior periods should be restated to the current measuring unit (see Chapter 16). *[IAS 34.B33]*.

In practice, interim reporting under IAS 34 can be onerous for an entity whose functional currency is that of a hyperinflationary economy. As shown in Examples 37.2 and 37.3 above, IAS 34 requires an interim report to contain many components, which are all restated at every interim reporting date.

The measuring unit used is the same as that as of the end of the interim period, with the resulting gain or loss on the net monetary position included in that period's net income. An entity may not annualise the recognition of gains or losses, nor may it estimate an annual inflation rate in preparing an interim financial report in a hyperinflationary economy. *[IAS 34.B34].*

IAS 29 applies from the beginning of the reporting period in which an entity identifies the existence of hyperinflation in the country in whose currency it reports. *[IAS 29.4].* Accordingly, for interim reporting purposes, IAS 29 should be applied from the beginning of the interim period in which the hyperinflation is identified. The Interpretations Committee clarified that adoption of IAS 29 should be fully retrospective, by applying its requirements as if the economy had always been hyperinflationary (see Chapter 16 at 9). *[IFRIC 7.3].*

It is less obvious though, as to how a parent, which does not operate in a hyperinflationary economy, should account for the restatement of a subsidiary that operates in an economy that becomes hyperinflationary in the current reporting period when incorporating it within its consolidated financial statements.

This issue has been clarified by paragraph 42(b) of IAS 21 which specifically prohibits restatement of comparative figures when the reporting currency is not hyperinflationary. This means that when the financial statements of a hyperinflationary subsidiary are translated into the non-hyperinflationary reporting currency of the parent, the comparative amounts are not adjusted.

Notwithstanding the above, some argue that in interim period reports of the subsequent year, the parent should adjust its comparative information for the corresponding interim periods which are part of the (first) full financial year affected by hyperinflation. This is because comparative interim information had been part of the full year financial statements, which were adjusted for hyperinflation.

In our view, the parent is allowed, but not required, to adjust the comparative interim information that relates to the first full financial year affected by hyperinflation, as illustrated in the example below:

Example 37.19: Accounting by the parent when a hyperinflationary subsidiary first applies IAS 29

A parent with 31 December year-end owns a subsidiary, whose functional currency is considered hyperinflationary from 31 July 2013 onwards. In preparing its interim consolidated financial statements for the quarter ended 31 March 2014, the parent consolidates this subsidiary in both the current and comparative interim periods.

In our view the parent is allowed, but not required, to adjust the comparative interim information (for the quarter ended 31 March 2013) in its 31 March 2014 interim financial report.

Whilst IAS 34 and IAS 29 are silent on the matter, a corollary of this approach suggests that when an economy stops being hyperinflationary, the entity should stop applying the requirements of IAS 29 during that interim period. However, in practice, it is difficult to determine when an economy stops being hyperinflationary. The characteristics indicating restored confidence in an economy (such as the population ceasing to store wealth in a more stable foreign currency) change gradually as sufficient time elapses to indicate that the three-year cumulative inflation rate is likely to stay below 100%. When the exit from hyperinflation can reasonably be identified, an entity should stop applying IAS 29 in that interim period. Prior interim periods should not be restated; instead, the entity should treat the amounts expressed in the measuring unit current as at the end of the previous reporting period as the basis for the carrying amounts in its subsequent interim reports *[IAS 29.38]* (see Chapter 16 at 7.2).

9.7 Provisions, contingencies and accruals for other costs

9.7.1 Provisions

IAS 34 requires an entity to apply the same criteria for recognising and measuring a provision at an interim date as it would at year-end. *[IAS 34.B4].* Hence, an entity should recognise a provision when it has no realistic alternative but to transfer economic benefits because of an event that has created a legal or constructive obligation. *[IAS 34.B3].* The standard emphasises that the existence or non-existence of an obligation to transfer benefits is a question of fact, and does not depend on the length of the reporting period. *[IAS 34.B4].*

The obligation is adjusted upward or downward at each interim reporting date, if the entity's best estimate of the amount of the obligation changes. The standard states that any corresponding loss or gain should normally be recognised in profit or loss. *[IAS 34.B3].* However, an entity applying IFRIC 1 – *Changes in Existing Decommissioning, Restoration and Similar Liabilities* – might instead need to adjust the carrying amount of the corresponding asset rather than recognise a gain or loss.

9.7.2 Other planned but irregularly occurring costs

Many entities budget for costs that they expect to incur irregularly during the year, such as advertising campaigns, employee training and charitable contributions. Even though these costs are planned and expected to recur annually, they tend to be discretionary in nature. Therefore, it is generally not appropriate to recognise an obligation at the end of an interim financial reporting period for such costs that are not yet incurred, as they do not meet the definition of a liability. *[IAS 34.B11].*

As discussed at 8.2.2 above, IAS 34 prohibits the recognition or deferral of costs incurred unevenly throughout the year at the interim date if recognition or deferral would be inappropriate at year-end. *[IAS 34.39].* Accordingly, such costs should be recognised as they are incurred and an entity should not recognise provisions or accruals in the interim report to adjust these costs to their budgeted amount.

Extract 37.32: Coca-Cola Hellenic Bottling Company S.A. (Q2, 2011)

Selected explanatory notes to the condensed consolidated interim financial statements (unaudited) [extract]

1. **Accounting policies** [extract]

Basis of preparation [extract]

Operating results for the first half of 2011 are not indicative of the results that may be expected for the year ended 31 December 2011 because of business seasonality. Business seasonality results from higher unit sales of the Group's products in the warmer months of the year. The Group's methods of accounting for fixed costs such as depreciation and interest expense are not significantly affected by business seasonality.

Costs that are incurred unevenly during the financial year are anticipated or deferred in the interim report only if it would also be appropriate to anticipate or defer such costs at the end of the financial year.

9.7.3 *Major planned periodic maintenance or overhaul*

The cost of periodic maintenance, a planned major overhaul, or other seasonal expenditures expected to occur after the interim reporting date should not be recognised for interim reporting purposes unless an event before the end of the interim period causes the entity to have a legal or constructive obligation. The mere intention or necessity to incur expenditures in the future is not sufficient to recognise an obligation as at the interim reporting date. *[IAS 34.B2].* Similarly, an entity may not defer and amortise such costs if they are incurred early in the year, but do not satisfy the criteria for recognition as an asset as at the interim reporting date.

9.7.4 *Contingent lease payments*

Contingent lease payments can create legal or constructive obligations that are recognised as liabilities. If a lease includes contingent payments based on achieving a certain level of annual sales (or annual use of the asset), an obligation can arise in an interim period before the required level of annual sales (or usage) is achieved. If the entity expects to achieve the required level of annual sales (or usage), it should recognise a liability as it has no realistic alternative but to make the future lease payment. *[IAS 34.B7].*

9.7.5 *Levies charged by public authorities*

When governments or other public authorities impose levies on entities in relation to their activities, as opposed to income taxes, it is not always clear when the liability to pay a levy arises and a provision should be recognised. In May 2013, the Interpretations Committee issued Interpretation 21 – *Levies*. The scope of the Interpretation is limited to provisions within the scope of IAS 37 and specifically need not be applied to emissions trading schemes. *[IFRIC 21.2, 6].*

The Interpretation requires that an activity within its scope, an entity should recognise a liability for a levy only when the activity that triggers payment, as identified by the relevant legislation, occurs *[IFRIC 21.8].* The Interpretation states that neither a constructive nor a present obligation arises as a result of being economically compelled to continue operating; or from any implication of continuing operations in the future arising from the use of the going concern assumption in the preparation of financial statements (see Chapter 27 at 6.8). *[IFRIC 21.9-10].*

The Interpretation states that the same recognition principles should be applied in the interim financial statements. Therefore, a liability for any levy expense should not be anticipated if there is no present obligation to pay the levy at the end of the interim reporting period. Similarly, a liability should not be deferred if a present obligation to pay the levy exists at the end of the interim period. *[IFRIC 21.31]*.

This is relatively simple when a levy is triggered on a specific day or when a specific event occurs. When a levy is triggered progressively, for example as the entity generates revenues, the levy is accrued over time. At any time in the year, the entity would have a present obligation to pay an amount of levy that would be based on revenues generated to that date and recognises a liability and an expense on that basis. *[IFRIC 21.11]*.

If a levy is triggered in full as soon as the entity commences generating revenues, the liability is recognised in full on the first day that the entity commences generating revenue. In this case, the entity does not defer any expense and amortise this amount over the year or otherwise allocate it to subsequent interim periods. The example below illustrates this situation. *[IFRIC 21.IE.1 Example 2]*.

Example 37.20: A levy is triggered in full as soon as the entity generates revenue

An entity has a calendar year end. In accordance with legislation, a levy is triggered in full as soon as the entity generates revenue in 2014. The amount of the levy is determined by reference to revenue generated by the entity in 2013. The entity generated revenue in 2013 and starts to generate revenue in 2014 on 3 January 2014.

In this example, the liability is recognised in full on 3 January 2014 because the obligating event, as identified by the legislation, is the first generation of revenue in 2014. The generation of revenue in 2013 is necessary, but not sufficient, to create a present obligation to pay a levy. Before 3 January 2014, the entity has no obligation. In other words, the activity that triggers the payment of the levy as identified by the legislation is the first generation of revenue at a point in time in 2014. The generation of revenues in 2013 is not the activity that triggers the payment of the levy. The amount of revenue generated in 2013 only affects the measurement of the liability.

In the interim financial report, because the liability is recognised in full on 3 January 2014, the expense is recognised in full in the first interim period of 2014. The expense should not be deferred until subsequent interim periods and shall not be anticipated in previous interim periods.

When the legislation provides that a levy is triggered by an entity operating in a market only at the end of the annual reporting period, no liability is recognised until the last day of the annual reporting period. No amount is recognised before that date in anticipation of the entity still operating in the market. In the interim financial reports, no liability for the levy expense in this case is recognised. Only if the entity reports for the last quarter of that year would the expenditure appear in an interim report. *[IFRIC 21.IE.1 Example 2]*.

These requirements provide a clear demonstration of what is meant by the concept of the 'year-to-date' basis in IAS 34 and discussed at 8 above. The Interpretations Committee considers IFRIC 21 to be consistent with the examples in IAS 34 discussed at 9.7.1-3 above. *[IFRIC 21.BC29]*. These examples do not include those which imply that there are circumstances in which the expectation of meeting a future obligation can be taken into account, such as in the case of employer payroll taxes and insurance contributions (see 9.3.1 above); when considering the effect of volume rebates and other contractual price changes (see 9.4.2 above); and in accounting for contingent lease payments (see 9.7.4 above).

9.8 Earnings per share

Earnings per share (EPS) in an interim period is computed in the same way as for annual periods. However, IAS 33 – *Earnings per Share* – does not allow diluted EPS of a prior period to be restated for subsequent changes in the assumptions used in those EPS calculations. *[IAS 33.65]*. This approach might be perceived as inconsistent to the year-to-date approach which should be followed for computing EPS for an interim period. For example, if an entity, reporting quarterly, computes diluted EPS in its first quarter financial statements, it cannot restate the reported diluted EPS subsequently for any changes in the assumptions used. However, following a year-to-date approach, the entity should consider the revised assumptions to compute the diluted EPS for the six months in its second quarter financial statements, which, in this case would not be the sum of its diluted EPS for first quarter and the second quarter.

10 USE OF ESTIMATES

IAS 34 requires that the measurement procedures followed in an interim financial report should be designed to ensure that the resulting information is reliable and that all material financial information that is relevant to an understanding of the financial position or performance of the entity is appropriately disclosed. Whilst estimation is necessary in both interim and annual financial statements, the standard recognises that preparing interim financial reports generally requires greater use of estimates than at year-end. *[IAS 34.41]*. Consequently, the measurement of assets and liabilities at an interim date may involve less use of outside experts in determining amounts for items such as provisions, contingencies, pensions or non-current assets revalued at fair values. Reliable measurement of such amounts may simply involve updating the previously reported year-end position. The procedures may be less rigorous than those at year-end. The example below is based on Appendix C to IAS 34. *[IAS 34.42]*.

Example 37.21: Use of estimates

Inventories	Full stock-taking and valuation procedures may not be required for inventories at interim dates, although it may be done at year-end. It may be sufficient to make estimates at interim dates based on sales margins.
Classifications of current and non-current assets and liabilities	Entities may do a more thorough investigation for classifying assets and liabilities as current or non-current at annual reporting dates than at interim dates.
Provisions	Determining the appropriate provision (such as a provision for warranties, environmental costs, and site restoration costs) may be complex and often costly and time-consuming. Entities sometimes engage outside experts to assist in the annual calculations. Making similar estimates at interim dates often entails updating of the prior annual provision rather than the engaging of outside experts to do a new calculation.

Pensions	IAS 19 requires an entity to determine the present value of defined benefit obligations and the fair value of plan assets at the end of each reporting period and encourages an entity to involve a professionally qualified actuary in measurement of the obligations. As discussed at 9.3.3 above, market values of plan assets as at the interim reporting date should be available without recourse to an actuary, and reliable measurement of defined benefit obligations for interim reporting purposes can often be extrapolated from the latest actuarial valuation.
Income taxes	Entities may calculate income tax expense and deferred income tax liability at annual dates by applying the tax rate for each individual jurisdiction to measures of income for each jurisdiction. Paragraph 14 of Appendix B (see 9.5.1 above) acknowledges that while that degree of precision is desirable at interim reporting dates as well, it may not be achievable in all cases, and a weighted-average of rates across jurisdictions or across categories of income is used if it is a reasonable approximation of the effect of using more specific rates.
Contingencies	The measurement of contingencies may involve the opinions of legal experts or other advisers. Formal reports from independent experts are sometimes obtained for contingencies. Such opinions about litigation, claims, assessments, and other contingencies and uncertainties may or may not also be needed at interim dates.
Revaluations and fair value accounting	IAS 16 allows an entity to choose as its accounting policy the revaluation model whereby items of property, plant and equipment are revalued to fair value. Similarly, IAS 40 – *Investment Property* – requires an entity to measure the fair value of investment property. An entity should revalue at the end of the interim reporting period, but may choose not to rely on professionally qualified valuers to the extent that is required at year-end.
Intercompany reconciliations	Some intercompany balances that are reconciled on a detailed level in preparing consolidated financial statements at year-end might be reconciled at a less detailed level in preparing consolidated financial statements at an interim date.
Specialised industries	Because of complexity, costliness, and time, interim period measurements in specialised industries might be less precise than at year-end. An example is calculation of insurance reserves by insurance companies.

Attention is given to items that are recognised at fair value. Although an entity is not required to use professionally qualified valuers at interim reporting dates, and may only update the previous year-end position, the entity is required to recognise impairments in the proper interim period.

11 RESTATEMENT OF PREVIOUSLY REPORTED INTERIM PERIODS

As discussed at 8.1 above, an entity should apply the same accounting policies as applied in the most recent annual financial statements as adjusted for accounting policy changes that are to be reflected in the next annual financial statements. *[IAS 34.28]*. One objective of IAS 34's rules on the adoption of new accounting policies is to ensure that a single accounting policy is applied to a particular class of transactions throughout the year. Another objective is to ensure consistency with IAS 8, under which a change in accounting policy is adopted retrospectively and prior period financial data are restated as far back as practicable. *[IAS 34.44].*

In the absence of any specified transitional provisions in a new IFRS or interpretation, IAS 34 requires a change in accounting policy to be reflected: *[IAS 34.43]*

(a) by restating the financial statements of prior interim periods of the current year, and the comparable interim periods of any prior years that will be restated in the annual financial statements under IAS 8; or

(b) when it is impracticable to determine the cumulative effect at the beginning of the year of applying a new accounting policy to all prior periods, by:

  (i) adjusting the financial statements of prior interim periods of the current year; and

  (ii) applying the new accounting policy prospectively from the earliest date practicable in comparable interim periods of prior years.

IAS 1 states that application of a requirement is 'impracticable' when the entity cannot apply it after making every reasonable effort to do so. *[IAS 1.7].*

While an entity may adopt a change in accounting policy during the year, it is generally not permitted to change an accounting policy, i.e. to apply the new accounting policy, from a date later than the beginning of the current year, for example, as at the start of the second quarter for an entity reporting quarterly. To do so allows two different accounting policies be applied to a particular class of transactions within a single year and makes interim allocation difficult, obscures operating results, and complicates the analysis and understandability of interim period information. *[IAS 34.45].* However, as noted in 8.1.2 above, in certain circumstances an entity is allowed or required to adopt an IFRS mid-year in a manner that over-rides the general requirements of IAS 8. If an entity prepares a complete set of financial statements, it should present a third statement of financial position. *[IAS 34.5(f)].* (See 3.1 above).

12 EFFECTIVE DATES AND TRANSITIONAL RULES

12.1 First-time presentation of interim reports complying with IAS 34

IAS 34 became effective for financial statements covering periods beginning on or after 1 January 1999; it did not contain any general transitional rules. *[IAS 34.46].* Therefore, an existing IFRS reporting entity must apply the requirements of IAS 34 in full and without any transitional relief when it first chooses (or is required) to publish an interim financial report prepared under IFRS.

For example, an entity that has already published annual financial statements prepared under IFRS and either chooses (or is required) to prepare interim financial reports in compliance with IAS 34 must present all the information required by the standard for the current interim period, cumulatively for the current year-to-date, and for comparable periods (current and year-to-date) of the preceding year. *[IAS 34.20]*. The absence of any transitional provisions requires such entities to restate previously reported interim financial information to comply with IAS 34 and to present information relating to comparative interim periods, such as in respect of segment disclosures or in relation to asset write-downs and reversals thereof, which might not previously have been reported.

12.1.1 Condensed financial statements in the year of incorporation or when an entity converts from its local GAAP to IFRS

The standard defines 'interim period' as a financial reporting period shorter than a full financial year *[IAS 34.4]* and requires the format of condensed financial statements for an interim period to include each of the headings and subtotals that were included in the entity's most recent annual financial statements. *[IAS 34.10]*.

However, IAS 34 provides no guidance for an entity that either is required or chooses to issue interim financial statements before it has prepared a set of IFRS compliant annual financial statements. This situation might arise in the entity's first year of its existence or in the year in which the entity converts from its local GAAP to IFRS. Whilst the standard does not prohibit the entity from preparing a condensed set of interim financial statements, it fails to specify how an entity would interpret the minimum disclosure requirements of IAS 34 when there are no annual financial statements to refer to.

In our view, the entity should consider making additional disclosures to recognise that a user of this first set of interim financial statements does not have the access otherwise assumed by the standard to the most recent annual financial report of the entity. Accordingly, the explanation of significant events and transactions and changes in financial position in the period should be more detailed than the update normally expected in IAS 34. *[IAS 34.15]*. In the absence of any specific regulatory requirements to which the entity is subject, the following are examples of additional considerations that would apply:

- since it is not possible to make a statement that the same accounting policies and methods of computation have been applied, *[IAS 34.16A(a)]*, the entity should disclose all those accounting policies and methods of computation in the same level of detail as it would in a set of annual financial statements. When the entity issues interim reports on a quarterly basis, the first quarter interim report should provide the abovementioned details; subsequent quarterly reports could refer to the details included in the first quarter report;
- similarly, the disclosure of the nature and amount of changes in estimates of amounts reported in prior periods will have to go into more detail than just the changes normally required to be disclosed; *[IAS 34.16A(d)]*
- mere disclosure of transfers between levels of the fair value hierarchy used in measuring the fair value of financial instruments, *[IAS 34.15B(k)]*, would not be meaningful unless put in the context of how those fair values are determined (e.g. methods used, any assumptions applied) and providing a detailed classification of all such financial instrument measurements using fair value hierarchy, based on the significance of the inputs used;

- rather than disclosing changes in the basis of segmentation or in the basis of measurement of segment profit and loss, *[IAS 34.16A(g)(v)]*, a full description will be necessary, as will the disclosure of segment assets and liabilities *[IAS 34.16A(g)(iv)]*, where such information is required to be disclosed in the annual financial statements *[IAS 34.16A(g)]*;
- more extensive disclosure than simply the changes since the last report date will be required for contingent liabilities and contingent assets; *[IAS 34.15B(m)]* and
- in the absence of a complete set of annual financial statements complying with IFRS, the entity should include each of the headings and subtotals in the condensed financial statements that it would expect to include in its first financial statements prepared under IFRS.

Entities that have converted from local GAAP to IFRS and have not yet published IFRS annual financial statements are subject to additional requirements under IFRS 1 – *First-time Adoption of International Financial Reporting Standards* – when presenting interim reports in accordance with IAS 34. Such requirements are discussed in detail in Chapter 5 at 6.6.

12.2 Consequential amendments to IFRIC 10 when first adopting IFRS 9

As discussed at 9.2 above, the IASB issued IFRS 9 in November 2009 (subsequently expanded and amended in October 2010), which made amendments to IFRIC 10. The amendment deletes references to equity instruments and financial assets carried at cost. With the adoption of IFRS 9, such financial assets would not be carried at cost and as a consequence, the determination of impairment and related reversals would not be relevant for such instruments in this context.

These amendments should be applied concurrently with the adoption of IFRS 9, which is mandatory for annual periods beginning on or after 1 January 2015 *[IFRS 9.7.1.1]*. The transitional arrangements for the adoption of IFRS 9 are discussed in Chapter 45 at 10.

References

1 *IASB Update*, April 2013, p.4
2 *IFRIC Update*, July 2013, p.10
3 *IASB Update*, May 2013, p.6; and IASB Agenda Paper 17: Annual Improvements to IFRSs – 2012-2014 cycle, Disclosure of information 'elsewhere in the interim financial report', May 2013.

Chapter 38 Agriculture

List of examples

Chapter 38 Agriculture

1 INTRODUCTION

IAS 41 – *Agriculture* – prescribes the accounting treatment for agricultural activity, from the initial recognition of a biological asset to the harvest of agricultural produce.

Practical difficulties arise when determining which assets are within the scope of the standard, particularly for arrangements that involve leases or concessions. However, it is the standard's application of the fair value model that is the most problematic and contentious.

For assets that are in-scope, IAS 41 requires the application of the fair value model to animals and plant life alike, with limited relief. Under this approach, a market price for a part-grown crop is presumed to exist (or is presumed to be reliably measureable if there is no such market price) and the part-grown crop must be valued at this price in the entity's financial statements. The fair value model is also applied to all biological assets regardless of whether they are consumed as part of the agricultural activity (consumable biological assets) or not (bearer biological assets).

During their June 2009 meeting, members of the IFRS Advisory Council observed that bearer biological assets such as rubber trees and vines do not produce offspring, but rather produce a flow of product, be that latex or grapes, in very much the same way as any other piece of plant and equipment. As a result of this discussion and subsequent discussions by the National Standard-Setters, the IASB acknowledged the concerns that had been raised regarding the application of the fair value model to bearer biological assets and added a limited scope project onto its agenda in September 2012.[1] As a result of this project, in June 2013, the IASB issued an exposure draft that proposed changes for a subset of bearer biological assets; specifically plants that met certain criteria. The proposed amendments are discussed further at 6 below. At the time of writing, the exposure draft was still open for comments, which were due by 28 October 2013.

2 OBJECTIVE, DEFINITIONS AND SCOPE

2.1 Objective

The stated objective of IAS 41 is to 'prescribe the accounting treatment and disclosures related to agricultural activity'. *[IAS 41 Objective]*.

2.2 Definitions

2.2.1 *Agriculture-related definitions*

IAS 41 defines *agricultural activity* as 'the management by an entity of the biological transformation and harvest of biological assets for sale or for conversion into agricultural produce or into additional biological assets'. *[IAS 41.5]*.

The standard states that 'agricultural activity' covers a wide range of activities, e.g. 'raising livestock, forestry, annual or perennial cropping, cultivating orchards and plantations, floriculture, and aquaculture (including fish farming)'. *[IAS 41.6]*. Nevertheless, these agricultural activities have certain common features:

'(a) *Capability to change* – Living animals and plants are capable of biological transformation;

(b) *Management of change* – Management facilitates biological transformation by enhancing, or at least stabilising, conditions necessary for the process to take place (for example, nutrient levels, moisture, temperature, fertility, and light). Such management distinguishes agricultural activity from other activities. For example, harvesting from unmanaged sources (such as ocean fishing and deforestation) is not agricultural activity; and

(c) *Measurement of change* – The change in quality (for example, genetic merit, density, ripeness, fat cover, protein content, and fibre strength) or quantity (for example, progeny, weight, cubic metres, fibre length or diameter, and number of buds) brought about by biological transformation "or harvest" is measured and monitored as a routine management function.' *[IAS 41.6]*.

Biological transformation under IAS 41 'comprises the processes of growth, degeneration, production, and procreation that cause qualitative or quantitative changes in a biological asset'. *[IAS 41.5]*. The standard explains that biological transformation results in the following types of outcomes:

'(a) asset changes through:

- (i) growth (an increase in quantity or improvement in quality of an animal or plant);
- (ii) degeneration (a decrease in the quantity or deterioration in quality of an animal or plant); or
- (iii) procreation (creation of additional living animals or plants); or

(b) production of agricultural produce such as latex, tea leaf, wool, and milk.' *[IAS 41.7]*.

IAS 41 defines the following additional terms that are used throughout the standard: *[IAS 41.5]*

- A *biological asset* is a living animal or plant.
- A *group of biological assets* is an aggregation of similar living animals or plants.
- *Agricultural produce* is the harvested product of the entity's biological assets.
- *Harvest* is the detachment of produce from a biological asset or the cessation of a biological asset's life processes.

The standard provides the following examples to illustrate the above definitions: *[IAS 41.4]*

Biological assets	Agricultural produce	Products that are the result of processing after harvest
Sheep	Wool	Yarn, carpet
Trees in a plantation forest	Felled trees	Logs, lumber
Plants	Cotton	Thread, clothing
	Harvested cane	Sugar
Dairy cattle	Milk	Cheese
Pigs	Carcass	Sausages, cured hams
Bushes	Leaf	Tea, cured tobacco
Vines	Grapes	Wine
Fruit trees	Picked fruit	Processed fruit

Costs to sell are the incremental costs directly attributable to the disposal of an asset excluding finance costs and income taxes.

2.2.2 General definitions

IAS 41 defines the general terms it uses throughout the standard as follows: *[IAS 41.8]*

- *Carrying amount* is the amount at which an asset is recognised in the statement of financial position.
- Government grants are as defined in IAS 20 – *Accounting for Government Grants and Disclosure of Government Assistance* (see Chapter 25).

With the introduction of IFRS 13 – *Fair Value Measurement*, the definitions of fair value and active market were deleted from IAS 41. IFRS 13 defines fair value as 'the price that would be received to sell an asset or paid to transfer a liability in an orderly transaction between market participants at the measurement date'. *[IFRS 13.9]*. Measuring fair value in accordance with IFRS 13 is discussed further at 4 below and in Chapter 14.

2.3 Scope

IAS 41 applies to accounting for biological assets, agricultural produce at the point of harvest and government grants involving biological assets measured at fair value less costs to sell. However to be within the scope of IAS 41, these items must relate to agricultural activity. *[IAS 41.1]*.

IAS 41 explicitly excludes the following assets from its scope: *[IAS 41.2]*

- land related to agricultural activity, which should be accounted for under either IAS 16 – *Property, Plant and Equipment* – or IAS 40 – *Investment Property* – and; *[IAS 41.B55-B57]*
- intangible assets related to agricultural activity, for instance the costs of developing new disease resistant crops, which should be accounted for under IAS 38 – *Intangible Assets*. *[IAS 41.B58-B60]*.

In June 2013, the IASB issued an exposure draft that proposed changes to the scope of IAS 41 for biological assets that met a proposed definition of bearer plants. A summary of the proposed changes are discussed at 6 below.

2.3.1 Biological assets outside the scope of IAS 41

Biological assets may be outside the scope of IAS 41 when they are not used in agricultural activity. For example, animals in a zoo (or game park) that does not have an active breeding programme and rarely sells any animals or animal products would be outside the scope of the standard. Another example is activities in the pharmaceutical industry that involve the culture of bacteria. Such activity would not fall within the scope of IAS 41. While the bacteria may be considered a biological asset, the development of a culture by a pharmaceutical company would not constitute agricultural activity.

Biological assets outside the scope of IAS 41 will normally fall within the scope of either IAS 16 or IAS 2 – *Inventories.*

2.3.2 Agricultural produce before and after harvest

IAS 41 only applies to agricultural produce (i.e. harvested crops) at the point of harvest and not prior or subsequent to harvest. Under IAS 41, unharvested agricultural produce is considered to be part of the biological asset from which it will be harvested. Therefore, before harvest, agricultural produce should not be accounted for separately from the biological asset from which it comes. Thus, for example, grapes on the vine should be accounted for as part of the vines themselves right up to the point of harvest.

Subsequent to harvest, agricultural produce is accounted for under IAS 2. *[IAS 41.3].* Under that standard the agricultural produce is initially recognised as inventory at its fair value less costs to sell, which becomes its cost for IAS 2 purposes. *[IAS 41.B45].*

2.3.3 Products that are the result of processing after harvest

IAS 41 does not deal with the processing of agricultural produce after harvest. The standard makes it clear that, even if the processing is considered 'a logical and natural extension of agricultural activity, and the events taking place ... bear some similarity to biological transformation, such processing is not included within the definition of agricultural activity'. For example, the processing of grapes into wine – a process in which yeast (a fungus) converts sugars into alcohol – is not deemed to be included within the definition of agricultural activity in the standard. *[IAS 41.3].* Similarly, cheese production would fall outside the definition of agricultural activity.

2.3.4 Leased assets

Leases involving biological assets are common in many jurisdictions, for example, the leasing of a vineyard, where the lessee rents the vineyard, including the land, vines and other assets, tends the vines and sells the grapes.

Whether or not a leased biological asset is within the scope of IAS 41 will depend on the specific facts and circumstances of each arrangement. A key determinant is the classification of a biological asset lease as either a finance lease or operating lease under IAS 17 – *Leases* (see Chapter 24 for a discussion regarding leases). *[IAS 41.B82(n)].*

For finance leases of biological assets:

- The lessee initially recognises the leased biological asset under IAS 17. Subsequently, the lessee measures and presents it under IAS 41 (for measurement purposes the leased biological asset is outside the scope of IAS 17). The lessee accounts for the lease liability in accordance with IAS 17. The lessee makes disclosures both under IAS 41 and IAS 17. *[IAS 41.B82(n)]*.
- The lessor accounts for the net investment in the lease (i.e. the lease receivable, not the biological asset) in accordance with IAS 17.

For operating leases of biological assets:

- The lessee accounts for the lease (i.e. the expensed lease payments, not the biological asset) in accordance with IAS 17.
- The lessor measures and presents the leased biological asset under IAS 41 (for measurement purposes the leased biological asset is outside the scope of IAS 17). The lessor accounts for other rights and obligations under the lease (e.g. lease income) in accordance with IAS 17. The lessor makes disclosures both under IAS 41 and IAS 17. *[IAS 41.B82(n)]*.

Biological asset lease arrangements may include the land to which the biological asset is attached. Any leased land would need to be separately accounted for under the relevant standard, for example IAS 16 or IAS 40, as it is explicitly excluded from the scope of IAS 41 (see 2.3 above).

In the example above, where the vines are leased under an operating lease, the arrangement would be within the scope of IAS 41. Therefore, the lessor must account for the leased vines (excluding any related land) under IAS 41 – both upon initial recognition and subsequently – at fair value less costs to sell. It is worth noting that paragraph 1 of IAS 41 requires the standard to be applied to biological assets when they relate to agricultural activity. In this case, the grapes are the agricultural produce and vines are managed, albeit by the lessee and not the lessor. Since IAS 41 does not specify who must do the managing, the definition of agricultural activity is met.

The IASB, jointly with the US FASB, is currently undertaking a project on lease accounting (see Chapter 24). The resulting standard is expected to include requirements that differ significantly from the current IAS 17. In the May 2013 exposure draft specifically excluded biological assets that are within the scope of IAS 41 from the proposed scope of the final leases standard. However, it is not yet clear whether these proposals will change who, lessee or lessor, accounts for a leased biological asset in accordance with IAS 41.

2.3.5 Concessions

A concession typically involves a government, or other controlling authority, granting land to an entity, but requiring that the land be used for a specific purpose, for example growing certain crops for a minimum period of time.

The treatment of each concession will be dependent on the specific facts and circumstances. However, if the concession requires an entity to undertake agricultural activity (see 2.2.1 above), the agricultural activity will be within the scope of IAS 41. The grant received may also be within the scope of the standard. However, the land granted would be within the scope of IAS 16 or IAS 40. The discussion at 3.3 below addresses the treatment of government grants related to biological assets.

3 RECOGNITION AND MEASUREMENT PRINCIPLES

3.1 Recognition

An entity recognises a biological asset or agricultural produce that is within the scope of IAS 41 only when: *[IAS 41.10]*

(a) it controls the asset as a result of past events;

(b) it is probable that future economic benefits associated with the asset will flow to the entity; and

(c) the fair value or cost of the asset can be measured reliably.

3.1.1 Control

In agricultural activity, an entity may evidence control by, for example, 'legal ownership of cattle and the branding or otherwise marking of the cattle on acquisition, birth, or weaning'. *[IAS 41.11]*.

3.2 Measurement

3.2.1 Biological assets

3.2.1.A Initial and subsequent measurement

A biological asset is measured on initial recognition and at the end of each reporting period at its fair value less costs to sell, unless an entity can demonstrate at initial recognition that fair value cannot be measured reliably. *[IAS 41.12]*. In the latter case, the entity measures the biological asset at historic cost less any accumulated depreciation and any accumulated impairment losses (see 3.2.4 below), unless fair value becomes reliably measureable.

3.2.1.B Subsequent expenditure

IAS 41 does not prescribe how an entity should account for subsequent expenditure in relation to biological assets, because the (then) IASC believed this to be unnecessary with a fair-value-based measurement approach. *[IAS 41.B62]*.

Such expenditure may be expensed as incurred or capitalised as additions to the related biological asset. However, under the fair value model, the biological asset will be re-measured at the end of each reporting period. As such, any amounts capitalised will only result in a reallocation between expenses and the fair value gain or loss for the biological asset. Therefore, an entity's policy in relation to subsequent expenditure will have no effect on its equity or net profit or loss, although it will affect:

- the reconciliation of changes in the carrying amount of biological assets;
- the classification of the expenditure in the income statement as either an expense or as part of the net gain or loss on biological assets; and
- the presentation of investments in biological assets in the statement of cash flows.

In our view, an entity should select an accounting policy for subsequent expenditure that is broadly consistent with the principles in other standards, such as IAS 16 and IAS 38. For example, in the case of a vineyard an entity may want to expense maintenance costs such as pruning, while adding capital expenditure such as planting new vines to the carrying value of the asset; though it must be understood that any such additions would be adjusted at each period end when the biological asset concerned is revalued to its new fair value.

3.2.2 *Agricultural produce*

Agricultural produce harvested from an entity's biological assets should initially 'be measured at its fair value less costs to sell at the point of harvest'. *[IAS 41.13]*. The standard presumes that an entity can always reliably measure this amount and hence does not permit valuation at historical cost. *[IAS 41.32, B43]*.

The value resulting from initial measurement is subsequently used as cost in applying IAS 2 (if the agricultural produce is to be sold), IAS 16 (if harvested logs are used for the construction of a building) or other applicable IFRSs. *[IAS 41.13, B8]*.

An important reason for requiring agricultural produce at the point of harvest to be measured at fair value was to ensure that the basis of measurement would be consistent with that of biological assets and to avoid inconsistent and distorted reporting of current period performance upon harvest of agricultural produce. *[IAS 41.B42]*.

3.2.3 *Gains and losses*

IAS 41 requires gains and losses arising on the initial recognition of a biological asset at fair value less costs to sell to be included in profit or loss for the period in which they arise. *[IAS 41.26]*. The standard warns that '[a] loss may arise on initial recognition of a biological asset, because costs to sell are deducted in determining fair value less costs to sell of a biological asset.' On the other hand, a gain may arise on the initial recognition of a biological asset (e.g. when a calf is born). *[IAS 41.27]*.

Subsequent to initial recognition, reported gains or losses essentially represent the difference between two fair values. As such, the standard effectively decouples profit recognition from a sales transaction. One consequence of this approach is to anticipate a realised profit, often by a matter of years for long-term crops such as trees.

The implications for initial recognition of agricultural produce are similar – an entity may need to recognise a gain or loss on agricultural produce upon harvesting, if the fair value of the harvested produce is different from the pre-harvest valuation. *[IAS 41.29]*. The standard requires that '[a] gain or loss arising on initial recognition of agricultural produce at fair value less costs to sell ... be included in profit or loss for the period in which it arises'. *[IAS 41.28]*.

3.2.4 Inability to measure fair value reliably

3.2.4.A Rebutting the presumption

Under IAS 41, there is a presumption that the fair value of all biological assets can be measured reliably. This presumption can only be rebutted on initial recognition for a biological asset (*not* agricultural produce). To be able to rebut the presumption, an entity must demonstrate that:

(a) quoted market prices for the biological asset are not available; and

(b) alternative fair value measurements for the biological asset are determined to be clearly unreliable. *[IAS 41.30]*.

Since IAS 41 requires that the fair value of a biological asset be measured in accordance with IFRS 13, an entity would need to consider the requirements of that standard in order to determine whether fair value can be reliably measured.

An entity that previously measured a biological asset at its fair value less costs to sell cannot revert to a cost-based measurement in a later period, even if a fair value can no longer be measured reliably. *[IAS 41.31]*. The standard assumes that reliable estimates of fair value would rarely, if ever, cease to be available. *[IAS 41.B36]*. Section 4.7 below discusses more fully some of the practical problems associated with determining fair value in the absence of a market price.

If it becomes possible at a later date to measure the fair value of a biological asset reliably, the entity is required to apply the fair value model to that asset from that date onwards. *[IAS 41.30]*. In developing the standard, the (then) IASC noted in this respect that 'in agricultural activity, it is likely that fair value becomes measurable more reliably as biological transformation occurs and that fair value measurement is preferable to cost in those cases'. Therefore, the IASC 'decided to require fair value measurement once fair value becomes reliably measurable'. *[IAS 41.B35]*.

IAS 41 presumes that the fair value of a non-current biological asset that 'meets the criteria to be classified as held for sale (or is included in a disposal group that is classified as held for sale) in accordance with IFRS 5 – *Non-current Assets Held for Sale and Discontinued Operations*' can always be measured reliably. *[IAS 41.30]*.

In situations where the cost model is initially applied and then fair value becomes reliably measurable, the question arises as to whether acquisition-related transaction costs (i.e. those that have been incurred by the entity on purchasing the asset) that have been capitalised can be taken into account when subsequently measuring the fair value component of 'fair value less costs to sell'. Fair value is a market-based measure and is defined in IFRS 13 as an exit price. The objective is to measure the price that would be obtained in a transaction between market participants to sell an asset, not the costs each party would incur in order to transact – those costs reflect the characteristics of the transaction and not of the asset being hypothetically sold. It would, therefore, be inappropriate to include acquisition-related transaction costs, particularly since a seller would not incur such costs. In addition, as discussed at 4.6.4.A below, IFRS 13 specifically states that transaction costs that would be incurred in a transaction to sell an asset are not part of fair value (that is, they are not added to or deducted from the exit price used to measure fair value). *[IFRS 13.25]*.

However, IAS 41 requires 'costs to sell' to be deducted from fair value, measured in accordance with IFRS 13, before recognition in the financial statements.

3.2.4.B The cost model

If on initial recognition an entity rebuts the presumption and demonstrates that fair value cannot be measured reliably, it applies the cost model to the biological asset, i.e. the asset is measured at cost less any accumulated depreciation and any accumulated impairment losses. *[IAS 41.30]*.

When determining cost, accumulated depreciation and accumulated impairment losses an entity needs to consider the requirements of IAS 2, IAS 16 and IAS 36 – *Impairment of Assets*. *[IAS 41.33]*. IAS 41 provides no further guidance on the application of the cost model or the extent to which entities should consider the requirements of these standards.

Both IAS 2 and IAS 16 establish frameworks within which to determine cost. In our view, the nature of the biological asset should be taken into consideration when determining which approach to use. Consumable biological assets that are to be harvested as agricultural produce or sold as biological assets, for example livestock to be slaughtered or held for sale, fish in farms or crops to be harvested, may be more consistent with inventories accounted for in accordance with IAS 2. Bearer biological assets, such as dairy cows, grape vines and fruit trees, may be more consistent with plant and equipment accounted for in accordance with IAS 16.

The nature of the biological asset may also be helpful in determining when to commence depreciation and the useful life of the asset. Paragraph 53 of IAS 16 requires depreciation to commence when an asset is available for use. *[IAS 16.53]*. Determining when a biological asset is available for use may be more obvious in relation to bearer biological assets. For example, a cow may be considered available for use as soon as it is sufficiently mature to produce milk. However, for consumable biological assets defining when an asset is available for use is less clear because the period between these assets reaching maturity and being sold or harvested is typically short. It could also be argued that entities do not hold consumable biological assets for use and, as such, applying a depreciation model may be inappropriate.

The last component of the cost model is the assessment of impairment in accordance with IAS 36. That standard requires an entity to determine the recoverable amount of an asset or cash-generating unit (CGU) and compare it to its carrying amount in order to determine whether the asset or CGU is impaired. Recoverable amount is defined by IAS 36 as the higher of either the value in use or fair value less costs of disposal of the asset or CGU (IAS 36 is discussed in Chapter 20). Entities that have demonstrated that fair value cannot be reliably determined for a biological asset should be careful to apply a consistent approach when determining the recoverable amount of an asset. As such, using a value in use approach to determine recoverable amount will be required.

An entity that uses the reliability exception (and therefore applies the cost model) should disclose certain additional information in its financial statements. This is discussed further at 5.3 below. *[IAS 41.B37]*.

3.3 Government grants

Government grants involving biological assets should only be accounted for under IAS 20 if the biological asset is 'measured at its cost less any accumulated depreciation and any accumulated impairment losses' (see Chapter 25 for a discussion of government grants). *[IAS 41.37-38]*. IAS 41 applies to government grants relating to biological assets accounted for at fair value less costs to sell and should be accounted for as follows.

An unconditional government grant related to 'a biological asset measured at its fair value less costs to sell shall be recognised in profit or loss when, and only when, the government grant becomes receivable'. *[IAS 41.34]*. An entity is therefore not permitted under IAS 41 to deduct a government grant from the carrying amount of the related asset. This would be inconsistent with a 'fair value model in which an asset is measured and presented at its fair value' because the entity would recognise even conditional government grants in income immediately. *[IAS 41.B66]*.

Any conditional government grant related to a biological asset measured at its fair value less costs to sell – including government grants that require an entity not to engage in a specified agricultural activity – should be recognised only when the conditions attaching to the grant are met. *[IAS 41.35]*. IAS 41 permits an entity to recognise a government grant as income only to the extent that it (i) has met the terms and conditions of the grant and (ii) has no obligation to return the grant. The following example, which is derived from IAS 41, illustrates how an entity should apply these requirements.

Example 38.1: Conditional government grants [IAS 41.36]

A government grant requires an entity to farm in a particular location for five years and requires the entity to return the entire government grant if it farms for less than five years. The government grant is not recognised as income until the five years have passed.

A government grant allows part of the government grant to be retained based on the passage of time. The entity recognises the government grant as income on a time proportion basis.

4 MEASURING FAIR VALUE LESS COSTS TO SELL

4.1 The interaction between IAS 41 and IFRS 13

The IASB issued IFRS 13 in May 2011, providing a single source of guidance on how to measure fair value. IFRS 13 applied prospectively and was mandatorily effective for annual periods that began on or after 1 January 2013.

While IFRS 13 specifies how to measure fair value, it does not specify what must be measured at fair value or when a fair value measurement must be performed. Therefore, an entity applies IAS 41 to determine what to measure at fair value less costs to sell and when to measure fair value (i.e. the measurement date). The entity then applies IFRS 13 to measure 'fair value', taking into consideration the specific requirements in IAS 41 (see 4.5 below). 'Costs to sell', measured in accordance with IAS 41, are then deducted.

As discussed at 5 below, disclosures in relation to the fair value measurement will need to be prepared in accordance with IFRS 13 and also IAS 41, to the extent that it requires additional agriculture-specific disclosures.

The following sections consider further the interaction between IFRS 13 and IAS 41 and highlight some of the key requirements of IFRS 13 relating to biological assets and agricultural produce, comparing them to the previous requirements in IAS 41. See Chapter 14 for a discussion regarding the requirements of IFRS 13.

4.2 Establishing what to measure

4.2.1 Unit of account

The unit of account identifies what is being measured for financial reporting purposes, i.e. the level of aggregation (or disaggregation) for presentation and disclosure purposes. For example, whether the information presented and disclosed in the financial statements is for an individual asset or for a group of assets.

The unit of account in IAS 41 is the individual biological asset or agricultural produce, for example, the standard applies to the individual trees in a forest, not the forest as a whole. As discussed at 4.2.2 below, the standard does permit grouping of assets. This is intended to facilitate measuring fair value, but this does not change the unit of account.

4.2.2 Grouping of assets

IAS 41 states that '[t]he measurement of fair value for a biological asset or agricultural produce may be facilitated by grouping biological assets or agricultural produce according to significant attributes; for example, by age or quality. An entity selects the attributes corresponding to the attributes used in the market as a basis for pricing'. *[IAS 41.15].*

For example, when undertaking a forestry valuation, an entity may group trees in the forest based on factors such as species, when and where the trees were planted and the expected yield.

4.3 When to measure fair value

In order to apply the requirements of IFRS 13, an entity needs to determine when to measure fair value, i.e. the measurement date. IFRS 13 relies on the standard that requires, or permits, the fair value measurement to specify this date – i.e. IAS 41 for biological assets and agricultural produce.

As discussed at 3.2.1.A above, biological assets are required to be measured at fair value less costs to sell at initial recognition and subsequently, on a recurring basis, at the end of each reporting period.

The fair value less costs to sell of agricultural produce is measured on the date that it is harvested (see 3.2.2 above).

4.4 Determining costs to sell

Costs to sell are defined in IAS 41 as 'the incremental costs directly attributable to the disposal of an asset, excluding finance costs and income taxes'. *[IAS 41.5].*

Costs to sell should include all costs that are necessary for a sale to occur but would otherwise not arise. However, costs already included within the fair value measurement, such as transportation costs, should be excluded from costs to sell. Examples of costs to sell could include brokers' and dealers' commissions, levies by regulatory agencies and commodity exchanges, transfer taxes and duties. *[IAS 41.BC3, B22]*.

4.5 Measuring fair value: IAS 41-specific requirements

4.5.1 Use of external independent valuers

IAS 41 does not require an entity to use an external independent valuer to determine the value of biological assets. In fact, the Board rejected a proposal to require external independent valuations because they are 'not commonly used for certain agricultural activity and it would be burdensome to require an external independent valuation. The Board believes that it is for entities to decide how to determine fair value reliably, including the extent to which independent valuers need to be involved'. *[IAS 41.B33]*. Furthermore, the Board also noted that requiring the disclosure of the extent to which the carrying amount of biological assets reflects a valuation by an external independent valuer would not be appropriate for the same reasons. *[IAS 41.B81]*.

4.5.2 Obligation to re-establish a biological asset after harvest

It is common in certain industries, particularly where a biological asset is physically attached to land, for an entity to have an obligation to re-establish a biological asset after harvest. The standard gives the example of an entity that has an obligation to replant the trees in forest after harvest.

IAS 41 does not permit an entity to include the costs of re-establishing a biological asset after harvest when using estimated future cash flows to measure fair value. *[IAS 41.22]*. This is consistent with the unit of account being the individual biological asset (see 4.2.1 above). For example, an entity that owns an orchard might consider its intention, or obligation, to replace its fruit trees in the future if it were measuring the fair value of the orchard as a whole. However, the entity would be required by IAS 41 to measure the individual fruit trees that are actually planted in the orchard on the measurement date. It would be inconsistent to consider replanting, since removal of an existing tree (in order to plant a new tree) would be the end of that asset's useful life.

The Interpretations Committee considered such obligations in May 2004 and confirmed its previous decisions that if an entity has an obligation to re-establish a biological asset after harvest, that obligation is attached to the land and does not affect the fair value of the biological assets currently growing on the land.

The problem of how to account for an obligation to replant was considered by the Board in 2007. Circumstances can arise where an entity is legally obliged (whether by law or contract) to replant a biological asset after harvest. The interaction of the fair value measurement basis of IAS 41, the prohibition on including the replanting costs in determining that fair value in paragraph 22 of IAS 41 and the potential recognition of a provision for the cost of replanting in accordance with IAS 37 – *Provisions, Contingent Liabilities and Contingent Assets* – when the biological asset is harvested, could lead to a net expense being recognised at the point of harvest. There is concern that this does not appropriately reflect the commercial reality. The Board made no decision on the matter and asked its staff to develop further possible solutions for later consideration.

Even in situations where there is a legal obligation to replant, an entity cannot consider replanting when measuring the fair value of a biological asset.

4.5.3 Forward sales contracts

When an entity enters into a contract to sell its biological assets or agricultural produce at a future date, the standard does not permit it to measure those assets at the contracted price, stating that 'the fair value of a biological asset or agricultural produce is not adjusted because of the existence of a contract'. *[IAS 41.16]*.

The (then) IASC considered whether it should require sales contracts to be measured at fair value, but concluded that no solution would be practicable without a complete review of the accounting for commodity contracts that are not in the scope of IAS 39 – *Financial Instruments: Recognition and Measurement*. *[IAS 41.B50-B54]*.

It follows from this that if an entity engaged in agricultural activity enters into forward sales contracts for its produce it will need to consider whether such contracts are within the scope of IAS 39. Paragraph 5 of IAS 39 states 'this standard shall be applied to those contracts to buy or sell a non-financial item that can be settled net in cash or another financial instrument, or by exchanging financial instruments, as if the contracts were financial instruments, with the exception of contracts that were entered into and continue to be held for the purpose of receipt or delivery of a non-financial item in accordance with the entity's expected purchase, sale or usage requirements'. *[IAS 39.5]*. Accordingly an agricultural commodity sales contract will be accounted for under IAS 39 by an entity which intends to net settle that contract even if it is also a producer of the underlying agricultural produce. Conversely a farmer who intends to settle a forward sales contract for barley by physical delivery would not account for the contract under IAS 39, but would treat it as an executory contract. This issue is discussed further in Chapter 41.

4.5.4 Onerous contracts

Although a forward sales contract scoped out of IAS 39 (see 4.5.3 above) is treated as an executory contract, IAS 41 notes that if the contracted price is lower than the fair value of the assets, the contract for the sale of a biological asset or agricultural produce may be an onerous contract, as defined in IAS 37, and if so, should be accounted for under that standard *[IAS 41.16]* (the accounting for onerous contracts is dealt with in Chapter 27).

However, IAS 41 provides no further guidance on the subject of when such a contract becomes onerous. The standard is also silent on what this might mean, given the fact that IAS 37 defines an onerous contract as 'a contract in which the unavoidable costs of meeting the obligations under the contract exceed the economic benefits expected to be received under it.' *[IAS 41.B50-B54]*. In other words, a contract that is not loss-making, but that has a contract price lower than the fair value of the produce concerned, is not automatically defined as onerous by IAS 37, yet seems to be regarded as onerous under IAS 41.

Nevertheless, it is our view that a contract to sell a biological asset at an amount that is below its fair value less costs to sell (and, therefore, its carrying amount) should be regarded as onerous under IAS 37.

4.5.5 Financing cash flows and taxation

IAS 41 does not permit an entity to include any cash flows for financing an asset or tax cash flows when using estimated future cash flows to measure fair value. *[IAS 41.22]*.

The exclusion of taxation is likely to be practically challenging if an entity uses an income approach to measure fair value. Valuers typically prepare post-tax calculations, discounting post-tax cash flows using a post-tax discount rate. If this approach is used to derive a pre-tax equivalent fair value, entities will need to ensure the assumptions related to tax are not entity-specific. As discussed at 4.6 below, IFRS 13 requires that assumptions used to measure fair value reflect what market participants would consider.

4.6 Measuring fair value: overview of IFRS 13's requirements

4.6.1 The fair value measurement framework

The objective of a fair value measurement is 'to estimate the price at which an orderly transaction to sell the asset or to transfer the liability would take place between market participants at the measurement date under current market conditions'. *[IFRS 13.B2]*. In order to measure the fair value of a biological asset or agricultural produce, an entity needs to determine all of the following:

(a) the particular asset that is the subject of the measurement (consistent with its unit of account – see 4.2 above);

(b) the valuation premise that is appropriate for the measurement (consistent with its highest and best use – see 4.6.2 below);

(c) the principal market (or in the absence of a principal market, the most advantageous market) for the asset or liability (see 4.6.3 below); and

(d) the valuation technique(s) appropriate for the measurement, considering the availability of data with which to develop inputs that represent the assumptions that market participants would use when pricing the asset and the level of the fair value hierarchy within which the inputs are categorised (see 4.6.3 and 4.6.4 below). *[IFRS 13.B2]*.

4.6.2 Highest and best use and valuation premise

IFRS 13 requires that the fair value of non-financial assets, such as biological assets and agricultural produce, take into account 'a market participant's ability to generate economic benefits by using the asset in its *highest and best use* or by selling it to another market participant that would use the asset in its highest and best use'. *[IFRS 13.27]*.

The objective in determining highest and best use is to identify the use by market participants that would maximise the value of the asset, either on its own or with other assets and/or liabilities. Therefore, in order to determine the highest and best use of a non-financial asset, an entity needs to make the assessment from the perspective of market participants (see 4.6.3 below).

Importantly, IFRS 13 starts with the presumption that the highest and best use is an asset's current use. Alternative uses are not considered unless market or other factors suggest that market participants would use that asset differently to maximise the value of that asset. *[IFRS 13.29]*. If such factors exist, an entity would only consider those alternative uses that are physically possible, legally permissible and financially feasible. Appropriately determining an asset's highest and best use is a critical step and can have significant implications on the measurement of fair value. Therefore, this assessment should be based on the weight of evidence available. Careful consideration will be needed to ensure consistent assumptions regarding the principal market (or in the absence of a principal market, the most advantageous market) and the participants in that market, since highest and best use is determined from the market participants' perspective.

Determining highest and best use is discussed further in Chapter 14. As discussed at 5.2 below, additional disclosures are required if an entity determines that the highest and best use of a non-financial asset is different from its current use.

Dependent on its highest and best use, the fair value of the non-financial asset will either be measured based on the value it would derive on a standalone basis or in combination with other assets or other assets and liabilities (known as the valuation premise). For example, as discussed at 4.6.2.A below, the highest and best use of an asset might be in combination with the land to which it is physically attached.

Even in situations where the valuation premise of a biological asset is 'in combination with other assets and/or liabilities', the objective of a fair value measurement is still to measure the price to sell the biological asset, not the combined group. IFRS 13 assumes that the market participants that would purchase the biological asset would use it in combination with those other assets and/or liabilities. That is, if the market participants already had those other assets and/or liabilities, what price would the market participants pay to acquire the biological asset? In reality. sales are unlikely to be structured in this way. Entities might need to sell the 'other assets and/or liabilities' in order to sell the biological asset (particularly if they are physically attached, as is discussed at 4.6.2.A below). However, regardless of how an entity might structure an actual sale, IFRS 13 contemplates a hypothetical sale and specifically states that, when the highest and best use is the use of the asset in combination with other assets and/or liabilities, a fair value measurement assumes that the market participant acquiring the asset already holds the complementary assets and the associated liabilities. *[IFRS 13.32]*.

In practice, an entity may need to measure the price to sell the biological asset by measuring the price for the combined assets and/or liabilities and then allocating that fair value to the various components. IFRS 13 does not specify what allocation approaches can or cannot be used. Therefore, an entity must use its judgement to select the most appropriate technique. Even if this approach is used, the objective is to measure the fair value of the biological asset assuming it is sold consistent with its unit of account, which for a biological asset is the individual asset. *[IFRS 13.32]*. This is discussed further at 4.6.2.A below.

4.6.2.A Biological assets attached to land

IAS 41 observes that biological assets are often physically attached to land, for example crops growing in a field. In many cases, there will be no separate market for biological assets in their current condition and location. The objective of a fair value measurement is to determine the price for the asset in its current form. However, as discussed at 4.7 below (see also section 5.2 in Chapter 14), if no market exists for an biological asset in its current form, but there is a market for the converted or transformed asset, an entity would adjust the price that would be received for the converted or transformed asset for the costs a market participant would incur to re-condition the asset (after acquiring the asset in its current condition) and the compensation they would expect for the effort in order to measure fair value.

IFRS 13 does not require a market to be observable or active in order to measure fair value. However, it is clear that, if there is a principal market for the asset, the fair value measurement represents the price in that market at the measurement date (regardless of whether that price is directly observable or estimated using another valuation technique). This price must be used even if a price in a different market is potentially more advantageous. *[IFRS 13.18]*. While the price need not be observable to measure fair value, the standard does require an entity to prioritise observable inputs in the principal (or in the absence of a principal market, the most advantageous) market over unobservable inputs.

If an income approach (such as a discounted cash flow approach) is used to measure the biological asset (excluding the land) and the land, to which the asset is physically attached, is owned by the entity, care is needed to ensure that fair value measurement is not overstated. This is because land owned by the entity would not derive any expected cash outflows. It is therefore common for entities to include a notional rental charge for the land, reflecting what would be paid to rent the land, using market participant assumptions.

IAS 41 suggests that where there is no separate market for biological assets in their current form and they are physically attached to land, an active market might exist for the combined assets, i.e. for the biological assets, land and land improvements. If this is the case, an entity could use the information regarding the combined assets to determine the fair value of the biological assets. *[IAS 41.25]*. IFRS 13 defines an active market as 'a market in which transactions for the asset or liability take place with sufficient frequency and volume to provide pricing information on an ongoing basis'. *[IFRS 13 Appendix A]*. Whether such a market exists for the combined assets is a matter of judgement, taking into consideration all the relevant facts and circumstances. However, an entity should have sufficient evidence to support such an assumption.

Importantly, the unit of account established by IAS 41 is an individual asset (see 4.2.1 above). Therefore, if fair value is measured for the combined assets, the total fair value would need to be allocated to each component in order to derive the fair value for the biological asset or agricultural produce (as is illustrated by Figure 38.1 below). As discussed at 4.6.2 above, IFRS 13 does not provide guidance on how to perform such an allocation. IAS 41 suggests the use of the residual method as one possible way to allocate the fair value between the biological assets and the land. However, this might be difficult to apply in practice as illustrated in Example 38.2 below. Therefore entities will need to apply judgement when determining the appropriate allocation of fair value.

Example 38.2: Biological assets attached to land

Entity A acquired a 10-hectare vineyard on 1 January 2014 for CU1,200. The purchase price of the vineyard was attributed as follows:

1 January 2014	*CU*
Purchase price	1,200
Land	(780)
Vineyard improvements	(130)
Grape vines	290

At the end of its financial year Entity A needs to determine the fair value of the grape vines in accordance with IAS 41 and invites two equally skilled professional valuers to determine the value of the grape vines.

31 December 2014	*Valuer 1* *CU*	*Valuer 2* *CU*
Fair value of an average 10-hectare vineyard	1,105	1,100
Adjustment for soil and climatic conditions	135	150
Estimated fair value of Entity A's vineyard	1,240	1,250
Fair value of the land	(830)	(825)
Fair value of vineyard improvements	(135)	(125)
Grape vines	275	300

Valuer 1 and Valuer 2 make a virtually identical assessment of the market values of the vineyard, the land and the vineyard improvements. Nevertheless, because the value of grape vines is calculated by subtracting all the other known elements from the total value of the vineyard, a noticeable difference arises in the valuation of the grape vines. In a similar vein, entities that use only one valuer need to be aware that even small changes in assumptions from period to period could have a significant impact on the valuation of biological assets and therefore reported profits or losses. For this reason, IFRS 13 requires extensive disclosures about assumptions used in determining fair value (as did IAS 41 previously).

In April 2012, the Interpretations Committee received a request to clarify the use of the residual approach, as discussed in paragraph 25 of IAS 41 (in light of the requirement in IFRS 13 to measure the fair value of non-financial assets based on their highest and best use). Specifically, the Committee was asked to consider the situation where a biological asset was physically attached to land and no separate market for the biological asset existed in its current condition and location. The submitter of the request assumed entities would apply paragraph 25 of IAS 41, measure the biological asset and land on a combined basis and use the residual approach to derive a fair value for the biological asset. The submitter was concerned about situations where the highest and best use of the biological asset is in combination with the land, but the value of the land could be higher if measured assuming some alternative use (such as property development). In these circumstances, the allocated fair value of the biological asset might be nil or negligible. The fact pattern was further complicated because it was assumed the land to which the biological asset was attached was measured using the cost model in accordance with IAS 16.[2]

The Committee elected not to take the issue onto its agenda, but noted that, in the development of IFRS 13, the IASB had considered the situation where the highest and best use of an asset in a group of assets is different from its current use.

However, 'IFRS 13 does not explicitly address the accounting implications if those circumstances arise and the fair value measurement of the asset based on its highest and best use assumes that other assets in the group need to be converted or destroyed'. The Committee also observed that this issue may affect non-financial assets within the scope of other standards, not just those within the scope of IAS 41.[3] The Committee asked the IASB to provide clarification of the accounting requirements for the issues it had considered. However, as outreach indicated the issue was not widespread, in May 2013, the IASB decided it could, instead, be considered for review in the Post-Implementation Review of IFRS 13.[4]

Determining the highest and best use of an asset requires judgement (see 4.6.2 above), but an entity should start with the presumption that the highest and best use is an asset's current use. As discussed above, paragraph 25 of IAS 41 is only relevant where there is no separate market for a biological asset in its current form and it is physically attached to land. In addition, that paragraph suggests an active market may exists for the combined assets (land and biological asset) and, therefore, that an observable price in that market for the assets (on a combined basis) could be used to derive fair value for the biological asset. *[IAS 41.25].* Selecting appropriate valuation techniques with which to measure fair value in accordance with IFRS 13 requires judgement. Some might use the residual approach to do this, as indicated in the submission. However, paragraph 25 of IAS 41 does not require the use of the residual approach; it is only mentioned as an example. The IASB reaffirmed this when they considered this matter in May 2013. They also noted that IFRS 13 encourages the use of multiple valuation techniques where appropriate.[5]

The outcome from a fact pattern such as the one the Committee discussed may be somewhat counterintuitive. However, the fact that the fair value of the land, in that situation, would not be recognised in the financial statements is, in our view, irrelevant to the measurement of fair value. The objective of a fair value measurement does not change regardless of whether it is recognised or unrecognised.

Figure 38.1: Applying paragraph 25 of IAS 41 to measure the fair value of a biological asset

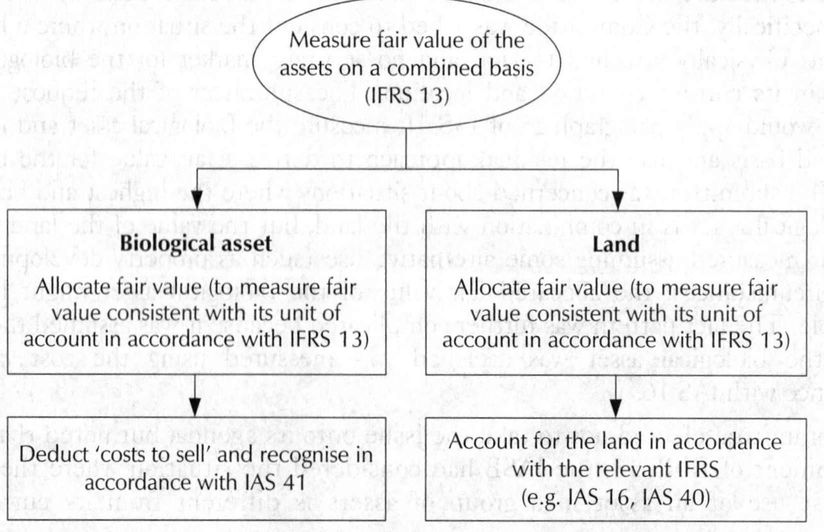

4.6.3 Selecting appropriate assumptions

Selecting the appropriate assumption with which to measure the fair value of biological assets and agricultural produce can often be difficult. According to IFRS 13, an entity should select assumptions that:

- market participants would use, i.e. they are not entity-specific;
- are consistent with the unit of account and characteristics of the asset, including an asset's condition and location and any restrictions on the use or sale of the asset;
- are consistent with an orderly transaction to sell the asset in the principal market, or in the absence of a principal market, the most advantageous market; and
- maximise the use of observable inputs and minimise the use of unobservable inputs (based on the fair value hierarchy, see Chapter 14).

Focusing on market participant assumptions is consistent with the previous requirements in IAS 41. However, IFRS 13 clarifies that the transaction to sell the asset would be between market participants, not between the entity and a market participant. In addition, assumptions should reflect a group of market participants, not an individual market participant. In order to select the appropriate assumptions, an entity would identify characteristics of market participants. At a minimum, IFRS 13 assumes that market participants will be independent of each other, knowledgeable about the asset, able and willing to enter into a transaction for the asset. Assumptions used in a fair value measurement would need to be consistent with those characteristics.

Selecting the appropriate market participants depends on the principal market for the asset or, in the absence of a principal market, the most advantageous market (see Chapter 14 for further discussion). IAS 41 previously referred to the most relevant market, typically the market the entity would normally transact in. There is a general presumption in IFRS 13 that the principal market is the one in which the entity would normally enter into a transaction to sell the asset, unless there is evidence to the contrary. However, on adoption of IFRS 13, entities should not assume 'most relevant market' in IAS 41 is the same as the principal market. In fact, the assessed highest and best use of the asset may require different markets to be considered.

4.6.3.A Condition and location

IAS 41 previously required an entity to take the present location and condition of a biological asset into account in determining its fair value. Fair value measured in accordance with IFRS 13 also takes into consideration an asset's condition and location.

This will have a direct impact on what is being measured. For example, entities measuring partly grown crops may also need to consider the fair value of the land in which they are planted (see 4.6.2.A above). It may also require an entity to consider alternative markets. For example, an entity that rears chickens may have to consider whether there is a market for immature chicks.

It is possible for a market to exist in one geographical area but not in another area. For example, transportation costs may limit the geographical size of the market for agricultural produce significantly, possibly to the point where a local cooperative or factory is the only buyer.

If no market exists for an asset in its current form, but there is a market for the converted or transformed asset, an entity adjusts the fair value for the costs a market participant would incur to re-condition the asset (after acquiring the asset in its current condition) and the compensation they would expect for the effort.

If the location of a biological asset or agricultural produce would require it to be transported to the market in order to sell it, transportation costs would be deducted from the market price in order to measure fair value, consistent with the previous requirements in IAS 41. Given the logistical problems and generally high costs of transporting living animals and plants, there could be many different fair values for identical biological assets depending on their location.

4.6.4 Valuation techniques in IFRS 13

IFRS 13 does not limit the types of valuation techniques an entity might use to measure fair value. However, it does require the valuation techniques to be consistent with one of three approaches: the market approach, the income approach and the cost approach.

Unlike the previous requirements in IAS 41, IFRS 13 does not prioritise the use of one valuation technique over another, or require the use of only one technique. Instead, IFRS 13 establishes a hierarchy for the inputs used in those valuation techniques, requiring an entity to maximise observable inputs and minimise the use of unobservable inputs (this is discussed further at 16 in Chapter 14). *[IFRS 13.74]*.

Previously, IAS 41 provided a hierarchy of valuation techniques for determining the fair value of a biological asset or agricultural produce:

(a) *An active market existed* – the quoted price in that market was the appropriate basis for determining the fair value of that asset.

(b) *No active market existed* – if an active market did not exist an entity used one or more of the following *market-determined prices or values* to estimate fair value *[IAS 41(2012).18]*:

 (i) the most recent market transaction price, provided the economic circumstances had not significantly changed;

 (ii) market prices for similar assets with adjustments to reflect differences; and

 (iii) sector benchmarks.

 Where no active market existed, an entity was required by IAS 41 to use all available market-determined prices or values since otherwise there was 'a possibility that entities may opt to use present value of expected net cash flows from the asset even when useful market-determined prices or values are available'. *[IAS 41.B30]*.

(c) *No active market existed and no market-based information was available* – only if an active market did not exist and there was no market-based information available on which to base an estimate of fair value, could an entity estimate fair value using a *discounted cash flows* method or *cost as an approximation of fair value*. *[IAS 41(2012).20,24]*.

In general, the approach in IFRS 13 will likely be consistent with previous requirements in IAS 41. For example, the best indication of fair value is still a quoted price in an active market. In addition, the use of techniques previously required by IAS 41 would be consistent with the approaches permitted by IFRS 13. However, since multiple techniques should be used when applicable, judgement will be needed to select the techniques that are appropriate in the circumstances. *[IFRS 13.63]*. Selecting appropriate valuation techniques is discussed further at 14 in Chapter 14.

4.6.4.A Cost as an approximation of fair value

The definition of fair value in IFRS 13 is not significantly different from the previous definition in IAS 41, which was, 'the amount for which an asset could be exchanged, or a liability settled, between knowledgeable, willing parties in an arm's length transaction'. *[IAS 41(2012).8]*. However, IFRS 13 clarifies that fair value is a current exit price, not an entry price. Therefore, while exit and entry prices may be identical in many situations, the transaction price (an entry price) is not presumed to represent the fair value of an asset or liability measured in accordance with IFRS 13 on its initial recognition.

IAS 41 indicates that cost may sometimes approximate fair value. The standard gives two situations where this might occur: *[IAS 41.24]*

- when little biological transformation has taken place since cost was initially incurred – fruit tree seedlings planted immediately prior to the end of a reporting period is given as an example; or
- when the impact of the biological transformation on price is not expected to be material – for example, during the initial phase of growth for a pine plantation with a 30-year production cycle.

Even in such situations, the objective is still to measure fair value in accordance with IFRS 13. Therefore, as with an entry price on initial recognition, an entity cannot presume that cost approximates fair value. Instead, it should ensure cost is materially consistent with a current exit price for the asset. For example, entities would need carefully consider which costs could be included in the entry price. IFRS 13 specifically states that transaction costs are not part of fair value (that is, they are not added to or deducted from the exit price), *[IFRS 13.25]*, therefore, we would not expect an entity to deduct such costs from the entry price – particularly as 'costs to sell' are deducted from fair value before being recognised in the financial statements. Nor would we expect entities applying a fair value model to include acquisition-related transaction costs within an entry price used to approximate fair value.

4.7 The problem of measuring fair value for part-grown biological assets

Entities may be required to measure their biological assets part way through the transformation process, particularly when the time to harvest is greater than 12 months. In these circumstances, there may not be an active market for the asset in its current condition and location. In the absence of an active market, preparers often use a discounted cash flow model to estimate fair value.

In these situations, a common question is whether an entity can take into consideration the future biological transformation when estimating the fair value of a biological asset.

As discussed at 4.6.3.A above, IFRS 13 makes it clear that the fair value of an asset considers characteristics of an asset, such as its current condition and location. An entity must consider this objective in determining an appropriate discount rate and estimating its future cash flows, which should be based on assumptions market participants would use. Therefore, if a market participant would consider the potential for future growth, the related cash flows and risks from additional biological transformation should be included in determining the appropriate fair value.

The original version of IAS 41 had caused confusion in this area, as it had required that the estimation of future cash flows 'exclude any increases in value from additional biological transformation and future activities of the entity'. *[IAS 41(2008).21]*. This seemed to suggest that the value of immature biological assets should be based on values in their current condition rather than recognising that part of the value must logically lie in their potential, given appropriate husbandry, to grow to full size. The IASB amended IAS 41 to clarify that entities should consider the risks associated with cash flows from additional biological transformation in determining the cash flows, the discount rate or some combination of the two provided a market participant would take the additional biological transformation into consideration.

While paragraph 21 of IAS 41 was subsequently deleted by the introduction of IFRS 13, this clarification is consistent with the requirements in that standard and is helpful in understanding its requirements in situations where prices are available in an active market for part-grown biological assets, but that market is not the principal market (or in the absence of a principal market, the most advantageous market).

IFRS 13 is clear that, if there is a principal market for the asset or liability, the fair value measurement shall represent the price in that market at the measurement date (regardless of whether that price is directly observable or estimated using another valuation technique). The price in the principal market must be used even if the price in a different market is potentially more advantageous. *[IFRS 13.18]*. Since an entity can consider the expected cash flows the asset can generate in its principal market, the entity is not permitted to use available prices in other active markets for part-grown biological assets. Even in situations where there is no principal market, once the most advantageous market has been selected, an entity would not look to other markets for available prices or use prices in the most advantageous market if market participants would not consider them.

This issue is illustrated by an extract from CESR's database of enforcement decisions published in April 2007 (Decision ref. EECS/0407-11) in relation to the fair value measurement requirements in IAS 41 (prior to the issuance of IFRS 13). Norwegian fish farmers had developed a practice of recording live immature fish at cost on the basis that they were unable to value them reliably in accordance with paragraph 30 of IAS 41. The Norwegian regulator took the view that slaughtered fish sold whole and gutted should be considered the same as live salmon under paragraph 18(b) of IAS 41(2012) and that it was possible to value the live immature fish based on the market price for slaughtered fish of the same size. Smaller fish are sold on the market because they are harvested with mature fish, however their value per kilo is significantly below that of mature fish and the Norwegian fish farming entities did not therefore believe that it was appropriate to use their market price as a basis for fair value. The regulator's decision was appealed to the Norwegian Ministry of Finance and the database reports the conclusion as follows:

> 'The Ministry of Finance upheld the decision of the enforcer, with some adjustments and additions. Most significantly, the final ruling upholds the enforcer's decision that slaughtered salmon which is sold whole and gutted is in an accounting sense to be considered as a similar asset of live salmon, according to IAS 41.18(b) and that this also applies to so-called immature farmed salmon. Hence, the observable prices of slaughtered salmon shall be used as a basis for determining the fair value of live immature salmon. The key amendment to the decision made by the Ministry of Finance is that it added certain comments relating to how the term "adjustments to reflect differences" in IAS 41.18(b) was to be applied. The adjustments should reflect the differences between the price of an immature salmon and the hypothetical market price in an active market for live immature salmon.'

As a result of this decision, the Norwegian entities were required to record immature salmon at fair value, rather than at cost, by making appropriate adjustments to available market prices for similar sized slaughtered fish.

While IFRS 13 has now replaced the requirements in paragraph 18(b) of IAS 41(2012) to which this decision related, the same approach could be used when measuring fair value in accordance with that standard. IFRS 13 prioritises the use of observable (Level 1) inputs for identical or similar items when measuring fair value. Therefore, in situations where an active market does not exist for the asset in its current form, entities might use prices for similar assets, for which observable prices do exist, as an input into the fair value measurement. As discussed in the Norwegian salmon example, an entity would need to identify any differences between the asset being measured at fair value and similar asset, for which observable market prices are available, and make the appropriate adjustments for those differences. Such adjustments could affect the categorisation of the fair value measurement as a whole within the fair value hierarchy. Categorisation within the hierarchy is done for disclosure purposes as it affects how much information must be disclosed about the fair value measurement (see 5.2 below). IFRS 13 requires that, '[i]f an observable input requires an adjustment using an unobservable input and that adjustment results in a significantly higher or lower fair value measurement, the resulting fair value measurement ... be categorised within Level 3 of the hierarchy'. *[IFRS 13.75]*. Categorisation within IFRS 13's fair value hierarchy is discussed further at 16 in Chapter 14.

5 DISCLOSURE

5.1 General

5.1.1 Statement of financial position

IAS 1 – *Presentation of Financial Statements* – requires biological assets to be presented separately on the face of an entity's statement of financial position (see Chapter 3). *[IAS 1.54]*. Agricultural produce after the point of harvest should be accounted for under IAS 2. That standard does not require agricultural produce to be disclosed separately on the face of the statement of financial position (see Chapter 22). The following example, which is derived from the Illustrative Examples to IAS 41, illustrates the requirement to disclose biological assets in the statement of financial position.

Example 38.3: Presentation of biological assets in the statement of financial position [IAS 41.IE1]

The statement of financial position below illustrates how a dairy farming business might present biological assets in its statement of financial position.

XYZ Dairy Ltd.
Statement of financial position

ASSETS	**31 December 20X1**	**31 December 20X0**
Non-current assets		
Dairy livestock – immature *	52,060	47,730
Dairy livestock – mature *	372,990	411,840
Subtotal – biological assets	425,050	459,570
Property, plant and equipment	1,462,650	1,409,800
Total non-current assets	**1,887,700**	**1,869,370**
Current assets		
Inventories	82,950	70,650
Trade and other receivables	88,000	65,000
Cash	10,000	10,000
Total current assets	**180,950**	**145,650**
Total assets	**2,068,650**	**2,015,020**
EQUITY AND LIABILITIES		
Equity		
Issued capital	1,000,000	1,000,000
Retained earnings	902,828	865,000
Total equity	**1,902,828**	**1,865,000**
Current liabilities		
Trade and other payables	165,822	150,020
Total current liabilities	**165,822**	**150,020**
Total equity and liabilities	**2,068,650**	**2,015,020**

* An entity is encouraged, but not required, to provide a quantified description of each group of biological assets, distinguishing between consumable and bearer biological assets or between mature and immature biological assets, as appropriate. An entity discloses the basis for making any such distinctions. (Bearer biological assets are those assets that self-regenerate, e.g. cows that bear calves).

The extract below from the financial statements of the Turners & Growers Group illustrates the proportion of total assets that biological assets can comprise in an agricultural business and that biological assets might be classified as both current and non-current assets. This extract also illustrates some of the other disclosure requirements of the standard discussed at 5.1.4 below.

Extract 38.1: Turners & Growers Limited and Subsidiary Companies (2012)

Balance Sheets
As at 31 December [extract]

	Notes	Group 2012 $'000	2011 $'000
Current assets			
Cash and cash equivalents	12	**15,994**	12,775
Trade and other receivables	13	**75,997**	86,547
Inventories	14	**43,103**	34,814
Taxation receivable		**3,498**	3,865
Biological assets	17	**1,111**	1,344
Non-current assets classified as held for sale	16	**16,712**	–
Total current assets		**156,415**	139,345
Non-current assets			
Trade and other receivables	13	**2,142**	3,556
Available-for-sale investments	18	**201**	345
Biological assets	17	**16,847**	30,276
Property, plant & equipment	19	**253,816**	275,517
Intangible assets	21	**12,960**	18,048
Investments in associates and joint ventures	24	**16,314**	15,730
Total non-current assets		**302,280**	343,472
Total assets		**458,695**	482,817

Notes to the Financial Statements
For the year ended 31 December [extract]

17 Biological Assets [extract]

	Notes	Group 2012 $'000	2011 $'000
Current			
Balance at 1 January		**1,344**	1,290
Capitalised costs		**26,545**	24,042
Change in fair value less costs to sell	7	**423**	(143)
Decreases due to harvest		**(27,201)**	(23,845)
Balance at 31 December		**1,111**	1,344
Non-current			
Balance at 1 January		**30,276**	19,019
Increases due to subsidiary acquisition	23	**–**	24,826
Increases due to purchases		**1,114**	–
Capitalised costs		**12,324**	11,791
Change in fair value less costs to sell – crop	7	**(935)**	(2,486)
Decrease due to harvest		**(10,715)**	(7,732)
Change in fair value less costs to sell – trees and vines	7	**(15,120)**	(14,888)
Decrease due to disposals		**(97)**	(254)
Balance at 31 December		**16,847**	30,276

At 31 December the biological assets were as follows:

	Hectares planted owned		Hectares planted leased		Production owned		Production leased	
	2012	2011	**2012**	2011	**2012**	2011	**2012**	2011
Tomatoes	**20**	20	**–**	–	**8,858,037**	9,043,823	**–**	–
Apples	**234**	234	**20**	20	**478,915**	577,562	**9,400**	19,663
Lemons	**97**	104	**5**	–	**1,252,469**	1,643,686	**41,289**	–
Navels	**–**	–	**20**	20	**–**	–	**550,110**	561,811
Mandarins	**54**	54	**16**	16	**879,110**	2,082,037	**276,904**	228,035
Kiwifruit	**52**	64	**44**	31	**291,309**	456,379	**334,831**	282,883
Blueberries	**11**	4	**–**	–	**–**	–	**–**	–

Production units:

- Tomatoes: kgs
- Apples: export tce (tray carton equivalent)
- Citrus (lemons, navels and mandarins): kgs for export, tag 1 and tag 2 grades
- Kiwifruit: class 1 trays
- Blueberries: no production in 2012

The Group's biological assets are stated at valuations completed by either independent valuers or management, with reference to current valuations prepared for management and are adjusted to reflect the location, plantings, age and varieties of biological assets and productive capacities of the orchards.

Biological asset valuations undertaken by independent registered valuers were:

- Duke & Cooke Ltd – Inglis Horticulture Nelson orchards and ENZA Hastings apple orchards
- Property Solutions (BOP) Ltd – Kerikeri kiwifruit, navel, mandarin, lemons and blueberry orchards

All external valuers used are members of the New Zealand Institute of Valuers.

Biological asset valuations undertaken by management include the valuation of current assets, being the tomato crop, at Status Produce Ltd.

Biological assets are categorised as bearer biological assets and are stated at fair value less estimated point-of-sale costs, with any resultant gain or loss recognised in the income statement. Fair value is based on the assets' present location and condition and therefore excludes the costs necessary to get the assets to market. Point-of-sale costs include all other costs that would be necessary to sell the assets. In the majority of cases biological assets have been valued on an income approach (discounted cash flows) with reference back to underlying market based valuations for land and buildings, to ensure the total combined carrying value of biological assets and fixed assets are at fair value. The independent valuer uses valuation techniques which are inherently subjective and involve estimation. Included in the biological asset valuation is a provision for the fair value of the existing crop on the biological asset.

The following valuation assumptions have been adopted in determining the fair value of the Group's biological assets:

(a) Discount rates ranging between 11-22% have been used in discounting the present value of expected cash flows, which approximates the Group's weighted average cost of capital adjusted for risk premium;

(b) Notional land rental costs have been included for freehold land;

(c) Orchards have been valued on a going concern basis;

(d) Inflation has been allowed on costs and revenues at rates of between 0-3%;

(e) Costs are based on current average costs and, where applicable, referenced back to industry standard costs. The costs are variable depending on the biological asset's location, planting, age and the varieties being assessed;

(f) Revenue is based on current pricing and expected levels of production, with an assessment made about the long-term future returns for each variety. Revenue is variable depending on the variety of the biological asset and represents the valuers and management's best judgement. The impact of changes in foreign exchange rates have been included in the forecast crop returns. The underlying price assumptions are as follows:

	Price range (before inflation)		
	2012	2011	
Tomatoes	**$2 - $5**	$2 - $5	kg
Apples	**$19 - $30**	$19 - $30	export tce (tray carton equivalent)
Lemons	**$1 - $3**	$1 - $3	kg
Kiwifruit	**$6 - $13**	$7 - $12	tray
Navels	**$1 - $2**	$1 - $2	kg
Mandarins	**$1 - $4**	$1 - $3	kg

Weighted average prices in 2012 are generally assumed to be at the lower end of the price ranges compared to 2011.

(g) Management have made assessments as to when the newly developed plantings will reach full production. Newly developed plantings are managed as part of the total plantings and therefore are not separately disclosed. The total average yield is dependent upon the variety of biological asset growth, as well as the underlying age and health of the biological assets.

(h) One kiwifruit orchard owned by Turners & Growers in Kerikeri has been identified as having PSA-V. Strict processes have been put in place to contain the bacteria to a local area and at this stage it does not appear to have spread elsewhere. PSA-V symptoms tend to be low over the hot summer months and do not show again until spring, so although continual assessment of the orchards is being undertaken, there will be a better indication as to whether it has spread further in the spring of 2013. Due to this positive PSA-V result and the possible spread of PSA-V, the value placed on kiwifruit vines has been reduced to zero. Valuation of kiwifruit orchard improvements and structures on Zespri Gold orchards have also taken into account the possibility of needing to regraft to a new, more resistent variety.

(i) Lemon trees have also reduced in value this year due to concerns over the ongoing profitability of the lemon operation. There has been a value placed on a new variety of lemon tree rootstock that produces more volume per tree than the older rootstock variety. The older rootstock variety has had no value placed on it.

The fair value of biological crops (tomatoes, apples, lemons, kiwifruit, mandarins and navels) at or before the point of harvest is based on the value of the estimated market price of the volumes produced, net of harvesting costs.

The primary financial risk which the Group is exposed to in respect of agricultural activity occurs due to the length of time between the cash outflow on the purchase, planting and maintenance of trees and vines and the cost of harvesting the fruit and receiving the cash from the sale of the fruit to third parties. This risk includes exposure to adverse movements in foreign exchange rates arising from sales to parties located overseas.

5.1.1.A *Current versus non-current classification*

IAS 1 requires an asset to be classified as current when: *[IAS 1.66]*

(a) the entity expects to sell, consume or realise the asset in its normal operating cycle;

(b) the asset is primarily for trading purposes;

(c) the entity expects to realise the asset within 12 months after the reporting period; or

(d) the asset is cash or a cash equivalent (as defined in IAS 7 – *Statement of Cash Flows*, see Chapter 36), unless it is restricted from being exchanged or used to settle a liability for at least twelve months after the reporting period.

If these criteria are not met, the asset is classified as non-current.

The classification of agricultural produce is usually consistent with an entity's assessment for its inventories, i.e. typically classified as a current asset because it will be sold, consumed or realised as part of the normal operating cycle.

The classification of biological assets typically varies based on the nature of the biological asset and the time it takes to mature.

For consumable biological assets that only have one harvest, classification will depend on when the asset will be harvested and sold. For example, livestock held for slaughter would likely be realised within 12 months after the end of the reporting period or as part of the normal operating cycle, and therefore would be classified as a current asset. Trees in a forest usually take more than 20 years to mature. Therefore, forests are usually classified as non-current.

Bearer biological assets, such as fruit trees, dairy cows or animals used for breeding, are often classified as non-current. Such assets usually provide multiple harvests, which may extend beyond one accounting period. Therefore, in order to classify the asset appropriately, an entity would need to consider the period over which it will derive future economic benefits from the asset, which is likely to be when the biological asset will be sold, replaced or removed. This is essentially consistent with determining the useful life of an item of property, plant and equipment in accordance with IAS 16.

Determining the appropriate classification may be less intuitive for consumable biological assets that have multiple harvests, e.g. sugar cane or bamboo. When the agricultural produce is harvested, generally all that is left are the roots, culms or similar. It might appear as if the biological asset has been harvested but it is the roots that are capable of producing additional biological assets and the classification of the biological asset should therefore focus on the useful life of the roots, consistent with the assessment for bearer biological assets.

In situations where biological assets are classified as non-current, there is some debate about whether a portion should be classified as current. Some believe that, particularly for bearer biological assets, the asset should be classified as non-current, consistent with the classification of property, plant and equipment under IAS 16. In this situation, an entity would probably only classify the asset as current when it is held for sale in accordance with IFRS 5 (see Chapter 4). Others argue that, since the unit of account in IAS 41 is the individual asset (see 4.2.1 above), a portion of a group of biological assets could be classified as current. The current portion would be comprised of biological assets that will be removed permanently (e.g. sold, up-rooted or otherwise removed) within 12 months after the end of the reporting period. Determining such a split may be more obvious for consumable biological assets with only one harvest, for example, the trees in a forest an entity expects to harvest within 12 months of the end of the reporting period. For other biological assets, care is needed to ensure that it is the final removal of the biological asset itself that is considered and not its agricultural produce. Examples of the final removal of such biological assets include dairy cows in a herd that an entity sells for slaughter and the removal of the root-system of sugar cane for replanting (rather than the harvest of the sugar cane). Regardless of which approach is used, an entity should be consistent from period to period across all similar types of biological assets. An entity should also assess whether its policy for classifying, or not classifying, a portion of its biological assets as current should be disclosed (see Chapter 3 for further discussion).

5.1.2 *Income statement*

IAS 1 is silent on the presentation of gains and losses on biological assets and agricultural produce in the income statement. IAS 41 requires that an entity disclose 'the aggregate gain or loss arising during the current period on initial recognition of biological assets and agricultural produce and from the change in fair value less costs to sell of biological assets'. *[IAS 41.40]*. The standard only requires disclosure of the aggregate gain or loss; it does not require or encourage disaggregating the gain or loss. *[IAS 41.B78-B79]*. Example 1 of the Illustrative Examples to IAS 41 illustrates gains on biological assets and agricultural produce presented near the top of the income statement, although it is not entirely clear from the example whether losses on biological assets should be presented in the same position or elsewhere in the income statement. *[IAS 41.IE1]*.

The extract below is from the combined and consolidated financial statements of Mondi Limited. The Mondi Limited group recognised changes in fair value less costs to sell in profit or loss but did not separately disclose that amount on the face of the financial statements. Instead, as is illustrated below, the change in the fair value less costs to sell of biological assets was separately disclosed in the notes to the financial statements.

Extract 38.2: Mondi Limited (2012)

Notes to the combined and consolidated financial statements for the year ended 31 December 2012 [extract]

1 Accounting policies [extract]

Agriculture

Owned forestry assets

Owned forestry assets are measured at fair value, calculated by applying the expected selling price, less costs to harvest and deliver, to the estimated volume of timber on hand at each reporting date. The estimated volume of timber on hand is determined based on the maturity profile of the area under afforestation, the species, the geographic location and other environmental considerations and excludes future growth. The product of these is then adjusted to present value by applying a market related pre tax discount rate.

Changes in fair value are recognised in the combined and consolidated income statement within other net operating expenses. At point of felling, the carrying value of forestry assets is transferred to inventory.

Directly attributable costs incurred during the year of biological growth and investments in standing timber are capitalised and presented within cash flows from investing activities in the combined and consolidated statement of cash flows.

3 Operating profit from continuing operations before special items [extract]

Underlying operating profit from continuing operations includes:

€ million	**2012**	2011
Depreciation of property, plant and equipment (see note 14)	(334)	(332)
Profit on disposal of tangible and intangible assets	4	–
Amortisation of intangible assets (see note 13)	(17)	(10)
Impairment of property, plant and equipment (excluding special items) (see note 14)	(4)	–
Operating lease charges (see note 2)	(38)	(56)
Research and development expenditure	(12)	(12)
Restructuring and closure costs (excluding special items)	(4)	(1)
Net foreign currency gains/(losses) (see note 7)	2	(4)
Green energy sales and disposal of emissions credits (see note 2)	76	84
Fair value gains on forestry assets (see note 15)	40	49
Felling costs (see note 15)	(64)	(65)

Total revenue from continuing operations, as defined under IAS 18, 'Revenue', consisting of Group revenue, sale of green energy and disposal of CO_2e credits, interest income and dividend income, was €5,887 million (2011: €5,832 million).

Other than depreciation and amortisation, and fair value movements on forestry assets which are disclosed above, there are no other significant non-cash items recorded within Group underlying operating profit.

15 Forestry assets

€ million	**2012**	2011
At 1 January	297	320
Capitalised expenditure	40	39
Acquisition of assets	20	3
Fair value gains[1]	40	49
Disposal of assets	(3)	–
Felling costs	(64)	(65)
Currency movements	(19)	(49)
At 31 December	**311**	297

Note:

1 The fair value of forestry assets is calculated on the basis of future expected cash flows discounted using a discount rate relevant in the local country, based on a pre tax real yield on long-term bonds over the last five years. All fair value gains originate from South Africa.

Forestry assets comprise forests with the maturity profile disclosed in the table below:

€ million	**2012**	2011
Mature	187	166
Immature	124	131
Total forestry assets	**311**	297

Mature forestry assets are those plantations that are harvestable, while immature forestry assets have not yet reached that stage of growth. Plantations are considered harvestable after a specific age depending on the species planted and regional considerations.

IAS 41 is not clear about how gains should be presented in the income statement. IAS 1 prohibits offsetting of income and expenses in the income statement. *[IAS 1.32]*. Therefore, if the sale of biological assets or agricultural produce meets the definition of revenue under IAS 18 – *Revenue*, i.e. it results in a gross inflow of economic benefits during the period arising from the ordinary activities of the entity, it should be presented on a gross basis in the income statement. However, if sales of non-current biological assets are incidental to the main revenue-generating activities of the entity they should be presented on a net basis. *[IAS 1.34]*. However, under IAS 41 the gross margin on agricultural produce sold shortly after harvest may be negligible, as the produce may have been previously carried at a valuation near to its sales price.

5.1.3 Groups of biological assets

The standard requires an entity to provide a narrative or quantitative description of each group of biological assets. *[IAS 41.41-42]*. An entity is encouraged to provide 'a quantified description of each group of biological assets, distinguishing between consumable and bearer biological assets or between mature and immature biological assets, as appropriate'. *[IAS 41.43]*. The standard suggests that an entity may separately disclose the carrying amounts of: *[IAS 41.43-44]*

- consumable biological assets (i.e. assets that are to be harvested as agricultural produce or sold as biological assets); and
- bearer biological assets (i.e. assets that are not consumable but rather are self-regenerating).

The standard continues by suggesting that an entity 'may further divide those carrying amounts between mature and immature assets. These distinctions provide information that may be helpful in assessing the timing of future cash flows'. *[IAS 41.43]*. Mature biological assets are defined by the standard as those assets 'that have attained harvestable specifications (for consumable biological assets) or are able to sustain regular harvests (for bearer biological assets)'. *[IAS 41.45]*. If an entity makes such distinctions, it should disclose the basis for making those distinctions. *[IAS 41.43]*.

5.1.4 Other disclosures

If not disclosed elsewhere in information published with the financial statements, an entity is required to describe:

'(a) the nature of its activities involving each group of biological assets; and

(b) non-financial measures or estimates of the physical quantities of:

  (i) each group of the entity's biological assets at the end of the period; and

  (ii) output of agricultural produce during the period'. *[IAS 41.46]*.

In addition, an entity shall disclose the following information:

(a) the existence and carrying amounts of biological assets whose title is restricted, and the carrying amounts of biological assets pledged as security for liabilities; *[IAS 41.49]*

(b) the amount of commitments for the development or acquisition of biological assets; *[IAS 41.49]*

(c) financial risk management strategies related to agricultural activity; *[IAS 41.49]*

(d) a reconciliation of changes in the carrying amount of biological assets between the beginning and the end of the current period, which includes: *[IAS 41.50]*

  (i) the gain or loss arising from changes in fair value less costs to sell;

  (ii) increases due to purchases;

  (iii) decreases attributable to sales and biological assets classified as held for sale (or included in a disposal group that is classified as held for sale) in accordance with IFRS 5;

  (iv) decreases due to harvest;

  (v) increases resulting from business combinations;

  (vi) net exchange differences arising on the translation of financial statements into a different presentation currency, and on the translation of a foreign operation into the presentation currency of the reporting entity; and

  (vii) other changes.

Fair value measurement disclosures are discussed at 5.2 below.

The standard also encourages, but does not require, an entity 'to disclose, by group or otherwise, the amount of change in fair value less costs to sell included in profit or loss due to physical changes and due to price changes', because this information is 'useful in appraising current period performance and future prospects, particularly when there is a production cycle of more than one year'. *[IAS 41.51, B74-B77]*. IAS 41 notes that physical change itself can be broken down further into growth, degeneration, production and procreation, but the standard does not specifically encourage disclosure of this information. *[IAS 41.52]*. The following example, which is derived from the standard, explains how an entity should go about separating the effect of physical changes from those of price changes.

Example 38.4: Physical change and price change [IAS 41.IE2]

A herd of ten 2-year-old animals was held at 1 January 2014. One animal aged 2½ years was purchased on 1 July 2014 for CU108, and one animal was born on 1 July 2014. No animals were sold or disposed of during the period. Per-unit fair values less costs to sell were as follows:

	1/1/2014	*1/7/2014*	*31/12/2014*
Newborn animal	–	CU70	CU72
½ year old animal	–	–	CU80
2 year old animal	CU100	–	CU105
2½ year old animal	–	CU108	CU111
3 year old animal	–	–	CU120

Fair value less costs to sell of herd at 1 January 2014:			
	(10 × CU100) =		CU1,000
Purchase on 1 July 2014:			
	(1 × CU108) =		CU108
Increase in fair value less costs to sell due to price change:			
	10 × (CU105 – CU100) =	CU50	
	1 × (CU111 – CU108) =	CU3	
	1 × (CU72 – CU70) =	CU2	
			CU55
Increase in fair value less costs to sell due to physical change:			
	10 × (CU120 – CU105) =	CU150	
	1 × (CU120 – CU111) =	CU9	
	1 × (CU80 – CU72) =	CU8	
	1 × CU70 =	CU70	
			CU237
Fair value less costs to sell of herd at 31 December 2014:			
	11 × CU120 =	CU1,320	
	1 × CU80 =	CU80	
			CU1,400

In January 2012, the Interpretations Committee considered a request for clarification in relation to paragraph 51 of IAS 41. The submitter was concerned that this paragraph may be contributing to an unacceptable application of the market approach to valuing biological assets. To remedy this, the submitter suggested that the disclosure be amended as part of annual improvements so that it would only be encouraged when the entity's biological assets are at the same level of biological transformation as those quoted in an active market. However, the Committee did not believe an amendment was needed, noting that paragraph 51 of IAS 41 addresses disclosures, not measurement. The Committee also pointed out that fair value measurement guidance is set out in IFRS 13, which is not affected by paragraph 51 of IAS 41.[6]

In addition to the above required and encouraged disclosures, the standard notes that agricultural activity is 'often exposed to climatic, disease and other natural risks. If an event occurs that gives rise to a material item of income or expense, the nature and amount of that item are disclosed in accordance with IAS 1' (see Chapter 3). For example, an entity may need to disclose events such as 'an outbreak of a virulent disease, a flood, a severe drought or frost, and a plague of insects'. *[IAS 41.53]*.

Many of the uncertainties and judgements inherent in the valuations that have to be made under IAS 41 are very clearly explained in the financial statements of Sappi Limited, as shown in the following extract.

Extract 38.3: Sappi Limited (2012)

Notes to the group annual financial statements
for the year ended September 2012 [extract]

2 Accounting Policies [extract]

2.3 Critical accounting policies and estimates [extract]

2.3.5 Plantations

Plantations are stated at fair value less estimated cost to sell at the harvesting stage.

In arriving at plantation fair values, the key assumptions are estimated prices less cost of delivery, discount rates, and volume and growth estimations. All changes in fair value are recognised in the period in which they arise.

The impact of changes in estimate prices, discount rates and, volume and growth assumptions may have on the calculated fair value and other key financial information on plantations is disclosed in note 10.

- **Estimated prices less cost of delivery**

The group uses a 12 quarter rolling historical average price to estimate the fair value of all immature timber and mature timber that is to be felled in more than 12 months from the reporting date. 12 quarters is considered a reasonable period of time after taking the length of the growth cycle of the plantations into account. Expected future price trends and recent market transactions involving comparable plantations are also considered in estimating fair value.

Mature timber that is expected to be felled within 12 months from the end of the reporting period are valued using unadjusted current market prices. Such timber is expected to be used in the short-term and consequently, current market prices are considered an appropriate reflection of fair value.

The fair value is derived by using the prices as explained above reduced by the estimated cost of delivery. Cost of delivery includes all costs associated with getting the harvested agricultural produce to the market, including harvesting, loading, transport and allocated fixed overheads.

- **Discount rate**

The discount rate used is the applicable pre-tax weighted average cost of capital of the business unit.

- **Volume and growth estimations and cost assumptions**

The group focuses on good husbandry techniques which include ensuring that the rotation of plantations is met with adequate planting activities for future harvesting. The age threshold used for quantifying immature timber is dependent on the rotation period of the specific timber genus which varies between 8 and 18 years. In the Southern African region, softwood less than eight years and hardwood less than five years are classified as immature timber.

Trees are generally felled at the optimum age when ready for intended use. At the time the tree is felled it is taken out of plantations and accounted for under inventory and reported as depletion cost (fellings).

Depletion costs include the fair value of timber felled, which is determined on the average method, plus amounts written off against standing timber to cover loss or damage caused by fire, disease and stunted growth. These costs are accounted for on a cost per metric ton allocation method multiplied by unadjusted current market prices. Tons are calculated using the projected growth to rotation age and are extrapolated to current age on a straight-line basis.

The group has projected growth estimation over a period of 8 to 18 years per rotation. In deriving this estimate, the group established a long-term sample plot network which is representative of the species and sites on which trees are grown and the measured data from these permanent sample plots were used as input into the group's growth estimation. Periodic adjustments are made to existing models for new genetic material.

The group directly manages plantations established on land that is either owned or leased from third parties. Indirectly managed plantations represent plantations established on land held by independent commercial farmers where Sappi provides technical advice on the growing and tendering of trees. The associated costs for managing the plantations are recognised as silviculture costs in cost of sales (see note 4).

10 Plantations [extract]

Sappi manages the establishment, maintenance and harvesting of its plantations on a compartmentalised basis. These plantations are comprised of pulpwood and sawlogs and are managed in such a way so as to ensure that the optimum fibre balance is supplied to its paper and pulping operations in Southern Africa.

As the group manages its plantations on a rotational basis, the respective increases by means of growth are negated by depletions over the rotation period for the group's own production or sales.

The group owns plantations on land that the group owns, as well as on land that the group leases. The group discloses both of these as directly managed plantations. With regard to indirectly managed plantations, the group has several different types of agreements with many independent farmers. The terms of the agreements depend on the type and specific needs of the farmer and the areas planted and range in duration from one to more than 20 years. In certain circumstances, the group provides loans to farmers that are disclosed as accounts receivable on the group balance sheet (these loans are considered, individually and in aggregate, immaterial to the group). If the group provides seedlings, silviculture and/or technical assistance, the costs are expensed when incurred by the group.

The group is exposed to financial risks arising from climatic changes, disease and other natural risks such as fire, flooding and storms as well as human-induced losses arising from strikes, civil commotion and malicious damage. These risks are covered by an appropriate level of insurance as determined by management. The plantations have an integrated management system that complies with FSC standards.

Changes in estimated prices, the discount rate, costs to sell and, volume and growth assumptions applied in the valuation of immature timber may impact the calculated fair value as tabled below:

US$ million	**2012**	2011
Market price changes		
1% increase in market prices	**4**	4
1% decrease in market prices	**(4)**	(4)
Discount rate (for immature timber)		
1% increase in rate	**(4)**	(4)
1% decrease in rate	**4**	4
Volume assumption		
1% increase in estimate of volume	**5**	6
1% decrease in estimate of volume	**(5)**	(6)
Costs to sell		
1% increase in costs to sell	**(3)**	(3)
1% decrease in costs to sell	**3**	3
Growth assumptions		
1% increase in rate of growth	**2**	1
1% decrease in rate of growth	**(2)**	(1)

5.2 Fair value measurement disclosures

IFRS 13 specifies the disclosures that are required for fair value measurements of biological assets and agricultural produce. Prior to the introduction of IFRS 13, IAS 41 required an entity to disclose:

(a) the methods and significant assumptions applied in determining the fair value of each group of agricultural produce at the point of harvest and each group of biological assets; *[IAS 41(2012).47]* and

(b) the fair value less costs to sell of agricultural produce harvested during the period, determined at the point of harvest. *[IAS 41(2012).48]*.

While these requirements have now been removed from IAS 41, they are subsumed within the disclosure requirements in IFRS 13. That standard requires substantially more information to be disclosed about fair value measurements, for example:

- the classification of a fair value measurement within the fair value hierarchy, i.e. Level 1, 2 or 3, and, for recurring fair value measurements, any transfers between levels in the hierarchy;
- a detailed reconciliation of movements for fair value measurements classified within Level 3 of the hierarchy, along with narrative sensitivity analysis; and
- the highest and best use of a non-financial asset if it differs from its current use, including why the non-financial asset is being used in a manner that differs from its highest and best use. *[IFRS 13.93]*.

Section 20 of Chapter 14 discusses IFRS 13's disclosure requirements in more detail.

5.3 Additional disclosures if fair value cannot be measured reliably

If an entity rebuts the presumption that fair value can be reliably measured on initial recognition of a biological asset and measures the asset at its cost less any accumulated depreciation and any accumulated impairment losses it is required to disclose the following information:

(a) if the entity holds such assets at the end of the period: *[IAS 41.54]*

   (i) a description of the biological assets;

   (ii) an explanation of why fair value cannot be measured reliably;

   (iii) if possible, the range of estimates within which fair value is highly likely to lie;

   (iv) the depreciation method used;

   (v) the useful lives or the depreciation rates used; and

   (vi) the gross carrying amount and the accumulated depreciation (aggregated with accumulated impairment losses) at the beginning and end of the period;

(b) if the entity held such assets at any point during the current period: *[IAS 41.55]*

   (i) any gain or loss recognised on disposal of such biological assets;

   (ii) the reconciliation required by paragraph 50 of IAS 41 (see 5.1.4 above) shall disclose amounts related to such biological assets separately;

(iii) that reconciliation shall include the following amounts included in profit or loss related to those biological assets:
- impairment losses;
- reversals of impairment losses; and
- depreciation;

(c) if the entity held such assets and their fair value became reliably measurable during the current period: *[IAS 41.56]*

(i) a description of the biological assets;

(ii) an explanation of why fair value has become reliably measurable; and

(iii) the effect of the change.

5.4 Government grants

An entity that has received government grants related to agricultural activity covered by IAS 41 is required to disclose the following information:

'(a) the nature and extent of government grants recognised in the financial statements;

(b) unfulfilled conditions and other contingencies attaching to government grants; and

(c) significant decreases expected in the level of government grants.' *[IAS 41.57]*.

6 POSSIBLE FUTURE DEVELOPMENTS

As discussed at 1 above, in June 2013 the IASB issued an exposure draft proposing the following changes to the accounting requirements for biological assets that meet the proposed definition of bearer plants (e.g. fruit trees, see 6.1 below):[7]

- bearer plants would be treated as property, plant and equipment in the scope of IAS 16 and would be subject to all the requirements of that standard (see 6.2.1 below);
- agricultural produce growing on bearer plants (e.g. fruit growing on a tree) would remain in the scope of IAS 41 (see 6.2.2 below); and
- government grants related to bearer plants would be accounted for in accordance with IAS 20, instead of IAS 41 (see 6.2.3 below).

The exposure draft did not include any proposed changes to the disclosure requirements in IAS 16 or IAS 41. However, the IASB specifically asked constituents for their views regarding disclosure. This included whether the fair value of bearer plants accounted for using the cost model should be disclosed and whether additional information about the bearer plant should be provided. Examples of such additional information could include age profiles and estimates of physical quantities.

6.1 Scope of proposed amendments and a definition of bearer plants

Only those biological assets that meet the proposed definition of bearer plants would be in the scope of the proposed amendments. All other assets that are currently within the scope of IAS 41 would be unaffected.

Bearer plants would be defined as plants that are:[8]

- used in the production or supply of agricultural produce;
- expected to bear produce for more than one period; and
- not intended to be sold as a plant or harvested as agricultural produce, except for incidental scrap sales.

All of the above criteria would need to be met for a plant to be considered a bearer plant.

Identifying a bearer plant may be obvious in many cases, for instance, grape vines, if the sole purpose is to grow grapes. The definition would also capture plants that are considered to be consumable today, such as the root systems of perennial plants (e.g. sugar cane or bamboo). However, the IASB specifically requested feedback from constituents on the inclusion of such root systems. The proposed definition would also exclude some plants that are currently considered bearers, e.g. a plant that yields more than one crop but has a productive life that is less than one period.

Plants that are held solely for sale (e.g. trees grown for lumber) would not be bearer plants. In addition, plants that have a dual use, bearing produce and being sold as either living plants or agricultural produce (beyond incidental scrap sales), would not meet the definition of bearer plants. This may be the case when an entity holds rubber trees to sell both the rubber milk and the trees as lumber. This proposed requirement is not aimed at situations where the agricultural produce has multiple uses (e.g. grapes sold as food or used to make wine). Instead, it seems to be aimed at plants that can be both consumable and bearers. In paragraph BC12 of the Basis for Conclusions to the Exposure Draft, it notes that the IASB had considered, but rejected, a predominant use model. In the IASB's view, 'a predominant-use model would be more difficult to apply than a no-alternative-use model because it requires additional judgement to be applied in order to determine the predominant use, and would need to address the consequences of reclassifications between IAS 16 and IAS 41 if the predominant use changes. [The IASB] also observed that, if the scope is restricted to biological assets that are only used as bearer plants, the need to apply this additional judgement and make reclassifications would be expected to be rare'.[9]

Bearer animals, like plants, may be held solely for the purpose of growing produce. However, the IASB explicitly excluded bearer animals from the scope of the proposed amendments because the Board believes that the proposed measurement model would become more complex if applied to these assets.[10]

6.2 Separating bearer plants from their agricultural produce

Prior to harvest, IAS 41 currently treats bearer plants and their agricultural produce as one asset (i.e. one unit of account). As discussed at 5.1.1.A above, these assets are generally presented as non-current based on their useful life. The exposure draft proposes to split the bearer plant and its agricultural produce into two assets (i.e. two units of account) with different accounting requirements. Bearer plants would likely still be presented as non-current. However, depending on how long it takes to mature, agricultural produce may be a current asset.

6.2.1 Proposed requirements for bearer plants

Under IAS 41, bearer plants are currently measured at fair value less costs to sell both at initial recognition and subsequently (unless, as discussed at 3.2.4 above, the measurement exception applies because fair value cannot be reliably measured). Under the proposed amendments, bearer plants would be subject to all of the recognition and measurement requirements in IAS 16 (see Chapter 18), including the following:

- before maturity, bearer plants would be measured at their accumulated cost, similar to the accounting treatment for a self-constructed item of plant and equipment before it is available for use; and
- entities would have a policy choice to measure their bearer plants, after they are mature, using either the cost model or the revaluation model. If the revaluation model is selected, revaluations would need to take place with sufficient regularity to ensure the carrying amount does not differ materially from the asset's fair value had it been measured at the end of the reporting period. Fair value changes would be recognised in other comprehensive income, rather than profit or loss.

Regardless of the subsequent measurement model selected, entities would need to determine the useful life of the bearer plant in order to depreciate it and re-evaluate the useful life each year. In addition, entities would need to assess, at the end of each reporting period, whether there are indicators that a bearer plant is impaired. If indicators exist, an impairment loss would be recognised if the carrying value is lower than the bearer asset's recoverable amount (being the higher of the asset's fair value less costs of disposal and its value in use).

While the proposed requirements would reduce the volatility in profit or loss for bearer plants, entities would still need to recognise any changes in the fair value of agricultural produce growing on the bearer plant, as discussed at 6.2.2 below.

Figure 38.2: Comparison of measurement requirements for bearer plants (assuming fair value can be reliably measured)

	Current Requirements	Proposed Requirements
At initial recognition	• Measured *together* with any agricultural produce attached (i.e. one unit of account) • Measured at fair value less costs to sell	• Would be measured *separately* from any related agricultural produce (i.e. two units of account) • Would be measured at cost, accumulated until maturity

	Current Requirements	Proposed Requirements
Subsequent measurement requirements	• Measured *together* with the agricultural produce until the point of harvest (see Figure 38.3) (i.e. one unit of account until the point of harvest) • Measured at the end of each reporting period at fair value less costs to sell • Changes are recognised in profit or loss	• Would be measured *separately* from any related agricultural produce (i.e. two units of account) • Would be measured at either: • Cost less any subsequent accumulated depreciation and impairment • Changes would be recognised in profit or loss Or • Fair value at each revaluation date less any subsequent accumulated depreciation and impairment • Revaluation adjustments (and impairment, to the extent it reverses previous revaluation increases) would be recognised in other comprehensive income; all other changes would be recognised in profit or loss

6.2.2 Proposed requirements for agricultural produce growing on bearer plants

Under IAS 41, entities currently treat a bearer plant and its agricultural produce as a single asset until the point of harvest. The proposed amendments would require an entity to recognise a bearer plant separately from its agricultural produce prior to harvest. Determining the timing of recognition may be difficult.

The agricultural produce would continue to be in the scope of IAS 41 and would be measured at fair value less costs to sell, with changes recognised in profit or loss as the produce grows. In the IASB's view, this proposed requirement would ensure that produce growing in the ground (e.g. wheat) and produce growing on a bearer biological asset (e.g. grapes) would be accounted for consistently. As a result, changes in the fair value of such agricultural produce would continue to be recognised in profit or loss at the end of each reporting period.

The proposed amendments are intended to address concerns raised regarding the cost, complexity and reliability of a fair value model in the absence of observable markets for these assets. However, if the IASB were to proceed with the proposed amendment, it could be challenging to apply in practice, for example, entities may need to track agricultural produce more closely in order to recognise and measure these assets separately from the related bearer plants. In addition, entities would need to determine appropriate fair value measurement methodologies (e.g. discounted cash flow techniques) to measure the fair value of these assets separately from the bearer plants on which they are growing, which may increase the complexity and subjectivity of the measurement.

Figure 38.3: Comparison of measurement requirements for agricultural produce growing on bearer plants

	Current Requirements	Proposed Requirements
At the end of each reporting period prior to harvest	• Measured *together* with the bearer plant (see Figure 38.2)	• Would be measured *separately* from the bearer plant at fair value less costs to sell
At the point of harvest	• Would be measured *separately* from the bearer plant at fair value less costs to sell	• Would be measured *separately* from the bearer plant at fair value less costs to sell (i.e. no change from current requirements)

6.3 Proposed requirements for government grants

Since bearer plants would be excluded from the scope of IAS 41, any related government grants would be in the scope of IAS 20 instead. Under IAS 20, government grants related to bearer assets would either be:

- recognised as deferred income and then recognised in profit or loss on a systematic basis over the useful life of the asset; or
- deducted in calculating the carrying amount of the asset and then recognised in profit or loss over the life of a depreciable asset as a reduced depreciation expense.

As discussed at 3.3 above, IAS 41 does not permit the second approach for government grants related to biological assets measured at fair value less costs to sell.

References

1 *IASB Update*, September 2012.
2 Agenda Paper 13, *Valuation of biological assets using a residual method,* IFRS Interpretations Committee Meeting, May 2012.
3 *IFRIC Update*, March 2013.
4 *IASB Update*, May 2013.
5 *IASB Update*, May 2013.
6 *IFRIC Update*, January 2012.
7 Exposure Draft ED/2013/8 *Agriculture: Bearer Plants, Proposed amendments to IAS 16 and IAS 41.*
8 ED/2013/8, proposed amendment to paragraph 5 of IAS 41.
9 Basis for Conclusions to ED/2013/8, para. BC12.
10 Basis for Conclusions to ED/2013/8, para. BC14.

Chapter 39 Extractive industries

List of examples

Chapter 39 Extractive industries

1 INTRODUCTION

1.1 Nature of extractive industries

'Extractive industries' were defined in the IASC's Issues Paper – *Extractive Industries* – published in November 2000 as 'those industries involved in finding and removing wasting natural resources located in or near the earth's crust'.[1] However, this chapter adopts a slightly narrower focus and concentrates on the accounting issues that affect mining companies and oil and gas companies.

Historically the IASB and its predecessor, the IASC, have avoided dealing with specific accounting issues in the extractive industries by excluding minerals and mineral reserves from the scope of their accounting standards. Currently, minerals and mineral reserves are excluded at least in part from the scope of the following standards:

- IAS 2 – *Inventories*; [IAS 2.3(a), 4]
- IAS 16 – *Property, Plant and Equipment*; [IAS 16.3(d)]
- IAS 17 – *Leases*; [IAS 17.2(a)]
- IAS 18 – *Revenue*; [IAS 18.6(h)]
- IAS 38 – *Intangible Assets*; [IAS 38.2(c)]
- IAS 40 – *Investment Property*; [IAS 40.4(b)] and
- IFRIC 4 – *Determining whether an Arrangement contains a Lease*. [IFRIC 4.4].

While these standards exclude 'minerals' from their scope, the exact wording of the scope exclusions differs between standards – see 3.1.1 below for more information. In addition, although minerals and mineral reserves themselves are excluded from the scope of many standards, assets used for the exploration and extraction of minerals are covered by existing IFRSs.

Many of the financial reporting issues that affect entities that operate in the extractive industries are a result of the environment in which they operate. Specific accounting issues arise because of the uncertainties involved in mineral exploration and extraction, the wide range of risk sharing arrangements, and government involvement in the form of mandatory participations and special tax regimes. At the same time, however, some of the business arrangements that are aimed at mitigating certain risks give rise to financial reporting complications. The financial reports of these entities need to reflect the risks and rewards to which they are exposed. In many cases, there are legitimate differences of opinion about how an entity should account for these matters.

The IASC's Issues Paper identified the following characteristics of activities in the extractive industries, which are closely related to the financial reporting issues that are discussed in this chapter:

- *High risks* – In the extractive industries there is a high risk that the amounts spent in finding new mineral reserves will not result in additional commercially recoverable reserves. In financial reporting terms this means that it can remain uncertain for a long period whether or not certain expenditures give rise to an asset. Further risks exist in relation to production (i.e. quantities actually produced may differ considerably from those previously estimated) and price (i.e. commodity prices are often volatile);
- *Little relationship between risks and rewards* – In the extractive industries a small expenditure may result in finding mineral deposits with a value of many times the amount of the expenditure. Conversely, large expenditures can frequently result in little or no future production. This has given rise to different approaches in financial reporting: (1) expense all expenditures as the future benefits are too uncertain, (2) capitalise all expenditures as the cumulative expenditures may be matched to the cumulative benefits, or (3) recognise the mineral reserves found at fair value;
- *Long lag between expenditure and production* – Exploration and/or development may take years to complete. During this period it is often far from certain that economic benefits will be derived from the costs incurred;
- *High costs of individual projects* – The costs of individual projects can be very high (e.g. offshore oil and gas projects and deep mining projects). Exploration expenditures that are carried forward pending the outcome of mineral acquisition and development projects may be highly significant in relation to the equity and the total assets of an entity;
- *Unique cost-sharing arrangements* – High costs and high risks, as discussed above, often lead entities in the extractive industries to enter into risk-sharing arrangements (e.g. joint arrangements, farm-out arrangements, carried interest arrangements, oilfield services arrangements and contract mining). These types of arrangements, which are much more common in the extractive industries than elsewhere, often give rise to their own financial reporting issues;
- *Intense government oversight and regulation* – The regulation of the extractive industries ranges from 'outright governmental ownership of some (especially petroleum) or all minerals to unusual tax benefits or penalties, price controls, restrictions on imports and exports, restrictions on production and distribution, environmental and health and safety regulations, and others'. Governments may also seek to charge an economic rent for resources extracted. These types of government involvement give rise to financial reporting issues, particularly when the precise nature of the government involvement is not obvious;

- *Scarce non-replaceable assets* – Mineral reserves are unique and scarce resources that an entity may not be able to replace in any location or in any form; and
- *Economic, technological and political factors* – While these factors are not unique to the extractive industries, the IASC's Issues Paper argues that they tend to have a greater impact on the extractive industries because:
  '(a) fluctuating market prices for minerals (together with floating exchange rates) have a direct impact on the economic viability of reserves and mineral properties. A relatively small percentage change in long-term prices can change decisions on whether or when to explore for, develop, or produce minerals;
  (b) there is a sharp impact from cost changes and technological developments. Changes in costs and, probably more significantly, changes in technology can significantly change the economic viability of particular mineral projects; and
  (c) in almost every country, mineral rights are owned by the state. In those countries where some mineral rights are privately owned, public reliance on adequate sources of minerals for economic and defence purposes often leads to governmental regulations and control. ... At other times, governmental policies may be changed to levy special taxes or impose governmental controls on the extractive industries.'

While it may be the case that the above factors affect the extractive industries more than others, to the extent that they also arise in the pharmaceutical, bio-technology, agricultural and software industries some of these risks give rise to further financial reporting issues. However, those industries are not affected by the combination of these circumstances to the same extent as is the case with the extractive industries. It is a combination of these factors, a lack of specific guidance in IFRS and a long history of industry practice and guidance from previous GAAPs that have given rise to a range of accounting practices in the extractive industries.

There is as yet no IFRS that addresses all of the specific issues of the extractive industries although attempts to devise such a standard have commenced. Having said this, draft proposals to date still do not address many of these specific issues.

1.1.1 Development of IFRS 6 – Exploration for and Evaluation of Mineral Resources

In December 2004, the IASB issued IFRS 6 – *Exploration for and Evaluation of Mineral Resources* – which addresses the accounting for one particular aspect of the extractive industries – being exploration and evaluation ('E&E'). IFRS 6 was issued as a form of interim guidance to clarify the application of IFRSs and the IASB *Conceptual Framework* to exploration and evaluation activities and to provide temporary relief from existing IFRS in some areas. The IASB decided to develop IFRS 6 because mineral rights and mineral resources are outside the scope of IAS 16 and IAS 38, exploration and evaluation expenditures are significant to entities engaged in extractive activities and there were different views on how these expenditures should be accounted for under IFRS. Other standard-setting bodies have had diverse accounting practices for exploration and evaluation assets which often differed from practices in other sectors with analogous expenditures. *[IFRS 6.IN1]*.

One of the IASB's goals in developing IFRS 6 was to avoid unnecessary disruption for both users and preparers. The Board therefore proposed to limit the need for entities to change their existing accounting policies for exploration and evaluation assets. As a result, IFRS 6 defines what E&E expenditures are, makes limited improvements to existing accounting practices for E&E expenditures, such as specifying when entities need to assess E&E assets for impairment in accordance with IAS 36 – *Impairment of Assets,* and requires certain disclosures.

E&E expenditures are 'expenditures incurred by an entity in connection with the exploration for and evaluation of mineral resources before the technical feasibility and commercial viability of extracting a mineral resource are demonstrable', while E&E assets are 'exploration and evaluation expenditures recognised as assets in accordance with the entity's accounting policy'. *[IFRS 6 Appendix A].*

The IFRS Interpretations Committee ('the Interpretations Committee'), formerly the IFRIC, has noted that the effect of the limited scope of IFRS 6 is to grant relief only to policies in respect of E&E activities, and that this relief did not extend to activities before or after the E&E phase. The Interpretations Committee confirmed that the scope of IFRS 6 consistently limited the relief from the hierarchy to policies applied to E&E activities only and that there is no basis for interpreting IFRS 6 as granting any additional relief in areas outside its scope.

The detailed requirements of IFRS 6 are discussed at 3 below.

1.1.2 Discussion Paper: Extractive Activities

On 6 April 2010 the IASB published the staff Discussion Paper – *Extractive Activities* (DP). The DP was developed by a research team comprising members of the Australian, Canadian, Norwegian and South African accounting standard-setters.[2] Although the IASB has discussed the project team's findings, the Board has yet to develop preliminary views or make any tentative decisions on the DP, and hence the DP only reflects the views of the project team. The DP addresses some of the financial reporting issues associated with exploring for and finding minerals, oil and natural gas deposits, developing those deposits and extracting the minerals, oil and natural gas. These are collectively referred to as 'extractive activities' or, alternatively, as 'upstream activities'.[3] The aim of the project is to create a single accounting and disclosure model that will only apply to upstream extractive activities in both the minerals and oil and gas industries. This represents a change from IFRS 6, which currently includes exploration and evaluation activities relating to minerals, oil, natural gas and similar non-regenerative resources within its scope. The project team decided against a broader scope in the DP as this would result in the need to develop additional definitions, accounting models and disclosures.[4]

The DP concluded that there were similarities in the main business activities, and the geological and other risks and uncertainties of both the minerals and oil and gas industries.[5] There were also similarities in the definitions of reserves and resources used by the Committee for Mineral Reserves International Reporting Standards (CRIRSCO) and the Society of Petroleum Engineers Oil and Gas Reserves Committee (SPE ORG).[6] The DP therefore proposed that there should be a single accounting and disclosure model that applies to all extractive activities (as defined).

While it has been generally acknowledged that the issues addressed in the DP are important, a significant number of respondents to the DP commented that the current scope did not address many of the more complex accounting issues where practice is diverse and greater consistency is required.

These issues include:

- the lack of guidance on complex areas such as farm-out and farm-in transactions (see 4.7.2);
- accounting for production sharing and royalty agreements (see 4.5 and 4.6); and
- the relationship between the proposals and IFRS 6.

The main proposals in the DP are summarised briefly below and then considered in more detail in the relevant sections of this chapter below.

1.1.2.A Definitions of reserves and resources

The DP explored a number of alternatives for defining reserves and resources. As the IASB does not have the required technical expertise to develop and maintain a comprehensive set of reserve and resource definitions, the DP proposed to rely on the following existing definitions of reserves and resources:

- minerals sector – *International Reporting Template for the Public Reporting of Exploration Results, Minerals Resources and Mineral Reserves* (CRIRSCO Template) established by the Committee for Mineral Reserves International Reporting Standards (CRIRSCO); and
- oil and gas sector – *Petroleum Resource Management System* (PRMS) established by the Society of Petroleum Engineers (in conjunction with other industry bodies).

This was on the basis that both of these are widely accepted and are comprehensive classification systems that cover many types of minerals and oil and gas. We believe, however, that if the IASB does decide to make use of the CRIRSCO Template and the PRMS it would be essential for the IASB to establish formal relationships with these bodies. This is because these definitions would form an integral part of an IFRS, and therefore it would be imperative for the Board to be appropriately involved in the maintenance of these definitions.

1.1.2.B Asset recognition

The DP proposed that legal rights (i.e. exploration rights and extraction rights) should form the basis of a mineral or oil and gas asset. An asset should be recognised when the legal rights are acquired. Associated with these legal rights is information about the (possible) existence of minerals or oil and gas, the extent and characteristics of the deposit, and the economics of their extraction. The project team believed that rights and information associated with minerals or oil and gas properties satisfy the asset recognition criteria. While such information does not represent a separate asset, the project team proposed that information obtained from subsequent exploration and evaluation activities and development works would be treated as enhancements of the asset represented by the legal rights.

When considering the appropriate unit of account (see 4.2 below), the DP proposed that the geographical boundary of the unit of account would be defined initially on the basis of the exploration rights held. As exploration, evaluation and development activities took place, the unit of account would contract progressively until it became no greater than a single area, or group of contiguous areas, for which the legal rights were held and which are managed separately and would be expected to generate largely independent cash flows. The project team's view was that the components approach in IAS 16 would determine the items that are accounted for as a single asset. However, an entity may decide to account for its assets using a smaller unit of account.

1.1.2.C Asset measurement

The DP considered both current value (e.g. fair value) and historical cost as potential measurement bases for minerals and oil and gas assets. Based on their findings, and taking the views of users and preparers into account, the project team concluded that minerals and oil and gas assets should be measured at historical cost and that detailed disclosures should be provided to enhance the relevance of the financial statements. The project team acknowledged that its choice of historical cost as the measurement basis was based to a large extent on doing the 'least harm'. In relation to impairment, it was considered that the IAS 36 impairment testing model was not feasible for exploration properties. Therefore, the DP concluded that exploration properties should only be tested for impairment whenever, in management's judgement, there is evidence that suggests that there is a high likelihood that the carrying amount of an exploration asset will not be recovered in full. This would require management to apply a separate set of indicators to such properties in order to assess whether their continued recognition as assets would be justified. In addition, further disclosures would be required in respect of the impairment of exploration properties due to the fact that management may take different views on the exploration properties. These would include separate presentation of exploration properties, the factors that lead to an impairment being recognised, and management's view as to why the remaining value of the asset or the other exploration assets is not impaired. This impairment assessment would need to be conducted separately for each exploration property.

1.1.2.D Disclosure

The DP proposed extensive disclosures aimed at ensuring users of financial reports could evaluate:

- the value attributable to an entity's minerals or oil and gas assets;
- the contribution of those assets to current period financial performance; and
- the nature and extent of risks and uncertainties associated with those assets.

The DP proposed detailed disclosures about the quantities of reserves and resources, and production revenues and costs. If the assets are measured at historical cost then detailed information should be disclosed about their current value and how it was determined. If, instead, the assets are measured at fair value then detailed information should be disclosed about that fair value and how it was determined.

US GAAP convergence: A number of the proposed disclosures differ from US GAAP. These include disclosures of:

- key reserve estimate assumptions and sensitivity analysis (not required by US GAAP); and
- proved and probable reserves (US GAAP only requires proved reserves, with an option to disclose probable reserves).

1.1.2.E *Publish What You Pay proposals*

A coalition of non-governmental organisations has been promoting, and continues to promote, a campaign called Publish What You Pay (PWYP), proposing that entities undertaking extractive activities should be required to disclose, in their financial reports, the payments they make to each host government. Specifically PWYP was recommending that its disclosure proposals should be incorporated into an eventual IFRS for extractive activities. This was because they regarded IFRS as offering the best mechanism for creating a global and enforceable standard that would generate comparable information. PWYP also proposed that disclosures should be provided on a country by country basis for other types of information including minerals and oil and gas reserve quantities, production volumes, production revenues, costs incurred in development and production, and key subsidiaries and properties.

Given PWYP's desire to have these disclosure requirements in an extractive activities IFRS, a section in the DP was dedicated to the PWYP proposals. The DP acknowledged that the disclosure of payments made to governments provides information that would be of use to capital providers in making their investment and lending decisions, but noted that providing this information might be difficult and costly for some entities. Therefore, the DP sought to develop an understanding (through feedback from respondents) of whether a requirement to disclose this information is justifiable on cost-benefit grounds.

It is worth noting that several jurisdictions have either issued, or are proposing to issue, rules to require mining and oil and gas companies to report certain payments to governments. These include the US Dodd Frank Act, the new European Union Accounting Directive and Transparency Directive (issued in July 2013), and proposed rules for Canada (which are contained in a recommendations paper issued by the Extractive Resource Revenue Transparency Working Group in June 2013). Australia is also considering a similar initiative. These are part of an overall push to increase the level of transparency of the activities of participants in extractive industries.

1.1.2.F *Status of Extractive Activities project*

As part of the IASB's 2011 agenda consultation process, the Extractive Activities project was included in the list of projects to be considered for inclusion on the IASB's active agenda for the following three years. After the outreach was completed, the IASB decided that this project would not be added to their active agenda. Instead it would become one of the nine priority research projects and would be combined with intangible assets and research and development activities. The commencement of these priority projects was expected to be staggered over an 18 month period. Nothing has started on the Extractive Activities/Intangibles project yet, nor have any timelines been posted on the IASB website. Given this, we do not expect anything significant to happen on this project for several years.

1.2 Upstream and downstream activities

Upstream activities in the extractive industries are defined as 'exploring for, finding, acquiring, and developing mineral reserves up to the point that the reserves are first capable of being sold or used, even if the enterprise intends to process them further'.[7] *Downstream activities* are 'the refining, processing, marketing, and distributing of petroleum, natural gas, or mined mineral (other than refining or processing that is necessary to make the minerals that have been mined or extracted capable of being sold)'.[8]

Thus, activities that are required to make the product saleable or usable are generally considered to be upstream activities. For example, the removal of water to produce dry gas would be an upstream activity, because otherwise the gas cannot be sold at all. However, refining crude oil is considered to be a downstream activity, because crude oil can be sold.

This chapter focuses on upstream activities in the extractive industries as they are primarily affected by the issues discussed above. However, downstream activities are discussed to the extent that they give rise to issues that are unique to the extractive industries (e.g. provisional pricing clauses) or are subject to the same issues as upstream activities (e.g. production sharing contracts).

1.2.1 Phases in upstream activities

Although there is not a universally accepted classification of upstream activities in the extractive industries, the IASC Issues Paper identified the following eight phases which other authors also commonly identify:[9]

(a) *Prospecting* – Prospecting involves activities undertaken to search for an area of interest, a geologic anomaly or structure that may warrant detailed exploration.[10] Prospecting is undertaken typically before mineral rights in the area have been acquired, and if the prospecting results are negative the area of prospecting generally will be abandoned and no mineral rights acquired.[11] However, sometimes it will be necessary to acquire a prospecting permit as the prospecting activities require access to the land to carry out geological and geophysical tests;[12]

(b) *Acquisition of mineral rights* – The acquisition phase involves the activities related to obtaining legal rights to explore for, develop, and/or produce wasting resources on a mineral property.[13] Legal rights may be acquired in a number of ways as discussed at 4.5 below;

(c) *Exploration* – Exploration is the detailed examination of a geographical area of interest that has shown sufficient mineral-producing potential to merit further exploration, often using techniques that are similar to those used in the prospecting phase.[14] In the mining sector, exploration usually involves taking cores for analysis, sinking exploratory shafts, geological mapping, geochemical analysis, cutting drifts and crosscuts, opening shallow pits, and removing overburden in some areas.[15] In the oil and gas sector, exploration involves techniques such as shooting seismic, core drilling, and ultimately the drilling of an exploratory well to determine whether oil and gas reserves do exist;[16]

(d) *Appraisal or evaluation* – This involves determining the technical feasibility and commercial viability of mineral deposits that have been found through exploration.[17] This phase typically includes:[18]

(i) detailed engineering studies and drilling of additional wells by oil and gas companies to determine how the reservoir can best be developed to obtain maximum recovery;

(ii) determination by mining companies of the volume and grade of deposits through drilling of core samples, trenching, and sampling activities in an area known to contain mineral resources;

(iii) examination and testing by mining companies of extraction methods and metallurgical or treatment processes;

(iv) surveying transportation and infrastructure requirements;

(v) conducting market and finance studies; and

(vi) making detailed economic evaluations to determine whether development of the reserves is commercially justified.

(e) *Development* – Development is the establishment of access to the mineral reserve and other preparations for commercial production. In the mining sector, development includes sinking shafts and underground drifts, making permanent excavations, developing passageways and rooms or galleries, building roads and tunnels, and advance removal of overburden and waste rock.[19] In the oil and gas sector the development phase involves gaining access to, and preparing, well locations for drilling, constructing platforms or preparing drill sites, drilling wells, and installing equipment and facilities;[20]

(f) *Construction* – Construction involves installing facilities, such as buildings, machinery and equipment to extract, treat, and transport minerals;[21]

(g) *Production* – The production phase involves the extraction of the natural resources from the earth and the related processes necessary to make the produced resource marketable or transportable;[22] and

(h) *Closure and decommissioning* – Closure means ceasing production, removing equipment and facilities, restoring the production site to appropriate conditions after operations have ceased and abandoning the site.[23]

The above phases are not necessarily discrete sequential steps. Instead, the phases often overlap or take place simultaneously. Nevertheless, they provide a useful framework for developing accounting policies in the extractive industries. Accounting for expenditures depends very much on the phase during which they are incurred; for example, as discussed further below, costs incurred in the prospecting phase cannot be recognised as assets, whereas most costs incurred in the construction phase should be capitalised.

1.3 Definition of key terms

The most important terms and abbreviations used are defined in this chapter when discussed or in the glossary at 7 below. However, alternative or more detailed definitions of financial reporting terms, and of mining and oil and gas technical terms and abbreviations, can be found in the following publications:

- *Issues Paper Extractive Industries*, IASC, November 2000;
- *Petroleum Resources Management System*, Society of Petroleum Engineers, 2007; and
- *Accounting for Oil and Gas Exploration, Development, Production and Decommissioning Activities*, Statement of Recommended Practice, UK Oil Industry Accounting Committee, June 2001.

IFRSs currently use the term 'minerals' and 'mineral assets' when referring to the extractive industries as a whole. This is used as a collective term to include both mining and oil and gas reserves and resources. In contrast, a distinction between the two industries was introduced in the Extractive Activities DP (discussed above at 1.1.2 above), where the term 'minerals' has been used to refer to the mining sector and the term 'oil and gas' has been used to refer to the oil and gas sector.

For the purposes of this chapter, consistency with the current wording in IFRSs will be maintained and therefore, unless stated otherwise, 'minerals' and 'mineral assets' will encompass both mining and oil and gas.

2 MINERAL RESERVES AND RESOURCES

This section discusses in some detail the underlying principles used by entities to estimate the quantity of recoverable mineral reserves and resources for both mining and oil and gas, that the entity owns or has a right to extract. At the commercial level, these estimates are considered of paramount importance by stakeholders in making investment decisions.

The importance of estimating reserves is matched by the difficulty in doing so, both technically and methodologically. For example, there is no firm consensus on which commodity prices should be used in determining commercially recoverable reserves (i.e. historical, spot or forward looking). This section therefore aims to provide an introduction to this subject, and to explain the main methods used to arrive at reserve estimates, including the valuation methods used once quantities of reserves have been estimated. In our view, without a sound grasp of this aspect, it is difficult to make an informed judgement as to how to account for mineral reserves.

Mineral reserves are often the most valuable assets of mining, and oil and gas companies and mineral reserve estimates are a very important part of the way mining companies and oil and gas companies report to their stakeholders. However, mineral reserves are generally measured under IFRS at their historical cost which, other than by coincidence, will not be their market value. Currently IFRS does not require disclosure of reserves, though certain national standards (e.g. US GAAP) and stock exchange regulators (e.g. US Securities and Exchange Commission) do. Notwithstanding there are no specific disclosure requirements, detailed reserve estimates are required in order to apply historical cost accounting under IFRS in:

- deciding whether to capitalise exploration and evaluation costs (see 3.2 below);
- calculating the annual depreciation, depletion and amortisation charge under the units of production method (see 4.9 below);
- calculating deferred stripping cost adjustments (applicable to mining companies only – see 6.1 below);
- determining impairment charges and reversals under IAS 36 (see 4.10 below);
- determining whether a gain or loss should be recognised on transactions such as asset swaps, carried interest arrangements and farm-in or farm-out arrangements (see 4.7 below);
- determining the fair value of acquired mineral reserves when applying the purchase method of accounting under IFRS 3 – *Business Combinations* (see 4.8 below); and
- estimating the timing of decommissioning or restoration activities (see 4.12 below).

Reserves reporting in the oil and gas sector and mining sector has been under development since the beginning of the twentieth century. However, reserve estimation techniques in the oil and gas sector and mining sector have developed largely independently as a result of the different nature of the reserves involved. Therefore, the terminology and definitions used in the oil and gas sector and mining sector are discussed separately at 2.2 and 2.3 below respectively. Disclosure is discussed at 2.4 below.

The international efforts to harmonise reserve estimation and reporting are discussed below.

2.1 International harmonisation of reserve reporting

The project team concluded in the Extractive Activities DP that the nature and extent of the similarities between the CRIRSCO Template (mining) and the PRMS reserve and resource definitions (oil and gas) indicate that these definitions are capable of providing a platform for setting comparable accounting and disclosure requirements for both mining and oil and gas activities. Therefore they recommended that the CRIRSCO template and the PRMS definitions of reserves and resources are suitable to use in a future IFRS for Extractive Activities. Nonetheless, there is some tension between the definition of an asset in the IASB's *Conceptual Framework* and the assumptions underlying the reserves and resources definitions.[24] The points of tension highlighted in the DP include: the CRIRSCO Template and the PRMS both make use of entity-specific assumptions that are applied to derive a reserve estimate, whereas IFRS typically requires that estimates should make use of economic assumptions that reflect market-based evidence, where available; and the CRIRSCO Template and the PRMS require that certain conditions must exist before a resource can be converted into a reserve. In contrast, management's intentions are not a feature of the *Conceptual Framework's* definition of an asset.

While the DP recommended the use of the CRIRSCO Template and PRMS, it also recommended that the alternative option of using the *United Nations Framework Classification for Fossil Energy and Mineral Resources* (UNFC) should be reconsidered if an Extractive Activities project is added to the IASB's active agenda.[25]

In January 2009, the SEC published its final rule – *Modernization of Oil and Gas Reporting (Release No. 33-8995)* – detailing its oil and gas reserves estimation and disclosure requirements. The primary objectives of the rule were to increase the transparency and information value of reserve disclosures and improve comparability among oil and gas companies, including comparability between domestic registrants and foreign private issuers. The rule became effective for registration statements filed on or after 1 January 2010, and for annual reports for fiscal years ending on or after 31 December 2009. Both the CRIRSCO and the Society for Mining, Metallurgy, and Exploration (SME) provided comments on this Release. In its comment letter, CRIRSCO called for the SEC to consider 'concurrent revisions to disclosure requirements relating to minerals exploration and mining as well as oil and gas',[26] while the SME noted that 'given the increasing overlap between oil and gas, and mining in such areas as tar sands and oil shales, the need for convergence should not be ignored when reviewing oil and gas rules.'[27] However, so far no progress has been made in achieving convergence between the SEC requirements and the various other requirements and differences still remain – these include:

- the SEC does not allow the term 'resources' to be used in reports (see 2.2 and 2.4.2 below);
- the SEC states that final or bankable feasibility studies need to be completed before new greenfield reserves can be declared;
- the SEC requirement for mining companies to use three year trailing average rather than forward looking commodity prices in reserve estimation under SEC Industry Guide 7; and
- the SEC requirement for oil and gas companies to use a 12-month average price instead of a year-end price in estimating reserves.

2.2 Petroleum reserve estimation and reporting

The '*SPE/WPC/AAPG/SPEE Petroleum Resources Management System*' (SPE-PRMS), which was published in 2007, is the leading framework for the estimation and reporting of petroleum reserves and resources. It was prepared by the Oil and Gas Reserves Committee of the Society of Petroleum Engineers (SPE) and reviewed and sponsored by the World Petroleum Council (WPC), the American Association of Petroleum Geologists (AAPG) and the Society of Petroleum Evaluation Engineers (SPEE). The definitions and guidelines in the SPE-PRMS, which are internationally used within the oil and gas sector, deal with:[28]

- classification and categorisation of resources;
- evaluation and reporting; and
- estimation of recoverable quantities.

As noted by the IASB, 'most of the major regulatory agencies have developed disclosure guidelines that impose classification rules similar to, but not directly linked to, the SPE-PRMS. Regulatory agencies typically mandate disclosure of only a subset of the total reserves and resources defined in the SPE-PRMS; for example, the SEC specifies that only Proved Reserves should be disclosed.'[29] Note that the SEC now allows for optional disclosure of probable reserves.

2.2.1 *Petroleum Resources Management System (SPE-PRMS)*

2.2.1.A *Basic principles and definitions*

The following diagram summarises the SPE-PRMS resources classification system:[30]

Figure 39.1

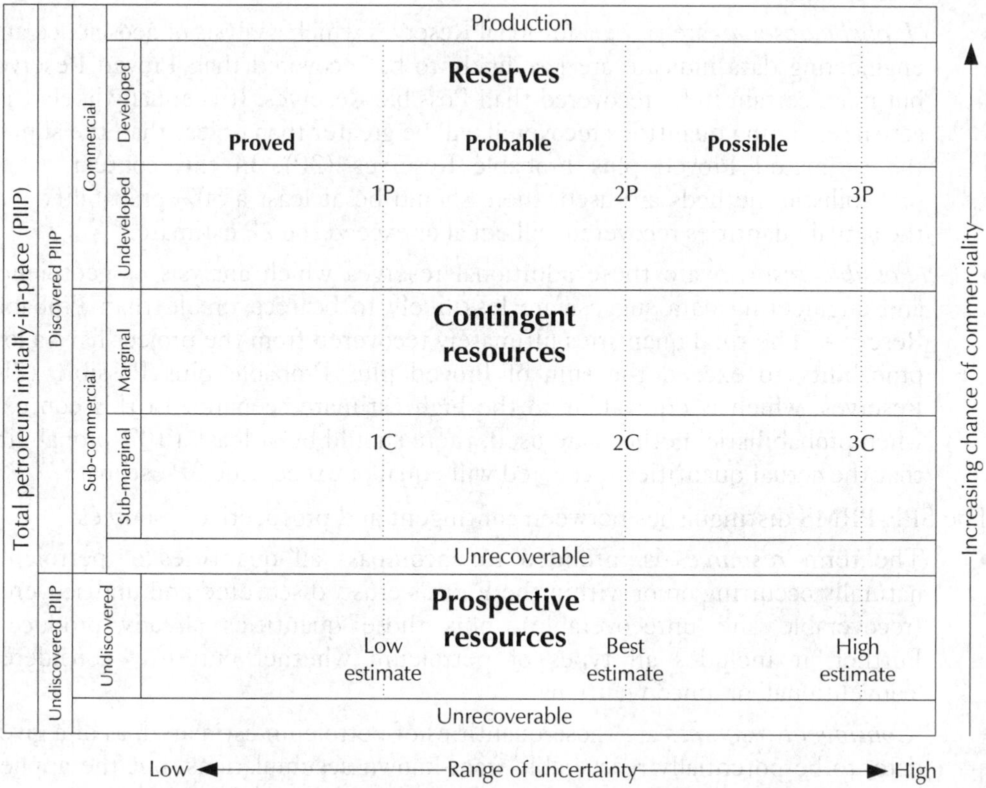

Total petroleum initially-in-place (PIIP)
Discovered PIIP
Commercial
Developed
Undeveloped
Production
Reserves
Proved **Probable** **Possible**
1P 2P 3P
Sub-commercial
Marginal
Sub-marginal
Contingent resources
1C 2C 3C
Unrecoverable
Undiscovered PIIP
Undiscovered
Prospective resources
Low estimate Best estimate High estimate
Unrecoverable
Low ◄— Range of uncertainty —► High
Increasing chance of commerciality

The *range of uncertainty* reflects a range of estimated quantities potentially recoverable, while the vertical axis represents the *chance of commerciality*, that is, the chance that the project will be developed and reach commercial producing status.[31]

The SPE-PRMS defines proved, probable and possible reserves as follows:

- '*Reserves* are those quantities of petroleum anticipated to be commercially recoverable by application of development projects to known accumulations from a given date forward under defined conditions. Reserves must further satisfy four criteria: they must be discovered, recoverable, commercial, and remaining (as of the evaluation date) based on the development project(s) applied. Reserves are further categorized in accordance with the level of certainty associated with the estimates and may be sub-classified based on project maturity and/or characterized by development and production status.'[32]
- '*Proved reserves* are those quantities of petroleum, which, by analysis of geoscience and engineering data, can be estimated with reasonable certainty to be commercially recoverable, from a given date forward, from known reservoirs

and under defined economic conditions, operating methods, and government regulations. If deterministic methods are used, the term reasonable certainty is intended to express a high degree of confidence that the quantities will be recovered. If probabilistic methods are used, there should be at least a 90% probability that the quantities actually recovered will equal or exceed the estimate.'[33]

- '*Probable reserves* are those additional Reserves which analysis of geoscience and engineering data indicate are less likely to be recovered than Proved Reserves but more certain to be recovered than Possible Reserves. It is equally likely that actual remaining quantities recovered will be greater than or less than the sum of the estimated Proved plus Probable Reserves (2P). In this context, when probabilistic methods are used, there should be at least a 50% probability that the actual quantities recovered will equal or exceed the 2P estimate.'[34]
- '*Possible reserves* are those additional reserves which analysis of geoscience and engineering data suggest are less likely to be recoverable than Probable Reserves. The total quantities ultimately recovered from the project have a low probability to exceed the sum of Proved plus Probable plus Possible (3P) Reserves, which is equivalent to the high estimate scenario. In this context, when probabilistic methods are used, there should be at least a 10% probability that the actual quantities recovered will equal or exceed the 3P estimate.'[35]

The SPE-PRMS distinguishes between contingent and prospective resources:

- The term *resources* is intended to encompass all quantities of petroleum naturally occurring on or within the Earth's crust, discovered and undiscovered (recoverable and unrecoverable), plus those quantities already produced. Further, it includes all types of petroleum whether currently considered 'conventional' or 'unconventional'.[36]
- '*Contingent resources* are those quantities of petroleum estimated, as of a given date, to be potentially recoverable from known accumulations, but the applied project(s) are not yet considered mature enough for commercial development due to one or more contingencies. Contingent Resources may include, for example, projects for which there are currently no viable markets, or where commercial recovery is dependent on technology under development, or where evaluation of the accumulation is insufficient to clearly assess commerciality. Contingent Resources are further categorized in accordance with the level of certainty associated with the estimates and may be sub-classified based on project maturity and/or characterized by their economic status.'[37]
- '*Prospective resources* are those quantities of petroleum estimated, as of a given date, to be potentially recoverable from undiscovered accumulations by application of future development projects. Prospective Resources have both an associated chance of discovery and a chance of development. Prospective Resources are further subdivided in accordance with the level of certainty associated with recoverable estimates assuming their discovery and development and may be sub-classified based on project maturity.'[38]

Total petroleum initially-in-place is that quantity of petroleum that is estimated to exist originally in naturally occurring accumulations. *Discovered petroleum initially-in-place* is that quantity of petroleum that is estimated, as of a given date, to be contained in known accumulations prior to production. *Undiscovered petroleum initially-in-place* is that quantity of petroleum estimated, as of a given date, to be contained within accumulations yet to be discovered.[39]

Production is the cumulative quantity of petroleum that has been recovered at a given date. *Unrecoverable* is that portion of Discovered or Undiscovered Petroleum Initially-in-Place quantities which is estimated, as of a given date, not to be recoverable by future development projects. A portion of these quantities may become recoverable in the future as commercial circumstances change or technological developments occur; the remaining portion may never be recovered due to physical/chemical constraints represented by subsurface interaction of fluids and reservoir rocks.[40]

2.2.1.B Classification and categorisation guidelines

The SPE-PRMS provides guidance on classifying resources depending on the relative maturity of the development projects being applied to yield the recoverable quantity estimates, as follows:[41]

Figure 39.2

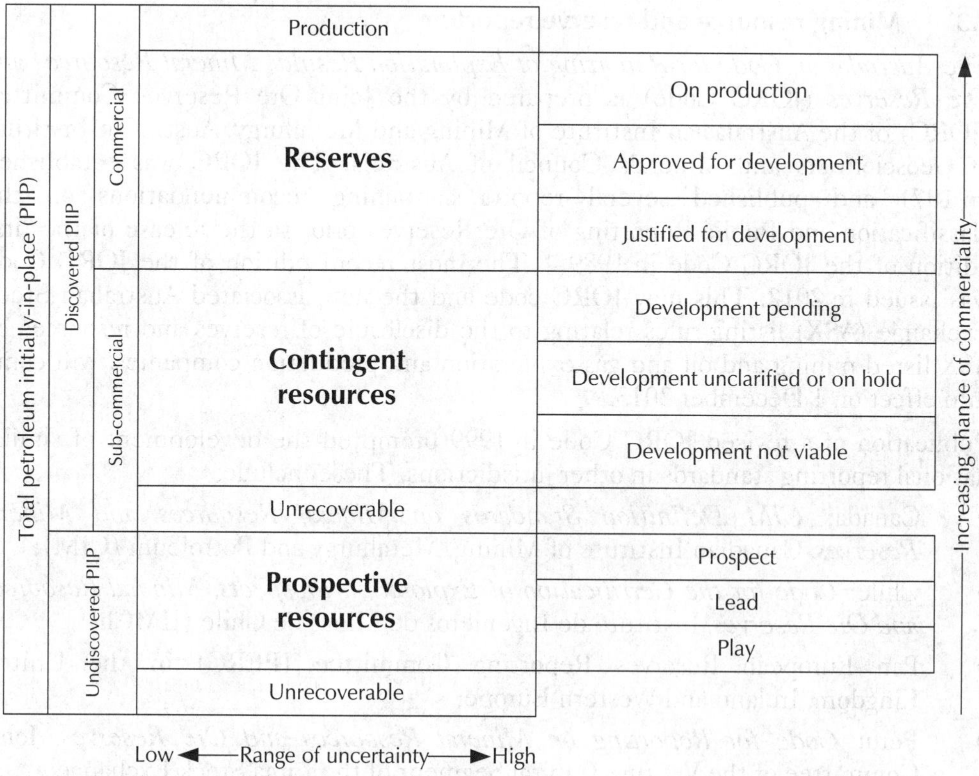

Total petroleum initially-in-place (PIIP)
Discovered PIIP
Commercial
Production
Reserves
On production
Approved for development
Justified for development
Sub-commercial
Contingent resources
Development pending
Development unclarified or on hold
Development not viable
Unrecoverable
Undiscovered PIIP
Prospective resources
Prospect
Lead
Play
Unrecoverable
Low ◀— Range of uncertainty —▶ High
Increasing chance of commerciality ▲

Project maturity may be indicated qualitatively by allocation to classes and sub-classes and/or quantitatively by associating a project's estimated chance of reaching producing status.

The SPE-PRMS also provides guidance on categorising resources, depending on the associated degrees of uncertainty, into the following cumulative categories:[42]

- proved, probable and possible (1P, 2P and 3P) for reserves;
- low, best and high (1C, 2C and 3C) for contingent resources; and
- low estimate, best estimate and high estimate for prospective resources.

Additionally, guidance is provided on categorisation of reserves and resources related to incremental projects, such as workovers, infill drilling and improved recovery.

2.2.1.C Evaluation and reporting guidelines

To promote consistency in project evaluations and reporting, the SPE-PRMS provides guidelines on the economic assumptions that are to be used, measurement of production, and resources entitlement and recognition.[43]

2.2.1.D Estimating recoverable quantities

Finally, the SPE-PRMS provides guidance on the analytical procedures, and on the deterministic and probabilistic methods to be used.

2.3 Mining resource and reserve reporting

The *Australasian Code for Reporting of Exploration Results, Mineral Resources and Ore Reserves* (JORC Code) is prepared by the Joint Ore Reserves Committee (JORC) of the Australasian Institute of Mining and Metallurgy, Australian Institute of Geoscientists and Minerals Council of Australia. The JORC was established 'in 1971 and published several reports containing recommendations on the classification and Public Reporting of Ore Reserves prior to the release of the first edition of the JORC Code in 1989.'[44] The most recent edition of the JORC Code was issued in 2012. This new JORC code and the new associated Australian Stock Exchange (ASX) listing rules relating to the disclosure of reserves and resources by ASX listed mining and oil and gas exploration and production companies, will come into effect on 1 December 2013.

Publication of a revised JORC Code in 1999 prompted the development of similar national reporting standards in other jurisdictions. These include:

- Canada: *CIM Definition Standards on Mineral Resources and Mineral Reserves*, Canadian Institute of Mining, Metallurgy and Petroleum (CIM);
- Chile: *Code for the Certification of Exploration Prospects, Mineral Resources and Ore Reserves*, Instituto de Ingenieros de Minas de Chile (IIMCh);
- Pan European Reserves Reporting Committee (PERC) in the United Kingdom, Ireland and Western Europe;
- Peru: *Code for Reporting on Mineral Resources and Ore Reserves*, Joint Committee of the Venture Capital Segment of the Lima Stock Exchange;

- South Africa: *South African Code for Reporting of Mineral Resources and Mineral Reserves*, South African Mineral Resource Committee (SAMREC); and
- United States: *Guide for Reporting Exploration Information, Mineral Resources and Mineral Reserves*, Society for Mining, Metallurgy, and Exploration (SME).

In July 2006 CRIRSCO first published a generic International Reporting Template for reporting mineral resources and mineral ore reserves, modelled on those of the JORC Code. This template is regularly updated and improved, with the latest update having occurred in May 2013. This reflects best practice national reporting standards but excludes national regulatory requirements. The template serves as a guide to national standard-setters that do not have a reporting standard or who want to revise their existing standard to an internationally acceptable form.[45] 'The system is primarily targeted at establishing international best practice standards for regulatory and public disclosures and combines the basic components of a number of national reporting codes and guidelines that have been adopted in similar forms by all the major agencies [other than] the US Securities and Exchange Commission (SEC). The classification is applied, with small modifications or extensions, by most mining companies for the purpose of internal resource management.'[46]

CRIRSCO has been participating in the activities of the IASB's Discussion Paper – *Extractive Activities* (see 2.1 above).

In the United States, public disclosures of mineral resources and mineral reserves are regulated by the SEC, which does not recognise the CRIRSCO guidelines. Unsurprisingly, some of the SEC requirements (Industry Guide 7) for public release of information are materially different from those applicable in other countries.[47] The SEC's Industry Guide 7 is discussed at 2.4.2 below.

2.3.1 CRIRSCO International Reporting Template (May 2013)

This section describes the main requirements of the CRIRSCO International Reporting Template (CRIRSCO Template) to the extent that they are relevant to financial reporting by mining companies.

2.3.1.A Scope

The main principles governing the operation and application of the CRIRSCO Template are transparency, materiality and competence. These are aimed at ensuring that the reader of a public report is provided with:[48]

- sufficient information that is clear and unambiguous (transparency),
- a report that contains all relevant information which investors and their professional advisers would reasonably require and would reasonably expect to find, to be able to form a reasoned and balanced judgement about the Exploration Results, Mineral Resources or Mineral Reserves being reported (materiality), and
- information that is based on work that is the responsibility of suitably qualified and experienced persons who are subject to an enforceable professional code of ethics and rules of conduct (competence).

A *public report* is a report 'prepared for the purpose of informing investors or potential investors and their advisors on Exploration Results, Mineral Resources or Mineral Reserves. They include, but are not limited to, annual and quarterly company reports, press releases, information memoranda, technical papers, website postings and public presentations'.[49] The CRIRSCO Template is applicable to all solid minerals, including diamonds, other gemstones, industrial minerals, stone and aggregates, and coal.[50] The CRIRSCO Template provides supplementary rules on reporting related to coal, diamonds and industrial minerals, due to the special nature of those types of deposit.

A public report should be prepared by a *competent person*, defined in the CRIRSCO Template as '... a minerals industry professional (NRO to insert appropriate membership class and organisation including Recognised Professional Organisations) with enforceable disciplinary processes including the powers to suspend or expel a member.'[51] (Note that NRO stands for 'national representative organisations'.)

2.3.1.B Reporting terminology

The general relationship between Exploration Results, Mineral Resources and Mineral Reserves can be summarised in the following diagram:[52]

Figure 39.3

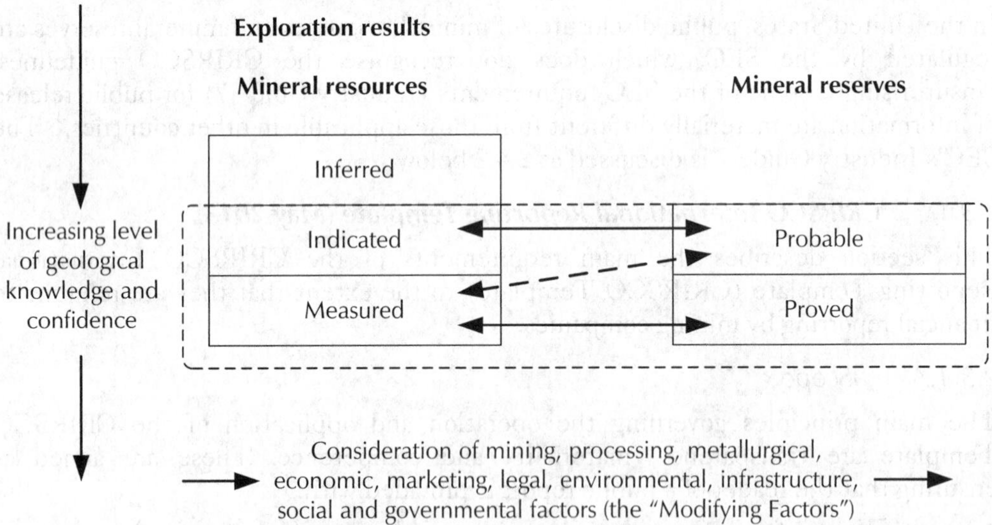

The terms in the above diagram are defined as follows.

Exploration Results include data and information generated by mineral exploration programmes that might be of use to investors but which do not form part of a declaration of Mineral Resources or Mineral Reserves.[53] The CRIRSCO Template specifically requires that any information relating to Exploration Results be expressed in such a way that it does not unreasonably imply that potentially economic mineralisation has been discovered.[54]

A *Mineral Resource* is a concentration or occurrence of solid material of economic interest in or on the Earth's crust in such form, grade, quality and quantity that there are reasonable prospects for eventual economic extraction. The location, quantity, grade, continuity and other geological characteristics of a Mineral Resource are known, estimated or interpreted from specific geological evidence and knowledge, including sampling. Mineral Resources are sub-divided, in order of increasing geological confidence, into Inferred, Indicated and Measured categories:[55]

- 'An *Inferred Mineral Resource* is that part of a Mineral Resource for which quantity and grade or quality are estimated on the basis of limited geological evidence and sampling. Geological evidence is sufficient to imply but not verify geological and grade or quality continuity. An Inferred Resource has a lower level of confidence than that applying to an Indicated Mineral Resource and must not be converted to a Mineral Reserve. It is reasonably expected that the majority of Inferred Mineral Resources could be upgraded to Indicated Mineral Resources with continued exploration.'[56]
- 'An *Indicated Mineral Resource* is that part of a Mineral Resource for which quantity, grade or quality, densities, shape and physical characteristics are estimated with sufficient confidence to allow the application of Modifying Factors in sufficient detail to support mine planning and evaluation of the economic viability of the deposit. Geological evidence is derived from adequately detailed and reliable exploration, sampling and testing and is sufficient to assume geological and grade or quality continuity between points of observation. An Indicated Mineral Resource has a lower level of confidence than that applying to a Measured Mineral Resource and may only be converted to a Probable Mineral Reserve.'[57]
- 'A *Measured Mineral Resource* is that part of a Mineral Resource for which quantity, grade or quality, densities, shape and physical characteristics are estimated with confidence to allow the application of Modifying Factors to support detailed mine planning and final evaluation of the economic viability of the deposit. Geological evidence is derived from detailed and reliable exploration, sampling and testing and is sufficient to confirm geological and grade or quality continuity between points of observation. A Measured Mineral Resource has a higher level of confidence than that applying to either an Indicated Mineral Resource or an Inferred Mineral Resource. It may be converted to a Proved Mineral Reserve or to a Probable Mineral Reserve.'[58]
- 'Modifying factors are considerations used to convert Mineral Resources to Mineral Reserves. These include, but are not restricted to, mining, processing, metallurgical, infrastructure, economic, marketing, legal, environmental, social and governmental factors.'[59]
- 'A *Mineral Reserve* is the economically mineable part of a Measured and/or Indicated Mineral Resource. It includes diluting materials and allowances for losses, which may occur when the material is mined or extracted and is defined by studies at Pre-Feasibility or Feasibility level as appropriate that include application of Modifying Factors. Such studies demonstrate that, at the time of reporting, extraction could reasonably be justified.'[60]

- 'A *Probable Mineral Reserve* is the economically mineable part of an Indicated, and in some circumstances, a Measured Mineral Resource. The confidence in the Modifying Factors applying to a Probable Mineral Reserve is lower than that applying to a Proved Mineral Reserve. A Probable Mineral Reserve has a lower level of confidence than a Proved Mineral Reserve but is of sufficient quality to serve as the basis for a decision on the development of the deposit.'[61]
- 'A *Proved Mineral Reserve* is the economically mineable part of a Measured Mineral Resource. A Proved Mineral Reserve implies a high degree of confidence in the Modifying Factors. A Proved Mineral Reserve represents the highest confidence category of reserve estimate.'[62]

The CRIRSCO Template contains more detailed guidance on how a competent person should decide on mineral resource and mineral reserve classification and contains a checklist and guideline for the preparation of public reports.

2.4 Disclosure of mineral reserves and resources

Mineral reserves are a significant element in communications by mining companies and oil and gas companies to their stakeholders. IFRS requires an entity to provide 'additional disclosures when compliance with the specific requirements in IFRSs is insufficient to enable users to understand the impact of particular transactions, other events and conditions on the entity's financial position and financial performance'. *[IAS 1.17(c)]*. Therefore, although IFRS does not specifically require it, disclosures regarding mineral resources and reserves will generally be necessary under IFRS to provide users with the information they need to understand the entity's financial position and performance. In the absence of specific guidance, entities should develop a method for communicating reserves that is consistent with the overall IFRS *Conceptual Framework*.

As noted in 2 above, entities have to use reserves data for a number of accounting purposes and the methodology should be consistent with the definitions in the IFRS *Conceptual Framework* for asset recognition. We believe that users of the financial statements need to be able to identify the methodology used to estimate reserves in order to understand an entity's financial statements. If management uses proven reserves for investment appraisal and uses these same reserves for depreciation and impairment calculations, this should be clearly identified in the reserves disclosure. Conversely, if management uses different reserves definitions for different purposes, that should be made clear in the financial statements.

As there is currently no guidance under IFRS relating to the disclosure of information about mineral reserves and resources, entities not subject to the requirements of a national regulator may wish to use the disclosure requirements of other standard-setters as a starting point in developing their own policies. The sections below discuss the disclosure requirements of several standard-setters for mineral reserve and resource quantities (see 2.4.1 and 2.4.2 below) and reserve values (see 2.4.3 below).

However, while disclosure of information about mineral reserves is clearly very useful, users of financial statements should be aware that there are many differences between different jurisdictions or even within those jurisdictions. Therefore, comparisons between entities may be difficult or even impossible. In particular, the following aspects are important:

- *Proven and probable reserves* – The definition of reserves can vary greatly, e.g. the UK Oil Industry Accounting Committee's Statement of Recommended Practice (OIAC SORP) permits disclosure of either 'proven and probable' or 'proved developed and undeveloped' reserves (see 2.4.1.A below), whereas Accounting Standards Codification (ASC) Topic 932-235-50 – *Extractive Activities – Oil and Gas – Notes to Financial Statements – Disclosure* – requires disclosure of 'proved reserves, proved developed reserves and proved undeveloped reserves'[63] (see 2.4.1.B below);
- *Commodity price* – The quantity of economically recoverable reserves may depend to a large extent on the price assumptions that an entity uses. Differences often arise because the entity:
  - uses its own long-term price assumption which, for example, is permitted under the OIAC SORP;
  - is required to use 12-month average prices, which is required by the SEC Release No. 33-8995 in the oil and gas sector; or
  - is required to use a three year trailing average, which is required under the SEC's Industry Guide 7 in the mining sector;
- *Royalties* – Royalties payable in-kind to the government or legal owner of the mineral rights may or may not be included in reserves;
- *Non-controlling interests* – Generally 'reserves' include all reserves held by the parent and its consolidated subsidiaries. While in many jurisdictions mining companies and oil and gas companies are required to disclose the reserves attributable to significant non-controlling interests, this is not always required;
- *Associates and other investments* – An entity may have economic ownership of reserves through investments in associates and joint arrangements, equity interests (see 4.4 below) or royalty yielding contracts (see 4.6 below). Such reserves are generally not included in consolidated reserves, but may need to be disclosed separately; and
- *Production sharing contracts and risk service contracts* (see 4.5 below) – Frequently the mining company or oil and gas company does not legally own the mineral reserves in the ground, i.e. the government retains legal ownership. A significant amount of judgement concerning the nature of the rights and economic interests of the entity may be required to determine whether the entity is the economic owner of any reserves. Depending on the reserve reporting framework that the entity is subject to, such 'economic' reserves may or may not be included in reserves.

Undoubtedly there are other differences between the disclosures of reserves required in different jurisdictions of which users of IFRS financial statements should be aware. As illustrated in the extract below from BP's 2006 financial statements, such differences in reserve definition may also affect IFRS financial reporting directly.

Extract 39.1: BP p.l.c. (2006)

Notes on financial statements [extract]

3 Oil and natural gas reserves estimates

At the end of 2006, BP adopted the US Securities and Exchange Commission (SEC) rules for estimating oil and natural gas reserves for all accounting and reporting purposes instead of the UK accounting rules contained in the Statement of Recommended Practice 'Accounting for Oil and Gas Exploration, Development, Production and Decommissioning Activities' (UK SORP). The main differences relate to the SEC requirement to use year-end prices, the application of SEC interpretations of SEC regulations relating to the use of technology (mainly seismic) to estimate reserves in the reservoir away from wellbores and the reporting of fuel gas (i.e. gas used for fuel in operations) within proved reserves. Consequently, reserves quantities under SEC rules differ from those that would be reported under application of the UK SORP.

The change to SEC reserves represents a simplification of the group's reserves reporting, as in the future only one set of reserves estimates will be disclosed. In addition, the use of SEC reserves for accounting purposes will bring our IFRS and US GAAP reporting into closer alignment, as well as making our results more comparable with those of our major competitors.

This change in accounting estimate has a direct impact on the amount of depreciation, depletion and amortization (DD&A) charged in the income statement in respect of oil and natural gas properties which are depreciated on a unit-of-production basis as described in Note 1. The change in estimate is applied prospectively, with no restatement of prior periods' results. The group's actual DD&A charge for the year is $9,128 million, whereas the charge based on UK SORP reserves would have been $9,057 million, i.e. an increase of $71 million due to the change in reserves estimates which was used to calculate DD&A for the last three months of the year. Over the life of a field this change would have no overall effect on DD&A but the estimated effect for 2007 is expected to be an increase of approximately $400 million to $500 million for the group.

2.4.1 Oil and gas sector

Many oil and gas companies are required to disclose information about reserve quantities in accordance with the rules and requirements of the stock exchange on which they are listed. However, those oil and gas companies that are not subject to the specific disclosure requirements of a stock exchange or other local regulator may wish to consider disclosing the information required under the UK Oil Industry Accounting Committee's Statement of Recommended Practice (OIAC SORP) (see 2.4.1.A below) or the US ASC 932-235-50 – *Extractive Activities – Oil and Gas – Notes to Financial Statements – Disclosure* (see 2.4.1.B below).

2.4.1.A OIAC SORP disclosure of commercial reserve quantities

The OIAC SORP requires disclosure, in a separate unaudited statement, of the net quantities of a company's interest in 'commercial reserves of crude oil (including condensate and natural gas liquids) and natural gas ... as at the beginning and end of each accounting period in total and by geographical area'.[64] Under the OIAC SORP, an entity should adopt one of the following definitions for its 'commercial reserves':

(a) proven and probable oil and gas reserves; or

(b) proved developed and undeveloped oil and gas reserves.

There should be a 50% probability that the actual quantity of recoverable reserves will be more than the amount estimated as proved and probable and a 50% probability that it will be less. The equivalent statistical probabilities for the proven component of proven and probable reserves are 90% and 10% respectively.[65] Regarding commercial reserves, the OIAC SORP specifies that:[66]

- net quantities of reserves include those relating to the company's operating and non-operating interests in properties;
- net quantities should not include reserves relating to interests of others in properties owned by the company, nor quantities available under long-term supply agreements;
- net quantities should only include amounts that may be taken by governments as royalties-in-kind where it is the company's policy to record as turnover the value of production taken as royalty-in-kind;
- if the company issues consolidated accounts, 100% of the net reserve quantities attributable to the parent company and 100% of the net reserve quantities attributable to its consolidated subsidiaries should be included, whether they are wholly owned or not; and
- if the company's consolidated accounts include investments that are accounted for by the equity method, the net oil and gas reserves of those investments should not be included in the disclosures of the company's reserves.

The OIAC SORP requires changes in the net quantities of commercial reserves during each accounting period to be disclosed as illustrated in Example 39.1 below.[67]

Example 39.1: Net commercial oil and gas reserve quantities

Net Commercial Oil and Gas Reserve Quantities for the year ended 31 December xxxx

	Total		Area A		Area B	
	Oil	**Gas**	**Oil**	**Gas**	**Oil**	**Gas**
Net commercial reserves, beginning of year:						
– commercial developed reserves	×	×	×	×	×	×
– commercial undeveloped reserves	×	×	×	×	×	×
	×	×	×	×	×	×
Changes during the year:						
– revisions of previous estimates	×	×	×	×	×	×
– purchases of reserves-in-place	×	×	×	×	×	×
– extensions, discoveries & other additions	×	×	×	×	×	×
– sales of reserves-in-place	(×)	(×)	(×)	(×)	(×)	(×)
– production	(×)	(×)	(×)	(×)	(×)	(×)
	×	×	×	×	×	×
Net commercial reserves, end of year:						
– commercial developed reserves	×	×	×	×	×	×
– commercial undeveloped reserves	×	×	×	×	×	×
	×	×	×	×	×	×
Company's share of net commercial reserves of associates and joint ventures at end of year *)	×	×	×	×	×	×

Of total net commercial oil and gas reserves at 31 December xxxx, × barrels of oil and y cubic feet of gas are attributable to non-controlling shareholders of certain subsidiaries.

*) The definitions of associates and joint ventures under UK GAAP are, however, different from those under IFRS.

The OIAC SORP requires the following additional information to be disclosed:

- the source of the estimates, together with a description of the basis used to arrive at net quantities;[68]
- changes in the net quantities of reserves of oil and gas during each accounting period should be reported. Changes resulting from each of the following should be shown separately, with supporting narrative explanation of significant changes:
  - revisions of previous estimates – revisions represent changes in previous estimates of commercial reserves either upward or downward resulting from new information (except for an increase in proved acreage) normally obtained from development drilling or production history or resulting from a change in economic factors or the application of improved recovery techniques
  - purchases of reserves-in-place
  - extensions, discoveries and other additions – additions to commercial reserves that result from (i) extension of the proved acreage of previously discovered (old) reservoirs through additional drilling in periods subsequent to discovery; and (ii) discovery of new fields with commercial reserves or new reservoirs of commercial reserves in old fields
  - sales of reserves-in-place
  - production
  - a supporting narrative explanation should be provided to describe the effect of significant unusual events (e.g. redeterminations of equity interests in unitised fields which would be included within 'purchases of reserves-in-place' or 'sales of reserves-in-place');[69]
- if a significant portion of the reserve quantities of the parent and its consolidated subsidiaries at the end of the year is attributable to consolidated subsidiaries in which there is a significant non-controlling interest, that fact and the approximate portion should be disclosed;[70]
- if the entity's consolidated accounts include investments that are accounted for by the equity method, the entity's share of those investments' net commercial reserve quantities as at the end of the year should be shown separately;[71] and
- reserves of oil and natural gas liquids should be stated in barrels and gas reserves in cubic feet.[72]

2.4.1.B ASC 932-235-50 disclosure of reserves

All entities engaged in significant oil and gas producing activities that report under US GAAP are required by ASC 932-235-50 to disclose supplementary information about proved oil and gas reserve quantities as follows:

'50-4 Net quantities of an entity's interests in proved oil and gas reserves, proved developed oil and gas reserves, and proved undeveloped oil and gas reserves of each of the following shall be disclosed as of the beginning and the end of the year:

a. Crude oil, including condensate and natural gas liquids. (If significant, the reserve quantity information shall be disclosed separately for natural gas liquids)
b. Natural gas
c. Synthetic oil
d. Synthetic gas
e. Other non-renewable natural resources that are intended to be upgraded into synthetic oil and gas

Net quantities of reserves include those relating to the entity's operating and nonoperating interests in properties. Quantities of reserves relating to royalty interests owned shall be included in net quantities if the necessary information is available to the entity; if reserves relating to royalty interests owned are not included because the information is unavailable, that fact and the entity's share of oil and gas produced for those royalty interests shall be disclosed for the year. Net quantities shall not include reserves relating to interests of others in properties owned by the entity.

50-5 Changes in the net quantities of an entity's proved reserves of oil and of gas during the year shall be disclosed. Changes resulting from all of the following shall be shown separately with appropriate explanation of significant changes:

a. Revisions of previous estimates. Revisions represent changes in previous estimates of proved reserves, either upward or downward, resulting from new information (except for an increase in proved acreage) normally obtained from development drilling and production history or resulting from a change in economic factors.
b. Improved recovery. Changes in reserve estimates resulting from application of improved recovery techniques shall be shown separately, if significant. If not significant, such changes shall be included in revisions of previous estimates.
c. Purchases of minerals in place.
d. Extensions and discoveries. Additions to proved reserves that result from either of the following:
    1. Extension of the proved acreage of previously discovered (old) reservoirs through additional drilling in periods subsequent to discovery
    2. Discovery of new fields with proved reserves or of new reservoirs of proved reserves in old fields.
e. Production.
f. Sales of minerals in place.

50-6 The disclosures of net quantities of proved reserves of oil and of gas and changes in them required by paragraphs 932-235-50-4 through 50-5 shall be presented in the aggregate and separately by geographic area (see the following paragraph) in which significant reserves (see paragraph 932-235-50-6B) are located. If an entity's proved reserves of oil and of gas are located entirely within its home country, the entity shall disclose that fact.

50-6A Any one of the following may constitute a geographic area, as appropriate for meaningful disclosure in the circumstances:

a. An individual country

b. A group of countries within a continent

c. A continent.

50-6B In determining whether reserves are significant:

a. An entity shall consider all facts and circumstances and not solely the quantity of reserves.

b. At a minimum, net quantities of reserves shall be presented in the aggregate and separately by geographic area and for each country containing 15 percent or more of an entity's proved reserves, expressed on an oil-equivalent-barrels basis.

Reserves shall include an entity's proportionate share of reserves of equity method investees.

50-7 Net quantities disclosed in conformity with paragraphs 932-235-50-4 through 50-6B shall not include oil or gas subject to purchase under long-term supply, purchase, or similar agreements and contracts, including such agreements with governments or authorities. However, quantities of oil or gas subject to such agreements with governments or authorities as of the end of the year, and the net quantity of oil or gas received under the agreements during the year, shall be separately disclosed if the entity participates in the operation of the properties in which the oil or gas is located or otherwise serves as the producer of those reserves, as opposed, for example, to being an independent purchaser, broker, dealer, or importer.

50-8 In determining the reserve quantities to be disclosed in conformity with paragraphs 932-235-50-4 through 50-7:

a. If the entity issues consolidated financial statements, 100 percent of the net reserve quantities attributable to the parent and 100 percent of the net reserve quantities attributable to its consolidated subsidiaries (whether or not wholly owned) shall be included. If a significant portion of those reserve quantities at the end of the year is attributable to a consolidated subsidiary or subsidiaries in which there is a significant noncontrolling interest, that fact and the approximate portion shall be disclosed.

b. If the entity's financial statements include investments that are proportionately consolidated, the entity's reserve quantities shall include its proportionate share of the investees' net oil and gas reserves.

c. If the entity's financial statements include investments that are accounted for by the equity method, the entity shall separately disclose the net reserve quantities required by paragraphs 932-235-50-4 through 50-7 for both of the following:

   1. Consolidated entities
   2. The entity's share of equity method investees.

   The entity may, in addition to separate disclosure, disclose a combined total for items (1) and (2) for each of the quantities required to be disclosed by this paragraph.

50-9 In reporting reserve quantities and changes in them, oil reserves and synthetic oil reserves and natural gas liquids reserves shall be stated in barrels, and gas and synthetic reserves in cubic feet.

50-10 If important economic factors or significant uncertainties affect particular components of an entity's proved reserves, explanation shall be provided. Examples include unusually high expected development or lifting costs, the necessity to build a major pipeline or other major facilities before production of the reserves can begin, and contractual obligations to produce and sell a significant portion of reserves at prices that are substantially below those at which the oil or gas could otherwise be sold in the absence of the contractual obligation.

50-11 An entity need not disclose the proved reserves in either of the following circumstances:

a. The government of a country containing reserves prohibits disclosing reserves in that country.

b. The government of a country containing reserves prohibits disclosing a particular field, and disclosing reserves in that country would have the effect of disclosing reserves in particular fields.

50-11A If a country's government prohibits disclosing the reserves in that country but does not prohibit including those reserves as part of a more aggregated total quantity of reserves (for example, the quantity of reserves disclosed for a group of countries within a continent or a continent), the entity shall include the reserves located in that country in total reserves disclosed for the most disaggregated geographic area that does not violate specific government prohibitions.

50-11B If a government restricts the disclosure of estimated reserves for properties under its authority, or of amounts under long-term supply, purchase, or similar agreements or contracts, or if the government requires the disclosure of reserves other than proved, the entity shall indicate that the disclosed reserve estimates or amounts do not include figures for the named country or that reserve estimates include reserves other than proved.'[73]

Example 39.2 below illustrates an extract from the disclosures required under ASC 932-235-55.[74]

Example 39.2: ASC 932-235-55-2 reserve disclosures (extract)

Reserve quantity information (a)
For the year ended December 31, 20X0

	Total	Total – by product		Continent A		Continent B – Country A		Other Countries in Continent B	
	All products	Oil	Syn Oil*	Oil	Syn Oil*	Oil	Syn Oil*	Oil	Syn Oil*
Proved developed and undeveloped reserves (consolidated entities only)									
Beginning of year		×	×	×	×	×	×	×	×
Revisions of previous estimates		×	×	×	×	×	×	×	×
Improved recovery		×	×	×	×	×	×	×	×
Purchases of minerals in place		×	×	×	×	×	×	×	×
Extensions and discoveries		×	×	×	×	×	×	×	×
Production		(×)	(×)	(×)	(×)	(×)	(×)	(×)	(×)
Sales of minerals in place		(×)	(×)	(×)	(×)	(×)	(×)	(×)	(×)
End of year		×(b)	×	×	×	×	×	×	×
Entity's share of proved developed and undeveloped reserves of investees accounted for by the equity method									
Beginning of year		×	×	×	×	×	×	×	×
Revisions of previous estimates		×	×	×	×	×	×	×	×
Improved recovery		×	×	×	×	×	×	×	×
Purchases of minerals in place		×	×	×	×	×	×	×	×
Extensions and discoveries		×	×	×	×	×	×	×	×
Production		(×)	(×)	(×)	(×)	(×)	(×)	(×)	(×)
Sales of minerals in place		(×)	(×)	(×)	(×)	(×)	(×)	(×)	(×)
Entity's share of reserves of investees accounted for by the equity method – end of year		×	×	×	×	×	×	×	×
Total consolidated and equity interests in reserves – end of year		×	×	×	×	×	×	×	×

Note: Total consolidated and equity interests in reserves – end of year is permitted, but is not required (see paragraph 932-235-50-8(c))

	Total	Total – by product		Continent A		Continent B – Country A		Other Countries in Continent B	
	All products	Oil	Syn Oil*	Oil	Syn Oil*	Oil	Syn Oil*	Oil	Syn Oil*
Proved developed reserves (consolidated entities only):									
Beginning of year		×	×	×	×	×	×	×	×
End of year		×	×	×	×	×	×	×	×
Proved undeveloped reserves (consolidated entities only):									
Beginning of year		×	×	×	×	×	×	×	×
End of year		×	×	×	×	×	×	×	×
Oil and gas subject to long-term supply, purchase, or other similar agreements with governments or authorities in which the entity participates in the operation of the properties where the oil and gas is located or otherwise serves as the producer of these reserves (consolidated entities only)									
Total under contract (quantity subject to agreement) – end of year		×	×			×	×		
Received during the year		×	×			×	×		

* Synthetic Oil

(a) Oil and synthetic oil reserves stated in barrels

(b) Includes reserves of X barrels attributable to a consolidated subsidiary in which there is an X percent noncontrolling interest.

Notes:

If applicable, reserve quantity information is required for gas and synthetic gas reserves, and other products by paragraph 932-235-50-4.

The table above discloses quantities of proved developed and undeveloped reserves, and oil and gas subject to long-term supply, purchase, or similar agreements with governments or authorities in which the entity participates in the operation of the properties where the oil and gas is located or otherwise serves as the producer of those reserves, attributable to consolidated entities (see paragraph 932-235-50-4 and 932-235-50-7). The entity shall disclose the same information for the entity's share of reserves of investees accounted for by the equity method, if applicable (see paragraph 932-235-50-8).

The table above discloses information for the total quantity of reserves for all products, in addition to disclosing the information by product. This disclosure is permitted, but is not required (see paragraph 932-235-50-4).

2.4.2 Mining sector

Many mining companies are required to disclose information about reserve quantities in accordance with the rules and requirements of the stock exchange on which they are listed. However, those mining companies that are not subject to the specific disclosure requirements of a stock exchange or other local regulator may wish to consider disclosing the information required under the US Securities and Exchange Commission's Industry Guide 7 – *Description of Property by Issuers Engaged or to Be Engaged in Significant Mining Operations.*

Mining companies that are subject to the SEC rules and regulations need to understand not only the content of Industry Guide 7, briefly outlined below, but also the current interpretation of this content by the SEC's staff. While many of the definitions may seem familiar, the SEC staff's interpretations may differ considerably from those of regulators in other countries.[75]

2.4.2.A SEC Industry Guide 7

I Definitions

Industry Guide 7 applies to all SEC registrants that are engaged or to be engaged in significant mining operations.[76] Some of the requirements of Industry Guide 7 for public release of information are materially different from those applicable in other countries. Under Industry Guide 7, the following definitions apply to registrants engaged or to be engaged in significant mining operations:

'(1) *Reserve.* That part of a mineral deposit which could be economically and legally extracted or produced at the time of the reserve determination. Note. Reserves are customarily stated in terms of "ore" when dealing with metalliferous minerals; when other materials such as coal, oil, shale, tar, sands, limestone, etc. are involved, an appropriate term such as "recoverable coal" may be substituted.

'(2) *Proven (Measured) Reserves.* Reserves for which (a) quantity is computed from dimensions revealed in outcrops, trenches, workings or drill holes; grade and/or quality are computed from the results of detailed sampling and (b) the sites for inspection, sampling and measurement are spaced so closely and the geologic character is so well defined that size, shape, depth and mineral content of reserves are well-established.

'(3) *Probable (Indicated) Reserves.* Reserves for which quantity and grade and/or quality are computed from information similar to that used for proven (measure) reserves, but the sites for inspection, sampling, and measurement are farther apart or are otherwise less adequately spaced. The degree of assurance, although lower than that for proven (measured) reserves, is high enough to assume continuity between points of observation.

'(4) (i) *Exploration Stage* – includes all issuers engaged in the search for mineral deposits (reserves) which are not in either the development or production stage.

(ii) *Development Stage* – includes all issuers engaged in the preparation of an established commercially minable deposit (reserves) for its extraction which are not in the production stage.

(iii) *Production Stage* – includes all issuers engaged in the exploitation of a mineral deposit (reserve).'[77]

II Mining operations disclosures

Under Industry Guide 7, a mining company should disclose the following information about each of the mines, plants and other significant properties that it owns or operates, or that it intends to own or operate:

'(1) The location and means of access to the property;

'(2) A brief description of the title, claim, lease or option under which the registrant and its subsidiaries have or will have the right to hold or operate the property, indicating any conditions which the registrant must meet in order to obtain or retain the property. If held by leases or options, the expiration dates of such leases or options should be stated. Appropriate maps may be used to portray the locations of significant properties;

'(3) A brief history of previous operations, including the names of previous operators, insofar as known;

'(4) (i) A brief description of the present condition of the property, the work completed by the registrant on the property, the registrant's proposed program of exploration and development, and the current state of exploration and/or development of the property. Mines should be identified as either open-pit or underground. If the property is without known reserves and the proposed program is exploratory in nature, a statement to that effect shall be made;

(ii) The age, details as to modernization and physical condition of the plant and equipment, including subsurface improvements and equipment. Further, the total cost for each property and its associated plant and equipment should be stated. The source of power utilized with respect to each property should also be disclosed.

'(5) A brief description of the rock formations and mineralization of existing or potential economic significance on the property, including the identity of the principal metallic or other constituents, insofar as known. If proven (measured) or probable (indicated) reserves have been established, state (i) the estimated tonnages and grades (or quality, where appropriate) of such classes of reserves, and (ii) the name of the person making the estimates and the nature of his relationship to the registrant.

'(6) If technical terms relating to geology, mining or related matters whose definition cannot readily be found in conventional dictionaries (as opposed to technical dictionaries or glossaries) are used, an appropriate glossary should be included in this report.

'(7) Detailed geographic maps and reports, feasibility studies and other highly technical data should not be included in the report but should be, to the degree appropriate and necessary for the Commission's understanding of the registrant's presentation of business and property matters, furnished as supplemental information.'[78]

In respect of the information required under (5) above, a mining company is required to comply with the following:

'1. It should be stated whether the reserve estimate is of in-place material or of recoverable material. Any in-place estimate should be qualified to show the anticipated losses resulting from mining methods and beneficiation or preparation.

'2. The summation of proven (measured) and probable (indicated) ore reserves is acceptable if the difference in degree of assurance between the two classes of reserves cannot be readily defined.

'3. Estimates other than proved (measured) or probable (indicated) reserves, and any estimated values of such reserves shall not be disclosed unless such information is required to be disclosed by foreign or state law; provided, however, that where such estimates previously have been provided to a person (or any of its affiliates) that is offering to acquire, merge, or consolidate with, the registrant or otherwise to acquire the registrant's securities, such estimates may be included.'[79]

III Supplemental information

Under Industry Guide 7, mining companies should provide the following supplemental information:

'(c)(1) If an estimate of proven (measured) or probable (indicated) reserves is set forth in the report, furnish:

(i) maps drawn to scale showing any mine workings and the outlines of the reserve blocks involved together with the pertinent sample-assay thereon.

(ii) all pertinent drill data and related maps.

(iii) the calculations whereby the basic sample-assay or drill data were translated into the estimates made of the grade and tonnage of reserves in each block and in the complete reserve estimate.

Instructions to paragraph (c)(1).

1. Maps and drawings submitted to the staff should include:

(a) A legend or explanation showing, by means of pattern or symbol, every pattern or symbol used on the map or drawing; the use of the symbols used by the U.S. Geological Survey is encouraged;

(b) A graphical bar scale should be included; additional representations of scale such as "one inch equals one mile" may be utilized provided the original scale of the map has not been altered;

(c) A north arrow on the maps;

(d) An index map showing where the property is situated in relationship to the state or province, etc., in which it was located;

(e) A title of the map or drawing and the date on which it was drawn;

(f) *In the event interpretive data is submitted in conjunction with any map, the identity of the geologist or engineer that prepared such data; and*

(g) *Any drawing should be simple enough or of sufficiently large scale to clearly show all features on the drawing.*

'(c)(2) Furnish a complete copy of every material engineering, geological or metallurgical report concerning the registrant's property, including governmental reports, which are known and available to the registrant. Every such report should include the name of its author and the date of its preparation, if known to the registrant.

Instruction to paragraph (c)(2).

1. *Any of the above-required reports as to which the staff has access need not be submitted. In this regard, issuers should consult with the staff prior to filing the report. Any reports not submitted should be identified in a list furnished to the staff. This list should also identify any known governmental reports concerning the registrant's property.*

'(c)(3) Furnish copies of all documents such as title documents, operating permits and easements needed to support representations made in the report.'[80]

2.4.3 Disclosure of the value of reserves

As part of its work on the Extractive Activities DP the IASB staff considered whether a disclosure-focused approach might be appropriate in an extractive industries financial reporting standard. It is in this context that the DP noted that, given the near unanimity of the feedback from users on the lack of relevance of either historical cost or current value accounting for reserves and resources, a disclosure-focused approach needed to be considered as one alternative in the discussion paper.[81]

One of the key issues to consider before developing a disclosure-focused approach is whether or not disclosure of the value of mineral reserves should be a requirement. A secondary issue is whether the mineral reserves should be disclosed at their fair value or at a standardised measure of value, similar to the requirement under ASC 932-235-50 (see 2.4.3.A below). This disclosure requirement is not uncontroversial, as the 'standardized measure of oil and gas' (often abbreviated to SMOG) does not represent the market value of an entity's proved reserves. However, the standardised measure of the value of oil and gas reserves greatly reduces the impact of management's opinion about future development on the value calculated, e.g. the method prescribes the discount rate and commodity price to be used. While this may not take into account relevant insights that management may have, the advantage is that comparability of the disclosures between entities is increased. As illustrated in Extract 39.2, some companies caution against over-reliance on these disclosures.

Extract 39.2: BP p.l.c. (2012)

Supplementary information on oil and natural gas (unaudited) [extract]

Standardized measure of discounted future net cash flows and changes therein relating to proved oil and gas reserves [extract]

The following tables set out the standardized measure of discounted future net cash flows, and changes therein, relating to crude oil and natural gas production from the group's estimated proved reserves. This information is prepared in compliance with FASB Oil and Gas Disclosures requirements.

Future net cash flows have been prepared on the basis of certain assumptions which may or may not be realized. These include the timing of future production, the estimation of crude oil and natural gas reserves and the application of average crude oil and natural gas prices and exchange rates from the previous 12 months. Furthermore, both proved reserves estimates and production forecasts are subject to revision as further technical information becomes available and economic conditions change. BP cautions against relying on the information presented because of the highly arbitrary nature of the assumptions on which it is based and its lack of comparability with the historical cost information presented in the financial statements.

It is clear that reaching agreement as to what constitutes useful and relevant disclosures about the value of mineral reserves is not straightforward and will be controversial. Still, in September 2008, the Board indicated support for the Extractive Activities DP to propose the disclosure of 'a current value measurement, such as a standardised measure of discounted cash flows, and the key assumptions necessary for a user to make use of that measurement. This would not be disclosed if the minerals or oil & gas assets are measured on the balance sheet at fair value or some other current value measurement. In that case, an entity would provide disclosures similar to those required in the US [by ASC 820-10-50-1, 2, 3 – *Fair Value Measurements and Disclosures*].'[82] Accordingly, the DP concluded that:

- if the assets are measured at historical cost then detailed information should be disclosed about their current value (either fair value or standardised measure) and how it was determined;
- if, instead, the assets are measured at fair value then detailed information should be disclosed about that fair value and how it was determined.

2.4.3.A ASC 932-235-50 – disclosure of standardised measure of oil and gas

All entities engaged in significant oil and gas producing activities that report under US GAAP are required by ASC 932-235-50 to disclose a standardised measure of discounted future net cash flows relating to proved oil and gas reserve quantities as follows:

'50-30 A standardized measure of discounted future net cash flows relating to an entity's interests in both of the following shall be disclosed as of the end of the year:

a. Proved oil and gas reserves (see paragraphs 932-235-50-3 through 50-11B)

b. Oil and gas subject to purchase under long-term supply, purchase, or similar agreements and contracts in which the entity participates in the operation of the properties on which the oil or gas is located or otherwise serves as the producer of those reserves (see paragraph 932-235-50-7).

The standardized measure of discounted future net cash flows relating to those two types of interests in reserves may be combined for reporting purposes.

50-31 All of the following information shall be disclosed in the aggregate and for each geographic area for which reserve quantities are disclosed in accordance with paragraphs 932-235-50-3 through 50-11B:

a. Future cash inflows. These shall be computed by applying prices used in estimating the entity's proved oil and gas reserves to the year-end quantities of those reserves. Future price changes shall be considered only to the extent provided by contractual arrangements in existence at year-end.

b. Future development and production costs. These costs shall be computed by estimating the expenditures to be incurred in developing and producing the proved oil and gas reserves at the end of the year, based on year-end costs and assuming continuation of existing economic conditions. If estimated development expenditures are significant, they shall be presented separately from estimated production costs.

c. Future income tax expenses. These expenses shall be computed by applying the appropriate year-end statutory tax rates, with consideration of future tax rates already legislated, to the future pretax net cash flows relating to the entity's proved oil and gas reserves, less the tax basis of the properties involved. The future income tax expenses shall give effect to tax deductions and tax credits and allowances relating to the entity's proved oil and gas reserves.

d. Future net cash flows. These amounts are the result of subtracting future development and production costs and future income tax expenses from future cash inflows.

e. Discount. This amount shall be derived from using a discount rate of 10 percent a year to reflect the timing of the future net cash flows relating to proved oil and gas reserves.

f. Standardized measure of discounted future net cash flows. This amount is the future net cash flows less the computed discount.

50-32 If a significant portion of the economic interest in the consolidated standardized measure of discounted future net cash flows reported is attributable to a consolidated subsidiary or subsidiaries in which there is a significant noncontrolling interest, that fact and the approximate portion shall be disclosed.

50-33 If the financial statements include investments that are accounted for by the equity method, the entity shall separately disclose the amounts required by paragraphs 932-235-50-30 through 50-32 for both of the following:

a. Consolidated entities

b. The entity's share of equity method investees.

The entity may, in addition to separate disclosure, disclose a combined total for items (a) and (b) for each of the amounts required to be disclosed by this paragraph.

...

50-35 The aggregate change in the standardized measure of discounted future net cash flows shall be disclosed for the year. If individually significant, all of the following sources of change shall be presented separately:

a. Net change in sales and transfer prices and in production (lifting) costs related to future production
b. Changes in estimated future development costs
c. Sales and transfers of oil and gas produced during the period
d. Net change due to extensions, discoveries, and improved recovery
e. Net change due to purchases and sales of minerals in place
f. Net change due to revisions in quantity estimates
g. Previously estimated development costs incurred during the period
h. Accretion of discount
i. Other – unspecified
j. Net change in income taxes.

In computing the amounts under each of the above categories, the effects of changes in prices and costs shall be computed before the effects of changes in quantities. As a result, changes in quantities shall be stated at prices used in estimating proved oil and gas reserves and year-end and costs. The change in computed income taxes shall reflect the effect of income taxes incurred during the period as well as the change in future income tax expenses. Therefore, all changes except income taxes shall be reported pretax.

50-35A If the financial statements include investments that are accounted for by the equity method, the entity shall separately disclose the amounts required by the preceding paragraph for both of the following:

a. Consolidated entities
b. The entity's share of equity method investees.

The entity may, in addition to separate disclosure, disclose a combined total for items (a) and (b) for each of the amounts required to be disclosed by this paragraph.

50-36 Additional information necessary to prevent the disclosure of the standardized measure of discounted future net cash flows and changes therein from being misleading also shall be provided.'[83]

These disclosures are illustrated in the extract below from the financial statements of TOTAL.

Extract 39.3: TOTAL S.A. (2012)

Section 10 – Supplemental oil and gas information (unaudited) [extract]

1.8 Standardized measure of discounted future net cash flows (excluding transportation)

The standardized measure of discounted future net cash flows relating to proved oil and gas reserve quantities was developed as follows:

- estimates of proved reserves and the corresponding production profiles are based on existing technical and economic conditions;

- the estimated future cash flows are determined based on prices used in estimating the Group's proved oil and gas reserves;
- the future cash flows incorporate estimated production costs (including production taxes), future development costs and asset retirement costs. All cost estimates are based on year-end technical and economic conditions;
- future income taxes are computed by applying the year-end statutory tax rate to future net cash flows after consideration of permanent differences and future income tax credits; and
- future net cash flows are discounted at a standard discount rate of 10 percent.

These principles applied are those required by ASC 932 and do not reflect the expectations of real revenues from these reserves, nor their present value; hence, they do not constitute criteria for investment decisions. An estimate of the fair value of reserves should also take into account, among other things, the recovery of reserves not presently classified as proved, anticipated future changes in prices and costs and a discount factor more representative of the time value of money and the risks inherent in reserves estimates.

(M€)	Consolidated subsidiaries					
As of December 31, 2010	**Europe**	**Africa**	**Americas**	**Middle East**	**Asia**	**Total**
Future cash inflows	65,644	142,085	42,378	14,777	41,075	305,959
Future production costs	(16,143)	(29,479)	(19,477)	(4,110)	(6,476)	(75,685)
Future development costs	(18,744)	(25,587)	(8,317)	(3,788)	(8,334)	(64,770)
Future income taxes	(20,571)	(51,390)	(3,217)	(2,541)	(7,281)	(85,000)
Future net cash flows, after income taxes	10,186	35,629	11,367	4,338	18,984	80,504
Discount at 10%	(5,182)	(16,722)	(8,667)	(2,106)	(11,794)	(44,471)
Standardized measure of discounted future net cash flows	**5,004**	**18,907**	**2,700**	**2,232**	**7,190**	**36,033**
As of December 31, 2011						
Future cash inflows	85,919	167,367	53,578	14,297	67,868	389,029
Future production costs	(18,787)	(31,741)	(22,713)	(3,962)	(12,646)	(89,849)
Future development costs	(21,631)	(22,776)	(11,548)	(3,110)	(11,044)	(70,109)
Future income taxes	(28,075)	(71,049)	(4,361)	(2,794)	(12,963)	(119,242)
Future net cash flows, after income taxes	17,426	41,801	14,956	4,431	31,215	109,829
Discount at 10%	(9,426)	(17,789)	(12,298)	(2,186)	(20,717)	(62,416)
Standardized measure of discounted future net cash flows	**8,000**	**24,012**	**2,658**	**2,245**	**10,498**	**47,413**
As of December 31, 2012						
Future cash inflows	93,215	177,392	58,140	16,474	70,985	416,206
Future production costs	(20,337)	(39,091)	(25,824)	(5,213)	(15,218)	(105,683)
Future development costs	(24,490)	(28,896)	(12,949)	(3,807)	(10,954)	(81,096)
Future income taxes	(27,393)	(68,017)	(4,456)	(2,732)	(12,641)	(115,239)
Future net cash flows, after income taxes	20,995	41,388	14,911	4,722	32,172	114,188
Discount at 10%	(10,549)	(17,731)	(11,608)	(2,227)	(19,969)	(62,084)
Standardized measure of discounted future net cash flows	**10,446**	**23,657**	**3,303**	**2,495**	**12,203**	**52,104**
Minority interests in future net cash flows as of (M€)						
As of December 31, 2010	273	344	–	–	–	617
As of December 31, 2011	–	558	–	–	–	558
As of December 31, 2012	**–**	**501**	**–**	**–**	**–**	**501**

(M€)					Equity affiliates	
	Europe	Africa	Americas	Middle East	Asia	Total
As of December 31, 2010						
Future cash inflows	–	1,814	22,293	59,472	–	83,579
Future production costs	–	(765)	(8,666)	(40,085)	–	(49,516)
Future development costs	–	(26)	(2,020)	(3,006)	–	(5,052)
Future income taxes	–	(349)	(5,503)	(2,390)	–	(8,242)
Future net cash flows, after income taxes	–	674	6,104	13,991	–	20,769
Discount at 10%	–	(203)	(3,946)	(7,386)	–	(11,535)
Standardized measure of discounted future net cash flows	**–**	**471**	**2,158**	**6,605**	**–**	**9,234**
As of December 31, 2011						
Future cash inflows	–	210	29,887	64,977	7,116	102,190
Future production costs	–	(95)	(17,393)	(39,800)	(2,683)	(59,971)
Future development costs	–	–	(1,838)	(2,809)	(1,297)	(5,944)
Future income taxes	–	(29)	(5,152)	(3,942)	(2,280)	(11,403)
Future net cash flows, after income taxes	–	86	5,504	18,426	856	24,872
Discount at 10%	–	(36)	(3,652)	(9,757)	(196)	(13,641)
Standardized measure of discounted future net cash flows	**–**	**50**	**1,852**	**8,669**	**660**	**11,231**
As of December 31, 2012						
Future cash inflows	–	2,103	27,439	64,234	9,390	103,166
Future production costs	–	(99)	(17,250)	(35,830)	(3,265)	(56,444)
Future development costs	–	–	(2,360)	(2,967)	(3,906)	(9,233)
Future income taxes	–	(392)	(3,353)	(5,430)	(648)	(9,823)
Future net cash flows, after income taxes	–	1,612	4,476	20,007	1,571	27,666
Discount at 10%	–	(1,087)	(2,978)	(10,316)	(955)	(15,336)
Standardized measure of discounted future net cash flows	**–**	**525**	**1,498**	**9,691**	**616**	**12,330**

1.9 Changes in the standardized measure of discounted future net cash flows

Consolidated subsidiaries (M€)	**2010**	**2011**	**2012**
Beginning of year	**25,802**	**36,033**	**47,413**
Sales and transfers, net of production costs	**(22,297)**	(27,026)	(28,552)
Net change in sales and transfer prices and in production costs and other expenses	**30,390**	44,315	7,382
Extensions, discoveries and improved recovery	**716**	1,680	1,357
Changes in estimated future development costs	**(7,245)**	(4,798)	(6,503)
Previously estimated development costs incurred during the year	**7,896**	9,519	11,809
Revisions of previous quantity estimates	**5,523**	1,288	2,719
Accretion of discount	**2,580**	3,603	4,741
Net change in income taxes	**(6,773)**	(16,925)	13,992
Purchases of reserves in place	**442**	885	299
Sales of reserves in place	**(1,001)**	(1,161)	(2,553)
End of year	**36,033**	**47,413**	**52,104**

Equity affiliates (M€)	2010	2011	2012
Beginning of year	**7,295**	**9,234**	**11,231**
Sales and transfers, net of production costs	(1,583)	(1,991)	(1,885)
Net change in sales and transfer prices and in production costs and other expenses	2,366	3,715	(743)
Extensions, discoveries and improved recovery	–	–	(25)
Changes in estimated future development costs	195	(383)	(495)
Previously estimated development costs incurred during the year	651	635	809
Revisions of previous quantity estimates	308	(749)	984
Accretion of discount	730	923	1,123
Net change in income taxes	(728)	(1,341)	1,314
Purchases of reserves in place	–	1,812	17
Sales of reserves in place	–	(624)	–
End of year	**9,234**	**11,231**	**12,330**

3 IFRS 6 – EXPLORATION FOR AND EVALUATION OF MINERAL RESOURCES

3.1 Objective and scope

The IASB's objective in developing IFRS 6, as noted at 1.1.1 above, was restricted to making limited improvements to existing accounting practices for exploration and evaluation expenditures (E&E expenditures). E&E expenditures are 'expenditures incurred by an entity in connection with the exploration for and evaluation of mineral resources before the technical feasibility and commercial viability of extracting a mineral resource are demonstrable', while E&E assets are 'exploration and evaluation expenditures recognised as assets in accordance with the entity's accounting policy'. *[IFRS 6 Appendix A]*.

IFRS 6 is limited to specifying the financial reporting for the exploration for and evaluation of mineral resources, which the standard defines as 'the search for mineral resources, including minerals, oil, natural gas and similar non-regenerative resources after the entity has obtained legal rights to explore in a specific area, as well as the determination of the technical feasibility and commercial viability of extracting the mineral resource'. *[IFRS 6.1, Appendix A]*. The standard also specifies when entities need to assess E&E assets for impairment in accordance with IAS 36 and requires certain disclosures.

An entity may not apply IFRS 6 to expenditures incurred before the exploration for and evaluation of mineral resources (e.g. expenditures incurred before the entity has obtained the legal rights to explore a specific area such as prospecting and acquisition of mineral rights) or after the technical feasibility and commercial viability of extracting a mineral resource are demonstrable (e.g. development, construction, production and closure). *[IFRS 6.5]*. Furthermore, it deals only with E&E expenditures and does not provide guidance on other sector-specific issues that may arise during the E&E phase.

Equipment used in the E&E phase e.g. property, plant and equipment and any other intangibles, such as software, are not in the scope of IFRS 6, instead they are in the scope of IAS 16 or IAS 38.

The IASB deliberately decided not to expand the scope of the standard as 'it did not want to prejudge the comprehensive review of the accounting for such activities' and it concluded 'that an appropriate accounting policy for pre-exploration activities could be developed from an application of existing IFRSs' or the *Conceptual Framework*. *[IFRS 6.BC7, BC10]*. A further, more practical, reason for not expanding the scope of IFRS 6 was that this would have required additional due process and possibly another exposure draft; consequently, in view of 'the many entities engaged in extractive activities that would be required to apply IFRSs from 1 January 2005, the Board decided that it should not delay issuing guidance by expanding the scope of the IFRS beyond the exploration for and evaluation of mineral resources'. *[IFRS 6.BC8]*.

3.1.1 Scope exclusions in other standards relating to the extractive industries

In the Basis for Conclusions on IFRS 6 the IASB confirmed that 'even though no IFRS has addressed extractive activities directly, all IFRSs (including International Accounting Standards and Interpretations) are applicable to entities engaged in the exploration for and evaluation of mineral resources that make an unreserved statement of compliance with IFRSs in accordance with IAS 1'. *[IFRS 6.BC6]*. However, certain aspects of activities that occur in the extractive industries that fall outside the scope of IFRS 6 are excluded from the scope of other standards.

Various standards exclude 'minerals' from their scope, but the exact wording of the scope exclusions differs from standard to standard. Therefore, it would be incorrect to conclude that the same aspects of the extractive industries' activities are excluded from the scope of these standards:

- IAS 2 – does not apply to the measurement of minerals and mineral products, 'to the extent that they are measured at net realisable value in accordance with well-established practices in those industries'. *[IAS 2.3(a), 4]*. The practice of measuring minerals and mineral products inventories at net realisable value is, in reality, relatively rare in many areas of the extractive industries;
- IAS 16 – does not apply to 'mineral rights and mineral reserves such as oil, natural gas and similar non-regenerative resources'. *[IAS 16.3(d)]*. In addition, the standard does not apply to 'the recognition and measurement of exploration and evaluation assets'. *[IAS 16.3(c)]*. Equipment used in extracting reserves is within the scope of IAS 16;
- IAS 17 – does not apply to 'leases to explore for or use minerals, oil, natural gas and similar non-regenerative resources'. *[IAS 17.2(a)]*. However, leases of assets used for exploration or evaluation activities are in the scope of IAS 17;
- IAS 18 – does not deal with revenue arising from 'the extraction of mineral ores'; *[IAS 18.6(h)]*

- IAS 38 – does not apply to 'expenditure on the exploration for, or development and extraction of, minerals, oil, natural gas and similar non-regenerative resources' or to the recognition and measurement of E&E assets; *[IAS 38.2(c)-(d)]*
- IAS 40 – does not apply to 'mineral rights and mineral reserves such as oil, natural gas and similar non-regenerative resources'; *[IAS 40.4(b)]* and
- IFRIC 4 – does not apply to arrangements that are, or contain, leases excluded from the scope of IAS 17. *[IFRIC 4.4]*.

3.2 Recognition of exploration and evaluation assets

3.2.1 Choice of accounting policy

When developing its accounting policy for E&E expenditures, IFRS 6 requires an entity recognising E&E assets to apply paragraph 10 of IAS 8 – *Accounting Policies, Changes in Accounting Estimates and Errors*. *[IFRS 6.6, BC19]*. Hence management should use its judgement in developing and applying an accounting policy that results in information that is relevant and reliable. *[IAS 8.10]*. However, IFRS 6 does provide an exemption from paragraphs 11 and 12 of IAS 8, *[IFRS 6.7, BC17]*, which 'specify sources of authoritative requirements and guidance that management is required to consider in developing an accounting policy for an item if no IFRS applies specifically to that item' (the so-called 'GAAP hierarchy', see Chapter 3 at 4.3). In developing such a policy, IFRS 6 imposes a number of significant constraints on an entity's choice of accounting policy because:

- an entity needs to specify which expenditures are recognised as E&E assets and apply that accounting policy consistently (see 3.3.1 below); *[IFRS 6.9]*
- expenditures related to the development of mineral resources should not be recognised as E&E assets (see 3.3.2 below); *[IFRS 6.10]* and
- the requirement to apply IAS 16, IAS 38 and IAS 36 after the E&E phase affects the choice of accounting policies during the E&E phase. In January 2006, the IFRIC clarified that 'it was clear that the scope of IFRS 6 consistently limited the relief from the hierarchy to policies applied to E&E activities and that there was no basis for interpreting IFRS 6 as granting any additional relief in areas outside its scope'.[84] For example, an entity may be able to apply the full cost method of accounting (see 5.2.2 below) during the E&E phase, but it will not be able to apply that policy after the E&E phase.

The IASB believed that waiving these requirements in IFRS 6 would 'detract from the relevance and reliability of an entity's financial statements to an unacceptable degree'. *[IFRS 6.BC23]*.

3.2.2 Transition to IFRS 6: are previous policies 'grandfathered'?

Entities active in the extractive industries have followed, and continue to follow, a large variety of accounting practices for E&E expenditure, which range 'from deferring on the balance sheet nearly all exploration and evaluation expenditure to recognising all such expenditure in profit or loss as incurred'. *[IFRS 6.BC17]*. As mentioned earlier, IFRS 6 provides an exemption from paragraphs 11 and 12 of IAS 8. The inference from this is that the standard 'grandfathers' all existing practices by not requiring these to have any authoritative basis. The Basis for Conclusions states that 'the Board decided that an entity could continue to follow the accounting policies that it was using when it first applied the IFRS's requirements, provided they satisfy the requirements of paragraph 10 of IAS 8 ... with some exceptions ...'. *[IFRS 6.BC22].* These exceptions in IFRS 6, described above, have a rather more profound impact than may be obvious at first sight and, in fact, instead of allowing previous national GAAP accounting policies, IFRS 6 effectively prohibits many of them.

3.2.3 Changes in accounting policies

The standard permits a change in an entity's accounting policies for E&E expenditures only if 'the change makes the financial statements more relevant to the economic decision-making needs of users and no less reliable, or more reliable and no less relevant to those needs'. *[IFRS 6.13, BC49].* In making such a change, an entity should judge the relevance and reliability using the criteria in IAS 8. The entity should justify the change by demonstrating that the change 'brings its financial statements closer to meeting the criteria in IAS 8, but the change need not achieve full compliance with those criteria'. *[IFRS 6.14].*

3.3 Measurement of exploration and evaluation assets

IFRS 6 draws a distinction between measurement at recognition (i.e. the initial recognition of an E&E asset on acquisition) and measurement after recognition (i.e. the subsequent treatment of the E&E asset).

3.3.1 Measurement at recognition

The standard requires that upon initial recognition, E&E assets should be measured at cost, *[IFRS 6.8]*, which is the same as the initial recognition requirements found in IAS 16, *[IAS 16.15]*, and IAS 38. *[IAS 38.24].* Therefore the question arises as to what may be included in the cost of an item. The standard contains considerable guidance on this matter, under the heading 'Elements of cost of exploration and evaluation assets'.

3.3.1.A Elements of cost of exploration and evaluation assets

The standard requires an entity to determine an accounting policy specifying which expenditures are recognised as E&E assets and apply the policy consistently. Such an accounting policy should take into account the degree to which the expenditure can be associated with finding specific mineral resources. Types of expenditure include:

(a) acquisition of rights to explore;

(b) topographical, geological, geochemical and geophysical studies;

(c) exploratory drilling;

(d) trenching;

(e) sampling; and

(f) activities in relation to evaluating the technical feasibility and commercial viability of extracting a mineral resource. *[IFRS 6.9].*

This list is not intended to be exhaustive.

In permitting geological and geophysical costs (G&G costs) to be included in the initial measurement of E&E assets, IFRS differs from US GAAP – ASC 932 – *Extractive Activities – Oil and Gas*, which does not permit capitalisation of G&G costs,[85] and may differ from the requirements under other national standards.

In the exposure draft that led to the standard, the IASB proposed that administration and other general overhead costs should be excluded from the initial measurement of E&E assets. However, in the light of inconsistencies between IAS 16 (which does not allow such costs to be capitalised) and IAS 2 and IAS 38 (which do permit capitalisation of such costs), the IASB decided that IFRS 6 would allow an accounting policy choice as to how to treat expenditures on administration and other general overhead costs; the chosen policy should be consistent with one of the treatments available under IFRSs i.e. expense or capitalise. *[IFRS 6.BC28]*.

Expenditures related to the development of mineral resources should not be recognised as E&E assets. Instead the IASB's *Conceptual Framework* and IAS 38 should be applied in developing guidance on accounting for such assets. *[IFRS 6.10]*. IFRS does not define 'development of mineral resources', but notes that 'development of a mineral resource once the technical feasibility and commercial viability of extracting the mineral resource had been determined was an example of the development phase of an internal project'. *[IFRS 6.BC27]*. While this is not a full definition, in practice this means that until a feasibility study is complete and a development is approved, accumulated costs are considered E&E assets and are accounted for under IFRS 6.

The standard specifically requires the application of IAS 37 – *Provisions, Contingent Liabilities and Contingent Assets* – to any obligations for removal and restoration that are incurred during a particular period as a consequence of having undertaken the exploration for and evaluation of mineral resources. *[IFRS 6.11]*. Although IFRS 6 did not make a corresponding amendment to the scope of IFRIC 1 – *Changes in Existing Decommissioning, Restoration and Similar Liabilities*, which applies to such liabilities when they are recognised in property, plant and equipment under IAS 16, we believe that the interpretation should also be applied in relation to E&E assets. However, if the E&E costs were originally expensed, then the future costs of any related removal and restoration obligations should also be expensed.

The extract below from Xstrata illustrates a typical accounting policy for E&E assets for a mining company.

Extract 39.4: Xstrata plc (2012)

Notes to the financial statements [extract]

6. Principal accounting policies [extract]

Exploration and evaluation expenditure

Exploration and evaluation expenditure relates to costs incurred on the exploration and evaluation of potential mineral reserves and resources and includes costs such as exploratory drilling and sample testing and the costs of pre-feasibility studies. Exploration and evaluation expenditure for each area of interest, other than that acquired from the purchase of another mining company, is carried forward as an asset provided that one of the following conditions is met:

- such costs are expected to be recouped in full through successful development and exploration of the area of interest or alternatively, by its sale; or
- exploration and evaluation activities in the area of interest have not yet reached a stage that permits a reasonable assessment of the existence or otherwise of economically recoverable reserves, and active and significant operations in relation to the area are continuing, or planned for the future.

Purchased exploration and evaluation assets are recognised as assets at their cost of acquisition or at fair value if purchased as part of a business combination.

An impairment review is performed, either individually or at the cash-generating unit level, when there are indicators that the carrying amount of the assets may exceed their recoverable amounts. To the extent that this occurs, the excess is fully provided against, in the financial year in which this is determined. Exploration and evaluation assets are reassessed on a regular basis and these costs are carried forward provided that at least one of the conditions outlined above is met.

Expenditure is transferred to mine development assets or capital work in progress once the work completed to date supports the future development of the property and such development receives appropriate approvals.

The extract below from BP illustrates an accounting policy for E&E assets for an oil and gas company.

Extract 39.5: BP p.l.c. (2012)

Notes on financial statements [extract]

1. Significant accounting policies [extract]

Oil and natural gas exploration, appraisal and development expenditure

Oil and natural gas exploration, appraisal and development expenditure is accounted for using the principles of the successful efforts method of accounting.

Licence and property acquisition costs

Exploration licence and leasehold property acquisition costs are capitalized within intangible assets and are reviewed at each reporting date to confirm that there is no indication that the carrying amount exceeds the recoverable amount. This review includes confirming that exploration drilling is still under way or firmly planned or that it has been determined, or work is under way to determine, that the discovery is economically viable based on a range of technical and commercial considerations and sufficient progress is being made on establishing development plans and timing. If no future activity is planned, the remaining balance of the licence and property acquisition costs is written off. Lower value licences are pooled and amortized on a straight-line basis over the estimated period of exploration. Upon recognition of proved reserves and internal approval for development, the relevant expenditure is transferred to property, plant and equipment.

Exploration and appraisal expenditure

Geological and geophysical exploration costs are charged against income as incurred. Costs directly associated with an exploration well are initially capitalized as an intangible asset until the drilling of the well is complete and the results have been evaluated. These costs include employee remuneration, materials and fuel used, rig costs and payments made to contractors. If potentially commercial quantities of hydrocarbons are not found, the exploration expenditure is written off as a dry hole. If hydrocarbons are found and, subject to further appraisal activity, are likely to be capable of commercial development, the costs continue to be carried as an asset.

Costs directly associated with appraisal activity, undertaken to determine the size, characteristics and commercial potential of a reservoir following the initial discovery of hydrocarbons, including the costs of appraisal wells where hydrocarbons were not found, are initially capitalized as an intangible asset.

All such carried costs are subject to technical, commercial and management review at least once a year to confirm the continued intent to develop or otherwise extract value from the discovery. When this is no longer the case, the costs are written off. When proved reserves of oil and natural gas are determined and development is approved by management, the relevant expenditure is transferred to property, plant and equipment.

3.3.2 *Measurement after recognition*

IFRS 6 allows either of two alternatives to be chosen as the accounting policy for E&E assets after initial recognition that it must apply consistently to all E&E assets.

The first is the 'cost model' whereby the item is carried at cost less impairment. *[IFRS 6.12].* Entities that apply the 'cost model' should therefore develop an accounting policy in the constraints of IFRS 6 (see 3.2.1 above). As a result an entity will either develop an accounting policy based on the successful efforts type of method or area-of-interest type of method (see 5.2.1 and 5.2.3 below) – that requires capitalisation of E&E costs pending evaluation; or develop a policy similar to the full cost type of method, which capitalises all E&E costs (successful and unsuccessful). Although it is not possible to continue using this method outside the E&E phase (see 5.2.2 below).

The alternative is the 'revaluation model', which is not defined in IFRS 6 itself. Instead, the standard requires an entity to classify E&E assets as tangible or intangible assets (see 3.4 below) and apply the IAS 16 revaluation model to the tangible assets and the IAS 38 revaluation model to the intangible assets (see Chapter 18 at 6 and Chapter 17 at 8.2). *[IFRS 6.12].* Practically what this means is that E&E classified as intangible assets may not be revalued, since the IAS 38 revaluation model may only be applied to homogeneous intangible assets that are traded in an active market. *[IAS 38.8, 72, 75, IFRS 6.BC29-BC30].*

3.3.3 *Capitalisation of borrowing costs*

IAS 23 – *Borrowing Costs* – requires capitalisation of borrowing costs that are directly attributable to the acquisition, construction or production of a 'qualifying asset' as part of the cost of that asset. *[IAS 23.8].* An E&E asset will generally meet the definition of a qualifying asset as it 'necessarily takes a substantial period of time to get ready for its intended use or sale'. *[IAS 23.5].* However, IAS 23 requires capitalisation of borrowing costs only when it is probable that they will result in future economic benefits to the entity and the costs can be measured reliably. *[IAS 23.9].* Unlike IAS 23, IFRS 6 permits capitalisation of E&E assets even when it is not probable that they will result in future economic benefits. Unless an entity's E&E project has resulted in the classification of mineral resources as proven or probable, it is unlikely that future economic benefits from that project can be considered probable. In these circumstances, it is consistent with the requirements of IFRS 6 and IAS 23 to capitalise an E&E asset but not capitalise borrowing costs in respect of it.

3.4 Presentation and classification

E&E assets should be classified consistently as either tangible or intangible assets in accordance with the nature of the assets acquired. *[IFRS 6.15].* For example, drilling rights should be presented as intangible assets, whereas vehicles and drilling rigs are tangible assets. A tangible asset that is used in developing an intangible asset should still be presented as a tangible asset. However, to the 'extent that a tangible asset is consumed in developing an intangible asset, the amount reflecting that consumption is part of the cost of the intangible asset'. For example, the depreciation of a drilling rig would be capitalised as part of the intangible E&E asset that represents the costs incurred on active exploration projects. *[IFRS 6.16, BC33].*

3.4.1 Reclassification of E&E assets

E&E assets should no longer be classified as such when 'technical feasibility and commercial viability of extracting a mineral resource are demonstrable'. *[IFRS 6.17].* Before reclassification, however, E&E assets should be assessed for impairment individually or as part of a cash-generating unit and any impairment loss should be recognised.

3.5 Impairment

As E&E assets do not generate cash inflows and there is insufficient information about the mineral resources in a specific area for an entity to make reasonable estimates of an E&E asset's recoverable amount, it is not possible to estimate either fair value less costs of disposal ('FVLCD') or value in use ('VIU'), the two measures of recoverable amount in IAS 36. The IASB therefore decided that under IFRS 6 the assessment of impairment should be triggered by changes in facts and circumstances. However once an entity had determined that an E&E asset is impaired, IAS 36 should be used to measure, present and disclose that impairment in the financial statements. This is subject to the special requirements with respect to the level at which impairment is assessed. *[IFRS 6.BC37].*

IFRS 6 makes two important modifications to IAS 36:

- it defines separate impairment testing 'triggers' for E&E assets; and
- it allows groups of cash-generating units to be used in impairment testing. *[IFRS 6.18-20].*

3.5.1 Impairment testing 'triggers'

E&E assets should be assessed for impairment when facts and circumstances suggest that the carrying amount of an E&E asset may exceed its recoverable amount. *[IFRS 6.18].* Under IFRS 6 one or more of the following facts and circumstances could indicate that an impairment test is required. The list is not intended to be exhaustive:

(a) the period for which the entity has the right to explore in the specific area has expired during the period or will expire in the near future, and is not expected to be renewed;

(b) substantive expenditure on further exploration for and evaluation of mineral resources in the specific area is neither budgeted nor planned;

(c) exploration for and evaluation of mineral resources in the specific area have not led to the discovery of commercially viable quantities of mineral resources and the entity has decided to discontinue such activities in the specific area; and

(d) sufficient data exist to indicate that, although a development in the specific area is likely to proceed, the carrying amount of the E&E asset is unlikely to be recovered in full from successful development or by sale. *[IFRS 6.20]*.

This list does not include finding that an exploratory or development well does not contain oil or gas in commercial quantities as an impairment indicator (i.e. finding a 'dry hole'). If finding a dry hole marks the end of budgeted or planned exploration activity, indicator (b) above would require impairment testing under IAS 36 and indicator (d) requires an entity to do an impairment test if it is unlikely that it will recover the E&E costs from successful development or sale.

3.5.2 *Specifying the level at which E&E assets are assessed for impairment*

When deciding the level at which E&E assets should be assessed rather than introduce a special cash-generating unit ('CGU') for E&E assets, IFRS 6 allows CGUs to be aggregated in a way consistent with the approach applied to goodwill in IAS 36 (see Chapter 20 at 4.2 for more detail). *[IFRS 6.BC40-BC47]*. Therefore, an entity should determine an accounting policy for allocating E&E assets to CGUs or to CGU groups for the purpose of assessing them for impairment. *[IFRS 6.21]*. Each CGU or group of CGUs to which an E&E asset is allocated should not be larger than an operating segment (which is smaller than a reportable segment) determined in accordance with IFRS 8 – *Operating Segments*. *[IFRS 6.21]*. See also Chapter 20 at 4.2.

Hence, the level identified by an entity for the purposes of testing E&E assets for impairment may be comprised of one or more CGUs. *[IFRS 6.22]*.

3.5.3 *Cash-generating units comprising successful and unsuccessful E&E projects*

IFRS 6 does not specifically address whether successful and unsuccessful E&E projects can be combined in a single CGU (which will occur under full cost accounting and may occur under area of interest accounting). There are some issues to consider before doing this:

- regardless of whether there is an impairment trigger (see 3.5.1 above), IFRS 6 requires E&E assets to be tested for impairment before reclassification when the technical feasibility and commercial viability of extracting a mineral resource are demonstrable. *[IFRS 6.17]*. That means that the successful conclusion of a small E&E project and its reclassification out of E&E would result in an impairment test of a much larger CGU and possible recognition of an impairment loss on that larger CGU;
- successful E&E projects should be reclassified as tangible or intangible assets under IAS 16 and IAS 38, respectively. *[IFRS 6.15]*. Therefore, a CGU comprising both successful and unsuccessful E&E projects would be subject to the

impairment triggers in both paragraph 20 of IFRS 6 and paragraphs 8 to 17 of IAS 36. This would significantly increase the frequency of impairment testing *[IFRS 6.20, IAS 36.8-17]*; and

- an entity should carefully consider the consequences of including several E&E projects in a CGU, because the unsuccessful conclusion of one project would usually trigger an impairment test of the entire CGU. *[IFRS 6.20]*.

3.5.4 Order of impairment testing

CGUs often contain other assets as well as E&E assets. When developing IFRS 6, ED 6 specifically stated that such other assets should be tested for impairment first, in accordance with IAS 36, before testing the CGU inclusive of the E&E assets.[86] However, IFRS 6 does not specifically address this topic. Despite this, we believe that as the impairment test is completed in accordance with IAS 36, and a similar approach is adopted as that applied to goodwill, the order of the impairment testing as set out in IAS 36 would apply. That is, an entity would test the underlying assets/CGU without the E&E assets first, recognise any write down (if applicable) and then test the CGU/CGU group with the E&E assets allocated.

3.5.5 Reversal of impairment losses

Any impairment loss on an E&E asset recognised in accordance with IFRS 6 needs to be reversed if there is evidence that the loss no longer exists or has decreased. The entity must apply the requirements specified in IAS 36 for reversing an impairment loss (see Chapter 20 at 6). *[IFRS 6.BC48, IAS 36.109-123]*.

In some circumstances an entity that recognises an impairment of an E&E asset must also decide whether or not to derecognise the asset because no future economic benefits are expected, as illustrated in Example 39.3 below.

Example 39.3: Reversal of impairment losses on E&E assets

Entity A's exploration activity in a specific area does not discover oil and/or gas reserves. Therefore, A recognises an impairment of the cash-generating unit and derecognises the related E&E assets.

Entity B's exploration activity in a specific area leads to the discovery of a significant quantity of reserves, but these are located in a complex reservoir. Therefore, at present the costs of extraction of the discovered reserves do not justify the construction of the required infrastructure. Nevertheless, B's management believes that the surrounding area has strong potential to yield other discoveries on other geological structures and it is considered possible that the required infrastructure will be constructed in the future, although at this stage management has no plans to undertake further exploration activity. Entity B recognises an impairment of the E&E assets, but since it expects future economic benefits the related E&E assets are not derecognised.

If an entity concludes that production is not technically feasible or commercially viable, that provides evidence that the related E&E asset needs to be tested for impairment. It is also possible that such evidence may indicate that no future economic benefits are expected from such assets and therefore any remaining assets should be derecognised. When considering the two examples above, in Entity A's situation, no oil and/or gas reserves were discovered and based on current plans, no future economic benefits were expected from the related E&E assets so they were derecognised. Whereas in Entity B's situation, while oil and/or gas reserves were discovered, extraction was not commercially viable at this stage. So while an impairment was recognised, the remaining assets were not derecognised as management did expect future economic benefits to flow from such assets.

Although IFRS 6 does not specifically deal with derecognition of E&E assets, the entity should derecognise the E&E asset because the asset is no longer in the exploration and evaluation phase and hence outside the scope of IFRS 6 and other asset standards such as IAS 16 and IAS 38 would require derecognition under those circumstances. Once derecognised, the costs of an E&E asset that have been written off cannot be re-recognised as part of a new E&E asset, so unlike an impairment, the write off is permanent.

3.6 Disclosure

To identify and explain 'the amounts recognised in its financial statements arising from the exploration for and evaluation of mineral resources', *[IFRS 6.23]*, an entity should disclose:

(a) its accounting policies for exploration and evaluation expenditures including the recognition of exploration and evaluation assets.

(b) the amounts of assets, liabilities, income and expense and operating and investing cash flows arising from the exploration for and evaluation of mineral resources. *[IFRS 6.24]*.

The extract below from Tullow Oil's 2012 financial statements illustrates the disclosures required by IFRS 6:

Extract 39.6: Tullow Oil plc (2012)

GROUP INCOME STATEMENT [extract]
Year ended 31 December 2012

	Notes	2012 $m	2011 $m
Continuing activities			
Sales revenue	2	**2,344.1**	2,304.2
Cost of sales		**(999.3)**	(930.8)
Gross Profit		**1,344.8**	1,373.4
Administrative expenses		**(191.2)**	(122.8)
Profit on disposal	9	**702.5**	2.0
Exploration costs written off	10	**(670.9)**	(120.6)
Operating profit	3	**1,185.2**	1,132.0

GROUP BALANCE SHEET [extract]
As at 31 December 2012

	Notes	2012 $m	2011 $m
ASSETS			
Non-current assets			
Intangible exploration and evaluation assets	10	**2,977.1**	5,529.7
Property, plant and equipment	11	**4,407.9**	3,580.3
Investments	12	**1.0**	1.0
Other non-current assets	15	**696.7**	313.5
Deferred tax assets	22	**4.9**	39.0
		8,087.6	9,463.5

GROUP CASH FLOW STATEMENT [extract]
Year ended 31 December 2012

	2012 $m	2011 $m
Cash flows from investing activities		
Disposal of exploration and evaluation assets	**2,568.2**	–
Disposal of oil and gas assets	**0.3**	–
Disposal of other assets	**1.3**	2.4
Purchase of subsidiaries	**–**	(404.0)
Purchase of intangible exploration and evaluation assets	**(1,196.6)**	(1,018.4)
Purchase of property, plant and equipment	**(652.8)**	(635.1)
Finance revenue	**1.3**	13.6
Net cash generated/(used) in investing activities	**721.7**	(2,041.5)

ACCOUNTING POLICIES [extract]
Year ended 31 December 2012
(k) Exploration, evaluation and production assets

The Group adopts the successful efforts method of accounting for exploration and appraisal costs. All licence acquisition, exploration and evaluation costs and directly attributable administration costs are initially capitalised in cost centres by well, field or exploration area, as appropriate. Interest payable is capitalised insofar as it relates to specific development activities. Pre-licence costs are expensed in the period in which they are incurred.

These costs are then written off as exploration costs in the income statement unless commercial reserves have been established or the determination process has not been completed and there are no indications of impairment.

All field development costs are capitalised as property, plant and equipment. Property, plant and equipment related to production activities are amortised in accordance with the Group's depletion and amortisation accounting policy.

NOTES TO GROUP FINANCIAL STATEMENTS [extract]
Year ended 31 December 2012
Note 10. Intangible exploration and evaluation assets [extract]

	2012 $m	*Restated 2011 $m
At 1 January	**5,529.7**	4,001.2
Acquisition of subsidiaries (note 9)	**–**	503.8
Additions	**1,340.9**	1,190.0
Disposals (note 9)	**(2,573.6)**	–
Amounts written-off	**(670.9)**	(120.6)
Transfer to assets held for sale (note 17)	**(28.4)**	–
Transfer to property, plant and equipment (note 11)	**(625.3)**	–
Currency translation adjustments	**4.7**	(44.7)
At 31 December	**2,977.1**	5,529.7

* Certain numbers shown above do not correspond to the 2011 financial statements as a result of a retrospective restatement as set out in note 33.

The amounts for intangible exploration and evaluation assets represent active exploration projects. These amounts will be written off to the income statement as exploration costs unless commercial reserves are established or the determination process is not completed and there are no indications of impairment. The outcome of ongoing exploration, and therefore whether the carrying value of exploration and evaluation assets will ultimately be recovered, is inherently uncertain.

> Included within 2012 additions is $67.2 million of capitalised interest (2011: $128.8 million). The Group only capitalises interest in respect of intangible exploration and evaluation assets where it is considered that development is highly likely and advanced appraisal and development is ongoing.
>
> Exploration costs written-off were $670.9 million (2011: $120.6 million), in accordance with the Group's successful efforts accounting policy. This requires that all costs associated with unsuccessful exploration are written-off in the income statement. Write-offs associated with unsuccessful exploration activities during 2012 in Guyana, Ghana, Sierra Leone, Côte d'Ivoire, Suriname, Tanzania, Uganda and new ventures activity and licence relinquishments totalled $300 million. As a result of the Group's review of the exploration asset values on its balance sheet compared with expected near-term work programmes and the relative attractiveness of further investment in these assets an additional write-down of $371 million has been made. The principal elements of these write-downs are: the Odum discovery in Ghana where acreage has been relinquished ($37 million); carried costs for Kudu in Namibia where progress towards commercialisation continues to be delayed ($160 million); undeveloped discoveries in Mauritania ($93 million) and exploration costs to date in Sierra Leone where interest remains, but a hub-class commercial discovery has yet to be made ($50 million).

An entity should treat E&E assets as a separate class of assets and make the disclosures required by IAS 16 and IAS 38 for tangible E&E assets and intangible E&E assets, respectively. *[IFRS 6.25, BC53]*.

3.6.1 Statement of cash flows

IAS 7 – *Statement of Cash Flows* – was amended (for annual periods beginning on or after 1 January 2010) to state that only expenditures that result in a recognised asset in the statement of financial position are eligible for classification as investing activities. *[IAS 7.16]*. The IASB specifically notes that 'the exemption in IFRS 6 applies only to recognition and measurement of exploration and evaluation assets, not to the classification of related expenditures in the statement of cash flows'. *[IFRS 6.BC23B]*. This means that an entity that expenses E&E expenditure will not be able to classify the associated cash flows as arising from investing activities.

4 PRACTICAL ISSUES IN THE EXTRACTIVE INDUSTRIES

4.1 Guidance under national accounting standards

Entities complying with IFRS do not have a free hand in selecting accounting policies – indeed the very purpose of a body of accounting literature is to restrict such choices. IAS 8 makes it clear that when a standard or an interpretation specifically applies to a transaction, other event or condition, the accounting policy or policies applied to that item should be determined by applying the standard or interpretation and considering any relevant implementation guidance issued by the IASB. *[IAS 8.7]*.

However, in the extractive industries there are many circumstances where a particular event, transaction or other condition is *not* specifically addressed by IFRS. When this is the case, IAS 8 sets out a hierarchy of guidance to be considered in the selection of an accounting policy (see Chapter 3 at 4.3).

The primary requirement of the standard is that management should use its judgement in developing and applying an accounting policy that results in information that is both relevant and reliable. *[IAS 8.10]*.

In making the judgement, management *should* refer to, and consider the applicability of, the following sources in descending order:

(a) the requirements in standards and interpretations dealing with similar and related issues; and

(b) the definitions, recognition criteria and measurement concepts for assets, liabilities, income and expenses in the *Conceptual Framework*. [IAS 8.11].

Management may also take into account the most recent pronouncements of other standard setting bodies that use a similar conceptual framework to develop accounting standards, other accounting literature and accepted industry practices, to the extent that these do not conflict with the sources in (a) and (b) above. [IAS 8.12].

The stock exchanges in Australia, Canada, South Africa, the United Kingdom and the United States have historically been home to the majority of the listed mining companies and oil and gas companies. Consequently it is organisations from those countries that have been the most active in developing both reserves measurement standards and accounting standards specifically for the extractive industries. In developing an accounting policy for an issue that is not specifically dealt with in IFRS, an entity operating in an extractive industry may find it useful to consider accounting standards developed in these countries. It should be noted, however, that the requirements in such guidance were developed under national accounting standards and may contradict specific requirements and guidance in IFRS that deals with similar and related issues, or may not all be consistent.

4.2 Unit of account

One of the key issues in the development of accounting standards and in the selection of accounting policies by preparers, is deciding the level at which an entity should separately account for assets, i.e. what is the 'unit of account'? The definition of the unit of account has significant accounting consequences, as can be seen in the example below.

Example 39.4: Unit of account – dry well

An oil and gas company concludes, based on a number of exploration wells, that oil and gas reserves are present. However, it needs to drill a number of delineation wells to determine the amount of reserves present in the field. The first delineation well that is drilled is a dry hole, i.e. no reserves are found.

There are two ways of looking at the cost of drilling the dry hole:

- the dry hole provides important information about the extent of the oil and gas reserves present in the oil field and should therefore be capitalised as part of the larger oil field; or
- the dry hole will not produce oil in the future and in the absence of future economic benefits the costs should be expensed immediately.

This example suggests that assets or actions that have no value or meaning at one level may actually be valuable and necessary at another level.

The unit of account plays a significant role in:

(1) recognition and derecognition of assets;

(2) determining the rate of depreciation or amortisation;

(3) deciding whether or not certain costs should be capitalised;

(4) undertaking impairment testing;
(5) determining the substance of transactions;
(6) application of the measurement model subsequent to recognition of the asset; and
(7) determining the level of detail of the disclosures required.

IFRS does not provide comprehensive guidance on either unit of account or the related concept of 'linkage' (i.e. whether the accounting treatment for two or more transactions or contracts differs depending on whether the contracts are accounted for separately or together). The decisions about the unit of account will consider, inter alia, cost/benefits and materiality, whether the items are capable of being used separately, their useful economic lives, whether the economic benefits that the entity will derive are separable and the substance of the transaction. To some degree the choice of the unit of account will depend on industry practice, as discussed below.

In Example 39.4 above, an individual dry hole might not be considered a separate asset because individual wells are typically not capable of being used separately, their economic benefits are inseparable, the wells are similar in nature and the substance of the matter can only be understood at the level of the project as a whole. In such a scenario, the costs of dry holes will typically be capitalised as the individual well is not considered to be a separate unit of account.

4.2.1 Unit of account in the extractive industries

In the extractive industries the definition of the unit of account is particularly important in: deciding whether or not certain costs may be capitalised; determining the rate of depreciation; and impairment testing. Historically entities in the extractive industries have accounted for preproduction costs using methods such as:

- successful efforts method;
- area-of-interest method; and
- full cost method.

These are discussed further at 5.2 below. A key issue under each of these methods is determining the appropriate unit of account, which is referred to in the industry as the 'cost centre' or 'pool'. In practice, entities would define their cost centres along geographical, political or legal boundaries or align them to the operating units in their organisation. The IASC's Issues Paper listed the following, commonly used, cost centres:[87]

(a) the world;
(b) each country or group of countries in which the entity operates;
(c) each contractual or legal mineral acquisition unit, such as a lease or production sharing contract;
(d) each area of interest (geological feature, such as a mine or field, that lends itself to a unified exploration and development effort);
(e) geological units other than areas of interest (such as a basin or a geologic province); or
(f) the entity's organisational units.

IFRS does not provide industry specific guidance on determining appropriate units of account for the extractive industries. Nevertheless, we believe that in determining the unit of account an entity should take the legal rights (see (c) above) as its starting point and apply the criteria discussed above to assess whether the unit of account should be larger or smaller. The other cost centres listed above might result in a unit of account that is unjustifiably large when viewed in the light of the criteria discussed above.

The definition of 'unit of account' was considered in the Discussion Paper – *Extractive Activities* (DP). While the DP would not need to be considered in the context of the IAS 8 hierarchy, it did draw attention to the fact that the selection of an appropriate unit of account might need to take into account the stage of the underlying activities. In particular, the DP proposed that '...the geographical boundary of the unit of account would be defined initially on the basis of the exploration rights held. As exploration, evaluation and development activities take place, the unit of account would contract progressively until it becomes no greater than a single area, or group of contiguous areas, for which the legal rights are held and which is managed separately and would be expected to generate largely independent cash flows'. The DP's view was that the components approach in IAS 16 would apply to determine the items that should be accounted for as a single asset. However, the DP suggested that an entity may decide to account for its assets using a smaller unit of account.

The thinking underlying the above proposal in the DP would be relevant in the following types of situations:

- certain transactions in the extractive industries (e.g. carried interests arrangements) result in the creation of new legal rights out of existing legal rights. Whenever this is the case, an entity needs to assess whether such transactions give rise to new units of account. If so, the accounting policies should be applied to those new units of account rather than the previous unit/s of account; and
- when an entity acquires a business that owns reserves and resources, it needs to consider whether it should define the unit of account at the level of the licence or separate ore zones or reservoirs within the licence.

Determining the unit of account is an area that requires a significant amount of judgement, which may need to be disclosed under IAS 1 – *Presentation of Financial Statements* – together with other judgements that management has made in the process of applying the entity's accounting policies and that have the most significant effect on the amounts recognised in the financial statements. *[IAS 1.122]*.

4.3 Functional currency

4.3.1 Determining functional currency

Determining functional currency correctly is important because it will, for example, affect volatility of revenue and operating profit resulting from exchange rate movements, determine whether transactions can be hedged or not and influence the identification of embedded currency derivatives. The movements may give rise to temporary differences that affect profit or loss. *[IAS 12.41]*. While under IAS 21 – *The Effects of Changes in Foreign Exchange Rates* – an entity can select any presentation currency, it does not have a free choice in determining its functional currency. Choice of functional currency is discussed in detail in Chapter 15 at 4; this section is a summary of the application of the requirements to the extractive industries. IAS 21 requires an entity to consider the following factors in determining its functional currency:

(a) the currency that mainly influences sales prices for goods and services (this will often be the currency in which sales prices for its goods and services are denominated and settled);

(b) the currency of the country whose competitive forces and regulations mainly determine the sales prices of its goods and services; and

(c) the currency that mainly influences labour, material and other costs of providing goods or services (this will often be the currency in which such costs are denominated and settled). *[IAS 21.9]*.

While the currency referred to under (a) above will often be the currency in which sales prices for its goods and services are denominated and settled, this is not always the case. The US dollar is used for many commodities as the contract or settlement currency in transactions (e.g. iron ore, oil), but the pricing of transactions is often driven by factors completely unrelated to the US dollar or the US economy (e.g. it may be influenced more by demand from the local economy or other economies such as China).

As the extractive industries are international, it is often difficult to determine the currency of the country whose competitive forces and regulations mainly determine the sales prices of its goods and services. Therefore, factor (b) above will often prove to be inconclusive when a particular product is produced in many different countries.

It will generally be fairly straightforward to identify the currency that mainly influences an entity's key inputs (i.e. factor (c) above). In developing countries an entity will often need to import a significant proportion of its key inputs (e.g. fuel, equipment and expatriate workers) and even local inputs in an economy with a high inflation rate will often be linked to the US dollar. In such a case, the local currency is less likely to be the main currency that influences an entity's key inputs. In most developed countries, however, the inputs tend to be denominated in the local currency, although some inputs (e.g. major items of equipment) may be denominated in another currency. As the extractive industries are capital intensive, the cost of equipment often far exceeds the operating expenses incurred. Equipment is often purchased in US dollars.

When the factors (a) to (c) above are mixed, as they often are in practice, and the functional currency is not obvious, management should use 'its judgement to determine the functional currency that most faithfully represents the economic effects of the underlying transactions, events and conditions'. *[IAS 21.12]*. If the above factors are inconclusive then an entity should also consider the following secondary factors:

- the currency in which funds from financing activities (i.e. issuing debt and equity instruments) are generated;
- the currency in which receipts from operating activities are usually retained; and
- the functional currency of the reporting entity that has the foreign operation as its subsidiary, branch, associate or joint venture. *[IAS 21.10, 11].*

After considering both the primary and secondary factors the functional currency may not be obvious because, for example, revenue is denominated in US dollars while virtually all expenses are denominated in the local currency. In that situation management may conclude that revenue, while denominated in US dollars, is in fact influenced by a basket of currencies. It is therefore possible that companies operating in a similar environment can reach different conclusions about their functional currency. Even in developed countries there is a general bias towards the US dollar as the functional currency.

Finally, IAS 21 requires an entity to determine separately the functional currency of each entity in a consolidated group. There is no concept of the functional currency of the group, only a presentation currency. Therefore, the functional currency of an operating subsidiary may differ from that of the group's parent and/or foreign sales company to which it sells its production. The factors taken into account in determining functional currency may differ for operating companies and for group entities that are financing or intermediate holding companies (see Chapter 15 at 4.2).

Although local statutory and tax requirements should be ignored in determining the functional currency, there may be a requirement to keep two sets of accounting records when an entity concludes that its local currency is not its functional currency.

The extract below from Rio Tinto illustrates a typical currency translation accounting policy of a mining company.

Extract 39.7: Rio Tinto Group (2012)

Notes to the 2012 financial statements [extract]

1 PRINCIPAL ACCOUNTING POLICIES [extract]

(d) Currency translation

The functional currency for each entity in the Group, and for JCEs and associates, is the currency of the primary economic environment in which that entity operates. For many entities, this is the currency of the country in which they are located. Transactions denominated in other currencies are converted to the functional currency at the exchange rate ruling at the date of the transaction. The accounting for hedged transactions is discussed in note (p) below. Monetary assets and liabilities denominated in foreign currencies are retranslated at year end exchange rates.

The Group's accounting policies for derivative financial instruments and hedge accounting are explained in more detail in note 1(p) (iii). The Group's financial statements are presented in US dollars, as that currency most reliably reflects the global business performance of the Group as a whole. On consolidation, income statement items for each entity are translated from the functional currency into US dollars at average rates of exchange where the average approximates the rate at the date of transactions. Statement of financial position items are translated into US dollars at year end exchange rates.

Exchange differences arising on the translation of the net assets of entities with functional currencies other than the US dollar are recognised directly in the foreign currency translation reserve. These translation differences are shown in the statement of comprehensive income with the exception of translation adjustments relating to Rio Tinto Limited's share capital which are shown in the Group statement of changes in equity.

Where an intragroup balance is, in substance, part of the Group's net investment in an entity, exchange gains and losses on that balance are taken to the foreign currency translation reserve. Except as noted above, or in note (p) below relating to derivative contracts, all other exchange differences are charged or credited to the income statement in the year in which they arise.

4.3.2 Changes in functional currency

IAS 21 requires management to use its judgement to determine the entity's functional currency so that it most faithfully represents the economic effects of the underlying transactions, events and conditions that are relevant to the entity. Note that IAS 21 requires the functional currency to be determined by reference to factors that exist *during* the reporting period. Therefore, an entity should ignore future developments in its business, no matter how likely those developments are. For example, even if an entity is convinced that in three years' time it will have revenues that will be denominated in US dollars, this is not a factor to be considered in determining its functional currency today. Consequently, a company may conclude that during the development phase of the project the local currency is its functional currency but that once production and sales commence the US dollar will become its functional currency.

This is illustrated in the extract below from Hochschild Mining's 2008 financial statements.

Extract 39.8: Hochschild Mining plc (2008)

Notes to the consolidated financial statements continued

For the year ended 31 December 2008 [extract]

36 Financial risk management [extract]

(a) Foreign currency risk [extract]

1 Minera Santa Cruz, one of the Group's subsidiaries which is the legal owner of the San José mine, had debts denominated in US dollars. As Minera Santa Cruz's functional currency was the peso during 2007, the translation of this loan into Pesos created a loss. Following the commencement of operations the Group was required to change the functional currency in Minera Santa Cruz to US dollars and as a result, these loans were no longer being exposed to foreign currency risk.

Once the functional currency is determined, the standard allows it to be changed only if there is a change in those underlying transactions, events and conditions. For example, a change in the currency that mainly influences the sales prices of goods and services may lead to a change in an entity's functional currency. *[IAS 21.36]*.

The extract below, from Angel Mining plc's financial statements, provides an example of a change in conditions that resulted in a change in functional currency. Accounting for a change in functional currency is discussed in Chapter 15 at 5.5.

Extract 39.9: Angel Mining plc (2010)

Notes to the financial statements

Year ended 28 February 2010 [extract]

1a. Basis of preparation – Change in functional currency

Previously, the directors considered the functional currency of the Company to be Sterling. In light of developments within the Company's operations and the nature of its funding, the directors have reassessed the functional currency of the Company and concluded that the currency of the primary economic environment in which Angel Mining operates is now the US dollar. The date of change from Sterling to US dollars has been taken as 1 March 2009. The key factors influencing this decision include the following:

(i) During the year, the Company acquired the Nalunaq license and mining assets. This will be the first producing mine for the Company. The consideration for these assets was paid in US dollars;

(ii) During the year, the Company sourced plant, machinery and employees with technical skills on a global basis. A significant proportion of these costs were based in US dollars. In prior years, the Company's costs had been incurred primarily in Sterling;

(iii) The Company's primary form of finance during the period was the long term and short term debt facilities provided by FBC. These facilities are all based in US dollars. During prior periods, the Company had been more heavily dependent upon equity finance which was denominated in Sterling;

(iv) The vast majority of the forms of finance which the Company has been pursuing and is likely to pursue going forward are US dollar based;

(v) Commencing during the year, one of the largest consumables used by the Company in its operations in Greenland was diesel fuel. Although the Company pays for its diesel in Danish Kroner, the price of diesel is determined globally and priced in US dollars; and

(vi) The resources that the Company is working to exploit are global commodities which are always priced in US dollars. When the Company begins producing, all its revenues will be dollar based.

The change in the Company's functional currency has been accounted for prospectively from 1 March 2009 in accordance with IAS 21. This change constituted a prospective change in accounting policy. The financial statements for 2009 have been prepared using Sterling as the functional currency and US dollars as the presentational currency.

The change in the presentational currency from Sterling to US dollar is and therefore is applied retrospectively in accordance with IAS 8 'Accounting Policies, Changes in Accounting Estimates and Errors' and therefore require comparative information to be restated and consequently, a third balance sheet is required to be presented in the financial statements.

The impact of this change in presentational currency for 2009, is as follows:

(i) The assets and liabilities for both the Group and the Company at 28 February 2009 have been translated using the closing rate for the same date of $1.426/£;

(ii) The consolidated income statement for 2009 has been translated using the average rate for the year ended 28 February 2009 of $1.771/£ on the basis that this average rate approximates the exchange rates on the dates of transactions; and

The resulting gain on retranslation from average to closing rate has been recognised in the consolidated statement of comprehensive income.

4.4 Investments in the extractive industries

Extractive industries are characterised by the high risks associated with the exploration for and development of mineral reserves. To mitigate those risks, industry participants use a variety of ownership structures that are aimed at sharing risks, such as joint investments through subsidiaries, joint arrangements, associates or equity interests. IFRS defines each of these as follows:

- *subsidiaries* – entities controlled by the reporting entity (see 4.4.1 below);
- *joint arrangements* – contractual arrangements of which two or more parties have joint control (see 4.4.2 below);
- *associates* – entities that, while not controlled or jointly controlled by the reporting entity, are subject to significant influence by it (see 4.4.4 below);
- *equity interests* – entities over which the reporting entity cannot exercise any control, joint control or significant influence (see 4.4.5 below); and
- *undivided interests* – participations in projects which entitle the reporting entity only to a share of the production or use of an asset, and do not of themselves give the entity any form of control, joint control or significant influence (see 4.4.6 below).

4.4.1 Investments in subsidiaries

In the extractive industries it is common to find that a parent company is not exposed to all the risks and rewards from its investments in subsidiaries. Instead, there are often significant non-controlling shareholders that share in the risks and rewards. Accounting for non-controlling interests is discussed in detail in Chapter 7 at 4. Furthermore, there sometimes exist put and/or call options over non-controlling interests that transfer some of the risks between the parent company shareholders and the non-controlling shareholders. This issue is discussed in detail in Chapter 7 at 5.

4.4.2 Investments in joint arrangements

Joint arrangements have always been, and continue to be, a common structure in the extractive industries. Such arrangements are used to bring in partners to source new projects, combine adjacent mineral licences, improve utilisation of expensive infrastructure, attract investors and help manage technical or political risk or comply with local regulations. The majority of entities operating in the extractive industries are party to at least one joint arrangement. However, not all arrangements that are casually described as 'joint arrangements' or 'joint ventures' meet the definition of a joint arrangement under IFRS.

Accounting for joint arrangements used to be governed by IAS 31 – *Interests in Joint Ventures.* This was superseded by IFRS 11 – *Joint Arrangements* – which was effective for annual periods beginning on or after 1 January 2013.

Under IAS 31, there were three broad types of joint ventures:

- jointly controlled operations (JCO);
- jointly controlled assets (JCA); and
- jointly controlled entities (JCE).

A JCO was a joint venture that involved the use of assets and other resources of the venturers, rather than the establishment of a corporation, partnership or other legal entity, or a financial structure, separate from the venturers themselves. Each venturer used its own property, plant and equipment and carried its own inventories. It also incurred its own expenses and liabilities, raised its own finance, and was only responsible for its own obligations. Activities may have been carried out by the venturer's employees alongside similar activities of the other venturer. The JCO agreement usually provided the basis for sharing the revenue from the joint product, and any common expenses incurred among the venturers.

JCAs were the most common form of joint venture in the extractive industries. They involved the joint control, and often joint ownership, of one or more assets contributed to, or acquired for, and dedicated to the purposes of, the joint venture. The assets were used to obtain benefits for the venturers, who may each have taken a share of the output from the assets and each borne an agreed share of the expenses incurred. Such ventures did not involve the establishment of an entity or financial structure separate from the venturers themselves, so that each venturer had control over its share of future economic benefits through its share in the jointly controlled asset.

A JCA was similar to an 'undivided interest', which is 'a fractional ownership interest in the entire area of the property. For example, if an entity owning 100 per cent of the working interest in a property sold a 50 per cent undivided interest to another party, the purchaser would own 50 per cent of the entire property, and the seller would own 50 per cent of the same property.'[88] This is called an 'undivided' interest because neither party owns a physically identifiable half of the property concerned. However, as discussed at 4.4.6 below, it is possible for an undivided interest not to be subject to joint control.

In contrast to a JCO or JCA, a JCE was a joint venture that involved the establishment of a separate corporation, partnership or other entity in which each venturer had an interest. The entity operated in the same way as any other entity, except that a contractual arrangement between the venturers established joint control over the economic activity of the entity.

Now under IFRS 11, there are only two types of joint arrangements – 'joint operations' and 'joint ventures'. Classification between these two types of arrangements is based on the rights and obligations that arise from the contractual arrangement:

Joint operation

- A joint operation is defined as 'a joint arrangement whereby the parties that have joint control of the arrangement have rights to the assets, and obligations for the liabilities, relating to the arrangement.' *[IFRS 11 Appendix A].*
- This term effectively replaces the terms 'jointly controlled operation' (JCO) and 'jointly controlled asset' (JCA) that were used in IAS 31.

For more information on accounting for joint operations under IFRS 11 refer to Chapter 12 at 6.

Joint venture

- A joint venture is defined in IFRS 11 as 'a joint arrangement whereby the parties that have joint control of the arrangement have rights to the net assets of the arrangement.' *[IFRS 11 Appendix A]*.
- Arrangements referred to as 'jointly controlled entities' (JCEs) under IAS 31 could either be joint operations or joint ventures under IFRS 11. This will depend upon the assessment of the rights and obligations of the arrangement.

For more information on accounting for joint ventures under IFRS 11 refer to Chapter 12 at 7.

An entity that is party to a joint arrangement must determine the type of joint arrangement by assessing its rights and obligations and account for those rights and obligations in accordance with that type of joint arrangement. *[IFRS 11.2]*.

An entity will need to have a detailed understanding of the specific rights and obligations of each of its arrangements to be able to determine the impact of this new standard.

Further details on IFRS 11 and its requirements are set out in Chapter 12.

4.4.3 Impact on the extractive industries

Given the prevalence of joint arrangements in the extractive industries, careful analysis of IFRS 11, in conjunction with the requirements of IFRS 10 – *Consolidated Financial Statements* – (see Chapter 6) and IFRS 12 – *Disclosure of Interests in Other Entities* – (see Chapter 13) will be required. Some specific areas to consider are set out below.

Under IFRS 11 joint control is defined as '...the contractually agreed sharing of control of an arrangement which exists only when the decisions about the relevant activities require the unanimous consent of the parties sharing control'. *[IFRS 11.7, Appendix A]*. IFRS 11 describes the key aspects of joint control as follows:

- *Contractually agreed* – contractual arrangements are usually, but not always, written, and set out the terms of the arrangements. *[IFRS 11.5(a), B2]*.
- *Control and relevant activities* – IFRS 10 describes how to assess whether a party has control, and how to identify the relevant activities. *[IFRS 11.8, B5]*.
- *Unanimous consent* – exists when the parties to an arrangement have collective control over the arrangement, but no single party has control. *[IFRS 11.9, B6]*.

The new requirements of this new definition of joint control relate to the assessment of control and relevant activities. The requirement for there to be unanimous consent is not new; however, additional guidance has been added to clarify when it exists.

4.4.3.A Determination of control – impact of changes to the consolidation standard

It is common in the extractive industries for one of the parties to be appointed as the operator or manager of the joint arrangement ('the operator'), to whom some of the decision-making powers might be delegated. Currently, many consider that the operator does not control a joint arrangement, but simply carries out the decisions of the parties under the joint venture (or operating) agreement (JOA), i.e. the operator acts as an agent. This view is based on the way in which these roles are generally established and referred to, or perceived, in the industries. Under the new standards, it may be possible to conclude that the operator actually controls the arrangement. This is because when decision-making rights have been delegated, IFRS 10 now provides new requirements on how to assess whether an entity is acting as principal or agent, which is then used to determine which party has control.

Careful consideration will be required to assess whether an operator acts as a principal (and, therefore, may potentially control the arrangement) or as an agent. In the former situation, the impact of determining that an operator controls an arrangement will depend upon the rights and obligations conveyed by the arrangement (see 4.4.3.A.I below for further discussion on this issue). In the latter situation, as an agent, the operator would always only recognise its own interests in the joint arrangement (the accounting for which will depend upon whether it is a joint operation or joint venture) and its operator/management fee.

The factors to be considered in making the assessment of principal versus agent include:

- Scope of the operator's decision-making authority;
- Rights held by others (e.g. protective, removal rights);
- Exposure to variability in returns through the remuneration of the operator; and
- Variable returns held through other interests (e.g. direct investments by the operator in the joint arrangement).

The following factors may be particularly relevant:

Rights held by others – If a non-operator party has a right to remove the operator that is substantive (e.g. it can be exercised without cause), then the operator would be an agent. However, if the exercise of that removal right requires agreement by more than one of the non-operator parties, then it is not conclusive as to whether the operator is a principal or an agent.

Variable returns held through other interests – When an operator holds other interests in a joint arrangement over and above the remuneration it receives for being the operator, this may indicate it is not an agent. It is common in the extractive industries for an operator also to have a direct financial interest in the joint arrangement. By virtue of holding this other interest, the standard indicates that decisions made by the operator may differ from those it would have made if it did not hold the other interest, and potentially may indicate the operator is acting as principal.

It is important to note that assessing whether an entity is a principal or an agent will require consideration of all factors collectively. See Chapter 6 at 6.1 for more details regarding the new principal versus agent requirements.

i Implications of control

The impact of controlling an arrangement depends on a number of factors.

The most important of these will be identifying and assessing the rights and obligations the contractual arrangement provides the parties, as well as assessing whether the arrangement is a business.

a) Identifying and assessing rights and obligations

- *Rights to the underlying assets and obligations for the underlying liabilities of the arrangement:* While the principal or agent assessment may lead to a conclusion that an operator has control, the fact that each party has specific rights to, and obligations for, the underlying assets and liabilities of the arrangement by virtue of the contract, means the operator does not control anything over and above its own direct interest in those assets and liabilities. Therefore, it still only recognises its interest in those assets and liabilities conveyed to it by the contractual arrangement.

  This accounting applies regardless of whether the arrangement is in a separate vehicle or not, as the contractual terms are the primary determinant of the accounting. Note that IFRS 11 defines a separate vehicle as 'a separately identifiable financial structure, including separate legal entities or entities recognised by statute, regardless of whether those entities have a legal personality.' *[IFRS 11 Appendix A]*.

  To explain this further, it is worth considering the two types of joint arrangements contemplated by IFRS 11 – one that is not structured through a separate vehicle (e.g. a contract alone) and one that is structured through a separate vehicle.

  No separate vehicle: The IASB acknowledged that while it is possible that the contractual terms of a joint arrangement not structured through a separate vehicle might give the parties rights only to the net assets of the arrangement, they expected this would be rare. *[IFRS 11.BC27]*. Instead, they considered it would be more common for the parties to have rights to, and obligations for, the underlying assets and liabilities of the arrangement.

  So in such a situation, even if the operator 'controlled' the arrangement, there is really nothing for it to control. This is because each party would continue to account for its rights and obligations arising from the contract e.g. it would apply IAS 16 to account for its rights to any tangible assets, IAS 38 to account for its rights to any intangible assets or IAS 39 – *Financial Instruments: Recognition and Measurement* – to account for its obligations for any financial liabilities etc. Additionally, an entity cannot consolidate a contract as the requirements of IFRS 10 only apply to entities and, in most circumstances, a contract does not create an entity.

  Separate vehicle: Some may initially conclude that if an operator controls an arrangement structured through a separate vehicle e.g. a company, it would automatically look to IFRS 10 and consolidate the arrangement, accounting for the interests of the other parties as non-controlling interests. However, in such situations, a contract still exists which gives the parties to the arrangement rights to, and obligations for, the underlying assets and liabilities of that arrangement. These rights and obligations should be accounted for first. That is, each party to the arrangement would recognise its respective share of the assets and liabilities (applying each IFRS as appropriate e.g. IAS 16, IAS 38, IAS 39 etc.).

From the perspective of the separate vehicle, what this means is that the rights to, and obligations for, its assets and liabilities have been contracted out to other parties (i.e. the parties to the contractual arrangement) and therefore there are no assets or liabilities left within the separate vehicle to recognise.

Consequently, from the perspective of the operator, who may be considered to control the separate vehicle, it would initially account for its rights and obligations arising from the contract, and then when it looks to consolidate the separate vehicle, there is nothing left to consolidate, as the separate vehicle is effectively empty.

The above analysis demonstrates that where parties to an arrangement genuinely have contractual rights to, and obligations for, the underlying assets and liabilities of the arrangement, concluding that an operator controls the arrangement does not change the accounting for either the operator or the non-operator parties.

- *Rights to the net assets of the arrangement:* As noted above, the IASB acknowledged that it would be rare for an arrangement not structured through a separate vehicle to provide the parties with rights to the net assets. Therefore it is considered that rights to the net assets of an arrangement would be more likely to only arise where the arrangement is structured through a separate vehicle. In this instance, the operator would consolidate the separate vehicle and recognise any non-controlling interest(s).

b) Is the arrangement a business?

The other relevant factor is whether the arrangement is a business, as this determines whether, upon obtaining control, the requirements of IFRS 3 apply. All of the requirements of IFRS 3 apply if the entity controls the arrangement where it has rights to the net assets, and that arrangement is a business. However, if that controlled arrangement is not a business, the entity identifies and recognises the individual assets acquired and liabilities assumed based on their relative fair value, and does not recognise any goodwill.

For arrangements where there are rights to the assets and obligations for the liabilities, it is not clear whether IFRS 3 applies and whether goodwill could or should be recognised. This issue was referred to the Interpretations Committee and is discussed further in Chapter 12 at 8.3.1.

II What are relevant activities?

Relevant activities are those activities of the arrangement which significantly affect the returns of the arrangement. Determining what these are for each arrangement will require significant judgement.

Examples of decisions about relevant activities include, but are not limited to:

- Establishing operating and capital decisions of the arrangement including budgets – for example, for an arrangement in the extractive industries, approving the capital expenditure programme for the next year; and
- Appointing and remunerating a joint arrangement's key management personnel or service providers and terminating their services or employment – for example, appointing a contract miner or oil field services provider to undertake operations.

For more information on identifying relevant activities, see Chapter 12 at 4.1.

III Meaning of unanimous consent

While the requirement for unanimous consent is not new, IFRS 11 does provide additional guidance that clarifies when unanimous consent exists, and over which activities it is required. Unanimous consent means that any party with joint control can prevent any of the other parties, or a group of parties, from making unilateral decisions about relevant activities.

For further discussion on unanimous consent, see Chapter 12 at 4.3.

In some extractive industries operations, decision-making may vary over the life of the project e.g. during the exploration and evaluation phase, the development phase or the production phase. For example, it may be agreed at the time of initially entering the contractual arrangement that during the exploration and evaluation phase, one party to the arrangement may be able to make all of the decisions, whereas once the project enters the development phase, decisions may then require unanimous consent. To determine whether the arrangement is jointly controlled, it will be necessary to decide (at the point of initially entering the contractual arrangement, and subsequently, should facts and circumstances change) which of these activities e.g. exploration and evaluation and/or development, most significantly affect the returns of the arrangement. This is because the arrangement will only be considered to be a joint arrangement if those activities which require unanimous consent are the ones that most significantly affect the returns. This will be a highly judgemental assessment.

For further information on the impact of different decision-making arrangements over various activities, see Chapter 12 at 4.1.

4.4.3.B Differences between joint ventures and joint operations

Once it has been established that there is joint control, joint arrangements are then classified as either joint operations or joint ventures. For more information on the requirements for classifying a joint arrangement as a joint operation or joint venture, see Chapter 12 at 5.

4.4.3.C Gross versus net – what should be recognised?

It is clear that a participant in a joint operation is required to recognise its rights to the assets, and its obligations for the liabilities (or share thereof), of the joint arrangement. Therefore it is important that an entity fully understands what these rights and obligations are and how these may differ between the parties.

I Operators of joint arrangements

Operators of joint arrangements may have a direct legal liability in respect of the entire balance of certain obligations arising from transactions related to the joint arrangement. These may include, but are not limited to, third party creditors, leases, employee liabilities, etc. They may also have a right of reimbursement (by virtue of the JOA) from the non-operator parties. The operator would be required to recognise 100% of such liabilities and would potentially recognise a receivable from the non-operator parties for their share of such liabilities. IFRS prohibits the offsetting of these liabilities against any receivables recognised in the statement of financial position. However, there is no effect on profit or loss if these costs are effectively being incurred on behalf of the non-operator parties, i.e. the operator is acting as agent, and such costs are directly recharged. This is because these recharges are considered to be a reimbursement which can be offset against the related expense in profit or loss.

While, in most circumstances, the ability or willingness of the non-operator parties to pay their share of the costs incurred by the operator will not be in doubt, particularly where cash calls are paid in advance, there may be instances where they are unable/unwilling to pay. Here the operator might not be able to recognise a corresponding receivable and reimbursement, and consequently, this would negatively impact its financial statements.

II Non-operators

Non-operators would recognise an amount payable to the operator, which would be recognised as a financial instrument under IAS 32 – *Financial Instruments: Presentation* – and IAS 39 or potentially a provision under IAS 37 and not under the standard which relates to the type of cost being reimbursed. For example, the non-operator's share of employee entitlements relating to the operator's employees who work on the joint project would not be recognised as an employee benefit under IAS 19 – *Employee Benefits.* In addition, the related disclosure requirements of IAS 19 would not apply, instead the disclosure requirements of other standards, e.g. IFRS 7 – *Financial Instruments: Disclosures* – would apply.

Note that the requirements of IFRS 9 – *Financial Instruments* – have not been considered in this chapter – see Chapter 45.

III Joint and several liability

It is also possible that there may be liabilities in the arrangement where the obligation is joint and several. That is, an entity is not only responsible for its proportionate share, but it is also liable for the other party's or parties' share(s) should it/they be unable or unwilling to pay. A common example of this in the extractives industries is restoration, rehabilitation and decommissioning obligations.

In these instances, each party not only takes up its proportionate share of the decommissioning/restoration obligation, it is also required to assess the likelihood that the other party/ies will not be able or willing to meet their share. The facts and circumstances would need to be assessed in each case, and any additional liability and disclosures would be accounted for, and disclosed, in accordance with IAS 37.

Any increase in the provision would be accounted for under IFRIC 1, if it related to a restoration or decommissioning liability that had both been included as part of an asset measured in accordance with IAS 16 and measured as a liability in accordance with IAS 37 (see 4.12.2 for more details). Such an addition to the asset would also require an entity to consider whether this is an indication of impairment of the asset as a whole, and if so, would need to test for impairment in accordance with IAS 36. Increases that do not meet the requirements of IFRIC 1 would be recognised in profit or loss.

4.4.3.D An entity does not have joint control or control?

The accounting treatment of an interest in a contractual arrangement that does not give rise to joint control or control depends on a number of factors most importantly the rights and obligations arising under the contractual arrangement.

I Identifying and assessing the rights and obligations

- *Rights to the underlying assets and obligations for the underlying liabilities of the arrangement:* Despite not having joint control (or control) the party still has rights to, and obligations for, the underlying assets and liabilities which are contained in a contractual arrangement. Therefore, it would continue to recognise its interest in those assets and liabilities.

  This accounting would apply regardless of whether the arrangement is in a separate vehicle or not, as the contractual terms are the initial (primary) determinant of the accounting.

  To explain this further, it is worth considering the two types of joint arrangements contemplated by IFRS 11 – one that is not structured through a separate vehicle (e.g. a contract alone) and one that is structured through a separate vehicle.

- **No separate vehicle:** As explained at 4.4.3.A.I above, an arrangement not structured through a separate vehicle (effectively those arrangements undertaken via contract alone) is considered to give the parties to that contractual arrangement rights to, and obligations for, the underlying assets and liabilities of the arrangement. Therefore, each party would continue to account for its rights and obligations arising from the contract e.g. it would apply IAS 16 to account for its rights to any tangible assets, IAS 38 to account for its rights to any intangible assets or IAS 39 to account for its rights to any financial assets and obligations for any financial liabilities, etc. The requirements of IAS 28 – *Investments in Associates and Joint Ventures* – would not apply as an associate is defined as an 'entity over which the investor has significant influence' (emphasis added), *[IAS 28.3]*, and in most circumstances, a contract does not create an entity.

  Separate vehicle: Some may initially consider that if an entity concludes it does not have control or joint control over an arrangement in a separate vehicle, then IAS 28 may apply (assuming that their percentage interest in the arrangement provided them with significant influence). However, similar to the situation discussed above regarding control, in such situations, there is still a contractual arrangement which gives the parties to the arrangement rights to, and obligations for, the underlying assets and liabilities of that arrangement. These rights and obligations should be accounted for first. Each party to the arrangement would recognise its respective share of the assets and liabilities (applying each IFRS as appropriate e.g. IAS 16, IAS 38, IAS 39 etc.).

The above analysis demonstrates that where parties to an arrangement genuinely have rights to, and obligations for, the underlying assets and liabilities of the arrangement by virtue of the contract they have entered into, concluding that an entity has neither control nor joint control over the arrangement does not change the accounting for that party.

- *Rights to the net assets of the arrangement:* Again, as noted above, rights to the net assets of an arrangement would be more likely to arise only where the arrangement is structured through a separate vehicle. In this instance, if the party is considered to have significant influence over the arrangement, it applies equity accounting to its interest in accordance with IAS 28. Otherwise it accounts for its interest under IAS 32 and IAS 39 at fair value through profit or loss or other comprehensive income, unless the investment was held for trading. Note that the requirements of IFRS 9 have not been considered in this chapter – see Chapter 45.

4.4.3.E Summary

Given the unique nature of the various arrangements that currently exist, and are emerging, in the extractive industries, an entity will need to analyse each contract individually to be able to complete this assessment. The difficulty of this task will be impacted by the number and complexity of the arrangements an entity has and also because an entity should (ideally) discuss and agree the accounting with other parties to the joint arrangement, to ensure consistency and manage regulatory risk. Robust systems and processes will need to be developed, not only to complete the initial assessment, but also to enable the ongoing assessment of current arrangements (should facts and circumstances change) and the assessment of new arrangements.

4.4.4 Investments in associates

An investor should apply the equity method in accounting for investments in associates, which are entities over which the investor can exercise significant influence (i.e. the investor has the power to participate in the financial and operating policy decisions of the investee but it does not have control or joint control over those policies). *[IAS 28.3]*. Significant influence is deemed to exist under IFRS when an investor holds between 20% and 50% of the voting rights in an investee. However, significant influence may also exist in limited circumstances when the investor holds an interest of less than 20% or more than 50% (see Chapter 11 at 4.2). Some arrangements that are aimed at establishing joint control over an entity do not meet the definition of a joint arrangement under IFRS 11. Those types of arrangement will, however, often give rise to significant influence and, therefore, the requirement to account for the investment as an associate.

4.4.5 Investments in financial assets

Small investments in the equity instruments of an entity over which the investor cannot exercise control, joint control or significant influence meet the definition of a financial asset under IAS 32. If the investor is exposed to risks other than credit risk, such investments do not meet the definition of 'loans and receivables' under IAS 39 and should, instead, be classified as either 'at fair value through profit or loss' or 'available for sale'. *[IAS 39.9]*. Note that the requirements of IFRS 9 have not been considered in this chapter – see Chapter 45.

4.4.6 Investments in undivided interests

Undivided interests are usually subject to joint control (see Chapter 12 at 4) and can, therefore, be accounted for as joint operations. However, some joint operating agreements (JOAs) do not establish joint control but are, instead, based on some form of supermajority voting whereby a qualified majority (e.g. 75%) of the participants can approve decisions. This situation usually arises when the group of participants is too large for joint control to be practical or when the main investor wants to retain a certain level of influence.

Such undivided interests cannot be accounted for as joint operations in the scope of IFRS 11 in the absence of joint control.

Entities enter into arrangements in which they buy and sell parts of undivided assets, e.g. carried interests (see 4.7.1.D below) and farm-in arrangements outside the E&E phase (see 4.7.2.C below). Although neither IAS 16 nor IAS 38 addresses part-disposals of undivided assets, it is industry practice to apply the principles in those standards when the vendor disposes of these interests in circumstances in which it can demonstrate that it neither controls nor jointly controls the whole of the original asset. In these circumstances, the principles of IAS 16 and IAS 38 are applied and the entity derecognises part of the asset, having calculated an appropriate carrying value for the part disposed of, and a gain or loss on disposal. See Chapter 17 at 9.5 and Chapter 18 at 7.3.

The appropriate accounting treatment by the investor depends on the nature of the arrangement:

- If the investor has rights to the underlying asset then the arrangement should be accounted for as a tangible or intangible asset under IAS 16 or IAS 38, respectively. The investor's proportionate share of the operating costs of the asset (e.g. repairs and maintenance) should be accounted for in the same way as the operating costs of wholly owned assets; or
- If the investor is entitled only to a proportion of the cash flows generated by the asset then its investment will generally meet the definition of a financial asset under IAS 32. As the investor is exposed to risks other than credit risk, such investments do not meet the definition of 'loans and receivables' under IAS 39 and should, instead, be classified as either 'at fair value through profit or loss' or 'available for sale'. *[IAS 39.9]*. Note that the requirements of IFRS 9 have not been considered in this chapter – see Chapter 45.

4.4.7 Operators of joint arrangements

A joint operating agreement may identify one participant as the operator or manager of the joint arrangement. An operator does not control the joint arrangement but acts within the financial and operating policies agreed by the participants in accordance with the contractual arrangement and delegated to the operator. However, if an entity described as an 'operator' has the power to govern (i.e. not merely to execute) the financial and operating policies of the economic activity then it controls the venture and it may have to consolidate the arrangement as a subsidiary.

See also 4.4.2 and 4.4.3 above for discussion of the impact of IFRS 11.

4.4.7.A Reimbursements of costs

An operator often carries out activities on behalf of the joint arrangement on a no gain, no loss basis. Generally these activities can be identified separately and are carried out by the operator in its capacity as an agent for the joint arrangement, which is effectively the principal in those transactions. The operator receives reimbursement of direct costs recharged to the joint arrangement. Such recharges are reimbursements of costs that the operator incurred as an agent for the joint venture and therefore have no effect on profit or loss in the statement of comprehensive income (or income statement) of the operator.

In many cases an operator also incurs certain general overhead expenses in carrying out activities on behalf of the joint arrangement. As these costs can often not be specifically identified, many joint operating agreements allow the operator to recover the general overhead expenses incurred by charging an overhead fee that is based on a fixed percentage of the total costs incurred for the year. Although the purpose of this recharge is very similar to the reimbursement of direct costs, the operator is not acting as an agent in this case. Therefore, the operator should recognise the general overhead expenses and the overhead fee in profit or loss in its statement of comprehensive income (or income statement) as an expense and income, respectively.

4.4.7.B Direct legal liability

The operator of a joint arrangement may have a direct legal liability to third party creditors in respect of the entire balance arising from transactions related to the joint arrangement.[89] IFRS prohibits the offsetting of such liabilities against the amounts recoverable from the other joint arrangement participants. *[IAS 1.32, IAS 32.42]*. The operator may therefore need to disclose, for example, some of the leases that it has entered into on behalf of the joint arrangement, if entered into in its own name.

4.5 Legal rights to explore for, develop and produce mineral properties

An entity can acquire legal rights to explore for, develop and produce wasting resources on a mineral property by:[90]

(a) purchasing of minerals (i.e. outright ownership);

(b) obtaining a lease or concession (see 4.5.1 below);

(c) entering into a production-sharing contract or production-sharing agreement (see 4.5.2 below);

(d) entering into a pure-service contract (see 4.5.3 below);

(e) entering into a service contract (also called a service agreement or risk service contract) (see 4.5.4 below); and

(f) entering into a joint operating agreement (see 4.5.5 below).

Although many of these are more commonly encountered in the oil and gas sector, which is reflected in many of the examples and illustrations below, they are not restricted to this sector and mining companies can and do enter into similar arrangements.

The IASC Issues Paper noted that 'in the mining sector, rights to explore for, develop, and produce minerals are often acquired by purchase of either the mineral rights alone (which does not include ownership of the land surface) or by purchase of both mineral rights and surface rights. In other cases, they are acquired through a right to mine contract, which grants the enterprise the rights to develop and mine the property and may call for a payment at the time the contract becomes effective and subsequent periodic payments. In the mining sector, rights to explore, develop, and produce minerals may also be acquired by mineral leases from private owners or from the government.'[91]

In the oil and gas sector entities usually obtain the rights to explore for, develop, and produce oil and gas through mineral leases, concession agreements, production-sharing contracts, or service contracts.[92] However arrangements similar to production sharing contracts are becoming more common in the mining sector. The type of legal arrangement used depends to a large extent on the legal framework of the country and market practice. The main features of each of these legal rights to access mineral reserves, except for the outright ownership of minerals, are discussed below.

The extract below from the financial statements of TOTAL illustrates the different types of legal arrangements that an oil and gas company may enter into to secure access to mineral reserves.

Extract 39.10: TOTAL S.A. (2012)

4 Risk factors [extract]

3. Other risks [extract]

3.7 Legal aspects of the Group's activities [extract]

3.7.1 Legal aspects of the Upstream segment's activities

TOTAL's Upstream segment conducts activities in various countries which are therefore subject to a broad range of regulations. These cover virtually all aspects of exploration and production operations, including leasehold rights, production rates, royalties, environmental protection, exports, taxes and foreign exchange rates. The terms of the concessions, licenses, permits and contracts governing the Group's ownership of oil and gas interests vary from country to country. These concessions, licenses, permits and contracts are generally granted by or entered into with a government entity or a state-owned company and are sometimes entered into with private owners. These arrangements usually take the form of concessions or production sharing contracts.

In the framework of oil concession agreements, the oil company owns the assets and the facilities and is entitled to the entire production.

In exchange, the operating risks, costs and investments are the oil Company's responsibility and it agrees to remit to the relevant State, usually the owner of the subsoil resources, a production-based royalty, income tax, and possibly other taxes that may apply under local tax legislation.

> The production sharing contract (PSC) involves a more complex legal framework than the concession agreement: it defines the terms and conditions of production sharing and sets the rules governing the cooperation between the Company or consortium in possession of the license and the host State, which is generally represented by a state-owned company. The latter can thus be involved in operating decisions, cost accounting and production allocation.
>
> The consortium agrees to undertake and finance all exploration, development and production activities at its own risk. In exchange, it is entitled to a portion of the production, known as "cost oil", the sale of which should cover all of these expenses (investments and operating costs). The balance of production, known as "profit oil", is then shared in varying proportions, between the Company or consortium, on the one hand, and with the State or the state-owned company, on the other hand.
>
> In some instances, concession agreements and PSCs coexist, sometimes in the same country. Even though there are other contractual models, TOTAL's license portfolio is comprised mainly of concession agreements.
>
> In every country, the authorities of the host State, often assisted by international accounting firms, perform joint venture and PSC cost audits and ensure the observance of contractual obligations.
>
> In some countries, TOTAL has also signed contracts called "risked service contracts", which are similar to production sharing contracts. However, the profit oil is replaced by risked monetary remuneration, agreed by contract, which depends notably on the field performance. Thus, the remuneration under the Iraqi contract is based on an amount calculated per barrel produced.
>
> Oil and gas exploration and production activities are subject to authorization granted by public authorities (licenses), which are granted for specific and limited periods of time and include an obligation to return a large portion, or the entire portion in case of failure, of the area covered by the license at the end of the exploration period.
>
> TOTAL pays taxes on income generated from its oil and gas production and sales activities under its concessions, production sharing contracts and risked service contracts, as provided for by local regulations. In addition, depending on the country, TOTAL's production and sale activities may be subject to a range of other taxes, fees and withholdings, including special petroleum taxes and fees. The taxes imposed on oil and gas production and sales activities may be substantially higher than those imposed on other industrial or commercial businesses.
>
> The legal framework of TOTAL's exploration and production activities, established through concessions, licenses, permits and contracts granted by or entered into with a government entity, a state-owned company or, sometimes, private owners, is subject to certain risks that, in certain cases, can reduce or challenge the protections offered by this legal framework.

4.5.1 Mineral leases and concession agreements

In most countries the government owns all mineral rights, but in some other countries mineral rights can also be directly owned by individuals. While these contracts are negotiated individually, and may therefore each be different, they typically share a large number of common features, which are discussed below:

(a) the *owner/lessor* of the mineral rights retains a *royalty interest*, which entitles it to a specified percentage of the mineral produced. The lessor is normally only required to pay for its share of the severance taxes and the costs of getting the production into a marketable state, but not for any exploration and development costs. The *royalty* is either payable in cash or payable in kind. Although the lessor is normally not interested in receiving its royalty in kind, the option of receiving the royalty in kind is often included for tax purposes;

(b) the lessee obtains a *working interest* under the mineral lease, which entitles it to explore for, develop, and produce minerals from the property as its cost. The working interest can be held by more than one party, in which case a *joint operating agreement* needs to be executed (see 4.5.5 below);

(c) upon signing of the mineral lease agreement the lessee typically pays the lessor a *lease bonus* or *signature bonus*, which is a one-off upfront payment in exchange for the lessor's signing of the mineral lease agreement;

(d) it is in the lessor's interest for the lessee to explore the property as quickly as possible. To ensure that the lessee does not delay exploration and development unnecessarily, the following terms are typically included:
   - most mineral leases define a *primary term* during which the lessee is required to commence drilling;
   - normally the lessee has a *drill or exploration obligation* that must be met within a certain period. However, by paying *delay rentals* the lessee can defer commencement of drilling or exploration; and
   - the mineral lease will remain in force once the obligatory drilling/exploration programme has been completed successfully and production commences, but the lease will be cancelled if activities are suspended for a prolonged period;

(e) most mineral leases provide that the lessee and the lessor have the right to assign their interest without approval to another party. This means that both the lessee and the lessor can create new rights out of existing rights (see 4.6 below);

(f) under many oil and gas lease contracts the lessee can be required to pay *shut-in royalties* when a successful well capable of commercial production has been completed, but production has not commenced within a specified time; and

(g) the lessor is typically not entitled to royalties on any minerals consumed in producing further minerals from a property.

4.5.1.A Concessionary agreements (concessions)

Concessionary agreements or concessions are mineral leases 'under which the government owning mineral rights grants the concessionaire the right to explore, develop, and produce the minerals'.[93] However, unlike a production sharing contract (see 4.5.2 below), under a concessionary agreement the extractive industries company retains title to the assets constructed during the term of the concession. Furthermore, the company bears all the risks and there is no profit sharing arrangement with the government. Rather, the government is entitled to a royalty computed in much the same way as a royalty under lease contracts.[94] In addition, depending on the country's fiscal policies, the government will typically also collect taxes such as duties, severance or production taxes, and income taxes.

In some jurisdictions the government may retain the option to participate in the project as a working interest owner in the property. In this case, the company initially holds 100% of the working interest. If the project is successful and reserves are found, the national oil company or entity representing the government becomes a working interest owner and will pay for its proportionate share of the investment.

4.5.2 Production sharing contracts

A production sharing contract (PSC) or production sharing arrangement (PSA) is a contract between a national oil company (NOC) or the government of a host country and a contracting entity (contractor) to carry out oil and gas exploration and production activities in accordance with the terms of the contract, with the two parties sharing mineral output.[95] While these arrangements have historically been more commonly found in the oil and gas sector, similar types of arrangements do exist in the mining sector.

In such countries the ownership of the mineral reserves in the ground does not pass to the contractor. Instead, the contractor is permitted to recover its costs and share in the profits from the exploration and production activities. Although the precise form and content of a PSC may vary, the following features are likely to be encountered:[96]

(a) the government retains ownership of the reserves and grants the contractor the right to explore for, develop, and produce the reserves;

(b) the government is often directly involved in the operation of the property, either by way of an *operating committee* that comprises representatives of the contractor and the government or NOC, or by requiring the contractor to submit its annual work programme and corresponding annual budget to the government or NOC for approval. The contractor is responsible to the NOC for carrying out operations in accordance with contract terms;

(c) upon signing of the PSC the contractor pays the government a *signature bonus*, which is a one-off upfront payment in exchange for the government's signing of the PSC;

(d) the contractor pays the government a *production bonus* upon commencement of production and when the average production over a given period first exceeds a threshold level;

(e) the government is entitled to a *royalty payment* that is calculated as a percentage of the net production (i.e. net of petroleum lost, flared or re-injected) and which is payable in kind or in cash at the option of the government. The royalty rate applicable is not necessarily a fixed percentage, but may depend on the production volume or destination of the production (e.g. different rates may apply to crude oil and gas that is exported);

(f) the contractor provides all financing and technology necessary to carry out operations and pays all of the costs specified;

(g) the contractor is typically required to bear all of the risks related to exploration and, perhaps, development (i.e. the government does not have a working interest during the exploration and development phases);

(h) the contractor is frequently required to provide infrastructure, such as streets, electricity, water systems, roads, hospitals, schools, and other items during various phases of activities. Additionally, the contract customarily requires the contractor to provide specified training of personnel. Infrastructure and training costs may or may not be recoverable from future production by the contractor;[97]

(i) the contractor may have a *domestic market obligation* that requires them to meet, as a priority, the needs of domestic oil and/or gas consumption in the host country. Alternatively, the contractor may be required to sell oil and/or gas to the NOC at the official oil or gas price;

(j) the contractor is normally committed to completing a *minimum work programme* in each of the phases of the project, which generally needs to be completed within a specified period. If the work is not performed, the contract may require the unspent amount to be paid in cash to the government;

(k) a PSC normally requires *relinquishment* of a certain percentage of the original contract area by the end of the initial term of the exploration period. A further reduction is typically required by the end of the exploration period. The government can negotiate a new contract with another party for the continued exploration of the surrendered acreage. Any data and information relating to the surrendered area often becomes the exclusive property of the government;

(l) equipment that is acquired for the development and production activities normally becomes the property of the government or NOC;

(m) operating costs and specified exploration and development costs are recoverable out of *cost recovery oil*, which is a specified percentage of production revenues after the royalty payment each year. The PSC specifies whether particular types of cost are recoverable or non-recoverable. Recoverable costs not recovered by the contractor in the current period can be carried forward to the following reporting period for recovery purposes;

(n) revenues remaining after royalty and cost recovery are called *profit oil*. Profit oil is split between the government and the contractor on a predetermined basis;

(o) many PSCs provide that the income tax to which the contractor is subject is deemed to have been paid to the government as part of the payment of profit oil (see 4.17.2 below); and

(p) some PSCs give the contractor the right to set up a decommissioning reserve fund which enables the contractor to recover the costs associated with future decommissioning and site restoration. In cases where the PSC terminates before the end of the life of the field, the government is typically responsible for decommissioning and site restoration.

Even in situations where the provisions of a PSC are fairly straightforward at first sight, it may be rather complicated to calculate the entitlement of each of the parties involved as is illustrated in the example below.

Example 39.5: Production sharing contract

An oil and gas company (contractor) entered into a PSC that includes the following terms:

- the oil and gas company pays for all exploration costs;
- the government is entitled to:
  - 15% royalty on the production;
  - severance tax of USD 2.50 per barrel;
  - USD 5 million production bonus when average production first exceeds 25,000 barrels per day; and
  - 10% of the profit oil;
- operating expenses are recoverable before exploration costs;
- development costs are recoverable after exploration costs;
- cost recovery oil is capped at 45% of the annual production; and
- the national oil company (NOC) and the contractor have a 51% and 49% working interest, respectively.

How should the production be allocated between parties, assuming the following for 2013?

- annual production in 2013 is 10 million barrels;
- recoverable operating costs in 2013 are USD 25 million;
- the average oil price in 2013 is USD 100/barrel (this amount is used to convert any amount calculated in monetary units i.e. USD, back into volumetric units i.e. barrels of oil;
- during 2013 average production exceeded 25,000 barrels per day for the first time;
- unrecovered exploration costs at the beginning of 2013 were USD 180 million; and
- unrecovered development costs at the beginning of 2013 were USD 275 million.

		Barrels	Contractor (49%)	NOC (51%)	Government
			bbls	bbls	bbls
Production in 2013	a	10,000,000			
Royalty 15% of 10,000,000 =	b	1,500,000			1,500,000
Severance tax 10,000,000 × $2.50 ÷ $100 =	c	250,000			250,000
Cost oil					
Operating costs $25,000,000 ÷ $100 =	d	250,000	122,500	127,500	
Exploration cost $180,000,000 ÷ $100 =	e	1,800,000	1,800,000		
Development cost $275,000,000 ÷ $100, but capped at 2,450,000	f	2,450,000	1,200,500	1,249,500	
Total cost oil 45% of 10,000,000 =	g	4,500,000			
Production bonus $5,000,000 ÷ $100 =	h	50,000			50,000
Profit oil: a – b – c – g – h =	i	3,700,000			
Government profit oil 10% of 3,700,000 =	j	370,000			370,000
Working interest in profit oil 3,700,000 – 370,000 =	k	3,330,000	1,631,700	1,698,300	
Total		10,000,000	4,754,700	3,075,300	2,170,000
Unrecovered development costs $275,000,000 – (2,450,000 × $100) =		$30,000,000	$14,700,000	$15,300,000	

The above example illustrates not only that calculating an entity's share in the production of the current period requires a detailed knowledge of the PSC's provisions, but also that calculating the contractor's share of the remaining reserves requires a number of assumptions.

The reserves and production that the parties are entitled to varies depending on the oil price. Had the average oil price in 2013 been $50/barrel the parties' entitlements would have been as follows: Contractor 5,540,400 barrels, NOC 2,019,600 barrels and Government 2,440,000 barrels. The quantity of reserves and production attributable to each of the parties often reacts to changes in oil prices in ways that, at first, might seem counterintuitive.

It is also worth noting that the type and nature of contracts emerging continue to evolve. New contracts emerging have some attributes of PSCs, but do differ from the traditional PSC. Therefore, determining the accounting implications of these contracts is becoming increasingly complex. This not only has an impact on the accounting for such contracts but also on whether, and the extent to which, the contractor entity is able to recognise reserves.

Reserves recognition involves a considerable amount of judgement. Each contractual arrangement needs to be analysed carefully to determine whether reserves recognition is appropriate. Such an analysis would include, at a minimum:

- The extent of risk to which the contractor party is exposed, including exploration and/or development risk;
- The structure of the contractor's reimbursement arrangements and whether it is subject to performance/reservoir risk or price risk;
- The ability for the contractor to take product in-kind, rather than a cash reimbursement only.

Other facts and circumstances may also be relevant in reaching the final assessment. Given the varying terms and conditions that exist within these contracts and the fact that they are continuing to change/evolve, each contract will need to be individually analysed and assessed in detail.

4.5.3 *Pure-service contracts*

'A pure-service contract is an agreement between a contractor and a host government that typically covers a defined technical service to be provided or completed during a specific period of time. The service company investment is typically limited to the value of equipment, tools, and personnel used to perform the service. In most cases, the service contractor's reimbursement is fixed by the terms of the contract with little exposure to either project performance or market factors. Payment for services is normally based on daily or hourly rates, a fixed turnkey rate, or some other specified amount. Payments may be made at specified intervals or at the completion of the service. Payments, in some cases, may be tied to the field performance, operating cost reductions, or other important metrics.

The risks of the service company under this type of contract are usually limited to non-recoverable cost overruns, losses owing to client breach of contract, default, or contractual dispute. These agreements generally do not have exposure to production volume or market price; consequently, reserves are not usually recognised under this type of agreement.'[98] Such a contract is generally considered to be a management contract that gives rise to revenue from rendering services and not income from the production of mineral. Therefore, the minerals produced are not included in the normal reserve disclosures of the contractor,[99] and the contractor bears no risk if reserves are not found. It is worth noting that such contracts do need to be assessed for embedded leases in accordance with the requirements of IFRIC 4. See Section 4.16.1 below for more information.

4.5.4 Risk service contracts

Unlike pure-service contracts, under a risk service contract (also called risked service agreement or at-risk service contract) a fee is not certain: an entity (contractor) agrees to explore for, develop, and produce minerals on behalf of a host government, but the contractor is at risk for the amount spent on exploration and development costs. That is, if no minerals are found in commercial quantities, no fee is paid.[100] Although a risk service contract (RSC) does not result in the contractor's ownership of the minerals in place, the contractor may be at risk for the costs of exploration and may have economic interest in those minerals. The IASC Issues Paper noted that in the case of risk service contracts:[101]

- the fee may be payable in cash or in minerals produced;
- the contract may call for the contractor to bear all or part of the costs of exploration that are usually recoverable, in whole or in part, from production. If there is no production, there is no recovery; and
- the contract may also give the contractor the right to purchase part of the minerals produced.

As noted in Extract 39.10 above from TOTAL's financial statements, risk service contracts are similar to PSCs in a number of respects. Although the precise form and content of a risk service contract may vary, the following features are common:

(a) the repayment of expenses and the compensation for services are established on a monetary basis;

(b) an RSC is for a limited period, after which the government or national oil company will take over operations;

(c) under an RSC the contractor does not obtain ownership of the mineral reserves or production;

(d) the contractor is normally required to carry out a minimum amount of work in providing the contracted services;

(e) the fee that is payable to the contractor covers its capital expenditure, operating costs and an agreed-upon profit margin; and

(f) ownership of the assets used under the contract passes to the government when the contractor has been reimbursed for its costs.

The SPE's *Guidelines for the Evaluation of Petroleum Reserves and Resources* notes in connection with risk service contracts that 'under the existing regulations, it may be more difficult for the contractor to justify reserves recognition, and special care must be taken in drafting the agreement. If regulations are satisfied, reserves equivalent to the value of the cost-recovery-plus-revenue-profit split are normally reported by the contractor.'[102]

The nature and terms and conditions of these risk service contracts continue to change over time. Therefore each contract will need to be analysed in detail to determine how it should be accounted for.

4.5.5 Joint operating agreements

When several entities are involved in a joint arrangement (e.g. joint ownership of a property, production sharing contract or concession) they will need to enter into some form of joint operating agreement (JOA). A JOA is a contract between two or more parties to a joint arrangement that sets out the rights and obligations to operate the property. Typically, a JOA designates one of the working interest owners as the operator and it governs the operations and sharing of costs between parties. A JOA does not override, but instead builds upon, the contracts that are already in place (such as production sharing contracts). In fact, many production sharing contracts require the execution of a JOA between the parties. A JOA may give rise to a joint arrangement under IFRS 11 (see 4.4.2 above).

4.6 Different types of royalty interests

4.6.1 Working interest and basic royalties

As discussed at 4.5.1 above, under a mineral lease the owner/lessor of the mineral rights retains a *basic royalty* interest (or non-operating interest), which entitles it to a specified percentage of the mineral produced, while the lessee obtains a *working interest* (or operating interest) under the mineral lease, which entitles it to explore for, develop, and produce minerals from the property.

If the owner of a working interest cannot fund or does not wish to bear the risk of exploration, development or production from the property, it may be able – if this is permitted by the underlying lease – to sell the working interest or to create new types of interest out of its existing working interest. By creating new types of non-operating interests, the working interest owner is able to raise financing and spread the risk of the development. The original working interest holder may either:

- retain the new non-operating interest and transfer the working interest (i.e. the rights and obligations for exploring, developing and operating the property); or
- carve out and transfer a new non-operating interest to another party, while retaining the working interest.

The following non-operating interests are commonly created in practice:[103]

- overriding royalties (see 4.6.2 below);
- production payment royalties (see 4.6.3 below); and
- net profits interests (see 4.6.4 below).

4.6.2 Overriding royalties

An *overriding royalty* is very similar to a basic royalty, except that the former is created out of the operating interest and if the operating interest expires, the overriding royalty also expires.[104] An overriding royalty owner bears only its share of production taxes and sometimes of the costs incurred to get the product into a saleable condition.

4.6.3 Production payment royalties

A *production payment royalty* is the right to recover a specified amount of cash or a specified quantity of minerals, out of the working interest's share of gross production. For example, the working interest holder may assign a production payment royalty to another party for USD 12 million, in exchange for a repayment of USD 15 million plus 12% interest out of the first 65% of the working interest holder's share of production. Production payments that are specified as a quantity of minerals are often called volumetric production payments or VPPs.

4.6.4 Net profits interests

A *net profits interest* is similar to an overriding royalty. However, the amount to be received by the royalty owner is a share of the net proceeds from production (as defined in the contract) that is paid solely from the working interest owner's share. The owner of a net profits interest is not liable for any expenses.

4.6.5 Revenue and royalties: gross or net?

Many mineral leases, concession agreements and production sharing contracts require the payment of a royalty to the original owner of the mineral reserves or the government. Under IAS 18 it is not entirely clear whether revenue should be presented net of royalty payments or not. Historically, many companies have presented revenue net of those royalties that are paid in kind as they never received any inflow of economic benefits. *[IAS 18.8].* However, an entity that is required to sell the physical product in the market and remit the net proceeds (after deduction of certain costs incurred) to the royalty holder, may be exposed to risks and rewards of ownership to such an extent that it is appropriate to present revenue on a gross basis and include the royalty payment within cost of sales.

Extracts 39.11 and 39.12 below, from the financial statements of Premier Oil and BHP Billiton respectively, illustrate typical accounting policies for royalties under IFRS.

Extract 39.11: Premier Oil plc (2012)

ACCOUNTING POLICIES [extract]

Royalties

Royalties are charged as production costs to the income statement in the year in which the related production is recognised as income.

Extract 39.12: BHP Billiton (2012)

9.1.6 Notes to Financial Statements

1 Accounting policies [extract]

Sales revenue [extract]

Revenue is not reduced for royalties and other taxes payable from the Group's production.

Extract 39.13 below, from the financial statements of Statoil, illustrates some of the complications that may arise in determining revenue when an entity sells product on behalf of the government.

> *Extract 39.13: Statoil ASA (2012)*
>
> **8.1 Notes to the Consolidated financial statements** [extract]
>
> **8.1.2 Significant accounting policies** [extract]
>
> **Transactions with the Norwegian State**
>
> Statoil markets and sells the Norwegian State's share of oil and gas production from the Norwegian Continental Shelf (NCS). The Norwegian State's participation in petroleum activities is organised through the State's direct financial interest (SDFI). All purchases and sales of the SDFI's oil production are classified as *Purchases [net of inventory variation]* and *Revenues,* respectively. Statoil ASA sells, in its own name, but for the Norwegian State's account and risk, the State's production of natural gas. This sale, and related expenditures refunded by the Norwegian State, are presented net in the Consolidated financial statements. Sales made by Statoil subsidiaries in their own name, and related expenditure, are however presented gross in the Consolidated financial statements where the applicable subsidiary is considered the principal when selling natural gas on behalf of the Norwegian State. In accounting for these sales activities, the Norwegian State's share of profit or loss is reflected in Statoil's *Selling, general and administrative expenses* as expenses or reduction of expenses, respectively.

The SPE-PRMS (see 2.2.1 above) notes that 'royalty volumes should be deducted from the lessee's entitlement to resources. In some agreements, royalties owned by the host government are actually treated as taxes to be paid in cash. In such cases, the equivalent royalty volumes are controlled by the contractor who may (subject to regulatory guidance) elect to report these volumes as reserves and/or contingent resources with appropriate offsets (increase in operating expense) to recognize the financial liability of the royalty obligation.'[105]

4.7 Risk-sharing arrangements

As discussed at 1.1 above, the high costs and high risks in the extractive industries often lead entities to enter into risk-sharing arrangements. The following types of risk-sharing arrangements are discussed in this chapter:

- carried interests (see 4.7.1 below);
- farm-ins and farm-outs (see 4.7.2 below);
- asset swaps (see 4.7.3 below);
- unitisations (see 5.1 below);
- investments in subsidiaries, joint arrangements and associates (see 4.4 above);
- production sharing contracts (see 4.5.2 above), which result in a degree of risk sharing with local governments; and
- risk service contracts (see 4.5.4 above).

4.7.1 Carried interests

Carried interests often arise when a party in an arrangement is either unable or unwilling to bear the risk of exploration or is unable or unwilling to fund its share of the cost of exploration or development. A carried interest is an agreement under which one party (the carrying party) agrees to pay for a portion or all of the pre-production costs of another party (the carried party) on a licence in which both own a portion of the working interest.[106] In effect, commercially, the carried party is trading a share of any production to which it is entitled in the future in exchange for the carrying party funding one or more phases of the project. In other words, the parties create a new interest out of an existing working interest. If the project is unsuccessful then the carrying party will not be reimbursed for the costs that it has incurred on behalf of the carried party. If the project is successful then the carrying party will be reimbursed either in cash out of proceeds of the share of production attributable to the carried party, or by receiving a disproportionately high share of the production until the carried costs have been recovered.[107]

4.7.1.A Types of carried interest arrangements

Carried interest arrangements tend to fall into one of the following two categories:

- *Financing-type arrangements* – The carrying party provides funding to the carried party and receives a lender's return on the funds provided, while the right to additional production acts as a security that underpins the arrangement; or
- *Purchase/sale-type arrangement* – The carried party effectively sells an interest or a partial interest in a project to the carrying party. The carrying party will be required to fund the project in exchange for an increased share of any proceeds if the project succeeds, while the carried party retains a much reduced share of any proceeds.

In practice, however, it is not always easy to determine in which category a particular carried interest arrangement falls, as is illustrated in the example below.

Example 39.6: Carried interests (1)

Scenario 1

The carrying party has proposed a $10 million project, which has a very high chance of succeeding. The carried party, which is unable to fund its share of the project, agrees that the carrying party is entitled to recover its cost plus 7% interest by giving it a disproportionately high share of the production. If the production from this project is insufficient to repay the initial investment, the carried party should reimburse the carrying party out of its share of production from other fields within the same licence.

Scenario 2

The carrying party has proposed a project that may cost up to $6 million, the outcome of which is uncertain. The carried party, which is unwilling to participate in the project, agrees that the carrying party is entitled to all production from the project until it has recovered three times its initial investment.

Scenario 3

The carrying party has proposed a project that may cost up to $5 million, which has a good chance of succeeding. The carrying party has a 60% interest in the licence and the carried party holds the remaining 40%. The carried party, which is unable to fund its share of the project, agrees that the carrying party is entitled to an additional 25% of the production until the carrying party has recovered its costs plus a 20% return.

Some of the indicators that a carried interest arrangement should be accounted for as a financing-type arrangement are that:

- the carried party is unable to fund its share of the project;
- the risks associated with the development are not significant, i.e. financing-type arrangements will be more common in the development stage; and
- the carrying party receives a return that is comparable to a lender's rate of return.

Indicators that a carried interest arrangement should be treated as a purchase/sale-type arrangement include:

- the carrying party and carried party have genuinely different opinions about the chances of success of the project, and the carried party could fund its share of the project if it wanted to;
- there are significant uncertainties about the outcome of the project. Purchase/sale-type arrangements are therefore more common in the E&E phase;
- the arrangement gives the carrying party voting rights in the project;
- there are significant uncertainties about the costs of the project, perhaps because it involves use of a new technology or approach;
- the carrying party could lose all of its investment or possibly earn a return significantly in excess of a lender's rate of return; and
- the carrying party can only recover its investment from the project that is subject to the arrangement and there is no recourse to other assets or interests of the carried party.

In Example 39.6 above, scenario 1 has the characteristics of a financing-type arrangement, while scenario 2 has those of a purchase/sale-type arrangement. However, when an arrangement (such as scenario 3) has financing-type and purchase/sale-type characteristics (e.g. as a result of the relative bargaining strength of the parties), an entity will need to analyse the arrangement carefully and exercise judgement in developing an appropriate accounting policy.

The following types of carried interest arrangements are discussed below:

- carried interest arrangements in the E&E phase (see 4.7.1.B below);
- financing-type carried interest arrangements in the development phase (see 4.7.1.C below); and
- purchase/sale-type carried interest arrangements in the development phase (see 4.7.1.D below).

4.7.1.B Carried interest arrangements in the E&E phase

While IFRS 6 should be applied to accounting for E&E expenditures, the standard does not address other aspects of accounting by entities engaged in the exploration for and evaluation of mineral resources. *[IFRS 6.4].* That leaves unanswered the question of whether carried interest arrangements can ever fall within the scope of IFRS 6. In the case of a purchase/sale-type carried interest arrangement the transaction, at least in economic terms, leads to the acquisition of an E&E asset by the carrying party and a disposal by the carried party. Therefore, we believe that purchase/sale-type carried interest arrangements would fall within the scope of IFRS 6. Hence an entity has two options: either to develop an accounting policy under IAS 8 as discussed at 4.7.1.D below, or to develop an accounting policy under IFRS 6 that is based on its previous national GAAP. In practice this usually means that:

- the carrying party accounts for its expenditures under a carried interest arrangement in the same way as directly incurred E&E expenditure (see 3.2 and 3.3 above); and
- the carried party may need to recognise a loss when the terms of the transaction indicate that the asset is impaired. However, to the extent that an arrangement is favourable, the carried party would – depending on its accounting policy – recognise the gain either in profit or loss or as a reduction in the carrying amount of the E&E asset.

On the other hand, a finance-type carried interest arrangement (which is generally not as common in the E&E phase) that has no significant impact on the risks and rewards that an entity derives from the underlying E&E working interest, may be more akin to a funding arrangement. As IFRS 6 deals only with accounting for E&E expenditures and assets, it is a matter of judgement whether or not the accounting for finance-type carried interest arrangements is considered to be outside the scope of IFRS 6. If an arrangement is considered to be outside the scope of IFRS 6, it might be sensible to account for it in the same way as finance-type carried interest arrangements that relate to projects that are not in the E&E phase (see 4.7.1.C below).

4.7.1.C Financing-type carried interest arrangements in the development phase

As financing-type carried interest arrangements do not result in the transfer of the economic risks and rewards of the underlying working interest between parties, such arrangements are not accounted for as a sale (purchase) by the carried party (carrying party). Instead these arrangements are in effect secured borrowings in which the underlying asset is used as collateral that provides an identifiable stream of cash flows.

These arrangements are most appropriately accounted for as giving rise to a financial asset for the carrying party and a financial liability for the carried party.

The carried party will continue to recognise the expenditure incurred in relation to its full share of the working interest prior to the execution of the carried interest arrangement, and a corresponding financial liability for the amount that it is expected to reimburse to the carrying party as the pre-production costs being met by the carrying party are incurred, irrespective of whether it is a non-recourse arrangement or not. The liability is accounted for as a loan at amortised cost under IAS 39, which means that the carried party should accrete interest on the liability and reduce the loan to the extent the carrying party recovers its costs. It should be noted, however, that the application of the effective interest rate method under IAS 39 requires adjustment of the carrying amount when the entity revises its estimates of the payments to be made. *[IAS 39.AG8].*

Conversely the carrying party should recognise a financial asset for the amount that it expects to recover as a reimbursement as the pre-production costs (which are being met by the carrying party) are incurred. Classification of this financial asset as a loan or receivable under IAS 39 is only possible when the carrying party expects to recover substantially all of its entire investment. *[IAS 39.9]*. This should normally be the case in financing-type carried interest arrangements. Note that the requirements of IFRS 9 have not been considered in this chapter – see Chapter 45.

This approach to accounting for carried interest arrangements might not be appropriate if there were more than an insignificant transfer of risk (without necessarily resulting in a purchase/sale-type carried interest arrangement). Many argue that the transfer of risk would suggest that:

- the carried party should recognise a provision under IAS 37 rather than a liability under IAS 39; and
- the carrying party should account for its right to receive reimbursement as an available-for-sale investment under IAS 39 or a reimbursement right under IAS 37.

4.7.1.D Purchase/sale-type carried interest arrangements in the development phase

The accounting suggested here for the carried party is the same as that required by paragraph 155 of the OIAC SORP in UK GAAP, which states that the disposal should be accounted for in accordance with the entity's normal accounting policy.

Historically, some entities have accounted for these types of transactions on a cash basis, i.e. the carried party does nothing and the carrying party accounts for its actual cash outlays. It is hard to see how this can be justified under IFRS.

In purchase/sale-type carried interest arrangements, the carried party effectively sells part of its interest in a project to the carrying party. For example, the carried party may sell part of its interest in the mineral reserves to the carrying party which, in exchange, is obliged to fund the remaining costs of developing the field. Consequently, the arrangement has two elements, the purchase/sale of mineral reserves and the funding of developments costs, which should be accounted for in accordance with their substance. Therefore, the carried party should:

- derecognise the part of the asset that it has sold to the carrying party, consistent with the derecognition principles of IAS 16 or IAS 38. *[IAS 16.67, IAS 38.112]*. Determining the amount to be derecognised may require a considerable amount of judgement depending on how the interest sold is defined;
- recognise the consideration received or receivable from the carrying party;
- recognise a gain or loss on the transaction for the difference between the net disposal proceeds and the carrying amount of the asset disposed of. Recognition of a gain would be appropriate only when the value of the consideration can be determined reliably. If not, then the carried party should account for the consideration received as a reduction in the carrying amount of the underlying assets; and
- test the retained interest for impairment if the terms of the arrangement indicate that the retained interest may be impaired.

In accounting for its purchase the carrying party should:

- recognise an asset that represents the underlying (partially) undeveloped interest acquired at cost in accordance with IAS 16 or IAS 38. *[IAS 16.15, IAS 38.21].* Cost is defined in these standards as 'the amount of cash or cash equivalents paid or the fair value of the other consideration given to acquire an asset at the time of its acquisition or construction or, where applicable, the amount attributed to that asset when initially recognised in accordance with the specific requirements of other IFRSs'; *[IAS 16.6, IAS 38.8]* and
- recognise a liability for the obligation to make defined payments on behalf of the carried party, which relate to the carried party's share of future investments.

The application of this approach is illustrated in Example 39.7 below.

Example 39.7: Carried interests (2)

An oil and gas company is developing an oil field in the North Sea. Assume that the company did not capitalise any E&E costs in relation to the field, but that by 1 January 2013 it had capitalised $250 million of costs in relation to the construction of property, plant and equipment. To complete the development of the oil field and bring it to production a further investment in property, plant and equipment of $350 million is required in the first half of 2013.

At 1 January 2013, the oil and gas company (the carried party) enters into a purchase/sale-type carried interest arrangement with a carrying party, which will fund the entire $350 million required for the further development of the field. Upon entering into the carried interest arrangement the carried party's entitlement to oil is expected to be reduced from 15,000,000 barrels of oil to 9,000,000 barrels of oil, i.e. its interest in the oil field and the related property, plant and equipment has been reduced to (9,000,000 ÷ 15,000,000 =) 60%. In practice, calculating the portion of the interest sold may require a considerable amount of judgement (e.g. in scenario 2 in Example 39.6 above it would not be straightforward to calculate the portion of the interest sold).

Both parties believe that the fair value of the oil field and related property, plant and equipment will be $1 billion once the remaining investment of $350 million has been made. Consequently, the fair value of the oil field and related property, plant and equipment at 1 January 2013 is ($1 billion – $350 million =) $650 million.

The fair value of the interest acquired (which comprises a portion of the oil field and a portion of the related property, plant and equipment) by the carrying party is (40% × $650 million =) $260 million. In exchange for its interest, the carrying party will pay $50 million in cash and undertakes to pay the remaining investments related to the carried party's interest.

The carried party accounts for the transaction as follows:

	$	$
Cash received from the carrying party	50	
Capital calls to be paid by the carrying party (60% × $350 million =) †	210	
Property, plant and equipment (40% × $250 million =)		100
Gain on sale (40% × ($650 million – $250 million) =)		160

† *The carried party has obtained the commitment from the carrying party to make certain payments on its behalf.*

If the carried party had recognised a loss on the interest sold, it would need to perform an impairment test on the interest retained.

The carrying party accounts for the transaction as follows:

	$	$
Assets acquired ($50 million + $210 million =) †	260	
Cash paid to the carried party		50
Capital calls payable on behalf of the carried party (60% × $350 million =) ‡		210

† *As discussed above, the cost of property, plant and equipment is defined as the fair value of the consideration. In an arm's length transaction the fair value of property, plant and equipment acquired is normally equal to the fair value of the consideration paid. The fair value of the portion of the oil field and the portion of the related property, plant and equipment acquired is (40% × $650 million =) $260 million.*

‡ *The carrying party has assumed a liability to make these payments on behalf of the carried party. The carrying party will also be required to pay (40% × $350 million =) $140 million for its own share of the future investments, but that amount is only recognised as a liability upon recognition of the related property, plant and equipment.*

The receivable recognised by the carried party and the corresponding liability recognised by the carrying party are reduced over the course of the construction of the assets to which they relate. The carrying party reduces the liability as it funds the carried party's share of the investment and the carried party recognises its share of the assets being constructed while reducing the balance of the receivable. The carrying party should recognise a provision under IAS 37 if the timing and amount of the liability are uncertain. *[IAS 37.10]*. However, if the carried interest arrangement requires payment of a fixed monetary amount then it could be argued that the liability meets the definition of a financial liability under IAS 32 that should be accounted for in accordance with IAS 39. *[IAS 32.11]*.

4.7.2 Farm-ins and farm-outs

A farm-out (from the viewpoint of the transferor) or a farm-in (from the viewpoint of the transferee) is defined in the OIAC SORP as 'the transfer of part of an oil and gas interest in consideration for an agreement by the transferee ("farmee") to meet, absolutely, certain expenditure which would otherwise have to be undertaken by the owner ("farmor").'[108] Farm-in transactions generally occur in the exploration or development phase and are characterised by the transferor (i.e. farmor) giving up future economic benefits, in the form of reserves, in exchange for a (generally) permanent reduction in future funding obligations.

Under a carried interest arrangement the carried party transfers a *portion* of the risks and rewards of a property, in exchange for a funding commitment from the carrying party. Under a farm-in arrangement the farmor transfers all the risks and rewards of a *proportion* (i.e. a straight percentage) of a property, in exchange for a commitment from the farmee to fund certain expenditures. Therefore, a farm-out represents the complete disposal of a *proportion* of a property and is similar to purchase/sale-type carried interest arrangements as discussed at 4.7.1.D above.

The following types of farm-in arrangements are separately discussed below:

- farm-in arrangements in the E&E phase (see 4.7.2.A below); and
- farm-in arrangements outside the E&E phase (see 4.7.2.B below).

4.7.2.A Farm-in arrangements in the E&E phase

IFRS 6 deals only with accounting for E&E expenditures and does not address other aspects of accounting by entities engaged in the exploration for and evaluation of mineral resources. *[IFRS 6.4]*. That leaves open the question of whether farm-in arrangements can ever fall within the scope of IFRS 6. However, as a farm-in arrangement leads to the acquisition of an E&E asset by the farmee and a disposal by the farmor, we believe that a farm-in arrangement would fall within the scope of IFRS 6. Hence an entity has two options: either to develop an accounting policy under IAS 8 as discussed at 4.7.2.B below; or to develop an accounting policy under IFRS 6. In practice many entities use the second option and apply an accounting policy to farm-in arrangements that is based on their previous national GAAP.

Accounting policies for farm-in arrangements in the E&E phase that are based on an entity's previous national GAAP will often require that:

- the farmee recognises its expenditure under the arrangement in respect of its own interest and that retained by the farmor, as and when the costs are incurred. The farmee accounts for its expenditures under a farm-in arrangement in the same way as directly incurred E&E expenditure; and
- the farmor accounts for the farm-out arrangement as follows:
  - the farmor does not record any expenditure made by the farmee on its behalf;
  - the farmor does not recognise a gain or loss on the farm-out arrangement, but rather redesignates any costs previously capitalised in relation to the whole interest as relating to the partial interest retained; and
  - any cash consideration received is credited against costs previously capitalised in relation to the whole interest with any excess accounted for by the farmor as a gain on disposal.

If an entity applies its previous GAAP accounting policy in respect of farm-in arrangements, we would expect the entity also to make the farm-in disclosures required by its previous GAAP.

Extract 39.16 at 4.7.2.C below shows Revus Energy's historical cost based accounting policy, under which no gain or loss is recognised, for farm-in transactions in the exploration phase.

4.7.2.B Farm-in arrangements outside the E&E phase: accounting by the farmee

A farm-in represents the complete acquisition of a *proportion* of a property. Therefore, the farmee should recognise an asset that represents the underlying (partially) undeveloped interest acquired at cost in accordance with IAS 16 or IAS 38, *[IAS 16.15, IAS 38.21]*, and recognise a liability that reflects obligations to fund the farmor's share of the future investment from which the farmee itself will not derive any future economic benefits.

Farm-in arrangements can be structured in numerous ways, some requiring payment of a fixed monetary amount while others are more flexible and state, for example, that capital expenditures over the next five years will be paid for by the farmee regardless of what those amounts may be. Accounting for these arrangements is uncertain. In some cases it could be argued that the liability meets the definition of a financial liability under IAS 32 and should be accounted for in accordance with IAS 39. In other scenarios, such as the latter example above (i.e., where the farmee pays all capital expenditure incurred over a five year period, regardless of the amount), some argue a provision under IAS 37 should be recognised as the timing and amount of the liability are uncertain. *[IAS 37.10]*. If an entity concludes that IAS 37 applies then there is usually a debate as to when a provision should be recognised as that standard is not clear. The issue of contingent consideration in the context of the acquisition of assets has been discussed by the Interpretations Committee (see 4.8.4 below) but they have been unable (so far) to reach consensus on initial recognition of such amounts. Specifically, they have been unable to agree which standard applies, that is whether IAS 37 applies or IAS 39 applies. Hence, different treatments will continue to be encountered in practice. The arrangements are illustrated below in the extract from Newcrest's 2009 financial statements.

Extract 39.14: Newcrest Mining Limited (2009)

29. Interests in Unincorporated Joint Venture Assets [extract]

(b) Acquisition of Interest in the Morobe Mining Joint Venture [extract]

During the year Newcrest acquired a 50% interest in the Papua New Guinea (PNG) gold assets of Harmony Gold Mining Ltd (Harmony) via unincorporated joint venture structures. The joint venture assets comprise:

- The Hidden Valley mining operation, a gold and silver project, expected to produce over 250,000 ounces of gold and 4 million ounces of silver per annum over a 14-year mine life;
- The highly-prospective Wafi-Golpu gold-copper deposit and its surrounding exploration tenements; and
- Extensive exploration tenements in the Morobe province of PNG.

The acquisition of the interest in the joint ventures comprised two stages:

- In the first stage, which was completed on 7 August 2008, Newcrest acquired an initial 30.01% interest for cash consideration of US$228.0 million (A$249.4 million) consisting of an initial payment of US$180.0 million together with a reimbursement to Harmony of US$48.0 million in project expenditure incurred between 1 January 2008 and 7 August 2008.
- The second stage represented a farm-in commitment for the remaining 19.99% interest. In this stage, Newcrest solely funded all project expenditure up to 30 June 2009 which totalled US$297.7 million (A$420.8 million).

4.7.2.C Farm-in arrangements outside the E&E phase: accounting by the farmor

In accounting for a farm-in arrangement the farmor should:

- derecognise the proportion of the asset that it has sold to the farmee, consistent with the principles of IAS 16 or IAS 38; *[IAS 16.67, IAS 38.112]*
- recognise the consideration received or receivable from the farmee, which represents the farmee's obligation to fund the capital expenditure in relation to the interest retained by the farmor;
- recognise a gain or loss on the transaction for the difference between the net disposal proceeds and the carrying amount of the asset disposed of. *[IAS 16.71, IAS 38.113]*. Recognition of a gain would be appropriate only when the value of the consideration can be determined reliably. If not, then the carried party should account for the consideration received as a reduction in the carrying amount of the underlying assets; and
- test the retained interests for impairment if the terms of the arrangement indicate that the retained interest may be impaired.

Under IAS 16 and IAS 38, the consideration receivable on disposal of an item of property, plant and equipment or an intangible asset is recognised initially at its fair value by the farmor. However, if 'payment for the item is deferred, the consideration received is recognised initially at the cash price equivalent. The difference between the nominal amount of the consideration and the cash price equivalent is recognised as interest revenue in accordance with IAS 18 reflecting the effective yield on the receivable.' *[IAS 16.72, IAS 38.116]*. Any part of the consideration that is receivable in the form of cash will meet the definition of a financial asset under IAS 32 and should be accounted for in accordance with IAS 39, *[IAS 32.11]*; either at amortised cost or fair value depending on how the farmor designates the receivable.

The extract below describes the farm-in transactions of Harmony Gold.

Extract 39.15: Harmony Gold Mining Company Limited (2009)

Directors' report [extract]

Disposals [extract]

Sale of interest in PNG to Newcrest

During the year, the group sold 50% of its interest in its PNG assets in Morobe Province to Newcrest. This took place in three stages, with the disposal of 30.01% for US$229 million (stage one) being completed on 31 July 2008. Stages two and three were completed by the end of quarters three and four of the financial year respectively with Newcrest having earned in a further 10% and 9.99% respectively in each of these stages.

Notes to the group financial statements [extract]

6 Profit of sale of property, plant and equipment [extract]

Included in the total for 2009 is R931 million (US$111.9 million) profit on sale of 50% of Harmony's gold and copper assets in Morobe Province, Papua New Guinea, to Newcrest Mining Limited (Newcrest) in terms of the Master Purchase and Farm-in agreement. The sale was concluded in three stages. On 31 July 2008, stage 1, being the sale of an initial 30.1% participating interest in the assets, was concluded at a profit of R416 million (US$57.9 million). The remaining 19.99% interest was sold in two further stages, resulting in a profit of R439 million (US$44.6 million) for the 10% interest of stage 2 and a profit of R76 million (US$9.9 million) for the 9.99% interest of stage 3. These stages were completed on 27 February 2009 and 30 June 2009 respectively. Refer to note 23.

23 Investment in joint venture [extract]

a) Papua New Guinea (PNG) Partnership agreement (50%)

On 22 April 2008, Morobe Consolidated Goldfields Limited and WafiMining Limited, subsidiaries of Harmony Australia, entered into a Master Purchase and Farm-in Agreement with Newcrest. This agreement provided for Newcrest to purchase a 30.01% participating interest (stage 1) and a further farm-in of an additional 19.99% participating interest in Harmony's PNG gold and copper assets, giving them a 50% interest. The total value of the transaction was estimated at US$530 million.

On 16 July 2008, the conditions to the Master Purchase and Farm-in agreement were finalised, which included regulatory and statutory approvals by the PNG Government. Stage 1 completion took place on 31 July 2008, and a total consideration of R1 792 million (US$229.8 million) was received on 7 August 2008, of which R390 million (US$50 million) was placed in a jointly controlled escrow account. This amount was subsequently released to Harmony following confirmation of approval of an exploration licence during September 2008 by the PNG mining authorities.

Harmony recognised a profit of R416 million (US$58 million) on the completion of stage 1, which represented a sale of a 30.01% undivided interest of Harmony's PNG gold and copper assets and liabilities comprising the joint venture.

During the farm-in period, Harmony agreed to transfer a further 19.99% interest to Newcrest in consideration for an agreement by Newcrest to meet certain expenditure which would otherwise have to be undertaken by Harmony. The interest to be transferred were conditional on the level of capital expenditures funded by Newcrest at certain milestones, and by the end of February 2009, Newcrest acquired another 10% through the farm-in arrangement. The final 9.99% was acquired by 30 June 2009.

At the date of completion of each party's obligations under the farm-in arrangement, Harmony derecognised the proportion of the mining assets and liabilities in the joint venture that it had sold to Newcrest, and recognised its interest in the capital expenditure at fair value. The difference between the net disposal proceeds and the carrying amounts of the asset disposed of during the farm-in arrangement amounted to a gain of R515 million (US$54 million), which has been included in the consolidated income statements for 2009.

The extract below from Revus Energy's 2007 financial statements shows the different accounting policies that it applies to farm-in transactions in the exploration phase and development phase.

Extract 39.16: Revus Energy ASA (2007)

Accounting principles [extract]

Acquisitions and divestments [extract]

Farm-ins generally occur in the exploration or development phase and are characterised by the transferor giving up future economic benefits, in the form of reserves, in exchange for reduced future funding obligations. In the exploration phase the Group accounts for farm-ins on a historical cost basis. As such no gain or loss is recognised. In the development phase, the Group accounts for farm-ins as an acquisition at fair value when the Group is the transferee and a disposal at fair value when the Group is the transferor of a part of an oil and gas property. The fair value is determined by the costs that have been agreed as being borne by the transferee.

4.7.3 Asset swaps

Asset exchanges are transactions that have challenged standard-setters for a number of years. For example, an entity might swap certain intangible assets that it does not require or is no longer allowed to use for those of a counterparty that has other surplus assets. It is not uncommon for entities to exchange assets as part of their portfolio and risk management activities or simply to meet demands of competition authorities.

The key accounting issues that need to be addressed are:

- whether such an exchange should give rise to a profit when the fair value of the asset received is greater than the carrying value of the asset given up; and
- whether the exchange of similar assets should be recognised.

In the extractive industries an exchange of assets could involve property, plant and equipment (PP&E), intangible assets, investment property or E&E assets, which are in the scope of IAS 16, IAS 38, IAS 40 and IFRS 6, respectively. Hence there are three possible types of exchanges (which will be discussed below), those involving:

(a) only E&E assets;

(b) only PP&E, intangible assets and investment property; and

(c) a combination of E&E assets, PP&E, intangible assets and investment property.

4.7.3.A E&E assets

Accounting for E&E assets, and therefore also accounting for swaps involving only E&E assets, falls within the scope of IFRS 6. *[IFRS 6.3]*. As that standard does not directly address accounting for asset swaps, it is necessary to consider its hierarchy of guidance in the selection of an accounting policy. IFRS 6 does not require an entity to look at other standards and interpretations that deal with similar issues, or the guidance in the IASB's *Conceptual Framework*. *[IFRS 6.7]*. Instead, it allows entities to develop their own accounting policies, or use the guidance issued by other standard-setters, thereby effectively allowing entities to continue using accounting policies that they applied under their previous national GAAP. Therefore, many entities, especially those which consider that they can never determine the fair value of E&E assets reliably, have selected an accounting policy under which they account for E&E assets obtained in a swap transaction at the carrying amount of the asset given up. An alternative approach, which is also permitted under IFRS 6, would be to apply an accounting policy that is based on the guidance in other standards as discussed below.

4.7.3.B PP&E, intangible assets and investment property

Three separate international accounting standards contain virtually identical guidance on accounting for exchanges of assets: IAS 16, IAS 38 and IAS 40. These standards require the acquisition of PP&E, intangible assets or investment property, as the case may be, in exchange for non-monetary assets (or a combination of monetary and non-monetary assets) to be measured at fair value. The cost of the acquired asset is measured at fair value unless:

(a) the exchange transaction lacks 'commercial substance'; or

(b) the fair value of neither the asset received nor the asset given up is reliably measurable. *[IAS 16.24, IAS 38.45, IAS 40.27]*.

For more information, see Chapter 18 at 4.4 (PP&E), Chapter 17 at 4.7 (intangible assets) and Chapter 19 at 4.6 (investment properties).

4.7.3.C Exchanges of E&E assets for other types of assets

An entity that exchanges E&E assets for PP&E, intangible assets or investment property needs to apply an accounting treatment that meets the requirements of IFRS 6 and those of IAS 16, IAS 38 or IAS 40. As discussed above, exchanges involving PP&E, intangible assets and investment property that have commercial substance should be accounted for at fair value. Since this treatment is also allowed under IFRS 6, an entity that exchanges E&E assets for assets within the scope of IAS 16, IAS 38 or IAS 40 should apply an accounting policy that complies with the guidance in those standards.

4.8 Acquisitions

4.8.1 Business combinations versus asset acquisitions

When an entity acquires an asset or a group of assets, careful analysis is required to identify whether what is acquired constitutes a business or represents only an asset or group of assets. Accounting for business combinations is discussed in detail in Chapter 9.

A business is defined in IFRS 3 as 'an integrated set of activities and assets that is capable of being conducted and managed for the purpose of providing a return in the form of dividends, lower costs or other economic benefits directly to investors or other owners, members or participants.' *[IFRS 3 Appendix A]*. Specifically IFRS 3: *[IFRS 3.BC18]*

- requires the integrated set of activities and assets to be 'capable' of being conducted and managed for the purpose of providing a return in the form of dividends, lower costs or other economic benefits directly to investors or other owners, members or participants. The focus on the capability to achieve the purposes of the business helps avoid the unduly restrictive interpretations that existed under the former guidance;
- clarifies the meaning of the terms 'inputs', 'processes' and 'outputs', which helps eliminate the need for extensive detailed guidance and the misinterpretations that sometimes stem from such guidance;
- clarifies that inputs and processes applied to those inputs are essential and that although the resulting outputs are normally present, they need not be present; and
- clarifies that a business need not include all of the inputs or processes that the seller used in operating that business if a market participant is capable of continuing to produce outputs, which helps avoid the need for extensive detailed guidance and assessments about whether a missing input or process is minor.

In summary, the definition of a business in IFRS 3 may include 'integrated sets of activities' that were previously not considered to be businesses. However, as discussed in Chapter 9 at 3.2.2, we believe that, in most cases, the acquired set of activities and assets must have at least some inputs and processes in order to be considered a business. If an acquirer obtains control of an input or set of inputs without any processes, we think it is unlikely that the acquired input(s) would be considered a business, even if a market participant had all the processes necessary to operate the input(s) as a business. The definition of a business under IFRS 3 is discussed in more detail in Chapter 9 at 3.2.

Determining whether a particular set of integrated activities and assets is a business will often require a significant amount of judgement as illustrated in Example 39.8 below.

Example 39.8: Definition of a business under IFRS 3

Oil and gas company C acquires a single oil exploration area where there are active exploration activities underway, oil has been found and the company is close to declaring reserves but implementation of the development plan has not yet commenced.

This may be a business under IFRS 3 as assets and processes have been acquired and a market participant is capable of producing outputs by integrating these with its own inputs and processes.

Mining company D acquires a development stage mine, including all inputs (i.e. employees, mineral reserve and property, plant and equipment) and processes (i.e. exploration and evaluation processes e.g. active drilling programmes etc.) that are required to generate output.

This meets the definition of a business under IFRS 3 because it includes inputs and processes even though there are currently no outputs.

Oil and gas company E acquires a group of pipelines (or a fleet of oil or gas tankers) used for transporting gas on behalf of customers and the employees responsible for operational, maintenance and administrative tasks transfer to the buyer.

This meets the definition of a business under IFRS 3 because it includes inputs, processes and outputs.

Mining company F acquires a mine that was abandoned 10 years ago. There are no activities currently occurring at the mine. The company plans to perform new geological and geophysical survey to determine whether sufficient economic reserves are present.

The abandoned mine does not meet the definition of a business because there are no processes acquired in addition to the assets purchased.

Oil and gas company G acquires a producing oil field, but the seller's on-site staff will *not* transfer to the buyer. Instead, oil and gas company G will enter into maintenance and oil field services contracts with different contractors.

A business need not include all of the inputs or processes that the seller used in operating that business if market participants are capable of continuing to produce outputs. If market participants can easily outsource processes to contractors then the oil field would be a business under IFRS 3.

4.8.1.A Asset purchase transactions

The acquisition of an asset, group of assets or an entity that does not constitute a business is not a business combination. In such cases the acquirer should identify and recognise the individual identifiable assets acquired and liabilities assumed. The cost of the acquisition should be allocated to the individual identifiable assets and liabilities on the basis of their relative fair values at the date of purchase. Such a transaction or event does not give rise to goodwill. *[IFRS 3.2(b)]*.

Any difference between the carrying amount of the assets and liabilities thus recognised and their tax base would not give rise to a recognised deferred tax asset or liability under IAS 12 – *Income Taxes* – as it would fall within the initial recognition exception under that standard (see Chapter 29 at 7.2). *[IAS 12.15, 24]*.

4.8.1.B Differences between asset purchase transactions and business combinations

The main differences between accounting for an asset purchase and a business combination can be summarised as follows:

- goodwill or a bargain purchase (previously referred to as negative goodwill) only arise in business combinations;
- assets and liabilities are accounted for at fair value in a business combination, while they are assigned a carrying amount based on their relative fair values in an asset purchase transaction;
- transaction costs should be recognised as an expense under IFRS 3, but can be capitalised on an asset acquisition; and
- in an asset purchase transaction no deferred tax will arise in relation to acquired assets and assumed liabilities as the initial recognition exception for deferred tax under IAS 12 applies.

4.8.2 Acquisition of an interest in joint operation that constitutes a business

One area where there is currently a lack of clarity when accounting for acquisitions of interests in joint operations (under IFRS 11) which constitute businesses is whether IFRS 3 applies. See Chapter 12 at 8.3.1 for further discussion on this.

4.8.3 Business combinations

4.8.3.A Goodwill in business combinations

Traditionally, many mining companies and oil and gas companies assumed that the entire consideration paid for upstream assets should be allocated to the identifiable net assets acquired, i.e. any excess of the consideration over the fair value of the identifiable net assets (excluding mineral reserves and resources) acquired would then have been included within mineral reserves and resources acquired and goodwill would not be recognised. However, goodwill could arise as a result of synergies, overpayment by the acquirer, or when IFRS requires that acquired assets and/or liabilities are measured at an amount that is not fair value (e.g. deferred taxation). Therefore it is not appropriate for mining companies or oil and gas companies to simply assume that, under IFRS, goodwill would never arise in a business combination and that any differential automatically goes to mineral reserves and resources. Instead, mineral reserves and resources and any exploration potential (if relevant) acquired should be valued separately and any excess of the purchase consideration over and above the supportable fair value of the identifiable net assets (which include mineral reserves, resources and acquired exploration potential), should be allocated to goodwill.

By virtue of the way IFRS 3 operates, if an entity were simply to take any excess of the consideration transferred over the fair value of the identifiable assets acquired to mineral reserves, they may end up having to allocate significantly larger values to minerals reserves than expected. This is because, under IFRS, an entity is required to provide for deferred taxation on the temporary differences relating to all identifiable net assets acquired (including mineral reserves), but not on temporary differences related to goodwill. Therefore, if any excess was simply allocated to mineral reserves, IAS 12 would give rise to a deferred tax liability on the temporary difference, which would create a further excess. This would then result in an iterative calculation in which the deferred tax liability recognised would increase the amount attributed to mineral reserves, which would in turn give rise to an increase in the deferred tax liability (see Chapter 29 at 7.2.2). Given the very high marginal tax rates to which extractive activities are often subject (i.e. tax rates of 60 to 80% are not uncommon) the mineral reserves might end up being grossed up by a factor of 2.5 to 5 (i.e. 1/(1 – 60%) = 2.5). Such an approach would only be acceptable if the final amount allocated to mineral reserves remained in the range of fair values determined for those mineral reserves. If not, such an approach would lead to excessive amounts being allocated to mineral reserves which could not be supported by appropriate valuations.

The extract below from Xstrata's financial statements illustrates a typical accounting policy for business combinations in which excess consideration transferred is treated as goodwill.

Extract 39.17: Xstrata plc (2012)

Notes to the financial statements [extract]

6. Principal accounting policies [extract]

Business combinations

On the acquisition of a subsidiary, the acquisition method of accounting is used, whereby the purchase consideration is allocated to the identifiable assets, liabilities and contingent liabilities (identifiable net assets) on the basis of fair value at the date of acquisition. Those mining rights, mineral reserves and resources that are able to be reliably valued are recognised in the assessment of fair values on acquisition. Other potential reserves, resources and mineral rights, for which in the directors' opinion values cannot be reliably determined, are not recognised. Acquisition costs are expensed.

When the cost of acquisition exceeds the fair values attributable to the Group's share of the identifiable net assets, the difference is treated as purchased goodwill, which is not amortised but is reviewed for impairment annually or where there is an indication of impairment. If the fair value attributable to the Group's share of the identifiable net assets exceeds the cost of acquisition, the difference is immediately recognised in the income statement.

Non-controlling interests represent the portion of profit or loss and net assets in subsidiaries that are not held by the Group and are presented in equity in the consolidated balance sheet, separately from the parent's shareholders' equity.

[...]

Similar procedures are applied in accounting for the purchases of interests in associates. Any goodwill arising on such purchases is included within the carrying amount of the investment in the associates, but not thereafter amortised. Any excess of the Group's share of the net fair value of the associate's identifiable assets, liabilities and contingent liabilities over the cost of the investment is included in income in the period of the purchase.

4.8.3.B *Impairment of assets and goodwill recognised on acquisition*

There are a number of circumstances in which the carrying amount of assets and goodwill acquired as part of a business combination and as recorded in the consolidated accounts, may be measured at a higher amount through recognition of notional tax benefits, also known as tax amortisation benefits (i.e. the value has been grossed up on the assumption that its carrying value is deductible for tax) or deferred tax (which can increase goodwill as described above). Application of IAS 36 to goodwill which arises upon recognition of deferred tax liabilities in a business combination is discussed in Chapter 20 at 5.2.1.

4.8.3.C Value beyond proven and probable reserves (VBPP)

In the mining sector specifically, the 'value beyond proven and probable reserves' (VBPP) is defined as the economic value of the estimated cash flows of a mining asset beyond that asset's proven and probable reserves.

While this term is directly relevant to the mining sector, the concept may be equally relevant to the oil and gas sector, i.e. the economic value of an oil and gas licence/area beyond the proven and probable reserves.

There are various situations in which mineralisation and mineral resources might not be classified as proven or probable:

- prior to the quantification of a resource, a mining company may identify mineralisation following exploration activities. However, it may be too early to assess if the geology and grade is sufficiently expansive to meet the definition of a resource;
- Acquired Exploration Potential (AEP) represents the legal right to explore for minerals in a particular property, occurring in the same geological area of interest;
- carrying out the required assessments and studies to obtain classification of mineral reserves can be very costly. Consequently, these activities are often deferred until they become necessary for the planning of future operations. Significant mineral resources are often awaiting the initiation of this process; and
- if an entity acquires a mining company at a time when commodity prices are particularly low, the mineral resources owned by the acquiree may not meet the definition of proven or probable reserves because extraction might not be commercially viable.

While the above types of mineralisation and mineral resources cannot be classified as proven or probable, they will often be valuable because of the future potential that they represent (i.e. reserves may be proven in the future and commodity price increases may make extraction commercially feasible).

IFRS 3 requires that an acquirer recognises the identifiable assets acquired and liabilities assumed that meet the definitions of assets and liabilities at the acquisition date. *[IFRS 3.11]*.

While the legal or contractual rights that allow an entity to extract minerals are not themselves tangible assets, the mineral reserves concerned clearly are. Under IFRS, mineral reserves are to be treated as tangible assets. The legal or contractual rights – that allow an entity to extract mineral reserves – acquired in business combinations should be recognised, without exception, at fair value.

Under IFRS, an entity that acquires mineral reserves and resources that cannot be classified as proven or probable, should account for the VBPP as part of the value allocated to mining assets, to the extent that a market participant would include VBPP in determining the fair value of the asset, rather than as goodwill.[109] In practice, the majority of mining companies treat mining assets and licences as tangible assets on the basis that they relate to minerals in the ground, which are themselves tangible assets. However, some entities present the value associated with E&E assets as intangible assets.

AEP would often be indistinguishable from the value of the mineral licence to which it relates. Therefore, the classification of AEP may vary depending on how an entity presents its mining assets and licences. If an entity presents them as tangible assets, they may be likely to treat AEP (or its equivalent), where applicable, as forming part of mineral properties, and hence AEP would be classified as a tangible asset. For an entity that classifies some of its mineral assets as intangible assets, e.g. E&E assets, then they may classify AEP as an intangible also.

Determining the fair value of VBPP requires a considerable amount of expertise. An entity should not only take account of commodity spot prices but also consider the effects of anticipated fluctuations in the future price of minerals, in a manner that is consistent with the expectations of a market participant. Generally, an entity should consider all available information including current prices, historical averages, and forward pricing curves. Those market participant assumptions typically should be consistent with the acquiring entity's operating plans for developing and producing minerals. The potential upside associated with mineral resources that are not classified as reserves can be much larger than the downward risk. A valuation model that only takes account of a single factor, such as the spot price, historical average or a single long-term price, without considering other information that a market participant would consider, would generally not be able to reflect the upward potential that determines much of the value of VBPP. Consequently, an entity may need to apply option valuation techniques in measuring VBPP.

The CRIRSCO reporting standards consider the geological definition of mineral resources that have not yet been tested for economic viability, which is the first category of VBPP. Valuation techniques used for this category include:

- Probability weighted discounted-cash flows
- Resource reserve conversion adjustment
- Comparable transactions
- Option valuation.

In relation to early mineralisation, the second category of VBPP, while it may represent a discovery, its true value will be determined by further appraisal/evaluation activities to confirm whether a resource exists. This category of VBPP is often grouped with the next (and final) category, being AEP, even though it has a higher intrinsic value, and is valued using:

- Cost based methods
- Budgeted expenditure methods
- Comparable sales
- Farm in/out values
- Sophisticated option pricing.

In relation to AEP, which is the final category of VBPP, the basis for its valuation varies from studying historic cost to the use of sophisticated option valuation techniques.

As VBPP does not provide current economic benefits, there is no need to allocate its cost against current revenue and hence no need for amortisation or depreciation. However, as part of the process of completing the acquisition accounting, an entity should form a view about how that value will ultimately be ascribed to future discoveries and converted into proven and probable reserves. Such methodologies might include a per unit (e.g. tonnes/ounces) basis or possibly an area (e.g. acreage) basis. VBPP would need to be tested for impairment under IAS 36 if, depending on the classification of VBPP, there is an indicator of impairment under that standard or IFRS 6. The VBPP may ultimately be impaired because it may never be converted into proven or probable reserves, but impairment may not be confirmed until the entity is satisfied that the project will not continue.

An impairment of VBPP should be recognised if its book value exceeds the higher of fair value less costs of disposal and value in use. In practice, there may not be a convenient method to determine the value in use. Hence, impairment testing will often need to rely on an approach based on fair value less costs of disposal.

Extract 39.18 below illustrates that AngloGold Ashanti does not subsume the 'value beyond proven and probable reserves' in goodwill but instead recognises it as part of the value ascribed to mineral resources.

Extract 39.18: AngloGold Ashanti Limited (2012)

GROUP – NOTES TO THE FINANCIAL STATEMENTS [extract]

For the year ended 31 December

1 Accounting Policies [extract]

1.3 Summary of significant accounting policies [extract]

Intangible assets [extract]

Acquisition and goodwill arising thereon

Where an investment in a subsidiary, joint venture or an associate is made, any excess of the consideration transferred over the fair value of the attributable Mineral Resource including value beyond proved and probable, exploration properties and net assets is recognised as goodwill. Goodwill in respect of subsidiaries is disclosed as goodwill. Goodwill relating to equity-accounted joint ventures and associates is included within the carrying value of the investment which is tested for impairment when indicators exist.

4.8.4 Asset acquisitions and conditional purchase consideration

There are various standards in which 'cost' is defined, with those of most relevance to the acquisition of an asset being IAS 16, IAS 38 and IAS 40. Cost is defined as 'the amount of cash or cash equivalents paid or the fair value of the other consideration given to acquire an asset at the time of its acquisition or construction or, where applicable, the amount attributed to that asset when initially recognised in accordance with the specific requirements of other IFRSs, e.g. IFRS 2 *Share-based Payment*'. *[IAS 16.6, IAS 38.8, IAS 40.5]*.

These requirements sometimes give rise to issues in situations where the purchase price is conditional upon certain events or facts. These issues can best be illustrated by an example.

Example 39.9: Asset acquisitions with a conditional purchase price

Scenario 1

Entity A agrees to buy a group of assets from Entity B for a total purchase price of $15 million. However, the purchase contract provides a formula for adjusting the purchase price upward or downward based on the report of a surveyor on the existence and quality of the assets listed in the contract.

Scenario 2

Entity C agrees to buy an exploration licence and several related assets from Entity D for a total purchase price of $35 million. However, Entity C would only be allowed to extract minerals in excess of 20 million barrels (or tonnes), upon payment of an additional consideration transferred of $12 million.

In scenario 1, we believe Entity A would be required to account for the fair value of the consideration transferred as determined at the date of acquisition. In contrast to the treatment under IFRS 3, there is no purchase price allocation or measurement period under IAS 16. However, suppose that three weeks after the initial accounting the surveyor reports that at the date of acquisition a number of assets listed in the contract were not present or were of inferior quality, the purchase price is therefore adjusted downwards to $14.5 million. Rather than recognising a profit arising from this adjustment, the entity should adjust the cost of the asset as the surveyor's report provides evidence of conditions that existed at the date of acquisition. *[IAS 10.3(a)]*.

In scenario 2 above, Entity C pays an additional $12 million in exchange for additional rights to extract minerals in excess of 20 million barrels (or tonnes) agreed upon in the initial transaction. At the date that Entity C purchases the additional rights it accounts for this as an additional asset acquisition. In more complicated scenarios, however, it might be necessary to assess whether the first and second acquisition should be accounted for together.

It is clear from the above two scenarios that changes in the facts and circumstances can have a significant effect on the accounting for conditional purchase consideration.

When considering asset acquisitions with contingent consideration, several issues need to be addressed. These include: how and when should the contingent element be accounted for, i.e. when a liability should be recognised and how it should be measured; whether the cost of the asset acquired includes an amount relating to the contingent element; and how the remeasurement (if any) of any liability recognised in relation to the contingent element should be accounted for. Should it be recognised as an adjustment to the cost of the asset acquired, or should it be recognised in profit or loss?

IAS 32 (as currently worded) is clear that the purchase of goods on credit gives rise to a financial liability when the goods are delivered (see Chapter 41 at 2.2.6) and that a contingent obligation to deliver cash meets the definition of a financial liability (see Chapter 41 at 2.2.3). Consequently, it would seem that given the current requirements of IFRS, a financial liability arises on the outright purchase of an item of property, plant and equipment or an intangible asset if the purchase contract requires the subsequent payment of contingent consideration, e.g. amounts based on the performance of the asset. Further, because there is currently no exemption from applying IAS 39 to such contracts, one might expect that such a liability would be accounted for in accordance with IAS 39, i.e. any measurement changes to that liability would flow through profit or loss. This would be consistent with the accounting treatment for contingent consideration arising from a business combination under IFRS 3 (see Chapter 41 at 3.7.1.A). However, this is not necessarily clear and for this reason the issue of how to account for contingent consideration in the acquisition of an item of PP&E was taken to the Interpretations Committee. See below for further discussion of this issue.

The current definition of cost in IAS 16 requires the cost of an asset on the date of purchase to include the fair value of the consideration given (if a reliable estimate can be made), such as an obligation to pay a contingent price. Note that not all would agree that all contingent payments are for the original asset and, indeed, the circumstances of a particular contract might support this. In addition to this issue, there is the issue of how to account for the remeasurement of the liability and whether changes should be recognised in profit or loss, or included as an adjustment to the cost of the asset.

In practice, contracts can be more complex than suggested above and often give rise to situations where the purchaser can influence or control the crystallisation of the contingent payments, e.g. where the contingent payments are dependent on the purchaser's future actions – such as those that take the form of production-based royalties. These complexities can raise broader questions about the nature of the obligations and, as in the case of royalty-based contingent payments, the appropriate accounting standard to apply initially, as well as how to account for subsequent adjustments to any liability that may have been recognised. To date, these complexities and lack of clarity as to the appropriate accounting have led to various treatments, including:

- the cost of the asset does not initially include any amount relating to the contingent element. Any subsequent payments made in relation to the contingent element are either adjusted against the cost of the asset (once paid) or recognised in profit or loss as incurred;
- the cost of the asset includes an estimate of the contingent consideration at the date of purchase. Subsequent changes in the liability relating to the contingent consideration are then recognised in profit or loss; or
- the cost of the asset includes an estimate of the contingent consideration at the date of purchase. Subsequent changes in the liability relating to the contingent consideration that do not reflect the passage of time are adjusted against the cost of the asset.

The first approach (which is relatively common in the extractive industries) considers that the applicable standard is IAS 37, and applies the concepts of obligating events, probability, contingencies and not providing for future operations. This means that nothing relating to the contingent payment is recognised at the date of purchase. The second approach applies the methodology in IFRS 3, while the third is based on IFRIC 1.[110]

Given this divergence in practice, this issue was referred to the Interpretations Committee in January 2011. The Committee and the IASB have discussed this issue several times over the last three years. They have been attempting to clarify how the initial recognition and subsequent changes in relation to such contingent consideration should be recognised.

In discussing this issue, they separated the contingent costs into two types – those that do not depend on the purchaser's future activity and those that do. For those costs that do not depend on the purchaser's future activity, the Interpretations Committee tentatively decided that the fair value of the contingent payments should be included in the initial measurement of the asset and an associated liability should also be recognised. The Committee could not reach a consensus on variable payments that depend on the purchaser's future activity. There was also some debate about whether the liability was in the scope of IAS 37 or IAS 39.

Despite not being able to reach consensus on the second type of variable payments, the Interpretations Committee proceeded to recommend to the IASB to amend IAS 16, IAS 38 and IAS 39 to deal with the subsequent measurement of liabilities in relation to variable payments not dependent on the purchaser's future activities.

At the IASB's July 2013 meeting, the Board noted that the initial accounting for variable payments affects their subsequent accounting. Given this, the Board recommended that the Interpretations Committee address both initial and subsequent recognition of both types of contingent payments at a later date and, as a result, the amendment was not finalised. The Board acknowledged that the leases exposure draft proposed yet another treatment of variable payments and recommended that the Committee wait for the comment letter responses before proceeding with their analysis.[111] As at the date of writing, the Interpretations Committee has not re-discussed the proposed amendment and its preliminary decision is not yet effective.

In the meantime, an entity must capitalise costs that meet the definition of an asset, although it may choose not to recognise these costs until incurred. For other variable costs, it has the option to either (i) not capitalise on initial recognition and expense variable payments or (ii) capitalise them at their fair value on initial recognition and recognise the changes in contingent consideration in profit or loss or as an asset if certain conditions are met. The accounting policy must be applied consistently.

This issue is also discussed in Chapter 17 at 4.5, Chapter 18 at 4.1.9 and Chapter 41 at 3.8.

4.8.5 Accounting for land acquisitions

Obtaining the legal rights to explore for, develop and produce minerals can be achieved in a number of ways, as outlined at 4.5 above. One of these ways is through the outright purchase of the minerals and the land on, or under, which the minerals are located. In undertaking such a transaction, it is not uncommon for an entity to pay an amount in excess of the intrinsic value of the land itself. In such a situation, an entity needs to ensure it appropriately allocates the purchase price between the fair value of the land and the fair value of the mineral or surface mining rights acquired. The amount allocated to land will be capitalised and not depreciated, whereas the amount allocated to the minerals or surface mining rights will form part of the total cost of mining assets and will ultimately be depreciated on a units of production basis over the economically recoverable reserves to which it relates.

4.9 Depreciation, depletion and amortisation (DD&A)

4.9.1 Requirements under IAS 16 and IAS 38

The main types of depreciable assets of mining companies and oil and gas companies are property, plant and equipment, intangible assets and mineral reserves, although the exact titles given to these types of assets may vary.

While 'mineral rights and expenditure on the exploration for, or development and extraction of, minerals, oil, natural gas and similar non-regenerative resources' are outside the scope of IAS 16 and IAS 38, any items of property, plant and equipment (PP&E) and other intangible assets that are used in the extraction of mineral reserves should be accounted for under IAS 16 and IAS 38. *[IAS 16.2, 3, IAS 38.2].*

For items of PP&E, various descriptions are used for such assets which can include producing mines, mine assets, oil and gas assets, producing properties. Whatever the description given, IAS 16 requires depreciation of an item of PP&E over its useful life. Depreciation is required to be calculated separately for each part (often referred to as a 'component'), of an item of PP&E with a cost that is significant in relation to the total cost of the item, unless the item can be grouped with other items of PP&E that have the same useful life and depreciation method. *[IAS 16.43, 45].*

The guidance in IAS 16 relating to parts of an asset does not apply directly to intangible assets as IAS 38 does not apply a 'parts' approach, or to mineral rights but we believe that entities should use the general principles for determining an appropriate unit of account that are outlined at 4.2.1 above. IAS 16's general requirements are described in Chapter 18 and IAS 38 is addressed in Chapter 17.

4.9.1.A Mineral reserves

In the absence of a standard or an interpretation specifically applicable to mineral reserves and their related expenditures, which are outside the scope of IAS 16 and IAS 38, management needs to develop an accounting policy for the depreciation or amortisation of mineral reserves in accordance with the hierarchy in IAS 8, taking into account the requirements and guidance in Standards and Interpretations dealing with similar and related issues and the definitions, recognition criteria and measurement concepts for assets, liabilities, income and expenses in the *Conceptual Framework. [IAS 8.11].* In practice, an entity will develop an accounting policy that is based on the depreciation and amortisation principles in IAS 16 and IAS 38, which deal with similar and related issues.

4.9.2 Assets depreciated using the straight-line method

The straight-line method of depreciation is generally preferred in accounting for the depreciation of property, plant and equipment. The main practical advantages of the straight-line method are considered to be its simplicity and the fact that its results are often not materially different from the units of production method if annual production is relatively constant.[112] In general the straight-line method is considered to be preferable for:

- assets whose loss in value is more closely linked to the passage of time than to the quantities of minerals produced (e.g. front-end loaders that are used in stripping overburden and production of minerals);
- assets that are unrelated to production and that are separable from the field or mine (e.g. office buildings);
- assets with a useful life that is either much longer (e.g. offshore platforms) or much shorter (e.g. drill jumbos) than that of the field or mine in which they are used;
- assets used in fields or mines whose annual production is relatively constant. However, if assets are used in fields or mines that are expected to suffer extended outages, due to weather conditions or periodic repairs and maintenance, then the straight-line method may be less appropriate; and
- assets that are used in more than one field or mine (e.g. service trucks).

If the production of a field or mine drops significantly towards the end of its productive life, then the straight-line method may result in a relatively high depreciation charge per unit of production in these latter years. In those cases, an entity may need to perform an impairment test on the assets involved.

The extract below indicates the assets to which BHP Billiton applies the straight-line method.

Extract 39.19: BHP Billiton (2012)

9.1.6 Notes to Financial Statements [extract]

1 Accounting policies [extract]

Depreciation of property, plant and equipment

The carrying amounts of property, plant and equipment (including initial and any subsequent capital expenditure) are depreciated to their estimated residual value over the estimated useful lives of the specific assets concerned, or the estimated life of the associated mine, field or lease, if shorter. Estimates of residual values and useful lives are reassessed annually and any change in estimate is taken into account in the determination of remaining depreciation charges. Depreciation commences on the date of commissioning. The major categories of property, plant and equipment are depreciated on a unit of production and/or straight-line basis using estimated lives indicated below. However, where assets are dedicated to a mine, field or lease and are not readily transferable, the below useful lives are subject to the lesser of the asset category's useful life and the life of the mine, field or lease:

- Buildings – 25 to 50 years
- Land – not depreciated
- Plant and equipment – 3 to 30 years straight-line
- Mineral rights and Petroleum interests – based on reserves on a unit of production basis
- Capitalised exploration, evaluation and development expenditure – based on reserves on a unit of production basis

4.9.3 Assets depreciated using the units of production method

When it comes to assets relating to mineral reserves, the units of production method is the most common method applied. 'The underlying principle of the units of production method is that capitalised costs associated with a cost centre are incurred to find and develop the commercially producible reserves in that cost centre, so that each unit produced from the centre is assigned an equal amount of cost.'[113] The units of production method thereby effectively allocates an equal amount of depreciation to each unit produced, rather than an equal amount to each year as under the straight-line method.

When the level of production varies considerably over the life of a project (e.g. the production of oil fields is much higher in the periods just after the start of production than in the final periods of production), depreciation based on a units of production method will produce a more equal cost per unit from year to year than straight-line methods. Under the straight-line method the depreciation charge per unit in the early years of production could be much less than the depreciation per unit in later years. 'That factor, coupled with the fact that typically production costs per unit increase in later years, means that the profitability of operations would be distorted if the straight-line method is used, showing larger profits in early years and lower profits in later years of the mineral resource's life. The higher cost per unit in later years is, in part, due to fewer units being produced while many production costs remain fixed and, in part, a result of many variable costs per unit increasing over time because reserves may be harder to extract, there may be greater equipment repairs, and similar other factors.'[114] Nevertheless, even under the units of production method, profitability often drops significantly towards the end of the productive life of a field or mine. When this happens an entity will need to carry out an impairment test and may need to recognise an impairment charge (see 4.10 below).

In general the units of production method is considered to be preferable for:

- assets used in fields or mines whose annual production may vary considerably over their useful economic life;
- assets whose loss in value is more closely linked to the quantities of minerals produced than to the passage of time (e.g. draglines used in the extraction of mineral ore);
- assets that are used in production or that are inseparable from the field or mine (e.g. wells and well heads);
- assets with a useful life that is the same as that of the field or mine in which they are used; and
- assets that are used in only one field or mine (e.g. overland conveyor belts).

Extract 39.19 above and Extract 39.20 below indicate the classes of asset to which BHP Billiton and Lonmin, respectively, apply the units of production method.

Extract 39.20: Lonmin Plc (2012)

Notes to the Accounts [extract]

1 Statement on accounting policies [extract]

Intangible assets

Intangible assets, other than goodwill, acquired by the Group have finite useful lives and are measured at cost less accumulated amortisation and accumulated impairment losses. Where amortisation is charged on these assets, the expense is taken to the income statement through operating costs.

Amortisation of mineral rights is provided on a units of production basis over the remaining life of mine to residual value (20 to 40 years).

All other intangible assets are amortised over their useful economic lives subject to a maximum of 20 years and are tested for impairment at each reporting date when there is an indication of a possible impairment.

Property, plant and equipment [extract]

Depreciation

Depreciation is provided on a straight-line or units of production basis as appropriate over their expected useful lives or the remaining life of mine, if shorter, to residual value. The life of mine is based on proven and probable reserves. The expected useful lives of the major categories of property, plant and equipment are as follows:

	Method	Rate	
Shafts and underground	Units of production	2.5%-5.0% per annum	20-40 years
Metallurgical	Straight line	2.5%-7.1% per annum	14-40 years
Infrastructure	Straight line	2.5%-2.9% per annum	35-40 years
Other plant and equipment	Straight line	2.5%-50.0% per annum	2-40 years

No depreciation is provided on surface mining land which has a continuing value and capital work in progress.

Residual values and useful lives are re-assessed annually and if necessary changes are accounted for prospectively.

The practical application of the units of production method gives rise to the following issues that require entities to exercise a considerable degree of judgement in determining the:

(a) units of production formula (see 4.9.3.A below);

(b) reserves base (see 4.9.3.B below);

(c) unit of measure (see 4.9.3.C below); and

(d) joint and by-products (see 4.9.3.D below).

As discussed at 4.9.3.B below, the asset base that is subject to depreciation should be consistent with the reserves base that is used, which may require an entity to exclude certain costs from (or include future investments in) the depreciation pool.

4.9.3.A Units of production formula

There are a number of different ways in which an entity could calculate a depreciation charge under the units of production method. The most obvious of these is probably the following formula:

$$\text{Depreciation charge for the period} = \text{Current period's production} \times \frac{\text{Cost of the asset at the beginning of the period} - \text{Cumulative depreciation and impairment at the beginning of the period}}{\text{Opening reserves estimated at the beginning of the period}}$$

The reserves estimate used in the above formula is the best estimate of the reserves at the beginning of the period, but by the end of the period a revised and more accurate estimate is often available. It could therefore be argued that in order to take into account the most recent information, the opening reserves should be calculated by adding the 'closing reserves estimated at the end of the period' to the 'current period's production'. However, reserves estimates might change for a number of reasons:

(a) more detailed knowledge about existing reserves (e.g. detailed engineering studies or drilling of additional wells which occurred after the commencement of the period);

(b) new events that affect the physical quantity of reserves (e.g. major fire in a mine); and

(c) changes in economic assumptions (e.g. higher commodity prices).

It is generally not appropriate to take account of these events retrospectively. For example, changes in reserves estimates that result from events that took place after the end of the reporting period (such as those under (b) and (c)) are non-adjusting events that should be accounted for prospectively in accordance with IFRS. *[IAS 8.32-38, IAS 10.3]*. Changes in reserves estimates that result from new information or new developments which do not offer greater clarity concerning the conditions that existed at the end of the reporting period (such as those under (a)) are not considered to be corrections of errors; instead they are changes in accounting estimates that should be accounted for prospectively under IFRS. *[IAS 8.5, 32-38]*.

In practice, many mining and oil and gas companies take new information and new developments into account from the beginning of their current reporting period (e.g. the beginning of the current quarter for quarterly reporters or the beginning of the year for those who report only annually). However, if the reporting period is sufficiently short or the change in mineral reserves is relatively insignificant then the impact of retrospective application from the beginning of the reporting period is unlikely to be material. Determining whether actual changes in reserves estimates should be treated as adjusting or non-adjusting events will depend upon the specific facts and circumstances and may require significant judgement.

Usually an entity will continue to invest during the year in assets in the depreciation pool (see 4.9.3.B below for a discussion of 'depreciation pools') that are used to extract minerals. This raises the question as to whether or not assets that were used for only part of the production during the period should be depreciated on a different basis. Under the straight-line method, an entity will generally calculate the depreciation of asset additions during the period based on the assumption that they were added (1) at the beginning of the period, (2) in the middle of the period or (3) at the end of the period. While method (2) is often the best approximation, methods (1) and (3) are generally not materially different when the accounting period is rather short (e.g. monthly or quarterly reporting) or when the level of asset additions is relatively low compared to the asset base.

The above considerations explain why the units of production formula that is commonly used in the extractive industries is slightly more complicated than the formula given above:

$$\text{Depreciation charge for the period} = \text{Current period's production} \times \frac{\text{Cost of the asset at the end of the period} - \text{Cumulative depreciation and impairment at the beginning of the period}}{\text{Closing reserves estimated at the end of the period} + \text{Current period's production}}$$

This units of production formula is widely used in the oil and gas sector by entities that apply US GAAP or the OIAC SORP. In the mining sector, however, both the first and the second units of production formulae are used in practice.

4.9.3.B Reserves base

An important decision in applying the units of production method is selecting the reserves base that will be used. The following reserves bases could in theory be used:

(a) proved developed reserves (see (a) below);

(b) proved developed and undeveloped reserves (see (b) below);

(c) proved and probable reserves (see (c) below);

(d) proved and probable reserves and a portion of resources expected to be converted into reserves (see (d) below); and

(e) proved, probable and possible reserves.

The term 'possible reserves', which is used in the oil and gas sector, is associated with a probability of only 10% (see 2.2.1 above). Therefore, it is not considered acceptable to include possible reserves within the reserves base in applying the units of production method.

It is important that whatever reserves base is chosen the costs applicable to that category of reserves are included in the depreciable amount to achieve a proper matching of costs and production.[115] For example, 'if the cost centre is not fully developed ... there may be costs that do not apply, in total or in part, to proved developed reserves, which may create difficulties in matching costs and reserves. In addition, some reserve categories will require future costs to bring them to the point where production may begin.'[116]

IFRS does not provide any guidance on the selection of an appropriate reserves base or cost centre (i.e. unit of account) for the application of the units of production method. The relative merits for the use of each of the reserves bases listed under (a) to (c) above are discussed in detail below.

(a) Proved developed reserves

Under some national GAAPs that have accounting standards for the extractive industries, an entity is required to use proved developed reserves as its reserves base for the depreciation of certain types of assets. An entity would therefore calculate its depreciation charge on the basis of actual costs that have been incurred to date.

However, the cost centre frequently includes capitalised costs that relate to undeveloped reserves. To calculate the depreciation charge correctly, it will be necessary to exclude a portion of the capitalised costs from the depreciation calculation. Example 39.10 below, which is taken from the IASC's Issues Paper, illustrates how this might work.

Example 39.10: Exclusion of capitalised costs relating to undeveloped reserves[117]

In an offshore oil and gas field a platform may be constructed from which 20 development wells will be drilled. The platform's cost has been capitalised as a part of the total cost of the cost centre. If only 5 of the 20 wells have been drilled, it would be inappropriate to depreciate that portion of platform costs, as well as that portion of all other capitalised costs, that are deemed to be applicable to the 15 wells not yet drilled. Only 5/20ths of the platform costs would be subject to depreciation in the current year, while 15/20ths of the platform costs (those applicable to the 15 undrilled wells) would be withheld from the depreciable amount. The costs withheld would be transferred to the depreciable amount as the additional wells are drilled. In lieu of basing the exclusion from depreciation on the number of wells, the exclusion (and subsequent transfer to depreciable amount) could be based on the quantity of reserves developed by individual wells compared with the estimated total quantity of reserves to be developed.

Similarly, an appropriate portion of prospecting costs, mineral acquisition costs, exploration costs, appraisal costs, and future dismantlement, removal, and restoration costs that have been capitalised should be withheld from the depreciation calculation if proved developed reserves are used as the reserves base and if there are undeveloped reserves in the cost pool.[118]

By withholding some of the costs from the depreciation pool, an entity is able to achieve a better matching of the costs incurred with the benefits of production. This is particularly important in respect of pre-development costs, which provide future economic benefits in relation to reserves that are not yet classified as 'proved developed'. However, excluding costs from the depreciation pool may not be appropriate if it is not possible to determine reliably the portion of costs to be excluded or if the reserves that are not 'proved developed' are highly uncertain. It may not be necessary to exclude any costs at all from the depreciation pool if those costs are immaterial, which is sometimes the case in mining operations.

As illustrated in Extract 39.21, Royal Dutch Shell, in reporting under IFRS, applies the units of production method based on proved developed reserves.

Extract 39.21: Royal Dutch Shell plc (2012)

Notes to the Consolidated Financial Statements [extract]

2 ACCOUNTING POLICIES [extract]

Property, plant and equipment and intangible assets [extract]

B – Depreciation, depletion and amortisation

Property, plant and equipment related to hydrocarbon production activities are depreciated on a unit-of-production basis over the proved developed reserves of the field concerned, except in the case of assets whose useful lives differ from the lifetime of the field, in which case the straight-line method is applied. Rights and concessions in respect of proved properties are depleted on the unit-of-production basis over the total proved reserves of the relevant area. Where individually insignificant, unproved properties may be grouped and depreciated based on factors such as the average concession term and past experience of recognising proved reserves.

Other property, plant and equipment and intangible assets are depreciated and amortised on a straight-line basis over their estimated useful lives, except for goodwill, which is not amortised. They include major inspection costs, which are depreciated over the estimated period before the next planned major inspection (three to five years), and the following:

Asset type	**Useful life**
Upgraders	30 years
Refineries and chemical plants	20 years
Retail service stations	15 years
Property, plant and equipment held under finance lease	lease term
Software	5 years
Trademarks	40 years

Estimates of the useful lives and residual values of property, plant and equipment and intangible assets are reviewed annually and adjusted if appropriate.

(b) *Proved developed and undeveloped reserves*

Another approach that is common under IFRS is to use 'proved developed and undeveloped reserves' as the reserves base for the application of the units of production method. This approach reflects the fact that it is often difficult to allocate costs that have already been incurred between developed and undeveloped reserves and has the advantage that it effectively straight-lines the depreciation charge per unit of production across the different phases of a project. For example, if the depreciation cost in phase 1 of the development is $24/barrel and the depreciation cost in phase 2 of the development could be $18/barrel, an entity that uses proved developed and undeveloped reserves as its reserves base might recognise depreciation of, say, $22/barrel during phase 1 and phase 2.

Application of this approach is complicated by the fact that phase 1 of the project will start production before phase 2 is completed. To apply the units of production method on the basis of proved developed and undeveloped reserves, the entity would need to forecast the remaining investment related to phase 2. The approach does not appear unreasonable at first sight, given that the proved reserves are reasonably certain to exist and 'the costs of developing the proved undeveloped reserves will be incurred in the near future in most situations, the total depreciable costs can also be estimated with a high degree of reliability'.[119] Nevertheless, the entity would therefore define its cost pool (i.e. unit of account) as including both assets that it currently owns and certain future investments. Although there is no precedent within IFRS for using such a widely defined unit of account, such an approach is not prohibited, while in practice it has gained a broad measure of acceptance within the extractive industries.

(c) *Proved and probable reserves*

The arguments in favour of using 'proved and probable reserves' as the reserves base in applying the units of production method are similar to those discussed at (b) above. The IASC's Issues Paper summarised the arguments in favour of this approach as follows:

> 'Proponents of [using "proved and probable reserves" as the reserve base] use the same arguments given for including proved undeveloped reserves and related future costs in calculating depreciation. They point out that in a cost centre in which development has only begun a large part of capitalised prospecting, mineral acquisition, exploration, and appraisal costs may apply to probable reserves. Often in this situation there are large quantities of probable reserves, lacking only relatively minor additional exploration and/or appraisal work to be reclassified as proved reserves. They argue that, in calculating depreciation, it would be possible to defer all costs relating to the probable reserves if either proved developed reserves only, or all proved reserves, were to be used as the quantity on which depreciation is based. They contend that using probable and proved reserves in the reserve base and including in the depreciable costs any additional costs anticipated to explore and develop those reserves provides more relevant and reliable information.'[120]

The main drawbacks of this approach are that estimates of probable reserves are almost certainly different from actual reserves that will ultimately be developed and estimates of the costs to complete the development are likely to be incorrect because of the potentially long time scales involved.[121] Nevertheless, this approach has also found a considerable degree of acceptance under IFRS among mining companies and oil and gas companies that were permitted to apply the approach under their national GAAP before (e.g. UK GAAP). Both Tullow Oil and Anglo American apply this approach, as illustrated in Extracts 39.22 and 39.23 below.

Extract 39.22: Tullow Oil plc (2012)

ACCOUNTING POLICIES [extract]

Year ended 31 December 2012

(l) Commercial reserves

Commercial reserves are proven and probable oil and gas reserves, which are defined as the estimated quantities of crude oil, natural gas and natural gas liquids which geological, geophysical and engineering data demonstrate with a specified degree of certainty to be recoverable in future years from known reservoirs and which are considered commercially producible. There should be a 50 per cent statistical probability that the actual quantity of recoverable reserves will be more than the amount estimated as proven and probable reserves and a 50 per cent statistical probability that it will be less.

(m) Depletion and amortisation – discovery fields [extract]

All expenditure carried within each field is amortised from the commencement of production on a unit of production basis, which is the ratio of oil and gas production in the period to the estimated quantities of commercial reserves at the end of the period plus the production in the period, generally on a field-by-field basis or by a group of fields which are reliant on common infrastructure. Costs used in the unit of production calculation comprise the net book value of capitalised costs plus the estimated future field development costs. Changes in the estimates of commercial reserves or future field development costs are dealt with prospectively.

Extract 39.23: Anglo American plc (2012)

Notes to the financial statements [extract]

1. ACCOUNTING POLICIES [extract]

Property, plant and equipment [extract]

Mining properties and leases include the cost of acquiring and developing mining properties and mineral rights. Mining properties are depreciated to their residual values using the unit of production method based on proven and probable ore reserves and, in certain limited circumstances, other mineral resources. Mineral resources are included in depreciation calculations where there is a high degree of confidence that they will be extracted in an economic manner. For diamond operations, depreciation calculations are based on mineral reserves and resources included in the Life of Mine Plan. Depreciation is charged on new mining ventures from the date that the mining property is capable of commercial production. When there is little likelihood of a mineral right being exploited, or the value of the exploitable mineral right has diminished below cost, an impairment loss is recognised in the income statement.

(d) Proved and probable reserves and a portion of resources expected to be converted into reserves

We observe in practice that some mining entities adopt a slightly different policy when depreciating some of their mining assets. They use proven and probable reserves and a portion of resources expected to be converted into reserves. Such an approach tends to be limited to mining companies where the type of mineral and the characteristics of the ore body indicate that there is a high degree of confidence that those resources will be converted into reserves.

Such resources can comprise measured, indicated and inferred resources, and even exploration potential. Determining which of those have a high degree of confidence of being extracted in an economic manner will require judgement. Such an assessment will take into account the specific mineralisation and the 'reserves to resource' conversion that has previously been achieved for a mine.

Such an approach is generally justified on the basis that it helps to ensure the depreciation charges reflect management's best estimate of the useful life of the assets and provides greater accuracy in the calculation of the consumption of future economic benefits.

Anglo American applies this approach, as illustrated in Extract 39.23 above, as does Rio Tinto, as illustrated in Extract 39.24 below.

Extract 39.24: Rio Tinto plc (2012)

Notes to the 2012 financial statements [extract]

1 PRINCIPAL ACCOUNTING POLICIES [extract]

(i) Depreciation and impairment [extract]

Units of production basis

For mining properties and leases and certain mining equipment, the consumption of the economic benefits of the asset is linked to the production level. Except as noted below, these assets are depreciated on a units of production basis.

In applying the units of production method, depreciation is normally calculated using the quantity of material extracted from the mine in the period as a percentage of the total quantity of material to be extracted in current and future periods based on proved and probable reserves and, for some mines, other mineral resources. These other mineral resources may be included in depreciation calculations in limited circumstances and where there is a high degree of confidence in their economic extraction.

An entity preparing its financial statements under IFRS will need to choose between using 'proved developed reserves', 'proved developed and undeveloped reserves', 'proved and probable reserves' and, for mining entities in relation to certain mines, 'proved and probable reserves and a portion of resources expected to be converted into reserves' as its reserves base. Each of these approaches is currently acceptable under IFRS. Preparers of financial statements should, however, be aware of the difficulties that exist in ensuring that the reserves base and the costs that are being depreciated correspond. Users of financial statements need to understand that comparability between entities reporting under IFRS may sometimes be limited and need to be aware of the impact that each of the approaches has on the depreciation charge that is reported. Given this, detailed disclosures are essential.

4.9.3.C Unit of measure

Under the units of production method, an entity assigns an equal amount of cost to each unit produced. Determining the appropriate unit by which to measure production requires a significant amount of judgement. An entity could measure the units of production by reference to physical units or, when different minerals are produced in a common process, cost could be allocated between the different minerals on the basis of their relative sales prices.

(a) Physical units of production method

If an entity uses the physical units of production method, each physical unit of reserves (such as barrels, tonnes, ounces, gallons, and cubic metres) produced is assigned a pro rata portion of undepreciated costs less residual value.

Example 39.11: Physical units of production method[122]

If an entity produces 100 units during the current period and the estimated remaining commercial reserves at the end of the period are 1,900 units, the units available would be 2,000. The fractional part of the depreciable basis to be charged to depreciation expense would be 100/2,000. Therefore, if the depreciable basis was 5,000 monetary units, the depreciation for the period would be 250 monetary units.

In applying the physical units of production method a mining company needs to decide whether to use either the quantity of ore produced or the quantity of mineral contained in the ore as the unit of measure.[123] Similarly, an oil and gas company needs to decide whether to use either the volume of hydrocarbons or the volume of hydrocarbons plus gas, water and other materials. When mining different grades of ore, a mining company's gross margin on the subsequent sale of minerals will fluctuate far less when it uses the quantity of minerals as its unit of measure. While a large part of the wear and tear of equipment used in mining is closely related to the quantity of ore produced, the economic benefits are more closely related to the quantity of mineral contained in the ore. Therefore, both approaches are currently considered to be acceptable under IFRS.

(b) Revenue-based units of production method

Another possible approach in applying the units of production method that may have been used by some entities previously is to measure the units produced based on the gross selling price of mineral.[124] Under the gross revenue approach the depreciation charge would be calculated by multiplying the depreciable cost base by:[125]

(a) the gross revenues from sale during the period, divided by

(b) the total of the gross revenues for the period plus the estimated future gross revenues to be derived from sale of the reserves remaining at the end of the period.

If an entity bases its forecast of future gross revenues on the average sales price for the current period, the depreciation charge calculated will be the same as that calculated using a physical unit of measure.

Nevertheless, given the substantial uncertainties that surround future commodity prices, application of a revenue-based units of production method was rarely considered acceptable in the past, and in fact, will now no longer be permitted. This is because as part of the 2011-2013 cycle of annual improvements the IASB approved an amendment to IAS 16 and IAS 38 to clarify that a revenue-based depreciation or amortisation method would not be appropriate.

4.9.3.D Joint and by-products

In the extractive industries it is common for more than one product to be extracted from the same reserves (e.g. copper mines often produce gold and silver; lead and zinc are often found together; and many oil fields produce both oil and gas). When the ratio between the joint products or between the main product and the by-products is stable, this does not pose any complications. Also, if the value of the by-products is immaterial then it will often be acceptable to base the depreciation charge on the main product. In other cases, however, it will be necessary to define a unit of measure that takes into account all minerals produced. The IASC's Issues Paper listed the following approaches in defining conversion factors for calculating such a unit of measure:[126]

'(a) physical characteristics:

   (i) based on volume: such as barrels, litres, gallons, thousand cubic feet or cubic metres;

   (ii) based on weight: such as tonnes, pounds, and kilograms; or

   (iii) based on energy content (British thermal units) of oil and gas;

(b) gross revenues for the period in relation to estimated total gross revenues of the current period and future periods (more commonly seen in the mining sector); and

(c) net revenues for the period in relation to total net revenues of the current and future periods'.

Calculation of a conversion factor based on volume or weight has the benefit of being easy to apply and can lead to satisfactory results if the relative value of the products is fairly stable. For example, some mining companies that produce both gold and silver from the same mines express their production in millions of ounces of silver equivalent. This is calculated as the sum of the ounces of silver produced plus their ounces of gold produced multiplied by some ratio of the gold price divided by the silver price. For example, if the gold price was $900 and the silver price was $12, this would provide a ratio of 1/75 – so the quantity of gold would be multiplied by 75 to determine the equivalent ounces of silver. However these ratios can change depending on the relationship between gold and silver.

Calculation of a conversion factor based on other physical characteristics is quite common in the oil and gas sector. Typically production and reserves in oil fields are expressed in millions of barrels of oil equivalent (mmboe), which is calculated by dividing the quantity of gas expressed in thousands of cubic feet by 6 and adding that to the quantity of oil expressed in barrels. This conversion is based on the fact that one barrel of oil contains as much energy as 6,000 cubic feet of gas. While this approach is commonly used, it is important to recognise two limiting factors: the actual energy conversion factor will not always be 1:6 but may vary between 1:5½ to 1:6½ and the market price of gas per unit of energy (typically BTU) is often lower than that of oil because of government price controls and the need for expensive infrastructure to deliver gas to end users.

An approach that is commonly used (more so in the mining sector than the oil and gas sector) in calculating a conversion factor when joint products are extracted, is to base it on gross revenues. As discussed at 4.9.3.C above, the main drawback of this method is that it requires an entity to forecast future commodity prices. Despite this drawback, there will be situations where no other viable alternative exists for calculating an appropriate conversion factor.

Finally, it is possible to calculate a conversion factor based on net revenue after deducting certain direct processing costs. An argument in favour of this method is that gross revenues do not necessarily measure the economic benefits from an asset. However, taken to an extreme this argument would lead down a path where no depreciation is charged in unprofitable years, which is clearly not an acceptable practice.

Accounting for the sale of joint products and by-products is addressed at 4.14.1 below.

4.10 Impairment of assets

The following issues require additional attention when a mining company or oil and gas company applies the impairment testing rules under IFRS:

- impairment indicators (see 4.10.1 below);
- future capital expenditure (see 4.10.2 below);
- identifying cash-generating units (see 4.10.3 below);
- projections of cash flows (see 4.10.4 below);
- cash flows from mineral reserves and resources and the appropriate discount rate (see 4.10.5 below);
- foreign currency cash flows (see 4.10.6 below); and
- commodity price assumptions (see 4.10.7 below).

The general requirements of IAS 36 are covered in Chapter 20.

4.10.1 Impairment indicators

IFRS 6 describes a number of situations in which an entity should test E&E assets for impairment, discussed at 3.5.1 above, while an entity should apply the impairment indicators in IAS 36 to assets other than E&E assets. The lists of impairment indicators in IFRS 6 and IAS 36 are not exhaustive. Entities operating in the extractive industries may also consider carrying out an impairment test in the following situations:[127]

- declines in prices of products or increases in production costs;
- governmental actions, such as new environmental regulations, imposition of price controls and tax increases;
- actual production levels from the cost centre or cost pool are below forecast and/or there is a downward revision in production forecasts;
- serious operational problems and accidents;
- capitalisation of large amounts of unsuccessful pre-production costs in the cost centre;
- decreases in reserve estimates;
- increases in the anticipated period over which reserves will be produced;
- substantial cost overruns during the development and construction phases of a field or mine; and
- adverse drilling results.

The extract below shows BHP Billiton's accounting policy for impairment testing.

Extract 39.25: BHP Billiton (2012)

9.1.6 Notes to Financial Statements [extract]

1 Accounting policies [extract]

Exploration and evaluation expenditure [extract]

Capitalised exploration and evaluation expenditure considered to be tangible is recorded as a component of property, plant and equipment at cost less impairment charges. Otherwise, it is recorded as an intangible asset (such as licences). As the capitalised exploration and evaluation expenditure asset is not available for use, it is not depreciated. All capitalised exploration and evaluation expenditure is monitored for indications of impairment. Where a potential impairment is indicated, assessment is performed for each area of interest in conjunction with the group of operating assets (representing a cash generating unit) to which the exploration is attributed. Exploration areas at which reserves have been discovered but require major capital expenditure before production can begin, are continually evaluated to ensure that commercial quantities of reserves exist or to ensure that additional exploration work is under way or planned. To the extent that capitalised expenditure is no longer expected to be recovered it is charged to the income statement.

Impairment of non-current assets

Formal impairment tests are carried out annually for goodwill. In addition, formal impairment tests for all assets are performed when there is an indication of impairment. The Group conducts annually an internal review of asset values which is used as a source of information to assess for any indications of impairment. External factors, such as changes in expected future prices, costs and other market factors are also monitored to assess for indications of impairment. If any such indication exists, an estimate of the asset's recoverable amount is calculated, being the higher of fair value less direct costs to sell and the asset's value in use.

If the carrying amount of the asset exceeds its recoverable amount, the asset is impaired and an impairment loss is charged to the income statement so as to reduce the carrying amount in the balance sheet to its recoverable amount.

Fair value is determined as the amount that would be obtained from the sale of the asset in an arm's length transaction between knowledgeable and willing parties. Fair value for mineral assets is generally determined as the present value of the estimated future cash flows expected to arise from the continued use of the asset, including any expansion prospects, and its eventual disposal, using assumptions that an independent market participant may take into account. These cash flows are discounted by an appropriate rate to arrive at a net present value of the asset.

Value in use is determined as the present value of the estimated future cash flows expected to arise from the continued use of the asset in its present form and its eventual disposal. Value in use is determined by applying assumptions specific to the Group's continued use and cannot take into account future development. These assumptions are different to those used in calculating fair value and consequently the value in use calculation is likely to give a different result (usually lower) to a fair value calculation.

In testing for indications of impairment and performing impairment calculations, assets are considered as collective groups and referred to as cash generating units. Cash generating units are the smallest identifiable group of assets, liabilities and associated goodwill that generate cash inflows that are largely independent of the cash inflows from other assets or groups of assets.

The impairment assessments are based on a range of estimates and assumptions, including:

Estimates/assumptions:		*Basis:*
• Future production	–	proved and probable reserves, resource estimates and, in certain cases, expansion projects
• Commodity prices	–	forward market and contract prices, and longer-term price protocol estimates
• Exchange rates	–	current (forward) market exchange rates
• Discount rates	–	cost of capital risk-adjusted appropriate to the resource

4.10.2 Future capital expenditure

IAS 36 defines recoverable amount as the higher of 'value in use' (VIU) and 'fair value less costs of disposal' (FVLCD). VIU is determined using a discounted cash flow (DCF) method. Although the standard permits an entity to take account of cash outflows required to make an asset ready for use, *[IAS 36.42]*, it does not allow inclusion of cash outflows relating to future enhancements of an asset's performance or capacity to which an entity is not committed. *[IAS 36.44]*. This may have a significant impact on relatively new assets and on fields or mines that will be developed over time. Note that while enhancement capital expenditure may not be recognised, routine or replacement capital expenditure necessary to maintain the function or current performance of the asset or assets in the CGU has to be included. Entities must therefore distinguish between maintenance and enhancement expenditure. This distinction may not be easy to draw in practice.

There are no such restrictions when determining fair value provided that it can be demonstrated that a market participant would be willing to attribute some value to the future enhancement and that the requirements of IFRS 13 – *Fair Value Measurement* – have been complied with. IFRS 13 is discussed in more detail in Chapter 14.

This is one reason why entities may choose to calculate the FVLCD of their assets using a DCF approach, as illustrated in Extract 39.25 above. The treatment of future capital expenditure is discussed in more detail in Chapter 20 at 4.4.1.

4.10.3 Identifying cash-generating units (CGUs)

An entity is required under IAS 36 to test individual assets for impairment. However, if it is not possible to estimate the recoverable amount of an individual asset then an entity should determine the recoverable amount of the CGU to which the asset belongs. *[IAS 36.66]*. A CGU is defined by the standard as the smallest identifiable group of assets that generates cash inflows that are largely independent of the cash inflows from other assets or groups of assets. *[IAS 36.6]*. In determining appropriate CGUs an entity will need to consider the following issues in particular:

(a) active markets for intermediate products;

(b) external users of the processing assets;

(c) fields or mines that are operated as one 'complex' through the use of shared infrastructure; and

(d) stand-alone fields or mines that operate on a portfolio basis.

These issues are discussed below.

4.10.3.A Markets for intermediate products

In vertically integrated mining operations the successive stages of the mining and production process are often considered to be one CGU as it is not possible to allocate net cash inflows to individual stages of the process. However, if there is an active market for intermediate commodities (e.g. bauxite, alumina and aluminium) then a vertically integrated mining company needs to consider whether its smelting and refining operations are part of the same CGU as its mining operations. If there is an active market for the output produced by an asset or group of assets, the assets concerned are identified as a separate CGU, even if some or all of the output is used internally. If extraction and smelting or refining are separate CGUs and the cash inflows generated by the asset or each CGU are based on internal transfer pricing, the best estimate of an external arm's length transaction price should be used in estimating the future cash flows to determine the asset's or CGU's VIU. *[IAS 36.70]*. See Chapter 20 at 4.1.1.

4.10.3.B External users of processing assets

When an entity is able to derive cash inflows from its processing assets (e.g. smelting or refining facilities) under tolling arrangements (see 6.4 below), the question arises as to whether or not those processing assets are a separate CGU. If an entity's processing assets generate significant cash inflows from arrangements with third parties then those assets are likely to be a separate CGU.

4.10.3.C Shared infrastructure

When several fields or mines share infrastructure (e.g. pipelines, railways, ports or refining and smelting facilities) the question arises as to whether the fields or mines and the shared infrastructure should be treated as a single CGU. Treating the fields or mines and the shared infrastructure as part of the same CGU is not appropriate under the following circumstances:

(a) if the shared infrastructure is relatively insignificant;

(b) if the fields or mines are capable of selling their product without making use of the shared infrastructure; and

(c) if the shared infrastructure is classified as a corporate asset, which is defined under IAS 36 as 'assets other than goodwill that contribute to the future cash flows of both the cash-generating unit under review and other cash-generating units'. *[IAS 36.6]*. In that case, the entity should apply the requirements in IAS 36 regarding corporate assets, which are discussed in Chapter 20 at 4.3.2.

However, if the conditions under (a) to (c) above do not apply then it may be appropriate to treat the fields or mines and the shared infrastructure as one CGU.

4.10.3.D Fields or mines operated on a portfolio basis

Mining companies and oil and gas companies sometimes operate a 'portfolio' of similar fields or mines, which are completely independent from an operational point of view. However, IAS 36 includes the following illustrative example.

Example 39.12: Single product entity [IAS 36 IE Example 1C]

Entity M produces a single product and owns plants A, B and C. Each plant is located in a different continent. A produces a component that is assembled in either B or C. The combined capacity of B and C is not fully utilised. M's products are sold worldwide from either B or C. For example, B's production can be sold in C's continent if the products can be delivered faster from B than from C. Utilisation levels of B and C depend on the allocation of sales between the two sites.

Although there is an active market for the products assembled by B and C, cash inflows for B and C depend on the allocation of production across the two sites. It is unlikely that the future cash inflows for B and C can be determined individually. Therefore, it is likely that B and C together are the smallest identifiable group of assets that generates cash inflows that are largely independent.

The same rationale could also be applied by a mining company that, for example, operates two coal mines on a portfolio basis. However, judgement needs to be exercised before concluding that it is appropriate to treat separate fields or mines as one CGU. This is particularly the case when the production costs of the output of fields or mines differ considerably, as it may not be appropriate to combine them into one CGU, thereby avoiding recognition of an impairment charge on the higher cost fields or mines.

4.10.4 Projections of cash flows

IAS 36 requires that in calculating VIU an entity base its cash flow projection on the most recent financial budgets/forecasts approved by management, excluding any estimated future cash inflows or outflows expected to arise from future restructurings or from improving or enhancing the asset's performance. The assumptions used to prepare the cash flows should be reasonable and supportable, which can best be achieved by benchmarking against market data or performance against previous budgets.

These projections cannot cover a period in excess of five years, unless a longer period can be justified. *[IAS 36.33(b)].* Entities are permitted to use a longer period if they are confident that their projections are reliable, based on past experience. *[IAS 36.35].*

In practice, most production or mining plans will cover a period of more than five years and hence management will typically make financial forecasts for a corresponding period. The use of such longer term forecasts may be appropriate where it is based on proved and probable reserves and expected annual production rates. Assumptions as to the level of reserves expected to be extracted should be consistent with the latest estimates prepared by reserve engineers; annual production rates should be consistent with those for a certain specified preceding period, e.g. five years; and price and cost assumptions should be consistent with the final period of specific assumptions.

The recoverable amount of an asset or a CGU is the higher of its FVLCD and its VIU. *[IAS 36.6].*

While IAS 36 does not impose any restrictions on how an entity determines the FVLCD of an asset or CGU, there are specific requirements in IFRS 13 as to how to determine fair value. IFRS 13 applies to almost all situations where a fair value measurement is required, and this includes the determination of FVLCD for impairment testing purposes. IFRS 13 is discussed in more detail in Chapter 14.

IFRS 13 defines fair value as the price that would be received to sell an asset or paid to transfer a liability in an orderly transaction between market participants at the measurement date and assumes such a transaction takes place under current market conditions. It is explicitly an exit price notion. FVLCD, like fair value, is not an entity-specific measurement, but is focused on market participants' assumptions for a particular asset or liability.

Before the issuance of IFRS 13, FVLCD in IAS 36 was already an exit value, but the requirements of IFRS 13 are different. For example, entities now have to consider the highest and best use (from a market participant perspective) to which the asset could be put. It is possible that a FVLCD calculation under IAS 36 (prior to the implementation of IFRS 13) may have been based on the existing use of an asset rather than its highest and best use. While this new requirement could (technically) result in a different fair value, it is generally presumed that an entity's current use of those assets or CGUs would be its highest and best use (unless market or other factors suggest that a different use by market participants would maximise the value of the asset).

Given this, we do not expect IFRS 13 to have a major impact, from a measurement perspective, on mining companies and oil and gas companies. Also, we do not expect major disclosure changes, as the disclosure requirements of IFRS 13 do not apply where an entity has calculated recoverable amount as FVLCD. However, an amendment to IAS 36 has been proposed to require additional disclosures consistent with certain disclosures required by IFRS 13.

While IFRS 13 introduces some new concepts, it does not limit or prioritise the valuation technique(s) an entity might use to measure fair value. An entity may use any valuation technique, or multiple techniques, as long as it is consistent with one of three valuation approaches: market approach, income approach and cost approach. However, IFRS 13 does focus on the type of inputs to be used and requires an entity to maximise the use of relevant observable inputs and minimise the use of the unobservable inputs.

Historically, many mining companies have calculated FVLCD using a DCF valuation technique. This approach differs from VIU in a number of ways. One of the key differences is that FVLCD would require an entity to use assumptions that a market participant would be likely to take into account rather than entity-specific assumptions. For example, as mining sector market participants invest for the longer term, they would not restrict themselves to a limited project time horizon. Therefore, the cash flow forecasts included in a FVLCD calculation may cover a longer period than may be used in a VIU calculation. Moreover, market participants would also take into account future expansionary capital expenditure related to subsequent phases in the development of a mining property in a FVLCD calculation, whereas this is not permitted in a VIU calculation. As illustrated in Extract 39.25 at 4.10.1 above, BHP Billiton uses this approach in determining the fair value less costs of disposal for its mineral assets.

The use of this type of DCF approach would continue to be acceptable under IFRS 13, provided the entity could demonstrate that the current use of the asset or CGU represented the highest and best use.

4.10.5 Cash flows from mineral reserves and resources and the appropriate discount rate

As discussed at 2.2 and 2.3 above, a significant amount of work is required before an entity can conclude that its mineral resources should be classified as mineral reserves. In practice, an entity may not have formally completed all of the detailed work that is required in order to designate mineral resources as mineral reserves. IAS 36 requires the cash flow projection used in calculating the VIU of assets to be based on 'reasonable and supportable assumptions that represent management's best estimate of the range of economic conditions that will exist over the remaining useful life of the asset'. *[IAS 36.33(a)].* Therefore, it may sometimes be appropriate under IAS 36 to take into account mineral resources that have not formally been designated as mineral reserves. However an entity would need to adjust the discount rate it uses in its VIU calculation for the additional risks associated with mineral resources for which the future cash flow estimates have not been adjusted. *[IAS 36.55].*

The requirements of IAS 36 for determining an appropriate discount rate are discussed in detail in Chapter 20 at 4.5.

4.10.6 Foreign currency cash flows

An entity in the extractive industries will often sell its product in a currency that is different from the one in which it incurs its production costs (e.g. silver production may be sold in US dollars while production costs are incurred in pesos). In such situations, impairment testing and calculating VIU under IAS 36 require that the foreign currency cash flows should first be estimated in the currency in which they will be generated and then discounted using a discount rate appropriate for that currency. An entity should translate the present value calculated in the foreign currency using the spot exchange rate at the date of the VIU calculation. *[IAS 36.54].* This is to avoid the problems inherent in using forward exchange rates, which are based on differential interest rates. Using such forward rates would result in double-counting the time value of money, first in the discount rate and then in the forward rate. *[IAS 36.BCZ49].*

This requirement, however, is more complex than it may initially appear. Effectively, this method requires an entity to perform separate impairment tests for cash flows generated in different currencies, but make them consistent with one another so that the combined effect is meaningful. This is an extremely difficult exercise to undertake. Many different factors need to be considered, including relative inflation rates and relative interest rates, as well as appropriate discount rates for the currencies in question. Because of this, the possibility for error is significant and the greatest danger lies in understating the present value of cash outflows by using a discount rate that is too high. Given this, it is important for entities to seek input from experienced valuers who will be able to assist them in dealing with these challenges.

For FVLCD calculations, the requirements relating to foreign currency are not specified other than they must reflect what a market participant would use when valuing the asset or CGU. In practice, entities that use a DCF analysis when calculating FVLCD will incorporate a forecast for exchange rates into their calculations rather than using the spot rate. A key issue in any forecast is the assumed timeframe over which the exchange rate may return to lower levels. This assumption is generally best analysed in conjunction with commodity prices in order to ensure consistency in the parameters used, i.e. a rise in prices will usually be accompanied by a rise in currency.

4.10.7 Commodity price assumptions

Forecasting commodity prices is never straightforward, because it is not usually possible to know whether recent changes in commodity prices are a temporary aberration or the beginning of a longer-term trend. Management usually takes a longer term approach to the commodity prices but these are not always consistent with the VIU rules. Given the long life of most mines and oil fields, an entity should not consider price levels only for the past three or four years. Instead, it should consider historical price levels for longer periods and assess how these prices are influenced by changes in underlying supply and demand levels. This requires an understanding of the industry marginal cost curves to determine at which price levels competitors are forced to reduce production as this will determine long-term minimum price levels in the industry. It will also require an understanding of whether or not new low cost producers are about to enter the market or new low cost mines/fields are about to commence production.

For actively traded commodities, there are typically forward price curves available and in such situations, these provide a reference point for forecast price assumptions. The commodity assumptions need to match the profile of the life of the mine or oil field. Spot prices and forward curve prices (where they are available as at the impairment testing date) are more relevant for shorter life mines and oil fields, while long-term price assumptions are more relevant for longer life mines and oil fields. Forecast prices (where available) should be used for the future periods covered by the VIU calculation. Where the forward price curve does not extend far enough into the future, the price at the end of the forward curve is generally held steady, or is often dropped to a longer term average price, where appropriate.

The future cash flows relating to the purchase or sale of commodities might be known from forward purchase or sales contracts. Use of these contracted prices in place of the spot price or forward curve price for the contracted volumes will generally be acceptable. However, it is possible that some of these forward contracts might be accounted for as derivatives contracts at fair value in accordance with IAS 39, and therefore the related assets or liabilities will be recognised in the statement of financial position. Such balances would be excluded from the IAS 36 impairment test. Given this, the cash flow projections prepared for the purposes of the IAS 36 impairment test should exclude the pricing terms associated with these forward contracts.

The commodity price is a key assumption in calculating the VIU and the FVLCD of any mine or oil field. Only in the context of impairment testing of goodwill and indefinite life intangible assets does IAS 36 specifically require disclosure of:

'(i) a description of each key assumption on which management has based its cash flow projections for the period covered by the most recent budgets/forecasts. Key assumptions are those to which the unit's (group of units') recoverable amount is most sensitive.

(ii) a description of management's approach to determining the value(s) assigned to each key assumption, whether those value(s) reflect past experience or, if appropriate, are consistent with external sources of information, and, if not, how and why they differ from past experience or external sources of information.' *[IAS 36.134(d)(i)-(ii), 134(e)(i)-(ii)]*.

In practice, considerable differences may exist between entities in their estimates of future commodity prices. Therefore, we recommend disclosure of the actual commodity prices used in calculating the VIU and the FVLCD of any mine or oil field, even though this is not specifically required by IAS 36 as these would generally be considered a significant judgement or estimate and hence would require disclosure under IAS 1. *[IAS 1.122, 125].* A possible approach to such disclosures is illustrated in the following extract from the financial statements of BP.

Extract 39.26: BP p.l.c. (2012)

Additional disclosures [extract]

Critical accounting policies [extract]

Recoverability of asset carrying values [extract]

For oil and natural gas properties, the expected future cash flows are estimated using management's best estimate of future oil and natural gas prices and reserves volumes. Prices for oil and natural gas used for future cash flow calculations are based on market prices for the first five years and the group's long-term price assumptions thereafter. As at 31 December 2012, the group's long-term planning assumptions were $90 per barrel for Brent and $6.50/mmBtu for Henry Hub (2011 $90 per barrel and $6.50/mmBtu). These long-term price assumptions are subject to periodic review and modification. The estimated future level of production is based on assumptions about future commodity prices, production and development costs, field decline rates, current fiscal regimes and other factors.

The extract below illustrates a similar type of disclosure by Randgold Resources, in this case as part of the disclosures on critical accounting estimates and judgements.

Extract 39.27: Randgold Resources Limited (2012)

Notes to the consolidated financial statements [extract]

3. Key accounting estimates and judgements [extract]

Gold price assumptions

The following gold prices were used in the mineral reserves optimisation calculations:

US$/oz	2012	2011
Morila	1000	1000
Loulo: open pit	1000	1000
Loulo: underground	1000	1000
Tongon	1000	1000
Kibali	1000	1000
Massawa	1000	1000
Gounkoto	1000	1000

Changes in the gold price used could result in changes in the mineral reserve optimisation calculations. Mine modelling is a complex process and hence is it not feasible to perform sensitivities on gold price assumptions.

4.11 Events after the reporting period

4.11.1 Reserves proven after the reporting period

IAS 10 – *Events after the Reporting Period* – distinguishes between two types of events:

- adjusting events after the reporting period being those that provide evidence of conditions that existed at the end of the reporting period ; and
- non adjusting events after the reporting period being those that are indicative of conditions that arose after the reporting period. *[IAS 10.3].*

This raises the question as to how an entity should deal with information regarding mineral reserves that it obtains after the end of its reporting period, but before its financial statements are authorised for issue i.e. finalised. For example, suppose that an entity concludes after the year-end that its remaining mineral reserves at that date were not 10 million barrels (or tonnes) but only 8 million barrels (or tonnes). As discussed at 4.9.3.A above, it may not always be entirely clear under IFRS whether such a change in mineral reserves should be treated as an adjusting event in accordance with IAS 10 (i.e. the new estimate provides evidence of conditions that existed previously) or as a change in estimate in accordance with IAS 8 (i.e. the new estimate resulted from new information or new developments).

If an entity believes that the change in the estimate of mineral reserves resulted from new information or new developments then it should account for that change prospectively from the date the new information becomes available. However, if such a change in mineral reserves is considered to be an adjusting event, only then should the entity base its depreciation, depletion and amortisation calculations under the units of production method on the most recent insight and base the calculation on the assumption that the remaining reserves at the end of the year were 8 million barrels (or tonnes). This assessment is highly judgemental and will depend upon the specific facts and circumstances associated with each individual event that occurs after the reporting period. Regardless of the approach it takes, an entity would need to consider whether the revision of the reserves estimate constitutes an impairment indicator.

4.11.2 Application of the acquisition method

If the initial accounting for a business combination can be determined only provisionally by the end of the period in which the combination is effected – because either the fair values to be assigned to the acquiree's identifiable assets, liabilities or contingent liabilities or the fair value of the combination can be determined only provisionally – the acquirer should account for the combination using those provisional values. Where, as a result of completing the initial accounting within twelve months from the acquisition date, adjustments to the provisional values have been found to be necessary, IFRS 3 requires them to be recognised from the acquisition date. *[IFRS 3.45].* Specifically IFRS 3 states that the provisional values are to be retrospectively adjusted to reflect new information obtained about facts and circumstances that existed as at the acquisition date and, if known, would have affected the measurement of the amounts recognised as at that date. This raises the question of how an entity should account for new information that it receives regarding an acquiree's reserves before it has finalised its acquisition accounting.

Example 39.13: Acquisition of an entity that owns mineral reserves

Entity A acquires Entity B for €27 million at 31 October 2012. At the time it assigned the following fair values to the acquired net assets:

	€ million
Mineral reserves (assuming reserves of 10 million barrels)	10
Other net assets acquired	5
Goodwill	12
Consideration transferred	27

At 30 June 2013, after conducting a drilling programme which commenced in March 2013, Entity A obtains information about the reserves (as at 30 June 2013), which when added to the production for the period (i.e. from 31 October 2012 to 30 June 2013) reveals that the mineral reserves at the date of acquisition were not 10 million barrels, as previously thought, but were only 8 million barrels.

Can Entity A revise its initial acquisition accounting to reflect the fact that the mineral reserves are only 8 million barrels, rather than 10 million?

The answer to this question is not straightforward and it is a matter of significant judgement which needs to be made based on the facts and circumstances of each individual situation.

IFRS 3 requires assets acquired and liabilities assumed to be measured at fair value as at the acquisition date. It then defines fair value as: the amount for which an asset could be exchanged, or a liability settled, between knowledgeable, willing parties in an arm's length transaction. The challenge with the new information obtained about the mineral reserves in Example 39.13 above is determining whether it provided new information about facts and circumstances that existed as at the acquisition date or whether it resulted from events that occurred after the acquisition date. As discussed in 4.9.3.A above, it is difficult to determine exactly what causes a reserve estimate to change i.e. whether the facts and circumstances existed at acquisition date or whether it was due to new events.

In Example 39.13, the new reserves information arose as a result of a drilling programme that commenced five months after the acquisition date and it is not entirely clear why the reserves estimate changed. One may therefore conclude that as entity A should be valuing the mineral reserves acquired on the basis of information that a knowledgeable, willing party *would and could* reasonably have been expected to use in an arm's length transaction at 31 October 2012, that this new information should not have an impact on the provisional accounting. This is on the basis that this new information was not available at acquisition date and could not reasonably have been expected to be considered.

Similarly, if entity A had concluded at 30 June 2013 that its internal long-term oil price assumption was $80/barrel instead of $60/barrel that would not have any effect on the acquisition accounting. Entity A should be valuing the mineral reserves on the basis of information that a knowledgeable, willing party *would* have used in an arm's length transaction at 31 October 2012; this may, of course, have been neither $80 nor $60.

The conclusion may differ however, if the drilling programme had been completed and the information was available at acquisition date, but due to the pressures of completing the transaction, entity A had not been able to assess fully or take into account all of this information e.g. it had not had time to properly analyse all of the information available in the data room. In this instance, it would be appropriate to adjust the provisional accounting.

4.11.3 Completion of E&E activity after the reporting period

As discussed at 3.5.1 above, IFRS 6 requires E&E assets to be tested for impairment when exploration for and evaluation of mineral resources in the specific area have not led to the discovery of commercially viable quantities of mineral resources and the entity has decided to discontinue its activities in the specific area. *[IFRS 6.20]*. An entity that concludes, after its reporting period, that an exploration and evaluation project is unsuccessful, should account for this conclusion as:

- a *non-adjusting event* if the conclusion is indicative of conditions that arose after the reporting period, for example new information or new developments that did not offer greater clarity concerning the conditions that existed at the end of the reporting period (one possible example may be drilling that only commenced after reporting date). The new information or new developments are considered to be changes in accounting estimates under IAS 8. Also, based on the information that existed at the reporting period, the fair value less costs of disposal of the underlying E&E asset might well have been in excess of its carrying amount; *[IAS 8.5]*
- an *adjusting event* if the decision not to sanction the project for development was based on information that existed at the reporting date. Failure to use, or misuse of, reliable information that was available when financial statements for those periods were authorised for issue and could reasonably be expected to have been obtained and taken into account in the preparation and presentation of those financial statements, would constitute an error under IAS 8. *[IAS 8.5]*.

Evaluating whether information obtained subsequent to the reporting period but before the financial statements are authorised for issue is an adjusting or non-adjusting events may require significant judgement. The conditions should be carefully evaluated based on the facts and circumstances of each individual situation.

4.12 Decommissioning and restoration/rehabilitation

The operations of entities engaged in extractive industries can have a significant impact on the environment. Decommissioning or restoration activities at the end of a mining or oil and gas operation may be required by law, the terms of mineral licences or an entity's stated policy and past practice. The associated costs of decommissioning, remediation or restoration can be significant. The accounting treatment for such costs is therefore critical. Different terms may be used, often interchangeably, to essentially refer to the same activity, e.g. restoration, remediation and rehabilitation. In this section we shall use the word restoration (to align to the wording in IFRS).

4.12.1 Recognition and measurement issues

4.12.1.A Initial recognition

Initial recognition of a decommissioning or restoration provision only on commencement of commercial production is generally not appropriate under IFRS, because the obligation to remove facilities and to restore the environment typically arises during the construction of the facilities, with some further obligations arising during the production phase. Therefore, a decommissioning or restoration provision should be recognised during the development or construction phase (see 1.2.1 above) of the project, i.e. before any production takes place, and should form part of the cost of the assets acquired or constructed. It may also be necessary to recognise a further decommissioning or restoration provision during the production phase (see 4.12.1.D below).

While the damage caused in the exploration phase may generally be immaterial, an entity should recognise a decommissioning or restoration provision where the damage is material and the entity will be required to carry out remediation. The accounting for such a provision will depend on how the related E&E costs have been accounted for. If the E&E costs are capitalised, the associated decommissioning costs should also be capitalised. However, if the E&E costs are expensed, any associated decommissioning or restoration costs should also be expensed.

Finally, even if decommissioning and restoration were not planned to take place in the foreseeable future (for example because the related assets are continually renewed and replaced), IAS 37 would still require a decommissioning or restoration provision to be recognised. However, in these cases the discounted value of the obligation may be comparatively insignificant.

4.12.1.B Measurement of the liability

As illustrated in Extract 39.28 below, measurement of a decommissioning or restoration provision requires a significant amount of judgement because:

- the amount of remedial work required will depend on the scale of the operations. In the extractives industries the environmental damage may vary considerably depending on the type and development of the project;
- the amount of remedial work further depends on environmental standards imposed by local regulators, which may vary over time;
- detailed decommissioning and remedial work plans will often not be developed until fairly shortly before closure of the operations;
- it may not always be clear which costs are directly attributable to decommissioning or restoration (e.g. security costs, maintenance cost, ongoing environmental monitoring and employee termination costs);
- the value of materials recovered during decommissioning or restoration may depend on commodity prices (e.g. gold recovered in processing a tailings pond; oil recovered from pipes etc.);
- the timing of the decommissioning or restoration depends on when the fields or mines cease to produce at economically viable rates, which depends upon future commodity prices and reserves; and
- the actual decommissioning or restoration work will often be carried out by specialised contractors, the cost of which will depend on future market prices for the necessary remedial work.

Many of the uncertainties above can only be finally resolved towards the end of the production phase, shortly before decommissioning and restoration are to take place. A significant increase in the decommissioning or restoration provision resulting from revised estimates could result in recognition of an additional decommissioning or restoration asset that is immediately impaired. Therefore, a significant increase in a decommissioning or restoration provision close to the end of the production phase is a trigger for impairment testing. Conversely, a decrease in the decommissioning or restoration provision could exceed the carrying amount of the related asset, in which case the excess should be recognised as a gain in profit or loss.

Accounting for decommissioning costs is discussed in more detail in Chapter 18 at 4.3.

4.12.1.C Discount rate

IAS 37 requires that where the effect of the time value of money is material, the amount of a provision should be the present value of the expenditures expected to be required to settle the obligation. *[IAS 37.45]*. The discount rate (or rates) to be used in arriving at the present value should be 'a pre-tax rate (or rates) that reflect(s) current market assessments of the time value of money and the risks specific to the liability. The discount rate(s) shall not reflect risks for which the future cash flow estimates have been adjusted.' *[IAS 37.47]*. There are a number of complications in applying these requirements that are discussed in Chapter 27:

- real discount rate or a nominal discount rate (see Chapter 27 at 4.3.1);
- adjusting cash flow estimates and discount rates for risk (see Chapter 27 at 4.3.2); and
- determining the pre-tax discount rate (see Chapter 27 at 4.3.4).

Although IAS 37 provides an entity with the option of reflecting risk either in the discount rate or in the cash flow estimates, entities generally use a risk free discount rate and reflect the risks in the cash flow estimates. Finally, the discount rate of a provision should be *reduced* to reflect an increase in risk (i.e. only a lower discount will result in a higher provision).

4.12.1.D Decommissioning or restoration costs incurred in the production phase

IAS 16 considers the initial estimate of the costs of dismantling and removing the item and restoring the site on which it is located to be part of the cost of an item of property, plant and equipment. *[IAS 16.16(c)]*. However, an entity should apply IAS 2 to the costs of obligations for dismantling, removing and restoring the site on which an item is located that are incurred during a particular period as a consequence of having used the item to produce inventories during that period. *[IAS 16.18]*. That means that such additional decommissioning or restoration costs resulting from production activities should be included in the cost of inventories, *[IAS 2.10]*, while decommissioning costs resulting from the construction of assets should be accounted for as discussed above. An entity that incurs abnormal amounts of costs (e.g. costs of remediation of soil contamination from oil spills or overflowing of a tailings pond) should not treat these as part of the cost of inventories under IAS 2, but expense them immediately. *[IAS 2.16]*.

4.12.2 Accounting for changes in decommissioning and restoration costs

IAS 16 is unclear about the extent to which an item's carrying amount should be affected by changes in the estimated amount of dismantling and site restoration costs that occur *after* the estimate made upon initial measurement. This issue is the subject of IFRIC 1 – *Changes in Existing Decommissioning, Restoration and Similar Liabilities* – issued in May 2004.

IFRIC 1 applies to any decommissioning or similar liability that has both been included as part of an asset measured in accordance with IAS 16 and measured as a liability in accordance with IAS 37. *[IFRIC 1.2]*. It deals with the impact of events that change the measurement of an existing liability. Such events include a change in the estimated cash flows, the discount rate and the unwinding of the discount. *[IFRIC 1.3]*.

IFRIC 1 differentiates between the treatment required depending upon whether the items of PP&E concerned are valued under the cost model or under the revaluation model of IAS 16. If the asset is carried at cost, changes in the liability are added to, or deducted from, the cost of the asset. Any deduction may not exceed the carrying amount of the asset and any excess over the carrying value is taken immediately to profit or loss. If the change in estimate results in an addition to the carrying value of the asset, the entity is required to consider whether this is an indication of impairment of the asset as a whole and test for impairment in accordance with IAS 36 (see 4.10 above and Chapter 20). *[IFRIC 1.5]*.

Where a reduction in a decommissioning or restoration obligation is to be deducted from the cost of the asset, the cost of the asset is the written down carrying value of the whole asset (comprising its construction costs and decommissioning or restoration cost). It is not just the value of the decommissioning or restoration asset originally recognised. Accordingly, we believe that it would not be appropriate to recognise any gain until the carrying value of the whole asset is extinguished. See Chapter 27 at 6.3.1 for more details.

If the related asset is carried at a revalued amount and changes in the estimated liability alter the revaluation surplus (i.e. the re-estimation takes place independently of the revaluation of the asset), then a decrease in the liability is credited directly to the revaluation surplus in equity, unless it reverses a revaluation deficit on the asset that was previously recognised in profit or loss, in which case it should be taken to profit or loss. Similarly, an increase in the liability is taken straight to profit or loss, unless there is a revaluation surplus existing in respect of that asset. *[IFRIC 1.6]*.

If the liability decreases and the deduction exceeds the amount that the asset would have been carried at under the cost model (e.g. its depreciated cost), the amount by which the asset is reduced is capped at this amount. Any excess is taken immediately to profit or loss. *[IFRIC 1.7]*. This means that the maximum amount by which an asset can be reduced is the same whether it is carried at cost or valuation.

Any change in the revalued amount must conform to the requirements of IAS 16 concerning revalued assets, particularly the requirement that they must be carried at an amount that does not differ materially from fair value (see Chapter 18 at 6 for the standard's rules regarding revaluations of assets). Such an adjustment is an indication that the carrying amount may differ from fair value and the asset may have to be revalued. Any such revaluation must, of course, take account of the adjustment to the estimated liability. If a revaluation is necessary, all assets of the same class must be revalued. *[IFRIC 1.7]*.

Any changes in estimate taken to the revaluation reserve in equity must be disclosed on the face of the statement of changes in equity in accordance with IAS 1 (see Chapter 3 at 3.3). *[IFRIC 1.6]*. Depreciation of the 'decommissioning asset' and any changes thereto are covered in Chapter 18 at 4.3. The unwinding of the discount must be recognised in profit or loss as a finance cost as it occurs. The allowed alternative treatment of capitalisation under IAS 23 is not permitted. *[IFRIC 1.8]*.

The extract below from Tullow Oil illustrates a typical accounting policy for decommissioning costs and the disclosure of decommissioning costs.

Extract 39.28: Tullow Oil plc (2012)

ACCOUNTING POLICIES [extract]

Year ended 31 December 2012

(n) Decommissioning [extract]

Provision for decommissioning is recognised in full when the related facilities are installed. A corresponding amount equivalent to the provision is also recognised as part of the cost of the related property, plant and equipment. The amount recognised is the estimated cost of decommissioning, discounted to its net present value, and is reassessed each year in accordance with local conditions and requirements. Changes in the estimated timing of decommissioning or decommissioning cost estimates are dealt with prospectively by recording an adjustment to the provision, and a corresponding adjustment to property, plant and equipment. The unwinding of the discount on the decommissioning provision is included as a finance cost.

NOTES TO GROUP FINANCIAL STATEMENTS [extract]

Year ended 31 December 2012

Note 22. Provisions [extract]

(i) Decommissioning costs and other provisions

	2012 $m	2011 $m
At 1 January	**440.8**	278.6
New provisions and changes in estimates	**60.4**	81.6
Acquisition of subsidiary	**–**	86.6
Decommissioning payments	**1.1**	(16.7)
Unwinding of discount (note 5)	**20.3**	20.9
Transfer to assets held for sale (note 17)	**(1.6)**	–
Currency translation adjustment	**10.9**	(10.2)
At 31 December 2012	**531.6**	440.8

The decommissioning provision represents the present value of decommissioning costs relating to the European and African oil and gas interests, which are expected to be incurred up to 2035. A review of all decommissioning estimates was undertaken by an independent specialist in 2010 which has been assessed and updated internally for the purposes of the 2012 financial statements.

Assumptions, based on the current economic environment, have been made which management believe are a reasonable basis upon which to estimate the future liability. These estimates are reviewed regularly to take into account any material changes to the assumptions. However, actual decommissioning costs will ultimately depend upon future market prices for the necessary decommissioning works required which will reflect market conditions at the relevant time. Furthermore, the timing of decommissioning is likely to depend on when the fields cease to produce at economically viable rates. This in turn will depend upon future oil and gas prices, which are inherently uncertain.

One matter that IFRIC 1 does not specifically address is the treatment of obligations arising after the asset has been constructed, for example as a result of a change in legislation. *[IFRIC 1.BC23]*. In our opinion, the cost of the related asset should be measured in accordance with the principles set out in IFRIC 1 regardless of whether the obligation exists at the time of constructing the asset or arises later in its life. For further discussion on this matter see Chapter 27 at 6.3.2.

4.12.3 Treatment of exchange differences

In most cases it will be appropriate for the exchange differences arising on provisions to be taken to profit or loss in the period they arise. However, it may be that an entity has recognised a decommissioning provision under IAS 37. One practical difficulty with such a provision is that due to the long period over which the actual cash outflows will arise, an entity may not know the currency in which the transaction will actually be settled. Nevertheless if it is determined that it is expected to be settled in a foreign currency it will be a monetary item. The main issue then is what should happen to any exchange differences. As discussed in Chapter 27 at 6.3, IFRIC 1 applies to any decommissioning or similar liability that has been both included as part of an asset and measured as a liability in accordance with IAS 37. IFRIC 1 requires, *inter alia*, that any adjustment to such a provision resulting from changes in the estimated outflow of resources embodying economic benefits (e.g. cash flows) required to settle the obligation should not be taken to profit or loss as it occurs, but should be added to or deducted from the cost of the asset to which it relates. Therefore, the requirement of IAS 21 to take the exchange differences arising on the provision to profit or loss in the period in which they arise conflicts with this requirement in IFRIC 1. It is our view that IFRIC 1 is the more relevant pronouncement for decommissioning purposes, therefore we consider that this type of exchange difference should not to be taken to profit or loss, but dealt with in accordance with IFRIC 1.

4.12.4 Deferred tax on decommissioning obligations

The exception in IAS 12 from recognising the deferred tax effects of certain temporary differences arising on the initial recognition of some assets and liabilities is generally referred to as the 'initial recognition exception'. Accounting for decommissioning obligations involves the initial recognition of an equal and opposite asset and liability which subsequently unwind on different bases. A strict interpretation of IAS 12 would be to argue that upon initial recognition, the tax base of both the decommissioning liability and the decommissioning part of the asset are nil. Therefore, no deferred taxation should be recognised relating to the deductible temporary difference on the decommissioning liability or the taxable temporary difference on the decommissioning part of the asset. However, the unrecognised deductible and taxable temporary differences will unwind at a different rate, which can result in significant fluctuations in the effective tax rate (see Example 29.18 in Chapter 29).

That leads some to argue that, as the asset and liability recognised on establishment of a decommissioning provision are the result of a single transaction, they should be regarded as effectively giving rise to a single (net) temporary difference of zero. This means that, as and when (net) temporary differences emerge after initial recognition, deferred tax may be recognised on those temporary differences, with the effect that the effective tax rate in profit or loss reflects the statutory rate actually applicable to the transaction as a whole.

Those who take this view might also argue that it is consistent with the implied, if not explicit, intention of the initial recognition exception that deferred tax should always be recognised unless it creates a 'day one' tax charge or credit in profit or loss.

In this case a 'day one' profit or loss is avoided by establishing an equal and opposite deferred tax asset and liability.

Others argue that this approach is not acceptable. The financial statements present a clearly separate asset and liability which do not meet any offset criteria. The 'initial recognition exception' should therefore be applied to the asset and liability separately and not as if the two comprised some form of single net asset or liability.

The Interpretations Committee considered this issue on two occasions in 2005, both in the context of finance leases, which raise identical issues. The *IFRIC Update* for April 2005 appeared to support the latter view:

> 'The IFRIC noted that initial recognition exemption applies to each separate recognised element in the balance sheet, and no deferred tax asset or liability should be recognised on the temporary difference existing on the initial recognition of assets and liabilities arising from finance leases or subsequently.'

However, only two months later, the Interpretations Committee added:

> 'The IFRIC considered the treatment of deferred tax relating to assets and liabilities arising from finance leases.
>
> 'While noting that there is diversity in practice in applying the requirements of IAS 12 to assets and liabilities arising from finance leases, the IFRIC agreed not to develop any guidance because the issue falls directly within the scope of the Board's short-term convergence project on income taxes with the FASB.'

It would therefore seem that, while the Interpretations Committee regards the analysis that the asset and liability must be considered separately as consistent with a literal reading of IAS 12, it accepts the alternative approach.

4.12.5 Indefinite life assets

While the economic lives of oil fields and mines are finite, certain infrastructure assets (e.g. pipelines and refineries) are continually being repaired, replaced and upgraded. While individual parts of such assets may not have an indefinite economic life, these assets may occupy a particular site for an indefinite period.

IAS 37 requires a decommissioning provision to be recognised when:

(a) an entity has a present obligation (legal or constructive) as a result of a past event;

(b) it is probable that an outflow of resources embodying economic benefits will be required to settle the obligation; and

(c) the entity can make a reliable estimate of the amount of the obligation. *[IAS 37.14]*.

Regardless of whether or not the related asset has an indefinite life, the decommissioning provision will normally meet the criteria under (a) and (b) above. While it might seem that a reliable estimate of the decommissioning provision cannot be made if the underlying asset has an indefinite life, 'indefinite' does not mean that the asset has an infinite life but that the life is long and has not yet been determined. IAS 37 presumes that:

> 'Except in extremely rare cases, an entity will be able to determine a range of possible outcomes and can therefore make an estimate of the obligation that is sufficiently reliable to use in recognising a provision.' *[IAS 37.25]*.

Therefore, it should be extremely rare for an entity to conclude that it cannot make a reliable estimate of the amount of the obligation. Even if an entity did conclude in an extremely rare case that no reliable estimate could be made, there would still be a contingent liability and the following disclosures would be required:

- a brief description of the nature of the contingent liability; and
- where practicable:
  - an estimate of its financial effect, measured under paragraphs 36-52 of IAS 37;
  - an indication of the uncertainties relating to the amount or timing of any outflow; and
  - the possibility of any reimbursement. *[IAS 37.26, 86].*

Finally, it should be noted that the discounted value of decommissioning costs that will only be incurred far into the future may be relatively insignificant.

4.12.6 Funds established or put aside to meet a decommissioning or restoration obligation

Some entities may participate in a decommissioning, restoration or environmental rehabilitation fund, the purpose of which is to segregate assets to fund some or all of the costs of decommissioning. IFRIC 5 – *Rights to Interests arising from Decommissioning, Restoration and Environmental Rehabilitation Funds* – was issued in December 2004 to address this issue. See Chapter 27 at 6.3.3 for more information.

Entities may also set aside cash, for example in an escrow account, for the purpose of meeting future decommissioning, rehabilitation or restoration obligations.

A common question raised is whether the decommissioning/restoration fund asset or cash held in escrow can be offset against the decommissioning, rehabilitation or restoration provision. For decommissioning or restoration fund assets, IFRIC 5 requires the contributor to a fund to recognise its obligations to pay decommissioning or restoration costs as a liability and recognise its interest in the fund separately, unless the contributor is not liable to pay decommissioning or restoration costs even if the fund fails to pay. *[IFRIC 5.7].* Accordingly, in most cases it would not be appropriate to offset the decommissioning / restoration liability and the interest in the fund. See Chapter 27 at 6.3.3.C for more information as to why they should be presented gross.

In relation to cash held in escrow, similar considerations would apply. While funds have been set aside to meet the obligation at some point in the future, they have not yet been applied to extinguish the decommissioning obligation. Therefore, the entity remains liable for the decommissioning costs and hence should continue to recognise the decommissioning / restoration provision.

4.13 Revenue recognition

4.13.1 Revenue in the development phase: Incidental revenue

Under IAS 16, the cost of an item of property, plant and equipment includes any costs directly attributable to bringing the asset to the location and condition necessary for it to be capable of operating in the manner intended by management. *[IAS 16.16(b)]*. However, during the construction of an asset, an entity may enter into incidental operations that are not, in themselves, necessary to bring the asset itself into the location and condition necessary for it to be capable of operating in the manner intended by management. The standard gives the example of income earned by using a building site as a car park prior to starting construction. A mining example may be income earned from leasing out the land surrounding the mine site to a local farmer to run his sheep on. Because incidental operations such as these are not necessary to bring an item to the location and condition necessary for it to be capable of operating in the manner intended by management, the income and related expenses of incidental operations are recognised in profit or loss and included in their respective classifications of income and expense. *[IAS 16.21]*. Such incidental income is not offset against the cost of the asset.

If the asset is *already in* the location and condition necessary for it to be capable of being used in the manner intended by management, then IAS 16 requires capitalisation to cease and depreciation to start. *[IAS 16.20]*. In these circumstances, all income earned from using the asset must be recognised as revenue in profit or loss and the related costs of the activity should include an element of depreciation of the asset.

4.13.2 Revenue in the development phase: Integral to development

The directly attributable costs of an item of property, plant and equipment include the costs of testing whether the asset is functioning properly, after deducting the net proceeds from selling any items produced while bringing the asset to that location and condition. *[IAS 16.17(e)]*. The standard gives the example of samples produced when testing equipment. There are other situations in which income may be generated wholly and necessarily as a result of the process of bringing the asset to the location and condition for its intended use.

The extractive industries are highly capital intensive and there are many instances where income may be generated prior to the commencement of production. Some mining examples include:

- During the evaluation i.e. when the technical feasibility and commercial viability are being determined, an entity may 'trial mine', to determine which method would be the most profitable and efficient in the circumstances, and which metallurgical process is the most efficient. Ore mined through trial mining may be processed and sold during the evaluation phase.
- As part of the process of constructing a deep underground mine, the mining operation may extract some saleable 'product' during the construction of the mine e.g. sinking shafts to the depth where the main ore-bearing rock is located.
- At the other end of the spectrum, income may be earned from the sale of product from 'ramping up' the mine to production at commercial levels.

Alternatively, an example in the oil and gas sector would be:

- Onshore wells are frequently placed on long-term production test as part of the process of appraisal and formulation of a field development plan. Test production may be sold during this time.

Some interpret IAS 16's requirement quite narrowly as only applying to income earned from actually 'testing' the asset, while others interpret it more broadly to include other types of pre-commissioning or production testing revenue.

We have noted that some income may be generated wholly and necessarily as a result of activities that are part of the process of bringing the asset into the location and condition for its intended use, i.e. the activities are integral to the construction or development of the mine or field. Some consider that, as income generated from incidental operations should be taken to revenue, income earned from activities that are integral to the development of the mine or field should be credited to the cost of the mine or field. This is because the main purpose of the activities is the development of the mine or field, not the production of ore or hydrocarbons. The income earned from production is an unintended benefit.

In our experience, practice in accounting for pre-commissioning or test production revenue varies. These various treatments have evolved as a result of the way in which the relatively limited guidance in IFRS has been interpreted and applied. In some instances, this has also been influenced by approaches that originated in previous and other GAAPs, where guidance was/is somewhat clearer.

The key challenge is usually not how to measure the revenue but how entities view this revenue and, more significantly, how to distinguish those costs that are directly attributable to developing the operating capability of the mine or field from those that represent the cost of producing saleable material. It can be extremely difficult to apportion these costs. Consequently, there is a risk of misstatement of gross profits.

Other GAAPs have either previously provided or continue to provide further guidance that has influenced some of the approaches adopted under IFRS. For example, the now superseded Australian GAAP (AGAAP) standard on extractive industries[128] and the UK guidance for the oil and gas industry (the OIAC SORP)[129] provided more specific guidance. The former clearly required, and the latter recommended, that any proceeds earned from the sale of product obtained during the exploration, evaluation or development phases should be treated in the same manner as the proceeds from the sale of product in the production phase, i.e. recognised in profit or loss as part of income.

AGAAP required the estimated cost of producing the quantities concerned to be deducted from the accumulated costs of such activities and included as part of costs of goods sold.[130] By contrast, the OIAC SORP was more specific and stated that an amount equivalent to the revenues should be both charged to cost of sales and credited against appraisal costs to record a zero net margin on such production.[131]

The various practices that are adopted and accepted include:

- all pre-commissioning/test production revenue is considered integral to the development of the mine or field and is therefore credited to the asset;
- only revenue genuinely earned from the testing of assets, e.g. product processed as a result of testing the processing plant and associated facilities, is credited to the associated asset, with all other revenue being recognised in profit or loss; or
- all pre-commissioning or test production revenue is recognised in profit or loss.

For entities that recognise pre-commissioning or test production revenue in profit or loss, various approaches are applied to determine the amount to be included in cost of goods sold and include:

- an amount equivalent to the revenues is charged to cost of sales and credited against the asset to record a zero net margin on such production (similar to the guidance in the OIAC SORP);
- a standard or expected cost of production is ascribed to the volumes produced, e.g. weighted average cost per tonne/barrel based on actual results over a historical period, e.g. the last two or three years; or for new mines or fields, the expected cost per tonne/bbl as set out in the business, mine or field plan, producing a standard margin;
- recognising only the incremental cost of processing the product; or
- recognising nothing in cost of goods sold.

The net effect of all of these approaches is that any excess of the total cost incurred over the amount recognised in profit or loss as cost of goods sold, is effectively capitalised as part of the asset. Note that the first approach, where cost of goods sold is recognised at the same amount as the revenue, produces the same net balance sheet and profit or loss result as if the revenue had been credited to the asset in its entirety.

In our view, while diverse treatments may be adopted and accepted, it is unlikely the third and fourth cost of goods sold approaches would be appropriate because they would not provide a fair reflection of the cost to produce the saleable product.

There is a significant degree of divergence as to how entities account for pre-commissioning revenue. It will be a matter of significant judgement as to what is incidental revenue that should be recognised in profit or loss, and what is integral revenue that should be recognised as a credit to the related asset. Significant judgement will also be required to determine when the asset is in the location and condition to be capable of operating as intended by management, i.e. when it is ready for its intended use. In the absence of specific guidance this divergence will continue. However, capitalisation (including recognising income as a credit to the cost of the asset) is to cease when the asset is ready for its intended use, regardless of whether or not it is achieving its targeted levels of production or profitability, or even operating at all.

4.13.3 Exchanges of inventories

Under IAS 18, when goods or services are exchanged or swapped for goods or services that are of a similar nature and value, the exchange is not regarded as a transaction that generates revenue. This can occur with commodities like oil and sometimes coal, where suppliers exchange or swap inventories in various locations to fulfil demand on a timely basis in a particular location. However, when goods are sold in exchange for dissimilar goods, the exchange is regarded as a transaction that generates revenue. *[IAS 18.12].*

Accounting for exchanges of inventories requires a degree of judgement particularly:

- when the inventories exchanged are not identical (e.g. swaps of slightly different products, possibly with an adjustment for the difference in quality); or
- there is some past practice of settling net in cash.

Furthermore, any receivable or payable balance does not entirely meet the definition of inventory in IAS 2 but is instead a non-monetary receivable or payable. The product receivable or payable is normally recorded at cost within current assets or liabilities.

Extract 39.29: TOTAL S.A. (2012)

Notes to the Consolidated Financial Statements [extract]

1) Accounting policies [extract]

D) Sales and revenues from sales [extract]

(i) Sale of goods [extract]

Exchanges of crude oil and petroleum products within normal trading activities do not generate any income and therefore these flows are shown at their net value in both the statement of income and the balance sheet.

4.14 Inventories

4.14.1 Sale of by-products and joint products

In the extractive industries it is common for more than one product to be extracted from the same reserves, e.g. copper is often found together with gold and silver. Products produced at the same time are classified as joint products or by-products and are usually driven by the importance of the different products to the viability of the mine. The same metal may be treated differently based on differing grades and quantities of products. In most cases where more than one product is produced there is a clear distinction between the main product and the by-products. In other cases the distinction may not be as clear.

The decision as to whether these are joint products or whether one is a by-product, is important, as it impacts the way in which costs are allocated. This decision may also affect the classification of sales of the various products.

4.14.1.A By-products

A by-product is a secondary product obtained during the course of production or processing, having relatively small importance when compared with the principal product or products.

IAS 2 prescribes the following accounting for by-products:

> '...When the costs of conversion of each product are not separately identifiable, they are allocated between the products on a rational and consistent basis. The allocation may be based, for example, on the relative sales value of each product either at the stage in the production process when the products become separately identifiable, or at the completion of production. Most by-products, by their nature, are immaterial. When this is the case, they are often measured at net realisable value and this value is deducted from the cost of the main product. As a result, the carrying amount of the main product is not materially different from its cost.' *[IAS 2.14]*.

By-products that are significant in value should be accounted for as joint products as discussed at 4.14.1.B below. Where they are not significant, sales of by-products are often treated as a negative cost, i.e. credited against cost of goods sold.

The extract below from AngloGold Ashanti's financial statements illustrates how insignificant by-products are deducted from costs of sales and how significant by-products are accounted for separately within inventories.

Extract 39.30: AngloGold Ashanti Limited (2012)

GROUP - NOTES TO THE FINANCIAL STATEMENTS [extract]

For the year ended 31 December

1 Accounting policies [extract]

1.3 Summary of significant accounting policies [extract]

Inventories [extract]

Inventories are valued at the lower of cost and net realisable value after appropriate allowances for redundant and slow moving items. Cost is determined on the following bases:

[...]

- by-products, which include uranium oxide and sulphuric acid, are valued on an average total production cost method. By-products are classified as a non-current asset where the by-products on hand exceed current processing capacity; [...]

Revenue recognition [extract]

Revenue is recognised at the fair value of the consideration received or receivable to the extent that it is probable that economic benefits will flow to the group and revenue and costs can be reliably measured. The following criteria must also be present:

[...]

- where a by-product is not regarded as significant, revenue is credited against cost of sales, when the significant risks and rewards of ownership of the products are transferred to the buyer. [...]

Although IAS 2 does not require extensive disclosures in respect of by-products, if amounts are material, disclosure of the following information, which many extractives companies provide on a voluntary basis, will greatly assist users:

- accounting policies applied to by-products;
- line items in the primary financial statements in which revenues and carried amounts have been disclosed;
- quantities of by-products sold; and
- average prices of by-products sold.

4.14.1.B Joint products

Joint products are two or more products produced simultaneously from a common raw material source, with each product having a significant relative sales value. One joint product cannot be produced without the other and the products cannot be identified separately until a certain production stage, often called the 'split-off point', is reached. Joint products are very common in both the oil and gas sector (e.g. crude oil when run through a refinery produces a variety of products) and the mining sector.

Joint products, by definition, are all significant in value and require that an entity allocate on a rational and consistent basis the costs of conversion that are not separately identifiable for each product. The IASC Issues Paper outlined two approaches that have found acceptance in practice:[132]

(a) *allocation on the basis of physical characteristics* – In the oil and gas sector, entities often combine quantities of oil and gas based on their relative energy content (i.e. 6,000 cubic feet of gas is roughly equal in energy to one barrel of oil). This method, however, does not take account of the fact that, for example, gas is cheaper per unit of energy than oil because it is more difficult to transport; and

(b) *allocation on the basis of relative values* – This approach is more common in the mining sector where often it is not possible to identify a relevant physical characteristic that can be used to combine quantities of different products. The drawback of this method is that it results in very similar profit margins for each of the joint products, which may not be reflective of the underlying economic reality (i.e. one of the joint products, if mined in isolation, might have a completely different profit margin).

Although it should be kept in mind that neither method is perfect, both approaches are currently permitted under IFRS. It is true also that whichever method is selected, it is unlikely to have a material effect on reported profit overall. The extract below illustrates the application of approach (b) by Anglo American.

Extract 39.31: Anglo American plc (2012)

NOTES TO THE FINANCIAL STATEMENTS [extract]
1. ACCOUNTING POLICIES [extract]
Inventory

Inventory and work in progress are measured at the lower of cost and net realisable value. The production cost of inventory includes an appropriate proportion of depreciation and production overheads. Cost is determined on the following bases:

- Raw materials and consumables are measured at cost on a first in, first out (FIFO) basis or a weighted average cost basis.
- Finished products are measured at raw material cost, labour cost and a proportion of manufacturing overhead expenses.
- Metal and coal stocks are included within finished products and are measured at average cost.

At precious metals operations that produce 'joint products', cost is allocated amongst products according to the ratio of contribution of these metals to gross sales revenues.

4.15 Major maintenance and turnarounds / renewals and reconditioning costs

Some assets (e.g. refineries, smelters and oil rigs) require major maintenance at regular intervals, which is often described as an overhaul or turnaround in the oil and gas sector and renewal or reconditioning in the mining sector. When an entity incurs further costs in relation to an item of property, plant and equipment, IAS 16 requires it to determine the nature of the costs. Where such costs provide access to future economic benefits they should be capitalised. Costs of day-to-day servicing costs (e.g. costs of labour and consumables, and possibly the cost of small parts) should be expensed as incurred. *[IAS 16.12]*. If the costs relate to the replacement of a part of the entire asset then the entity derecognises the carrying amount of the part that is replaced and recognises the cost of the replacement part. *[IAS 16.13]*. However, the part need not represent a physical part of the asset. When a major inspection, renewal or reconditioning project is performed, its cost should be recognised in the carrying amount of the item of property, plant and equipment and any remaining carrying amount of the cost of the previous inspection/renewal (which will be distinct from physical parts) is derecognised. This is not affected by whether the entity identified the cost of the previous inspection when the item was acquired or constructed. *[IAS 16.14]*. See Chapter 18 at 3.3.1.

Subsequent costs that meet the recognition criteria should therefore be capitalised even if the costs incurred merely restore the assets to their original standard of performance. However, under IAS 37 an entity cannot provide for the costs of planned future maintenance (e.g. turnarounds, renewals/reconditions) as is illustrated by Example 39.14, based on Example 11A in IAS 37. *[IAS 37 Appendix C]*.

Example 39.14: Refurbishment costs – no legislative requirement

A furnace has a lining that needs to be replaced every five years for technical reasons. At the end of the reporting period, the lining has been in use for three years.

Under IAS 37 no provision should be recognised as there is no present obligation. The cost of replacing the lining is not recognised because, at the end of the reporting period, no obligation to replace the lining exists independently of the company's future actions – even the intention to incur the expenditure depends on the company deciding to continue operating the furnace or to replace the lining. Instead of a provision being recognised, the depreciation of the lining takes account of its consumption, i.e. it is depreciated over five years. The re-lining costs then incurred are capitalised with the consumption of each new lining shown by depreciation over the subsequent five years.

Even a legal requirement to refurbish does not make the costs of a turnaround/renewal a liability under IAS 37, because no obligation exists independently of the entity's future actions – the entity could avoid the future overhaul expenditure by its future actions, for example by selling the refinery or the asset that is being renewed/reconditioned. *[IAS 37 IE Example 11B]*.

The extract below from BP illustrates a typical accounting policy for repairs, maintenance and inspection costs under IFRS.

Extract 39.32: BP p.l.c. (2012)

Notes on financial statements [extract]

1. Significant accounting policies [extract]

Property, plant and equipment [extract]

Expenditure on major maintenance refits or repairs comprises the cost of replacement assets or parts of assets, inspection costs and overhaul costs. Where an asset or part of an asset that was separately depreciated is replaced and it is probable that future economic benefits associated with the item will flow to the group, the expenditure is capitalized and the carrying amount of the replaced asset is derecognized. Inspection costs associated with major maintenance programmes are capitalized and amortized over the period to the next inspection. Overhaul costs for major maintenance programmes, and all other maintenance costs are expensed as incurred.

Turnarounds/renewals can have a considerable impact on financial performance because of additional costs incurred and lower revenues. Therefore fairly detailed information is generally disclosed about turnaround costs incurred in the past and turnarounds planned in the future.

Extract 39.33: BP p.l.c (2012)

Business review: Group overview [extract]

Our performance [extract]

Safety [extract]

We continued our programme of major upstream turnarounds, with 30 turnarounds completed in 2012. We expect to carry out up to 22 further turnarounds in 2013.

Downstream [extract]

Refinery operations were strong this year, with Solomon refining availability of 94.8%. (See refining availability on page 74.) Utilization rates were at 88% despite a relatively high level of turnaround activity in 2012.

Business review: BP in more depth [extract]

Profit or loss for the year [extract]

Compared with 2010, in 2011 there were higher realizations, higher earnings from equity-accounted entities, a higher refining margin environment and a stronger supply and trading contribution, partly offset by lower production volumes, rig standby costs in the Gulf of Mexico, higher costs related to turnarounds, higher exploration write-offs, and negative impacts of increased relative sweet crude prices in Europe and Australia, primarily caused by the loss of Libya production and the weather-related power outages in the US.

Risk factors [extract]

Strategic and commercial risks [extract]

Major project delivery – our group plan depends upon successful delivery of major projects, and failure to deliver major projects successfully could adversely affect our financial performance.

Successful execution of our group plan depends critically on implementing the activities to deliver the major projects over the plan period. Poor delivery of any major project that underpins production or production growth and/or any other major programme designed to enhance shareholder value, including maintenance turnaround programmes, could adversely affect our financial performance. Successful project delivery requires, among other things, adequate engineering and other capabilities and therefore successful recruitment and development of staff is central to our plans.

4.16 Long-term contracts and leases

Given the nature of the extractive industries, mining companies and oil and gas companies regularly enter into a wide range of long-term contracts. These may relate to the provision of services or the sale of goods. There are a number of potential issues to be addressed when considering the accounting for these arrangements. One of these is whether the contract contains any embedded derivatives. This is discussed in more detail in 4.18.2.C below. The other issues are discussed below.

4.16.1 Embedded leases

IFRIC 4 notes that there are arrangements that do not take the legal form of a lease but that convey rights to use items for agreed periods of time in return for a payment or series of payments. *[IFRIC 4.1]*.

The Interpretation focuses on the accounting implications of the following, all of which are forms of arrangements found in the extractive industries and in all of which an entity (the supplier) conveys a right to use an asset to another entity (the purchaser), together with related services or outputs:

- outsourcing arrangements;
- arrangements where suppliers of network capacity enter into contracts to provide purchasers with rights to capacity; and
- take-or-pay and similar contracts, in which purchasers must make specified payments regardless of whether they take delivery of the contracted products or services (e.g. where purchasers are committed to acquiring substantially all of the output of a supplier's power generator). *[IFRIC 4.1]*. See 4.16.2 below.

Other types of agreements common in the extractive industries and which would need to be assessed for the existence of embedded leases include:

- service arrangements – such as contract mining services arrangements or oilfield services arrangements;
- throughput arrangements (which may take the form of a take-or-pay arrangement);
- tolling contracts (see 6.4 below);
- contractor facilities located on the mining company's or oil and gas company's property;
- energy-related or utility contracts, e.g. gas, electricity, telecommunications, water; or
- transportation/freight services contracts.

The Interpretations Committee concluded that an arrangement of one of these types could be within the scope of IAS 17 if it met the definition of a lease, e.g. if it conveyed to the lessee the right to use an asset for an agreed period of time in return for a payment or series of payments. *[IFRIC 4.BC2]*. IAS 17 applies to the lease element of the arrangement notwithstanding the related services or outputs because IAS 17 applies to 'agreements that transfer the right to use assets even though substantial services by the lessor may be called for in connection with the operation or maintenance of such assets.' *[IAS 17.3]*. This is regardless of the fact that the arrangement is not described as a lease and is likely to grant rights that are significantly different from those in a formal lease agreement. The detailed requirements of IFRIC 4 are discussed in Chapter 24 at 2.1.

GDF SUEZ has an accounting policy addressing IFRIC 4.

Extract 39.34: GDF SUEZ (2012)

Notes to the consolidated financial statements [extract]

NOTE 1 SUMMARY OF SIGNIFICANT ACCOUNTING POLICIES [extract]

1.4 Significant accounting policies [extract]

1.4.9 Leases [extract]

1.4.9.3 Accounting for arrangements that contain a lease

IFRIC 4 deals with the identification of services and take-or-pay sales or purchasing contracts that do not take the legal form of a lease but convey rights to customers/suppliers to use an asset or a group of assets in return for a payment or a series of fixed payments. Contracts meeting these criteria should be identified as either operating leases or finance leases. In the latter case, a finance receivable should be recognized to reflect the financing deemed to be granted by the Group where it is considered as acting as lessor and its customers as lessees.

The Group is concerned by this interpretation mainly with respect to:

- some energy purchase and sale contracts, particularly where the contract conveys to the purchaser of the energy an exclusive right to use a production asset;
- certain contracts with industrial customers relating to assets held by the Group.

The IASB has an ongoing project on leasing. Under the current proposal, a lessee will recognise an asset representing its right-to-use the leased asset for the lease term (the 'right-of-use' asset) and a liability for its obligation to make lease payments for all existing and new leases with a maximum possible lease term greater than 12 months. For more information on the current proposal, see Chapter 24 at 10.

4.16.2 Take-or-pay contracts

A 'take-or-pay' contract is an agreement between a buyer and seller in which the buyer will pay a specified amount even if the product or service is not provided. Take-or-pay contracts for the supply of gas are particularly common, because entities developing gas fields need to make very significant investments in infrastructure such as pipelines, liquefaction plants and shipping terminals, to make transport of gas to the end-consumer economically viable. In order to raise the funds to finance such investments, it is crucial to know that there is a profitable market for the gas, as it cannot easily be diverted and sold in an alternative market or to an alternative customer.

While take-or-pay contracts perhaps most commonly involve the supply of gas, they can also include other arrangements such as contracts for pipeline capacity or LNG regasification facilities. Take-or-pay contracts also are used in the mining sector, though less frequently than in the oil and gas sector. Often take-or-pay contracts permit the purchaser to recover payments for quantities not taken, by allowing the purchaser to take more than the minimum in later years and to apply the previously paid-for undertake amount towards the cost of product taken in the later years.[133]

The following issues need to be considered in accounting for take-or-pay contracts:

- *Structured entities* – If a take-or-pay contract transfers the majority of the risks and rewards from the development of a mine or gas field to the customer, it is necessary to consider whether the entity developing the gas field has, in effect, become a structured entity of that customer (see Chapter 6 at 4.4.1);

- *Embedded leases* – Take-or-pay contracts are often for a very significant portion of the output of the gas field that it relates to. Therefore, as illustrated in Extract 39.34 above, the operator and customer need to consider whether the take-or-pay contract contains a lease of the related assets (see 4.16.1 above);
- *Embedded derivatives* – As illustrated in Extract 39.35 below, the price of gas sold under take-or-pay contracts is often based on a 'basket' of fuel prices and/or inflation price indices. If there is an active market for gas then this often means that an embedded derivative needs to be separated from the underlying host take-or-pay contract (see 4.18.2 below);
- *Guarantees* – Lenders are often willing to provide funding for the development of a gas field only if the operator can present a solid business case, which includes a 'guaranteed' stream of revenue from a reputable customer. In such cases, the take-or-pay contract acts as a form of credit enhancement or possibly as a guarantee. The operator and customer may need to consider whether the take-or-pay arrangement includes a guarantee that should be accounted for such under IAS 39 (see Chapter 41 at 3.4);
- *Make-up product and undertake* – A customer that fails to take the specified volume during the period specified must nevertheless pay for the agreed-volume. However, a take-or-pay contract sometimes permits the customer to take an equivalent amount of production (makeup product) at a later date after the payment for the guaranteed amount has been made (see 4.16.2.A below).

Extract 39.35 below from the financial statements of GDF SUEZ gives an overview of some of these important terms and conditions that exist in take-or-pay contracts.

Extract 39.35: GDF SUEZ (2012)

2 Risk Factors [extract]

2.3 OPERATING RISKS [extract]

2.3.1 PURCHASES AND SALES [extract]

2.3.1.1 Long-term gas supply contracts [extract]

The Group has built up a portfolio consisting largely of long-term take-or-pay contracts, by which the seller agrees to serve the buyer in the long-term in exchange for a commitment by the latter to pay minimum amounts regardless of whether it takes delivery or not. However, these clauses are accompanied by flexibility measures (see Section 1.3.1.6.1 "Central Western Europe").

Most long-term purchase contracts are indexed to oil products. However, with the emergence of gas marketplaces, spot gas prices have changed independently of oil prices.

Negotiations in recent years have enabled the market indices to be taken into account in long-term contracts and/or the differential between the contract price and marketplace price to be reduced. They have also led to increased frequency of price revisions. However, a situation in which the gas price on the markets remains lower than fuel-indexed contract prices in the long term could have a significant impact on Group performance if the negotiation process for long-term contracts does not enable satisfactory rebalancing.

1 Presentation of the Group [extract]

1.3 DESCRIPTION OF BUSINESS LINES [extract]

1.3.1 ENERGY EUROPE BUSINESS LINE [extract]

1.3.1.6 Description of the activities [extract]

1.3.1.6.1 Central Western Europe

Gas Supply Gas Optimization

Gas purchases [extract]

GDF SUEZ Gas Supply brings to the Group one of the largest, most diversified and flexible contract portfolios in Europe, representing a real competitive edge in the natural gas market in Europe.

It consists largely of long-term contracts lasting about 20 years. As of December 31, 2012, the average residual term of these long-term contracts (weighted by volume) was 13.3 years. This portfolio is balanced through purchases in short-term markets through GDF SUEZ Trading. GDF SUEZ Gas Supply thus adjusts its supplies to the Group's requirements by optimizing its purchasing costs.

According to market practice, the long-term purchase contracts include take-or-pay clauses, according to which the buyer agrees to pay for minimum gas volumes each year, whether or not delivery occurs (except in the event of supplier default or *force majeure*). Most contracts also stipulate flexibility clauses: these are compensation mechanisms that allow volumes already paid for but not taken to be carried over to a subsequent period (make-up) or limited volumes to be deducted from the take-or-pay obligation, when the volumes taken over the course of previous years exceeds the minimum volumes applicable to these years (carry forward).

The price of natural gas under these contracts has historically been indexed to the market price of energy products (mainly oil products). In addition, these contracts provide for periodic revisions of price and indexing formula to account for market changes. Finally, most contracts provide for the possibility of adjusting prices in exceptional circumstances, over and above the periodic reviews.

In certain cases, it is possible to change other contractual provisions in response to exceptional events affecting their economic balance (hardship clause).

The parties are then required to negotiate in good faith and can, in the event of disagreement, revert to arbitration.

GDF SUEZ constantly seeks to match its portfolio to the market situation. This entails drawing up new contracts and performing price reviews. In a context marked by the decoupling of oil prices, on which the long-term contracts are indexed, from those of the gas sold in the market place, GDF SUEZ Gas Supply has pursued negotiations with all its principal suppliers to reduce the spread and improve competitiveness of these contracts in the new market conditions.

At December 31, 2012, references to the price of gas sold on the marketplace concerned more than a third of the volumes in the long-term contract portfolio in Europe.

4.16.2.A Make-up product and undertake

Under some take or pay arrangements, a customer who is required to pay for the product not taken will often have no right of future recovery. The customer should recognise an expense equal to the payment made, while the operator recognises the same amount as revenue. However, if the substance of the relationship between the operator and customer is such that a renegotiation of the arrangement is probable then it may be more appropriate for the operator to recognise the penalty payment as deferred revenue. The customer, however, should still recognise an expense in this case as it does not have a legal right to receive reimbursement or makeup product.[134]

The accounting is different when a customer that is required to pay for product not taken has a right to take makeup product in the future. In that case the operator would recognise deferred revenue equal to the amount paid for the 'undertake' as it represents an obligation to provide the product in the future. The operator only recognises revenue in accordance with IAS 18 once the make-up product has been taken by the customer. *[IAS 18.14(a)]*. Only once the make-up period has expired or it is clear that the purchaser has become unable to take the product, would the liability be eliminated and revenue recognised.[135] The customer would normally recognise a prepaid amount representing the make-up product that it is entitled to receive in the future. However, if the customer is entitled to more make-up product than it can sell, it may need to recognise an impairment charge.

Extract 39.36 below illustrates how Tullow Oil as an operator accounts for undertakes.

> *Extract 39.36: Tullow Oil plc (2012)*
>
> **ACCOUNTING POLICIES** [extract]
>
> Year ended 31 December 2012
>
> **(g) Revenue** [extract]
>
> Sales revenue represents the sales value, net of VAT and overriding royalties, of the Group's share of liftings in the year together with tariff income. Revenue is recognised when goods are delivered and title has passed.
>
> Revenues received under take-or-pay sales contracts in respect of undelivered volumes are accounted for as deferred income.

4.17 Taxation

As mentioned at 1.1 above, one of the characteristics of the extractive industries is the intense government involvement in their activities, which ranges from 'outright governmental ownership of some (especially petroleum) or all minerals to unusual tax benefits or penalties, price controls, restrictions on imports and exports, restrictions on production and distribution, environmental and health and safety regulations, and others'.[136]

Mining companies and oil and gas companies typically need to make payments to governments in their capacity as:

- owner of the mineral resources;
- co-owner or joint arrangement partner in the projects;
- regulator of, among other things, environmental matters and health and safety matters; and
- tax authority.

The total payment to a government is often described as the 'government take'. This includes fixed payments or variable payments that are based on production, revenue, or a net profit figure; and which may take the form of fees, bonuses, royalties or taxes. Determining whether a payment to government meets the definition of income tax is not straightforward.

IAS 12 should be applied in accounting for income taxes, defined as including:

(a) all domestic and foreign taxes which are based on taxable profits; and

(b) taxes, such as withholding taxes, which are payable by a subsidiary, associate or joint arrangements on distributions to the reporting entity. *[IAS 12.1-2]*.

As discussed in Chapter 29 at 4.1, it is not altogether clear what an income tax actually is. In the extractive industries the main problem with the definition in IAS 12 occurs when:

(a) a government raises 'taxes' on sub-components of net profit (e.g. net profit before financing costs or revenue minus allowed costs); or

(b) there is a mandatory government participation in certain projects that entitle the government to a share of profits as defined in a joint operating agreement.

A considerable amount of judgement is required to determine whether a particular arrangement falls within the definition of 'income tax' under IAS 12 or whether it is another form of government take. From a commercial perspective the overall share of the economic benefits that the government takes is much more important than the distinction between its different forms. In practice, most governments receive benefits from extractive activities in several different ways, as discussed below. Governments can choose any of these methods to increase or decrease their share of the benefits.

However, under IFRS the distinction is crucial given the considerable differences in the accounting treatments and disclosures that apply to income taxes, other taxes, fees and government participations. For example, it will affect where these amounts are presented in the profit or loss, e.g. in operating costs or income tax expense; and it will determine whether deferred tax balances are required to be recognised and the related disclosures provided.

4.17.1 Excise duties, production taxes and severance taxes

Excise duties, production taxes and severance taxes result in payments that are due on production (or severance) of minerals from the earth. Depending on the jurisdiction and the type of mineral involved, they are calculated:

(a) as a fixed amount per unit produced;

(b) as a percentage of the value of the minerals produced; or

(c) based on revenue minus certain allowable costs.

4.17.1.A Production-based taxation

If the tax is based on a fixed amount per unit produced or as a percentage of the value of the minerals produced, then it will not meet the definition of an income tax under IAS 12. In these cases the normal principles of liability recognition under IAS 37 apply in recognising the tax charge.

Another issue that arises is whether the tax should be presented as a cost of production or whether it should be deducted in arriving at revenue. Given that excise duties, production taxes and severance taxes are aimed at taxing the production of minerals rather than the sale of minerals, they are considered to be a tax on extractive activities rather than a tax collected by a mining company or oil and gas company on behalf of the government. Based on this argument the tax should be presented as a production cost.

However, it could also be argued, particularly when the excise duty, production tax or severance tax is payable in kind, that the mining company or oil and gas company never receives any of the benefits associated with the production of the associated minerals. Hence, it would be more appropriate to present revenue net of the production or severance tax as it is in substance the same as a royalty payment. For this reason, revenue is generally presented net of excise duties, as illustrated by Extract 39.37 below from the financial statements of Royal Dutch Shell.

Extract 39.37: Royal Dutch Shell plc (2012)

Notes to the Consolidated Financial Statements [extract]

2 ACCOUNTING POLICIES [extract]

Revenue recognition

Revenue from sales of oil, natural gas, chemicals and all other products is recognised at the fair value of consideration received or receivable, after deducting sales taxes, excise duties and similar levies, when the significant risks and rewards of ownership have been transferred, which is when title passes to the customer. For sales by Upstream operations, this generally occurs when product is physically transferred into a vessel, pipe or other delivery mechanism; for sales by refining operations, it is either when product is placed onboard a vessel or offloaded from the vessel, depending on the contractually agreed terms; and for wholesale sales of oil products and chemicals it is either at the point of delivery or the point of receipt, depending on contractual conditions.

Revenue resulting from the production of oil and natural gas properties in which Shell has an interest with partners in joint ventures is recognised on the basis of Shell's working interest (entitlement method). Revenue resulting from the production of oil and natural gas under production-sharing contracts is recognised for those amounts relating to Shell's cost recoveries and Shell's share of the remaining production. Gains and losses on derivative contracts and the revenue and costs associated with other contracts that are classified as held for trading purposes are reported on a net basis in the Consolidated Statement of Income. Purchases and sales of hydrocarbons under exchange contracts that are necessary to obtain or reposition feedstock for refinery operations are presented net in the Consolidated Statement of Income.

4.17.1.B Petroleum revenue tax (or resource rent tax)

Determining whether a petroleum revenue tax (or resource rent tax) is a production- or profit-based tax is often not straightforward. Example 39.15 describes the petroleum revenue tax in the United Kingdom.

Example 39.15: Petroleum revenue tax[137]

Petroleum revenue tax (PRT) is a special tax that seeks to tax a high proportion of the economic rent (super-profits) from the exploitation of the UK's oil and gas. PRT is a cash-based tax that is levied on a field-by-field basis: in general, the costs of developing and running a field can only be set against the profits generated by that field. Any losses, e.g. arising from unused expenditure relief, can be carried back or forward within the field indefinitely. There is also a range of reliefs, including:

- oil allowance – a PRT-free slice of production;
- supplement – a proxy for interest and other financing costs;
- Tariff Receipts Allowance (TRA) – participators owning assets, for example pipelines, relating to one field will sometimes allow participators from other fields to share the use of the asset in return for the payment of tariffs, and TRA relieves some of the tariffs received from PRT;
- exemption from PRT for gas sold to British Gas under a pre-July 1975 contract; and
- cross-field relief for research expenditure.

PRT is currently charged at 50% on profits after these allowances. For a limited period, safeguard relief then applies to ensure that PRT does not reduce the annual return in the early years of production of a field to below 15% of the historic capital expenditure on the field.

PRT was abolished on 16 March 1993 for all fields given development consent on or after that date. This was part of a package of PRT reforms which also included the reduction of the rate of PRT from 75 per cent to 50 per cent and the abolition of PRT relief for Exploration and Appraisal (E&A) expenditure.

The UK PRT is similar to an income tax in that the tax is a percentage of revenue minus certain costs. However, there are also a number of other features that are not commonly found in income taxes or in some other resource rent taxes:

- the oil allowance is a physical quantity of oil that is PRT exempt in each field, subject to a cumulative maximum over the life of the field; and
- the tax is levied on individual oil fields rather than the entity owning the oil field as a whole.

There are many different types of petroleum revenue taxes (or resource rent taxes) around the world, some of which are clearly not income taxes, while others have some of the characteristics of an income tax. In determining whether a particular production tax meets the definition of an income tax under IAS 12, an entity will need to assess whether or not the tax is based on (or closely enough linked to) net profit for the period. If it does not meet the definition of an income tax, an entity should develop an accounting policy under the hierarchy in IAS 8.

Practice is mixed, which means that while some entities may treat a particular petroleum revenue tax (or resource rent tax) as an income tax under IAS 12 and hence provide for current and deferred taxes (see Extract 39.38 below), others may consider the same tax to be outside the scope of IAS 12.

Extract 39.38: Woodside Petroleum (2012)

Notes to and forming part of the Financial Report [extract]

For the year ended 31 December 2012

1. Summary of significant accounting policies [extract]

z) Tax [extract]

Petroleum Resource Rent Tax (PRRT)

PRRT is considered, for accounting purposes, to be a tax based on income. Accordingly, current and deferred PRRT expense is measured and disclosed on the same basis as income tax.

As illustrated in Extract 39.39 below, BHP Billiton assesses resource rent taxes and royalties individually to determine whether they meet the definition of an income tax or not.

Extract 39.39: BHP Billiton (2012)

9.1.6 Notes to Financial Statements [extract]

1 Accounting policies [extract]

Taxation [extract]

Royalties and resource rent taxes are treated as taxation arrangements when they have the characteristics of a tax. This is considered to be the case when they are imposed under government authority and the amount payable is calculated by reference to revenue derived (net of any allowable deductions) after adjustment for temporary differences. For such arrangements, current and deferred tax is provided on the same basis as described above for other forms of taxation. Obligations arising from royalty arrangements that do not satisfy these criteria are recognised as current provisions and included in expenses.

4.17.2 Grossing up of notional quantities withheld

Many production sharing contracts provide that the income tax to which the contractor is subject is deemed to have been paid to the government as part of the payment of profit oil to the government or its representative (e.g. the designated national oil company) (see 4.5.2 above). This raises the question as to whether an entity should be presenting current and deferred taxation arising from such 'notional' income tax, which is only deemed to have been paid, on a net or a gross basis.

Example 39.16: Grossing up of notional quantities withheld

Entity A is the operator of an oil field that produces 10 million barrels of oil per year. Under the production sharing contract between entity A and the national government, entity A and the government are entitled to 4,000,000 and 6,000,000 barrels of oil, respectively. The production sharing contract includes the following clause:

> 'The share of the profit petroleum to which the government is entitled in any calendar year in accordance with the production sharing contract shall be deemed to include a portion representing the corporate income tax imposed upon and due by entity A, and which will be paid directly by the government on behalf of entity A to the appropriate tax authorities.'

Assuming the following facts, how should entity A account for the income tax that it is deemed to have paid in 2013:

- the normal corporate income tax rate in the country in which entity A operates is 40%;
- entity A made a net profit of USD 30 million in 2013; and
- the average oil price during the year was USD 50/barrel.

Gross presentation

Entity A's profit after 40% corporate income tax was USD 30 million. Therefore, its profit before tax would have been USD 50 million (i.e. USD 30 million ÷ (100% – 40%)). In other words, the government is deemed to have paid corporate income tax of USD 20 million on behalf of entity A. Therefore, the government is deemed to have taken 400,000 barrels (i.e. USD 20 million ÷ USD 50/barrel) out of entity A's share of the production. Hence, entity A's share of production before corporate income tax was 4,400,000 barrels (i.e. 4,000,000 barrels + 400,000 barrels).

Net presentation

Under the net presentation approach, entity A ignores the corporate income tax that was deemed to have been paid by the government because it is not a transaction that entity A was party to *or* because the deemed transaction did not actually take place.

The disadvantage of presenting such tax on a gross basis is that the combined production attributed to the entity and that attributable to the government exceeds the total quantity of oil that is actually produced (i.e. in the above example the government and entity A would report a combined production of 10.4 million barrels whereas actual production was only 10 million barrels). Similarly, if the reserves were to be expressed on the same basis as revenues, the reserves reported by the entity would include oil reserves that it would not actually be entitled to.

On the other hand, if the host country has a well-established income tax regime that falls under the authority of the ministry of finance and the production sharing contract requires an income tax return to be filed, then the entity would have a legal liability to pay the tax until the date on which the national oil company or the ministry responsible for extractive activities (e.g. the ministry of mines, industry and energy) pays the tax on its behalf. In such cases it may be appropriate to present revenue and income tax on a gross basis.

4.18 Financial instruments

4.18.1 Normal purchase and sales exemption

Contracts to buy or sell non-financial items generally do not meet the definition of a financial instrument because the contractual right of one party to receive a non-financial asset or service and the corresponding obligation of the other party do not establish a present right or obligation of either party to receive, deliver or exchange a financial asset. For example, contracts that provide for settlement only by the receipt or delivery of non-financial items (e.g. forward purchase of oil or a forward purchase of copper) are not financial instruments. However, some of these contracts are traded in a standardised form on organised markets in the same way as derivative financial instruments. The ability to buy or sell a commodity contract for cash does not alter the characteristics of the contract and make it into a financial instrument. *[IAS 32.AG20].*

IAS 32 and IAS 39 should generally be applied to those contracts to buy or sell a non-financial item that can be settled net as if the contracts were financial instruments, whether this be in cash, another financial instrument, or by exchanging financial instruments, unless the contracts were entered into and continue to be held for the purpose of the receipt or delivery of a non-financial item in accordance with the entity's expected purchase, sale or usage requirements. *[IAS 32.8, IAS 39.5].*

Contracts that fall within this exemption, which is known as the 'normal purchase or sale exemption', 'executory contract exemption' or 'own-use exemption', are accounted for as executory contracts. An entity recognises such contracts in its statement of financial position only when one of the parties meets its obligation under the contract to deliver either cash or a non-financial asset. *[Framework.4.46].*

There are various ways in which a contract to buy or sell a non-financial item can be settled net, including:

(a) the terms of the contract permit either party to settle it net;

(b) the ability to settle the contract net is not explicit in its terms, but the entity has a practice of settling similar contracts net (whether with the counterparty, by entering into offsetting contracts or by selling the contract before its exercise or lapse);

(c) for similar contracts, the entity has a practice of taking delivery of the underlying and selling it within a short period after delivery for the purpose of generating a profit from short-term fluctuations in price or dealer's margin; and

(d) the non-financial item that is the subject of the contract is readily convertible to cash, e.g. precious metals or base metals quoted on the London Metal Exchange are considered to be readily convertible to cash.

The IASB views the practice of settling net or taking delivery of the underlying and selling it within a short period after delivery as an indication that the contracts are not normal purchases or sales. Therefore, contracts to which (b) or (c) apply cannot be subject to the normal purchase or sale exception. Other contracts that can be settled net are evaluated to determine whether this exemption can actually apply. *[IAS 32.9, IAS 39.6, BC24]*.

A written option to buy or sell a non-financial item that can be settled net in cash or another financial instrument, or by exchanging financial instruments, in accordance with (a) or (d) should be accounted for under IAS 39 and does not qualify for use of the normal purchase or sale exemption. *[IAS 39.7]*.

The conditions associated with the use of the normal purchase or sale exemption often pose problems for mining companies and oil and gas companies because, historically, they have settled many purchase and sales contracts on a net basis.

A further problem may arise when a mining company or oil and gas company holds a written option for the purpose of the receipt or delivery of a non-financial item in accordance with the entity's expected purchase, sale or usage requirements – because IAS 39 would require such contracts to be accounted for as derivative financial instruments.

Finally, from time to time mining companies and oil and gas companies may need to settle contracts for the sale of commodities on a net basis because of operational problems. Such a situation would mean that the company would need to treat those contracts as derivative financial instruments under IAS 39. Where this situation is caused by a unique event beyond management's control, a level of judgement will be required to determine whether that would prevent the company from applying the own use exemption to similar contracts. This should be assessed on a case by case basis.

Judgement will also be required as to what constitutes 'similar contracts'. The definition of similar contracts in IAS 39, *[IAS 39.6]*, considers the intended use for such contracts. This means that contracts identical in form may be dissimilar due to their intended use, e.g. own purchase requirements versus proprietary trading. If the intended use is for normal purchase or sale, such an intention must be documented at inception of the contract. A history of regular revisions of expected purchase or sale requirements could impair the ability of a company to distinguish identical contracts as being dissimilar.

The extract below from AngloGold Ashanti's 2008 financial statements illustrates how this could affect an entity's reported financial position. (Note that in October 2010, AngloGold Ashanti removed the last of its gold hedging instruments and long-term sales contracts.)

Extract 39.40: AngloGold Ashanti Limited (2008)

Risk management and internal controls [extract]

Risks related to AngloGold Ashanti's operations [extract]

AngloGold Ashanti uses gold hedging instruments and has entered into long-term sales contracts, which may prevent the company from realising potential gains resulting from subsequent commodity price increases in the future. AngloGold Ashanti's reported financial condition could be adversely affected as a result of the need to fair value all of its hedge contracts.

AngloGold Ashanti has used gold hedging instruments to protect and fix the selling price of some of its anticipated production. The use of such instruments prevents full participation in subsequent increases in the market price for the commodity with respect to covered production. Since 2001, AngloGold Ashanti has been reducing its hedge commitments through hedge buy-backs (limited to non-hedge derivatives), deliveries into contracts and restructuring in order to provide greater participation in a rising gold price environment. As a result of these measures, AngloGold Ashanti has, and expects to continue to have, substantially less protection against declines in the market price of gold as compared with previous years.

AngloGold Ashanti continues to use gold hedging instruments to fix the selling price of a portion of its anticipated gold production and to protect revenues against unfavourable gold price and exchange rate movements. While the use of these instruments may protect against a drop in gold prices and exchange rate movements, it will do so for only a limited period of time and only to the extent that the hedge remains in place. The use of these instruments may also prevent AngloGold Ashanti from fully realising the positive impact on income from any subsequent favourable increase in the price of gold on the portion of production covered by the hedge and of any subsequent favourable exchange rate movements.

In 2008, AngloGold Ashanti used part of the proceeds from its $1.7 billion rights offer to undertake a major restructuring of the hedge book. This hedge restructuring resulted in hedge commitments reducing by 5.29 million ounces (or 47%) from 11.28 million ounces as at 31 December 2007 to 5.99 million ounces as at 31 December 2008. Although this hedge restructuring has significantly reduced the exposure to the hedge book, a rising gold price may result in a gap between the spot price and AngloGold Ashanti's received price of gold for ounces still hedged, and this may continue as AngloGold Ashanti closes out its existing hedge positions by delivering into contracts.

A significant number of AngloGold Ashanti's forward sales contracts are not treated as derivatives and fair valued on the financial statements as they fall under the normal purchase sales exemption. Should AngloGold Ashanti fail to settle these contracts by physical delivery, then it may be required to account for the fair value of a portion, or potentially all of, the existing contracts in the financial statements. This could adversely affect AngloGold Ashanti's reported financial condition.

As the global financial crisis continues, some of AngloGold Ashanti's hedge counterparties may either be unable to perform their obligations under the applicable derivative instrument or in certain cases elect to terminate their contracts early in 2010, which may result in the company being called upon to immediately meet any obligation under the hedge contracts with such hedge counterparties. This could adversely affect AngloGold Ashanti's financial condition.

4.18.2 Embedded derivatives

A contract that qualifies for the normal purchase and sale exemption still needs to be assessed for the existence of embedded derivatives. An embedded derivative is a component of a hybrid or combined instrument that also includes a non-derivative host contract; it has the effect that some of the cash flows of the combined instrument vary in a similar way to a stand-alone derivative. In other words, it causes some or all of the cash flows that otherwise would be required by the contract to be modified according to a specified interest rate, financial instrument price, commodity price, foreign exchange rate, index of prices or rates, credit rating or credit index, or other underlying variable (provided in the case of a non-financial variable that the variable is not specific to a party to the contract). *[IAS 39.10]*.

The detailed rules and requirements regarding the separation of embedded derivatives, and the interpretation and application of those requirements, are discussed in Chapter 42. A number of issues related to embedded derivatives that are of particular importance to the extractive industries are discussed at 4.18.2.A to 4.18.2.D below.

4.18.2.A Foreign currency embedded derivatives

The most common embedded derivatives in the extractive industries are probably foreign currency embedded derivatives which arise when a producer of minerals sells these in a currency that is not the functional currency of any substantial party to the contract, the currency in which the price of the related commodity is routinely denominated in commercial transactions around the world or a currency that is commonly used in contracts to purchase or sell non-financial items in the economic environment in which the transaction takes place. *[IAS 39.AG33(d)]*. A more detailed analysis of these requirements can be found in Chapter 42 at 5.2.1.

4.18.2.B Provisionally priced contracts

Sales contracts for certain commodities (e.g. copper and oil) often provide for provisional pricing at the time of shipment, with final pricing based on the average market price for a particular future period. The final sales price is often based on the average market prices during a subsequent period (the 'quotational period'), the price on a fixed date after delivery or the amount subsequently realised by the smelter or refiner, net of tolling charges.

Price adjustment features contained in non-cancellable contracts that are based on quoted market prices for a date subsequent to the date of shipment or delivery (e.g. the spot price three weeks after shipment or the average spot price for the month of shipment) are considered to be embedded derivatives that require separation under IAS 39, because the forward price at which the contract is to be settled is not closely related to the spot price. *[IAS 39.11, AG30(e)]*. The non-financial contract for the sale or purchase of the product, e.g. copper or oil, at a future date would be treated as the host contract, while the exposure to the price movements from the date of sale to the end of the quotational period would be treated as an embedded derivative.

If the contract is cancellable without penalty before delivery, the price adjustment feature does not meet the definition of a derivative because there is no contractual obligation until delivery takes place.

If the contract is not cancellable, there will be a contractual obligation, but until delivery, the embedded derivative would be considered to be closely related to the host commodity contract and does not need to be recorded separately.

When the embedded derivative is separated from the host contract, the host contract will normally meet the revenue recognition criteria – in particular the requirement that revenue can be measured reliably – at the date that the product is delivered. *[IAS 18.14]*.

Changes in the fair value of the embedded derivative should be recognised in profit or loss for the period. While gains or losses from embedded derivatives should normally be presented together with those from other derivatives, many companies include adjustments of provisionally priced contracts within revenue, presumably on the grounds of materiality or as a matter of industry practice.

Antofagasta is an example of a mining company that discloses the effects of provisional pricing in its financial statements in considerable detail, including the quantities of minerals that are subject to provisional prices.

Extract 39.41: Antofagasta plc (2012)

Notes to the Financial Statements [extract]

2 Principal accounting policies [extract]

f) Revenue recognition [extract]

Revenue represents the value of goods and services supplied to third parties during the year. Revenue is measured at the fair value of consideration received or receivable, and excludes any applicable sales tax.

A sale is recognised when the significant risks and rewards of ownership have passed. This is generally when title and any insurance risk has passed to the customer, and the goods have been delivered to a contractually agreed location or when any services have been provided.

Revenue from mining activities is recorded at the invoiced amounts with an adjustment for provisional pricing at each reporting date, as explained below. For copper and molybdenum concentrates, which are sold to smelters and roasting plants for further processing, the invoiced amount is the market value of the metal payable by the customer, net of deductions for tolling charges. Revenue includes revenues from the sale of by-products.

Copper and molybdenum concentrate sale agreements and copper cathode sale agreements generally provide for provisional pricing of sales at the time of shipment, with final pricing based on the monthly average London Metal Exchange ("LME") copper price or the monthly average market molybdenum price for specified future periods. This normally ranges from 30 to 120 days after delivery to the customer. Such a provisional sale contains an embedded derivative which is required to be separated from the host contract. The host contract is the sale of metals contained in the concentrate or cathode at the provisional invoice price less tolling charges deducted, and the embedded derivative is the forward contract for which the provisional sale is subsequently adjusted. At each reporting date, the provisionally priced metal sales together with any related tolling charges are marked-to-market, with adjustments (both gains and losses) being recorded in revenue in the consolidated income statement and in trade debtors in the balance sheet. Forward prices at the period end are used for copper concentrate and cathode sales, while period-end average prices are used for molybdenum concentrate sales due to the absence of a futures market.

25 Financial instruments and financial risk management [extract]

d) Embedded derivatives – provisionally priced sales [extract]

Copper and molybdenum concentrate sale agreements and copper cathode sale agreements generally provide for provisional pricing of sales at the time or month of shipment, with final pricing being based on the monthly average London Metal Exchange copper price or monthly average molybdenum price for specified future periods. This normally ranges from one to five months after shipment to the customer.

Under IFRS, both gains and losses from the marking-to-market of open sales are recognised through adjustments to revenue in the income statement and to trade debtors in the balance sheet. The Group determines mark-to-market prices using forward prices at each period end for copper concentrate and cathode sales, and period-end monthly average prices for molybdenum concentrate sales due to the absence of a futures market for that commodity in the majority of the Group's contracts.

[...]

i) Copper concentrate

The typical period for which sales of copper concentrate remain open until settlement occurs is a range of approximately three to five months from shipment date.

At 31 December 2012 sales totalling 203,400 tonnes remained open as to price, with an average mark-to-market price of 359.6 cents per pound compared with an average provisional invoice price of 359.3 cents per pound.

At 31 December 2011 sales totalling 201,600 tonnes remained open as to price, with an average mark-to-market price of 344.7 cents per pound compared with an average provisional invoice price of 347.9 cents per pound.

ii) Copper cathodes

The typical period for which sales of copper cathodes remain open until settlement occurs is approximately one month from shipment date.

At 31 December 2012, sales totalling 13,400 tonnes remained open as to price, with an average mark-to-market price of 358.9 cents per pound compared with an average provisional invoice price of 360.2 cents per pound.

At 31 December 2011, sales totalling 12,600 tonnes remained open as to price, with an average mark-to-market price of 344.5 cents per pound compared with an average provisional invoice price of 345.9 cents per pound.

4.18.2.C Long-term supply contracts

Long-term supply contracts sometimes contain embedded derivatives because of a desire to shift certain risks between contracting parties or as a consequence of existing market practices. The fair value of embedded derivatives increases as a function of the duration of the contract. Hence the fair value of embedded derivatives in long-term supply contracts is often highly material to the entities involved. For example, in the mining sector electricity purchase contracts sometimes contain price conditions based on the commodity that is being sold, which provides an economic hedge for the mining company. In the oil and gas sector the sales price of gas is at times based on that of electricity, which provides an economic hedge for the utility company that purchases the gas.

As can be seen in the following extract from BHP Billiton's 2007 financial statements, the pricing terms of embedded derivatives in purchase (sales) contracts often match those of the product that the entity sells (purchases).

Extract 39.42: BHP Billiton (2007)

Notes to Financial Statements [extract]

28 Financial instruments [extract]

Embedded derivatives

Derivatives embedded in host contracts are accounted for as separate derivatives when their risks and characteristics are not closely related to those of the host contracts or have intrinsic value at inception and the host contracts are not carried at fair value. These embedded derivatives are measured at fair value with gains or losses arising from changes in fair value recognised in the income statement.

Contracts are assessed for embedded derivatives when the Group becomes a party to them, including at the date of a business combination. Host contracts which incorporate embedded derivatives are entered into during the normal course of operations and are standard business practices in the industries in which the Group operate.

The following table provides information about the principal embedded derivatives contracts:

	Maturity date 2007	2006	Volume 2007	2006		Exposure price
Commodity Price Swaps						
Electricity purchase arrangement (a)	31 Dec 2024	31 Dec 2024	240,000	240,000	MWh	Aluminium
Electricity purchase arrangement (a)	30 June 2020	30 June 2020	576,000	576,000	MWh	Aluminium
Gas sales (b)	31 Dec 2013	31 Dec 2013	1,195,572	1,428,070	'000 therms	Electricity
Commodity Price Options						
Finance lease of plant and equipment (b)	31 Dec 2018	30 Dec 2018	38.5	39.5	mmboe	Crude Oil
Copper concentrate purchases and sales (b)	31 Dec 2007	31 Dec 2006	52	41	'000 tonnes	Copper
Lead concentrate purchases and sales (b)	31 Dec 2007	1 January 2007	11	67	'000 tonnes	Lead
Zinc concentrate purchases and sales (b)	31 Dec 2007	2 January 2007	51	6	'000 tonnes	Zinc
Silver concentrate sales (b)	31 Dec 2007	–	4,604	–	'000 ounces	Silver

(a) The volumes shown in these contracts indicate a megawatt volume per hour for each hour of the contract.

(b) The volumes shown in these contracts indicate the total volumes for the contract.

4.18.2.D Development of gas markets

If there is no active local market in gas, market participants often enter into long-term contracts that are priced on the basis of a basket of underlying factors, such as oil prices, electricity prices and inflation indices. In the absence of an active market in gas, such price clauses are not considered to give rise to embedded derivatives because there is no accepted benchmark price for gas that could have been used instead.

An entity that applies IAS 39 is required under IFRIC 9 – *Reassessment of Embedded Derivatives* – to assess whether an embedded derivative is required to be separated from the host contract and accounted for as a derivative when the entity first becomes a party to the contract and subsequent reassessment is generally prohibited (see Chapter 42 at 7). *[IFRIC 9.7].* Therefore, when subsequently an active gas market develops, an entity is not permitted to separate embedded derivatives from existing gas contracts, unless there is a change in the terms of the contract that significantly modifies the cash flows that otherwise would be required under the contract. However, if the entity enters into a new gas contract with exactly the same terms and conditions, it would be required to separate embedded derivatives from the new gas contract.

Judgement is required in determining whether there is an active gas market in a particular geographic region and the relevant geographic market for any type of commodity.

The extract below from BP shows that the fair value of embedded derivatives in long-term gas contracts can be quite significant.

Extract 39.43: BP p.l.c (2012)

Notes on financial statements [extract]

33 Derivative financial instruments [extract]

Embedded derivatives [extract]

The group has embedded derivatives, the majority of which relate to certain natural gas contracts. Prior to the development of an active gas trading market, UK gas contracts were priced using a basket of available price indices, primarily relating to oil products, power and inflation. After the development of an active UK gas market, certain contracts were entered into or renegotiated using pricing formulae not directly related to gas prices, for example, oil product and power prices. In these circumstances, pricing formulae have been determined to be derivatives, embedded within the overall contractual arrangements that are not clearly and closely related to the underlying commodity. The resulting fair value relating to these contracts is recognized on the balance sheet with gains or losses recognized in the income statement.

All the commodity price embedded derivatives relate to natural gas contracts, are categorized in level 3 of the fair value hierarchy and are valued using inputs that include price curves for each of the different products that are built up from active market pricing data. Where necessary, these are extrapolated to the expiry of the contracts (the last of which is in 2018) using all available external pricing information. Additionally, where limited data exists for certain products, prices are interpolated using historic and long-term pricing relationships.

[...]

The following table shows the changes during the year in the net fair value of embedded derivatives, within level 3 of the fair value hierarchy.

		$ million
	2012 Commodity price	2011 Commodity price
Net fair value of contracts at 1 January	**(1,417)**	(1,607)
Settlements	**375**	301
Losses recognized in the income statement	**(6)**	(106)
Exchange adjustments	**(64)**	(5)
Net fair value of contracts at 31 December	**(1,112)**	(1,417)

The amount recognized in the income statement for the year relating to level 3 embedded derivatives still held at 31 December 2012 was a loss of $6 million (2011 $106 million loss relating to embedded derivatives still held at 31 December 2011).

The fair value gain (loss) on embedded derivatives is shown below.

			$ million
	2012	2011	2010
Commodity price embedded derivatives	**347**	190	(309)
Other embedded derivatives	**–**	(122)	–
Fair value gain (loss)	**347**	68	(309)

4.18.3 Volume flexibility in supply contracts

It is not uncommon for other sales contracts, such as those with large industrial customers, to contain volume flexibility features. For example, a supplier might enter into a contract requiring it to deliver, say, 100,000 units at a given price as well as giving the counterparty the option to purchase a further 20,000 units at the same price. Very often such a supply contract is readily convertible to cash as parties to the contract can settle the contract on a net basis, as discussed at 4.18.1 above. For example, precious metals or base metals quoted on the London Metal Exchange are considered to be readily convertible to cash, whereas bulk materials without spot prices (e.g. coal and iron) are generally not considered to be readily convertible to cash. However, with increasing levels of liquidity in certain commodities, this view may need to be reconfirmed/rechallenged before concluding that this remains the case.

If the customer has access to markets for the non-financial item and, following the guidance of the Interpretations Committee the supplier might consider such a contract to be within the scope of IAS 39 as it contains a written option (see Chapter 41 at 4.2). However, some would say that the supplier could split the contract into two separate components for accounting purposes: a forward contract to supply 100,000 units (which may qualify as a normal sale) and a written option to supply 20,000 units (which would not). Arguments put forward include:

- the parties could easily have entered into two separate contracts, a forward contract and a written option; and
- it is appropriate to analogise to the requirements for embedded derivatives and separate a written option from the normal forward sale or purchase contract because it is not closely related.

Although these arguments are not universally accepted, we believe that there is merit in them.

This issue is discussed in more detail in Chapter 41 at 4.2.4 and 4.2.5.

5 PRACTICAL ISSUES IN THE OIL AND GAS SECTOR

This section explores some of the practical issues commonly faced by oil and gas companies in applying IFRS to their operations.

5.1 Unitisations and redeterminations

5.1.1 Unitisations

A unitisation arrangement is 'an agreement between two parties each of which owns an interest in one or more mineral properties in an area to cross-assign to one another a share of the interest in the mineral properties that each owns in the area; from that point forward they share, as agreed, in further costs and revenues related to the properties'.[138] The parties pool their individual interests in return for an interest in the overall unit, which is then operated jointly to increase efficiency.[139] Once an area is subject to an unitisation arrangement, the parties share costs and production in accordance with their percentages established under the unitisation agreement. The unitisation agreement does not affect costs and production associated with non-unitised areas within the original licences, which continue to fall to the original licensees.[140]

IFRS does not specifically address accounting for a unitisation arrangement. Therefore, the accounting for such an arrangement depends on the type of asset that is subject to the arrangement. If the assets subject to the arrangement were E&E assets, then the transaction would fall within the scope of IFRS 6, which provides a temporary exemption from IAS 8 (see 3.2.1 above). An entity would be permitted to develop an accounting policy for unitisation arrangements involving E&E assets that is not based on IFRS. However, unitisations are unlikely to occur in the E&E phase when technical feasibility and commercial viability of extracting a mineral resource are not yet demonstrable.

The first step in developing an accounting policy for unitisations is setting criteria for determining which assets are included within the transaction. Particularly important is the assessment as to whether the unitisation includes the mineral reserves themselves or not. The main reason for not including the mineral reserves derives from the fact that they are subject to redetermination (see 5.1.2 below).

The example below, which is taken from the IASC's Issues Paper, illustrates how a unitisation transaction might work in practice.

Example 39.17: Unitisation[141]

Entities E and F have carried out exploration programs on separate properties owned by each in a remote area near the Antarctic Circle. Both entities have discovered petroleum reserves on their properties and have begun development of the properties. Because of the high operating costs and the need to construct support facilities, such as pipelines, dock facilities, transportation systems, and warehouses, the entities decide to unitise the properties, which means that they have agreed to combine their properties into a single property. A joint operating agreement is signed and entity F is chosen as operator of the combined properties. Relevant data about each entity's properties and costs are given as follows:

Party E	
Prospecting costs incurred prior to property acquisition	€8,000,000
Mineral acquisition costs	€42,000,000
Geological and geophysical exploration costs (G&G)	€12,000,000
Exploratory drilling costs:	
Successful	€16,000,000
Unsuccessful	€7,000,000
Development costs incurred	€23,000,000
Estimated reserves, agreed between parties (in barrels)	30,000,000

Party F	
Prospecting costs incurred prior to property acquisition	€3,000,000
Mineral acquisition costs	€31,000,000
Geological and geophysical exploration costs (G&G)	€17,000,000
Exploratory drilling costs	
Successful	€24,000,000
Unsuccessful	€4,000,000
Development costs incurred	€36,000,000
Estimated reserves, agreed between parties (in barrels)	70,000,000

Ownership ratio in the venture is to be based on the relative quantity of agreed-upon reserves contributed by each party (30% to E and 70% to F). The parties agree that there should be an equalisation between them for the value of pre-unitisation exploration and development costs that directly benefit the unit, but not for other exploration and development costs. That is, there will be a cash settlement between the parties for the value of assets (other than mineral rights) or services that each party contributes to the unitisation. This is done so that the net value contributed by each party for the specified expenditures will equal that venturer's share of the total value of such expenditures at the time unitisation is consummated. Thus, the party contributing a value less than that party's share of ownership in the total value of those costs contributed by all the parties will make a cash payment to the other party so that each party's net contribution will equal that party's share of total value. The agreed amounts of costs to be equalised that are contributed by E and F are:

Expenditures made by:	E	F	Total
	€	€	€
Successful exploratory drilling	12,000,000	12,000,000	24,000,000
Development costs	18,000,000	30,000,000	48,000,000
Geological and geophysical exploration	4,000,000	14,000,000	18,000,000
Total expenditure	34,000,000	56,000,000	90,000,000

As a result of this agreement, F is obliged to pay E the net amount of €7,000,000 to equalise exploration and development costs. This is made up of the following components:

(a) €4,800,000 excess of value of exploratory drilling received by F (€16,800,000 = 70% × €24,000,000) in excess of value for successful exploratory drilling contributed (€12,000,000); plus

(b) €3,600,000 excess of value of development costs received by F in the unit (€33,600,000 = 70% × €48,000,000) in excess of the value of development costs contributed by F (€30,000,000); and less

(c) €1,400,000 excess of value of G&G costs contributed by F (€14,000,000) over the value of the share of G & G costs owned by F after unitisation (€12,600,000 = 70% × €18,000,000).

Although the reserves are unitised in the physical sense (i.e. each party will end up selling oil or gas that physically came out of the reserves of the other party), in volume terms the parties remain entitled to a quantity of reserves that is equal to that which they contributed. However, the timing of production and the costs to produce the reserves may be impacted by the unitisation agreement. The example below explains this in more detail.

Example 39.18: Reserves contributed in an unitisation

Entities A and B enter into a unitisation agreement and contribute Licences A and B, respectively. The table below shows the initial determination, redetermination and final determination of the reserves in each of the fields.

	Initial determination		Redetermination		Final determination	
	mboe		mboe		mboe	
Licence A	20	40.0%	19	37.3%	21	38.9%
Licence B	30	60.0%	32	62.7%	33	61.1%
	50	100.0%	51	100.0%	54	100.0%

Although Licences A and B were unitised, ultimately Entity A will be entitled to 21 mboe and Entity B will be entitled to 33 mboe, which is exactly the same quantity that they would have been entitled to had there been no unitisation.

To the extent that the unitisation of the mineral reserves themselves lacks commercial substance (see 4.7.3.B above), it may be appropriate to exclude the mineral reserves in accounting for an unitisation. Where the unitisation significantly affects the risk and timing of the cash flows or the type of product (e.g. an unitisation could lead to an exchange of, say, gas reserves for oil reserves) there is likely to be substance to the unitisation of the reserves.

If the assets subject to the unitisation arrangement are not E&E assets, or not only E&E assets, then it is necessary to develop an accounting policy in accordance with the requirements of IAS 8. Unitisation arrangements generally give rise to joint control over the underlying assets or entities:

(a) if the unitisation arrangement results in joint control over a joint venture then the parties should apply IFRS 11 (see Chapter 12) and IAS 28 (see Chapter 11) and provide the relevant disclosures in accordance with the requirements contained in IFRS 12 (see Chapter 13); or

(b) if the unitisation arrangement gives rise to a joint operation or results in a swap of assets that are not jointly controlled, then each of the parties should account for the arrangement as an asset swap (see 4.7.3 above).

Under both (a) and (b) above, a party to an unitisation agreement would report a gain (or loss) depending on whether the fair value of the interest received is higher (or lower) than the carrying amount of the interest given up.

5.1.2 Redeterminations

The percentage interests in an unitisation arrangement are based on estimates of the relative quantities of reserves contributed by each of the parties. As field life progresses and production experience is gained, many unitisation agreements require the reserves to be redetermined, which often leads the parties to conclude that the recoverable reserves in one or perhaps both of the original properties are not as previously estimated. Unitisation agreements typically require one or more 'redeterminations' of percentage interests once better reservoir information becomes available. In most cases, the revised percentage interests are deemed to be effective from the date of the original unitisation agreement, which means that adjustments are required between the parties in respect of their relative entitlements to cumulative production and their shares of cumulative costs.[142]

Unitisation agreements normally set out when redeterminations need to take place and the way in which adjustments to the percentage interests should be effected. The OIAC SORP describes the process as follows:

'(a) Adjustments in respect of cumulative "capital" costs are usually made immediately following the redetermination by means of a lump sum reimbursement, sometimes including an "interest" or uplift element to reflect related financing costs.

(b) Adjustments to shares of cumulative production are generally effected prospectively. Participants with an increased share are entitled to additional "make-up" production until the cumulative liftings are rebalanced. During this period adjusted percentage interests are applied to both production entitlement and operating costs. Once equity is achieved the effective percentage interests revert to those established by the redetermination.'[143]

An adjustment to an entity's percentage interest due to a redetermination is not a prior period error under IFRS. *[IAS 8.5]*. Instead, the redetermination results from new information or new developments and therefore should be treated as a change in an accounting estimate. Accordingly, a redetermination should not result in a fully retrospective adjustment.

Redeterminations give rise to some further accounting issues which are discussed below.

5.1.2.A Redeterminations as capital reimbursements

Under many national GAAPs redeterminations are accounted for as reimbursement of capital expenditure rather than as sales/purchases of a partial interest. Given that this second approach could result in the recognition of a gain upon redetermination, followed by a higher depreciation charge per barrel, it has become accepted industry practice that redeterminations should be accounted for as reimbursements of capital expenditure under IFRS. Both approaches are illustrated in Example 39.19 below.

In addition a redetermination gives rise to a number of questions, for example, how should the entities account for:

- the adjustment of their share in the remaining reserves;
- the 'make-up' oil obligation; and
- their revised shares in the decommissioning liabilities.

The 'make-up' oil obligation and the revised shares in the decommissioning liabilities are discussed further following the example below.

Example 39.19: Redetermination (1)

Entities A and B have a 10% and 90% percentage interest in a unitised property, respectively. On 1 January 2013, after three years of operations, their interests in the property are redetermined. The relevant data about each entity's interest in the property are as follows:

	A	B	Total
Percentage interest after initial determination	10%	90%	100%
Percentage interest after redetermination	8%	92%	100%
Initial reserves in 2010 (million barrels of oil equivalent)	100 mboe	900 mboe	1000 mboe
Total production from 2010 to 2012	30 mboe	270 mboe	300 mboe
Remaining reserves at 31/12/2012 before redetermination	70 mboe	630 mboe	700 mboe
Reserves after redetermination at 1/1/2013	56 mboe	644 mboe	700 mboe
'Make-up' oil: 300 mboe × (10% – 8%) =	–6 mboe	6 mboe	–
Total entitlement at 1/1/2013	50 mboe	650 mboe	700 mboe
	$	*$*	*$*
Exploration and development asset at 1/1/2010	400	3,600	4,000
Units of production depreciation:			
$400 ÷ 100 mboe × 30 mboe =	120		120
$3,600 ÷ 900 mboe × 270 mboe =		1,080	1,080
Exploration and development asset at 31/12/2012 before redetermination	280	2,520	2,800

	A	B	Total
Total investment based on 'initial determination': A: 10% of $4,000 = $400 and B: 90% of $4,000 = $3,600	400	3,600	4,000
Total investment based on redetermination: A: 8% of $4,000 = $320 and B: 92% of $4,000 = $3,680	320	3,680	4,000
Reimbursement of exploration and development costs	80	–80	–
Decommissioning asset at 1/1/2009	100	900	1,000
Units of production depreciation:			
$100 ÷ 100 mboe × 30 mboe =	30		30
$900 ÷ 900 mboe × 270 mboe =		270	270
Decommissioning asset at 31/12/2012 before redetermination	70	630	700
Decommissioning provision at 1/1/2010	100	900	1,000
Accreted interest from 1/1/2010 to 31/12/2012	20	180	200
Decommissioning provision at 31/12/2012 before redetermination	120	1,080	1,200
Reimbursement of decommissioning costs	–24	24	–
Decommissioning provision at 1/1/2013: A: 8% of $1,200 = $96 and B: 92% of $1,200 = $1,104	96	1,104	1,200

There are different ways in which an entity might interpret the effect of a redetermination on the exploration and development asset:

(a) Reimbursement of capital expenditure; or

(b) Sale/purchase of a partial interest.

Reimbursement of capital expenditure

Under this approach, the redetermination is treated as a reimbursement of capital expenditure and the 'make-up' oil is accounted for prospectively. This would lead entity A to make the following journal entries:

	$	$
Dr Cash	80	
Cr Exploration and development asset		80

The reimbursement of exploration and development costs is accounted for as a reduction in the exploration and development asset.

The overall impact on the statement of financial position of both Entities A and B is summarised in the table below:

	A	B	Total
	$	$	$
Exploration and development asset at 31/12/2012 before redetermination	280	2,520	2,800
Reimbursement of exploration and development costs	–80	80	–
Exploration and development asset at 1/1/2013 after redetermination	200	2,600	2,800

Before the redetermination both A and B would record depreciation of the exploration and development asset of $4/barrel (i.e. A: $400 ÷ 100 mboe = $4/barrel and B: $3,600 ÷ 900 mboe = $4/barrel). After the redetermination the depreciation of the exploration and development asset is still $4/barrel for both A and B (i.e. A: $200 ÷ 50 mboe = $4/barrel and B: $2,600 ÷ 650 mboe = $4/barrel).

Sale/purchase of a partial interest

The second approach, which is sometimes advocated, is to treat the redetermination as the equivalent of a sale or purchase of part of an interest.

	$	$
Dr Cash	80	
Cr Exploration and development asset: (8% – 10%) ÷ 10% × $280 =		56
Cr Gain on disposal of exploration and development asset		24

The reimbursement of exploration and development costs is accounted for as a partial disposal of the exploration and development asset.

However, Entity B will treat its entire payment of $80 to Entity A as the cost of the additional 2% interest that it 'acquired' in the redetermination. The overall impact on the statement of financial position of both Entities A and B is summarised in the table below:

	A	**B**	**Total**
	$	$	$
Exploration and development asset at 31/12/2012 before redetermination	280	2,520	2,800
Reimbursement of exploration and development costs	–56	80	–
Exploration and development asset at 1/1/2013 after redetermination	224	2,600	2,824

After the redetermination the depreciation of exploration and development asset for Entity A is ($224 ÷ 50 mboe =) $4.48/barrel and for Entity B is ($2,600 ÷ 650 mboe =) $4/barrel.

5.1.2.B 'Make-up' oil

As indicated in Example 39.19 above, Entity B would be entitled to 6 mboe of 'make-up' oil out of Entity A's share of the production. This raises the question whether Entity A should recognise a liability for the 'make-up' oil and whether Entity B should recognise an asset for the 'make-up' oil that it is entitled to.

'Make-up' oil is in many ways comparable to an over- or underlift of oil, because after the redetermination it appears that Entity A is effectively in an overlift position (i.e. it has sold more product than its proportionate share of production) while Entity B is in an underlift position (i.e. it has sold less product than its proportionate share of production).

IFRS does not directly address accounting for underlifts and overlifts (as discussed at 5.4 below) or accounting for 'make-up' oil following a redetermination. Consequently, an entity that is entitled to receive or is obliged to pay 'make-up' oil will need to apply the hierarchy in IAS 8 to develop an accounting policy. Therefore, an entity might develop either an accounting policy that is:

(a) similar to the 'entitlements method' (see 5.4.2 below) and account for a 'make-up' oil asset or liability that is similar to an underlift asset or and overlift liability; or

(b) based on the accounting standards of another standard-setter with a similar conceptual framework, such as US GAAP or UK GAAP, in which case the entity would not recognise an asset or liability and account for the 'make-up' oil prospectively.

Under many unitisation agreements, entities are required to give up oil only to the extent that there is production from the underlying field. Proponents of method (b) therefore argue that in the absence of future production, Entity A would have no obligation to deliver oil or make another form of payment to the other parties under the unitisation agreement. In those cases, the 'make-up' oil obligation would not meet the definition of financial liability under IAS 32 or that of a provision under IAS 37. They would also argue that Entity B cannot recognise an asset, because its right to 'make-up' oil only arises because of a future event (i.e. the future production of oil).

5.1.2.C Decommissioning provisions

Another effect of a redetermination is that it may increase or decrease an entity's share of the decommissioning liability in relation to the project, as illustrated in the example below.

Example 39.20: Redetermination (2)

Assuming the same facts as in Example 39.19 above, how should Entities A and B account for the change in the decommissioning provision?

Under IFRIC 1 – *Changes in Existing Decommissioning, Restoration and Similar Liabilities* – the change in a decommissioning provision should be added to, or deducted from, the cost of the related asset in the current period. However, if a decrease in the liability exceeds the carrying amount of the asset, the excess should be recognised immediately in profit or loss. *[IFRIC 1.5].*

This would lead Entities A and B to make the following journal entries:

	$	*$*
Entity A		
Dr Decommissioning provision	24	
Cr Decommissioning asset		24
Entity B		
Dr Decommissioning asset	24	
Cr Decommissioning provision		24

The decommission asset is adjusted in accordance with IFRIC 1 for the change in the decommissioning provision.

If Entity A had recognised a gain of $24 upon the reduction of the decommissioning liability, this would have resulted in an increase in the depreciation of the decommissioning asset from ($100 ÷ 100 mboe =) $1/barrel to ($70 ÷ 50 mboe =) $1.40/barrel. The IFRIC 1 approach avoids this although it increases the depreciation of the decommissioning asset slightly to ($56 ÷ 50mboe =) $1.12/barrel, as the decommissioning provision is also affected by the accretion of interest. Nevertheless, the approach required by IFRIC 1 is largely consistent with the treatment of a redetermination as a reimbursement of capital expenditure in Example 39.19 above.

5.2 Exploration and evaluation costs

There are several methods adopted by oil and gas companies to account for exploration and evaluation (E&E) costs. These include successful efforts, full cost and area of interest accounting. These methods have evolved through the use of previous GAAPs and industry practice. While these terms and methods (or similar methods) are commonly used in the sector, none of these is specifically referred to in IFRS.

In this section, we explore each of these methods and consider to what extent they are compliant with the requirements of IFRS.

5.2.1 Successful efforts method

The successful efforts methods that have been developed by different accounting standard-setters are generally based on the successful efforts concept as set out in US GAAP, under which generally only those costs that lead directly to the discovery, acquisition, or development of specific, discrete mineral reserves are capitalised and become part of the capitalised costs of the cost centre. Costs that when incurred fail to meet this criterion are generally charged to expense in the period they are incurred. Some interpretations of the successful efforts concept allow entities to capitalise the cost of unsuccessful development wells.[144]

Under the successful efforts method an entity will generally consider each individual mineral lease, concession, or production sharing contract as a cost centre.

When an entity applies the successful efforts method under IFRS, it will need to account for prospecting costs incurred before the E&E phase under IAS 16 or IAS 38. As economic benefits are highly uncertain at this stage of a project, prospecting costs will typically be expensed as incurred. Costs incurred to acquire undeveloped mineral rights, however, should be capitalised under IFRS if an entity expects an inflow of future economic benefits.

To the extent that costs are incurred within the E&E phase of a project, IFRS 6 does not prescribe any recognition and measurement rules. Therefore, it would be acceptable for such costs to be recorded as assets and written off when it is determined that the costs will not lead to economic benefits or to be expensed as incurred if the outcome is uncertain. Deferred costs of an undeveloped mineral right may be depreciated over some determinable period, subject to an impairment test each period with the amount of impairment charged to expense, or an entity may choose to carry forward the deferred costs of the undeveloped mineral right until the entity determines whether the property contains mineral reserves.[145] However, E&E assets should no longer be classified as such when the technical feasibility and commercial viability of extracting mineral resources are demonstrable. *[IFRS 6.17]*. At that time the asset should be tested for impairment under IAS 36, reclassified in the statement of financial position and accounted for under IAS 16 or IAS 38. If it is determined that no commercial reserves are present, then the costs capitalised should be expensed. Costs incurred after the E&E phase should be accounted for in accordance with the applicable IFRSs (i.e. IAS 16 and IAS 38).

While some elements of the successful efforts method as applied under certain national GAAPs are prohibited under IFRS, IFRS only requires relatively minor modifications to the method. Therefore the essence of the approach – that costs are capitalised pending evaluation – is acceptable under IFRS.

The following extract from the financial statements of Premier Oil illustrates a typical successful efforts method accounting policy applied under IFRS.

Extract 39.44: Premier Oil plc (2012)

ACCOUNTING POLICIES [extract]

Oil and gas assets [extract]

The company applies the successful efforts method of accounting for exploration and evaluation (E&E) costs, having regard to the requirements of IFRS 6 – 'Exploration for and Evaluation of Mineral Resources'.

(a) Exploration and evaluation assets

Under the successful efforts method of accounting, all licence acquisition, exploration and appraisal costs are initially capitalised in well, field or specific exploration cost centres as appropriate, pending determination. Expenditure incurred during the various exploration and appraisal phases is then written off unless commercial reserves have been established or the determination process has not been completed.

Pre-licence costs

Costs incurred prior to having obtained the legal rights to explore an area are expensed directly to the income statement as they are incurred.

Exploration and evaluation costs

Costs of E&E are initially capitalised as E&E assets. Payments to acquire the legal right to explore, costs of technical services and studies, seismic acquisition, exploratory drilling and testing are capitalised as intangible E&E assets.

Tangible assets used in E&E activities (such as the group's vehicles, drilling rigs, seismic equipment and other property, plant and equipment used by the company's exploration function) are classified as property, plant and equipment. However, to the extent that such a tangible asset is consumed in developing an intangible E&E asset, the amount reflecting that consumption is recorded as part of the cost of the intangible asset. Such intangible costs include directly attributable overhead, including the depreciation of property, plant and equipment utilised in E&E activities, together with the cost of other materials consumed during the exploration and evaluation phases.

E&E costs are not amortised prior to the conclusion of appraisal activities.

Treatment of E&E assets at conclusion of appraisal activities

Intangible E&E assets related to each exploration licence/prospect are carried forward, until the existence (or otherwise) of commercial reserves has been determined subject to certain limitations including review for indications of impairment. If commercial reserves have been discovered, the carrying value, after any impairment loss, of the relevant E&E assets, is then reclassified as development and production assets. If, however, commercial reserves have not been found, the capitalised costs are charged to expense after conclusion of appraisal activities.

(b) Development and production assets

Development and production assets are accumulated generally on a field-by-field basis and represent the cost of developing the commercial reserves discovered and bringing them into production, together with the E&E expenditures incurred in finding commercial reserves transferred from intangible E&E assets, as outlined in accounting policy (a) above.

The cost of development and production assets also includes the cost of acquisitions and purchases of such assets, directly attributable overheads, finance costs capitalised, and the cost of recognising provisions for future restoration and decommissioning.

Depreciation of producing assets

The net book values of producing assets are depreciated generally on a field-by-field basis using the unit-of-production method by reference to the ratio of production in the year and the related commercial reserves of the field, taking into account future development expenditures necessary to bring those reserves into production.

Producing assets are generally grouped with other assets that are dedicated to serving the same reserves for depreciation purposes, but are depreciated separately from producing assets that serve other reserves.

Pipelines are depreciated on a unit-of-throughput basis.

5.2.2 Full cost method

The full cost method under most national GAAPs requires all costs incurred in prospecting, acquiring mineral interests, exploration, appraisal, development, and construction to be accumulated in large cost centres, e.g. individual countries, groups of countries, or the entire world.[146] However, although an entity is permitted by IFRS 6 to develop an accounting policy without reference to other IFRSs or to the hierarchy, as described at 3.2.1 above, IFRS 6 cannot be extrapolated or applied by analogy to permit application of the full cost method outside the E&E phase. This was confirmed by the Interpretations Committee in January 2006.[147]

There are several other areas in which application of the full cost method under IFRS is restricted because:

- while the full cost method under most national GAAPs requires application of some form of 'ceiling test', IFRS 6 requires – when impairment indicators are present – an impairment test is to be performed in accordance with IAS 36;
- IFRS 6 requires E&E assets to be classified as tangible or intangible assets according to the nature of the assets. *[IFRS 6.15]*. In other words, even when an entity accounts for E&E costs in relatively large pools, it will still need to distinguish between tangible and intangible assets; and
- once the technical feasibility and commercial viability of extracting mineral resources are demonstrable, IFRS 6 requires E&E assets to be tested for impairment under IAS 36 (although in accordance with IFRS 6 E&E assets can be allocated to CGUs or groups of CGUs (which may include producing CGUs), provided certain criteria are met – see 3.5.2 above for further information), reclassified in the statement of financial position and accounted for under IAS 16 or IAS 38. *[IFRS 6.17]*. That means that it is not possible to account for successful and unsuccessful projects within one cost centre or pool.

For these reasons it is not possible to apply the full cost method of accounting under IFRS without making very significant modifications in the application of the method. An entity might want to use the full cost method as its starting point in developing its accounting policy for E&E assets under IFRS. However, it will rarely be appropriate to describe the resulting accounting policy as a 'full cost method' because key elements of the full cost method are not permitted under IFRS.

In July 2009, the IASB published an amendment to IFRS 1 – *Additional Exemptions for First-time Adopters* (Amendments to IFRS 1), which introduced a first-time adoption exemption for first-time adopters that accounted under their previous GAAP for 'exploration and development costs for oil and gas properties in the development or production phases ... in cost centres that include all properties in a large geographical area' (i.e. the full cost method).[148] Under the exemption, a first-time adopter may elect to measure oil and gas assets at the date of transition to IFRSs on a deemed cost basis (see Chapter 5 at 5.5.3), but does not permit continued application of the previous GAAP accounting policy.

Cairn Energy, which had originally wanted to apply the full cost method of accounting under IFRS, decided after the Interpretations Committee clarification in January 2006 to apply the successful efforts method.

Extract 39.45: Cairn Energy PLC (2006)

Restatement of 2004 Results from UK GAAP to IFRS

Updated 28 February 2006 [extract]

Introduction [extract]

Cairn originally released restated IFRS results for prior periods on 8 September 2005 and its interim 2005 results under IFRS on 20 September 2005. Both sets of results were prepared on the basis of the Group's continued application of its full cost accounting policy for oil and gas assets to both the exploration and appraisal activity phase and to those in the development and production phase. When these results were authorised for issue, the Board were aware that, owing to a lack of clarity in the authoritative literature, no consensus had been reached amongst the UK oil industry and the accounting profession on the status of full cost accounting policies under IFRS beyond the exploration and appraisal phase. As noted in the restatement document, this point was referred to the Agenda Committee of the International Financial Reporting Interpretations Committee ("IFRIC") to request clarification. The Agenda Committee subsequently issued guidance that the scope of IFRS 6 "Exploration for and Evaluation of Mineral Resources" is limited to exploration and appraisal activities and that accounting policies for development and production activities are to be based on the provisions of other existing IFRS.

Following this clarification from the IFRIC Agenda Committee, Cairn has reviewed its oil and gas accounting policy for both exploration and appraisal and development/producing assets. Cairn has decided to adopt a successful efforts based accounting policy for the Group's 2005 Annual Report and Accounts and has updated its restatement of prior periods to reflect this change in policy. The revised accounting policy is detailed in Note 1.

The key implications for Cairn's financial statements on adopting this policy are as follows:

- Costs of unsuccessful wells initially capitalised within exploration assets are expensed in the Income Statement in the period in which they are determined unsuccessful;
- depletion of development/producing assets is now performed on a field by field basis although fields within development areas can be combined where appropriate; and
- impairment testing for development/producing assets is now performed on each cash generating unit – this is usually, but not always, the development area.

5.2.3 *Area-of-interest method*

The area-of-interest method is an accounting concept by which 'costs incurred for individual geological or geographical areas that have characteristics conducive to containing a mineral reserve are deferred as assets pending determination of whether commercial reserves are found. If the area of interest is found to contain commercial reserves, the accumulated costs are capitalised. If the area is found to contain no commercial reserves, the accumulated costs are charged to expense.'[149]

Some consider the area-of-interest method to be a version of the successful efforts method that uses an area-of-interest, rather than an individual licence, as its unit of account. Others believe that the area-of-interest method is more akin to the full cost method applied on an area-of-interest basis.[150] 'Under the area-of-interest concept, all costs identified with an area of interest would be deferred and capitalised if commercial reserves are later determined to exist in the area. However, costs incurred up to the point that an area of interest is identified (prospecting costs) are often charged to expense by those who consider that they are applying the area-of-interest concept. ... Costs of individual unsuccessful activities incurred on a specific area of interest, such as drilling an exploratory well that finds no reserves, are accumulated as part of the total cost of the area of interest.'[151]

While IFRS 6 will often not permit all aspects of an area-of-interest method defined by a national GAAP, an entity that uses relatively small areas of interest may be able to implement the method in a meaningful way under IFRS. The area-of-interest method is more common in the mining sector than in the oil and gas sector. Still, there are some entities that apply the method to oil and gas activities.

Extract 39.46: BHP Billiton (2012)

9.1.6 Notes to Financial Statements [extract]
1 Accounting policies [extract]
Exploration and evaluation expenditure [extract]

Exploration and evaluation activity involves the search for mineral and petroleum resources, the determination of technical feasibility and the assessment of commercial viability of an identified resource. Exploration and evaluation activity includes:

- researching and analysing historical exploration data;
- gathering exploration data through topographical, geochemical and geophysical studies;
- exploratory drilling, trenching and sampling;
- determining and examining the volume and grade of the resource;
- surveying transportation and infrastructure requirements; and
- conducting market and finance studies.

Administration costs that are not directly attributable to a specific exploration area are charged to the income statement. Licence costs paid in connection with a right to explore in an existing exploration area are capitalised and amortised over the term of the permit.

Exploration and evaluation expenditure (including amortisation of capitalised licence costs) is charged to the income statement as incurred except in the following circumstances, in which case the expenditure may be capitalised:

- In respect of minerals activities:
  - the exploration and evaluation activity is within an area of interest which was previously acquired in an asset acquisition or in a business combination and measured at fair value on acquisition, or
  - the existence of a commercially viable mineral deposit has been established.
- In respect of petroleum activities:
  - the exploration and evaluation activity is within an area of interest for which it is expected that the expenditure will be recouped by future exploitation or sale; or
  - exploration and evaluation activity has not reached a stage which permits a reasonable assessment of the existence of commercially recoverable reserves.

Capitalised exploration and evaluation expenditure considered to be tangible is recorded as a component of property, plant and equipment at cost less impairment charges. Otherwise, it is recorded as an intangible asset (such as licences). As the capitalised exploration and evaluation asset is not available for use, it is not depreciated. All capitalised exploration and evaluation expenditure is monitored for indications of impairment. Where a potential impairment is indicated, assessment is performed for each area of interest in conjunction with the group of operating assets (representing a cash generating unit) to which the exploration is attributed. Exploration areas at which reserves have been discovered but require major capital expenditure before production can begin, are continually evaluated to ensure that commercial quantities of reserves exist or to ensure that additional exploration work is under way or planned. To the extent that capitalised expenditure is no longer expected to be recovered it is charged to the income statement.

> **Application of critical accounting policies and estimates** [extract]
>
> **Exploration and evaluation expenditure**
>
> The Group's accounting policy for exploration and evaluation expenditure results in certain items of expenditure being capitalised for an area of interest where it is considered likely to be recoverable by future exploitation or sale or where the activities have not reached a stage which permits a reasonable assessment of the existence of reserves. This policy requires management to make certain estimates and assumptions as to future events and circumstances, in particular whether an economically viable extraction operation can be established. Any such estimates and assumptions may change as new information becomes available. If, after having capitalised the expenditure under the policy, a judgement is made that recovery of the expenditure is unlikely, the relevant capitalised amount will be written off to the income statement.

5.3 Well workovers and recompletions

Well workovers or recompletions are often required when the producing oil sands become clogged and production declines, or other physical or mechanical problems arise.[152] Workover costs that relate to the day-to-day servicing of the wells (i.e. primarily the costs of labour and consumables, and possibly the cost of small parts) should be expensed as incurred. However, as discussed at 5.4 above, costs incurred to restore a well to its former level of production should be capitalised under IFRS, but an entity should derecognise any relevant previously capitalised well completion costs. However, to the extent that an entity can forecast future well workovers, it will need to depreciate the original well completion costs over a shorter economic life. Conversely, if an entity unexpectedly incurs well workover costs, it may need to consider whether those additional costs result in the need to perform an impairment test.

5.4 Overlift and underlift – revenue recognition

In jointly owned operations it is often not practical for each participant to take in kind or to sell its exact share of production during a period. In most periods some participants in the jointly owned operations will be in an overlift position (i.e. they have taken more product than their proportionate entitlement) while other participants may be in an underlift position (i.e. they have taken less product than their proportionate entitlement). Such lifting imbalances are usually settled in one of three ways:[153]

- in future periods the owner in an underlift position may sell or take product in excess of their normal entitlement, while the owner in an overlift position will sell or take less product than the normal entitlement;
- cash balancing may be used, whereby the overlift party will make a cash payment to the underlift party for the value of the imbalance volume; or
- if the co-owners have joint ownership interests in other properties, they may agree to offset balances in the two properties to the extent possible.

The two methods of accounting for underlifts and overlifts that are commonly used in the oil and gas sector are (a) the sales method and (b) the entitlements method.[154]

5.4.1 Sales method

Under the *sales method*, revenue is the value of what a participant sells or the value of all product that has been transferred to its downstream activity.[155] Although revenue arising from the extraction of mineral ores is outside the scope of IAS 18, *[IAS 18.6(h)]*, the sales method is similar to the revenue recognition approach in IAS 18. This is because revenue is only recognised when an entity has transferred ownership of the goods and the amount of revenue can be measured reliably.

A drawback of the sales method is that when an imbalance occurs it gives rise to a mismatch between expenses and revenue. This mismatch arises because the participants' share of expenses for the period is often equal to its ownership percentage, while its revenues are based on actual sales. There are two approaches to dealing with the effects of such mismatches:

(a) *Accrue or defer expenses* – It has been argued that an overlift participant should accrue for future expenses that are not matched by corresponding future revenues. Conversely, an underlift participant should defer expenses and match them against future catch-up production. Therefore, an overlift liability would be accounted for as accrued production costs, while an underlift asset would be accounted for as a prepaid cost at the lower of the amount of accrued production costs or net realisable value. However, as IFRS does not require matching of revenue and expenses, it seems that accrued (deferred) expenses would not meet the definition of a liability (asset) under the IASB's *Conceptual Framework*;

(b) *No adjustment* – Not accounting for the effects of imbalances has been justified on the grounds that the amounts involved are immaterial, or operating costs for the period should be expensed as incurred because they relate to the period's production activity and not to the revenues recognised.[156]

5.4.2 Entitlements method

Under the *entitlements method*, net revenue reflects the participant's share of production regardless of which participant has actually made the sale and invoiced the production. This is achieved by applying one of the following approaches in dealing with imbalances between actual sales and entitlements:[157]

(a) *Adjusting revenue* – The excess of product sold during the period over the participant's ownership share of production from the property is recognised by the overlift party as a liability and not as revenue.[158] Conversely, the underlift party would recognise an underlift asset and report corresponding revenue. As the participant's share of expenses for the period is generally equal to its ownership percentage, there is no need to make any further adjustments;[159] or

(b) *Adjusting cost of sales* – This version of the entitlements method, which is the recommended approach under the UK OIAC SORP, requires the cost of sales to be adjusted to take account of an asset or liability that reflects the lifting imbalance. If the adjustments are recorded at the market value of the product then it results in recognition of gross profit on an entitlements basis, while at the same time permitting revenues to be shown at the actual invoiced amount.

It is important for an entity to define clearly the measurement point for determining its 'share of production' and to apply that definition consistently. While it is possible to measure production at the well head, in practice production is often measured at the point where product is transferred into a pipeline or from a floating production, storage and offloading (FPSO) vessel into a ship.

5.4.3 *Settlement*

5.4.3.A *Cash balancing*

If participants have the right to settle imbalances on a cash basis then an underlift asset (overlift liability) clearly meets the definition of a financial asset (financial liability) under IFRS and should be accounted for under IAS 39. Depending on the designation of the financial asset or financial liability, it should be measured either at amortised cost or at fair value. The fair value in such cases would equal the cash settlement amount that participants are entitled to or required to pay.

5.4.3.B *Physical settlement*

If settlement of imbalances takes place physically by adjusting future liftings or providing a quantity of product from another source, it is not immediately obvious at what value the asset or liability should be recognised.

An overlift liability generally meets the definition of a provision under IAS 37 as the timing and amount of the settlement are uncertain and are not payable in cash but in kind. In applying IAS 37 the amount recognised as a provision should be 'the best estimate of the expenditure required to settle the present obligation at the end of the reporting period', *[IAS 37.36]*, which is 'the amount that an entity would rationally pay to settle the obligation at the end of the reporting period'. *[IAS 37.37]*.

An underlift asset that gives an entity the right to receive a quantity of product from another party is equivalent to a prepaid commodity purchase (and also similar to product borrowing). Therefore, it is reasonable to account for such underlift assets in the same way and apply the guidance in IAS 2 by analogy. Therefore, an underlift asset can be measured either at the lower of cost or net realisable value or at net realisable value in accordance with well-established industry practice. *[IAS 2.3(a), 9]*.

5.4.4 *Facility imbalances*

Imbalances that are similar to overlifts and underlifts can also arise on facilities such as pipelines when a venturer delivers more or less product into a pipeline than it takes out in the same period. The resulting accounting issues arising are similar to those concerning overlifts and underlifts.

5.4.5 *Overlift and underlift in practice*

IFRS does not address accounting for underlifts and overlifts directly; hence an entity that applied the hierarchy in IAS 8 could consider guidance from a number of sources: *[IAS 8.12]*

- Under US GAAP, ASC 932-10-S99-5 – *Extractive Activities – Oil and Gas – Overall – SEC Materials – General* – does not express a preference for the sales method or the entitlements method. In practice, it seems that of those companies that apply the sales method under US GAAP a large majority do not make adjustments for operating expenses related to imbalances;[160] and

- The OIAC SORP under UK GAAP recommended that entities apply the entitlements method and adjust cost of sales for the effect of underlifts and overlifts.

As illustrated in the extracts below, in practice both the entitlements method and the sales method are used under IFRS.

Extract 39.47: BG Group plc (2012)

Principal accounting policies [extract]

Revenue recognition [extract]

Revenue associated with exploration and production sales (of natural gas, crude oil and petroleum products) is recorded when title passes to the customer. Revenue from the production of natural gas and oil in which BG Group has an interest with other producers is recognised based on the Group's working interest and the terms of the relevant production sharing contracts (entitlement method).

Extract 39.48: Statoil ASA (2012)

8.1 Notes to the Consolidated financial statements [extract]

8.1.2 Significant accounting policies [extract]

Revenue recognition

Revenues associated with sale and transportation of crude oil, natural gas, petroleum and chemical products and other merchandise are recognised when risk passes to the customer, which is normally when title passes at the point of delivery of the goods, based on the contractual terms of the agreements.

Revenues from the production of oil and gas properties in which Statoil shares an interest with other companies are recognised on the basis of volumes lifted and sold to customers during the period (the sales method). Where Statoil has lifted and sold more than the ownership interest, an accrual is recognised for the cost of the overlift. Where Statoil has lifted and sold less than the ownership interest, costs are deferred for the underlift.

Revenue is presented net of customs, excise taxes and royalties paid in-kind on petroleum products. Revenue is presented gross of in-kind payments of amounts representing income tax.

Sales and purchases of physical commodities, which are not settled net, are presented on a gross basis as revenue and cost of goods sold in the statement of income. Activities related to trading and commodity-based derivative instruments are reported on a net basis, with the margin included in revenue.

5.5 Trading activities by oil and gas companies

Many oil and gas companies engage in oil and gas trading (e.g. crude oil cargos) and they may either take delivery of the product or resell it without taking delivery. Even when an entity takes physical delivery and becomes the legal owner of a crude oil cargo or contents of a storage tank, it may still only be as part of its trading activities. Such transactions do not fall within the normal purchase and sales exemption (see 4.18.1 above) when 'the entity has a practice of taking delivery of the underlying and selling it within a short period after delivery for the purpose of generating a profit from short-term fluctuations in price or dealer's margin'. *[IAS 32.9(c), IAS 39.6(c)]*. In that case, the purchase and sales contracts should be accounted for as derivatives within the scope of IAS 39.

The extract below from the financial statements of BP illustrates an accounting policy that an entity can apply in accounting for trading activities.

> *Extract 39.49: BP p.l.c. (2012)*
>
> **Notes on financial statements** [extract]
>
> **1. Significant accounting policies** [extract]
>
> **Revenue** [extract]
>
> Revenue arising from the sale of goods is recognized when the significant risks and rewards of ownership have passed to the buyer, which is typically at the point that title passes, and the revenue can be reliably measured.
>
> Revenue is measured at the fair value of the consideration received or receivable and represents amounts receivable for goods provided in the normal course of business, net of discounts, customs duties and sales taxes.
>
> Physical exchanges are reported net, as are sales and purchases made with a common counterparty, as part of an arrangement similar to a physical exchange. Similarly, where the group acts as agent on behalf of a third party to procure or market energy commodities, any associated fee income is recognized but no purchase or sale is recorded. Additionally, where forward sale and purchase contracts for oil, natural gas or power have been determined to be for trading purposes, the associated sales and purchases are reported net within sales and other operating revenues whether or not physical delivery has occurred.

5.6 Inventories

5.6.1 Pipeline fill and cushion gas

In certain industries, for example the petrochemical sector, certain processes or storage arrangements require a core of inventory to be present in the system at all times. For example in order for a crude oil refining process to take place, the plant must contain a certain minimum quantity of oil. This can only be taken out once the plant is abandoned and could then only be sold as sludge. Similarly, underground gas storage caves are filled with gas; but a substantial part (25%) of that gas can never be sold as its function is to pressurise the cave, thereby allowing the remaining 75% to be extracted. Even though the gas will be turned around on a continuing basis, at any one time 25% of it will never be available to sell and cannot be recouped from the cave. Finally, long distance pipelines contain a significant volume of gas that keeps them operational.

It is our view that if an item of inventory is not held for sale or consumed in a production process, but is necessary to the operation of a facility during more than one operating cycle, and its cost cannot be recouped through sale (or is significantly impaired), this item of inventory should be accounted for as an item of property, plant and equipment under IAS 16 rather than as inventory under IAS 2. This applies even if the part of inventory that is deemed to be an item of property, plant and equipment (PP&E) cannot be separated physically from the rest of inventory.

These matters will always involve the exercise of judgement, however, in the above instances, we consider that:

- the deemed PP&E items do not meet the definition of inventories;
- although it is not possible to physically separate the chemicals involved into inventory and PP&E categories, there is no accounting reason why one cannot distinguish between identical assets with different uses and therefore account for them differently. Indeed, IAS 2 does envisage such a possibility when discussing different cost formulas; *[IAS 2.25]*
- the deemed PP&E items are necessary to bring another item of PP&E to the condition necessary for it to be capable of operating in the manner intended by management. This meets the definition of the costs of PP&E in IAS 16 upon initial recognition; *[IAS 16.16(b)]* and
- recognising these items as inventories would lead to an immediate loss because these items cannot be sold or consumed in a production process, or during the process of rendering services. This does not properly reflect the fact that the items are necessary to operate another asset over more than one operating cycle.

By contrast, core inventory that is not necessary to operate the asset and that is recoverable (e.g. gas in a pipeline) is considered to be held for sale or to be consumed in the production process or process of rendering services. Therefore such gas is accounted for as inventory.

The extract below from the financial statements of GDF SUEZ shows how cushion gas is accounted for as a tangible asset that is depreciated over its economic life.

Extract 39.50: GDF SUEZ (2012)

Notes to the consolidated financial statements [extract]

NOTE 1 SUMMARY OF SIGNIFICANT ACCOUNTING POLICIES [extract]

1.4 Significant accounting policies [extract]

1.4.5 Property, plant and equipment [extract]

1.4.5.1 Initial recognition and subsequent measurement [extract]

Cushion gas

"Cushion" gas injected into underground storage facilities is essential for ensuring that reservoirs can be operated effectively, and is therefore inseparable from these reservoirs. Unlike "working" gas which is included in inventories, cushion gas is reported in property, plant and equipment. It is measured at average purchase price plus regasification, transportation and injection costs.

1.4.10 Inventories [extract]

Gas inventories

Gas injected into underground storage facilities includes working gas which can be withdrawn without adversely affecting the operation of the reservoir, and cushion gas which is inseparable from the reservoirs and essential for their operation (see the section on property, plant and equipment).

Working gas is classified in inventory and measured at weighted average purchase cost upon entering the transportation network regardless of its source, including any regasification costs.

Group inventory outflows are valued using the weighted average unit cost method.

An impairment loss is recognized when the net realizable value of inventories is lower than their weighted average cost.

5.6.2 *Carried at fair value*

Inventories should be measured at the lower of cost and net realisable value under IAS 2. However, IAS 2 does not apply to the measurement of minerals and mineral products, to the extent that they are measured at net realisable value in accordance with well established practices in those industries. *[IAS 2.3(a)]*. There is also an exception for commodity broker traders who measure their inventories at fair value less costs to sell. When such inventories are measured at fair value less costs to sell, changes in fair value less costs to sell are recognised in profit or loss in the period of the change. *[IAS 2.3(b)]*.

Both these scope exemptions are relevant to the oil and gas sector. An oil and gas company that wishes to use the exemption relating to minerals and mineral products outlined above would need to demonstrate that valuation at net realisable value was a well-established practice in its industry, which may be difficult to do for base inventory.

The commodity broker trader exemption above is commonly used by oil and gas companies that engage in oil and gas trading. The extract below from the financial statements of BP illustrates a typical accounting policy for an oil and gas company that makes use of this exemption.

Extract 39.51: BP p.l.c. (2012)

Notes on financial statements [extract]

1. Significant accounting policies [extract]

Inventories

Inventories, other than inventory held for trading purposes, are stated at the lower of cost and net realizable value. Cost is determined by the first-in first-out method and comprises direct purchase costs, cost of production, transportation and manufacturing expenses. Net realizable value is determined by reference to prices existing at the balance sheet date.

Inventories held for trading purposes are stated at fair value less costs to sell and any changes in net realizable value are recognized in the income statement.

Supplies are valued at cost to the group mainly using the average method or net realizable value, whichever is the lower.

5.6.3 *Recognition – work in progress*

Oil and gas companies often do not separately report work in progress inventories of either oil or gas. As is noted in the IASC Issues Paper 'the main reason is that, at the point of their removal from the earth, oil and gas frequently do not require processing and they may be sold or may be transferred to the enterprise's downstream operations in the form existing at the time of removal, that is, they are immediately recognised as finished goods. Even if the oil and gas removed from the earth require additional processing to make them saleable or transportable, the time required for processing is typically minimal and the amount of raw products involved in the processing at any one time is likely to be immaterial.'[161] However, if more than an insignificant quantity of product is undergoing processing at any given point in time then an entity may need to disclose work in progress under IAS 2. *[IAS 2.8, 37]*.

6 PRACTICAL ISSUES IN THE MINING SECTOR

6.1 IFRIC 20 – Stripping Costs in the Production Phase of a Surface Mine

In surface mining operations it is necessary to remove overburden and other waste materials to gain access to ore from which minerals can be extracted. It is generally accepted that the costs of removal (also known as stripping) of overburden and waste materials during the development of a mine, i.e. before production commences, should be capitalised as part of the investment in the construction of the mine. For these purposes the 'mine' is considered to be an asset that is separate from the 'mineral rights and mineral reserves', which are outside the scope of IAS 16. *[IAS 16.3(d)].*

Until the guidance provided by IFRIC 20 – *Stripping Costs in the Production Phase of a Surface Mine* – issued by the Interpretations Committee in October 2011 there was no consensus regarding the treatment of stripping costs that were incurred during the production phase. IFRS was not clear on whether stripping costs were to be treated as costs of inventory under IAS 2 or as a period cost, or capitalised as an asset. In practice three approaches were used: expensing production stripping costs as incurred, capitalising production stripping costs as cost of inventory and deferral of production stripping costs.

6.1.1 Scope of IFRIC 20

IFRIC 20 was issued in October 2011 and applies to annual periods beginning on or after 1 January 2013.

IFRIC 20 considers the different types of stripping costs encountered in a surface mining operation. These costs are separated into those incurred in the development phase of the mine (i.e. pre-production) and those that are incurred in the production phase. *[IFRIC 20.2, 3].*

Generally those costs that are incurred in the development phase of the mine would be capitalised as part of the depreciable cost of building, developing and constructing the mine, under the principles of IAS 16. Ultimately these capitalised costs are depreciated or amortised on a systematic basis, usually by using the units of production method, once production commences. The stripping costs incurred in the development phase of a mine are not considered by the Interpretation. The Interpretations Committee considered that there was little divergence in practice when accounting for these costs. *[IFRIC 20.BC5].*

The Interpretation applies to all waste removal (stripping) costs that are incurred during the production phase of a surface mine (production stripping costs). *[IFRIC 20.2].* It does not apply to oil and natural gas extraction and underground mining activities. Also, it does not address the question of whether oil sands extraction is considered to be a surface mining activity and therefore whether it is in scope or not. *[IFRIC 20.BC4].*

Despite the importance of the term 'production phase', this is not defined in the Interpretation, or elsewhere in IFRS. The determination of the commencement of the production phase not only affects stripping costs, but also affects many other accounting issues in the extractive industries, described in more detail above. These include the cessation of the capitalisation of other costs, including borrowing costs (see 3.3.3 above), the commencement of depreciation or amortisation (see 4.9 above), and the treatment of certain pre-production revenues (see 4.13 above).

The Interpretation acknowledges that stripping activity undertaken during the production phase may create two benefits – the first being the extraction of ore (inventory) in the current period and the second being improved access to the ore body to be mined in a future period. Where the benefits are realised in the form of inventory produced, the production stripping costs are to be accounted for in accordance with IAS 2. Where the benefit is improved access to ore to be mined in the future, these costs are to be recognised as a non-current asset, if the required criteria are met (see 6.1.2 below). The Interpretation refers to this non-current asset as the 'stripping activity asset'. *[IFRIC 20.8]*.

6.1.2 Recognition criteria – stripping activity asset

IFRIC 20 states that an entity must recognise a stripping activity asset if, and only if, all of the following criteria are satisfied:

(a) it is probable that the future economic benefit (improved access to the ore body) associated with the stripping activity will flow to the entity;

(b) the entity can identify the component of the ore body for which access has been improved; and

(c) the costs relating to the stripping activity associated with that component can be measured reliably. *[IFRIC 20.9]*.

Instead of being a separate asset, the stripping activity asset is to be accounted for as an addition to, or as an enhancement of, an existing asset. This means that the stripping activity asset will be accounted for as part of an existing asset. *[IFRIC 20.10]*. IFRIC 20 does not specify whether the stripping activity asset is a tangible or intangible asset. Instead it simply states that it should be classified as tangible or intangible according to the nature of the existing asset of which it is part – so it will depend upon whether an entity classifies its mine assets as tangible or intangible.

The Interpretation considers that the stripping activity asset might add to or improve a variety of existing assets, such as, the mine property (land), the mineral deposit itself, an intangible right to extract the ore or an asset that originated in the mine development phase. *[IFRIC 20.BC10]*. In most instances, entities classify their producing mine assets as tangible assets; therefore it is likely that the stripping activity assets will also be classified as tangible assets.

Entities that had previously presented their capitalised stripping costs as an asset separate from their mine assets or mining rights, for example, if they had presented these as part of other current or non-current assets, such amounts (which qualify to be carried forward at transition) will need to be reclassified to form part of the mining related assets (either tangible or intangible) upon adoption of IFRIC 20 and will be presented within non-current assets. See 6.1.5 for more details on transition.

6.1.3 Initial recognition

The stripping activity asset is to be initially measured at cost. This will be the accumulation of costs directly incurred to perform the stripping activity that benefits the identified component of ore, plus an allocation of directly attributable overhead costs. *[IFRIC 20.12]*. Examples of the types of costs that the Interpretations Committee expects to be included as directly attributable overhead costs are items such as salary costs of the mine supervisor overseeing that component of the mine, and an allocation of rental costs of any equipment hired specifically to perform the stripping activity. *[IFRIC 20.BC12]*.

Some incidental operations may take place at the same time as the production stripping activity that are not necessary for the production stripping activity to continue as planned. The costs associated with these incidental operations are not to be included in the cost of the stripping activity asset. *[IFRIC 20.12]*. An example provided in the Interpretation is the building of an access ramp in the area in which the production stripping activity is taking place. These ancillary costs must be recognised as assets or expensed in accordance with other IFRSs.

6.1.3.A Allocating costs between inventory and the stripping activity asset

If the costs of waste removal can be directly allocated between inventory and the stripping activity asset, then the entity should allocate those costs accordingly. However, the Interpretation acknowledges that it may be difficult in practice to identify these costs separately, particularly if inventory is produced at the same time as access to the ore body is improved. This is likely to be very common in practice. Where this is the case, the Interpretation permits an entity to use an allocation approach that is based on a relevant production measure as this is considered to be a good indicator of the nature of benefits that are generated for the activity taking place in the mine. *[IFRIC 20.13]*.

In determining an appropriate allocation basis, the Interpretation provides a (non-exhaustive) list of some of the possible metrics that could be used. These include:

- cost of inventory produced compared with expected cost;
- volume of waste extracted compared with expected volume, for a given volume of ore production; and
- mineral content of the ore extracted compared with expected mineral content to be extracted, for a given quantity of ore produced. *[IFRIC 20.13]*.

The Interpretation states that an allocation basis which uses sales value or relative sales value is not acceptable. *[IFRIC 20.BC15]*.

The production measure is calculated for each identified component of the ore body. Application of this allocation methodology effectively involves a comparison of the expected level of activity for that component with the actual level of activity for the same component, to identify when additional activity may have occurred and may be creating a future benefit.

Where the actual level of activity exceeds the expected level of activity, the waste removal activity incurred at the expected level and its associated costs would then form part of the cost of inventory produced in that period. Any excess of actual activity over the expected level (and the associated costs of such excess activity) needs to be considered to determine whether it represents a stripping activity asset.

It is important to note that where actual stripping levels exceed those expected for the identified component, this will not automatically result in the recognition of a stripping activity asset. An entity will need to assess whether the removal of such additional waste has actually resulted in a future economic benefit, i.e. improved access to future ore. If not, such costs should not be capitalised as an asset, but instead recognised in profit or loss in the period incurred. For example, the mining of an unexpected fault or dyke should not be capitalised but instead expensed as incurred.

Where actual waste removal activity is less than the expected level of activity, only the actual waste removed and its associated costs, not the expected costs, will form part of the cost of inventory produced in that period. This is because continuing to recognise waste costs at the expected level would require an entity to recognise a deferred stripping liability. This is not permitted under IFRIC 20 or generally under IFRS because, in the absence of a legal or constructive obligation to continue to the mine the deposit, such costs would not satisfy the criteria to be recognised as a liability.

It is worth noting that while some of the allocation approaches set out in the Interpretation are similar to the life-of-mine average strip ratio approach used by many entities prior to the introduction of IFRIC 20, there are differences.

The key difference is that the level at which the expected level of activity is to be determined when calculating the relevant production measure is likely to be lower than that used for the life-of-mine average strip ratio approach. The life-of-mine average strip ratio approach uses the entire ore body, whereas IFRIC 20 requires this to be determined for each component of the ore body, which is expected to be a subset of the ore body. See 6.1.3.B below for further discussion about how to determine a component.

The other difference relates to the way in which any stripping activity asset is recognised in profit or loss. Under the life-of-mine average stripping ratio approach, a portion of the deferred stripping asset is recognised in profit or loss when the actual stripping ratio falls below the expected average life of mine strip ratio. Under IFRIC 20 however, the stripping activity asset is to be depreciated or amortised over the useful life of the identified component of the ore body that becomes more accessible. The units of production (UOP) method is to be used unless another method is more appropriate. *[IFRIC 20.15]*.

It is important to note that the calculation of the expected production measure for each component will not only need to be done on transition to IFRIC 20, but it will also need to be reviewed and updated if there are material changes to the mine plan for that component (for example due to differences in actual versus budgeted performance or changes in future mining plans resulting from other factors, e.g. changes in commodity prices or increases in costs). Should these changes impact the expected production measure for the remaining life of the component, then the IFRIC 20 calculations will need to be updated and applied on a prospective basis. The calculation of the expected production measures will also be required if and when new components commence production.

Example 39.21: Allocating costs between inventory and the stripping activity asset

Scenario A – actual performance measure exceeds the expected performance measure

The following example illustrates how an entity would allocate costs between inventory and the stripping activity asset where the actual performance measure exceeds the expected performance measure for a component in a particular period.

Assume Entity A had a mine which comprised two separate pits which were accessing the one ore body. For the purposes of IFRIC 20, each pit was identified as a component. Pit 1 had a total life of three years and at reporting period end, had been in production for one year. Pit 2 had a total life of five years but production had not yet commenced.

At the commencement of production from pit 1, the company had forecast the following mining and stripping activity:

Expected ore to be extracted over the 3 years	1,000 tonnes
Expected volume of waste to be extracted over the 3 years	3,000 tonnes

During the current period, the following had occurred in relation to the production from pit 1:

Cost incurred for mining activity	\$13,000,000 (a)
Actual tonnes of ore removed	100 tonnes (b)
Actual tonnes of waste removed	1,200 tonnes (c)
Average cost per tonne in year 1 = (a) / [(b)+(c)]	\$10,000

The company has determined that it is not practically possible to identify separately what portion of the waste removal costs leads to the extraction of inventory and what portion to improved access to future ore. This is because these two activities were occurring simultaneously as there were multiple shovels in operation in multiple parts of the component and a single haulage fleet was used.

Given this, the company has decided that it will allocate costs by comparing the actual volume of waste and ore extracted (the actual strip ratio) in the period with the expected volume of waste and ore (expected strip ratio) for the life of the component i.e. for pit 1.

The allocation of the actual waste removal costs incurred will involve the following steps:

Step 1: Calculate the expected strip ratio for pit 1

Expected volume of waste to be extracted / expected volume of ore to be extracted
= 3,000 tonnes / 1,000 tonnes
= 3.00 (expected strip ratio)

This means that for every 1 tonne of ore extracted over the life of pit 1, the company expects (on average) to remove 3 tonnes of waste.

Step 2: Calculate the additional waste extracted compared to the expected waste extracted for the actual volume of ore extracted

Actual volume of ore extracted × expected strip ratio
= 100 tonnes × 3 tonnes
= 300 tonnes

Actual volume of waste extracted in year 1 = 1,200 tonnes

Additional waste extracted in year 1 = actual waste extracted less expected waste to be extracted
= 1,200 tonnes – 300 tonnes
= 900 tonnes of additional waste was extracted

Step 3: Allocate mining costs between inventory and the stripping activity asset

Stripping activity asset

Additional waste tonnes removed × cost per tonne

= 900 tonnes × $10,000

= $9,000,000

Inventory

Total mining costs incurred less costs allocated to the stripping activity asset

= $13,000,000 – $9,000,000

= $4,000,000

This comprises:

(1) The cost of extracting the inventory tonnes

= 100 × $10,000

= $1,000,000

Plus:

(2) The cost of waste removal allocated directly to inventory (which was allocated at the expected level of 3:1)

= 300 tonnes × $10,000

= $3,000,000

Scenario B – actual strip ratio is less than the expected strip ratio

Assume the same basic fact pattern as per Scenario A above, but with different actual mining results for pit 1 in the current period:

Cost incurred for mining activity	$13,000,000 (a)
Actual tonnes of ore removed	1,200 tonnes (b)
Actual tonnes of waste removed	100 tonnes (c)
Average cost per tonne in year 1 = (a) / [(b)+(c)]	$10,000

The company has determined that it is not practically possible to identify separately what portion of the waste removal costs leads to the extraction of inventory and what portion to improved access to future ore. This is because these two activities were occurring simultaneously as there were multiple shovels in operation in multiple parts of the component and a single haulage fleet was used.

Given this, the company has decided that it will allocate costs by comparing the actual volume of waste and ore extracted (the actual strip ratio) in the period with the expected volume of waste and ore (expected strip ratio) for the life of the component i.e. for pit 1.

The allocation of the actual waste removal costs incurred will involve the following steps:

Step 1: Calculate the expected strip ratio for pit 1

Expected volume of waste to be extracted / expected volume of ore to be extracted

= 3,000 tonnes / 1,000 tonnes

= 3.00 (expected strip ratio)

This means that for every 1 tonne of ore extracted over the life of pit 1, the company expects (on average) to remove 3 tonnes of waste.

Step 2: Calculate the additional waste extracted compared to the expected waste extracted for the actual volume of ore extracted

Actual volume of ore extracted × expected strip ratio

= 1,200 tonnes × 3 tonnes

= 36,000 tonnes

Actual volume of waste extracted in year 1 = 100 tonnes

During the current period the actual strip ratio was only 0.0833. As this is less than the expected strip ratio, as explained above, there is no additional waste removed during the period.

Step 3: Allocate mining costs between inventory and the stripping activity asset

Stripping activity asset

As the actual strip ratio was below the expected strip ratio, no additional waste was removed during the period; therefore there is no amount to be added to the stripping activity asset.

Inventory

As the actual amount of waste removed during the current period is less than the expected level of waste for the life of the component, and there is no amount to be allocated to the stripping activity asset, then the total mining costs for the period will be allocated to inventory.

= $13,000,000

This comprises:

(1) The cost of extracting the inventory tonnes

= 1,200 × $10,000

= $12,000,000

Plus:

(2) The cost of waste removal allocated directly to inventory (which is allocated based on the actual waste tonnes removed during the period)

= 100 tonnes × $10,000

= $1,000,000

6.1.3.B *Identifying the component of the ore body*

One of the critical steps an entity needs to undertake when applying IFRIC 20 is to identify the various components of the ore body. This is necessary for several reasons:

(a) production stripping costs can only be capitalised as an asset if the component of the ore body for which access has been improved, can be identified;

(b) to allocate stripping activity costs between inventory and the stripping activity asset, an entity needs to determine the expected level of activity for each component of the mine; and

(c) the stripping activity asset is required to be depreciated or amortised on a systematic basis, over the expected useful life of the identified component of the ore body that becomes more accessible as a result of the stripping activity.

Limited guidance is provided in the Interpretation relating to the identification of components, although it does appear the Interpretations Committee expected a component to be a subset of the whole ore body. This view is supported in several sections of IFRIC 20.

- A 'component' refers to the specific volume of the ore body that is made more accessible by the stripping activity; the identified component of the ore body would typically be a subset of the total ore body of the mine; and a mine may have several components, which are identified during the mine planning stage. *[IFRIC 20.BC8]*.
- The depreciation or amortisation requirements state that the expected useful life of the identified component of the ore body that is used to depreciate or amortise the stripping activity asset will differ from the expected useful life that is used to depreciate or amortise the mine itself and the related life-of-mine assets, unless the stripping activity provides improved access to the whole of the ore body. *[IFRIC 20.BC17]*.

Identification of the various components of an ore body requires significant management judgement. While the Interpretations Committee considers that an entity's mine plan will provide the information required allowing these judgements to be made with reasonable consistency, this may not be a straightforward exercise, and it will be particularly challenging for the more complex mines.

In practice, the identification of components of an ore body is a complex process which requires a significant amount of management judgement. This is because ore bodies vary significantly in shape and size and are more haphazard than often illustrated in simple examples. Management may identify components in a number of different ways. These could include identifying discrete components in the mine plan, such as phases, sections, push backs, cutbacks, lay backs, blocks, etc. examining annual production plans; or examining push back campaigns. Whatever approach is adopted, it is essential that the components are recognisable to those who are responsible for mine planning as they will be the ones who will need to track progress as ore is removed and will need to update the assessment of components should the mine plan change. Given this, practice has revealed that when identifying the components of an ore body, it is essential that input is obtained from those who best understand the mine plan, i.e. the mining engineers and operational personnel.

The identification of components will not only need to be done on transition to IFRIC 20 but it will also need to be reassessed and updated (if necessary) whenever there are material changes to the mine plan. Given this, an entity will need to establish systems, processes, procedures and controls to ensure it is able to identify when material changes to the mine plan have occurred that would require the IFRIC 20 calculations to be updated. Identification of components will also be required when an entity commences production on a new component of the ore body or in relation to a new ore body.

6.1.4 Subsequent measurement

After initial recognition, the stripping activity asset must be carried at its cost or revalued amount less depreciation or amortisation and less impairment losses, in the same way as the existing asset of which it is a part. *[IFRIC 20.14]*. The stripping activity asset is to be depreciated or amortised on a systematic basis, over the expected useful life of the identified component of the ore body that becomes more accessible as a result of the stripping activity. *[IFRIC 20.15]*.

The Interpretation effectively requires the units of production method to be applied unless another method is more appropriate. *[IFRIC 20.15]*. The expected useful life of the identified component that is used to depreciate or amortise the stripping activity asset will differ from the expected useful life that is used to depreciate or amortise the mine itself and the related life-of-mine assets, unless the stripping activity provides improved access to the whole of the ore body (this is expected to be rare). *[IFRIC 20.16]*.

Consistent with the units of production method used for other mining assets, the calculation of the units of production rate will be completed when a stripping activity asset is first recognised. It will then need to be reviewed (and if necessary, updated) at the end of each reporting period, or when the mine plan changes. The new units of production rate will be applied prospectively.

Given the depreciation or amortisation of the stripping activity asset represents the consumption of the benefits associated with the stripping activity asset, and those benefits are realised by the extraction of the ore to which the stripping activity asset relates (i.e. the ore for which access was improved by the removal of this waste in prior periods), this depreciation or amortisation effectively represents part of the cost of extracting that ore in future periods. In accordance with IAS 2, such costs should be included in the cost of that subsequent ore. What this effectively means is that the depreciation or amortisation of the stripping activity asset should be recapitalised as part of the cost of the inventory produced in those subsequent periods. Then once the inventory is sold, those costs will be recognised in profit or loss as part of cost of goods sold.

6.1.5 Effective date and transition

IFRIC 20 is effective for annual periods beginning on or after 1 January 2013. The Interpretation is to be applied prospectively to production stripping costs incurred on or after the beginning of the earliest period presented. *[IFRIC 20.A1, A2]*.

If an entity has any existing stripping related asset balances as at the beginning of the earliest period presented that arose due to stripping activity undertaken during the production phase, it is not required (or permitted) to go back and recalculate this in accordance with the requirements of IFRIC 20. Instead, it must determine the extent to which there remains an identifiable component of the ore body with which the stripping activity asset can be associated. Where such an identifiable component(s) remains, the entity must reclassify this asset as part of an existing asset to which the stripping activity relates. This assessment effectively requires an entity to determine whether, and what portion (if any) of, the existing asset balance can be attributed to ore yet to be extracted.

Any portion of the existing asset balance that can be attributed to an identifiable component is to be carried forward at the transition date and must be depreciated or amortised over the remaining expected useful life of the identified component of the ore body to which each existing asset balance relates. *[IFRIC 20.A3]*.

To the extent that any portion of the existing asset balance relates to ore that has already been extracted, or if an entity cannot identify the component of the ore body to which that existing asset balance relates, it must write off that portion of the asset and include it in opening retained earnings at the beginning of the earliest period presented. *[IFRIC 20.A4]*.

6.1.6 Disclosures

There are no specific disclosure requirements in IFRIC 20. However, the general disclosure requirements of IAS 1 are relevant, e.g. the requirements to disclose significant accounting policies, *[IAS 1.117]*, and significant judgements, estimates and assumptions. *[IAS 1.125]*. For many entities, it is likely that the accounting policy for stripping costs would be considered a significant accounting policy which would therefore warrant disclosure, as would the judgements, estimates and assumptions they make when applying this policy.

The extract below from Rio Tinto illustrates an IFRIC 20 accounting policy disclosure.

Extract 39.52: Rio Tinto plc (30 June 2013 – interim financial statements)

30 June 2013 half year media release – condensed financial statements [extract]

Accounting policies [extract]

Updated 'Deferred Stripping' accounting policy

In order to qualify for capitalisation as a stripping activity asset, post-production stripping costs must meet three criteria:

– It must be probable that economic benefit will be realised in a future accounting period as a result of improved access to the ore body created by the stripping activity; and

– It must be possible to identify the 'component' of the ore body for which access has been improved; and

– It must be possible to reliably measure the costs that relate to the stripping activity.

A 'component' is a specific volume of the ore body that is made more accessible by the stripping activity. It will typically be a subset of the larger ore body that is distinguished by a separate useful economic life.

When the cost of stripping related to development which has a future benefit is not distinguishable from the cost of producing current inventories, i.e. there is a mixture of waste being removed to extract ore in the current period as well as waste being removed to allow extraction of ore in future periods, the stripping costs are allocated to each activity based on a relevant production measure. Generally, the measure would be calculated based on a ratio ('Ratio') obtained by dividing the tonnage of waste mined for the component for the period either by the quantity of ore mined for the component or by the quantity of minerals contained in the ore mined for the component. In some operations, the quantity of ore is a more appropriate basis for allocating costs, particularly, where there are important co-products. Stripping costs incurred in the period related to the component are deferred to the extent that the current period Ratio exceeds the life of component Ratio. The stripping activity asset is depreciated on a 'units of production' basis based on expected production of either ore or contained mineral over the life of the component unless another method is more appropriate.

The life of component Ratio is based on proved and probable reserves of the mine (and for some mines, other mineral resources) and the annual mine plan; it is a function of the mine design and therefore changes to that design will generally result in changes to the Ratio. Changes in other technical or economic parameters that impact on reserves may also have an impact on the life of component Ratio even if they do not affect the mine design. Changes to the life of component Ratio are accounted for prospectively.

It may be the case that subsequent phases of stripping will access additional ore and that these subsequent phases are only possible after the first phase has taken place. Where applicable, the Group considers this on a mine by mine basis. Generally, the only ore attributed to the stripping activity asset for the purposes of calculating the life of component Ratio and for the purposes of amortisation is the ore to be extracted from the originally identified component.

Deferred stripping costs are included in "Mining properties and leases" within property, plant and equipment or within "Investments in equity accounted units", as appropriate. Amortisation of deferred stripping costs is included in net operating costs or in the Group's share of the results of its equity accounted units, as appropriate.

In the first year of adoption, the disclosure requirements in IAS 8 relating to the initial application of a new standard or interpretation must be provided. See Chapter 3 at 5.1.2.A for more information. Extract 39.53 below is an example of the qualitative disclosures made by Rio Tinto in relation to the initial application of IFRIC 20 (additional qualitative disclosures were also provided which have not been included below).

Extract 39.53: Rio Tinto plc (30 June 2013 – interim financial statements)

30 June 2013 half year media release – condensed financial statements [extract]

Accounting policies [extract]

IFRIC 20 'Stripping Costs in the Production Phase of a Surface Mine'

In open pit mining operations, it is necessary to remove overburden and other waste materials in order to access ore from which minerals can be extracted economically. The process of removing overburden and waste materials is referred to as stripping.

The Group capitalises pre-production stripping costs incurred during the development of a mine (or pit) as part of the investment in construction of the mine (or pit). These costs are subsequently amortised over the life of the mine (or pit) on a units of production basis. This accounting treatment is unchanged by the implementation of IFRIC 20 which specifies the accounting for post-production stripping costs only.

The Group's accounting policy for post-production stripping costs for 2012 and previous years was to defer costs where this was the most appropriate basis for matching the costs against the related economic benefits and the effect was material. Implementation of IFRIC 20 has changed the way in which the Group accounts for post-production stripping costs and resulted in a write-off to retained earnings on implementation.

IFRIC 20 is not fully retrospective; the impact of adoption is calculated as at 1 January 2011 and comparatives are restated from that point.

On implementation of IFRIC 20 capitalised post-production stripping costs could only be carried forward if they could be identified with a remaining component of the orebody for the relevant Business Unit. A net amount of US$0.7 billion was therefore written off these capitalised costs (pre-tax and non-controlling interests) which reduced retained earnings at 1 January 2011 by US$0.4 billion post tax and non-controlling interests.

The Group's accounting policy under IFRIC 20 is given on page 51. The Group's criteria for identifying separate operations as disclosed in the 2012 annual report are unchanged.

It should be noted that the accounting policy referred to in the final paragraph of Extract 39.53 is reproduced above as Extract 39.52.

6.2 Revenue recognition

6.2.1 *The recognition of revenue at the completion of production*

Under some circumstances, mining companies can recognise revenue once the production of the commodity has been completed.

Clearly, the uncertainty surrounding the cost of production is removed when the product is completed; it is therefore necessary to evaluate the remaining uncertainties in order to determine whether or not completion of production can be used as the critical event for revenue recognition. Where the entity has entered into a firm contract for the production and delivery of a product, the sales price will have been determined and the selling costs will have already been incurred. Consequently, provided that both the delivery expenses and the bad debt risk can satisfactorily be assessed, it may be appropriate to report revenue on this basis. One application of this practice is the completed contract method of recognising revenue on construction contracts, under which revenue is recognised only when the contract is completed or substantially completed.

It has also become accepted practice in a limited number of industries to recognise revenue at the completion of production, even though a sales contract may not have been entered into. This practice has been adopted, for example, in the case of the production of certain minerals and mineral products, provided that the following criteria are met:

(a) the minerals have been extracted;

(b) sale is assured under a forward contract or a government guarantee or an active market exists and there is a negligible risk of failure to sell; and

(c) the market price is determinable and stable. *[IAS 2.3(a), 4]*.

The historical cost principles of IAS 2 do not apply mandatorily to inventories held by 'producers of agricultural and forest products, agricultural produce after harvest, and minerals and mineral products, to the extent that they are measured at net realisable value in accordance with well-established practices in those industries.' *[IAS 2.3(a)]*. However, in order to be able to apply this scope exemption, changes in net realisable value must be recognised in profit or loss in the period of the change. *[IAS 2.3(a), (6)]*. It is important to note that the valuation of inventory at net realisable value under these circumstances is permitted only if this approach is adopted in accordance with well-established industry practice.

The US FASB's Concepts Statement 5 – *Recognition and Measurement in Financial Statements of Business Enterprises* – refers to such assets as being 'readily realisable' (since they are saleable at readily determinable prices without significant effort), and acknowledges that revenue may be recognised on the completion of production, provided that they consist of interchangeable units and quoted prices are available in an active market that can rapidly absorb the quantity held by the entity without significantly affecting the price.[162] The accounting treatment for this basis would be to value closing stock of items such as minerals and mineral products at net realisable value (i.e. sales price less estimated selling costs), and to expense the related production costs.

6.2.2 *Sale of product with delayed shipment*

From time to time, a mining entity may enter into a sales arrangement where the purchaser pays a significant portion of the final estimated purchase price but then requests delayed shipment, for example, because of limited storage space. These sales can sometimes also be referred to as 'in store sales'.

Revenue can be recognised in relation to such sales if it is probable delivery will be made and if: a) the product is specifically identified as belonging to the purchaser; b) it is available for immediate delivery; and c) is held at the purchaser's risk. In many cases, the product is usually physically segregated from other product and is clearly marked as belonging to the purchaser and hence it is therefore not available for sale to other parties. In addition, acknowledgement of the arrangement by both the mining entity and purchaser must be evidenced in the form of a formal agreement between the parties and the usual payment terms apply.

6.2.3 Forward-selling contracts to finance development

Mineral exploration and development is a highly capital intensive business and different financing methods have arisen. In recent years, obtaining financing for these major mining projects has become increasingly difficult, as equity markets have become tighter and loan financing more difficult to obtain. Some increasingly common structured transactions involve the owner of the mineral interests, i.e. a mining entity (the producer) selling a specified volume of future production from a specified property(ies) to a third party 'investor' for cash.

A common example would be a precious metal streaming arrangement with a streaming company (the investor). Here the producer receives an upfront cash payment and (usually) an ongoing predetermined per ounce payment for part or all of the by-product precious metal (the commodity) production – ordinarily gold and/or silver, which is traded on an active market. By entering into these contracts, the mining entity is able to access funding by monetising the non-core precious metal, while the investor receives the production of precious metals without having to invest directly in, or operate, the mine.

These arrangements can take many forms and accounting for such arrangements is incredibly complex. There is no specific guidance for accounting for these types of streaming arrangements under IFRS. Generally, the accounting for these streaming arrangements by the producer is either:

(a) a financial liability (i.e. debt) in accordance with IAS 39, when the arrangement establishes a contractual obligation for the producer to deliver cash or another financial asset;

(b) a sale of a mineral interest and a contract to provide services such as extraction, refining, etc., in accordance with IAS 18, when the arrangement effectively transfers the risks and economic benefits of ownership from the producer to the investor; or

(c) a commodity contract, outside the scope of IAS 39, only when the arrangement is an executory contract to deliver an expected amount of the commodity in the future to the investor from the producer's own operation (i.e. it meets the 'own-use' exemption). If the commodity contract does not meet the own-use exemption, the arrangement will be in scope of IAS 39.

In each classification, the producer must assess and determine whether the arrangement contains separable embedded derivatives. That is, the producer would need to determine whether the arrangement contained a component or terms which had the effect that some of the cash flows of the combined instrument (being the arrangement) vary in a similar way to a stand-alone derivative (i.e. an embedded derivative).

When determining the accounting for such arrangements, the following matters would be taken into consideration:

- **Financial liability:** A key factor in determining whether the contract is a financial liability is whether the contract establishes a contractual obligation for the producer to make payments in cash or another financial asset, *[IAS 32.16(a)]* – that is, whether the arrangement has more of the characteristics of debt.

- **Sale of a mineral interest:** When the nature of the arrangement indicates that the investor's investment is more akin to an equity interest in the project (rather than debt), this may indicate that the producer has essentially sold an interest in a property to the investor in return for the advance. In such a situation, the arrangement would be classified as a sale of a mineral interest.

  To apply this accounting, an entity would have to be able to demonstrate that the criteria in relation to the sale of an asset in IAS 16 and IAS 18 have been satisfied; that the investor bears the risks and economic benefits of ownership related to the output (a mineral interest); and agrees to pay for a portion or all of the production costs of extracting and/or refining its new mineral interest to the producer. Some of the relevant risks include production risk (which party bears the risk the project will be unable to produce output or will have a production outage), resource risk (which party bears the risk the project has insufficient reserves to repay the investor), and price risk (which party bears the risk the price of the output will fluctuate).
- **Commodity contract:** A producer and an investor may agree to enter such an arrangement where both parties have an expectation of the amount of the commodity to be delivered under the contract at inception (for example, based on the reserves) and that there may or may not be additional resources. On the basis that the reserves will be delivered under the contract (and the contract cannot be net settled in cash), the advance would be considered a deposit for the commodity to be delivered at a future date. In this case, the arrangement is a commodity contract that falls outside the scope of IAS 39, but only if the contract will always be settled through the physical delivery of the commodity which has been extracted by the producer as part of its own operations (i.e. it meets the 'own-use exemption').

  To determine if the own-use exemption applies and continues to apply, the key tests are whether the contract will always be settled through the physical delivery of a commodity (that is, not in cash and would not be considered to be capable of net settlement in cash), and that the commodity will always be extracted by the producer as part of its own operations. This means that there is no prospect of the producer settling part, or the entire advance, by purchasing the commodity on the open market or from a third party.

As noted above, regardless of the classification, each contract would still need to be assessed for the existence of any embedded derivatives.

Whether the arrangement constitutes debt, a sale of mineral interest or a sale of a commodity, is subject to significant judgement. Each arrangement will have very specific facts and circumstances that will need to be understood and assessed, as different accounting treatments may apply in certain circumstances. In many cases, the route to determining the classification will be a non-linear and iterative process.

6.3 Inventories

Inventories of mining companies usually include:

- run-of-mine ore;
- work in progress (crushed ore, ore-in-circuit); and
- finished goods (concentrate, metal).

Inventories should be measured at the lower of cost and net realisable value under IAS 2. However, IAS 2 does not apply to the measurement of minerals and mineral products, to the extent that they are measured at net realisable value in accordance with well established practices in those industries. *[IAS 2.3(a)]*. There is also an exception for commodity broker traders who measure their inventories at fair value less costs to sell. When such inventories are measured at fair value less costs to sell, changes in fair value less costs to sell are recognised in profit or loss in the period of the change. *[IAS 2.3(b)]*. This is discussed in relation to oil and gas companies at 5.6.2 above.

Various cost methods are acceptable under IFRS and include specific identification, weighted average costs, or first-in first-out (FIFO). Last-in first-out (LIFO) is not permitted under IFRS.

Issues that mining companies commonly face in relation to inventory include:

- point of recognition (see 6.3.1 below);
- cost absorption in the measurement of inventory;
- method of allocating costs to inventory, e.g. FIFO or weighted average;
- determination of joint and by-products and measurement consequences (see 4.14.1 above); and
- accounting for stockpiles of long-term, low grade ore (see 6.3.2 below).

6.3.1 *Recognition of work-in-progress and ore in circuit*

Inventory is recognised when it is probable that future economic benefits will flow to the entity and the asset has a cost or value than can be reliably measured. It has become accepted practice in the mining sector to recognise work in progress at the point at which ore is broken and the entity can make a reasonable assessment of quantity, recovery and cost.[163]

Extract 39.54 from the financial statements of Harmony Gold Mining illustrates the need for judgement in determining when work in progress can be recognised.

Extract 39.54: Harmony Gold Mining Company Limited (2012)

Notes to the group financial statements [extract]

2 Accounting policies [extract]

2.10 Inventories

Inventories which include bullion on hand, gold in process, gold in lock-up, ore stockpiles and stores and materials, are measured at the lower of cost and net realisable value after appropriate allowances for redundant and slow moving items. Net realisable value is the estimated selling price in the ordinary course of business less the estimated cost of completion and the estimated cost necessary to perform the sale.

Cost of bullion, gold in process and gold in lock-up is determined by reference to production cost, including amortisation and depreciation at the relevant stage of production. Ore stockpiles are valued at average production cost. Stockpiles and gold in lock-up are classified as a non-current asset where the stockpile exceeds current processing capacity and where a portion of static gold in lock-up is expected to be recovered more than 12 months after balance sheet date.

Gold in process inventories represent materials that are currently in the process of being converted to a saleable product. Conversion processes vary depending on the nature of the ore and the specific mining operation, but include mill in-circuit, leach in-circuit, flotation and column cells, and carbon in-pulp inventories. In-process material is measured based on assays of the material fed to process and the projected recoveries at the respective plants. In-process inventories are valued at the average cost of the material fed to process attributable to the source material coming from the mine, stockpile or leach pad plus the in-process conversion costs, including the applicable depreciation relating to the process facility, incurred to that point in the process. Gold in process includes gold in lock-up which is generally measured from the plants onwards. Gold in lock-up is estimated as described under the section dealing with critical accounting estimates and judgements (refer to note 3.9). It is expected to be extracted when plants are demolished at the end of their useful lives, which is largely dependent on the estimated useful life of the operations feeding the plants. Where mechanised mining is used in underground operations, in-progress material is accounted for at the earliest stage of production when reliable estimates of quantities and costs are capable of being made. Given the varying nature of the group's open pit operations, gold in process represents either production in broken ore form or production from the time of placement on heap leach pads.

Consumables are valued at weighted average cost.

Measurement issues can arise in relation to work-in-progress for concentrators, smelters and refineries, where significant volumes of product can be located in pipes or vessels, with no uniformity of grade. Work-in-progress inventories may also be in stockpiles, for example underground, where it is more difficult to measure quantities.

Processing varies in extent, duration and complexity depending on the type of mineral and different production and processing techniques that are used. Therefore, measuring work-in-progress, as it moves through the various stages of processing, is difficult and determining the quantities of work-in-progress may require a significant degree of estimation. Practice varies in this area, which is a reflection of the genuine differences mining companies face in their ability to assess mineral content and predict production and processing costs.

Extract 39.55 below from the financial statements of Anglo Platinum illustrates the complexity involved in making such estimates.

Extract 39.55: Anglo Platinum Limited (2012)

PRINCIPAL ACCOUNTING POLICIES [extract]

For the year ended 31 December 2012

Critical accounting estimates [extract]

Metal inventory

Work-in-progress metal inventory is valued at the lower of net realisable value and the average cost of production or purchase less net revenue from sales of other metals, in the ratio of the contribution of these metals to gross sales revenue. Production costs are allocated to platinum, palladium, rhodium and nickel (joint products) by dividing the mine output into total mine production costs, determined on a 12-month rolling average basis. The quantity of ounces of joint products in work-in-progress is calculated based on the following factors:

- The theoretical inventory at that point in time which is calculated by adding the inputs to the previous physical inventory and then deducting the outputs for the inventory period.
- The inputs and outputs include estimates due to the delay in finalising analytical values.
- The estimates are subsequently trued up to the final metal accounting quantities when available.
- The theoretical inventory is then converted to a refined equivalent inventory by applying appropriate recoveries depending on where the material is within the production pipeline. The recoveries are based on actual results as determined by the inventory count and are in line with industry standards.

Other than at the Precious Metal Refinery, an annual physical count of work-in-progress is done, usually around February of each year. The Precious Metal Refinery is subject to a physical count usually every three years. The annual physical count is limited to once per annum owing to the dislocation of production required to perform the physical inventory count and the in-process inventories being contained in tanks, pipes and other vessels. Once the results of the physical count are finalised, the variance between the theoretical count and actual count is investigated and recorded. Thereafter the physical quantity forms the opening balance for the theoretical inventory calculation. Consequently, the estimates are refined based on actual results over time. The nature of the production process inherently limits the ability to precisely measure recoverability levels. As a result, the metallurgical balancing process is constantly monitored and the variables used in the process are refined based on actual results over time.

Ore in circuit at the end of a reporting period can be very difficult to measure as it is generally not easily accessible. The value of materials being processed should therefore be estimated based on inputs, throughput time and ore grade. The significance of the value of ore in circuit will depend on the type of commodity being processed. For example, precious metals producers may have a material value in process at reporting period end.

6.3.2 *Stockpiles of low grade ore*

Mining companies often stockpile low grade ore that cannot be economically processed at current market prices or to give priority to the processing of higher grade ore. Low grade ore stockpiles may not be processed for many years until market prices or technology have improved or until no higher grade ore remains available. Extract 39.56 below from AngloGold Ashanti illustrates that stockpiles of low grade ore may be held for many years.

Mineralised waste that is stockpiled in the hope, but without the expectation, that it may become economical to process in the future should be accounted in the same way as overburden and other waste materials (see 6.1 above). Low grade ore that is stockpiled with the expectation that it will be processed in the future should be accounted for in the same way as high grade ore. However, if the cost of the low grade ore exceeds its net realisable value, an entity should recognise an impairment charge that it might need to reverse at some point in the future if (and when) commodity prices were to increase.

If and when processing of low grade ore becomes economically viable and management intends to process the stockpile in the future, the ore should be accounted for as non-current inventory under IAS 2. Such stockpiles should be measured at the lower of cost and net realisable value. *[IAS 2.9, 30].* In allocating production costs to the low grade ore stockpile and in subsequently assessing net realisable value, an entity should be mindful that:

(1) the commodity price at the reporting date may not be representative of the price that can realistically be expected to prevail when the ore is expected to be processed. The assumptions as to the long-term commodity prices used in the estimate of the sales proceeds and the expected timing of realisation, should generally be consistent with those used in the Life of Mine Plan and other models that would be used for valuation and impairment purposes;

(2) the costs of processing may change in the future because of inflation, technological changes and new environmental regulations; and

(3) the time value of money reduces the net realisable value. Therefore, application of a discount factor to the future cash flows associated with the sales proceeds and conversion costs may be appropriate to reflect the time value of money. The net realisable value of a stockpile which is not expected to be sold for a very long period of time, determined based on the discounted future cash flows, will typically be very low.

The extract below shows how AngloGold Ashanti accounts for ore stockpiles.

Extract 39.56: AngloGold Ashanti Limited (2012)

GROUP - NOTES TO THE FINANCIAL STATEMENTS [extract]

For the year ended 31 December

1 Accounting policies [extract]

1.2 Significant accounting judgements and estimates [extract]

Stockpiles, metal in process and ore on leach pad

Costs that are incurred in or benefit the production process are accumulated as stockpiles, metals in process and ore on leach pads. Net realisable value tests are performed at least annually and represent the estimated future sales price of the product, based on prevailing and long-term metals prices, less estimated costs to complete production and bring the product to sale.

Stockpiles and underground metals in process are measured by estimating the number of tonnes added and removed from the stockpile and from underground, the number of contained gold ounces based on assay data, and the estimated recovery percentage based on the expected processing method. Stockpile and underground ore tonnages are verified by periodic surveys.

Estimates of the recoverable gold on the leach pads are calculated from the quantities of ore placed on the pads based on measured tonnes added to the leach pads, the grade of ore placed on the leach pads based on assay data and a recovery percentage based on metallurgical testing and ore type.

Although the quantities of recoverable metal are reconciled by comparing the grades of ore to the quantities of gold actually recovered (metallurgical balancing), the nature of the process inherently limits the ability to precisely monitor recoverability levels. As a result, the metallurgical balancing process is constantly monitored and engineering estimates are refined based on actual results over time.

> Variations between actual and estimated quantities resulting from changes in assumptions and estimates that do not result in write-downs to net realisable value are accounted for on a prospective basis.
>
> The carrying amount of inventories (excluding finished goods and mine operating supplies) for the group at 31 December 2012 was \$1,383m (2011: \$1,060m).
>
> **1.3 Summary of significant accounting policies** [extract]
>
> **Inventories** [extract]
>
> Inventories are valued at the lower of cost and net realisable value after appropriate allowances for redundant and slow moving items. Cost is determined on the following bases:
>
> [...]
>
> - ore stockpiles are valued at the average moving cost of mining and stockpiling the ore. Stockpiles are classified as a non-current asset where the stockpile exceeds current processing capacity;
>
> [...]

The extract below illustrates the disclosure of an impairment of stockpiled ore (in 2008) and then disclosures relating to the reversal of impairment of stockpiled ore.

> *Extract 39.57: Kazakhmys PLC (2008 and 2010)*
>
> **Notes to the consolidated financial statements** [extract]
>
> **7. IMPAIRMENT LOSSES – 2008** [extract]
>
> **(d) Kazakhmys Copper and MKM inventories**
>
> Impairment of inventories includes an amount of \$73 million and \$15 million in respect of Kazakhmys Copper and MKM, respectively. For Kazakhmys Copper, the impairment primarily relates to the impairment of stockpiled ore which is not going to be processed in the foreseeable future as its processing is uneconomic at current commodity price levels. Within MKM, a provision has been recognised to record inventory at the lower of cost and net realisable value. This primarily relates to finished goods held in stock at the end of the year which have been written down reflecting the fall in copper price in December.
>
> **8. IMPAIRMENT LOSSES – 2010** [extract]
>
> **(b) Kazakhmys Copper inventories**
>
> Included within the provisions against inventories is an impairment loss of \$15 million relating to general slow moving inventory, and a reversal of a previous impairment against certain stockpiled ore of \$18 million. In 2008, it was envisaged that the stockpiled ore would not be processed in the future as this would have been uneconomic at the prevailing commodity prices. However, during 2010 certain of these stockpiles were processed and the previous impairment reversed.

6.3.3 Heap leaching

Heap leaching is a process which may be used for the recovery of metals from low grade ore. The crushed ore is laid on a slightly sloping, impermeable pad and leached by uniformly trickling a chemical solution through the heaps to be collected in ponds. The metals are subsequently extracted from the pregnant solution. Although heap leaching is one of the lowest cost methods of processing, recovery rates are relatively low.

Despite the estimation and measurement challenges associated with heap leaching, ore loaded on heap leach pads is usually recognised as inventory. An entity that develops an accounting policy for heap leaching needs to consider the following:

- the metal recovery factor is relatively low and will vary depending on the metallurgical characteristics of the material on the heap leach pad. The final (actual) recovery is therefore unknown until leaching is complete. Therefore, an entity will need to estimate the quantity of recoverable metal on each of its heap leach pads, based on laboratory test work or historical ore performance;
- the assayed head grade of ore added to the heap;
- the ore stockpiles on heap leach pads are accounted for as inventories that are measured at cost under IAS 2. As the valuable metal content is leached from these ore stockpiles, the cost basis is depleted based upon expected grades and recovery rates. The depletion charge should be accounted as the cost of production of work in progress or finished goods;
- the level at which the heap leach pads are measured – that is, whether they are measured separately, in groups or in total. The preferred approach is to consider each pad separately (where possible) because this reduces the expected volatility in ore type to more manageable levels; and
- ore stockpiles on heap leach pads from which metals are expected to be recovered in a period longer than 12 months are classified as non-current assets.

The extracts below from the financial statements of AngloGold Ashanti and Goldcorp illustrate the issues that an entity will need to consider in developing an accounting policy for heap leaching.

Extract 39.58: AngloGold Ashanti Limited (2012)

GROUP - NOTES TO THE FINANCIAL STATEMENTS [extract]
For the year ended 31 December
1 Accounting policies [extract]
1.3 Summary of significant accounting policies [extract]
Inventories [extract]

Inventories are valued at the lower of cost and net realisable value after appropriate allowances for redundant and slow moving items. Cost is determined on the following bases:

...

- heap leach pad materials are measured on an average total production cost basis. The cost of materials on the leach pad from which metals are expected to be recovered in a period longer than 12 months is classified as a non-current asset.

Extract 39.59: Goldcorp (2012)

Notes to the Consolidated Financial Statements

For the Years Ended December 31, 2012 and 2011 [extract]

3. SUMMARY OF SIGNIFICANT ACCOUNTING POLICIES [extract]

(m) Inventories and stockpiled ore [extract]

Finished goods, work-in-process, heap leach ore and stockpiled ore are measured at the lower of average cost and net realizable value. Net realizable value is calculated as the estimated price at the time of sale based on prevailing and long-term metal prices less estimated future costs to convert the inventories into saleable form and estimated costs to sell.

Ore extracted from the mines is stockpiled and subsequently processed into finished goods (gold and by-products in doré or concentrate form). Costs are included in work-in-process inventory based on current costs incurred up to the point prior to the refining process, including applicable depreciation and depletion of mining interests, and removed at the average cost per recoverable ounce of gold. The average costs of finished goods represent the average costs of work-in-process inventories incurred prior to the refining process, plus applicable refining costs.

The recovery of gold and by-products from certain oxide ore is achieved through a heap leaching process at the Peñasquito, Los Filos, Marigold and Wharf mines. Under this method, ore is stacked on leach pads and treated with a chemical solution that dissolves the gold contained within the ore. The resulting "pregnant" solution is further processed in a plant where the gold is recovered. Costs are included in heap leach ore inventory based on current mining and leaching costs, including applicable depreciation and depletion of mining interests and refining costs, and removed from heap leach ore inventory as ounces of gold are recovered at the average cost per recoverable ounce of gold on the leach pads. Estimates of recoverable gold on the leach pads are calculated based on the quantities of ore placed on the leach pads (measured tonnes added to the leach pads), the grade of ore placed on the leach pads (based on assay data), and a recovery percentage (based on ore type).

6.4 Tolling arrangements

In the mining sector it is common for entities to provide raw material to a smelter or refiner for further processing. If the raw material is sold to the smelter or refiner, the mining company recognises revenue in accordance with IAS 18. However, under a 'tolling' arrangement a mining company supplies, without transferring ownership, raw material to a smelter or refiner which processes it for a fee and then returns the finished product to the customer. Alternatively, the mining company may sell the raw material to the smelter or refiner, but is required to repurchase the finished product. In the latter two situations, no revenue should be recognised when the raw material is shipped to the smelter or refiner as there has not been a transfer of the risks and rewards. An entity should carefully assess the terms and conditions of its tolling arrangements to determine:

- when it is appropriate to recognise revenue;
- whether those arrangements contain embedded leases that require separation under IFRIC 4 (see 4.16.1 above);
- whether the tolling arrangement is part of a series of transactions with a joint arrangement; and
- whether the toll processing entity is a structured entity that requires consolidation under IFRS 10 (see Chapter 6 at 4.4.1 for more information).

The extract below describes a tolling arrangement between Norsk Hydro and one of its joint arrangements.

Extract 39.60: Norsk Hydro ASA (2012)

Notes to the consolidated financial statements [extract]

Note 26 – Investments in jointly controlled entities [extract]

Aluminium Norf GmbH (Alunorf) located in Germany is the world's largest rolling mill and is owned by Hydro and Hindalco Industries (50 percent each). Alunorf produces flat rolled products from raw material from the partners based on a tolling arrangement. Sales from Alunorf to Hydro amounted to NOK 1,423 million in 2012 and NOK 1,475 million in 2011. Hydro's capital and financing commitments are regulated in the Joint Venture agreement. Hydro's financing commitment based on its interest is NOK 109 million as of December 31, 2012. Alunorf is part of Rolled Products.

6.5 Hedging sales of metal concentrate

In the mining sector metals are often sold in the form of a concentrate that comprises two or more metals and impurities. The metal content of concentrate varies depending on the mine and grade of ore being mined. The sales price of concentrate is typically determined from the quantity of each metal contained in the concentrate, multiplied by the market price for refined metal (often the price at the London Metal Exchange (LME)), minus various charges and deductions, which reflect the fact that the metal sold is not refined. Charges and deductions vary by contract and typically comprise refining and treatment charges, price participation clauses, transportation, impurity penalties, etc.

If an entity hedges the price risk of only one of the metals in the concentrate, the question arises whether, for hedge accounting purposes, the entity can designate as the hedged item, the sale of that individual metal, or instead, the sale of the concentrate as a whole. Paragraph 82 of IAS 39 requires that a non-financial asset is 'designated as a hedged item (a) for foreign currency risks, or (b) in its entirety for all risks, because of the difficulty of isolating and measuring the appropriate portion of the cash flows or fair value changes attributable to specific risks other than foreign currency risks'. *[IAS 39.82]*.

The terms and conditions of each sales contract need to be considered carefully in determining whether individual metals or only the concentrate as a whole can be designated as a hedged item. If each of the metals contained in a concentrate is sold at a price that is determined independently of the price of any other metal in the concentrate then, for the purposes of hedge accounting under IAS 39, we believe that each metal may be viewed as a separate non-financial asset instead of a risk-component of the concentrate as a whole.

Consequently, in these circumstances, the sale of each individual metal can be hedged separately. The price of each individual metal is the total price established under the sales contract for that metal, i.e. including the adjustments of the market price for refined metal for the various deductions and charges. This means that the entity is hedging the price for the unrefined metal that is dissolved in the concentrate, e.g. LME, less the various charges and deductions. This could lead to some hedge ineffectiveness. Designating only the part of the price that is linked to the market price for refined metal, e.g. the LME part of the pricing formula, would constitute the designation of a risk component of a non-financial item that is prohibited by paragraph 82 of IAS 39 (even if the pricing of the metal is separate). The current IFRS 9 hedge accounting proposals would change this. See Chapter 49 for more information on IFRS 9's hedge accounting proposals. These considerations also apply from the perspective of an entity that purchases metals in the form of a concentrate.

This approach is conceptually no different from hedging the contents of a box that contains a number of non-financial assets, each of which is priced at fair value and itemised separately on the invoice. The approach clearly differs from hedging jet fuel with crude oil based derivatives because in that case the underlying of the hedging instruments may only be a risk component of the jet fuel (for which paragraph 82 of IAS 39 prohibits designation as the hedged item on a risk components basis) but not a separate content of a box that you can take out (like the individual metal that is extracted from the concentrate).

6.6 Impairment of assets

6.6.1 Low mine profitability near end of life

Most mining plans aim to maximise the net present value of mineral reserves by first extracting the highest grade ore with the lowest production costs. Consequently, in most mining operations the grade of the ore mined steadily declines over the life of the mine which results in a declining annual production, while the production costs per volume of ore e.g. tonne, gradually increases as it becomes more difficult to extract the ore. From an economic perspective, a mining company will generally continue to mine as long as the cash inflows from the sale of minerals exceed the cash cost of production. Therefore, a mining company with a positive net cash flow will continue to mine even if it does not fully recover the depreciation of its property, plant and equipment and mineral reserves, as is likely to occur towards the end of the life of a mine. In part this is the result of the depreciation methods applied:

- the straight-line method of depreciation allocates a relatively high depreciation charge to periods with a low annual production;
- a units of production method based on the quantity of ore extracted allocates a relatively high depreciation charge to production of lower grade ore; and
- a units of production method based on the quantity of minerals produced allocates a relatively high depreciation charge to production of minerals that are difficult to recover.

Each of these situations is most likely to occur towards the end of the life of a mine. It could be argued that the methods of depreciation most commonly used in the mining sector do not allocate a sufficiently high depreciation charge to the early life of a mine when production is generally most profitable. An entity should therefore be mindful of the fact that relatively small changes in facts and circumstances can lead to an impairment of mining assets.

6.6.2 Impairment testing requirements

Following on from the discussion in 6.6.1 above, from an impairment perspective, the impairment tests in the early years of the life of a mine will often reveal that the mine is cash flow positive and is able to produce a recoverable amount that is sufficient to recoup the carrying value of the mine, i.e. the mine is not impaired. However, when the impairment tests are conducted in later years, while the mine may still be cash flow positive, i.e. the expected cash proceeds from the future sale of minerals still exceed the expected future cash costs of production and hence management will continue with the mining operations, as margins generally reduce towards the end of mine life, the impairment tests may not produce a recoverable amount sufficient to recoup the remaining carrying value of the mine. Therefore the mine will need to be impaired.

It is possible, when preparing the impairment models for a mine, for an entity to identify when (in the future) the remaining net cash inflows of the mine may no longer be sufficient to recoup the remaining carrying value of the mine, that is when compared to the way in which the mine assets are expected to be depreciated over the remaining mine life. However, provided the recoverable amount as at the date of the impairment test exceeds the carrying amount of the mine, there is no requirement to recognise any possible future impairment. It is only when the recoverable amount actually falls below the carrying amount that an impairment must be recognised. See 4.6 for more information.

6.7 Block caving – depreciation, depletion and amortisation

Given the nature of mining operations, determining the appropriate unit of account has always been a matter requiring considerable judgement for mining entities. See 4.2 above for further discussion. This issue is particularly relevant when assessing how to account for new mining techniques. For example, block cave mining is one such mining technique that is being increasingly proposed or used for a number of deposits worldwide.

Block cave mining is a mass mining method that allows for the bulk mining of large, relatively lower grade, ore bodies for which the grade is consistently distributed throughout. The word 'block' refers to the layout of the mine – which effectively divides the ore body into large sections, with areas that can be several thousand square metres in size. This approach adopts a mine design and process which involves the creation of an undercut by fracturing the rock section underneath the block through the use of blasting. This blasting destroys the rock's ability to support the block above. Caving of the rock mass then occurs under the natural forces of gravity (which can be in the order of millions of tonnes), when a sufficient amount of rock has been removed underneath the block. The broken ore is then removed from the base of the block. This mine activity occurs without the need for drilling and blasting, as the ore above continues to fall while the broken ore beneath is removed. Broken ore is removed from the area at the extraction level through the use of a grid of draw points. These effectively funnel the broken ore down to a particular point so that it can be collected and removed for further processing.

Block caving has been applied to large scale extraction of various metals and minerals, sometimes in thick beds of ore but more usually in steep to vertical masses. Examples of block caving operations include Northparkes (Australia), Palabora (South Africa), Questa Mine (New Mexico) and Freeport (Indonesia).[164]

Block cave mining does require substantial upfront development costs, as initial underground access followed by large excavations (undercutting), must be completed to gain access and initially 'undermine' the block that is to cave. In addition, large underground and above ground haulage and milling infrastructure must be constructed to extract and then process the ore that a successful cave will generate.

One of the key issues to be addressed is how these substantial upfront development costs, in addition to the ongoing development costs associated with each block (i.e. to extend the undercutting beneath each new block and construct the draw points for each block) should be treated for depreciation or amortisation.

Generally these costs are depreciated or amortised on a units of production basis – therefore in determining useful life, it is necessary to determine what the appropriate reserves base should be for each of these costs. For example, in relation to the costs associated with initially going underground and constructing the main haulage tunnel which will be used to access and extract the reserves from the entire ore body, the useful life associated with such assets may be the reserves of the entire ore body.

In relation to the costs associated in constructing the milling infrastructure, it is possible that such assets may be used to process ore from multiple ore bodies. Therefore, the useful life of such assets may be the reserves of multiple ore bodies. However, this will depend upon the specific facts and circumstances of the particular development.

For those costs associated with each individual block e.g. the undercutting costs directly attributable to each block and the costs associated in constructing the draw points for that block, the appropriate reserves base may potentially only be those to be extracted from that particular block, which may only be a component of the entire ore body.

The approach adopted by each entity will be determined by the specific facts and circumstances of each mine development, such as the nature of the block cave mining technique employed and how the associated assets will be used. Such an assessment will require entities to exercise considerable judgement.

6.8 Care and maintenance

At certain times, a mining operation may be suspended because of a change in circumstances, which may include a weakening of global demand for the commodity, lower prices, higher costs, changes in exchange rates or changes in government policy. Such changes mean that continuing with production or further development becomes uneconomical. Instead of permanently shutting down and abandoning the mine, the operations and development are curtailed and the mine is placed on 'care and maintenance'. This can happen either in the development phase or the production phase.

A decision to put a mine on care and maintenance would be an indicator of impairment (see 4.10.1 above). An impairment test would need to be conducted and if the recoverable amount of the CGU is less than the carrying amount, an impairment loss would need to be recognised.

While the mine remains in care and maintenance, expenditures are still incurred but usually at a lower rate than when the mine is operating. A lower rate of depreciation for tangible non-current assets is also usually appropriate due to reduced wear and tear. Movable plant and machinery would generally be depreciated over its useful life. Management should consider depreciation to allow for deterioration. Where depreciation for movable plant and machinery had previously been determined on a units of production basis, this may no longer be appropriate.

Management should also ensure that any assets for which there are no longer any future economic benefits, i.e. which have become redundant, are written off.

The length of the closure and the associated care and maintenance expenditure may be estimated for depreciation and impairment purposes. However, it is not appropriate to recognise a provision for the entire estimated expenditure relating to the care and maintenance period. All care and maintenance cost is to be expensed as incurred.

Development costs amortised or depreciated using the units of production method would no longer be depreciated. Holding costs associated with such assets should be expensed in profit or loss in the period they are incurred. These may include costs such as security costs and site property maintenance costs.

The costs associated with restarting a mine which had previously been on care and maintenance should only be capitalised if they improve the mine beyond its original operating capabilities. Entities will need to exercise significant judgement when performing this assessment.

7 GLOSSARY

The glossary below defines some of the terms and abbreviations commonly used in the extractive industries.[165]

Abandon	To discontinue attempts to produce oil or gas from a well or lease, plug the reservoir in accordance with regulatory requirements and recover equipment.
Area-of-interest method	An accounting concept by which costs incurred for individual geological or geographical areas that have characteristics conducive to containing a mineral reserve are deferred as assets pending determination of whether commercial reserves are found. If the area of interest is found to contain commercial reserves, the accumulated costs are capitalised. If the area is found to contain no commercial reserves, the accumulated costs are charged to expense.
Barrels of oil equivalent (BOE)	Using prices or heating content, units of sulphur, condensate, natural gas and by products are converted to and expressed in equivalent barrels of oil for standard measurement purposes.

British Thermal Unit (BTU)	A measure of the amount of heat required to raise the temperature of one pound of water one degree Fahrenheit at the temperature at which water has its greatest density (39 degrees Fahrenheit).
Bullion	Metal in bars, ingots or other uncoined form.
Carried interest	An agreement by which an entity that contracts to operate a mineral property and, therefore, agrees to incur exploration or development costs (the carrying party) is entitled to recover the costs incurred (and usually an amount in addition to actual costs incurred) before the entity that originally owned the mineral interest (the carried party) is entitled to share in revenues from production.
Carried party	The party for whom funds are advances in a carried interest arrangement.
Carrying party	The party advancing funds in a carried interest agreement.
Concession	A contract, similar to a mineral lease, under which the government owning mineral rights grants the concessionaire the right to explore, develop, and produce the minerals.
Cost recovery oil	Oil revenue paid to an operating entity to enable that entity to recover its operating costs and specified exploration and development costs from a specified percentage of oil revenues remaining after the royalty payment to the property owner.
Customer smelter	A smelter which processes concentrates from independent mines. Concentrates may be purchased or the smelter may be contracted to do the processing for the independent company.
Delay rental	Annual payments by the lessee of a mineral property to the lessor until drilling has begun.
Delineation well	A well to define, or delineate, the boundaries of a reservoir.
Development well	A well drilled to gain access to oil or gas classified as proved reserves.

Downstream activities	The refining, processing, marketing, and distributing of petroleum, natural gas, or mined mineral (other than refining or processing that is necessary to make the minerals that have been mined or extracted capable of being sold).
Dry gas	Natural gas composed of vapours without liquids and which tends not to liquefy.
Dry hole	An exploratory or development well that does not contain oil or gas in commercial quantities.
Entitlements method	A method of revenue recognition by which a joint venturer records revenue based on the share of production for the period to which that venturer is entitled.
Exploratory well	A well drilled to find and produce oil or gas in an unproved area, to find a new reservoir in a field previously found to be productive of oil or gas in another reservoir, or to extend a known reservoir.
Farm out and farm in	An agreement by which the owner of operating rights in a mineral property (the farmor) transfers a part of that interest to a second party (the farmee) in return for the latter's paying all of the costs, or only specified costs, to explore the property and perhaps to carry out part or all of the development of the property if reserves are found.
Full cost method	An accounting concept by which all costs incurred in searching for, acquiring, and developing mineral reserves in a cost centre are capitalised, even though a specific cost clearly resulted from an effort that was a failure
Geological and geophysical costs (G&G)	Costs of topographical, geological, geochemical, and geophysical studies.
Infill drilling	Technical and commercial analyses may support drilling additional producing wells to reduce the spacing beyond that utilised within the initial development plan. Infill drilling may have the combined effect of increasing recovery efficiency and accelerating production.
Joint operating agreement (JOA)	A contract between two parties to a sharing arrangement that sets out the rights and obligations to operate the property, if operating interests are owned by both parties after a sharing arrangement.

Overlift or underlift	Overlift is the excess of the amount of production that a participant in a joint venture has taken as compared to that participant's proportionate share of ownership in total production. Underlift is the shortfall in the amount of production that a participant in a joint venture has taken as compared to that participant's proportionate share of ownership in total production.
Production sharing contract (PSC)	A contract between a national oil company or the government of a host country and a contracting entity (contractor) to carry out oil and gas exploration and production activities in accordance with the terms of the contract, with the two parties sharing mineral output.
Profit oil	Revenue in excess of cost recovery oil and royalties.
Recompletion	The process of re-entering a previously completed well to install new equipment or to perform such services necessary to restore production.
Redetermination	A retroactive adjustment to the relative percentage interests of the participants in a field that is subject to an unitisation agreement.
Risk service contract	A contract by which an entity agrees to explore for, develop, and produce minerals on behalf of a host government in return for a fee paid by the host government.
Royalty	A portion of the proceeds from production, usually before deducting operating expenses, payable to a party having an interest in a lease.
Sales method	A method of revenue recognition by which a joint venturer records revenue based on the actual amount of product it has sold (or transferred downstream) during the period. No receivable or other asset is recorded for undertaken production (underlift) and no liability is recorded for overtaken production (overlift).
Stripping ratio	The ratio of tonnes removed as waste relative to the number of tonnes of ore removed from an open pit mine.
Successful efforts method	An accounting concept that capitalises only those upstream costs that lead directly to finding, acquiring and developing mineral reserves, while those costs that do not lead directly to finding, acquiring and developing mineral reserves are charged to expense.

Take-or-pay contracts	An agreement between a buyer and seller in which the buyer will still pay some amount even if the product or service is not provided. If the purchaser does not take the minimum quantity, payment is required for that minimum quantity at the contract price. Normally, deficiency amounts can be made up in future years if purchases are in excess of minimum amounts.
Unitisation	An agreement between two parties, each of which owns an interest in one or more mineral properties in an area, to cross-assign to one another a share of the interest in the mineral properties that each owns in the area; from that point forward they share, as agreed, in further costs and revenues related to the properties.
Upstream activities	Exploring for, finding, acquiring, and developing mineral reserves up to the point that the reserves are first capable of being sold or used, even if the entity intends to process them further.
Workovers	Major repairs, generally of oil and gas wells.

References

1 IASC Issues Paper, *Issues Paper Extractive Industries*, IASC, November 2000, 1.5.
2 Discussion Paper DP/2010/1, *Extractive Activities*, IASB, April 2010, P6.
3 DP/2010/1, 1.1.
4 DP/2010/1, P1.4-1.5.
5 DP/2010/1, 1.9.
6 DP/2010/1, 1.10.
7 IASC Issues Paper, 1.16.
8 IASC Issues Paper, 1.18.
9 IASC Issues Paper, 2.3.
10 IASC Issues Paper, 2.5.
11 IASC Issues Paper, 2.6.
12 IASC Issues Paper, 2.10.
13 IASC Issues Paper, 2.12.
14 IASC Issues Paper, 2.24.
15 IASC Issues Paper, 2.26.
16 IASC Issues Paper, 2.27.
17 IASC Issues Paper, 2.29.
18 IASC Issues Paper, 2.29, 2.30.
19 IASC Issues Paper, 2.32.
20 IASC Issues Paper, 2.34.
21 IASC Issues Paper, 2.36.
22 IASC Issues Paper, 2.38.
23 IASC Issues Paper, 2.42.
24 Discussion Paper DP/2010/1, para. 2.48.
25 Discussion Paper DP/2010/1, para. 2.23.
26 *Comments on SEC File No. S7-29-07 'Concept Release on Possible Revisions to the Disclosure Requirements Relating to Oil and Gas Reserves'*, The Committee for Mineral Reserves International Reporting Standards, 12 February 2008, p. 1.
27 *Comments on SEC File No. S7-29-07 'Concept Release on Possible Revisions to the Disclosure Requirements Relating to Oil and Gas Reserves'*, The Society for Mining, Metallurgy, and Exploration, Inc., 4 February 2008. p. 1-2.
28 SPE-PRMS, *Petroleum Resources Management Systems*, Society of Petroleum Engineers, 2007.
29 IASB Agenda Paper 13A, *Comparison of Petroleum and Minerals Reserves and Resource Classification Systems*, IASB, 22 June 2007, p. 3-4.
30 IASB Agenda Paper 13A, p.8 and SPE-PRMS, Figure 1-1.

31 SPE-PRMS, p. 2-3.
32 SPE-PRMS, p. 2-3.
33 SPE-PRMS, p.10-11.
34 SPE-PRMS, p.10-11.
35 SPE-PRMS, p.10-11.
36 SPE-PRMS, p. 2-3.
37 SPE-PRMS, p. 2-3.
38 SPE-PRMS, p. 2-3.
39 SPE-PRMS, p. 2-3.
40 SPE-PRMS, p. 2-3.
41 SPE-PRMS, p. 6-9.
42 SPE-PRMS, p. 9-13.
43 SPE-PRMS, p. 13-19.
44 JORC Code, Australasian Code for Reporting of Exploration Results, Mineral Resources and Ore Reserves, Joint Ore Reserves Committee of the Australasian Institute of Mining and Metallurgy, Australian Institute of Geoscientists and Minerals Council of Australia (JORC), 2004, para. 1.
45 Weatherstone, p. 5.
46 IASB Agenda Paper 13A, p. 3.
47 J. M. Rendu, *Reporting Mineral Resources and Mineral Reserves in the United States of America – Technical and Regulatory Issues*, 20-25 August 2006, p. 2.
48 CRIRSCO Template, *International Reporting Template for the public reporting of exploration results, mineral resources and mineral reserves*, CRIRSCO, May 2013, 3.
49 CRIRSCO Template, 4.
50 CRIRSCO Template, 5.
51 CRIRSCO Template, 8 and 11.
52 CRIRSCO Template, Figure 1.
53 CRIRSCO Template, 18.
54 CRIRSCO Template, 20.
55 CRIRSCO Template, 21.
56 CRIRSCO Template, 22.
57 CRIRSCO Template, 23.
58 CRIRSCO Template, 24.
59 CRIRSO Template, 12.
60 CRIRSCO Template, 30.
61 CRIRSCO Template, 31.
62 CRIRSCO Template, 32.
63 Pre codification FAS 69, *Disclosures about Oil and Gas Producing Activities an amendment of FASB Statements 19, 25, 33, and 39*, FASB, November 1982, para. 10.
64 OIAC SORP, *Statement of Recommended Practice – Accounting for Oil and Gas Exploration, Development, Production and Decommissioning Activities,* UK Oil Industry Accounting Committee (OIAC), 7 June 2001, para. 246.
65 OIAC SORP 12.
66 OIAC SORP, 247, 250.
67 OIAC SORP, Appendix 4.
68 OIAC SORP 248.
69 OIAC SORP 249.
70 OIAC SORP 250.
71 OIAC SORP 250.
72 OIAC SORP 251.
73 ASC 932-235-50, *Extractive Activities – Oil and Gas – Notes to Financial Statements – Disclosure*, 50-4 to 50-11B.
74 ASC 932-235-55-2, *Extractive Activities – Oil and Gas – Notes to Financial Statements – Implementation Guidance and Illustrations.*
75 Rendu, p. 9 and 10.
76 Industry Guide 7, *Description of Property by Issuers Engaged or to be Engaged in Significant Mining Operations*, Securities and Exchange Commission, Securities Act Release No. 33-6949, effective 13 August 1992.
77 Industry Guide 7, (a).
78 Industry Guide 7, (b).
79 Industry Guide 7, (b)(5)
80 Industry Guide 7, (c)
81 IASB Agenda Paper 15C, *Possible principles for a historical cost accounting model that accompanies decision-useful disclosures of minerals and oil & gas reserves and resources*, IASB, 22 June 2007, 6.
82 *IASB Update*, September 2008, p. 3.
83 ASC 932-235, *Extractive Activities – Oil and Gas – Notes to Financial Statements – Disclosure*, 50-30 to 50-33, 50-35 to 50-36.
84 *IFRIC Update*, January 2006, p. 3.
85 ASC 932-720-25-1, *Extractive Activities – Oil and Gas – Other Expenses – Recognition..*
86 ED 6, *Exploration for and Evaluation of Mineral Resources*, IASB, January 2004, 14.
87 IASC Issues Paper, 6.3.
88 IASC Issues Paper, 13.21.
89 OIAC SORP para 144.
90 IASC Issues Paper, 2.12.
91 IASC Issues Paper, 2.13.
92 IASC Issues Paper, 2.14.
93 IASC Issues Paper, 2.21.
94 IASC Issues Paper, 2.21.
95 IASC Issues Paper, Glossary.
96 IASC Issues Paper, 2.19.
97 IASC Issues Paper, 12.12(b).
98 *Guidelines for the Evaluation of Petroleum Reserves and Resources – A Supplement to the SPE/WPC Petroleum Reserves Definitions and the SPE/WPC/AAPG*

Petroleum Resources Definitions, Society of Petroleum Engineers, 2001, p. 120.
99 IASC Issues Paper, 12.68.
100 IASC Issues Paper, 12.69.
101 IASC Issues Paper, 2.23.
102 *Guidelines for the Evaluation of Petroleum Reserves and Resources – A Supplement to the SPE/WPC Petroleum Reserves Definitions and the SPE/WPC/AAPG Petroleum Resources Definitions*, Society of Petroleum Engineers, 2001, p. 120.
103 D. R. Jennings, J. B. Feiten and H. R. Brock, *Petroleum Accounting, Principles, Procedures, & Issues*, 5th edition, Professional Development Institute, Denton (Texas), p. 165-169.
104 IASC Issues Paper, 12.9.
105 SPE-PRMS, p. 18.
106 OIAC SORP 149.
107 OIAC SORP 150.
108 OIAC SORP 16.
109 ASC 930-805-30-1 *Extractive Activities – Mining – Business Combinations – Initial Measurement* (pre-codification EITF 04-3, *Mining Assets: Impairment and Business Combinations*, EITF, March 2004).
110 *IFRIC Update*, January 2011.
111 *IASB Update*, July 2013
112 IASC Issues Paper, 7.13.
113 IASC Issues Paper, 7.19.
114 IASC Issues Paper, 7.20.
115 IASC Issues Paper, 7.36.
116 IASC Issues Paper, 7.39.
117 IASC Issues Paper, 7.41.
118 IASC Issues Paper, 7.42.
119 IASC Issues Paper, 7.46.
120 IASC Issues Paper, 7.49.
121 IASC Issues Paper, 7.50.
122 IASC Issues Paper, 7.23.
123 IASC Issues Paper, 7.24.
124 IASC Issues Paper, 7.25.
125 IASC Issues Paper, 7.26.
126 IASC Issues Paper, 7.61.
127 IASC Issues Paper, 9.26.
128 AASB 1022 *Accounting for the Extractive Industries* (now superseded).
129 Oil Industry Association Committee Statement of Recommended Practice *Accounting for Oil and Gas Exploration, Development, Production and Decommissioning Activities* (July 2001).
130 AASB 1022 Accounting for the Extractive Industries (now superseded) para 62
131 Oil Industry Association Committee Statement of Recommended Practice *Accounting for Oil and Gas Exploration, Development, Production and Decommissioning Activities* (July 2001) para 127
132 IASC Issues Paper 7.61-7.68.
133 IASC Issues Paper, 10.26.
134 IASC Issues Paper, 10.23.
135 IASC Issues Paper, 10.24.
136 IASC Issues Paper, 1.27.
137 HM Revenue & Customs website, www.hmrc.gov.uk, *International – Taxation of UK oil production.*
138 IASC Issues Paper, 12.14.
139 OIAC SORP 175.
140 OIAC SORP 176.
141 IASC Issues Paper, 12.14.
142 OIAC SORP 177-178.
143 OIAC SORP 179-180.
144 IASC Issues Paper 4.18.
145 IASC Issues Paper 4.20.
146 IASC Issues Paper 4.45.
147 *IFRIC Update*, January 2006, p. 3.
148 Amendments to IFRS 1, *Additional Exemptions for First-time Adopters*, IASB, July 2009, D8A.
149 IASC Issues Paper 4.16(b).
150 IASC Issues Paper 4.36.
151 IASC Issues Paper 4.39.
152 IASC Issues Paper 6.64.
153 IASC Issues Paper 10.27.
154 IASC Issues Paper 10.29, 10.32. OIAC SORP 114-121.
155 IASC Issues Paper 10.29.
156 IASC Issues Paper 10.29.
157 IASC Issues Paper 10.32.
158 IASC Issues Paper 10.32.
159 IASC Issues Paper 10.32.
160 IASC Issues Paper 10.29.
161 IASC Issues Paper 11.17.
162 SFAC No. 5, *Recognition and Measurement in Financial Statements of Business Enterprises*, FASB, December 1984, paras. 83-84.
163 IASC Issues Paper 11.9-11.16.
164 Global infomine www.technology.infomine.com / reviews – "Block caving".
165 IASC Issues Paper, Glossary of Terms.

Index of extracts from financial statements

Index of standards

Conceptual Framework

IFRS 1

IFRS 1 (2012)

IFRS 2

IFRS 3

IFRS 4

IFRS 5

IFRS 6

IFRS 7

IFRS 7 (Draft)

IFRS 8

IFRS 9

IFRS 9 (Draft)

IFRS 10

IFRS 11

IFRS 12

IFRS 13

IAS 1

IAS 2

IAS 7

IAS 8

IAS 10

IAS 11

IAS 12

IAS 16

IAS 17

IAS 18

IAS 19

IAS 20

IAS 21

IAS 23

IAS 28

IAS 29

IAS 32

IAS 33

IAS 34

IAS 36

IAS 37

IAS 38

IAS 39

IAS 40

IAS 41

IFRIC 1

IFRIC 10

IFRIC 12

IFRIC 13

IFRIC 14

IFRIC 15

IFRIC 16

IFRIC 17

IFRIC 18

IFRIC 19

IFRIC 20

IFRIC 21

SIC-7

SIC 10

SIC 15

SIC 25

SIC 27

SIC 29

SIC 31

SIC 32

Index

Notes